杨良宜 杨大明 杨大志 | 著

合约的履行、弃权与禁反言

Performance of Contract, Waiver and Estoppel

法律出版社
LAW PRESS · CHINA
北京

作者简介

杨良宜 现为全职国际商事仲裁员，在过去四十年中处理了大量国际商事、海事、贸易领域的案件，熟悉亚洲地区及国际的有关实务，曾在中国香港特区、英国、新加坡、马来西亚、澳大利亚、奥地利、美国、韩国以及中国内地的仲裁案件中担任仲裁员，作出超过六百份的仲裁裁决书。

现任中国国际经济贸易仲裁委员会（China International Economic and Trade Arbitration Commission）国际咨询委员会（International Advisory Board）委员、丹麦哥本哈根波罗的国际海事协会（Baltic & International Maritime Council）文件委员会副主席、香港国际仲裁中心（Hong Kong International Arbitration Centre）名誉主席、新加坡海事仲裁员协会（Singapore Chamber of Maritime Arbitration）常务委员会（General Committee）成员、马来西亚吉隆坡仲裁中心（Kuala Lumpur Regional Centre for Arbitration）国际咨询委员会（International Advisory Board）成员以及韩国商事仲裁院（Korean Commercial Arbitration Board）国际仲裁委员会（International Arbitration Committee）成员。曾任香港国际仲裁中心主席、亚太仲裁组织（Asia Pacific Regional Arbitration Group）主席、法国巴黎国际商会国际仲裁庭（ICC International Court of Arbitration）香港代表、英国特许仲裁员学会（Chartered Institute of Arbitrators）东亚分会主席。

联系方式：philipyang@ biznetvigator. com

个人网站：www. yangliangyee. com

杨大明 现为欧华律师事务所香港办事处合伙人以及诉讼与监管业务部负责人，主要业务包括商业诉讼和仲裁。在处理涉及国际贸易和商品、合资企业和股东纠纷、国际投资和离岸项目以及科技相关的国际商业纠纷方面拥有丰富经验。同时，具有在中国香港、新加坡和英国伦敦等各地处理仲裁纠纷的丰富经验，涉及范围广泛的辖区、管辖法律和仲裁机构，包括北京仲裁委员会、中国国际经济贸易仲裁委员会、香港国际仲裁中心、国际商会、伦敦国际仲裁法院、伦敦海事仲裁协会、斯德哥尔摩商会、新加坡国际仲裁中心等。

2013 年，当选为上海市政协委员，并被任命协助上海发展成为国际仲裁中心。2015 年，作为领导小组成员之一向中国（上海）自由贸易试验区提交了有关“打造上海为航空航运融资租赁中心”的方案，并获评 2016 年“年度优秀提案”。2017 年，被

《钱伯斯亚洲太平洋》(Chambers Asia Pacific)评为争议解决在华仲裁领域的领先律师。2016/2017年,被《商法》(China Business Law Journal)杂志评为"The A List 法律精英100强"之一。

联系方式:ernest_yang@ hotmail. com

杨大志 现为高伟绅律师事务所香港分所金融市场部门的合伙人。专长于处理场外衍生品交易和各类结构化产品,包括股权和信用挂钩产品、结构型重新组合证券、与基金挂钩的衍生品以及ISDA净额结算及套期保值交易。入选《钱伯斯亚洲太平洋》(Chambers Asia Pacific)律师名录,并因其在场外衍生品监管改革方面的丰富经验获得特别肯定与认可。经常为监管机构、行业组织以及各类客户就涉及场外衍生品的报告义务、清算义务和(非清算型产品的)保证金义务等方面提供专业意见与帮助。

2007年,在英国取得律师资格;2013年,在中国香港取得律师资格。在加入高伟绅律师事务所香港分所之前,曾在伦敦主流国际律师事务所与美国顶尖律师事务所的结构性金融产品部门工作。

联系方式:terry. yang@ cliffordchance. com

序 言 一

这是笔者第三本也是最后一本关于英美合约法(因为历史原因,也是国际商务游戏规则)的书,另外两本是《损失赔偿与救济》与《合约的解释:规则与应用》。虽然这三本书的内容并没有囊括或重点针对英美合约法的所有课题,如非法与公共政策(illegality & public policy)、复原与不当得利(restitution & unjust enrichment)、法律冲突(conflict of law)等,但相信已经基本包括了所有重要与和实践相关的课题,并有详细介绍。由于所有商业关系都是由一个个合约串联起来,因此,掌握了合约法,就是掌握了商法。

这本书针对的内容是合约的履行。合约的履行比订立合约更具有危险性。笔者上一本《合约的解释:规则与应用》强调了订立对自己有利的合约非常重要,比对方懂得少,就可能签了一个"要命"的商业合约(sign your life away)。这也是发展中国家的公司/企业在与发达国家的公司/企业订立合约时常出的问题。现在,越来越多的中国公司/企业在订立合约时愿意雇佣称职与专业的律师参与谈判,更不用说很多合约还存在标准格式(standard form),如中国船厂普遍使用的日本造船格式(SAJ Form),条文相对清楚明确,如果改动不多,应是对中国船厂有利。但合约的履行则不同,合约期长达几年、十几年甚至几十年的合约并不罕见。在这么长的时间里,要雇佣律师参与履行的每个步骤显然不现实。而且履行期间,需要公司大量员工共同参与,双方之间的交往与互动多了,就很容易从中找出可能构成违约/毁约、弃权或禁反言的言行。

法律在判断禁反言时为了法律的肯定性,让所有人都能有所适从,只能有统一的标准。如果不知道这个法律标准,导致轻重掌握不好,就会带来严重的后果。笔者曾见过一些对中国公司非常有利的合约,因为中方在履行中做出过火的言行而构成违约/毁约,不仅保不住合约,还要赔偿对方损失。也见过不少中国公司/企业面对对方违约却忍气吞声,有关言行构成弃权与/或禁反言,失去了原本对自己有利的合约条文。在有责任与有必要说清楚时,保持沉默本身就可能属于明确无误的陈述/承诺,构成禁反言。要知道究竟何时应该出声,何时应该沉默,就必须了解法律规定一方说清楚的责任的情况。

总而言之,只有掌握这方面的法律,才能在履行中依法办事与轻重掌握地恰到好处,最大限度地保护自己的权利。这也不仅是合约权利,还有其他方面的权利。如本书第十章是介绍对民事诉讼/仲裁过程中的法律权利的弃权与禁反言,这对中国越来越庞大的律师群体特别是涉外律师群体特别重要。掌握法律在这方面的统一标准，还可以有理有据地应对一些常见的争议。例如，在笔者近期的一个仲裁中，中方向外国买方提供设备，买方安装后出现问题，向中方投诉。中方为了友好或声誉，很快以白纸黑字承诺将设备修好，但结果修不好。根据有关的买卖合约，中方对此没有责任，但买方就抓住中方曾经同意将设备修好的说法，双方就中方是否因这个承诺承担责任与赔偿损失，开始了仲裁。在掌握了本书的内容后，读者就会知道正确的答案。

在履行合约时，除非双方达成正式的更改（要满足一定的要件），否则就必须严格遵照合约的规定。在订约自由下，商业合约的规定会是千变万化。笔者见到不少公司/企业的员工在履行时根本不看合约，只以自己认为“合理”或习惯性的方式履行。这种履行方式如果不符合合约规定，就属于违约，要承担责任。例如，工程合约规定了一些设备/材料的付运期，但由于知道对方工程进度慢，暂时用不上这些设备/材料，为了对方可以节省仓储费用，主动推迟付运。这种单方面“更改”合约就属于典型的违约/毁约，让对方可以从合约中脱身与/或索赔损失。在没有约因/对价构成合约正式更改的情况下，想要改变合约的履行方式，唯一能依赖的就是对方曾做出可以构成弃权与/或禁反言的言行。本书中还有相当多的例子，笔者就不在此一一介绍。

现在，中国经济发展平稳迅速，随着在国际商业社会扮演着越来越重要的角色，磨炼的机会也很多，可以说是学习与成长的黄金机会。当然机会永远与风险并存，所以笔者也希望读者居安思危，因为危机感是极佳的推动力。

在过去的四十多年来，笔者在精神层面一直很满足，也很荣幸能通过举办讲座与写书，将自己对英美商法的了解、经验与感悟完整与有系统地分享给中国青年、商业与法律从业人士，希望对他们有所帮助。如今的国际商业社会越来越复杂，相关的法律也快速发展以配合实务需要。笔者相信，这三本合约法相关的书籍在五年内就需要进行更新与补充。但笔者已经年近古稀，精力有限，将来想要再更新这些书籍，也可能心有余而力不足。因此，笔者很高兴两个儿子杨大明与杨大志加入本书作为共同作者。他们在笔者写作期间不断提供意见与想法，也希望他们将来能将这套合约法的书发扬光大，不断补充。

另外，还有很多朋友在写作期间提供了帮助与提出意见与建议，在此无法一一感谢。他们建议我将对“estoppel”一词的翻译从“禁止翻供”改为“禁反言”。为了帮助中国读者理解，笔者在本书中使用了“禁反言”。

最后要感谢笔者公司团队的司嘉女士与贡航先生帮助本书的审阅、校对与提出宝贵意见，以及在笔者三本合约法书籍中都作为主力负责录入整理与研究内容的王可心女士。

杨良宜

2017 年 11 月

序　言　二

Success is a journey, not a destination. It requires constant effort, vigilance and reevaluation.

——Mark Twain

成就是一个旅途，不是一个目的地。这是需要不断的努力，警觉以及重新评估。

——马克·吐温

以我多年为中国企业处理对外纠纷的经验而言，最近十年中国企业在签订大型合约时比前十年更谨慎，对合约条款会非常小心，也经常会聘用专业的律师处理合约谈判、草拟与签订的过程。看到中国企业这方面的发展，我感到很鼓舞与喜悦。

但是，很多企业认为法务部或外部律师小心谨慎地谈好和签好一份大型、多年期的合约后，就可以放松，然后把合约放到柜底里，与合作伙伴就是世界上最好的朋友，什么都可以说。这种企业往往在这么想以及这么做之后，会发现执行合约的过程并不是这么简单。他们在履行合约的过程中，很容易透过有意或无意的行为更改或放弃了法务或外部律师辛辛苦苦在合约争取回来的权利。

我常常协助客户处理这类的案件，所以非常开心与荣幸再次有机会与父亲合作，参与撰写这本书。这也让我有机会从协助中国企业解决这种问题的角度，将我处理的案件和经验与大家分享。我衷心希望这些经验可以鼓励中国企业在合约执行当中，不要认为高枕无忧而是要不断地努力，保持警觉以及重新评估，知道尽早找公司法务或外部律师参与以应对履行中发生的问题。

我也特别高兴可以和弟弟杨大志合作，大志一直都是我们家庭的骄傲。这次我们可以从不同的专业角度为这本书做贡献，非常有意义。在这一次协助父亲写书时，在自己人生走到目前所积累的阅历与经验的基础上，我越来越对父亲多年的决心，即把整套国际商业游戏规则变为中国人与中国企业拥有的财富，感到非常佩服。我现在有两个年纪还很小的孩子，深深感受到要平衡多方面带来的时间压力，但还是以不动摇的决心往目标走，我希望以父亲作为我终生的榜样。

最后，我希望我的两个孩子——婉淇和祺乐，在人生的旅途上会不断地努力、警觉以及重新评估。

杨大明

2017 年 11 月

序　言　三

在伦敦求学并从事法律职业近十年后，我于 2010 年回到香港。过去 7 年里，我有幸见证了两起令我印象极其深刻的事件。

第一是中国在世界舞台上的崛起。中国人焕发出一种真切的欢欣鼓舞和积极乐观的精神面貌，这和我离开遭受金融危机重创后的伦敦时所目见的情绪形成了鲜明对比。我深切地希望，我们可以继续保有这样的自信，并继续进步和发展。

第二则是我终于有机会亲身感受我父亲毕生从事的事业是如何影响、帮助他人的。在过去这些年里，无论我去哪里出差，上海、北京或是其他地方，都会遇见曾经研习过我父亲的著作、聆听过他的讲座或以其他方式接收过我父亲智识的律师；这种智识也传承给我，并使我受益至今。少年时代，我只能记起父亲每每写作至深夜，并时常在中国不同的城市举办讲座。最终有幸亲见他所做的一切带来的影响，我由衷感到高兴。

近年来，我很大一部分时间都在为中国公司海外业务的扩张提供法律服务；这些海外扩张既包括在英国设立办公室、在欧洲收购子公司，也包括在美国进行投资。在业务扩张的过程中，客户面临的最大挑战之一，即是如何适应国际商事法律的体系和规则（如我父亲指出，往往为英国法）。

我还记得有一次给一家大型中国公司做法律培训，当时我在培训上向大家解释发生违约时对基础证券进行估值的合约条文。这一条文十分复杂和精细。一名听众点评指出，如果进行这样详细的约定，当事人会丧失在按照估值条文所得出的估值对其不利时与对方进一步协商的余地；因此，在合约中只简单地约定一方违约时双方将就估值进行协商，更为可取。我非常理解这位听众的顾虑，但在国际商法实践中，就估值机制提前做出详尽安排以避免发生争议时冗长而昂贵的诉讼，具有十分重要的意义。此外，针对这一看法马上可以提出两个重要的问题。首先，任何的商业合约只是订约当事人的明示约定，合约写得简单并不代表针对相关的问题没有法律的默示地位。碰到厉害的对手，他在知道法律默示地位对他有利的情况下，会任由中方简单约定。这样，如果协商不成最后需要诉讼解决，就会对中方不利。其次，在一个复杂的国际交易中，合约写得详细主要是为了将来履行时可以减少双方再协商的时间与成本，并通过合约管理与理解提高合约顺利履行完毕的几率。

对正在寻求全球化发展的中国企业来说，缺乏对国际商法的了解以及与国际商法实践的背离，是极其危险的。另外，需要着重强调的是，境外监管部门也日渐从法律及监管的角度对中国公司进行更严密的监察。这些都表明，为了真正地在世界舞台站稳脚跟，中国公司需要按照世界舞台的"游戏规则"行事。

能与父亲共同撰写他职业生涯最重要的作品之一，对我具有非凡的意义。我已有幸承继父亲的姓氏，但我也殷切期望自己能从他身上汲取更多的学识与人生智慧，更重要的是，承继他乐于给予的精神。

杨大志

2017 年 11 月

目　　录

第一章　违约令合约终止

1. 中国公司/企业最危险的合约终止方法：违约/毁约(repudiation)

英国法律的大精神是合约订立后就不轻易允许其中一方逃避合约责任去提前或在履行中途终止合约。如 Roskill 大法官在 The"Hansa Nord" (1975) 2 Lloyd's Rep. 445 先例中的名言："Contracts are made to be performed and not to be avoided according to the whims of market fluctuation."

但偏偏商业合约特别是涉及一些金额庞大并且市场波动幅度很大与很快的业务，如商品、土地等买卖与航运，不利的一方想通过终止合约去逃避合约责任的诱因就特别大，所以这一类争议与案例也特别多。合约由于不涉及违约的"受阻"(frustration)而提前或在履行中途终止的情况很少。[1] 绝大部分合约会提前或在履行中途终止都涉及违约，这往往会带来非常庞大的损失索赔。所以，违约令合约终止(discharge of contract by breach)是合约法的一个重要课题，中国公司/企业与诉讼律师必须要熟悉。

涉及真正违约，合约条文或责任要构成"条件条文"(condition)，令无辜方以对方违反该合约条件条文终止一个合约并不容易，因为通过法律(普通法与立法)或合约明示条文确定的合约条件条文，通常不多。合约条文要构成"中间条文"(innominate/immediate term)而且违约造成了严重后果，可让无辜方终止合约也不容易而且不能事前肯定。

现实中最容易造成违约导致合约被终止的就是"预期违约"(anticipatory breach)中的"拒绝性违约"(renunciatory breach)，也就是违约方通过语言或行为或两者都有，显示了将不会依照合约履行的意图。违约方拒绝履行合约也可以是已经到期应该履行的合约责任，这样，如果拒绝是涉及重要的合约责任，也会有导致合约被终止的同样后果。通常在一个中长期合约的履行期间，如果违约方通过言行拒绝履行合约，这会涉及真正违约(拒绝履行已经到期的合约责任)，但也同时涉及预期违约(因

---

〔1〕 即使合约发生受阻，如果涉及诉讼，就表示有一方不同意是受阻。如果诉讼的结果是不构成受阻，就等于有一方违约/毁约。所以受阻的先例也无可避免涉及违约令合约终止的争议。

为合约还有一段时间才能履行完毕所有将来的责任)。这种既有真正也有预期违约的拒绝,均可称为"违约/毁约"(repudiatory breach)。[2] 正如 Porter 勋爵在 Heyman v. Darwins (1942) AC 356 先例中说:all these acts (of renunciation, impossibility or failure of performance) may be compendiously described as repudiation..."

Denning 勋爵在 The"Hansa Nord"先例说:"The word 'repudiation' should be confined to those cases of an anticipatory breach, but it is also used in connection with cases of an actual breach going to the root of the contract: see Heyman v. Darwins Ltd. ..."

Wilberforce 勋爵在 The "Nanfri" (1979) 1 Lloyd's Rep. 201 (HL) 先例所说:"However it makes no difference whether the conduct of the owners amounted to an actual breach, or anticipatory breach for, as my noble and learned friend has so clearly demonstrated, their conduct was repudiatory."

英国合约法的一些著名先例,如 The "Hong Kong Fir" (1962) 2 QB 26 先例, The "Golden Victory" (2007) 2 Lloyd's Rep. 164 先例等,都是长期租约在履行中途被单方面终止。虽然涉及真正违约,但由于将来的履行也被同时终止,所以也涉及预期违约并需要对将来的预期损失(expectation loss)[3] 做出估计要违约方赔偿。

1.1　违约/毁约的例子

可以说拒绝性违约与违约/毁约,在合约订立后与整个履行过程中都可能与经常在发生。这种违约也经常会混杂了真正违约与预期违约,由于对两种违约是否能导致合约被终止的考验(tests)基本一致,所以也不需要细分。

这方面的案例经常涉及的合约类别往往数量众多与标的金额很大,如雇佣合约。这种争议在双方当事人,也就是雇主与雇员之间无时无刻不在发生。例如,雇主无理辞退员工或将员工降职,或是员工总是迟到早退、旷工甚至直接"失踪",这种严重违反雇佣合约的言行都属于违约/毁约。而一些跨国公司/企业的高级管理人员的雇佣合约,一旦发生争议,涉及的金额可能高达几千万甚至上亿美元。

涉及国际货物买卖(尤其是商品买卖)是另一个数量众多与标的金额很大的合约类别,有很多著名的有关违约/毁约的先例。除了这种合约数量众多与标的金额很大之外,商品买卖的市场波动也是很大与很快,如 2014 年开始的原油价格从约一百美元在几个月后就跌到约三十美元一桶,任何要承担市场损失的一方,都会想办法合法从合约中脱身,如果不成功(很有可能不成功)就会构成违约/毁约。例如,在一个国际货物买卖合约中,卖方如果告知 FOB 买方不必派船来装港,因为没货可装,除非

---

[2] 在一个完整合约中(见本书第二章第 8 段),即使违约方表示只拒绝履行现在的责任而不拒绝履行将来的合约责任,也依然属于违约/毁约。因为虽然一个完整合约会有不同的阶段,但彼此之间不独立,必须完成前一个阶段才能完成下一个阶段,因此,如果违约方拒绝履行这一阶段的合约责任就等于拒绝履行将来的合约责任。

[3] 参见杨良宜:《损失赔偿与救济》,法律出版社 2013 年版,第二章第 3 段。

买方加价。这是预期违约,因为卖方拒绝履行的是提供货物的将来合约责任。但如果 FOB 买方不接受,坚持要卖方履约,并持续指示租进的船舶开往装港并递交准备就绪通知书,而期间施加其他压力,如向卖方启动仲裁。如果这些行动逼使卖方回心转意,在装港提供货物装船,就等于根本没有发生过拒绝性违约或违约/毁约。而如果卖方不回心转意,船舶到了装港后,卖方仍然坚持不提供货物装船,这就会把拒绝性违约变为真正违约的违约/毁约。

拒绝性违约与违约/毁约另一种形式是双方在本质上比较善意,只是对合约条文的解释或者合约履行中的一些行为是否构成弃权/禁反言等有不同的理解,并各持己见与坚持对方要按自己的理解履行现有或将来的合约责任。这种坚持如果不能马上解决(通过和解或即时仲裁等)而导致最后双方互相指称对方违约/毁约,并令合约被终止,最后的审理显然只会有一方的理解正确,这等于不正确理解的一方与他所坚持的立场导致合约被终止,他也就是违约方。

不涉及真正违约,纯粹是预期违约(只针对将来的合约责任)的一个主要与典型类别的争议,就是合约是否存在。一方坚持还在谈判或是双方根本没有订约的意图,但另一方坚持已经达成合约。在这种争议中,由于一方坚持没有合约存在,显然他根本不会履行任何合约责任,另一方就要找替代的生意并别无其他选择地接受对方的拒绝性违约而终止合约(如果有合约存在)。一旦最后被判合约的确存在,坚持没有合约存在的一方就会构成拒绝性违约。[4] 这种争议非常多,在仲裁就是"管辖权"(jurisdiction)的争议,而这个争议一经过裁定,往往也同时决定了双方在实质责任(substantive liability)方面的争议,即是否拒绝性违约。这种争议如果涉及的是中长期合约,"预期损失"(expectation loss)计算出来会很惊人。笔者经手的仲裁案件中就常有此类争议。笔者有涉及的 Covington Marine Corp v. Xiamen Shipbuilding Industry Co. (2006) 1 Lloyd's Rep. 745 先例,也是这类合约是否存在的争议,具体案情与分析可看笔者《合约的解释:规则与应用》一书第二章之 13.3 段。在仲裁中,笔者所在的仲裁庭根据事实认定并没有合约存在,但可惜上诉到法院后,仲裁庭的裁决被推翻。而造船合约涉及的 4 艘船舶,违约/毁约的厦门船厂所面对的损失显然是很大一笔金额。

在 2008 年"金融海啸"之前,航运市场高涨,中国很多钢厂为了确保货物(主要是矿砂与煤炭)的付运,订立了很多中长期的包运合约(COA)。然而在 2008 年后,航运市场大跌,中国钢厂就想要从包运合约中脱身。这类的案件发生很多,笔者近期就在两个涉及包运合约的仲裁中担任仲裁员。

可先简单介绍第一个仲裁案件的案情。一家中国钢厂与船公司订立了长达 10

---

〔4〕 在《合约的解释:规则与应用》(杨良宜著,法律出版社 2015 年版)一书第二章第 2 段提到,构成有效合约的要求并不多,加上英国法院或仲裁庭普遍倾向支持存在一个合约而不是否定它,所以很容易就会让不小心或不熟悉合约法的商业人士掉进他以为还没有合约但实际上已经受到约束的陷阱。

年的包运合约。之后，船公司指定X轮作为履行这一包运合约的唯一船舶，除非该X轮短暂不能营运，船东可以指定替代船舶。包运合约履行得不太顺利，部分原因是X轮在不同的港口不断被扣船，并在2013年7月被拍卖给了第三方，并在11月被拆废钢。2014年2月24日，中国钢厂通过律师向船公司做出了终止合约通知，指称船公司不可能或拒绝履行合约，中国钢厂接受船公司的预期违约并终止合约。船公司在2月25日回复表示，2008年后市场大跌，这个合约利润很高，他们不会不继续履行。虽然X轮已经被拍卖，但他们完全可以替代船舶履行。中国钢厂的终止合约通知才属于违约/毁约，被船公司接受。之后双方开始仲裁，争议的焦点就是中国钢厂在2月24日的终止合约通知是否合法。

中国钢厂的立场是：(1)因为船公司在2013年11月申请破产，并且履行包运合约的唯一船舶X轮已经被拍卖并拆废钢，所以船公司不可能(impossible)继续履行合约，是预期违约；(2)船公司没有或拒绝履行包运合约的行为，构成违约/毁约或拒绝性违约。这些行为包括在2013年5月X轮被扣船后，船公司当时并没有指定替代船舶履约，允许X轮在中国钢厂不知情的情况下被拍卖并在之后被拆废钢，从2013年6月直到合约被终止前没有与中国钢厂就履行进行任何沟通等。

船公司的抗辩是：(1)合约存在"误名"(misnomer)，真正的合约方并不是船公司而是另一家巴拿马公司，所以船公司申请破产不会影响包运合约的履行，但这没有被仲裁庭接受。[5] (2)船公司可以替代船舶履行包运合约，并非不可能履行合约。但这也不被仲裁庭接受，因为根据合约X轮是履行这包运合约的唯一船舶。X轮被转卖并拆废钢，明显不属于X轮短暂不能营运(X轮已经永远不能营运)的例外情况。(3)船公司之前的违约不重要，不足以让中国钢厂终止合约。这不被仲裁庭接受，仲裁庭考虑了所有的事实后认为，船公司在X轮被转卖之前与之后的行为，虽然单独看来并不足够构成拒绝性违约，但加在一起可以变为重要，让中国钢厂作为无辜方可以合理推断船公司不愿意或不能够履行将来的合约责任，构成拒绝性违约。

在该仲裁，最后判是中国钢厂胜诉，这有如下原因：第一，包运合约中规定了X轮是唯一履行的船舶，如果没有这个规定，中国钢厂拒绝船公司指定替代船舶就可能会造成违约/毁约甚至拒绝性违约。第二，一般来说，要证明合约不可能被履行很困难。该仲裁中，X轮是被拆废钢，否则即使包运合约中规定了X轮是唯一履行的船舶，并且X轮被转卖，也不代表船公司不能将船舶租回继续履约。[6] 第三，包运合约在2014年2月24日被终止前，中国钢厂就聘用了称职律师来处理与船公司的争议。包括在之前的付运中，X轮不断被扣船需要另找替代船舶，钢厂虽然同意了以替

---

〔5〕 关于误名可看笔者的《提单与其他付运单证》(大连海事大学2016年版)第三章第3段，本章不再详述。

〔6〕 这与在本章之4.2段提到的 Omnium D'Enterprises v. Sutherland (1919) 1 KB 618 先例的情况类似。

代船舶履行，但在通讯往来中明确写明同意只针对该次付运，避免了产生“弃权”（waiver）或“共识性禁反言”（estoppel by convention）的问题。

在另一个仲裁案件中，原告船公司与被告中国钢厂在2007年10月15日订立了5年共20个航次的包运合约。到2011年年底，合约只履行了11个航次。双方在2012年1月签订了附录一，约定在2012、2013与2014年各履行3个航次。但在履行了4个航次之后，中国钢厂没有再提供货物。在2008年“金融海啸”后不久，船公司经济出现困难，并于2013年申请破产。外国清盘人开始仲裁，声称中国钢厂违约/毁约或拒绝性违约，并索赔高达上千万美元的损失。外国清盘人认为责任与损失方面都已经很清楚，向仲裁庭申请做出一个“中间裁决”（interim award）[7]。中国钢厂及时委任了律师做出抗辩，反对这一中间裁决的申请，证明中国钢厂无论是在责任还是损失方面都有可争辩的立场（arguable case）。

首先在责任方面，中国钢厂的立场是船公司将近十亿美元的欠债，加上合约终止前船公司其他的不当言行，显示了其不愿意或不能够继续履行剩余的5个航次，属于预期违约的拒绝性违约。中国钢厂作为承租人没有宣告剩余5个航次的装货期限（laycan）的行为，实质上是中国钢厂以行动或不行动接受[8]了这一预期违约。

在损失方面，中国钢厂依赖了The “Mihalis Angelos”（1970）2 Lloyd's Rep. 43、The “Golden Victory”（2007）2 Lloyd's Rep. 164、Flame SA v. Glory Wealth Shipping Pte Ltd.（2013）2 Lloyd's Rep. 653等先例，认为损失的计算是让船公司回复到合约被履行的地位。如果中国钢厂没有违约/毁约（假设中国钢厂在责任方面败诉），船公司也必须证明其可以继续履行合约。而在2013年与2014年，以船公司的经济状况根本提供不了船舶行走这5个航次，所以只有“名义损失”（nominal damages）。笔者所在的仲裁庭接受了中国钢厂的抗辩，认为不应该做出中间裁决。最后这个仲裁双方达成和解。

1.2　违约/毁约对中国公司/企业的危险

拒绝性违约与违约/毁约对中国商人特别危险。这可以从如下方面探讨；

第一个方面是中国商人经常在一开始“以和为贵”、忍气吞声，[9]后来积累的怨气又突然爆发，做出一些不相称、过火与坚决的言行。这样轻重掌握不好的言行造成的结果就是之前持续的忍气吞声，往往已造成“弃权”（waiver）与“禁反言”（estoppel），或是错失了可先一步接受对方的拒绝性违约而终止合约令自己变为无辜方的机会。后来爆发的言行在英国法下很容易构成拒绝性违约，精明的外商（特别是希望从合

---

〔7〕 关于中间裁决，做法上类似法院的简易判决（summary judgment），可参见The “Kostas Melas”（1981）1 Lloyd's Rep. 18等先例。

〔8〕 可参见本章第7段。

〔9〕 有争议时不表明自己的立场而让步只会被对方视为示弱，导致得寸进尺，也有失去中国商人本来在合约有的权利的危险，因为忍气吞声会构成“弃权”（waiver）或“禁反言”（estoppel），尤其是“共识性禁反言”（estoppel by convention）。

约中合法脱身)就会抓紧机会马上接受并终止合约。这样失去令自己成为无辜方的中国商人,就反过来变成违约方,非但不能索赔自己的损失,还要向对方做出可能金额庞大的赔偿。

第二个方面是中国商人通常不了解国际贸易中普遍适用的英国法。在面对危险时不认为需要咨询法律地位,贸然行事。常常在该坚持立场时不断让步,而不该坚持的立场却寸步不让。因此,中国商人相比外国商人有更大的可能性被法院/仲裁庭判是对法律地位的理解错误,言行构成拒绝性违约或者违约/毁约。

第三个方面涉及证据。现在英国法律对于拒绝性违约与违约/毁约的定义已经很明确,只会根据每个案件的不同事实做出判决/裁决。在这种案件中,最后胜负的关键就是对事实的认定,即所谓的"facts sensitive"。事实的认定就会涉及证据,包括书面证据与口头证据。纯粹或主要依据事实认定决定胜负的案件,笔者认为结果比较不肯定并难以预测。中国商人对证据方面的掌握往往特别薄弱。例如,一些重要的通讯往来没有保留文件证据;一些重要的问题只在电话中做出沟通,事后也不会再发邮件等确认电话内容(特别是对自己有利的部分留下文书记录);没有记录员工使用电脑情况(如收发的所有邮件等)的系统,即使有,也没有进行相关培训;员工离职时没有留下在职期间与对方沟通记录(如QQ、微信等记录)的副本等。如果依赖口头证据,中国的证人经常在开庭盘问时不知道应该如何应对。

总而言之,针对这一种预期违约或违约/毁约的案件,中方很容易败诉。近年中国企业惨痛的经验是在2008年"金融海啸"后,船价暴跌,中国船厂被外国船东大量弃船。在两千多个涉及上万艘新造船舶的伦敦仲裁中,除个别一两个外,中国船厂几乎全军覆没。其中有不少就是涉及中国船厂被外国船东指称预期违约或违约/毁约。[10] 船价暴跌后,外国船东会想方设法不合作与找麻烦,中国船厂通常就是一开始忍气吞声后来爆发,掉入外国船东的陷阱,被对方借机合法终止合约。一般的说法是归咎于航运市场太差,但笔者认为这些造船合约都是在市场高涨时订立,船价很高,船厂是看准了市场,在接下来的几年都不会受到航运市场下跌的影响。如果能保住这些合约不让外国船东轻易脱身,中国船厂就会在航运低潮时赚大钱。中国的造船业也应该可以更强大,甚至达到世界垄断地位。

本章会针对预期违约下的两种情况:拒绝性违约(renunciatory breach)与失去履约能力(disablement)进行介绍。特别是拒绝性违约,本章会进行更加深入的探讨,因为这种情况发生的最多。其中有不少情况会与真正违约的违约/毁约(repudiatory breach)一并介绍,因为有些情况很难区分。而只要违约/毁约被无辜方接受并终止合约,就是本章的题目——违约令合约终止。

---

〔10〕 其中包括由杨大明律师处理且为少数中国船厂胜诉的 Primera Maritime(Hellas) v. Jiangsu Eastern Heavy Industry Co. (2014) 1 Lloyd's Rep. 255 先例。

2. 预期违约(future breach / anticipatory breach)

首先可节录对这一重要课题的权威说法。在《Chitty on Contracts》(第 32 版, 2015 年)一书之 24 - 022 段,说:"**Anticipatory breach.** If, before the time arrives at which a party is bound to perform a contract, he expresses an intention to break it, or acts in such a way as to lead a reasonable person to the conclusion that he does not intend to fulfil his part, this constitutes an 'anticipatory breach' of the contract and entitles the other party to take one of two courses. He may 'accept' the renunciation, treat it as discharging him from further performance, and sue for damages forthwith, or he may wait till the time for performance arrives and then sue..."

《Chitty on Contracts》(第 32 版,2015 年)一书之 24 - 026 段中说:"**Anticipatory breach.** Anticipatory breach of contract may be constituted by impossibility[11] as well as by renunciation[12], and similar principles apply to both..."

另可节录《Halsbury's Law of England》(第 5 版,2012 年)第 546 页相关段落如下:

"560. **Repudiation and anticipatory breach**. Instead of merely failing to provide due performance at the stipulated time, one party (A) may put himself in breach by evincing an intention, by words or conduct, of repudiating his obligations under the contract in some essential respect. It has been said that repudiation is a serious matter, not to be lightly found or inferred. Such repudiation may occur at the time fixed for performance or before that time, in the latter case it is known as 'anticipatory breach'.

Repudiation will give the innocent party (B) the right to treat the contract as discharged and claim damages. It may be express or implied.

561. **Repudiation must go to the root of the contract.**[13] Not every refusal by A to perform a part of the contract amounts to a repudiation which entitles the other party (B) to treat the contract as at an end; there must be a refusal to perform something which goes to the root or essence of the contract. Thus it is not just any delay in breach of contract which amounts to a repudiation, but only such delay as would frustrate the adventure.

The question whether the refusal to perform part of the contract amounts to a repudi-

---

〔11〕 见本章第 4 段。

〔12〕 见本章第 3 段。

〔13〕 见本章之 3.5 段。

ation of the whole contract depends on the construction of the contract and the circumstances of the case. The test is the same for both repudiation and anticipatory breach. If the agreement is an entire contract, the test is applied to repudiation of any part of it...

563. **Continuing ability to perform.**〔14〕 Unwillingness and inability by A to perform are often difficult to disentangle, for inability may lie at the root of unwillingness. If, therefore, A puts it out of his power to perform or acts in a manner which leads the other reasonably to assume that he will be unable to perform, the other party (B) may be entitled to terminate the contract, even though the disability is not necessarily permanent and A (the defaulting party) may subsequently be in a position to perform the contract. This may be so even though the inability is not deliberate, or even if it extends to part only of A's obligation.

Impossibility of performance created by the act or default of a party of itself constitutes a ground for termination; but in a case of apparent inability to perform, the innocent party will usually rely on the apparent inability as constituting an anticipatory repudiation by conduct, since he will not then be required to show that performance was in fact impossible at the stipulated time."

本章接下来会针对预期违约下的两种主要类别分段进行具体分析。但不妨先举一个假设的例子说明不同类别的预期违约,让读者更加容易理解。例如,中国商人与外国某著名足球队订了一个合约——7 月 2 日在北京举行表演赛,约定几位明星球员必须上场。但在 6 月中的一次会面中,外国足球队的负责人对中国商人说决定不来了。这显然是预期违约的拒绝性违约,这种预期违约可以称为明示的拒绝(explicit renunciation)。

第二种情况,双方在 6 月中的一次社交活动中遇见,其中也包括了双方共同的朋友周先生。外国足球队的负责人对周先生说:"我们球队 7 月 2 日将在欧洲某地有一场很重要的赛事,必须参加。"中国商人也同时在场。这也是预期违约的拒绝性违约,可称为是默示的拒绝(implicit renunciation)。

第三种情况,球员的签证需要 14 个工作日,但中国商人得知在 6 月 20 日还没有收到申请,这显然来不及。这样,可以从外国足球队的行动合理推算是一个预期违约,违约的类别是不可能(impossibility)或失去履约能力(disablement)。

上述的情况也可能有各种不同的变化。如第二种情况,中国商人听到球队在欧洲有比赛,很可能会追问北京的表演赛怎么办,外国足球队的负责人就可能会把默示的拒绝变为明示的拒绝。

---

〔14〕 见本章第 4 段。

3. 预期违约之一:拒绝性违约(renunciatory breach)

这种违约是违约方通过言行显示了他拒绝履行"将来的合约责任"(future contractual obligation),这就给对方或无辜方一个选择权,也就是接受并终止合约的机会。笔者处理的很多案件,包括金额很大的案件,中国商人常常被对方指称在分寸没掌握好的电文、电话或者会议中有过拒绝性违约的言行。此处例举一个近期审理完毕的仲裁案件,希望能警示对中国企业的危险性。案情涉及中国一间大型药厂与欧洲公司订立了合作协议,共同研发与生产一种医疗设备,将来由欧洲公司在世界各地出售。但在履行与研发的过程中遇到了很大困难,导致双方合作关系难以为继。在一次双方在中国举行的会议中,欧洲公司指称中国药厂提出要终止合约。欧洲公司在会议后的两三天,以电文确认中国药厂在较早的会议中要终止合约,并在最后加了一句——欧洲公司希望之后会再有合作机会。而中国药厂没有回应,特别是没有指出欧洲公司的电文中提到的情况是不正确的。不久后,欧洲公司就通过律师文书正式向中国药厂表示接受"拒绝性违约"(renunciatory breach),并很快启动了香港仲裁程序,索赔一笔金额巨大的损失。在开庭时,中国药厂在证人证言中指称其在会议中没有确实地说过坚决不履行,只是提出建议与询问,这显然不是拒绝性违约。中国证人还指出,这个终止合约的建议是欧洲公司诱导并率先提出,双方才进行讨论的。显然,欧洲公司不同意这一说法。笔者作为仲裁员之一也知道,中国药厂证人所说的完全有可能发生,另一方面,笔者也知道中国商业人士言行往往轻重掌握不好。最后,笔者与另外两位外国仲裁员经过合议之后,一致同意中国药厂在责任方面败诉。[15]毕竟中国证人在盘问时表现得很不好,如对讲话过火的严重性并不了解。更重要的是,欧洲公司有很明确的会议后的文件证据(即上面提到的电文)证明与记录了会议中所讲的内容,中国公司没有马上回应。在开庭的证人证言中指称当场文书记录(contemporanious written record)并不正确,往往不会被仲裁庭接受。

3.1 拒绝性违约的定义

"拒绝履约"(renunciation)在《Chitty on Contracts》(第32版,2015年)之24-018段的定义如下:"A renunciation of a contract occurs when one partyby words or conduct evinces an intention not to perform, or expressly declares that he is or will be unable to perform, his obligations under the contract in some essential respect. The renunciation may occur before or at the time fixed for performance. An absolute refusal by one party to perform his side of the contract will entitle the other party to treat himself as discharged, as will also a clear and unambiguous assertion by one party that he will be una-

〔15〕 中国药厂在损失计算方面运气好得多,这在本章之10.2段有详述。

ble to perform when the time for performance should arrive. Short of such an express refusal or declaration, however, the test is to ascertain whether the action or actions of the party in default are such as to lead a reasonable person to the conclude that he no longer intends to be bound by its provisions. The renunciation is then evidenced by conduct."

很多有关的先例对拒绝性违约有大同小异的定义,笔者只节录 Donaldson 大法官在 The "Hermosa"(1982) 1 Lloyd's Rep. 570 先例[16]总结的四个方面:"(a) Dissolution of a contract upon the basis of renunciation is a drastic conclusion which should only be held to arise in clear cases of a refusal to perform contractual obligations in a respect or respects going to the root of the contract. (b) The refusal must not only be clear, but must be absolute. Where a party declares his intention to act or refrain from acting in a particular way on the basis of a particular appreciation of his obligations, either as a matter of fact or of law, the declaration gives rise to a right of dissolution only if in all the circumstances it is clear that it is not conditional upon his present appreciation of his obligations proving correct when the time for performance arrives. (c) What does or does not amount to a sufficient refusal is to be judged in the light of whether a reasonable person in the position of the party claiming to be freed from the contract would regard the refusal as being clear and absolute?... (d) the conduct relied upon is to be considered as at the time when it is treated as terminating the contract, in the light of the then existing circumstances. These circumstances will include the history of the transaction or relationship. Later events are irrelevant, save to the extent that they may point to matters which the parties should have considered as hypothetical possibilities at the relevant time."

另在 The "Pro Victor" (2010) 2 Lloyd's Rep. 158 先例,[17] Flaux 大法官就根据以上的总结定义拒绝性违约说:"The critical question is thus whether, by its words or conduct, a party has evinced an intention not to perform the contract, which a reasonable person in the position of the other, innocent, party would regard as clear and absolute. As that last proposition in The Hermosa demonstrates, that question is to be judged at the time of termination of the contract, having regard to all the circumstances, including the history of the contractual relationship."

可见拒绝性违约只需要是合约一方(可称为违约方)对另一方显示了意图(evinces an intention)——他再也不愿意(unwilling)或不能够(unable)依照合约办事,或是除非以违约方单方面的条件办事。这显示可以通过语言(口头或书面),也可以通过行动(或不行动),只要另一方作为一个合理人士(法官或仲裁员)客观来

---

〔16〕 这将在本章之 9.3 段有详细介绍。

〔17〕 这将在本章之 9.6 段有详细介绍。

看,违约方是再也不愿受合约约束。

怎样是语言的显示呢？每一个先例都会有不同,而且往往也不会只是根据一两句话。但不妨先简单举几个笔者熟悉的国际货物买卖与航运的例子如下:(1)卖方书面或口头通知买方市场大涨,[18]他不会交货,除非合约价格每吨多加 10 元美元。(2)反之,买方书面或口头通知卖方市场下跌,他不开信用证,不会要货,除非减价。或是买方投诉上次交付的货物质量不好,其他合约下即将付运的货物也不要了。(3)承租人在一份期租合约扣下一部分租金,船东提出抗议并通知承租人他命令船长不再签发提单,或者威胁承租人如果下令船舶往东开,则船长会往西开,直到所有欠的租金付清。(4)船舶开往装港途中,承租人/发货人书面通知船东没有货装,船舶不必前来装港。(5)船舶开往装港途中,承租人说我要履约,但船舶将要在装港等待半年后才会有货装,我也无能为力,这是不可抗力。可如果船舶真的在装港等上半年,这延误已经可以构成受阻延误。这样,是属于"没有履约能力"(inability)的拒绝。(6)船东指称承租人指定的装港不安全,船舶拒绝前往或进港。

什么又是行动的显示呢？行动或不行动虽然比不上书面的明确与肯定,但也可以构成拒绝履行。在《Contractual Duties: Performance, Breach, Termination and Remedies》(2011 年)一书之 6 – 016 段介绍说:"**Types of conduct or inaction**: There are various types of conduct or inaction which might be relied on to support the inference of renunciation. There might be: an absolute failure or refusal to act; or failure or refusal to act fully; or a failure or refusal to act other than on unjustified terms now proposed, or perhaps insisted upon, where these are inconsistent with the true agreement. It can thus involve indicating, that 'I will not be doing this at all', 'I will not be doing this in full'; or 'I will not be performing as originally agree because I intend to carry out the contract in my way, even though this might be substantially inconsistent with the contract."

在下面会介绍的 Mersey Steel & Iron Co. Ltd. v. Naylor, Benzon & Co. (1881 – 2) LR 9 Q. B. D. 648 先例,Bowen 大法官提到一些会或不会构成拒绝性违约的违约行为,如在一个长期合约,违约方不支付一笔或多笔分期付款。这显然本身是违约行为,但这个行为能否让无辜方认为违约方显示了意图他再也不会按照合约办事,进而可以终止合约？Bowen 大法官说这要看每个先例的不同情况而定:"Non – payment of itself is certainly not necessarily evidence of an intention no longer to be bound by the contract, but I do not say there might not be circumstances under which the Court would be entitled to draw that inference from it."

在 The "Pro Victor"先例,Flaux 大法官就把承租人(违约方)的不行动,也就是不

---

[18] 卖方(或买方)如果拒绝履行买卖合约,即使不说出来往往背后也是这个原因。否则,即使交付的货物质量不好,买方大可以索赔金钱损失,何必终止一个货价订得低利润大的合约?

回应船东对他是否会履行合约做出的询问或最后通牒(ultimatum),视为行动或不行动的拒绝性违约。一般而言,以行动拒绝履行合约通常都会涉及真正违约,如在买卖合约,约定的时间到了,但买方没有开出信用证或是卖方没有做出付运。这都是违反条件条文而构成是"违约/毁约"(repudiatory breach)。但如果开出信用证或做出付运是将来的合约责任,就很少会是违约方以行动来显示拒绝,通常会以语言。而语言如果不完全明确,可以把当时的情况与违约方的其他行动来整体考虑。通常,如果只能以违约方的行动构成拒绝性违约为由终止合约,是不太容易成功。毕竟语言容易把话说死,但很少会有行动可以清楚与不可扭转地显示将来不会履行。估计在早期通讯不太容易,行为的拒绝比语言拒绝更多。在 Mersey Steel & Iron Co. Ltd. v. Naylor, Benzon & Co. 先例,George Jessel 大法官说:"There may, indeed, be a case where one party says in so many words that he does not intend to go on with the contract, but generally you must infer the intention from the acts of the parties."

但在今天通讯如此容易的情况下,绝大部分涉及拒绝性违约的案件都是根据或主要根据语言上的拒绝。如在 The "Bulk Uruguay" (2014) 2 Lloyd's Rep. 66 先例,涉及一个三年半的期租合约,租约允许通过亚丁湾,而当时由于海盗的风险,不少船东是有保留。在该先例中,船东实际上是二船东,在与原船东的租约中,是需要取得原船东的批准才可以行走亚丁湾。但在这一先例的期租合约,虽然租约还有 Conwartime 2004(战争条文)与 Bimco Piracy Clause(海盗条文),但最后仲裁庭对租约整体解释还是认为承租人可以无条件行走亚丁湾。该船舶在交船的第一个航次要通过亚丁湾从菲律宾去大西洋,二船东取得原船东的批准去行走,但原船东声明这批准只针对这一航次。二船东就把同样的话转给承租人,说明以后行走亚丁湾要拿到原船东的批准。估计承租人是借机想从这个亏本的租约中脱身,就接受了二船东的拒绝性违约,并终止了租约。幸亏在该先例的租约仲裁庭的多数裁决是二船东这句话不足以显示其不愿意或不能够履行将来的合约责任,而且在全球营运的期租合约中,即使拒绝行走亚丁湾也不重要,[19]不能让承租人终止合约。

不止在笔者熟悉的领域,针对其他各种类别的合约履行说错话都会有同样的风险。如在 Dymocks Franchise Systems (NSW) Pty Ltd. v. Todd (2002) UKPC 50 先例,涉及书店的特许经营,特许经销商(franchisee)在发给授权方(franchisor)的传真中拒绝支付特许经营费(franchise fee)甚至威胁以后都不会支付的语言,以及表示将来不会参加任何授权方要求的推广活动的语言,被枢密院判是拒绝性违约。在苏格兰的 Miller Fabrications Ltd. v. J & D pierce (Contracts) Ltd. (2010) CSIH 27 先例,案情涉及建造合约,法院判是分分承包商要看到分承包商的银行信誉参考(bank reference)才会继续工作的语言构成拒绝性违约。

拒绝性违约有时也会表现为合约方没有能力(inability/unable)履约,这也会通

---

〔19〕 见本章之3.5段。

过违约方的语言或行动显示。正如 Delvin 大法官在 Universal Cargo Carriers Corp. v. Pedro Citati (1957) 1 Lloyd's Rep. 174 先例[20]所说:"Since a man must be both ready and willing to perform, a profession by words and conducts of inability is by itself enough to constitute renunciation."在拒绝性违约的构成上,合约一方显示不能够(inability)履约与其不愿意(unwilling)履约本质上并无区别。如合约一方对另一方说"I would like to but cannot"(我很愿意履约但不能),这无异于说"I will not"(我不会履约)。

这种拒绝性违约也是通过违约方的语言通常比较容易成立。但如果只能以违约方的行动(或不行动)构成拒绝性违约为由终止合约,是不太容易成功。因为行动往往不够明确与不能扭转(irrevocable)去说明违约方拒绝履行将来的合约责任。如在 Universal Cargo Carriers Corp. v. Pedro Citati 先例,船东指称承租人的行动与不行动(如没有指定发货人接受准备就绪通知书、没有备妥货物装船等)显示了他将来不能提供货物装船。船东以这构成拒绝性违约为由终止租约,但被法院判是不足够去显示。

另在 The "Hermosa"[21]先例,承租人指称船东的行为(如船舶状况不妥、修理延误、不允许承租人派检查员上船、不告知承租人有关修理的安排等)显示了船东将来不能履行该两年的期租合约,并终止租约。但这也被法院判是不足够去显示船东拒绝性违约。

上述提到的这种通过言行显示将来没有能力履约(inability to perform)的拒绝与本章第 4 段论及的"不可能"(impossibility)履行有相似之处,但其实有区别。主要在于,前者的判定须以所谓的预期违约发生时无辜方所掌握的事实与违约方的言行为依据,而不论对方此种不能履约(inability)的情况事后直至应该履约时是否有所改变。而后者的判定,即对方是否真正"不可能"(impossibility)履约,则须以当时及其后所发生的所有事实为准,这将在本章之 4.2 段有论述。

最明显与肯定的例子是违约方通过语言说明他没有能力履约,如卖方告知 FOB 买方没有货物付运,买方不必派船前往装港。这句话可能只是威胁希望提高货价,或是卖方自己收到错误的信息,而事实上装港完全有货可装。但买方依然可以依赖卖方的语言提前终止买卖合约,因为买方可否这样做纯粹看拒绝时的证据,也就是卖方的语言。至于后来卖方在抗辩时拿出证据证明他在装港有货装,在拒绝性违约中不加以考虑。但如果拒绝性违约不成立,因为证据不足去显示违约方拒绝履行,如 Universal Cargo Carriers Corp. v. Pedro Citati 先例,这样本来会败诉的买方就可能有一个替代诉因,根据事后找到的证据证明卖方根本没有货装,是第二种预期违约之"不可能"(impossibility)履约。

---

[20] 在本章之 3.5.2 段会有详细介绍。

[21] 在本章之 9.3 段有详细介绍。

3.2 构成拒绝性违约的用字要明确决绝

这方面可节录两位法官的名言,以显示其要求。首先是 Coleridge 勋爵在 Freeth & Anr. v. Burr (1873 – 74) L. R. 9 C. P. 208 先例中说:"... whether the acts or conduct of the one do or do not amount to an intimation of an intention to abandon and altogether torefuse performance of the contract."另是在 Mersey Steel & Iron Co. Ltd. v. Naylor, Benzon & Co. (1884) L. R. 9 App. Cas. 434 先例,Selborne 伯爵也说:"... an absolute refusal to perform the contract, such as would amount to a rescission if he (the guilty party) had the power to rescind."

比较近期的是 Wilberforce 勋爵在著名的 Woodar Investment Development Ltd. v. Wimpey Construction UK Ltd. (1980) 1 WLR 277 先例说:"... repudiation is a drastic conclusion which should only be held to arise in clear cases of a refusal to perform obligations. ..."

可见,用字上决绝(final)与不可扭转(irrevocable)才构成拒绝性违约。这表示在争议时,双方互施压力,也不要把话说死,尤其是在知道自己的立场不一定正确的情况下。例如,只说"考虑"或"将会",这不是"拒绝"。因为"考虑"之后,将来可能会回心转意去履约。又如,只提出一些解决当前问题的建议,一般也不被当做拒绝。即使这建议不太可能被对方接受(如建议对方/买方加价 20%,因为货价涨了,提供货物有困难),因为没有说死,对方如果不接受,也不会继续履行。当然这并不代表如果在履行的过程中遇到困难,如市场急剧变化,不应该与对方协商与谈判。只是在协商与谈判的过程中要小心,避免需要承担"次要合约责任"(secondary obligation),就是对这一违约产生的损失向无辜方做出金钱上的赔偿。正如 Devlin 大法官在 Universal Cargo Carriers Corp. v. Pedro Citati (1957) 1 Lloyd's Rep. 174 先例里描述的"artful enough to conceal his state of mind or obstinate enough not to admit his inability"。有水平的合约方在确实没有办法履行合约的困境时,会让对方明白自己的困难和立场,但仔细分析又留有余地,有机会去争辩不是决绝与不能扭转。如果不警觉与水平不够,很可能会掉进陷阱,从占据有利地位的一方变为违约方。如直白说"我不再履行了,大家有机会再合作",只会让自己在违约/毁约的责任毫无可抗辩之处,在将来的诉讼中也肯定处于十分被动与不利的地位。

这种争议涉及分析与推敲违约方的言行是否构成拒绝性违约或违约/毁约,在本章介绍的很多有关拒绝性违约的先例中会涉及。在这里只先介绍三个先例以显示重要性。第一个是 The"Lutetian" (1982) 2 Lloyd's Rep. 140 先例。该先例是关于船东在期租合约中撤船(这是代表终止租约的行为)的争议。船东如果说"我撤船",这是错误的言行,并会构成拒绝性违约。但如果船东说"我将(shall)撤船",这只是表达对"将来"的意图,有可能会改变与没有说死。该先例中,Bingham 大法官说:"Mr. Hallgarten(承租人大律师) contended that the Owners' telex... was repudiatory because it was properly to be read as an unconditional announcement that the vessel was or would be withdrawn ... The language used by the Owners was, however, this: 'We confirm that we shall withdraw the vessel from Charterers' service as per our telex of 18th July 1980. ' While I am not altogether surprised at the Charterers' reactions, the Owners are in my view entitled to rely on the fact that the intention was expressed in the future, not the present, tense, and further on the fact that they expressly referred to their earlier telex which had concluded: 'Failing your payment(指租金) **we shall exercise our right of withdrawing the vessel** without any further notice. ' I cannot accordingly construe the later telex as meaning that the vessel was withdrawn, or that it would be withdrawn, whether or not the full sum was paid within the three-day period. "(加黑部分是笔者的强调)

另一个是上诉庭的 The "Hazelmoor" (1980) 2 Lloyd's Rep. 351 先例,该先例涉及一艘二手船舶的买卖。买卖合约是在 1977 年 10 月 21 日订立,买方在 1977 年 11 月 8 日支付了 10% 的定金。但之后船价大跌,在 1978 年 1 月 19 日,买方写信给卖方说在融资方面(通常船东需要银行融资才能支付剩下的 90% 船价)遇到了问题:"... use every endeavor to secure alternative finance and if successful inform sellers accordingly, however, our recent experience does not give us any great encouragement at least in the immediate future."

卖方回信要求买方尽力取得融资,并且允许买方转卖给任何其他的人士。在该先例看来,买卖双方原来不想很快转卖该船舶给其他外国买方。显然,如果可以马上转售该船舶,即使市场下跌导致转卖的船价有亏损,买方也只需要支付中间的差价,这笔金额显然较低。当然,这样买方既没有船又要支付一大笔钱,可以说"赔了夫人又折兵",但这是他看错市场的代价。

1978 年 1 月 26 日,买方的回复中提到希望能找到下一手买家,说:"... Our immediate consideration is to endeavor to solve the situation whereby (卖方) are in no way financially affected by our present position ... The obvious way to achieve a financially satisfactory answer... is to resell the vessel at a price which will result in(卖方) receiving the full purchase price ... and we thank(卖方) for advising us to do so."

但到了 1 月 27 日与 2 月 1 日,卖方通过电传与信件表示接受买方的预期违约,并在市场上试图出售 Hazelmoor 轮给其他的买家。2 月 3 日,买方否认其有任何的违约/毁约言行,并指称是卖方错误终止合约,并要求卖方退还 10% 船价的定金。到了 2 月 20 日,卖方把 Hazelmoor 轮以不到原合约一半的船舶价格出售给了新买方。卖方开始诉讼程序,指称买方 1 月 19 日与 1 月 26 日的信件显示了买方不愿意继续履行的意图,构成拒绝性违约并要求买方赔偿损失。一审法院与上诉庭都判是买方 1 月 19 日与 1 月 26 日的信件不构成拒绝性违约。上诉庭的 Megaw 大法官分析 1 月 19 日的信件,说:"I would hold, in agreement with Mr. Justice Lloyd, that on that ground, apart from any other, the letter of Jan. 19 at the time when it was received did not give rise, and could not fairly or sensibly have been treated by the plaintiffs(卖方)

as giving rise, to a right to treat the contract as having been repudiated in anticipation by an assertion of inability to perform."

针对1月26日的信件,Megaw大法官说:"If I am right in the view which I have expressed that the plaintiffs in their letter of Jan. 24 were accepting as honest, and were encouraging the defendants to continue in, their encouraging the defendants to continue in, their declared intention to use every endeavor to secure alternative finance, there was nothing that I can see in the defendants' letter of Jan. 26 to suggest that the defendants (买方), during the lapse of two days, had abandoned their intention or had become disabled from performing it, or that the plaintiffs, as reasonable persons, should have so understood."

Megaw大法官接着说:"Is it then a clear, or a permissible, inference from these letters that the defendants were saying, expressly or by implication, that they would not be able to fill the unquantifiable gap – to provide the balance between the contract price less £ 21,500 and the resale price whatever it might be – from their own resources or any resources that they could find and use? I do not see how any such conclusion could be drawn; certainly not as being shown clearly and unequivocally by the letters. ... The plaintiffs have to show that the defendants themselves clearly asserted their inability to perform – to find the necessary money when it should become due to be paid. I think they fall short of showing any such thing."

要小心的是,违约方如果在用字上只是提出要求或没有说死,往往不一定构成拒绝性违约。在Jaks v. Cera Investment (1998) 2 Lloyd's Rep. 89先例,涉及一个已经开出的信用证,受益人是买卖合约的卖方(原告)。1995年8月23日,开证银行(被告)通过代理人(通知银行)告诉卖方,在开证人/买方的要求下取消该信用证,并要求受益人尽快同意,说:"At applicant's(买方)request we herewith cancel above – mentioned documentary credit ... Please urgently obtain beneficiaries agreement with cancellation of the credit and confirm this agreement to us by tested telex."

通知银行把开证银行的电文转发给了受益人,说:"Attached is copy telex from Belgium(开证银行是比利时的)requesting cancellation of the letter of credit of US $2,970,000 in your favour. Please confirm your agreement ...."

9月4日,开证银行又追问受益人说:"We refer to our message dated 23rd August requesting cancellation of your letter of credit ... Please inform us about the present status of our request of cancellation for said letter of credit."

9月12日,受益人回复开证银行,实质上是接受了违约/毁约,说:"Reference your fax dated 23rd August 1995 ... We hereby confirm that we do not agree to cancel this credit... The credit was established subject to ... UCP 500. Please take guidance from article 9d(1) which clearly stipulates that letter of credit cannot be unilaterally cancelled by the issuing bank. Hence we have been asked by the beneficiary(这是因为该信用证被转让,所以另有分卖方的受益人)of the credit to convey to you that your action in cancelling the credit was ultra vires. By your action you have precluded the beneficiary from completing the shipment in time, plus they have suffered financial losses and demand that an amount of US $ 195,000 be paid to compensate the loss which has taken place due to cancellation of the letter of credit. . . ”

之后受益人的卖方向开证银行提起诉讼,要求英国法院作出“简易判决”(summary judgment)。但这被英国高院拒绝,认为开证银行的语言并不足够构成拒绝性违约。Moore-Bick 大法官说:“The authorities show that repudiation is not lightly to be inferred and that it is necessary for the Court to find a clear and unequivocal refusal to perform. They also make it clear that an ambiguous statement will not do, and nor in my judgment will a statement which merely casts doubt, even grave doubt, on the party’s willingness to perform. . . Taken alone the defendants’ telex in my view is not so clear as to amount to an absolute refusal to perform. I accept that it is unfortunately worded, and perhaps unfortunately constructed, but read as a whole it seems to me that it is inviting the beneficiaries’ agreement to cancellation. It is not stating an unequivocal refusal to perform. ”

毕竟现在拒绝性违约(特别是通过不当/错误的语言)的情况实是太多了,大部分情况是被利用来终止合约。而且,这方面如果了解不深,没有合约法概念,英文水平不足的人士危险很大。在一个高利润的长期合约中,他们很容易被对方激怒或是诱导,导致不知轻重的讲错话。这即会被对方利用,“接受”了拒绝性违约后才慢慢另谈新条件来重新订立原合约,或是干脆赖掉。这终止的理由不是受阻,也不是破坏条件条文,而往往就是预期违约/拒绝性违约。

3.3　拒绝性违约是否为违约的疑点

这一问题经常受到质疑。真正违约也就是违反了合约中做出的承诺,这是已经发生的事实(past fact)。相比之下,拒绝性违约就会有疑问。违约方到底违反了哪一个合约承诺,毕竟合约承诺的是将来的事情。即使能够完全明确(对将来的事情不可能做到),到将来真正需要履行时,违约方也不会履行,从而构成真正违约,也很难说为什么这一将来的违约可以在无辜方“接受”(accept)后提前与加速(accelerate)变成一个现在的违约并且可以提前索赔损失。毕竟,发生拒绝性违约言行时与承诺的合约责任需要履行时总会有一段时间。在这段时间里,违约方可能回心转意,或只是吓唬人,最终还是乖乖履行合约责任。[22] 也可能在期间发生一些事情导致合约“受阻”(frustration)而自动终止,[23] 根本不会有真正违约发生。

〔22〕 见 Norwest Holst v. Harrison (1985) ICR 668 (CA)先例。

〔23〕 见 Avery v. Bowden (1855) 119 ER 647 先例。

另一个质疑是拒绝性违约,也就是发生了违约方的言行,一贯说法是本身根本不是违约,也不会是"诉因"(cause of action)。直到无辜方接受了这一拒绝,才会把这一拒绝变为违约或"拒绝性违约"(renunciatory breach)。这才带来有一个无辜方可以索赔损失的诉因。这方面权威性的判决与说法很多,其中最有名的就是Asquith大法官在Howard v. Pickford Tool Co. Ltd. (1951) 1 KB 417先例中所说,较早前没有被无辜方接受的预期违约就好像"没有发生过的镜花水月"(a thing writ in water)。

但这样就十分奇怪并且与一般大家理解的违约不同。违约应该属于单方面的行为,违约方单方面不履行合约责任或没有按照合约履行就构成违约。怎么会是需要通过无辜方接受才会把违约方的行动"变为"(convert)违约,而如果无辜方不接受就等于违约方的不当言行就不算违约呢?难怪Simon勋爵在Heyman v. Darwin (1942) AC 356先例就节录了Scrutton大法官在Golding v. London & Edinburgh Insurance Co. , Ltd. (1932) 43 Lloyd's Rep. 487先例中的疑问:"I have never been able to understand, what effect the repudiation of one party has unless the other party accepts the repudiation."

这一疑问甚至一些近期的先例还在探讨或试图自圆其说,如有说法是违约方拒绝的言行实际上是一个违约,只是针对损失的诉因直到无辜方接受之后才明确。Dillon大法官在Tilcon Ltd. v. Land & Real Estate Investments Ltd. (1987) 1 WLR 46 (CA)先例中说:"The election to treat the contract as repudiated as a result of those facts is a matter going to remedy rather than a fresh fact necessary to complete a new cause of action."Rix大法官在Manx Electricity Authority v. J P Morgan Chase Bank (2003) EWCA Civ 1324先例中,也对构成违约的言行与索赔损失的诉因进行了区分。而索赔损失的诉因是在无辜方接受了拒绝后才出现。

但即使是一些自圆其说的说法也不完全讲通,因为的确有不少接受拒绝性违约去终止合约也没有索赔损失。有可能是无辜方并没有损失,只是借这个机会从合约中脱身。但现代的说法就接近真正违约了,而违反的是条件条文或违反了中间条文并造成严重后果,这导致无辜方除了可以索赔金钱损失外的额外权利,也可以"选择"(elect)是否"确认"(affirm)或"取消"(cancel)合约。换言之,拒绝性违约需要"接受"(acceptance)去完成合约的终止,这与真正违约的"选择"(election)同义。至于两种不同类别的违约,需要通过无辜方接受或选择取消才会终止合约,完全可以理解。否则,如果一旦发生拒绝性违约或严重的真正违约,合约就像"受阻"(frustration)一样自动终止,就会太善待违约方,让他主宰合约终止的单方面权利。这严重违反英国普通法下法律默示与政策性的说法,就是违约方不能通过自己的过错获利。毕竟,会有不少情况无辜方不愿意接受或选择终止合约,因为没有办法证明金钱损失或是无辜方因为各种原因必须让这个合约履行下去。毕竟,面对一个拒绝性违约的无辜方,完全可以不接受并向法院申请"履约指令"(specific performance):Khatijabai

Jiwa Hasham v. Zenab (1960) AC 316 先例。这个问题在这里只是稍作解释,稍后在本章之3.11段会有详论。根据同样的道理,无辜方也可以向法院申请"禁令"(injunction),这在近期的 Berkeley Community Villages Ltd. v. Pullen (2007) EWHC 1330 (Ch)先例有支持的说法。

但两种违约还是有不同,如果不接受拒绝性违约就根本不存在索赔损失,而"没有发生过的镜花水月"这句名言还是经常被引用。但在真正违约,如果无辜方确认合约或不做出任何选择,他对较早前的违约的事实还是可以索赔金钱的损失,[24]唯一失去的只是取消合约的权利。所以,拒绝性违约不是真正违约,而应是另外一个类别。

但拒绝性违约的法律地位在普通法中已经根深蒂固,不可能否定。不止是英国,已经有无数涉及这一课题的先例(部分会在接下来进行介绍),其他普通法国家也有许多明确的先例甚至是立法。例如,新西兰的《Contractual Remedies Act》之 Section 7 (3)(c),说:"Subject to this Act, but without prejudice to subsection (2), a party to a contract may cancel it if—...(c) it is clear that a term in the contract will be broken by another party to that contract."

在美国《Uniform Commercial Code》之 Article 2 – 610,说:"When either party repudiates the contractwith respect to a performance not yet due the loss of which will substantially impair the value of the contract to the other, the aggrieved party may...(c) in either case suspend his own performance ..."

不只是普通法,一些大陆法系很有影响的国际公约或国际认可的合约法原则也有同样的说法,如中国也承认的《联合国国际货物销售合同公约》(CISG,1980年)第五章第一节。[25]

---

〔24〕 只是针对较早违约所带来的直接损失,而不包括合约被终止的将来"估计利润"(loss of profit)或"交易损失"(loss of bargain)或"预期损失"(expectation loss)。

〔25〕 "第一节预期违反合同和分批交货合同第71条(1)如果订立合同后,另一方当事人由于下列原因显然将不履行其大部分重要责任,一方当事人可以中止履行责任:(a)他履行责任的能力或他的信用有严重缺陷;或(b)他在准备履行合同或履行合同中的行为。(2)如果卖方在上一款所述的理由明显化以前已将货物发运,他可以阻止将货物交给买方,即使买方持有其有权获得货物的单据。本款规定只与买方和卖方间对货物的权利有关。(3)中止履行责任的一方当事人不论是在货物发运前还是发运后,都必须立即通知另一方当事人,如经另一方当事人对履行责任提供充分保证,则他必须继续履行责任。第72条(1)如果在履行合同日期之前,明显看出一方当事人将根本违反合同,另一方当事人可以宣告合同无效。(2)如果时间许可,打算宣告合同无效的一方当事人必须向另一方当事人发出合理的通知,使他可以对履行责任提供充分保证。(3)如果另一方当事人已声明他将不履行其责任,则上一款的规定不适用。第73条(1)对于分批交付货物的合同,如果一方当事人不履行对任何一批货物的责任,便对该批货物构成根本违反合同,则另一方当事人可以宣告合同对该批货物无效。(2)如果一方当事人不履行对任何一批货物的责任,使另一方当事人有充分理由断定对今后各批货物将会发生根本违反合同,该另一方当事人可以在一段合理时间内宣告合同今后无效。(3)买方宣告合同对任何一批货物的交付为无效时,可以同时宣告合同对已交付的或今后交付的各批货物均为无效,如果各批货物是互相依存的,不能单独用于双方当事人在订立合同时所设想的目的。"

另在《The Principles Of European ContractLaw 2002》，相关部分节录如下："［Article 8:103 – Fundamental Non-Performance］A non-performance of an obligation is fundamental to the contract if：（a） strict compliance with the obligation is of the essence of the contract；or（b） the non – performance substantially deprives the aggrieved party of what it was entitled to expect under the contract，unless the other party did not foresee and could notreasonably have foreseen that result；or（c） the non – performance is intentional and gives the aggrieved party reason to believe thatit cannot rely on the other party's **future performance.** "（加黑部分就是针对预期违约）

在《UNIDROIT Principlesof International Commercial Contract 2010》，相关部分节录如下："ARTICLE 7.3.3 （ANTICIPATORY NON – PERFORMANCE）Where prior to the date for performance by one of the parties it is clear that there will be a fundamental non – performance by that party，the other party may terminate the contract. "

3.4 拒绝性违约的历史

上诉庭的 Hochster v. De la Tour（1853）118 ER 922 先例是拒绝性违约的第一个权威性先例，并带来了之后的无数先例。在这之前也不是没有这方面的先例，但法院并没有深入考虑，并创立这种类别违约的理论。这就是如果合约一方在履约前提前向另一方说"我不干了"，这句话是否有后果？毕竟这句话很可能只是赌气，只要等到真正需要履约时，他完全有可能改变想法并履行合约。但在 Hochster v. De la Tour 先例，明确了这句话或类似的言行可以有严重后果，也就是创立了这一"拒绝性违约"（renunciatory breach）的理论。正如 Flaux 大法官在 The "Pro Victor"（2010）2 Lloyd's Rep. 158 先例提到这一段历史，说："I said that it was after Hochster v. De la Tour that renunciation established itself as the favourite，because until then it was not certain that a man who said 'I will not perform' would be held to his word. In Hochster v. De la Tour it was argued that he could change his mind，and that the fact that at one time he said he was not ready and willing did not necessarily mean that he would be unwilling when the time for performance came. Hochster v. De la Tour established that a renunciation，when acted upon，became final. Thus，if a man proclaimed by words or conduct an inability to perform，the other party could safely act upon it without having to prove that when the time for performance came the inability was still effective. "

在 Hochster v. De la Tour 先例中有提及一些早期的案例。其中在 Planche v. Colburn（1831）131 ER 305 先例，案情涉及被告与原告订立合约出版书籍，当原告完成全部的书稿后，被告会支付 100 英镑。在原告已经做了很多工作但尚未完成书稿时，被告修改了出版计划，计划将原告写的这本书在另一个面对完全不同的读者的系列丛书中出版。被告表示，如果原告不同意，他就不会支付 100 英镑或者对原告已做工作支付任何报酬。原告拒绝接受修改的出版计划，并起诉被告要求已做工作的赔偿。法院及陪审团最后判是被告要向原告支付 50 英镑。但在该先例，这 50 英镑的赔偿到底是因为违约、债务还是按劳计酬(quantum meruit),并不清楚。并且该先例也没有涉及任何被告支付100英镑(或其他金额)的责任能否在需要履行之前就被视为违约的争论,因此也没有创立任何拒绝性违约的理论。

不久之后,Parke B 大法官在 Phillpotts v. Evans(1839)151 ER 200 先例与 Ripley v. McClure(1849)154 ER 1245 先例更是提到在需要履行的日期前拒绝履行的言行本身并不是违约,也不代表什么。这两个先例的情况在今天的国际货物买卖也经常会发生,案情涉及在货物运送途中,买方告诉卖方拒绝收货。卖方没有接受或理会这个拒绝,船舶开去了卸港要求买方收货,买方依然拒绝,这就从一个拒绝性违约变为了"不履行"(non - performance)的真正违约。因为如果买方不合作,卖方就交不了货,合约也就履行不下去,这与较早在运送途中的拒绝很不一样。Parke B 大法官在 Phillpotts v. Evans 先例说这个拒绝性违约是"空的"(nullity),另在 Ripley v. McClure 先例的判词中针对之前的拒绝性违约说:"... to constitute a breach of the contract, a refusal at any time was insufficient; that it must be a refusal after the arrival of the cargo; and that the supposed refusal in July, ... which was long before the contract to buy became absolute, was no breach, and nothing more than an expression of an intention to break the contract, not final, and capable of being retracted."

Hochster v. De la Tour 先例的案情很简单,被告在1852年4月12日与原告订立合约,雇佣原告作为3个月的信差去欧洲,开始履约的日期是6月1日。但在5月1日,被告通知原告说有改变,不再需要他的服务。原告在5月22日提起诉讼,但在6月1日之前,原告就已经找到了另一份有同样报酬的替代工作,但这替代的工作从7月4日才开始。在法院,原告胜诉并获得期间(6月1日到7月4日)的损失赔偿。在该先例中,主要的争议来自原告,即法律究竟是否可以让违反一个将来才需要履行的合约承诺提前变为违约(whether in law it is possible to break a contract before the day for its performance comes)。显然直到那时,还没有权威先例支持这一看法。在该先例中,Campbell 勋爵不接受作为无辜方的原告只能等到合约需要被履行的一刻,并认为有个很重要的政策性理由可以提前允许原告终止合约并减少损失,说:"Instead of remaining idle and laying out money in preparations which must be useless, he(无辜方的原告)is at liberty to seek service under another employer, which would go in mitigation of the damages to which he would otherwise be entitled for a breach of the contract."

Campbell 勋爵也不接受被告的说法,就是他拒绝的言行只是一个"终止合约的要约"(offer to rescind)。也就是原告如果接受,就等于双方同意终止合约。显然这不涉及任何损失的赔偿,纯粹是根据双方的意愿令合约产生与终止的问题。而如果原告不接受,合约继续存在并需要履行,毕竟原告可能回心转意。显然这一说法对无辜方的原告很不公平,如果原告接受这一要约,就等于失去了索赔金钱损失的权利。而如果原告不接受这一要约,要到合约需要履行的6月1日被告还是坚持不履行,也就是变为一个真正违约时,才能索赔损失。这显然不符合 Campbell 勋爵认为要允许原告提前终止合约并减少损失的政策性理由。

最后 Campbell 勋爵创立了"默示承诺"(implied promise)[26]的说法,并指称被告拒绝的言行违反了这一默示承诺,可让允许无辜方提前终止合约,说:"Where there is a contract to do an act on a future day, there is a relation constituted between the parties in the meantime by the contract, and that **they impliedly promise that in the meantime neither will do any thing to the prejudice of the other inconsistent with that relation.**"(加黑部分就是所谓的默示承诺或默示条件,而违约方一旦做出拒绝的言行,就是违反了有关合约的默示承诺或条件。)

在该先例中,Campbell 勋爵看来也认同要构成拒绝性违约必须要原来合约终止,让无辜方不需要再履行他将来需要承担的合约责任,才可以索赔损失。虽然该先例没有针对这些具体分析,但笔者认为这样的说法也是理所当然。第一,如果预期违约的说法是因为政策上要无辜方减少损失,显然需要让原来的合约终止后,他才能这样做。例如在该先例,寻找一份替代的工作。如果原来的合约没有终止,无辜方还是受到约束并需要准备履行,减少损失与避免浪费就无从说起。第二,也是通过终止合约才让违约方有诉因去索赔损失。如果合约还存在时,无辜方就可以索赔损失,到了合约应该履行的一天,违约方还是不履行,岂不是无辜方可以再索赔一次损失?又或者是到了合约应该履行的一天,违约方回心转意去履行,违约方是否可以向无辜方要回之前支付的损失?这显然说不通。总而言之,Campbell 勋爵在该先例的判法,为拒绝性违约或者整个预期违约要无辜方接受终止合约才能索赔损失埋下了种子。接下来的 Avery v. Bowden (1855) 119 ER 647 先例中,Campbell 勋爵对这一说法有了定论。

在 Avery v. Bowden 先例,案情涉及程租合约,要求一艘悬挂英国旗的船舶在 Odessa港装货,船舶是在 1854 年 3 月 11 日抵达装港。但在接下来的几天内,船长与承租人在装港的代理的通讯中被告知,没有货物在装港,要求船舶开航。到了 4 月 1 日,英国(船旗国)与俄罗斯宣布开战,这显然是即时导致租约受阻(frustration)而自动终止。船长还是继续要求与等待货物,并在 4 月 17 日开航。而当时约定的装货时间还没有届满,所以承租人不严格算是已经真正违约。船东事后向承租人索赔损失,主要是依赖被告的代理人在 3 月中告知船长没有货物并要求船舶开航。Campbell 勋爵在一审判是代理人的言行并不严格是拒绝性违约,换言之原告的船东败诉,因为租

[26] 在当时的年代,默示地位或条文很随意地被法院强加在合约,使合约变得更加合理。但后来,就开始有先例收紧,必须满足各种要求才会进行默示,如在 The "Moorcock" (1889) 14 PD 64 先例,要求必须(necessary)增加这一默示才能令合约有商业效力(business efficacy),否则不应该默示。如果以今天对默示地位的要求来判,Hochster v. De la Tour 先例不一定可以满足,或即使可以默示,违反的后果也不一定与拒绝性违约一致。但这已经是历史,不再重要。关于默示条文的具体介绍,请看笔者《合约的解释:规则与应用》第七章。

约是由于英国与俄罗斯开战造成受阻而自动终止。这一判决之后也被上诉庭支持。被告另一个争议是，即使3月中代理人的言行是可以构成拒绝性违约，船东也没有接受并终止合约。这被 Campbell 勋爵接受，说："According to our decision in Hochster v. De La Tour (2 E. & B. 678), to which we adhere, if the defendant, within the running days and before the declaration of war, had positively informed the captain of The 'Lebanon'（船名）that no cargo had been provided or would be provided for him at Odessa, and that there was no use in his remaining there any longer, the captain might have treated this as a breach and renunciation of the contract; and thereupon, sailing away from Odessa, he might have loaded a cargo at a friendly port from another person; whereupon the plaintiff would have had a right to maintain an action on the charter party to recover damages equal to the loss he had sustained from the breach of contract on the part of the defendant. The language used by the defendant's agent before the declaration of war can hardly be considered as amounting to a renunciation of the contract: **but, if it had been much stronger, we conceive that it could not be considered as constituting a cause of action after the captain still continued to insist upon having a cargo in fulfilment of the charter party**."（加黑部分是笔者的强调）

这一"随口说说"（obiter dictum）很快就被接受为英国的法律：Barrick v. Buba (1857) 140 ER 536；Danube & Black Sea Railway & Kustendjie Harbour Co. Ltd. v. Xenos (1863) 142 ER 753 等先例。另在 Wilkinson v. Verity (1870－71) LR 6 CP 206 先例，案情涉及一个受托人侵占了托管的货物，在没有委托人的授权或知情下把货物出售给第三人，并拒绝把货物退还给委托人。Willes 大法官也是依赖了 Campbell 勋爵的"随口说说"，判受托人的侵占行为不构成违约直到被委托人所接受："of itself a violation and breach of the contract unless and until it was treated as such by the bailor."所以，6年时效的开始是要到了真正违约，也就是托管届满但受托人拒绝把货物退还给委托人才起算。

这一拒绝性违约必须要被无辜方接受的说法在 Frost v. Knight (1871－72) LR 7 Ex 111 先例，被 Cockburn 大法官总结如下：

"The promisee, if he pleases, may treat the notice of intention as inoperative, and await the time when the contract is to be executed, and then hold the other party responsible for all the consequences of non-performance[27]: but in that case he keeps the contract alive for the benefit of the other party as well as his own; he remains subject to all

〔27〕 无辜方可以不理会违约方拒绝履行合约的意图，如果等到合约需要履行时，违约方仍不履行合约，无辜方就可以要求违约方承担不履行合约的责任。

his own obligations and liabilities under it〔28〕, and enables the other party not only to complete the contract, if so advised, notwithstanding his previous repudiation of it, but also to take advantage of any supervening circumstance which would justify him in declining to complete it.〔29〕

On the other hand, the promisee may, if he thinks proper, treat the repudiation of the other party as a wrongful putting an end to the contract, and may at once bring his action as on a breach of it〔30〕; and in such action he will be entitled to such damages as would have arisen from the non - performance of the contract at the appointed time, subject, however, to abatement in respect of any circumstances which may have afforded him the means of mitigating his loss.〔31〕"

在 Johnstone v. Milling (1886) 16 QBD 460 (CA)先例,上诉庭进一步说:"A renunciation of a contract, or, in other words, a total refusal to perform it by one party before the time for performance arrives, does not, by itself, amount to a breach of contract but may be so acted upon and adopted by the other party as a rescission of the contract as to give an immediate right of action.... a declaration of intention by the promisor not to carry out the contract ... is not in itself and unless acted on by the promisee a breach of the contract; and that it only becomes a breach when it is converted by force of what follows it into a wrongful renunciation of the contract."

3.5 拒绝履行的是否需要是重要的合约责任

如果是"真正违约"(actual breach),要区分违约方违反的是"条件条文"(condition)、"保证条文"(warranty)或是"中间条文"(innominate term)与有否造成严重后果。众所周知,如果违反的是条件条文或违反中间条文并造成严重后果,无辜方就会有终止合约的选择权。但如果违反的只是保证条文或者违反中间条文没有造成严重后果,无辜方就只能索赔损失。〔32〕违反条件条文对商业人士最大的好处就是肯定性与可预测性。换言之,只要知道对方违反了条件条文,不论个别案件的后果严重与否,都可以安心地行使终止合约的权利。但在今天的合约责任,被法律(包括立法)与/或合约明确为条件条文的责任并不多,大量存在的是中间条文。在 1962 年 The "Hong Kong Fir"(1962) 2 QB 26 先例明确下来的中间条文,被视为属于一种"等着

〔28〕 但如果无辜方确认合约继续存在,那么不仅违约方需要继续履行自己的合约责任,无辜方也同样需要继续履行自己的合约责任。

〔29〕 虽然违约方之前曾经拒绝履行合约,但违约方仍可以回心转意选择继续履行合约,并且可以依赖后来发生的合法理由(如果有,如无辜方之后违约/毁约、合约受阻等)不再履行合约。

〔30〕 另一方面,无辜方也可以选择接受违约方的违约/毁约并终止合约,然后开始诉讼程序索赔违约/毁约的损失。

〔31〕 无辜方可以获得违约方拒绝履行造成的损失,但同时无辜方有减少损失的责任。

〔32〕 见杨良宜的《损失赔偿与救济》一书。

看结果”的规定(wait and see rule)。即要在每一个不同案件发生了违反中间条文,然后看它造成的后果。在很多有关的先例中,大同小异的说法是如果违约的后果导致无辜方严重地失去整个合约的利益(deprives the innocent party the whole benefit of the contract),或是触及了合约的根基(it goes so much to the root of the contract),或是使合约在商业上不可能继续履行(makes further commercial performance of the contract impossible),无辜方除了索赔金钱损失外,还可以终止合约。如在 The “Hong Kong Fir”先例中,判船舶适航的问题是属于中间条文。这表示直到真正发生了这种违约,才根据每个案子不同的案情判断到底违约的结果是否足够严重,达到合理让无辜方终止合约。例如,除了要看到底是什么不适航,即使是严重的船舶失修,但当时因为航运市场低落令船舶准备抛老锚,显然船舶的不适航就不会有严重后果。

违约方只是“显示了意图”(evinces an intention)将来拒绝履行合约或部分合约责任。由于针对的是将来的合约责任,不容易进行区分。违约方拒绝履行的到底是条件条文还是保证条文还比较容易区分,但如果拒绝履行的是中间条文,就无法估计将来如果发生,会否造成严重后果可让无辜方终止合约。当然,如果违约方是拒绝履行整个合约,这就等于合约中不论重要与否的条文都不会履行,这就不需要再进行区分,而是一个明显的拒绝性违约。例如,船东说我再也不维修船舶,这明显表达了拒绝履行部分合约责任。但事情发展下去也难说,可能顺顺利利、根本不维修船舶也可完成这份租约。

曾有说法是事无大小,违约方如果拒绝履行都会让无辜方终止合约。如在 Aktieselskabet Pitwood v. J. W. Baird & Co. Ltd. (1926) 24 Lloyd's Rep. 282 先例,法院判是:“If a man states he is not going to comply with the contractual stipulations, or any of them, and states so in advance, the other party is entitled to say: ‘Very well you are only going to perform something which I never agreed: I am going to treat myself as no longer bound.’ **It seems to me quite irrelevant that the party affecting to repudiate the contract is dealing with a matter which he thinks relatively unimportant, or which may in fact be unimportant.**”(加黑部分是笔者的强调)

但这一说法已经不再被接受。在 The “Nanfri” (1978) 1 Lloyd's Rep. 581 先例,一审的 Kerr 大法官就明确了这一点,说:“But Mr. Mustill(承租人代表大律师)... relied on two older decisions, one of the Privy Council and one of the Court of Appeal ... These are Clausen v. Canada Timber and Lands Ltd. (1923) 4 D. L. R. 751... and Aktieselskabet Pitwood v. J. W. Baird & Co. Ltd. (1926) 24 Ll. L. Rep. 282 ... Neither of these appears ever to have been judicially considered, nor are they referred to in any of the standard text – books. There was no time for lengthy argument on these cases before me, but I think that their approach is difficult, if not impossible, to reconcile with the approach in the Ross T. Smyth, James Shaffer, Sweet & Maxwell and Decro – Wall cases. In particular the Pitwood case suggests that an intimation by one party to commit what Lord Justice Atkin refers to as ‘only a little breach’ is nevertheless by itself sufficient to constitute a repudiation. I do not think that this accords with the modern view as illustrated in the cases to which I have referred; nor perhaps with the emergence of ' innominate terms', which are neither necessarily ' conditions' nor ' warranties' but whose character and effect depend on their gravity and consequences in all the circumstances: see Hongkong Fir Shipping Co. Ltd. v. Kawasaki Kisen Kaisha Ltd. , [1961] 2 Lloyd's Rep. 478. Nor do I think that this approach can be reconciled with the statement of Lord Wright in the Ross T. Smyth case in 1940 which I have already cited, where he refers to an honest misapprehension which is open to correction. The approach of the Court of Appeal in the Pitwood case would also appear to lead to the conclusion that an intimation that a party proposes to do something which on the true construction of the contract amounts to a' little breach' can be treated as a repudiation, whereas the actual breach would not. I think that I should follow the modern authorities. If a party can be seen to have the intention of performing the contract, but misconstrues it in a way which is not unreasonable, and in a respect which does not go to the roots of the contract but can be compensated by damages, then I do not think that he should be held to have repudiated the whole contract more or less accidentally."

3.5.1 拒绝履行的须是合约重要责任的权威说法

现在的说法是,拒绝的须是合约重要(substantial)与基本性(fundamental)责任才会构成拒绝性违约。针对这一点,《Chitty on Contracts》(第32版,2015年)一书之24-018段说:"... If one party evinces an intention not to perform or declares his inability to perform some, but not all, of his obligations under the contract, then the right of the other party to treat himself as discharged depends on whether the non-performance of those obligations will amount to a breach of a condition of the contract or deprive him of substantially the whole benefit which it was the intention of the parties that he should obtain from the obligations of the parties under the contract then remaining unperformed.[33] Words or conduct which do not amount to a renunciation will not justify a discharge."

另在《Halsbury's Law of England》(第5版,2012年)第546页说:"561**. Repudiation must go to the root of the contract.** Not every refusal by A to perform a part of the contract amounts to a repudiation which entitles the other party (B) to treat the contract as at an end;[34] there must be a refusal to perform something which goes to the root or

---

[33] 如果合约一方显示他不愿意或不能够履行部分但不是所有的合约责任,则合约另一方能否终止合约取决于不履行合约责任是否属于违反条件条文,或会剥夺其主要的合约利益。

[34] 并非合约方A拒绝履行任何合约责任都会构成违约/毁约,令对方B可以终止合约。因此,不是所有的延误履行合约都属于拒绝履行的违约/毁约,延误必须达到令合约受阻的程度。这方面最有代表性的是Universal Cargo Carriers Corp. v. Pedro Citati (1957) 1 Lloyd's Rep. 174先例,在本章之3.5.2段有介绍。

essence of the contract.[35] Thus it is not just any delay in breach of contract which amounts to a repudiation, but only such delay as would frustrate the adventure.[36]"

同样说法的先例有很多,如 Buckley 大法官在 Decro – Wall International SA v. Practitioners in Marketing Ltd. (1971) 1 WLR 361 先例也说:"Each party to an agreement is entitled to performance of the contract according to its terms in every particular, and any breach, however slight, which causes damage to the other party will afford a cause of action for damages; but not every breach, even if its continuance is threatened throughout the contract or remainder of its subsistence, will amount to a repudiation. **To constitute repudiation, the threatened breach must be such as to deprive the injured party of the benefit to which he is entitled under the contract.** The measure of the necessary degree of substantiality has been expressed in variety of ways in the cases. It has been said that **the breach must be an essential term**, or of **a fundamental terms of the contract**, or that it **must go to the root of the contract**. Various tests have been suggested. I venture to put the test in my own words as follows: 'will the consequences of the breach be such that it would be unfair for the injured party to hold him to the contract and leave him to his remedy in damages as and when a breach or breaches may occur?' If this would be so, then a repudiation has taken place."(加黑部分是笔者的强调)

Diplock 勋爵在 The "Afovos" (1983) 1 Lloyd's Rep. 335 先例也有同样的说法:"The doctrine of anticipatory breach is but a species of the genus repudiation and applies only to fundamental breach. If one party to a contract states expressly or by implication to the other party in advance that he will not be able to perform a particular primary obligation on his part under the contract when the time for performance arrives, the question whether the other party may elect to treat the statement as a repudiation depends upon whether the threatened non – performance would **have the effect of depriving that other party of substantially the whole benefit** which it was the intention of the parties that he should obtain from the primary obligations of the parties under the contract then remaining unperformed. If it would not have that effect there is no repudiation, and the other party cannot elect to put an end to such primary obligations remaining to be performed. **The non-performance threatened must itselfsatisfy the criteria of a fundamental breach**... Similarly where a party to a contract, whether by failure to take timeous action or by any other default, has put it out of his power to perform a particular primary obligation, the right of the other party to elect to treat this as a repudiation of the contract by

---

〔35〕 拒绝履行的必须触及合约的根基或是合约的重要部分。

〔36〕 因此不是所有的延误履行合约都属于拒绝履行的违约/毁约,延误必须达到令合约受阻的程度。

conduct depends upon whether the resulting **non-performance would amount to a fundamental breach**."(加黑部分是笔者的强调)

至于要达到上面所讲的"essential breach"或"fundamental breach"到底要有怎样的严重性,一般来说是与中间条文是否有严重后果的考验一样,需要严重至允许终止合约的程度。这可节录《Halsbury's Law of England》(第5版,2012年)第539页,如下:

"**555. General requirement of substantial failure to perform.** The general requirement to be met before there is a right to terminate for defective performance is that the breach in question amounts to a substantial failure to perform. This may be expressed in a number of ways (which are also employed to determine whether there has been a repudiation), such as whether the breach goes to the root of the contract, or frustrates the purpose of the innocent party in making the contract, or deprives the innocent party of substantially the whole benefit of the contract, but such expressions provide no indication of precisely when a breach will be found to have reached the necessary level of seriousness.

Among the factors which the courts may take into account are the following:

(1) the extent of the failure to perform when assessed against the performance undertaken; thus, the court did not regard the failure to perform as substantial where one (the sixteenth) out of a potential 66 instalments of goods was defective; by contrast, it was a substantial failure where a buyer refused without justification to accept one of two instalments of oil. Such cases may also be analysed as turning on repudiation by the party in default;

(2) where a failure to perform has created uncertainty as to future performance, for example where the buyer fails to pay a deposit. Again, such cases may also be analysed as turning on repudiation by the party in default;

(3) whether, if the innocent party is confined to damages, that would be an adequate remedy;

(4) the fact that a breach is deliberate is not of itself sufficient but it is a factor which may taken into account as evidence of an intention no longer to be bound by the contract, and support a claim of repudiation.

The courts may decline to find that a failure to perform was substantial if the innocent party has an ulterior motive for termination[37], or termination would result in the unjust enrichment of the innocent party.

〔37〕 这一句的说法与本章之3.6.1段最后节录的《Halsbury's Law of England》(第5版,2012年)第556页脚注18有不同。另可见本章之3.6.2段有关无辜方主观知道违约方的言行并非拒绝履行。

Where, under an express provision for termination for breach, the breach must first reach a certain level of seriousness, or termination is subject to a period of notice to remedy the breach, a breach falling below that level or without the opportunity to remedy is 'unlikely' to amount to a repudiatory breach."

最后一提的是,拒绝性违约是否必须针对合约重要与基本性责任才会构成,也不是没有不同意见。如英国法律委员会曾在1993年关于《Contract Code》的建议(最终没有立法)中说:"Thus if a decorator, who has contracted with a householder to paint all the rooms in his new house and to return twelve months later to do any necessary touching up to them, announces upon the completion of the initial painting that he has no intention of returning to do the touching up, why should not the householder have to wait a year before suing for damages for breach? Accordingly, even where a party's anticipated breach is not sufficiently substantial [to constitute a ground for termination], the Code ... [should allow] the other party to sue immediately while at the same time completing his own performance, if indeed he has not already completed it."

3.5.2 拒绝履行合约中不重要的责任不能使无辜方终止合约

很早就已经有先例判是如果违约方拒绝履行的只是合约中一些不太重要的责任,无辜方不能以此为由终止合约。在 Johnstone v. Milling (1886) 16 QBD 460 (CA)先例,房东表示他没有能力修理屋宇,这被判是不构成拒绝性违约,因为并没有影响整个约因/对价(go to the whole consideration)。在 Ellis & Co's Trustee v. Dixon - Johnson (1924) 2 Ch 451 (CA)先例,涉及一个股票经纪在没有授权且过早的情况下处理了小量的存放在他手里的股票,也是有同样的判法。

在较近期的 Universal Cargo Carriers Corp. v. Pedro Citati(1957)1 Lloyd's Rep. 174 先例中,更是对这一点有明确的判决。该先例也涉及常见的争议,就是租约下的船舶去了装港没有货装。有关的船舶 Catherine M. Goulandris 轮根据一个基于金康租约的程租合约去了伊拉克 Basrah 装港,准备装运6000吨废钢去南美。船舶在1951年7月12日抵达装港,但船长与船东代理没办法与承租人指定的发货人接触。这导致船东在7月18日把船舶另出租给从印度装矿砂去美国的一个替代航次。承租人于7月24日在美国的纽约法院(船东的管理人在美国)禁止船舶出租作其他用途。这一法院的命令于7月27日在双方同意下撤销,双方事后把有关的争议提交伦敦仲裁。而船东的立场是承租人拒绝履行合约,所以他是有权终止租约并把船舶在7月18日出租给其他承租人,并索赔有关的损失。船东的指控是包括:(1)承租人违反了租约的重要条文:没有指定接受准备就绪通知书(notice of readiness)的发货人;没有指定码头;没有提供货物;不能在约定的装货期内装完货;(2)承租人显示了拒绝履行租约的意图,属于预期违约,而船东接受了承租人的预期违约。

在伦敦仲裁,独任仲裁员判是承租人没有在合理时间内指定发货人是违反合约,但这不是条件条文。但承租人的行为(因为承租人口头没有做出任何拒绝)对船东来说足够构成拒绝性违约,包括没有指定发货人,船东调查也发觉岸上没有货待装等。但去了高院,Devlin 大法官认为所有准备待装的责任,包括货物要在约定的装货期内装完,[38]都只是属于保证条文而不是条件条文,所以不足以让船东有权终止租约。Devlin 大法官的判决被总结说:"No time being stipulated for carrying out the obligations preliminary to loading the cargo, such obligations had to be carried out so that the main duty of loading would be completed within the time prescribed; and that as, on the facts found, the cargo could not have been loaded in the lay time remaining after July 18, the charterer was in breach; but that such breaches were breaches of warranty and did not ipso facto entitle the owners to rescind."

至于没有在合理时间履行合约责任,Devlin 大法官说如果涉及保证条文,需要延误至合约受阻而不能只是不合理,才能终止合约,也就是判仲裁庭根据不合理延误判船东可以取消租约是错误:"An aggrieved party was nevertheless entitled to rescind if the delay in carrying out such obligation was so grave as to go to the root of the contract, i. e., such as to frustrate the object of the venture... accordingly, as it was clear from the award that the arbitrator had accepted 'reasonable time' as something less than the period required for frustration, he was wrong in finding that the delay was long enough to justify rescission."

船东也提出了另一替代的争议,即在 7 月 18 日,即使承租人没有拒绝履行合约(evince an intention not to perform),他也无法在租约受阻前履行合约,也就是不可能(impossible)履约的说法。虽然船东争辩说,他提供的证据已经足够推断承租人是不可能履约,但 Devlin 大法官认为仲裁庭认定的事实还不足够,并把裁决书"发还"(remit)给仲裁庭。这一先例也提出了上诉,但只是针对是否应该发还裁决书的问题。

在 Mersey Steel & Iron Co. Ltd. v. Naylor, Benzon & Co. (1881 – 2) LR 9 Q. B. D. 648 先例,上诉庭的 Bowen 大法官提到两种经常会出现的情况是否会构成违约/毁约或拒绝性违约。一种是违约方不支付合约规定的款项,另一种是货物买卖的分批付运但违约方不付运其中部分。Bowen 大法官这样说:[39]"Non – delivery of a single parcel would not be necessarily, of course, sufficient to intimate that the person who does not deliver intends no longer to be bound, but I am far from saying that non – delivery of a single parcel might not in particular contracts, and under particular circumstances, be sufficient. So as to non – payment. Non – payment of itself is certainly not

〔38〕 一般的延误,如未能在装货期内装完货物的违约,只是有金钱赔偿作为救济。双方通常约定"滞期费"(demurrage)的赔偿,若没有约定,则是"船期延误赔偿"(damage for detention)。这种延误不会让无辜方的船东有权终止租约,把船舶开走。

〔39〕 贵族院([1884] L. R. 9 App. Cas. 434)没有否定这个说法。

necessarily evidence of an intention no longer to be bound by the contract, but I do not say there might not be circumstances under which the Court would be entitled to draw that inference from it."

以下笔者会针对这两种常见的情况分别探讨。

3.5.3　没有准时或拒绝做出支付合约款项是否重要的探讨

首先看有关违约方没有准时做出支付或拒绝做出支付的情况。这种情况也很难说到底是否重要,要看每一个案件的不同情况,例如,其中一个重要的考虑是什么为本质的支付?如果支付涉及分期付款,除非有明示条文把准时支付提升为条件条文,一般被视为不重要。这导致违约方如果没有支付一两期或更多的分期付款或租金,[40]不一定被视为违反条件条文并构成违约/毁约。同样的道理,如果违约方告知无辜方他没有办法准时支付下一期的分期付款或租金,也不一定会构成拒绝性违约。这方面的先例不少,包括早期与近期的,笔者介绍部分代表性的先例。

第一个是 Withers v. Reynolds (1831) 109 ER 1370 先例,在该先例,买方不愿意对每一次付运的货物支付货款,而是要在倒数第二次付运后才一起支付。法院判是买方的行为是在没有获得卖方同意也没有合法理由的情况下,根本性地改写了合约,把原来规定要求支付现款变成了信贷(credit)。卖方可以认为买方的行为是拒绝履行。

第二个是 Decro-Wall International SA v. Practitioners in Marketing Ltd. (1971) 1 WLR 361 先例,英国独家经销商每次都迟付货款给法国生产商。上诉庭判是该独家经销商没有显示拒绝履行的意图。因为虽然每次都迟付,但法国生产商从来都没有担心过对方不付钱。而且英国法律中延误支付并非是重要(time is not of essence),所以,虽然英国独家经销商不断违约,但违约没有触及合约的根基,不构成拒绝性违约。

近期的有 Dalkia Utilities Services Plc. v. Celtech International Ltd. (2006)1 Lloyd's Rep. 599 先例,涉及一个15年分期付款的合约。期间违约方因为经济困难,没有支付3期分期付款,但高院的 Christopher Clarke 大法官判这不足以构成违约方拒绝履约或违约/毁约,说:"A party may be in repudiatory breach as a result of breaches that he has committed or indicated that he will commit or a combination of the two. As to the

---

[40]　例如涉及期租合约的租金支付,在 The "Brimnes" (1972) 2 Lloyd's Rep. 465 先例,一审的 Brandon 大法官认为多次迟交租金不属于违约/毁约,说:"The question whether the charterers' conduct in this respect was repudiatory or not is a question of fact and of degree. ... I am not satisfied that, on an objective view, their conduct in relation to late payment, although persisted in over a long time, went so far as this. For this reason I am not preparted to hold that the charterers repudiated the contract, so as to entitle the shipowners to treat it as at an end."上诉庭([1974] 2 Lloyd's Rep. 241)也支持了这个判决。这也不只是航运,其他合约的租金,如房屋的租金也是如此:Lombard North Central v. Butterworth (1987) 1 QB 527 先例。

former, Celtech(违约方)failed to pay the instalments due in respect of April, May and June. As to the latter, it never said that it would not perform its financial obligations under the agreement. But it made plain that it was in financial difficulties, was facing insolvency, and could not presently honour its obligations under the agreement as they fell due. It asked for a 6 month moratorium on the instalments due in respect of April, May and June upon the footing that it would make monthly payments of about £ 60,000 in order to satisfy them... I do not regard Celtech as having renounced or repudiated the agreement. The failure to pay the three instalments by 12th August 2003 did not amount to a breach of condition, nor did that failure, coupled with the statements made about its financial difficulties (in particular its inability 'presently' to pay) indicate that it intended to perform, or could only perform, in such a manner as would deprive Dalkia(无辜方) of substantially the whole benefit of the contract. Celtech did not evince an intention never to pay, although it skirted close to the wind by indicating, no doubt as a lever in the negotiations, that 'the current scenario can only lead Celtech International to bankruptcy' (23rd July) and that it was 'facing insolvency' (1st August)."

稍后在本章之6.2段会提到更近期有关分期付款的 Januzaj v. Valilas (2014) EWCA Civ 436 先例与其他有关期租合约下的租金支付的先例,看来英国法院开始重视没有支付只是延误或将不会支付的事实区分,而后者会被视为重要并会构成拒绝性违约的行为。

但如果支付的款项本质不同,加上有关合约的条文把准时支付明确为条件条文,违约方没有支付或拒绝支付,就会构成违约/毁约或拒绝性违约。在另一个近期的 The "Aktor" (2008) 2 Lloyd's Rep. 246 先例,案情涉及一艘二手船舶的买卖(以著名的挪威船舶买卖标准格式 NSF 93 为模板),有关的条文可节录如下:

"... the Sellers have agreed to sell, and ... [the Buyers] have agreed to buy ... the Vessel, on the following terms and conditions:

1. Purchase Price US $ 8,400,000 CASH ...

2. Deposit

As security for the correct fulfilment of this Agreement the Buyers shall pay a deposit of 10% ... of the Purchase Price within 3 ... banking days from the date of this Agreement being signed ... This deposit shall be placed with Sellers nominated Bank in Singapore and held by them in an interest earning joint account for the Sellers and the Buyers, to be released in accordance with joint written instructions of the Sellers and the Buyers. Interest, if any, to be credited to the Buyers. Any fee charged for the opening / holding the said account shall be borne equally by the Sellers and the Buyers.

3. Payment

The said Purchase Price together with extra payment for bunkers ROB and for luboils, against delivery documents . . . shall be paid in full free of bank charges to Sellers nominated bank ondelivery of the vessel, but not later than 3 banking days after the Vessel is in every respect physically ready for delivery . . .

. . .

13. Buyers' default

Should the Purchase Price not be paid in accordance with Clause 3, the Sellers have the right to cancel the Agreement in which case the deposit together with interest earned shall be released to the Sellers. . ."

但还没有交船(delivery)与过户(closing)前,双方就有了一个争议。卖家认为根据买卖合约的第 3 条,买方需要支付全数 840 万美金的船价加上燃油与银行手续费到卖方指定的希腊银行。如果买方没有全数支付,就违反了条件条文,卖方可以根据第 13 条取消合约并没收定金。但买方认为他只需要支付 90% 的船价加上燃油与银行手续费到希腊银行,因为在交船的一天同时签好一份指示新加坡银行把这笔 10% 的定金发放给卖方,也就完成了合约支付的责任。显然这对买方来说的好处就是可以减轻资金压力,毕竟船价的 10% 也不是小数目。

在二手船舶买卖通常的做法,可节录 Robert Goff 大法官在 The "Selene G" (1981) 2 Lloyd's Rep. 180 先例所说的:"The purchase money is paid, in normal circumstances, by the payment of 90 per cent of the price plus the release of the 10 per cent deposit from the deposit account on the authority of the buyers. Alternatively it could, in theory (and may sometimes in fact) be paid by payment of 100 per cent of the purchase price followed by a release of the deposit to the buyers by the sellers. But whichever way it is paid, in my judgment, the deposit of the 10 per cent of the price in no way constitutes a payment of purchase money or of part of the purchase money."

需要注意的是,Robert Goff 大法官在最后一句是说明 10% 的定金并非是支付船价的部分,两者的本质不同。但通常在二手船买卖,的确做法是买方只需要支付 90% 的船价加上把定金发放给卖方,但这只适用于存放定金与支付 90% 船价的是同一间银行的情况。在这一先例中,存放定金的是一家新加坡银行,但支付船价的是希腊银行。这里卖方抗拒买方的提议与坚持是有一定道理的,正如 Christopher Clarke 大法官在判决中说:"The parties cannot have contemplated that the sellers would be bound to make delivery of a valuable vessel without payment in full of the purchase price in accordance with the terms of the contract. Crediting the Sellers with some or all of the purchase price otherwise than at the place stipulated for payment would be likely to prevent redemption at the time of payment and out of the payment of any mortgage on the vessel, as would ordinarily be expected; and would expose the Sellers to the risk involved in transferring the monies from the non – contractual place, where or from which the Buyers purported to make payment, to the place agreed. Monies that pass through the banking system may become unavailable to the payee because of claims to the money, or claims to freeze the money, by banks or others."

买方也争辩说即使他错误理解有关买卖合约的条文与法律地位,这也不是一个重要条文,毕竟卖方肯定会收到全部船价。这方面可以节录如下:"The Buyers' third ground of appeal is that, even if they are wrong on the first two points, nevertheless the obligation to make payment in full at NBG, Piraeus was not a condition of the contract and the arbitrators erred in law in finding that it was. The Buyers' obligations in respect of the price covered a number of matters: what the price was, when it should be paid, how it should be paid, and where it should be paid. Some breaches of those obligations, such as a refusal to pay the full amount would entitle the Sellers to terminate. Others would not. Here there was no question of the Buyers not paying in full, or not paying when the vessel was ready for delivery. The only issue was as to where the 10% should be paid. The obligation to pay 10% at NBG, Piraeus, if that was what the Buyers were bound to do, is an innominate term. If the Buyers were wrong in saying that they were entitled to pay by releasing the deposit in Singapore, the Sellers would be entitled to recover any proved loss resulting from the 10% payment being made there and not at NBG, Piraeus. But they would not be entitled to throw up the whole contract."

但 Christopher Clarke 大法官不同意,认为根据 Bunge v. Tradax (1981) 2 Lloyd's Rep. 1 先例,全部准时支付船价是条件条文。所以在这一先例中,买方向卖方坚持只支付 90% 船价是构成了拒绝性违约,这被卖方接受,卖方除可以终止买卖合约外,也可以没收 10% 的定金。

3.5.4 分期交付或供应货物涉及部分违约是否重要的探讨

Bowen 大法官提到的另一个常见的情况是货物的交付或供应,这也会包括提供服务。在一些大宗货买卖或长期买卖/供应合约,经常会约定分期进行货物的交付或供应,甚至货价的结算也是针对每一期货物个别计算。这种中长期的合约经常由于各种理由发生违约,如卖方因为市场或供应短缺,没有或拒绝按时交付或供应。又或是卖方个别的交付或供应的货物是货不对版。反过来也有可能是买方没有按时支付已经交付的货物/已经提供的服务,正如上面介绍的 Dalkia Utilities Services Plc. v. Celtech International Ltd. (2006) 1 Lloyd's Rep. 599 先例。这带来的问题是,在这种可分开(divisible 或 severable)的合约中,[41] 如果拒绝履行可分开的部分合约责任,是否可被视为拒绝履行整个合约?这可节录《Halsbury's Law of England》(第 5 版,2012 年)第 547 页,如下:"Thus, if in a contract for the sale of goods to be delivered by instalments, which are to be separately paid for, the seller makes defective deliveries in respect of one or more instalments or the buyer neglects or refuses to take delivery of, or

---

[41] 关于完整(entire)或可分开合约的课题可看本书第二章第 8 段。

to pay for, one or more instalments, it is a question in each case, depending on the terms of the contract and the circumstances of the case, whether the breach is a repudiation of the whole contract, or whether it is a severable breach giving rise to a claim for compensation but not to a right to treat the whole contract as repudiated. **The main tests in deciding this issue are the ratio quantitatively which the breach bears to the contract as a whole and the degree of probability or improbability that such a breach will be repeated.** In relation to payment, if the breaches are such as to destroy the innocent party's confidence in the defaulting party's creditworthiness the breach will be treated as going to the root of the contract."

前述加黑部分是 Hewart 勋爵在 Maple Flock Co. Ltd. v. Universal Furniture Products (Wembley) Ltd. (1934) 1 KB 148 先例所说,是否为违约/毁约或拒绝性违约最重要的考虑是违约部分在整个合约数量上的比例。如在该先例中,判是其中一批货物货不对版不会构成对将来66 批货物的拒绝性违约。但相反在 Warinco AG v. Samor SpA (1979) 1 Lloyd's Rep. 450 CA 先例,总共只有两批石油,买方没有合理理由地拒绝接受第一批货物即被判是构成对整个合约的拒绝性违约。另一个重要考虑是这种违约会重复的可能性,正如 Bigham 大法官在 Millars' Karri and Jarrah Co. v. Weddel, Turner & Co. (1908) 14 Com Cas 25 先例中说:"If the breach is of such a kind or takes place in such circumstances as reasonably to lead to the inference that similar breaches will be committed in relation to subsequent deliveries, the whole contract may there and then be regarded as repudiated and may be rescinded."

英国已经有立法针对这个问题,在 1979 年《英国货物销售法》之 Section 31(2)规定:"Where there is a contract for the sale of goods to be delivered by stated instalments, which are to be separately paid for, and the seller makes defective deliveries in respect of one or more instalments, or the buyer neglects or refuses to take delivery of or pay for one or more instalments, it is a question in each case depending on the terms of the contract and the circumstances of the case whether the breach of contract is a repudiation of the whole contract or whether it is a severable breach giving rise to a claim for compensation but not to a right to treat the whole contract as repudiated."

这方面也介绍两个很早期的先例。首先是 Freeth & Anr. v. Burr (1873 – 74) L. R. 9 C. P. 208 先例。在该先例中,卖方卖给买方 250 吨生铁。其中 125 吨在 2 个星期内付运,其余 125 吨在 4 个星期内付运,货款在付运后 14 天内支付。之后市场不断上涨,卖方直到 6 个月后才付运了第一批 125 吨生铁。买方不肯支付货款,理由是因为卖方延误付运,他不得不另以更高价格购买替代货物,这批生铁的货款应与买方的损失抵销(set off)。另外,买方坚持卖方要付运剩下的 125 吨生铁。卖方没有做出付运,并声称买方拒绝支付第一批生铁的货款的行为是拒绝性违约。买方有能力支付货款是没有争议,而且事实上买方最后也做出了支付。法院判是买方拒绝支付第一批生铁货款的行为不构成拒绝性违约,因此,卖方不能以此理由终止合约而不付运第二批生铁,买方可以向卖方索赔他不付运第二批生铁的损失。Coleridge 大法官解释说:"... the mere non-payment for the first portion of the iron contracted for, unattended by any other act on the part of the purchasers, did not put an end to the contract so as to disentitle the purchasers to maintain an action for the non-delivery of the second portion, but only gave the seller a remedy by cross – action."

Keating 大法官也认为事实背景并不支持买方有拒绝履行的意图,说:"... looking at all the circumstances of this case – a rising market; a failure on the part of the defendant to deliver the iron according to the terms of the contract; a series of deliveries in small quantities long after the times for delivery provided for by the contract; and a refusal on the part of the plaintiffs to pay for the iron delivered, not only accompanied by remonstrances, but with a requisition to the seller to fix a day for the delivery of a certain quantity..."

第二个是 Mersey Steel & Iron Co. Ltd. v. Naylor, Benzon & Co. (1884) L. R. 9 App. Cas. 434 先例,案情涉及 5000 吨钢材的买卖。合约规定从 1881 年 1 月起每个月付运 1000 吨钢材,买方在每次付运后的 3 天内支付货款。卖方在 1 月做出了付运但数量大约只有合约约定的一半,买方在到期支付前,得知卖方正面临破产。买方的律师错误地建议说在这种情况,买方要获得法院命令再支付比较安全。于是买方拒绝支付货款并要求卖方向破产法院申请命令。卖方回复说,买方拒绝支付货款是拒绝履行合约,卖方不再需要履行合约责任。买方写信给刚被委任的卖方清盘人要求赔偿 1 月的付运中短缺的部分造成的损失,并清楚表示愿意继续履行合约以及接受其余 4 批的钢材,甚至可以考虑放弃索赔损失。卖方清盘人拒绝继续履行合约,并向买方提起诉讼,要求支付已经付运的钢材的货价,指称买方违约/毁约或拒绝性违约。但贵族院拒绝接受卖方清盘人的主张,认为买方的违约并不重要。Blackburn 勋爵说:"So far from the respondents(买方) saying that when the iron was brought in future they would not pay for it, they were always anxious to get it, and for a very good reason, that the price had risen high above the contract price. There was a statement that for reasons which they thought sufficient they were not willing to pay for the iron at present; and if that statement had been an absolute refusal to pay, saying, 'Because we have power to do wrong we will refuse to pay the money that we ought to pay,' I will not say that it might not have been evidence to go to the jury(早年的民事案件是由陪审团认定事实问题) for them to say whether it would not amount to a refusal to go on with the contract in future, for a man might reasonably so consider it. But there is nothing of that kind here; it was a bona fide statement, and a very plausible statement... Mr. Cohen(卖方代表律师) contended that whenever there was ... a breach of a material part of the contract... it necessarily went to the root of the matter. I cannot agree with that at all...

There was a delay in fulfilling the obligation to pay the money, it may have been with or without good reason (if that would have made any difference), but it did not go to the root or essence of the contract..."

3.5.5 不重要的违约或拒绝履行重复发生是否可以累积变为重要

因为有一个违约或拒绝履行的必须是重要(substantial)才能让无辜方终止合约,所以有不少先例质疑能否把过去曾发生多次的不重要(insubstantial)违约加在一起,看违约方会否持续拒绝将来同样的合约责任并变为重要,足以终止合约。这方面首先是 Donaldson 大法官在 The"Hermosa"(1982)1 Lloyd's Rep. 570 先例说:"Finally, there is the argument... that it is permissible to add together the actual breaches and the conduct which threatened further breaches in the future to yield a state of affairs amounting to a repudiation, even if the individual elements were not in themselves repudiatory. **Whether actual and anticipated breaches can be treated as cumulative** in this way has yet to be decided. I need say nothing about the matter here. I have rejected the argument on renounciatory breach, not because the breach which Nitrates anticipated was insubstantial, but because the conduct of MTC and the owners did not justify a firm inference that there would be a further breach. This being so, there is nothing to add to the actual breaches which had already occurred."(加黑部分是笔者的强调)

该先例会在本章稍后的9.3段进一步介绍,在这里只说船舶期租给了承租人两年,但交船后一直有问题,包括船舱漏水导致货损、修理的延误导致承租人失去了分租约、船舶发生碰撞事故、船东拒绝承租人上船检查、船东不理睬承租人有关修理的最后通牒等一连串不幸与不愉快事件,双方关系很差。于是承租人终止租约,指称船东的言行(主要是行为,船东没有说过什么拒绝履行的话)构成拒绝性违约。但这被判是不足以合理推断船东不会去维修保养并改善船舶的情况,所以船东不构成拒绝性违约可让承租人接受终止租约。Donaldson 大法官说如果船东真正有拒绝维修船舶与解决各种问题,已经是拒绝履行合约重要责任,所以不需要再考虑把它们(船舶不适航、没有尽快维修保养船舶等的违约)加在一起看是否足以使船东构成拒绝性违约。

但稍后有不少先例就这一问题明确了这方面应该加以考虑,特别是一些长期的服务性或工程合约。过去曾发生多次的不重要违约加在一起可以作为背景去推断合约将来的履行是否会持续有问题,从而预测将来会有一个时刻,所有这些问题加在一起达到重要的地步。当然这不是简单的数学问题,这些不重要违约必须性质上是类似或者有一定关联性,而不能风马牛不相及,才能累积。相关先例有:Lewis v. Motorworld Garages Ltd. (1986) ICR 157 (CA); Rice (T/A the Garden Guardian) v. Great Yarmouth Borough Council (2000) All ER (D) 902 (CA); Omilaju v. Waltham Forest LBC (No. 2) (2004) EWCA Civ 1493; The "Pro Victor" (2010) 2 Lloyd's Rep. 158 等。

Lewis v. Motorworld Garages Ltd. 与 Omilaju v. Waltham Forest LBC 两个先例都涉及雇佣合约(employment contract)。这两个先例都是判雇主的违约,即使个别来看不重要,但可以加起来变为重要而构成违约/毁约或拒绝性违约,进而可以让雇员合法终止雇佣合约。反过来,雇员的违约也可以这样加起来考虑。这里顺便一提,雇佣合约在现代社会显然是数量极大并经常会发生争议的合约类别。因为违约/毁约或其中一方的言行构成拒绝性违而导致雇佣合约终止的情况经常发生。例如,一位雇员被雇主突然辞退,雇员会声称这是无理辞退,如果成立,显然是雇主违约/毁约。相反,如果雇主抗辩说事实上是雇员在辞退前的违约或言行构成违约/毁约或拒绝性违约可以成立,就变成雇主接受雇员的违约/毁约或拒绝性违约去终止雇佣合约。这种先例很多,雇佣合约在这一课题与其他合约一样,唯一主要的不同之处是在发生违约/毁约的情况下,普通法一贯的说法是雇佣合约自动终止,而不必无辜方接受才终止:Vine v. National Dock Labour Board (1956) 2 Lloyd's Rep. 567; Sanders v. Ernest A Neale Ltd. (1974) 3 All ER 327 等先例。这一说法也可以理解,从一个角度来看,雇佣合约是自然人提供服务,特别是涉及双方的互信(trust and confidence)关系的默示地位,所以法院一般不会做出"履约指令"(specific performance)。这种情况下,如果硬要雇佣双方维持雇佣关系,一般也不会有好结果。另一个角度来看,雇佣合约是要双方合作才能够履行,这与单方面已经足够履行的合约不同。在后者,如果违约方拒绝履行,但无辜方单方面可履行,法律就允许无辜方选择不接受违约/违约,自行履行完毕,以"债务"(debt)的方式向违约方收取合约报酬。[42] 在履行合约期间也不存在无辜方需要减少损失的问题。这种先例有著名的 White and Carter (Councils) Ltd. v. McGregor (1962) AC 413 先例与 The "Aquafaith" (2012) 2 Lloyd's Rep. 61 先例等。而雇佣合约是要双方合作,雇员没有雇主的合作,也进不去办公楼/工厂;雇主没有雇员的合作,也找不到人来上班。所以,没有被无辜方接受的预期违约就好像"没有发生过的镜花水月"(a thing writ in water)的说法不适用在雇佣合约。有不少案例判是被雇主无理辞退的雇员不能安坐在家里拒绝接受雇主的违约/毁约,然后索赔期间累积的工资。相反,作为无辜方的雇员是需要减少损失,如找一份替代工作:Goodman v. Pocock (1850) 15 QB 576; Hochster v. De la Tour (1853) 118 ER 922; Denmark Productions Ltd. v. Boscobel Productions Ltd. (1969) 1 QB 699 等先例。但这一说法在最近的一些先例,包括 Societe Generale (London Branch) v. Geys (2012) UKSC 63 的最高院先例,有了改变。在该先例中,雇主可以提前 3 个月通知雇员终止雇佣合约,或在终止雇佣合约时支付一笔赔偿金作为 3 个月通知的替代。雇主在 2007 年 11 月底口头通知了雇员结束雇佣合约,并在 12 月中支付了一笔赔偿金。[43]

---

〔42〕 这一课题在本章之 8.4 段会有详论。

〔43〕 在本章之 6.3 段提到,明示条文对如何终止有关的合约有一些实质性的要求,都需要严格遵守。雇主因为没有根据合约在做出通知的同时支付赔偿金,所以通知无效,变为违约/毁约。

雇员在12月底知道收到了一笔钱,并估计是赔偿金,但并不能肯定。2008年1月初,雇主向雇员做出了书面确认终止雇佣合约并支付了该笔赔偿金。法院判是雇员在2007年11月底确认了雇佣合约继续存在,雇佣合约直到2008年1月初才根据相关条文被正式终止。因为雇佣合约是在2008年1月而非2007年12月终止,雇员可以多获得几百万英镑的赔偿。[44] 这样看来,最高院的判法是雇佣合约与其他合约没有不同,违约方的预期违约要被无辜方接受才能终止合约,而不是自动终止。但最高院这个4:1的多数意见很有争议性。而关于雇佣合约的终止与赔偿的问题很复杂,除了案例还有很多立法针对,但因为与中国公司/企业的关系不大,本书不详细阐述。

另在Rice (T/A the Garden Guardian) v. Great Yarmouth Borough Council这一上诉庭先例,涉及Great Yarmouth市政府与原告公司订立管理维护协议,包括地面维护,体育设施的管理(包括板球场、足球场、保龄球绿地、推杆课程等),市政公园、花园、儿童游乐场的绿化与维护。合约是在1996年2月14日订立,为期4年。在1996年5月与6月,市政府发出了一系列的"违约通知"(notice of default),包括花坛没有完成布置,板球场与保龄球绿地的状况不佳,没有及时为9月开始的新赛季修剪足球场的草坪等。一审法院的法官认为这些违约通知有些是有效的,有些是无效的,还有些虽然是有效但针对的只是一些微不足道的违约。市政府在8月2日正式终止了合约。市政府没有支付到期款项,并决定向原告索赔损失。在12月30日,原告提起诉讼,要求市政府支付到期款项与赔偿合约被错误终止的损失。

该先例主要有两个争议,第一个是市政府能否根据合约条文终止合约。相关合约条文可节录如下:

"Clause 23 Termination ...

23.2　If the contractor:

23.2.1　commits a breach of any of its obligations under the Contract; ... the Council may, without prejudice to any accrued rights or remedies under the Contract, terminate the Contractor's employment under the Contract by notice in writing having immediate effect."

市政府的争辩是条文中的"any breach"指的是任何违约,不论大小,市政府都可以终止合约。但这不被上诉庭接受,这也不奇怪,在航运租约就早已经有类似的判法。在NYPE 46格式就有一句与承租人没有准时预付租金并列的"发生任何违约"(any breach of this Charter Party),船东就有权撤船与终止期租合约。这在贵族院的The "Antaios" (1984) 2 Lloyd's Rep. 235先例,判这个违约只是指一些严重的违约,而不是任何微不足道的违约都可以终止期租合约。毕竟,这种轻微的违约不断会发生,动辄可以终止就不会有中长期租约这回事了。Diplock勋爵也是在该先例说了一句名言,如果在一个商业合约中,文字上的分析会带来商业上荒谬的结果,前者就应

[44] 对雇主来说,要多支付这几百万英镑很不幸,因为如果雇主根据相关条文做出通知,原本不必支付。

该服从后者(... if detailed semantic and syntactical analysis of words in a commercial contract is going to lead to a conclusion that flouts business common sense, it must be made to yield to business common sense)。[45]

另一个争议是能否将原告之前多个不重要的违约加在一起变为重要,使市政府可以拒绝性违约终止合约。针对这个争议,上诉庭认为虽然可以加在一起考虑,并做出一个合理的估计是否将来重要的合约责任违约方是不愿意或不能够履行。但上诉庭认同一审法院判是原告的违约依然没有达到重要的程度,也就是市政府败诉。Hale 法官说:"These contracts are, however, like building contracts in that the accumulation of past breaches is relevant, not only for its own sake, but also for what it shows about the future. **In my view, the judge was right to ask himself whether the cumulative breaches were such as to justify an inference that the contractor would continue to deliver a substandard performance.** However, I would agree with Mr Smith that the inference should be that the council would thereby be deprived of a substantial part of the totality of that which it had contracted for that year, subject to the additional possibility that some aspects of the contract were so important that the parties are to be taken to have intended that depriving the council of that part of the contract would be sufficient in itself. That is not what the judge found in this case."(加黑部分是笔者的强调)

在 The "Pro Victor"先例(案情在本章之9.6段有介绍),针对能否把过去曾发生多次的不重要违约加在一起来看,Flaux 说:"First, Mr Phillips(违约方代表大律师) submits that if, as he says is the case (for reasons I will elaborate below), the claimant (无辜方)cannot establish that individual e – mails or pieces of conduct were renunciatory, the claimant cannot add those words and conduct together to make a renunciation. As he put it, if the individual bricks are not renunciatory, Miss Hopkins(无辜方代表大律师) cannot use them to build a wall of renunciation. In the light of the test set out in the authorities to which I have referred, it seems to me this is wrong in principle. The court has to look at the totality of the relevant words and conduct relied upon, in the light of all the circumstances, including the history of the contractual relationship, to determine whether at the time that the claimant purports to accept the words and conduct as renunciatory, the defendant has evinced an intention not to perform, as at that time. Furthermore, particular words or conduct taken in isolation may appear equivocal, but taken with other words and conduct may become unequivocal in terms of amounting to a renunciation. That proposition is of some application in the present case, as will appear."

最后,笔者介绍一个涉及中国船厂的仲裁。该民营上市船厂曾是中国数一数二的大船厂,现在已经破产。该造船合约中的买方是德国船东,船价是8000万美元,但

---

〔45〕 见《合约的解释:规则与应用》第一章之6.5段。

"金融海啸"后市场大跌,船舶的价格跌为3000万美元。船舶建造过程中一切顺利,看情况可以准时交船,即使有延误,也不会拖过"死亡日期"。但德国船东不甘心自己承担5000万美元的差价,所以派了一位没有披露身份的律师与检验师(surveyor)到船厂,由律师每天发邮件给船东,船东再向船厂做出不满意通知(notice of complaints)。由律师发邮件给船东的主要目的是确保可以享受律师与客户之间的特免权(privilege),[46]如有些检验师觉得有点毛病但也可以接受的问题,船东也会添油加醋做出通知。这些律师与客户(船东)之间通信往来享受特免权,可以不必披露,不会对最后仲裁庭的判决产生影响。总之,船东做出了500多个不满意通知,根据船厂的口头证据,船厂对其中绝大部分都做了相应的工作,只是没有留下书面证据。船厂对船东的行为一直不以为意,直到接近交船时,船东不肯接船并声称船厂违约/毁约,才发觉大事不妙,聘用了杨大明律师。杨大明律师立即找了独立验船师上船检查,希望证明船厂已经完成了船东要求的工作,只是很多工作随着造船工程进行已经无法再看出本来的缺陷(如果有)是否已经被补救,或投诉的所谓"缺陷"根本不正确。另一个证据就是船级社上船检验后,对船舶质量满意。另是德国船东拒船后,船厂将船舶转卖给了另一家附属公司,营运一年多一切正常,质量没有问题。但仲裁庭的多数意见不接受船厂的争辩,认为虽然没有任何一个单独的不满意通知中提及的缺陷是严重至构成船厂拒绝性违约,但加在一起的严重性足以达到拒绝性违约的程度。

3.6　拒绝性违约一方的真正意图是否重要

经常见到一些被指称是拒绝性违约的被告会抗辩说,他不可能有拒绝履行合约责任的意图。这里先明确,违约方主观(subjective)的意图是不会被考虑,毕竟这意图是其他人不知道的。一直以来的说法是客观(objective)看违约方的言行是否构成拒绝性违约,不理会违约方主观的意图或善意。这客观去看也就是指做出审理的法院或仲裁庭对有关的言行会否构成拒绝性违约的看法。在The "Nanfri"(1978)1 Lloyd's Rep. 581先例,一审的Kerr大法官说:"Mr. Mustill(无辜方大律师) submitted that the actual intention and bona fides of the guilty party is irrelevant; what matters is his outward conduct. If he is in breach or intimates that he will not perform the contract according to its terms, then his subjective state of mind will not help him. With this I agree..."

3.6.1　市场情况显示违约方不可能想拒绝履行有关合约

这样看来,违约方的实际言行才是最重要,法院或仲裁庭也不会跳出违约方实际的言行去看其他周围的环境以推断违约方的主观意图。否则很有可能是根据当时的市场,违约方不可能有意图拒绝履行这个有高价值/高利润的合约,言行过火只是不小心与/或不懂法律。例如,2008年之后,船价大跌,中国船厂在伦敦有2000多个仲

---

〔46〕见本书第十章第12段。

裁,几乎是全军覆没。其中不少败诉案件涉及拒绝性违约而被外国船东趁机接受去终止造船合约。但根据当时的市场情况,这些造船合约对船厂十分珍贵,船厂按道理不可能拒绝履行。但这不会被考虑,主要还是对船厂被指称是拒绝性违约的言行本身作出客观的判决。在 The "Nanfri" (1979) 1 Lloyd's Rep. 201 (HL)先例,船东也有同样的争议,说:"Having regard to the state of the market, no right - minded charterer would think that it was(这里指船东拒绝履约去签发运费预付的提单)……"但这不被上诉庭([1978] 2 Lloyd's Rep. 132)的 Goff 大法官接受,说:"The answer is similarly ineffective. By the same test, what did their conduct evince? Surely as the umpire concluded: The conduct of the Owners did not constitute an absolute refusal to perform the Charter-parties, but did constitute an intention to perform the Charter-parties in a fundamentally different manner."

贵族院的 Wilberforce 勋爵说:"It is irrelevant that it was in the owners' real interest to continue the charters rather than to put an end to them. If a party's conduct is such as to amount to a threatened repudiatory breach, his subjective desire to maintain the contract cannot prevent the other party from drawing the consequences of his actions."

在稍后的 Woodar Investment Development Ltd. v. Wimpey Construction UK Ltd. (1980) 1 WLR 277 先例,Wilberforce 勋爵说:"It isclear in the first place that, subjectively, the appellants, in 1974, wanted to get out of the contract. Land prices had fallen, and they thought that if the contractwere dissolved, they could probably acquire it at a much lower price. **But subjective intention is not decisive**: it supplied the motive for serving the noticeof rescission: there remains the question whether, objectively regarded, theirconduct showed an intention to abandon the contract."(加黑部分是笔者的强调。注意文字上是指"非决定性",而不是说肯定无关。在本章稍后的 3.6.2 段提到的 Eminence Property Developments Limited v. Kevin Christopher Heaney [2010] EWCA Civ 1168 先例中,Etherton 大法官就是根据这一点去支持他的看法。)

同样的道理下,无辜方的主观意图也不重要。例如,终止合约对无辜方非常有利,如上面提到的外国船东在市场下跌的情况下,抓到中国船厂的不当言行就趁机从造船合约中脱身,从而把市场下跌的风险转嫁给了中国船厂。只要中国船厂的不当言行的确可以构成违约/毁约或拒绝性违约,外国船东的主观意图与期望从中能得到的巨大利益,也不在考虑之列。这可部分节录《Halsbury's Law of England》(第 5 版,2012 年)第 556 页脚注 18 如下:"... the innocent party is entitled to terminate notwithstanding that his principal motive is to escape from a bad bargain: Cunliffe v. Harrison (1851) 6 Exch 901..."

但这方面也有点不同说法,在下一段会做进一步介绍。

3.6.2 无辜方主观知道违约方的言行并非拒绝

一般而言,这种情况感觉上不会少见,但很少有这方面的证据,所以也不会提出这方面的争议。但笔者感觉不会少见是因为经常见到一些案件是水平差的一方被高水平的对方诱导做出一个违约/毁约的言行。这样,所谓的无辜方在心底里是知道违约方的言行不代表拒绝履行,但无辜方不会承认,也无法证明。

但有极少数的情况可推断无辜方不可能把违约方的不当言行视为拒绝,如违约方错误的言行是一个明显不过的笔误(clerical mistake),或是无辜方的证人在开庭被盘问时自己承认没有把违约方的不当言行视为拒绝。这方面没有有关的先例,但近期的两个先例都有涉及这一问题,并倾向去加以考虑。

首先是 Eminence Property Developments Limited v. Kevin Christopher Heaney (2010) EWCA Civ 1168 先例,案情将在稍后有详细介绍。在该先例,无辜方可以很明显看出违约方并非想拒绝履行,而只是有一个笔误,但无辜方没有指出,并利用这个文书错误接受违约方的拒绝终止合约。针对这一点,Etherton 大法官说:"Thirdly, all the circumstances must be taken into account insofar as they bear on an objective assessment of the intention of the contract breaker. This means that motive, while irrelevant if relied upon solely to show the subjective intention of the contract breaker, may be relevant if it is something or it reflects something of which the innocent party was, or a reasonable person in his or her position would have been, aware and throws light on the way the alleged repudiatory act would be viewed by such a reasonable person. So, Lord Wilberforce in Woodar (at p. 281D) expressed himself in qualified terms on motive, not by saying it will always be irrelevant, but that it is not, of itself, decisive."

在 The "Pro Victor" (2010) 2 Lloyd's Rep. 158 先例,无辜方的证人在盘问时承认并没有把违约方的不当言行视为拒绝。Flaux 大法官没有针对这个问题做出任何决定,因为没有必要。但倾向于要将无辜方主观认知加以考虑,并做出详细的分析如下:

"Mr Phillips(违约方代表大律师) submitted that, where the claimant's(无辜方) subjective state of mind was that it did not consider that the defendant's(违约方) words and conduct evinced an intention not to perform, but only that it was unlikely that the defendant would be able to perform, the claimant could not rely upon the defendant's words and conduct as amounting to renunciation entitling the claimant to terminate the contract, even if objectively the words and conduct were renunciatory.[47] Mr Phillips candidly accepted that there was no authority which bore directly upon this point, although he drew my attention to passages in the speeches of the House of Lords in Forslind v. Bechely –

〔47〕 违约方代表大律师认为即使客观来看违约方的言行可以构成拒绝履行,但如果无辜方主观上(这是通过较早前的盘问显示)并没有将其视为拒绝履行合约,而只是认为违约方有可能不会履行,这不足以构成违约/毁约。

Crundell 1922 SC（HL）173 which he submitted supported his analysis.〔48〕. . .

Lord Shaw said this：'If, in short, A, a party to a contract, acts in such a fashion of ignoring or not complying with his obligations under it, B, the other party, is entitled to say："My rights under this contract are being completely ignored and my interests may suffer by non – performance by A of his obligations, and that to such a fundamental and essential extent that I declare he is treating me as if no contract exists which bound him". The accent of the psychology is not upon the mind of the person who is defiant or heedless of his obligation, but as Lord Herschell put it, upon the mind of the person who is suffering from the defiance. '〔49〕

This passage in particular seems to support the proposition that the innocent party must have subjectively considered that the other party was renouncing the contract. However other passages from the speeches of their Lordships（specifically Viscount Haldane at 179 and Lord Dunedin at 190）seem to support the objective approach to renunciation.〔50〕It is also fair to say that the reference in Lord Shaw's speech to Lord Herschell is to a speech in an earlier case in the House of Lords, Carswell v. Collard（1893）20 R（HL）47, another passage from which Lord Shaw quotes earlier in his speech：'Of course the question was not what actually influenced [the innocent party], but what effect the conduct of the [other party] would be reasonably calculated to have upon a reasonable person. '〔51〕

At first blush that might suggest that only the objective question of whether the words or conduct evince an intention not to perform is relevant, but in my judgment taking that short judgment in Carswell v. Collard as a whole, what Lord Herschell was actually saying supports Mr Phillips' proposition that not only must the words and conduct be objectively evincing an intention not to perform but the innocent party must subjectively believe that to be the case.〔52〕

Miss Hopkins（无辜方代表大律师）submitted that to make an entitlement to accept a renunciation as terminating the contract depend upon the subjective intention of the in-

〔48〕　违约方代表大律师承认没有这方面的先例，但有一个早期贵族院先例的说法是支持他这一观点。

〔49〕　这是引用了Shaw勋爵在该先例的说法，并被指是支持违约方代表大律师的主张，就是需要看无辜方主观如何看待违约方这一不当言行。

〔50〕　但在该先例，Haldane勋爵与Dunedin勋爵的观点就是要客观看待违约方拒绝的言行。

〔51〕　Shaw勋爵是依赖了Herschell勋爵在较早前的贵族院先例Carswell v. Collard的说法。

〔52〕　Flaux大法官在分析了较早的贵族院的说法之后，同意支持违约方大律师的主张。不仅要客观看违约方是否显示了拒绝履行的意图，也要看无辜方是否主观也这样认为。

nocent party was not only contrary to the objective theory of the English law of contract,[53] but would present practical difficulties, specifically, in the case of a corporate claimant, which individual's state of mind was relevant for the purpose of determining whether, subjectively, the claimant considered the defendant's words and conduct evinced an intention not to perform the contract.[54]

I do not accept Miss Hopkins' submission that the conclusion that for an entitlement to rescind a contract for renunciation to arise the words or conduct should not only be objectively renunciatory, but the claimant should subjectively consider the words and conduct renunciatory, would somehow subvert the objective approach which English law adopts to contract. It seems to me that there is an analogy to be drawn between renunciation and (non-fraudulent) misrepresentation. Just as a claimant must show both actual reliance on or inducement by a misrepresentation as well as that such reliance or inducement was objectively reasonable, so it seems to me a claimant who contends that the defendant has renounced the contract should have to show not only that the words or conduct were objectively evincing an intention not to perform but that the claimant subjectively believed that to be the case. The passages which Mr Phillips highlighted from Viscount Finlay and Lord Shaw in Forslind and Lord Herschell's speech in Carswell v. Collard seem to me to support the analogy.[55]

Furthermore, the practical difficulties to which Miss Hopkins alluded are no more difficult to solve than in any other case in which the court is concerned with the knowledge or state of mind of a corporate entity. The relevant knowledge or state of mind is that of whoever is an 'agent to know' on behalf of the company. In the present case, the relevant state of mind is that of Mr Yang.[56]"

看来目前英国法律针对这方面还没有明确的先例,但显然是有认同的说法。这表示代表经常被指称拒绝履行合约的中国公司/企业的律师,可能会值得在开庭审理时盘问无辜方的主要证人有关其主观如何看待相关的不当言行。有水平的证人恐怕

---

〔53〕 无辜方代表大律师认为如果支持这一主张,会违反英国法下一贯以来客观看待违约/毁约的言行的立场。

〔54〕 并且会带来操作上的困难,尤其是在无辜方是公司的情况下,个别证人作为公司的雇员的主观看法也不一定能代表公司法人。

〔55〕 简单来说,Flaux 大法官不同意无辜方代表大律师认为如果支持这一主张,会违反了英国法下一贯以来客观看待违约/毁约的言行的立场的说法。Flaux 大法官将无辜方看待违约方拒绝履行的言行,与依赖"误述"(misrepresentation)进行了类比,认为情况是类似。

〔56〕 Flaux 大法官也不同意无辜方代表大律师说认定公司法人的主观想法有困难的情况。在本先例,证人杨先生的主观想法足以代表无辜方的公司法人。证人杨先生在争议发生时是新加坡公司的租船部经理,在作证时是韩国母公司法律与保险部经理。

不会被套出对违约方有利的证言,但对付水平不高的证人就可能会有机会了。

3.6.3 客观看待违约方的言行是否构成违约/毁约

针对以上所讲“客观”看违约方的言行还有很多先例,可另介绍在 Woodar Investment Development Ltd. v. Wimpey Construction UK Ltd. (1980) 1 WLR 277 先例,Keith 勋爵引用了 Bowen 大法官在 Johnstone v. Milling (1886) 16 QBD 460 (CA)先例的判决,节录如下:“The matter is to be considered **objectively**: ‘The claim being for wrongful repudiation of the contract it was necessary that the plaintiff's language should amount to a declaration of intention not to carry out the contract, or that it should be such that the defendant was justified in inferring from it such intention. We must construe the language used by the light of the contract and the circumstances of the case in order to see whether there was in this case any such renunciation of the contract.’”

较近期的可节录 Aikens 大法官在 Gulf Agri Trade v. Aston Agro Industrial (2008) 2 Lloyd's Rep. 376 先例中说:“... it is necessary to ask the question: what, **objectively**, is the intention of the party who has done something which is said to be a repudiation of the contract? Is it (**objectively**) that party's intention to abandon or repudiate the contract or not? This is a question of fact, to be determined by the fact finding tribunal from all the relevant evidence available.”

换言之,笔者在本章一开始就有强调双方有了争议时,言行要注意轻重,如果说得太轻,会被对方认为是示弱而达不到目的。同样,如果不表明自己的立场而让步,也会被认为是示弱,而且可能构成“弃权”(waiver)或“禁反言”(estoppel),对将来的履行造成对自己不利的影响。但如果说得太重,就会构成拒绝性违约的危险,尤其是不要把话说死。例如,跟对方说“我是这样的立场,无论你接不接受”(take it or leave it);或是带有威胁性言行类似“我会摧毁你的业务”(I will ruin your business)、“你的钱或你的命”(your money or your life)的效果。这种过火言行的问题之一是与解决有关的争议是“不成比例”(disproportionate),这种不成比例的威胁很容易就被视为违约/毁约。在 The “Nanfri”先例就涉及船东威胁不会签发提单,尤其是运费预付的提单,就被法院判是有类似的效果。Denning 勋爵说:“That stroke by the owners was a pistol at the head of the charterers. If the owners carried out their threat – for that is what it was – it would mean disaster for the charterers.”

至于什么是轻重掌握得好与合法的威胁,好的例子是告知对方会在 7 天或某个期限内启动仲裁(如果合约有仲裁条文),甚至向对方做出仲裁通知。外国公司通常都是以采取法律行动/开始诉讼威胁对方,也经常成功迫使对方让步。中国公司/企业也可以“以其人之道,还治其人之身”。

3.6.4 违约方诚实的误解的例外

但客观看违约方的言行显示出的意图也往往会面对一个例外情况,就是违约方

“诚实的误解”(honest misapprehension)以为他在合法行使合约权利。这个说法也等于违约方“善意”(bona fide)坚持他的立场,但事后不幸被证明是错误也不被视为违约/毁约(包括真正违约或是拒绝性违约)。估计有这些说法的原因是合约双方经常对合约的条文(无论是明示或默示)有不同的理解。而双方各执己见,认为自己的观点才是正确。即使是由法院来决定,也可能在上诉过程中不断被推翻,而最后有了定论不可避免只会是一方胜诉一方败诉。英国法律不希望合约不被履行并动辄被提前终止,正如 Wright 勋爵在 T. D. Baily Son & Co. v. Ross. T. Smyth & Co. Ltd. (1940) 67 Lloyd’s Rep. 147 先例中说:“Repudiation is a serious matter, not to be lightly found or inferred.”所以,有了诚实的误解说法,也是希望合约双方能够避免太多与太轻易以拒绝性违约终止合约的案件。毕竟,合约一方的言行虽然会是不当/错误,但可能会成功以诚实的误解抗辩。在该先例中,Wright 勋爵说如果违约方是诚实的误解,无辜方不能以此终止合约,否则无辜方会自己变为违约方:“I do not say that it is necessary to show that the party alleged to have repudiated should have an actual intention not to fulfil the contract. He may intend in fact to fulfil, but may be determined to do so only in a manner substantially inconsistent with his obligations, and not in any other way. **However, a mere honest misapprehension, especially if open to correction, does not justify a charge of repudiation.**”(加黑部分是笔者的强调)

在 Sweet & Maxwell Ltd. v. Universal New Services Ltd. (1964) 2 QB 699 先例,上诉庭一致认为依赖对合约善意但错误的解释不属于毁约(reliance on bona fide but mistaken construction isnot repudiation)。其中,Harman 大法官说:“... I do not think that a person who maintains his view of the construction of what is, after all, a not very perspicuous document is repudiating because he says ‘my view of it is this, and this I will do’ and the other man says ‘well, my view is different.’ Let them go to the court and have the matter determined as they can. But to seize upon an attitude of that sort and call it repudiation in order to serve an object which was then of course dear to the hearts of the plaintiffs, who wanted to get rid of this deed, is not in my opinion justified...”

另是在 James Shaffer Ltd. v. Findlay Durham & Brodie (1953) 1 WLR 106 (CA) 先例,也是涉及经销商与生产商之间就合约的解释产生争议,最后生产商终止合约。一审法院判是经销商违约/毁约,生产商胜诉。但上诉至上诉庭,判是经销商对合约的错误解释是善意,而且并不是愚蠢与不合理的理解。Morris 大法官说:“They took an erroneous view, but not one which was impossible or stupid, in regard to one clause of the contract; they had done their best; they had met difficulties which were unexpected both by them and by the plaintiffs; it was a sorry position for both sides, but I do not consider that the defendants had repudiated their contract.”

这里值得一提的是,上诉庭的 Singleton 大法官判生产商败诉的主要理由是,双方如果对合约的解释有了争议,可以去英国法院很快拿到一个即时判决,决定谁的观点正确。但生产商并没有这样做,而是冒险终止合约。

3.6.4.1 诚实误解带来的不肯定

这样,也导致英国法律在这方面并不肯定,毕竟判断是否是诚实的误解应该涉及违约方的主观意图。但判断违约方在拒绝时的主观意图并不可能。而到了审理时,违约方为了避免严重的后果,在口头证据肯定会说自己虽然做出了拒绝的言行,但是内心是善意的或是基于诚实的误解。毕竟他想的是什么不会留下证据,能够留下证据的只有外在的言行,这都是每一个别案件的事实问题(matter of facts)。

也有其他的原因不能轻易接受违约方这种诚实的误解的抗辩,很多是其自己水平太差、不懂,而所谓误解的条文解释其实很直白与明确,作为一个合格的业务人士根本应该知道正确的法律地位。在法律而言,是不能接受无知、误解为理由,令有罪变无罪,违约变不违约。特别是涉及违约/毁约的案件,合约往往已经被终止,如果判违约方没有违约/毁约,就等于要判无辜方违约/毁约。

所以,虽然有说法是拒绝性违约的法律已经十分清楚,正如在 The "Nanfri" (1979) 1 Lloyd's Rep. 201 贵族院先例, Wilberforce 勋爵说:"Was this breach, or threatened breach, repudiatory or not? I shall not set out at any length the numerous authorities on anticipatory breach: this is one of the more perspicuous branches of the law of contract and the modern position is clear."但由于每个案件的事实都不一样,而且诚实的误解对事实方面的界线并不明确,所以导致对哪些违约方坚持对自己的法律地位诚实的误解会构成违约/毁约以及哪些并不会构成违约/毁约的区分有实际困难。在《Halsbury's Law of England》(第5版,2012年)第548页,就提到对法律地位的诚实的误解不一定(not necessarily)会构成违约/毁约,说:"Where the parties genuinely differ as to the meaning of the contract a party will not necessarily be treated as having repudiated if he refuses to perform except according to his own bona fide interpretation of the contract, although that interpretation turns out to be erroneous."

接下来的脚注就列举了一些数目看来是均等的诚实的误解构成与不构成违约/毁约的先例。构成违约/毁约的有:Ross. T. Smyth & Co. Ltd. v. T. D. Baily Son & Co. (1940) 67 Lloyd's Rep. 147; Evans Marshall & Co. Ltd. v. Bertola SA and Independent Sherry Importers Ltd. (1976) 2 Lloyd's Rep. 17; The "Nanfri"; Agrokor AG v. Tradigrain SA (2000) 1 Lloyd's Rep. 497; Dalkia Utilities Services Plc. v. Celtech International Ltd. (2006) 1 Lloyd's Rep. 599 等先例。不构成违约/毁约的有:Consorzio Veneziano di Armamento e Navigazione v. Northumberland Shipbuilding Co. Ltd. (1919) 88 LJKB 1194, CA; Peter Dumenil & Co. Ltd. v. James Ruddin Ltd. (1953) 2 All ER 294, CA; James Shaffer Ltd. v. Findlay Durham & Brodie (1953) 1 WLR 106 (CA); Cunliffe - Owen v. Teather and Greenwood (1967) 3 All ER 561; Sweet & Maxwell Ltd. v. Universal News Services Ltd. (1964) 2 QB 699, CA; The "Fairport" (1966) 2 All ER 1026; Woodar Investment Development Ltd. v. Wimpey

Construction UK Ltd. (1980) 1 WLR 277, HL; Orion Finance Ltd. v. Heritable Finance Ltd. (1997) 5 CL 123, CA; Gulf Agri Trade v. Aston Agro Industrial (2008) 2 Lloyd's Rep. 376 等先例。

在《Chitty on Contracts》(第32版,2015年)之24－019与24－020段说:"The courts have struggled to reconcile the latter proposition(善意) with their reluctance to conclude that a party who has acted in good faith but was mistaken has thereby repudiated the contract... The result of this tension is that the cases are not at all easy to reconcile and have been said to be 'highly fact sensitive'. The test that is applied by the courts can, however, be set out in straightforward terms: it is whether, looking at all the circumstances objectively, that is from the perspective of a reasonable person in the position of the innocent party, the contract breaker has clearly shown an intention to abandon and altogether refuse to perform the contract. It is the application of this test to the facts of individual cases which has proved to be less than straightforward. All of the circumstances must be taken into account insofar as they bear on an objective assessment of the intention of the contract breaker...."

3.6.4.2　违约方的言行是根据律师的建议

违约方为了加强诚实的误解的抗辩,还经常会提出其对合约的理解是咨询过称职的律师。但这样的抗辩显然有问题,毕竟律师也会犯错,即使是同一个律师事务所的律师,水平也有区别,不能说咨询过律师就自动变为诚实的误解了。要避免因为律师的错误建议而导致做出违约/毁约的言行,首先要当事人自己有判断能力,知道谁是有水平的律师,可以得到相对正确的答案,从而降低这方面的风险。

在早期,有过先例判是违约方的言行是先咨询过称职律师,显示了其善意,所以不构成拒绝性违约。这在 Mersey Steel & Iron Co. Ltd. v. Naylor, Benzon & Co. (1884) L. R. 9 App. Cas. 434 先例,贵族院认为首先违约方的行为是想要完成合约,而非拒绝履行合约,第二违约方是善意与依赖律师意见,因此判是违约方的行为不构成拒绝性违约。

但在后来的先例,这一说法不再被接受。首先是 Denning 勋爵在 The"Nanfri"拒绝这个抗辩,该案中的违约方是听了律师(一家英国著名的海事律师所)的意见而做出这一被判是违约/毁约的言行,指出:"... they (违约方) said that they were under an honest misapprehension as to their rights which was open to correction ... I have yet to learn that a party who breaks a contract can excuse himself by saying that he did it on the advice of his lawyers..."另 Woolf 勋爵在 Vaswani v. Italian Motors (Sales & Services) Ltd. (1996) 1 WLR 270 先例也说:"Nor is conduct, if it is repudiatory, excused because it occurs in consequence of legal advice, as may be the case with the sellers' actions in this case."

3.6.4.3 根据英国近期先例对诚实的误解例外的总结

针对诚实的误解的不肯定，可以贵族院的 The "Nanfri"(1979) 1 Lloyd's Rep. 201 (HL)先例与 Woodar Investment Development Ltd. v. Wimpey Construction UK Ltd. (1980) 1 WLR 277 先例为例。在两三年的时间内，贵族院做出了两个看起来完全相反的判决。这两个判决会在稍后详细介绍。

不妨先节录在《Contractual Duties：Performance，Breach，Termination and Remedies》(2011 年)一书之 6-068 至 6-070 段针对这个复杂的情况做出的总结：

"**A party's mistaken but good faith statement that his non-performance is justified**:[57] In general, where a party mistakenly believes that he is required to perform, his statement that he will not perform will constitute renunciation.[58] (Similarly, if instead of a renunciation, his good faith conduct is inconsistent with the continuation of the contract, this will be a case of repudiatory breach).[59] The law on this topic is evolving. But the following propositions summarise recent judicial examination of this thorny matter:[60]

(a) Prima facie X's good faith proposed serious non-compliance with the contract will constitute a renunciation if X was not in fact justified under the contract inresiling in this way: 'The Nanfri' (1979);[61]

(b) However, such good faith proposed serious non-compliance will not justify the other party in terminating the contract if:[62]

(1) It is obvious to Y that X has made an erroneous step, in purported compliance with the contract and the true position is apparent to Y; and (b) it is obvious to Y that, once Y points out the error to X, X will quickly step back in line, and resume fidelity to the contract: Eminence Property Developments Ltd. v. Heaney (2010); or[63]

---

〔57〕 标题是"违约方善意但错误理解合约的法律地位"。

〔58〕 一般来说，如果合约一方需要履行合约或其中一个重要责任，但被他错误理解，他声称他不会履行就会构成拒绝性违约。

〔59〕 类似的，即使违约方诚实/善意的言行，但与有关合约持续履行下去相违背，这也是违约/毁约。

〔60〕 这一问题还是不断在发展，没有太明确的分水线。但总结这个困难的问题的近期先例，可以得出以下的结论。

〔61〕 第一，根据 The "Nanfri"(1979) 1 Lloyd's Rep. 201 (HL)先例，违约方表面看来是善意但涉及了严重不履行合约的言行，如果事后被判定是错误理解合约/法律的地位，会构成违约/毁约。

〔62〕 善意但涉及严重的不履行合约的言行，在以下的三种情况将不会构成违约/毁约，对方不能以此终止合约。

〔63〕 第一种情况可称为"清楚的误解"(transparent error)，即无辜方的 Y 可以清楚看到违约方的 X 做出错误/不当的言行，很容易指出或做出纠正。典型的例子就是违约方声称他根据合约的某一条文计算出一笔款项要求无辜方支付，但无辜方估计违约方漏了合约的另外一条也是有关的条文或明显看到计算错误，如果马上向违约方指出就会让他改正。这方面的 Eminence Property Developments Limited v. Kevin Christopher Heaney(2010) EWCA Civ 1168 先例会稍后介绍。

(2) X's proposed serious non - compliance might easily have been challenged by Y, whereupon it would have been possible for C to make clear whether he was wishing to present to Y a 'take - it - or - to - leave - it' ultimatum: Vaswani v. Italian Motors (Sales & Services) Ltd. (1996); or[64]

(3) X and Y are agreed that the matter must be tested legally (by a court, arbitrator, or perhaps by some other mechanism) and that, if the relevant point is held against him, X will abide by the contract: Woodar Investment Development Ltd. v. Wimpey Construction UK Ltd. (1980).[65]

However, approach (iii), just mentioned, presupposes that there is 'time and space' to resolve this disputed matter.[66] As the Court of Appeal observed in James Shaffer Ltd. v. Findlay Durham & Brodie (1953), modern practice has failed to maintain the speedy practice of the early twentieth century Commercial Court, when disputed questions of repudiation or renunciation were often taken to court within a few days of the

---

〔64〕 第二种情况可称为"有责任澄清对方的言行是否代表最后立场"(duty to invite clarification whether position adopted is last word)。这种情况往往指无辜方其实很容易对违约方错误的言行做出质疑,这样无辜方会在客观来看合理与很容易做到的情况下向对方澄清是否不管对错都会坚持。在一定程度上,这与第一种情况差不多,但会针对一些相对来说没有这么明显并可以马上纠正的明显错误(obvious mistake)。笔者随意举个例子,无辜方估计违约方坚持的立场看来会是漏了考虑双方在订立合约后另外同意过的修改或附件,这就可能表示无辜方应该向违约方澄清他的立场。而如果违约方的言行不是最后立场,就可以进一步提出这方面的质疑。这方面的 Vaswani v. Italian Motors (Sales & Services) Ltd. (1996) 1 WLR 270, PC 先例会在稍后介绍。

〔65〕 第三种情况可称为"马上解决争议"(immediate dispute resolution)。这种情况是指双方很容易马上解决有关的争议,而不需要各持己见。这种情况甚至会是由违约方先提出,显然是为了避免他的言行如果事后被认为错误/不当,会有构成违约/毁约的风险。但只要有关的争议可以马上解决,由无辜方提出也是无妨。而如果违约方拒绝合作,他的言行就有更大的可能会构成违约/毁约。这方面主要的先例就是 Woodar Investment Development Ltd. v. Wimpey Construction UK Ltd. (1980) 1 WLR 277,会在稍后介绍。

〔66〕 针对第三种情况,需要一些先决条件。其中最重要的是,有关争议是否可以马上由第三人(法院或仲裁庭)解决。显然,如果是一个复杂的争议并涉及事实的认定,这就很难很快做出判决或裁决。相反,如果双方的争议只是相对独立的法律观点(通常就是指合约条文的解释),就容易马上由第三人做出"宣示"(declaration)判决或裁决。显然,在一个复杂的争议中,加上有关争议当时的情况没有时间解决(如一批马上会腐烂的货物要做出处理,但买卖双方之间有争议),即使违约方提出马上解决,无辜方可以完全合理地回答说:"我不知道你为什么有这样的提议,这根本不可行,我们也根本没有时间通过这样的办法来解决我们之间的争议。"另一个条件就是双方必须合作,毕竟如果双方不合作去同意省略大部分的诉讼程序,是不可能很快拿到判决/裁决。所以,如果争议的双方有一方不合作,如违约方向无辜方提出马上解决争议,或无辜方向违约方提出同样的建议,但被对方拒绝,可以说拒绝的一方在最后的判决或裁决就有较高的危险败诉。既然需要双方合作,即使有关的合约有一些比较耗时的解决争议办法,如一个机构仲裁,单是启动与委任仲裁员就可能要几个月的时间。提出马上解决争议的一方完全可以提议双方同意针对目前的争议去临时仲裁(*ad hoc*)并委任独任仲裁员,或去英国法院。显然如果对方不合理地拒绝,也是有危险将来会因此而败诉。

relevant events. In the James Shaffer case Singleton LJ also noted the speedy 'referral' of a disputed renunciation in the Spettabile case (1919).[67]

Honest error concerning contractual rights is no defence to renunciation if time does not permit disputable point to be investigated at relative leisure or the actual breach takes immediate effect: The innocent party will be entitled to terminate for breach, even though the defaulting party acts in good faith, if either: (i) a threatened form of serious default takes place, where there is no real opportunity to consult outside agencies to resolve the impasse; or (ii) the guilty party commits a serious default (including failure to perform) which takes effect immediately."[68]

3.7 证明违约方将来不会履行的举证

很自然,证明违约方的言行显示其不愿意或不能够按照合约规定履行将来的重要合约责任,举证责任是在无辜方。也已经提到这些证据是在违约方被指称拒绝履行合约时(或之前的违约历史),但不理会后来的事实或证据(如证明违约方完全可以履行)。正如 Donaldson 在 The"Hermosa" (1982) 1 Lloyd's Rep. 570 先例,说:"This assessment must be carried out with regard to the circumstances prevailing at the time of the decision to terminate and not by reference to subsequent information."

Flaux 大法官在 The"Ekha"(2010) 1 Lloyd's Rep. 543 先例也说:"What must be established (apart from the other requirements of repudiation) is quite simple ... namely that on the balance of probabilities the party in question cannot perform his obligations."

无辜方是否容易满足这个举证责任,是根据每个案例不同的案情而有所不同。如果指控违约方拒绝履行将来的合约责任是根据他的行为,特别是要把之前的违约或不合作的行为加在一起看待时,无辜方的举证责任就会很不容易满足。相反,如果违约方拒绝履行合约是白纸黑字写明,主要是文书解释,那么无辜方的举证责任就可以很轻松满足。对违约方而言,他是无法做出抗辩说这些话并不代表他内心的想法。

---

〔67〕 英国法院在 20 世纪初经常省略中间的程序,在几天内作出这种即时判决。但上诉庭在 James Shaffer Ltd. v. Findlay Durham & Brodie(1953) 1 WLR 106 (CA)先例也提到,现在这种即时判决越来越少,估计与现在的国际贸易几乎都使用仲裁来解决争议有一定关系。而这种即时判决,几乎也只在英国法院见到。部分原因是很多国家法院的法官对国际贸易的情况没有这么熟悉,在没有时间进行研究与依赖专家证人的情况下,很难即时作出判决。但在商业仲裁中,这种"即时仲裁"(instant arbitration)的做法依然大量存在,仲裁方面著名的 The "Nema" (1981) 2 Lloyd's Rep. 239 先例就涉及一个即时仲裁。笔者也曾经多次作为独任仲裁员处理过类似紧急的争议,并在两三天内作出了裁决。但即时仲裁一般只是海事或国际贸易中处理紧急争议的做法,对其他类别的商业活动能否适用即时仲裁,笔者认为不会有问题。近年来大部分机构的仲裁规则都规定了"紧急仲裁员"(emergency arbitrator)的做法以处理"中间措施"(interim measures),笔者认为紧急仲裁员处理的争议不见得比即时仲裁处理的实质法律争议简单。

〔68〕 《Contractual Duties: Performance, Breach, Termination and Remedies》(2011 年)一书根据现有的案例进行总结,在大部分情况下,违约方诚实的误解或善意并不是有效的抗辩。

毕竟,这是一个客观的考验,没有人知道他说话时到底在想什么。但笔者的确会看见一些公司轻率地说出一句过火的话,就导致丢失了价值高达数千甚至上亿美元的合约,或要面对同样金额的索赔。这是十分可惜但又不会有人可怜的,孔子就曾经说过"一言兴邦,一言丧邦"。

3.7.1　举证责任:平衡的可能性

至于证明违约方的言行显示了他不愿意或不能够按照合约规定履行将来的重要合约责任的举证程度,应该是与其他民事诉讼一样,是根据"平衡的可能性"(balance of probability),也就是违约方有51%以上的机会不会履行将来合约的重要责任。在不少先例,都有提到类似的举证程度。如在 Maple Flock Co. Ltd. v. Universal Furniture Products (Wembley) Ltd. (1934) 1 KB 148 先例,Hewart 大法官认为除非违约方再次违约的可能性是"实务上可忽略不计"(practical negligible);在 The "Hermosa" 先例说是要"合理可能"(a reasonable probability);在 Alfred C Toepfer International GmbH v. Hagrani Export SA (1993) 1 Lloyd's Rep. 360 (Com Ct)先例,Saville 大法官说是"根据平衡的可能性"(on the balance of probabilities);在 Polymers v. Imerys (2008) EWHC 344 (Comm)先例,Burton 大法官说是要"更可能"(more likely than not);在新西兰的 Ken & Ken Corp Ltd. v. Kenji Umezaki (2005) NZHC 479 先例,针对相关立法[69]中"清楚"一词,Baragwanath 大法官说不需要"不可避免"(inevitability)而只要"合理可能"(sensible probability)。

但在《Contractual Duties: Performance, Breach, Termination and Remedies》(2011年)一书之7-077段,是说更重要的是无辜方要举证的程度是让法院或仲裁庭看到有清楚与有说服力的可能违约方将来不会履行:"The better approach, which is supported by English law, is this: whether it ca n be responsibly and convincingly said by X (无辜方) that Y(违约方) was definitely destined to fail to perform. Nothing short of a clear and convincing case of such prospective inability should suffice."

对笔者来说,不论是平衡的可能性或是证明清楚与有说服力的可能本质上都一样,反正无辜方就是要有足够证据说明违约方将来不愿意或不可能履行的可能性更大。提供足够证据显然是无辜方与其律师的责任,但还会有其他控制不了的因素。例如,个别法官与仲裁庭由于其不同背景甚至是潜在的偏见,看待同样的证据却得出不同的结论,特别是针对将来是否会发生的事。这里还会有危险是在审理时,法官或仲裁员都会知道后来实际上发生的事,在判断无辜方在当时认为对方将来不愿意或不能够履行是否合理时,很难不受到影响。但即使当时是合理的预测,也有可能被事后发生的事证明是错误的。如在 The "Hermosa" (1982) 1 Lloyd's Rep. 570 先例,案情在本章之9.3段将有详细介绍,这里不再重复。只说在判断船东不合作与沉默的行为是否让承租人合理判断他将来不愿意或不能够履行租约时,很难说仲裁庭与法

[69] 见本章之3.3段。

院（虽然 Donaldson 大法官在该先例强调了这方面）有否被诉讼中证明的船东确实在进行修理的事实影响。相反，如果事后证明船东并没有修理甚至船舶根本修不好而需要拆船，承租人较早的接受船东拒绝性违约而终止租约会否有更大可能被视为英明，答案或许对某些警觉性没有这么高的仲裁员或法官会有不同。

3.7.2 不同类别的预期违约举证方面的不同

这可以本章第 2 段举的外国足球队在 7 月 2 日到北京举行表演赛的假设为例。在第一种明示拒绝（explicit renunciation）的情况中，这是最清楚明确与肯定的拒绝性违约，中国商人作为受害方完全可以把外国足球队负责人的语言（当然最好留下文书记录）作为表见价值（face value），即他说什么就真正表示什么。而第二种默示拒绝（implicit renunciation），就比较不肯定。因为即使外国足球队在欧洲有重要赛事，有较大可能去不了北京，但除非球队明确说不去北京，否则也不能肯定球队拒绝或不可能履行与中国商人的合约。这与其他商业合约经常发生的同时承诺两个有直接冲突的合约（conflict of engagement）[70] 相似，如一货两卖或一船两租。但这在英国法下不足以被视为构成预期违约：Toepfer v. Itex Itagrani (1993) 1 Lloyd's Rep. 360 先例。

至于第三种情况（一定程度上第二种情况也类似），是最不容易清楚与有说服力地证明外国足球队将来不可能或没有能力履行。正如《Contractual Duties: Performance, Breach, Termination and Remedies》（2011 年）一书之 7－086 至 7－087 段所说："... because requires clear inability to perform: a likely failure to perform is not enough. Thus in ... the claim that future performance is in fact impossible is one which requires a very high level of proof. The law prudently inclines in favour of the party whose future performance is in question. This is because life is full of examples of people pulling off a last－minute success. In the vernacular, this is described as a 'narrow scrape', a 'close－run thing', or escaping liability 'by the skin of one's teeth'. Conversely, the other party should not be encouraged to make gloomy prognostications: premature declarations of hopelessness where there is still a decent glimmer of hope. By contrast, confronted by a case of explicit renunciation... the law respects a party's right to take this at face－value as a cancellation...."

例如，第三种情况没有及时申请签证，如果中国商人以此为由指称外国足球队预期违约并索赔损失，如前期准备的费用、场地安排的费用、已经出售票务安排退款的行政费用、可能数额庞大的利润损失等，就可能会面临外国足球队各种抗辩。例如，14 个工作日只是一般的程序，但加急就不需要这么久。或是在外国的中国大使馆已经承诺会及时协助，保证球队可以按时去北京参加比赛。甚至可能因为这个表演赛是国家元首访华的附属活动，所以签证流程与平时不同。总之会有各种抗辩，中国商

〔70〕 这个课题可见本章之 4.3 段。

人只是证明即使有这种抗辩，外国足球队不能到北京的可能性比不来的可能性要大还不足够，必须要清楚地证明外国足球队不可能或没有能力履约。

3.7.3　不得以事后的证据影响有否拒绝性违约的判断

已经在本章之3.7.1段有强调，拒绝性违约不能以事后的证据影响对无辜方接受对方的言行的一刻是否合理的判断。在本段会对这重要的一点进一步探讨。拒绝性违约作为主要与最常见的预期违约类别，就是为了让无辜方可以根据事前违约方的言行客观与合理地估计他将来不愿意或不能够履行。为了商业的肯定性以及对无辜方通过接受去终止合约的决定公平，就不能以事后的证据与事实去影响，即使这一合理的估计事后证明是错误的。

这方面重要的说法可先节录Devlin大法官在Universal Cargo Carriers Corp. v. Pedro Citati（1957）1 Lloyd's Rep. 174先例的总结，如下：

"In my opinion the arbitrator was right. Indeed, I do not really know what is meant by interpreting conduct in the light of later events. I think that the question or the finding embodies a confusion between the principle illustrated by Forslind v. Bechely – Crundall (1922) SC (HL) 173 and that laid down in The Savona [1900] P 252 and Embiricos v. Sydney Reid & Co. , [1914] 3 KB 45 and which is most fully formulated by Lord Sumner in Bank Line Ltd. v. Arthur Capel & Co. [1919] AC 435 as follows: 'The question must be considered at the trial as it had to be considered by the parties, when they came to know of the cause and the probabilities of the delay and had to decide what to do. On this the judgments in the above cases substantially agree. **Rights ought not to be left in suspense or to hang on the chances of subsequent events. The contract binds or it does not bind, and the law ought to be that the parties can gather their fate then and there.** What happens afterwards may assist in showing what the probabilities really were, if they had been reasonably forecasted, but when the causes of frustration have operated so long or under such circumstances as to raise a presumption of inordinate delay, the time has arrived at which the fate of the contract falls to be decided.'

The Forslind case is based on the simple and well – known principle that a man may speak by his deeds as well as his words. It is not peculiar to anticipatory breach; a contract can, for example, be made by conduct as well as be broken by it. Lord Sumner's principle is a device by which **for commercial purposes a man may be entitled to act on information which he has and be protected even if it turns out to be unreliable or untrue. It depends on likelihood and a forecast of future events.** But conduct, it seems to me, can only be interpreted in the light of the events that are known to the interpreter at the time."（加黑部分是笔者的强调）

在Nottingham Building Society v. Eurodynamics Systems Plc.（1995）FSR 605先例，上诉庭的Peter Gibson大法官也说："（后来才发觉的）internal communings of the

(被指称拒绝履行方) are not relevant to the question whether there has been a repudiation by(被指称拒绝履行方), as the objective observer in the position of(无辜方) would not have seen any of these documents, and would have had to reach a conclusion on repudiation from what was revealed by the(当场的) correspondence and at meetings with the(被指称拒绝履行方)."

在 The "Ekha" (2010) 1 Lloyd's Rep. 543 先例,案情在本章之 4.3 段有介绍,Flaux 大法官也说:"I agree ... which is that, in considering whether words and conduct are clear and unequivocal for the purposes of the doctrine of renunciation, you can only look at the words and conduct at the time of the termination of the contract, and cannot seek to make what was equivocal unequivocal, by reference to subsequent events after the termination of the contract."

3.8 最后通牒能起到的作用

如果一方没有明确的语言或者行动显示他不愿意或不能够继续履行合约,而只是不合作或沉默,另一方(也就是无辜方)不肯定对方是否不再履行,从而陷入很被动与不肯定的地位。因为如果贸然终止合约,但最后被判是对方的言行不足以构成拒绝性违约或违约/毁约,就会变为自己违约/毁约而要面对对方的损失索赔。在这种情况下,无辜方通常会做出最后通牒(ultimatum),要求对方在一个期限(deadline)前确认是否履行,否则就会当作他拒绝履行去终止合约。根据不同的案情,无辜方这样做可能是真心想知道对方是否愿意继续履约。而如果对方不履约,他可以尽快减少损失,甚至已经有替代的业务可以接手,损失会是很少或基本没有。但也有可能是无辜方只是担心违约方的言行还不够明确能构成拒绝性违约或违约/毁约,于是在这最后通牒中设下陷阱,希望对方能够明确回复一句不再履约,这样他就可以安心终止合约。

但这种最后通牒是否有作用存在疑问,英国法律没有要求对方(违约方)对这种最后通牒必须做出回应。换言之,对方完全可以继续不合作或保持沉默。

这可见 The "Hermosa" (1982) 1 Lloyd's Rep. 570 先例,承租人给的最后通牒被判是改变不了法律地位,因为它不过是言辞强硬地要求船东保证会履行,但被指称是违约方的船东在法律上没有必要理睬。正如 Mustill 大法官所说:"... had no legal status and was no more than a strongly worded demand for assurance..."

从合约法来分析,英国法律的地位也完全可以理解。单方面要求对方回应,对方是否必须回应是要看合约的要求。一般来说,很少会有合约明示要求对方回应所谓的最后通牒,变成无辜方只能依赖合约有这一默示责任。但无论是法律的默示还是事实的默示,[71]要求都很高。如事实的默示,就要求必须加上才会使合约有商业效力,这显然达不到。而另一个条文必须能够清楚地表达出来的要求,也很难做到。因

〔71〕 这课题可看杨良宜《合约的解释:规则与应用》一书第七章。

为不同的最后通牒内容千变万化，期限的要求也可长可短。

但这一英国法律的地位看来与国际上的公约或原则并不相符，甚至另一个重要的普通法国家——美国，在这方面的法律地位也不一样。在《Restatement (Second) of Contract》，相关部分可节录如下：

"251. When a Failure to Give Assurance May Be Treated as aRepudiation

(1) Where reasonable grounds arise to believe that the obligor will commit abreach by non – performance that would of itself give the obligee a claim for damagesfor total breach under § 243, **the obligee may demand adequate assurance of dueperformance** and may, if reasonable, **suspend any performance** for which he has notalready received the agreed exchange until he receives such assurance.

(2) **The obligee may treat as a repudiation the obligor's failure to provide within areasonable time such assurance of due performance as is adequate in the circumstances of the particular case.**"[加黑部分显示了无辜方可以通过最后通牒要求对方保证会履行(或不履行)合约，如果违约方不回应，无辜方可视为违约/毁约。加黑部分也说无辜方可以暂时中断他对该合约的履行，[72] 直至收到违约方保证他会履行合约。]

在《联合国国际货物销售合同公约》(CISG, 1980 年)、《The Principles of European Contract Law 2002》与《UNIDROIT Principles of International Commercial Contract 2010》都有相关的条文，但本段不再节录。

另一方面，英国普通法也从善如流，开始与美国或国际的说法靠近。在近期的 The "Pro Victor" (2010) 2 Lloyd's Rep. 158 先例，案情将在本章之 9.6 段详细介绍。在这里只是针对最后通牒的作用，在该先例，无辜方的船东在终止合约前根据律师的建议发了一封电邮给违约方的承租人，内容如下：

"We refer to Charterers' message earlier.

It is clear from Charterers' last message and their previous message that they do not intend to perform the charterparty...

Charterers are now saying that they wish to carry an alternative cargo .. from India to East Coast Africa on a time charter basis. They are not entitled to do so under the charterparty which has been agreed.

---

[72] 英国法律也不认同无辜方可以暂时中断其对该合约的履行。英国法律是没有"和稀泥"的情况，无辜方要么接受违约方的拒绝终止合约，如果不终止合约，就不能以对方违约为由暂时中断履行自己在该合约的责任。Staughton 大法官在 Eurotunnel v. Balfour Beauty (1992) 2 Lloyd's Rep. 11 先例，说："It is well established that if one party is in serious breach, the other can treat the contract as altogether at all end, but there is not yet any established doctrine of English law that the other party may suspend performance, keeping the contract alive."但通过"禁反言"(estoppel)的说法在有限度的情况下，无辜方可以暂时中断履行自己的部分合约责任，这可见本章之 3.10.2 段的详论。

As we say, it is clear to us that Charterers do not intend to perform their obligations under the charterparty. Therefore, unless Charterers confirm unequivocally and unconditionally by [0900 Singapore time] tomorrow, 29 August 2008 that they will provide a full cargo for loading and discharging in accordance with their obligation in the charterparty, then we will (1) assume that Charterers do not intend to perform the charterparty and (2) treat Charterers' conduct asrepudiating the charterparty.

Owners' rights are fully reserved in the meantime."

船东第一次发送电邮时疏忽,将律师的意见与建议部分,包括草拟的这封电邮一起发送给了承租人,这导致承租人回来澄清这封电邮。接下来,船东只是把律师草拟的邮件,也就是上述节录的部分,抽出来重发了一次,唯一改动就是把要求回应的期限从 2008 年 8 月 29 日的 9 时变为 15 时。但承租人没有回应,接下来船东就终止租约。其中针对这一最后通牒是否有作用,Flaux 大法官认为承租人如果愿意与能够履行合约,完全可以很简单地回应船东。而如果不回答,就更是明确构成了拒绝性违约。Flaux 大法官说:

"In those circumstances, I consider that it was perfectly legitimate for the claimant (船东) to send the email which it did asking for confirmation that the defendant (承租人) would load cargo in Karachi. This was a natural reaction on the part of the claimant to what was undoubtedly an uncertain situation as regards the defendant's precise intention.

I was unimpressed by the evidence of Captain Skarvelis (承租人证人) to the effect that he did not consider that the claimant had any right to seek such confirmation, which was somehow 'uncontractual' and that he found this sort of email 'irritating'. Whatever the strict contractual position ... I am quite satisfied that the claimant was justified in asking the question given the uncertainty as at the time that the email was sent. ... if the defendant did still intend to load the cargo in Karachi, it would have been the simplest thing in the world for Captain Skarvelis to have vented his spleen by responding to the effect that of course the defendant intended to load the cargo in Karachi ...

... it was perfectly obvious that the claimant was giving the defendant a last chance to state clearly and unequivocally that it would perform the charterparty. Although the timescale was tight and it was the middle of the night in New York, Captain Skarvelis was aware of the message and was sending emails. As with the earlier messages from the claimant asking for confirmation that the defendant intended to perform, if the defendant had been ready, willing and able to perform, it would have been a very straightforward thing to confirm this, however irritating Captain Skarvelis found the claimant's emails.

However there was in effect a refusal on the part of the defendant to provide that confirmation. Mr Phillips (承租人代表大律师) submitted that silence would not suffice for renunciation, because it is equivocal. I do not accept that submission, as it seems to me it must depend on the context. **Renunciation may be by words or conduct and where one party is seeking confirmation that the other will perform, a failure to give the confirmation may be renunciatory, especially if, as in the present case, it is preceded by other conduct which is renunciatory.**"(加黑部分是笔者的强调)

这样看来,目前在英国法律下,无辜方在终止合约前做出最后通牒是重要,更不用说有时合约会明示合并《联合国国际货物销售合同公约》或《UNIDROIT Principlesof International Commercial Contract 2010》。而对另一方来说,如果无辜方做出的最后通牒要求很多,不回应还可以解释。但如果无辜方只是简单要求一个不再履行或保证履行的确认,不回应就很可能被法院或仲裁庭认为是显示了不愿意或不能够继续履行的意图。

不回应就代表违约方保持沉默,而沉默通常不被视为代表违约/毁约。但会有情况可以被推断是违约方不愿意履行合约,其中应该包括不回应最后通牒。在 Stocznia v. Latco (2001) 1 Lloyd's Rep. 537 先例,针对无辜方的船厂给违约方的船东两个通知要求履行造船合约,但船东没有回应的情况,一审的 Thomas 大法官认为可以推断船东是拒绝履行,说:"The question therefore is whether the breach was a continuing one and amounted to repudiatory conduct. In my view it was. As I have set out, the yard(船厂)pressed for performance on April 19, 1994 and May 4, 1994; there was no response. It does not seem to me that the failure to respond can make a difference; if, for example Latreefers(船东)had replied and said they were not going to perform, then there would clearly have been a new repudiatory act. Can it make a difference that they were silent in the face of a demand for performance, if the inference from silence was their continuous refusal to perform? As that is the inference I draw, I do not think it can make a difference, as by not responding in the circumstances of this case they were making clear that they were not going to perform."

3.9 一方已履行合约是否适用拒绝性违约

顾名思义,"一方已履行合约"(executed contract)是指其中一方已经履行了自己的全部合约责任,只剩下另一方去履行他的合约责任,这通常是根据合约剩下的责任只有支付一笔钱。因此,一份"待履行合约"(executory contract)在其中一方已经履行了自己的全部合约责任后会变成一份一方已履行合约。例如,在一个货物买卖合约中,卖方已经交付了货物,只剩下买方支付全部或剩余货款。这时这份买卖合约就成为了一份一方已履行合约。

预期违约可能发生在一份待履行合约是确定无疑,因为双方都有将来的合约责任需要履行,其中一方很有可能做出言行显示不愿意或不能够履行将来的合约责任。预期违约的说法适用的合理理由之一是在一个待履行的合约,一旦违约方拒绝履行,无辜方也可以不用再花时间与金钱履行其合约责任,无须等到合约规定的履行时间已过而违约方仍然没有履行(真正违约发生之后)再减少损失,这就可以避免造成浪费。如在一个 FOB 买卖,买方订约后不久告知卖方他不会要这票货,也不会派船去装港。卖方接受预期违约后就不必再花钱花精力去备货待装:Vitol SA v. Beta Renowable SA (2017) EWHC 1734 (Comm)先例。

但在一个一方已履行的合约,这个理由就说不通。毕竟在这种合约中,只有一方需要履行将来的合约责任。即使是适用预期违约的说法,也只适用在这一方的合约方。而他需要履行的将来合约责任,如支付一笔款项,往往有明示条文针对。这样,如果通过预期违约的拒绝性违约提前终止合约并加速可以要求提前支付这笔款项,看来说不通。在加拿大的早期先例 Melanson v. Dominion of Canada General Insurance Co. (1934) 2 DLR 459,新布伦瑞克最高院就提到这点并判是预期违约不适用在一方已履行合约,说:"The distinction [between executory and executed contracts] is a reasonable one ... But in case of an executed contract where the defendant(违约方) simply says he will not, under any circumstances pay a sum of money when it falls due there is no possible reason for accelerating the payment and no hardship upon the plaintiff in not doing so..."

在英国的 Moschi v. Lep Ari Services Ltd. and ors. (1973) AC 331 先例,债务人没有按照合约规定向债权人分期还款,债权人接受了债务人的违约/毁约并索赔损失(包括已到期但未付的分期还款与将来才需要支付的分期还款)。在该先例中,债权人已经履行了其所有的合约责任,相关的合约是一份一方已履行合约。贵族院一致判是债权人可以终止合约,即贵族院认为预期违约(针对将来才需要支付的分期还款)适用在一方已履行合约。

近期的 The "STX Mumbai" (2015) SGCA 35 新加坡先例也确认预期违约适用在待履行合约与一方已履行合约。在该先例中,原告(燃油供应商)向被告(STX Mumbai 轮船东)提供燃油,合约规定船东要在 30 日内做出支付。在合约规定期限前的 3 天,原告向被告要求当天内做出支付。原告要求被告提前做出支付是因为被告所属集团的经济状况十分糟糕,包括原告向另一艘被告所属集团拥有的船舶提供燃油但没有获得支付,被告的母公司在首尔法院申请破产。第二天,也就是合约规定期限前的 2 天,原告开始"对物诉讼"(in rem action)并扣船。原告的理由是燃油供应合约已经因为被告的预期违约被终止,被告没有在原告要求支付的当天做出支付,这显示被告预期违约/拒绝履行将来的合约责任的意图。又或者是当时的情况显示被告不可能在合约规定期限内支付这笔燃油费用。原告这样做可能希望比首尔法院正式批准破产早一步。被告向法院申请撤销诉讼(strike out the writ)并放船,因为诉因明显站不住脚。高院支持了被告的申请,认为被告没有预期违约,破产并不自动代表违约/毁约,并且预期违约不适用于一方已履行合约。但这个决定在上诉法院被改变,上诉庭判预期违约适用于一方已履行合约,并且虽然破产并不自动代表违约/毁

约，但在一定情况下可以显示有预期违约。〔73〕

但在美国普遍判是预期违约不适用于一方已履行合约，见：General American Tank Car Corp v. Goree（No 2114）296 F 32（4th Cir 2924）；Phelps v. Herro137 A. 2d 159（Court of Appeals of Maryland）；Thomas v. Ocean Technology，Inc. United States District Court，E. D. North Carolina，Eastern Division，May 29，2009（unreported）；McGregor v. National Steak Processors，Inc. United States District Court，N. D. Oklahoma，July 20，2012（unreported）等先例。在加拿大也有不少先例认为预期违约不适用于一方已履行合约，见：Long Island R. Co. v. Northville Indus. Corp. 362 N. E. 2d 558（1977）；Islip U－Slip LLC v. Gander Mountain Co. 2 F. Supp. 3d 296（2014）等先例。澳大利亚的 Mackenzie v. Rees（1941）65 CLR 1 先例也是类似的判法。

3.10　无辜方于违约方拒绝履行合约期间是否需要履行其合约责任

这已经在本章之3.4段提到，如果违约方做出拒绝性违约，无辜方不接受，则合约不会终止而需要持续履行。这已经是清楚明确的法律，没有被无辜方接受的预期违约就好像“没有发生过的镜花水月”（a thing writ in water）。这也表示无辜方不能因为对方做出拒绝性违约，一方面不接受违约去终止合约，另一方面又在期间暂时中断履行其自己的合约责任。除非是合约有明示条文规定可以这样做，〔74〕英国法律不承认无辜方有这一法律权利。正如 Staughton 大法官在 Eurotunnel v. Balfour Beauty（1992）2 Lloyd's Rep. 11 先例所说：“It is well established that if one party is in serious breach，the other can treat the contract as altogether at all end, but there is not yet any established doctrine of English law that the other party may suspend performance，keeping the contract alive.”

这种常会发生的情况是违约方拒绝履行，但无辜方努力想维持这一合约，就会面对两难处境。如在 CIF 买卖合约，合约的条件与价格对卖方很有利，所以卖方很希望这一合约获得履行。更会是在买方做出拒绝性违约时，卖方有关的货物已经生产得差不多，不做出付运给买方，就连已经生产好的货物都很难处置（如无法转售）。在这种情况下，卖方肯定是不会很快与干脆地接受并终止合约，而是哀求或威逼利诱，希望买方回心转意。但在这期间，卖方总会觉得心里没底，不敢租船与做出付运。如果贸然租船，就会面对另一个合约的履行要负责。而如果贸然付运，货物到了卸港买方也不接受，卖方损失会更大。显然，卖方会暂时中断履行，既不租船也暂时不付运，

---

〔73〕　有关破产与倒闭的有关课题，可看本章之4.4段。

〔74〕　如在期租合约最普遍被使用的标准格式 NYPE（在最近有了2015年新版本），第11（d）条文说：“At any time while hire is outstanding，the Owners shall，without prejudice to the liberty to withdraw，be entitled to withhold the performance of any and all obligations hereunder and shall have noresponsibility whatsoever for any consequences thereof，and Charterers hereby indemnify theOwners for all legitimate and justifiable actions taken to secure their interests，and hire shallcontinue to accrue and any extra expenses resulting from such withholding shall be for theCharterers' account.”

直到买方回心转意或买方的拒绝变得更加明确与肯定为止。但这样卖方就可能错过合约规定的付运期,这是条件条文。英国法律没有无辜方可以暂时中断履行的说法,就给了买方机会可以反过来说卖方违约/毁约,终止合约。在 Stocznia v. Latco (2002) 2 Lloyd's Rep. 436 先例,上诉庭的 Rix 大法官就把无辜方两难的情况总结如下:"In my judgment, there is of course a middle ground between acceptance of repudiation and affirmation of the contract, and that is the period when the innocent party is making up his mind what to do. If he does nothing for too long, there may come a time when the law will treat him as having affirmed. If he maintains the contract in being for the moment, while reserving his right to treat it as repudiated if his contract partner persists in his repudiation, then he has not yet elected. As long as the contract remains alive, the innocent party runs the risk that a merely anticipatory repudiatory breach, a thing "writ in water" until acceptance, can be **overtaken by another event which prejudices the innocent party's rights under the contract - such as frustration or even his own breach.** He also runs the risk, if that is the right word, that the party in repudiation will resume performance of the contract and thus end any continuing right in the innocent party to elect to accept the former repudiation as terminating the contract."(加黑部分是笔者的强调)

3.10.1 无辜方不接受拒绝性违约但事后因自己违反合约履行而变成违约方

这种案例可先介绍澳大利亚的 Bowes v. Chaleyer (1923) 32 CLR 159 先例,该先例的案情是在 1920 年 3 月 8 日,买方向卖方购买 1780 码的丝绸。合约规定一半尽快交付,另一半两个月后交付。买卖合约订立后不久,买方拒绝履行合约。但卖方还是在 10 月 21 日、11 月 17 日与 12 月 13 日做出了付运。买方分别在 1921 年 1 月 19 日、1 月 25 日与 1 月 27 日再度拒货。卖方只能将货物拍卖,并以买方的违约/毁约向其索赔差价。买方的抗辩是,卖方没有接受买方的拒绝履行并终止合约,但自己也没有按照合约的规定付运(没有分成两等份付运,付运也没有相隔两个月)是违反了买卖合约的条件条文。所以买方合法拒货并终止了合约。澳大利亚高院支持了买方的主张,Higgins 大法官说:"It is clear, . . . , the defendant gave absolute and unequivocal notice to the plaintiff that he would not accept the goods—would not perform the contract. The plaintiff then had a right of election: he could have concurred with the defendant in rescinding the contract, and bring an action for the breach; or he could have treated the notice as inoperative, and proceed with the contract. The plaintiff chose the latter course; and thereby he remained subject to all his own obligations under the contract, and the defendant remained in a position to take advantage of any failure of the plaintiff to do his part. A door must be either open or shut; a contract must either subsist or be at an end. This contract was not at an end; and the question remains, has the plaintiff failed to fulfil the conditions which would entitle him to payment from the defendant."

另一个是 The "Simona"(1988) 2 Lloyd's Rep. 199 (HL)先例,在该先例承租人以金康格式租了 Simona 轮,租约的销约期是 7 月 9 日。但在 7 月 2 日,船东因为延误要求承租人延长销约期,但承租人则回应说取消租约。显然在这一情况下,船东只是要求,并不代表拒绝履行租约,反而是承租人的回应要终止租约。船东并没有借这个机会接受,船依然开往装港 Durban,并在 7 月 7 日抵达。但船东有其他货物的装载作业,直到 7 月 9 日还没完成。船东向承租人询问装船时间,但承租人在 7 月 12 日取消租约。船东向承租人提出索赔(空仓费),说承租人在 7 月 2 日拒绝履行并构成违约/毁约。贵族院判是没有被接受的拒绝性违约,无辜方还是需要履行其合约责任,而租约也是继续存在。这等于船东没有在销约期前递交准备就绪通知书,承租人就可以合法终止租约。

3.10.2 弃权与禁反言对无辜方自己违反合约履行的救济

上述无辜方两难的情况经常发生,如何可以找到一个合理的方式让无辜方不会变为违约方?这在 The "Simona"(1988) 2 Lloyd's Rep. 199 (HL)先例就已经有了答案,就是无辜方可以根据违约方的"禁反言"(estoppel)言行[应该是属于陈述性禁反言(estoppel by representation)]作为理由否定违约方的争辩,Ackner 勋爵是这样说:"It is always open to A, who has refused to accept B's repudiation of the contract, and thereby kept the contract alive, to contend that in relation to a particular right or obligation under the contract, B is estopped from contending that he, B, is entitled to exercise that right or that he, A, has remained bound by that obligation. If B represents to A that he no longer intends to exercise that right or requires that obligation to be fulfilled by A and A acts upon that representation, then clearly B cannot be heard thereafter to say that he is entitled to exercise that right or that A is in breach of contract by not fulfilling that obligation. On my view of the meaning of the words of the contract, the plaintiff has failed to have the goods shipped in halves, with an interval of two months; and the defendant is entitled to say, 'what you offered to me is not that for which I bargained—non haec in fœdera veni.' It is not for Courts to weigh the importance of conditions which parties choose to put into their contracts; the failure here must be treated as being as fatal as if the contract were for pigskins and the tender were of sheepskins."

这样,如何和 Bowes v. Chaleyer (1923) 32 CLR 159 先例与 The "Simona"先例协调呢?笔者看来就是在这两个先例,无辜方自己违反了合约独立的条件条文,导致被原来的违约方反咬一口。但这些违约,包括货不对板与错过销约期,是与违约方的拒绝性违约毫无关系,所以陈述性禁反言不适用。禁反言要求必须无辜方依赖了(reliance)违约方的言行,并导致无辜方受到损害性影响(prejudice)。显然,在买方拒绝接受货物导致 CIF 卖方不敢租船与做出付运,这就与买方的拒绝有直接关系,完全可以适用禁反言的说法。

3.10.3 权威说法与有关先例/笔者的仲裁案件

禁反言的说法在一些权威书籍都写得很清楚,在《Chitty on Contracts》(第32版,2015年)之24-002段,说:"A contract remains in force until it has been terminated for breach so that a contracting party who has not elected to terminate the contract remains bound to perform its obligations unless the effect of the other party's breach is to prevent performance of the innocent party's obligation becoming due."在24-012段,也说:"Nevertheless, it may be that there are certain circumstances in which the innocent party may be released form performance of one or more of his obligations under the contract, notwithstanding the fact that he has not accepted the wrongdoer's repudiation. The first arises where **the repudiating party has, by words or conduct, represented to the innocent party that he will no longer require performance of a particular obligation under the contract, and the innocent party acts upon that representation. In such a case the repudiating party will be estopped from contending that the innocent party still remains bound by that obligation.** Secondly, where the repudiating party by means of a breach of contract or other default, prevents the innocent party from performing his obligations under the contract he cannot rely upon that non-performance to reduce or eliminate his liability. Finally, where the repudiating party stipulates for a mode of performance which is at variance with the terms of the contract and the innocent party attempts to comply with the new stipulation, the repudiating party cannot rely on a failure by the innocent party to perform his original obligations where the failure is attributable to his attempt to comply with the fresh stipulations."(加黑部分是笔者的强调)

货物买卖合约经常会有这种争议,在《Benjamin's Sale of Goods》(第8版,2014年)第9-018段与9-019段,也同样说:"Where the repudiation is not accepted by the seller, the contract is kept alive for the benefit of both parties; the seller remains subject to all the obligations and liabilities under it and takes the risk that he will, when the time for performance arrives, be unable to perform the contract in accordance with its terms or at all, or that some other event will occur which releases the buyer from liability. Since the seller continues to be bound to deliver the goods in accordance with the contract, it is a good defence to liability for the buyer to show that, notwithstanding his refusal to accept the goods, the seller has failed or is unable to perform his obligations under the contract in some fundamental respect at the time appointed for their performance. Even if the buyer persists in his refusal to accept, he does not thereby waive performance by the seller of the conditions precedent devolving on him ... Nevertheless, even where the seller has not accepted the buyer's repudiation, there may be circumstances where a refusal to accept, persisted in by the buyer, may release the seller from performance of one or more of his obligations, under the contract. The first is **where the buyer has, by words or**

conduct, represented to the seller that he will no longer require performance of that obligation, and the seller acts upon that representation..."(加黑部分是笔者的强调)

有关的先例也有很多,如在 Sinason – Teicher Inter – American Grain Corporation v. Oilcakes and Oilseeds Trading Co. Ltd. (1954) 1 WLR 935 先例,Devlin 大法官指出:"The buyers had kept the contract alive, but it does not mean that if the buyer chooses to keep the contract alive he is obliged to behave in precisely the same way as if the seller had not repudiated. That is to confuse two things. It is plainly established by Braithwaite v. Foreign Hardwood Co. [1905] 2 KB 543; 21 TLR 413 that that is not the case. If the seller's repudiation is such that he displayed an attitude which showed that he was, in effect, saying to the buyer, 'Although you are keeping the contract alive you can take up or perform your next obligation whatever it may be, tender your documents as much as you like, I cannot accept them,' the buyer is relieved from the obligation of making an empty and formal tender. He may, if he wishes for his own purposes, keep the contract alive and still claim that he is relieved from the obligation of making an empty and formal tender. The attitude of the sellers as shown in their cables was plain. They were not saying to the buyers in the period that elapsed between September 10 and 16: 'If you tender your document now we will look at it and see if it is all right.' What they were saying was: 'We have cancelled on September 10 and we stand on the fact that we cancelled on that date.' That made it plain that they were waiving any obligation on the buyers' part to trade during that period."

在澳大利亚的 Foran v. Wight (1989) 168 CLR 385 先例,Brennan 大法官说:"... more frequently, the facts will show no more than that the party to whom the intimation is given abstains from tendering performance in reliance on the intimation that he need not trouble to perform and that it will be useless for him to do so. It would be inequitable for A(违约方), having induced B(无辜方)to abstain from tendering performance, to assert that B's failure to tender performance when the time for completion arrives is a breach of contract by B or constitutes a failure to fulfil a condition on which A's obligation depends. The basis on which a party is dispensed from tendering performance is that an equity is raised against the party giving the intimation which is satisfied by treating him as though he had prevented the innocent party from tendering performance: see Waltons Stores (Interstate) Ltd. v. Maher (1988) 164 CLR 387. ... In my view, an equity created by estoppel arising from an intimation by A that he does not intend to perform which conveys to B that performance by him would be nugatory absolves B 'from tendering further performance unless and until A gives reasonable notice that he is once again able and willing to perform'."

再介绍香港终审法院鲍志金常任法官(Bokhary PJ)在 Kensland Realty Ltd. v. Whale View Investment Ltd. and another (2001) 4 HKCFAR 381 先例说:"However, the statement of principle by Lord Ackner in Fercometal cited above was expressed in reference to an argument that, when one party (the guilty party) repudiates his obligations under a contract and the other party (the innocent party) does not accept the repudiation and affirms the continued existence of the contract, the innocent party 'is absolved from tendering further performance under the contract while the repudiatory attitude is maintained.' His Lordship rejected that argument..."

最后介绍一个新的先例,在 Vitol SA v. Beta Renowable SA (2017) EWHC 1734 (Comm)先例中,案情涉及一个生物燃料(biofuel)的 FOB 买卖。但在付运期之前,卖方 Beta 电邮告知买方 Vitol 无法提供货物,之后 Vitol 没有明确接受这一违约/毁约,但开始向 Beta 索赔合约与市场的差价。Beta 的抗辩是,在合约仍继续存在的情况下,Vitol 自己没有在买卖合约规定的最后期限前指定船舶,而在 FOB 买卖,买方准时派船是卖方提供货物的先决条件(condition precedent)。一审法院判 Beta 败诉,不认为 Vitol 需要在知道 Beta 无法提供货物的情况下去租船并指定船舶。Carr 大法官说:"where to both parties' knowledge, the Contract could not and would not be performed by Beta, the condition precedent contended for does not thus arise."

另举一个笔者近期的香港仲裁案件。案情涉及硅片的买卖,合约规定"FOB Shanghai Airport",即卖方将货送往上海机场,由买方接收后做出付运去目的地。之后双方产生了争议,买方写信给卖方,表示如果合约价格不能按照市场价格计算(大幅度减价),他们会暂停履行合约。这是一个拒绝性违约,但卖方显然没有接受。双方之后有一些电邮往来的谈判,而卖方也没有继续按照合约的期限发货去上海机场。之后,卖方将准备送往上海机场给买方的货物以较低的价格转卖,并开始仲裁向买方索赔损失。但买方抗辩说卖方没有终止合约,也没有向买方按照合约交货,属于违约,不能向买方索赔损失。仲裁庭在分析了上述节录的权威书籍与判例后,认为买方的说法不能成立,要赔偿卖方的损失。

3.11 针对拒绝性违约能否向法院或仲裁庭申请履约指令或禁令

这个问题在本章之 3.3 段已经提到,如果一方拒绝履行合约,无辜方可以向法院申请履约指令(specific performance)或禁令(injunction)。这里涉及的疑问在 Khatijabai Jiwa Hasham v. Zenab (1960) AC 316 先例就已经有了答案,这就是一个还没有被接受的预期违约,本身虽然不是诉因(或可以索赔的诉因),因为没有被无辜方接受的预期违约就好像"没有发生过的镜花水月",但不影响可以申请履约指令。英国枢密院根据加拿大的类似判法,同意做出履约指令。判例说明了原因之一是这并非索赔金钱的损失,不严格需要法律认可的诉因。履约指令是"衡平法"(equity),而衡平法的救济只需要是显示了需要衡平法院伸出援手的情况。此外,履约指令一般分两个部分,第一个部分是"宣示"(declaration),第二部分是具体的指令(consequential directions)。而针对宣示,这不过是法院表达了其对这种争议(即使涉及将来的合约责任)的权威性看法。而针对预期违约,如果后来的确发生了真正违约,法院就可以不必再等待重启新的诉讼,而可以马上做出具体的指令。这种履约指令,法院不会强制一方当事人比合约规定的时间更早履行。如果在期间合约受阻,这一宣示判决/裁决可以向法院/仲裁庭申请做出改变,甚至可能在开始的宣示判决/裁决中,已经针对了这一变数说明会自动无效。

Khatijabai Jiwa Hasham v. Zenab 先例涉及非洲 Nairobi 土地的买卖,被告在签署了土地买卖合约几分钟后,就拒绝承认这一合约。结果在合约规定的交接前的两三个星期,原告(买方)向法院申请履约指令。这种先例还有:McGibbon v. Popoff (1977) 4 WWR 685 (BCSC);加拿大的 Roberto v. Bumb (1943) 2 DLR 613 (Ontario CA), Kloepfer Wholesale Hardware & Automotive Co. v. Roy (1952) 2 SCR 465 (SCC);澳大利亚的 Turner v. Bladin (1951) 82 CLR 463 (HCA)等。有趣的是,这些先例都涉及土地买卖,显示了这种争议经常在发生而且金额庞大,值得采取法律行动。对履约指令而言,更重要的是,土地买卖通常可以取得这种救济,不像其他的货物买卖,如商品买卖,会被法院视为金钱赔偿的救济已经足够,通常不会再做出履约指令,这可看杨良宜的《损失赔偿与救济》一书第十二章之4.5段。

有关履约指令的做法,在杨良宜的《损失赔偿与救济》一书第十二章有详论,这里不再重复。显然这也不表示法院或仲裁庭一旦涉及预期违约就会做出履行指令,毕竟很多情况金钱赔偿已经足够,在这些情况下,法院或仲裁庭就不愿意做出履约指令。另一种情况是预期违约涉及违约方明确表示他没有办法履行将来的责任,如没钱履行,而且很有可能事实也是如此,这样做出履约指令是将违约方逼上梁山。

在同样的原则下,无辜方也可以针对拒绝性违约向法院或仲裁庭申请“禁令”(injunction):Denmark Productions Ltd. v. Boscobel Productions Ltd. (1969) 1 QB 699 (CA); Decro – Wall International SA v. Practitioners in Marketing Ltd. (1971) 1 WLR 361; Berkeley Community Villages Ltd. v. Pullen (2007) EWHC 1330 (Ch)等先例,在杨良宜的《损失赔偿与救济》一书第十二章之1.1段也有提到。

所以稍早提到的三个关于禁令的先例,只有 Berkeley Community Villages Ltd. v. Pullen)涉及土地买卖。在该先例中,相关协议规定原告可以开发被告的土地,被告之后想将土地卖给第三人,原告向法院申请禁令禁止被告这样做。但在 Denmark Productions Ltd. v. Boscobel Productions Ltd. 先例,案情是被告与英国一个乐队订立了经纪合约,拥有乐队作品的专属销售权,并收取乐队40%的收入。之后被告与原告订立合约,约定共同管理乐队,承诺将支付给原告乐队10%的收入,并会将乐队作品的销售权转让给原告。后来双方关系恶化,原告向法院申请禁令禁止被告将作品销售给除原告外的任何人。在 Decro – Wall International SA v. Practitioners in Marketing Ltd. 先例,案情在本章之3.5.3段已经有简单介绍,只说卖方声称买方违约,不再是其独家经销商。但买方不承认责任,并向法院申请禁令禁止卖方找任何其他经销商。

4. 预期违约之二:不可能履行(impossibility)

这是一方(违约方)自己做的事令他将来无法再履约,所以即使他什么也没做、也没说,可以说没向合约的对方(无辜方)显示不履行将来的合约责任,也可构成“违约/毁约”(repudiatory breach)。这也是针对将来履约的责任,亦属“预期违约”(anticipatory breach)的另一种。

可先节录权威书籍《Chitty on Contracts》(第32版,2015年)一书之24-029段的说法:

“**Impossibility**. Where one party has, by his own act or default, disabled himself from performing his contractual obligations in some essential respect, the other party will be entitled to treat himself as discharged.[75] The inability to perform his contractual obligations must be established on the balance of probabilities...[76]

The inability to perform need not be due to a deliberate act...[77]

So, where a person undertook to transfer certain furniture, but before he could do so a judgment creditor took the furniture in execution and sold it, his inability to perform, though not due to his own deliberate act, constituted a breach of the agreement.[78] However, where part only of one party's obligations are rendered impossible of performance, the other party will not be able to treat himself as discharged unless the resulting non-performance would amount to a breach of condition or would deprive him of substantially the whole benefit of the contract.[79]”

4.1 不可能履行与合约受阻的关系

上述介绍的因为合约一方(违约方)的行为或过错导致合约的重要部分无法履行,也经常被称为“breach by frustration”。这是因为合约受阻也是针对合约无法履行。但真正的合约“受阻”(frustration)针对的情况是合约双方都没有过错或责

---

〔75〕 如果因为合约一方(违约方)的行为或过错导致合约的重要部分无法履行,另一方(无辜方)就可以终止合约。

〔76〕 违约方是否可以履行,要根据所有的证据以平衡的可能性判断。

〔77〕 但违约方不需要故意才须负责,这在接下来的先例有清楚说明。

〔78〕 在 Keys v. Harwood (1846) 2 CB 905 先例,涉及一批家具的买卖。但卖方交付之前,由于他在一个判决债务下的债权人向法院申请强制执行,这批家具被强制取走拍卖,卖方肯定无法交货。虽然卖方的行为不是故意,依然属于预期违约。

〔79〕 但除非违约方不可能履行的是条件条文或合约的重要责任,无辜方不能终止合约。这与本章之3.5段介绍的另一种预期违约“拒绝性违约”(renunciatory breach)需要是一个重要的合约责任是同样的道理。

任,[80]而是有其他外来的原因导致了合约无法履行。所以在真正的合约受阻,合约自动终止,[81]也不存在合约双方之间可以向对方索赔损失:Hirji Mulji v. Cheong Yue S. S. Co. Ltd. (1926) AC 497, 509 先例与 BP v. Hunt (1979) 1 WLR 783 先例。

这可节录《Chitty on Contracts》(第 32 版,2015 年)一书之 24 - 029 段,如下:"**Impossibility and frustration**. Similar tests have been applied to determinate whether or not a contract has become impossible of performance by reason of the default of one party as have been applied to determine whether there has been a mutual discharge of the contract by reason of the doctrine of frustration."

这里可举一些简单的例子说明两者之间的区别。如一个房屋的买卖,在卖方交接之前,房屋被烧毁。如果房屋被烧毁是因为卖方疏忽,如没有检查出电路老化,属于卖方预期违约。但如果房屋被烧毁与卖方无关,如被闪电劈中着火,则属于合约受阻。

4.2　证明不可能履行的困难

无辜方要证明对方(违约方)不可能履行合约责任并不容易,毕竟很多事情只要肯花时间与金钱总可以办到,正如那句名言"nothing is impossible"。但如果可能履行的概率实在太小,只能说在理论上存在一定的可能性也不会被法院接受。在《Chitty on Contracts》(第 32 版,2015 年)一书之 24 - 031 段提到 Omnium D'Enterprises v. Sutherland (1919) 1 KB 618 先例,说:"... So where a shipowner agreed to charter a ship ... but ... sold her to another person, it was held that he had put it out of his power to perform the agreement and the charterer was entitled to sue for damages forthwith. It was argued for the shipowner that he might have bought back the ship in time to fulfill the contract, but this was regarded as too speculative a possibility; ..."

该先例的案情涉及原船东把一艘有租约在身的船舶出售给买方,买卖合约说明船舶是"free from any charter engagement"(没有租约在身)。面对承租人的起诉与索赔损失,船东否认他是违约/毁约,不可能去履行该租约,因为他可以向新船东租回来,再以二船东(也是船东)的身份去继续履行对承租人的租约。但法院不接受这一说法,说这是以不肯定(新船东不一定肯回租)来替代不可能履行(船舶已卖掉)的事实:"substituting a chance for a certainty."

本章之 3.1 段已经提到不可能履行与将来没有能力履行(inability to perform)的拒绝有相似之处,但也有区别。其主要区别在于,前者要证明事实,即对方是否真正"不可能"(impossibility)履约,则须以当时及其后所发生的所有事实为准。而对后者的判定须以当时无辜方所掌握的事实与违约方的语言和行动为依据,而不管对方此种显示出不能履约(inability)的情况事后一直至应该履约时有否改变。对于不可能

〔80〕 见本书第二章之 7.5 段。

〔81〕 见本书第二章第 8 段。

履行，推断对方在将来不可能履行并不足够，而需要去以后来发生的事实证明。正如Delvin大法官在Universal Cargo Carriers Corp. v. Pedro Citati (1957) 1 Lloyd's Rep. 174先例所说："An anticipatory breach must be proved in fact and not in supposition."又说："... on the basis of impossibility of performance, ... the determination is to be made in the light of all the events – whether occurring before or after the critical date."

在该先例中，Delvin大法官也举例显示"不可能"不容易成立。一位男士答应将娶一位A女士（双方有婚约），但结婚前不久，他另娶了B女士。表面看来，该男士对A女士的婚约明显是"不可能"在应娶嫁时履约，即使马上跟B女士离婚，也不会这么快办妥。但谁知道呢，B女士突然死亡？正如Delvin对方说："Suppose, for example, that a man promises to marry a woman on a future date ... and... before that date arrives he marries another... the aggrieved party may sue at once. One reason alleged in support of such action ... is that the defendant has, before the day, rendered it impossible for him to perform... but this does not necessary follow; for, prior to the date... the first wife may have died."

当然，在以上两例中，即把船舶卖掉与另娶B女士，也可不只依赖"不可能"，只需加上违约方的言行显示"拒绝履约"（renunciation）。那样对无辜方会更明确稳妥，因为指证违约方不愿意或没有能力履约只需根据当时的情况，无须受以后可能发生的事情验证约束（如B女士事后突然死亡）。即将该男士娶了B女士视为拒绝性违约的行为，而同时以Omnium D'Enterprises v. Sutherland先例认为年轻的B女士突然死亡的概率实在太低，也构成不可能履约。

4.3 不可能履行情况之一：同时承诺两个有直接冲突的合约

同时承诺两个有直接冲突的合约（conflict engagement）的情况时有发生。曾有一个案例，中国的船公司早期因为权利分配不清晰，同一艘船舶总公司与分公司都可以出租，如果双方没有良好的沟通，就会出现一艘船舶同时出租给两个承租人的情况。也会有其他原因导致一方被夹在两个有直接冲突的合约中，本章之7.2段将会提到笔者处理过的案子就是很好的例子。如果无辜方不小心或不懂，在接受违约方的预期违约终止有关合约前，就另订立一个替代合约，就会出现这种不幸的情况。这样，违约方一定要选择一个合约违约，不可能同时履行两个租约。但是无辜方能否以不可能履行为由提前终止合约？答案是否定的，毕竟履行其中一个合约的概率仍有50%。无辜方也无法证明不可能履行的是他的合约，而非另一个。否则，岂不是两个合约的无辜方都可以以不可能为由终止合约，违约方最后什么也保不住？

涉及同时承诺两个有直接冲突的合约著名先例是Toepfer v. Itex Itagrani (1993) 1 Lloyd's Rep. 360。在该先例中，卖方出售了约2.1万吨玉米给买方（Toepfer），买方又转售了给第三人的分买方，都是以FOB条件交易。分买方派了2万多吨载重量的Danobar Tanabe轮来南美的装港，但原来分买方另有一个买6100吨玉米的FOB合约，也指定（nominate）这条船来装运。这样，两票货根本装不下，如装了

6100 吨的玉米,船舶剩下的载重只有约 1.54 万吨,而不是合约的 2.1 万吨。知悉这个情况后,卖方以此为由"接受"买方的违约/毁约并终止合约,说这行为(虽是分买方所做的,但对卖方而言,是买方负责)构成"不可能履行"。

但仲裁庭与上诉的 Saville 大法官都不同意,认为这只是显示买方可能有机会不可能履行而已,但不是明确不可能。例如,分买方稍后不装另外合约的 6100 吨,即使这是在另一合约的违约/毁约。Saville 大法官说:"On the present case, however, the mere fact that the sub – buyers had contracted to load other goods on the vessel did not, in itself, establish that the buyers could not perform—at most that established that the buyers might not be able to perform... in the present case there was only a chance that the buyers would be unable to perform...Quite apart from the foregoing, the arbitrators have found as a fact that had matters continued (that is to say had the sellers not purported to accept the buyers' repudiation of the contract), then the Sub – buyers would have allowed 21,000 tons to be loaded upriver under the contract, even if this meant that they had to resile from their obligations (of the other contract)."

看来,在该先例中,卖方行动得太快,太早肯定买方不可能履行,结果变成自己违约/毁约。卖方要是多等一会,可能买方真会是不可能履行。

另一个例子是更近期的 The "Ekha" (2010) 1 Lloyd's Rep. 543 先例。在该先例中,Seadrill 将一架自升式钻井平台(jack – up drilling rig)名为 Ekha,出租给俄罗斯最大的天然气开采集团 Gazprom,用来在孟加拉湾钻井开采油气。双方在 2005 年 9 月 10 日订立租约,租约中并没有写明合约期限,但双方估计 45 天可以完成工程。但在开始钻井前,平台的脚架损坏,被迫要去新加坡修理。在修理期间,Seadrill 与另一家石油公司 Premier Oil 进行了接触,承诺修理完毕后就会直接为 Premier Oil 服务。虽然双方没有正式签订合约,但 Ekha 在修理的同时也进行了升级,以满足 Premier Oil 的要求。Ekha 完成修理与升级后,预计无法在 2006 年 5 月季风季节(估计会影响工程)开始前返回孟加拉湾。2006 年 5 月 16 日,Gazprom 写信给 Seadrill,声称由于 Seadrill 的预期违约,包括操作时的疏忽导致平台的脚架损坏,合约被终止。而 Seadrill 否认其预期违约,并指称 Gazprom 终止合约的行为才是预期违约。Seadrill 在 2006 年 7 月 10 日接受了 Gazprom 的预期违约,并向 Gazprom 索赔 2005 年 11 月到 2006 年 7 月的租金与其他损失。Gazprom 的抗辩是,Ekha 损坏是由于 Seadrill 在操作过程中疏忽,这带来严重的延误,这已经足够重要让 Gazprom 终止合约。但这一抗辩不成立,因为时间的延误并非是条件条文,虽然延误到季风季节的来临,但这仍不足以构成受阻延误。

Gazprom 的另一个抗辩是,即使不能以此终止合约,Seadrill 在修理过程中与 Premier Oil 接触并承诺修理完毕后直接为其工作的行为,属于拒绝性违约或预期违约的不可能履行。针对不可能履行,Flaux 大法官也是判不成立,说:"However, unless and until the contract with Gazprom was terminated on one ground or another, I can see no earthly reason in commercial terms why Seadrill would make some formal or contractual arrangement with Premier Oil that it might not be able to keep. . . . I would still have held that there was no renunciation even if (contrary to my findings) Seadrill had made a binding contractual commitment at some point in the period January to April 2006 (as Mr Rainey [Gazprom 代表大律师] urged me to find) to Premier Oil to go to work for it in Indonesia after the works completed in the yard. This is because, although the effect of that commitment would have been that Seadrill had clashing contractual commitments, until the rig came out of the yard she was not available to either Gazprom or Premier Oil. It was only when she came out of the yard in June 2006 that (assuming at that stage Gazprom had still wanted the rig) Seadrill would have had to choose between those clashing-commitments. Until then, it could not be said Seadrill had renounced the contract with Gazprom. A submission to that effect was rejected in Alfred C Toepfer International GmbH v. Itex Itagrani Export SA [1993] 1 Lloyd's Rep. 360, as was a further submission that by entering a clashing contractual commitment, the defendant had put it out of its power to perform the contract and thus repudiated the contract because of impossibility of performance."

4.4 不可能履行情况之二:清盘倒闭

在现在的商业社会,经常会遇见公司破产清盘,[82]这时合约的另一方就会处于十分不利与被动的地位。例如,根据合约向对方提供了服务或是交付了货物,但收不到钱,只能成为一个"普通债权人"(ordinary trade creditor)。在这种情况下就会有疑问是,如果一方宣布破产,合约的另一方是否可将对方的这一言行当做预期违约而终止合约不再履行?答案是否定的,因为破产公司的"清盘人"(liquidator)会履行对该公司有利润的合约。这可节录《Chitty on Contracts》(第 32 版,2015 年)之 20 - 032 段如下:"**Contracts not terminated by bankruptcy.** A contract is not determined by the bankruptcy of one of the parties thereto. Ordinarily the benefit of any contract made by the debtor passes to his trustee in bankruptcy as part of his property, subject to the

---

〔82〕 这里应将破产清盘与公司解散(dissolution of company)进行区分。公司解散意味着公司不再存在,所有的合约都不会被履行,已经进行中的所有的法律程序也都会停止。这与公司还存在债务偿还安排(scheme of arrangement)不同。当公司清盘(wind up),清盘人(liquidator)会控制公司所有资产,卸弃(disclaim)所有有繁苛条件的资产(onerous property),如无利可图的合约。根据 Tanning Research Laboratories Inc. v. O' Brien (1990) HCA 8 先例,清盘人替代了合约方的位置。如果清盘人卸弃了合约,就属于违约/毁约,合约另一方可以无抵押债权人(unsecured creditor)的身份获得赔偿。显然,如果是有利可图的合约,清盘人也会替代合约方去履行,而赚取的利润会在之后分摊给公司的债权人。另一种要进行区分的是破产管理人(receiver/administrator)替代了公司董事会的位置。虽然接管人不能卸弃无利可图的合约,但公司永远可以选择违约/毁约,而另一方也只能以无抵押债权人的身份获得(部分或极少的)赔偿。

trustee's right to disclaim unprofitable contracts, and if it is an executory contract, the trustee may complete it and receive the benefit for the estate, he may give receipts and, with the permission of the creditors' committee, exercise various powers, e. g. even to the bankrupt, sell the bankrupt's business (in a proper case even to a company promoted by himself and the creditors' committee) or make any compromise of an action or claim."

当然法律总会有例外,如在货物买卖,如果卖方知道买方破产,而货物还在付运途中,卖方有权"终止付运"(stoppage in transit)并要求"承运人"(carrier)不能把货物交给买方。卖方也可以在卸港或交货前留置货物,即使买卖合约是信贷交易(sale on credit)。这些都有立法的规定,即1979年英国《货物销售法》的Section 41(1)(c),可节录如下:"Subject to this Act, the unpaid seller of goods who is in possession of them is entitled to retain possession of them until payment or tender of the price in the following cases:—...(c) where the buyer becomes insolvent."

这在《Chitty on Contracts》(第32版,2015年)一书之20-033段也说:"... The vendor may also exercise the right of lien even though he has agreed to give the buyer credit, and would not therefore have had any lien in the absence of insolvency of the buyer. So also, the seller's right of stoppage in transit only arises if the buyer is insolvent. ..."

另一个例外涉及个人履约有特别的重要性,如在雇佣合约,雇主破产,雇员就权终止合约:Reid v. Explosives Co. Ltd. (1887) LR 19 QBD 264 (CA)先例。

所以有不少中长期的合约,特别是合约的履行会严重受到其中一方破产的影响,如工程合约,通常合约会加上一条明示条文,说明如果一方(如在造船合约的船厂)在合约履行中破产,另一方就有权终止合约:Perar BV v. General Surety & Guarantee Co. Ltd. (1994) 43 Con LR 110 (CA)先例。当然在订约自由下,写法千变万化,在Perar BV v. General Surety & Guarantee Co. Ltd. 先例,涉及的条文是:

"27.2 In the event of the Contractor having an administrative receiver, as defined in the Insolvency Act 1986, appointed the employment of the Contractor under this Contract **shall be forth with automatically determined** but the said employment may be reinstated and continued if the Employer and the Contractor [and] receiver shall so agree.

27.4 In the event of the employment of the Contractor under this Contract being determined under clauses 27.1, 27.2 or 27.3 and so long as it has not been reinstated and continued, the following shall be the respective rights and duties of the Employer and the Contractor."

在该工程合约中,履约期间承建商被债权人通过法院委任的行政管理人(administrative receiver)接管,根据《Insolvency Act 1986》,这是公司清盘前必要步骤,看能否挽救。工程合约根据上述节录的条文被终止,而且没有再变回有效(reinstate)。雇主受该事件的影响而蒙受损失,所以向承建商提供履约担保(performance bond)的担保人索赔这笔钱。该履约担保的文字是针对承建商如果有过错(default)并且不做出赔偿,担保人就会赔偿这笔损失,最高的限额是 137 万英镑。这样,雇主与作为被告的担保人之间的争议就是到底这一工程合约的终止是否由于承建商的过错,这就表示要争议承建商被行政管理人接管是否构成违约/毁约,也表示这一合约是违约令合约终止(discharge by breach)。但在上诉庭,判承建商被行政管理人接管不构成预期违约的行为,而这个情况也已经有第 27.2 条文明示针对,所以合约的自动终止是根据这一条文,不涉及承建商的违约或过错。其中 Peter Gibson 大法官是这样说:

"... there was an anticipatory breach of contract on the contractor going into administrative receivership. He pointed out that going into insolvency may be a repudiation of a contract, because of the insolvent party's inability further toperform the obligations under the contract. He submitted that such an anticipatory breach caused damage which the employer could recover under the bond. This is a claim that, notwithstanding the operation of cl 27.2, there remains a right in the employer to proceed against the contractor at common law for a breach. Of course, an anticipatory breach is not an actual breach. There is no term in this contract that the contractor should not have an administrative receiver appointed of it.

In my judgment, the answer to this submission lies in the fact to which I have already adverted, that cl 27.2 was intended by the parties to be an exclusive code. Thereby the parties to the contract contracted out of allowing a claim to be made in respect of the contractor becoming insolvent in any of the ways indicated in that paragraph. Instead, the parties agreed that the consequences of the contractor becoming insolvent were to be those specified in cl 27.4... Accordingly, I cannot accept this submission either."

另 Staughton 大法官也同意,说:"I can accept that the appointment of an administrative receiver will in some cases amount to a repudiation or renunciation. But that result does not occur in this case, because the contract provides otherwise. It provides that the employment of the contractors shall automatically be determined, and that the employers have no option to continue the contract. It also provides that there shall then be an accounting under cl 27.4. It is not open to the employers to treat the appointment of the administrative receiver in this case as an anticipatory breach of contract."

这样看来,如果涉及破产清盘的情况,除非另外有言行(特别是来自有权控制该破产公司的人士,如清盘人),显示了其不愿意或不能履行,否则只是根据公司宣布破产这个行动说是对方预期违约是不足够的:Edinburgh Grain Ltd. (in liquidation) v. Marshall Food Group Ltd. 1999 SLT 15 (CSOH)先例。在该苏格兰先例中,涉及粮食买卖合约,买方决定破产,并电话通知卖方说他已经停止经营,这是最终决定,所以他不能继续履行合约。之后,法院委任了临时清盘人,买方给清盘人发了一封传真,表达他认为卖方之前已经拒绝履行合约。清盘人以传真要求买方澄清他是否要终止合约并要求支付已经付运的粮食的货款。但买方认为,卖方已经拒绝履行合约并被买方接受,所以,买方有权将需要支付的货款与卖方拒绝履行造成的损失进行抵销。清盘人开始诉讼,买方主要的抗辩/反索赔是卖方之前的电话已经显示了其不能继续履行合约,这是拒绝性违约(renunciatory breach)。买方另一个替代抗辩是卖方的破产显示了他/清盘人不可能继续履行合约(impossibility)。法院最后判是卖方之前的电话已经显示了其不能够继续履行合约,是拒绝性违约。但对不可能履行的替代抗辩,法院判是不成立。

另一个更明确也是笔者很熟悉的较早期先例是加拿大的 The "Sanko Iris" and "Sanko Venus" (1987) 1 Lloyd's Rep. 487 先例。该先例的原告是当时日本很大的一家船公司 Sanko。Sanko 在几年前航运市场好的时候雄心勃勃,发展势头迅猛,建造与租入了上百艘船舶。但之后航运市场暴跌,Sanko 的经济立即出现问题,并在 1985 年 8 月 12 日向日本法院申请破产。该先例涉及的是 Sanko 与加拿大的木材公司 Eacom 的包运合约(COA),从温哥华运木材去美国东岸港口。8 月 13 日,履行包运合约其中一个航次的 Sanko Iris 轮完成前一批货物的卸载并将 Eacom 的货物装上了船舶。但在离开美国纽约前,被装卸工人扣船。Sanko 也得知下一个卸港 Bridgeport 要求必须提前支付相关费用才会让 Sanko Iris 轮靠泊卸货。8 月 15 日,Sanko Iris 轮的原船东通知 Eacom(对原船东来说就是分承租人),因为 Sanko 不支付租金,他已经终止了与 Sanko 的租约。此外,船东留置分租约下的运费(即 Eacom 要支付给 Sanko 的运费)。[83] 8 月 12 日,履行包运合约另一个航次的 Sanko Venus 轮在温哥华准备装货,但装卸工人向 Eacom 表示除非另有可信赖的人士提供担保或提前支付其费用,他们不会为 Sanko Venus 轮装货。为了解决眼前的问题,Eacom 表示愿意提供资金支持,但 Sanko 必须保证 Sanko Venus 轮不再被延误或受到阻碍。但直到 8 月 19 日,法院委任了临时管理人,Sanko 才能提供担保,期间 Eacom 已经在 8 月 16 日租入了另一艘替代船舶。8 月 29 日,Eacom 接受了 Sanko 的预期违约,终止了包运合约。Sanko 指称 Eacom 错误终止了包运合约,并索赔损失。Sanko 的立场是,Eacom 并不能因为 Sanko 破产就终止包运合约,事实上 Sanko 可以履行,临时管理人也愿意履行。发生在 Sanko Iris 轮与 Sanko Venus 轮的延误/阻碍不属于违约,即使属于违约也没有影响包运合约的根基。Macdonald 大法官不支持 Sanko 的立场,判 Sanko 以行动拒绝履行合约,说:"When inability to perform in the future is indicated by something that a party to a contract does or fails to do, the other party will invariably rely, as Eacom does here, upon renunciation by conduct rather than upon impossibility, because renunciation is easier to establish and once established, is final."

MacDonald 大法官认为 Eacom 有权怀疑 Sanko 不能履行包运合约下将来的责

〔83〕 关于留置运费这一课题与相关做法,请看杨大明的《期租合约》一书第四十篇之 40.4.1 至 40.4.7 段。

任,只要这一怀疑是合理的,即使后来的变化显示这一怀疑不正确。MacDonald 大法官的判决被总结如下:"Eacom had the right in law to doubt Sanko's future ability to perform the COA provided that its decision was reasonable on Aug. 29, 1985."

4.5 拒绝性违约与不可能履行一并作为替代理由

总结以上的介绍,无辜方根据对方的言行显示了其没有能力履行合约或不可能履行合约而合法终止合约,安全的做法还是把两个争议同时作为替代理由。在本章之4.3 段介绍的同时承诺两个有直接冲突的合约或是 4.4 段介绍的破产,或其他同样性质的情况,都应该把拒绝履行与不可能履行一并作为替代理由。而两者之间,已经在本章之4.2 段提到,拒绝履行作为终止合约的理由会比不可能履行容易成立得多。但需要注意的是,首先拒绝履行要涉及违约方事前的言行,无辜方甚至需要在终止合约前制造有利的证据,如在本章之3.8 段介绍的最后通牒(ultimatum)。在终止合约后,也需要收集证据,确认违约方不可能履行的情况有否发生变化,是否有新的证据证明违约方确实不可能履行。在开始诉讼后,也要注意不要在文书请求中漏了其中一个作为替代理由。

在《Chitty on Contracts》(第 32 版,2015 年)一书之 24 - 030 段有建议说:"**Impossibility and renunciation.** In most cases where the impossibility created by one party has manifested itself by conduct, the innocent party will rely upon renunciation by conduct rather than impossibility, because renunciation is so much easier to establish.[84] Renunciation is to be preferred because the innocent party need only show that the conduct of the party in default was such as to lead a reasonable man to believe that he did not intend, or was not able, to perform his promise; whereas if the innocent party relies upon impossibility he must show that the contract was in fact impossible of performance due to the other party's default.[85] Nevertheless the innocent party would be well advised to rely on both grounds for treating the contract as at an end, because: (1) renunciation may not, for some reason, be open to him; and (2) if he has misinterpreted the conduct of the other party and so rescinded for an inadequate reason he may still fall back on impossibility if it should subsequently appear that the other party was in fact incapable of perform-

---

〔84〕 在大多数案件中,一方不可能履行合约责任都只是由行为显示出来的,因为如果违约方是加上语言,无辜方就根本可以根据对方的话的表见价值构成拒绝性违约终止合约。通常,无辜方更倾向于依赖"以行为拒绝履行"而不是"不可能履行",因为前者容易证明得多。

〔85〕 更倾向于依赖"拒绝履行"是因为无辜方只需要证明违约方的行为会使一个合理人士认为其不愿意或不能履行将来的合约责任。但如果无辜方依赖"不可能履行",就必须证明因为违约方的行为,在事实上已经不可能履行将来的合约责任。

ing his promise.[86]"

无数的先例有同样的说法，只节录 Delvin 大法官在 Universal Cargo Carriers Corp. v. Pedro Citati (1957) 1 Lloyd's Rep. 174 先例中说："... **renunciation has since the decision in Hochster v. De la Tour (1853) 2 E&B 678 established itself as the favourite. The disadvantage of the other is that the party who elects to treat impossibility as an anticipatory breach may be running a serious risk.** Suppose, for example, that a man promises to marry a woman on a future date... and that before the date arrives he married another. The aggrieved party may sue at once. 'Once reason alleged in support of such an action', Campbell CJ observed in Hochster v. De la Tour, 'is, that the defendant has, before the day, rendered it impossible for him to perform the contract at that day, ..."（加黑部分是笔者的强调）

5. 错误拒绝履行合约能否以另一个事后才发觉的合法理由补救

以错误理由或不给理由拒绝履行合约的事情经常发生，这在中国公司/企业发生得特别多。一种情况是，违约方告诉对方一些根本不合法的理由去拒绝履行合约，如说市场不好，公司资金异常困难，已经尽了最大努力履行，但下一批货物我不会接受。同时，讲一些哀求的话，如哀求对方不要把事情升级，顾全将来的合作机会。在笔者看来，这些根本没有用。[87]

另一种情况是，一方以看似合法的理由拒绝履行合约，但因为后来的变化，不论是发现更多的证据，或是拿到更多的法律意见，或是有了新的案例，甚至是经过审理，发现理由不足够，以前已经发生了的拒绝履行的行为构成违约/毁约。

也有很多不同的情况，但总而言之，很少会有情况是一方拒绝履行合约时，讲明现有的所有合法理由。至于因为后来才发觉或才出现的合法理由，更是不可能在拒绝履行时说出来。

这显然会带来一个很现实的后果，即对方认为讲明的理由根本站不住脚或根本

---

〔86〕 当然无论如何，无辜方在诉讼中应该同时依赖这两个理由作为替代（alternative reason）来显示合约已经被终止，理由在于：第一，"拒绝履行"可能因为某些原因不适用；第二，如果他错误理解了违约方的言行，导致终止合约的理由不足够，那么还有机会证明违约方事实上不可能履行合约责任。这种做法在本章之 3.5.2 段提到的 Universal Cargo Carriers Corp. v. Pedro Citati (1957) 1 Lloyd's Rep. 174 先例就有显示。

〔87〕 哀求对方非但不会有效果，更会在后来的诉讼中使自己处于更加不利的地位。即使称职律师能找到合法理由解释拒绝履行合约的言行，当场白纸黑字写明的不合法理由也会让法院或仲裁庭有了敌意。

没有理由,就会在接受拒绝履行去终止合约后提起诉讼并索赔损失。这也解释了中国公司/企业为什么面对这么多索赔,并需要委任律师并做出抗辩。如果委任的律师称职并有水平,往往会发觉有其他根本没有提到或想到的合法理由可以拒绝履行。问题是可否"事后诸葛亮"地以一个或多个事后挑出来的合法理由补救?如上述提到的破产的例子,一方合约方以对方破产不可能履行为由终止合约。这事后被判是错误,如在 The "Sanko Iris" and "Sanko Venus" (1987) 1 Lloyd's Rep. 487 先例中,Sanko 可以继续履行,Eacom 终止包运合约是早了一些。但 Eacom 事后仍以终止时,不论早或晚,当时而言根据 Sanko 的言行,是可以得出合理的估计 Sanko 不能够履行包运合约将来的责任。如果能够说服仲裁庭或法院这是一个合理的估计,Eacom 就可以在拒绝性违约胜诉,即使最初以 Sanko 破产为由终止包运合约是不足够的理由。或是相反,在 Universal Cargo Carriers Corp. v. Pedro Citati(1957) 1 Lloyd's Rep. 174 先例,Devlin 大法官判是违约方在装港的不行动并非拒绝履行重要的合约责任,不构成拒绝性违约。但如果无辜方能通过事后的证据证明违约方确实最后不可能履行(在装港不能提供货物装船),也可以加上不可能履行的理由作为补救。

5.1 英国法律允许以事后才发觉的合法理由补救

英国法律的大原则是可以事后才发现的合法理由进行补救,毕竟这种事情发生得太多。这甚至可以反映在诉讼程序,也就是直到做出判决/裁决前,双方都可以更改(amend)文书请求。这一适用在所有违约令合约终止(discharge by breach)的合约法原则在两个早期的先例的说法是经常被引用的,一个是 Taylor v. Oakes Roncoroni & Co. (1922) 27 Com Cas 261 先例,Greer 大法官说:"It is a long established rule of law that a contracting party, who, after he has become entitled to refuse performance of his contractual obligations, gives a wrong reason for his refusal, does not thereby deprive himself of a justification which in fact existed, whether he was aware of it or not."

另一个是在 British and Beningtons Ltd. v. North Western Cachar Tea Co. Ltd. (1922) 13 Lloyd's Rep. 67 先例,Sumner 勋爵说:"I do not think that the case, as reported, lays it down that a buyer, who has repudiated a contract for a given reason which fails him, has, therefore, no other opportunity of defence either as to the whole or as to part, but must fail utterly. If he had repudiated, giving no reason at all, I suppose all reasons and all defences in the action, partial or complete, would be open to him. His motives certainly are immaterial, and I do not see why his reasons should be crucial."

这一法律大原则也在权威的合约法书籍有总结,《Chitty on Contracts》(第 32 版,2015 年)一书之 24 - 014 段说:"**No reason or bad reason given.** The general rule is well established that, if a party refuses to perform a contract, giving a wrong or inadequate reason or no reason at all, he may yet justify his refusal if there were at the time facts in existence which would have provided a good reason, even if he did not know of them at the time of his refusal. Thus when an employee brings an action against his employer, alleging that he has been wrongfully dismissed, the employer can rely on information acquired after the dismissal when seeking to justify the dismissal. The general rule is the subject of a number of exceptions. **First**, a party cannot rely on a ground which he did not specify at the time of his refusal to perform 'if the point which was not taken could have been put right'. **Secondly**, a party may be precluded by the operation of the doctrines of waiver or estoppel from relying on a ground which he did not specify at the time of his refusal to perform. **Thirdly**, a party may be held to have accepted the goods so that he is no longer able to justify his refusal to perform. However, there does not appear to be any separate principle which would preclude a party from setting up a different ground simply because it would be unfair or unjust to allow him to do so."

5.2 有关先例介绍

这一合约法原则在很多先例都有适用,只介绍少数的著名先例。如在 The "Mihalis Angelos"(1970) 2 Lloyd's Rep. 43 先例,案情涉及一艘希腊船舶程租给当时的北越政府(承租人)去海防装货,租约规定船舶预计在 7 月 1 日备妥可以装货(expect to load on 1st July 1965)与销约期是 7 月 20 日。由于船舶延误,船东赶不上销约期之前抵达海防港装货。但承租人在 7 月 17 日告知船东由于"不可抗力"(force majeure)终止租约,因为越战期间铁路被美国飞机炸毁,导致承租人没有办法把货物运到海防港装船。船东指承租人违约/毁约并向承租人索赔损失。但实际上,船东如果继续履行租约也只会多花费用如燃油费用,把船舶开去海防港,然后被承租人以错过销约期终止租约。上诉庭的 Denning 勋爵等大法官判承租人没有违约/毁约,船舶租预计在 7 月 1 日备妥可以装货是条件条文,船东违反了条件条文,虽然承租人使用了不可抗力的错误理由,〔88〕但不影响他终止租约的有效性。Edmund Davies 大法官说:"... I would be for holding that clause 1 in the present case imported a condition. That the owners were in breach of it is common ground. It is equally undisputed that if, as I think, the circumstances entitled the charterers to repudiate on July 17, the fact that they did so by reliance on an untenable plea of force majeure does not invalidate their act of cancellation."

另在 The "John S. Darbyshire" (1977) 2 Lloyd's Rep. 457 先例,案情涉及一个 1 年的期租合约,租约有一个特别的后续条件(condition subsequent/condition precedent to performance)〔89〕规定承租人要对前两次的试用航次感到满意,才需要继续履行。第一次试用航次就出现了问题,但在两个试用航次跑完后,承租人告诉船东由于

---

〔88〕 不可抗力是错误理由是因为不可抗力是大陆法的概念,英国法没有这个说法,必须要有明示条文针对。详见杨良宜的《合约的解释:规则与应用》第十三章之 1 段。

〔89〕 关于合约的先决条件与后续条件,请见笔者《合约的解释:规则与应用》一书第八章。

经济原因,所以终止租约。[90] 这导致船东开始仲裁并向承租人提出索赔,逼使承租人在这一诉讼要求英国法院做出宣告期租合约没有订立或生效。在 Mocatta 大法官的随口说说(obiter)中提到,尽管承租人是以错误的理由终止了租约,但依然可以另一个事后才发现的合法理由补救,说:"... although the plaintiffs gave a bad reason for not performing the charter at the time, they were and are entitled now to relay upon any good reason available to them at the time to justify their refusal to perform this charter."

5.3 不能事后补救的例外情况

在稍早节录的《Chitty on Contracts》中的段节中就已经提到了三种大原则不适用的情况。可以说,第一种与第二种情况本身十分接近,这就是在个别的案件中,如果一方在拒绝履行合约时给错误的理由或不给理由,事后再补救会造成对对方不公平的情况。在这种情况下,就可以"弃权"(waiver)或"禁反言"(estoppel)禁止拒绝履行的一方事后提出合法理由进行补救。在 South Caribbean Trading Ltd. v. Trafigura Beheer BV (2005) 1 Lloyd's Rep. 128 先例,Colman 大法官说:"... It is clear from the decision of the Court of Appeal in Glencore v. Lorico (1997) 2 Lloyd's Rep. 386 that where one party is in repudiatory breach of a contract because of what may be conveniently described as conduct A and the other party purports to accept that the contract was terminated by reason of conduct B (which is not a repudiatory breach) it is subsequently open to the innocent party to justify his termination of the contract on the wrong grounds as valid acceptance of conduct A as repudiatory... The exception to the general rule in Taylor v. Oakes Roncoroni & Co. that termination of a contract for repudiatory breach on an invalid ground is effective as a termination provided that a valid ground existed at the time did not apply. They are that the rule will not apply if the repudiatory breach could have been cured had the valid ground been given: see Heisler v. Anglo-Dal Ltd. (1954) 1 WLR 1273 and in cases where the conduct of the innocent party gives rise to a waiver or estoppel."

看来,这与刚提到的在诉讼过程中直到判决/裁决前,通常的说法是双方都可以更改文书请求,除非对对方造成不利影响(prejudice)是同样的道理。以下会举一些相对近期与商业有关的先例对这两种例外进行介绍。

5.3.1 例外情况之一:合法理由应该在拒绝履行时向对方提出

在 Heisler v. Anglo – Dal Ltd. (1954) 2Lloyd's Rep. 5 先例,案情涉及 300 吨铝锭的买卖,卖方承诺在买方提供信用证后,30 天内做出付运并提供 10% 货价的担保以确保做出付运。买方的银行通知卖方,只要收到 10% 货价的担保就会开出信用证。卖方做出个人担保,但买方坚持要卖方在 4 天内提供银行或其他第三人的担保。卖方没有提供第三人的担保,买方指卖方拒绝性违约,买方接受并终止了合约。卖方

[90] 正如稍早所讲,中国的公司/企业也经常使用这个不合法的理由。

提起诉讼,索赔买方错误终止合约造成的损失。一审与上诉庭都判卖方胜诉,卖方提供的个人担保已经满足合约条件,买方无权要求提供银行或其他第三人的担保。

在该先例,买方的一个替代争议是卖方给出的担保是无效的,因为担保涉及外汇需要财政部批准,[91]因此,有一个默示条件是卖方提供担保时必须同时提供财政部的批准,但在该先例中卖方显然没有。所以即使买方以错误的理由终止合约,之后也可以担保无效的合法理由补救。但这争议不被上诉庭接受,因为如果在当时而不是事后提出,卖方可以申请财政部的批准。上诉庭的 Somervell 大法官说:

"Mr. Pritt(买方代表大律师), on behalf of the defendants, then submitted that the 'guarantee' was valueless because the payment of the dollars referred to would require Treasury permission and the condition of permission should have accompanied the document. I am not satisfied that contractually such permission had to accompany the document, but I am clear that the point cannot now be taken. It was not taken in the correspodence at the time, and in the letter which I have read the defendants demanded the bankers' or approved guarantee, but were not raising the question of Treasury sanction. Mr. Pritt relied on the principle which will be found stated by Greer J. in Taylor v. Oakes, Roncoroni & Co. : 'It is a long established rule of law that a contracting party, who, after he has become entitled to refuse performance of his contractual obligations, gives a wrong reason for his refusal, does not thereby deprive himself of a justification which in fact existed, whether he was aware of it or not.'

This rule is, however, subject to a proviso. **If the point not taken is one which if taken could have been put right, the principle will not apply.** This has, I think, clear application here. The plaintiff was producing his document before he was under any obligation to do so. If the defendants had accepted it **subject to the provision of a Treasury permission it might have been obtained**; further, the plaintiff could have said that he was not bound to produce any guarantee until the defendants obtained from the bankers confirmation of the letter of credit. It is doubtful if they could ever have done so, but if they had **this might itself have assisted the plaintiff in getting Treasury permission.** I think, therefore, assuming the point was a good one, that it fails on the ground that it was not taken and is not one which can now be relied on."(加黑部分是笔者的强调)

5.3.2　例外情况之二:弃权与/或禁反言

在 Andre et Cie v. Cook Industries (1987) 2 Lloyd's Rep. 463 先例中,是 1973 年密西西比河泛滥影响大豆收成并造成美国本土供应紧张,导致美国政府禁止出口大豆时带来无数著名案例之一。[92] 在该先例中,双方于 1973 年 5 月 25 日订立 CIF 买

[91] 中国也有类似的要求,担保必须经外汇管理局批准才有效。

[92] 其他先例可见杨大明的《国际货物买卖》第六章之 8.5.3.5 段。

卖合约,货量是200吨大豆,合约根据的是GAFTA 100标准格式。6月27日,美国政府全面禁止大豆出口。7月2日,禁止放宽到可以出口每个已经订立合约未履行部分的40%。7月5日,卖方通知买方因为美国政府的行政措施,他们只能付运合约货量的40%。7月18日,卖方再向买方发了类似意思的电传。买方在当日回复接受40%的大豆,双方对这40%的大豆的交付没有争议。之后在8月8日,估计美国政府不再禁止大豆出口,卖方又向买方做出了三份划归通知(notice of appropriation),[93]总量加起来刚刚超过合约货量的60%。三份提单日期是7月17日,表示货物是在该日装船付运。8月9日(估计是市场价格下跌),买方回复说卖方已经交付了40%,他们不再接受新的付运。卖方指称买方违约/毁约并开始仲裁(仲裁中间停了10年),最后一路上诉到上诉庭。上诉庭认为主要有两个争议。第一个就是双方7月的电传往来是否构成对合约的更改(variation),把原来200吨大豆的买卖更改为80吨左右?针对这一争议,上诉庭判是不构成对合约的更改,卖方在7月5日与18日的电传只属于告知买方情况,根本没有改变原本合约的货量。换言之,买方根据合约更改拒绝卖方划归的60%货量的大豆的理由不成立,构成违约/毁约。这就带来第二个争议,是买方事后在仲裁中才提出,就是以卖方延迟做出划归通知为由拒绝卖方划归的60%货量的大豆(虽然在终止合约时并没有提出这个理由)? GAFTA 100标准格式合约中有条文规定,卖方必须在提单日期后10日内做出划归通知,除非涉及一连串的买卖(string sales)。这是因为在这种大豆贸易,一连串的买卖经常会涉及三四十个转卖。这表示第一个卖方(往往也是发货人)向他的买方做出划归通知,的确是可以做到提单日期后的10日内。但第一位买方把有关货物转卖给下一位买方,显然就不一定赶得上在10日内。而排到很后的中间商,更加没有办法给他的买方在10天内做出划归通知。所以,GAFTA 100标准格式的条文针对一连串的买卖,中间的卖方或贸易商只需要在收到上一手卖方的划归通知后在当天转给下一手的买方,就没有违反合约的条件条文。在该先例种,划归通知是在该三份提单日期后22日后(7月17日到8月8日)才做出。这划归通知显然超出了GAFTA 100标准格式规定的10日,除非卖方能证明这是一连串的买卖。但由于买方在拒货时或有关的合理时间内没有提出,相隔这么久才提出导致了卖方根本不可能证明这是一连串的买卖(有关的文件档案或证人全部失去),让表面看来是延误的划归通知变为有效(validated by proof of string)。Parker大法官说:"We agree with the Sellers; if proof of string is required by a buyer, he must ask for it at the relevant time, and we consider that 11 years after the event is too late to raise a point which can only be proved or disproved by reference to records existing at the time, and such records are unlikely to be available more than 10 years after the event. ... In addition, since the notices were late on the face of

〔93〕 关于划归通知(notice of appropriation / declaration of shipment)可见杨大明的《国际货物买卖》第六章,这是买卖合约的条件条文。

them, WE Find that the Buyers Waived their rights to demand proof of string by waiting until it was too late to produce such proof."

下一个是 Glencore v. Lorico (1997) 2 Lloyd's Rep. 386 先例,案情涉及一个25000 吨小麦的 FOB 买卖。1993 年 3 月 24 日,买方将信用证的草稿发给了卖方,其中结汇的付运文件是要求提单要注明"运费预付"(freight pre – paid)。[94] 3 月 25 日,卖方回复说信用证的写法并不符合合约规定并草拟了一个新版本的信用证,要求买方按照这个草拟的新版本开信用证,其中只要求提单注明"运费按照租约支付"(freight payable as per charterparty)。[95] 3 月 29 日,买方将修改后的信用证电传给了卖方,显示接受了卖方的其他修改,但并没有删去对提单要注明"运费预付"的要求。之后,卖方没有再回复。3 与 31 日,卖方表示由于买方指定的船舶没有在 3 月 29 日到达,所以买方要承担 7 美金/吨的罚金(这是卖方与上一手卖方的合约规定)。卖方也通过经纪人要求将支付方式从信用证支付改为预付一笔折扣后的货价(prepayments of goods against a discount in the price)。买方回复说,他们之间的合约从来没有关于罚金的规定,卖方不装货是违约/毁约。4 月 2 日,卖方表示除非买方支付每吨 7 美金的罚金与预付货价,否则不会装货。双方之后还有些通讯往来,总之最后双方互指对方违约/毁约并导致合约终止。接下来,双方开始仲裁并最后上诉到上诉庭,上诉庭要解决的是两个主要争议:第一,FOB 买方能否在买卖合约没有明示规定下,坚持在信用证上要求卖家必须交出提单有"运费预付"的标注才能在信用证下获得支付?第二,如果不行,卖方能否以买方坚持在信用证上要求提单有"运费预付"的标注作为其拒绝装货的替代合法理由,如果卖方要求买方支付罚金与预付货价否则不会装货是不合法的理由?

上诉庭判是作为 FOB 买方,在没有明示条文规定下不能坚持在信用证上要求提

〔94〕 虽然在法律报告中没有解释,但笔者对这方面的理解估计问题出在买方把货物以 CIF 或 CFR 转卖。这样,在转售的合约与信用证就会要求买方提供一份"运费预付"的提单。但在买方与卖方的 FOB 买卖,是由买方派船与作为承租人支付运费给船东,与 FOB 卖方没有关系。所以,要求 FOB 卖方交出一份运费预付的提单会对卖方造成困难。即使在该先例,买方向卖方保证一定会尽快支付运费给船东,让船东不会拒绝签发"运费预付"提单给卖方。但这不足以让卖方安心,因为如果市场下跌,买方想赖皮不支付运费给船东,或是买方作为承运人与船东在运费的支付的确有争议,都会导致卖方无法或延误才能取到运费预付提单,向银行根据信用证要求支付货款。一般来说,这种以 FOB 买入并在之后以 CIF/CFR 转售的中间商很多都是有经验的跨国贸易商,船舶也是由他们租进付运。他们往往会在租约中强制要求船东签发第二套提单(switch bill of lading),也就是第一套提单是给 FOB 卖方的"运费按照租约支付"提单,第二套提单是给 CIF/CFR 买方的"运费预付"提单。但问题是,如果并非由这个中间商租船并且租约中也没有写明,船东就不会愿意出第二套提单。也会有情况是中间商不知道有这个做法,这样就会像本先例一样要求 FOB 卖方交出"运费预付"的提单,否则在信用证就无法结汇。正如本先例的判决,这是不合法与构成违约/毁约,可让卖方终止合约并索赔损失。

〔95〕 关于这一课题与这两个有关运费的注明的区别,请看笔者的《提单与其他付运单证》(2016 年)第四章之 2.3.3 段与第六章之 7.5 段。

单有“运费预付”的标注，这属于违约/毁约。卖方没有回复并不能显示其同意了信用证的写法。之后卖方要求买方支付罚金与预付货价否则不装货，单独来看是明确地拒绝履行合约并且不合法（uncontractual）。但因为买方较早时坚持在信用证上要求提单有“运费预付”的标注的行为构成了拒绝性违约，一并来看就可以把卖方的不合法要求作为对买方违约/毁约的接受，合法终止原买卖合约（虽然这个合法理由在当时没有提出），并在一个新的合约提出新的条件。Evans 大法官说：

“‘It is a long established rule of law that a contracting party, who, after he has become entitled to refuse performanceof his contractual obligations, gives a wrong reason for his refusal, does not thereby deprive himself of a justificationwhich in fact existed, whether he was aware of it or not’. [per Greer J. in Taylor v. Oakes, Roncoroni & Co. (1922) 127 LT 267 at 269].

... ‘The rule is, however, subject to a proviso. If the point not taken is one which if taken could have been put right, theprinciple will not apply’. [per Somervell L. J. in Heisler v. Anglo – Dal Ltd. (1954) 1 W. L. R. 1273 at 1278]....

The sellers' demand for an increased price etc. on1 April was undoubtedly a refusal to perform the contract, even though if viewed in isolation from the buyers'previous failure to open a conforming letter of credit it was an anticipatory rather than an actual breach. If thebuyers' breach is included in the perspective, the refusal was justified by it and the sellers' failure to refer to itthen does not necessarily preclude them from relying on it now (the basic rule). The Heisler v. Anglo – Dalqualification in my judgment does not apply, because by 1 April the time for contractual performance of thebuyers' letter of credit obligation had passed. I do not see how the sellers' refusal to perform the contract couldeither extend the time for performance by the buyers or amount to a waiver of their right to refuse performance, if such a right existed.

I would add that in any event the buyers' language in their response on 29 March was peremptory ('themaximum we can') and there was no further indication from them, either before or after 1 April, that the freightpre – paid terms of the letter of credit could or might be deleted. On the Board's findings, therefore, the possibilityof such a change was entirely speculative...”

5.3.3 例外情况之三：接受付运单证或货物

至于《Chitty on Contracts》（第 32 版，2015 年）一书之 24 – 014 段提到的第三种例外情况，首先可见英国 1979 年《货物销售法》之 Section 35，如下：“The buyer is deemed to have accepted the goods — (a) when he intimates to the seller that he has accepted them, or (b) when the goods have been delivered to him and he does any act in relation to them which is inconsistent with the ownership of the seller.... (4) The buyer is also deemed to have accepted the goods when after the lapse of a reasonable time he retains the goods without intimating to the seller that he has rejected them."

在 Panchaud Freres S. A. v. Etablissements General Grain Co.（1970）1 Lloyd's Rep. 53 先例,[96]案情涉及 CIF 卖方倒签提单,但交出的付运文件中的一份品质证书(certificate of quality)写明了货物是在付运期后装运。[97]但买方不知道是疏忽没看到两份付运文件的矛盾之处,或是因为当时市场价格有利所以就"睁一只眼闭一只眼",接受了这套付运文件,这也等于是《货物销售法》之 Section 35(1)的情况。之后货物到达卸港,买方以货物的件数(number of bags)不符合提单描述为由拒货,这可能是因为这时市场价格下跌。之后在双方的仲裁中,仲裁庭支持了买方在卸港拒货的立场。这看来是错误的裁决,因为后来卖方上诉至 Committee of Appeal of London Corn Trade Association Ltd.,买方就意识到货物件数不符合提单描述,也就是货物短卸,应该是向船东/承运人而不是向卖方索赔。[98] 这导致买方第一次提出了他可以根据另一个合法与正确的理由拒货,也就是卖方倒签提单,此时已经是 3 年后。而卖方声称这是新的诉因,并且已经超过了时效。之后卖方一路上诉到上诉庭,上诉庭判是买方不能事后以倒签提单为由拒货,因为买方在接受付运文件时就应该已经知道倒签提单的情况,事实上,货物是在付运期后才付运,但当时买方接受了这套付运文件,而没有选择接受卖方的违约/毁约拒货。Denning 勋爵说:"The basis of it is that a man has so conducted himself that itwould be unfair or unjust to allow him to depart from a particular state of affairs which another has taken to besettled or correct."

Winn 大法官也完全同意 Denning 勋爵的判法,说:"In my own judgment it does not seem possible in this case to say affirmatively that therewas here ... anything which, within the scope of the doctrine as hitherto enunciated, could be described as an estoppel... what one has here is something perhaps in our law not yet wholly developed as a separate doctrine- which is morein the nature of a requirement of fair conduct-a criteria of what is fair conduct between the parties. There may be aninchoate doctrine stemming from the manifest convenience of consistency in pragmatic affairs, negativing any liberty-to blow hot and cold in commercial conduct."

Winn 大法官希望创造一个新说法(emerge a separate doctrine),这是因为根据当时弃权或禁反言的类别,还没有明确在这种事实情况中哪一种可以配套。但这个观点并没有获得支持。

Denning 勋爵在之后的 Berg v. Vanden（1977）1 Lloyd's Rep. 499 先例中提到 Panchaud Freres S. A. v. Etablissements General Grain Co. 先例,说:"... a case where

---

〔96〕这先例发展出的 Panchaud 原则在本书第三章第 6 段有详细介绍。

〔97〕付运期是买卖合约的条件条文,这就导致卖方如果延误付运经常倒签提单来欺骗买方与银行的恶习。这方面的问题可看杨大明的《国际货物买卖》第二章之 9.4.11 段。

〔98〕这可看笔者的《提单与其他付运单证》(2016 年)一书第五章之 10 段与第六章之 7.3 段。

there was a waiver by one person of his strict right – or an estoppel – whatever you like tocall it – whereby a person cannot go back on something he has done. ”

同样是在 Berg v. Vanden 先例,Roskill 大法官也认为并没有产生一个新的原则或说法,说:“... the so-called principles laid down by this Court in the Panchaud ... this Court then laid down no new principles of law. It merely applied well-established principles of law to theparticular facts of that case, and those principles ... are no more than if in the course of the working out of a contractone party by his conduct leads the other party to think that he will not insist on the strict performance of a particularterm in the contract so that the other party alters his position, the former party will not be permitted to resile and toseek to insist upon strict performance-at least without notice. ”

最后 Evans 大法官在 Glencore v. Lorico 先例总结如下:“(1) Panchaud Freres is authority for the application of the common law rule of acceptance, now established in-section 35 of the Sale of Goods Act, in the comparatively limited circumstances of a case where a c. i. f. buyeraccepts documents but rejects or purports to reject the goods. (2) The decision can equally be said to represent a form of ‘estoppel by conduct’, but there is no ‘separatedoctrine’ derived from Panchaud Freres alone. (3) Like all other forms of estoppel or waiver, the facts must justify a finding that there was an unequivocalrepresentation made by one party, by conduct or otherwise, which was acted upon by the other. (4) When the facts do justify that finding, it is likely to be regarded as ‘unfair and unjust’ for the party whichmade the representation to a contrary effect, to rely upon its contractual rights. (5) Without such a representation, no estoppel or waiver can arise, and there is no general rule that what theCourt or Tribunal may perceive as ‘unfairness or injustice’ has the same effect. (6) Panchaud Freres and subsequent cases illustrate the possible scope of an estoppel or waiver in circumstancessuch as these, but they do not reveal a further exception to the basic rule, that a party is entitled to rely uponhis contractual rights. (7) Unfairness and injustice, however, will always be relevant where the Court is required to exercise adiscretionary power e. g. where a party seeks leave to raise a fresh matter by way of amendment or at alate stage of the proceedings before it ... ”

5.3.4 例外情况之四:拒绝性违约不得以后来发觉的合法理由补救

在本章之3.7.3段已经有介绍,拒绝性违约只能根据违约方当时的言行估计他是否不愿意或不能够履行将来的合约责任,而不能受事后的证据与事实影响。这就带来一个疑问,就是本段所讲的大原则即可以事后发觉的合法理由补救,是否只适用在真正违约与预期违约的不可能履行,但不适用在拒绝性违约?这不能一概而论,因为如果一方显示了他不愿意或不能够履行将来的合约责任的言行是发生在合约被终止前,并且这言行是另一方知道或可以知道,那么即使另一方以错误的理由甚至没有理由终止合约,事后也可以对方拒绝性违约的合法理由补救,也就是大原则适用。而且这种情况经常发生,另一方在面对对方提起的诉讼,指定了称职的律师,就很有可能找出一个或多个合法理由进行补救。但如果一方不愿意或不能够履行将来的合约责任的言行根本在当时不会让另一方知道,而是在事后的诉讼中通过文件披露才发觉,这大原则看来就不适用。这也可以理解,拒绝性违约是无辜方根据违约方的言行合理估计他不愿意或不能够履行将来的合约责任。如果在终止合约时,一方根本不可能知道有这样的言行存在,就无法合理估计对方不愿意或不能够履行将来的合约责任,即无法构成拒绝性违约,变成错误终止合约的一方违约/毁约。

这种情况出现在 The "Ekha"(2010) 1 Lloyd's Rep. 543 先例,具体的案情已经在本章之 4.3 段有介绍,不再重复。只针对 Gazprom 在文件披露过程中才发现 Seadrill 与 Premier Oil 进行了接触,能否以 Seadrill 的行为属于拒绝性违约进行补救?这争议在该先例中是不相关,因为 Flaux 大法官已经判 Seadrill 与 Premier Oil 在当时没有达成合约,即使达成合约也不代表 Seadrill 不可能履行。但因为双方花了大量时间与精力在这个争议,Flaux 大法官还是进行了针对,说:

"Mr Jacobs(Seadrill 代表大律师)advanced two reasons why the principle could not apply to a case such as the present. First he relied on the proposition that a man's words and conduct are to be judged at the time, not by subsequent events, to support a submission that it was not open to Gazprom to trawl through disclosure by Seadrill of documents concerning its dealings with Premier Oil, years after the event, to establish something which is deemed to have been a renunciation....

Mr Jacobs advanced two reasons why the principle could not apply to a case such as the present. First he relied on the proposition that a man's words and conduct are to be judged at the time, not by subsequent events, to support a submission that it was not open to Gazprom to trawl through disclosure by Seadrill of documents concerning its dealings with Premier Oil, years after the event, to establish something which is deemed to have been a renunciation....

In my judgment, it follows that, since **the words and conduct now alleged by Gazprom to have been renunciatory were not known to Gazprom at the time of the purported termination on 16 May 2006, there was not objectively speaking a repudiatory breach by reason of renunciation in existence at that date.** No amount of 'deemed knowledge' through the application of the Boston Deep Sea Fishing principle can remedy the **complete absence of the essential ingredient of renunciation, namely communication to or at least knowledge of Gazprom at the time of what are said to have been renunciatory words or conduct**."(加黑部分是笔者的强调)

6. 违约/毁约与合约明示条文的关系

6.1 明示条文允许合约一方或双方终止合约

不少商业合约都会有明示条文针对在一方合约方有违反某一些合约责任时，另一方有权终止合约。针对的违约通常在英国法下是不被视为可以让终止合约的条件条文或估计会造成严重后果的中间条文。换言之，针对的违约通常只是保证条文。例如，针对的是违约方没有准时支付到期的款项，或是延误履行一些合约的承诺。也会有一些明示条文是与违约没有关系，反正就是允许其中一方或双方在某种情况下，可以通过通知选择终止合约。

涉及其中一方违约可让对方终止合约的明示条文有很多不同形式，如在 Dalkia Utilities Services Plc. v. Celtech International Ltd.（2006）1 Lloyd's Rep. 599 先例，相关合约有条文说："In the event of the CLIENT being in material breach of its obligations to pay the CHARGES the COMPANY shall have the right to terminate this Agreement immediately."

这看来是与期租合约中的租金必须准时与足数支付，否则船东可以撤船的措辞/文字虽然不一样，但目的一致。又或是房屋的租金，在 Lombard North Central v. Butterworth（1987）1 QB 527 先例，有条文明示准时支付租金是租约的重要部分，也是有同样的目的。事实上，房屋的租赁合约经常会有一条"没收条文"（forfeiture clause），针对租客的各种违约事项，也会包括不准时与/或不支付租金，允许房东终止租约并收回房屋。在融资合约中，客户与银行的借贷合约中经常明示规定了一连串的违约事项（events of default），并写明一旦发生这些违约事项，银行就可以终止合约，包括要求所欠债务变为即时清还。

不涉及其中一方违约，但可让一方终止合约的条文也有很多。其中一种是"长青条文"（evergreen clause），会出现在一些估计会是长期或很难估计期限的合约。例如，发电厂或其他的供应商，订立合约向一个工厂供电或供应其他的物料。又或是一方作为另一方生产的产品的独家经销商，在市场上推广与销售该产品。由于将来在履行过程中会有变化导致其中一方想从合约中脱身，就会根据长青条文的要求向另一方做出通知，合约就会在几个月不等的时间后终止。在订约自由下，这种长青条文还可以根据每个合约不同的情况做出针对，如通知终止合约的权利，必须要过了一段时间后才能行使，以保证合约不会刚开始生效不久，只是前期投入还没有收到利润，就被对方终止合约。另一种不涉及对方违约的是"不可抗力条文"（force majeure clause），如在国际粮油买卖经常使用的 GAFTA 标准格式合约中，就有条文保护 CIF/CFR 的卖方，如果在装港发生了不可抗力事件，导致没有办法提供货物装船，卖方就可以做出通知，将提供货物的付运期延长。但如果过了一段时间，如 21

天,这不可能抗力的事件仍然存在,卖方还是没有办法提供货物,买方就有权终止买卖合约。

这种明示条文可以有千变万化的写法,也经常会同时针对条文如果被依赖终止合约的救济,如一方要支付另一方一笔“议定赔偿”(liquidated damages),或是合约自动终止不存在可以索赔金钱损失,或是一方可以没收定金或要退回定金给另一方等。反正在订约自由下,双方想要怎样写都可以。这种争议很多,通常属于对明示条文的解释的课题。〔99〕

6.2 明示条文与违约/毁约(真正违约与预期违约)互相重叠或矛盾

不可避免会有情况是合约明示条文与违约/毁约(包括真正违约与预期违约)互相重叠或产生矛盾。例如,如果明示条文有针对某一种违约并写明无辜方怎样根据条文的要求才能终止合约,普通法的违约/毁约是否还可以适用?表面看来这是不难明白,在笔者的《合约的解释:规则与应用》一书多处提到,明示条文超越默示条文。另是,可否让无辜方在终止合约的同时依赖合约的明示条文以及普通法的违约/毁约?毕竟两种终止合约的办法有不同的救济。再一种重叠的情况是,如果一方以普通法的违约/毁约终止合约,但事后发觉错误,能否以明示条文补救?或是相反,一方以明示条文终止合约,但事后发觉明示条文并没有针对这种违约,或者没有严格按照条文的要求办事,又或者明示条文规定的救济办法对自己不利(如只能索赔名义损失或有限的议定赔偿),能否以普通法的违约/毁约补救?

进一步分析这种重叠或发生矛盾的情况,不妨先举一个简单的例子,在期租合约(房屋租赁也是同样道理)中,承租人必须准时与足数预先支付租金,否则船东可以撤船,〔100〕会有好几种情况可以与普通法的违约/毁约重叠或起矛盾。

---

〔99〕 可见杨良宜《合约的解释:规则与应用》一书。

〔100〕 在期租合约最常被使用的 NYPE 标准格式(最近有了 2015 年新版本),第 11 条是关于租金的支付,可节录如下:“(a) Payment Payment of Hire shall be made without deductions due to Charterers' bank charges so as to bereceived by the Owners or their designated payee into the bank account... in the currency stated in Clause 10 (Rate of Hire; Hold Cleaning; Communications; Victualing andExpenses), in funds available to the Owners on the due date, fifteen (15) days in advance, and forthe last fifteen (15) days or part of same the approximate amount of hire, and should the same notcover the actual time, hire shall be paid for the balance day by day as it becomes due, if sorequired by the Owners. The first payment of hire shall be due on delivery. (b) Grace PeriodWhere there is failure to make punctual payment of hire due, the Charterers shall be given by theOwners three (3) Banking Days (as recognized at the agreed place of payment) written notice torectify the failure, and when so rectified within those three (3) Banking Days (as recognized at theagreed place of payment and the place of currency of the Charter Party) following the Owners' notice, the payment shall stand as punctual. (c) WithdrawalFailure by the Charterers to pay hire due in full within three (3) Banking Days of their receiving anotice from Owners under Sub – clause 11(b) above shall entitle the Owners, without prejudice toany other rights or claims the Owners may have against the Charterers: (i) to withdraw the Vessel from the service of the Charterers; (ii) to damages, if they withdraw the Vessel, for the loss of the remainder of the Charter Party.”

第一，承租人提前告诉船东，因为经济困难与航运市场十分低落，以后不会再支付租金。这是典型的以语言拒绝履行重要的合约承诺或责任，看来船东就可以拒绝性违约去接受并终止租约。至于有关的明示条文，由于文字上是针对真正违约，也就是承租人在最后的期限没有预付租金，并没有针对拒绝性违约，所以法律的默示地位并没有被明示条文超越，看来船东可以接受并终止合约而不必理会租约里面的有关条文与要求的步骤，如做出通知。

第二，承租人提前告诉船东，下一个租金的预付最后期限是承租人所在地的假期，所以他要过了假期再支付。这样看来也是违约合约，因为合约要求必须在最后期限前支付。表面看来这与第一种情况差不多，也是以语言拒绝履行合约，但拒绝的只是下一期租金不会准时支付，而不是像第一种情况以后不再支付。所以，看来达不到本章之3.5段介绍的拒绝的必须是合约重要责任的要求。这样看来，如果船东还是希望撤船就不能依赖普通法的拒绝性违约，而需要忍耐，直到承租人没有在合约规定的最后期限前支付租金，他在严格按照有关条文的要求行事后撤船。

第三，承租人没有在合约规定的最后期限前支付租金，船东想趁机终止合约，但没有按照租约要求行事。例如，没有做出反技术性通知（anti-technicality clause notice），[101]或是做出的通知与租约要求不符。这样，就变为没有严格依照明示条文撤船的船东违约/毁约。在这种情况下，船东能否以普通法下的违约/毁约作为补救？这就要看准时支付租金在普通法下是条件条文或是保证条文/中间条文。根据英国法下一贯的先例，准时支付租金是不重要的中间条文：The "Brimnes"（1974）2 Lloyd's Rep. 241 先例。但这个一贯被接受的法律地位在30年后的 The "Astra"（2013）2 Lloyd's Rep. 69 先例被质疑。Flaux 大法官针对同样的 NYPE 条文，判是条件条文，如果违反该条文本身，就构成违约/毁约。在这种情况下，再在 NYPE 加一条明示条文允许船东撤船就变得没有必要。但同时间另有其他有关租金准时支付的判法与该先例不一致。

在 Januzaj v. Valilas（2014）EWCA Civ 436 先例，案情涉及原告租用被告的设备开展牙医业务，但有3个月没有支付租金，导致被告终止合约，而原告以被告错误终止合约为由索赔损失。上诉庭一致判准时支付租金不是条件条文，但在原告的行为是否构成拒绝性违约上存在争议。上诉庭的 Underhill 大法官认为3个月没有支付租金的行为属于违约/毁约，但 Floyd 大法官与 Arden 认为不属于违约/毁约，主要是根据一审法官对原告最后会支付租金的认定。这样看来，分界线应是如果虽然迟延但租金预计最后还是会支付，就不属于违约/毁约，而如果租金很有可能最终不会支付，就属于违约/毁约。也就是说，行为是否构成拒绝性违约取决于法官/仲裁员对事实的认定，这就会带来很大的不确定。

在这种先例判决不一致的情况下，航运人士普遍还是认为期租合约下的租金没

---

〔101〕 这一课题可见杨大明《期租合同》一书第18篇。

有准时预付只属于违反中间条文,船东如果想终止合约只能依赖 NYPE 下的明示条文。而最普遍被使用的 NYPE 46 与 NYPE 93 格式被解释是船东可以根据条文撤船,但由于不是普通法的违约/毁约(虽然 The "Astra" 先例说是违约/毁约,但已经被否定)而不可以索赔撤船后的损失。由于这方面的法律不肯定,所以包括 BIMCO 在内的航运组织在 NYPE 2015 格式加上了 11(c)(ii)条说明船东除了撤船,还可以索赔取消租约后所带来的损失,其中包括了剩下租期的"交易损失"(loss of bargain)。

但 The "Astra" 先例后的 Spar Shipping AS v. Grand China Logistics Holding (Group) Co. Ltd. (2016) EWCA Civ 982 先例,一审([2015] EWHC 718)判决拒绝跟从 The "Astra" 先例的说法,而回到了 The "Brimnes" 先例的法律地位。这样,英国高院之间就有了不同看法,带来了更大的不确定。这也是上述所讲的 NYPE 2015 要以明示条文确定这个不同意见的原因。但在 NYPE 2015 格式推出后,上诉庭在该先例做出了支持一审法院的判决,也就是一定程度上这个法律地位重新确定下来,无须再理会 The "Astra" 的高院先例。

第四,假设 The "Astra" 先例仍然有法律效力或是将来最高院在其他先例判英国普通法的地位是准时支付租金是条件条文,这表示承租人不准时与足数支付就构成了违约/毁约。也同时假设双方适用的是 NYPE 46 或 NYPE 93 格式,不像 NYPE 2015 明示允许船东索赔撤船后的所有损失。这样,如果船东根据有关明示条文撤船后,发觉自己有损失(如剩下租期的交易损失或要完成已签发提单的航次),能否同时以承租人违约/毁约作为诉因索赔损失,即使租约的明示条文下没有这个权利?如果可以,会否因为船东撤船是根据明示条文做出通知,构成了对租约存在的确认(affirm),而被视为对普通法违约/毁约的诉因的弃权?这些问题在上诉庭有关造船的 Stocznia Gdynia SA v. Gearbulk Holdings Ltd. (2009) 1 Lloyd's Rep. 461 先例有针对,稍后会分段介绍。

6.3　重叠或矛盾情况之一:明示条文有针对并写明无辜方如何终止合约

如果终止合约是根据明示条文,明示条文对如何终止有关的合约有一些实质性的要求,如需要在哪一天做出怎样内容的通知,以及在发生了怎样的事情(如另一方违约)才能做出通知等,都需要严格遵守。正如 Hoffmann 勋爵在 Mannai Investment Co. Ltd. v. Eagle Star Life Assurance Co. Ltd. (1997) AC 749 先例说:"If the clause had said that the notice had to be on blue paper, it would be no good serving a notice on pink paper, however clear it might have been that the tenant wanted to terminate the lease."

这方面的例子很多,笔者这里只举两个与笔者熟悉的业务有关的先例。在绝大部分租约中(有时也会出现在货物买卖合约针对 FOB 买方派船去装港的期限),就经常有一条销约期条文(cancellation clause),说明船舶在某一天没有抵达装港,承租人(或卖方)就有权终止租约(或买卖合约)。如在 The "Mihalis Angelos" (1970) 2 Lloyd's Rep. 43 先例中,虽然船东可以肯定无法在销约期前抵达装港,但一审法院与上诉庭的多数意见还是判承租人不能根据该条文提前终止租约。上诉庭的多数意见被总结如下:“The defendants(承租人)were not entitled to cancel before July 20 under clause 11 in that the option under that clause was only exercisable when the condition was fulfilled.”

另在期租合约,由于船东对船准时支付租金的重视,但英国法律下不明确视其为重要,[102]所以在船东的坚持下,一般的期租合约都有明示条文提升准时支付租金以让船东有权终止租约,也就是撤船。但这样的明示条文也带来机会让船东取巧,就是在航运市场高涨时,船东等待机会,一旦承租人迟延(甚至只是 1 分钟)或少支付租金,就马上行使终止租约的权利去撤船。承租人的反击是在期租合约加上一条“反技术取巧条文”(anti – technicality notice),要求在承租人仍未支付租金时,船东在撤船前必须先给出 48 小时或不等时间的通知,让承租人有机会补救。有关这些问题带来许多英国重要的先例,在杨大明的《期租合同》一书第十八篇有详细介绍。其中介绍的 The “Afovos” (1983) 1 Lloyd’s Rep. 335 先例,就涉及了预期违约的问题。

这个先例的案情如下:承租人的银行把钱电汇予船东收款银行——芝加哥第一国民银行(First Chicago Bank)。但由于该银行的电传号码有改动,并忘记了更改国际电传号码登记册(directory),结果承租人银行根据登记册旧电传号码做出通知把钱汇出,而原来旧电传号码已改配予一家疏浚公司所用。汇钱银行亦没有小心复核对方回号(answerback),以为已把钱汇出。结果,船东当然是到期收不到租金撤回了该船舶。事后,经过调查事实真相并在法庭上所有的证据均呈堂,法院认为其实双方均有错误。承租人银行没有核实对方电传回号,而船东银行却错在没有更改国际电传号码登记册。结果法院判船东胜诉。由于承租人银行没有核实对方电传回号违反了一般电传操作最基本的行为守则,所犯错误的程度较大,故此船东可险中获胜。

但这一先例还有一个争议并涉及预期违约,这就是船东向承租人做出一个反技术取巧条文下的通知是否有效。根据该租约的明示条文,船东需要在收不到承租人支付的租金的违约后才能做出这个通知。租金是在 1979 年 6 月 14 日到期支付,但在该天的 16 时 40 分,船东就做出了通知。显然,当天还没有结束,船东的通知看来是过早,而过早的通知在法律上被视为“空与无效”(null and void)。但从现实的角度看,到了那个时间,银行就开始下班,不可能再收到承租人支付的租金。所以,承租人没有准时支付租金的违约已经非常明显,要等到当天结束也就是子夜,看来是有点多余。但法律上是明确过了子夜一天才结束,届时才可以说承租人违反了支付租金的责任,船东才可以做出通知。这就逼使船东提出另一个替代的预期违约的诉因,这预期违约倒不是拒绝性违约,而是不可能(impossibility),因为承租人不可能在当天银行下班后支付给船东租金。

但这一争议在上诉庭与贵族院被拒绝,原因是如果船东要依赖租约的第 5 条文

[102] 见 The “Brimnes” (1974) 2 Lloyd’s Rep. 241 先例。

(允许船东撤船)与第 31 条文(反技术取巧条文),就必须严格按照条文的规定行事,包括准时而不是提早做出通知。而这一明示条文也排除了法律默示的地位,包括预期违约。而如果船东不依赖明示条文,而是想依赖法律默示的预期违约,带来的问题就是涉及的违约必须是重要。但延误支付租金如果撇开了第 5 条文,并非是重要。以上的说法首先可以节录 Hailsham 勋爵所说:"To escape from this meaning, Counsel for the appellant sought to rely on the doctrine of anticipatory breach. But this is not the basis on which cl. 31 stood to be invoked, or upon which an actual brach of cl. 5 can be said to have occurred. No doubt if there had been a total repudiation of the whole contract the appellants could have elected to treat the contract as at an end. But then they would not have required to invoke cl. 31 to do so or to give 48 hours notice of their election. A breach of cl. 5 occurred, and could only occur, at a particular moment of time, and it was only on the occurrence of that breach that, on the true constraction of the charter, notice could be given under cl. 31. There is no reason, in my judgment, to place the moment of time at which 'punctual payment' ceased to be possible at any moment earlier than midnight on June 14, 1979."

Diplock 勋爵也说:"Similarly where a party to a contract, whether by failure to take timeous action or by any other default, has put it out of his power to perform a particular primary obligation, the right of the other party to elect to treat this as a repudiation of the contract by conduct deponds upon whether the resulting non-performance would amount to a fundamental breach. Clearly, in the instant case delay in payment of one semi-monthly instalment of hire would not."

6.4　重叠或矛盾情况之二:明示条文有否超越/否定普通法的违约/毁约

显然如果明示条文超越甚至否定了普通法的违约/毁约,后者就不适用。当然是否有这样的结果是要看合约条文具体的写法,一般来说很不容易,更不用说经常会有些草拟得好的合约条文会说明保留普通法的权利。如在 Laing Management Ltd. v. Aegon Insurance Company (UK) Ltd. (1996) 86 BLR 70 先例,相关的合约条文可节录如下:"20.2　Without prejudice to any other legal or equitable right orremedy which the Contractor would otherwise possess hereunder or as a matter of Law, the Contractor shall be entitled to terminate all or part of the subcontract work at any time for any of the following reasons, specifying the date and extent to which the subcontract work is terminated:...20.2.2　If a receiver ... of any of the property or income of the sub-contractor is appointed."

这是因为法院或仲裁庭在解释有关的明示条文时会认为双方通常不会有订约意图去否定这一重要的英国法律下的权利,就是对方违约/毁约时可以接受并终止合约。正如 Moore-Bick 大法官在 Stocznia Gdynia SA v. Gearbulk Holdings Ltd. (2009) 1 Lloyd's Rep. 461 先例中说:"The court is unlikely to be satisfied that a party to a contract has abandoned valuable rights arising by operation of law unless the terms of the contract make it sufficiently clear that that was intended. The more valuable the right, the clearer the language will need to be."

在《Chitty on Contracts》(第32版,2015年)之24-032段,说:"**No anticipation of express right to terminate.** Where it is alleged that one party has, by his own act or default, disabled himself form performing his contractual obligations at some future time and the contract also contrains an express provision giving to the innocent party the right to terminate the contract in certain circumstances, care must be taken to establish the basis upon which the innocent party seeks to terminate the contract. Where the basis for the decision to terminate is the express right to determine the contract, the requirements of the clause containing the right to terminate must be complied with. On the other hand, where reliance is placed on the inability of the party to perform his obligations under the contract at some future time, it must be demonstrated that the inability to perform relates to some essential aspect of the obligations of the party in breach. To be entitled to terminate, the innocent party must establish that he had a right to terminate on one or other ground. Where he can establish neither ground, he cannot justify his decision to terminate by combining the two grounds so as to apply the doctrine of anticipatory breach to the contractual right to terminate. It is not possible to anticipate a contractual right to terminate. Either the conditions necessary to exercise the right have been satisfied or they have not."

在 Stocznia Gdynia SA v. Gearbulk Holdings Ltd. 先例,涉及三艘散货船的建造,造船合约是与一般造船合约相同针对造船厂如果过了死亡日期(drop dead date),船东就可以取消合约并将预付的船价取回。这笔钱一般是有银行提供的还款担保(refund guarantee)。该造船合约针对"死亡日期"(drop dead date)的条文很长,这里不全部节录,只说中间一段规定除了预付的船价与利息,船东不能索赔其他损失,说:"The Purchaser shall not be entitled to claim any other compensation and the Seller shall not be liable for any other compensation for damages sustained by reason of events set out in this Article and/or direct consequences of such events other than liquidated damages specified in this Article."

该先例的船厂是著名的波兰船厂,但由于经济出了问题破产,并在2003年1月就停止了工作,而合约的死亡日期是在8月15日。双方后来谈判不果,船东在11月7日终止合约,并根据明示条文取回了预付船价与利息。但当时看来航运市场是在上涨,所以只是把预付船价与利息退还给船东不足以补偿他的损失,于是船东根据船厂违约/违约的行为(已经被仲裁庭裁定)向船厂索赔交易损失。这带来两个重要的问题,第一个就是本小段针对的,明示条文也同样针对造船延误过了死亡日期,是否超越了普通法的违约/毁约,毕竟违约/毁约就是指船厂造船的延误。第二个问题是下一小段会针对的,两个诉因是否可以同时提出。

在第一个问题中,船厂的争议本质上就是明示条文已经针对造船延误的情况,明示条文超越默示条文,既然明示条文已经有了一个针对性的完整方案(complete code),普通法的违约/毁约就被超越。但代表船东的争议是解释任何合约条文必须要合理与符合商业常识。如果按照船厂的说法,就会带来在船价暴涨时,船厂会干脆停工转去建造其他能够赚大钱的船舶,然后拖过了"死亡日期"让船东自己选择是否弃船。如果船东选择弃船,只能在还款担保下取回预付船价与利息。

高院与上诉庭都不接受船厂的争议,判决涉及解释合约的有关条文。其中重要的考虑是船东的争议的确比较合理,而船厂的说法就会是违反了 Diplock 勋爵在 The "Antaios"(1984) 2 Lloyd's Rep. 235 先例说的,如果在一个商业合约中,文字上的分析会带来商业上的不合理,前者就应该服从后者:"While deprecating the extension of the use of the expression 'purposive construction' from the interpretation of statues to the interpretation of private contracts, I agree with the passage I have cited from the arbitrator's award and I take this opportunity of restating that, if a detailed semantic and syntactical analysis of words in a commercial contract is going to lead to a conclusion that flouts business common sense, it must be made to yield to business common sense."

另一个重要考虑是整体考虑造船合约特别是第 5.9 条文,针对如果船东没有准时支付预付船价的情况,船厂除了有终止造船合约的权利外,还可以索赔其他的损失包括交易损失,也就是有权把建造中的船舶完成后转售给其他船东。显然,如果市场下跌,需要以低价出售,船厂就会有交易损失。法院的考虑就是两条同样是针对对方延误的违约(第 5.9 条针对支付船价的延误,第 10 条针对造船的延误)允许合约一方终止合约的条文,第 5.9 条文允许船厂在终止合约后索赔其他的损失包括交易损失,而第 10 条文不允许船东索赔交易损失,这整体看来是不合理。因此,法院判是除非有更明确的文字写明,否则不能假设这是双方的订约意图。

针对明示条文的第 10 条有否超越普通法的违约/毁约,上诉庭的 Moore-Bick 大法官说:"The primary purpose of Article 10(针对延误与死亡日期的条文)in the present case is to provide an agreed measure of compensation for breaches of contract by way of delay in delivery and deficiencies in capacity and performance which, although important, do not go to the root of the contract. ... However, they have also agreed that there comes a point at which the delay or deficiency is so serious that it should entitle Gearbulk (船东) to terminate the contract. In my view they must be taken to have agreed that at that point the breach is to be treated as going to the root of the contract. In those circumstances the right to terminate the contract cannot sensibly be understood as anything other than embodying the parties' agreement that Gearbulk has the right to treat the contract as repudiated ... In paragraph 88 of his judgment in Stocznia Gdanska S. A. v. Latvian Shipping Co. [2002] EWCA Civ 889, [2002] 2 Lloyd's Rep. 436 Rix L. J. expressed the view that where contractual and common law rights overlap it would be too harsh to regard the use of a contractual mechanism of termination as ousting the common law mechanism, at any rate against a background of an express reservation of rights. In this case I would go further. In my view it is wrong to treat the right to terminate in accordance with the terms of the contract as different in substance from the right to treat the contract as discharged by reason of repudiation at common law. In those cases where the contract gives a right of termination they are in effect one and the same."

针对明示条文的第 10 条有否排除船东因为船厂违约/毁约索赔交易损失的权利,Moore-Bick 大法官说:"It is true that it would have the benefit of a demand guarantee under which it could be sure of recovering its money quickly, but it would recover nothing in respect of the bargain represented by the contract itself. That would be in marked contrast to the position of the Yard if it were to terminate the contract under Article 5.9. Moreover, it would mean that the Yard could at any time refuse to perform the contract without any liability other than to refund instalments of the price. That does not strike me as the kind of agreement that would be likely to commend itself to any purchaser... **The court is unlikely to be satisfied that a party to a contract has abandoned valuable rights arising by operation of law unless the terms of the contract make it sufficiently clear that that was intended. The more valuable the right, the clearer the language will need to be... I agree that Article 10 does not exclude Gearbulk's right to recover damages at common law for the loss of its bargain.**"(加黑部分是笔者的强调)

6.5 重叠或矛盾情况之三:终止合约是根据明示合约或是违约/毁约

在 Stocznia Gdynia SA v. Gearbulk Holdings Ltd. (2009) 1 Lloyd's Rep. 461 先例,涉及船东作为买方根据造船合约的第 10 条做出通知终止合约。由于有三艘船,所以三个通知是在不同时间做出的,但内容是大同小异,只节录其中一份的部分内容如下:

"Dear Sir

...

The provisions of Article 3.1 of the above Contract provide that the Delivery Date of the Vessel was 3 March 2003. The provisions of Article 10.1(b) provide that if delivery of the Vessel is delayed beyond the Delivery Date by more than 150 days then we will be entitled to terminate the Contract. 150 days from 3 March 2003 was 1 August 2003. Accordingly from that date we have been entitled to terminate the Building Contract pursuant to the provisions of Article 10.1(b).

Further, the provisions of Article 10.1(c) provide that, in the event that the Vessel is not delivered by you to us on or prior to 15 August 2003 then we will be entitled to terminate the Contract. The Vessel was not delivered to us on or before that date and accordingly from that date we also have been entitled to terminate the Building Contract pursuant to the provisions of this Article.

We hereby give you notice that we hereby exercise our rights of termination under both of Article 10.1(b) and 10.1(c) and call upon you, in accordance with the provisions of Article 5.10 to repay to us immediately the predelivery instalment that we have paid to you in respect of this Vessel in the amount of US $1,323,400 ... together with interest thereon calculated at the rate of 1 month LIBOR per annum, US $ 127,519.47."

可以看出,通知是根据合约的第10条文,完全没有提到普通法下的违约/毁约,直到船东为了索赔其他损失如交易损失,才在诉讼中提出。这样的做法类似本章第5段介绍的以错误的理由终止合约,事后以合法的理由补救。但这里的问题是,一旦违约方的言行构成预期违约,无辜方可以选择接受并终止合约,也可以选择拒绝不接受并确认合约继续存在与有效,而没有被接受的预期违约就好像没有发生过的镜花水月。在该先例中,船厂根据合约条文做出通知终止合约并向银行根据还款担保取回预付船价与利息的行为是否构成对合约的确认?而如果构成对合约的确认,就等于放弃了接受普通法下的违约/毁约的权利。一审法院([2008] 2 Lloyd's Rep. 202)的Burton大法官判是船东做出的通知构成对合约的确认,说:"The terms of the letters terminating each of the contracts, combined with the fact that the purchaser(船东)claimed on the refund guarantee, had the effect that the purchaser elected to terminate the contract in accordance with its terms, and consequently affirmed the contract. The purchaser did not simply make a claim and obtain recovery against the yard; it enforced the contractual provisions which enabled it to obtain a secured sum against a third party, the guarantor, by virtue of an entitlement only available under the contract."

但到了上诉庭,一审法院的判决被推翻。进一步解释前,可以先简单介绍有关选择原则(principle of election)。[103] 在英国法律中,针对合约方如果出现了两个不同甚至对立的权利或方向要做出选择,就必须在合约规定或合理的时间内,通过言行做出其中一个选择。这个权利可以是来自合约或来自法律的默示,可以举一些经常见到的例子。如来自合约,在本章之6.1段介绍的所有明示条文在条件成熟时都允许一方或双方终止合约。而该合约方必须在合约规定或法律默示的合理时间内做出选择是否终止合约,否则会对对方造成不公平与不肯定。如果该合约方没有在合约规定或法律默示的合理时间内做出选择,则会被视为对选择终止合约的权利弃权(waiver by election)。再多举一个与违约没有关系但同样选择原则适用的例子,就是一个房屋的租赁合约是3年,但有关合约另有一个明示选择权(option)让租客可以多延长3年。这就表示租客必须要在合约规定的明示时间或法律默示的合理时间内

---

[103] 这在本书第三章第3段有详论。

做出选择,否则也视为构成弃权。至于法律的权利,最典型就是违约方违反了一个条件条文,无辜方就根据普通法有一个终止合约的权利。但这一权利不会永远存在,无辜方不及时做出选择就是弃权。至于什么是及时,这法律地位一般不会说死,总之是合理时间。什么是合理时间,就要根据每个不同性质的案件做出认定,通常就是要尽快以免造成对违约方不公平与不肯定。例如,有关案件涉及的标的的市场波动很大与很快,如商品与股票买卖,这合理时间就会很短,甚至只有一两个工作日。原因是怕无辜方用这个机会等待市场走向相对明确哪样对他有利才做出选择。但如果有关的案件涉及一个大型工程的合约,无辜方如果选择终止合约会涉及很多事后工作,显然合理时间就会长一些,让无辜方可以调查清楚是否可行再做出选择。

有关选择原则,在此只节录一个权威性的定义,即 Goff 勋爵在 The "Kanchenjunga" (1990) 1 Lloyd's Rep. 391 先例中说:"In the present case, we are concerned with an election which may arise in the context of a binding contract, when a state of affairs comes into existence in which one party becomes entitled, either under the terms of the contract or by the general law, to exercise a right, and he has to decide whether or not to do so. His decision, being a matter of choice for him, is called in law an election. Characteristically, this state of affairs arises where the other party has repudiated the contract or has otherwise committed a breach of the contract which entitles the innocent party to bring it to an end, or has made a tender of performance which does not conform to the terms of the contract. . . . In all cases, he has in the end to make his election, not as a matter of obligation, but in the sense that, if he does not do so, the time may come when the law takes the decision out of his hands, either by holding him to have elected not to exercise the right which has become available to him, or sometimes by holding him to have elected to exercise it."

已经提到在 Stocznia Gdynia SA v. Gearbulk Holdings Ltd. 先例,上诉庭改变了一审法院的判决,原因是上诉庭认为选择原则在该先例中不适用。根据还款担保取回预付船价与利息和索赔交易损失这两个权利完全可以分开与互补,并不存在矛盾与对立。虽然这个终止合约的通知只是引用了造船合约第 10 条以及根据还款担保取回预付船价与利息。但如果没有这个条文,船厂违约/毁约,船东依然可以根据普通法终止合约,取回预付船价与利息,另加上索赔交易损失。因此,船东现在根据普通法下的违约/毁约向船厂索赔交易损失不存在双重赔偿的问题。Moore-Bick 大法官说:

"The exercise by Gearbulk of the right to treat the contract as terminated under Article 10.1(b) and 10.1(c) was intended to and did operate to discharge the contract with the same consequences as if it had been discharged by repudiation in accordance with the general law. In the first place, Gearbulk's letters exercising its right to terminate the contracts for Hulls 24 and 25 were wholly inconsistent with an election to affirm them, so there can be no doubt that the contract in each case was discharged...

Moreover, I am quite unable to accept that the exercise by Gearbulk of its right to recover instalments of the contract price ... involved an election on its part to affirm the contract. ... On discharge of a contract of this kind a buyer who has paid the whole or part of the price in advance is entitled, in the absence of any agreement to the contrary, to recover what he has paid by reason of a total failure of consideration. He therefore has a right to recover in restitution any payments he has made in respect of the price, a right which is quite distinct from any right he may have (if he is the injured party) to recover damages for the loss of his bargain. In the present case the parties made specific provision for the repayment of instalments and Gearbulk could not, of course, recover both under the contract and in restitution; to do so would result in double recovery. In fact, however, Gearbulk is not seeking to recover the advance payments since it has already done so. There is no inherent inconsistency, however, in recovering instalments of the price under Article 10 and recovering damages for loss of bargain at common law.

...Taking into account the contract as a whole I am left in no doubt that the parties intended Article 10. 7 to provide a remedy additional to those that would ordinarily be available to Gearbulk on termination of the contract."

那么船东终止合约的通知既然不被视为对普通法下终止合约的弃权(因为选择原则不适用),能否同时被视为普通法下对船厂违约/毁约的接受?上诉庭判是可以,Moore – Bick 大法官说:"It must be borne in mind that all that is required for acceptance of a repudiation at common law is for the injured party to communicate clearly and unequivocally his intention to treat the contract as discharged... If the contract and the general law provide the injured party with alternative rights which have different consequences... he will necessarily have to elect between them and the precise terms in which he informs the other party of his decision will be significant, but where the contract provides a right to terminate which corresponds to a right under the general law (because the breach goes to the root of the contract or the parties have agreed that it should be treated as doing so) no election is necessary. In such cases it is sufficient for the injured party simply to make it clear that he is treating the contract as discharged...

In the present case ... the breaches on the part of the Yard which entitled Gearbulk to terminate the contracts were in each case sufficient to amount to a repudiation...It was quite unequivocal as to Gearbulk's intention to treat the contract as discharged and that was all that was necessary."

总而言之,如果终止合约的通知(notice of termination)是依赖允许终止合约的明示条文,并且该明示条文的解释是这种违约的完整方案(complete code),或者该明示条文针对的救济方案可被视为包括了普通法违约/毁约的损失或与普通法违约/毁约的损失计算不一致,[104]这就会把该通知视为无辜方选择了确认(affirm)合约存在,并以合约的明示条文获得救济。

相反,如果根据合约明示条文终止合约与以普通法的违约/毁约终止合约,两者的救济没有矛盾与对立而只是互补,正如 Stocznia Gdynia SA v. Gearbulk Holdings Ltd. 先例,终止合约的通知不视为做出任何选择,而被视为同时对违约/毁约的接受。毕竟,接受违约/毁约去终止合约没有任何形式的要求,既可以是以语言,也可以是以行动。

7. 接受(acceptance)或确认(affirmation)

拒绝性违约(renunciatory breach)需要无辜方"接受"(accept)才能构成违约,使合约被终止。但有很多先例与权威书籍针对违约/毁约(包括拒绝性违约与真正违约)说是无辜方有权"选择"(elect)终止合约。看来,"接受"与"选择"没有什么区别,反正都是在本章之6.5段与本书第三章第3段提到的选择原则(principle of election)适用。估计"接受"的说法是早期为了与在 Hochster v. De la Tour (1853) 118 ER 922 先例提出但没有被接受的"offer to rescind"的说法对应,既然有违约方的要约,也必须要有无辜方的无条件接受,才能终止合约。但一般在违约/毁约的情况下,无辜方想终止合约,这两个称呼是通用的,本书也不会做出区分。

7.1 权威说法/定义

在进一步探讨这一课题前,不妨先节录权威的《Chitty on Contracts》(第32版,2015年)之24-013段,说:

"**Acceptance of repudiation**. Where there is an anticipatory breach, or the breach of an executory contract, and the innocent party wishes to treat himself as discharged, he must 'accept the repudiation'.[105] An act of acceptance of a repudiation requires no particular form. It is usually done by communicating the decision to terminate to the party in default, although it may be sufficient to lead evidence of an: 'unequivocal overt act which is inconsistent with the subsistence of the contract without any concurrent manifes-

---

[104] 如支付一笔议定赔偿,或是一个针对合约终止后双方如何分摊或做出支付的方案。在 Dalkia Utilities Services Plc. v. Celtech International Ltd. (2006) 1 Lloyd's Rep. 599 先例,合约的第15.5条文规定:"On a termination of this Agreement by the CLIENT ... the following shall apply: (i) The CLIENT shall pay the COMPANY the TERMINATION SUM as specified in Schedule D. (ii) On receipt of such payment stipulated under clause 15.5. (i) the LEASE shall terminate. For theavoidance of doubt, the CLIENT shall keep the INTERIM ENERGY PLANT and the NEW PLANT."法院判是合约终止后根据该条文下的方案与接受普通法下的违约/毁约在结果上有很大不同,无辜方必须做出选择。

[105] 不论是一个真正违约或预期违约,无辜方必须要接受才能终止合约。

tation of intent directed to the other party. '[106]

In an appropriate case an acceptance of a repudiation may take the form of reliance on a contract term which entitles the innocent party to terminate the contract. Where the conduct of the party in breach is such as to entitle the innocent party to terminate either pursuant to a term of the contract or under the general law,[107] the innocent party is not required to elect between its two rights to terminate and so can be treated as having terminated the contract both under the appropriate term of the contract and in accordance with its rights at common law.[108] Unless and until the repudiation is accepted the contract continues in existence for ' an unaccepted repudiation is a thing writ in water'.[109] Acceptance of a repudiation must be clear and unequivocal and mere inactivity or acquiescence will generally not be regarded asacceptance for this purpose.[110] But there may be circumstances in which a continuing failure to perform will be sufficiently unequivocal to constitute acceptance of a repudiation. It all depends on ' the particular contractual relationship and the particular circumstances of the case'. An example of a failure to perform which has been suggested as sufficient to constitute an acceptance is the following: ' Postulate the case where an employer at the end of the day tells a contractor that he, the employer, is repudiating the contract and that the contractor need not return the next day. The contractor does not return the next day or at all. It seems to me that the contractor's failure to return may, in the absence of any other explanation, convery as decision to

〔106〕 接受违约/毁约不需要任何特别的形式。通常是会通过文字或语言告诉违约方,但也可以通过举证来证明一个清楚无误与公开的行动显示了无辜方不再视为与违约方之间有合约存在:State Trading Corp of India Ltd. v. M. Golodetz Ltd. (1989) 2 Lloyd's Rep. 277; The "Santa Clara" (1993) 2 Lloyd's Rep. 301 (QB); Enfield London BC v. Sivanandan (2004) EWHC 672 (QB)等先例。

〔107〕 如果在一个特定的违约/毁约,合约的明示条文与普通法都允许无辜方终止合约,无辜方可以根据合约明示条文终止合约,这并不被视为在合约明示条文与普通法权利中做出了选择。这可见本章第6段,特别是6.5段介绍的 Stocznia Gdynia SA v. Gearbulk Holdings Ltd. (2009) 1 Lloyd's Rep. 461先例。

〔108〕 无辜方无须在合约明示条文与普通法权利中做出选择,但这是假设无辜方在明示条文下的权利与普通法下的权利不存在矛盾与对立。如果存在矛盾与对立,就必须在两者之中做出选择并在终止合约时通知对方。这可见本章之6.5段,有关的先例还有 Stocznia v. Latco (2002) 2 Lloyd's Rep. 436 (CA)与 Vivergo Fuels Ltd. v. Redhall Engineering Solutions Ltd. (2013) EWHC 4030 (TCC)等。

〔109〕 不被接受的预期违约就好像没有发生过的镜花水月。

〔110〕 接受必须清楚无误,不行动与沉默一般会被视为不足够。因为无辜方一行动或一开口正反都有可能。

treat the contract as at an end.'[111]

... Once a repudiation has been accepted, the acceptance cannot be withdrawn.[112] If the parties thereafter resume performance of the contract, their rights are governed by a new contract, even if the term remains the same.[113]"

接受与确认明显是两个矛盾与对立的权利,根据选择原则,或者是接受了违约方的违约/毁约,或者是确认了合约继续存在与有效。这可节录权威书籍《Chitty on Contracts》(第32版,2015年)之24-003段如下:"**Affirmation.** Where the innocent party, being entitled to choose whether to treat the contract as continuing or to accept the repudiation and treat himself as discharged, elects to treat the contract as continuing, he is usually said to have 'affirm' the contract.[114] He will not be held to have elected to affirm the contract unless, first, he has knowledge of the facts giving rise to the breach, and, secondly, he has knowledge of his legal right to choose between the alternatives open to him.[115] When deciding whether the innocent party has affirmed the contract, a court is not conducting a 'mechanical exercise' but is exercising a judgment. The acceptance of the repudiation must be 'real', that is to say, there must be a 'conscious intention to bring the contract to an end, or the doing of something that is inconsistent with its continuation'.[116] Affirmation may be express or implied. It will be implied if, with knowledge of the breach and of his right to choose, he does some unequivocal act from

---

〔111〕 但在某些情况下,无辜方持续性地不履行合约可能会被视为足够清楚无误显示了无辜方接受了违约/毁约。在 The "Santa Clara" (1993) 2 Lloyd's Rep. 301 (QB)先例举了一个假设的例子,某天,雇主对合同工说你明天不用再来上班了,这明显属于违约/毁约,第二天甚至之后合同工都没有再回公司工作,也没有其他解释(如期间生病),这可被视为清楚无误地接受了雇主的违约/毁约。

〔112〕 违约/违约一被接受,合约即被终止,不能撤回。道理是很简单,已经"死亡"的合约是不能单方面使之复生。

〔113〕 经常会有情况是合约根据违约/毁约被终止后,双方通过"无损害"(without prejudice)的谈判让原合约恢复履行,但只是对价(如货价或租金)或其他原合约的条文有所变动。原因是机灵的无辜方往往会借这个机会从对其不利的合约中脱身,之后改变条件重新继续履行。这种情况在国际货物买卖与租约中经常发生。而无损害就代表双方在期间去法院或仲裁庭对有关的违约/毁约是否成立与被无辜方接受做出判决/裁定,双方无损害的协议通常会说明如果判决/裁决对违约方不利,就以谈判后的新合约为准。如果判决/裁决对无辜方不利,就以原合约为准,也就是"复生"(reinstate)原合约,好像什么事情也没有发生过。这种游戏对机灵的无辜方只会有好处,不会有坏处。败诉了也只是损失一些律师费用,不存在需要赔偿金钱的损失。例如,在本章之9.1段介绍的 The "Nanfri" (1979) 1 Lloyd's Rep. 201 (HL)先例就是这种安排。

〔114〕 无辜方有权决定是认为合约继续存在,或接受违约方的违约/毁约去终止继续履行合约责任。当无辜方选择认为合约继续存在时,一般被称为他"确认"(affirm)了合约。

〔115〕 除非无辜方知道违约方违约,并且知道他可以选择确认或终止合约,无辜方不会被认为确认了合约。

〔116〕 在决定无辜方是否确认了合约时,法院不能过于僵化去看双方的言行。无辜方必须"真正"接受了违约方的违约/毁约,也就是显示了终止合约的意图,或做出了一些与合约继续存在有矛盾的事情(如在违约的卖方知悉的情况下,无辜方的买方开始在市场试图买入替代货物)。

which it may be inferred that he intends to go on with the contract regardless of the breach or from which it may be inferred that he will not exercise his right to treat the contract as repudiated.[117] Affirmation must be total：the innocent party cannot approbate and reprobate by affirming part of the contract and disaffirming the rest, for that would be to make a new contract. Equally a party cannot affirm the contract for a limited period of time and then abrogate it on the expiry of that period of time.[118] Mere inactivity after breach does not of itself amount to affirmation, nor (it seems) does the commencement of an action claiming damages for breach.[119] The mere fact that the innocent party has called on the party in breach to change his mind, accept his obligations and perform the contract will not generally, of itself, amount to an affirmation[120]：'... the law does not require an injured party to snatch at a repudiation and he does not automatically lose his right to treat the contract as discharged merely by calling on the other to reconsider his position and recognize his obligation.'

But if the innocent party unreservedly continues to press for performance or accepts performance by the other party after becoming aware of the breach and of his right to elect, he will be held to have affirmed the contract.[121] Reliance upon a term of the contract (such as a term giving a party the right to claim a refund) will not be held to amount to an affirmation, at least in the case where the party who is alleged to have affirmed the contract has made it clear that it was treating the contract as discharged.[122]"

7.2 及时接受违约/毁约的重要性

无辜方接受违约方的违约/毁约要及时(timely)与尽快,并让违约方知道。这也比较公平,否则,岂非会有一个中长期的合约一方对另一方说:"你一年前曾拒绝履行合约,你记不记得?当时我不'接受'终止合约是因为市场对我有利或环境不允许我这样做,但现在不一样了,所以我保留至今才选择终止合约。"这明显不能接受,所以行使选择要及时。正如在 McComick v. National Motor & Accidenct Insurance Union Ltd. (1934) 49 Lloyd's Rep. 362 先例,Scrutton 大法官说:"You are not bound

---

〔117〕 确认合约可以明示或默示让违约方知道无辜方的选择。如果在无辜方知道违约发生并知道自己有选择权的情况下做出一些明确无误的行为,从中可以推断即使违约方违约,他仍希望继续履行合约,或可以推断他不会行使终止合约的选择权,就可以认定无辜方选择确认合约。

〔118〕 确认必须是确认所有合约责任继续存在:无辜方不能确认部分合约责任继续存在,而剩余的不存在,因为这会构成一个新合约。同样,无辜方不能确认合约在一段时间内继续存在,但过了这段时间就不再存在。这可见 Norwest Holst v. Harrison (1985) ICR 668 (CA)先例,将在本章之7.3.1段有介绍。

〔119〕 而无辜方仅仅是在违约后保持沉默或不行动,或是开始诉讼索赔损失,一般不构成确认合约。

〔120〕 无辜方仅仅是试图让违约方改变主意继续履行合约,一般来说不构成确认合约。

〔121〕 但是如果无辜方在毫无保留下持续要求违约方继续履行合约,就可能会构成确认合约。

〔122〕 依赖合约条文(如要求退还款项),至少在无辜方已经明确合约被终止的情况下,不构成确认合约。

the moment the statement is made to make up your mind up at once; you are entitled to a reasonable time to consider – to a reasonable time to make enquiries. ”

Roskill 大法官也在 The"Avisfaith"（1969）2 Lloyd's Rep. 257 先例说："Then he must exercise that right（指选择权）either, if no time limit is provided, within a reasonable time, or if a time limit is provided, then within the time limit so provided. ”

是否接受对方拒绝履行的选择不像合约选择权，不可能约定一个期限行使。所以，无辜方接受对方拒绝履行必须在合理时间内，一过合理时间即算是因选择而弃权（waiver by election），[123]放弃了接受违约/毁约去终止合约的权利，并会被视作确认（affirm）合约，特别是在有其他行为来配合的情况下。

什么是合理时间，要看每个不同合约的性质与个别案件的事实。在涉及标的的市场波动很大与很快的案件中，如商品与股票买卖，这合理时间就会很短，甚至只有一两个工作日。原因是怕无辜方用这个机会等待市场走向相对明确哪种对他有利才做出选择是否接受去终止合约。显然，这会是对违约方构成损害，如他不知道合约是否会被终止就不采取相应的行动。例如，违约方（假设是买方）趁价格还没有涨得太多，在市场买入替代的货物或股票。又如，合约的本质对时间方面很紧张，甚至有条文说明时间规定是重要（time of essence），这样合理时间也会很短。但如果有关的案件涉及一个大型工程的合约，无辜方（不论是雇主或是承建商）如果选择终止合约会涉及很多事后工作，显然合理时间就会长得多，让无辜方可以调查清楚是否可行，再做出选择。这可节录《Chitty on Contracts》（第 32 版，2015 年）之 24 – 002 段下的脚注 14，说："The length of time given to the innocent party will depend in part upon the nature of the contract. Where time is of the essence of the contract or the contract has been entered into a volatile market, the time allowed is likely to be relatively short. But where there is no particular urgency, or the situation is a complex one, the innocent party may be a given a longer period of time in which to make up its mind: Force India Formula One Team Ltd. v. Etihad Airways PJSC [2010] EWCA Civ 1501.[124]"

至于个别案件的不同事实，会要考虑很多方面，如当时是否涉及长假、公司结构与做出重要决定的程序、有否涉及双方订约时都知道的合约链（接受会需要来自合约链的最后一环）等。另是接受对方的拒绝是一个重大决定，花上一两个工作日去寻求法律意见也应是合理：The"Scaptrade"（1981）2 Lloyd's Rep. 425 先例。如果是一个复杂的法律问题与涉及庞大的金额，甚至会有更长的时间允许寻求多个大律师意见。总体来说，是否接受对方的违约/毁约的选择容许的合理时间会比较宽松，大概是因为违约方的拒绝履行一日不撤回，就是一直存在的事实。但笔者作为仲裁员还是经常遇到一些案件，要被迫与其他两位仲裁员做出不同的少数意见。例如，在一

---

〔123〕 可见本书第三章之 3.4 段。

〔124〕 该先例涉及 F1 车队的赞助合约，法院判是赞助商 3 个月后做出选择仍在合理时间内。

个涉及造船合约的伦敦仲裁,中国船厂延误,过了"死亡日期",但外国船东过了一个半月明确了航运市场下跌后才终止合约。仲裁庭的多数判终止合约是在合理时间内,但笔者不同意。这虽然不是根据违约/毁约,而是根据造船合约的终止合约条文,但选择原则(principle of election)的道理是一样。最近也有一个新加坡仲裁涉及货物买卖,CFR卖方由于加拿大东岸遇上大风雪带来装货的延误,导致卖方租用的船舶在充裕的时间抵达装港,但无法在付运期装船。结果船舶装了货往卸港开的途中,卖方根据买卖合约中的不可抗力条文(在仲裁判是不能保护卖方,原因是卖方没有根据条文的要求及时向卖方做出通知)要求买方接受这批货物,并延长信用证的付运期。但买方迟迟不回应,结果过了约35天才指称卖方过了付运期是违反条件条文,构成违约/毁约并终止买卖合约。期间有关货物的市场价格大跌,导致卖方需要以很低的价格把船上的这批货物转卖给第三人而蒙受庞大损失。笔者也不同意其他两位仲裁员的多数裁决判35天仍是及时。可见,什么是合理时间是很不稳定与见仁见智的事情。

无辜方接受违约方的违约/毁约要及时与明确无误,可先简单介绍一个笔者早期处理过的案件以显示其重要性。笔者代表的中国公司作为承租人租了一条10万吨的美国船东的油轮,从大连装货去美国。但订约后不久,承租人被发货人告知没有货装,承租人只好转告美国船东说没有货装,船不必来大连。美国船东马上回应说坚持要承租人履约,并且威胁如果承租人想终止租约必须赔偿其35万美元。承租人一看这份电传就害怕了,并马上来找笔者。笔者建议不再讲话并摸清船东的底,如油轮会否在高雄(该油轮上一个航次的卸港)延误而过了颇紧的销约期,但很快发觉并没有延误。笔者也在租船市场摸底,并知悉船东在找替代租约,据闻很快找到了一个租约去新加坡装货。从市场被报道的替代租约的运费来看,船东是有损失。事实上,他也在追问承租人是否接受35万美元的赔偿。油轮从高雄开航时,笔者也从代理人处知悉油轮清关是去新加坡,不是大连。在算好时间(整件事也只发生在几天内),估计船舶转向回头开去大连(万一市场消息不准,这替代租约仍未确实,所谓"firmly fixed")也再赶不上销约期,笔者为承租人草拟了一个电传回复船东说:"因为你坚持我要履约,加上我不愿意接受赔偿35万美元之数目,我只好努力在大连安排装货来履约。你曾说船舶经已从高雄开航,并会在某天抵达大连,不知最新船期如何,也可去安排装货。"船东马上指称承租人已经拒绝履行合约,所以他已经找了替代租约。而笔者就回应说船东一直坚持承租人履约否则要索赔35万美元,从来没有接受较早前的拒绝,所以确认(affirm)了租约的存在。由于现在船东在没有终止原租约的情况下履行了替代租约,这变为船东自己拒绝性违约并被承租人接受。这事件最后不了了之,船东不敢提起索赔,最终承租人也不必赔。

读者可能会有疑问,船东如果去大连调查发现根本没有待装的这批油,能否证明承租人"不可能"(impossible)履行而违约?首先,要证明不可能履行十分困难,船东查到大连没有这批待装的石油也不代表什么。承租人完全可以争辩说:"本来我是要安排的,但你说不来我就不安排了,毕竟安排起来确实很困难,所以之前我才会说是没货装。”而且,如果船舶到了大连发现没有货装,也不代表船东就可以终止合约了。双方在租约中已经规定了装卸时间与滞期费,船舶在大连等待装货的时间,承租人只需要支付滞期费。除非延误达到了英国法下的“受阻延误”(frustration delay)的程度,船东不能说承租人没有提供货物是真正违约并终止租约。[125] 而要达到受阻延误,时间可能会长达3个月甚至半年,证明在这么长的时间内承租人都不可能履行非常难。其次,就算能够证明承租人不可能履行,这也是一个预期违约,必须要无辜方也就是船东接受才能明确是一个违约,所以对责任的认定也没有帮助。但如果承租人起诉船东违约,在计算损失时,会变成无法证明自己有任何真正损失,只能获得象征性赔偿,这也就是 The “Mihalis Angelos”(1970)2 Lloyd’s Rep. 43 先例的情况。从笔者处理的这个案件也可以看出,拒绝性违约很容易发生与证明,但相对来说,要证明另一种预期违约的不可能履行就困难得多。

另一个类似的例子是 Yukong Line Ltd. of Korea v. Rendsburg Investment Corporation(1996)2 Lloyd’s Rep. 604 先例,但这一先例中的船东的运气要好得多。在该先例中,1995 年 6 月 8 日,Yukong 的船期租了 3 年给 Rendsburg。之后市场下跌,1996 年 1 月 23 日,Rendsburg 的承租人在船东交船前就已经发了一份电文交给船东说:“... Regret to say that charterers for reasons beyond their control are unable to perform any further. ”这是清楚无误的拒绝性违约。Yukong 在 1 月 24 日回应说:“... It is really upset to receive notice of non – performance from charterers. Charterers’ cancellation of charterparty is totally unacceptable and charterers are strongly requested to honour their contractual obligations according to the charterparty... In ease of non – performance all damages, loss and any other costs incurred directly or indirectly to be for charterers’ responsibility and liability. ”

同时,Yukong 发出 20 天的交船前通知(notice of delivery)。在 1 月 29 日,Yukong 根据租约条文再发出 12 天的交船前通知。但承租人一直不理睬,终于在 2 月 1 日,Yukong 看无望挽救,接受了承租人的拒绝履约,终止租约,并发出了以下的电文:

“We refer to your fax dated 23rd January 1996 and your advice that charterers will not perform their obligations under terms of the charterparty.

Despite our repeated requests that charterers confirm they will fulfil their contractual obligations and take delivery of the vessel in accordance with the terms of the charterparty, charterers have failed to do so.

Charterers are therefore in repudiatory breach of the charterparty and we have no option but to accept their breach as repudiation of the contract. ”

---

[125] 这正是 Universal Cargo Carriers Corp. v. Pedro Citati(1957)1 Lloyd’s Rep. 174 先例的决定。

Rendsburg 是说 Yukong 在 1 月 24 日与 29 日(12 天交船通知)是明确选择“确认”租约的存在,所以 1 月 23 日的拒绝已成为过去,变成 Yukong 在 2 月 1 日“接受”这个已成过去的拒绝根本不对,是 Yukong 自己拒绝性违约。

Moore – Bick 大法官判是:(1) 要说无辜方已选择了“确认”合约,必须是明确无误的(irrevocable and unequivocal)。(2) 在 1 月 24 日与 29 日的交船通知,只是在 Yukong 仍未决定选择之前的租约要求下的“行政做法”(administrative matters),本身不足够明确肯定让 Rendsburg 认为 Yukong 已最后选择确认租约。(3) 在 1 月 24 日 Yukong 的电文用字上也只能是个抗议,并请求承租人收回拒绝履行的行为,否则面对损失索赔。用字上不能说明确无误表达 Yukong 已最终正式选择是确认租约。(4) 所以,Yukong 可在 2 月 1 日(看来,事件的发展仍算是合理时间内,虽然双方对此没有争辨)接受拒绝,终止租约并索赔损失。

应该说 Moore – Bick 大法官的判决符合商业做法。因为除非是无辜方想取巧(如市场对其终止合约有利),他总会想挽救这一合约的履行。如果动辄说其已选择了确认合约,并非是好事。当然,Yukong 可在电文上使用更明确的用字,例如:(1)在1 月 24 日的电文中注明“无损害”(without prejudice,这可防止打官司时要披露),并在要求承租人尊重合约之处,说明是:“This is without prejudice to our right to accept your repudiation which we will let you know in due course.”(2)在 1 月 24 日与 29 日的交船前通知,也应是与(1)一样说明,除了不必在抬头中注明无损害。说明也可以是:“This notice of delivery should not be taken as the owners having elected the affirmation of the charter-party.”

总结上述两个例子,对方一拒绝履行,若是市场对无辜方有利,或是对方是经济不稳、信用不妥的公司,无辜方不要拖泥带水,应尽快明确接受。因为如果过了合理时间,或是言行中表达了选择确认合约,将来不一定再有机会终止合约,对方可能不再第二次拒绝履行。

反正即使是无辜方不对违约方绝望,或仍想做这票生意,也可接受终止合约再继续与对方谈判下去,迫使对方履约(同意重新订立原合约,所谓 re-instatement of contract),否则起诉索赔损失。这样做在有些情况下安全多了,无辜方也可进可退,可另外要求新的合约条文,如对方给予银行或母公司担保,因为这是在谈判一个新合约。

另可一提,笔者感觉判断是否明确与及时接受的程度,与不同案情给法官及仲裁员的不同感觉很有关系。要是无辜方实是在取巧,法官及仲裁员不自觉中会对其判得严格。相反,他若是真无辜,则会判得不严格。但毕竟对这种事实的判断合理与否,经常会看到仲裁员对有关的业务不太熟悉,甚至对这方面的法律掌握也不太好,所以有摇摆不定的情况,带来诉讼结果的不确定。

7.3　接受必须清楚无误并即时终止合约

7.3.1　什么是清楚无误

无辜方的接受必须清楚无误并即时终止合约,这可以 Norwest Holst v. Harrison

(1985) ICR 668 (CA)先例为例进行解释。在该先例中,被告聘用原告为首席工程师与董事,合约每年一续,结束合约需要提前12个月通知。1982年6月14日,原告被通知从7月1日开始,他不再担任董事的职位并被派往一个偏远的办事处。6月17日,原告回复了一封标题"无损害"(without prejudice)的信件,说他认为根据被告6月14日的信件,他的工作到6月30日结束。原告同时要求被告支付12个月的工资和福利(因为没有提前12个月通知)与根据相关法律规定裁员要支付的金额。双方之后有一些通讯往来并进行了一次会议。6月24日或25日,被告正式撤回6月14日的信件。但原告坚持雇佣合约已经被终止,并要求被告赔偿损失。法院要决定的争议是原告有否清楚无误地接受了被告的拒绝履行?上诉法院一致判是原告没有清楚无误地接受,原因主要是原告6月17日信件上"无损害"的标题以及该信件的倒数第二段,说:"With respect your letter was indefinite on a number of points, and I would ask you to contact me immediately if you feel I have misunderstood what has been said or if further discussion would assist an amicable resolution of the matter."针对这两部分内容,Cumming – Bruce大法官说:

"I do not take the view that this letter, headed as it was 'without prejudice', should have been fairly regarded by the recipient company as an unequivocal acceptance of the repudiation thereby determining the contract. I take the view that he was communicating his strong objection to the course proposed by the company in stating that he was ready to enter into discussions about it, and there was time for discussion between 17 June and 30 June.

If that is right, there was no unequivocal acceptance of the repudiation and on 24 June the company were entitled to withdraw their threat because there was sufficient anticipatory element in their breach to confer on them a locus poenitentiae at any time before acceptance was communicated."

除了原告6月17日的信件中的上述两部分内容,Buckley大法官还提出了认为并不是"接受"的另一个原因。原告6月17日的信件中说雇佣合约到6月30日结束。Buckley大法官认为无辜方的接受除了必须清楚无误外,也必须立即终止合约。换句话说,无辜方不能接受违约方的拒绝履行说:"到×月×日,我们的合约继续,但之后合约终止。"Buckley的判决可节录如下:"The effect of an acceptance of an anticipatory repudiation must, in my view, be the immediate termination of the contract. By accepting repudiation, the innocent party elects to treat the contract as abrogated at the moment when he exercises his election. He cannot, in my judgment, affirm the contract for a limited time down to some future date and treat it as abrogated only from that future date.... He(原告)is, in my opinion, affirming the contract in respect of the period from 14 to 30 June and that is wholly inconsistent with the view that he was unequivocally accepting the repudiation as something which upon acceptance would abrogate the contract."

总结上述先例所讲,无辜方的接受首先必须清楚无误。这样双方才能明确自己的法律地位,并采取相应的行动。这与订立合约的谈判时接受要约的情况类似,简单说"我接受"是最明确不过,再在后面加一些描述反而可能造成争议,毕竟涉及解释的问题。如果想要在"我接受"之外继续强调自己的立场,加上的内容也必须与"接受"的后果一致,如说"我从明天起就不再上班,并且会开始找新的工作"。但在该先例中,"无损害"的标题就显示了原告想要谈判的意图,而倒数第二段更加强了这种意图。原告还想要谈判就说明不是最终与不能扭转(irrevocable)的决定。

其次,无辜方必须即时终止合约,而不能说合约在一段时间后终止。这也可以理解,较早已经提到没有被无辜方接受的预期违约就好像"没有发生过的镜花水月"(a thing writ in water)。在合约被终止前,违约方都可以回心转意去履行合约,除非被禁反言。而合约一旦终止,违约方(甚至无辜方)就没法回头,因为已经"死亡"的合约是不能单方面使之复生(what is dead is dead)。如果无辜方可以接受违约方的违约/毁约并决定在一段时间后合约才终止,那么违约方能否在这段时间内回心转意(就像在该先例发生的情况一样)?再一个问题是,在这段时间内无辜方与违约方应该继续履行合约,这很容易就构成了对合约继续存在的确认,导致与无辜方接受违约/毁约并终止合约有解释不通的矛盾。在 The "Fortune Plum" (2013) 2 Lloyd's Rep. 618 先例也有涉及这方面的争议。

最后一个问题是,已经允许无辜方在合约规定的履行时间之前提前终止合约,如果再允许无辜方决定什么时间合约继续,什么时间合约终止会是对无辜方过于优待了。例如,合约规定某个阶段违约方要支付一大笔钱给无辜方,但违约方在应该支付之前一段时间拒绝继续履行合约并且获得无辜方的接受。但如果无辜方可以同时决定合约稍后在违约方应该支付这笔钱之后终止,那么这笔钱就变为债务而非损失。[126]

7.3.2 接受可以通过任何形式表示

无辜方接受违约方的拒绝履行并终止合约的意图,可以通过任何形式的语言或行动向违约方直接或间接表示,只要是清楚无误。正如 Steyn 勋爵在 The "Santa Clara" (1996) 2 Lloyd's Rep. 225 (HL)先例说的:"For present purposes I would accept as established law the following propositions. (1) Where a party has repudiated a contract the aggrieved party has an election to accept the repudiation or to affirm the contract: Fercometal S. A. R. L. v. Mediterranean Shipping Co. S. A. [1989] A. C. 788. (2) An act of acceptance of a repudiation requires no particular form: acommunication does not have to be couched in the language of acceptance. It is sufficient that the communication or conduct clearly and unequivocally conveys to the repudiating party that that aggrieved party is treating the contract as at an end. (3) It is rightly conceded by counsel

---

〔126〕 债务与损失的重要分别可见杨良宜《损失赔偿与救济》一书第十一章。

for the buyers that the aggrieved party need not personally, or by an agent, notify the repudiating party of his election to treat the contract as at an end. It is sufficient that the fact of the election comes to the repudiating party's attention, e. g. notification by an unauthorised broker or other intermediary may be sufficient..."

在 Stocznia v. Latco (2001) 1 Lloyd's Rep. 537 先例,一审的 Thomas 大法官说:"It is clear that no particular form or formality is required for the acceptance of a repudiation. Although the letters referred to the termination under cl. 5 of the contract, they made it clear that the yard considered the contract at an end and neither party was under an obligation of any further performance. If the yard had a right to terminate for repudiation, the fact that they did not set that out does not in my view make any difference, as it is well established that a party terminating a contract can rely on grounds other than those he gives. The important matter is that the letters unequivocally stated that the contractual obligations were at an end. I therefore conclude that there was an acceptance by the yard."

至于无辜方的接受是否清楚无误让违约方知道其选择是终止或是确认合约,要根据不同的合约关系与不同的事实背景决定:The "Santa Clara"先例。而且,要客观来看而不考虑无辜方的主观意图。

通过语言使用"接受"(acceptance)与"终止合约"(termination 或 rescind)的文字当然是再明确不过,但并不是必须。无辜方的行动(只要直接或间接让违约方知悉)往往也足够能体现出他是否有清楚无误地接受违约方的拒绝履行。例如,将合约的标的(一票货物、名画、房产的买卖)等转卖给第三人显然显示了无辜方将原合约视为被终止;或是一个装修的合约,房东联系另一个装修公司来进行装修也显示了他将原合约视为被终止;又或是在一个 FOB 买卖合约中,船舶开到了装港,卖方通知买方没有货装,买方通知船舶离开,这也显示了买方将买卖合约视为被终止。同样,无辜方的行为也可能显示出无辜方是确认了合约继续存在。例如,房东拒绝履行租约,但租客继续住在房子里并交房租,租客就不能说自己已经接受了房东的拒绝履行:Johnstone v. Milling(1886) 16 QBD 460 (CA)先例;如果无辜方向法院要求履约指令(specific performance)更是显示了无辜方"确认"(affirm)了合约继续存在:Garnac Grain v. Faure (1962) AC 1130 (HL)先例。

7.3.3 沉默/不行动与持续性不履行合约责任能否构成接受?

问题是无辜方的沉默与不行动(这在一个待履行合约[executory contract]就表示无辜方不再履行他的合约责任[127])是否属于清楚无误地接受并终止合约?一般来说,答案是否定的,因为沉默与不行动算不上是清楚无误。正如 Goff 大法官在 The

---

[127] 这与本章之 3.10.2 段提到的确认合约后,无辜方暂时中断履行合约并以弃权与禁反言作为抗辩的情况有所不同。

"Leonidas D"（1985）2 Lloyd's Rep. 18 先例指出："In the absence of special circumstances, silence and inaction by a party to a reference are, objectively considered, just as consistent with his having inadvertently forgotten about the matter; or with his simply hoping that the matter will die a natural death if he does not stir up the other party; or with his office staff, or his agents, or his insurers, or his solicitors, being appallingly slow."

另在 State Trading Corp of India Ltd. v. M. Golodetz Ltd.（1989）2 Lloyd's Rep. 277 先例，上诉庭的 Kerr 大法官说："What is commonly referred to as an acceptance of a repudiation must be communicated to the party in breach or at least overtly evinced... The decision of the High Court of Australia in Holland v. Wiltshire（1954）90 C. L. R. 409 shows that an unequivocal overt act which is inconsistent with the subsistence of the contract may be sufficient, without any concurrent manifestation of intent directed to the other party. **But saying and doing nothing at all, other than a continuing failure to perform, cannot constitute an acceptance of a repudiation even if the grounds for such an acceptance then exist. Such conduct would be equivocal and equally consistent with a decision not to exercise the right to treat the contract as repudiated.**"（加黑部分是笔者的强调）

但在 The "Santa Clara"（1996）2 Lloyd's Rep. 225（HL）先例，这只是沉默与不行动并不足以构成接受并终止合约的说法受到了质疑。在该先例中，上诉庭推翻了高院的判决而贵族院又推翻了上诉庭的判决，认为沉默与不行动在某些特殊的情况下可以构成接受。该先例的案情涉及一个 CIF 的丙烷买卖合约，合约价格是 400 美元/吨。但在船舶要装货时，市场跌至约 170 美元/吨。买方（Vitol）肯定是想赖掉这份合约，他的借口是货物装船将会是错过付运期（这借口后来在仲裁被裁决不成立，原因是事实上装完货时还在付运期内）。Vitol 在 1991 年 3 月 8 日发了一份传真给卖方（Norelf）说："We are advised that the vessel is not likely to complete loading... until sometime on the 9th March-well outside the agreed contractual period. In view of the breach of condition we must reject the cargo and repudiate the contract."这份电传显然构成了预期违约的拒绝性违约，它明确显示了 Vitol 拒绝履约。

但之后 Norelf 没有采取任何行动履行或确认合约。根据合约，Norelf 需要在货物装船后尽快交出提单给 Vitol，而 Vitol 需要在提单日期的 30 日内支付货款。事实上，Norelf 并没有交出提单，在 3 月 15 日，Norelf 将货物在市场以 170 美元转卖。4 个月后，Norelf 开始仲裁向 Vitol 索赔 100 万美元损失。Norelf 声称他收到买方电传之后的沉默与不行动，也就是没有交出提单，代表已经接受了 Vitol 的预期违约。仲裁庭判是 Norelf 的不行动属于有效的接受，Vitol 以"单纯地不履行合约或不行动能否构成接受"这个法律问题提起上诉。一审法院（[1993] 2 Lloyd's Rep. 301）的 Phillips 大法官判是可以构成接受，但这被上诉法院（[1995] 2 Lloyd's Rep. 128）推翻。到了贵族院，上诉庭的判决再次被推翻，贵族院支持了 Phillips 大法官的判法。Steyn

勋爵说："**An act of acceptance of a repudiation requires no particular form：a communication does not have to be couched in the language of acceptance. It is sufficient that the communication or conduct clearly and unequivocally conveys to the repudiating party that that aggrieved party is treating the contract as at an end**... It is now possible to turn directly to the first issue posed, namely whether non – performance of an obligation is ever as a matter of law capable of constituting an act of acceptance. On this aspect I found the judgment of Phillips J. entirely convincing. One cannot generalise on the point. **It all depends on the particular contractual relationship and the particular circumstances of the case.** But, like Phillips J., I am satisfied that a **failure to perform may sometimes signify to a repudiating party an election by the aggrieved party to treat the contract as at an end**... Taking the present case as illustrative, it is important to bear in mind that the tender of a bill of lading is the pre – condition to payment of the price. Why should an arbitrator not be able to infer that when, in the days and weeks following loading and the sailing of the vessel, the seller failed to tender a bill of lading to the buyer he clearly conveyed to a trader that he was treating the contract as at an end? ... Sometimes in the practical world of businessmen an omission to act may be as pregnant with meaning as a positive declaration."(加黑部分是笔者的强调)

Steyn 勋爵在 The "Santa Clara"先例举了两个特殊的情况解释无辜方沉默与不行动同样可以让违约方知道其已经接受了违约/毁约并终止合约。一个例子是雇佣合约，雇主对合同工说"你明天不用再来上班了"，这属于违约/毁约。第二天甚至以后的日子直到合同工向雇主提出索赔损失，他都没有再回公司工作，也没有其他解释(如期间生病)，这客观来看是可以被视为清楚无误地接受了雇主的违约/毁约。就算是以雇主的角度看，也是合同工接受了不用再来上班的告知。

另一个例子是买卖合约下，卖方必须取得出口证才能装船，但买方在装船前就错误拒绝这批货物。买方也知道卖方因此没有向当局申请出口证(因为这个申请需要买方的帮助与提供资料)。显然，作为违约方的买方是知道卖方虽然是沉默与不行动，但是接受了该买卖合约的终止。

在这个先例中，Norelf 作为 CIF 卖方没有按照买卖合约在装货期后尽快交出提单要求 Vitol 在 30 日内支付货价，这是 Vitol 完全知道的不行动，客观来看，他完全知道 Norelf 是接受了他的违约/毁约，所以没有履行(交出提单)。

Steyn 勋爵同意在绝大部分正常的情况下，无辜方需要清楚无误接受违约方的违约/毁约，但会有特殊与例外情况可以将沉默与不行动视为接受。虽然是两个不同的课题，但合约的订立也会在特殊与例外的情况下，即使一方沉默与不行动，也被视为接受了合约的订立：Rust v. Abbey Life Assurance Co. Ltd. (1979) 2 Lloyd's Rep. 334 先例。

7.4　确认合约能否被扭转?

上文已经提到无论是接受违约/毁约或是确认合约继续存在都是不可扭转(irrevocable),特别明确是接受会导致合约被终止,而已经“死亡”的合约是不能单方面令其“复生”(what is dead is dead)。但确认合约继续存在是否明确不能被扭转就有疑问,因为可以被解释为无辜方确认合约的言行经常发生。合约一方拒绝履行合约,大部分情况是市场情况发生了改变,对违约方不利。这样在大部分的违约/毁约案件中,无辜方往往是希望合约能够继续履行,不会在违约方违约/毁约时马上干脆利落地接受。通常的情况是,无辜方会希望通过哀求或向违约方施加压力等手段,令违约方回心转意去履行合约。但往往会到了一个时间点是无辜方接受违约方是确实不会履行合约,除非无辜方做出重大且无法接受的让步的事实。这样,如果无辜方可以被挑出一些较早的言行解释为是确认合约,而且如果确认是不能被扭转,岂非无辜方之后发觉无望时都不能改变立场去接受并终止合约?看来,为了配合商业上的现实做法,不应该太轻易解释无辜方的言行属于确认合约。英国的法律针对这一种现实的常见情况,有以下的几种办法。

7.4.1　不应该太轻易解释无辜方的言行属于确认合约

在本章之7.3.2段已经提到,接受可以通过任何形式表示,确实也是同样道理。确认可以很明确,如无辜方向法院或仲裁庭申请履约指令,强制违约方执行。或者清楚明确向违约方说“你必须要履行,我不接受你的违约/毁约”。危险的是确认可以通过无辜方的言行去默示,正如在 W. E. Cox Toner (International) Ltd. v. Crook (1981) IRLR 443 先例,Browne-Wilkinson 大法官说:

“... Mere delay by itself (unaccompanied by any express or implied affirmation of the contract) does not constitute affirmation of the contract; but if it is prolonged it may be evidence of an implied affirmation.

Affirmation of the contract can be implied. Thus, it the innocent party calls on the guilty party for further performance of the contract, he will normally be taken to have affirmed the contract since his conduct is only consistent with the continued existence of the contractual obligation. Moreover, if the innocent party himself does acts which are only consistent with the continued existence of the contract, such act will normally show affirmation of the contract...”

从上述说法马上可以看到危险之处,无辜方哀求或向违约方施加压力要求他履行就可能已经构成确认合约,更不用说无辜方自己同时可能还会履行部分合约责任,以向对方施加压力。例如,因为市场下跌,CIF 买方通知卖方说不要这批货了,也不会开信用证(letter of credit),而卖方则回信要求买方开信用证,甚至表示他要去市场上租船。根据 Browne – Wilkinson 大法官的权威说法,这既让违约方继续履行合约,再加上自己也履行了部分合约责任,是应该被解释为确认合约。但现实中如果市场还是在下跌,买方不会回心转意,所以迟早卖方会要接受违约/毁约,然后索赔损失。

但这样在后来的诉讼中,买方就会挑出这些言行是确认合约,但之后卖方没有履行合约进行付运,反而变为卖方违约/毁约。

所以法院有一些权威说法说解释确认合约应该尽量严格,如在 Yukong Line Ltd. of Korea v. Rendsburg Investment Corporation(1996)2 Lloyd's Rep. 604 先例,Moore - Bick 大法官警告说法院或仲裁庭不应该太僵化(unduly technical approach)解释无辜方的言行是否构成确认合约,说:"... the Court should generally be slow to accept that the injured party has committed himself irrevocably to continuing with the contract in the knowledge that if, without finally committing himself, the injured party has made an unequivocal statement of some kind on which the party in repudiation has relied, the doctrine of estoppel is likely to prevent any injustice being done."

权威书籍《Chitty on Contracts》(第 32 版,2015 年)之 24 - 003 段也说:"... the law does not require an injured party to snatch at a repudiation and he does not automatically lose his right to treat the contract as discharged merely by calling on the other to reconsider his position and recognize his obligation."

判断无辜方是否选择确认合约的另一个考验是从其言行推断他做出选择时是否知道自己的权利。毕竟,根据 The "Kanchenjunga"(1990)1 Lloyd's Rep. 391 先例,无辜方必须知道自己的权利,才能构成因选择而弃权(waiver by election)。显然,无辜方必须知道自己的权利,才能接受违约/毁约并终止合约。但针对无辜方确认了合约的情况,如果无辜方说"你必须要履行,我不接受你的违约/毁约",那显然他是知道自己的权利。但无辜方很少会这样说清楚,而是拖拖拉拉并有各种言行,因此判断是否确认合约就比接受违约/毁约困难得多。而其中一个重要的判断方法就是看,是否有证据或根据当时的情况与无辜方的言行推断他是否知道自己的权利并做出选择。这方面可节录 Mance 大法官在 Insurance Corp of the Channel Islands v. Royal Hotel Ltd.(1998)Lloyd's Rep. I. R. 151 先例所说,如下:"Where the circumstances justify an avoidance and the choice is to avoid, the requirement of an unequivocal communication creates no problem. The claim to avoid demonstrates of itself at one and the same time awareness of the choice and its making. Where it is said there has been an election to affirm rather than to avoid, the position is more problematic. Is it sufficient for affirmation that there is knowledge and a communication (by words or conduct) which, assuming such knowledge, demonstrates an unequivocal choice? Or must the communication itself or the surrounding circumstances demonstrate such knowledge to the other party? In principle, it seems to me that the latter approach is correct in the context of affirmation. The communication itself or the circumstances must demonstrate objectively or unequivocally that the party affirming is making an informed choice."

Yukong Line Ltd. of Korea v. Rendsburg Investment Corporation 先例的案情在本章之 7.2 段有详细介绍,这里不再重复。只说在承租人拒绝履行之后,船东除了施加压力希望承租人回心转意外，还同时做出了20天的交船通知。这一交船通知被违约方的承租人说是确认了租约。这不被 Moore - Bick 大法官接受，说无辜方的船东做出的20天交船通知是无辜方在对方拒绝履行后最自然的反应，只是一个行政做法，不应该被视为选择了不可扭转地确认租约存在："Consideration of this kind are perhaps most likely to arise when the injured party's initial response to the renunciation of the contract has been to call on the other to change his mind, accept his obligations and perform the contract. That is often the most natural response and one which, in my view, the Court should do nothing to discourage... the owners' telex of Jan. 24 giving 20 days' notice for the delivery of the vessel was essentially concerned with administrative matters... it did not carry the implication that the owners intended to continue with the charter notwithstanding the charterers' repudiation and so could not be understood as an unequivocal election to affirm the contract."

有趣的是 Moore - Bick 大法官分析时没有将确认合约与接受要约进行类比，而是与"禁反言"（estoppel）的说法联系在一起，说："In my view, the Court should generally be slow to accept that the injured party has committed himself irrevocably to continuing with the contract in the knowledge that if, without finally committing himself, the injured party has made an unequivocal statement of some kind on which the party in repudiation has, **the doctrine relied of estoppel is likely to prevent any injustice being done**."（加黑部分是笔者的强调）

在本书稍后的章节会介绍禁反言的问题，其中多次提到重要的 The "Kanchenjunga"贵族院先例，Goff 勋爵对一直以来被混为一谈的"弃权"（waiver）与禁反言做出区分。针对弃权，弃权方必须知道自己的权利，他在两个相对立的权利中选择了一个，就代表对另一个弃权。而针对禁反言，提出禁反言的一方必须证明自己依赖了对方的言行并蒙受损害。在 Yukong Line Ltd. of Korea v. Rendsburg Investment Corporation 先例，船东如果在知道自己的权利的情况下，不能扭转地选择了确认租约，就会构成"因选择而弃权"（waiver by election）。但已经提到，法院不应该太轻易接受无辜方选择确认合约而放弃接受违约/毁约的权利。

由于在该先例中，双方没有争议禁反言，所以 Moore - Bick 大法官只是简单提了一句说，通过禁反言可以防止任何不公平的决定。笔者不妨进一步解释，如果无法决定船东的言行是否属于清楚无误的陈述或承诺确认租约，就可以看承租人即违约方的反应与怎样解读船东的言行。如果承租人解读为船东确认租约，就会做出依赖并因此蒙受损害。例如，根据船东的交船通知订立了另一个分租约，而在没有认定船东确认租约的情况下，承租人不会这样做。这样，就可以更肯定地把船东的交船通知视为确认租约或构成禁反言。而如果承租人根本没有做出任何依赖，也就是根本没有将船东的交船通知解释为确认租约，或是持续坚持拒绝履行租约。

在 Carillion JM Ltd. v. Bath & North East Somerset Council（2009）EWHC 166

(TCC)先例,案情涉及工程合约,法院在没有口头证据的情况下,不愿意以初步争议(preliminary issue)决定雇主给承建商要求按照工程师指示进行工程是否构成确认合约。这也显示了法院同意 Moore - Bick 大法官的说法,认为解释无辜方的言行是否构成确认合约要谨慎,必须听取口头证据并全面理解。Coulson 大法官说:"... affirmation of the contract would be implied 'where the injured party acts in a way which is consistent only with a decision to keep the contract alive or where he exercises his rights which would **only** be available to him if the contract had been affirmed'. The repeated use of the word 'only' identifies the relatively high hurdle that a party relying on an affirmation argument must get over, and, speaking for myself, I would not be happy about reaching a conclusion that the injured party affirmed the existence of a contract without hearing any oral evidence."

在 Stocznia v. Latco (2001) 1 Lloyd's Rep. 537 先例,也有同样的争议。详细的案情在本章之 8.4.1.1 段有介绍,这里只说在船东违约/毁约后,船厂没有接受反而在第三与第四艘船舶(后来在第五与第六艘船舶也是如此)做手脚去安放龙骨,并向船东做出通知与要求支付 20% 船价。这显然是履行合约的言行,船东在后来的诉讼中说这属于确认合约,而在船东保持沉默的情况下,船厂不能单方面改变立场终止合约。一审的 Thomas 大法官说:"When the yard(无辜方的船厂) served the keel - lying notices in respect of vessels 3 & 4, in my view on the evidence I have heard, the yard were not making an unconditional affirmation nor, in my view, was their position so understood by Latreefers(违约方的船东). At the time of service of those keel - laying notices in April, 1994, the yard's position was clear, they still had some hope that Latreefers might still perform and served the keel - laying notices for that purpose, but if Latreefers did not perform, the yard would bring the contracts to an end."

看来对无辜方而言,最安全的办法是在对方违约/违约后试图挽救合约的存在,不论是哀求或向违约方施加压力,最好对所有的言行写明无辜方的权利"无损害"(without prejudice)。而针对有些言行,如无辜方的卖方督促违约方的买方开信用证,可以尽量设定一个期限,一旦过了期限,就可以终止合约。

最后笔者介绍两个涉及国际货物买卖的仲裁案件,笔者是仲裁员,两个案件的裁决发生在半年不到的时间内,其胜负就取决于到底无辜方有否确认合约的存在。但两个仲裁案件的结果笔者都不认同,其中一个笔者也做出了不同意见。

第一个案件就是在本章之 7.2 段提到的新加坡仲裁,有关 CFR 卖方由于加拿大东岸遇上大风雪带来装货的延误,导致卖方租用的船舶在充裕的时间抵达装港,但无法在付运期装船。这等于卖方违反了买卖合约的条件条文,由于货物已经装船付运,卖方(背后是美国公司)也没有弄虚作假倒签提单(back-date bill of lading),而只是问买方是否接受这批货物,如果接受,就延长信用证的付运期。已经提到买方约 35 天后才指称卖方过了付运期是违反条件条文,构成违约/毁约并终止买卖合约。期间有关货物的市场价格大跌,导致卖方需要以很低的价格把船上的这批货物转卖给第三人而蒙受庞大损失。但事实上在这35天发生了一些事情,包括买方曾经要求卖方减货价到一个卖方不能接受的价格,但是这是双方无损害的谈判,对仲裁庭没有影响。但买方的其他言行对仲裁庭有影响,首先是卖方开航不久曾经询问买方要求如何签发提单,而买方要求签发三套不同货物数量的提单(估计是有不同分买方)。另是较后期的通讯往来就是买方问卖方如果延长信用证的付运期,所需要的费用卖方是否愿意承担,而卖方很快就确认他愿意。在不久后,买方要求卖方提供这三套提单的副本。在后期,卖方一直追问买方有关修改信用证的消息,但买方没有回应。结果在35天后,买方告知卖方终止买卖合约。

对笔者来说,整体来看,买方的这些言行都可以构成买方确认买卖合约继续存在,特别是在考虑到35天的不合理延误。卖方在后期一直追问买方有关修改信用证的消息,也加强了笔者的看法,即卖方根本就是依赖了买方的言行,以为问题已经解决,并且因此蒙受了损害,没有在市场进一步下跌之前转卖。这样看来,即使是从禁反言的角度,也应该成立。但很可惜买方委任的仲裁员在每个方面都不同意笔者的看法,而首席仲裁员在起初同意笔者有关一两个方面(如卖方同意了承担修改信用证的费用与35天的延误等),但最后改变初衷并同意另一位仲裁员,导致最后裁决判卖方败诉。以下只节录其中比较有关两段裁决书决定,如下:"Bearing in mind that the Respondent was only responding to the Claimant under timepressure from the Claimant to reply the same day on how the bill of lading was to besplit, that exchange of 3 January 2014 could not be taken as an unequivocalrepresentation that the Respondent had chosen to affirm the Contract. It was a limitedimmediate response to an administrative question by the Claimant... Therefore, none of the communications relied by the Claimant on splitting the bill oflading, the copy of the bill of lading or the amendments of the L/C was acommunication in clear and unequivocal terms that the Respondent elected to affirmthe Contract. The Claimant was probably justifiably frustrated by the Respondent'srefusal to confirm amendment of the L/C, but that is not the same as saying that theRespondent had affirmed the Contract."

笔者不能接受这裁决或可以与多数意见协调,所以最终做出了简单的不同意见,大致如下:

"It is accepted that if the Claimant/Seller had breached a condition of the Contract in failing to ship cargo on/before 31 December 2012 and the 3 – day's delay could not be extended for failing to prove a force majeure event or alternatively, failing to serve prompt notice, then the Respondent/Buyer, as an innocent party, would be faced with an 'election'. Namely, to elect whether to terminate or to keep alive (affirm) the Contract.

My co-arbitrators held that the Respondent's belated decision to cancel and the matters or conducts set out above did not amount to an affirmation. They relied on Chitty on Contracts (31st edition) at 24 – 003, the material part can be set out as follows: '(v) affirmation will be implied if, with knowledge of the breach and of his right to choose, the innocent party does some **unequivocal act**, from which it may be inferred that he intends to go on with the contract regardless of the breach and from which it may be inferred that he will not exercise his right to treat the contract as repudiated." (my emphasis)'

I disagree. If these conducts or acts by the Respondent did not amount to an 'unequivocal act of affirmation', they are then logically to be inferred as an 'unequivocal act of cancellation' in a situation of an election. I cannot see how it is possible.

Lastly, I should add in Chitty on Contract 31st Ed. Para. 24 – 005, it further said: 'There are, however, circumstances here the innocent party may be deprived of his right to treat the contract as repudiated ... For example, there will be circumstances where, even in the absence of an actual election, the innocent party will be regarded as having made its election, and decided not to terminate, when **a reasonable time has passed and it has not sought to bring the contract to an end**.' (bold letters are my emphasis)

As a shipping man, I am used to an election to cancel a contract has to be made by the innocent party (shipowner in charterparties) within no more than 1/2 days in well – known cases like The "Laconia" (1977) 1 Lloyd's Rep. 315; The "Mihalios Xilas" (1979) 2 Lloyd's Rep. 303; The "Balder London" (1980) 2 Lloyd's Rep. 489; The "Scaptrade" (1981) 2 Lloyd's Rep. 425; etc. Iappreciate the shipping market is volatile and this must be one of the reasons behind in thosecases. But themarket for the cargo in this case, iron ore pallets, should be equally volatile."

另一个仲裁案件涉及航次期租(TCT),有关的航次涉及中国买方以 FOB 向印尼卖方购买木质纸浆。众所周知,印尼的货源不可靠,往往由于各种原因,船舶到了印尼装港没有货装,因此,对派遣船舶去印尼装货的 FOB 买方很危险。在这个案件也是如此,后来提供的证据显示印尼卖方事实上没有这批木质纸浆备妥可以装船。但印尼卖方用了外国公司的技巧,船舶抵达印尼装港后,委任了一位独立的印尼检验师上船检测,并做出报告说船舱不清洁,不适合装载这批货物。并在后来以无法在买卖合约的付运期内备妥装货为由,终止了买卖合约。但在船舶被印尼卖方指称船舱不清洁的同时,船东马上通过互保协会(P & I Club)委任了一位独立的国际检验师上船检测,该检测报告说船舱适合装一般的货物,虽然不适合装要求清洁程度很高的特定货物。至于租约链则是中国 FOB 买方委任了一家外国船公司作为承租人(charterer)以 TCT 租进船舶。印尼买方终止合约后,承租人也只能指称船舱不清洁取消了 TCT,在印尼装港还船。船东回复以下电邮抗议说:

"Dear Sir,

Surprise and regret to know below, but sorry, we can notaccept your such arrangement, the reason of redelivery isdefinitely not acceptable, please note the reason of un-cargoworthinessis not suitable for any special shipper'srequirement like this wood pulp. As per normal shippingpractice, the cargo hold should be clean and free of smell andprevious cargo residues and without any loose scale andconstruction defects only. We and our crew had done ourutmost to cooperate on this issue, the failure of passing the cargo holdis not on owner/crew' side.

As owner we hereby declare she is still under your Time Charter, and hold youfully execute the CP without fail!"

十几天后,船东看到一直保持沉默的承租人不会再履行TCT,加上也找到了替代租约,就命令船舶离开印尼装港开往马来西亚装货去日本。之后,蒙受严重损失的船东开始仲裁向承租人索赔,并委任笔者作为仲裁员。该租约的仲裁条文是典型的伦敦海事仲裁做法,即只是由双方当事人各自委任仲裁员,如果两位仲裁员不能达成一致意见,则委任一位"公断人"(umpire)以独任仲裁员的身份做出裁决。

笔者认为争议的强弱在这个案件十分明显,租约(根据NYPE 46标准格式)只是写明可以装载一般货物(Vessel on her delivery to be ready to receive cargo with clean-swept holds),并没有承诺可以装载木质纸浆。根据互保协会委任的国际检验师的检验报告,船东并没有违约。而即使是违约,船舱清洁也只属于保证条文,多花一些时间与金钱就可以解决问题,承租人不能以此终止TCT。但承租人在仲裁中提出了一个争议,指称在订立TCT前曾经向船东询问有关船舱情况,而船东提供了另一艘姐妹船的船舱照片给承租人,这构成了"误述"(misrepresentation),所以,承租人可以根据这一理由终止TCT。笔者对这点无法接受,因为船东是在电文明确说明了这是姐妹船的船舱照片,一般思维的承租人都应该知道这不能作准。但笔者和另一位承租人指定的仲裁员意见不同,也没有办法说服对方,于是共同委任了一位英国大律师作为公断人。两位当事人委任的仲裁员各自向该英国大律师详尽解释了自己对误述与否的看法,该英国大律师是最终同意了笔者在误述这方面的看法,认为不构成误述。

但笔者对后来裁决的结果感到十分意外的是,该英国大律师还是判船东败诉,无法成功索赔损失。因为其裁决判船东上述节录的电邮构成了对TCT的确认,所以在租约继续存在的情况下,船东私下离开印尼装港将船舶开往马来西亚装货去日本的行为属于违约/毁约,从原本的无辜方变为违约方。裁决书的相关部分可节录如下:"The e-mail from(船东)could not be in clearer terms. Owners wererejecting the re-delivery of the Vessel and had gone so far as to 'declare' thatthe Vessel 'is still under yr TC, and hold you fully execute the CP withoutfail!' In my view, this is an affirmation of the C/P and a clear rejection of Charterers' repudiatory breach."

笔者对英国大律师针对合约确认的裁决感到意外是笔者与另一位承租人指定的仲裁员都不觉得这是大问题,所以没有太多这方面的争议。如果这是一个三位仲裁员组成的仲裁庭并且知道他（会变为首席仲裁员）是这样的看法，笔者肯定会向该英国大律师指出根据 Moore - Bick 大法官在 Yukong Line Ltd. of Korea v. Rendsburg Investment Corporation 先例的说法（包括笔者做出的分析）与下一小段会介绍的“第三种选择”的说法，不能僵化地根据 Browne - Wilkinson 大法官的传统说法判断是否构成确认。毕竟整体来看，完全可以将船东的电邮解释为一个简单的抗议，要求对方重新考虑，也是无辜方的正常反应。但过了十几天，外国船公司作为承租人一直保持沉默没有任何会继续履行租约的迹象，[128] 或对船东的电邮有所依赖，导致船东在找到替代租约后离开印尼装港。整体解释船东的言行，是不能解释为受害的船东在知道自己的权利后选择确认合约，并在之后违约/毁约将船开走，变为违约方，要自己承受庞大的损失。

虽然认定无辜方是否有确认合约继续存在是事实问题，而且同样的证据下不同的仲裁员会得出不同的结论，正如 Teare 大法官在 The “Fortune Plum” (2013) 2 Lloyd’s Rep. 618 先例中拒绝干预仲裁庭在裁决书对无辜方确认合约继续存在的认定，认为是事实问题，说：“I am therefore unable to say that the correct application of the law of affirmation to the facts of this case must inevitably lead to only one answer, namely, that there had been no affirmation. It follows that it cannot be concluded that the tribunal must have misunderstood the principles it directed itself to apply and so must have erred in law. It is not for the court to substitute for the tribunal’s answer the answer it might have given had it been the tribunal of fact...”

但在上述介绍的两个仲裁案件中，笔者与共同仲裁员在同样的文件证据下得出完全不同的结论，毕竟还是很令人困扰的。

7.4.2 接受与确认之外的第三种选择

一直以来是说无辜方只有两个选择，或者接受并终止合约，或者确认合约继续存在与有效，正如 Ackner 勋爵在 The “Simona” (1988) 2 Lloyd’s Rep. 199 先例所说：“When A wrongfully repudiates his contractual obligations in anticipation of the time for their performance, he presents the innocent party B with two choices. He may either affirm the contract by treating it as still in force or he may treat is as finally had conclusively discharged. There is no third choice...”

但上诉庭的 Rix 大法官在 Stocznia v. Latco (2002) 2 Lloyd’s Rep. 436 先例提出有第三种选择的说法，也就是在违约方违约/毁约后，无辜方有一段缓冲期决定是否接受违约/毁约。在这段期间，无辜方继续履行合约（在该先例就是做出安放龙骨的通知），但并不影响接受违约方违约/毁约的权利。Rix 大法官说：“It is clear therefore that during the period when the yard was serving its notices up to the time of purporting

---

〔128〕 这可见 Teare 大法官在本章之 7.4.3 段介绍的 The “Fortune Plum” (2013) 2 Lloyd’s Rep. 618 先例提到的，在决定违约方是否持续违约/毁约时的一个测试。

to exercise its contractual rights of rescission the respective contracts remained alive. The question is whether the keel laying notices were an unequivocal affirmation of them. If they had been served under cover of a letter which had expressly warned Latreefers that it was being given a last chance to perform, and that failing due payment the yard would exercise its rights of rescission, I do not think that the use of a contractual mechanism for terminating the contracts is inconsistent with reliance on repudiatory conduct for effecting a common law acceptance of an anticipatory breach. Where contractual and common law rights overlap, it would be too harsh a doctrine to regard the use of a contractual mechanism of termination as unequivocally ousting the common law mechanism, at any rate against the background of an express reservation of rights."

在《Chitty on Contracts》(第32版,2015年)之24-002段对这第三种选择总结如下:

"**A middle ground.** An innocent party, faced by a repudiatory breach, is therefore given a choice: he can either treat the contract as continuing ('affirmation' of the contract) or he can bring it to an end ('acceptance of repudiation'). He must 'elect' or choose between these options. Further, it is sometimes said that there is no other option open to the innocent party; that is to say, there is no 'middle way' or 'third choice'. This is true in the sense that there is no '... third choice, as a sort of via media, to affirm the contract and yet be absolved from tendering further performance unless and until [the breaching party] gives reasonable notice that he is once again able and willing to perform.'

But the proposition that there is no middle way can be over-stated. There is a sense in which there is a middle way open to the innocent party in that he is given a period of time in which to make up his mind whether he is going to affirm the contract or terminate. ...

The length of the period given to the innocent party in order to make up his mind will very much depend upon the facts of the case. The period may not be a long one because a party who does nothing for too long may be held to have affirmed the contrat. The length of time will also depend upon the time at which the innocent party's obligations fall due for performance. A contract remains in force until it has been terminated for breach so that a contracting party who has not elected to terminate the contract remains bound to perform his obligations unless the effect of the other party's breach is to prevent performance of the innocent party's obligation becoming due."

看来这第三种选择也谈不上是选择,反正无辜方迟早要选择是接受并终止合约或是确认合约继续存在。事实上,只要法院与/或仲裁庭不轻易将无辜方的言行解释为确认合约,并且在解释接受是否及时与清楚无误时在恰当的案件尽量宽松(但要小心不让无辜方在市场上取巧),也无须有这第三种选择。

7.4.3 持续违约/毁约的情况

就算无辜方没有接受违约方最早的违约/毁约,确认合约继续存在,在某些案件他还是有机会扭转这一确认,改为选择接受并终止合约。这在违约方持续违约/毁约(continuous repudiation)的情况经常会发生。举一个简单的例子,在订立买卖合约不久后市场突然暴跌,买方对卖方说除非你减价,我将不会开信用证。卖方之后做了很多事情希望能挽救这个合约,即使不宽松解释这些言行,并认为是属于确认合约,但只要后来买方重复一次要卖方减价(如说少减一点,因为市场在回升)才愿意开信用证,这就属于一个新的违约/毁约,可以被卖方接受并终止合约。即使违约的买方不重复一次,只是保持沉默与不行动,这从全局来看也可以推断是持续拒绝履行。已经在本章之3.8段提到,一审的Thomas大法官在Stocznia v. Latco(2001)1 Lloyd's Rep. 537先例就是这样的判法。

持续违约/毁约最常见是发生在预期违约,但如果涉及真正的违约,例如在本章稍早的7.2段与7.4.1段提到的新加坡仲裁,货物已经过了买卖合约的付运期还未装船,就不存在持续违约/毁约的情况。

有关这一持续违约/毁约,无辜方即使确认了较早的违约/毁约,也可以改变主意接受新的违约/毁约的说法,在很多先例都有提到。比较近期的有Yukong Line Ltd. of Korea v. Rendsburg Investment Corporation(1996)2 Lloyd's Rep. 604; Safehaven Investments Inc. v. Springbok Ltd.(1996)71 P & CR 59; Stocznia v. Latco(2002)2 Lloyd's Rep. 436(CA); The "Fortune Plum"(2013)2 Lloyd's Rep. 618等先例。

简单节录Moore – Bick大法官在Yukong Line Ltd. of Korea v. Rendsburg Investment Corporation先例中说:"Although the injured party is bound by his election once it has been made, the fact that he has affirmed the contract does not of course preclude him from treating it as discharged on a subsequent occasion if the other party again repudiates it."

在Safehaven Investments Inc. v. Springbok Ltd.先例,Sumption大法官说:"It does not follow from this analysis that the innocent party may in all cases change his mind after affirming the contract. If, after he had affirmed it, the repudiating party's conduct suggested that he proposed to perform after all, then the previous party's repudiation is spent. It has no further legal significance. If on the other hand, the repudiating party persists in his refusal to perform, the innocent party may later treat the contract as being at an end. The correct analysis in this case is not that the innocent party is terminating on account of the original repudiation and going back on his election to affirm. It is that he is treating the contract as being at an end on account of the continuing repudiation reflected in the other party's behaviour after the affirmation. . . . Once the innocent party has affirmed, he must go on performing. He must then be able to point to behaviour that amounts to a repudiation after the affirmation either by way of some fresh conduct amounting to repudiation or by way of the continuing refusal to perform amounting to repudiation. I cannot see any reason why the innocent party must wait until there is an actual repudiatory breach. . . ”

在 Stocznia v. Latco 先例，Rix 大法官针对预期违约与真正违约的不同说：“It seems to me that an affirmation of a repudiatory actual breach may differ from an affirmation of a merely anticipatory repudiatory breach in that the former breach is complete at the time it occurs whereas the latter breach looks to the future. An affirmation of an actual breach may therefore be said to leave nothing outstanding for the future, in that the worst has already occurred, whereas an affirmation of an anticipatory breach still leaves the future open. Prima facie an election or waiver looks to the past, even if it is possible, in a very clear case, to waive one's rights for the future too. . . . It also occurs to me that even in the case of an actual repudiatory breach, where the breach is of a continuing nature, such as a failure to pay or to deliver, an affirmation at one stage is not necessarily an irrevocable affirmation for all time in the future. If it were otherwise, the law could not have developed the doctrine of Rickards v. Oppenhaim. ”

最后在 The “Fortune Plum” 先例，无辜方的船东在承租人的违约/毁约（延误与没有支付租金）后，延误作出撤船的决定，而希望先把货物卸下。承租人抗辩说船东这是确认（affirm）了租约的存在，之后就不能再接受并撤船。仲裁庭支持了承租人的抗辩，但 Teare 大法官推翻了仲裁庭的裁决，并告诫仲裁庭说在认定无辜方确认了租约后，仍要看违约方之后的言行有否改变立场，如果没有，就可以当做一个持续性的违约/毁约，并可以被无辜方接受：“Where, following a renunciation or anticipatory breach of contract, the innocent party affirmed the contract but the renunciation continued, the innocent party might thereafter accept the continuing renunciation as terminating the contract. The tribunal of fact had to carefully consider whether there were words or conduct after affirmation which demonstrated that the renunciation of the contract was continuing, so that a later acceptance of the continuing renunciation would be a legitimate termination. ”

7.5　双方相继违约/毁约

在《Chitty on Contracts》（第 32 版，2015 年）一书之 24 – 015 段，说：“Where both parties are alleged to have committed a breach of contract, and it is asserted that each breach (taken independently) gives rise to a right to terminate further performance of the contract, regard must be had to the order in which the breaches occurred.[129] Where one

---

〔129〕 如果双方相继违约/违约，则都会给对方机会终止合约（假设这两个违约/毁约相互独立），要考虑这两个违约/毁约发生的顺序。

party (A) breaches the contract and that breach is followed by a breach by the other party (B) then, assuming both breaches are repudiatory, the breach by Party A will give party B the right to terminate future performance of the contract.[130] If B exercises that right and accepts the repudiation his subsequent failure to perform his obligations under the contract will not constitute a breach of contract.[131] The position is rather more complex if B does not accept the breach and then himself commits a repudiatory breach of the contract. In such a case can A accept the breach and terminate performance of the contract or does the fact that he has previously repudiated the contract prevent him from exercising his option to terminate?[132] It is suggested that, in such a case, the effect of B electing to affirm the contract is to leave the primary obligations of both parties unchanged. The contract therefore remains in existence for the benefit of A as well as for B so that A should be free to elect to terminate the contract[133]... So unless the obligation of A to perform is a condition precedent to B's obligation to perform, the fact that A is in breach of contract should not act as a barrier to A's ability to terminate on the ground of B's breach."[134]

在 STC v. Golodetz (1989) 2 Lloyd's Rep. 277 先例,案情涉及食糖买卖合约,买方承诺在合约订立后 7 天内开信用证,而卖方在合约订立后 7 天内承诺提供履约担保(performance bond guarantee)以及将来会从买方(印度国有公司)回购等于食糖价值 60% 的其他商品的担保(counter-trade PBG)。合约涉及的食糖已经装上 Sara D 轮,是一票浮动货物(floating cargo),但在合约订立后没几天,Sara D 发生火灾,造成了这票食糖变为推定全损。但这损失按照英国法律是买方的损失,因为货物装船后运输期间的损失都是由买方承担,即使买卖合约是运输期间订立。[135] 买方的损失只能向保险公司要求赔付。当时卖方已经提供了履约担保,但还没有提供回购担保,而买方还没有开信用证。卖方催促买方开信用证(这等于要求买方支付货款),买方没有理会(显然因为食糖已经变为全损)。双方谈判无果,卖方以买方没有在合约规定的时间内开信用证是违约/毁约为由,终止合约。之后双方开始仲裁索赔货价,买方

---

〔130〕 如果 A 违约/毁约,然后 B 违约/毁约,A 的违约毁约令 B 有权终止合约,不需要履行将来的合约责任。

〔131〕 如果 B 接受了 A 的违约/毁约并终止合约,则他之后没有履行合约权利不属于违约/毁约。道理很简单,合约已经终止,B 当然无须在履行合约责任。

〔132〕 但如果 B 没有接受 A 的违约/毁约,并在之后自己违约/毁约,情况就会复杂得多。A 是否有权接受 B 的违约/毁约并终止合约?或是 A 之前自己的违约/毁约使其无权这么做?

〔133〕 B 选择确认合约继续存在,就表示双方原本的合约责任不变,合约对 A 与 B 来说都是继续存在,所以如果 B 违约/毁约,A 完全可以选择终止合约。

〔134〕 除非 A 没有履行的合约责任是 B 履行其合约责任的先决条件,A 之前违约/毁约的事实不影响其以 B 违约/毁约为由终止合约的权利。

〔135〕 参见杨大明的《国际货物买卖》第六章。

显然抗拒,双方的争议一路上诉到上诉庭。在上诉庭,主要有两个争议,第一个是卖方在合约订立后7天内提供回购担保是否是条件条文;第二个是如果是条件条文,买方能否以卖方的违约作为抗辩他自己没有开信用证的违约。[136] 针对第一个争议,Kerr大法官认为没有在合约订立后7天内提供回购担保不属于违反条件条文。这也就是说第二个争议不再需要判决,但因为双方花费了大量时间争辩,Kerr大法官还是做出了针对:

"The fact that in the present case both parties had committed breaches before one of them elected to treat the contract as repudiated appears to me to make no difference whatever; nor the fact that (assumedly) both had been breaches of condition. If A is entitled to treat B as having wrongfully repudiated the contract between them and does so, then it does not avail B to point to A's past reaches of contract, whatever their nature. A breach by A would only assist B if it was still continuing when A purported to treat B as having repudiated the contract and if the effect of A's subsisting breach was such as to preclude A from claiming that B had committed a repudiatory breach. In other words, Bwould have to show that A, being in breach of an obligation in the nature of a condition precedent, was therefore not entitled to rely on B's breach as a repudiation.

Thus, take the present case. If the sellers' obligation to open the counter – trade PBG had been a condition precedent to STC's(买方)obligation to open the letter of credit, then the sellers would obviously not have been entitled to treat STC's failure to open the letter of credit as a wrongful repudiation so long as they themselves had not opened the counter – trade PBG. But this is not the position here. Neither obligation was dependent upon the other and both had to be performed concurrently, within seven days of the conclusion of the contract. Since both obligations are (assumedly) in the nature of conditions, both parties had an equal right, so long as the other party's obligation remained unperformed, to treat the other party as having wrongfully repudiated."

上述第二段Kerr大法官是解释如果卖方提供回购担保是买方开出信用证的先决条件,如开出信用证是卖方需要提供货物与在付运期做出付运的先决条件一样,则卖方不能指责买方没有在7天内开出信用证是违反条件条文,因为卖方自己违反了先决条件。但在本案件不是这个情况,回购担保与开出信用证是独立的合约责任,并不互相依赖。所以,如果两个合约责任都是条件条文,违反双方有了同等的权利去终止合约,就要看是谁先接受了对方的违约。但在本先例中,Kerr大法官已经判提供回购担保并非是条件条文,所以说是第二个争议,其实不需要去针对。

---

[136] 这明确是条件条文,也是卖方需要提供货物与做出付运的先决条件:Dexters Ltd. v. Schenker & Co. (1923) 14 Lloyd's Rep. 586 等先例。

8. 选择接受是否是无辜方毫无节制的权利

选择接受与否是无辜方的权利,这是毫无疑问。针对一般的合约关系,都会是涉及双方都需要履行合约责任,所以如果违约方通过言行向无辜方说明他不会履行将来的合约责任,这就是一个典型的预期违约。而如果无辜方不接受,这个将来的合约责任迟早会变成到期需要履行的合约责任,如果违约方依然不履行,这就变了真正违约。如果这个不履行针对的是合约的重要责任或者是剩余的所有合约责任,没有违约方的合作,无辜方也往往履行不下去,这样不存在无辜方选择接受与否的问题,合约非要终止不可。举一个简单的例子,如果卖方在付运期前坚持合约不存在或说因为货价暴涨将不会提供货物,这就存在买方是否接受这个预期违约去终止合约的问题。但如果已经过了合约的付运期,卖方还是有同样的坚持或是在一个 FOB 买卖合约下,不提供货物给 FOB 买方的船舶装船,这样就不存在无辜方的买方是否接受的问题,纯粹是卖方不履行的真正违约,合约非要终止不可。

但这一无辜方没有制约的权利(unfettered right)也带来了很大的矛盾,可先谈如下方面。

8.1 无辜方的考虑

无辜方选择接受与否要考虑的因素有很多,如市场上是否有更好的替代的生意。如果没有,无辜方倒不如盯着违约方去履行,毕竟一选择接受,无辜方是要马上减少损失,而如果不能减少,又何必接受。在货物买卖中,就经常有买方盯着违约方的卖方交货,即使卖方不断地拒绝履行,因为市场紧张,不容易找到替代货物。买方甚至会考虑向法院申请“履约指令”(specific performance),但这不容易成功。买方的坚持会持续到合约交货的最后一天,但卖方仍然拒绝交货,买方才不得不放弃希望。

就算有替代的生意,如果不是更好/更赚钱,也表示无辜方在所难免会有损失,将来需要向违约方索赔。但索赔损失毕竟是困难、昂贵与费时的,往往需要通过诉讼才能从违约方逼出这笔钱。而如果不接受违约/毁约,合约继续存在,会有情况可让违约方在合约下应该支付的钱变为债务,即使无辜方还是需要通过诉讼才能逼出这笔债务,但会比索赔损失容易得多。[137] 如不存在太多的争议,[138] 以及往往可以通过法院的简易判决(summary judgment)[139] 或仲裁的中间裁决(interim/partial award)[140]

---

〔137〕 关于损失与债务的区别,可见杨良宜的《损失赔偿与救济》一书第十一章。

〔138〕 有关损失计算的众多与复杂的争议,可见杨良宜的《损失赔偿与救济》一书。相比之下,合约被履行而带来的债务,就根本没有什么可争议的。例如,损失计算下无辜方必须合理减少损失就十分有争议与不肯定,但合约的履行以及产生的债务根本不涉及减少损失,一切照合约的规定。

〔139〕 如 Stocznia v. Latco (1998) 1 Lloyd's Rep. 609 (HL)等先例。

〔140〕 如 The "Kostas Melas" (1981) 1 Lloyd's Rep. 18 等先例。

逼违约方做出支付。

这方面还会涉及更复杂的考虑，即违约方将来是否有财力做出赔偿，或有关的合约是否有第三人的担保、担保的范围等。以程租合约为例，假设在已经订了租约但船舶仍未开往装港时，承租人说我没有货给你装。这样，如果承租人是皮包公司，船东就会有顾虑，如果确认合约继续存在，无辜方的船东就非要跑这个去装港的航次不可。而如果到了装港，承租人还是没有货装，这个去装港的航次的时间与费用就浪费了。虽然理论上将来可以向承租人索赔，但承租人是皮包公司很可能赔不起。因此，即使市场上没有更好的替代，船东也会选择接受并终止租约，至少可以省下这白跑一次装港的时间与费用，不扩大损失。但如果承租人在租约下有提供母公司甚至银行的担保，考虑就会有不同。船东在市场没有更好的替代生意/租约的情况下，乐意跑这个去装港的航次，反正财力雄厚的母公司和银行担保赔偿有关的损失。然而，有了担保也不代表万事大吉，还必须小心担保的范围。如果担保的只是支付运费，承租人没有货装就不能让船东赚取运费，这表示第三人的担保就起不了作用。而如果担保的是租约的履行（performance guarantee），情况又会不同。如果不是程租而是期租，也同样有这种复杂的考虑。例如，承租人支付租金的责任有第三人或银行担保，这样，除非市场可让船东赚取更高的租金，否则没有诱因去撤船与接受承租人的违约/毁约，反正只要租约持续，每过15日就会有租金欠下，可根据担保要求第三人或银行支付这笔债务。

其他复杂的考虑还有很多，不能一一列举，只多提一种是无辜方要考虑如果不接受并确认合约继续存在，自己能否履行合约。已经在本章之7.2段提到，如果无辜方确认合约继续存在，之后自己又违约/毁约，就可以让对方合法脱身甚至索赔损失。这种风险还包括合约会遇上受阻而自动终止，虽然合约受阻的风险远远比不上无辜方自己可能违约/毁约。在The "Mihalis Angelos" (1970) 2 Lloyd's Rep. 43先例，精明的船东明知自己赶不上销约期，于是在承租人先一步表示没有货装之后，马上接受并终止租约。这样至少在责任方面，船东自己将来也无法履行的事实就一笔勾销。反面例子是笔者经历过2008年"金融海啸"后航运市场大跌的年代，有中国船厂在明知船舶建造已经延误，有极大危险无法在"死亡日期"前完成工程的情况下，有机会是外国船东因为经济或融资银行的问题延误支付分期船价（这在造船合约经常被明示规定为条件条文），船厂就应该抓住机会脱身。这样船厂不仅可以没收部分船价，还可以向船东索赔利润损失（虽然船东经常是皮包公司，但船厂会有船东母公司或银行的履约担保）。而即使船厂是希望保住这个造船合约（也处于保得住工人的就业等考虑），也可以在终止合约后与外国船东无损害谈判，使合约再变为有效（re-instate），但把"死亡日期"押后至一个较宽松与安全的日期。有可能同时需要对船价做出一些让步，但这个让步有限，因为船厂是处于有利与强势的谈判地位。但笔者发现中国船厂由于不了解法律地位，选择了一味让步，往往对这种先一步接受船东违约/毁约的好机会弃权。而合约继续履行下去，事后因为过了"死亡日期"被船东弃船,并要退还全部预付船价与利息。

8.2 违约方的考虑

经常会有情况是违约方做出拒绝性违约的言行是逼不得已,因为他实际上没办法履行,而需要尽快终止合约并愿意向无辜方做出金钱上的赔偿,只希望无辜方尽快减少损失。例如,与房东订立一个两年的租约,但租客住满一年后因家事或工作上的变动而不得不退租。毕竟虽然是违约/毁约,但是如果被房东接受,那么只需要赔偿真正损失,也就是市场租金与该租约租金的差价。在市场高涨的今天,房东很可能根本没有损失或即使有也很有限,总好过让房子空着而白交一年租金。或是为了申请批文需要与检验机构订立合约做某种检验,但在开始进行检验前发现申请该批文根本不需要这份检验报告。这时违约/毁约并被检验机构接受,要赔偿的也不过是检验机构的利润,这总好过白交检验费以拿到一份没用的检验报告。这就带来"有效益违约"(efficient breach)的说法,也被英国法律所鼓励,因为不仅在经济上对两方都有利,而且可以减少社会资源的浪费。所以,英国法院对这种有效益违约的情况,金钱赔偿损失已经是足够的救济,不会做出"履约指令"(specific performance)。[141]

有关有效益违约的说法在 Co-operative Insurance Society Ltd. v. Argyll Stores (Holdings) Ltd. (1996) Ch. 286 先例也有提到,上诉庭的 Millet 大法官说:"... Modern economic theory supports ... an award of damages reflects normal commercial expectations and ensures a more efficient allocation of scarce economic resources. The defendant will break his contract only if it pays him to do so after taking the payment of damages into account; the plaintiff will be fully compensated in damages; and both parties will be free to allocate their resources elsewhere."

贵族院([1998] AC 1)的 Hoffmann 勋爵也说:"From a wider perspective, it cannot be in the public interest for the courts to require someone to carry on business at a loss if there is any plausible alternative by which the other party can be given compensation. It is not only a waste of resources but yokes the parties together in a continuing hostile relationship."

但上述违约方的考虑可以看出与无辜方有毫无节制的权利(unfettered right)选择是否接受有严重的矛盾。如果房东与检验机构不接受而选择确认合约并继续履行,那违约方就惨了,并会面对可能数额庞大的损失,对社会而言,也显然会造成不必要的资源浪费。所以,有看法是无辜方不应该有毫无节制的选择权去确认合约。如在 White and Carter (Councils) Ltd. v. McGregor (1962) AC 413 先例,Keith 勋爵说:"If it is right it would seem that a man who has contracted to go to Hongkong at his own expense and make a report, in return for remuneration of £ 10,000, and who, before the date fixed for the start of the journey and perhaps before he has incurred any ex-

---

[141] 有关有效益违约可见杨良宜的《损失赔偿与救济》第五章之10.4段与第十二章之4.1段。

pense, is informed by the other contracting party that he has cancelled or repudiates the contract, is entitled to set off for Hongkong and produce his report in order to claim in debt the stipulated sum. Such a result is not, in my opinion, in accordance with principle or authority, and cuts across the rule that where one party is in breach of contract the other must take steps to minimise the loss sustained by the breach."

8.3　法律肯定性与合理性的平衡

从上述看来,这里涉及法律肯定性(certainty)与合理性(包括整体看让无辜方任意坚持无用的履行是否合理)的平衡。可以说,这两者的平衡很难掌握。如果要法律的肯定,显然是坚持无辜方有毫无节制的选择权去确认合约继续存在与有效。但有时违约方(不论是预期违约还是违约/毁约)是逼不得已,客观来看,无辜方坚持合约的履行很不合理。甚至有一个极端情况是,即使违约方向无辜方提议马上有替代生意接上,并同意支付替代与原合约之间的差价去赔偿无辜方的损失,但无辜方仍然对违约方说"我就是不合理,偏要你好看",坚决不肯接受违约/毁约。这肯定是不能接受,否则就会造成虽然因为金钱赔偿已经完成足够的救济,无辜方无法在法院申请到履约指令(specific performance),但通过确认合约可以达到同样效果的情况。无辜方白纸黑字讲这种赌气的话在现实中也比较少见,毕竟无辜方就算在心里这样想,也不会表现出来。因此,把分界线划在这里意义不大。而如果把分界线划在无辜方不接受是否合理,也会带来法律不肯定的问题,因为每一个案件双方对合理与否都有争。而这里涉及无辜方需要很快决定接受并终止合约或确认合约,如果法律不肯定,对无辜方甚至双方不是好事。正如Reid勋爵在White and Carter (Councils) Ltd. v. McGregor (1962) AC 413先例说:"It might be, but it never has been, the law that a person is only entitled to enforce his contractual rights in a reasonable way, and that a court will not support an attempt to enforce them in an unreasonable way. One reason why that is not the law is, no doubt, because it was thought that it would create too much uncertainty to require the court to decide whether it is reasonable or equitable to allow a party to enforce his full rights under a contract."

事实上,无论分界线划在哪里都会造成合约的不肯定。正如Lloyd大法官在The "Alaskan Trader" (No. 2) (1983) 2 Lloyd's Rep. 645先例,说:"On the point of uncertainty, it is of course true that the existence of a fetter on the right to claim hire, even if it only be exercised in extreme cases, necessarily introduces an element of uncertainty. Thus it can be said with force that bankers[142] need to know where they are when accepting an assignment of charter hire as security for their loan. On the other hand, absolute certainty can never be attained. Mr. Cooke(承租人代表大律师) gave as an example the

---

〔142〕 该先例涉及租金被转让给了银行,如果船东非要接受承租人的违约/毁约并只能索赔损失,银行就无法获得租金的支付,令船东向银行转让的担保失去了价值。

doctrine of frustration which may import a degree of uncertainty into commercial contracts of all kinds ... ”

可以说长久以来,合约法的肯定性与合理性(包括经济上有效益)这两个政策上的考虑存在正面冲突。传统上英国合约法更强调与重视肯定性,如上诉庭的 Goff 大法官在 The “Scaptrade” (1983) 1 Lloyd’s Rep. 146 先例中说:“It is of the utmost importance in commercial transactions that, if any particular event occurs which may affect the parties’ respective rights under a commercial contract, they should know where they stand. The Court should so far as possible desist from placing obstacles in the way of either party ascertaining his legal position, if necessary with the aid of advice from a qualified lawyer; because it may be commercially undesirable for action to be taken without delay, action which may be irrecoverable and which may have far - reaching consequences. It is for this reason, of course, that the English Courts have time and again asserted the need for certainty in commercial transactions – for the simple reason that the parties to such transactions are entitled to know where they stand, and to act accordingly... The policy which favours certainty in commercial transactions is so antipathetic to the form of equitable intervention ... ”

在 White and Carter (Councils) Ltd. v. McGregor 这一重要与富有争议的先例,贵族院的多数意见(即判决中说明原因的 Reid 勋爵与 Hobson 勋爵)也强调了其决定主要是因为肯定性。Reid 勋爵加了一个例外情况,即除非违约方没有“合法利益”(legitimate interest)。这样,有了这个分界线等于也带来了不肯定以及很多后来的先例,这方面后文详述。

但无辜方是否有毫无节制的选择权去确认合约的问题之前一直不是很尖锐,因为大部分合约都需要双方合作才能让无辜方履行下去并赚取合约的约因/对价,如稍早提到的雇佣合约:Masood v. Zahoor (2008) EWHC 1034 (Ch)等先例。在上述检验报告的例子也一样,如果违约方不提供样本等信息,检验机构即使确认合约存在检验,也进行不下去,也就无法赚取合约规定的报酬。另一个例子可以是定制机器,如果买方不提供具体的参数,卖方无法制造机器。即使卖方已经有参数,在机器建造完毕后,没有买方告知交货方式与地址,卖方也无法交付这台机器,也就无法赚取合约的货价。所以,往往如果一方违约/毁约,无辜方到了违约方真正需要合作才能履行时就非要接受不可。这直到 White and Carter (Councils) Ltd. v. McGregor 先例涉及一个无辜方可以单方面履行下去并赚取合约约因/对价的合约,才令这一分界线的问题变得尖锐,这重要的先例会在下一段介绍。

8.4 White and Carter (Councils) Ltd. v. McGregor 先例

在 White and Carter (Councils) Ltd. v. McGregor (1962) AC 413 这一富争议的先例,广告公司与停车场老板的代表订立合约,为该停车场做 3 年的广告。在同一天,停车场老板写信给广告公司要求终止合约,说是他的代表理解错了他的意思。这种情况错误订下了合约也不少见,在订立后很快就拒绝履行。但广告公司拒绝终止合约并在5个月后开始根据合约展示广告。合约规定:"In the event of an instalment ... being due for payment, and remaining unpaid for a period of four weeks or in the event of the advertiser being in any way in breach of this contract then the whole amount due for the 156 weeks or such part of the said 156 weeks as the advertiser shall not yet have paid shall immediately become due and payable."

停车场老板拒绝支付任何已到期的款项,广告公司开始诉讼要求支付合约下的全部金额。该先例中特殊的事实是,广告公司的履行并不需要对方的合作。最终这个枢密院先例[143]以3:2的多数意见判是广告公司可以不接受对方的违约/毁约,并成功赚取合约约因/对价,否则会带来不肯定。Hodson勋爵说:"It may be unfortunate that the appellants have saddled themselves with an unwanted contract causing an apparent waste of time and money... but there is no equity which can assist the respondent. It is trite that equity will not rewrite an improvident contract where there is no disability on either side. There is no duty laid upon a party to a subsisting contract to vary it at the behest of the other party so as to deprive himself of the benefit given to him by the contract. To hold otherwise would be to introduce a novel equitable doctrine that a party was not to be held to his contract unless the court in a given instance thought it reasonable so to do. In this case it would make an action for debt a claim for discretionary remedy. This would introduce an uncertainty into the field of contract which appears to be unsupported by authority in English law..."

White and Carter (Councils) Ltd. v. McGregor先例被人批评的主要原因之一是,它不仅没有避免还鼓励了无用的合约履行,导致社会资源的浪费与经济上没有效益。但看来,这虽然是政策上的考虑,但重要性比不上合约法的肯定性。只要合约写得清清楚楚,英国法院一般不愿意行使其衡平法权利(equitable jurisdiction)去改变合约的规定。例如,N. Strauss御用大律师作为暂委法官在Ministry of Sound (Ireland) Limited v. World Online Limited (2003) EWHC 2178 (Ch)先例举了一个例子说:"The decision in White and Carter has been criticized, mainly on the ground that the performance of unwanted contractual services is wasteful... However, such a situation is hardly uncommon. For example, if a company leases expensive equipment, with no right to sub-lease, and then has no further use for it, there is no way in which it can force the owner, before the end of the period of the lease, to accept the return of the equipment and minimize its loss by leasing it to another available customer whom it has found, however estimable. It would remain liable for the rent for the full period..."

---

〔143〕 这虽然是苏格兰上诉到枢密院的先例,涉及苏格兰的法律,但这一所谓的"White & Carter Principle"在很多后来的英国先例被依从,所以也可视为英国的法律。

但 Reid 勋爵提到了有两个相关的例外情况,可以说这就是分界线。这两种情况就是:

"It could only be supported on one or other of two grounds. It might be said that, because in most cases the circumstances are such that an innocent party is unable to complete the contract and earn the contract price without the assent or co – operation of the other party, therefore in cases where he can do so he should not be allowed to do so. I can see no justification for that.

The other ground would be that there is some general equitable principle or element of public policy which requires this limitation of the contractual rights of the innocent party. It may well be that, if it can be shown that a person has no legitimate interest, financial or otherwise, in performing the contract rather than claiming damages, he ought not to be allowed to saddle the other party with an additional burden with no benefit to himself. If a party has no interest to enforce a stipulation, he cannot in general enforce it: so it might be said that, if a party has no interest to insist on a particular remedy, he ought not to be allowed to insist on it. And, just as a party is not allowed to enforce a penalty, so he ought not to be allowed to penalise the other party by taking one course when another is equally advantageous to him."

在 Reid 勋爵的两个相关例外,第一个例外就是如果合约不是单方面可以履行而需要双方合作。第二个例外是首次提出的无辜方没有"合法利益"(legitimate interest)[144] 坚持履行这个对违约方毫无用处的合约并赚取约因/对价而不索赔金钱的损失,他就不能这样做。在这里一提的是,在近期的 Societe Generale (London Branch) v. Geys (2012) UKSC 63 先例,Sumption 勋爵在分析了该先例后,多加了一个例外(虽然最高院的其他大法官不同意),说:"The contract is incapable of specific performance, with the result that that co – operation cannot be compelled."但这一例外的确站不住脚,除了与第一个例外十分接近外,履约指令的衡平法救济也在笔者的《损失赔偿与救济》一书第十二章有详论。只简单一提,履约指令的救济是否能被给予,除了金钱的赔偿是否足够外,还有很多重要的考虑,如对相互性原则的要求、法院或仲裁庭能否监督等。这与无辜方有否无节制权利选择是否接受对方的违约/毁约的考虑是两回事。

接下来的段节会分析这两种相关例外。

8.4.1 例外之一:合约不是单方面可以履行而需要双方合作

这一例外已经在本章之 3.5.5 段有提及,即需要双方合作才能履行并赚取约因/

---

[144] 该先例是 3:2 的多数意见,合法利益的说法是 Reid 勋爵提出但没有获得其他两位大法官的认同。这带来这一个说法是 Reid 勋爵的随口说说(obiter)或是判决的部分(ratio)。但没有 Reid 勋爵的认同是不会有多数意见的判决,所以还是被后来的先例接受合法利益是该先例的部分判决。

对价的合约,没有被接受的预期违约是“没有发生过的镜花水月”的名言不完全适用。在本章稍早的第 8 段,也有类似的说法。举个简单的例子,如果有人请一位画家给他画肖像画,但是在画家作画前因为某些原因改变了主意,那么因为画家没有对方的合作没有办法完成肖像画并赚取报酬,只能接受对方的违约/毁约,索赔损失。但是如果画的不是肖像画而是某一处名胜的风景画,那么无须对方的合作,画家就可以单方面履行合约,画完后要对方根据合约支付报酬。但是这种情况下,因为画家确认合约继续存在,客户必须支付全部的报酬换取一张他根本不需要的画。这是造成了社会资源的浪费,但根据“White & Carter principle”,画家可以这样做。

即使在 White and Carter (Councils) Ltd. v. McGregor (1962) AC 413 先例,如果案情有一点改变,就马上变为需要违约方的合作才能赚取约因/对价。例如,N. Strauss QC 大法官在 Ministry of Sound (Ireland) Limited v. World Online Limited (2003) EWHC 2178 (Ch)先例举了 White and Carter (Councils) Ltd. v. McGregor 先例的两种变化:“Therefore, if the advertiser had been in a position to prevent the display of advertisements, for example, by withholding material which was to form part of the advertisements, in the absence of a decree of specific performance, which the court would not have granted, the contractor could not fulfil the contractual pre - condition to payment. This would be so whether the advertiser was seeking to terminate the contract or was merely delaying it for some reason. . . . To take another illustration, suppose in White and Carter the advertiser had been able to prevent performance on some sites, for example because they were on his land, to which he could refuse admittance, but not on other sites, there seems to be no reason why the contractor should not have displayed the advertisements where he was able to, and claimed the contractual price of 2s per week for those advertisements, and damages in respect of the others if he could prove loss.”

8.4.1.1　大多数类别的合约的履行需要双方合作

幸好大多数类别的合约是需要双方合作才能履行,没有违约方的合作(或在违约方的阻碍之下),无辜方无法履行合约并赚取约因/对价。无辜方可能不需要对方的合作就可以履行部分合约,但要赚取约因/对价,合约或相关法律往往规定了必须满足一些需要违约方合作(至少不阻碍)才能满足的先决条件。

例如,建筑合约/工程合约明显需要双方合作。如果地产商或雇主不让承建商进入他的产业,承建商就无法工作。即使根据合约无须履行完整个合约才能赚取约因/对价,而是每完成一个阶段并拿到建筑师的证明便可以获得地产商或雇主支付相应的金额,但如果承建商连工地都进不去,显然无法继续履行下去。

雇佣合约也是如此,除了履行需要双方的合作外,这种合约也涉及了雇主与雇员之间的互信关系。所以,一直以来的说法是雇佣合约其中一方违约/毁约,合约就自动终止,无须无辜方的接受,而无辜方只能索赔损失。经常发生的一种情况是雇主无理解雇雇员,这是典型的违约/毁约,但雇员只能接受这个现实去减少损失(找其他的工作),不能索赔雇佣合约剩下期限的工资。这可节录 Gunton v. Richmond - upon - Thames London Borough Council (1981) Ch 448 先例,上诉庭的 Brightman 大法官说:"An employee's remedy, if he is unlawfully dismissed by his employer, is damages. He cannot obtain an order for specific performance because it is not available to compel performance of a contract of service against an unwilling employer.... It is clear beyond argument that a wrongfully dismissed employee cannot sue for his salary or wages as such, but only for damages. It is also, in my view, equally clear that such an employee cannot assert that he still retains his employment under the contract. If a servant is dismissed and excluded from his employment, it is absurd to suppose that he still occupies the status of a servant. Quite plainly he does not. The relationship of master and servant has been broken, albeit wrongfully by one side alone. The same would apply to a contract for services, such as an agency."

这种判法的先例有很多,最早在 Archard v. Hornor (1828) 172 ER 451 先例,较近期的有 Vine v. National Dock Labour Board (1956) 2 Lloyd's Rep. 567; Francis v. Municipal Councillors of Kuala Lumpur (1962) 1 WLR 1411; Ridge v. Baldwin (1964) AC 40; Sanders v. Ernest A Neale Ltd. (1974) ICR 565 等先例。在 Sanders v. Ernest A Neale Ltd. 先例,Donaldson 大法官说雇佣合约的违约/毁约不涉及无辜方要接受:"terminates the contract without the necessity for acceptance by the injured party."

但近期也有不同看法,就是无辜方接受才能终止雇佣合约,否则就变为违约方可以决定什么时候终止合约。这除了严重违反英国合约法的主导思想,即不能让违约方因为自己的错误获利[145]外,也的确会有被违约方滥用的情况。例如,根据雇佣合约,员工在该公司工作 10 年后可以获得一笔丰厚的奖金,但雇主(违约方)在 9 年 11 个月的时候将员工无理解雇。虽然该员工事后可以索赔损失,但已经多次提到索赔损失是远远比索赔债务复杂与不确定。除了证明损失的各种困难外,如果该员工运气好找到一份更好的工作,这好处就要做出扣减。其实早在 Temple v. Prescott (1773) [在《The Oxford History of the Laws of England》(2010 年)一书 13 卷之 645 页提到]先例,Mansfield 勋爵就是这样判,只是这个先例后来没有被依从。但在比较近期的 Gunton v. Richmond - upon - Thames London Borough Council 先例,法院的多数意见也是这样的看法。更近期的是贵族院的 Societe Generale (London Branch) v. Geys (2012) UKSC 63 先例,案情在本章之 3.5.5 段有介绍。由于不同说法都有先例支持,而且先例很多,[146]在 Boyo v. Lambeth LBC (1994) ICR 727 (CA)先例,上

[145] 见杨良宜《合约的解释:规则与应用》一书第四章第 10 段。

[146] 涉及高层员工的雇佣合约被终止后争议的金额可能很大,达到上千万甚至上亿美元,所以打官司花费的律师费不是问题。

诉庭的 Staughton 大法官说:"(雇佣合约这方面的法律是)distinctly lacking in rhyme and reason."

雇佣合约的法律地位也影响一些相关提供服务的合约,如在 Denmark Productions Ltd. v. Boscobel Productions Ltd. (1969) 1 QB 699 先例,案情涉及一个流行乐队与经理人之间的合约,在本章之3.11段有介绍。这里就涉及无辜方的经理人是否可以坚持不接受违约/毁约,让合约持续下去并获得部分利润,或只能索赔合约被终止带来的预期损失。上诉庭判是这个合约与雇佣合约一样自动终止,不存在无辜方接受才能终止合约,Salmon 大法官说:"It has long been well settled that, if a man employed under a contract of personal service is wrongfully dismissed, he has no claim for remuneration due under the contract after the repudiation. His only money claim is for damages for having been prevented from earning his remuneration: Goodman v. Pocock; French v. Brookes; Fewings v. Tisdal. A managing director, for example, engaged at £ 10,000 a year, who has ten years of his service agreement to run, is dismissed without cause. He cannot sit in the sun for ten years drawing his salary on the basis that he is ready, able and willing to serve as managing director if only the company would allow him todo so. His sole money claim is for damages and he must do everything he reasonably can to mitigate them."

针对货物买卖合约,也是需要双方合作才能履行。即使无辜方(如买方)不接受违约方的违约/毁约,也只能局限于预期违约(如订立买卖合约后不久,因为市场暴升,卖方告诉买方将不会交货)。如果到了货物应该付运的一天,卖方还是不愿意履行,买方也只能接受并终止合约,不存在可以自己单方面将合约履行完毕。买方违约/毁约也一样,如果卖方根据合约向买方交货,但买方无理拒货,这属于违约/毁约。但卖方不能以债务的形式索赔这笔货价,因为一般买卖合约的明示或默示条文都要求直到卖方将货物的财产权转移给买方后,才能赚取货价。虽然是因为买方的阻碍才无法转移财产权,但反正卖方单方面不能履行。卖方只能在买方违约/毁约后接受并减少损失,也只能索赔买方无理拒货的损失(如果合约没有规定议定赔偿):澳大利亚的 Plaimar Ltd. v. Waters Trading Co. Ltd. (1945) 72 C. L. R 304 先例。

但同样也是属于货物买卖合约(虽然混杂了工程合约的因素),造船合约就会不同。在 Hyundai Heavy Industries Co. Ltd. v. Papadopoulos and Others (1980) 2 Lloyd's Rep. 1 先例,Fraser 勋爵说:"(造船合约)did not require the vendor to perform any work or incur any expense on the subjects of sale."但看来这一说法也不完全正确,因为不少造船合约的规定是大部分的船价要到了船厂交船之前才会支付。这样,如果买方的船东不合作,作为卖方的船厂根本交不了船。例如,船东如果不派船员接收船舶,交接时需要的一份名为"protocol of delivery and acceptance"的文件证明都没有人签字。但是,造船合约的预付船价(根据造船工程的进展)的赚取就不一定需要船东的合作。

在 Stocznia v. Latco (1998) 1 Lloyd's Rep. 609 (HL)先例,涉及船东向原告的波兰船厂订了6艘冷藏船的造船合约。这6份合约条文一致,对船价的支付主要分四期。第一期是在签署造船合约时支付5%,第二期是在船厂通知船东有关的船舶安放龙骨时支付20%,第三期是船舶下水时再支付25%,其余在交船时支付。但合约订立后不久,冷藏船的市场就开始下跌,这造成船东向银行融资与日常营运有困难,船东被迫与船厂谈判,但不成功。[147] 于是,船东决定不支付下一期船价,对经济困难的船厂施加压力,以利再次谈判,之后也将驻在船厂的总管撤走。而造船工作还是在进行,船厂在第一艘与第二艘船舶安放了龙骨,并通知船东要求船东支付20%的船价。显然,船东拒绝支付,船厂就根据合约针对船东不支付分期船价的明示条文终止合约。之后,船厂也很快向英国法院(合约同意英国法律)申请"简易判决"(summary judgment)并成功取得。但船厂对剩下的4艘船舶也使用同样的手段,但由于没有空的干坞,船厂采取的做法是将第一艘与第二艘已安放好龙骨的船舶上的编号(Hull No.)铲掉,换成第三艘与第四艘船舶的编号,然后请船级社来确认,证明龙骨已经安放,然后通知船东要求支付20%的船价。之后针对第五艘与第六艘也是同样的手法,向英国法院申请简易判决,要求支付这4艘船舶20%的船价。但没有成功,法院判是船厂在没有船东同意的情况下,不能随意更改船舶的编号。Lloyd勋爵说,船厂的行为是做了一场戏,使他可以在只安放两根龙骨的情况下获得6艘船舶20%的船价(an artifice to enable the plaintiffs to recover six keel - laying instalments when they had laid only two keels)。但看来如果该船厂有足够的空置干坞将6艘船舶全部分开,分别安放龙骨,并向法院申请20%船价的简易判决不会有问题,只要船厂不要太早接受船东的违约/毁约并终止造船合约。

8.4.1.2 租约

至于与国际货物买卖密切相关的租船合约,在这一课题有很多先例,显示了这个行业经常有这方面的争议。首先要理解如下不同的租约:第一种是光船租(demise/bareboat charter),第二种是程租(voyage charter),第三种是期租(time charter)。这三种租约的不同,在杨大明的《期租合同》一书有详尽介绍,不再重复。首先有关光船租,明确的是这种租约的履行需要双方合作。在 The "Puerto Buitrago" (1976) 1 Lloyd's Rep. 250 的上诉庭先例,就是针对光船租。这先例也在 The "Aquafaith" (2012) 2 Lloyd's Rep. 61 先例被上诉庭总结如下:"The position was differentin the case of a demise charter, where possession of the vessel was given to thedemise charterer so that, as soon as possession was retaken by the owner, the latter(承租人) could no longer be entitled to hire under the demise charter."

---

[147] 不成功一点不奇怪,船东要求船厂减价是狮子大开口:合约船价扣减20%,余价改为交船后分期付款而不是根据合约规定在交船时付清,另要船厂延长交船期。看来是要求船厂承担冷藏船市场下跌的恶果,船厂显然不会接受。

至于一个程租,也明显需要双方合作。如果船东违约/毁约,很多情况会是承租人根本没有船舶可以将货物做出付运。而如果承租人违约/毁约,船舶到了装港也不会有货物装船或不知道明确是哪个卸港。所以也不存在无辜方,如船东可以单方面履行整个航次去赚取运费。当然如果涉及预期违约,会有承租人告诉船东不需要来装港,因为没有货物,无辜方的船东不需要承租人的合作可以将船开往装港。但这也只是将损失扩大,本质没有改变,就是他不能单方面履行去赚取运费作为债务要求承租人支付。早在 Smith v. Wilson (1807) 8 East 437 先例,法院就判是在承租人不给装货指示的情况下,船东根本无法运载货物到达目的地卸港去赚取运费。

至于期租合约,一贯的看法也是需要双方合作才能履行,有说法是期租合约是一个服务合约(service contract),由船东向承租人提供营运的服务,与雇佣合约一样,一般法院也不会做出履约指令。期租合约一般是由船东提供船舶、船员、维修保养与供应,承租人要提供燃油、支付港口使费与做出营运命令与指令。但这一看法在一个近期的先例有了改变。在 The "Aquafaith" 先例,案情涉及中国江苏沙钢集团下的沙钢船务有限公司(Shagang Shipping Co. Ltd.)在航运好景时长期期租(长达5年)了该艘船舶,显然租约的租金偏高。但到了 2011 年 7 月 6 日,沙钢船务作为承租人决定提早还船,并通知船东在船舶完成航次并在中国卸货后,马上把船交还。但船东拒绝接受这一违约/毁约并开始了伦敦仲裁,其间船舶停在卸港等待进一步消息。伦敦仲裁的仲裁庭判是船东需要接受承租人提早还船的违约/毁约,并在终止租约后在航运市场找其他租约以减少损失,最后向承租人索赔有关的损失。看来仲裁庭认同期租的本质是需要双方合作才能履行并赚取租金。

但船东不服,上诉至法院,这一裁决被英国高院推翻。Cooke 大法官分析了所有有关的先例,从 White and Carter (Councils) Ltd. v. McGregor (1962) AC 413 先例开始与接下来的 The "Puerto Buitrago"; The "Odenfeld" (1978) 2 Lloyd's Rep. 357; The "Alaskan Trader" (No. 2) (1983) 2 Lloyd's Rep. 645; The "Dynamic" (2003) 2 Lloyd's Rep. 693; Stocznia v. Latco (1996) 2 Lloyd's Rep. 132 与 Reichman v. Beveridge (2006) EWCA Civ 1659 先例。Cooke 大法官判仲裁庭错误认为 White and Carter (Councils) Ltd. v. McGregor 先例不适用,判期租合约是与该先例的合约本质一样,可以单方面履行合约,也就是船东不需要承租人的合作去赚取租金并把租约履行完毕。他是这样说:"The question, to my mind, is very simple. Could the owners claim hire from the charterers under this time charter without the need for the charterers to do anything under the charter? The answer is yes. If the charterers failed to give any orders, the vessel would simply stay where it was, awaiting order but earning hire. Although the master is under the orders of the charterer, the master and crew are the servants of the owners and the ship is available to the charterers for any order they wish to give. Hire continues to be earned. Although the charterers are obliged under the terms of the charter to provide and pay for fuel, should the bunkers run out whilst awaiting orders, it is open to the owners to stem the vessel and to charge that to the charterers' account. In order to complete their side of the bargain, the owners do not need the charterers to do anything in order for them to earn the hire in question. The earning of hire after purported redelivery was not dependent on any performance by the charterers of their obligations."

Cooke 大法官以上的说法看来与以前的先例很不一样，如在 The "Alaskan Trader" (No. 2)先例，Lloyd 大法官认为期租合约与雇佣合约的性质类似，需要双方的合作才能履行，说："I consider that the analogy of a contract between Master and servant applies more closely to a timecharter than the analogy of a simple debt. The owner supplies the vessel and crew; the Charterer supplies fuel oil, pays disbursements and gives orders."

但 Cooke 大法官的说法是承租人不合作，不提供燃油，船东可以在燃油短缺时自己安排加油，然后向承租人要求支付。显然其他的费用，如港口费用，船东也可以这样做。但问题是这种越俎代庖的做法，显然不是租约的规定，也不是承租人的要求。在笔者看来，似乎有把期租合约说成船东不需要承租人的合作也可以提供服务并赚取租金的意思。这样，期租合约可以被解释是与 White and Carter (Councils) Ltd. v. McGregor 先例一样，笔者担心如果这样宽松解释，大多数类别的合约需要双方合作才能履行的说法可能会受到冲击，会有更多合约可以被解释为单方面就可以履行。

针对期租合约，笔者许多年来一贯的看法与提供的意见是即使承租人不按照合约的要求还船，船东也非要接受这个违约/毁约不可，并尽快减少损失与将来索赔损失(如果有的话)。承租人提早还船除了因为市场下跌想尽快脱身外，还可能有很多其他原因造成坚持不当的还船。例如，期租中最后航次的卸港距离租约规定的还船地点有距离，如卸港在波斯湾，但租约的还船地约定在中国。承租人会有很大的诱因不理会租约的规定，卸完货物就坚持还船，不愿意花钱空放去中国还船。船东接受违约/毁约后，找到下一个航次的租约去欧洲方向，就不会有损失，并且整个做法对双方都有利。而如果下一个租约是去中国方向，那么从波斯湾去中国这一段路就是损失，可以向承租人提出索赔。再如，承租人常常会遇到要将船舶在船舶营运期间的损坏(如承租人雇佣的小工造成装卸货物带来的损坏)在还船前修妥的问题。按照期租合约一般的规定，承租人必须把船舶修好后再还船。所以，承租人如果坚持不修妥就还船会构成违约/毁约。但问题是还船地点可能无法安排修理或修理费用高昂，如在美国。这样，估计船舶(假设是散货船)的营运很有可能将会去中国这种修理又便宜又好的地方，船东可以将船舶修好后向承租人索赔损失。除非船舶的损坏根本是船级社不会批准继续营运，否则承租人都会希望去还船，即使这是违约/毁约。但是在上述的情况下，会否按照 The "Aquafaith"先例的判法，船东可以坚持不接受承租人的不当还船，令租约继续存在，而船东也可以继续在僵持期间赚取租金。看来，谨慎的承租人需要考虑在租约中加多几条有针对性的明示条文，以保护自己如果需要不当还船，船东非要接受不可并减少损失。

笔者一贯的看法(现在看来有偏差)是根据权威的《Time Charters》一书，该书从第1版到第5版(2003年),针对这个问题是说:"it seems clear that once it becomes clear that there is no room for a change of mind by the charterers, the courts are likely to insist that the owners accept the re-delivery and sue for damages – assuming that damages will be an adequate remedy."但到了第6版(2008年),就没有了这句话。看来在The"Aquafaith"先例后,第7版针对这一问题会有很不一样的说法。

8.4.1.3　赚取约因/对价没有需要违约方合作才能满足的前提条件

笔者在本章之8.4.1.1段已经提到大多数类型的合约都需要双方合作才能履行,这表示无辜方不能自己通过不接受违约/毁约履行有关的合约责任。但很明显无辜方坚持不接受违约方的违约/毁约不会是为了赌气,而往往是想让合约继续存在,然后根据合约规定要求违约方到期支付部分或全部约因/对价,这就可以避免索赔损失的麻烦与风险。一种可能存在的情况是,虽然无辜方没有对方的合作无法履行合约的部分或全部责任,但合约的规定是针对部分(甚至全部)约因/对价的支付,并不需要违约方的合作。以本章之8.4.1.1段提到的Stocznia v. Latco (1998) 1 Lloyd's Rep. 609 (HL)先例为例,如果分期船价的支付并不是取决于造船进程,而是规定在某一个时间就需要支付(当然一般合约不会这样规定,因为到了具体的时间,造船进度如何很难控制),那么时间一到,对无辜方的船厂而言,这分期船价就赚取并自动变为债务。船厂唯一不要做的就是在这个时间之前接受船东的违约/毁约并终止造船合约。

在Ministry of Sound (Ireland) Limited v. World Online Limited (2003) EWHC 2178 (Ch)先例,原告是非常有名的俱乐部品牌,被告是一家网络服务商。原告同意利用"Ministry of Sound"的品牌推广被告的网络服务。这包装与销售由被告提供的访问盘(Access CDs),并且在自己的网站上维护与宣传在购买了访问盘后可以使用的由被告提供的网络服务。而被告向原告支付200万美金与每期20万美金的8期分期付款。合约期为2年,于2002年2月结束。但从2000年8月开始,被告就不再提供访问盘,原告也因此不再包装与销售访问盘。在2001年9月,被告拒绝支付最后一期分期付款。原告仍然在自己的网站上维护与推广被告的网络服务(不接受被告的违约/毁约),并向法院申请最后一期分期付款的简易判决。被告声称原告无权获得最后一期分期付款,因为从2000年8月开始,原告就不再包装与销售访问盘,这方面的工作显然是没有被告的合作无法履行。N. Strauss QC大法官判是被告需要支付这笔分期付款,主要的理由是根据合约规定,最后一期分期付款应在2001年10月3日支付,而并非取决于之前的合约责任的履行(主要是包装与销售了多少张访问盘)。所以,即使被告的阻碍导致原告无法履行这部分的合约责任,不影响到了2001年10月3日,被告就必须支付最后一期分期付款。而如果被告认为原告从2000年8月开始就不再包装与销售访问盘属于违约,可以提出反索赔损失(如果有)。

货物买卖一般需要双方合作才能履行并赚取约因/对价,但这也不一定。有部分的长期供应与买卖合约规定在某一天(或一个期限内)要支付分期货价,而不是取决于卖方的某一次或某几次交货。在这种合约规定下,如果买方到期拒绝支付,即使期间没有没有任何交货,卖方仍可以向法院通过简易判决要求买方支付货价。而买方如果对没有交货有争议,也是反索赔损失的问题,不能混为一谈。这情况看来也不少见,所以 1979 年《货物销售法》之 Section 49(2)规定说:"49 Action for price.... (2) Where, under a contract of sale, the price is payable on a day certain irrespective of delivery and the buyer wrongfully neglects or refuses to pay such price, the seller may maintain an action for the price, although the property in the goods has not passed and the goods have not been appropriated to the contract."

8.4.1.4 合约不是单方面可以履行的例外

法律难免有例外情况,在 Decro – Wall International SA v. Practitioners in Marketing Ltd. (1971) 1 WLR 361 先例,简单的案情在本章之 3.5.3 段已经有介绍。法国生产商拒绝履行合约后,英国独家经销商不接受对方的违约/毁约并确认合约继续存在,也同时向英国法院申请禁令禁止法国生产商寻找其他英国经销商。为了撤销禁令,法国生产商向法院做出担保在合约合法终止前不另委任其他人作为在英国的经销商。之后双方开始诉讼,法国生产商声称英国独家经销商不准时支付货价是违约/毁约,法国生产商是合法终止合约。而英国独家经销商则声称法国生产商错误终止合约,并且不接受这个违约/毁约。法国生产商在这一点上败诉,这就变成法国生产商自己违约/毁约。这带来另一个争议就是英国独家经销商是否有权不接受违约/毁约并确认合约继续存在。法国生产商的立场是英国独家经销商要履行合约并赚取约因/对价(即从法国生产商购买货物然后转售给英国的消费者之间的差价),显然是要双方合作,如果他不供应货物给英国独家经销商,英国独家经销商没有办法自己履行下去。但是法院认为,当时英国市场业务很好,法国生产商不可能不向英国独家经销商供货,放弃英国的市场。并且法国生产商已经在法院做出担保,如果找其他经销商,就会构成"藐视法院"(contempt of court),这是刑事犯罪。所以,不怕违约方不合作让无辜方不能履行去赚取约因/对价。上诉庭的 Salmon 大法官说:"They(法国生产商)could now, of course, cut off supplies before July 1971(合约到期时间). The undertaking(向法院做出的保证) however ensures that they could obtain no advantage from adopting such a course. Indeed if they did so they would probably lose the benefit of the market built up for them by the defendants(英国独家经销商)in the United Kingdom and increase the damages which are to be assessed by the official referee. For these reasons I would leave the findings of the judge undisturbed and dismiss the appeal."

8.4.2 例外之二:无辜方没有合法利益去确认合约

Reid 勋爵在 White and Carter (Councils) Ltd. v. McGregor(1962) AC 413 先例中提出"合法利益"(legitimate interest)的另一个例外情况。换言之,即使合约可以让无辜方单方面履行部分或全部合约责任去赚取约因/对价,但如果符合第二个例外,无辜方还是不能确认合约继续存在。但 Reid 勋爵在 White and Carter(Councils)

Ltd. v. McGregor 先例没有对什么是合法利益做出定义或解释。在该先例,原告的代表大律师举例如果一家公司委任了专家出具报告,但该专家在什么工作还没开始时反悔并告知专家不再需要报告了,该专家能否不接受违约/毁约,确认合约继续存在,把一份可能昂贵但完全无用的报告完成? Reid 勋爵只针对这个例子给了一个有关合法利益的模糊答案,说是该专家可能不可以这样做,特别是坚持履行合约对无辜方的利益是极微小(de minimis)或欠缺:"If I may revert to the example which I gave of a company engaging an expert to prepare an elaborate report and then repudiating before anything was done, it might be that the company could show that the expert had no substantial or legitimate interest in carrying out the work rather than accepting damages: I would think that the de minimis principle would apply in determining whether his interest was substantial, and that he might have a legitimate interest other than an immediate financial interest. But if the expert had no such interest then that might be regarded as a proper case for the exercise of the general equitable jurisdiction of the court."

但分界线在哪里仍是不清楚,需要看在该先例后的其他先例,特别是不少有关租约的先例。在 The "Puerto Buitrago" (1976) 1 Lloyd's Rep. 250 的上诉庭先例,案情有关光船租,并需要双方合作才能履行租约责任并赚取租金。由于第一个例外的测试也过不了,所以没有必要针对合法利益这一方面的问题。但 Denning 勋爵有提到说:"... in a case where the plaintiff ought, in all reason, to accept the repudiationand sue for damages provided that damages would provide an adequate remedy forany loss suffered by him."

这个说法看来对合法利益的要求很宽松,就是只要金钱的赔偿是足够的救济,无辜方就要接受违约/毁约。看来这是法院另一种衡平法救济(equitable remedy),即履约指令,其中一个主要的要求是类似,就是如果金钱赔偿的救济已经足够,法院通常不会做出履约指令。但在这么宽松的说法下恐怕无辜方可以自由选择接受违约/毁约或确认合约存在的权利事实上是很局限,没有太大价值。

接下来在 The "Odenfeld" (1978) 2 Lloyd's Rep. 357 先例,Kerr 大法官说:"... any fetter on the innocent party's right of election whether or not to accept a repudiation will only be applied in extreme cases, viz. where damage would be an adequate remedy and where an election to keep the contract alive would be wholly unreasonable."

在该先例,Kerr 大法官虽然认为应该对无辜方选择是否接受的权利有所限制,但认为除了金钱赔偿的救济已经足够外,还需要无辜方坚持不接受违约/毁约完全不合理。在该先例中,Kerr 大法官认为金钱赔偿的救济不足够,因为在违约/毁约时该租约还剩下六年半的租期,这么长的租期的预期损失(expectation loss)计算是很复杂且困难。

在 The "Alaskan Trader" (No. 2) (1983) 2 Lloyd's Rep. 645 先例中,船舶在一个两年的期租中营运了10个月后,主机严重损坏,需要好几个月的时间修理。这导致承租人对船东说"我再也不要这艘船了"。但船东没有接受并进行了昂贵的修理，船舶在大约5个半月后修妥并要求承租人接船。承租人拒绝履行并把租约视为已经终止，这导致船舶在Piraeus港等待承租人的命令长达8个月之久，直到租约期满。期间，承租人在抗议下继续支付船东租金。而到了租约期满还船后不久就开始仲裁，承租人要求船东退还这8个月的租金。承租人指船东是没有合法利益坚持租约的履行，而应该接受承租人的违约/毁约。在该先例中，判是船东的确没有合法利益而应该接受承租人的违约/毁约。这接受是指修船完毕后承租人还是坚决不接受该船舶，而在修理前承租人说不要这艘船的违约/毁约，判是船东不必接受。这个判法看来是受到Kerr大法官在The"Odenfield"先例所说的随着时间逝去，双方的法律地位会有改变的说法的影响。这改变就是无辜方的船东在同一个违约/毁约下，在之前是可以不接受，但在后来会变为不接受是不现实与不合理。Kerr大法官说："... the passage of time might in itself alter the legal position of the parties, because an insistence to treat the contract as still in being might in time become quite unrealistic, unreasonable and untenable."

而针对合法利益这一课题，独任仲裁员认为船东不接受承租人的违约/毁约是错误，因为他没有合法利益。Lloyd大法官说："... the arbitrator is here ... saying that a time charter is more analogous to a contract between master and servant than a simple debt, i. e., that it is a contract which calls for co-operation between both parties. He is also saying – 'the Charterers were also able to satisfy me – that the Owners had no legitimate interest in pursuing their claim for hire as distinct from damages... In addition to arguing that what Lord Reid had said about legitimate interest was ... in any event obiter... Mr Colman（船东代表大律师）submitted that Lord Reid was, quite simply, wrong. It seems to me that it would be difficult for me to take that view in the light of what was said by all three members of the Court of Appeal in The Puerto Buitrago ... or Mr. Justice Kerr's language in The Odenfield ('wholly unreasonable, quite unrealistic, unreasonable and untenable'), there comes a point at which the Court will cease, on general equitable principles, to allow the innocent party to enforce his contract according to its strict legal terms. How one defines that point is obviously a matter of some difficulty; for it involves drawing a line between conduct which is merely unreasonable ... and conduct which is wholly unreasonable... But that there is such a point seems to me to have been accepted ...."

Lloyd大法官等于确认了有一条分界线，到了某个地步，法院会根据衡平法的精神干预合约的肯定性，不允许无辜方坚持合约的履行。即到达某个地步，合理性超越了肯定性。但到底需要到达怎样的地步，这分界线的划分就很困难。并且，仅仅是不合理并不不足够，必须要达到完全不合理（wholly unreasonable）的程度，Lloyd大法官也说必须是在十分极端的案件中，法院才会干预。

在 Stocznia v. Latco (1996) 2 Lloyd's Rep. 132 (CA)先例,Staughton 大法官对合法利益做出了一个相对宽松的解释:"If the yard were entitled to consult only their own interests, plainly they did have such an interest: keeping these contracts open would, on this hypothesis, enable them to claim the keel – laying installments. But that cannot be the right test. To be a legitimate interest, the innocent party must have reasonable grounds for keeping the contract open bearing in mind also the interests of the wrongdoer."

在 The "Dynamic"(2003) 2 Lloyd's Rep. 693 先例,针对合法利益,Simon 大法官总结了以下三点说:"1. The burden is on the contract breaker to show that the innocent party has nolegitimate interest in performing the contract rather than claiming damages. 2. This burden is not discharged merely by showing that the benefit to the otherparty is small in comparison to the loss to the contract breaker. 3. The exception to the general rule applies only in extreme cases: where damageswould be an adequate remedy and where an election to keep the contract alivewould be unreasonable."

在 Reichman v. Beveridge (2006) EWCA Civ 1659 先例中,案情有关写字楼的租赁,被告是租客,向原告的房东租了写字楼作为其律师事务所的办公场所,为期 5 年。但租用了两年多后,被告停止营业,再也不需要租用写字楼,被告也就不再支付租金。这导致房东开始诉讼,向被告追偿欠下的租金,但被告抗辩指房东应该在没有收到租金的早期将写字楼收回,并再次出租以减少损失,然后只能向被告索赔之间的差价,而不是所有欠下的租金。被告的争辩不被上诉庭接受,其中 Lloyd 大法官在参考了较早前的先例,包括他自己判的 The "Alaskan Trader" (No. 2)先例,认为在完全不合理与金钱的赔偿已经足够的救济的情况下,无辜方才不能选择确认合约,说:"There is, therefore, a very limited category of cases in which, although the innocent party to a contract has not accepted a repudiation by the other party, and although the innocent party is able to continue to perform all his obligations under the contract despite the absence of co – operation from the other party, nevertheless the court will not allow the innocent party to enforce his full contractual right to maintain the contract in force and sue for the contract price. The characteristics of such cases are that an election to keep the contract alive would be wholly unreasonable and that damages would be an adequate remedy, or that the landlord would have no legitimate interest in making such an election."

最后在 The "Aquafaith"(2012) 2 Lloyd's Rep. 61 先例,Cooke 大法官判是如果说受害方再也没有合法利益,就必须符合如下条件:一是金钱赔偿已经是足够的救济;二是无辜方的行为是完全不合理或荒谬/反常的。Cooke 大法官这样说:"He(指仲裁员)understood the nature of the test when eliminating from his consideration anything other than that part of the speech of Lord Reid (这是指 White & Carter 先例中的 Reid 勋爵)which referred to 'no legitimate interest'. He ignored what was said by Lord Reid about the irrelevance of reasonableness in itself, and he ignored all the subsequent explanations of the meaning of ‘legitimate interest’, by reference to the need for the contract breaker to show that damages were an entirely adequate remedy and that the conduct on the part of the innocent party was beyond all reason, wholly unreasonable or, to use my expression perverse.”

针对该先例,Cooke 大法官认为金钱的赔偿对船东而言不是足够的救济,因为承租人经济出现问题,将来索赔损失相比追偿租金更加没有把握,说:“It is plain from the arbitrator's recitation of the submissions made by the parties that the owners had submitted that damages were an inadequate remedy because the charterers were in financial difficulty. The owners were therefore at risk of the charterers directing their limited funds to meet obligations to other parties, whilst delaying payment of any sums owing to the owners until the end of the charterparty and the assessment of what was due in damages. Instead of paying hire up front, semi-monthly in advance, with all the cashflow implications of that, the charterers wished to compel the owners to trade the vessel in mitigation of loss and leave themselves liberty to argue about the quantum of damages at the end of the relevant period and pay whatever they could at that stage...”

至于无辜方的船东的行为(拒绝接受承租人的违约/毁约)是否完全不合理或荒谬/反常? Cooke 大法官也不认为是。因为当时的市场实在太差,船舶去航运市场营运以减少损失显然不是太容易的事情。Cooke 大法官认为船东在终止合约后自己去市场营运相比租约仍然存在,让承租人自己去转租(期租合约都有条文允许这样做),结果没有什么不一样。所以,没有必要在船东身上强加市场营运以减少损失的“责任”,而船东拒绝这样做也谈不上是完全不合理或荒谬/反常的。

根据以上先例,看来合法利益的考验主要是金钱的赔偿是否为足够的救济、完全不合理(wholly unreasonable)、极端例子等。否则,无辜方选择接受对方的违约/毁约或确认合约继续存在的权利是不受限制(unfettered)。

以下可分别进行介绍。

8.4.2.1 无辜方能否造成不必要的浪费与应否减少损失

White and Carter (Councils) Ltd. v. McGregor(1962) AC 413 先例被人批评最多的一点是无辜方如果有权坚持不接受违约/毁约,会造成不必要的浪费。枢密院的两位大法官(Keith 勋爵与 Morton 勋爵)做出少数意见也主要是从这方面考虑。Keith 勋爵说:“I find the argument advanced for the appellants(无辜方的广告公司)a somewhat startling one. If it is right it would seem that a man who has contracted to go to Hongkong at his own expense and make a report, in return for remuneration of £ 10,000, and who, before the date fixed for the start of the journey and perhaps before he has incurred any expense, is informed by the other contracting party that he has cancelled or repudiates the contract, is entitled to set off for Hongkong and produce his report in order to claim in debt the stipulated sum. Such a result is not, in my opinion, in accordance with principle or authority, and cuts across the rule that where one party is in breach of contract the other must take steps to minimise the loss sustained by the breach."

但在本章之8.3段已经提及,传统上英国合约法一直偏向肯定性是超越了合理性。White and Carter (Councils) Ltd. v. McGregor 先例的多数意见即权威性的判决强调了肯定性的重要,是超越了是否会造成不必要的浪费的考虑。N. Strauss QC 大法官在 Ministry of Sound (Ireland) Limited v. World Online Limited (2003) EWHC 2178 (Ch)先例举了一个会造成不必要的浪费但合约还是必须严格执行的例子,支持 White and Carter (Councils) Ltd. v. McGregor 先例的判决,说:"The decision in White and Carter has been criticized, mainly on the ground that the performance of unwanted contractual services is wasteful... However, such a situation is hardly uncommon. For example, if a company leases expensive equipment, with no right to sub-lease, and then has no further use for it, there is no way in which it can force the owner, before the end of the period of the lease, to accept the return of the equipment and minimize its loss by leasing it to another available customer whom it has found, however estimable. It would remain liable for the rent for the full period..."

N. Strauss QC 大法官的例子是说,如果一家公司租用了很昂贵的机器,并且根据合约无权转租,但之后发现用不上,只能把机器闲置,但租金还是要继续支付。在租期结束前,该公司不能强迫无辜方接受退回的机器,并要在市场上转租给许多其他需要的人士以减少损失。当然,双方可以进行谈判,私下同意违约方将机器转租等,但这并非是合约的规定,也不是法律要考虑的问题。

看来,除非是达到 Reid 勋爵说的无辜方的利益极微小(de minimis),相比造成的浪费与无辜方的利益是完全不成比例的程度,否则英国法院不会以衡平法干预。

与能否造成不必要的浪费并提的,是无辜方是否需要减少损失。[148] 如果无辜方选择接受违约/毁约,则要减少损失毫无疑问。但如果无辜方选择不接受违约/毁约,则合约继续存在,无辜方应该严格按照合约规定履行(除非有本章之3.10.2提到的禁反言的例外情况)。根据英国合约法在合约被终止后,无辜方才存在减少损失的责任,而既然合约没有被终止,无辜方也谈不上有减少损失的责任。在 The "Alaskan Trader" (No.2) (1983) 2 Lloyd's Rep. 645 先例,Lloyd 大法官提到美国的法律在这方面有所不同,无论预期违约有否被接受,无辜方都要减少损失,说:"In America the courts take the uncomplicated view that whether the repudiation is accepted or not, the innocent party is always obliged to mitigate his damages: see Williston on Contracts (3rd edn, 1968) Vol. Ⅱ, § 1301, Corbin on Contracts (1951) Vol. 4, § 983 and Professor A L Goodhart 'Measure of damages when a contract is repudiated' (1962) 78 LQR 263 at 267."

---

〔148〕 有关减少损失的课题,可见杨良宜的《损失赔偿与救济》一书第五章。

这方面的美国法律看起来很有吸引力，但笔者对实际操作有疑问。如果不接受违约/毁约令合约继续存在，无辜方如何才能减少损失呢？以 Reichman v. Beveridge (2006) EWCA Civ 1659 先例为例，如果在写字楼的租赁合约继续存在的情况下要求无辜方的房东减少损失，那么房东或许可以向租客介绍其他有意向租用写字楼的人士并同意让租客分租。但这实际上是对合约的更改，如果租客不合作，房东自己办不到，所以还是依赖私下协议而不是严格按照合约履行。而且分租给其他人士也不需要无辜方代劳，违约方的租客自己也可以找代理这样做。如果租赁合约不允许分租，租客可以向房东要求批准。这也是靠私下协议，顶多如果房东粗暴拒绝，可能会增加房东完全不合理的争议的分量。The "Aquafaith" (2012) 2 Lloyd's Rep. 61 先例也是如此，船东确认期租合约继续存在，抛锚等待承租人的命令。如果要求无辜方的船东减少损失，难道他要去市场上寻找分租约吗？如果船东真的去市场上寻找并订立分租约会令无辜的船东自己变成违约方，因为同时有了两个起直接冲突的合约。总而言之，如果无辜方无论是否接受违约/毁约都要求他减少损失，感觉上很难做到或等于剥夺了无辜方拒绝接受违约/毁约的权利。

8.4.2.2　金钱的赔偿是否为足够的救济

要限制无辜方决定是否接受违约/毁约的权利，首先必须证明金钱的赔偿已经为足够的救济。这一点几乎不存在争议，在本章稍早的 8.4.2 段节录的不同先例的说法中基本都有提到。例如，在 The "Puerto Buitrago" (1976) 1 Lloyd's Rep. 250 的上诉庭先例中，Denning 勋爵说无辜方要接受违约/毁约，只要"damages would provide an adequate remedy for any loss suffered by him"。在 Kerr 大法官 The "Odenfeld" (1978) 2 Lloyd's Rep. 357 先例，Simon 大法官在 The "Dynamic" (2003) 2 Lloyd's Rep. 693 先例，Lloyd 大法官在 Reichman v. Beveridge (2006) EWCA Civ 1659 先例，Cooke 大法官在 The "Aquafaith" (2012) 2 Lloyd's Rep. 61 先例，都是必须为"damage would be an adequate remedy"的极端案件。这也十分合理，如果金钱的赔偿不是足够的救济，就没有理由强迫无辜方必须吃亏，因为一旦终止合约，就只能获得金钱赔偿的救济。

在 The "Odenfeld"先例中，Kerr 大法官认为金钱并不是足够的救济，因为该租约还剩下六年半，损失计算会十分复杂与困难。另在 Decro – Wall International SA v. Practitioners in Marketing Ltd. (1971) 1 WLR 361 先例，Salmon 大法官也是因为损失计算困难而认为金钱赔偿不是足够的救济，说："If the plaintiffs were released from it, they and the concessionaires they appointed in breach of their contract with the defendants would be left free to take advantage of this breach and enjoy the fruits of the time, effort and money which the defendants have expended during the last three years in creating and building up a thriving market for the plaintiffs' goods in the United Kingdom. Damages in such a case are very difficult to prove and I do not believe that they would by themselves be an adequate remedy. To release the plaintiffs from this undertaking would therefore be a positive encouragement to contract - breakers."

在 Reichman v. Beveridge 先例中，法院也认为金钱的赔偿不是足够的救济，因为根据英国法律，房东收回写字楼后，不一定可以索赔将来的房租损失，Lloyd 大法官说："If it is still the law of England that damages for the loss of future rent cannot be recovered after the landlord has taken back possession of the premises following a tenant's default, as seems to me to be the case, then damages cannot be an adequate remedy for the landlord in the circumstances suggested by Mr Gauntlett, and one of the conditions for the intervention of equity so as to fetter the landlord's ability to hold the tenant to the lease is not satisfied. Even if it is not clear that this is the position under English law, the uncertainty of the position at law would be relevant to the reasonableness or otherwise of the landlord's conduct. The landlord could not be criticised for wishing to avoid embarking on litigation which might have to go to the House of Lords before the point was settled."

8.4.2.3　完全不合理

已经在本章之 8.3 段提到，合理与否是一个十分广泛的概念，在每一个案件中都可以争论，要法院对无辜方选择是否接受违约/毁约的权利进行干涉，仅仅为不合理不足够，违约方必须证明无辜方不接受违约/毁约的行为是完全不合理（wholly unreasonable）。但不合理与完全不合理很难区分，Lloyd 大法官在 The "Alaskan Trader"（No.2）（1983）2 Lloyd's Rep. 645 先例中说："How one defines that point is obviously a matter of some difficulty; for it involves drawing a line between conduct which is merely unreasonable ... and conduct which is wholly unreasonable..."

而在 The "Dynamic"（2003）2 Lloyd's Rep. 693 先例，Simon 大法官更是认为"完全"这两个字根本不代表什么，说："Although, the use of the qualifying word 'wholly' in the expression 'wholly unreasonable' by Kerr J in The Odenfeld, properly emphasised that the rule was general and the exception only applied in extreme cases but added nothing to the test."

因此，笔者认为不如说是只有在极端的案件中（extreme case），法院或仲裁庭能够找到其他好的原因（additional good reason），才会行使衡平法管辖权去干预无辜方选择是否接受违约/毁约的合约法权利。

在无数合理与否的争议中，笔者只针对上述段节已经提到的先例进行探讨。首先是针对租约，在 The "Puerto Buitrago"（1976）1 Lloyd's Rep. 250 先例，本章之 8.4.1.2 段已经提到光船租约需要双方合作才能赚取租金，所以，船东必须接受承租人的违约/毁约。但这不是唯一的原因，另一个原因是船东如果确认租约是完全不合理。该先例的案情是一个一年半的光船租约，履行了六个月后就因为严重的损坏（部分是承租人要负责），船舶就要拖去德国 Kiel 港并必须进行修理，才能继续营运。但当时的船价只有 100 万美元，可是在当地进行修理需要 200 万美元（承租人承认其中 40

万美元的修理由他负责)。这导致承租人终止租约,但船东坚持不接受违约/毁约。这被法院视为完全不合理,上诉庭的 Denning 勋爵指出允许船东确认租约的存在就代表了"while the vessel lies idle and useless for want of repair or to repair it at a cost twice as much as its value"。

The "Alaskan Trader"(No. 2)先例的案情已在本章之 8.4.2 段有介绍,这里不再重复。在该先例中,判是在修理前承租人说不要这艘船的违约/毁约,船东不必接受。而修船完毕后,承租人还是坚决不接受该船舶,船东不接受就是完全不合理,因为在当时船东再坚持租约继续存在已经没有意义。换言之,对同一个承租人的违约/毁约随着时间流逝,船东坚持不接受让船舶停在希腊 Piraeus 港等待承租人的命令长达 8 个月之久,造成严重的浪费,会从合理变为完全不合理。

判断是否完全不合理的另一个角度是无辜方是否有真正的其他选择(如替代的生意),甚至比违约方有更好的选择去减少浪费。显然,如果无辜方根本没有其他选择,就没有理由要其接受违约/毁约去终止合约。所以在 The "Odenfeld"(1978)2 Lloyd's Rep. 357 先例中,Kerr 大法官判这一艘大油轮在当时低迷的市场找不到类似的租约,所以,船东不接受程租人的违约/毁约并非完全不合理。在 The "Dynamic" 先例也有同样的争议,即在船舶被承租人在美国港口扣押的情况下,无辜方的船东接受违约/毁约也无法在市场租给其他人士。

已经在本章之 8.4.1.2 段提到,承租人提早还船除了因为市场下跌想尽快脱身之外,还可能是其他与市场无关的原因所造成。例如,最后一个航次的卸港在波斯湾,而还船地点在中国,租期还剩下 20 天,但承租人坚持在波斯湾提早还船。如果无辜方的船东坚持不接受,让船舶停在波斯湾去赚取这 20 天的租金,承租人就有可能争辩说船东应该接受违约/毁约,并减少损失找下一个租约。承租人或许可以证明在当时他在租船市场根本找不到前往中国方向的货物,而即使找到航次,也不能在 20 天内完成。相反,如果船东接受违约/毁约终止租约,再去租船市场就很容易找到下一个租约,因为船东自己营运就再也没有时间与地点的限制,而当时市场上有很多去欧洲或美洲的租约或是中长期的期租合约,所以不接受违约/毁约完全不合理。

另一种情况是违约方与无辜方同样可以减少浪费,首先是在 Reichman v. Beveridge(2006)EWCA Civ 1659 先例,租客争辩说无辜方的房东应该收回写字楼并在市场出租减少损失,但 Lloyd 大法官判是房东不接受违约/毁约不是完全不合理。因为租客同样可以找其他人士将写字楼转租,只要房东没有不合理地拒绝同意(unreasonably withhold its consent)。而如果房东不合理地拒绝同意,就会增加租客说房东不接受是完全不合理的抗辩分量。至于在 The "Aquafaith"(2012)2 Lloyd's Rep. 61 先例中,合约中有转租条文,沙钢作为承租人完全可以将船舶转租减少浪费,甚至不需要船东的同意。所以,沙钢争辩说船东应该接受违约/毁约,然后把船舶在市场营运以减少损失的说法,法院不接受。可以说,The "Aquafaith" 的判法根据 Reichman v. Beveridge 先例的说法完全可以理解。

如果涉及无辜的第三人,这也肯定会带来影响。例如在 The "Odenfeld"先例中,涉及一个 10 年的期租,船东并且把租金"转让"(assign)给了原告的金融公司(finance company)。这种做法在 20 世纪七八十年代十分流行,香港与希腊很快就出现大批国际知名的船东,如董浩云与包玉刚先生能够快速扩充其船队就是通过这种做法。这就是找到一个长期租约,然后再找银行或金融公司融资造新船或买二手船,提供的担保就是这个长期租约的租金将会转让给银行或金融公司来还债。银行最关心的不是新船的船价(因为波动很厉害),而最关心与最重要的担保就是这一份长期租约,包括年期足够将债务还清以及承租人的信誉与实力。在疯狂的年代,银行或金融公司甚至会借给船东 100% 到 120% 的船价,船东几乎可以白手起家,唯一需要做的就是要找到一个有信誉的承租人并愿意给其一个长期租约,所谓的"bankable charter"。回到 The "Odenfeld"先例,本质上也是这样的做法,特殊之处是租约不是固定的租金,而是租金每两年根据油轮市场调整一次。看来承租人很有经验与小心,知道好景不长(good time never last long)。但这样的租约显然不会是一个"bankable charter",所以为了能从金融公司获得融资,船东与承租人做了私下安排(side letter arrangement),即租约规定的租金固定(而且当时油轮市场很好,租金相对很高)并且转让给原告的金融公司。但如果之后根据油轮市场调整的租金低于租约的租金,船东就向承租人补足差价。由于在租约订立时,船东也是一家有信誉与有实力的船公司,承租人同意了这一安排。但几年后,油轮市场开始暴跌,船东也开始资金短缺,不支付差价给承租人。这导致承租人以船东的违约/毁约为由,接受并终止他们之间的租约与私下安排。也由于租约的终止,承租人也停止支付租金给原告。这就带来了诉讼,即原告的金融公司作为"受让人"(assignee)向第一被告的承租人(债务人)与第二被告的船东索赔欠下的租金。有关违约/毁约的责任方面,Kerr 大法官判租约与私下安排(side letter)是独立与分开的合约,各自针对不同的合约责任。所以,船东对承租人违反了私下安排不代表对租约的违约/毁约。这样,对租约而言就变为承租人自己对船东违约/毁约。由于船东在原告的要求下不接受承租人的违约/毁约,这表示这一租约从来没有被终止,承租人需要一直支付租金给受让人的原告。这就带来另一个争议,即船东作为无辜方应否接受承租人的违约/毁约去减少损失,或船东是否有合法利益确认这个租约继续存在。Kerr 大法官认为船东完全有这个选择权。理由之一就是本章之 8.4.2 段提到的在违约/毁约时该租约还剩下六年半的租期,这么长的租期损失计算很不容易。而另一个理由就是会影响原告的金融公司(笔者估计 Kerr 大法官对船东与承租人这种接近欺骗金融公司的行为不认同),说:"The plaintiffs(金融公司)were at all material requiring Occidental(船东) to holdthe defendants(承租人)to the charter. To have accepted the defendants' repudiation would have involved breaches of these covenants(融资合约,内中有条文要求船东尽力保持租约). Then there are other considerations. To have accepted the repudiation would clearly have caused damage to the plaintiffs, who were an entirely innocent party. I do not see how

Occidental could reasonably be said to have been under a duty to the defendants, the party in repudiation, to break their contracts with the plaintiffs and to cause injury to the plaintiffs. Even if the concept of a duty to mitigate damages is relevant in this context, I cannot think for one moment that the duty would go as far as this. The existence of the loan agreement and of the assignment were known to the defendants and had been in the contemplation of both parties from the time when the charter was concluded."

最后再举一个例子是笔者作为仲裁员曾经处理过的租约争议,涉及承租人(CIF卖方)程租了一艘船舶去印度装煤去中国。该船舶在新加坡开航后空放去印度装港,但船舶刚从新加坡开航,承租人就知道因为内陆的矿场水灾(租约没有相关的免责条文),在几个月内都不会有这票货物,于是马上坚决告诉船东船舶不必开往印度而尽快找其他租约减损。但船东不理会,一直把船舶开到印度装港并等待一段时间后才开走,在印尼找到了替代租约去日本。承租人违约/毁约的责任方面应该没有争议,因为一直没有这票货物。但船东是否应该在一开始就接受承租人的拒绝性违约,而没有合法利益去确认租约继续存在导致损失严重扩大?索赔的损失包括新加坡空放到印度装港再回去印尼港口的时间与使费(特别是昂贵的燃油),金额很大。在这一争议中,承租人的做法看来是很精明。他在违约/毁约后不断将市场信息告知船东,如市场报告显示印度装港附近没有租船的生意,而新加坡附近的生意很多,可以作为替代租约减少损失。而通讯往来中也显示了船东对承租人的要求与提供替代租约的资讯不加理会。承租人是以一家实力不足的公司出面租船,承租人也曾经愿意提供母公司的担保赔偿船东运费的差价或损失,[149] 只要船东肯接受违约/毁约并减损。考虑到这些事实与证据,仲裁庭最后以多数意见同意,金钱的赔偿是足够的救济,以及船东不接受承租人的违约/毁约完全不合理。

关于是否合理的争议无法尽举,每一个案件根据不同的事实都可能有不同的结果。Keith 大法官在 White and Carter (Councils) Ltd. v. McGregor (1962) AC 413 先例中做出的少数意见中,举了一个支持其看法的例子(在本章之 8.2 段节录),专家坚持来香港做一份无用的报告。表面看来确实不合理,但如果事实稍微发生一点改变或补充,如已经预订的飞机与酒店不能取消,这已经增加了专家声称有合法利益的争辩的分量。或者更重要的是,如果这份报告对该专家的名誉或学术研究有重要意义,有关的报告在一个香港举办的国际会议也已经广泛被宣称,专家如果突然不出现会带来猜疑。这样,该专家有合法利益去确认合约继续存在,这理据在笔者看来就很强。而即使专家报告对委托的公司没有用,他也必须承担这个合约的后果去支付 1 万英镑。

8.4.2.4 合法利益的总结

已经在本章之 8.3 段与 8.4.2.3 段提到,合理与否是一个十分广泛、空泛与富争

---

[149] 这方面可见在 The "Aquafaith" (2012) 2 Lloyd's Rep. 61 先例,法院将承租人沙钢船务的经济困难视为船东将来索赔金钱赔偿是不足够保障。

议性的概念,针对同一个事实与证据,每个人从不同的角度看,可能会有不同的判断。法官或仲裁员是被要求根据双方提供的证据与争辩客观认定是否合理,所以,当事人在发生争议时要保存与创造证据显示自己的合理与对方的不合理,并找称职的律师向法院或仲裁庭展示有说服力的案情。但不可避免法院或仲裁庭(甚至不同成员之间)还是有自己的看法,笔者四十多年前开始接触伦敦波罗的交易所的海事仲裁,就已经有几位著名的海事仲裁员各自有很明确的标签,一些是看法偏向船东,另一些是看法偏向货方或承租人。这些著名的仲裁员不会是道德有问题或不懂自己的定位,而纯粹是因为其经历(如长期为船东服务)而有了不自知的偏向(imputed bias)。但笔者认为这种不自知的偏向远比不上另一种更严重的即文化差异(cultural difference)所带来的偏向。这种偏向在国际仲裁中广泛存在,甚至在很多社会问题中存在。由于国际仲裁绝大部分是西方的仲裁员,不少人对中国或亚洲的文化完全不了解甚至有误解。所以,争议一涉及是否合理,中国公司/企业在对抗西方公司时往往就会不利。这表示中国公司/企业在针对这方面的问题时,需要做更多的预防与对抗手段。简单的预防手段首先是合约条文要订得好,以及一旦发生争议要保存与创造证据显示自己的合理与对方的不合理,无论自己是无辜方或是违约方。至于对抗的手段则涉及诉讼技巧,这不是这本书所要针对,不去赘述。但显然可以看到,中国公司/企业在考虑仲裁庭的组成时,仲裁庭的成员对中国文化的了解与接受就是十分重要的因素。

合约条文针对这一问题要订得好,在订约自由下可以有各种不同的写法。例如,在一个昂贵与长期的合约中,如果中国公司/企业知道履行的过程中可能有变数(针对这方面应该考虑得悲观一些,毕竟二三十年的合约履行中间没有变数是不可能的),导致履行有变化需要双方谈判改变合约。简单在合约中写明遇到不可抗力事件(如政府干预)双方要谈判改变合约会有危险是属于“协议将来达成协议”(agreement to agree),[150]因为太不肯定而无效。所以为了肯定有效,可以在合约中写明如果发生变数,双方要进行谈判改变合约,如 3 个月还是无法达成协议,中方可以做出通知合约在 3 个月或半年不等后终止。毕竟,在终止合约后双方仍然可以继续谈判,但中国公司会处于进可攻退可守的有利地位。如果外方抗拒,因为需要 3 年或 5 年才能收回投入的成本,那么中方可以在谈判中做出让步,说在合约履行一定的期限后才能提前做出通知终止合约。毕竟这种不可抗力的变数有更大的可能是在合约履行的中后期发生。这样的好处是,即使中方预期违约,没有根据合约规定终止合约,需要承担的损失也只是外方在合约规定的 3 个月或半年或一年不等时间的损失,而不是剩下的合约期的所有损失(可能是天文数字)。原因有两个,一是计算损失以违约方最低合约责任为准,[151]二是本章第 5 段提到的错误拒绝履行合约可以合法理由补

---

〔150〕 关于协议将来达成协议,可见杨良宜的《合约的解释:规则与应用》一书第三章之 12.1.3 段。

〔151〕 见杨良宜的《损失赔偿与救济》一书第十章。

救。所以,合约如果有条文允许中国公司作为违约方在任何情况下做出通知令合约被终止,这就是合约履行的最低责任。而即使中国公司粗暴地违约/毁约,由于同时合约允许做出通知令合约终止,就可以这个合法理由补救。

又或是在合约中约定如果中方违约(包括预期违约或违约/毁约),赔偿不超过一定金额。但要注意的是,如果需要双方合作才能赚取约因/对价的合约,[152]这样的限制赔偿金额的条文可以起到一定的作用,逼外方尽快接受违约/毁约以减少损失。而如果是单方面就可以履行的合约,外方只要选择不接受违约/毁约,继续履行并赚取约因/对价,这条文就没有用武之地。因此,如果是单方面可以履行的合约,还需要有针对性的条文,如中方可以通过做出通知终止合约。

国际粮油买卖经常使用的 GAFTA 或是 FOSFA 标准合约有一条名为"GAFTA/FOSFA Default Clause"的条文,明示规定以违约/毁约的一天计算损失。这表示违约方一旦拒绝履行合约,无辜方在货价持续下跌的市场不能通过拖延去接受违约/毁约,把普通法计算损失的一天延后,令违约方蒙受更大的损失。该条文相关部分可节录如下:"The damages awarded against the defaulter shall be limited to the difference between the contract price and the actual or estimated market price on the day of default."在杨良宜的《损失赔偿与救济》一书第十六章之 1.6 段也介绍了一些有关该条文的实例。

总而言之,订约自由下合约的写法是千变万化,每个合约的性质针对的方面不同,每个合约方"戴的帽子"也不同,不能尽举。而且也不会中方提出要求外方就接受,在谈判过程中也会有阻力。但只要中方了解这方面的法律地位,自然会想到最保护自己也是当时情况下能达到最好结果的方案。

最后节录 Yukong Line Ltd. of Korea v. Rendsburg Investment Corporation (1996) 2 Lloyd's Rep. 604 先例对无辜方选择接受违约/毁约或确认合约的各方面总结如下,其中每一点都已经在以上段节有详细针对:

"(i) A renunciation of the contract by one party prior to the time for performance is not itself a breach but it gives the other party, the injured party, the right to treat it as a breach in anticipation and thus to treat the contract as discharged immediately. In other words, if a person says he will not perform, the law allows the other to take him at his word and act accordingly.(在预期违约,无辜方有权力提早终止合约。)

(ii) In such a case the injured party is not ordinarily bound to treat the contract as discharged; the law gives him a choice. He may treat the contract as discharged or he may disregard the repudiation and treat the contract as continuing in full effect, notwithstanding what has occurred. He can, in other words, elect to affirm it.(无辜方有权选择终止或确认合约。)

---

[152] 见本章之 8.4.1 段。

(iii) If the injured party elects to affirm the contract, both parties' rights and obligations under it remain completely unaffected; the renunciation is 'writ in water'...(一选择确认合约继续存在,原先的拒绝性违约就好像没有发生过的镜花水月。)

(iv) The choice placed before the injured party is between inconsistent rights, and once the choice has been made and communicated to the other party of the contract, it is irrevocable. Unlike estoppel, election does not depend upon any change in position by the party to whom it is communicated.(一旦选择并通知违约方,就不能再改变。)

(v) Although the injured party is bound by his election once it has been made, the fact that he has affirmed the contract does not of course preclude him from treating it as discharged on a subsequent occasion if the other party again repudiates it.(如果违约方有一个新的违约/毁约,无辜方会有一个新的理由去接受并改变较早前的确认。)

(vi) The injured party will not be treated as having elected to affirm the contract in the face of the renunciation unless it can be shown that he knew of the facts giving rise to his right to treat the contract as discharged and of his right to choose between affirming the contract and treating it as discharged.(无辜方要知道了违约/毁约,明确了他的地位,才可看他做出什么选择。)

(vii) A binding election requires the injured party to communicate his choice to the other party in clear and unequivocal terms. In particular, he will not be held bound by a qualified or conditional decision.(这选择,不论是终止或肯定合约,应是明确无误,没有拖泥带水,让违约方知道。)

(viii) Election can be express or implied and will be implied where the injured party acts ina way which is consistent only with a decision to keep the contract alive or where he exercises rights which would only be available to him if the contract had been affirmed.(行使这选择可以明示或默示,但行为上不要与选择有矛盾不符之处,令违约方无所依从。)"

9. 权威先例介绍

9.1 先例之一:The "Nanfri"

The "Nanfri" (1979) 1 Lloyd's Rep. 201 这个著名的先例涉及三艘船舶,船东是一家著名的挪威船公司。三艘船舶建造完毕之后就长期(6年)期租给了一家著名的加拿大承租人(也是船公司),当时的市场价格很高,所以租金也很可观。加拿大承租人把三艘船舶用来分租与用来履行他与一家美国著名粮商的包运合约,主要是从美加的大湖港口装粮去欧洲。这些货物的买卖是CIF,运费会由发货人预先支付,所以"运费预付"(freight prepaid)的提单是必要的。后来由于航运市场下跌,双方的关系也比较紧张。在出争议的时间段,承租人指称船舶在航次中的航速与耗油不符合租约的要求,并不断扣减部分租金后才做出支付。这种在期租中经常会发生的所谓“航速与耗油量争议”(performance claim),在杨大明的《期租合约》一书第四篇之4.4.9段有详论。船舶如果航速慢或耗油多,也往往表示或多或少船东要负责部分承租人的扣减金额。但这种争议与很多其他争议一样,承租人最初计算并提出索赔时总会是对他最有利的情况。所以,涉及承租人扣减的租金,在还没有最后决定实际应扣减多少金额(这种争议处理起来需要一定的时间,因为涉及很多技术性问题)之前,通常会偏高,估计在这个先例也不例外。还有一个问题,在当时,英国法律对租金能否对这种争议提前做出扣减还不是太明确。笔者还记得当时有不少说法是期租合约的租金与程租合约的运费类似,由于历史原因,运费属于法律上神圣(sacred)与不可侵犯(without deduction),必须如数支付。除了租约以明示条文规定可以对运费或租金做出扣减外,租金像运费一样不能单方面做出扣减。直到这一先例,明确了期租合约的租金与程租合约的运费不同,而是与岸上合约支付租金的情况类似,可以允许“衡平法抵销”(equitable set-off)。这种抵销也包括了航速与耗油量争议的扣减,只要承租人的金额是合理与善意的计算出来,即使扣多了也没有关系,可以在最后法院或仲裁庭决定之后再归还。所以在该先例中,船东坚持自己的法律立场就是承租人不能在租金做出扣减,但结果被判是错误地理解了英国法律地位,笔者在当时也觉得船东有点冤枉。当然,最后船东因为违约/毁约成立而被取消了三艘船舶的高利润租约也是由于他根据英国律师(也包括纽约律师)的意见所做出的言行,看来是反应完全不成比例。双方当时已经因为承租人对航速的扣减开始了伦敦仲裁,但由于这种仲裁需要一定时间,所以船东不耐烦。挪威船东也不像亚洲船东,在市场下跌时为了珍惜高利润的租约会忍气吞声,特别承租人扣减的租金金额也不高。但该挪威船东却不断抗议与向承租人争辩不应该继续扣减租金,但承租人不加理会仍在每一期租金扣减,即使之前的扣减已经在进行伦敦仲裁。挪威船东于是根据律师意见向承租人做出通知,表示撤回 Nanfri 轮、Benfri 轮与 Lorfri 轮承租人签发提单的授权,[153] 特别是不会签发运费预付的提单。该通知可节录如下:“The Masters of the Benfri, Nanfri and Lorfri are being instructed to withdraw all direct or implied authority to Charterers or its agents to sign bills of lading. Please present all bills of lading to the Master for signature. Note that the Masters will not sign any bill of lading (1) endorsed ‘freight prepaid’ or (2) ...”

当时 Nanfri 轮已经挂靠了美国 Toledo 港码头并且即将装完一船大豆的货,可以说是马上要签发运费预付的提单。而另两艘船舶,Benfri 轮还没有卸完货,但之后会去美国的 Duluth 港装货,Lorfri 轮正在芝加哥装货。这一言行在法院看来的确是不成比例与过火,被 Denning 勋爵形容为拿枪指着承租人的头说“你要钱还是要命”。

---

〔153〕 期租合约一般都有明示条文授权承租人代船长签发提单,包括该先例的 Baltime 标准格式合约。

之后,承租人给船东电文,要求船东改变主意,并提出把扣减的租金存放在一个共同的银行账号,等待伦敦仲裁裁决的结果。但这被船东拒绝,坚持承租人要退还扣减的租金,并指称不断在赚取的租金已经足够承租人作为伦敦仲裁结果的担保。这导致了以下承租人的回电指称船东的言行构成违约/毁约,承租人接受马上终止这三份租约:"It is a matter of regret to us that we have had no satisfactory response to our message of this morning, particularly against the background of our inability to employ the vessel without the co – operation or assistance of her Master and the Owners. Owners, by their conduct, have clearly evinced an intention not to be bound by the terms of the charter and we accept the totality of their conduct as a repudiation of the charter and we accept such repudiation without prejudice to any rights that we may have including our claim for damages. Accordingly we consider the charter terminated effective immediately ..."

在该先例中,最后法院判是船东认为不能扣减租金的法律地位是错误。但笔者认为,即使船东的法律地位正确,即租金不能做出这种扣减或在该先例承租人过多的扣减,这个船东过火与不成比例的言行仍然会导致船东构成违约/毁约。

显然在该先例中,船东如果做出的言行并不过火而且不影响租约的履行,就不会带来这么严重的后果。例如,最正规的言行是采取法律行动或者开始仲裁,但这在该先例中,仲裁已经开始进行,所以不管用。另一个可能的言行是冻结承租人的资产或是扣押承租人的船舶。前者的行动不会成功,因为承租人是一家著名的一流承租人(first class charterer),面对这种财力雄厚的人士,根本不可能成功申请到"冻结令"(freezing injunction)。至于扣押承租人的船舶,应该完全可行,但这也是只能拿到担保,而不能像船东的要求承租人把扣减的租金全数退还,还是需要等待最后伦敦仲裁的结果。船东也可以威胁承租人在卸港对货物进行留置,但这会带来面对收货人的困难,特别是提单有了批注是运费预付,加上即使能够留置货物,还是只能取得担保。这样看来,船东在该先例唯一能做的,也是合法与最安全的,就是尽快推进伦敦仲裁并早日取得结果。至于期间的延误,船东可以获得利息的赔偿。至于有了裁决后,面对一流的承租人,也不必害怕变不了金钱。

9.2 先例之二:Woodar Investment Development Ltd. v. Wimpey Construction UK Ltd.

Woodar Investment Development Ltd. v. Wimpey Construction UK Ltd. (1980) 1 WLR 277 这个著名先例涉及一个土地买卖的合约———幅在英国 14 亩的土地用来发展。该在 1973 年 2 月 21 日签订的合约有一条特殊的条文是允许买家在三种情况下终止合约,而最后一种情况是:"(在买卖双方完成交接前发生了)... (iii) Any Authority having a statutory power of compulsory acquisitionshall have commenced to negotiate for the acquisition by agreementor shall have commenced the procedure required by law for the compulsoryacquisition of the property or any part thereof."

在 1974 年 3 月 20 日,估计因为土地价格下跌,买方给卖方一个终止合约的通知

(notice of rescission),说明理由是环境部强制征收其中2.3亩的土地。事实上,政府做出了强制征收土地令是在1973年,环境部早在1970年已经宣布想征收这2.3亩的土地,换言之,双方在1973年2月订立该合约时就已经完全知道。这在一审的法院被判是合约条文中的"shall have commenced"表示该条文只适用在合约订立后才开始的强制征收程序,也就是该条文在该先例的情况中不适用。

这样剩下的就是终止合约的通知是否构成"违约/毁约"的言行,并且被卖方接受去终止该土地买卖合约。在贵族院,多数意见判是买方的言行只是一个诚实的误解。至于做出的终止合约通知,充其量只是一份保留买方可以在法院判决如果对其有利的情况下终止合约的权利的中性文件。其中多数意见的Wilberforce勋爵是这样说:

"This gives rise to the first issue in this appeal: whether, by invoking Special Condition E(a)(iii), and in the circumstances, the appellants(买方)are to be taken ashaving repudiated the contract. The respondents(卖方)so claim, and assert that theyhave accepted the repudiation and are entitled to sue the appellants fordamage.

My Lords, I have used the words 'in the circumstances' to indicate, as Ithink both sides accept, that in considering whether there has been a repudiationby one party, it is necessary to look at his conduct as a whole. Does this indicatean intention to abandon and to refuse performance of the contract? In thepresent case, without taking the appellants conduct generally into account, the respondents' contention, that the appellants had repudiated, would be adifficult one. So far from repudiating the contract, the appellants were relying onit and invoking one of its provisions, to which both parties had given theirconsent. And unless the invocation of that provision were totally abusive, orlacking in good faith, (neither of which is contended for), the fact that it hasproved to be wrong in law cannot turn it into a repudiation. At the lowest, thenotice of rescission was a neutral document consistent either with an intention topreserve or with an intention to abandon the contract, and I will deal with it onthis basis—more favourable to the respondents. In order to decide which iscorrect the appellants' conduct has to be examined."

贵族院多数意见的判法看来主要是依赖了该先例在一审被认定的事实。在买方做出通知之前,买方与卖方的代表Cornwall先生曾经有一次会面。Cornwall先生被告知买方有做出终止合约通知的意向。Cornwall先生说,如果买方做出这个通知,卖方会将买方告上法院,并让法官来决定买方能否终止合约。Cornwall先生还说,他会接受买方的通知只是买方全面与谨慎的自我保护,并不会认为这是敌意的行为。之后,买方做出终止合约通知,卖方的律师回信表示卖方不接受该通知的有效性并开始诉讼程序。Cornwall先生之后写信给买方提到了诉讼程序,并认为双方都应该等待法院对买方根据该条文终止合约是否有效的决定。接着Cornwall先生又写了一封信说毫无疑问双方都要遵守法院的决定。Wilberforce勋爵将这些证据的相关性总结如下:"My Lords, I cannot find anything which carries the matter one inch beyond, on Wimpey's part, an expressed reliance on the contract [condition E (a) (iii)], on Woodar's side an intention to take the issue of the validity of the notice (nothing else) to the courts, and an assumption, not disputed by Wimpey, that both sides would abide by the decision of the court. This is quite insufficient to support the case for repudiation... My Lords, in my opinion, it follows, as a clear conclusion of fact, that the appellants manifested no intention to abandon, or to refuse future performance of or to repudiate the contract. And the issue being one of fact, citation of other decided cases on the other facts is hardly necessary. I shall simply state that the proposition that a party who takes action relying simply on the terms of the contract, and not manifesting by his conduct an ulterior intention to abandon it, is not to be treated as repudiating it is supported by James Shaffer Ltd. v. Findlay Durham & Brodie [1953] 1 W. L. R. 106 and Sweet & Maxwell Ltd. v. Universal News Services Ltd. [1964] 2 Q. B. 699."

在该贵族院的先例,Salmon 勋爵与 Russell 勋爵持相反意见。其中 Salmon 勋爵的意见可部分节录如下:

"I do not recall that any of these definitions of a repudiation of a contract have ever until now, been questioned. The fact that a party to a contract mistakenly believes that he has the right to refuse to perform it cannot avail him. Nor is there any authority for the proposition that if a party to a contract totally refuses to perform it, this refusal is any the less a repudiation of the contract because he honestly but mistakenly believes that he is entitled by a condition of the contract to refuse to perform it.

It would indeed be unfortunate if the law were otherwise. A mistake in the construction of a contractual condition, even such a glaringly obvious mistake as the present can apparently easily be made especially perhaps when the market price has fallen far below the contract price. It is acknowledged in this case that the mistake was an honest one. If, however, a case arose in which a mistake of this kind was alleged to be an honest mistake, but not acknowledged to be so, it would be extremely difficult, if not impossible to prove the contrary."

9.3　先例之三:The "Hermosa"

在 The "Hermosa"(1982) 1 Lloyd's Rep. 570 先例,原船东期租给 MTC,MTC 又以二船东身份转租给智利承租人 CNSC,租期是两年,交船时间是 1974 年 12 月。第一个航次从智利去荷兰,就有海水进入船舱而导致货损。在 1975 年 1 月 16 日卸完货后,船舶要开去法国敦刻尔克修理。由于修理的延误(直到 3 月 27 日),CNSC 因此失去一笔原来安排的从欧洲装货回航到智利的生意,需要在修理后空放回智利装港。但在 4 月 18 日,Hermosa 轮在空放航次中又发生了碰撞,被迫在加勒比海的古拉索修理。修理不断延误,过了三个多月,船舶还没修好。船舶在欧洲修理时,CNSC

曾经要求上船检查,但被原船东拒绝。这导致 CNSC 十分怀疑原船东到底在干什么以及是否想以及会把船舶修理好。结果,CNSC 向古拉索法院取得命令,强制上船检查。检查后发觉船舶的状况确实不妥,特别如舱盖(hatchcover)的状况以及在期间原船东需要做的工作没有太多进展等。CNSC 认为原船东不会进行修理,或者修理也不会令人满意,就通过电传与二船东 MTC 交涉(显然 MTC 会把有关电传转给原船东),但没有结果。这导致在 8 月 15 日,CNSC 向 MTC 做出最后通牒(ultimatum),要求原船东在 10 天内开始进行修理,并在完成修理后允许上船检查,否则将把 MTC 视为拒绝履行合约去终止该租约。但原船东没有回应,因此,作为二船东的 MTC 也无法回应 CNSC。于是在 8 月 29 日,CNSC 就终止了与 MTC 的租约。MTC 曾经希望 CNSC 回心转意,但没有成功,所以 MTC 也接受了 CNSC 的违约/毁约。

而事后证明,原船东虽然不合作与没有回应,但在事发时,他是在同一家哥伦比亚修船厂谈判对船舶进行永久性修理的合约,尤其是对舱盖的修理。在达成协议后,船舶在 8 月 27 日开航并于 8 月 30 日抵达哥伦比亚修船厂。完成修理后 7 个星期,船舶也进行了检查,被证明状况良好。

显然在这个先例中,CNSC 不能争辩预期违约的"不可能"(impossibility),因为事实证明这个船舶是完全可能履约的。CNSC 也不能争辩预期违约的语言上"拒绝履约"(renunciation),因为原船东没有说过不修理,显然 MTC 也不会转达。而唯一能争辩并令 CNSC 终止合约合法化的,就是行为上的拒绝。

高院的 Mustill 大法官与上诉庭都判 CNSC 败诉。Donaldson 大法官在该案例说:"We sympathise with (CNSC) sense of anger and frustration, in the non-legal sense of the word. We can understand the rise in their corporate blood pressure which no doubt followed... But as Lord Wilberforce said in Woodar's case, repudiation is a drastic conclusion which should only be held to arise in clear cases of a refusal to perform obligations. (CNSC) should have continued to press for definite information as to the owners' and MTC's intentions. They struck too soon. As events turned out, had they waited they would have realised that they could not strike at all."

显然以 MTC(原船东)的行动与否作为拒绝履行,需要十分明确的证据。在此先例中,CNSC 终止的理由显然有危险。首先,船舶不适航、不妥只是保证条文,不是严重到可构成条件条文去终止租约:The"Hong Kong Fir"(1961)2 Lloyd's Rep. 478 先例。如果说 MTC(原船东)曾说过一些可构成拒绝的语言,如"你不加租金,我不修理"或"我资金短缺,暂时无法进行修理"等,CNSC 的地位就会强得多。MTC(原船东)只是不讲话而已,沉默不代表否定,他真的开口可能会说"我马上修理",怎可当做拒绝履行?看来,CNSC 行动得太早与太快,它应该通过向 MTC(原船东)施加各种压力与造成麻烦,以求套出一句拒绝性违约的语言。

至于修理延误导致 CNSC 作为承租人在商业上很难营运这艘船舶,但这是一个两年的期租,所以即使修理很慢与很多延误,CNSC 还是无法说剩下的租期已经是让他重大地失去了整个租约的利益。正如 Mustill 大法官在一审说:"In the present case although Nitrates' enjoyment of the charter had been curtailed by a very exasperating course of events, it had not been curtailed to such an extent as to make it possible to say that they had lost substantially the whole benefit of the charter."

至于 CNSC 给的最后通牒,也改变不了法律地位,因为它不过是言辞强硬地要求 MTC(原船东)保证会履行。如 Mustill 大法官所说:"... had no legal status and was no more than a strongly worded demand for assurance..."这也正确,否则每一方以后动辄就给最后通牒,"我限你在 5 秒钟之内明确告知修船,否则我当作拒绝履行合约",这就麻烦了。[154]

9.4 先例之四:Vaswani v. Italian Motors (Sales & Services) Ltd.

Vaswani v. Italian Motors (Sales & Services) Ltd. (1996) 1 W. L. R. 270 先例涉及在香港的一辆法拉利汽车的买卖。买卖合约规定基准价格是 179500 英镑(这笔钱在订立合约的 1989 年估计可以买几栋豪宅),但同时规定卖方在一定情况下可以在交付汽车时调整/提高最终的价格。相关条文可节录如下:

"Sterling £ 179,500 at contract signing, subject to clause noted hereunder. (Inclusive of first registration tax at prevailing 90 per cent. rate).

(The price appearing upon this document is based upon the manufacturer's current price, specification and present freight and exchange rates. The price is subject to adjustment should there be any change in the manufacturer's current price or freight rates prior to shipment or should there be any change in exchange rates prior to delivery or in any of the other cases set out in condition[s] 4 and 5 on the reverse hereof and the price ruling at the date of delivery will be invoiced.)(这一段是红字标注)...

4(a) If, for any reason whatsoever, the manufacturers should make any changes in their specifications or models or should discontinue the production of the model/s sold under this contract so that the sellers are unable to make delivery thereof, the sellers shall not thereby incur any liability to **the buyer but shall, in any such case, deliver to the buyer the current model/s closest in line to the model ordered which is available for delivery in Hong Kong and the buyer shall be bound to take delivery and to pay the purchase price for the new model (including any increase by reason of an increase in the manufacturer's price or other circumstances referred to in condition 5 hereof) provided that the total price for the model delivered shall not be more than 15 per cent. higher than the price specified on the face of this contract.** (b) Discontinuance by the manufacturer of production of the model ordered shall not operate to terminate the contract or give the buyer any right of rescission if the sellers are able to make delivery of

---

[154] 可见本章之 3.8 段稍有不同的说法。

the model ordered and the buyer shall be obligated to accept delivery of the model ordered on the terms and conditions hereof notwithstanding such discontinuance and/or the introduction of a new model. (c) If the manufacturers should make any changes in their specifications or models or should discontinue production of the model ordered and the seller is unable to make delivery of the model ordered or another available model which is close in line thereto, this contract shall be cancelled and the deposit shall be refunded to the buyer without interest, costs or compensation. . . .

5. In the event of war, war – like operations, civil commotion, strikes, floods, **currency exchange fluctuations** or any other circumstances beyond the control of the sellers resulting in changes in the cost to the seller of the goods, ready for delivery in Hong Kong, **the seller shall be entitled to adjust the price to reflect the amount of all such changes.**"(加黑部分是有关争议的条文)

买方是一个年轻人,但这个买卖是由他父亲处理,并由他父亲出资支付了25%的定金,即44875英镑。在汽车可以付运后,卖方要求买方支付剩下的168141.66英镑,该金额是根据当时同样的法拉利汽车的售价218800英镑计算出来的。买方在当时没有对提高的价格提出异议,但因为改变计划打算不在香港居住,所以不想完成交易。卖方坚持要买方完成交易,并提出会帮助买方找其他有钱的买方将汽车转卖,还做出了限时折扣的要约,但这要约没有被买方接受。之后,买方曾经承诺会支付剩下的金额,但后来并没有支付。卖方最后通知买方除非交易在某个时间前完成,卖方会认为合约被终止并根据合约第8条文没收定金。

买方最后也没有支付剩下的金额,卖方转卖了汽车并没收了定金。买方新换的律师第一次提出卖方没有权利提高价格到218800英镑,要求支付才交付汽车是构成拒绝性违约。双方进行了谈判,但在还没有结果的时候,买方向法院提起诉讼要求卖方退还定金,理由是卖方误述与拒绝履约。一审法院判是误述不成立,这一点在之后没有被上诉。针对卖方是否有权提高价格到他要求的金额,一审法院判卖方根据有关买卖合约没有权利这样做,并且判卖方拒绝履行,需要退回定金。卖方上诉到上诉庭,上诉庭对买卖合约做出不同的解释,一致判是卖方有权提高价格到他要求的金额。上诉庭的Penlington大法官还说,即使卖方没有权利这样做,他也是善意的,不构成拒绝性违约。

最后买方上诉到英国枢密院,相关的争议有两个,第一个是卖方是否有权提高价格到他要求的金额,这是对买卖合约的解释。第二个是如果卖方没有权利这么做,卖方坚持要买方支付、转卖与没收定金的行为就属于拒绝履行,并且被买方接受了。

针对第一个争议,枢密院综合解释了合约条文,最后支持了买方的观点,认为卖方只能在某些特定的情况下升高价格。在本先例中,卖方只有权提高22127英镑,而不是39300英镑。但针对第二个争议,Woolf勋爵分析了Woodar Investment Development Ltd. v. Wimpey Construction U. K. Ltd. (1980) 1 W. L. R. 277, The "Nanfri"

(1979) 1 Lloyd's Rep. 201 等先例,认为卖方对合约条文诚实的误解不构成拒绝履行,说:

"If the sellers had demanded the payment of the correct sum then they would have had the right to forfeit the deposit and resell the car. The sellers having demanded a sum in excess of that due their primary argument is based on the proposition that it does not amount to a repudiation of a contract to assert a genuinely held but erroneous view as to the effect of the contract. ...

While therefore here the request for the payment of an excessive price would not in itself amount to a repudiation, if the conduct relied on went beyond the assertion of a genuinely held view of the effect of the contract the conduct could amount to a repudiation. This is the positionif the conduct is inconsistent with the continuance of the contract. Then the bona fide motives of the party responsible do not prevent the conduct being repudiatory. ...

Nor is conduct, if it is repudiatory, excused because it occurs in consequence of legal advice as may be the case with the sellers' actions in this case. ...

In this case while the sellers did indicate to the buyer that he should pay a sum which was excessive or the deposit would be forfeited they never went so far as to indicate to the buyer that it would be purposeless to pay the correct sum as required by condition 8. This was not therefore a case like The Norway (1865) 3 Moo. P. C. C. N. S. 245 where the sellers had made it clear that it was pointless to tender a lesser sum. All they had done was to put forward their calculation which had gone unchallenged. There was nothing to prevent the buyer paying the sum he calculated was due. Until he at least tendered the sum he considered was due the sellers were not required to deliver the vehicle. However in fact the buyer never called for delivery by the sellers. This was no doubt because he had made no further payment and never intended to attempt to test their willingness to deliver. The sellers did not threaten 'a breach of the contract with serious consequences'... and there was no conduct by them which was totally inconsistent with the continuance of the contract until after the buyer had made it clear that he was not going to make any further payment. This being the situation their Lordships are of the opinion the sellers did not repudiate the contract."

枢密院在上述节录最后一段就说明了根据这一先例的事实,不构成拒绝性违约的原因。毕竟在商业合约的履行中,一方算错了应向对方收取的金额的事情经常发生。如果一旦算错了金额,就属于拒绝性违约可让对方终止合约,岂不是天下大乱。在本先例中,卖方算出一个金额要求买方支付并提车完全符合合约的履行,只是金额上算错了。如果卖方曾经说过一些过火的话,如"少给一分钱,我也不会把汽车给你",情况可能会有不同。而买方如果在得知卖方要求的金额后曾经提出异议,但卖方依然坚持他错误的计算,或是曾经试图支付他认为正确的金额并要求卖方将车辆交给他,但仍被拒绝,这情况也可能会不同。毕竟如果买方提出异议,卖方很可能会同意改为正确的金额。但在本先例中,买方没有这么做,而是在卖方终止合约后才提出异议。所以整体来看,枢密院不支持买方的立场。

9.5 先例之五:Eminence Property Developments Limited v. Kevin Christopher Heaney

Eminence Property Developments Limited v. Kevin Christopher Heaney (2010) EWCA Civ 1168 先例也是涉及土地买卖,原告出售给被告(Heaney 先生是一个发展商)13 套房子并在 2007 年 12 月 10 日同时为每一套房子签订了一份合约。合约规定买卖双方交易完成的日期是房子完成建筑可以入住,当时估计是 2008 年 12 月 4 日。有关合约的条文是:

"6.8.2 The parties are to complete, the contract within ten working days of giving a notice to complete, excluding the day on which the notice is given. For this purpose, time is of the essence of thecontract...

7.5 Buyer's failure to comply with notice tocomplete.

7.5.1 If the buyer fails to complete in accordance with a notice to complete, the following terms apply:

7.5.2 The seller may rescind the contract, and if he does so:

(a) he may

(i) forfeit and keep any deposit and accrued interest

(ii) resell the property and any chattels included in the contract

(iii) claim damages ..."

在 2008 年"金融海啸"后,市场暴跌,买方财政上有困难,无法找到融资来完成这个交易。所以买方就要求减价,但卖方没有做出让步,双方的谈判也没有结果。2008 年 12 月 5 日,卖方根据第 6.8.2 条文,通过其律师做出了要求完成交易的通知(notice to complete)。在该通知中,卖方也指出如果买方不准时完成交易,会带来第 7.5 条文的严重后果。通知也在最后一段提到了完成交易的一天是 2008 年 12 月 15 日,说:"We calculate the final date for completion under the notice is 15th December 2008."

这显然是个错误,因为第 6.8.2 条文所要求的是 10 个工作日,所以完成交易最后的日期不是 12 月 15 日,而应该是 12 月 18 日。收到这个通知,买方没有向卖方指出这一明显的错误。这可能是买方自己也没有发觉,或更可能是发觉了但等待卖方下一步的行动,看卖方是否犯错。结果卖方果然犯错,在 12 月 17 日向买方做出终止合约的通知(notice of rescission),说:"Further to the expiry of the notice to complete served under condition 6.8 of the Standard Conditions of Sale 4th edition (The Standard Conditions) you have failed to complete the purchase of the above property. Pursuant to

7.5 of the Standard conditions please treat this letter as formal notice of rescission of the Agreement for sale dated 10th December 2007. Your clients deposit has been forfeited along with accrued interest and our client is entitled to damages for breach of contract, including but not limited to the remainder of the deposit payable under the contract."

买方的律师看来是有准备,马上接受卖方的违约(因为马上接受就可以立即终止合约,怕卖方发觉错误撤回)。该接受的回函如下:

"1.3. The Notices to Complete that were served by you required completion of the contracts on or before 18 December 2008, which is the date 10 working days after service of the Notices to Complete (assuming it was deemed served on 5 December rather than 8 December for the purpose of standard condition 1.3).

1.4. The act of rescinding contracts under cover of your letters of 17th December 2008 constitutes a repudiatory breach of contract. Our client accepts your clients' repudiatory breach of contract and elects to rescind the contracts and is discharged from them.

1.5. Please remit, by return, our client's deposits together with any interest accrued on those deposits."

卖方争辩说终止合约通知只是一个预先通知,直到交易最后日期过后才生效,但这不被买方接受,这就带来诉讼。在一审中,法院判是卖方12月17日的终止合约通知的确是构成了违约/毁约,说:"In those circumstances my conclusion is that Eminence (卖方) committed a repudiatory breach of the contract by their letter of 17th December 2008 and that that breach was accepted by the letter dated 18th December 2008 sent by Foot Anstey (买方) and that the contract has therefore been determined, and I answer the preliminary issue accordingly."

卖方上诉至上诉庭,上诉庭推翻一审并批评说,一审只注意12月17日的文字/措辞而没有充分考虑整个案件的事实背景。上诉庭主要的理由是卖方的错误是一个明显的错误,买方完全可以看到并知道如果向卖方提出,卖方肯定会马上做出改变,而不可能继续坚持自己的立场不履行合约。Etherton大法官其中部分的理由可节录如下:

"(4)... In the present case, as a reasonable person in Mr Heaney's (买方代表) position would have realised, there was a simple error of calculation by Eminence's solicitors, analogous to a clerical error, which, once pointed out, would have been (as it was) conceded immediately. The consequence of pointing it out, as the reasonable person would have appreciated, was that the rescission notices would have been treated, as they were in law, as ineffective, and Eminence would have waited until the expiry of the notices to complete before deciding whether or not to treat the contracts as at an end...

(5) It is, in my judgment, impossible clearly to find on those facts an intention by Eminence to abandon and altogether to refuse to perform the contacts, which, in view of

the state of the market, had become highly advantageous to Eminence and onerous to Mr Heaney. On the contrary, the obvious inference from those facts is that Mr Heaney and his solicitors were only too well aware that Eminence very much wanted to enforce the contracts, either by completing them or by rescinding them and exercising the other remedies conferred by them, in either case in accordance with the contractual terms.

(6) The error of the Recorder(一审法官) was to concentrate on the rescission notices without taking into account all the circumstances. To do so results in a lack of reality..."

9.6 先例之六:The "Pro Victor"

The "Pro Victor" (2010) 2 Lloyd's Rep. 158 先例是一个类似案情经常发生的租船案例。承租人租了船舶(无论是程租或是航次期租)后有关的付运出了问题,导致承租人被迫要告诉船东不需要来装港,从而构成拒绝性违约。或是船舶到了装港,但被承租人告知没有货物装,进而构成违约/毁约。通常的做法是,船东接受拒绝性违约或是违约/毁约,然后去市场寻找其他的替代航次。如果蒙受损失,就会向违约方的承租人通过租约的仲裁条文提起索赔。但在仲裁中,承租人不会坐以待毙,所以会有各种不同的抗辩,根据每个案件尽量挑毛病。在本先例中,抗辩是承租人并没有明确的拒绝履行合约,是船东自己过早做出反应。

本先例的案情是一艘油轮通过程租合约去 Karachi 装石油产品去中国台湾地区、韩国与日本。租约是在 2008 年 8 月 17 日订立,但不久之后,承租人曾经给过船东一些提议去装载其他的货物,但双方最后没有达成任何协议。可以说,这是一个显示了承租人之前的货物出现问题的迹象。结果船舶准时在 8 月 27 日抵达装港 Karachi,抛锚并给了"准备就绪通知书"(notice of readiness)准备装货。但随即船东代理被承租人的装港代理告知,因为买卖合约下的买方突然不再需要这批货,承租人不再需要这条船,因为没有货装。在 8 月 28 日,在船东代理人的追问之下,承租人的代理人发了第一封电邮,如下:

"Due to circumstances beyond charterers control, it **may** become necessary to declare force major [sic].

Charterers have offered owner two possible alternatives in order to assist owners to mitigate the situation.

Charterers will consider releasing the vessel from its current charter in order to permit owner to seek other business with owner and charterer agreeing to a mutual cancellation.

Please discuss with owners and obtain their agreement for a mutual cancellation of reference charter."(加黑部分是笔者的强调)

船东就回应说这封电邮等同宣布不履行。承租人发送了第二封电邮:

"... Charterers reject owners declaration of non - performance.

Owners have been advised that Charterers have the means to mitigate any alleged losses of Owners by taking the vessel on time charter from Karachi at $18,000 per day for trip via port or ports with redelivery Singapore/S. Korea range with estimated duration of 45/60 days wog.

Charterers have cargo to load promptly from west coast India to east cost [sic] Africa hence fromAG going east.

If Owners really interested in mitigating losses, they will agree to charterers proposal above.

On completion of time charter, owners and charterers will be able to calculate Owner's position of alleged losses.

Charterers sincerely regret current circumstances and are doing everything possible to maintain a good relationship with Owners for ongoing business as discussed with your Mr. Se Un Kim in Athens.

Urgent for owners to agree to charterers proposal of time charter in order not to lose the cargo from west coast India and AG..."

接下来的通讯往来是船东的代理在第二封电邮之后接到了承租人代理的电话，说承租人没有买方没有办法继续履行原来的租约。在8月29日，船东要求承租人在新加坡时间下午3点前明确与无条件确认会根据原租约提供货物。承租人并没有给出这样的确认。在8月29日新加坡时间下午6点25分，船东终止租约并开航。针对承租人是否已经明确的拒绝履行合约，Flaux大法官针对第一封电邮说承租人并非说死，无法扭转地拒绝履行合约："Taken overall, I accept Mr Phillips'（违约方代表大律师）submission that this email is equivocal in the sense that it does not state clearly and unequivocally that the defendant cannot or will not perform the charterparty. Furthermore, Mr Yang（无辜方的主要证人）did not see it as such.[155] In cross-examination he said that he saw this email as the defendant saying that it would probably not be able to perform, which is insufficient to amount to renunciation."

除了船东证人杨先生自己不认为承租人是无法扭转地拒绝履行合约外，承租人在第一封电邮中的用字是"may"，也没有把话说死。而邮件接下来的内容是想要同船东达成协议走另一个航次，或者让船东在市场上找替代租约，双方共同取消。这明显不属于拒绝，因为承租人并没有说死是无论船东同意与否都不再履行。

Flaux大法官针对第二封电邮的说法不同，认为是拒绝履行，说：

"However, in my judgment the second email from Captain Skarvelis（承租人租船部的负责人）sent at 1724 hours Singapore time on 28 August 2008 is a different matter. In circumstances where the claimant had stated that it regarded the first email as a declara-

---

[155] 见本章之3.6.2段。

tion of non – performance, the situation had become very serious, as Captain Skarvelis accepted in evidence. The situation cried out for a clear statement from the defendant that it was ready, willing and able to perform the charterparty. Again, as before, if it had been ready, willing and able to perform, it would have been very easy to state that in terms. Captain Skarvelis' assertion in cross – examination that it was not necessary to do so because that was the effect of the opening words: 'charterers reject owners declaration of non – performance' was unconvincing.

The rest of the email seems to me to be saying not that the defendant(承租人)will perform the charter but that to mitigate their loss the claimant(船东)should agree to the defendant's proposal for a 45 – 60 day time charter at US $ 18,000 a day. This seems to have been a variant of Proposal 2(这是上面提到的船舶还没有到装港前,承租人曾经向船东提议装载其他货物,但没有被船东接受), but unlike when that proposal was made, the defendant was not saying 'if we cannot agree this proposal, we will revert to the original charter, which I will then perform'. The statement in the email 'if owners really interested in mitigating losses, they will agree to charterers' proposal' is inconsistent with an intention to perform the charterparty if the proposal was not agreed. Mr Yang said he saw this email as a threat and, in my judgment, he was right to do so.

Furthermore, the statement: 'charterers sincerely regret current circumstances' looks like and is an apology for not being able to perform. Captain Skarvelis' attempt to explain this away as a reference to the claimant trying to put the vessel on subs to Glencore was pure invention which was completely incredible.

Viewed in the overall context of where matters stood on 28 August 2008, to which I have already referred, I consider that this email was renunciatory..."

最后 Flaux 大法官说即使他对第二封电邮的结论是错误的,接下来承租人代理给船东代理的电话就也再清楚不过是拒绝性违约或违约/毁约:"However, even if that conclusion were wrong, matters did not rest there. In particular, soon after this email was received, Sky Kim(船东代理)received the phone call from Mr Hermon(承租人代理)(clearly passing on what he had been told by Mr Karamanos) saying that the defendant had lost its buyer and would be unable to proceed with the charterparty, a message which Mr Kim relayed to Mr Yang. In my judgment that was a clear express renunciation of the charterparty."

9.7 先例之七:Wuhan Ocean Economic v. Hansa Murcia

Wuhan Ocean Economic v. Hansa Murcia (2013) 1 Lloyd's Rep. 273 先例是中国船厂在伦敦两千多个仲裁中极个别胜诉的案件之一。在该先例中,中国船厂与德国船东在 2008 年"金融海啸"之前订立造船合约,显然是一个对中国船厂利润十分丰厚的合约。在 2007 年 6 月 7 日,船厂提供了中国进出口银行签发的还款担保(refund guarantee)，可部分节录如下："This Letter of Guarantee shall remain in force until the Vessel has been delivered to and accepted by [the Buyers] or refund has been made by the Seller or ourselves (the Export Import Bank of China) or until **June 30th 2010**, whichever occurs earliest, after which you are to return it to us by airmail for cancellation. In case arbitration initiated by either Seller or Buyer before delivery of the Vessel, the validity of this guarantee shall be extended to 60 calendar days after the final arbitration award is issued."(加黑是还款担保的最后限期，但注意最后的一句是如果启动了仲裁，还款担保就会自动延期。)

之后造船发生延误，2009 年 12 月 22 日，双方同意延迟交船至 2011 年 10 月 31 日，并签订了附录四，可部分节录如下："1. The Buyer and Seller agree that the Vessel shall be delivered to the Buyer on 31st October 2011, which shall be the Delivery Date... 3. The Seller does undertake to extend the validity of the Refund Guarantee dated 7th June 2007 of Export Import Bank of China... until 31 May 2012."

笔者估计中国船厂为了取得这一延迟交船是付出了代价，即把原来的船价减到 2009 年年底的市场价格。但在当时，船价也曾短暂稳定甚至轻微上涨，估计德国船东在船厂减价的情况下，愿意延迟交船。但之后船价继续下跌，德国船东再度想从该合约中脱身与弃船。于是在 2010 年 6 月 28 日，以还款担保没有根据附录四延期为由，向船厂做出了终止合约通知："You have failed to obtain the extension of the Refund Guarantee and evinced an intention of not so doing and are therefore in repudiatory breach of the Shipbuilding Contract (as amended). We, on behalf of the Buyers, hereby accept your repudiatory breach as terminating the... Contract and give you formal notice of the Buyers final and irrevocable cancellation of the above mentioned Shipbuilding Contract."

第二天，也就是 6 月 29 日，德国船东开始了仲裁程序，以取得裁决书向中国进出口银行根据还款担保取回预付船价与利息。

后来中国船厂提供的证据证明，事实上在 4 月 23 日就已经向中国进出口银行提出了申请，并且多次派人催促，最后在 6 月 29 日取得延期。需注意的是，原来的还款担保是在第二天即 6 月 30 日才到期。期间，虽然中国船厂没有告知德国船东有关他的努力去延长还款担保，但也没有任何的言行显示不愿意或不能够取得还款担保延期。从案情的事实与有关证据看来，难以接受中国船厂有任何违约，不论是拒绝性违约或是真正违约。仲裁庭接受中国船厂没有言行足以构成拒绝性违约，但有真正违约，就是没有在合理时间内取得还款担保的延期，而这是重要的责任。

仲裁庭的理据是造船合约与附录四中都没有明示规定船厂应该在什么时间内取得延期，附录四只是明示了中国船厂需要延长还款担保的期限，显然这是需要在 6 月 30 日之前。仲裁庭判是因为还款担保对船东十分重要，认定合理时间应是 6 月 16 日之前(这是一个事实认定的问题，高院不可以改变)。船厂没有在 6 月 16 日取得延期已经是真正违约，但到了 6 月 23 日，船厂依然没有取得延期，这个延误已经达到合约根基而变得重要,因此船东可以船厂违约/毁约为由终止造船合约。

仲裁庭的裁决有关部分节录如下:

"i)The Refund Guarantee was an extremely important provision for the Buyers since it provided third party security from a bank in respect of a breach of contract by the Sellers and the latter's inability to meet their financial obligations. The four instalments of the purchase price payable prior to delivery all fell to be paid if and only if the Buyers had received the Refund Guarantee covering the relevant instalment.

ii)The contract itself was silent as to the date by which the Sellers should procure the Refund Guarantee.

iii)It would be unreasonable and uncommercial to expect the Buyers to bear the risk of losing the security of the Refund Guarantee by having to wait for an extension of the guarantee until shortly before its expiry, particularly because the Contract provided that the Refund Guarantee had to be in place before the payment of instalments which were advances under the contract repayable in the event of defined rights of cancellation.

iv)It was necessary to imply a term into the Contract as a matter of business necessity, because the Contract was silent and in order to protect the Buyers' security, that the Seller should fulfil its obligation to obtain the extension of the Refund Guarantee within a reasonable time, having regard to all the circumstances of the case. Such a term was 'precise and obvious'."

在这一方面,高院也确认了仲裁庭的裁决,虽然在另外一个方面推翻了仲裁员对中国船厂不利的裁决。即德国船东在6月29日开始了仲裁,这就自动令还款担保延期。所以,虽然中国船厂没有在合理时间内取得延期,这个违约变得无关紧要。

但笔者对仲裁庭与高院确认中国船厂违反了默示条文没有在合理时间取得延期,有很大保留。估计笔者如果是仲裁庭成员之一,很有可能做出不同意见。原因如下:

1. 既然仲裁庭不认为这是拒绝性违约,而是真正违约,在考虑证据方面应不一样,这在本章之3.7.3段有详论。如果是拒绝性违约,仲裁庭不应该考虑船厂事后披露的证据,如早在4月份就已经申请延期,并在6月29日已经取得延期。但对于真正违约,仲裁庭就应该将所有的证据都加以考虑,既然船厂证明早在4月份已经申请延期并且确实在还款担保到期前取得延期,就不应该再凭空认定合理时间是6月16日。毕竟合理本身就是十分有弹性的词,每个人都有自己认为的合理。这样,事实证明还款担保即使取得延期,就没有理由再强加其他主观认为合理的时间。

2. 更重要的是,笔者认为这一判法与其他先例不一样,特别是国际货物买卖的信用证。如果造船合约中还款担保对船东十分重要,信用证对卖方的重要性只会有过之而无不及。针对买方什么时候需要开出信用证,有很多著名的先例,但笔者没有看到在这个案件中被引用。在杨大明的《国际货物买卖》一书第十章之1.4.5段有介绍许多有关的先例，针对明示条文要求开出信用证的时间（这纯粹是解释的问题）与没有明示的情况下法律默示的时间。笔者只节录《Benjamin's Sale of Goods》（第9版，2014年）一书之23－059段如下："**Conclusion.** The authorities provide a measure of guidance on the inference to be drawn in cases of sales of goods to be shipped on a date to be determined during a future shipment period. Where the seller controls the precise shipment datem the credit must be open no later than the commerncement of the shipment period. Although there is some support for a requirement that the credit be open a reasonable time beforehand, the resultant uncertainty recognized by Diplock J., albeit in a different context, militates strongly against such a rule. It is, therefore, suggested that, **in the absence of contrary intention, the appropriate inference to be drawn from the provision for shipment on a date controlled by the seller within a prescribed shipment period is that the credit should be open by the commencement of that period.** Where the buyer controls the precise shipment date, it is difficult to formulate a default rule by reference to a reasonable time before the relevant date without introducing undersirable uncertainty. The case law accordingly favours a fixed date rule, the date being the commencement of the shipment period. There appears to be no reason, however, why the buyer should be placed in repudiatory breach by failing to provide the seller with assurance of payment by a date that has no sensible connection with the timetable for contractual performance."（加黑部分是笔者的强调）

9.8　先例之八：Downing v. Al Tameer Establishment & Anor

众所周知，在独立原则（separation principle）下，仲裁协议是与主合约分开的独立合约，即使仲裁协议通常只是主合约针对争议解决的条件。在这个说法下，主合约的适用法不代表也是仲裁协议的适用法，虽然这是在考虑仲裁协议的适用法时会有影响：Deutsche Schachtbau v. Shell International Petroleum Co. Ltd.（1990）1 AC 295；Naviera Amazonica Peruana SA v. Cia Internacional de Seguros del Peru（1988）1 Lloyd's Rep. 116（CA）等先例。这些课题都在笔者《仲裁法——从1996年英国仲裁法到国际商务仲裁》第二章有详论。

因此，主合约发生拒绝性违约或违约/毁约（repudiatory breach）并被对方接受，应该不会影响独立的仲裁协议有效性。合约方仍要根据仲裁协议的要求，解决双方之间的争议，即由仲裁庭裁定违约/毁约是否成立。在一定程度上，这类似本书第二章第8段介绍的可分开（severable 或 divisible）合约，即使发生违约/毁约的争议（也包括如否受阻的争议），也只影响部分合约，而不会令整个合约被终止。但根据Downing v. Al Tameer Establishment & Anor（2002）EWCA Civ 721先例，这个说法看来不一定准确。

在该先例中，原告（估计是个美国人）发明了一款油水分离器并取得专利，但由于缺乏资金，无法商业化，包括打开市场与大量生产。在寻找资金支持的过程中，他认识了一位来自沙特阿拉伯的有钱人。原告与这个有钱人的公司(被告)订立了一个五五分的联营合约,合约的适用法是英国法。合约另有一条仲裁条文,但看来拟定得不太完善,没有提到仲裁地在哪里。订立合约后不久,被告在不同机构安排对该油水分离器做出了检验,但结果不尽如人意。被告于是后悔与原告订立了合约并且否认双方存在合约关系。原告委任了一个美国律师向被告施压,而被告也委任了自己的律师,并在与原告律师的通信中几度否认双方存在合约关系。其中被告律师在1995年6月22日的电文中说:"... we have made it perfectedly clear in the past that our clients do not accept that they have or have had at any time any contractual relationship with you. Theyhave no intentionofdealing with you andyou should consider this matter closed."

1996年7月24日,被告律师再次回复说:"... Your client has asserted on a number of occasions that our client is in breach of contract. We have pointed out to Mr Downing that we do not share his view. Indeed, we do not consider that our client has any contractual relationship with your client. We do not have instructions to accept service of proceedings nor do we have instructions to make any settlement proposals to you ... Any proceedings will be vigorously defended and our client would likely pursue your client for the not insubstantial expenses it has been put to in dealing with your client's claims in the past and present."

最后在1997年2月13日,被告律师回复说:"Our clients deny any contractual relationship between them and your client. If there had been such a contractual relationship it would appear that your client would have committed a fundamental and repudiatory breach some years ago."

1997年2月17日,原告在英国法院做出告票(writ)并送达沙特阿拉伯的被告。被告委任英国律师,并根据1996年《仲裁法》之section 9要求法院中止诉讼程序。而原告做出的抗辩则是原告已经接受了被告对仲裁协议的违约/毁约,仲裁协议被终止。一审法庭与上诉庭都支持原告的地位,确认被告律师在1995年6月22日与1996年7月24日的两封信构成对仲裁协议的拒绝性违约。而原告在2月17日做出告票并附上申索起诉书(statement of claim)属于以行动接受了被告的违约/毁约。

上诉庭的Potter大法官说:"That being so, in our view the judge was right to hold that the letter of 22 June 1995 amounted to a repudiatory breach of the agreement to arbitrate. The letter was written against the background of a scrupulous effort by the claimant to rely upon and implement Clause 13 of the contract in his letters of 29 November 1994 and 14 December 1994. In the latter, he had sought to set arbitration proceedings in motion by inviting the defendants to submit their choice of arbitrators, which request had been ignored. The question was taken up again by the U. S. lawyers in their letter of January 1995 but apparently ignored save that by a 'missing' telefax it appears that a point was taken that there was no agreement with the claimant: see the first paragraph of his solicitors' letter of 16 February 1995 which, by its second paragraph, again relied on Clause 13. That letter too was ignored. Finally, the claimant, on 15 June 1995, again expressly requested the defendants to co – operate by putting forward the names of arbitrators, only to receive a response denying any contractual relationship and stating in unqualified terms that the defendants 'have no intention of dealing with you further' (i. e. in relation to their obligation to arbitrate)."

在笔者看来,该先例的危险之处是被告律师在 1995 年 6 月 22 日与 1996 年 7 月 24 日的两封信中根本没有提到仲裁协议,只针对了主合约的履行。所以,如果最后判双方存在合约关系,判被告违约/毁约没有问题,但如果同时说被告对仲裁协议违约/毁约,似乎是太轻易就否定了仲裁协议。相比之下,很多言行是比这两封信件更能说明构成了对仲裁协议的违约/毁约。例如,原告委任了仲裁员并向被告做出仲裁通知,但被告坚持双方没有仲裁协议并拒绝委任仲裁员。被告甚至可能向仲裁机构写信否认有仲裁条文,而仲裁机构往往回复说这是仲裁庭管辖权的问题,留待将来由仲裁庭裁定,目前不影响仲裁庭的组成。

这对中国公司危险的地方在于,中国公司在国际仲裁中做被告的机会远大于做原告的机会,而该先例的回复也经常发生,这样就很容易被精明的外国公司说是对仲裁协议违约/毁约。当然绝大部分情况下对方不会接受,因为在《纽约公约》下,针对中国公司的仲裁裁决书比法院判决更容易在中国被执行。但会有情况是与中国公司的合约中的仲裁条文对外国公司不利,如在中国仲裁机构仲裁。加上该中国公司在英国有资产或分公司,不用担心执行,那么外国公司就可能用这一招取巧,在英国法院开始诉讼。

仲裁协议不是很容易构成违约/毁约,可以让对方接受并终止。在 BDMS Ltd. v. Rafael Advanced Defence Systems (2014) 1 Lloyd's Rep. 576 先例与 Trunk Flooring Ltd. v. HSBC Asset Finance (UK) Ltd. (2015) NICA 68 先例,都涉及被告拒绝支付国际商会(ICC)仲裁中被要求摊分的预付款。根据 ICC 仲裁规则,原告可以选择代为支付(然后通过仲裁庭的中间裁决将这笔钱要回来)并继续推进仲裁。而如果原告不愿意代为支付,根据 ICC 仲裁规则,就会被视为撤回仲裁请求。如果之后原告想重新索赔损失,可以开始另一个 ICC 仲裁。总之,这两个先例中法院都判拒绝支付预付款充其量只是仲裁程序上不合作,并非是对仲裁协议的违约/毁约。而且原告有上述所讲的解决办法(代为支付),所以被告的"违约"也不能说是在导致原告失去了整个合约的利益(deprives the innocent party the whole benefit of the contract)或是达到了合约的根基(it goes so much to the root of the contract)或是令仲裁协议不可能继续履行(makes further commercial performance of the contract impossible)。

10. 接受违约/毁约后无辜方无须证明其愿意与能够履行以及损失计算

这方面可先看权威书籍《Chitty on Contracts》(第32版,2015年)之24－024段:"If the breach is accepted, the innocent party is relieved from further performance of his obligations under the contract.[156] He is likewise relieved from proving, in any action against the party in default, that he was ready and willing at the date of the renunciation to perform the contract in accordance with its terms.[157] It follows that it is no defence to liability in such an action to show that, if the contract had not been renounced, the innocent party would not at the time fixed for performance have been able to perform it,[158] although proof of such inability to perform might possibly be material in the assessment of damages.[159]"

这段话在近期的 Acre 1127 Ltd. v. De Montfort Fine Art (2011) EWCA Civ 87 与 Flame SA v. Glory Wealth Shipping Pte Ltd. (2013) 2 Lloyd's Rep. 653 先例都有被引用,并且被法院认同。Teare 大法官是这样说:"I was not referred to this decision (这是指 Acre 1127 Ltd. v. De Montfort Fine Art 先例) but it appears to be relevant. Tomlinson LJ (with whom Jackson and Maurice Kay LJJ agreed) referred to Chitty on Contracts, 30th ed (2008), para 24－023 which stated that following an accepted repudiation which relieved the innocent party from the need to prove his readiness and willingness to perform his obligations **it could not be a defence to liability to show that if the contract had not been renounced the innocent party would not have been able to perform his obligations, but added that 'proof of such inability to perform might possibly be material in the assessment of damages'.** Tomlinson LJ said at para 52 that an inability to perform must be material to the assessment of damages and that **loss of profit cannot be recovered where it is posited on performance which would not have taken place.**"(加黑部分是笔者的强调)

---

〔156〕 如果无辜方接受了违约/毁约,他就再也不需要履行合约剩下的责任。同样,违约方也不需要履行合约余下的责任,但这只是指首要合约责任,取而代之的就是次要的合约责任,即要以金钱赔偿使无辜方回复到合约被履行的地位。关于首要合约责任与次要合约责任,可看杨良宜的《损失赔偿与救济》一书第十一章之1.1段。

〔157〕 无辜方与违约方的诉讼中也再也不需要证明他是能够与愿意履行合约剩下的责任。

〔158〕 这表示违约方不能在责任方面提出一个抗辩就是无辜方自己也没有能力履行合约的责任。

〔159〕 但这方面的证明会对损失的计算重要,即违约方面对无辜方的部分或全部损失可以提出抗辩是无辜方自己没有能力履行合约并赚取所谓的损失。

10.1　接受违约/毁约后无辜方无须证明其愿意与能够履行

这个问题看起来像是责任方面的问题，但实际上在本章之 7.5 段介绍过，如果合约双方有相继违约/毁约的行为，决定谁是无辜方与谁是违约方，还是如"击剑"(swordplay)，以谁先接受对方的违约/毁约为准。即使违约方能够证明无辜方自己也无法履行合约（不论是由于其违约/毁约或是根据合约条文），无辜方与违约方也不会互换，但这个问题是无辜方在接受违约/毁约并终止合约后能否再索赔损失的大前提。这可以通过著名的 The "Mihalis Angelos" (1970) 2 Lloyd's Rep. 43 先例帮助理解。简单的案情在本章之 5.2 段已经介绍，上诉庭判是船东在租约承诺"预计在 7 月 1 日备妥可以装货"(expect ready to load) 是条件条文，船东的违约是构成了违约/毁约。承租人可以根据这一合法理由接受并终止租约，虽然承租人在当时是以错误的理由不可抗力终止租约。但抛开这一点，在该先例还有替代争议是承租人可否以船东不可能赶上在不同条文的销约期(cancelling date)为由终止租约。上诉庭的多数意见判是不可以，合约条文应该解释为直到船舶在销约期后抵达，承租人才需要行使其"选择权"(option)保留或终止租约。承租人不能以船东预期违约为由提前行使其选择权去终止合约。也就是说，在这个替代争议中，承租人提前终止租约是违约/毁约，船东事实上无法在销约期前抵达装港不影响船东是无辜方。但在船东索赔损失时，由于船东无法在销约期前抵达而被承租人取消是注定会发生(predestined to happen)，所以船东实质上不会有任何损失，满足不了索赔任何损失的大前提。Megaw 大法官说："If the contractual rights which he has lost were capable by the terms of the contract of being rendered either less valuable or valueless in certain events, and if it can be shown that those events were at the date of acceptance of the repudiation, predestined to happen, then in my view the damages which he can recover are not more than the true value, if any, of the rights which he has lost, having regard to those predestined events."

在 Marplace (512) Ltd. v. Chaffe Street (2006) EWHC 1919 (Ch) 先例，Lawrence Collins 大法官总结说："Where a guilty party has repudiated a bilateral contract, the innocent party is relieved from proving that it was ready and willing to perform the contract in accordance with its terms. . . . this presumption would not (or be very unlikely to) assist ... where: (1) The principle is subject to an exception where, by something that is predestined to happen at the time of the guilty party's breach, the innocent party could not perform its obligations ... (2) Even where the principle operates, the innocent party must prove its loss."

当然这个注定会发生的事情（一般距离真正会发生的时间很近）很难证明，并非民事诉讼中的"平衡的可能性"(balance of probability)。正如 Denning 勋爵所说，这个注定会发生的事情是要"beyond doubt"，所以这种案件也不太多，违约方一般指称无辜方事后/履行会有很多变数（特别是远期的）是不足够的。即使违约方证明发生成数颇高,但这就是不肯定。对其加以考虑,是以“不肯定替代肯定”(substituting a chance for a certainty)。而肯定的是,违约方的违约/毁约导致了无辜方眼前的损失。

但也不是没有这种注定会发生案件,这在笔者的《损失赔偿与救济》一书第十章有介绍,这里不再重复,只讲一个笔者经历过的仲裁案件。该案件涉及期租合约下,船舶被承租人转租去欧洲装一票很清洁的货物。船舶在装港被分承租人以船舱不清洁为由终止分租约,导致承租人也借机同时终止与船东的期租合约。当时航运市场下跌,承租人想要脱身可以理解。但承租人是否合法就有很大的疑问,毕竟分租约的航次租约明确说明是装这一票很清洁的货物,有关条文与期租合约很不相同。期租合约是根据 NYPE 46 标准格式,条文只规定船舶需要在交船与事后的维修保养去装载一般货物(Vessel on her delivery to be ready to receive cargo with clean - swept holds),并没有承诺可以装这一票很清洁的货物,所以承租人在欧洲装港以船舱有锈、不能装载一票很清洁的货物为由终止租约,并不合法。至于船舱有锈,需要维修保养才能继续营运,充其量只是允许停租,而不是终止租约。但责任虽然明确,船东向承租人索赔的预期损失(剩下的租期租约租金与市场价格的差价)面对了“注定会发生”的抗辩。承租人的争议是船东不能满足索赔损失的大前提,因为在该欧洲装港进行维修保养清除船舱的锈迹,即使是达到一般货物的清洁程度,需要岸上工人工作 14 日以上的时间。而租约中有一条规定停租 14 日以上,承租人就可以终止租约。换言之,就像 The “Mihalis Angelos”先例一样,租约是注定会被取消的。但这一抗辩最后没有被仲裁庭接受,因为船东也举了很多其他假设证明这并非是注定。例如,可以不计成本地加班加点在 14 日内完成工作,或是只完成暂时性工作足够满足一般货物,或是开航到邻近工人更多的欧洲港口完成工作之后再返回装港等。

10.2　接受违约/毁约后无辜方针对损失计算必须证明其愿意与能够履行

上一段貌似与这一段很接近,甚至看来是有点矛盾。即使无辜方满足了可以索赔损失的大前提,到了真正核算部分或全部的损失(assessment of damages)时,无辜方还是必须根据平衡的可能性去证明其愿意与能够履行。毕竟无辜方如果不能履行,他就不会有真正损失,或者损失与违约方的违约/毁约没有因果关系。这一要求是考虑到两个原则:一是无辜方必须能够根据平衡的可能性证明其损失的基本原则,二是在 The “Golden Victory”(2007) 2 Lloyd’s Rep. 164 先例〔160〕后,是越来越强调“赔偿原则”(compensatory principle)。

这一课题涉及很多先例,甚至大家有一些不同的说法。在近期的 Flame SA v. Glory Wealth Shipping Pte Ltd. (2013) 2 Lloyd’s Rep. 653 先例中,Teare 大法官对以前的先例进行了总结与协调,并得出英国法律在这方面的结论。在该先例中,Flame 是承租人,他与作为二船东的 Glory Wealth 订立了包运合约,在 2009 年到 2011 年的

---

〔160〕 关于 The “Golden Victory”(2007) 2 Lloyd’s Rep. 164 先例,杨良宜的《损失赔偿与救济》一书第十三章第 6 段有详细针对。

三年之间运6个航次的煤炭。Flame履行了开始的4个航次,但第五与第六个航次承租人就没有宣告装货期限(laycan)。这导致了Glory Wealth也无法派船去履行。Glory Wealth指称Flame拒绝宣告装货期限是违约/毁约,并且接受去终止包运合约与索赔损失。Flame的抗辩主要不是在责任,而是在损失方面。Flame指称在"金融海啸"后市场暴跌,导致很多船舶经营人(operator)的经济状况迅速变坏,包括Glory Wealth。由于Glory Wealth是二船东,他需要在航运市场租船去履行,但在履行第五与第六个航次的当时,Glory Wealth在租船市场已经名誉扫地,船东一般不愿意租船给这种承租人。所以,Flame指称Glory Wealth根据平衡的可能性是不可能履行这两个航次,所以不会蒙受真正损失,而只能索赔"名义损失"(nominal damages)。

作为无辜方的Glory Wealth在法院做出的反驳只是一个法律问题(至于Glory Wealth能否在航运市场租到船舶是事实问题,这是仲裁庭的决定),即无辜方在违约/毁约下除了终止合约外还要索赔损失,是否需要证明他能够履行将来的合约责任?该先例就表示Glory Wealth必须证明如果Flame宣告了装货期限,他能够及时去航运市场租船履行包运合约。这也证明由于Flame没有宣告违约/毁约,Glory Wealth就不能赚取第五与第六个航次的运费。

仲裁庭接受Glory Wealth的说法,判在无辜方接受违约/毁约后,违约方不能要求无辜方证明他将来可以履行并因此有损失:"the 'contract - breaker' must prove that at the time when the innocent party accepted the repudiatory breaches, said innocent party was already in breach. The tribunal found that it was not open to the 'contract - breaker' to allege that the innocent party still bore the burden of proving its loss on the balance of probabilities if it had accepted the repudiatory breach of the 'contract - breaker'."

但这一法律问题的裁定被上诉至高院,并且被Teare大法官推翻。双方都对这一法律问题做出了全面的争辩,以及讨论了之前的有关先例,包括Braithwaite v. Foreign Hardwood Co. Ltd.(1905) 2 KB 543; Taylor v. Oakes Roncoroni & Co.(1922) 27 Com Cas 261; British & Beningtons Ltd. v. North Western Cachar Tea Co. Ltd.(1922) 13 Lloyd's Rep. 67; Brett v. Schneideman Bros Ltd.(1923) NZLR 938; Continental Contractors Ltd. v. Medway Oil and Storage Co. Ltd.(1925) 23 Lloyd's Rep. 124; YP Barley Producers Ltd. v. EC Robertson Pty Ltd.(1927) VLR 194; Esmail v. J Rosenthal & Sons Ltd.(1964) 2 Lloyd's Rep. 447; The "Mihalis Angelos"(1970) 2 Lloyd's Rep. 43; Gill & Duffus SA v. Berger & Co. Inc.(No 2)(1984) 1 Lloyd's Rep. 227; The "Simona"(1986) 1 Lloyd's Rep. 171(QB); North Sea Energy Holdings NV v. Petroleum Authority of Thailand(1997) 2 Lloyd's Rep. 418; Chiemgauer Membran und Zeltbau GmbH v. New Millennium Experience Co. Ltd.(2002) BPIR 42与重要的贵族院先例The "Golden Victory"。

在Flame SA v. Glory Wealth Shipping Pte Ltd. 先例,承租人的主要争辩可节录如下:"The importance(The 'Golden Victory'的贵族院先例)which the majority attributed to the compensatory principle . . . is relied on by Mr Hancock(Flame 代表大律师)in this case. He says that if the COA had not been repudiated by the charterers(Flame)and had remained on foot, it would have been terminated by the charterers on the grounds that the owners(Glory Wealth)were, by reason of their financial difficulties, unable to provide any vessels to carry the charterers' cargoes and so no freight would have been earned by the owners. The compensatory principle requires that to be taken into account when deciding whether the owners have proved that they have sustained substantial damages as a result of the charterers' repudiation of the COA."

这被 Teare 大法官接受并推翻仲裁庭的裁决,说:

"Since the court is concerned with a question as to the assessment of damages the court must have regard to the compensatory principle which underlies the assessment of damages. For the reasons expressed earlier in this judgment that principle, illustrated by The Mihalis Angelos and The Golden Victory, supports Mr Hancock's submission. . . However, the importance ascribed to the compensatory principle in The Golden Victory is a powerful argument for applying it in the present case.

The assessment of loss necessarily requires a hypothetical exercise to be undertaken, namely, an assessment of what would have happened had there been no repudiation. That enables the true value of the rights which have been lost to be assessed. The innocent party is claiming damages and therefore the burden lies on that party to prove its loss. That requires it to show that, had there been no repudiation, **the innocent party would have been able to perform his obligations under the contract. If the court were to assume that the innocent party would have been able to perform, rather than to consider what was likely to have happened in the event that there had been no repudiation, the court might well put the innocent party in a better position than he would have been in had the contract been performed.** The assessment of damages does require an assumption to be made, . . . When assessing what the innocent party would have earned had the contract been performed the court must assume that the party in breach has performed his obligations."(加黑部分是笔者的强调)

Teare 大法官上述的第二段就说出了他对英国法律的结论。核算损失需要假设如果没有这个违约/毁约会发生怎样的情况,这样才可以核算出无辜方失去的权利的真正价值。无辜方现在提出索赔,当然就有责任证明其损失。这需要显示如果没有发生违约/毁约,无辜方就可以履行其合约责任。如果法院只是假设无辜方可以履行,而不考虑如果没有发生违约/毁约下无辜方是否真正可以履行,就有可能使无辜方处于比合约被履行更有利的地位。所以当计算损失需要做出假设时,要假设如果违约方履行了其合约责任,无辜方可以赚取的约因/对价。

另举一个例子是本章第 3 段提到的有关中国药厂的仲裁,中国药厂在责任方面败诉,但中国药厂委任了水平很高的律师与十分有说服力的医疗设备专家证人,最后成功说服仲裁庭合约履行下去,欧洲公司也赚不到钱。所以,欧洲公司索赔的一笔很大金额的"预期损失"(expectation loss)与"机会损失"(loss of chance)[161] 被驳回(dismiss),只成功向中国公司取回一笔相对低很多的金额作为"依赖损失"(reliance loss),[162] 也就是欧洲公司花费在这一合作协议的费用。

10.3 无辜方计算损失的一天

有关计算损失的一天在杨良宜的《损失赔偿与救济》一书第十三章已经有详细的针对。真正违约的损失相对容易,无论无辜方是否接受,以哪一天的损失为准的争议不大。但在预期违约(anticipatory breach)中就会比较麻烦,因为如果无辜方不接受违约/毁约,合约就继续存在,也不涉及损失计算的问题。但不接受违约/毁约就会有无辜方是否单方面可以履行、[163] 有否合法利益[164] 等的问题,这会影响损失的计算。而如果无辜方最终选择接受违约/毁约,就会影响是以哪一天的损失为准。是以违约方做出预期违约言行的一天计算损失?以无辜方接受并终止合约的一天计算损失?以根据合约规定将来应该履行的一天计算损失?还是以这一段时间内对违约方最有利的一天计算损失?这可首先节录权威书籍《Chitty on Contracts》(第 32 版,2015 年)一书之 26 - 088 段,如下:

"... The general rule is that damages for breach of contract should be assessed as at the date when the cause of action arose, viz the date of the breach (which rule usually applies where substitute performance is readily available in the market): 'But this is not an absolute rule: if to follow it would give rise to injustice the court has power to fix such other date as may be appropriate in the circumstances.'[165]

Two departures from this principle require special note. First, if one party commits an anticipatory repudiation of the contract and the other elects to accept the repudiation and terminate the contract, the innocent party comes under a duty to mitigate at the date of termination.[166] Secondly, if, after a breach, the innocent party reasonably continues to treat the contract as in force, damages may be assessed as at the later date 'when (otherwise than by his default) the contract is lost', viz when performance becomes im-

---

[161] 参见杨良宜的《损失赔偿与救济》一书第六章第 4 - 7 段。

[162] 参见杨良宜的《损失赔偿与救济》一书第二章第 4 段。

[163] 参见本章之 8.4.1 段。

[164] 参见本章之 8.4.2 段。

[165] 损失一般应以违约一天计算(尤其是在相关标的有市场价格的情况下),但这也不是绝对的规则,为了公平,在适当的情况下,法院有权决定其他时间去计算损失。

[166] 第一种情况是违约方预期违约,无辜方选择接受并终止合约,无辜方从合约被终止的一天开始有减少损失的责任。

possible, or when innocent party terminates the contract.[167]... The assessment of damages by the cost of substitute performance or by the cost of a reasonable attempt to mitigate are other situations where the time for assessment may be postponed after the date of breach.[168]"

以国际货物买卖为例,因为这是最有代表性、发生争议最多与有最多先例的商业合约类型。国际货物买卖主要是指商品(如石油、矿砂、散粮、煤炭、食糖、钢材等)的CIF与FOB买卖。这种合约类型在全球订立的数目最多,并且因为操作比一般的货物买卖困难(包括国际性与和复杂的航运、保险息息相关),一旦发生争议就往往涉及很复杂的事实与法律问题。加上市场价格波动很大,每一天的价格都可能天差地别,所以往往会出现买卖双方订立合约后的第二天,就已经是一方千方百计想从合约中脱身,而另一方则拼命要保住合约的情况。因此,经常会出现违约/毁约并导致合约的终止,而针对损失计算,以哪一天的市场价格为准就显得十分关键。

以上所讲可先节录《Chitty on Contracts》(第32版,2015年)一书之26-162段,说:"**Anticipatory breach**. The measure of damages available when there has been an anticipatory breach by either the buyer or the seller was considered above. The innocent party may refuse to accept the repudiation and in that case the damages will normally be measured by the difference between the contract price and the market price at the date the goods should have been delivered or accepted. That is also the prima facie measure if the innocent party accepts the repudiation; however, he comesunder a duty to mitigate his loss and if he should have mitigated by making a substitute transaction, his damages will be measured by the market price at the date on which he should have made that transaction.[169]"

首先针对买方的预期违约拒绝接受货物,在《Chitty on Contracts》(第32版,2015年)一书之26-103段说:"... If the seller accepts the buyer's anticipatory repudiation, he is thereupon obliged to take reasonable steps to mitigate his loss; but if the seller does not accept the anticipatory repudiation he does not have any duty to mitigate unless and

---

[167] 第二种情况是如果在违约方违约/毁约后,无辜方合理确认合约继续存在,损失可能会以之后合约履行变为不可能(通常就是指没有违约方的合作就履行不下去)的一天,或是无辜方选择终止合约(看来是要持续性违约或有新的违约)的一天。

[168] 根据无辜方在违约/毁约后找到的替代履行所付出的代价与/或合理减少损失所付出的代价计算损失,也属于可以违约/毁约后被视为合适的一天进行损失计算的情况。

[169] 如果无辜方(无论卖方或买方)拒绝接受违约方的违约/毁约,则损失一般是根据合约规定应该交付(或接受)货物的一天的市场价格与合约价格之间的差价计算。这也是无辜方接受违约方的违约/毁约后计算损失的表面规则,但是因为无辜方这时存在减少损失的责任,所以,如果他应该在市场上寻找替代生意(如无辜方的卖方转售其手中被拒的货物,而无辜方的买方去市场买入替代货物)以减少损失,损失就以他应该这么做的一天的市场价格计算。

until the buyer actually commits a breach of contract. After the innocent party has terminated the contract, however the rules on mitigation will apply to any claim for damages he makes; [170] ... Moreover, once there has been an actual breach the rule on mitigation may in effect require the innocent party to terminate: if he waits an unreasonably long time before going into the market to make a replacement purchase or sale, he may find that the damages will be assessed by the date at which he should have acted. This may result in him receiving less than his full loss. [171]"

另在44 - 380与44 - 381段有更详细的针对,说:

"**Anticipatory breach by the buyer: repudiation accepted.** Where the buyer commits an anticipatory breach by repudiating, before the date fixed for delivery, his obligation to take delivery of the goods the seller has an option: he may either accept the repudiation and so treat it forthwith as a breach, or he may continue to treat the contract as binding and thus not accept the repudiation as a breach. [172] If the seller accepts the buyer's anticipatory repudiation, he may sue immediately for damages for breach of contract: but in those situations in which there is an available market for the goods, the relevant date for ascertaining the market price remains prima facie (and subject to any requirement of mitigation) the date fixed for delivery, since that is when the contract ought to be performed. [173] If the action is heard before the date for delivery arrives, the court should attempt to estimate what the market price is likely to be at that future date. [174] But if the seller does accept the buyer's anticipatory repudiation, he is forthwith subject to the rules on mitigation and must take reasonable steps to minimise his loss. Where the seller should have mitigated by reselling, the relevant market price is that existing at the date he ought reasonably to have resold, not that at the date of the repudiation, nor that at the

---

〔170〕 如果卖方接受了买方的违约/毁约,就有了减少损失的责任。而如果卖方没有接受,也就代表买卖合约仍然存在,他没有任何责任减少损失,直到买方真正违约并让卖方再也无法履行下去。

〔171〕 另外如果买方真正违约,减少损失的原则会在事实上要求无辜方的卖方尽快接受:如果他等待太久,过了合理的时间才在市场上进行替代的买卖去减少损失,他可能会面临的情况是损失以他应该行动的一天计算,如果有关的市场持续下跌就无法取回全部损失。

〔172〕 如果买方在合约规定的交货日期之前违约/毁约,拒绝接受货物,卖方可以选择接受违约/毁约并终止合约,或者不接受并确认合约继续存在。

〔173〕 如果卖方接受了买方的违约/毁约,他可以马上向买方索赔损失。但如果涉及市场规则适用,计算损失的一天是合约规定要履行的一天(合约规定的交货日期),因为在那一天买方还是持续不接受有关货物就构成了真正违约,而卖方也无法再履行下去。但这只是表面规则,要与减少损失的责任相互协调。

〔174〕 如果诉讼进行的很快,在合约规定的交货日期前就审理,就表示法院或仲裁庭需要估计将来在该日的市场价格会是多少以计算损失,这往往需要依靠专家意见证据。

date when the repudiation is accepted.〔175〕

Repudiation not accepted. If the seller does not accept the buyer's anticipatory repudiation, he may continue to treat the contract as binding on both himself and the buyer, and wait until the date fixed for delivery before he tenders the goods: if the buyer then fails to accept the goods, the seller thereupon should mitigate his loss by taking reasonable steps (viz in normal circumstances by reselling forthwith).〔176〕 Where there is an available market for the goods, the relevant market price will be that at the date fixed for delivery: if the seller did not accept the buyer's anticipatory repudiation, a higher or a lower market price at the date of the repudiation, or at any date during the period up to the date fixed for delivery, is irrelevant, because the rules of mitigation do not apply until the date of the actual breach.〔177〕 Of course, during the interval the contract is kept alive for the benefit of both parties: the buyer may change his mind and accept the goods when tendered; or the seller may decide to accept the repudiation (before it has been retracted by the buyer) whereupon the rules of mitigation will forthwith apply to the seller; or the obligations of the parties may be determined by the occurrence of a frustrating event; or the buyer may exercise a right under the contract to cancel it.〔178〕"

而针对卖方拒绝交货或付运的情况,在44－393与44－394段有详细针对,说:

"**The seller's anticipatory repudiation: repudiation accepted.** Where the seller, before the date fixed for delivery of the goods, repudiates his liability under the contract, the buyer has a choice. If he treats the repudiation as an immediate breach of contract, the relevant date for taking the market price is, prima facie, and subject to the rules on mitigation, the due date for delivery-not the date of the repudiation nor the date of the

〔175〕 但一旦接受了违约/毁约并终止合约,无辜方的卖方就有了减少损失的责任。如果卖方应该转卖手上被拒的货物去减少损失,就应该以他应该转卖一天的市场价格为准,而并非买方违约/毁约的一天或卖方接受的一天的市场价格。

〔176〕 如果卖方没有接受买方的违约/毁约而确认合约继续存在,而等到合约规定交货的一天(如CIF买卖,货物抵达卸港待卸的一天),买方仍拒绝接受货物,卖方就应该采取合理措施减少损失(一般就是转卖)。

〔177〕 如果有市场存在,应以合约规定交货的一天的市场价格计算损失。因为如果卖方没有接受买方的违约毁约,合约继续存在,则在买方真正违约之前,卖方都不存在减少损失的责任,所以,从违约方违约/毁约的一天到合约规定交货的一天期间内的市场价格波动都无关。

〔178〕 当然在这段时间内,合约对双方来说都继续存在:买方可以对较早的预期违约回心转意接受货物(毕竟下跌的市场会有回转的迹象);卖方可以在买方回心转意之前选择接受违约/毁约,在这种情况下,卖方就有减少损失的责任;合约存在的期间可能因为受阻而终止或可能出现一个合法理由令买方可以终止合约。

buyer's acceptance of the repudiation.[179] If the buyer's claim is heard before the date for delivery arrives, the court must attempt to estimate what the market price is likely to be at that date, e. g. by taking into account the current trend of the market.[180] However, under the rules of mitigation the buyer must, following his acceptance of the repudiation, take reasonable steps to reduce his loss, e. g. by buying substitute goods inthe market.[181] If the seller fails to produce evidence to show that the buyer ought reasonably to have bought substitute goods at a time earlier than the date fixed for delivery under the contract, the buyer's damages should be calculated with reference to the market price at that date. But where the seller can prove that the buyer should have mitigated his loss by repurchasing before the due date, the relevant market price is that existing at the date the buyer ought reasobably to have bought the substitute goods.[182] However, if the buyer accepts the anticipatory repudiation but does not in fact mitigate by repurchasing in the market when he ought reasonably to have done so, the market price may fall betweenthat date and the date fixed for delivery: it has been held that in these circumstances the buyer's damages will be assessed by reference to the lower price at the later date.[183]

Repudiation not accepted. If the buyer chooses not to accept the seller's anticipatory repudiation, it is treated as a 'nullity' and the contract continues to bind both parties: the buyer will then await the date fixed for delivery, and the seller will commit a breach of contract only if he then fails to deliver. Thus, the seller may change his mind before the due date and (without breach of contract) fulfil his contractual obligation by delivering on that date; or the contract may be terminated without a breach by the seller, e. g. by the seller exercising a right under the contract to cancel it, or be discharge by frustra-

---

〔179〕 如果卖方在合约规定的交货日期之前违约/毁约,拒绝交付货物,买方可以选择接受违约/毁约并终止合约,或者不接受并确认合约继续存在。如果买方接受了卖方的违约/毁约,计算损失是以合约规定要交货的一天(如在 CIF 买卖,就是卖方在合约付运期最后的一天),而不是卖方违约/毁约的一天(提前告知买方他将不会交付货物),也不是买方接受的一天的市场价格。但这只是表面规则,要与减少损失的责任相互协调,如无辜方的买方在卖方违约/毁约的一天接受并终止合约,但在合约规定的交货的一天前就已经能够在市场买入替代货物去减少损失,损失计算就应该以该替代货物的价格为准。

〔180〕 如果诉讼进行的很快,在合约规定的交货日期前就审理,就表示法院或仲裁庭需要估计将来在该日的市场价格会是多少以计算损失,如考虑当时的市场趋势等,这往往需要依靠专家意见证据。

〔181〕 但一旦买方接受了卖方的违约/毁约,他就有减少损失的责任,如在市场上买入替代货物。

〔182〕 如果卖方无法证明买方应该合理在合约规定交货的一天之前买进替代货物,则买方的损失以合约规定交货的一天的市场价格计算。但如果卖方可以证明买方应该在合约规定的交货的一天前在市场上买入替代货物减少损失,则就以买方应该在市场上买入替代货物的一天的市场价格计算损失。

〔183〕 然而如果买方接受了卖方的违约/毁约,但没有在应该在市场上买入货物减少损失时这么做,而之后直到合约规定应该交货的一天市场持续下跌,则无辜方的买方的损失就应该以合约规定应该交货的一天的市场价格计算。

tion. The rules on mitigation do not apply to the buyer until the seller commits an actual breach, and thus the buyer's damages are assessed with reference to the market price at the date of the breach.[184]"

〔184〕 如果买方不接受卖方的违约/毁约，则这个违约/毁约就是"空的"或是"没有发生过的镜花水月"，合约继续对双方有效。买方会等到合约规定应该交货的最后一天，如果卖方依然拒绝交货，则买方也就无法继续坚持卖方履约，卖方也就是真正违约。因此，在这段时间内，卖方可以回心转意，合约也可能因为与卖方违约无关的原因被终止（合约受阻或卖方有了一个合法理由可以终止合约）。卖方真正违约前，买方都没有减少损失的责任，买方的损失应该以真正违约一天的市场价格计算。

第二章 合约受阻

“合约受阻”(frustration)的课题在杨良宜《合约的解释:规则与应用》一书第十三章之1.1段有提到,但内容很少,主要目的是引出对不可抗力条文(*force majeure* clause)的介绍,所以在本章会进行全面的介绍。

1. 受阻与共同错误的密切关系

合约受阻与“共同错误”(common mistake or mutual mistake)[1]是一脉相承的概念,正如Phillips勋爵在The“Great Peace”(2002) 2 Lloyd's Rep. 653先例所说:“At the time of Bell v. Lever Bros Ltd. (1932) AC 161 the law of frustration and common mistake had advanced hand in hand on the foundation of a common principle. Thereafter frustration proved a more fertile ground for the development of this principle than common mistake, and consideration of the development of the law of frustration assists with the analysis of the law of common mistake.”

关于这两个说法的相似性,也可以见Phillips勋爵在The“Great Peace”先例提出

---

〔1〕 有关订约时双方共同错误(common mistake)或单方面错误(unilateral mistake)导致合约无效,在杨良宜《合约的解释:规则与应用》一书第三章之13.3段有详论,笔者在这里不再重复。在此只节录《Chitty on Contracts》(第32版,2015年)一书之3-001段:“**Type of mistake.** The doctrine of mistake in the law of contract deals with two rather different situations. In the first, there is some mistake or misunderstanding in the communications between the parties which prevents there being an effective agreement (for instance, if the parties misunderstand each other) or at least means that there is no agreement on the terms apparently stated (for instance, if one party in an offer states terms which the other party knows the first party does not intend, but nevertheless the other purports to accept). The first category of mistake which can generally be referred to as ‘mistake as to the terms or identity’, includes ‘mutual misunderstanding’, where each is mistaken as to the terms intended by the other, and ‘unilateral mistake’, where only one of the parties is mistaken, over the terms of the contract or the identity of the other party. In the second situation, the parties are agreed on the terms of the contract but have entered it under a shared and **fundamental misapprehension as to the facts** or the law. Cases in this category are now usually referred to as ‘common’ mistake, for normally **the mistake is legally relevant only if both parties have contracted as under some misapprehension.**”(最后两句加黑部分是笔者的强调)

的现代构成共同错误需要满足的五个要件,这与构成合约受阻的要件很类似:[2]"... the following elements must be present if common mistake is to avoid a contract: (i) there must be a common assumption as to the existence of a state of affairs; (ii) there must be no warranty by either party that that state of affairs exists; (iii) the non – existence of the state of affairs must not be attributable to the fault of either party; (iv) the non – existence of the state of affairs must render performance of the contract impossible; (v) the state of affairs may be the existence, or a vital attribute, of the consideration to be provided or circumstances which must subsist if performance of the contractual adventure is to be possible.[3]"

共同错误与合约受阻的主要区别是共同错误发生的时间是在订约前并会令合约自始无效(void *ab initio*),所以关系到的是合约构成(formation of contract)的问题。而合约受阻,也是本章节所要详论的,是发生在合约生效后的任何时间,并会令该完全有效与履行了部分(甚至是大部分)的合约自动终止,所以关系到的是合约履行(performance of contract)。

这以英皇加冕典礼取消导致的一连串先例为例。在本章多处提到的 Krell v. Henry (1903) 2 KB 740 先例,被判是合约受阻。但在 Griffith v. Brymer (1903) 19 TLR 434 先例的案情也涉及租用房间观看加冕典礼,但因为合约是在典礼取消的消息公布之后才订立,所以被判是因为对事实的共同错误而无效。

Phillips 勋爵在 The "Great Peace" 先例也说:"Circumstances where a contract is void as a result of common mistake are likely to be less common than instances of frustration ..."

根据报道出来的先例,合约受阻的先例确实远远多于共同错误。部分原因是上述提到的只有在十分有限的情况下才能适用共同错误的说法,因为法律是倾向于支持而不是毁掉表面看来有效的合约。笔者认为另一个更明显的原因是,共同错误的说法只涉及双方订立合约前相对较短的时间,尤其是在现代通讯技术十分发达的情况下,让双方对事实或法律有一个会令合约自始无效的共同错误不太可能。但合约受阻会涉及相对长得多的时间,如果在合约履行期间(可能长达几年甚至更长)的任何时间出现了严重的突发事件(supervening event),任何一方都可以争辩合约因为受阻而自动终止。

总结而言,笔者可以节录《Chitty on Contracts》(第 32 版,2015 年)一书之 23 – 002

[2] 参见本章第 7 段。

[3] 构成共同错误必须满足五个要件:(1)双方订约时共同假设有一个情况存在;(2)这一情况的存在并没有任何一方做出了保证;(3)这一情况其实并不存在,也并非是其中一方的过错所导致(如一栋房屋在交易成交前发生的火灾并非卖方疏忽或恶意造成);(4)不存在的情况导致合约无法履行;(5)这一情况是约因/对价的重要部分,或必须存在才能令有关合约的履行可以执行。

段所说:"**Frustration and mistake.** Although the doctrine of frustration has some affinity with common mistake, in that both doctrines are essentially concerned with the allocation of risk of an unforeseen event which makes contractual performance more onerous or even impossible, it is customary to treat the two doctrines separately on the ground that common mistake is concerned with a common misapprehension which was present at the date of entry into the contract, where frustration is solely concerned with events which occur after the date of formation of the contract."

共同错误的典型例子之一就是在双方不知道的情况下合约标的物灭失,如合约标的是一栋房屋,但双方在谈判后并马上要签约前,在双方不知道的情况下,该房屋被烧毁。显然双方稍后才订立的买卖合约中的房屋根本不再存在,合约自始无效。正如 Atkin 勋爵在 Bell v. Lever Bros Ltd.(1932)AC 161 先例中所说:"So the agreement of A and B to purchase a specific article is void if in fact the article had perished before the date of sale. In this case, though the parties in fact were agreed about the subject – matter, yet a consent is nullified. As codified in the Sale of Goods Act the contract is expressed to be void if the seller was in ignorance of the destruction of the specific chattel.〔4〕 I apprehend that if the seller with knowledge that a chattel was destroyed purported to sell it to a purchaser, the latter might sue for damages for non – delivery〔5〕 ..."

但如果同样的标的物(如房屋、船舶、飞机等)灭失的意外发生在买卖合约已经订立但卖方尚未交货之时,就属于受阻,合约会因为标的物的灭失而自动终止,卖方不需要继续履行合约或承担违约的赔偿责任。

除了合约标的物实质上(physically)灭失导致合约无效(如果是共同错误)或不可能履行(如果是合约受阻),还有情况是法律上(legally)不可能。如在 Oom v. Bruce(1810)12 East 225 先例,根据有关的法律,战争会令相关的保险合约变为非法(通敌),但双方在订立保险合约时并不知道爆发了战争。法院判是这个共同错误令保险合约无效,被保险人可以根据"复原"(restitution)〔6〕原则从保险人处取回已经支付的保费。

会有情况是希望从合约中脱身的一方并不确定有关的突发事件是在哪一天发生,如战争在哪一天爆发,或是令有关合约非法或不能履行的法律或命令具体在哪一天生效。这样一来,如果合约刚好在这段时间订立,他也不能确定有关的突发事件到底是发生在订立合约之前,令合约因共同错误而无效,还是发生在订立合约之后,令

---

〔4〕 1979 年《货物销售法》之 section 7(1)。

〔5〕 如果不是双方在订约时均不知道合约标的物灭失,而是有一方知道(在买卖合约下通常会是卖方),这不是共同错误,合约不会无效。这样一来,卖方因为合约标的物灭失而交不出货属于违约/毁约,要面对卖方对损失的索赔。

〔6〕 参见本书第五章第 4 段。

合约受阻而自动终止。因此为了保险,共同错误与合约受阻会作为替代争议被一并提出:Amalgamated Investment & Property Co. Ltd. v. John Walker & Co. Ltd.(1977) 1 WLR 164; Dany Lions Ltd. v. Bristol Cars Ltd. (2014) 1 Lloyd's Rep. 281 等先例。

换言之,在合约受阻的说法下,合约有效存在毫无疑问。合约受阻只是减轻了 Paradine v. Jane (1647) Aleyn 26 先例确定的履行合约的绝对责任(absolute performance),在特定的情况下,可以提早终止合约(discharge a contract),任何一方都不用继续履行合约,也不需要承担违约的赔偿责任。在 The "Super Servant Two" (1990) 1 Lloyd's Rep. 1 先例,Bingham 大法官提到合约受阻的说法的目的是:"... to give effect to the demands of justice, to achieve a just and reasonable result, to do what is reasonable and fair, as an expedient to escape from injustice where such would result from enforcement of a contract in its literal terms after a significant change in circumstances."

2. 合约承诺的严格或绝对责任

要了解受阻概念,必须先明白英国法律下对合约承诺方(promisor)[7]的严格或绝对责任。这方面最主要先例早自 Paradine v. Jane (1647) Aleyn 26 先例,法院说:"when the party by his own contract creates a duty or charge upon himself, he is bound to make it good, if he may, notwithstanding any accident by inevitable necessity, because he might have provided against it by his contract."

在 Paradine v. Jane 先例,涉及拖欠土地租金的争议。一位农民租用了地主的土地耕种,按照约定该农民按期应交纳一定的租金。但是在发生争议这一年,由于敌方率领的军队占领了这块土地并将该农民从这块土地上驱逐了出去,致使该农民无法耕种,自然颗粒未收,从而不能交纳租金。地主在法院开始诉讼,追讨拖欠的租金,而农民则以他被敌军从这块土地上驱逐出去完全不是他能控制的,不应该还需要履行合约责任或承诺抗辩。法院最后判农民败诉,需要支付拖欠的租金。显然,当年还没有受阻的说法,否则该农民不会败诉。

即使合约方承诺了一些不可能完成的事,也是如此,正如 Holt 大法官在 Thornborow v. Whitacre (1705) 92 ER 270 先例中所说:"where a man will for a valuable consideration undertake to do an impossible thing, though it cannot be performed, yet he shall answer damages."

法院的观点是作为被告的合约方既然承诺了不可能完成的事,就必须为自己自

〔7〕 商业合约通常双方都相互做出多个承诺,需要履行并承担责任。

己的愚蠢付出代价(the defendant ought to pay something for his folly)。因此,合约并不会因为合约承诺从一开始就不可能履行而无效,除非该承诺不仅仅是不可能履行,而是达到了可笑的地步。JJ Powell 先生在《Essay upon the Law of Contracts and Agreements》(London, J Johnson and T Whieldon, 1790)中举例说:"to overturn Westminster Hall with his finger; or to make the Thames overflow Westminster Hall; or to drink up the sea; or touch the sky with his hand."

这种合约中双方相互做出的承诺会有各种类型。例如,在一个简单的 CIF 或 FOB 国际买卖合约(实际是一个付运合约,卖方的承诺只是在装港付运有关货物)中,卖方会承诺备妥货物,付运期内装货,取得出口证与其他有关付运文件,准时结汇,货物要符合各种明示或默示条件或保证条文等。而买方会承诺准时开信用证(付运期之前或合约规定的签约后 7 天不等),准时派船允许卖方在付运期之前有足够时间装妥货物(FOB 买卖),派的船舶不能超龄与船舱要干净等。

如果买方没法准时开出信用证,就是违约/毁约(repudiatory breach),要面对卖方索赔损失与/或卖方会选择终止合约。即使买方的承诺不可能履行,如承诺一旦订立了买卖合约,就在一天之内开出信用证,但合约是在周六下午订立,这仍然是买方违约。如果买方违约是因为市场下跌想要赖,要承担违约责任赔偿卖方损失应是理所当然。但也有可能信用证开不出在买方主观来看有合理原因,如银行搞错了,或是总公司干预令最后买方的信用证延误开出,或连续几天台风令银行不开门,甚至是买方国家突然收紧外汇等各种原因。在英国履行合约是严格/绝对责任的说法下,无论是什么原因都一样是违约,买方要对卖方的损失负责。在货物市场上涨时,卖方也可以此违约/毁约乘机终止买卖合约,因为准时开信用证是条件条文(condition):Pavia & Co. SpA v. Thurmann - Nielsen (1952) 1 Lloyd's Rep. 527 等先例。

一旦清楚了英国法律对合约下承诺的起点(starting point),就会觉得其大精神非常合理、肯定与实用。因为如果要在每个案件中追究合理与否(这可能会涉及非常广泛甚至是没有边际的考虑因素),岂非事事都需要打官司才能有结果?毕竟这样一来,即使争议的事实十分类似,只是其他可能是无关的方面有所不同(如当时市场涨跌)都会导致不同的判决结果。而且法官或仲裁员不是神仙,怎么能肯定他们一定能找出全面"合理"的判决裁决?合约双方当事人肯定对当时的合理与否有不同说法,否则也不会有争议了。不肯定的法律会令人感到无法可依,才是最不合理的法律。

虽然履行合约是严格/绝对责任,但正如 Paradine v. Jane 先例所说的,英国法律完全允许订约自由。所以,如果买方自忖准时开信用证会有外汇管制可能,或出现他无法控制的错误/延误如银行雇员搞错等,他完全可以在订约时加入一条不可抗力条文(*force majeure* clause)或履行困难条文(hardship clause)或其他类似的条文避免责任。毕竟这对卖方也公道,订约时如果知道会面对这种风险,他可以拒绝订约,或是做出其他保障(如对有些风险投保)等。这种减轻或是豁免合约承诺的严格责任也经常见到，几乎每份合约都会有。这可以是广泛的免责条文(exemption/exception clause)或不可抗力条文，也可能只是针对性的条文，如说明因下列原因无法准时开出信用证，买方不必负责或可以延长履行期限等。

3. 合约受阻的历史

但上一段的解释，却无法配合一种情况，即履约中发生了一些客观来说双方订约时根本无法预见的突发事件或意外。既然无法预见，如何能要求双方订约时写明风险？所以在19世纪末，开始有一些先例容许一个合约中没有明示针对的风险令合约终止，而且不算任何一方违约，这即是合约受阻概念的产生。因此，合约受阻在合约法中算是相对近期的说法。这几个重要的先例是 Taylor v. Caldwell (1863) 3 B & S 826 先例、Jackson v. Union Marine Insurance Co. Ltd. (1874) LR 10 CP 125 先例与 Krell v. Henry (1903) 2 KB 740 先例。

在 Taylor v. Caldwell 先例，被告向原告出租 Surrey Gardens 与 Music Hall(当时最大的铁制结构音乐厅，可以容纳10000名听众并可以在阳台与游廊上多容纳2000名听众)来作为演奏之用。合约说明每场演奏100镑租金，共4晚。谁知在演出前7天，音乐厅意外被烧毁。虽然 Surrey Gardens 仍在，但双方订约的基础(为了举办音乐会)显然已是无法再执行。而原告为了这场演奏已付出代价(如广告费)，所以起诉被告，指后者没有履约提供 Music Hall。但法院判这合约已因火灾的突发事件无法履行(impossible to perform)而受阻。

Jackson v. Union Marine Insurance Co. Ltd. 先例将合约受阻说法的适用从合约标的物灭失(如 Taylor v. Caldwell 先例)拓展到商业活动无法进行。该先例的案情有关一条船舶出租跑一个从 Newport 装货去旧金山的航次。在去 Newport 途中，船舶意外搁浅，令船舶重新浮起需要6周，此外还要修理大半年，本来是1872年1月的航次要延误至8月。应该是因为运费市场上涨，承租人要求即使是迟至8月，船东也要履约，毕竟租约中即使有销约期条文也是承租人的选择权，不是船东的。所以，船东是否在严重延误后仍要履约只能看是否受阻了。法院判是受阻，因为8月的航次根本与原先订约的1月的航次是两码事(performance radically different from that originally contemplated)。

而 Krell v. Henry 先例是因英皇得病取消英皇加冕典礼而导致的一连串先例之一。这一系列先例涉及为了观看爱德华七世的加冕典礼，有人提前以高价在沿途租好了房间或预定了站位，但谁知爱德华七世病倒，于是取消了加冕典礼。已经提前订立了合约的观众声称合约受阻，另有不知道爱德华七世病倒取消加冕典礼的消息的观众声称后来才订立的合约因错误而无效，法院支持了他们的说法。在 Blakeley v. Muller & Co. (1903) 19 TLR 186 先例，Alverstone 勋爵针对合约受阻说："where there was a contract to do a thing, not in itself unlawful, and the parties when entering into the contract must have contemplated the occurrence of a specified event or the continued existence of a specified thing as the foundation of what was to be done, and the performance became impossible from some cause for which neither party was responsible, and the party sued had not contracted or warranted that the event or thing, the non – occurrence or non – continued existence of which had caused the contract not to be possible of performance, should take place or continue to exist, then the parties were excused from further performance of the contract."

其他普通法国家也有合约受阻的说法,如美国早年合约法的权威书籍《Corbin on Contracts》第6卷(1951),s. 1356,第388页说:"... Many short – term leases have been made, in which the purpose of the lessee was to conduct a liquor saloon, a purpose known to the lessor and one which gave to the premises a large part of its rental value. Then followed the enactment of a ... prohibitory law preventing the use of the premises for the expected purpose. The prohibition law does not make it impossible or illegal for the lessee to keep his promise to pay the rent ... but it frustrates his purpose of using the premises for a liquor saloon in the reasonable hope of pecuniary profit. If the terms of the lease are such that the lessee is restricted to this one use, it has been held in a considerable number of cases that his duty to pay rent is discharged.〔8〕"

4. 合约受阻说法的依据:默示条文的考验

在 Taylor v. Caldwell (1863) 3 B & S 826 先例,法院根据默示条文〔9〕的概念在英国法下发展出了合约受阻的说法。高院的 Blackburn 大法官说:"... as subject to an implied condition that the parties shall be excused in case, before breach, performance becomes impossible from the perishing of the thing, without default of the contractor... The principle seems to us to be that, in contracts in which the performance depends on the continued existence of a given person or thing, a condition is implied that the impossibility of performance arising from the perishing of the person or thing shall excuse the performance. In none of these cases is the promise other than positive, nor is there any express stipulation that the destruction of the person or thing shall excuse the performance; but that excuse is by law implied, because from the nature of the contract it is ap-

〔8〕 1920年美国颁发禁酒令,导致大量双方都知道是为了开设酒吧的短租因非法而无法履行。这被判是租约受阻而自动终止,租客不必再支付租金。

〔9〕 关于默示条文可见杨良宜《合约的解释:规则与应用》第七章。

parent that the parties contracted on the basis of the continued existence of the particular person or chattel."

这是指事实的默示(implied by facts),也就是假设双方在订约时,有一个好事第三人(officious bystander)问如果将来发生这种突发事件(supervening event)怎么办,双方会异口同声地回答当然是合约自动终止。

F. A. Tamplin SS Co. Ltd. v. Anglo - Mexican Petroleum Products Co. Ltd. (1916) 2 AC 397 先例也跟从了这个默示条文的考验。该先例的案情涉及 60 个月的期租合约。第一次世界大战开始后,船舶被英国海军征用。当时租约期还剩 3 年,船东要求法院判租约受阻,但承租人坚持租约仍然存在。贵族院最后判是租约中并不存在默示条文是如果船舶被征用一段时间,双方就不需要继续履行租约,因此不会构成租约受阻。Loreburn 勋爵说:"... a Court can and ought to examine the contract and the circumstances in which it was made, not of course to vary, but only to explain it, in order to see whether or not from the nature of it the parties must have made their bargain on the footing that a particular thing or state of things would continue to exist. And if they must have done so, then a term to that effect will be implied, though it be not expressed in the contract... An examination of those decisions confirms me in the view that, when our Courts have held innocent contracting parties absolved from further performance of their promises, it has been upon the ground that there was an implied term in the contract which entitled them to be absolved. Sometimes it is put that performance has become impossible and that the party concerned did not promise to perform an impossibility. Sometimes it is put that the parties contemplated a certain state of things which fell out otherwise. In most of the cases it is said that there was an implied condition in the contract which operated to release the parties from performing it, and in all of them I think that was at bottom the principle upon which the Court proceeded. ... Were the altered conditions such that, had they thought of them, they would have taken their chance of them, or such that as sensible men they would have said 'if that happens, of course, it is all over between us'?"

另有一些其他理论作为合约受阻的依据,但不太重要甚至已经被否定不能作为合约受阻的依据,这可节录《Chitty on Contracts》(第 32 版,2015 年)一书之 23 - 017 段,如下:"Various other theories have been put forward in an attempt to provide a coherent basis for the doctrine of frustration. ... some judges have maintained that the doctrine seeks to give effect to the demands of justice, but these statements cannot be invoked to justify the conferral upon the courts of a wide - ranging discretion to re - write the parties' bargain in the name of 'fairness and reasonableness'.[10] Another theory which has been invoked is that both parties have been discharged from further performance of their contractual obligations because of a total failure of consideration; but this rationalization has been rejected by the House of Lords.[11] The final theory put forward by Lord Haldane in Tamplin SS Co. Ltd. v. Anglo-Mexican Petroleum Products Co. Ltd. (1916) 2 AC 397 and Goddard J in Tatem Ltd. v. Gamboa (1939) 1 KB 132 is that the doctrine is based on 'the disappearance of the foundation of the contract'. The difficulty with this theory lies in ascertaining the 'foundation' of the contract, the inquiry would appear to be one based on the construction of the contract[12] and, if this is so, it is not easy to see how it differs from the construction theory.[13]"

近几十年来发展出的所谓现代合约受阻法律依据的主要是合约解释,即找出合约真正的意思(what in fact is the true meaning of the contract)。这与合约责任有了根本性改变的说法十分类似。笔者可简单节录这方面的权威先例,首先是在 British Movietonews Ltd. v. London & District Cinemas Ltd. (1952) AC 166 先例,Simon 勋爵认为通过解释合约,可以显示双方订立时没有同意在后来发生了出人意表意料的完全不同的情况,双方仍愿意受该合约的约束,说:"If... a consideration of the terms of the contract, in the light of the circumstances existing when it was made, shows that they never agreed to be bound in a fundamentally different situation which has now unexpectedly emerged, the contract ceases to bind at that point - not because the court in its discretion thinks it just and reasonable to qualify the terms of the contract, but because on its true construction it does not apply in that situation."

在著名的 Davis Contractors Ltd. v. Fareham Urban District Council (1956) AC 696 先例,Radcliffe 勋爵判是通过解释合约的承诺,可以得出结论,即在受阻的情况下,已经不是订约时做出的合约承诺,说:"... frustration occurs whenever the law recognises that without default of either party a contractual obligation has become incapable or being performed because the circumstances in which performance is called for would render it a thing radically different from that which was undertaken by the contract. Non haec in foedera veni. It was not this that I promised to do."

Reid 勋爵也认为要解释合约条文看是否足够广泛包括突发事件带来的完全不

---

〔10〕 一些法官主张合约受阻是为了保证公平,但英国法律是很明确法院没有为了保证公平合理就更改合约的裁量权。

〔11〕 贵族院在 National Carriers Ltd. v. Panalpina (Northern) Ltd. (1981) AC 675 先例否定了因为完全得不到约因/对价的好处,所以双方都不再需要履行合约的说法。

〔12〕 另一个说法是合约根基消失,但这个说法的困难之处在于必须先确定什么是合约根基,这取决于对合约的解释。

〔13〕 这样一来,这个说法与合约解释的说法并没有区别。

同的情况，如果不能，合约就要终止，说：“... there is no need to consider what the parties thought or how they or reasonable men in their shoes would have dealt with the new situation if they had foreseen it[14]. The question is whether the contract which they did make is, on its true construction, wide enough to apply to the new situation: if it is not, then it is at an end.”

最后在 National Carriers Ltd. v. Panalpina (Northern) Ltd. (1981) AC 675 先例，Simon 勋爵说：“... a number of theories have been advanced to clothe the doctrine of frustration in juristic respectability, the two most in favour being the ‘implied term theory’ (which was potent in the development of the doctrine and which still provides a satisfactory explanation of many cases) and the ‘theory of a radical change in obligation’ or ‘construction theory’ (which appears to be the one most generally accepted today).”

5. 合约受阻说法的依据：合约责任的根本性改变的考验

上一段已经提到贵族院在 National Carriers Ltd. v. Panalpina (Northern) Ltd. (1981) AC 675 先例否定了默示条文可以用来支持合约受阻的说法。该先例涉及原告将一个仓库租给被告 10 年，车辆只能通过一条街道前往仓库。而因为该仓库对面的一个废弃的维多利亚式仓库状况十分危险，政府将这条街道封闭了。从政府封闭这条街道到拆除废弃仓库重新开放大约需要 20 个月，在此期间这个被租用的仓库可以说对被告毫无作用，也就没有支付租金。之后原告开始诉讼索赔被告拖欠的租金，而被告则认为因为政府封闭街道，该租约受阻自动终止。贵族院的 Hailsham 勋爵说：“... the ‘implied term’ or ‘implied condition’ theory on which Blackburn J. plainly relied in Taylor v. Caldwell, as applying to the facts of the case before him. To these it is admirably suited. The weakness, it seems to me, of the implied term theory is that it raises once more the spectral figure of the officious bystander intruding on the parties at the moment of agreement. In the present case, had the officious bystander pointed out to the parties in July 1974 the danger of carrying on the business of a commercial warehouse opposite a listed building of doubtful stability and asked them what they would do in the event of a temporary closure of Kingston Street pending a public local inquiry into a proposal for demolition after the lease had been running for over five years, I have not the least idea what they would have said, or whether either would have entered into the lease at all.”

---

〔14〕 这等于否定了默示条文可以用来支持合约受阻的说法。

默示条文（事实的默示）的考验经常被质疑操作起来太过人为与刻意，甚至有时候可以说是有弄虚作假的成分。正如 Hailsham 勋爵在该先例指出的，即使假设在订约时有一位好事第三人（officious bystander）问了这个问题（如果前往仓库的街道 Kingston Street 被封闭 20 个月会有什么影响），双方也不大可能会异口同声说应立即终止合约。如果合约方预见了这种不可能预见的情况，可能不会订立这个合约或会在合约中加上保留（reservation）、限制（qualification）或赔偿（compensation）的条文：Denny, Mott & Dickson Ltd. v. James B Fraser & Co. Ltd.（1944）AC 265 先例。

因此，默示条文的考验被合约责任根本性改变的考验替代，这可节录《Chitty on Contracts》（第 32 版，2015 年）一书之 23 – 012 段如下："The test which found favour with the House of Lords in Davis Contractors Ltd. v. Fareham U. D. C.（1956）AC 696 and in later cases may be formulated as follows：If the literal words of the contractual promise were to be enforced in the changed circumstances, would performance involve a fundamental or radical change from the obligation originally undertaken? . . ."

《Chitty on Contracts》（第 32 版，2015 年）一书接下去在 23 – 013 段说："**Confirmation of the test.** In subsequent cases the House of Lords has expressly upheld the Davis Contractors Ltd. v. Fareham U. D. C.（1956）AC 696 formulation of the test for frustration. In National Carriers Ltd. v. Panalpina（Northern）Ltd. , Lord Simon restated the test as follows：'Frustration of a contract takes place when there supervenes an event（without default of either party and for which the contract makes no sufficient provision）which so significantly changes the nature（not merely the expense or onerousness）of the outstanding contractual rights and/or obligations from what the parties could reasonably have contemplated at the time of its execution that it would be unjust to hold them to the literal sense of its stipulations in the new circumstances；in such case the law declares both parties to be discharged from further performance.'."

在著名的 The "Nema"（1981）2 Lloyd's Rep. 239 先例，Diplock 勋爵再次确认了合约责任根本性改变的考验，说："The legal concept of frustration, as my noble and learned friend, Lord Roskill, points out, can be expressed in the short and simple language used by Lord Radcliffe in Davis Contractors Ltd. v. Fareham Urban District Council［1956］A. C. 696. Whether a particular event or series of events have made further performance something radically different from that which was undertaken by the contract involves, as is indicated by Lord Radcliffe's adverb and its oft – used variant 'fundamentally,' a question of degree upon which, though faced with the same facts, different opinions may not unreasonably be held by different men."

6. 关于合约受阻的部分著名判决的说法

在这方面,可节录一小部分先例的著名判决(部分是重复节录)如下:

第一,在 Davis Contractors Ltd. v. Fareham Urban District Council (1956) AC 696 先例,Radcliffe 勋爵说:"frustration occurs whenever the law recognises that, without default of either party, a contractual obligation has become incapable of being performed because the circumstances in which performance is called for would render it a thing radically different from that which was undertaken by the contract, Non haec in foedera veni. It was not this that I promised to do.... it is not hardship or inconvenience or material loss itself which calls the principle of frustration into play, There must be as well such a change in the significance of the obligation that the thing undertaken would, if performed, be a different thing from that contracted for."

第二,在 BP v. Hunt (1979) 1 WLR 783 先例,Goff 大法官说:"... it is well established that if a contract is frustrated, it is forthwith determined as a matter of law. It follows that, as a matter of law, the legal relationship between the parties under the contract so frustrated comes to an end ..."

较早时,Delvin 大法官在 Universal Cargo Carriers Corp. v. Pedro Citati (1957) 1 Lloyd's Rep. 174 先例说:"while the application of the doctrine of frustration is a matter of law, the assessment of a period of delay sufficient to constitute frustration is a matter of fact."

第三,在 National Carriers Ltd. v. Panalpina (Northern) Ltd. (1981) AC 675 先例,Simon 勋爵说:"Frustration of a contract takes place when there supervenes an event (without default of either party and for which the contract makes no sufficient provision) which so significantly changes the nature (not merely the expense or onerousness) of the outstanding contractual rights and/or obligations from what the parties could reasonably have contemplated at the time of its execution that it would be unjust to hold them to the literal sense of its stipulations in the new circumstances; in such case the law declares both parties to be discharged from further performance."

第四,在 The "Super Servant Two" (1990) 1 Lloyd's Rep. 1 先例,Bingham 大法官列出五条合约受阻的基本原则如下:

(1)合约受阻的原意是为了减轻普通法下严格与绝对的要求履行合约承诺的责任(literal performance of absolute promises),达到合理与公平的结果:"to give effect to the demands of justice, to achieve a just and reasonable result, to do what is reasonable and fair, as an expedient to escape from injustice where such would result from enforcement of a contract in its literal terms after a significant change in circumstances. ”

(2)合约受阻是把合约“杀死”(kill the contract and discharge the parties from further liability under it),所以必须尽量局限其使用(keep within very narrow limits and ought not to be extended)。

(3)合约受阻令合约立即自动终止(brings a contract to an end forthwith, without more and automatically)。所以,一旦合约受阻,并不需要一方或合约双方同意,或是要宣告(declare)才能终止合约。

(4)合约受阻必须是外来因素而非合约方自己的行为令原先的合约责任大变(essence of frustration is that it should not be due to the act or election of the party seeking to rely on it and it must be some outside event or extraneous change of situation)。

(5)想依赖合约受阻而不履行的一方必须对产生受阻的情况没有任何责任或过错(a frustrating event must take place without blame or fault on the side of the party seeking to rely on it)。

第五,在 The “Kyla” (2013) 1 Lloyd’s Rep. 565 先例,Flaux 大法官也提到了现代受阻说法的基本原则与要件,说:

“. . . I propose to consider the principles of the modern law of frustration. An authoritative summary of the applicable principles is to be found in the judgment of Bingham LJ in The ‘Super Servant Two’ . . . Certain propositions, established by the highest authority, are not open to question:

1. The doctrine of frustration was evolved to mitigate the rigour of the common law’s insistence on literal performance of absolute promises. . . The object of the doctrine was to give effect to the demands of justice, to achieve a just and reasonable result, to do what is reasonable and fair, as an expedient to escape from injustice where such would result from enforcement of a contract in it literal terms after a significant change in circumstances . . .

2. Since the effect of frustration is to kill the contract and discharge the parties from further liability under it, the doctrine is not to be likely invoked, must be kept within very narrow limits and ought not to be extended . . .

3. Frustration brings the contract to an end forthwith, without more and automatically . . .

4. The essence of frustration is that it should not be due to the act or election of the party seeking to rely on it. . . A frustrating event must be some outside event or extraneous change of situation . . .

5. A frustrating event must take place without blame or fault on the side of the party seeking to rely on it . . . ”

7. 合约受阻的大原则与要件

根据上一段节录的著名判决中的说法,可简单总结合约受阻的一些大原则与要件并分段介绍。

7.1 合约受阻是法律问题,但仍需要仲裁员认定事实

合约受阻是法律问题与事实问题的混合。在 Tsakiroglou & Co. Ltd. v. Noblee Thorl G. m. b. H. (1961) 1 Lloyd's Rep. 329 先例,法院认为尽管最终决定是否构成合约受阻是法律问题,但结论很大程度还是依赖知悉商业惯常做法的商业人士对有关事实的理解与认定。在《Chitty on Contracts》(第 32 版,2015 年)一书之 23 – 015 段,说:"... It has several times been emphasised in the House of Lords that 'that conclusion is almost completely determined by what is ascertained as to mercantile usage and the understanding of mercantile men'[15]. Hence, the court should seldom interfere with an arbitrator's application of the test to particular facts:'... when it is shown on the face of a reasoned award that the appointed tribunal has applied the right legal test, no reasonable person could have reached that conclusion. It ought not to interfere merely because the court thinks that upon those facts and applying that test, it would not or might not itself have reached the same conclusion, for to do that would be for the court to usurp what is the sole function of the tribunal of fact.[16]'."

Roskill 勋爵在 The "Nema" (1981) 2 Lloyd's Rep. 239 先例也说,法院不能仅是因为合约受阻是法律问题,就以自己的观点改变仲裁庭对有关事实的认定。

在 The "Mary Nour" (2008) 2 Lloyd's Rep. 526 CA 先例,[17] Moore – Bick 大法官说:"... Everything, he(卖方代表大律师) submitted, depends on the circumstances of the case and whether the test propounded by Lord Radcliffe in Davis v. Fareham is satisfied. He submitted that there is high authority in the form of the observations of Lord Roskill in... The 'Nema'... that where frustration is in issue the court should generally accept the arbitrators' conclusion. However, the issue of frustration arises in a wide range of different factual circumstances. At one end of the scale there are cases, of which The

---

〔15〕 Radcliffe 勋爵在 Tsakiroglou & Co. Ltd. v. Noblee Thorl G. m. b. H. (1961) 1 Lloyd's Rep. 329 先例(第 124 段)所说。

〔16〕 Roskill 勋爵在 The "Nema" (1981) 2 Lloyd's Rep. 239 先例所说。

〔17〕 在该先例,买方想要向墨西哥进口大量水泥,这显然会影响当地的水泥企业联合组织 Cemex 的利益。卖方知道这一点,但仍与买方订立了 FOB 买卖合约。之后因为 Cemex 的阻挠,卖方无法供货,于是声称合约受阻。

'Nema' is a prime example, in which the question is essentially one of fact and degree,[18] calling for the evaluation of a range of factors which a commercial tribunal is particularly well equipped to undertake. At the other there are cases which call for the application of established principles to a clearly defined event rendering performance impossible.[19] Such cases give rise to a clear – cut issue of law. The present case falls very much towards the latter end of the scale, requiring little more than the application of established principles to the particular facts of the case. Accordingly, although I accept that the court must accept loyally the findings of fact made by the arbitrators, I do not think it need be unduly inhibited by the arbitrators' conclusion that the facts they have found are sufficient to satisfy the legal test for frustration.[20]"

例如,经常遇到的对有关事实的估计与认定是因战争、法律的改变或其他突发事件会带来多长延误,与会对有关合约的履行造成什么程度的影响。鉴于今天对仲裁裁决的上诉不易,所以,受阻与否或何时受阻经常是仲裁员说了算数。而只要是仲裁员没有错误理解与适用合约受阻的大原则/大精神,法院一般也不干预裁决结果。

7.2 受阻事件要在订约后发生且原则上是双方订约时不能预见的

7.2.1 受阻事件不一定是双方订约时不能预见的说法

传统上受阻事件(frustrating event)是订约时不能预见的,并在订约后发生令合约方的合约责任或承诺与订约时的共同目的有根本性的改变。在 Krell v. Henry (1903) 2 KB 740 先例,Williams 大法官说:"The test of frustration seems to be whether the event which causes the impossibility was or might have been anticipated ..."

在早期的 Walton Harvey Ltd. v. Walker and Homfrays Ltd. (1931) 1 Ch 274 先例中,被告与原告订立合约同意原告在其酒店上展示广告,但合约期尚未结束,酒店就被政府强制收购并拆毁。但法院判合约没有受阻,因为双方(至少是被告)在订立合约前就知道酒店可能被政府收购。

这看来是表明不可预见或不可预测是构成合约受阻的重要要件。进一步说,如果所谓的受阻事件在合约中有明示条文针对,就表示该事件在订约时是可以预见的,否则双方不会有所规定。应该通过解释合约的大原则找出双方的约定,而合约受阻的说法很有可能不适用。而如果有关的事件能够预见,正确的做法是双方在合约中规定如何分配风险与/或善后。在订约自由下,可以有各种约定,包括但不限于合约

---

〔18〕 如果将合约受阻先例按照其中事实问题与法律问题孰轻孰重分布,其中一端是延误,是否构成合约受阻主要取决于每个案件的不同事实与延误的程度。对这方面事实的认定由商业仲裁员做出十分适合,法院应该尊重。

〔19〕 而另一端是合约标的物的全损,如在 Taylor v. Caldwell (1863) 3 B&S 826 先例中,音乐厅被完全烧毁,事实无可争议,只需要适用有关的法律原则看能否构成合约受阻。

〔20〕 虽然法院要尊重与支持仲裁庭对事实的认定(如估计延误多久),但不代表法院受到仲裁庭对认定的事实是否满足受阻的法律要件/考验的决定的约束。

被终止：Walton Harvey Ltd. v. Walker and Homfrays Ltd. 先例。

以 CIF 买卖为例，卖方所承诺的履约责任包括：(1)将货物运到装港，安排装船与租船将货物付运到目的地；(2)为航次风险投保；(3)将货物发票、提单与保单正本交出给买方。如果买卖的特定货物(specific goods)在装港仓库里发生意外被烧毁，买卖合约会因为受阻而自动终止，毕竟卖方无法履行其上述的承诺。但如果该货物付运后船舶开到半途，船舶发生意外全损，则合约不会受阻而自动终止。原因是 CIF 买卖合约作为付运合约，其中往往明示或默示[21]了货物装船后风险就转移给了买方，即在合约中规定了如何分配风险与/或善后，超越了普通法下的合约受阻的说法。在 Manbre Saccharine Co. Ltd. v. Corn Products Co. Ltd. (1919) 1 KB 198 先例，McArdle 大法官说："In my opinion it is also clear that he can make an effective tender even though he possess at the time of tender actual knowledge of the loss of the ship or goods. For the purchaser in case of loss will get the documents he bargained for; and if the policy be that required by the contract, and if the loss be covered thereby, he will secure the insurance moneys. **The contingency of loss is within and not outside the contemplation of the parties to a c. i. f. contract.**"(加黑部分是笔者的强调)

已经提到 CIF/CFR 卖方的首要履约责任或承诺是将货物付运，但这方面经常会出现差错，导致履行困难与/或延误。例如，自然灾害或其他阻碍导致无法供应货物，或是法律限制出口(美国在 1973 年的大豆出口禁令导致的一连串先例)等。卖方需要用多种方式保护自己。例如，相比于合约受阻，卖方希望有更灵活、宽松与有弹性的方式保护自己，如可以在发生突发事件后等待一段时间看事态的发展情况等。因此，买卖合约中往往会加入不可抗力条文(*force majeure* clause)[22]针对一些卖方因突发事件导致无法在付运期(shipment period)内及时供货付运的情况。这些不受双方控制的将来的突发事件会包括战争、装港政府干预、不可预见的坏天气等，并规定如果发生这些事件，卖方可以向买方做出通知延长付运期(一个月或三个月不等)。只有之后不可抗力事件仍然持续，买方或双方才可以取消合约。

在 PJ van der Zijden Wildhanded NV v. Tucker & Cross Ltd. (1975) 2 Lloyd's Rep. 240 先例，案情涉及将中国冻兔肉运到鹿特丹的 CIF 买卖，有关的不可抗力条文是："Should the sellers fail to deliver... or to effect shipment in time by reason of war, flood, fire or storm, heavy snow or any other causes beyond their control, the time of

[21] 1979 年《货物销售法》之 section 20 中规定："(1) Unless otherwise agreed, the goods remain at the seller's risk until the property in them is transferred to the buyer, but when the property in them is transferred to the buyer the goods are at the buyer's risk whether delivery has been made or not. (2) But where delivery has been delayed through the fault of either buyer or seller the goods are at the risk of the party at fault as regards any loss which might not have occurred but for such fault. (3) Nothing in this section affects the duties or liabilities of either seller or buyer as a bailee or custodier of the goods of the other party."

[22] 参见杨良宜《合约的解释：规则与应用》一书第十三章第 1 段。

shipment might be extended, or alternatively a part or whole of the contract might be cancelled but the sellers have to furnish the buyers with a certificate attesting such event or events."

如果发生了该不可抗力条文中列出的突发事件如洪水或大雪,导致卖方无法在付运期内做出付运,而卖方选择终止合约,这是在条文下终止合约,而不是因为合约受阻而自动终止(即使合约受阻的说法可以适用)。当然,如果卖方想依赖该条文终止合约,也必须根据该条文的规定提供这些突发事件的证明。

不只是明示条文,合约默示条文也会规定一些突发事件发生后风险如何分配。在 Amalgamated Investment & Property Co. Ltd. v. John Walker & Co. Ltd. (1977) 1 WLR 164 先例中,案情涉及土地/房屋买卖。订约后不久,买卖的建筑被加入了政府的保护文物名单,因此无法拆掉重新发展,这导致土地/房屋价格急跌,并与从前有云泥之别。法院判是这不属于合约受阻,因为在英国法下买方应该知道有这些风险并愿意承担,说:"anybody who buys property knows, that there are all kind of hazards which have to be taken into consideration. There is the obvious hazard of planning permission. There is the hazard of fiscal and legislative changes. There is the hazard of existing legislation being applied to the property under consideration - compulsory purchase, for example."

因此,Lawton 大法官认为买卖双方在订约时应该考虑到合约标的物的建筑可能随时被加入名单,并会造成不能拆除去重新开发的限制,因此,买方在买之前就已经要求卖方告知该建筑是否在名单上(在该先例中,建筑于订立合约时还不在保护文物的名单上)。Lawton 大法官总结说:"all that adds up... to indicting that those who deal in property nowadays appreciate the existence of these kind of risks. At common law anyone entering in to a contract for the purchase of real property had to accept the risk of damage to the property after the contract had been made. Damage to the property nowadays can arise from causes other than fire and tempest. Financial loss can arise from government intervention. **This is a risk which people have to suffer. In my judgment, from the very outset the purchasers had to take the risk of the very thing happening which did happen, namely, that after the contract had been made, the property which was the subject matter of that contract would be listed ...**"(加黑部分是笔者的强调)

7.2.2 即使受阻事件是可预见的,但合约条文不完整、足够与明确,仍不能排除合约受阻

现在的法律已经很清楚,不可预见或不可预测不再是构成合约受阻的重要要件。在当今的商业社会,几乎所有的合约中都加入不可抗力条文(*force majeure* 条文)或履行困难条文(hardship clause),其中往往会列出一长串不受双方控制的将来的突发事件,如战争、政府干预、地震、火山爆发、不可预见的坏天气等。如果这些事件都被

解释为可以预见从而不会令合约受阻，这些年就不会有这么多合约受阻的先例了。

除了不可抗力条文，多数合约也会包括免责条文(exception/exclusion clause)，规定对战争、政府行为、地震、火山爆发、天意等免责。例如，NYPE 46(一种被广泛使用的期租合约标准格式)在第17条文免责条文中就有针对战争、政府禁止、海上伤亡等事件。被合并进租约第24条文的1936年《美国海上运输法》(US Carriage of Goods by Sea Act 1936)内也有对这些将来的突发事件有所规定。但这种广泛的、一般性的、印在标准格式的事件，能否算是双方订约时已经预见并有所订明，所以以后发生极其严重的战事或自然灾害令合约/租约无法履行也不能适用受阻的说法？看来并非如此。

因此在《Chitty on Contracts》(第32版，2015年)一书之23－059段，就认为不可预见只是表面(*prima facie*)规则，或者说是不太重要的要件说："... While an unforeseen event will not necessarily lead to the frustration of a contract, a foreseen event will generally exclude the operation of the doctrine. The inference that a foreseen event is not a frustrating event is only a prima facie one and so can be excluded by evidence of contrary intention.〔23〕 Thus, it is a question of construction of the contract whether the parties intended their silence to mean that the contract should continue to bind in that event, or whether they intended the effect of the event, if it occurs, to be determined by any relevant legal rules.〔24〕 If one party foresaw the risk, but the other did not, it will be difficult for the former to claim that the occurrence of the risk frustrates the contract.〔25〕 On the other hand, a contract may be frustrated by supervening illegality, notwithstanding the fact that the war which has brought about the supervening illegality was foreseen.〔26〕"

---

〔23〕 一个不可预见的事件并不一定会导致合约受阻，而一个已经预见的事件会导致合约受阻的说法被排除。但这只是一个表面规则，如果有证据显示双方有相反的订约意图，就不适用。

〔24〕 重点是双方预见了该事件但没有在合约中针对的意图是仍须由相关的法律决定。The "Eugenia" (1963) 2 Lloyd's Rep. 381 先例是苏伊士运河封闭导致的一连串案例之一，订约时双方也曾预见会发生战争并导致苏伊士运河封闭，并且谈判如何分摊这个风险。但谈不拢，又不想不做这笔生意，毕竟运河封闭也不是一定会发生，所以，双方决定如果订约后确实发生苏伊士运河封闭的事件，后果让律师处理(leave it to the lawyers to sort out)。Denning 勋爵说这些事实不会影响该租约的受阻能否成立。

〔25〕 如果一方预见了有关事件发生的风险而另一方没有，前者很难成功声称合约因为该事件而受阻。例如，在一个买卖合约中，卖方预见了他将交付的货物有因法律改变而禁止出口的风险，但买方不知道有此风险，那么卖方想要声称合约受阻就有困难。这也可以理解，毕竟这种情况有点卖方设好陷阱等着买方踏入的意思。如果买方也能事先知道这个风险，他可以用同一笔钱向其他更可靠的渠道，包括不同国家的出口商购买。

〔26〕 另一方面，如果法律突然改变，合约可能因为变为非法而受阻，即使导致法律发生改变的战争是完全可以预见也不会影响受阻的成立，如"二战"爆发导致与德国公司订立的合约因为通敌而变为非法并马上受阻。

普通法下针对这一点也有很多著名的说法,在 The "Molton" (1938) 61 Lloyd's Rep. 149 先例,Goddard 大法官说:"... when one uses the expression 'unforeseen circumstances' in relation to frustration of the performance of a contract one is really dealing with circumstances which are unprovided for, circumstances for which... the contract makes no provision."

Denning 勋爵在著名的 The "Eugenia" (1963) 2 Lloyd's Rep. 381 先例也说:"It has frequently been said that the doctrine of frustration only applies when the new situation is 'unforeseen' or 'unexpected' or 'uncontemplated', as if that were an essential feature. **But it is not so**. The only thing that is essential is that the parties should have made no provision for it in their contract. The only relevance of it being 'unforeseen' is this: If the parties did not foresee anything of the kind happening, you can readily infer they have made no provision for it: whereas, if they did foresee it, you would expect them to make provision for it. But cases have occurred where the parties have foreseen the danger ahead, and yet made no provision for it in the contract."(加黑部分是笔者的强调)

的确有不少受阻的案件,如战争爆发的影响,在订约时可能局势已经十分紧张,战争一触即发,很难说双方在订约时完全预见不到。

在《Chitty on Contracts》(第 32 版,2015 年)一书之 23-061 段的脚注 289 以员工死亡为例说,员工的死亡可以预见(死亡本身无法避免,只是迟早问题),但如果发生仍会导致雇佣合约受阻:"Many events are foreseeable but neither party assumes the risk of their occurrence. Death is the classic example. The death of an employee during the currency of his employment contract is a foreseeable event but it operates to discharge the contract of employment because neither party assumes the risk of its occurrence."

因此,真正的考虑应是双方是否已经在合约中针对某个可以预见的突发事件,包括其类别、范围与严重程度,完整规定了双方应该如何分配风险与/或善后。[27] 如果没有,合约受阻的说法就没有被合约规定取代。换句话说,如果合约中有空隙(gap)没有针对某个将来发生的突发事件与如何善后,合约受阻的说法仍然可以适用。《The Law of Contract in Singapore》(2012 年)一书之 19-025 段将这方面说得很清楚,可节录如下:"The reason **why** it is open for the courts to find that a contract has been discharged by frustration is, therefore, because it has found, as a matter of construction of the contract, that the contract makes **neither express nor implied** provision as to the contracting parties' mutual rights and obligations arising out of the contract in

---

〔27〕 这在 The "Super Servant Two" (1990) 1 Lloyd's Rep. 1 先例是说:"full and complete provision for all of the effects of the supervening (frustration)"另在 The "Florida" (2007) 1 Lloyd's Rep. 1 先例是说:"full and complete provision for all of the effects of supervening illegality which ..."

light of the supervening event that has occurred. That is to say, **a contract may only be discharged by frustration where there is a gap in the contractual allocation of the risks of gains and losses** arising from non – performance of the contract in light of the state of affairs following occurrence of the supervening event in question."(加黑部分是笔者的强调)

7.2.3 对合约的解释

重复上一段所讲,如果受阻事件在合约中有针对,但订得不完整、足够与明确,有空隙,仍不能阻止合约受阻的适用。但如果条文订得完整明确,将受阻事件如果真的发生分配风险与/或善后订清楚,则受阻的说法再不适用。

订约自由下双方可在合约中订明将来发生受阻事件如何分配风险与/或善后。可简单举两个例子:

1. 在国际货物买卖合约,有条文说明有关货物如果被出口国禁止(原本可能会是受阻事件),卖方应去其他邻近出口国另找类似的替代货物付运,这是针对可能出现的装港的法律发生变化的意外事件,提供替代履行方式避免合约受阻说法的适用。

2. 如果在 1980 年至 1988 年的两伊战争中,其中一艘被关在阿拉伯河内的船舶的租约有一条条文说明如果船舶被拘(detained)或被关,承租人要再继续多付 6 个月租金才能终止租约,合约受阻的说法就不适用。

一般来说,一条一般性(general)或标准格式内的不可抗力条文不足以排除合约受阻,毕竟该广泛的条文不可能针对每一类事件(如战争或政府干预)中的每一种情况。不可抗力条文中针对的可以延长履行的期限或推迟履行时间的不可抗力事件,应被解释为一般人士所理解会影响合约顺利履行的事件。不在一般人士理解内的突发事件,如大战爆发或是遇到极端坏天气,可能不仅仅是短暂影响合约履行,而是直接令合约无法履行。

可举两个例子如下。在 The "Playa Larga" (1983) 2 Lloyd's Rep. 171 (CA)先例中,案情有关皮诺切特将军领导的军方政府在美国的支持下于 1973 年 9 月 11 日推翻了民选政府,这导致古巴与智利立即断交,古巴颁布法律(1256 号立法)冻结了智利官方与政府的所有资产,并禁止运糖到智利。在该先例中,相关的买卖合约下还有部分食糖没有付运,仲裁庭与法院判是虽然有关合约的合约方是智利私人公司,但控股的是智利国有企业,继续履行合约在古巴是非法的,所以合约受阻,不需要继续履行。在有关的合约下,有条文规定如果出现战争或政府干预等事件,可以延长付运期,如果事件的影响超过了延长的付运期,买方有终止合约的选择权。这是一条非常广泛与一般性的条文,目的是在因为双方都无法控制的原因导致卖方错过了付运期的情况下,保护卖方/货方。在该先例中,这种条文不足以排除合约受阻的说法,Ackner 大法官说:"Law 1256 rendered further performance on both sides illegal by Cuban law and was enacted because of the disintegration of relations between the two states.(合约条文)is clearly concerned with matters affecting delivery of the goods to the shipping port. It relates essentially to the seller's ability to perform. It provides what should happen where force majeure events prevent the seller shipping within the specified period. It contemplates a temporary interruption, which, after due notification to the buyer, is followed by extending the shipping period. Then, if the shipment is still prevented by the end of the extended period, it gives to the buyer the option of cancelling the contract. (合约条文) is not directed at events which strike at the contract as a whole and renders further performance by either party unthinkable. (合约条文) was not designed to deal with the situation which occurred in this case, as is apparent when one considers the provision which it makes for the giving of notices by the seller to the buyer of the event relied upon and the detailed provisions concerning the exercise by the buyer of the option. We accordingly agree with the learned judge that (合约条文) cannot have been intended by the parties to be an exclusive code of procedure for relieving the seller from liability in the situation with which we are concerned."

另一个例子是 The "Evia" (1982) 2 Lloyd's Rep. 307 的贵族院先例。该先例涉及一个期租合约,承租人命令船舶在古巴装糖去伊拉克的巴士拉港。但在 1979 年 9 月 22 日卸完货后,两伊战争爆发,导致阿拉伯河封闭,船舶无法开航。[28] 该租约第 21 条文可部分节录如下:"(A) unless the consent of the owners be first obtained [was] not to be ordered nor continue to any place... which will bring her within a zone which is dangerous as a result of any war. (B) should the vessel approach... such zone... (1) the owners [were] to be entitled to insure the vessel ... the charterers to make a refund to owners of the premium on demand ... (2) notwithstanding the terms of Clause 11 hire to be paid for all time lost including any lost owning to the action of the crew in refusing to be exposed to such risks."

这是 Baltime 标准合约内的一条印本条文,承租人不能在没有船东同意的情况下命令船舶开往有战争危险的地区。(B)部分说如果下令去这种地区(如在船东同意下),船东就可以为船舶加保战争险,而加保的保费(premium)是要承租人承担。另是即使遇上第 11 条文内允许承租人停租的情况(包括船员拒绝听从命令,如因港内危险而拒绝进港),承租人在战区内还是需要支付所有的租金。

一审([1981] 2 Lloyd's Rep. 613)的 Goff 大法官不认为第 21 条文可以排除合约受阻的说法,而后来的上诉庭([1982] 1 Lloyd's Rep. 334)与贵族院都支持这一判法。Goff 大法官是这样说:

"Now the question which arises on this issue in the case is whether, on a true construction of the clause in its context, it continued to apply in the events which occurred, and so had the effect of excluding frustration. The Court has however to exercise care be-

---

[28] 两伊战争导致阿拉伯河封闭带来的一连串先例将会在本章之 12.3.3 段介绍。

fore concluding that a clause is intended to apply in circumstances which would, apart from the clause, have the effect of frustrating a contract. Obviously, there are contractual provisions which may be held to apply after frustration; but frustration presupposes the occurrence of an event which effects so radical a change in the contractual adventure that, on a true construction of the contract, it ceases to bind the parties. This being so, it is dangerous just to look at the clause and to consider whether on its literal meaning it applies in the event which has occurred; the decision of the House of Lords in Bank Line Ltd. v. Arthur Capel & Co. (1919) AC 435 provides an ample warning against the adoption of such an approach.

When I look at cl. 21(b), I observe that it provides that 'notwithstanding the terms of Clause 11 hire to be paid for all time lost ...' ...

The relevant part of cl. 21(b) is therefore concerned to prevent the application of the off hire clause in the circumstances specified in cl. 21. It provides that, in this circumstances, the vessel will not, despite cl. 11, go off hire; on the contrary, hire is to continue to be paid. Now hire is of course payable in accordance with the terms of the charter; and the obligation to pay hire presupposes that the charter continues to bind. As I read cl. 21(b), it is not concerned to legislate for the consequences of frustration, or to exclude frustration ..."

Goff 大法官认为法院在解释有关条文排除了合约受阻的说法时必须非常谨慎。毕竟可以构成合约受阻的突发事件,必须根本性地改变双方订约时的合约责任与承诺。因此,只看字面的意思就解释有关的条文针对了该突发事件,从而排除了合约受阻的说法会十分危险。在该先例中,第 21(b)条文只是说如果前往战区,涉及停租的第 11 条文就不适用。也就是说,针对的只是能否停租的问题,而只有合约没有受阻时才存在停租的问题,租约一旦受阻就会自动终止,自然无须再支付租金。因此,Goff 大法官认为该第 21 条文没有针对也不能排除合约受阻的说法。

这样一来,不可抗力条文中列出的事件很多在适当情况下仍可以构成合约受阻。看来这主要是根据突发事件的不同性质、严重程度与影响,看能否被解释为已经被包括在双方的合约内。

但针对以明示条文订明将来发生受阻事件如何分配风险与/或善后,有两点需要特别注意。首先,法院或仲裁庭会对合约的约定做出非常严格与局限(narrow)的解释,条文中的措辞/用字必须非常清楚明确与有针对性,才能超越法律默示地位(即合约受阻的说法),但这种争议在国际商业社会还是经常会发生。

《Chitty on Contracts》(第 32 版,2015 年)一书之 23 - 058 段总结说:"A clause in the contract which is intended to deal with the event which has occurred will normally preclude the application of the doctrine of frustration. Frustration is concerned with unforeseen, supervening events, not events which have been anticipated and provided for in the contract itself. Thus the effect of a force majeure clause or a hardship clause may be to shut out the doctrine of frustration because the contract, on its proper construction, will be held to have covered the event which has occurred... **But the courts are likely to construe such clauses narrowly and insist that the provision for the event be 'full and complete' before the conclusion is reached that frustration is excluded.**〔29〕**The more catastrophic the event, the less likely it is that a clause will be held to cover the event which has occurred, unless particularly clear words are used.**〔30〕Similarly, the fact that a force majeure clause makes provision for an extension of time on the occurrence of one or the stipulated events may indicate to the court that the clause was confined in its application to events which are capable of resolution within that particular time-frame: an event which renders further performance of the contract 'unthinkable' may therefore not fall within the scope of the clause.〔31〕Further, the clause may not make complete provision for all the legal issues arising from the event.〔32〕For example, a clause may excuse one party from the consequence of delay, in the sense that it prevents the delay from constituting a breach of contract, but this does not necessarily exclude the operation of doctrine of frustration so as to enable that party to hold the other party to the contract when delay occurs. An express provision in the contract cannot, however, exclude frustration by supervening illegality where this would be against public policy.〔33〕"

---

〔29〕参见 Bank Line Ltd. v. Arthur Capel & Co.（1919）AC 435；The "Florida"（2007）1 Lloyd's Rep. 1；Bunge SA v. Kyla Shipping Co. Ltd.（2013）1 Lloyd's Rep. 565 等先例。

〔30〕参见 Metropolitan Water Board v. Dick, Kerr & Co. Ltd.（1918）AC 119；Pacific Phosphate Co. Ltd. v. Empire Transport Co. Ltd.（1920）36 TLR 750；The "Penelope"（1928）31 Lloyd's Rep. 96；Fibrosa Spolka Akcyjina v. Fairbairn Lawson Combe Barbour Ltd.（1943）AC 32；Denny, Mott & Dickson Ltd. v. James B Fraser & Co. Ltd.（1944）AC 265；The "Evia"（1982）2 Lloyd's Rep. 307；The "Sea Angel"（2007）2 Lloyd's Rep. 517 CA 等先例。这背后的逻辑也可以理解，如合约中规定发生任何延误都由 A 负责，但在合约还有 10 年需要履行时发生了灾难性的突发事件，面临无限期的延误。这种灾难性的延误不可能是 A 与 B 在订约时同意所有延误由 A 负责时的想法。因此，不能排除合约受阻说法的适用。

〔31〕参见 The "Playa Larga"（1983）2 Lloyd's Rep. 171（CA）先例。接下去是举例说有合约条文说明对一方的延误免责，这是为了避免他因为延误而违约，但不代表想排除会令合约受阻的延误。

〔32〕参见 Bank Line Ltd. v. Arthur Capel & Co.（1919）AC 435 先例。接下去是举例说有合约条文说明对一方的延误免责，这是为了避免该方因为延误而违约。但这不代表即使发生了可令合约受阻的延误，因为该条文的存在而无法适用合约受阻的说法。

〔33〕只有通敌这一种例外是合约不能订明的，如订约后，英国向德国宣战（"一战"），则有关合约马上受阻而自动终止。而合约另有规定去避免这种受阻（如另规定延期履行）也会因违反公共政策而无效：Ertel Bieber & Co. v. Rio Tinto Co. Ltd.（1918）AC 260；Islamic Republic of Iran Shipping Lines v. Steamship Mutual Underwriting Association（Bermuda）Ltd.（2011）1 Lloyd's Rep. 195 等先例。但在本段稍早也有提到进出口限制导致合约非法的情况是可以通过合约条文排除合约受阻说法的适用：Johnson Matthey Bankers Ltd. v. State Trading Corp of India（1984）1 Lloyd's Rep. 427 等先例。

（加黑部分是笔者的强调）

在 Metropolitan Water Board v. Dick, Kerr & Co.（1918）AC 119 先例,[34]合约涉及水库的建设。相关合约中有一条条文针对一连串会延误工程的事件规定可以延长完工时限,其中的用字是十分广泛与概括的“whatsoever and howsoever occasioned”。但之后因为政府干预工程停止,法院判是合约依然受阻。可见一般性的用字无论多么广泛,都很难在发生了灾难性的突发事件后排除合约受阻的说法。

因为有订约自由,所以针对同一个突发事件（如战争、地震、海啸等）,会有大部分合约受阻,个别合约因为写法不同而不受阻。而受阻的合约也可能因为合约的不同与/或实际履行不一样,导致受阻的日期不同。例如,在本章第 11 段介绍的 The “Kyla”（2013）1 Lloyd's Rep. 565 先例中,船舶已经在商业上全损,但因为保险的船价（期租合约中规定船东要购买这保险金额）远远高于发生事故时的船价,所以判是船舶不构成推定全损（constructive total loss）,合约无法受阻变成船东拒绝履行合约。但如果在租约链中的一个程租或期租合约中没有要求船东（实际上是二船东或三船东等）购买保险,就会在同一个突发事件下因为构成船舶推定全损是受阻：见 Moss v. Smith（1850）9 CB 94；Blane Steamships Ltd. v. Minister of Transport（1951）2 Lloyd's Rep. 155；The “Badagry”（1985）1 Lloyd's Rep. 395 CA 等先例。

除明示条文外,不同类别合约的法律默示条文也要注意。在本章之 7.2.1 段介绍的 Amalgamated Investment & Property Co. Ltd. v. John Walker & Co. Ltd.（1977）1 WLR 164 先例中,上诉庭改变了一审的判决,判合约没有受阻,因为买方应该承担建筑在保护文物名单上的风险。这显然是根据法律默示条文的说法,而法律默示要考虑对某类合约是否合理与政策性的问题。这样一来,如果事实发生改变,默示的条文也会不同。例如,在英国这种古老建筑很多的地方,政策性默示买方应承担这种风险是合理的。但是在一些较新的城镇,可能除了个别建筑,买方在其他的建筑不会想到有这种风险,政策性让买方承担这种风险没有必要,合约会因为有关建筑被列入了政府的保护文物名单而受阻。

尤其是在 The “Sea Angel”（2007）2 Lloyd's Rep. 517 CA 先例之后,Rix 大法官提到了决定是否构成合约受阻的困难与需要考虑多种因素（multi - factorial）,[35]更会导致在同样的受阻事件发生后,因为合约不同的背景/语境或双方对有关情况的了解等对能否构成合约受阻产生影响,所以,即使是在合约链中也有部分合约受阻,而部分合约无法受阻。

7.2.4　显示如果合约条文不完整、足够与明确不能排除受阻说法的先例

合约条文不完整与不明确,不能排除合约受阻的适用的先例可举以下几个例子：

1. 在 Bank Line Ltd. v. Arthur Capel & Co.（1919）AC 435 先例中,租约有条文

[34]　案情将在本章之 7.3.2.2 段介绍。

[35]　参见本章第 11 段。

明示说明如果船舶在租约期内被政府征用,承租人有终止租约的选择权(option)。[36] 之后,Quito 轮被政府征用多月,没法交船给承租人以开始一个 12 个月的期租。当时市场高涨,承租人起诉船东不交船并索赔损失。贵族院判是合约受阻的说法仍适用,承租人的选择权只可被适用于明知政府征用时间很短,即不可能是受阻的情况。在这种情况下,承租人可以根据租约条文行使选择权,立即终止租约。但租约没有针对如果承租人没有行使选择权而延误又严重到可以构成受阻时双方的合约责任。在受阻的说法下,租约自动终止,不存在需要行使选择权才能终止租约。

2. 在 The "Molton" (1938) 61 Lloyd's Rep. 149 先例中,该船舶被租来运载西班牙的难民去法国,租金很高,而租约期只是 30 日。但船舶在起租后不久就被敌方(佛郎哥将军)扣留(seize),一直扣了 2 个月。Goddard 大法官说即使双方订约时已预见有此扣留危险,仍不妨碍该租约的根基已毁(seizure destroyed the foundation of the charter),所以租约应在被扣的一日(7 月 14 日)受阻,船东不能要求承租人支付租金至 2 个月后被释放并开去法国还船为止。

3. 在 The "World Sky" (1961) 2 Lloyd's Rep. 496 先例中,这一 7 年的期租有一条文容许船东在任何时间替换另一艘替代船舶履行。World Sky 轮在搁浅后全损,因租约规定的租金相比市场价格很有吸引力,所以船东想用另一艘替代船舶继续这个租约。法院判 World Sky 轮全损后,租约已经受阻自动终止,包括容许以替代船舶履行的条文,无法再独自复生。在该先例中,如果条文的写法是"即使在原船沉没全损情况下,船东仍有权在 10 日内另找一条替代船舶履行",则合约受阻的说法不再适用。World Sky 轮的全损因为已有约定的完整机制针对,不会构成受阻而令租约自动终止。正如 Haldane 大法官在 Bank Line Ltd. v. Arthur Capel & Co 先例所说:"What is clear that where people enter into a contract which is dependent for the possibility of performance on the continued availability of the subject matter and that availability comes to an unforeseen end by reason of circumstances over which its owner had no control, the owner is not bound **unless it is quite plain that he has contracted to do so.**"(加黑部分是笔者的强调)

4. Wong Lai Ying and Investment v. Chinachem Investment Ltd. (1979) 13 BLR 81 (PC)先例的案情有关香港的房屋买卖。合约中 Chinachem 作为开发商与卖方,应在 18 个月内完成建筑并交房给买方。7 个月后,工程发生山泥倾泻(landslip)以致建筑停顿。之后,因整个地盘不稳定,建筑足足三年半没有动工。虽然合约中有一条允许因各种原因延误而延长交房时间的条文,但因它只局限在 365 日内的延长,所以也不适用。这样一来,双方争议的主要条文是第 22 条文:"It is further agreed that notwithstanding anything herein contained should ... any unforeseen circumstances beyond the vendor's control arise whereby the vendor becomes unable to sell... the vendor shall

[36] 这个课题可看本书第三章之 3.3.3 段。

be at liberty to rescind this Agreement forthwith..."香港法院的两审虽然都认同山泥倾泻是受阻意外,但高院与上诉庭对第22条文适用与否,是否已有说明如何分配风险与/或善后有不同意见。按理说这第22条文说明是针对"卖方/发展商无法控制与不可预见的情况",从字面上看应可以包括。否则难道要说明"山泥倾泻,引至地盘不稳定"才能算吗?但枢密院判,虽然字面上看来够广泛,该条文仍不能排除合约受阻的适用。Scarman勋爵说:"the unforeseen character of the event is not in dispute. Clause 22 cannot, in their Lordships' opinion, be construed as making provision for the possibility of this particular unforeseen contingency."

5. 另一个著名先例是The "Nema"(1981) 2 Lloyd's Rep. 239先例,具体的案情将在本章之8.2段介绍。在该先例中,独任仲裁员Donald Davis先生判相关的程租合约(C. Ore 7标准格式)可分为1979年与1980年两个季度,1979年这一季度的租约因为加拿大的Sorel港罢工而受阻。但这在高院([1980] 2 Lloyd's Rep. 83)被Goff大法官推翻,而之后的上诉庭([1980] 2 Lloyd's Rep. 339)与贵族院又推翻了高院的判决。在该先例的程租合约中,第27条文针对了装港Sorel港罢工的情况,说:"In the event of **any general strike**, riot, insurrection, revolution or war, **which may prevent shipment of titanium slag under this charter**, the owners in the event of no cargo being loaded, have the option of cancelling this charter or if any cargo has been loaded they have the right to proceed on the voyage with the cargo so loaded."(加黑部分是笔者的强调)

该第27条文的措辞/用字和目的与1994年金康格式(包括之前的版本)的罢工条文(General Strike Clause)大致相同。这种条文是为了保护船东,如果装港发生了罢工不能装货,船舶无须遥遥无期地在装港等下去。另是如果货物装到一半遇上了罢工而无法继续装货,这时要取消租约开走已经太迟,船东可以将已经装船的货物送到目的地港口,而不会因为没有付运全部货物而违约。但第27条文是一条广泛的标准条文,并没有考虑与针对The "Nema"先例的情况。更准确地说,双方没有针对这种罢工会造成租约下的剩余航次无法履行的情况。因此贵族院最后判是1979年这一季度的租约因为罢工而受阻。

6. 在The "Florida"(2007) 1 Lloyd's Rep. 1先例中,案情涉及一个程租合约。在船舶到达装港前,尼日利亚(卸港)政府宣布禁止进口植物油。因此,承租人以租约受阻为由终止租约。租约中有一条自由条文(liberty clause),相关部分可节录如下:"In any situation whatsoever and wheresoever occurring and whether existing or anticipated before commencement of or during the voyage, which... is likely to give rise to risk of capture, seizure, detention... delay or disadvantage to or loss of the Vessel or any part of her cargo... the Owners may before loading or before the commencement of the voyage... require the shipper... to take delivery of the cargo at the port of shipment..."Tomlinson大法官认为关键的问题是该条文针对进口货物变成非法的情况

有否提供了完整的分配风险与/或善后机制，说："the question is whether clause 29(a) of this charter made full and complete provision for the effects of supervening illegality which, even before a cargo had been brought forward for loading, made discharge at the contractual destination impossible." 只有该条文为针对进口货物变成非法的情况提供了完整的机制，合约受阻的说法才不再适用。该先例相关的条文只规定了货物已经装船或至少已经运到装港等待装船的情况下，承租人有权选择替代方式履行租约。该先例发生的这种船舶还没有到达装港的情况显然没有被针对，合约受阻的说法仍然可以适用。

7. 最后笔者可节录 Rix 大法官在近期的 The "Sea Angel" (2007) 2 Lloyd's Rep. 517 CA 先例所说：

"There were lengthy submissions before us from both parties as to the role in the doctrine of frustration of the fact that a risk might be foreseen or foreseeable. We had cited to us numerous passages from a major work of broad, detailed and exceptional scholarship by Professor Sir Guenter Treitel QC, his Frustration and Force Majeure (2nd edn, 2004). Similar submissions in reliance on this work were made to the judge. Mr Hamblen's(承租人代表大律师) summary of Professor Treitel's thesis as relevant to present purposes is that **foreseeability of a risk may be a weak or inconsequential factor** to take into account, **unless the three tests of kind, extent, and degree are met**. As to kind and extent, both the type and the extent or length of the interference or delay must be foreseeable; as to degree, the degree of foreseeability has to be very high.[37]

The significance of foreseen or of unforeseen but foreseeable events is in my judgment well, if briefly, summarised in Chitty on Contracts (29th edn, 2004) at paras. 23-057/8. Paragraph 23-057 which deals with foreseen events can be seen to make the point that there is no rule of exclusion, at best some prima facie indications.

Thus: 'While an unforeseen event will not necessarily lead to the frustration of a contract, a foreseen event will generally exclude the operation of the doctrine. The inference that a foreseen event is not a frustrating event is only a prima facie one and so can

---

〔37〕 著名的 Treitel 教授是说在考虑受阻的说法是否适用时，可否预见某一个风险只是一个不重要或非结论性的因素。只有有关风险的性质与类别、对合约履行影响的程度与延误的长度都可以预见，并且可预见性很高时，才可以排除受阻说法的适用。举一个简单的例子，船舶被政府征用(requisition)的情况时不时会发生，在相关的租约的不可抗力条文或免责条文中通常会提及。但这并不代表合约受阻的说法不再适用，法院或仲裁庭必须考虑征用的性质，如政府只是因为发生了自然灾害临时征用船舶运粮到灾区，还是因为发生了战争要长期甚至是无限期征用；合约是一个航次的程租合约，还是几年的长期租约等。如果不可抗力条文只是简单提到了"征用"一词，很有可能不能超越合约受阻的说法。而如果有关条文有详细针对，如征用超过 6 个月双方才能终止租约，即使船舶被征用时就可以预见会有很长一段时间也不会令租约受阻自动终止，而必须等到 6 个月后。

be excluded by evidence of contrary intention.'

However, there is no finding in terms that the detention by KPT(港口当局) which occurred in this case was actually foreseen (or unforeseen) even by Tsavliris(承租人), merely that unreasonable detention by port authorities is a 'risk of the industry', and as such foreseeable. In such circumstances it is para. 23 - 058 which is perhaps particularly pertinent, which reads: '**Event foreseeable but not foreseen.** When the event was foreseeable but not foreseen by the parties, it is less likely that the doctrine of frustration will be held to be inapplicable.[38] Much turns on the extent to which the event was foreseeable.[39] The issue which the court must consider is whether or not one or other party has assumed the risk of the occurrence of the event.[40] The degree of foreseeability required to exclude the doctrine of frustration is, however, a high one[41]: ... 'foreseeability' will support the inference of risk - assumption only where the supervening event is one which any person of ordinary intelligence would regard as likely to occur[42], or... the contingency must be 'one which the parties could reasonably be thought to have foreseen as a real possibility'."(加黑部分是笔者的强调)

7.3 受阻事件必须为外来的突发事件令整个合约无法履行或是与订约时的共同目的有根本性区别

如果订约一方承诺了一些他根本做不到的事(agreed to impossibility),如一条情况极差的老船出租去装清洁的货,要求的船舶状态是这条船无法达到的,这不是受阻,因为根本没有一个突发的受阻事件在订约后出现导致这合约/租约无法履行。"傻瓜"或不小心的船东在以上情况实是违约,要面对承租人的索赔。这也不会是"共同错误"(common mistake),因为订约时不存在双方对一个已经存在的事实或情况(existence of a state of affairs)有错误理解。最多只是一方对另一方承诺或保证了他做不到的事,而另一方充其量是半信半疑,觉得不妨一试:Dany Lions Ltd. v. Bristol Cars Ltd. (2014) 1 Lloyd's Rep. 281 先例。

7.3.1 合约无法履行

合约无法履行(impossible to perform)的情况可以分为两大类,第一大类是外来的突发事件导致合约实质上无法履行(physical impossible),这又可以细分为若干小类:

1. 合约标的物全毁,这一类突发事件导致的受阻相对来说争议性不大,虽然还要

---

〔38〕 如果双方没有预见一个可以预见的事件,合约受阻的说法不适用的可能性就会降低。

〔39〕 当然这很大程度上取决于该事件的可预见性。

〔40〕 法院必须考虑其中一方是否假设了该事件可能会发生并承担这一风险。

〔41〕 该事件要有很高的可预见性才可以排除合约受阻说法的适用。

〔42〕 只有该事件是任何智力正常的人士都认为有可能发生,才能说是有足够的可预见性,可以说合约方已经假设了该事件发生的风险。

看有关合约的条文与内容：本章第3段介绍的Taylor v. Caldwell（1863）3 B &S 826先例与本章之7.2.4段介绍的The“World Sky”（1961）2 Lloyd's Rep. 496先例等。

2.另一类相对简单的实质无法履行是自然人死亡，这一般涉及雇佣合约（无论是雇员或是自然人的雇主死亡）或服务合约。类似的如果自然人不是死亡，而是失去了履行合约的能力（可以是体力或脑力），合约同样会受阻。而如果雇主是一家有限公司而不是一个自然人，情况就会不同，即使公司破产合约也不会受阻，因为会有信托人（trustee）履行该合约，如同是一个法律规定的转让（assignment by operation of law）。这可节录《Chitty on Contracts》（第32版，2015年）一书之20－032段：“**Contracts not terminated by bankruptcy.** A contract is not determined by the bankruptcy of one of the parties thereto. Ordinarily the benefit of any contract made by the debtor passes to his trustee in bankruptcy as part of his property, subject to trustee's right to disclaim unprofitable contracts, and, if it is an executory contract, the trustee may complete it and receive the benefit for the estate; he may give receipts and, with the permission of the creditors' committee, exercise various powers, e. g. he may sue on the contract, assign the right of action to creditors or even to the bankrupt, sell the bankrupt's business (in a proper case even to a company promoted by himself and the creditor's committee), or make any compromise of an action or claim.”

凡事都有例外情况，在仲裁中，普通法国家通常都有立法明确当事人死亡不会使仲裁条文失效。英国的诉讼更重视诉讼事由或诉因（cause of action）的存在与否。因此，即使诉讼主体（自然人或公司法人）在诉讼中变为不存在（死亡或破产），只要诉讼事由或诉因仍然存在，诉讼都可以继续进行下去。相应的因诉讼主体死亡，法律有对应的更换诉讼参与人的相关规定，如公司法人破产往往会由法院指定破产管理人，自然人死亡也会有继承人或是财产管理人。当然，如果自然人一点财产也没有，其死亡后，即使有胜诉判决也无法执行，这种情况也时有发生。毕竟如果该自然人（或公司法人）没有财产，即使没有死亡（或破产），实际上也无法执行。而与法院判决有所不同的是，仲裁庭的管辖权来自仲裁协议。因此，与自然人之间的仲裁协议和其他与自然人订立的合约一样，因为自然人的死亡而无法履行，即合约受阻。因此，需要通过立法条文来改变普通法的地位，令仲裁条文不会由于自然人死亡而受阻，达到与法院审理同样的效果。1996年英国《仲裁法》之section 8规定：“**Whether agreement discharged by death of a party.** (1) Unless otherwise agreed by the parties, an arbitration agreement is not discharged by the death of a party and may be enforced by or against the personal representatives of that party. (2) Subsection (1) does not affect the operation of any enactment or rule of law by virtue of which a substantive right or obligation is extinguished by death.”

香港《仲裁条例》第22条与新加坡《仲裁法》第5条等也有同样的规定。

3.货物买卖合约，卖方受到外来的突发事件的影响无法提供货物。这在杨大明的《国际货物买卖》一书第六章有详细介绍,不再重复。只简单说,如果一个买卖机器设备的合约,机器设备在交货前被烧毁,就会构成合约受阻。另在英国古老的 Re an arbitration between Shipton, Anderson & Co. and Harrison Brothers & Co. (1915) 3 KB 676 先例中,涉及的是一批小麦的买卖,但因为“一战”,小麦被英国政府征收,导致卖方无法交货,法院判合约受阻。一般来说,国际货物买卖的 CIF/FOB 的付运合约中一般不会指明是哪一票货,只会规定货物的规格。因此,即使卖方有意愿以某一票货物履行合约,而这票货物被烧毁也无法构成合约受阻,因为卖方理论上完全可以另一票符合合约规格的货物履行。但这也不绝对,如在 Howell v. Coupland (1876) 1 QBD 258 先例中,在双方的买卖合约中明确写明是某一块土地上出产的 200 吨土豆,这等于说明了是哪一票货。而该年这块土地土豆歉收,法院判是合约受阻。上诉庭的 Coleridge 勋爵说:“The true ground, as it seems to me, on which the contract should be interpreted, and which is the ground on which, I believe, the Court of Queen's Bench proceeded, is that by the simple and obvious construction of the agreement both parties understood and agreed, that there should be a condition implied that before the time for the performance of the contract the potatoes should be, or should have been, in existence, and should still be existing when the time came for the performance ... It was not an absolute contract of delivery under all circumstances, **but a contract to deliver so many potatoes, of a particular kind, grown on a specific place, if deliverable from that place.** On the facts the condition did arise and the performance was excused.”(加黑部分是笔者的强调)

第二大类是外来的事件导致合约法律上无法履行(legal impossible),Macmilan 勋爵在贵族院的 Denny, Mott & Dickson Ltd. v. James B Fraser & Co. Ltd. (1944) AC 265 先例说:“It is plain that a contract to do what it has become illegal to do cannot be legally enforceable. There cannot be a default in not doing what the law forbids to be done.”

针对国际货物买卖合约,这是付运合约(shipment contracts),最常见的就是政府颁布了出口禁令导致合约非法,卖方因此无法在付运期内履行。或是发生战争时与敌国公司订立的合约都会因通敌而变为非法,无法履行。在土地/房屋的买卖合约中,如果政府突然没收了该土地/房屋或是设为保护区禁止买卖等,都会导致合约受阻。本章第 3 段提到的 1920 年美国颁发禁酒令导致的一连串案例,大量双方都知道是为了开设酒吧而订立的短租因非法而无法履行,这被判是租约受阻而自动终止,租客不必再支付租金。

7.3.2 合约的共同目的被毁

第二类受阻的合约的共同目的/意愿被毁(common purpose of contract destroyed),也已经举了不少先例。如在本章第 3 段介绍的 Krell v. Henry (1903) 2 KB 740 先例(英皇加冕典礼取消的先例),本章之 7.2.4 段介绍的 The “Molton” (1938)

61 Lloyd's Rep. 149 先例等。

7.3.2.1　不可能履行与共同目的被毁之间的关系

共同目的被毁也被称为“共同目的不可能达成”(impossibility of common purpose)或“履行不实际”(impracticability to perform)。在 Treitel 教授的《Frustration and Force Majeure》(第 2 版,2004 年)一书第 309 页说:“Frustration of purpose is, in a sense, the mirror – image of impracticability.〔43〕 The typical contract is an arrangement under which one party agrees to supply a thing or a service or some other facility to the other, and the latter agrees to pay a sum of money for it. In cases of impossibility, the contract is discharged because the supervening event has made it impossible for the former party to supply the thing, service or facility,〔44〕 but the cases of alleged impracticality, there is no such impossibility, but the normal position is that the supplier argues that the cost of providing the thing, service or facility has risen, or that other difficulties of so doing have increased, to such an extent that he should be discharged. In cases of alleged frustration of purpose it is normally the recipient of the thing, service or facility who argues that the contract should be discharged.〔45〕His own obligation, being merely one to pay money, cannot have become impossible, nor has any impossibility affected the obligation of the supplier, which can still be performed. But the recipient's case is that the contract should be discharged because the supplier's performance is no longer of any use to the recipient for the purpose for which both parties had intended it to be used.〔46〕 This was the ground of discharge recognised in the ‘coronation cases’ (eg. Krell v. Henry [1903] 2 KB 740)... Frustration of purpose thus resembles impracticability in that it can lead to discharge of contracts in cases failing short of impossibility; and for this reason the doctrines are sometimes regarded as equivalents, or are confused with each other.〔47〕 But they differ in that generally in cases of impracticability discharge is claimed by the supplier of the thing, service or facility which is to be supplied under the contract, while in cases of frustration of purpose it is the recipient who claims that the contract has been

---

〔43〕 合约目的受阻其实就是合约履行不实际。

〔44〕 在一个典型的合约下,一方同意向另一方提供货物、服务或设备,而后者同意为此支付一定的金钱。合约因为不可能履行而受阻,是指因为外来的突发事件导致前者无法提供货物、服务或设备。

〔45〕 而合约履行不实际的情况一般是合约并非不可能履行,但一方声称提供货物、服务或设备的成本升高,或是其他方面的困难增多到他应被视为不需要继续履行的程度。合约目的受阻的情况一般是接受货物、服务或设备的一方争辩他不再需要继续履行合约。

〔46〕 接受方的合约责任只是付钱,很难有情况导致他不可能付钱,而供应方不可能履行也不影响接受方付钱。接受方的争辩往往是供应方的履行对接受方来说已经无法起到与双方在订立合约时的目的,合约应被视为终止。

〔47〕 合约目的受阻类似合约履行不实际,可以让在合约并非不可能履行的情况下自动终止。因此,有说法是这两者是相同的,也会被混为一谈。

discharged.[48]"

7.3.2.2 确定什么是共同目的

从上述 Treitel 教授所讲可以看出，共同目的被毁与履行不实际没有区别，这相比合约不可能履行争议性更大。除了事件的严重程度能否导致共同目的被毁或是履行不实际会产生争议外，不少人对什么才是共同目的也有误解。如在一个典型的国际货物买卖合约中，有关的货物是大宗货，如果合约订立后出口国突然做出禁令禁止出口，往往导致市场价格急升。卖方显然不想继续履行合约而会声称合约受阻，这也有一定道理，毕竟政府的禁令导致合约变为非法。但这有很多变数，如出口禁令并不是完全禁止出口，卖方仍然可以申请许可[49]或可以找到属于禁令例外情况的货物，只是价格高得多。或者卖方可以在市场上购买已经装船的浮动货物（floating cargo），只是价格也很高。又或者这个出口禁令只是暂时，而相关的合约有一条不可抗力条文让卖方可以做出通知以延长付运期。以上各种情况都说明合约没有遇上法律上不可能履行（legal impossibility）的情况，而最多只是履行不实际。但这主要是对卖方来说不实际，如原本是赚钱的合约变成大亏本，而履行的做法上也苛刻了很多。这在本质上与将在本章之7.4段介绍的苏伊士运河封闭的先例相同，不应该构成受阻。因为这只是卖方单方面的合约目的被毁（赚不到钱甚至亏本），而对买方来说合约目的（收到货物）并没有被毁。毕竟必须是合约的共同目的被毁才能构成受阻，而在商业社会中，绝少会见到有合约说明必须保证一方有多少收益，并当做合约的主要目的。

要进一步分析合约的共同目的，可与本章第1段介绍的“共同错误”（common mistake）进行类比，重点是必须是共同的而不是单方面的。共同错误（不论是对订约时存在的事实或法律有了共同的错误理解）会导致合约空与无效（null and void），因为双方没有真正的订约意图（true *consensus ad idem*）。而共同目的（common purpose）被毁的受阻是后来的突发事件（无论涉及事实或法律）也必须与双方真正的订约意图有关系。也就是通过解释合约找出原本的合约责任与承诺，并与发生突发事件后的合约责任与承诺进行对比，看是否发生根本性的改变。[50] 如果发生根本性的改变，也就是双方对发生突发事件后的合约责任没有真正的订约意图。

这就可以更好地理解 Radcliffe 勋爵在 Davis Contractors Ltd. v. Fareham Urban District Council（1956）AC 696 先例针对这方面的著名判决：“It is not hardship or inconvenience or material loss itself which calls the principle of frustration into play. There must be as well such a change in the significance of the obligation that the thing undertaken would, **if performed, be a different thing from that contracted for.**”（加黑部分是笔者的强调）

---

〔48〕 一般来说，履行不实际是供应方提出，而合约目的受阻是接受方提出。

〔49〕 有关许可或批准，可见本章之12.2.2段。

〔50〕 见本章第5段。

这种情况经常发生,特别是针对延误。一般来说,大家的感觉是延误时间的长短才是至关重要,如果是长时间的延误就可以构成受阻,短时间的延误就不会构成受阻。但这样的说法并不准确,重点还是看该延误是否令合约责任发生根本性的改变,即合约的共同目的是否被毁。如在本章多次提到的 The "Nema" (1981) 2 Lloyd's Rep. 239 先例中,虽然延误相对来说不算太长,但因为会遇上大湖冰封,所以构成1979 年这一季度的租约受阻。另外,如果合约中就订明了货物是为了赶上在圣诞季销售(如圣诞帽等),则很短时间的延误可能就导致合约的共同目的被毁,构成合约受阻。

在 Metropolitan Water Board v. Dick, Kerr & Co. (1918) AC 119 先例中,被告为原告建造水库,合约规定工程要在 6 年内完成。与大多数类似工程的合约一样,有关合约也有条文规定在一些突发事件下(包括战争),被告完成工程的时限可以延长。

在 1914 年 8 月 4 日,也就是合约订立后没几个月,"一战"爆发。政府当局在1916 年 2 月强制要求水库所有工程停工,工人与设备转到其他地方制造军火。水库已经建造的部分与施工现场使用的设备也被强制征收。但显然双方针对合约是否受阻有争议, 1916 年 5 月,原告开始诉讼程序,申请法院做出合约仍然对被告有约束力的宣告(declaratory judgment)。

贵族院判是在政府当局的命令后,合约立即自动终止。因为这命令会造成无限期的延误(indefinite delay),这与双方订立合约时可以接受的完工时限可以延长是不同的性质。Finlay 勋爵说:"... though the works when constructed may last for centuries, the process of construction was to last for six years only. It is obvious that the whole character of such a contract for construction may be revolutionized by the indefinite delay; such as that which has occurred in the present case, in consequence of the prohibition."

Finlay 勋爵接受即使之后建造水库的工程可以复工,也是在 6 年合约期中的大部分已经过去的时候。而到那个时候,履行合约的条件包括人工与材料的价格都会完全不同(absolutely different)。因此,即使复工,也会是一个替代的新合约而非保持原合约不变(not to maintain the original contract, but to substitute a different contract for it)。

另在本章之 7.2.4 段介绍的 The "Molton" (1938) 61 Lloyd's Rep. 149 先例中,Goddard 大法官说:"if the foundation of the contract goes, either by the destruction of the subject-matter or by reason of such long interruption or **delay that the performance is really in effect that of a different contract**... then the performance of the contract is regarded as frustrated."(加黑部分是笔者的强调)

在 Sir Lindsay Parkinson & Co. Ltd. v. Commissioners of Works (1949) 2 KB 632 先例中,Asquith 大法官说:"... fundamental enough to transmute the job the contractor had undertaken into a job of a different kind, which the contract did not contemplate and to which it could not apply."

在 British Movietonews Ltd. v. London & District Cinemas Ltd. (1952) AC 166 先例中,Simon 勋爵说:"if... a consideration of the terms of the contract, in the light of the circumstances existing when it was made, shows that they never agreed to be bound **in a fundamentally different situation** which has now unexpectedly emerged, the contract ceases to bind at that point – not because the court in its discretion thinks it just and reasonable to qualify the terms of the contract, but **because on its true construction it does not apply in that situation**."(加黑部分是笔者的强调)

7.3.2.3 单方面目的或多个目的部分被毁是不足够

根据普通法的法律地位,在很局限的情况下单方面错误(unilateral mistake)也可以令合约变为空与无效。因为如果合约履行不顺利,一方往往可以提出其在订立合约时有单方面的错误,如算错成本、看错市场走势等。这些单方面的错误在现实中数不胜数,不可能导致合约空与无效,否则订立合约就没有意义,任何一方找个理由就可以脱身。只有在一方将另一方的身份搞错(这往往涉及另一方欺诈性误述),[51]或是虽然表面看来双方是达成一致想法(*ad diem*)但实际上是"鸡同鸭讲",[52]即双方没有真正的订约意图,单方面错误才可以令合约空与无效。但不像共同错误,单方面错误与合约受阻的说法没有什么关联,不存在"单方面目的被毁"的受阻,必须是共同目的被毁才能构成合约受阻。

在《The Law of Contract in Singapore》(2012 年)一书之 19 – 066 段,说:"Unlike the case with common mistake and instances of frustration of purposes common to both contracting parties, it is suggested that extension of the rationale for common law unilateral mistake to instances of frustration of purposes held unilaterally by one of the contracting parties is inappropriate... **One might reason, therefore, that mere impracticality of the purposes of one of the contracting parties ought not to give rise to a discharge of the contract for reasons of frustration.** In other words, it is arguable that a contract may be discharged because of **common** purposes of the contracting parties are 'frustrated' – and that **the position is different when there is no such commonality of purpose.**"(加黑部分是笔者的强调)

除了不能是单方面的目的(unilateral purpose),要构成共同目的被毁而受阻,被毁的共同目的必须是唯一或至少是主要的目的,只是合约的部分目的被毁(partial failure of purpose)是不足够。如在英皇加冕的一系列先例中,Krell v. Henry (1903)

---

〔51〕 在本书第五章之 10.2.1 段与杨良宜《合约的解释:规则与应用》一书第三章之 13.3.7.1 段有详细介绍。

〔52〕 在本书第五章之 10.2.2 段与杨良宜《合约的解释:规则与应用》一书第三章之 13.3.7.2 段有详细介绍。

2 KB 740 先例的共同目的被毁，正如 Vaughan Williams 大法官说："In my judgment the use of the rooms was let and taken for the purpose of seeing the Royal procession. It was not a demise of the rooms, or even an agreement to let and take the rooms. It is a licence to use rooms for a particular purpose and none other. And in my judgment the taking place of those processions on the days proclaimed along the proclaimed route, which passed 56A, Pall Mall, was regarded by both contracting parties as the foundation of the contract..."

但另一个 Herne Bay Steamboat Co. v. Hutton (1903) 2 KB 683 先例被判是合约的部分目的被毁是不足够构成受阻。在该先例中，有关的合约涉及租用一艘游艇，其中写明合约是为了两个目的，一是观看英皇检阅舰队（naval review），二是租用游艇在舰队周边巡航与观赏舰队威势一天（a day's cruise round the fleet）。而由于英皇生病，显然第一个目的受阻，但第二个目的还是可以达成。所以上诉庭判合约没有受阻，Vaughan Williams 大法官说："Mr. Hutton, in hiring this vessel, **had two objects in view: first, of taking people to see the naval review, and, secondly, of taking them round the fleet.** Those, no doubt, were the purposes of Mr. Hutton, but it does not seem to me that because, as it is said, those purposes became impossible, it would be a very legitimate inference that the happening of the naval review was contemplated by both parties as the basis and foundation of this contract, so as to bring the case within the doctrine of Taylor v. Caldwell."（加黑部分是笔者的强调）

7.3.2.4　共同目的必须十分狭窄与局限

虽然很多涉及合约受阻的先例都有一方合约方希望依赖共同目的被毁的理由令合约自动终止，但其中成功被判受阻的相对较少，因为有说法是共同目的必须十分狭窄与局限。在 North Shore Ventures Ltd. v. Anstead Holdings Inc. (2010) 2 Lloyd's Rep. 265 先例中，[53] 案情与俄罗斯著名的金融寡头别列佐夫斯基（Boris Berezovsky）有关。其公司即原告（North Shore）以很高的利息贷款 5000 万美元给被告（Anstead Holdings），并同时要被告的两位俄罗斯股东做出个人担保。该贷款合约第 2.2 条文说这笔钱是 Anstead Holdings 用作与俄罗斯的肉制品与石油买卖的业务。应 Anstead Holding 其中一位股东的要求，这笔钱汇到了瑞士的一家银行。但由于别列佐夫斯基被瑞士当局调查有关洗钱的非法活动，导致其中 1800 万美元冻结了 4 年后才被 Anstead Holdings 取出。后来 Anstead Holdings 也归还了大部分的钱，但还欠 3500 万美元（主要是利息）时就宣告破产。于是 North Shore 开始诉讼，向被告与做出个人担保的股东（第二与第三被告）追讨这笔欠下的钱。这两位股东提出了一连串的抗辩，其中包括他们的个人担保因为瑞士银行冻结了 1800 万美元这个突发事件

[53] 该先例虽然之后被上诉庭（[2011] 2 Lloyd's Rep. 45）推翻，但根据其他方面的理由，没有针对合约受阻这一点。

受阻,但这在一审法院被 Newey 大法官根据各种理由否定。两位股东声称合约受阻的理由之一是因为1800 万美元被冻结,所以 Anstead Holding 无法将这笔钱用作肉制品与石油买卖的业务,属于合约的共同目的受阻。但 Newey 大法官不接受这一说法,认为共同目的必须十分狭窄与局限,North Shore 在借钱给 Anstead Holdings 时是根本不会理会这笔钱的最终用途,谈不上将这笔钱用作肉制品与石油买卖的业务是借贷合约的基础(foundation)。另外这笔钱在冻结时依然会为 Anstead Holdings 赚取利息,并可以进行外汇交易。Newey 大法官说:"Subsequent cases have, moreover, warned that frustration in general, and Krell v. Henry in particular, should not be extended. In Maritime National Fish Ltd. v. Ocean Trawlers Ltd. [1935] AC 524, Lord Wright, giving the judgment of the Privy Council, said (at 529) that Krell v. Henry was 'certainly not one to be extended'. In J. Lauritzen AS v. Wijsmuller BV (The 'Super Servant Two') [1990] 1 Lloyd's Rep. 1, Bingham LJ said (at 8): 'Since the effect of frustration is to kill the contract and discharge the parties from further liability under it, the doctrine is not to be lightly invoked, must be kept within very narrow limits and ought not to be extended'."

法院判共同目的必须十分狭窄与局限的逻辑也很容易理解,一直以来,英国法院就强调要支持而不是否定合约的有效性。如果合约双方认为在某些情况下有必要终止合约,应该在合约中写明,如通过不可抗力条文(*force majeure* clause)或履行困难条文(hardship clause),法院不会轻易主动"杀死"双方订立的合约。

7.3.3 外来的突发事件必须严重影响合约才会构成受阻

笔者这里可举若干例子做出说明:

1. 在 Leiston Gas Co. v. Leiston – cum – Sizewell Urban District Council (1916) 2 KB 428 先例中,原告与被告订立合约为被告提供煤气灯照明服务,包括煤气灯设备与其他硬件设施,连接煤气灯与原告在当地的煤气总管,对煤气灯与其他设备的维修保养等工作。而被告做出的约因/对价就是每个季度为这些服务支付费用。这个合约从 1911 年 8 月开始,为期 5 年。但在合约履行三年多后,由于"一战"爆发,政府当局在战时通过立法《Defence of the Relm Regulations》(No. 1307 of 1914)下令灯火管制,以防止敌军的轰炸。在政府进行灯火管制之后,原告仍在进行一些日常的维护等工作,只是除了 1915 年第一季度有 26 日是亮灯的之外,其余时间因为政府禁止没有亮灯。之后原告开始诉讼,要求被告支付拖欠 3 个季度的费用。被告的抗辩是因为政府的灯火管制,所以合约受阻自动终止。但这不被上诉庭接受,上诉庭认为只有部分合约责任无法履行,而其他的合约责任可以履行,因此不构成受阻。Reading 勋爵说:"The decision in this case must depend on the true effect of the contract. Under the contract the plaintiffs undertook to perform various services for the defendants in return for an agreed rate of payment to be made quarterly by the defendants for every quarter in the five years duration of the contract. These services included the provision and erection

and maintenance of the column lamps and other plant for the supply of gas as stipulated, and the defendants agreed to make those payments extending over five years as the remuneration to the plaintiffs, not only for supplying and lighting the gas for the lamps, but also for providing and erecting and maintaining the plant. In fact the plaintiffs had performed the various services under the contract for nearly three and a half years before the event under discussion happened. The column lamps remain their property under the contract, and the defendants have had the advantage of them throughout the three and a half years. **They have used them even in the three quarters of** 1915, not indeed to the full extent, as the lamps were not lighted except for the twenty-six days of the first quarter, but to the extent that they remained there connected with the main and would be lighted **whenever the prohibition by the military authority was relaxed or withdrawn**. Upon these facts I cannot hold that the performance of the contract had become unlawful, or that the venture was frustrated by the act of the Executive in forbidding the lighting of the lamps. **Part of the performance of the contract had become unlawful, but another part of the contract, which cannot be regarded as a trivial part, was lawful and could be performed. In these circumstances the defendants are not justified in treating the contract as at an end, or in refusing to make the payments as agreed by them.**"(加黑部分是笔者的强调)

2. 在 E. B. Aaby's Rederi A/S v. Lep Transport, Ltd. (1948) 81 Lloyd's Rep. 465 先例中,案情涉及运输羊毛的程租合约。但在付运之前,存放在仓库里的 1816 捆羊毛被大火烧到剩下 48 捆。Sellers 大法官认为羊毛并没有全部被烧毁,剩下的 48 捆也谈不上极微小(*de minimis*)。至于只是运 48 捆羊毛经济上不划算(因为同意支付的是一次过的运费),并不是合约受阻的理由。

3. 在 The "Zuiho Maru" (1977) 2 Lloyd's Rep. 552 先例中,案情涉及沙特阿拉伯在 70 年代石油禁运时下令石油公司减产 1/10,这导致 Zuiho Maru 轮少装了 7% 的货物(原油)。在抗辩船东索赔的亏舱费(deadfreight)时,承租人指原租约已因石油禁运而受阻,而真正履行的航次虽然只装了 93% 的货物,但属于新安排,与原租约无关。Kerr 大法官不同意租约受阻,因为受影响太轻微,说:"Without resort to any definition of the nature of a frustrating event, it is self-evident that any short – fall of this kind could never be capable of giving rise to frustration, because there is nothing like a sufficiently fundamental change of circumstances."

4. 一般船舶被政府征用是延误遥遥无期(indefinite delay),会是很明显的租约受阻的例子:Hirji Mulji v. Cheong Yue S. S. Co. Ltd. (1926) AC 497 先例。但如果对租约的影响并不严重,征用期不长,后果就不一样了。在 The "Silveroak" (1958) 1 Lloyd's Rep. 290 先例中,有关租约长达 30 个月。起租 17 个月后,船舶被英国政府(船旗国)征用,估计为期 3 至 4 个月。这表示征用后,期租仍有约 10 个月租期可用,法院判是租约并没有受到严重影响,受阻不成立。

5. 根据以上案例可以推断,若期租尚余半年,而船舶遇上意外要修理一两个月或更长(但不是长达半年),都不足构成受阻。

6. 一般罢工(strike)不会被认为严重至影响合约的履行,因为劳资谈判常会有突破,历史上很少会有太严重的僵局。但如果遇上特殊情况,如租约只剩下 3 个月,而且冬天快要来临,大湖马上要封闭,而罢工看来会延续下去。正如 Roskill 勋爵在 The "Nema" (1981) 2 Lloyd's Rep. 239 先例中说:"It was not suggested that a strike could never bring about frustration of an adventure. But it was pointed out that most attempts to invoke strikes as a cause of frustration have in the past failed. The 'Penelope' (1928) P. 180 is almost the only example of success, and in that case the underlying reasoning of the judgment is far from easy to follow, even though the decision may well be correct... I see no reason in principle why a strike should not be capable of causing frustration of an adventure by delay."

7. 在上一段介绍的 North Shore Ventures Ltd. v. Anstead Holdings Inc. (2010) 2 Lloyd's Rep. 265 先例中,Newey 大法官拒绝受阻说法的另一个理由是 5000 万美元的贷款中,被瑞士当局冻结的 1800 万美元只占 36%,不够严重令合约受阻。

7.4 多花钱、多花时间以及赚钱变亏本都不足以令合约受阻

在 Tennants (Lancashire) Ltd. v. CS Wilson & Co. Ltd. (1917) AC 495 先例中,Loreburn 勋爵说:"the argument that a man can be excused from performance of his contract when it becomes commercially impossible... seems to me a dangerous contention which ought not to be admitted unless the parties have plainly contracted to that effect."

这一点在本章第 6 段提到的 Davis Contractors Ltd. v. Fareham Urban District Council (1956) AC 696 先例已是明确。该案涉及建造商原先估计的 8 个月建造 78 栋房子,但因工人短缺等意外事件延误了 14 个月,建造商亏大本。于是他想依赖合约受阻,令其"额外时间"的工作可另外议价而不受原合约的约束,但贵族院不同意。

在这一点上,航运方面最好的例子是一连串因苏伊士运河 1967 年封闭[54]而导致的案例。在这些案例中,船东纷纷想依赖合约/租约受阻,因为原本运费(或租金)很低,而苏伊士运河封闭后,市场暴涨,要是能在原租约脱身,船东可以发大财。并且如果要履行,原本是经苏伊士运河现在要绕经好望角(路程长一倍),要多花时间与

---

〔54〕 这是指在 1976 年 6 月的"六日战争"(Six - Day War),以色列于 6 月 5 日先发制人,突击埃及、叙利亚与约旦,并成功把整个埃及空军摧毁,在接下去的陆地战争中掌握了制空权。接着,以色列快速向西奈半岛与戈兰高地进攻,一直打到苏伊士运河才无法前进,这也导致了长达十多年的苏伊士运河的封闭。直到 1978 年以埃达成达成和平协议,即著名的"戴维营协议",以色列从西奈半岛分阶段撤军,埃及才能取回苏伊士运河,并在清雷后重新开放给国际航运使用。

燃油,而运费仍照旧,这可要亏大本了。但看来这严重的突发事件并不能令合约受阻,因为租约可以履行(绕经好望角),合约共同目的(走一个航次,如 The "Eugenia" [1963] 2 Lloyd's Rep. 381 先例[55]从意大利 Genoa 去印度)也没有被毁,这一装一卸实质(physically)上与法律上(legally)都仍是完全可能履行,只是船东要多花时间与燃油并亏大本了。

相关苏伊士运河封闭先例有:The "Eugenia"; The "Captain George K" (1970) 2 Lloyd's Rep. 21; 美国的 Glidden Co. v. Hellenic Lines Ltd. 275 F. 2d. 253 (2d Cir. 1960); Transatlantic Financing Corp. v. U. S. 363 F. 2d. 312, 1966 AMC 1717 (D. C. Cir. 1966); American Trading & Production Corp. v. Shell Int'l Marine Ltd. 453 F. 2d 939 (2d Cir. 1972)等。

同类的先例中唯一有不同结果的是 The "Massalia" (1960) 1 Lloyd's Rep. 594 先例,因为该租约中有一条文说:"Captain also to telegraph to(承租人)on passing Suez Canal."

但在 The "Eugenia"先例中,Denning 勋爵已否定了 The "Massalia"先例的判法,认为法院将这一条文看得过重,把通过苏伊士运河提升为合约的重要部分之一或合约的共同目的,以至于苏伊士运河一封闭,该合约就无法履行或共同目的被毁是不恰当。但 The "Eugenia"先例没有否定如果租约有一条条文说明通过苏伊士运河是唯一路线(only route),甚至说明这是先决条件如"it is a pre - condition of this charter that the vessel can transit Suez Canal without impediment",则受阻的理论仍可适用,因为运河封闭令这唯一路线无法履行与共同目的被毁。

同样的问题也在大量的 CIF/FOB 买卖合约中出现。如在 Tsakiroglou & Co. Ltd. v. Noblee Thorl G. m. b. H (1961) 1 Lloyd's Rep. 329 先例中,案情涉及一个 CIF 买卖。因为卖方要以高价才能租到船舶来履约将货物付运,所以争辩运河封闭令合约受阻,双方都不用再履约与做出赔偿。有关的判决自然是买卖合约没有受阻。

正是因为苏伊士运河封闭不能构成合约受阻,所以,不少买卖合约的不可抗力条文(*force majeure* clause)会写明如果运河封闭,双方可选择终止合约(option to terminate):见 Ewan McKendrick QC (Hon)编写的《Force Majeure and Frustration of Contract》(第 2 版,1995 年)一书第二章与 Cartoon 先生的《Drafting an Acceptable Force Majeure Clause》(1978) J. B. L. 230 一文。

在买卖合约中,货价上升或提供服务的成本升高不构成合约受阻的先例还有很多,这方面可节录权威的《Benjamin's Sale of Goods》(第 9 版,2014 年)一书第 6 - 055 段,如下:"**Contract becomes unprofitable for seller.** The fact that a contract of sale has

[55] 该先例涉及更早的一次苏伊士运河封闭。埃及的纳赛尔总统在 1956 年 7 月将运河收归国有,带来英法联军的攻击并导致埃及封闭运河。

become, because of a rise in prices or costs or by the occurrence of an extraneous event, unprofitable for the seller is insufficient to frustrate the contract.[56] Although it has been suggested that it would be possible for a court to find that ' a serious and sudden depreciation of monetary value, could disrupt the intended equivalent of performances on either side' and bring about a radical change in the obligation sufficient to frustrate contract, the better view is that a devaluation of the currency in which the price is expressed or the effect of inflation on the profitability of a fixed-price contract (even if of long duration) are risks which must be bound by the seller.[57]"

最后要一提的是2008年"金融海啸"后航运市场大跌,下挫95%以上,很多承租人(包括不少中国钢厂)试图以合约受阻为由避免继续履行一些租约或包运合约(COA),但都不成功。在 Classic Maritime Inc. v. Lion Diversified Holding Berhad (2010) 1 Lloyd's Rep. 59 先例中,案情涉及2008年8月中订立的2个航次的包运合约准备去运矿砂。这导致承租人很大的压力,甚至也没有能力在卸港贮存与生产这些即将付运的矿砂。而承租人也在2008年11月取得了卖方的同意,押后付运矿砂,即不再需要船东履行这一包运合约。这无可避免地导致了承租人以合约受阻与不可抗力为由拒绝履行包运合约,而船东也接受了违约/毁约,并在英国法院申请了简易判决(summary judgment)。而承租人就要求英国法院中止(stay)审理,因为在包运合约中有一条仲裁条文。针对承租人合约受阻与不可抗力的抗辩,虽然法院认为因为涉及事实的争议,不适合在简易判决的申请中做出决定,但明言承租人成功令合约受阻的可能性不高。

---

〔56〕 参见 Instone (S) & Co. Ltd. v. Speeding Marshall & Co. Ltd. (1916) 33 TLR 202(由于战争的影响加上矿工被征兵,煤炭价格上升了88%); Tennants (Lancashire) Ltd. v. CS Wilson & Co. Ltd. (1917) AC 495(案情涉及氯化镁的供应合约,英国市场上的氯化镁大部分来源于德国,"一战"爆发后,市场短缺,价格上升); Hulton (E) & Co. Ltd. v. Chadwick & Taylor Co. Ltd. (1918) 34 TLR 230(履行合约的原材料价格上升); Beves & Co. Ltd. v. Farkas (1953) 1 Lloyd's Rep. 103(案情涉及从奥地利出口木材到汉堡或鹿特丹的FOB买卖,原本奥地利政府会给奥地利公司许可让它可以较低的价格出口木材,但因为木材价格上涨,奥地利政府在双方订立合约后付运前撤回了许可,卖方要履约,就要从其他地方高价购买木材); Tsakiroglou & Co. Ltd. v. Noblee Thorl G. m. b. H. (1961) 1 Lloyd's Rep. 329(案情涉及从苏丹运花生到汉堡的CIF买卖,因为苏伊士运河关闭,卖方要花高价才能租到船,变成要亏本); Exportelisa SA v. Rocco Giuseppe & Figli Soc Coll (1978) 1 Lloyd's Rep. 433(因为阿根廷法律的变化,卖方不得不以高昂的价格向军政府购买粮食,而这个价格远远超出了卖方转卖的价格); Tandrin Aviation Holdings Ltd. v. Aero Toy Store (2010) 2 Lloyd's Rep. 668(案情涉及私人飞机的买卖,买方声称因为经济环境发生了重大的逆转,所以无法接收飞机)等先例。

〔57〕 在新加坡的 Glahe International Expo AG v. ACS Computer Pte Ltd. (1999) 1 SLR(R) 945 先例中,苏联解体后,卢布贬值严重,一个以卢布结算的买卖合约原本很赚钱,结果换成美金就大亏本,新加坡上诉庭判这不构成合约受阻。

7.5　受阻事件的产生不涉及任何一方的责任或过错或出自他的原因

这方面有许多先例，部分已经在本章较早的段节提及，只简单节录少数权威说法，如下：

1. 在 Maritime National Fish Ltd. v. Ocean Trawlers Ltd.（1935）AC 524 先例，Wright 勋爵说："The essence of frustration is that it should not be due to **the act or election** of the party seeking to rely on it."（加黑部分是笔者的强调）

2. 在 The "Eugenia"（1963）2 Lloyd's Rep. 381 先例，Denning 勋爵说："The second question is whether the charterparty was frustrated by what took place. The arbitrator has held it was not. The judge has held that it was. Which is right? One thing that is obvious is that the charterers cannot rely on the fact that the Eugenia was trapped in the canal; **for that was their own fault. They were in breach of the war clause in entering it. They cannot rely on a self – induced frustration**, see Maritime National Fish Ltd. v. Ocean Trawlers Ltd. ［1935］AC 524."（加黑部分是笔者的强调）

3. 在 The "Super Servant Two"（1990）1 Lloyd's Rep. 1 先例，Bingham 大法官说："whether the frustrating event relied upon is truly an outside event or extraneous change of situation or whether it is an event which the party seeking to rely on it **had the means and opportunity to prevent but nevertheless caused or permitted to come about**."（加黑部分是笔者的强调）

4. 在更近期的 The "Sea Angel"（2007）2 Lloyd's Rep. 517 先例，Rix 大法官说："Two classic modern statements of the incidence of frustration are to be found in the dicta of Lord Radcliffe in Davis Contractors Ltd. v. Fareham Urban District Council［1956］AC 696 at 729 and Lord Simon of Glaisdale in National Carriers Ltd. v. Panalpina (Northern) Ltd.［1981］AC 675 at 700. Lord Radcliffe said: '... frustration occurs whenever the law recognises that **without default of either party** a contractual obligation has become incapable of being performed because the circumstances in which performance is called for would render it a thing radically different from that which was undertaken by the contract."（加黑部分是笔者的强调）

这大原则/大精神也是理所当然，因此一个船东故意凿沉船（scuttle），虽然合约/租约标的物全损，但并不能令合约受阻，而只会是船东自己违约/毁约（repudiatory breach），承租人或货方等都可以向船东索赔损失。这种自己导致的受阻（self – induced frustration）实质是违约。

但不是船东自己凿沉船这种极端情况，而涉及合约一方的错误（default）或疏忽（negligence）或他的选择（election）或行为（act）而导致合约无法继续履行，也不能构成受阻。

按理说，受阻事件必须是外来因素导致情况改变（outside event or extraneous change of situation），一方的犯错或疏忽应该无法构成合约受阻。所以，船舶不适航引致船货全损,船东不能依赖提单合约受阻而脱身:Monarch Steamship v. Karlshamns Oljefabriker (1949) AC 196 先例。承租人错误下令船舶去不安全港口也不能依赖租约受阻脱身:The "Eugenia" 先例。但如果这错误或疏忽在合约中免责,情况就不一样了。在早期的 The "Carron Park" (1890) 15 P. D. 203 先例中,James Hannen 大法官说:"but negligence for which he is not responsible is as foreign to him as to the person who has suffered by it."

另在相对近期的 Constantine v. Imperial Smelting (1941) 70 Lloyd's Rep. 1 先例中,Wright 勋爵说:"Exceptions, however, may be important... as excluding fault if the frustrating event was induced by what, apart from the exception, would be an actionable breach of contract."

所以,即使船舶全损是船员航行过错与疏忽(negligence in navigation)导致,往往也不影响受阻的成立,因为海上运输合约(租约或提单等)所合并的《海牙规则》/《海牙—维斯比规则》通常对航行过错与疏忽免责。

但要注意的是,针对受阻的说法,疏忽或者更严重的过失是否免责(毕竟在订约自由下可以有"一边倒"的广泛免责)并非真正关键的问题,正如上述所节录的 Bingham 大法官在 The "Super Servant Two"先例所说,真正的问题想依赖合约受阻的一方是否能有办法或机会避免。

所以,合约一方的选择或行为而导致合约无法履行是无法构成合约受阻,笔者可举如下几个先例:

1. 在 The "St. Cuthbert" (1935) 51 Lloyd's Rep. 299 先例中,案情有关五只渔船只申请到三张证书,而承租人自己选择不指定一张证书给 St. Cuthbert 轮,导致它不能合法捕鱼。贵族院判这是自己导致的受阻,即违约,合约受阻的说法不能成立。

2. 在 The "Zuiho Maru" (1977) 2 Lloyd's Rep. 552 先例中,少装 7% 的石油实是在石油禁运减产后,石油公司与承租人之间协议的配给(ration)做法,即使受阻能够成立,也应属于自己导致的受阻。

3. 在 The "Super Servant Two"先例中,案情涉及把钻油台自日本拖到荷兰的拖带合约。合约说明使用 Super Servant Two 轮或是其姊妹船 Super Servant One 轮[Super Servant One or Super Servant Two in Wijismuller's(船东)option]。后者其实另有工作安排,所以船东的意图是使用前者来进行拖带。但在船东指定(nominate)Super Servant Two 轮之前,该船舶沉没。船东希望依赖受阻不履行合约与不做出赔偿,但法院判这是船东自己选择不使用 Super Servant One 轮履行合约,所以只是自己导致的受阻。Hobhouse 大法官说:"Where the promisor has alternative modes of performing the contract and one becomes impossible, that does not make it impossible for him to perform the contract. If the impossibility only comes about because the promisor makes some choice or election, then it is that choice or election which causes the alleged impossibility, not any antecedent event."

有关合约下的选择权在本书第三章之3.3段有介绍,即可以区分为合约选择权(contract option)与真正(或商业)选择权(true option or business option)两类。两者主要的区别是合约选择权只是一个以多种方式履行的合约承诺。其中任何一种方式都不属于首要合约责任(primary contract duty/obligation),但它们加在一起是首要合约责任。而真正(或商业)选择权只有一个首要责任或履行方式,但合约规定有选择权的一方可以选择以替代方式履行合约(substitute contract duty/obligation)。如果他通过宣告(declaration / notice)做出了选择(election),替代的履行方式成为了首要合约责任,原本约定的履行方式就消失了。但如果有选择权的一方没有做出选择,原本的首要合约责任就是合约唯一的履行方式,商业选择权消失。

在该先例中,相关合约的写法很明显是一个合约选择权,因为不能说以两艘姐妹船中的任何一艘履行是首要合约责任,因此,除非两艘船舶都沉没,其中任何一艘船舶沉没都不会令合约受阻。这也是合约选择权虽然表面看来对有选择权的一方有好处但有时也会带来困难之处,即如果有选择权的一方原本希望的履行方式(在该先例中就是以 Super Servant Two 轮履行拖带合约)变为不可能,就必须以另一种履行方式(以 Super Servant One 轮)履行,而不会因为受阻而合约自动终止。[58]

而如果合约的写法不同,如说明合约以 Super Servant Two 轮履行,但船东有选择权以 Super Servant One 轮替代履行,而船东没有行使选择权,则当 Super Servant Two 轮沉没后,合约受阻。或者合约的写法是以 Super Servant One 轮履行,但船东有选择权以 Super Servant Two 轮替代履行,而船东在其沉没前也确实行使了选择权宣告他指定 Super Servant Two 轮履行,合约就会受阻。因为一经宣告,就是最终确定,不能再改,如同 Super Servant Two 轮是拖带合约中唯一的拖带船:The "Trado" (1982) 1 Lloyd's Rep. 157 先例。

8. 受阻令合约自动终止

在本章第6段提到,受阻与否不必一方或双方做出宣告,合约甚至会在双方当时不自觉下实已自动终止。Roskill 勋爵在 National Carriers Ltd. v. Panalpina (Northern) Ltd. (1981) AC 675 先例强调说:"Its operation does not depend on the action or inaction of the parties."

在 Hirji Mulji v. Cheong Yue S. S. Co. Ltd. (1926) AC 497 先例中,船舶在交船前被政府征用(requisition),船东以为征用期不会长,还不断与承租人商讨延长交船时间,承租人也同意。谁知征用越拖越长,最后长达两年。贵族院判是船舶一被征

---

〔58〕 这也可见在本书第三章之3.3.2.2段介绍的 Reardon Smith Line Ltd. v. Ministry of Agriculture, Fisheries and Food (also known as Vancouver Strike Cases) (1963) 1 Lloyd's Rep. 12 先例。

用,租约已是受阻。虽然双方当时还以为征用时间不会久,所以同意某些条件,但这是无关(irrelevant),不影响租约已经自动终止。

8.1 合约可否分开令部分受阻?

这是一个重要的课题,因为影响的不止是受阻,也包括了本书第一章所讲的违约/毁约(repudiatory breach)。这也包括了合约条文,如有权终止合约的条文、免责条文或不可抗力条文,到底影响整个合约或只是局限在部分合约。

这就带来了完整合约(entire contract)或是可分开的合约(divisible contract)的说法。可以说,大部分合约都是完整合约,即使其履行涉及不同的阶段(stage),如一个涉及多个连续航次(每一航次接上一航次)的程租合约。这种完整合约如果涉及受阻的争议,受阻成立就会导致整个合约自动终止。在早期的 The “Kamouraska” (1920) 4 Lloyd’s Rep. 434 先例中,法院判一个期租不能分开来受阻,要么整个租约受阻,要么不受阻(it either does or does not destroy the whole contract)。该期租合约的租约期长达 7 年,并且有选择权可以延长 3 年,即总共 7 至 10 年。这个期租合约也很独特,每年只有在美加大湖不冰封的时间,该船舶才需要让承租人用来运煤。在租约期间,该船舶被政府征用一段时间,但征用完毕后,期租合约仍有余下的租期。而双方的争议并非剩下的租约是否要继续履行,而是征用这段时间租约是否部分受阻。原因是政府征用期间给了赔偿,估计这笔赔偿很可观,因此船东声称在这段时间租约受阻,政府的赔偿应归船东。而承租人则声称征用期间租约没有受阻,承租人要支付租金,而政府的赔偿应归承租人。

而如果是一个合约,但整体解释是可分开的合约责任,这样一来,如果发生受阻事件可能判部分受阻:The “Nema” (1981) 2 Lloyd’s Rep. 239 先例。

可以举个简单的例子,如果一个涉及 6 个航次的包运合约(contract of affreightment / COA)规定了航次是一个接一个履行,并且只针对第一个航次写明了销约期条文(cancellation clause),这就是一个典型的完整合约。如果船舶错过了销约期,承租人取消的是整个包运合约,而不仅仅是第一个航次。但如果包运合约的写法不同,如规定了每个月一次付运,每次付运都有分别的销约期条文,这就有可能属于一个可分开的合约。如果船舶错过了第一次付运的销约期,承租人就只能取消第一个航次。

再举一个涉及 6 批货的买卖合约的例子,如果买方拒绝开出信用证(letter of credit),这是违反了合约的条件条文(condition),卖方如果选择了终止合约,就是这个完整合约一起终止,而不只是针对第一批货。但如果买卖合约可以分开,卖方即使接受了买方的违约/毁约,也只能取消第一批货。

合约受阻的说法也是一样,笔者(杨良宜)早年曾经参与过一个涉及两个从澳大利亚装货到印尼的航次的案子。履行第一个航次的船舶在空放去装港期间沉没。当时因为市场高涨,承租人要求船东另派一艘船舶履行该合约。笔者认为承租人的要求很没有道理,如果船东需要再派一艘船舶,就等于船东的航行风险的免责没有任何作用。另一个问题是,即使船东再派一艘船舶,也赶不上销约期/货物的付运期,这就涉及合约更改,但这必须双方同意并存在约因/对价。在笔者看来,如果该合约是一个完整合约,履行第一个航次的船舶沉没,整个合约就受阻而自动终止。即使该合约是一个可分开(severable or divisible)的合约,至少第一个航次也会受阻。

在 Larrinaga v. Soc. Franco – Americaine des Phosphates (1923) 14 Lloyd's Rep. 457 先例中,案情涉及一个 6 个航次的包运合约(COA),首先三个自美国去欧洲的航次因战争无法履行,但船东拒绝跑余下的三个航次。原因也很容易猜到,大战后需要大量重建而船舶吨位又有所减少等,所以航运市场高涨,原本的运费对船东来说不划算。双方的主要争议是承租人是否有权要求船东派船付运剩下的三个航次的磷酸盐。贵族院判是包运合约没有受阻,船东必须履行。船东拒绝履行是违约/毁约,要面对承租人对损失的索赔。

这类争议主要是因为订约自由,所以合约会有各种写法,而不同的写法与解释会导致有些合约虽然有不同的履行阶段但仍是一个完整合约,每一阶段都相互有牵连。但有些是可分开履行的合约,互不牵连。正如 Sumner 勋爵在 Larrinaga v. Soc. Franco – Americaine des Phosphates 先例中所说:"**The charter – party provides for six separate voyages, each being a distinct commercial adventure. There is no reason why a single contract should not provide for many adventures, nor why these adventures should not be entirely independent of one another.** That the voyages are to be made at fixed and regular intervals; that the cargo is to be always of the same material; that the port of loading and discharge, the rate of freight and the contractual terms are to be the same throughout, only show that the adventures are severally as like one another as possible, not that they are not several adventures ... The argument always gets back to the same question, namely, **whether this is a contract for six separate adventures or for one composite adventure, carried out in six stages.**"(加黑部分是笔者的强调)

8.2 如何区分完整合约与可分开的合约

首先可节录在 The "Nema" (1980) 2 Lloyd's Rep. 83 先例中,一审的 Goff 大法官说:"Various terms are to be found in the reports and in the books-entire contracts, severable contract contracts, divisible contracts, severable adventures,. Various meanings have been ascribed to these terms, I propose to use these terms in the following manner:(1) **An entire contract** is a contract which provides expressly or impliedly that a party must perform his part in full before he can recover any part of the price or other consideration due to him under the contract.[59] The classic example of such a contract is to be found in Cutter v. Powell (1795) 6 T. R. 320; another example is a contract to carry goods by sea for freight payable on delivery at the contractual destination. Such a contract is to be contrasted with **a severable contract** which is a single contract which is not

[59] 在本章稍后的 8.3.1 段会有进一步介绍。

entire, and which therefore provides expressly or impliedly that payment of the price or furnishing of any other consideration is due from time to time as contractual performance is rendered. A typical example is a modern building contract on the R. I. B. A. form.[60]

(2) **A divisible contract** is a transaction (which may loosely be called a contract) contained in one document, which is divisible into separate and distinct contracts.[61] In such a case, there is one transaction and one contractual document, but a number of contracts – because the contractual document provides for a number of contractual adventures which are wholly independent of each other and so should properly be regarded as independent contracts. It follows that the term 'divisible contract', though convenient, is self – explanatory, because strictly speaking there is not one contract which is divided-on the contrary, there is one transaction, contained in one contractual document, which provides for a number of contracts. Such as contract is to be contrasted with an indivisible contract, which is a contract which, although it may provide for performance in a series of instalments, does not provide for sufficiently independent contractual adventures to enable the transaction to be divided into separate contracts."

上述节录的 Goff 大法官的说法中同时提到了"severable contract"与"divisible contract",这两者之间没有什么区别,只是用字不同。在《Chitty on Contracts》(第32版,2012年)一书之21 – 038段的标题就同时使用了"severable"与"divisible"两个词:"**Divisible (or severable) Obligations.** The question whether an obligation is entire or divisible depends on its construction in the light of all the circumstance. ..."

在 The "Nema"先例的一审,Goff 大法官说:"... in my judgement, where a single contractual document provides for what Lord Atkinson called: 'six wholly distinct, separate, and severable adventures between which there was no interdependence in the sense that the carrying out of any one of them was made to depend in any way upon the carrying out or abandonment of any of the others ...' That this transaction has in law no different effect from a divisible contract as I have described it, viz. a single transaction, contained in one contractual document, which provides for a number of contracts. In both cases, exception clauses excusing performance, and cancelling clauses, will be considered independently; anticipatory repudiation or fundamental breach, will be considered in relation to each adventure or separate contract independently; and likewise so will frus-

---

〔60〕 这是指英国 Royal Institute of Building Architects 针对工程合约的标准格式。工程/建造合约通过条文变为一个可分开的合约,而不再是一个完整合约,将会在本章是8.3.2段有详细介绍。

〔61〕 这种可分开的合约有很多典型的例子,如造船合约,船厂与买方船东会订立一个框架合约(framework contract),在该合约下建造4艘船舶,而双方之后可能会对每艘船舶再追加一个合约。这个框架合约就是一个典型的可分开的合约。另一个常见的例子是长期供应或买卖合约,货物可以是20万吨的镍矿或10万吨的钢材,双方同意每月一次付运,价格另议,付运期由买方决定等。

tration. It probably all comes down to a matter of terminology."

这里是说主要的考验是一份表面好像是完整合约的内容是否涉及若干不同的任务或合约承诺。如果它们之间是像 Atkinson 勋爵在 Larrinaga v. Soc. Franco – Americaine des Phosphates (1923) 14 Lloyd's Rep. 457 先例所说的6个航次是完全独特、独立与分得开的任务或航次,约因/对价也分得开,互不牵连,履行任何一个任务的成败都不影响另一个任务的履行,这样一来,这种合约就是可分开的合约(无论是被称为 severable contract 还是 divisible contract)。而只要是可分开的合约,无论免责条文或是取消合约条文,还是预期违约或违约/毁约,都应该独立分开考虑与适用在不同的任务。而受阻的说法也是同样的道理。

造船合约中船厂与买方船东订立的框架协议是一个典型的可分开的合约。分批供应的买卖合约根据不同的写法可能是完整合约,也可能是可分开的合约,有关的考验还是看分批付运这些货物之间是否会相互影响。例如,如果合约规定第二批货物在第一批货物付运后一个月内付运,第三批货物在第二批货物付运后一个月内付运,则该合约就应该属于一个完整合约。如果卖方因为不可抗力无法供货,想依赖合约中的不可抗力条文,或是错过了销约期,买方想终止合约,或是发生了受阻事件,影响的都是整个合约,而不仅仅是这一次付运。而如果合约中规定的是每个月进行一次付运,每次付运都有自己的销约期,很有可能就属于分得开的合约。买方无论是因为不可抗力或是受阻事件无法供货,或是违约/毁约,都只针对这一次付运,而不会影响之后的付运。这也不只是在国际货物买卖合约中,在造房子的建筑合约、购买飞机、钻油平台或大型机械的合约等中,都可能面对区分这一交易是完整合约还是可分开的合约。

完整合约或是可分开的合约取决于对有关合约文件的解释。[62] 但对合约文件的解释很多情况下其实是取决于法官或仲裁员对该合约文件的整体印象,因此常常会出现上诉后判决不断被推翻的情况。本段多次提到的 The "Nema" 先例就是很好的例子,在该先例中,独任仲裁员 Donald Davis 先生判相关的程租合约(C. Ore 7 标准格式)可分为 1979 年与 1980 年两个季度,也就是可分开的合约。但这在高院被 Goff 大法官推翻,而之后的上诉庭([1980] 2 Lloyd's Rep. 339)与贵族院([1981] 2 Lloyd's Rep. 239)又推翻了高院的判决。

可先介绍该先例的简单案情,该程租合约是从加拿大 Quebec 省的 Sorel 港装运钛矿(titanium)去英法港口的 6 至 7 个连续航次。由于 Sorel 港是在大湖区,冬季时会被冰封,所以第一个航次的销约期是 1979 年 4 月 30 日,而针对最后的航次,也有一个 1979 年 12 月 5 日的销约期。后一个销约期是给承租人一个选择权,让他可以因为大湖冰封在即而取消 1979 年季度余下的航次。

---

[62] 参见 Appleby v. Myers (1867) L. R. 2 C. P. 651; Regent OHG Aisestadt und Barig v. Francesco of Jermyn Street Ltd. (1981) 3 All ER 327; Smales v. Lea (2011) EWCA Civ 1325 等先例。

但之后双方又订了一个附件(addendum),在1980年同样履行6至7个连续航次。有关的文字可节录如下:"... 3(a) it is further hereby mutually agreed that this Charter Party is extended for a subsequent 7 (seven) further cargoes to be lifted in the period commencing layday 1st April 1980 / cancelling 30th April 1980, Charterers having the right of cancelling any voyages for which the vessel has not presented by 31 December, 1980."即连续航次的程租可分为1979年与1980年两个季度,第一季度是1979年的4月到12月。之后因为大湖冰封让船东自己经营,直至1980年的4月至12月再交船开始1980年的7个航次。

1979年6月6日,Sorel港开始有工业行动——罢工。Nema轮完成第一个航次后,于6月20日抵达Sorel港。罢工持续,而在之后漫长的等待装货期间,承租人也尽量安抚船东。如同意与签订附件三,从1979年7月1日起,在滞期费(demurrage)外每天额外给船东2000美元,另曾经允许船东私下行走一个短航次。显然当时的航运市场高涨,承租人尽量安抚船东,而船东也想私下营运以在市场上赚取更高的运费。

到了8月16日,船东私下找了一个估计需要45到50日的航次。承租人知悉后马上委任英国律师在英国法院申请禁令(租约适用英国法与伦敦仲裁)。显然承租人知道无法说服船东,也不再愿意进一步安抚船东,所以采取这一法律行动。英国法院要求双方马上根据仲裁协议开始仲裁程序解决争议,于是双方委任了Donald Davis先生作为独任仲裁员进行即时仲裁(instant arbitration)。虽然仲裁程序进行得很快,也没有中间程序,但还是在9月26日才开庭。当时Sorel港的罢工依然没有什么变化,[63]而船东在仲裁中就提出了程租合约受阻。Davis先生在10月3日做出裁决

---

〔63〕 在20世纪五六十年代,即使在西方先进国家,船舶的装卸(除了油轮)也完全靠人力(labor - intensive)的作业,所以码头装卸工人人数众多,工会势力庞大,也经常遇上罢工。而这些罢工往往持续很长一段时间,给航运带来很大不便。但从20世纪70年代开始,船舶的装卸已经开始以机械化操作替代人力作业,加上散装货物有了越来越大的散装船(specialized bulk carrier)以及班轮货物有了集装箱船(containers),使码头装卸工人数量大量减少,而工会的势力也相应降低。加上西方部分国家的政府开始通过改法/立法打压工会的势力,这种发展表示困扰航运界与外贸界的码头工人罢工问题在最近二十年已经几乎不存在了。但由于罢工不像战争,期间劳资双方通常都会谈判并单方面发放乐观的消息,令罢工很难构成受阻。这可节录Goff大法官在The "Nema"先例所说:"Furthermore, on the authorities it is notoriously difficult for a strike to have the effect of frustrating a charter - party-see, e. g. Reardon Smith Line Ltd. v. Ministry of Agriculture, Fisheries and Food, [1961] 1 Lloyd's Rep. 385... In other cases in which delay has occurred which, in comparison with the contractual adventure, was more serious than in the present case, the contract has been held not to be frustrated: see, e. g. The 'Angelia', [1972] 2 Lloyd's Rep. 154. In one case only, so far as I am aware, has a strike been held to have the effect of frustrating a charter - party. That was The 'Penelope', [1928] 31 Ll. L. Rep. 96.; but in that case, which was concerned with a charter - party for as many consecutive voyages as could be performed within a period of 12 months, the general strike and its consequences prevented contractual performance for a period of over seven months - an interruption substantially more severe than that in the present case."

书，判 1979 年这一季度已经受阻，而受阻的一天是 1979 年 9 月 29 日。但 Davis 先生没有决定双方在程租合约的附件二同意延长的 1980 年这一季度是否受阻。换言之，Davis 先生是把该租约包括附件视为是可分开的合约。这里的问题是租约中的两个季度是否可分开，至于每个季度的 6 至 7 个航次没有争议，因为是持续的航次，也应是很明确不能分开。

这一即时仲裁的裁决根据刚生效的 1979 年英国《仲裁法》被批准上诉到法院，[64] 而在一审，Goff 大法官推翻了 Davis 先生的裁决，判该租约包括附件是一个完整合约，不能部分受阻。Goff 大法官的原因是："As against consideration of this kind, it is to be remembered that this contract was in form of consecutive voyage charter – party, extended for a second season on terms which affected the first season. The fact that there was a gap in performance between the two seasons seems to have been no more than a physical necessity, imposed by the climatic conditions at the loading port. Furthermore, cl. 8 of Addendum 2 shows that the manner of performance of the contract so far as it related to the 1979 season might affect the parties' obligations in respect of the 1980 season. In these circumstances, **I ask myself, can the parties' obligations in relation to each season by regarded as entirely separate and independent?... I find it difficult to accept**, for example, that it would be open to either party to repudiate his obligation to perform during the first complete season, while insisting on performance by the other party during the second. Again, supposing that a revolution or war had occurred in August 1979, and was likely to prevent shipment for some months, possibly extending into 1980; it appears to me that the question whether the owners were entitled to cancel the contract under cl. 27 [65] would be considered in relation to the contract as a whole – **not** first in relation to the 1979 season, and **then independently** in relation to the 1980 season. To my mind, considerations of this kind, together with the form of the addendum and the terms in which the charter-party was extended to includes in 1980, point strongly to **the conclusion that the charter-party and addenda comprised one indivisible contract**."（加黑部分是笔者的强调）

但 Goff 法官的判决在上诉庭与贵族院被推翻，认为该程租合约与附件是可分开

---

〔64〕 The "Nema"先例中的裁决书被批准上诉在贵族院被 Diplock 勋爵严厉批评，认为这种即时仲裁不应被批准上诉，并对高院将来针对上诉批文的申请如何行使裁量权做出了指引，即著名的"Nema guidelines"。"Nema guidelines"把裁决书中的法律问题一分为二：第一种是一次过（one – off）的法律问题，这种能获上诉批文的机会接近零。第二种是有广泛影响的法律观点，如解释一份重要标准合约格式的其中一条条文等，这种能获上诉批文的机会较高。在 1996 年《仲裁法》中，"Nema guidelines"已被合并进 Section 69（3），成为立法的部分。这可见笔者《仲裁法：从 1996 年英国仲裁法到国际商务仲裁》一书第四章之 2.3.5.4 段。

〔65〕 该程租合约的第 27 条文给船东一个商业选择权，在一些意外事故（包括罢工）下终止租约。

的合约,等于支持了 Davis 先生的仲裁裁决。这可节录贵族院的 Roskill 勋爵的判决,说:"My Lords, two considerations seem to me to point strongly to the independence and against the interdependence of the two adventures. The first is that clause 3 (a) of addendum no. 2 provides completely new and different cancelling dates for the 1980 adventure from those in clauses 10 and 38 of the charterparty of November 2, 1978, for the 1979 adventure.[66] Secondly, the possible interposition of the substitute voyage for which paragraph 8[67] of the addendum no. 2 provides, is to take place (in events which did not in fact happen) first open water 1980, a date which is not linked with either April 1 or 30, 1980, which are, respectively, commencing and cancelling lay days under clause 3 (a of addendum no. 2). This seems to me to be a further indication of the independent nature of the obligations for which addendum no. 2 provides. My Lords, on this question I find the reasoning of Templeman L. J. [1980] Q. B. 547... entirely persuasive and convincing and I respectfully adopt it. Like the learned Lord Justice, I wholly decline to join the two adventures together in the manner which appealed to Robert Goff J."

总而言之,解释合约确实存在不肯定之处,在 The "Nema"先例中,高院、上诉庭与贵族院的大法官解释合约条文时有不同的重点与分析,从而得出了完全相反的结论。

由于大部分合约都是完整合约(entire contract),并且一旦受阻就会影响整个合约,接下来的段节会针对完整合约的履行与支付做进一步介绍。

8.3　完整合约责任只履行了部分

在被报道的先例中,法院倾向于认为一次过付钱(lump - sum payment)的合约[68]

---

〔66〕 程租合约的第 10 条文规定了第一个航次的销约期是 1979 年 4 月 30 日。而针对最后的航次,也有一个 1979 年 12 月 5 日的销约期。而第 38 条文规定了最后的航次的销约期是 1979 年 12 月 5 日。虽然该租约规定了要行走 6 至 7 个航次,但船舶会有延误,或者可能出现意外等,如果船舶在 1979 年 12 月 5 日之后抵达 Sorel 港,由于冰封有可能提早开始,承租人就有取消之后航次的选择权。在附件二的 3(a)条文针对 1980 年这一季度规定了新的销约期,这在 Roskill 勋爵看来,有力显示了租约与附件下的这两个季度是完全独立与可分开。

〔67〕 该条文的写法是:"8. If charterers have to charter another vessel to lift a Sorel cargo of slag with loading prior to presentation of 'Nema' for her second lifting owners to remain obligated to perform a replacement voyage in 1979 if possible, otherwise FOW 1980, at the rate of freight applicable for 1979 per item 5 above."简单说,附件二不止延长了租约并加上了 1980 年季度的 7 个航次,也针对了 Sorel 罢工对 1979 年季度的第二个航次的影响,包括承租人同意让 Nema 轮私下行走一个短航次。而第 8 段就是要求船东以 1979 年季度的较低运费多履行一个替代的航次,如果时间上不允许在 1979 年履行,就在 1980 年一开始解冻(FOW 或 first open water)时履行。

〔68〕 完整合约也被叫做一次过付钱合约,如果一方的约因/对价只是一笔钱,也就是分不开,无论另一方的约因/对价中的任务多么独立,都不能叫做可分开的合约,因为另一方完成其中一项任务后,合约中没有规定相应的约因/对价。

存在一个默示条文,即只有当一方完全履行了其全部的合约责任后,另一方才有付钱的责任。[69] 这可节录《Chitty on Contracts》(第32版,2015年)一书之21-028段说:"**Entire and divisible obligations.** A contract is said to be 'entire' when complete performance by one party is a condition precedent to the liability of the other; in such a contract the consideration is usually a lump sum which is payable only upon complete performance by the other party (hence, the reference is sometimes to a 'lump-sum contract'). The opposite of an 'entire contract' is a 'divisible contract', which is separable into parts, so that different parts of the consideration may be assigned to severable parts of the performance, e. g. an agreement for payment pro rata."

稍后的21-029段对完整合约责任与完整合约进行了区分,说:"... Yet the phrase 'entire contract' is a misleading one in that the real issue in the cases is whether the 'obligation of the party in default is entire', not whether the contract itself is entire."

在《Halsbury's Laws of England》(第4版)第9卷之1145段,说:"An entire contract is one where the complete performance of one party is a condition precedent to his right to call for the performance of the other party's obligation. Where the contractor undertakes to complete the works and the contract on its true construction is entire, the employer is entitled to insist on completion before his obligation to pay arises. If the building contractor leaves the work unfinished to a substantial degree he cannot claim a corresponding percentage to the contract sum or recover on a quantum meruit basis for that part of the work he has completed; moreover, he will be liable in damages to the employer for breach of contract. Nevertheless, if he can show that he has substantially completed the works (even though some minor items might remain unfinished) he will be entitled to claim payment. Where a contractor agrees to do the work for a lump sum he cannot recover any part of that sum until the work is complete, unless there is a provision in the contract for payment by instalments.[70]"

---

〔69〕 参见 Appleby v. Myers (1867) L. R. 2 C. P. 651; Jesse v. Roy (1834) 1 Cr M & R 316; The "Madras" (1898) P. 90; Sumpter v. Hedges (1898) 1 QB 673; Forman & Co. Proprietary Ltd. v. Liddesdale (1900) AC 190; Small & Sons Ltd. v. Middlesex Real Estates Ltd. (1921) W. N. 245; Heywood v. Wellers (1976) 1 QB 446 等先例。

〔70〕 现在的合约,如建筑合约,常常会规定工程完成至某一阶段,雇主就要做出分期付款:Smales v. Lea (2011) EWCA Civ 1325 等先例。在该先例中,上诉庭的 Jackson 大法官说:"In modern construction of contracts and contracts of retainer for professional services, it is relatively unusual for the client to have no obligation to make any payment unless and until the contractor or the professional firm has performed every single one of the obligations undertaken. It does, of course, happen in some cases, but in my judgment the case before this court is not such a case."

8.3.1 普通法下部分履行一个完整合约责任无权获得支付

在英国法下,如果一方没有完全履行其合约责任,无权对已经履行的部分获得任何支付:Cutter v. Powell (1795) 6 T. R. 320; Bolton v. Mahadeva (1972) 1 WLR 1009 等先例。Cutter v. Powell 先例是这方面最早的先例,案情是船长与船员 Cutter 先生订立合约履行有关的航次。该本质上是雇佣合约的有关条文说:"Ten days after the ship 'Governor Parry,' myself master, arrives at Liverpool, I promise to pay to Mr. T. Cutter the sum of thirty guineas, provided he proceeds, continues and does his duty as second mate in the said ship from hence to the port of Liverpool."但 Cutter 先生不幸在航次中途死亡。之后他的遗属向船长(雇主)索赔有关金额,但被法院驳回。其中 Ashhurst 大法官说:"And as it is entire, and as the defendant's promise depends on a condition precedent to be performed by the other party, the condition must be performed before the other party is entitled to receive any thing under it."

这在《Chitty on Contracts》(第 32 版,2015 年)一书之 21 - 031 段说:"**Partial performance of entire obligations.** Where a party has performed only part of an entire obligation it can normally recover nothing, neither the agreed price, since it is not due under the terms of the contract, nor any smaller sum for the value of its partial performance, since the court has no power to apportion the consideration. . . . Thus, where an employee is engaged for a fixed period for a lump sum, but fails to complete the term for a reason other than breach of contract by the employer, e. g. frustration, the common law rule is that he can recover nothing. In the famous case of Cutter v. Powell (1795) 6 T. R 320, a seaman was to be paid a lump sum when he completed the voyage; he died before completion of the voyage and it was held that his executor could not cover pro tanto wages because it was an 'entire contract'. . ."

但如果另一方在有选择的情况下接受了这部分履行,在特定情况下可以推断(infer)双方已经达成了新的默示合约(implied contract),[71] 原本的被承诺方需要对原合约的部分履行做出支付。至于支付的金额,由于在完整合约不会有针对,所以接受了部分履行的被承诺方在按劳计酬(*quantum meruit*)的说法下,为已经完成的工作做出部分支付。

在 Sumpter v. Hedges (1898) 1 QB 673 先例,上诉庭的 Chitty 大法官说:"In the case of goods sold and delivered, it is easy to show a contract from the retention of the goods; but that is not so where work is done on real property."

Collins 大法官也说:"If the plaintiff had merely broken his contract in some way so as not to give the defendant the right to treat him as having abandoned the contract, and the defendant had then proceeded to finish the work himself, the plaintiff might perhaps

---

〔71〕 这课题可见《合约的解释:规则与应用》一书第七章第 11 段。

have been entitled to **sue on a quantum meruit on the ground that the defendant had taken the benefit of the work done.** But that is not the present case. There are cases in which, though the plaintiff has abandoned the performance of a contract, it is possible for him to raise **the inference of a new contract to pay for the work done on a quantum meruit** from the defendant's having taken the benefit of that work, but, in order that that may be done, **the circumstances must be such as to give an option to the defendant to take or not to take the benefit of the work done.** It is only where the circumstances are such as to give that option that there is any evidence on which to ground the inference of a new contract. Where, as in the case of work done on land, the circumstances are such as to give the defendant no option whether he will take the benefit of the work or not, then one must look to other facts than the mere taking the benefit of the work in order to ground the inference of a new contract. In this case I see no other facts on which such an inference can be founded."(加黑部分是笔者的强调)

也就是说,在一个完整合约的建筑合约中,雇主接受了承建商/承包商未完成的工作并不一定有对已经完成的工作根据按劳计酬做出支付的返还性责任。例如,承建商/承包商在雇主土地上的工程建到一半就撤走了,雇主不得不接受这个未完成的工程,并自己花钱完成。雇主(土地所有人)不可能丢下工程不管,让它一直保持烂尾的状态。这样一来,就谈不上雇主有接受部分履行的选择权。但如果雇主使用了承建商/承包商撤走时留下来的材料完成工程,承建商/承包商可以索赔并取回这些材料的合理价值。因为雇主可以选择是使用这些材料还是退回给承建商/承包商。[72]

类似的,如果涉及一些物品的维修,所有人接受了没有修完就被退回的物品本身并不能默示所有人同意了对已经完成的维修工作做出部分支付:Forman & Co. Proprietary Ltd. v. Liddesdale (1900) AC 190 先例。毕竟对所有人来说,谈不上可以选择接受还是拒绝这个部分履行。

8.3.2 普通法地位被立法或合约条文改变

举例说,1870 年《Apportionment Act》改变了在合约下支付薪资(wage)与薪水(salary)的法律地位,其中 section 2 规定:"... all rents, annuities, dividends, and other periodical payments in the nature of income... shall... be considered as accruing from day to day, and shall be apportionable in respect of time accordingly."

根据 1870 年《Apportionment Act》之 section 5,"年金"(annuities)一词包括了薪水与养老金(pensions),根据之后的先例的判法,薪资也被包括在内:Moriarty v. Regent's Carage Co. Ltd. (1921) 1 KB 423; Item Software (UK) Ltd. v. Fassihi (2004) EWCA Civ 1244 等先例。

---

〔72〕 参见 Sumpter v. Hedges (1898) 1 QB 673 先例。

另可举货物买卖合约为例，如果货物数量不够，买方可以拒绝收货。但如果买方选择收货，就必须按照合约规定的单价做出支付，这可见1979年《货物销售法》之section 30(1)规定："**Delivery of wrong quantity.** (1) Where the seller delivers to the buyer a quantity of goods less than he contracted to sell, the buyer may reject them, but if the buyer accepts the goods so delivered he must pay for them at the contract rate..."

另在1979年《货物销售法》之section 31(2)规定，如果货物是分批交付，买方能否以某一批或几批货物数量不够或有瑕疵为由终止合约，要看有关的合约条文与具体的案情："Where there is a contract for the sale of goods to be delivered by stated instalments, which are to be separately paid for, and the seller makes defective deliveries in respect of one or more instalments, or the buyer neglects or refuses to take delivery of or pay for one or more instalments, it is a question in each case depending on the terms of the contract and the circumstances of the case whether the breach of contract is a repudiation of the whole contract or whether it is a severable breach giving rise to a claim for compensation but not to a right to treat the whole contract as repudiated."

在Regent OHG Aisestadt und Barig v. Francesco of Jermyn Street Ltd. (1981) 3 All ER 327先例中，卖方在交付某批货物时，数量少了1件，买方以此为由拒绝了所有货物并终止合约。卖方在法院向买方索赔，法院判section 31(2)适用，只是少交了1件货物不构成对整个合约的违约/毁约，买方错误终止合约，要赔偿卖方的损失。

通过明示合约条文改变或超越普通法规则的例子也很多。最常见的例子是建筑或工程合约中往往有条文规定每完成一个阶段的工作，雇主就要支付一笔分期付款，这笔钱也是由承建商/承包商所赚取。承建商/承包商完成一个阶段的工作是雇主支付这笔分期付款的前提条件。这里可节录Sundra Rajoo拿督（吉隆坡区域仲裁中心[KLRCA]秘书长）的《Construction Law in Malaysia》（2012年）一书第281页，如下：

"**Payment upon completion.** Progress payments are not applicable in contracts considered in law to be 'entire contract'. The court in Cutter v. Powell [1795] 6 TR 320 defined an 'entire contract' as one in which neither party can demand performance by the other unless he himself either has performed his obligations, or is otherwise ready and willing to do so ....

It is a general rule that in an entire contract, only complete performance will entitle the contractor to payment and no entitlement to payment will arise until the work is substantiallycompleted ... Under the doctrine of substantial performance, the contractor is entitled to payment upon the achievement of practical completion of the works unless the contract stipulates expressly to the contrary.

Synonymous with the labels 'payment at practical completion' and 'payment on handing over', this method of paying the contractor crystallizes on the achievement of practical or substantial completion and/or the handing over of the works to the employer;

the precondition to payment being the achievement and certification of the said milestone by the contract administrator . . .

The contractor is then paid a lump sum figure . . . ”

以上所介绍的虽然是马来西亚的法律,但与英国法的地位相同,引用的也是英国的先例。如果合约规定的是“实际完成后支付”(payment at practical completion)或“工程完成交给雇主后支付”(payment on handing over),即一个完整合约,承建商/承包商需要完成他承诺的全部责任,雇主才需要最后“一次过”付钱,而不会是根据工程时间/进度按部就班地付钱(progress payment)。而期间如果遇上受阻的突发事件导致合约自动终止,即使承建商/承包商的工作已经大部分完成,雇主还是不需要做出任何支付。

因为有订约自由,如果承建商/承包商希望根据工程时间/进度获得支付以减轻经济压力,试图把一个完整合约变为或在 1943 年《Law Reform (Frustration Contract) Act》立法下被当作可分开的合约,完全可以在合约中写明。Sundra Rajoo 拿督介绍了若干根据工程时间/进度进行支付的方式:

1. 定期支付(periodic payment)。这是指每过一段时间,如每月、每季度等,根据工程进度做出支付。每次支付的金额取决于合约管理者(contract administrator,可以是工程师、建筑师等)定期签发的中间证书(interim certificate)。中间证书只是大致估计承建商/承包商完成的工作的价值以及根据合约总金额应相应支付的金额,并且可以在之后的临时证书中做出改动。整个程序大致是承建商/承包商申请获得定期支付,建筑本值顾问(cost consultants)测量与估价,之后合约管理者签发相关的中间证书。这是马来西亚的本地建筑工程经常使用的一种支付方式。这种支付方式会令雇主承担大部分的经济压力,减少承建商/承包商现金流紧张的风险。

当然,合约规定定期支付并不代表把完整合约变成可分开的合约。毕竟承建商/承包商的合约责任难以区分,不会因为雇主定期做出支付就变为可分开。但这种定期支付方式的好处是,一旦合约受阻,1943 年《Law Reform (Frustration Contract) Act》立法[73]就可以适用。其中 section 2(4)规定:“(4) Where it appears to the court that a part of any contract to which this Act applies can properly be severed from the remainder of the contract, being a part wholly performed before the time of discharge, or so performed except for the payment in respect of that part of the contract of sums which are or can be ascertained under the contract, the court shall treat that part of the contract as if it were a separate contract and had not been frustrated and shall treat the foregoing section of this Act as only applicable to the remainder of that contract.”

估计法院或仲裁庭在适当的案情下,会允许承建商/承包商保留已经定期支付的

---

〔73〕 当然,如果是涉及马来西亚的工程与法律,相关的立法就是 1956 年《Civil Law Act》之 section 16(4)。

金额,当作这部分的承诺可以分开。毕竟承建商/承包商已经干活了且花费了金钱,不需要因为一个完整合约尚未履行完毕就中途受阻,而要将已经收取的钱退还给雇主。

2. 阶段支付(stage payment)或里程碑支付(milestone payment)。这种支付办法也是随着工程进度进行支付,但不是根据一段时间内完成的工作,而是只有当承建商/承包商完成了某个阶段的工作(如打了地基)或者说某个里程碑工作之后,才能获得支付。雇主与承建商/承包商在订立合约时会约定不同的阶段与相应要支付的金额。之后每一次中间支付(interim payment)都会被认为是合约总金额的分阶段付款。一般来说,这种支付方式会被认为是可分开的(severable)。在一些统包合约(package deal contract)、专业服务合约(如顾问咨询服务)、涉及一些重复工作的合约与总金额较小的合约中,常常会使用这种支付方式。

3. 预付(advance payment)。这可以是提前支付部分或全部的金额。如果雇主的信誉或经济状况堪忧,承建商不愿意承担完成工程后无法获得足额支付甚至分文无取的风险,就可能会要求雇主做出预付。如果是一个小工程,涉及的钱不多,合约也可能规定预付。

最后举一个程租合约〔74〕的例子,普通法的起点是把货物运抵目的地准备交货时,船东才可以赚取运费。早在 Dakin v. Oxley (1864) 15 CB (NS) 646 先例,Willes 大法官就明确了这一点,说:"... the true test of the right to freight is the question whether the service in respect of which the freight was contracted to be paid has been substantially performed; and according to the law of England, as a rule freight is earned by the carriage and arrival of the goods ready to be delivered to the merchant, though they may be in a damaged state when they arrive. If the shipowner fails to carry the goods for the merchant to the destined port, the freight is not earned. If he carries part, but not the whole, no freight is payable in respect of the part not carried, and freight is payable in respect of the part carried unless the charterparty makes the carriage of the whole a condition precedent to the earning of any freight – a case which has not within our experience arisen in practice ..."

根据上述原则,如果货物没有运抵目的地,很明显船东不能赚取运费。普通法下,也不存在半途放弃航次可收取照比例运费(pro rata freight)。也就是说,对完整合约的部分履行是不会获得约因/对价的支付。例如,易变质的货物快变坏,船长被迫在半途港作为紧急代理人拍卖货物,船东是不会获得按比例支付的运费:Vlierbloom v. Chapman (1844) 13 M & W 230 先例。或更常见的在半途遇上海难,船变为推定全损(constructive total loss)。如此一来,租约受阻自动终止,但由于未将货物运抵目的地不能赚取运费(即使已经距离目的地很近),船东仍不能要求承租人照比

〔74〕 有关程租合约受阻后预付运费的问题,可参见本章之 10.5.1 段。

例支付运费。

随着国际货物付运买卖合约(shipment sales contract,这是以 CIF/CFR 买卖为主)的盛行(虽然相比 FOB 买卖,数量上还是少得多),大部分的程租合约已经以明示的条文超越了这一对船东不利的普通法地位。毕竟,在 CIF/CFR 中,买卖承租人或货方都需要一套注明是运费预付(freight pre - paid)的提单。这样一来,船东也顺理成章地要求运费预付才肯签发这种提单。但要注意的是,明示条文必须清楚无误才能超越法律默示的地位。在 The "Lorna 1" (1983) 1 Lloyd's Rep. 373 先例中,相关的运费条文的写法是:"Freight non-returnable cargo and/or vessel lost or not lost to be paid... to the owners as follows—75% ... within...5 days after Master signed bills of lading and the balance after right and true delivery of the cargo and receipt of documents from discharging ports."

船舶在 1977 年 12 月 6 日装货并签发了提单。但起航后,船舶在 12 月 11 日沉没。双方(船东与承租人)对沉没令租约受阻而自动终止没有任何异议,问题是船东能否根据上述条款追讨 75% 的运费。Donaldson 大法官认为该条文的写法不足以超越普通法的默示地位,说:"Freight is the consideration payable for the carriage of the goods to and their delivery at the destination. In the absence of special contractual provisions, it is earned only upon the delivery of the goods at their destination. Forms of words appropriate to alter this position are well known, e. g. , 'Freight to be considered earned on shipment'."

根据上述 Donaldson 大法官的说法,如果相关条文的写法是"Freight to be considered earned on shipment"或类似 The "Karin Vatis" (1988) 2 Lloyd's Rep. 330 先例"freight deemed earned as cargo loaded"的写法,就会是足以超越普通法的地位,让预付的运费不受到航次中途受阻的影响。

8.3.3　大部分履行的说法

已经提到部分履行一个完整合约责任是无法获得任何对价的支付。在早期的 Appleby v. Myers (1867) L. R. 2 C. P. 651 先例中,案情涉及原告与被告订立合约,在被告的厂房里建造机械并负责两年的维修,被告将在机械建成后做出支付。但机械建造到一半时,在并非任何一方过错的情况下意外发生了大火,将建造了一半的机械、材料与厂房一起烧毁。原告向法院要求被告支付建造了一半的机械的价格。但法院判合约受阻,双方都不需要继续履行,而因为原告没有履行完这一完整合约责任,所以不能获得任何支付。

这会带来履约方的困境,特别是建筑或工程合约,经常会有一些尚未完成/令人满意之处(无论是一些零碎的工作没有完成或是已经完成的工作有缺陷)。但有先例判是雇主不能以此为由,拒绝做出支付。在第一个明确这种说法的 H. Dakin & Co. , Ltd. v. Lee (1916) 1 KB 566 的上诉庭先例中,Cozens-Hardy 勋爵说:"But to say that a builder cannot recover from a building owner merely because some item of the work has been done negligently or inefficiently or improperly is a proposition which I should not listen to unless compelled by a decision of the House of Lords. Take a contract for a lump sum to decorate a house; the contract provides that there shall be three coats of oil paint, but in one of the rooms only two coats of paint are put on. Can anyone seriously say that under these circumstances the building owner could go and occupy the house and take the benefit of all the decorations which had been done in the other rooms without paying a penny for all the work done by the builder, just because only two coats of paint had been put on in one room where there ought to have been three?”

所以有了一个大部分履行(substantial performance)即可让履约方要求对方付钱/支付对价的说法。在 Hoenig v. Isaacs (1952) 2 All ER 176 先例中,Denning 大法官针对这个大部分履行的说法如何操作总结说:“... When a contract provides for a specified sum to be paid on completion of specified work, the courts lean against a construction of the contract which would deprive the contractor of any payment at all simply because there are some defects or omissions.〔75〕 The promise to complete the work is, therefore, construed as a term of the contract, but not as a condition. It is not every breach of that term which absolves the employer from his promise to pay the price, but only a breach which goes to the root of the contract, such as an abandonment of the work, when it is only half done. Unless the breach does go to the root of the matter, the employer cannot resist payment of the price.〔76〕 He must pay it and bring a cross-claim for the defects and omissions, or alternatively, set them upon in diminution of the price. The measure is the amount which the work is worth less by reason of the defects and omissions, and is usually calculated by the cost of making them good.〔77〕”

这种大部分履行案件也不只是在建筑或工程合约,更早期的 William Thomas & Sons v. Harrowing SS Co. (1915) AC 58 先例涉及的就是租约。相关的程租合约规定将货物送到目的地港口后,承租人“一次过”支付一笔运费。但船舶在卸港外因为坏天气发生意外导致全损,货物只被救回了三分之二并送至目的地。贵族院判船东可以获得全部的运费,理由之一就是大部分货物已经被交付(a substantial part of the cargo had been delivered)。

---

〔75〕 如果合约规定完成特定工作后才需要做出支付,法院不会倾向于解释为工作有任何瑕疵或遗漏,另一方就可以完全不用做出任何支付。

〔76〕 完成工作的承诺应被视为合约的条文之一,而不是条件条文。并不是所有承建商/承包商对该承诺的违反都可以让雇主不再需要履行其做出支付的承诺。除非当对该承诺的违反已经严重至影响到合约的根基,如工程做到一半就离开,否则雇主不能拒绝支付。

〔77〕 但雇主可以对瑕疵或遗漏提起反索赔,或与需要支付的金额进行抵销。至于反索赔或抵销的金额,一般是瑕疵或遗漏导致的价值减少的部分,或是进行弥补的金额。关于抵销(set - off)的课题,读者可参阅杨良宜《损失赔偿与救济》一书第十一章之1.6段。

这可节录《Chitty on Contracts》(第32版,2015年)一书之21－034段,说:

"**The effects of substantial performance.** . . . it must be conceded that there is some authority which supports the existence of a doctrine of substantial performance in relation to entire contracts. On this view, upon completion of substantial performance, the part performer will be entitled to claim the price, subject to a counterclaim for damages. This so－called doctrine of substantial performance may be excluded by an express provision of the contract; 'each case turns on the construction of the contract', and 'it is always open to the parties by express words to make entire performance a condition precedent' (to payment). . . . What is 'substantial performance' will depend upon the nature of the contract and all the circumstances; if the contractor abandons performance, or does work entirely different in kind from that contracted for, it is clearly a case of substantial non－feasance and the contractor may recover nothing. Similarly, a builder who abandons work under a lump－sum contract can recover nothing, but if the work is substantially completed, and it is only in some minor details that the workmanship falls below the contractual specifications, the builder may recover the agreed price, less a deduction based on the cost of making good the defeats or omissions: 'In considering whether there was substantial performance. . . it is relevant to take into account both the nature of the defects and the proportion between the cost of rectifying them and the contract price.'[78]

The rule applies to unimportant matters of non－feasance as well as to unimportant matters of misfeasance. Notwithstanding these dicta it is suggested that there ought to be no room in English law for a doctrine of substantial performance: rather the court should inquire whether the particular obligation which is the subject matter of the litigation is entire. If it is not, non－performance of a part of that obligation should not, of itself, be a bar to an action to recover the price; but it is, and the obligation has not been completely performed, it should not be possible for the part performer to bring an action on the contract to recover the price."

在Hoenig v. Isaacs先例中,原告是一个室内与家具设计师,与被告订立合约,以750英镑的价格为被告提供室内装修、设计并安装家具的服务。原告完成工作后,被告声称衣柜门需要更换、书架太短要重新做等,而这两样改正需要超过55镑,因此不愿意做出支付。法院判原告胜诉,因为他已经大部分履行了合约。

之后在Kiely & Sons Ltd. v. Medcraft (1965) 109 Sol Jo 829先例中,原告给被告粉刷房屋,之后双方产生争议,原告向法院要求被告支付合约中约定的520英镑。但被告认为原告干得太差,不属于履行了完整合约责任,无权获得支付。一审法院判是弥补被告粉刷工作上的瑕疵需要200英镑,原告可以获得剩下的320英镑。被告

〔78〕 Cairns大法官在Bolton v. Mahadeva (1972) 1 WLR 1009先例所说。

上诉,理由之一就是如果被告的工作需要200英镑弥补,则不能说已经大部分履行了一个约因/对价是520英镑的合约。上诉庭判是否已经大部分履行不是严格从数学上计算。法院要根据每个案件不同的事实,包括瑕疵的程度,决定合约责任是否已经大部分被履行,这是程度的问题。

在较近期的Bolton v. Mahadeva (1972) 1 WLR 1009先例中,案情涉及以650镑的价格为被告的房屋安装供热与热水系统。安装完毕后,被告投诉工作做得不好,主要是冒烟与供热的温度不足,修好大约需要174英镑。被告认为这是一个完整合约,因此拒绝支付。在一审中,原告胜诉,法院判原告已经大部分履行的合约。但在上诉庭推翻了这个判决,其中Cairns大法官提到判决是否大部分履行主要看两方面,一是缺陷的性质是否重要,二是补救的费用与合约约因/对价的对比:"In considering whether there was substantial performance I am of opinion that it is relevant to take into account both the nature of the defects and the proportion between the cost of rectifying them and the contract price. It would be wrong to say that the contractor is only entitled to payment if the defects are so trifling as to be covered by the de minimis rule."

8.3.4 导致部分履行的原因

一个完整合约(entire contract)只被部分履行并且无法获得任何约因/对价的支付的情况很多。毕竟一个复杂的合约(如工程合约)要一切顺利才能获得支付,而正如本书介绍的,履行合约有各种困难。

无法全部履行一个完整合约的原因大致可分为以下三类:

1. 被另一方妨碍,不能完整履行。在合约中有默示条文规定,合约双方必须合作令另一方可以完成合约承诺,[79]也不能因自己的错误获利。[80] 因此,如果是因为一方的妨碍令合约不能完整履行,另一个无辜方可以索赔损失以回复到合约被完整履行的地位或要求另一方为部分履行做出合理支付。[81] 在《Chitty on Contracts》(第32版,2015年)一书之21-037段,说:"**Defendant preventing complete performance.** If the other party to the contract wrongfully prevents the claimant from completing its performance, the claimant may either recover damages for breach of contract, or alternatively sue upon a quantum meruit to recover a reasonable remuneration for its partial performance."

2. 履行方自己的错误导致无法完整履行。这本质上属于违约,在本章稍早的7.5段已经有所介绍,属于所谓的自己导致的合约受阻(self-induced frustration)。因为这是履行方违约/毁约,在复原大原则下(compensatory principle),需要赔偿无辜方的损失,令无辜方回复到合约被完整履行的地位。

---

〔79〕 参见杨良宜《合约的解释:规则与应用》一书第七章之10.2段。

〔80〕 参见杨良宜《合约的解释:规则与应用》一书第七章之10.3段。

〔81〕 参见杨良宜《损失赔偿与救济》一书。

3. 合约受阻导致无法完整履行。在 Cutter v. Powell（1795）6 T. R. 320 先例中，案情涉及一位水手在航程半途去世，即没有履行一个完整合约的承诺与责任，因此赚不到“一次过”的报酬。这属于该雇佣合约受阻，虽然在当时并没有合约受阻的说法。如果合约受阻的说法适用，一旦受阻事件发生，合约自动终止，双方都不需要继续履行已经被部分履行的合约责任，这也表示已经被部分履行的完整合约无法获得任何支付。

9. 受阻后合约被终止的法律后果

受阻后合约被终止的法律后果是，受阻前已付应付的钱可被保留，以后要付的钱也不必再履行。这普通法的地位按理说合情合理，因为一个合约一旦受阻便自动终止，双方不再需要履行将来的合约责任。正如 Wright 勋爵在 Fibrosa Spolka Akcyjina v. Fairbairn Lawson Combe Barbour Ltd.（1943）AC 32 先例中所说：“In my opinion, the contract is automatically terminated **as to the future**, because at that date its performance becomes impossible in fact in circumstances which involve no liability for damages for the failure on either party.”（加黑部分是笔者的强调）在《Chitty on Contracts》（第32 版，2015 年）一书之 23 – 071 段也说：“**Contract discharged automatically.** At common law frustration does not rescind the contract ab initio：it brings the contract to an end forthwith, without more and automatically, in the sense that it releases both parties from any further performance of the contract. A court does not have the power at common laws to allow the contract to continue and to adjust its terms to the new circumstances.”

但其实这地位与后果会导致不公平与严苛的结果，正如上诉庭的 Chandler v. Webster（1904）1 KB 493 先例所说，虽然合约受阻令双方都不再需要继续履行将来的合约责任，但这不影响在受阻事件发生之前的合约责任与承诺。因为在订约自由下，双方完全可以约定一方提前支付全部约因/对价。如果合约规定的支付时间早于受阻发生的时间，即使原告还没有做出支付，也不会受合约受阻的影响。在 Chandler v. Webster 先例中，原告与被告订立合约租阳台观看英皇加冕典礼，根据相关合约规定，原告要提前支付 141 英镑的租金。合约规定支付的时间早于典礼取消（发生受阻事件）的时间。当时原告已经支付了 100 英镑（还剩 41 英镑没有支付）。在诉讼中，原告要求被告退回这 100 英镑，而被告就反索赔没有支付的 41 英镑。法院判合约受阻而自动终止，但以前欠下的债务仍要支付，所以被告反索赔 41 英镑成功。这样判法对原告很不公平，他在合约受阻的情况下仍要支付所有租金，但由于合约受阻而无法享用原先租用的阳台与房间。否则原告即使不能观礼，也可用来晒一天太阳或开个派对。

而在另一个涉及英国加冕的 Krell v. Henry（1903）2 KB 740 先例中，因为相关合约规定一部分租金是在典礼取消后再支付，所以这部分在合约受阻后可以免除支付。这样一来，变成合约如何规定付款为决定性因素。而受阻事件又是针对突发与一般不可预见的意外，因此，双方在订约时根本无法针对受阻事件做出较合理与公平的分摊，只能听天由命。

这带来立法的呼声，因此在1939年，法律改革委员会（The Law Revision Committee）做出了名为《Seventh Interim Report (Rule in "Chandler v. Webster")》（Cmnd. 6009）的报道，并最终带来了1943年的《Law Reform (Frustration Contract) Act》立法。

在立法前不久，Chandler v. Webster 先例严苛的法律地位实际上就已经被贵族院的 Fibrosa Spolka Akcyjina v. Fairbairn Lawson Combe Barbour Ltd. 先例改变。在该先例相关的 CIF 买卖中，英国卖方以4800英镑的价格向波兰买方出售一种机器。根据合约，波兰买方要先支付1/3给英国卖方，剩下的2/3在英国卖方交出付运单证后再支付。波兰买方支付了1000英镑给英国卖方。但在英国卖方将机械造好之前，"二战"爆发，波兰目的地港被纳粹德军占领，买卖合约变为非法而受阻。

波兰买方于是要求英国卖方返还之前支付的1000英镑，但被英国卖方拒绝，于是双方开始诉讼。与 Chandler v. Webster 先例不同，在该先例中，贵族院判波兰买方可以取回这1000英镑，因为他完全得不到对价的好处（total failure of consideration）。这个完全得不到对价的好处的说法适用在合约一开始就被取消（rescind *ab intio*）的情况，如本章开头提到的共同错误（common mistake）、非法（illegality）或胁迫（duress）等情况，也适用在合约中途受阻的情况。这个判法与 Chandler v. Webster 先例不同。

但即使有了 Fibrosa Spolka Akcyjina v. Fairbairn Lawson Combe Barbour Ltd. 先例，普通法的地位还是不能令人满意，如：（1）如果只是"部分得不到对价好处"（partial failure of consideration），该先例的判法就不适用，也就是仍会导致不公平的情况：Whincup v. Hughes（1871）LR 6 CP 78 先例。例如，当时制造的机器（或其他货物或服务）已经交付了一部分给波兰买方。（2）波兰买方要求英国卖方退回已经到手的1000镑是依据完全得不到对价的好处。这说法与公平合理无关，普通法也不会理会在个别不同案情是否公平合理。这样一来，英国卖方不能在1000英镑中扣除制造机器半途已花费的成本后再退还给原告。（3）如果涉及的不是买卖合约而是提供服务的合约，并且要在完成整个服务后才能获得支付。合约受阻后，提供服务的一方无法对受阻前已经提供的服务获得任何支付。这本质与上一段一样，只涉及更复杂的问题，如需要对做出了部分的服务估价，这份服务有否为对方带来好处。如果有，提供服务的一方能否提出一个复原的索赔，类似在本章之8.3.1段提到的要求对方按劳计酬（*quantum meruit*）做出支付？

在《Chitty on Contracts》（第32版，2015年）一书之23－073段总结说："**Defects in the common law.** Although the result in Fibrosa represented an improvement . . . the common law remained in a less than satisfactory state. Three principal defects were apparent. The **first** was that the payer could only recover money paid upon a total failure of consideration; a partial failure of consideration did not give rise to a right of recovery. The **second** was that the House of Lords was of the opinion that the payee could not set off against the money to be repaid any expenditure which had been incurred in the performance of the contract. The **third** defect arose in relation to a claim by a provider of services. Where the frustrating event destroyed the work which had been done and payment was due only on the completion of the work, then the service provider was not entitled to bring a restitutionary claim to recover payment in respect of the work which he had done prior to the frustration of the contract."

因为普通法无法解决这些问题,所以有了 1943 年的《Law Reform (Frustration Contract) Act》立法想做出改善。

10.《Law Reform (Frustration Contract) Act》的介绍

在 BP v. Hunt (1979) 1 WLR 783 先例中,Goff 大法官指出 1943 年立法的宗旨是防止一方因为合约受阻占对方便宜而不当得利,说:"Fundamental principle underlying the Act itself is prevention of the unjust enrichment of either party to the contract at the other's expense."Goff 大法官也说该立法是设法允许双方公平分摊合约受阻所带来的损失:"real basis of the Act is that it is designed to provide a flexible machinery for the adjustment of loss."

需要注意的是,该立法没有针对合约是否受阻的问题,所以判断合约是否受阻仍要根据原本的普通法地位与先例。

10.1 立法适用的情况

该立法之 section 1 (1) 说:"Where a contract governed by English law has become impossible of performance or been otherwise frustrated, and the parties thereto have for that reason been discharged from the further performance of the contract, the following provisions of this section shall, subject to the provisions of section two of this Act, have effect in relation thereto."

针对 section 1(1),有两点需要注意:第一,只有合约的实体法是英国法时,该立法才会适用。所以,即使合约规定了去伦敦仲裁,但明示或默示了实体法是外国法律,该立法仍不适用。例如,合约规定了实体法适用新加坡法,该立法就不适用。但新加坡有《Frustrated Contracts Act》(Cap 115,1985 Rev Ed)的类似立法,该立法与英国 1943 年立法几乎完全相同。而香港也有《Law Amendment and Reform (Consolidation) Ordinance》(Cap 23)之 section 16 的类似立法。第二,1943 年立法说明适用情况是合约变为(become)不能履行而受阻,所以在合约不是“变为”而是一开始就不能履行,即共同错误（common mistake）的情况,该立法也不适用。另外,如果合约是因为条文中(如不可抗力条文)规定的事项而不能履行或被终止,而不是因为发生了受阻事件而自动终止,该立法也不适用。

10.2　针对受阻前支付的金钱

立法的 section 1(2)是针对受阻前支付的金钱,希望在退还这笔钱的同时,让双方能够公平分摊受阻带来的损失,说:“All sums paid or payable to any party in pursuance of the contract before the time when the parties were so discharged（in this Act referred to as ‘the time of discharge’）shall, in the ease of sums so paid, be recoverable from him as money received by him for the use of party by whom the sums were paid, and, in the ease of sums so payable, cease to be payable: Provided that, if the party to whom the sums were so paid or payable incurred expenses before the time of discharge in, or for the purpose of, the performance of contract, the court may if it considers it just to do so having regard to all the circumstances of the case, allow him to retain or, as the case may be, recover the whole or any part of the sums so paid or payable, not being an amount in excess of the expenses so incurred.”

针对 Section 1(2),可以先强调以下几点:(1)该条文容许合约一方向对方取回在受阻前已支付的钱(sums so paid)。(2)该条文容许合约受阻前已到期应付款(sums so payable)的一方尚未支付,则再不必付(cease to be payable)。换言之,在 Chandler v. Webster（1904）1 KB 493 先例中,原告不必再支付被告反索赔的 41 英镑。(3)该条文不像 Fibrosa Spolka Akcyjina v. Fairbairn Lawson Combe Barbour Ltd.（1943）AC 32 先例要在一方“完全得不到对价的好处”时才适用。(4)该条文与 Fibrosa Spolka Akcyjina v. Fairbairn Lawson Combe Barbour Ltd. 先例不同的一点是,容许收钱的一方先扣除其为了履行该合约而花费(for the purpose of the performance of contract)的使费(incurred expenses),再将剩下的钱退还给对方。而合约订立以前已花的钱不包括在内,合约受阻之后所继续支付[82]或花的钱(如果有)也不包括在内。另外,该立法条文只是允许将受阻前已支付的钱扣除使费再归还。如果已付的钱很多,而使费很少,这当然没有问题。但如果只付了很小一笔钱,但使费很多,收钱的一方最多也只是不需要退还任何钱,而不能再要求对方支付不足的部分。此外,Section 1（4）也允许包括合理的固定使费（overhead）。但 section 1(5)是说如果双方或其

[82] 会有支付方在不知道受阻的情况下继续做出支付,这笔钱可以在普通法的对事实的错误(mistake of fact)的说法下把钱要回来: Barclays Bank Ltd. v. W J Simms Son & Cooke（Southern）Ltd.（1980）QB 677 先例。即使支付方知道受阻的事实,但拿不准根据法律是否构成受阻也可以在对法律的错误(mistake of law)的说法下把钱要回来,总之与该 1943 年的立法无关: Kleinwort Benson Ltd. v. Lincoln City Council（1999）2 AC 349 先例。

中一方针对合约受阻终止带来的损失有保险,这些保险的好处不加以考虑。

但扣除自己的使费再将已经收到的钱(如果有剩余)退还给另一方最有争议的一点,就是扣除多少钱。简单的做法就是扣钱的一方自己证明在合约受阻前的使费,如 A 曾经支付了 5 万美元,B 可以证明自己的使费是 2 万美元,将剩下的 3 万美元退还。但这个做法的不公平之处是,必须双方都没有错才可以构成合约受阻,原本的普通法地位是要求 B 将 5 万美元全数退回,即要他承担 2 万美元的损失。而在该 1943 年立法下,B 可以将 2 万美元扣除后,将 3 万美元还给 A,这样一来等于 A 承担了这 2 万美元的损失。因此,有人认为这样解读该立法的规定并不公平,更公平的做法是 B 只能扣除这 2 万美元的一半,将剩下的 4 万美元还给 A。再复杂一点的情况是两方都有使费,但因为 A 向 B 支付了 5 万美金,所以,B 可以扣除使费后再退还,而 A 的使费就要自己承担,这也不公平。因此,有人提议说应该让法官或仲裁员将两方使费一起考虑之后,再决定一个公平(just)的扣除金额。[83]

这方面可节录《Chitty on Contracts》(第 32 版,2015 年)一书之 23-081 段:

"Although the payee may now be entitled to set off against a claim by the payer 'the amount of any expenses incurred before the time of discharge... in, or for the purpose of the performance of the contract', it is difficult to establish the basis upon which the payee is entitled to seek to bring his expenditure into account. The consequence of this is that it is difficult, if not impossible, to ascertain with any confidence the amount which the payee will be entitled to retain. Various views have been put forward. **First**, it has been argued that the loss caused by the frustrating event should be divided equally between the parties on the ground that the: 'situation with which the Act is concerned is the familiar one in which one of two parties has to suffer loss for which neither is responsible.'

And that in the 'normal case' the just course 'would be to order the retention or repayment of half the loss incurred. **Secondly**, it has been argued that the payee should be entitled to retain the full amount of the expenditure incurred in the performance of the contract; a view supported by the English Law Revision Committee and which also seems to receive some support from the judgment of Robert Goff J. in BP v. Hunt who argued

---

〔83〕 加拿大的类似立法《Frustrated Contracts Act (British Columbia) 1974》中就说明平分双方的使费:"5 (2) Subject to section 6, every party to a contract to which this Act applies is entitled to restitution from the other party or parties to the contract for benefits created by the party's performance or part performance of the contract... (4) If the circumstances giving rise to the frustration or avoidance cause a total or partial loss in value of a benefit to a party required to make restitution under subsection (2), that loss must be apportioned equally between the party required to make restitution and the party to whom the restitution is required to be made."

that the proviso constituted a ‘statutory recognition of the defence of change of position’[84] although this rationalization is controversial. The **third view** is that the court in deciding what is ‘just’ is exercising a broad discretion, which discretion is not confined to the entitlement to bring expenditure into account but extends to the proportion of the repayment which the payee can retain or recover and that therefore this discretion would be unduly circumscribed by the adoption of either of the other two views. These three views were considered by Garland J. in Gamerco SA v. I. C. M. /Fair Warning (Agency) Ltd. (1995) 1 WLR 1226 who concluded that he could see:‘... no indication in the Act, the authorities of the relevant literature that the court is obliged to incline towards either total retention or equal division. Its task is to do justice in a situation which the parties had neither contemplated nor provided for, and to mitigate the possible harshness of allowing all loss to lie where it has fallen ...’

The emphasis is thus placed on the ‘broad nature’ of the discretion which the court enjoys and the imperative to do justice on the facts of the case.”

上述节录的《Chitty on Contracts》(第 32 版,2015 年)一书之 23 - 081 段的最后提到了 Gamerco SA v. ICM/Fair Warning (Agency) Ltd. (1995) 1 WLR 1226 先例与 Garland 大法官的判决,该先例的案情涉及著名的摇滚乐队枪炮与玫瑰(Guns N' Roses)1992 年的欧洲巡演。原告是一家西班牙的流行音乐演唱会承办商(pop concert promoter),与被告订立合约承办枪炮与玫瑰 7 月 4 日在马德里的演唱会。原告原本已经获得政府的批文并租了场馆,但在 6 月 30 日,工程师报告该场馆不安全,于是政府在 7 月 1 日禁止使用该场馆,并取消了演唱会批文。原告紧急寻找替代场馆,但不成功,最后只能取消演唱会。当时双方为了履行该合约花了一定的钱,其中被告的使费约为 5 万美元,而原告的使费高达 45 万美元。

在演唱会被取消即合约终止前,根据合约的规定,原告应该支付 70 多万美元,但因为银行方面的问题,只支付了 40 多万美元。原告认为,在这种情况下合约受阻,根据 1943 年《Law Reform (Frustrated Contracts) Act》之 section 1(2),要求取回预付的 40 多万美元。而被告则认为,原告有保证场馆安全与保证政府批文持续有效的严格责任,原告违约/毁约要赔偿损失。

法院判是该合约下原告只需要尽合理努力取得批文,场馆因为不安全被停止使用属于受阻事件,原告在 1943 年立法下不需要支付合约受阻前到期尚未支付的 30 多万美元,并有权取回预付的 40 多万美元。但针对被告可以扣减的具体金额,高院的 Garland 大法官在考虑了其他不同扣减的做法后,对 1943 年立法之 section 1(2)的解读是倾向于法院有广泛的裁量权,应把两方的使费都纳入考虑以决定公平的金额。高院最后判是被告要返还原告全部的 40 多万美元,不能做出任何扣减。

[84] 这课题可参见本书第五章第 4 段。

这种广泛的裁量权当然有好处，可以做到尽量对合约双方都公平，但坏处是一旦法院有这种广泛的裁量权，必然导致不肯定。说到底，这问题还是出在1943年立法没有写清楚甚至是没有把这问题想透。

有关1943年立法之section 1(2)可另介绍一个更近期的先例，在DVB Bank v. Shere Shipping Co. Ltd. and others (2013) EWHC 2321 (Ch)先例中，案情涉及2006年DVB带头的财团贷款给伊朗的国有公司Shere Shipping，并由Shere Shipping背后的另外两家大型伊朗国有公司做担保人。这笔贷款是用来购买4艘船舶，但不久之后联合国就对伊朗实施制裁，导致Shere Shipping在2011年因为所有的美元账户都被冻结而无法偿还贷款。DVB向英国法院申请简易判决(summary judgment)，而被告除了Shere Shipping外，还包括作为担保人的两个公司。被告做出的抗辩有若干方面，包括欧盟对有关联合国制裁的立法所用的措辞，这与受阻无关，只是被告的这个抗辩失败。而与受阻有关的争辩之一是这个制裁可以令贷款合约的承诺(偿还贷款)被暂时中止(suspend)，这个争辩也不被高院接受，毕竟合约的承诺是严格或绝对责任。而最关键的受阻争议就是联合国的制裁与欧盟的立法是否导致贷款合约无法履行下去而受阻，这看来被高院接受。但即使是受阻，也带来了1943年立法的适用。所以DVB可以根据section 1(2)向被告取回以前做出但尚未偿还的贷款。Simon大法官这样说：

"It follows that ... the repayment obligations are incapable of being performed indefinitely due to the Regulations, the result is not that this obligation is 'suspended'. On this hypothesis, what has occurred is a supervening event (without the fault of either party and for which the contract does not provide) which has significantly changed the nature of the contractual obligations in a way which could not have been anticipated at the time the contract was made. In short the contract has been frustrated, see for example National Carriers Ltd. v. Panalpina (Northern) Ltd. [1981] AC 675 Lord Simon of Glaisdale at 700 and J Lauritzen AS v. Wijsmuller BV [1990] 2 Lloyd's Rep. 1, Bingham LJ at 8.

In such circumstances, and by the operation of s. 1 of the Law Reform (Frustrated Contracts) Act 1943... the Lenders would be entitled to recover and the Borrowers would be bound to repay the amount of the loans. Although the Borrowers have asserted in §15 of the Reply to Defence and Counterclaim that they are entitled to deduct certain expenses, they have not explained the basis on which they are entitled to do so, nor have they quantified such expenses."

结果Simon大法官就接受了DVB的申请，向被告做出了简易判决。

10.3　针对受阻前获得的非金钱的服务与好处

1943年立法之section 1(3)是针对一方受阻前获得的非金钱的服务与好处："Where any party to the contract has, by reason of anything done by any other party thereto in, or for the purpose of, the performance of the contract, obtained a valuable benefit (other than a payment of money to which the last foregoing subsection applies) before the time of discharge, there shall be recoverable from him by the said other party such sum (if any), not exceeding the value of the said benefit to the party obtaining it, as the court considers just, having regard to all the circumstances of the case and, in particular,— (a) the amount of any expenses incurred before the time of discharge by the benefited party in, or for the purpose of, the performance of the contract, including any sums paid or payable by him to any other party in pursuance of the contract and retained or recoverable by that party under the last foregoing subsection, and (b) the effect, in relation to the said benefit, of the circumstances giving rise to the frustration of the contract."

Section 1(3)与 section 1(2)的针对有所不同,是让提供服务的一方根据"复原"(restitution)原则要求另一方返还其服务成本与使费。这与本章之 8.3.1 段提到的如果一方接受了另一方的部分履行,就要做出按劳计酬(*quantum meruit*)的支付的道理类似,但在该段已经提到,如果所谓接受部分履行的一方谈不上是自己选择接受了部分履行,而是不得不接受,就不用做出支付。在合约受阻的情况下,接受服务并获得好处的一方谈不上选择接受了另一方的部分履行,而是因为出现受阻事件不得不接受。因此,section 1(3)介入改变了普通法地位,希望在发生受阻事件后,双方都可以向对方寻求复原。

这方面的计算十分复杂与富有争议性,其中部分原因是不像 section 1(2)针对的受阻前支付的金钱要退还是清楚明确,获得的服务或好处的价值很难确定。什么才可以叫做好处?怎样确定服务或好处的具体金额?例如,可能提供服务的一方在合约受阻前花费了很多金钱与做了大量工作,但另一方的好处不多或在受阻事件中失去。根据 section 1(3),获得服务或好处的一方返还的钱不能超过他获得的好处,即在这种情况下,提供服务的一方无法取回其所有的成本与使费。一个简单的例子是室内装修的合约,装修公司在前期花钱找人设计、购买了材料等,结果刚开始正式的装修工作,合约就因为法律改变而受阻。这时可以说房屋业主获得的好处很少,即使估价后全额还给装修公司,对装修公司来说也不足够。更不用说装修进行到一半甚至快进行完时,房屋被火烧毁,合约受阻。但这样一来,房屋业主获得的服务与好处已经在大火中一并失去,装修公司一分钱都拿不回来。另外,好处应该在什么时间点进行计算?是在受阻的一天或是以后?如果该服务带来的好处要在很长一段时间之后才能显示出来要怎么办?有不少说法认为该立法写得很差,针对这些方面的问题没有做出任何指引。这可节录《Chitty on Contracts》(第 32 版,2015 年)一书之 23-084 段:"... This is the most controversial and difficult provision in the Act, caused in large part by the failure of the draftsman to provide a definition of what constitutes a 'benefit' and to identify with sufficient precision the time at which the benefit is to be valued. In

BP v. Hunt, Robert Goff J. held that the proper approach to the construction of the subsection is a three – stage one. At the first stage the valuable benefit must be identified; at the second stage the benefit must be valued; and at the third stage the court must consider the award of a just sum."

可能也是因为该立法条文写得太差,而这方面的问题也十分不明朗,在 BP v. Hunt (1979) 1 WLR 783 先例前,35 年来都没有涉及该立法之 section 1(3)的先例。该先例涉及的金额很大,一直上诉到贵族院,但针对的都是其他争议,也就是说,只有一审的 Goff 大法官针对该立法之 section 1(3)有一定指引,包括上一段节录的内容中提到的这一复原原则要分三个阶段考虑。笔者可先简单介绍该先例的案情。

10.3.1　BP v. Hunt 先例

在 BP v. Hunt (1979) 1 WLR 783 先例中,Hunt 先生在 1957 年 12 月 18 日获得利比亚国王的特许(concession),在一块土地上开采石油。然而 Hunt 先生因为资金的问题,无法在特许要求的时间内开始钻油,于是在 1960 年 6 月与 BP 石油公司订立了一个名为"farm – in agreement"的合约,将特许的权利转让(assign)给 BP 一半,由 BP 负责提供开采石油的技术、设备与资金,而 BP 也同意在开采出石油后按照一定比例给 Hunt 先生现金与石油。之后,这块土地上果然开采出石油并且产量很高,于是在 1963 年,BP 决定开始建造必要的设备,铺设管道等。1967 年年初,工程全部完成,管道也全部铺设完毕。期间,BP 与 Hunt 先生都有石油的收益。

然而在 1969 年 9 月 1 日,利比亚发生政变,卡扎菲成为利比亚的最高领导人。从 1970 年开始,卡扎菲政府就开始向各石油公司施加压力并在 1971 年 12 月通过立法将 BP 的石油利益收归国有。1973 年的 6 月,也把 Hunt 先生的特许收回。后来在英国政府的支持下,BP 与卡扎菲政府达成和解协议,BP 可以收回所有在利比亚的设备的账面价值,但作为受让人的特许利益就无法获得任何赔偿。[85] 卡扎菲政府与 Hunt 先生也达成协议以提供一定数量的石油作为赔偿。

之后 BP 在英国法院开始诉讼,要求 Hunt 先生根据 1943 年《Law Reform (Frustrated Contracts) Act》之 section 1(3)向 BP 做出复原的支付或赔偿。BP 在受阻即 1971 年 12 月前,为了履行合约,花费了至少数亿美元。这方面履行的工作包括钻探、发现石油与估计产量、对油田设施的设计与建设、铺设油管将石油运到港口出口等。

这毫无疑问给 Hunt 先生带来了好处,因为没有 BP 的履行,Hunt 先生一桶油也拿不到,并且因为他无法在特许规定的时间内开始钻油,很可能特许也保不住。这一半的特许权益的好处原本可以是天文数字,虽然因为受阻事件价值大减,但至少令 Hunt 先生有权与卡扎菲政府达成和解协议。问题是这些好处的价值如何计算。

这里可节录对 Goff 大法官判决的总结,如下:

---

〔85〕 显然在 1965 年《华盛顿公约》下,利比亚可能会面对 BP 的天价索赔。

"That, in considering whether to make an award under section 1 (3) of the Act of 1943, the court has to apply the following principles:

(a) The court has first to ascertain whether the defendant has, by reason of something done by BP in, or for the purpose of, the performance of the contract, obtained a valuable benefit (other than a payment of money) before the time of discharge. That benefit has to be identified, and valued; and forms the upper limit of any award. The benefit so identified should not be equaled with the services rendered by BP, but may in an appropriate case be the end product of those services. The benefit is to be valued as at the date of frustration; but no allowance is to be made for the 'time value of money', i. e. the notional benefit derived from the fact that Mr. Hunt has had the use of the product of BP's contractual performance over a period of time before the frustrating event occurred. From the benefit as so valued, there has to be deducted the amount of any expenditure incurred by Mr. Hunt before the time of discharge in, or for the purpose of, the performance of the contract; and there has to be taken into account the effect, in relation to the benefit, of the circumstances giving rise to the frustration of the contract.

(b) The court has next to assess a just sum to award to BP in respect of his performance. In considering the assessment of such sum, the court may have regard to the contract consideration as providing evidence of the appropriate level of remuneration; in many cases, it will be unjust to award more than the contract consideration, or a rateable part of it.

(c) The amount to be awarded to BP will be the just sum, unless the benefit obtained by the defendant, valued on the principles stated above, is less, in which event the award will be limited to the amount of that benefit.

That, applying the foregoing principles to the plaintiffs' claim (a) Mr. Hunt's benefit was the enhancement in the value of his share in the concession; but that benefit was greatly reduced by the effect of the circumstances giving rise to the frustration of the contract, and was thereby limited to the benefit of the oil obtained by him from the concession and the benefit of his settlement with the Libyan Government. Furthermore, only half of the benefit derived from BP contractual performance, the other half deriving from Mr. Hunt's ownership of the concession. On this basis, Mr. Hunt benefit was valued at U. S. $84,951,000 (net of reimbursement oil). (b) If the just sum to be awarded to BP were to be assessed in U. S. dollars it would be assessed at U. S. $35,403,146."

10.3.2 考虑 section 1(3)下公平的金额的三个阶段

至于稍早提到的 Goff 大法官认为这一复原原则要分三个阶段考虑,即第一个阶段确定有哪些属于好处,第二个阶段给这些好处估价,第三个阶段根据这个估价行使裁量权认定公平的金额。

第一个阶段可节录《Chitty on Contracts》(第32版,2015年)一书之23-085段的解释:"**Identification of the benefit.** The 'benefit', which must of course be non-monetary, could consist of either the 'end product' of the services or the services themselves. Robert Goff J. concluded, as a matter of construction rather than one of principle, that 'in appropriate case' it was the end product which was to be regarded as the benefit. It is not clear when it would not be 'appropriate' to regard the end product as the benefit but there are a number of situations in which it has been argued that the benefit should be identified with the service itself. The general rule is therefore that regard must be had to the end product of the services when identifying the benefit. But there are at least two situations in which it is appropriate to have regard to the services themselves when identifying the benefit. The first case arises where the service, by its very nature, does not result in an end product, for example, 'where the services consist of doing such work as surveying, or transporting goods'. Where there is no end product the court must simply ascertain the benefit which the defendant has obtained by virtue of the claimant's contractual performance, which benefit can only be measured by reference to the value of the services performed by the claimant under the contract. The second case arises where the services performed result in an end product which has no objective value, in which case the benefit must also be measured by reference to the value of the services provided under the contract ..."

Goff大法官认为确定什么是好处时,大多数合约不应考虑服务本身的价值,而应该考虑服务的成果(end product)的价值。换言之,看服务为对方带来的实质的好处。但至少在两种情况下只能考虑服务本身的价值。第一种情况是服务的性质决定了并没有所谓的成果,如一些附属性的合约,在合约下要提供的服务是测量或搬运货物。因为该服务本质上不会有成果,法院或仲裁庭只能考虑服务本身的价值。第二种情况是服务的成果没有客观的价值。典型的例子是装修公司根据房屋业主的要求装修房屋,而业主的品位很奇怪,随着装修工作的进行,房屋的价值可能不仅没有升高反而降低了。在这种情况下,法院或仲裁庭也只能考虑服务本身的价值。在笔者看来还有第三种情况,如在BP v. Hunt (1979) 1 WLR 783先例中,如果合约受阻前BP钻探了三分之二的土地都没有发现石油,之后合约受阻,虽然表面看Hunt先生没有实质的好处,但之后如果Hunt先生仍然保留特许要继续钻探石油,就只需要钻探剩下三分之一的土地。还会有其他各种情况,笔者就不再一一猜测。

第二个阶段可节录《Chitty on Contracts》(第32版,2015年)一书之23-087段的解释:"**Valuing the benefit.** Once the benefit has been identified, the court must then value it. The conclusion that it is the end product and not the services themselves which are to be regarded as the benefit gives rise to considerable difficulties in valuing the benefit because there is no necessary relationship between the services and the end product. A small service may result in an end product of great value, while a service of great value may result in an end product of no or minimal value. If the benefit is only partly attributable to the claimant's performance, the court should apportion the value of the benefit accordingly. The wording of the subsection does not permit the court to account of the time value of money so that the benefit is valued at the date of the frustrating event without regard to the money which the defendant may have obtained by selling the benefit before the date of the frustrating event ..."

大多数合约应考虑服务的成果而不是服务本身的价值，这就带来了对好处估价的难度。因为服务的成果与服务本身的价值即使有关联，也不是成正比的。价值很低的服务的成果可能价值很高，价值很高的服务的成果可能反而价值很低。如果对方获得的好处只是部分因为原告提供的服务，法院就可以按比例计算原告的服务给另一方带来的好处的价值。该 1943 年立法之 section 1(3)的用字显示了法院或仲裁庭在估价时不应该考虑时间因素，这不涉及是否公平的问题，而是对立法条文措辞/用字的解释。因此，法院或仲裁庭在对这些好处进行估价时，应以受阻的一天为准，而不考虑如果被告在受阻事件发生之前将前期获得的好处转卖能得到的价值。

第三个阶段可节录《Chitty on Contracts》(第 32 版，2015 年)一书之 23 - 090 段的解释："**The just sum.** The final step is for the court to assess the 'just' sum to be awarded to the claimant. Robert Goff J. held that the aim of the court in assessing the just sum ought to be the 'prevention of the unjust enrichment of the defendant at the plaintiff's expense' but the Court of Appeal preferred a broader, discretionary approach, stating that 'what is just is what the trial judge thinks is just' and that an appellate court is not entitled to interfere with the assessment of the just sum by the trial judge 'unless it is so plainly wrong that it cannot be just'. This appears to leave the assessment of the just sum at the complete discretion of the trial judge. There are, however, certain factors which are clearly of relevance in the assessment of the just sum. The first is that the value of the benefit acts as a ceiling on the sum which the court can aware so that the 'just sum' cannot be greater than the value of the benefit obtained. The second is that the contractual allocation of risk is likely to be an important factor in the assessment of the just sum. It is 'likely' that in most cases the claimant's claim will be limited to a rateable proportion of the contract price so that s. 1(3) cannot be used to escape the consequences of a bad bargain. The first point is that the process of assessing the just sum may bear some resemblance to the inquiry conducted by the court in an action for a quantum meruit or a quantum valebant."

Goff 大法官认为决定公平的金额时主要还是要防止一方不当得利，但上诉庭认为一审法官有更广泛的裁量权。一审法官觉得公平就是公平，上诉庭的法官不能做出更改，除非一审法官的决定实在太离谱，不可能被认为是公平的金额。这样一来，什么是公平的金额完全是一审法官说了算。当然,虽然一审法官有十分广泛的裁量权,还是有些情况要纳入考虑。首先,section 1(3)明确规定了公平的金额不能超过对方因为服务而获得的好处。其次,在决定公平的金额时,合约的规定如何分配风险也是重要的考虑。另是在绝大多数情况下,提供服务的一方还只是获得一定比例的合约的约因/对价,不能利用 section 1(3)逃避原本是亏本的生意。这可以举一个简单的例子,A 与 B 订立合约,以 2000 万元的价格为 B 提供服务。当合约受阻时,A 已经花了 3000 万元(等于这注定是亏本的合约),而给 B 带来的好处高达 5000 万元。如果不考虑合约的约因/对价是 2000 万元,法官可能会认为公平的金额是 2500 万元。但这样一来,就会造成一个可笑的局面,即合约受阻后 A 可以拿到的钱比全部履行了合约还多。所以,为了避免 A 利用 section 1(3)逃避这个亏大本的生意,法官在决定公平的金额时需要考虑合约下约因/对价的金额。总体来说,法院在决定公平的金额时的做法与决定按劳计酬(*quantum meruit*)或按值付价(*quantum valebant*)的金额时的做法类似。

10.4　合约明示排除 1943 年立法的适用

为了避免像 Hunt 先生这样需要退还一大笔钱的危险,在一些是由一方承担了大部分履行责任的类别的合约,而另一方的履行责任主要是做出支付时,另一方就要小心 1943 年立法之 section 1(3)的适用。如建筑或工程合约,履行责任基本在承建商/承包商,如果是本章之 8.3.2 段介绍的按照工程时间/进度做出支付(progress payment),这方面的问题还不明显。但如果是"一次过"付钱的完整合约,合约受阻自动终止后双方都不再需要履行,因为雇主是被迫而不是自己选择接受了承建商/承包商的部分履行,所以普通法下不必再做出任何支付。[86] 但 section 1(3)改变了这一普通法地位,让雇主要为已经完成的工作支付公平的金额。这看来公平合理,但在上一段已经提到,在 section 1(3)下法官有十分广泛的裁量权,这必然会带来不肯定。这样一来,合约受阻后双方很难有谈判达成和解的基础,最后不得不开始昂贵的诉讼。因此在这一类合约中,接受服务的一方(如雇主)会希望以合约明示条文排除 1943 年立法之 section 1(3)的适用。[87] 该 1943 年立法允许合约明示排除 section 1(3)的适用,在 section 2(3)说:"Where any contract to which this Act applies contains any provision which, upon the true construction of the contract, is intended to have effect in the event of circumstances arising which operate, or would but for the said provision operate, to frustrate the contract, or is intended to have effect whether such circumstances arise or not, the court shall give effect to the said provision and shall only give effect to the foregoing section of this Act to such extent, if any, as appears to the court to be consistent

---

[86] 参见本章之 8.3.1 段。

[87] 当然,提供服务的一方如果懂得法律就不会无条件同意排除 section 1(3)适用的条文,而是会通过谈判以明示条文规定合约受阻后双方都能接受的方案。

with the said provision. ”

但要注意的是,合约的明示条文必须清楚明确才能超越法律默示地位,希望通过明示条文排除立法的适用更会被严格解释。所以,排除 1943 年的《Law Reform (Frustration Contract) Act》立法特别是 section 1(3)的适用很困难,并且会被严格解释。这可节录《Chitty on Contracts》(第 32 版,2015 年)一书之 23 – 093 段:“A court will be particularly reluctant to imply a term that the parties have made provision for the consequences of a frustrating event. But a clause which provides that one contracting party is under an obligation to maintain insurance against the consequences of the frustrating event would appear to be effective to exclude the operation of the Act so that the party upon whom the obligation to insure is imposed cannot bring a claim under the Act. However the fact that a contract is entire and that the contract provides that payment is not due until the work is complete or until a date which is after the date of the frustrating event does not ‘automatically preclude an award of damages under s. 1(3) and it is only: ‘... if upon a true construction of the contract the plaintiff has contracted on the terms that he is to receive no payment in the event which has occurred, will the fact that the contract is ‘entire’ have the effect of precluding an award under the Act. ”

在 BP v. Hunt (1979) 1 WLR 783 先例中,双方曾经在通信中同意说:“6. It is specifically understood and agreed that Mr Hunt shall have no personal liability to repay the sums required in the operating agreement and this letter agreement to be advanced by BP for Mr Hunt’s account or paid to Mr Hunt, but BP’s right to recover any such sums which BP is required to pay or advance for Mr Hunt’s account shall be limited to recovery solely out of three – eighths of Mr Hunt’s half of the production ... ”

但 Robert Goff 大法官认为这只是针对合约内容,而没有针对合约受阻的情况的意图,说:“on its true construction, clause 6 of the letter agreement was only applicable in its contractual context, and was not intended to apply in the event of frustration ... ”

10.5 《Law Reform (Frustration Contract) Act》不适用的合约

1943 年立法之 Section 2 (5) 说明在以下的合约不适用:“This Act shall not apply – (a) to any charterparty, except a time charterparty or a charterparty by way of demise, or to any contract (other than a charterparty) for the carriage of goods by sea;or(b) to any contract of insurance-save as provided by sub – section (5) of the foregoing section; or(c) to any contract to which section 7 of the Sale of Goods Act 1979 (which avoids contract for the sale of specific goods which perish before the risk has passed to the buyer) applies, or to any other contracts for the sale, or for the sale and delivery, of specific goods, where the contract is frustrated by reason of the fact that the goods have perished. ”

立法不适用的合约类别基本上是海事/海商合约(maritime contracts),可见海商法在英国商法中重要与独特的历史地位。规定不适用背后的原因可节录《Chitty on Contracts》(第32版,2015年)一书之23-096段:"**Contracts excluded from the Act.** Section 2(5) provides that the Act does not apply to four types of contract: (a) 'any charterparty, except a time charterparty or a charterparty by way of demise';[88] (b) 'any contract for the carriage of goods by sea' (since commercial practice has developed well-known rules for insurance against the risks of these contracts);[89] (c) 'any contract of insurance' (since there is a well-established principle that no part of a premium is legally recoverable where the subject matter of the risk ceases to exist before the period of the insurance expires[90]); (d) any contract for the sale of specific goods which perish, whether or not the risk passed to the buyer before the date of perishing. (Any other contract for the sale of goods will be governed by the Act, as will a contract for the sale of specific goods which is frustrated otherwise than by the 'perishing' of the goods).[91]"

此外也可节录另一本权威书籍中对1943年立法不适用的合约更详尽的解释。在《Goff & Jones, The Law of Unjust Enrichment》(第9版,2016年)一书之15-62至15-64段,说:

"**Advance freight.** Section 2(5)(a) preserves the common law rules on payment of freight in advance under voyage charterparties, under which the right to retain such freight was not conditional on the successful completion of the voyage. In this respect, the Act follows the recommendations of the Law Revision Committee, which, despite being highly critical of the advance freight rules, regarded them as being too well established to be abolished. Strong criticism of the rules seems to be misplaced, because they actually reflect the agreed basis on which the payment was made and are, therefore, consistent with the general principles of failure of basis. However, by enacting the 1943 legislation after the House of Lords' decision in Fibrosa Spolka Akcyjina v. Fairbairn Law-

---

[88] 1943年立法不适用在程租合约而只适用在期租合约与光船租约的原因,是针对程租合约已经有很多历史悠久与稳定的先例规定了预付运费的法律地位,即所谓的"advanced freight rule",所以1943年的立法决定不改变已经历史悠久与十分稳定的法律地位。这方面会在本章之10.5.1段与10.5.2段有详细介绍。

[89] 1943年立法也不适用在海上货物运输的合约,这种合约也就是很多商业人士熟悉的提单(bill of lading),也包括其他海运单(seaway bill)等。有关这一类别的合约可见笔者《提单与其他付运单证》(2016年)一书。背后的原因也是这类合约针对海上突发事件导致货物消失或损坏如何通过保险分配风险,有历史悠久与十分稳定的做法与法律地位(包括1924年《海牙规则》)。

[90] 这在英国1906年《Marine Insurance Act》之section 84(3)(a)规定:"... but if the risk is not apportionable, and has once attached, the premium is not returnable."这也表示无论是船舶或货物一旦开始有了风险,即使开航后很快遇上突发事件而灭失,被保险人也不能通过依赖1943年立法向保险人取回保费,因为1906年立法排除了保险合约。

[91] 不同类别的货物买卖合约是否适用该1943年立法,会在本章之10.5.3有详细介绍。

son Combe Barbour Ltd.（1943）AC 32, the decision was taken to replace failure of basis as the test for the return of payments following a frustrating event. The retention of failure of basis for advance payments of freight in voyage charterparties is, therefore, open to criticism as creating an anomaly.

Insurance. The 1943 Act does not apply to contracts of insurance. The relevant common law rules governing the recovery of insurance premium are discussed elsewhere. In the absence of any discussion in the report oif the Law Revision Committee it is difficult to know why the regime introduced by the 1943 Act was thought to be unsuitable. Possibly, as with the exception for payment of advance freight under voyage charterparties, it was thought that commercial practice in relation to insurance was too well settled to be disturbed by legislative reform. At any rate, there is no obvious reason of principle why insurance contracts would be unsuitable for the kind of treatment that the 1943 Act gives to other types of contract.

Sale of goods. Contracts governed by the Sale of Goods Act 1979 s. 7 are excluded from the 1943 Act, as are contracts for the sale of specific goods where the contract has been frustrated by the perishing of the goods. Section 7 of the 1979 Act provides that:

'Where there is an agreement to sell specified goods and subsequently the goods, without any fault on the part of the seller or buyer, perish before the risk passes to the buyer, the agreement is avoided.'

As Glanville Wiklliams observed, s. 2(5)(c) of the 1943 Act:

'... seems to be a somewhat involved way of saying that the Act does not apply to any contract for the sale of specific goods that perish, whether the risk passed to the buyer before the date of the perishing or not.'

Discussion of the precise extent of this exception is beyond the scope of this work, but its effect is that, where such contracts are frustrated by the perishing of the goods, the general common law principles of failure of basis will apply. Contracts for the sale of generic goods, or for the sale of specific goods where the goods have not perished, by contrast, fall within the 1943 Act."

10.5.1　立法不适用的合约：程租合约

已经提到程租合约（voyage charterparty）本身，特别是针对运费，已经有了历史悠久与稳定的预付运费规则（advance freight rule）。在解释这个规则之前，可以先简单介绍程租合约是服务性合约，承租人/货方租船将货物从一个港口运到另一个港口。租约的合约责任或承诺主要是由船东履行，承租人/货方在将货物装船后，唯一的合约责任就是在船舶抵达卸港后支付运费。程租合约是很明确的完整合约，履行的不同阶段（如空放航次、装港装货、满载航次、中途加燃油、卸港交货等）无法独立分开。如果运输途中发生了意外事件导致租约受阻，即使船舶已经距离卸港很近，船东也不能得到任何支付,不存在按比例赚取运费的说法。这一普通法的地位在本章之 8.3.2 段已经介绍,这里不再重复。

另一提的是,程租合约有很长的历史,早期的海上运输也是风险很高,因此遇上海难等突发事件导致租约受阻的机会很大。这样一来,因为船舶与货物无法抵达卸港,船东经常无法赚取运费。为了保障自己,船东也经常要为尚未赚取的运费投保。如果 1943 年立法适用,船东可以根据 section 1(3)在受阻后要求承租人或货方为已经做出的服务支付按劳计酬的一笔钱,不必再为运费投保,反而会扰乱这一贯的做法。

另是当时没有电汇等支付方式,所以船舶在装港(特别是在外国)经常会资金短缺,无法为船舶供应食物、饮水以及其他必需品。这导致船东经常要求承租人/货方在装货时或装货后做出部分或全部运费的预付,让船东有资金完成这个航次。但承租人预付的钱需要区分究竟是预付运费(advance freight)还是融资(loan)给船东。这有很大区别,因为在英国法下的预付运费规则(advance freight rule),船东收到预付的运费后,即使航次中途受阻,即船舶与货物到不了卸港,这笔钱也不需要退还给承租人。但如果是融资给船东,即使后来航次受阻,船东还是要把这笔借贷的钱退还给承租人。这两种在装港预付的区别,可见 Selborne 勋爵在贵族院的 Allison v. Bristol Marine Insurance Co. (1875) 1 App. Cas. 209 先例所说:"The peculiar of English Mercantile Law, that an **advance on account of freight** to be earned, made at the commencement of the voyage, is, in the absence of any stipulation to the contrary, **an irrevocable payment at the risk of the shipper** of the goods, and not **a loan repayable by the borrower** if freight to that amount be not earned."(加黑部分是笔者的强调)

至于在装港预付的钱究竟是预付运费或融资,就需要通过对有关租约的解释确定。例如,在 Manfield v. Maitland (1821) 4 B & Ald 582 先例中,租约中只说明承租人要在装港预付一笔钱,但没有说明是否为预付运费。后来航次在半途遇上突发事件而受阻,判是船东需要退还承租人这笔钱。

笔者接下来要介绍的是英国法律下的预付运费规则。在《Voyage Charters》(第 4 版,2014 年)一书之 13.87 段,说:"Where the freight is payable in advance, such as on shipment or on sailing from the loading port, or on signing bills of lading, it is irrevocable by the charterer even if the contract is subsequently frustrated by the loss of the ship or the cargo or by the impossibility of performing the voyage. This long - stand rule, which is peculiar to voyage charters, and which forms **an exception to the general rule relating to advance payments under contracts which are subsequently discharged by frustration**, was affirmed by the House of Lords in Allison v. Bristol Marine Insurance Co. (1875) 1 App. Cas. 209, ... The original justification for the rule was thought to be that the parties should be able to know at whose risk the freight is, so that the party at risk can insure his interest. However, the rule has been extended to the case where the failure to complete the voyage is caused by risks not normally insured against ...”(加黑部分是笔者的强调)

换言之,预付运费规则与其他一般合约的情况很不一样,前者的支付不受后来程租合约受阻而无法完成航次的影响,反正船东无需退还给承租人。但其他一般的合约如果半途受阻,而其中一方已经支付了一笔钱,不论是何种名义下的支付(即使是类似程租合约预付运费一样的预付款),他可以根据普通法下完全得不到对价的好处(total failure of consideration)的理由取回预付的钱:Fibrosa Spolka Akcyjina v. Fairbairn Lawson Combe Barbour Ltd. (1943) AC 32 先例。这个预付运费规则本意是让船东与承租人/货方明确谁需要承担责任,让他可以去购买保险(freight insurance),但现在即使是一些通常不会承保的风险(如因法律的改变去不了卸港)导致合约受阻,该规则仍然适用。

涉及预付运费规则的早期先例不少,如在 Andrew v. Moorhouse (1814) 5 Taunt 435 先例中,案情涉及从伦敦到南非好望角的程租合约。船东在合约谈判时提出如果承租人愿意在装港伦敦支付,运费是 5 英镑/吨,而如果承租人选择在卸港支付,运费就是 7 英镑/吨,结果承租人选择了 5 英镑/吨。之后,船舶与船上的货物在开航后发生全损,承租人拒绝支付 5 英镑/吨的运费。法院判是承租人必须支付,因为这笔钱应在伦敦支付,在程租合约受阻之前就已经欠下。

另在 Hicks v. Shield (1857) 7 E & B 633 先例与 Tamvaco v. Simpson (1866) LR 1 CP 363 先例中,程租合约有不同的写法,并显示了运费的风险要由承租人承担,如说明在装港预付的钱要让承租人扣除购买保险的保费。这样一来,在运费预付规则之下,程租合约在半途受阻,这笔预付的钱也不必退还给承租人。

由于 CIF/CFR 买卖的普遍性,通常付运单证(特别是提单)还需要注明运费预付(freight prepaid),因此,程租合约预付运费还是惯常的做法。但在今天的程租合约下,提到运费预付规则的已经不多。这主要是因为以下两点改变:(1)汇钱已经十分方便,不需要区分预付的钱究竟是预付运费还是融资给船东。(2)现在大部分程租合约都会使用标准格式,其中会有条文清楚写明预付运费应被视为已经赚取(earned on shipment),无论货物是否消失(cargo lost or not)。如在贵族院的 The “Dominique” (1989) 1 Lloyd’s Rep. 431 先例中有关租约的写法是:“freight shall be prepaid within 5 days of signing and surrender of final bills of lading, **full freight shall be deemed to be earned on signing bills of lading**, discountless and **non - returnable, vessel and/or cargo lost or not lost**.”(加黑部分是笔者的强调)

因为运费的具体金额要等全部装货完毕才能确定,加上承租人汇钱给船东也需要时间,所以运费预付的条文中往往也会规定几天(如 5 天或更长)后再做出支付。这样一来,如果船舶在开航后 5 天内沉没,而租约仅仅写明 5 天后支付,因为租约受阻时还没有到履行预付运费责任的时间,所以承租人不用做出支付。但如果是在支付日期后才发生受阻,则承租人预付的运费不能再向船东取回。但如果条文的写法有关键性的不同,写明是"freight deemed earned on signing of bills of lading"或"freight deemed earned on shipment",就表示要预付的运费在装港开航时已经欠下,只是时间上允许5天后再做出支付,即使租约受阻也不影响:The "Lorna 1"(1983)1 Lloyd's Rep. 373; The "Karin Vatis"(1988)2 Lloyd's Rep. 330等先例。

首先,在The "Lorna 1"先例,有关租约的运费条文是:"16. Freight non-returnable cargo and/or vessel lost or not lost to be paid... to the owners as follows-75%... within 5... days after Master signed bills of lading and the balance after right and true delivery of the cargo and receipt of documents from discharging ports."船舶在1977年12月6日装了矿砂并签发了提单。但开航后,船舶在12月11日沉没。双方对这沉没令程租合约受阻而自动终止没有任何异议,问题是船东能否追讨应该是预付的75%的运费?

船东所争辩的这预付的75%的运费应是在签发提单或货物付运时已欠下,只是因为国际汇款需要时间,所以给承租人5天的时限做出支付而已。在受阻前已欠下的钱(属于债务),自然仍要清偿。但这点不被上诉庭接受,Donaldson大法官说:"Freight is the consideration payable for the carriage of the goods to and their delivery at the destination. In the absence of special contractual provisions, it is earned only upon the delivery of the goods at their destination. Forms of words appropriate to alter this position are well known, e.g., 'Freight to be considered earned on shipment'."

另在The "Karin Vatis"先例中,有关租约订得对船东有利,95%的运费是在提单签发3天内付,余下的5%运费则在交货后20天内付,并且说明是"freight deemed earned as cargo loaded"。船舶在半途沉没,双方接受船东可以保留而不必退还已付清的95%运费。但问题是船东对余下的5%也想追索,声称"freight deemed earned as cargo loaded"是指全部运费,也明确了赚这笔运费的约因/对价只是付运,所以,货物一装上船承租人已欠下全部运费,而如何付95%与5%只是针对付款的方法(manner of payment),不影响受阻前已存在的付钱责任(accrued obligation to Pay)。仲裁员与高院是判承租人不必付5%运费,因为船货从未抵达卸港交货。但上诉庭接受了船东的争辩,推翻了高院的判决。

上诉庭的最后判决也不无商榷之处。即使是全部运费已在受阻前欠下,但毕竟受阻已令同意的付款方法无法履行(incapable of performance)。加上余下5%运费会有调整卸货量之用,而卸货量(outturn)一般比提单货量少,表示这5%余下运费在正常情况下也不必付足。总之从这先例来看,"freight deemed earned as cargo loaded(shipped)"的写法的条文对承租人来说十分危险。即使在船舶开出装港后立即遇上受阻事件,也非要给船东敲一笔,根本无法借助1943年立法公平分摊损失。

10.5.2 立法适用的合约:期租与光租

期租合约在本质上与程租合约有很大不同,期租合约也不严格是占有船舶,而只是将有关船舶的经营权从船东处"租用"过来。正如Reid勋爵在The "London Explorer”（1971）1 Lloyd’s Rep. 523 先例中所说：“Under a time charter there is no hiring in the true sense... the chartered vessel remains in the possession of the owners, and the master and crew remain the owners’ servants. What the charterer gets is a right to have the use of the vessel.”另在 The“Hill Harmony”（2001）1 Lloyd’s Rep. 147 先例中，Hobhouse 大法官也有类似的说法：“（船东）transfers the right to exploit the earning capacity of the vessel to the time charterer.”

而光船租约与期租类似，都在一段时间内拥有船舶的经营权。只是在光船租约下，船长与船员都由承租人雇佣，相比期租多了对船舶的实际占有权。Evans 大法官在 The“Giuseppe Di Vittorio”（1988）1 Lloyd’s Rep. 136 先例说：“When then is the demise charter? Its hallmarks, as it seems to me, are that the legal owner gives the charterer sufficient of the rights of possession and control which enable the transaction to be regarded as a letting – a lease, or demise, in real property terms – of the ship. Closely allied to this is the fact that the charterer becomes the employer of the master and crew. Both aspects are combined in the common description of a ‘bareboat’ lease or hire arrangement.”

相比程租，光租（与期租）不存在预付运费规则（advance freight rule），光租本质上也与岸上的房屋租赁合约没有不同，1943 年《Law Reform（Frustration Contract）Act》立法适用。

首先，期租合约与光船租约一般属于完整合约。在 The“Kamouraska”（1920）4 Lloyd’s Rep. 434 先例中，[92] 该期租合约的租约期长达 7 年，并且有选择权可以延长 3 年，即总共 7 至 10 年。在租约期间，该船舶被政府征用一段时间。针对在征用期间租约是否部分受阻，法院判期租不能分开来受阻，要么整个租约受阻，要么不受阻（it either does or does not destroy the whole contract）。也就是说，无论租约期有多长，期租合约（与光船租约）都会被视为一个完整合约（entire contract），一旦受阻，就是整个租约受阻。事实上，如果承租人没有准时支付租金令船东选择撤船，也是整个租约被终止，而不只是影响没有准时支付租金的这段时间。

而这也带来期租合约受阻后提前支付的租金如何处理的问题。普通法的地位是在合约下尚未到期要做出支付的，受阻后不必再做出支付。相反，如果对于已经到期要做出支付的，必须做出支付。如果承租人已经支付，船东可以保留。如在 Lloyd Royal v. Stathatos（1917）34 TLR 70 先例中，上诉庭拒绝了承租人希望取回提前支付的租金的请求。但在 Fibrosa Spolka Akcyjina v. Fairbairn Lawson Combe Barbour Ltd.（1943）AC 32 先例后，普通法的地位发生了改变，承租人可以完全得不到对价的好处（total failure of consideration）为由要求船东退还提前支付的租金。虽然这个说法在期租合约不一定适用，但至少有危险是一个三年的租约在两年后受阻，承租人

〔92〕 具体的案情可见本章之 8.1 段。

以完全得不到对价的好处为由要求船东归还已经支付的租金。

在1943年立法生效后（已经提到该立法适用在期租合约与光船租约），普通法地位发生了改变以保障船东：(1)在租约受阻前已经支付的租金需要退还，根据租约应付未付的租金也不用再支付。但根据 section 1(2)，[93]法院或仲裁庭有裁量权在考虑船东为了履行租约的花费（船东的固定成本）后，让船东保留公平的金额。(2)同时，船东可以在1943年立法之 section 1(3)[94]下针对合约受阻前提供的服务要求"复原"(restitution)。法院或仲裁庭可以在适合的案情下可以要求承租人支付相当于船舶实际履行天数的租金。(3)在该1943年立法 section 2(4)，[95]允许法院或仲裁庭在适当的案情下将合约已经履行的部分当做(treated as if)可以与因为受阻而无法继续履行的部分分开。例如，租约规定每个月或半个月支付租金，法院或仲裁庭可以假设受阻之前的部分与受阻之后的部分可以分开，船东可以保留受阻之前已经支付的租金。

针对船舶沉没的受阻事件，一些期租合约的标准格式（如航运市场被最广泛使用的NPYE标准格式）会明确排除1943年立法（根据 section 2[3]这是被允许）与/或普通法的适用，规定船东要返还预付但尚未赚取的租金。在NYPE 1946标准格式第16条（102与103行）说："16. That should the Vessel be lost, money paid in advance and not earned (reckoning from the date of loss or being last heard of) shall be returned to the Charterers at once..."

最后一提的是，现在十分盛行的航次期租（Time Charter Trip，简称TCT），在做法上是以期租方式租用船舶行走一个装卸的航次。由于它有点"四不像"，既有程租的特征，也有期租的特征，所以带来了很多争议，包括是程租或是期租、租期的长短、船舶在航次中能否多次装卸等。这些先例包括：Scottish Navigation v. Souter (1917) 1 KB 222; Temple Steamship v. Sovfracht (1945) 79 Lloyd's Rep. 1 (HL); The "Democritos" (1976) 2 Lloyd's Rep. 149 (CA); The "Rijn" (1981) 2 Lloyd's Rep. 267; The "World Symphony" (1991) 2 Lloyd's Rep. 251; The "Aragon" (1975) 1 Lloyd's Rep. 628; The "Doric Pride" (2006) 2 Lloyd's Rep. 175; The "Wisdom C" (2014) EWHC 1884 (Comm); The "Wehr Trave" (2016) EWHC 583 (Comm)等先例。

但看来较近期的先例应该明确这是期租，毕竟TCT通常使用是NYPE标准格式，所以1943年立法适用。这可节录Popplewell大法官在The "Wisdom C"先例所说如下：

"... A time charter is not [a voyage charterparty]: the owner does not agree to carry goods from and to specific or nominated ports, but rather to make the vessel and

---

〔93〕 参见本章之10.2段。

〔94〕 参见本章之10.3段。

〔95〕 参见本章之8.3.2段，这里与建筑或工程合约的定期支付(periodic payment)是一样的道理。

her crew available to the charterer, in return for hire, as a means for the charterer to transport goods. The defining characteristic of a time charter is that the vessel is under the directions and orders of the charterer as regards its employment. It is the charterer who determines what voyages the vessel is to undertake and what cargo it is to carry, within the geographical and other constraints contained in the particular charterparty clauses... What matters is that the charterparty is not in nature an undertaking by the owner to carry goods, but an undertaking by the owner to make available to the charterer a vessel and crew for the latter to employ in transporting goods.

This is as true of a **trip time charter**, such as the charterparty in this case, as of a term time charter. Although the length of the period of hire is limited by a trip defined within a geographical range (and sometimes, though not in this case, by a maximum duration), **the nature of the contract for the duration of the period remains that of making the vessel and her crew available to the charterers as a means for the charterers to transport goods, not a contract for carriage of the goods by the owners.**"(加黑部分是笔者的强调)

10.5.3 立法不适用的合约:特定货物的灭失

1943 年《Law Reform (Frustration Contract) Act》立法之 Section 2 (5) 说明在以下的合约不适用:"(c) to any contract to which section 7 of the Sale of Goods Act 1979 (which avoids contract for the sale of specific goods which perish before the risk has passed to the buyer) applies, or to any other contracts for the sale, or for the sale and delivery, of specific goods, where the contract is frustrated by reason of the fact that the goods have perished."

在 1979 年英国《货物销售法》之 section 7 是说:"Where there is an agreement to sell specific goods and subsequently the goods, without any fault on the part of the seller or buyer perish before the risk passes to the buyer, the agreement is avoided."

可以看到上述立法之 Section 2 (5)(c)规定的立法不适用的情况都是针对特定货物,[96]因此,首先要知道什么是特定货物(specific goods)。根据 1979 年《货物销售法》之 section 61(1),特定货物是指在订立买卖合约时已经明确并且双方同意的货物(goods identified and agreed upon at the time a contract of sale is made)。

这样就表示在国际货物买卖,绝少涉及特定货物的买卖而绝大多数是未确定货物(unascertained goods)或将来货物(future goods)。也就是在订立买卖合约时,货物还没有存在或生产出来,双方只能以对货物的描述订立合约。特定货物或现货(present goods)的买卖通常只是岸上才会发生。除了买卖合约,即使是租船合约也通常不会明确并且双方同意要运输的货物。如在 E. B. Aaby's Rederi A/S v. Lep

〔96〕 杨大明的《国际货物买卖》一书称为"具体货物",可与"特定货物"视为同义。

Transport, Ltd.（1948）81 Lloyd's Rep. 465 先例中，承租人租了 Faro 轮去装运一批已经存放在仓库的羊毛。但期间仓库发生大火，羊毛被烧毁。承租人企图依赖程租合约受阻，并说明这批运输的羊毛是特定货物，原因是临时租船（spot charter），所以订约时船东知道是这批已经存放在仓库的羊毛。显然如果不是特定货物而只是为了运输羊毛，即使承租人自己的意图是付运存在仓库里的羊毛，羊毛烧毁也无法导致租约受阻。这道理与在本章第 6 段介绍的 The "Super Servant Two"（1990）1 Lloyd's Rep. 1 先例是一致的。但 Sellers 大法官不接受这是特定货物，因为没有证据说明双方是明确与同意，租约中也没有划归这票羊毛的货物。

所以笔者只说 1943 年立法对特定货物的买卖不适用，而只适用在未确定货物或将来货物的买卖合约，这也表示包括了国际货物买卖，如 CIF 或 FOB 的付运合约。

这方面可节录《Benjamin's Sale of Goods》（第 9 版，2014 年）一书之 6 – 059 段，说："The consequence of frustration of a contract of sale of goods governed by English law are in principle governed by the common law as modified by the provisions of the Law Reform（Frustrated Contracts）Act 1943. But this Act exempts from its operation: '... any contract to which section 7 of the Sale of Goods Act 1979... applies, or ... any other contract for the sale, or for the sale and delivery, of specific goods, where the contract is frustrated by reason of the fact that the goods have perished.' The reference to s. 7 of the 1979 Act is clear, but the remainder of this provision is enigmatic. Cases where specific goods perish would, apart from s. 7, normally not give rise to frustration, but be determined as questions of risk. ... **The Act of 1943 will, however, apply to cases where a contract for the sale of unascertained goods is frustrated, and where a contract for the sale of specific goods is frustrated otherwise than by the fact that the goods have perished.** ..."（加黑部分是笔者的强调）

本章第 9 段介绍的 Fibrosa Spolka Akcyjina v. Fairbairn Lawson Combe Barbour Ltd.（1943）AC 32 先例，涉及的就是未确定与将来货物的 CIF 买卖（订立合约时机器还不存在）。如果该先例发生在今天，1943 年立法之 section 1(2) 就会适用，英国卖方在退回波兰买方预付的货价时可以扣除自己的使费或是法院或仲裁庭认为的公平金额。

11. 合约受阻的考虑因素

根据上一段介绍的合约责任与承诺有否根本性改变（或合约解释）的考验，要决定是否构成合约受阻，第一步就是解释原本的合约责任与承诺是什么，最后再与新情况下的合约责任对比，看后者是否与前者相近还是有根本性的改变。

关于考虑是否构成合约受阻的步骤，《Chitty on Contracts》（第 32 版，2015 年）一书之 23 - 014 段说："Both Lords Reid and Radcliffe in Davis Contractors emphasized that the first step was to construe '... the terms which are in the contract read in the light of the nature of the contract, and of the relevant surrounding circumstances when the contract was made.' From this construction the court should reach an impression of the scope of the original obligation, that is, the court should ascertain what the parties would be required to do in order to fulfill their literal promises in the original circumstances. This impression will depend on the court's estimate of what performance would have required in time, labour, money and materials, if there had been no change in the circumstances existing after the occurrence of the event alleged to have frustrated the contract, and ascertain whether what would be the obligation of the parties if the words of the contract were enforced in the new circumstances. Having discovered what was the original 'obligation' and what would be the new 'obligation', if the contract were still binding on the new circumstances, the last step in the process is for the court to compare the two obligations in order to decide whether the new obligation is a 'radical' or 'fundamental' change from the original obligation. It is not simply a question whether there has been a radical change in the circumstances, but whether there has been a radical change in the 'obligation' or the actual effect of the promises of the parties construed in the light of the new circumstances. Was 'performance... fundamentally different in the commercial sense'?"

很多合约受阻的先例中涉及商业活动无法进行，即是否因为某一特定或一连串的突发事件令继续履行合约与原本的合约责任与承诺的有根本性的（radically，或 Radcliffe 勋爵所说的"fundamentally"）改变。这是程度的问题，因此不同的人有不同的看法也很正常。

在 The "Sea Angel"（2007）2 Lloyd's Rep. 517 CA 先例中，Rix 大法官提到决定是否构成合约受阻的困难与需要考虑多种因素。这些因素包括合约的内容与其背景/语境，双方订约时对将来情况的理解、期望与想法，特别是针对有关突发事件的风险由谁承担或如何分摊等。这些要从双方的表述中尽量客观地找出。另一方面的因素是突发事件的性质、程度与对履行的影响，客观来看，双方对这种将来突发事件导致的新情况下应该如何履行是否有过想法等。因为合约受阻涉及风险应如何分摊，不止包括合约的明示或默示条文，也包括很难确定的双方在订约时的想法，因此，要考虑多方面因素确定是否构成受阻十分困难。"根本性改变"的考验可以看出合约受阻的说法不容易成立。仅仅是成本增加、延误或履行责任变得很严苛不足以构成合约受阻，必须是新的履行责任与承诺相比订约时双方的共同想法已经发生了根本性改变。Rix 大法官说："In my judgment, the application of the doctrine of frustration requires a multifactorial approach. Among the factors which have to be considered are the terms of the contract itself, its matrix or context, the parties' knowledge, expectations, assumptions and contemplations, in particular as to risk, as at the time of contract, at any rate so far as these can be ascribed mutually and objectively, and then the nature of the supervening event, and the parties' reasonable and objectively ascertainable calculations as to the possibilities of future performance in the new circumstances. Since the subject matter of the doctrine of frustration is contract, and contracts are about the allocation of risk, and since the allocation and assumption of risk is not simply a matter of express or implied provision but may also depend on less easily defined matters such as 'the contemplation of the parties', the application of the doctrine can often be a difficult one. In such circumstances, the test of 'radically different' is important: it tells us that the doctrine is not to be lightly invoked; that mere incidence of expense or delay or onerousness is not sufficient; and that there has to be as it were a break in identity between the contract as provided for and contemplated and its performance in the new circumstances."

在 The "Kyla" (2013) 1 Lloyd's Rep. 565 先例中,Kyla 轮在装货码头停泊时与另一艘船舶碰撞并受损。维修大概需要 900 万美元,但是该船舶的市场价格只有 575 万美元。因此,该船舶可以说已经推定全损(constructive total loss)[97]或者商业全损(commercial total loss),从经济方面考虑船东花钱把船修好完全不合逻辑。一直都有说法是商业全损与真正全损(physically total loss)一样会令租约(无论是光租、期租还是程租)受阻。[98] 这可节录 Coghlin Wilford 与 Kimball 的《Time Charters》(第 6 版,2008 年)一书之 26.14 段,如下:"A time charter will be frustrated or terminated not only by the actual total loss of the chartered ship, but also if she is so badly damaged that she has effectively been destroyed as a commercial ship or rendered unfit for the charter with no prospect of being made again fit: see Blane Steamships v. Minister of Transport (1951) 2 Lloyd's Rep. 155 (CA), a demise charter case. It is suggested that a time charter will also be frustrated or terminated by the constructive total loss of the chartered ship if she is abandoned by her owners to their underwriters."

因此,Kyla 轮的船东声称租约受阻,但承租人不接受这一说法。虽然 Kyla 轮确实已经不再存在,但如果船东没有成功证明租约受阻,则不能继续履行合约属于违约/毁约(repudiatory breach),船东要赔偿承租人 400 万美元的损失。

该先例的主要争议是租约中是否针对了因不可预见的突发事件导致船舶推定全损的情况,如果有,就应该适用租约条文而不是法律默示的合约受阻的说法。相关期租合约采用了 NYPE 46 标准格式,该标准格式中有一条条文规定船东在整个租约期

---

〔97〕 推定全损的定义可见 1906 年《Marine Insurance Act》之 section 60(1)。

〔98〕 如 Moss v. Smith (1850) 9 CB 94; Blane Steamships Ltd. v. Minister of Transport (1951) 2 Lloyd's Rep. 155; The "Badagry" (1985) 1 Lloyd's Rep. 395 CA 等先例。

内都应该保证有保险(船壳与机器)。但其中还有第41条附加条文(rider clause)规定:

"41.1 Owners warrant that throughout the currency of this C/P the vessel shall be fully covered by leading insurance companies... acceptable to the Charterers against Hull and Machinery... Cost of such cover to be at the sole expense of the Owners ...

41.3 Insurance full style and value

Hull and Machinery: US $ 16,000,000 London, Norway and USA Markets ..."

可以注意到船舶的保险价值(insured value)是1600万美元,远远高于575万美元的市场价格。但在航运市场低落时期这是常事,船舶建造时可能市场高涨,因此当时的船舶价格要高得多。而船东也不能调低船舶的保险金额,因为可能在银行有约1600万美元的贷款(loan)或抵押(mortgage),银行不会同意船东将保险价值调低到575万美元;否则,万一船舶出事,银行可能无法收回钱。毕竟只要船舶还在营运而不在市场上出售,是否暂时性船价触底并没有什么影响(除了心理上的影响)。

但为了避免一旦证明了推定全损(如在该先例中,船东要花900万美元修理市价575万美元的船舶显然不合理),船东就可以要求保险公司赔付保险价值(在该先例中是1600万美元),所以几乎所有的保单都会有条文针对,令船东在市场低落时以推定全损向保险公司理赔更加困难。这种条文的写法一般是:"In ascertaining whether the vessel is a constructive total loss, the insured value shall be taken as the repaired value ... No claim for constructive total loss based upon the... repair of the vessel shall be recoverable hereunder unless such cost would exceed the insured value ..."

实践中,很多类似的情况下,船东会与保险公司(银行可能会参与,也可能不会,取决于是否有贷款以及贷款尚未还清的金额)谈判,达成一个双方都能接受的协议全损赔偿(compromised total loss),而不是花一大笔钱修理一艘价格很低的船舶或"残骸"。

在The "Kyla"先例中,双方主要的争议就是租约中的第41条文对受阻说法的适用是否有影响。显然,如果将维修的900万美元与保险价值1600万美元相比较,Kyla轮并没有推定全损。在仲裁中,独任仲裁员Simon Rainey QC判第41条文对受阻说法的适用没有影响。因为从该条文并不能推断出船东保证会在船壳与机械保险下,以最高不超过1600万美元维修船舶。船东在该条文中也没有保证会以保险的保险价值达成特定的目的(打捞与维修船舶)。

但上诉到高院,Simon Rainey QC的裁决被推翻。在劳氏法律报告中将Flaux大法官的判决总结如下:"Following The "Sea Angel" (2007) 2 Lloyd's Rep. 517, the modern law of frustration had moved away from deciding the issue through the application of inflexible rules dependent upon one factor (eg cost versus value), to a multi-factorial approach; Clause 41 was a comprehensive insurance provision. The opening words made it clear that the Owner was warranting that the full hull and machinery cover would be in place throughout the C/P, so that the insurance would be available to cover the cost of repairs up to the insured value. Thus, Cl. 41 made it impossible for the Owner to say that what had occurred amounted to something radically different from what was contemplated. The C/P had allocated to the Owner the risk that if a casualty occurred, the ship required repair, where the repair costs was within the insured value. The C/P was not frustrated."

12. 常见的受阻事件类型

通过上面介绍的先例可以看出构成合约受阻的突发事件可以有葛洪,笔者不再重复,只是针对部分常见的突发事件类型进行若干总结与补充。

首先可节录《Chitty on Contracts》(第32版,2015年)一书之21-020-021段:"... The cases may be classified by reference either to the different types of frustrating events (such as a change in the law or subsequent illegality, outbreak of war, cancellation of an expected event or delay, or by reference to particular categories of contracts where frustration has been invoked (such as personal contracts, charterparties, sale and carriage of goods, building contracts, leases, and contracts for the sale of land) ... the following events may be taken as illustrations of the kind of events which have been held, in the circumstances of particular contracts, to bring the doctrine of frustration into operation: destruction by fire or other cause of the subject matter of the contract,[99] an explosion or stranding disabling a ship,[100] requisitioning of the subject matter of the contract by the government,[101] seizure of a ship[102] or expropriation of an oil concession by a foreign government,[103] incapacity or death of a person obliged to perform personal services,[104] and delay suffi-

〔99〕 参见 Taylor v. Caldwell (1863) 3 B&S 826; Appleby v. Myers (1867) L. R. 2 C. P. 651; Turner v. Goldsmith (1891) 1 QB 544; The "Maira" (No. 2) (1985) 1 Lloyd's Rep. 300; (1986) 2 Lloyd's Rep. 46 (CA) 等先例。

〔100〕 参见 Joseph Constantine S. S. Line Ltd. v. Imperial Smelting Corp Ltd. (1942) AC 154; Jackson v. Union Marine Insurance Co. Ltd. (1874) LR 10 CP 125 等先例。

〔101〕 参见 Metropolitan Water Board v. Dick, Kerr & Co. (1918) AC 119; White & Cater Ltd. v. Garbis Bay Garage Ltd. (1941) 2 All ER 633 等先例。

〔102〕 参见 Tatem Ltd. v. Gamboa (1939) 1 KB 132 先例。

〔103〕 参见 BP v. Hunt (1981) 1 WLR 232 (CA)(被贵族院[1983] 2 AC 352 支持)先例。

〔104〕 参见 Hall v. Wright (1858) 120 ER 688; Graves v. Cohen (1930) 46 T. L. R. 121; Condor v. The Barron Knights Ltd. (1966) 1 WLR 87; Marshall v. Harland & Wolff Ltd. (1972) 1 WLR 899; Hebden v. Forset & Son (1973) ICR 607; Hart v. A R Marshall & Sons (Bulwell) Ltd. (1977) 1 WLR 1067; Notcutt v. Universal Equipment Co. (London) Ltd. (1986) 1 WLR 641; GP Sharp & Co. Ltd. v. McMillan (1988) I. R. L. R. 632 等先例。

ciently long to frustrate the commercial adventure of the parties.[105] On the other hand, mere inconvenience, or hardship, or financial loss involved in performing the contract, or delay which is within the commercial risk undertaken by the parties, has been held insufficient to frustrate particular contracts."

这些事件可分为如下类型:第一类是在本章之7.3.1段提到的实质上无法履行(physical impossible),第二类是同样在本章之7.3.1段提到的法律上不能履行。

12.1 常见类别之一:实质上无法履行

由于本章之7.3.1段已经介绍,这里不再重复。只说在同样造成合约实质上无法履行的事件下,也会因为合约中对风险由谁承担或如何分摊有不同的规定,而导致部分合约可以受阻,而部分合约不能受阻。

以最典型的商业交易的国际货物买卖合约为例,关于合约的风险与受阻在杨大明的《国际货物买卖》一书第六章有详细介绍。这里只简单列举几种典型变化介绍。

同样是突发事件(无论是火灾或是天灾)导致货物实质上灭失,在不同的情况下就会有不同结果:

1. 货物做出付运之后灭失。CIF/FOB买卖合约是付运合约(shipment contract),如果卖方已经将货物装船付运,卖方的履约责任就已经告一段落。货物的风险自动转移给买方:The "Julia" (1949) 82 Lloyd's Rep. 270; The "Galatia" (1980) 1 Lloyd's Rep. 453先例。在The "Julia"先例,Porter勋爵判是货物在付运后损坏,不论买卖合约是在付运前还是付运后(这是因为在付运途中货物经常通过转让提单转卖)订立,都属于买方的风险。这不会构成受阻,即使有关的CIF合约通常写明卸港,这只是为了让卖方可以租船与支付到卸港的运费。这方面可见杨大明的《国际货物买卖》一书第六章之8.5.4段。

2. 货物在CIF卖方已经做出付运但还来不及做出划归通知(notice of appropriation)或付运通知(declaration of shipment)时灭失。这种情况就有点复杂,因为国际货物买卖(尤其是大宗货买卖)往往都是未确定货物,如果没有通过划归通知确定合约下的货物,就有机会让卖方在市场波动时取巧。这方面内容较多,就不在此详论,具体可见杨大明的《国际货物买卖》一书第六章之8.5.5段。

3. 货物在装港岸上灭失。在买卖合约下,提供货物是卖方的合约责任与承诺,如果货物灭失导致卖方无法提供货物,理论上卖方可以依赖合约受阻的说法。但一般来说,国际货物买卖往往都是未确定货物,所以即使卖方计划用来履行合约的货物灭失,也不会构成合约受阻:The "Super Servant Two" (1990) 1 Lloyd's Rep. 1先例。

---

[105] 怎样的延误才能构成合约受阻取决于合约的性质、延误结束后合约还需要多久履行完毕等因素,这对房屋租赁合约、建筑/工程合约与船舶租约特别重要。针对租约,导致延误的可能是船舶搁浅、被政府征用、发生暴动被扣押、苏伊士运河关闭、罢工、战争、坏天气、无法预见的劳工短缺、常规航线或港口封闭等。

但总会有例外情况，如果在 FOB 买卖合约下，因为买方迟延派船，导致卖方备好的货物要在岸上多放几天，而货物在此期间灭失，这应属于买方的责任。这是典型的自己导致的受阻（self – induced frustration），实质是违约/毁约，不会构成真正意义上的受阻。这方面可见杨大明的《国际货物买卖》一书第六章之 8.5.3.7 段。

4. 上述针对的都是付运合约的情况，在订约自由下，如果买卖合约属于交货合约（delivered contract）或是合约中写明卖方负责在卸港交货，则卖方的合约责任与承诺就是将货物运到卸港交给买方。如果因为突发事件导致划归了的货物在去卸港的途中灭失，在适当的情况下可以构成合约受阻。

12.2　常见类别之二：法律上不能履行

12.2.1　合约订立之后法律发生变化

今天的法律数不胜数，也经常在修改或增加内容，如金融法、竞争法、环境法、税法、劳工法等，都会严重影响某些商业合约的履行。如果合约在履行过程中因为法律发生改变而导致暂时或永久性无法履行，显然会构成合约受阻。这里可先节录《Chitty on Contracts》（第 32 版，2015 年）一书之 23 – 022 段所说：“**Subsequent Legal changes.** A subsequent change in the law or in the legal position affecting a contract is a well – recognised head of frustration; . . . In the leading case of Baily v. De Crespigny (1869) L. R. 4 QB 180, a lessor was held not liable for an alleged breach of his covenant that neither he nor his assigns would build on a piece of land adjoining the demised premises, when a railway company, under its powers derived from a subsequent statute, compulsorily acquired the land and erected a station on it. In delivering the judgment of the court, Hannen J. said: ‘The legislature by compelling him to part with his land to a railway company, whom he could not bind by any stipulation, as he could an assign chosen by himself, has created a new kind of assign, such as was not in the contemplation of the parties when the contract was entered into. To hold the defendant responsible for the acts of such an assignee is to make an entirely new contract for the parties’.”

除了上述《Chitty on Contracts》一书所介绍的有关土地租约的 Baily v. De Crespigny (1869) L. R. 4 QB 180 先例，可另介绍 Islwyn BC v. Newport BC (1994) E. L. R. 141 先例。该先例的案情涉及三个市政府订立合约在新开的学校里建造一个文娱中心，上课时间由学生使用，课余时间可以由市民使用。三个市政府还共同成立了一个委员会，负责文娱中心的建造、营运与资金。之后，Newport 市政府想从合约中脱身，理由之一就是合约受阻。因为在 1986《Education (No. 2) Act》生效后，其中的 section 42 规定，如果学校内的文娱中心要向公众开放，文娱中心必须由学校的管理机构管理，继续由三个政府共同成立的委员会管理是违法。但这不被法院接受，因为在 section 42 下，政府的教育机构可以要求学校的管理机构将对文娱中心的管理授权给委员会。所以，有关的立法并没有令合约无法履行，因此不能构成受阻。

涉及服务性的合约可举 Marshall v. Glanvill and Another (1917) 2 KB 87 先例为

例。案情是 1915 年被告的布商委任原告作为其在苏格兰的代表推广业务，并在他们之间的合约中说明被告要给原告谈判成功的生意 7.5% 的佣金。但在履行期间，英国出台了《Military Service Act》，并在 1916 年 7 月 12 日强制原告参军（空军）。但原告还是在 7 月 12 日至 7 月 16 日的 4 天内做了两单生意，所以向被告索赔 7.5% 的佣金。但被告以合约已经在 7 月 12 日受阻为由拒绝，因为原告根据立法被强制参军，导致无限期地无法履行他们之间的合约。这个说法被法院支持，合约受阻。

再举一个例子是 Studholme v. South Western Gas Board (1954) 1 WLR 313 先例，律师和一家燃气公司有长期的预聘合约（retainer agreement），但之后的 1948 年《Gas Act》将燃气公司收归国有，法院判预聘合约受阻。

总结而言，如果在履行期间，法律或政府命令导致合约暂时或永久性无法履行，会构成合约受阻。

12.2.2 英国法下突发性变为非法

本小段与下一小段介绍的突发性变为非法（supervening illegality）本身是很大的课题，本章主要针对受阻，所以只简单涉及非法这个课题。

不妨先节录《Chitty on Contracts》（第 32 版，2015 年）一书之 23 - 024 段所说："**Supervening illegality.** It is now customary to treat supervening illegality as an instance of frustration, in that it is similar to frustration by a subsequent change in the law. Apart from the effect of an outbreak of war upon a contract, e. g. with a person who thereby becomes an alien enemy, many wartime cases illustrate the power of the Government under statutory authority to forbid, whether temporarily or permanently, the performance of a contract, and so to frustrate it[106]. . . "

看来，本小段与上一小段主要的区别是，前者涉及合约履行期间法律改变令整个合约本身变为非法而受阻，这非法也往往涉及英国的公共政策。最常见的例子就是战争时期，政府有权力暂时或永久性地否定某些合约的有效性并禁止履行。如在"一战"与"二战"期间，与德国的公司订立商业合约就是通敌。

由于突发性变为非法会是十分严重的类别，如通敌，在公共政策下会禁止订约自由。例如，双方在合约中有明示条文针对这种突发事件就延长而非终止合约的履行，这种条文会不被接受。最著名的先例是 Ertel Bieber & Co. v. Rio Tinto Co. Ltd. (1918) AC 260，在"一战"前英国与德国公司订立的铁矿买卖合约由于战争爆发而突发性非法。但买卖合约有一条遇到这种情况可以延长履行的条文，被贵族院判是无效，不能阻止合约受阻而自动终止。公共政策之一的考虑就是如果让德国方面知道战争结束后马上会有铁矿供应，德国方面就会更加安心地使用现有储备。Sumner 勋爵说："What the law forbids is impossible of performance to those who owe obedience

---

〔106〕 接下去的内容不再节录，因为是有关已在本章之 7.3.2.2 段介绍的 Metropolitan Water Board v. Dick, Kerr & Co. (1918) AC 119 先例，该先例涉及"一战"。

to that law, and this higher public obligation discharges any private obligation to the contrary... If upon public grounds the law interferes with private executory contracts on the outbreak of war by dissolving them, how can it be open to a subject for his private advantage to withdraw his contract from the operation of the war and to claim to do what the law rejects, to suspend merely where the law dissolves?"

接下来在类似案情的 Fried Krupp Aktiengesellashaft v. Orconera Iron Ore Co. (1918) 88 L. J. Ch. 304 先例也是同样的判法,即"一战"的爆发令合约立即受阻。但贵族院的大法官之一有一点保留,原因是该供应铁矿砂的合约还有99 年,按理说"一战"不会持续这么久。[107]

要注意的是,在许多突发性变为非法的情况下,不论是禁运或是通敌,都会有特殊的例外情况被政府当局允许,这就涉及批文(permit)或许可(licence)。如在 Re Mahmoud and Ispahani (1921) 2 KB 716 先例中,有关的突发性非法是政府在1919 年做出的名为"Seeds, Oils and Fats Order"的命令导致。该命令禁止任何人买卖某些商品,除非取得政府许可。有关的命令是:"A person shall not... buy or sell or otherwise deal in, any of the articles specified in the schedule hereto... **except under and in accordance with the terms of a licence**."

如果有这种批文或许可的可能性,英国法律默示要求履行的一方在依赖合约因突发性非法而受阻前,需要尽力申请批文或许可。如果无法成功,才可以依赖受阻。在 Dalmia Dairy Industries Ltd. v. National Bank of Pakistan (1978) 2 Lloyd's Rep. 223 先例一审,Kerr 大法官说:"... settled law in England... that a supervening prohibition of some contractually undertaken obligation, which can be overcome by obtaining a licence, will only frustrate a contract at once if the person affected by the prohibition can show that no licence could in any event have been obtained. If this is uncertain, then his obligation is to use his best endeavours to obtain the necessary licence, and the contract then only becomes frustrated if and when all such efforts have failed."

即使在和平时期,也会有这种突发性的非法,如在 Islamic Republic of Iran Shipping Lines v. Steamship Mutual Underwriting Association (Bermuda) Ltd. (2011) 1 Lloyd's Rep. 195 先例中,案情涉及联合国因为伊朗发展核武器而对伊朗的禁令,导致英国在2008 年订立了《Counter - Terrorism Act》。在该立法下,财政部在2009 年10 月12 日做出命令(Financial Restrictions [Iran] Order 2009, SI 2009/2725),限制英国法律管辖的公司或机构与被列入名单的伊朗公司或组织(包括伊朗国家船公司,因为涉嫌运载核燃料)有财政或商业上的往来。该先例中的被告是一家著名的船东互保协会,而船东互保协会是保障船东营运带来的各种责任与赔偿,其中包括油污

[107] 这可与本章稍后的12.3 段举的长期房屋租赁合约很难受阻的例子比较。

(包括船用燃油发生污染)责任。[108] 在这些国际公约的签约国,一般的做法都是需要船舶向港口当局或有关当局[如美国的海事局(Federal Maritime Commission)]证明有认可的责任保险(通常就是在国际船东互保协会投保),显示即使出了油污事故也有保险,所以赔得起。

伊朗国家船公司也就是本先例的原告的船队向被告的互保协会投保,财政部在该2009年的命令下有权豁免一些特定的交往并签发许可(licence),其中较早的许可是允许被告在一段时间内可以继续向原告提供责任保险。第三个也是本案争议的许可是财政部在10月30日做出,导致被告为原告提供的大部分责任保险变为非法。

而在10月31日即一天后,碰巧原告的Zoorick轮在中国港口发生了严重事故,船舶推定全损并同时发生严重的燃油污染。但被告认为其没有责任,因为保险合约在10月30日就因为财政部命令变为非法而受阻。整个案件涉及非常复杂的争议,其中原告与被告与财政部的通讯往来,包括澄清10月30日命令的内容也作为背景/语境被一并考虑。高院的Beatson大法官对财政部10月30日命令的解释是被告允许为原告提供《燃油公约》下因为燃油污染造成的责任的保险。而原告已经向被告支付了保费(根据传统互保协会的承保年度,从2月20日开始),而且无法取回,所以即使10月30日的命令导致大部分的责任保险非法,不让被告承担油污责任并不公平。Beatson大法官的部分判决可节录如下:

"Under the contract of insurance the Club(被告)insured IRISL(原告)against the full range of P & I risks within Class 1 of its Rules. It is common ground that at midnight on 30 October (i. e. before the Casualty) it became unlawful for the Club to insure IRISL in respect of all risks apart from those required to be insured by reason of the provisions of the Bunkers Convention. I have concluded that paragraph 6 of the 30 October Licence permitted it to continue to provide IRISL with insurance cover and to meet all claims in respect of those risks. The next question is whether, notwithstanding this, the contract of insurance was frustrated at midnight on 30 October 2009.

In 1948 Lord McNair deplored the tendency to include impossibility arising from supervening illegality within the conception and terminology of frustration: see Legal Effects of War (3rd ed. 1948) 134. Today it is (see Chitty on Contracts 30th ed, 23 – 024) 'customary to treat supervening illegality as an instance of frustration'. But it is also well recognised that when considering supervening illegality, the court is concerned not only with allocating or distributing the loss caused by the supervening event and 'reaching a solution which may do justice between the contracting parties'. The court

[108] 关于油污责任可见杨良宜《损失赔偿与救济》一书第八章第7段与《海事法》第三章。早期的国际公约针对的油污责任只是油轮,但由于干货轮的燃油(bunker)也会造成污染,所以有了2008年《燃油公约》。

‘is also concerned with the public interest that the law is observed’: see Sir Guenter Treitel, Frustration and Force Majeure 2nd ed. 8 – 002 and 8 – 003.”

12.2.3 外国法下合约的履行变为非法

12.2.3.1 合约适用英国法但在外国履行

这里有两种情况,第一种情况是合约虽然适用英国法,但在外国履行,而外国的法律改变令履行变为非法。这种情况很多,主要是因为许多国际上的商业合约都会明示或默示适用英国法。但这种合约的履行往往与英国本土无关。这样一来,如果合约的履行根据履行地的法律突然变为非法,英国法律是否会承认这非法导致合约无法履行而受阻?这在国际货物买卖很常见,如在本章之7.2.3段提到的The“Playa Larga”(1983) 2 Lloyd’s Rep. 171 (CA)先例。古巴与智利断交并颁布法律(1256号立法)禁止运糖到智利。有关的食糖买卖合约适用英国法并有一条伦敦仲裁条文。仲裁庭与法院尊重履行地的法律并判继续履行合约在古巴是非法,所以合约受阻,不需要继续履行。

这方面可节录《Chitty on Contracts》(第32版,2015年)一书之23 – 027段所说:“**Supervening illegality under a foreign law.** Where a contract governed by English law as its applicable law is to be performed abroad, and that performance becomes illegal by the law of the place of performance (lex loci solutionis), the contract will not, according to common law rules, be enforced in England. The principle of frustration by supervening illegality operates where the change in the lex loci solutionis occurs after the formation of the contract but before its performance. For the principle to apply, performance must include the doing in a foreign country of something which the laws of that country make it illegal to do.... A party relying on frustration by the lexi loci solutionis must show that the illegality covered the whole of the period within which performance was due; thus where a foreign export control regulation prohibits performance of a contract during only part of the contract period, the exporters were held liable for failure to perform during the time no prohibition existed. But a contract governed by English law is not frustrated where the lex loci solutionis, without making performance illegal, merely excuses a party from performance in full. Equally a contract governed by English law is not frustrated because the party liable to perform would, by his performance, contravene the law of the place of his residence, or of which he is a national (if that law is neither the applicable law nor the lexi loci solutionis) nor does it suffice that the act of performance is unlawful by the law of the country in which the act happens to be done.[109]”

根据以上《Chitty on Contracts》一书所讲,履行地的法律突然变为非法导致合约

---

[109] Tamil Nadu Electricity Board v. ST – CMA Electric Co. Private Ltd. (2008) 1 Lloyd’s Rep. 93 先例(第47段)。

受阻有一些例外情况。首先希望依赖合约受阻的一方必须证明在合约允许履行的整个时间段内,履行合约都是非法(illegality covered the whole period of the contract)。这很容易理解,无论是履行地是英国还是外国,有关的突发事件必须足够严重(而不能是短暂与部分影响)才能令合约受阻,这可见本章之7.3.3段。在Ross T Smyth & Co.(Liverpool)Ltd. v. WN Lindsay(Leith)Ltd.(1953)1 WLR 1280先例中,案情涉及买卖合约,合约规定的付运期是1951年10月至11月。10月20日,意大利下令从11月1日起禁止蚕豆出口。仲裁员判合约受阻,但上诉到法院后,这个裁决被推翻。Devlin大法官认为卖方可以在10月20日至31日付运,并非无法履行(卖方来不及付运是另一回事),所以卖方违约。

而如果履行地的法律并非令履行非法,而只是令履行的一方有理由不完全履行其合约责任与承诺,合约不会受阻。在Jacobs, Marcus & Co. v. The Crédit Lyonnais(1884)12 QBD 589先例中,案情涉及两家在伦敦的公司订立了买卖合约,从阿尔及利亚运货到伦敦。因为阿尔及利亚的出口限制,被告的卖方无法付运全部的货物。被告的抗辩是阿尔及利亚(合约的履行地)当时适用法国法,而根据法国法下不可抗力(*force majeure*)的说法,卖方有理由不全部履行合约。法院判是合约的适用法是英国法,卖方在合约的履行地法律(法国法)下可以根据不可抗力的说法不全部履行合约是不会构成合约受阻。

另在Ralli Bros v. Compannia Naviera Sota y Aznar(1920)2 KB 287先例中,案情有关从印度装运麻布到西班牙的巴塞罗那的程租合约,适用法是英国法。程租合约的背后是买卖合约。英国的卖方与西班牙收货人同意这是CIF买卖,但运费各付一半。程租合约也有同样的条文,说明船东一半的运费在离开印度装港时在伦敦支付,而其余的运费在卸港向收货人收取。船舶在1918年12月28日抵达卸港,但不久前西班牙有了一个规定麻布进口最高能够支付的运费的立法,这导致船东向英国承租人要求补足运费。该先例没有提出租约受阻的问题,而上诉庭判如果合约履行的部分在外国变为非法,就无须履行,也可以免责。Sterndale勋爵说:"I think on principle and on authority that the charterers are not bound to perform that part of the contract, that is, the payment of freight above the maximum allowed by Spanish law, which has become illegal by the law of the place of its performance."

但要注意的是,如果不是适用法(英国法)或履行地的法律导致履行非法,而是合约方的常住地(place of residence)或国籍国(a national)的法律令合约变为非法,这不会令合约受阻。举例说,A国与B国交恶而变为敌国,而A国与B国的公司在较早前订立合约,适用法是英国法,而合约的履行是在C国。这样合约就不会受阻,而是涉及违约的问题。在Kleinwort Sons & Co. v. Ungarische Baumwolle Industrie Aktien-Gesellschaft(1939)2 KB 678(这先例的判法在Kahler v. Midland Bank [1950] AC 24先例被贵族院多数大法官认同)先例中,原告是伦敦的一家银行,接受了一家匈牙利公司签发的汇票(bills of exchange)。[110] 汇票是在1938年4月4日由一家匈牙利银行交给原告,同时交给原告的还有匈牙利公司会在到期日前一天做出支付的保证与匈牙利银行的担保。在同一天,匈牙利银行又单独写信给原告,提醒原告注意匈牙利公司作为出票人(drawer)的保证与银行的担保的前提都是匈牙利当时的外汇交易规定允许它们这样做。之后汇票到期时,匈牙利法律规定如果没有匈牙利国家银行的同意,向外国做出支付是非法。该先例有关的支付没有获得匈牙利国家银行的同意,因此匈牙利公司与银行没有在汇票到期前向原告做出支付。原告开始诉讼要求匈牙利公司与银行支付汇票金额与利息。法院判是有关合约的适用法是英国法,合约的履行地是英国,尽管被告履行合约会违反匈牙利的法律,英国法院还是可以执行有关的合约。

在 Fox v. Henderson Investment Fund Ltd. (1999) 2 Lloyd's Rep. 303 先例中,有关的案情不涉及商业合约。原告的Fox先生在伦敦有两笔基金,并由被告作为基金经理人管理。1996年2月,Fox先生与他太太在美国离婚,Fox太太在美国法院申请要求Fox先生披露财产的命令,但Fox先生没有理会。1997年1月17日,代表Fox太太的律师将美国法院的命令寄给基金经理人。3月16日,Fox先生要求被告将基金套现,并将钱寄到他巴哈马的账户。Fox先生的这个做法显然是希望转移财产,让Fox太太与她的律师拿不到这笔钱,但在4月1日,被告在电话里将这件事告诉了Fox太太的律师,事后也将这件事写信告诉Fox太太的律师。这导致Fox太太马上在英国法院申请冻结令(Mareva injunction 或 freezing injunction),分别在4月3日与4月4日将这些钱冻结起来。这最终令Fox先生蒙受损失,于是Fox先生起诉被告违反了基金管理合约的机密的责任。而该先例并非是判决被告是否有责任,而是被告向法院要求撤销Fox先生的诉讼。这其中就涉及非法的问题,根据美国法律,不遵守法院命令显然是非法。但在该先例有关合约的适用法是英国法,基金管理的履行地也是英国,而钱要寄到的巴哈马也是中立国。因此,虽然在美国不遵守法院命令是非法,美国的法院命令没有跨国的作用。被告不能以在美国是非法为由不履行自己的合约责任。因此,法院根据 Kleinwort Sons & Co. v. Ungarische Baumwolle Industrie Aktien – Gesellschaft 先例,判是表面看来原告是有诉因,驳回了被告的请求。

最后,如果合约没有明示或默示规定履行地,而只是履行的一方选择了该地履行,则合约在履行地变为非法不会构成合约受阻。在 Tamil Nadu Electricity Board v. ST – CMS Electric Co. Private Ltd. (2008) 1 Lloyd's Rep. 93 先例中,案情涉及被告向原告提供电力与能源的长期合约,合约期长达30年,履行的地点是印度的泰米尔纳德邦(Tamil Nadu)。被告是一家印度注册的公司,并在印度拥有一个发电厂,但背后的资金是来自美国、瑞士与荷兰的公司,而原告是当地政府的电力部门。双方的合

---

〔110〕 在信用证出现之前,汇票是一种常见的支付手段。在信用证被广泛使用之后,现在使用汇票的已经不多。

约条文不太常见,首先合约的17.8条说明合约的适用法是印度法,但15(2)条是一条ICC仲裁条文,仲裁地点是伦敦,仲裁的适用法是英国法并排除了印度仲裁法的适用。供应合约下的收费要根据包括不同因素的公式进行计算,并且如果计算出来的结果高出合约中规定的最高价格,则需要中央电力局(Central Electricity Authority)的批准。中央电力局是根据印度1948年《Indian Electricity Supply Act》成立的法定机构。但在2003年,印度通过了新的《Indian Electricity Act》立法。在该立法下,中央电力局这个机构虽然存在,但无权批准价格。法律的改变导致双方有不同的看法,原告认为应该交给另一个名为Tamil Nadu Electricity Commission的继承机构决定,但被告认为没有中央电力局的批准,合约价格纯粹是根据双方的协议,如果无法达成协议,就交由仲裁庭决定。僵持之下,被告在伦敦开始ICC仲裁,要求仲裁庭做出原告一定要支付超出最高价格部分的宣告。而原告向法院申请了禁令,禁止ICC仲裁继续推进,并声称仲裁庭没有管辖权。原告的理由是供应合约本身的适用法是印度法,履行地是印度,而根据印度法,没有中央电力局批准价格就会由另一个机构批准,所以由ICC仲裁庭决定是非法的。这可节录Cooke大法官的部分判决如下:"TNEB(原告)submits that, under the 2003 Act, all questions arising in connection with determination of the Tariff payable by TNEB to ST – CMS(被告)must, as a matter of Indian law, be determined by the state Electricity Regulation Commission alone (the SERC), here the Tamil Nadu Commission (the TNERC). Consequently, in its submission, the determination of ACC(Actual Capital Costs) which, it is common ground between the parties on any basis of calculation, forms a component in determining Tariff payments, is now within the exclusive jurisdiction of the TNERC and the arbitrators have no jurisdiction to determine it, or any consequences flowing from it. ..."

但Cooke大法官不接受这个争辩,因为仲裁条文是独立的协议,并且明示适用法是英国法,所以没有理由受印度法的影响。至于在实体法的争议,如应该由谁批准或决定合约价格,这是仲裁庭的管辖范围,法院不会干涉。Cooke大法官说:"The fallacy in this argument is that to which I have already referred. Whatever the changes in the substantive law of India, which constitutes the proper law of the PPA, and whatever Indian issues of policy inform those changes, that cannot affect the proper construction of the separate arbitration agreement which is governed by English law and which will take no account of such changes unless matters of English public policy so require."

原告的另一个争议是即使ICC仲裁判原告要向被告做出支付,在印度执行时都会因为非法而无法执行:"Payment of any sums ordered to be paid by the arbitrators would, in TNEB's submission, be illegal and give rise to offences in India punishable with penal sanctions falling on the directors as well as TNEB and ST-CMS."

但这也不被Cooke大法官接受,因为虽然大家的想法是在印度做出支付,供应合约中并没有任何规定说原告一定要在印度,而不能在其他地方支付这笔钱,因此Ralli Bros v. Compannia Naviera Sota y Aznar 先例的判决不适用。Cooke 大法官说："For the principle to be applicable, however, it is necessary that performance includes the doing in a foreign country of something which the laws of that country make it illegal to do (emphasis added). It not enough that an act of performance is unlawful by the law of the country in which it happens to be done, or that the contract is contrary to public policy, according to the law of the place of performance (see Dicey, Morris and Collins, 14th edition at paragraph 32 – 145, by reference to Lemenda Trading v. African Middle East Petroleum Co. Ltd. [1988] QB 448 at 455 – 456). The act must be unlawful by the law of the country in which, according to its express or implied terms, the contract has to be performed, as the decisions in Kahler (ibid) and Reggazoni v. Sethia Ltd. [1956] 2 QB 490 make clear.... There is an implied term in any arbitration agreement to perform any valid award made pursuant to the agreed arbitration procedure (see AEGIS Ltd. v. European Reinsurance Co. of Zurich [2003] 1 WLR 1041 (PC), per Lord Hobhouse, at paragraph 9). No provision in the PPA(电力与能源供应合约) was however relied on by TNEB as obliging TNEB to make Tariff payments specifically in India and nowhere else, nor to pay any sum awarded there, as opposed to anywhere else. Although, no doubt, the parties would have expected that payment would be made in India, whether Tariff payments or payment under an award, there would appear to be no requirement to that effect. In these circumstances there can be no agreement requiring performance of the arbitration agreement in India, to which the Ralli Bros principle can apply."

最后要介绍的是在 Tamil Nadu Electricity Board v. ST – CMS Electric Co. Private Ltd. 先例提到的 Lemenda Trading v. African Middle East Petroleum Co. Ltd. (1988) QB 448 先例。在该先例中,被告同意给原告一定的佣金,让原告利用其"个人关系"(实际上就是贪污受贿)确保被告可以更新其与卡塔尔国家石油公司的原油供应合约。但被告在更新了供应合约后拒绝支付佣金,理由是其与原告之间的合约违反卡塔尔的公共政策(不能以个人关系得利),所以无法执行。双方合约的适用法是英国法而不是卡塔尔法,因此原告在英国法院提起诉讼。尽管原告通过贪污受贿令被告更新合约违反了卡塔尔的公共政策,但卡塔尔并没有法律条文规定这样做是非法。Phillips 大法官将合约在履行地非法与违反履行地的公共政策进行了区分,认为英国法院不会仅仅因为违反了履行地的公共政策而令适用英国法的合约不能执行。Phillips 大法官说:"There is a clear distinction between acts which infringe public policy and acts which violate provisions of law. I have been referred to no decided case that supports the proposition that the English courts should, as a matter of comity, refuse to enforce an English law contract on the sole ground that performance would be contrary to the public policy of the country of performance. The public policy of Qatar cannot, of itself, constitute any bar to the enforcement of the agreement in this case. It may, however, be a relevant factor when considering whether the court ought to refuse to enforce the agreement in this case under principles of English public policy."

虽然在该先例中，因为贪污受贿同时违反了英国的公共政策，原告最终还是败诉，无法要求被告支付这笔佣金，但要清楚的是，有时违反了履行地的公共政策或者道德准则并不代表同时违反了英国的公共政策或国际认可的公共政策。这样一来，如果合约只是违反了履行地的公共政策或道德准则，并不是在履行地非法，本小段的说法就不适用。

12.2.3.2　合约适用外国法并在外国履行

第二种更复杂的情况是合约明示或默示适用外国法（A 国）并在外国履行（B 国），但在英国诉讼中，最常见的例子就是合约中有一条伦敦仲裁条文。这样如果 A 国的法律突发性令合约变为非法或该合约在 B 国变为非法，合约能否受阻？这看来取决于合约的适用法（A 国法律）对合约在履行地（B 国）变为非法的情况如何规定。在诉讼中，这往往就需要双方提供外国法律的专家意见。

而英国加入欧盟后，因为欧盟法律的影响，这方面的问题变得更为复杂（英国脱欧后会有新的困难）。正如《Chitty on Contracts》（第 32 版，2015 年）一书之 23 - 029 段解释说：

"**Applicable law is a foreign law.** It is uncertain, as a matter of common law, whether illegality by the lex loci solutionis as such has any effect in an English court if the law applicable to the contract is not English but a foreign law, and the place of performance is outside England. **In such cases, the effect of illegality by the lexi loci solutionis would seem to be a matter for the applicable law, subject to the rules of English public policy.**

However, art. 9(3) of the Rome I Regulation now provides that effect may be given to the overriding mandatory provisions of the law of the country where the obligations arising out of the contract have to be or have been performed, in so far as those overriding mandatory provisions render the performance of the contract unlawful. The word 'may' is important in this context. A court is not required to give effect to the lex loci solutionis; it is given a discretion to do so. In exercising that discretion the court is directed to have regard to the 'nature and purpose' of the provisions which render performance unlawful and to consider 'the consequences of their application or non - application'."（加黑部分是笔者的强调）

可以著名的先例 Dalmia Dairy Industries Ltd. v. National Bank of Pakistan (1978) 2 Lloyd's Rep. 223 作为介绍。该先例涉及印度的 Dalmia 公司向巴基斯坦公司（由 Maneckji 先生控制）出售两个水泥厂，而巴基斯坦公司要在约 3 三年时间内向 Dalmia 供应水泥。被告的巴基斯坦国家银行为 Maneckji 向印度卖方做出担保。虽然买卖合约明示适用巴基斯坦法律,担保合约的适用法是印度法并有一条 ICC 仲裁的仲裁条文,仲裁地是瑞士的日内瓦。巴基斯坦公司或者说 Maneckji 先生完全没有向 Dalmia 供应水泥。Dalmia 开始瑞士仲裁并获胜,于是在英国向巴基斯坦国家银行要求执行裁决书(显然是因为在伦敦有分行)。在英国法院中与本章介绍的受阻有关的争议是印巴在 1965 年 9 月 5 日开战,两个国家变为敌国,这样双方之间的担保合约与仲裁协议是否都因为变为非法而受阻。而如果仲裁条文受阻,就表示仲裁庭没有管辖权做出裁决。显然因为担保合约与仲裁条文的适用法是印度法,所以是否非法根据印度法律判断。而印度有关这方面法律是《Indian Contract Act》,英国法院解释有关的法律规定并非严格不允许履行,而是需要政府批准。而在该先例中,印度公司是在拿到印度政府的批准后才开始 ICC 仲裁,因此合约不是非法,裁决书也可以执行。

上诉庭的 Megaw 大法官说:"Mr. Justice Kerr found that the English common law of trading with the enemy would not now be held by the Supreme Court to be part of the law of India .... In English common law, the effects of the outbreak of war include making it a criminal offense to 'trade with the enemy' and abrogating certain contracts involving such ' 'trading'.... But on the analysis of the working of s. 56 (of the Indian Contract Act, 1962) which we have set out earlier in this judgment, and which is accepted by both parties, its only relevance (if it applies at all) would be as creating a 'source of illegality'. The question whether or not the arbitration agreement was avoided would in Indian law still depend entirely on s. 56.

Further, in English common law trading with the enemy is not unlawful if it is permitted by a license from the Crown. Mr Lall(巴基斯坦国家银行的印度法专家证人) took the view that if English common law is applicable in India, permission by the Indian government would be regarded as having the same effect as a licence from the Crown in English law. We think this must be right in principle and logic.

In our judgement, therefore, even if the English common law of trading with the enemy did apply in India it would not affect our conclusions.... Before Mr Justice Kerr the main controversy seems to have been whether, in deciding when a contract 'becomes void' by virtue of s. 56, one should apply what was described in shorthand as a 'wait and see test' or a 'probabilities test'. The 'wait and see test' is that in general one waits until the time comes for the 'act' to be done under the contract and sees whether it is then impossible or unlawful. The 'probabilities test' is that when the 'event' which might create impossibility or illegality happens one looks forwards to the time when the 'act' will have to be done under the contract and decides whether it will probably then be impossible or unlawful or not... Mr. Justice Kerr held that in Indian law the right test is the 'wait and see test'... But he also held that whichever test was applied Dalmia succeeded in this case. If the 'wait and see test' was applied, the 'act' of commencing the arbitration proceedings was not unlawful when the time came for it to be done, **because before then Dalmia had obtained the necessary 'authority' from the Indian government**... If the 'probabilities test' was applied, it was always probable that they would obtain the necessary 'authority' before the 'act' had to be done."(加黑部分是笔者的强调)

12.3 受阻实例之三:延误(delay)

延误导致合约受阻的例子在本章多处提到,特别是对房屋租赁合约、船舶租约、工程合约、长期供应合约等类别的合约。一般的说法是如果延误的程度可以令合约共同目的(common purpose)被毁,则合约就会受阻。延误经常会与突发事件导致合约在实质上或法律上无法履行有重叠。因为很多情况是这个实质上或法律上无法履行只是暂时性而非永久性,即只会造成对合约履行的延误。例如,如果房屋或特定货物灭失,这就是永久性无法履行合约。但如果标的物被征用或战争等导致合约无法履行,通常也只是暂时性。

延误能否构成受阻,要看延误的性质、估计延误的长度与对有关合约履行的影响。在《Chitty on Contracts》(第32版,2015年)一书之23-035段说:"**Delay.** It is often a difficult matter to decide whether a contract has been frustrated by an event or change in circumstances which causes unexpected delay in its performance.... To frustrate a contract, the delay must be abnormal, in its cause, its effects, or its expected duration, so that it falls outside what the parties could reasonably contemplate at the time of contracting. The fact that the delay was caused by 'a new and unforeseeable factor or event' is a relevant matter. **The probable length of the delay must be assessed in relation to the nature of the contract, and to the expected duration of the contract after the delay is expected to end.**"(加黑部分是笔者的强调)

另在涉及租约的 Anglo-Northern v. Jones (1917) 2 KB 78 先例,Bailhache 大法官说:"The main consideration is the probable length of the total deprivation of use of the vessel as compared with the unexpired portion of the charterparty."

除了造成延误的突发事件性质与严重程度,还必须将估计的延误长度与合约剩下的合约期进行比较,看是否足够令合约共同目的被毁。例如,同样是3个月的延误,如果期租合约还剩下10年,就很难说构成了受阻;但如果合约只剩下4个月,就会构成受阻。又如一个国际货物买卖合约,付运期是12月1日至7日,但在11月发生了一宗突发事件导致货物不能出口。这虽然是暂时性,但估计在12月7日前不会解决,这就足够令该买卖合约受阻。

在 The "Silveroak" (1958) 1 Lloyd's Rep. 290 先例中,涉及一个30个月的期租合约,但在履行了17个月之后,Silveroak 轮被政府征用,但估计征用的时间只是3至4个月,而后来也的确如此。换言之,船舶可以在有关的期租合约再履行10个月。

Diplock 大法官判是租约没有受阻。

但在 Cricklewood Property and Investment Trust Ltd. v. Leightons Investment Trust Ltd. (1945) AC 221 贵族院先例中,案情涉及房屋租赁。众所周知英国的房屋租赁合约可能长达 99 年,这与香港短租的做法很不一样。这样虽然战争会令大部分合约受阻,但在这种长期的房屋租赁合约下就不一定。在该先例中,双方在 1936 年订立了一个 99 年的租约,之后"二战"爆发。租客声称租约受阻,但由于租约还剩 90 年,被贵族院否定。Simon 子爵说:"The lease at the time had more than ninety years to run, and though we do not know how long the present war, and the emergency regulations which have been made necessary by it, are going to last, the length of the interruption so caused is presumably a small fraction of the whole term."

这样看来,虽然英国法下合约受阻的说法适用于房屋长期租赁合约,但由于租约期实在太长,合约受阻很难成立。

12.3.1　商业活动必须马上知道突发事件能否令合约受阻

发生突发事件导致延误时,一开始是不知道会延误多久。而商业活动是不可能等到延误结束再看到底延误了多久,能否构成受阻。毕竟如果突发事件导致其中一方拒绝或无法履行,如果合约没有受阻,他就会是违约/毁约。这可见 Scrutton 大法官在 Embiricos v. Sydney Reid & Co. (1914) 3 KB 45 先例所说:"Commercial men must not be asked to wait till the end of a long delay to find out from what in fact happens whether they are bound by a contract or not."另在 Anglo – Northern v. Jones (1917) 2 KB 78 先例中,Bailhache 大法官也说:"... the parties must have the right to claim that the charterparty is determined by frustration as soon as the event upon which the claim is based happens...."

12.3.2　估计延误的长度的困难

估计延误的长度以决定延误能否构成受阻很困难。在突发事件发生时估计会造成多久的延误,这就涉及多方面的因素。

第一,突发事件的性质是否决定了会造成无限期的延误。如一旦战争爆发,什么时候结束很难说。虽然历史上有一些闪电结束的战争,但大部分战争往往是一开始一方(甚至中立国)认为可以速战速决,结果被拖入了持久战。典型的例子是 1980 年开始的两伊战争,导致大量船舶被关在阿拉伯河无法离开,这将在本章之 12.3.3 段有详细介绍。而一般来说,罢工会造成的延误相对较短,谈判双方也常会放出乐观消息,造成受阻的可能性就相对较低,除非有关的合约有其特点,如 The "Nema" (1981) 2 Lloyd's Rep. 239 先例。同样的道理,地震或火山爆发造成的延误常常是无限期,相比暴雨或水灾造成的延误更容易构成合约受阻。正如 Wright 勋爵在 Denny, Mott & Dickson Ltd. v. James B Fraser & Co. Ltd. (1944) AC 265 先例所说:"If there is a reasonable probability from the nature of the interruption that it will be of indefinite duration, they ought to be free to turn their assets, their plant and equipment and their business operations into activities which are open to them, and to be free from commitments which are struck with sterility for an uncertain future period."

第二,突发事件刚发生时,信息往往不全面。例如,战争一开始小道消息或假消息满天飞,或者有些国家对天灾有关的情况报喜不报忧等。因此,要等上一段时间才能对延误的程度有比较准确的估计。这会导致即使最后合约因为突发事件造成的延误而受阻,受阻的时间也不是突发事件发生的一天,这会在本章稍后的12.3.3段介绍。

第三,这些涉及延误导致合约受阻的案件在一两年之后的审理时往往已事过境迁,有关的突发事件到底造成了多长时间的延误已经十分明确,法院或仲裁庭可以根据事实事后判断能否构成受阻。但这种事后做法是必须抗拒,还是要客观看突发事件发生后合约方根据当时的有关事实情况做出的延误估计是否合理。正如Summer勋爵在Bank Line Ltd. v. Arthur Capel & Co.(1919)AC 435先例说:"The question must be considered at the trial as it had to be considered by the parties when they came to know of the cause and the probabilities of the delay and to decide what to do."因此如果对延误的估计当时看是准确,但事后证明错误,合约受阻不应该被否定。例如,在受阻当时的消息是战事一定会十分漫长,但一个月后情况急转直下,处于弱势的一国投降,是不会影响一个月前根据当时的情况估计的延误已经令合约受阻。

第四,要估计有关延误的长度与能否构成受阻,需要对有关的行业操作熟悉,根据案件的事实综合所有因素做出全面的考量,因此,这是一个十分适合由商业仲裁员做出的决定。虽然在同样的突发事件下,受影响的几个合约在不同的仲裁庭有不同的判法,但这很正常与合理,只要仲裁员没有错误理解与适用合约受阻的大原则/大精神,法院不会干预裁决结果。

在The "Nema"先例,Roskill勋爵说:"... where the effect of that event is to cause delay in the performance of contractual obligations, it is often necessary to wait upon events in order to see whether the delay already suffered and the prospects of further delay from that cause, will make any ultimate performance of the relevant contractual obligations 'radically different,' to borrow Lord Radcliffe's phrase, from that which was undertaken by the contract. But, as has often been said, business men must not be required to await events too long. They are entitled to know where they stand. **Whether or not the delay is such as to bring about frustration must be a question to be determined by an informed judgment based upon all the evidence of what has occurred and what is likely thereafter to occur. Often it will be a question of degree whether the effect of delay suffered, and likely to be suffered, will be such as to bring about frustration of the particular adventure in question. Where questions of degree are involved, opinions may and often legitimately do differ.** Quot homines, tot sententiae. The required informed judgment must be that of the tribunal of fact to whom the issue has been referred. That tribunal, properly informed as to the relevant law, must form its own view of the effect of that delay and answer the critical question accordingly. ... In my judgment he made his findings of fact with reference to considerations of that kind, and he duly reached his conclusion. Another arbitrator might have reached a different conclusion for clearly there were many points which had to be taken into consideration both ways. But I am quite unable to say that the conclusion which Mr. Davis(独任仲裁员)reached was one which he was not, on the facts which he found, fully entitled to reach."(加黑部分是笔者的强调)

12.3.3 确定哪天可以构成受阻的困难

确定合约到底在哪天受阻也很困难,因为以该天的事实情况估计延误的长短甚至是否是无限期等。而突发事件常常一开始并不严重,随着事件越演越烈,每天估计的延误时间会不一样。有可能某天的估计不足以构成受阻,但再过一个星期的估计就会有不同。

以两伊战争为例,两伊战争一开始应是1980年9月17日,伊拉克的萨达姆正式宣布废除与伊朗签订的《阿尔及尔协议》,阿拉伯河归伊拉克所有,这被国际上视为宣战。之后,伊拉克便对阿拉伯河上航行船只严加检查。9月22日,伊拉克不准巴士拉(Basrah)港口内船舶开航,并对伊朗空袭。9月23日,萨达姆向伊朗大举进攻,有人认为伊朗会溃败,战事几天内就会结束。但在10月7日,萨达姆的攻势被顶住,伊拉克开始防守,令国际间首次认识到这场战争并不会速战速决。联合国召开会议并通过了促使两国停战的决议,之后派遣曾任瑞典首相的Olof Palme先生作为特使在两伊之间进行停火协调,试图让两国允许被困的中立国船舶离开巴士拉,但最后失败。然而正式失败前仍是断断续续似乎有转机让船舶可以离开,反正是时好时坏的消息。

好几十条船被关在阿拉伯河内并导致了一连串的先例,其中受阻的日期各不相同:The "Evia" (1982) 2 Lloyd's Rep. 307(1980年10月4日受阻);The "Agathon" (1982) 2 Lloyd's Rep. 211(10月17日受阻);The "Lucille" (1983) 1 Lloyd's Rep. 387(虽然10月23日就完成卸货但在12月9日才受阻);The "Wenjiang" (1983) 1 Lloyd's Rep. 400(11月24日受阻);The "Chrysalis" (1983) 1 Lloyd's Rep. 503(11月24日受阻)等。

可见在同一事件下,不同租约受阻的时间相差可达两个月以上(部分没有报道的先例受阻的时间可能更晚)。这在经济上有极大差别,承租人要多给两个月的租金(或滞期损失)、港口费用、燃油、高昂的加保费等。这个差别可能是因为个别租约的长短不一样(如在The "Agathon"先例,租约快到期还船);双方的做法不一样(如有的船舶早已卸清货,而有的船舶延误多时承租人仍在安排卸货);双方的观点/看法(expectation)不一样(如双方争辩的是11月或12月某天才是受阻,仲裁员总不能自作主张以10月7日替代);双方呈堂的证据的优劣不同;仲裁员有不同的背景,所以有不同的感受与裁决等。因此最后判决/裁决的受阻时间并不一致,甚至相差甚远也就不足为奇了。

正如 Roskill 勋爵在 The "Evia"先例说:"... that where questions of degree are involved opinions may, and often do, legitimately differ. I am not in the least surprised at this difference of opinion. The charter-parties in question may well have been of differing characteristics and of different lengths. The discharge of cargo may have been completed on a different date. The several masters, officers and crew may have left their ships on different dates. A host of different factors may have arisen ..."

在 The "Nema" (1981) 2 Lloyd's Rep. 239 先例中,Roskill 勋爵也有类似的说法:"In others, where the effect of that event is to cause delay in the performance of contractual obligations, it is often necessary to wait upon events in order to see whether the delay already suffered and the prospects of further delay from that cause will make any ultimate performance of the relevant contractual obligations 'radically different'... from that which has been undertaken by the contract."

也就是说,不是一发生构成受阻的突发事件(如战争),合约即在双方自己也不知悉的情况下因受阻自动终止。即使事后来看这突发事件确实造成了漫长的延误,绝对可以令一般的受影响合约全部受阻,在当时双方也一定要等待事态的发展(to wait upon events)来衡量到哪天是延误将会令有关合约的责任与承诺与订约时有了根本性的不同。

在笔者(杨良宜)涉及的 The "Wenjiang"先例中,案情涉及一个 11 至 13 个月的期租合约。当船舶因为两伊战争被困在阿拉伯河时,租约期大约还剩下 6 个月。双方的争议之一是合约受阻的日期,这会是从 9 月 22 日开始后的任何一天。但双方在英国高院的争议已经局限在 10 月 7 日还是 11 月 24 日。Bingham 大法官认为应该是 11 月 24 日,并分析了这两天的不同情况。如 11 月 24 日的情况才显示了战争肯定不会很快结束,包括联合国的和平特使也是这样认为。而以该天计算租约期只剩下了几个月,即使和谈有成果也令该期租合约有了根本性的不同。Bingham 大法官说:

"... I look upon the conflict just as I would in any other event which might lead to the frustration of the contract. In so doing, I have to be mindful of the important consideration regarding the probable length of the total deprivation of the use of the vessel as compared with the unexpired duration of the Charterparty. On this test I do not think that the Charterparty could have been frustrated by October 7, bearing in mind that the contract had about 6 months to run and there being the possibility that the vessel might be released within a period which would fall short of any period required for the deprivation/expiration principle to be relevant. I also have to be mindful of the change of obligation theory which, in turn, generally militates against a short delay as being capable of amounting to frustration. Therefore, I am discarding October 7 as a date for the frustration of the contract and I now move on to consider November 24.

By November 24 it appeared clear that there would be no rapid end to the war; even the special United Nations peace envoy had come to this conclusion. The Charterers had been deprived of the use of the vessel for about 2 months and there was prospective deprivation of at least another 2 months if one allowed for negotiations to be completed for the release of foreign vessels, and the clearing of the river for navigational purposes. The combination of the two types of deprivation resulted in a likely period of interruption amounting to 4 months, thus leaving about 2 months only for any possible performance of the contract if one takes the lesser period for which the Charterers were entitled to exercise an option. When the conflict broke out the contract had about 6 months to run so that, by November 24, the likely period of deprivation amounted to two – thirds of the outstanding period for performance; surely this made the performance of the contract radically different from that which had been undertaken."

13. 不可抗力条文与履行困难条文的重要性

现代的商业社会瞬息万变，一个中长期（甚至只是一两年）合约会受到很多意想不到的外来因素的影响，如人工与原材料价格暴涨、政府干预、法律改变、气候变化等。因此，在中长期合约或合约的履行责任主要在一方（如 CIF 买卖中的卖方，造船合约中的船厂，建筑或工程合约中的承建商等）的合约中，加入一条拟定得完善的不可抗力条文（*force majeure* clause）与/或履行困难条文（hardship clause）以保障自己很有必要。

关于不可抗力条文，杨良宜《合约的解释：规则与应用》一书第十三章第 1 段有详细介绍，这里不再重复。不可抗力条文主要针对履约期间的情况出现双方不可以完全合理预见与不想接受的重大改变（change of circumstance）应如何应对，怎样调整与分摊风险。而履行困难条文主要针对经济方面，如遇上人工或原材料涨价、汇率发生大幅度变化、通货膨胀等情况，一方可以提出调整合约价格的要求，并规定如果双方无法同意调整的价格，应交由第三方（往往是仲裁员）决定。

不可抗力条文与履行困难条文的好处主要有三点。第一，因为不可抗力条文是明示条文，只要拟定得完整与明确就有肯定性。一旦发生不可抗力条文中列明的事件，合约方就可以根据条文的规定做出通知终止合约或延长履行期或调整合约价格等。而合约受阻很困难，可以导致受阻的突发事件很局限，要考虑的因素也太多，所以发生突发事件后能否构成合约受阻是不肯定。

第二，不可抗力条文针对的突发事件往往比受阻的说法更广泛。一些令情况发生了重大改变的突发事件会被合约双方视为不可抗力，但不足以构成合约受阻，如相对严重的延误或市场有重大波动。这可以著名的 Intertradex v. Lesieur (1978) 2 Lloyd's Rep. 509 先例为例,案情涉及一个 CIF 买卖,货物是 800 吨的非洲马里的花生渣(Mali groundnut expeller)。但由于在 Koulikoro 榨油厂受到供电系统损坏的影响与火车运送花生去工厂时受到干预,卖方只能交大约 500 吨货物。事发时,该商品市场价格猛涨,买方向卖方索赔损失。卖方的抗辩之一是买卖合约中的第 22 条不可抗力条文,可节录如下:"Sellers shall not be responsible for delay in shipment of the goods or any part thereof occasioned by any... breakdown of machinery... or any cause comprehended in the term 'force majeure'."

英国法院判合约没有受阻,但卖方可以依赖不可抗力条文。Denning 勋爵说:"First as to frustration: I do not think the board(GAFTA 的上诉仲裁庭) were right in finding that the contracts were frustrated. The events were not sufficient to warrant any finding of frustration. There was the breakdown of machinery at the factory. There was difficulty getting raw material down by rail. Such events are commonplace in the world of affairs. If a party desires to avoid such consequences, he must insert a stipulation to excuse him... Second as to clause 22: it gives an exemption in case of force majeure... If the breakdown of machinery at Koulikoro had been proved to be by itself an effective cause of the non-delivery, the notices (of force majeure) would have been good..."

第三,受阻后法律地位不一定令人满意(如合约自动终止或可分开的合约部分受阻),而在订约自由下,不可抗力条文可以有各种写法。例如,并不是直接"杀死"合约,而是等待一段时间,让双方可以继续观察事态。如果延误超过了 3 个月(或半年不等),任何一方可以终止合约等。这种中间选择对商业人士来说更灵活并且有弹性。

第三章　合约更改、弃权与禁反言

1. 简　　介

本章主要介绍“弃权”(waiver)的说法与有关课题，但实际上弃权与“更改”(variation)和“禁反言”(estoppel)这些说法息息相关，甚至分不开。有关更改的课题，因为内容较少，也会在本章一并介绍。另也会在最后介绍公平交易的“Panchaud 原则”，虽然这一说法普遍不被接受，但由于是英国法律的一部分，所以也在本章介绍。而禁反言是很大的课题，因此会在本书其他章节对不同类别的禁反言进行详细介绍。本章只简单介绍禁反言的基本原则，以帮助理解禁反言与弃权的区别。

弃权、更改与禁反言这些说法都是针对双方订立合约后在履行时的大量言行交往与互动。如果一方没有严格根据合约条文履行合约（无论是否严重）就属于违约。在诉讼前的谈判或在诉讼中，双方（特别是被指称为违约的一方）经常会挑出违约前或违约后对方曾经有过与现在诉讼中的指控不一致(inconsistent)的言行，这可以构成更改、弃权与/或禁反言。在诉讼中，违约方会以这三个替代理由进行抗辩，说明原来的合约条文已经通过双方的言行有所改变或不再适用，所以不存在违约。如果能够成功，他就可以避免成为违约方，所以这也被人称为违约方“最后的防线”(doctrines of last resort)。[1] 其中 Denning 勋爵在许多案例中都有提到更改、弃权与禁反言之间息息相关与可以互换来形容同一事实情况：Charles Rickards Ltd. v. Oppenheim (1950) 1 KB 616 at 623; Plastimoda Societa Per Azioni v. Davidsons (Manchester) Ltd. (1952) 1 Lloyd's Rep. 527; Woodhouse AC Israel Cocoa Ltd. SA v. Nigerian Produce Marketing Co. Ltd. (1971) 1 Lloyd's Rep. 25 (CA); WJ Alan & Co. Ltd. v. El Nasr Export and Import Co. (1972) 1 Lloyd's Rep. 313 等先例。

在无数有同样说法的先例，笔者只节录 Potter 大法官在近期的 The “Happy Day” (2002) 2 Lloyd's Rep. 487 上诉庭先例的说法：“Although variation, waiver and estoppel by representation are traditionally treated as virtually interchangeable pleas in support of the assertion that, on the basis of particular facts, a party has lost or may not now en-

---

〔1〕 而在本章第 6 段介绍的公平交易的“Panchaud 原则”更是最后的防线。

force his rights under a written contract, they are by no means synonymous.[2] In particular (a) a variation alters the obligations to be performed under the original contract, whereas waiver and estoppel are conduct on the part of one party which does not alter the terms of the contract but merely affects the remedies in respect of a breach of those terms by the other party...; (b) because the same formalities apply to a variation as to the formation of an original contract, a plea of variation must sustain analysis in terms of offer, acceptance and certainty of terms.[3]"

这方面的法律之所以变得越来越复杂,种类越来越多,适用范围越来越广(尤其是禁反言),是因为在商业社会订立合约与发生合约关系的情况越来越多,不断出现一些特殊的案件与言行,而法院认为有关的言行不公正或不合情理,要做出救济,就需要在法律中创造新的说法以解决问题并达致公正。但另一方面,法律又需要为新创出来的这个说法设定边界(borderline)与适用的先决条件(pre-condition),以期在公平(合理性)与肯定性之中找到平衡。因此,为了应对在商业与社会中频频出现的各种情况与言行,法律就不断创新,在保证肯定性的基础上,又对个别案件保持弹性与做到公平。在很长一段时间内,法院也没有深究这种不当与/或出尔反尔的言行做出救济的说法,通常只是很笼统地说是弃权与禁反言。但在最近三四十年,不论是法院或是一些法律学者都开始重视这一方面。这表现在区分弃权与禁反言,将禁反言进行分类与细化,不同的类别适用在不同的情况与言行,并规定构成这些类别需要满足的要件(不同类别的禁反言的要件有重叠也有不同)。

在这里可以先对更改、弃权与禁反言的边界与区分做简单的介绍。首先更改是属于合约的范畴,所以必须双方同意(consent)。这与订立合约的要求一样,需要有要约、接受、约因/对价、订约意图。针对某些特定类别的合约还会有一些格式上的要求,如必须是书面。这种严格的格式要求在早期的立法都会有规定,如 1677 年《Statute of Fraud》与 1893 年《货物销售法》。现在的《货物销售法》已经不再有相关规定,但仍会有国际货物买卖合约或其他类别的商业合约明示规定所有更改必须以书面的形式做出才有效。

而弃权与禁反言属于合约履行的范畴,不需要满足构成合约更改的一些要求。弃权与禁反言针对的是弃权方或被禁止方在合约履行中做出的不当言行所带来的法律后果。这两个说法可以说是合约法中非常复杂与困难的部分,而且法院与仲裁庭也经常无法辨别其微妙的区分而造成混淆。在这里只提重要的区分之一,就是弃权

---

〔2〕 尽管传统上一贯认为更改、弃权与禁反言之间可以互换用来支持一方的立场,即根据事实指称对方失去或不能执行其在合约下的权利。但这三者其实并不相同。

〔3〕 特别是(a)更改改变了原来的合约责任,而弃权或禁反言没有改变合约条文,只是一方(弃权方或被禁反言方)的言行影响了他向另一方索赔损失的权利;(b)因为构成更改的要素与构成原合约的要素相同,更改必须分析有否要约、接受、条文的肯定性等。

是强调客观去看弃权方应该知道(knowledge)[4]自己有这个权利,然后才会涉及弃权,而禁反言则强调一方做出的言行被对方依赖并蒙受损害(detrimental reliance)[5]。

可以第一章无辜方有权选择接受(accept)违约方的违约/毁约(repudiatory breach)或确认(affirm)合约继续存在为例解释更改、弃权与禁反言的应用。如果无辜方期间与违约方达成新协议并趁机改变原合约条文,这就是典型的更改。但如果有关合约有明示条文规定通过书面才可以更改,而双方只是口头同意,则更改无效。[6] 这样,违约方可以提出无辜方早前的言行构成对接受违约/毁约终止合约的权利的弃权作为替代争议。弃权的说法并不受到合约法的约束,属于普通法发展起来的说法,属于一般法律(general law),因此不受明示条文规定的影响。而如果因为无辜方较早的言行令违约方相信对方已经确认了合约继续存在,并做出依赖进而蒙受了不利或损失,就可以同时以禁反言作为替代抗辩。由此可以看出这三个理由互相交叉,有时会作为替代争议一起出现。

可以再举一个经常发生的例子,双方对债务(debt)或损失(damages)达成和解协议(settlement agreement),这属于订立了新的合约,或对原合约的更改。但和解协议是否有效有时会存疑,[7]因为如果这个协议从表面看只对一方有利,即债务人减轻了还债的负担,而债权人减少其他应该获得支付的金额,因此不存在约因/对价(consideration)。而如果是对损失达成的和解协议还可以解释,因为合法地通过诉讼索赔损失总要面对一定的诉讼风险(litigation risk),对无辜方的约因/对价就是他不再需要承担风险与垫付律师费用。但对债务达成的和解协议就不存在这样的约因/对价,债务人也就不能用合约更改作为抗辩。这就带来了危险是债务人根据双方达成的和解协议支付了部分债务,以为已经从债务中脱身,但债权人赖皮持续追讨剩余的部

---

〔4〕 Peyman v. Lanjani (1985) 1 Ch. 457 CA; The "Kanchenjunga" (1990) 1 Lloyd's Rep. 391; The "Superhulls Cover" Case (No. 2) (1990) 2 Lloyd's Rep. 431 等先例。

〔5〕 The "Kanchenjunga" (1990) 1 Lloyd's Rep. 391 先例。

〔6〕 但在近期的 Globe Motors Inc. v. TRW Lucas Variety Electric Steering Ltd. (2016) EWCA Civ 396 先例与 MWB Business Exchange Centres Ltd. v. Rock Advertising Ltd. (2016) EWCA Civ 553 先例,上诉庭判是订约自由的大原则超越了合约中明示条文对书面更改的要求,合约双方完全可以新的协议改变原本的合约规定(更改必须以书面形式做出)。可以说在这两个先例之后,这种明示条文的作用有所减弱。但话虽如此,这种更改必须以书面形式做出的明示条文在商业交易中还是有很重要的作用,如果合约中有这种条文,合约双方会更谨慎地记录他们同意的对合约的更改。依赖口头协议让法院认定双方已经达成一致(meeting of mind),同意改变原本的合约地位会更困难,需要更多的证据才能满足平衡的可能性的要求。在 Spring Finance Ltd. v. HS Real Company LLC (2011) EWHC 57 (Comm)先例,Mackie QC 大法官说:"there could in theory be an oral variation, notwithstanding a clause requiring that to be in writing, but that the court would be likely to require strong evidence before reaching such a finding."

〔7〕 对这方面的介绍可见本章之 2.4.3 段。

分，并指称较早前达成的协议无效。这样，债务人可以债权人较早前同意以部分债务作为全面和解的言行构成弃权作为抗辩。而如果债务人由于依赖了这一同意或承诺而蒙受损失，如将本来可以用来还债的钱挪作他用而需要举债支付这部分债务或因此与另一个合约方同时对同一笔债务达成和解，他还可以同时以禁反言作为抗辩。这方面可节录《Chitty on Contracts》（第 32 版，2015 年）之 4 – 081 段，如下："**Variation which can benefit only one party**... In some situations of this kind, it is settled that there is no consideration.〔8〕 Where, for example, after a debt has fallen due, the creditor promises to accept part payment of it in full settlement, the mere part payment does not constitute consideration for the variation, though the creditor's promise may have a limited effect as a waiver...〔9〕"

这种案件的数量很多，无法尽举，主要还是要分析双方的言行，根据事实决定是否构成更改、弃权或禁反言。每个先例的案情都不同，所以先例之间也不能完全套用。但笔者觉得还是有必要举一些常见的例子进行介绍。而被报道的先例中最常见的例子是国际货物买卖/商品买卖以及与之有密切关系的信用证与航运。

第一个是 Continental Grain Export Corporation v. S. T. M. Grain Ltd.（1979）2 Lloyd's Rep. 460 先例。这是 1973 年密西西比河河水泛滥影响大豆收成并造成美国本土供应紧张，美国政府从而禁止出口大豆时无数著名案例之一。〔10〕 在该先例中，合约双方在 1 月 5 日订立租约买卖 4000 吨美国大豆，货物是在 5 月、6 月、7 月、8 月分四次付运，每次 1000 吨。卖方并非发货人，而只是买卖合约链中的一个合约下的卖方。6 月到 10 月，美国政府做出了一系列对大豆出口的限制。7 月 2 日，美国政府允许出口每个已经订立合约的未履行部分的 50%。针对 6 月的付运，7 月 3 日，卖方向买方发出以下有关的电传说："Please mail immediately following letter to [sellers]: We refer to the recently announced export control regulations for soyabeans issued by the U. S. Dept. of Commerce and hereby confirm our agreement to accept in complete fulfilment of captioned contract delivery of such quantities as the U. S. Dept. of Commerce agrees to licence for export under the export regulations in effect. Further please note that sellers are unable to execute any portion of this contract due to lack of receipt of above letter making it impossible to obtain an export licence sellers are not responsible for any claims due to late shipment."

7 月 11 日，买方根据卖方的要求，写信说："We refer to the recently announced Export Control Regulations for Soyabeans issued by the US Dept. of Commerce and hereby

---

〔8〕 发生争议后，双方达成的和解可能只有一方受益，从而没有约因/对价。

〔9〕 例如，债权人承诺债务人只需要他支付部分债务，这和解并不存在约因/对价，但债权人的承诺可能会构成弃权。

〔10〕 其他先例可见杨大明《国际货物买卖》第六章之 8.5.3.5 段。

confirm our agreement to accept in complete fulfilment of captioned contract delivery of such quantities as the US Dept. of Commerce agree to licence for export under the export regulations in effect."

7 月 23 日与 24 日，卖方向买方交付了约 500 吨大豆，提单日期是 7 月 12 日。而卖方从来没有交出 6 月份的提单并且没有证据显示卖方曾经试图购买 6 月份已经装船的浮动货物（floating cargo）。7 月 26 日，买方声称卖方递交的提单超过了合约的付运期是违约/毁约，所以买方拒绝接受提单。8 月 24 日，卖方声称买方在 7 月 11 日的信件中已经接受了部分的货物以及延误付运，所以拒货是违约/毁约。在诉讼中，卖方提出了合约更改、或双方订立了新合约、或弃权/禁反言这三个替代争议。

但这都不被法院接受，针对上述节录的两份双方最主要的通讯往来，Goff 大法官不认为足以构成对原买卖合约的更改或订立了新合约，说："First, I am satisfied that there was no binding contract between the parties, whether in the form of an accord and satisfaction〔11〕 or otherwise... It did not, in my judgment, constitute a binding contract, first because I do not read the correspondence as constituting any variation of the contract terms, and secondly because, on the findings of fact, no consideration was furnished by the sellers for any promise by the buyers to take less than the full contract quantity... It follows that the sellers' submission that there was a binding agreement fails."

而针对弃权/禁反言的替代争议，Goff 大法官指出卖方主要是依赖禁反言，但证据显示卖方并没有依赖过买方的言行，说："Second, the sellers cannot succeed on the grounds of waiver or estoppel. In point of fact, as appeared from Mr. Grace's（卖方代表大律师）argument, they were invoking not waiver but the doctrine of equitable estoppel, and to invoke that doctrine they have to prove not only the buyers represented that they would not enforce their strict legal rights under the contract, but also that in all the circumstances it would be inequitable for the buyers to be permitted to go back upon that representation... This latter requirement... that there was no evidence that the sellers ever relied on the action of the buyers or these documents or passed them or their contents on to their own sellers, Kruse（发货人）."

第二个是 Est. Soules v. International Trade Development Co. Ltd. (1980) 1 Lloyd's Rep. 129 的上诉庭先例，案情涉及 27 万吨美国小麦的 C&F（现在的 CFR）买卖。被告的卖方是属于国际粮商路易达孚集团的下属公司，而原告的法国公司虽然在这个合约是买方，但实际上货物最后是转卖给埃及公司。所以这票数量庞大的美国小麦分了多次付运，最后都是去埃及卸港。根据有关的买卖合约，支付货款是以信

---

〔11〕 "accord and satisfaction"与更改的说法一样，只不过更改发生在违约前，而"accord and satisfaction"发生在违约后，所以可以被称为"release"。

用证。而这种商品的买卖显然价格是根据重量,买卖合约(根据 GAFTA 30 标准格式)也有一条条文说明以装港正式的检验报告的重量为准,说:"Quantity: Weight final at shipment as per certificate of weight."该正式的检验报告也同时证明质量,说:"Quality and Condition final at loading as per Official Inspection certificates."

但到了最后一次付运,买方提出了一个争议。而这个争议实际应该是埃及分买方提出的,就是卖方开出的发票上的重量超出实际付运的重量。装港的检验报告计算重量的方法不符合合约的规定,因此卖方不能根据该检验报告的重量开出发票并据此在信用证下获得支付。买方声称多支付的金额高达约 50 万美金。装港的检验报告不符合合约的规定,这在仲裁中已经被认定。卖方对买方的索赔所做出的抗辩是,买方直到最后一次付运才提出这个争议,而之前的言行构成合约的更改、弃权或禁反言。

卖方声称买方开出信用证并做出支付的行为构成了对合约的更改。而即使不构成更改,买方通过银行接受这套单证并做出支付的行为也构成了选择的弃权。又或是这个行为构成衡平法禁反言。上诉庭的 Megaw 大法官简单总结卖方的争辩说:"... that is, that, even if the original contract was not amended in the way in which the sellers seek to say it was amended, nevertheless there was an election by the buyers; or an equitable estoppel arises which prevents the buyers from taking the point that the certificates which were in fact provided by the sellers in relation to each shipment under this contract were certificates which did not conform with the provisions of the contract. As amended by the letter of credit, it was to be a certificate of an 'Official Laboratory'. The certificates which were in fact tendered... were certificates issued by a laboratory called the Thionville Laboratory of New Orleans... according to the finding of the Board of Appeal (GAFTA 仲裁上诉庭)... were not 'official' certificates for the purpose of this contract..."

首先,有关合约更改的争议涉及有关结汇文件中检验报告的数据与签发机构与买卖合约中的规定有所不同,这就涉及买方接受结汇文件并做出支付的行为是否构成对合约条文中对信用证下需要提交的检验报告的规定的更改。一审的 Goff 大法官认为这是构成对合约的更改,说:"A contract for the sale of goods providing for payment under a letter of credit might be amended if the parties agreed to a letter of credit in terms materially different from the original contract; and there the letter of credit which was operated by the parties and which must be taken to have been agreed to by them was in terms materially different to the original contract..."

Goff 大法官认为信用证的结汇文件与原合约的规定存在重大的实质改变,所以构成对原合约的更改。但这在上诉庭被推翻,Lawton 大法官说:"I can see no intention on anybody's part, from what passed between the parties, that the final decision as to what should be in the letter of credit should in any way alter the general provisions of that part of the contract which came under the heading of 'Quality'. There was merely a series of telex messages suggesting alternative titles for certificates and sources of certificates. There is nothing, in my judgment, to indicate that it was intended that 'Quality' should be dealt with otherwise than in accordance with that provision of the contract which was in these terms."

在笔者看来,一审与上诉庭虽然做出了不同判决,但道理其实是一样的。毕竟构成有效合约更改的言行可以是千变万化,所以如果买卖双方有明确的更改意图并在言行中显示出来,没有理由阻止双方通过对信用证的改变去同时改变原买卖合约。但一般来说,信用证是不构成对买卖合约的有效更改。毕竟信用证的唯一目的是保证卖方可以在货物付运后顺利结并取得货价。在市场上升或关系良好时,如果卖方提出一些针对信用证要求的付运单证的更改,买方在自己的利益不受损害以及在开证银行可以接受的情况下,一般都会迁就,即使这并不严格遵照买卖合约的规定。但这种做法,一般也很难解读为买方与卖方是在同时达成协议更改买卖合约。

由于卖方提出的合约更改的抗辩在上诉庭不能成功,所以就要考虑另一个替代争辩,即弃权。卖方指称买方接受这些检验报告就构成了"因选择而弃权"(waiver by election),但这也被上诉庭否定,判是买方在接受这些检验报告时是不知道他的权利。此外,即使买方选择了不拒绝这些检验报告而构成了弃权,但不能进一步说买方这样做也放弃了索赔损失(多支付了货价)的权利。Megaw 大法官是这样说:"I also regard the submission as being wholly untenable. True, the buyers could have rejected these documents on each occasion when they were presented. But if they do not reject them, either because (as was the case here) they did not know at the time of the matters which gave rise to invalidity, or because, knowing that they could reject, they nevertheless decide not to do so, there is no basis on which it can be said that merely by electing not to reject the documents they have in any way given up their right to claim damages in respect of whatever damage may have been caused to them by the breach of contract involved in the tendering or wrong documents."

至于"衡平法禁反言"(equitable estoppel)或"承诺性禁反言"(promissory estoppel)的替代争辩,卖方声称买方(或分买方)在卖方递交文件时没有拒绝,而是接受了检验报告并做出了支付。如果买方不接受文件而提出抗议,卖方本可以提供正确的文件,因此买方被禁反言,不能事后指称检验报告不正确。但这不被一审法院与上诉庭接受,原因是作为禁反言,被禁反言的一方必须要做出言行,导致对方依赖并蒙受损害。但在这一案件中,接受检验报告并做出支付的是结汇银行。而众所周知,银行开出信用证给卖方是独立的支付货款合约,与买卖合约没有关系。而银行在信用证下也不会被视为开证人买方的代理人,所以银行对作为受益人的卖方做出的言行不会约束买方。Megaw 大法官说:"... that there was what is called an equitable or 'promissory' estoppel, or as it has been referred to on various occasions in the course of these proceedings, a waiver. It is said that the buyers, through their sub – buyers, raised no objection to the documents when they were tendered... they took them; they allowed payment to be made by the banks under the credits... therefore, the buyers ought to be treated as being estopped... The learned judge(一审的 Goff 大法官) dealt with that proposition, again, quite shortly and, as I think, entirely correct. He said: '... there are no findings of fact in the award supporting the submission of the sellers that any such representation was made by the buyers. I am quite satisfied that the action of the bank under the letter of credit cannot constitute any such representation by the buyers. It cannot be said that the bank were in any sense agents of the buyers for the purpose of making any such representation...'"

所以在该先例中,被告的卖方所提出的抗辩,即更改、弃权与禁反言全部被上诉庭否定。这也表示在信用证下多支付了货款的买方可以成功向卖方取回这约 50 万美元的损失以及利息。

2. 更改(variation)

这里主要介绍的更改是双方同意的更改(consensual variation)。众所周知,构成有效的更改的要件与构成合约(formation of contract)的要件相同,包括要约(offer)、接受(acceptance)、订约意图(intention to contract)、约因/对价(consideration)等。此处不再一一详细针对这些要件,相关内容可见杨良宜所著的《国际商务游戏规则——英国合约法》一书第二章、第三章以及其他更新与更详尽的有关书籍。如果双方是正式的书面更改,如通过合约附录(addendum)、补充协议等形式,这经常会是经过双方的深思熟虑与详细的谈判,甚至会有律师的参与。所以这种正式的书面更改一般都能满足有效更改的要件。

但在履约过程中因发生违约行为双方产生争议后,在争议违约责任时经常可以找出在较早履行合约期间存在其中一方对所指控的违约行为做出过让步或双方就该违约行为达成过一致的言行。这样抗辩一方就会提出双方曾经同意更改合约,而在新合约下其不再是违约。如果通过这种言行所构成的非正式(informal)的更改不能满足构成合约更改的要件,就需要"弃权"(waiver)与"禁反言"(estoppel)的说法来进行补充。例如,在一个简单的国际货物买卖合约中,经常发生买方没有按照买卖合约准时与准确地开出信用证,卖方催促与表示买方过期一周开出信用证也可以接受。这就会有争议是这两三个简单的通信往来能否构成对原买卖合约的有效更改(延长原来开出信用证的时限)。如果不能,卖方的让步是否构成弃权与禁反言。

对于更改的要件,合约双方在很久以前无法做到以书面形式做出与存在约因/对价这两个要求是非常常见的。1893 年《货物销售法》要求超过 10 英镑的合约更改就必须以书面形式做出。而这个立法对商业社会的影响很大,毕竟在当时(甚至是现在)货物销售合约是数量最多的商业合约,所以弃权与禁反言的说法作为补充就很重要。因为在国际货物买卖合约中,卖方要求迟一个月付运或是买方要求迟几天支付货价的情况并不少见,在弃权与禁反言说法的补充下,双方只是口头同意而没有做出书面更改就无关紧要,不会造成太大的影响。而在今天,因为无法达到以书面形式做出与存在约因/对价的情况已经减少,1979 年的《货物销售法》已经不再有更改必须以书面形式做出的要求,而在本章稍后的 2.4.3 段也可以看出对约因/对价的要求在逐渐放宽。因此,在某些情况下,依赖合约更改就已经足够,而无需依赖弃权或禁反言。但有时将合约更改与弃权或禁反言进行区分还是必要,因为合约更改是永久性(除非双方在更改时写明或后来再次更改回原合约),而弃权或禁反言往往是暂时性的,可以通过做出通知回复到原来的地位。

2.1　单方面更改

一般来说,合约不可以单方面更改(unilateral variation),因为单方面更改属于违反原来双方同意的合约。而如果单方面试图更改的条文重要,可能会构成"拒绝性违约"(renunciatory breach);如果单方面坚持,更会最后构成违约/毁约,而被对方接受并终止合约。

但会有情况是合约订立时给予一方单方面更改的权利,如货物买卖合约中在一定情况下允许卖方提高价格(price escalation clause),贷款合约规定贷款人/银行有权单方面改变利率等。这种允许单方面更改权利的条文,也经常出现在消费者合约中,但已经在目前的立法下受到管制。英国《Unfair Terms in Consumer Contracts Regulations 1999》(SI 1999/2083) Schedule 2 列举了因不公平而无效的条文,其中有针对单方面更改合约的内容如下:"(j) enabling the seller or supplier to alter the terms of the contract unilaterally without a valid reason which is specified in the contract; (k) enabling the seller or supplier to alter unilaterally without a valid reason any characteristics of the product or service to be provided; (l) providing for the price of goods to be determined at the time of delivery or allowing a seller of goods or supplier of services to increase their price without in both cases giving the consumer the corresponding right to cancel the contract if the final price is too high in relation to the price agreed when the contract was concluded..."

2.2　协议允许自动更改

协议允许自动更改还会出现在其他比较局限的情况。第一种是合约合并了一些规则,如某仲裁机构的规则。而在合约履行期间发生争议需要仲裁时发现订约时同意的仲裁规则已经有了修订,而从新规则生效后,该仲裁机构会根据新规则管理所有案件。这种情况下,扯皮的一方就会争议说必须要根据合约同意时的旧规则进行仲裁,如果根据新规则就属于违反了仲裁条文。但已经有案例判是在这种情况下,对该合约条文的合理解释可以自动更改为适用新规则。在杨良宜的《仲裁法——从 1996

年英国仲裁法到国际商务仲裁》一书,就在第一章之 2.12 段提到了一些有关先例。

2.3 协议必要更改

第二种情况可称为合约由于必要(necessity)去更改,这种情况也是很少出现。最著名的就是 1973 年密西西比河泛滥影响大豆收成造成美国本土供应紧张,进而导致美国政府禁止出口大豆而出现的著名案例。大豆买卖一般都是合约链(string of contracts),有时中间的转卖甚至达几十次。而货物一般被控制在为数不多的大型国际贸易商手中。美国全面禁止出口以后,不受影响的就只有已经装船的浮动货物(floating cargo),但数量肯定十分有限。掌握着这些浮动货物的大型贸易商就陷入了两难的境地。如果没有这些浮动货物,他们手中的很多合约都会因为"受阻"(frustration)[12]而自动终止。但因为有这些浮动货物,所以并非完全不能履行合约,合约不会受阻。而这些浮动货物的数量又肯定不够履行所有合约,如果将大豆交付给 A,就无法交付给 B,同时也无法在与 B 的合约下提出合约因为受阻而自动终止的抗辩,就需要赔偿没有交货的损失。因此,最好就是法律允许他们把手上的浮动货物按比例交付给所有的买方,也算是合法履行了合约责任,即合法更改合约,将相关的货物数量减低。显然买卖合约不会有这方面的明示规定,因为在订约时想不到会发生这种情况。禁止出口后,众多的卖方与买方也不可能一一达成协议以做出更改。在很多因密西西比河泛滥而产生的争议案件中,有两个先例判这是合理的做法与法律可以默示合约更改。首先是 Goff 大法官在 Westfalische Central – Genossenschaft GmbH v. Seabright Chemicals Ltd., Unreported March 1979 先例说:"... it is, in my judgment, proper to consider the widely asserted proposition that such a seller is under an obligation to apportion his available stock pro rata among his several purchasers. In my judgment, there is no rule as such. No term to that effect can generally be implied into the contract; and such a rule is too rigid to reflect accurately the principle of causation. No doubt, if apportionment pro rata is carried out it will generally be regarded as reasonable; but it will not invariably be required – for example, if the quantity available is too small to be sensibly apportioned among the relevant purchasers; or has storage problems or a perishable product require one purchaser to be preferred to another; or (perhaps) if a ship already chartered and tendered were reasonably to be loaded; and there may be other cases."

Goff 大法官也解释了从买方角度分析卖方可以按比例交货给若干不同买方的合理性,说:"In the absence of any term to the contrary, the buyer under a contract containing such a clause must contemplate that the seller has other customers besides himself, and must also contemplate that the seller will take reasonable steps to fulfil the needs of other customers."

---

〔12〕 关于合约受阻,可见本书第二章。

另在 Bremer v. Continental Grain (1983) 1 Lloyd's Rep. 269 先例中，一审的 Mustill 大法官是这样说："Where, under a contract in the present form, the seller has contractual commitments to more than one buyer, under contracts in identical terms save as to price and quantity, and where without actionable fault on his part he has insufficient goods available to supply all his buyers, a reasonable and sufficient mode of performance is to distribute the goods rateably between all the buyers."

上诉庭的 Ackner 大法官说："Bremer Handels(卖方) would have had to satisfy the arbitrators, or the board on appeal, that a proportional distribution of goods between the buyers would have been at least a reasonable method of allocating any available goods between buyers, although not necessarily the only method. The question of how the goods should have been distributed is a question of fact on which there were no findings, since they had not been provided with any relevant material."

这样假设合约是 1000 吨大豆的 CIF 买卖，但根据这个按比例交付的做法，卖方可能只要交付 200 吨就算履行了合约责任，而且价格与其他条件照旧。从这个角度看，就是对合约数量的更改。虽然涉及双方同意的更改往往不会这么简单，如价格与其他条件通常也会有相应的改变，甚至双方谈不拢。

只看以上两个先例的判法，这种按比例交付的做法只适用在一连串的合约并且合约有同样的条文[13]的情况，这样根据必要更改的适用就会非常局限。但其实在其他更广泛类别的合约，也有同样的说法。如涉及供应合约，如果在供应方没有过错的情况下货物短缺，这个按比例供应的做法也可能适用：Tennants (Lancashire) Ltd. v. CS Wilson & Co. Ltd. (1917) AC 495 先例与 Sainsbury Ltd. v. Street (1972) 1 WLR 834 先例。在前一个先例中，Haldane 男爵有提到供应合约下这种做法可以是合法。在后一个先例中，案情涉及买卖双方订立合约购买被告农场将来的小麦收成，数量大概 275 吨，付运期是 1970 年的 8 月到 9 月。但卖方的农场失收(卖方没有过错以及根据合约可以免责)，收成只有 140 吨。当时市场上涨，卖方把这 140 吨的小麦卖给了第三人。于是买方向卖方索赔 140 吨的差价并且最后胜诉。看来这是法院把原本买卖合约的 275 吨更改为 140 吨，并判是卖方仍必须履行。

在 Hall v. Wright (1858) 120 ER 688 先例提到了 Lawrence v. Twentiman 1 Roll. Abr. 450, Condition (G), pl. 10 先例，后者涉及一个建筑合约，双方约定在某个时间段内建造一栋房屋。但在合约规定的时间段中，待建的房屋所在区域鼠疫感染严重。法院判是在该区域鼠疫感染期间，建造合约的工作可以暂停。这看来又是法律根据必要的情况下做出对合约的更改。

2.4 双方同意更改

最常见的是通过双方同意更改合约条文。传统上英国法院的看法是，更改合约

---

〔13〕 通常是商会(如 GAFTA、FOSFA 等)所拟定的标准格式合约。

与订立新合约的要求相同,要有要约(offer)、接受(acceptance)、约因/对价(consideration)、订约意图(intention to contract)。在 Goss v. Lord Nugent (1883) 110 ER 713 先例,法院说:"By the general rules of the common law... it is competent to the parties at any time before breach of it, by a new contract not in writing, either altogether to waive, dissolve, or annul the former agreements, or in any manner add to, or subtract from, or vary or qualify the terms of it and thus to make a new contract..."

所以要有效地更改合约必须满足三个要件:第一,双方要有一个有效与持续的合约作为基础;第二,双方必须同意更改的内容;第三,双方都必须受益与/或蒙受损害,即要有约因/对价。上述三个要件可在以下做进一步的解释。

2.4.1 要件之一:有一个有效与持续的合约

第一个方面可以想到如果一个合约已经被终止或履行完毕,就没有什么需要更改。但这个问题也会带来有趣的争议,这里可以两个先例为例。第一个是 Royal Exchange Assurance v. Hope (1928) Ch 179 先例。在该先例中,Barker 先生生前为自己买了一份人寿保险,有效期到 1926 年 7 月 31 日。1925 年 8 月,Barker 先生将保险利益转让(assign)给了被告 Hope(案件报道中没有提到两人的关系),并做出了正式的转让通知给保险人 Sun Life。然而,在保险到期前不久,Barker 先生将保险延期到 1926 年 10 月 31 日,但忘了同时将延期的保险利益再次通知转让给 Hope。Barker 先生在 1926 年 10 月 1 日去世,由于保险人不明确应该支付保险利益给谁:Barker 的遗嘱执行人或是 Hope。这导致 Barker 的遗嘱执行人作为原告要求法院做出宣告,事实上有两份保险合约,第一份的利益被转让给了被告,但第二份没有,而第一份保险合约也因为期限被更改而被第二份新合约所替代。所以,被告不应获得保险利益。但法院根据事实判是延期属于对原保险合约的更改,所以转让利益给 Hope 并没有改变。法院表示如果 Barker 先生是在原保险合约到期后再延期保险,这就是一个完全的新合约,情况就会有很大不同。

第二个是 Shell UK Ltd. v. Revenue & Customs (2007) UKSPC 0624 先例。在该先例中,Shell 在 1975 年订立了一个北海 Brent 地区油气的长期供应合约。2002 年,Shell 订立了一个新的为期 10 年的供应合约。1975 年的合约根据立法规定免税,而新合约,如果确实是一个完完全全的新合约,则无法免税。如果 2002 年的合约只是对 1975 年合约的更改,可被视为从 1975 年起生效,而依然可以享受免税政策。法院最终根据对有关立法的解释而拒绝合约更改的说法,这也可看出有一个有效与持续的合约的重要性。

2.4.2 要件之二:双方必须同意

第二个要件是双方必须同意更改的内容,这与订立合约需要有清楚无误的要约与毫无保留的接受类似。在订约自由下,合约双方可以同意做出任何更改,唯一的限制就是《Contract (Rights of Third Parties) Act 1999》。如果在原合约双方有订约意图提供合约利益给第三人，就不能以事后更改的方式影响第三人的合约利益。[14]举个简单的例子，如果房屋买卖合约中约定卖方要给中介一定的佣金，买卖双方就不能事后同意更改有关条文去取消或减少支付佣金。

虽然合约的更改一般都只会涉及简单的一两个方面，但如果比较复杂，合约双方必须在所有方面达成一致（这种情况经常需要把所有双方同意的内容以附录的形式记录）。这也与订立合约时需要双方同意所有在谈判中曾经提出并想达成协议的条文是一样的道理。而如果合约方不止两方，则每一个合约方都必须同意，更改才能生效：Campbell v. Christie (1817) 171 ER 573 先例。

同样，"胁迫"(duress)、"非法"(illegality)或"错误"(mistake)等会令双方的合约有缺陷而无效的理由，也适用在合约更改。其中胁迫，尤其是经济上的胁迫发生的较多：The "Universe Sentinel" (1983) 1 AC 366；Atlas Express Ltd. v. Kafco (Importers and Distributors) Ltd. (1989) QB 833 等先例。如卖方威胁买方说有关的商品市场上涨，除非买方同意提高买卖合约的货价，否则不会交货。买方如果同意，这不一定构成胁迫，因为买方完全可以在市场上买入替代货物并索赔损失。但如果案情发生改变，FOB 卖方在买方派遣的船舶已经在装港靠泊与必须要装货的情况下，威胁买方除非提高买卖合约的货价，否则不会交货装船。由于这会导致买方除了接受卖方的要求没有别的合理选择，这一更改就有可能会因为胁迫而无效。

2.4.3　要件之三：要有约因/对价

第三个要件是要有"约因/对价"(consideration)。[15] 法律上认可的约因/对价(something of value in the eye of law)，经典的定义是在 Currie v. Misa (1875) L. R. 10 Ex. 153 先例所讲的，对被承诺人有损害或对承诺人有利益(either some detriment to the promisee [in that he may give value] or some benefit to the promisor [in that he may receive value])。没有约因/对价的日常随意的(informal)、单方面施予的(gratuitous)、没有回报(return)的承诺多如牛毛，都不可以通过法律去法院执行。在全面待履行的合约(executory contract)双方都向对方做出可以量化为金钱的承诺，并且同时从对方的承诺获益，都是有得有失，所以没有经济价值的约因/对价极少会发生。但在履行时，对合约的更改就常有这方面问题。例如：

1. 市场上涨时卖方要求增加货价，买方同意，这提高货价的追加协议有否约因/对价？如果有，是什么？毕竟按照原来的买卖合约，卖方就应该交货，他根本没有做出任何回报以交换买方单方面提高货价的施与。造船合约也属于货物买卖合约，在 The "Atlantic Baron" (1979) 1 Lloyd's Rep. 89 先例中，由于航运好景与经济上扬，市场上的船价与造船成本上涨，韩国船厂要求船东多付 300 万美元才肯依照原造船合约交新船。

---

〔14〕　关于第三人利益的课题，可见杨良宜的《损失赔偿与救济》一书第七章。

〔15〕　这在本书第四章之 12.1.2 段有进一步介绍。

2. 在航次期租或程租合约，特别是在航运市场不景气的情况下，船东经常会在付运途中面临困难。如果再遇上承租人倒闭，没有支付船东每 15 天一次的租金，就更是雪上加霜。由于在装港船长已经签发了“运费预付”(freight prepaid)的提单，发货人(CIF 卖方)也支付了预付运费给承租人，所以承租人的倒闭就导致船东要自己将剩下的航次完成。在航运市场好的时候，承租人倒闭的情况比较少，万一倒闭，船东也有足够的资金承受这一损失。但在航运不景气时，这种情况就很多，而船东自己也没有足够的资金完成航次，这就逼使船东向提单持有人求助，往往就是敲收货人一笔，要他在“运费预付”的提单下多付一次全部或部分的运费。作为 CIF 的买方，为了顺利收到货物，会被迫同意多付一次运费。但问题是这一更改(在运费已经预付的提单合约下多支付一次运费)有否约因/对价？如果有，是什么？收货人可否在货物抵达卸港并卸下后拒付，或付了后要求船东归还？这种案件很多，其中被报道的著名先例有 The “Proodos C” (1980) 2 Lloyd’s Rep. 390；The “Alev” (1989) 1 Lloyd’s Rep. 138 等。

3. 在工程合约中，经常有承包商以低价中标，但在履行的过程中因为各种原因发现亏本，雇主可能出于不同的原因同意加价。如担心工程烂尾影响其他工程，或一时高兴觉得承包商的价格实在太低，对他做出馈赠主动要求加价等。但这加价部分是否有约因/对价？

4. 商业社会中的和解协议很多，可探讨和解协议是否有约因/对价。和解协议最通常要针对的是其中一方向另一方提出的索赔，索赔的损失一般是在审理后才能确定金额(unliquidated damages)。但也有可能索赔一笔债务(debt)。也经常会有情况是同一诉讼中索赔的总金额部分是债务，部分是损失。如一个造船合约，如果作为买家的船东没有支付一两期到期的预付船价，而令船厂终止合约。船厂向船东索赔的就是这到期没有支付的船价与因为市场下跌蒙受的损失。在诉讼中处理债务与损失也很不一样，如船厂会先要求英国法院出“简易判决”(summary judgment)要求船东支付债务，而损失则留待之后的判决。在仲裁也是同样，船厂会先要求仲裁庭就债务做出“中间裁决”(interim award)，而损失则留待将来争辩与开庭后做出“最终裁决”(final award)。

由于损失的计算十分复杂，也极少有诉讼案件原告可以成功取回索赔的所有损失，除非被告缺席。绝大部分在笔者经历过的案件，损失会被部分甚至大幅度驳回，原因可能是证明不了，或是订约时不可预见，或是因果关系中断，或是原告作为无辜方没有减少损失等。[16]

所以，如果和解协议针对的是损失，由被告支付部分损失，而原告放弃诉讼，不论协议有否说清楚这是约因/对价，都可以被视为法律可接受的约因/对价。有争议的是债务，因为债务在理论上没有争辩，通过法院或仲裁庭迟早可以连同利息取回。但

---

〔16〕 这些课题可见杨良宜《损失赔偿与救济》一书。

在现实中，通过被告支付部分债务来达成和解的协议也经常有，但这就带来是否有约因/对价的问题。在笔者看来，这也是有约因/对价，如原告尽快取回部分的债务，就可以避免被告在诉讼中倒闭等风险。另是对任何商业机构，早一点取回部分的债务可以帮助现金流，也可以比较安心。

2.4.3.1　部分支付债务的和解协议没有约因/对价的法律地位

但英国普通法的发展并不是这样解释，早在 Pinnel's Case（1603）5 Coke's Rep. 117a 先例，Edward Coke 大法官就已经说："payment of a lesser sum on the [due] day in the satisfaction of a greater cannot be any satisfaction of the whole."这所谓的"Pinnel's Case 规则"在贵族院的 Foakes v. Beer（1882）9 App Cas 605 先例被接受。但在这一先例中，贵族院的法官们也有不同意见，Blackburn 勋爵是这样说："conviction that all men of business, whether merchants or tradesmen, do every day recognize and act on the ground that prompt payment of part of their demand may be more beneficial to them than it would be to insist on their rights and enforce payment of the whole. Even there the debtor is perfectly solvent, and sure to pay at last, this is often so. Where the credit of the debtor is doubtful it must be more so."

在苏格兰，法律认同 Blackburn 勋爵的不同意见，并早在 1937 年通过立法解决这个问题。这在英国的《The Statute of Frauds and the Doctrine of Consideration》的第六份报告（Cmnd 5449）有提到，立法委员会建议取消约因/对价："... we have no hesitation in recommending that legislation should be passed to give effect to it. This legislation would have the additional value of removing the logical difficulty involved in finding consideration for the creditors' promises in a composition with creditors when not under seal. It would be possible to enact only that actual payment of the lesser sum should discharge the obligation to pay the greater, but we consider that it is more logical and more convenient to recommend that the greater obligation can be discharged either by a promise to pay a lesser sum or by actual payment of it, but that if the new agreement is not performed then the original obligation shall revive."

但英格兰没有相关的立法，普通法的地位不明确。在较近期的 Williams v. Roffey Bros. & Nicholls Ltd.（1991）1 QB 1 上诉庭先例中（稍后会有详细介绍），更加被视为与 Foakes v. Beer 先例有直接冲突。照理说，Foakes v. Beer 是贵族院先例，应该约束 Williams v. Roffey Bros. & Nicholls Ltd. 的判决，但记录显示在后者的审理中，双方大律师没有提出这个先例，所以法院也没有考虑。有关这方面的矛盾，稍后会进一步探讨。[17]

2.4.3.2　不相称的约因/对价

在英国法律下，约因/对价只要存在而不必足够或相称（adequacy of considera-

---

〔17〕 另也可见本书第四章之 12.1.6 段。

tion)。约因/对价不相称的情况经常发生,如船舶在当时市场出租得太便宜(这可能有船东与承租人之间贪污舞弊的嫌疑,[18]或是双方有特别关系甚至是属于同一个集团)。或是,国际货物买卖买方支付的货价比当时市场价格高得多(这可能涉及各种理由,包括用这个办法套汇或洗钱)。造成这种情况,还可能是有错误、误述、胁迫、欺诈行为或吃亏的一方无知等。

针对错误、误述、胁迫、欺诈等行为,合约法有专门的机制否定这种订约时有缺陷的承诺或协议,所以不必以约因/对价是否相称来做出干预。而在现实中,最常见的是因无知而在国际商业活动中经常吃哑巴亏,英国法律是不加理会的。英国法律针对一方无知有救济(如保护消费者),但可惜不会适用在国际商业活动。以前的衡平法法院与现代合并后的法院一直以来有不少针对不合情理(unconscionable)的合约或合约条文的判决。[19] Fry v. Lane (1888) 49 CH. D. 312 先例给予一个买了太过昂贵货物的人救济,法官指该人士是穷而且无知(a poor and ignorant man)。这衡平法做法也延展到岸上的房产买卖:Cresswell v. Potter (1978) 1 WLR 255;Blackhouse v. Blackhouse (1978) 1 WLR 243。但在国际商贸中的承诺与合约,法律是不可能接受有一方需要给予这种救济的。

也因为约因/对价不必相称,只要存在即可,这就带来名义上的约因/对价的做法。这种"一元约因/对价"的合约表面上有约因/对价,实质上是施予(gratuitous),但由于在形式上符合约因/对价的要求,法律将其视为有效并可以通过法院或仲裁庭执行。在个别商业活动中,可能有立法禁止名义上的约因/对价,如为了防止公司负责人以名义上的约因/对价的承诺出售公司资产,影响小股东的利益,《Law of Property Act 1926》之 Section 205 (1)(xxi) 说:"valuable consideration does not include a nominal consideration in money."其他还有《Companies Act 1985》之 ss. 103,320;《Insolvency Act 1986》之 ss. 238,239,423 等。

约因/对价不必是金钱或是可以量化为金钱,只要是有实质的利益或损害即可。例如,合约双方发生争议并导致损失的索赔时,在诉讼前或诉讼期间达成的和解协议,一般都是以一方放弃诉讼为约因/对价。英国法律接受原告放弃诉讼索赔是认可的约因/对价:The "Attika Hope" (1988) 1 Lloyd's Rep. 439 等众多先例。

2.4.3.3 Williams v. Roffey Bros 先例对约因/对价的放宽

较早时提到多支付一笔钱给对方,要求对方履行本应履行的现有的合约责任,属于没有有价值的约因/对价。直到 Williams v. Roffey Bros. & Nicholls Ltd. (1991) 1 QB 1 先例后,才有了重大改变。该先例中,A 向雇主总包了一座有 27 个单元的大楼的翻新工程。A 把其中的木工部分分包给 B(分承包商)进行,分包工程的费用为 2 万镑。开工后,A 发现 B 陷入财政困难,而且 2 万镑的费用也确实太低,所以怕 B 不

---

〔18〕 如著名的 Fiona Trust & Holiding Corp & ors. v. Privalov & ors. (2008) 1 Lloyd's Rep. 254 先例。

〔19〕 本书第四章之 8.2 段有进一步介绍。

能按期完成工作。如果发生延误，A 是会在总包的工程合约下被雇主罚款。所以，A 主动向 B 承诺增加 1 万多镑的费用，鼓励与方便 B 继续工作。法院判这承诺有约因/对价，事后 A 必须支付这笔额外的 1 万多镑。

这一上诉庭的先例对“更改”(variation)这个课题很重要，因为之前的例子都涉及只有一方得益。之前一贯的说法是这会被视为没有约因/对价而无法构成有效的更改。在这个先例之后，这个问题就可以大幅度减少。如较早前提到的针对债务的和解协议的问题，在贵族院的 Foakes v. Beer 先例被判是没有约因/对价。但在 Williams v. Roffey Bros. & Nicholls Ltd. 的上诉庭先例后，支付部分债务也可以解释为有约因/对价。由于两个先例都有效，关于部分支付债务的和解协议是否有效，英国法律就有了不肯定。这估计也导致 Williams v. Roffey Bros. & Nicholls Ltd. 先例没有太多后来的先例跟从。

2.4.3.4　不同判法的 In re Selectmove Ltd. 先例

在近期的 In re Selectmove Ltd. (1995) 1 WLR 474 上诉庭先例，案情涉及债权人与债务人达成协议只需要偿还债务的本金而不需要支付利息，但这协议不被承认，因为没有约因/对价。显然上诉庭是跟从了贵族院的 Foakes v. Beer (1882) 9 App Cas 605 先例。而针对 Foakes v. Beer 先例与 Williams v. Roffey Bros. & Nicholls Ltd. (1991) 1 QB 1 先例之间的矛盾，上诉庭看来是认为这一问题最终要由贵族院(现在是最高院)或通过立法才能解决。Peter Gibson 大法官是这样说：“It would in effect leave the principle in Foakes v. Beer without any application. When a creditor and a debtor who are at arm's length reach agreement on the payment of the debt by instalments to accommodate the debtor, the creditor will no doubt always see a practical benefit to himself in so doing... Foakes v. Beer was not even referred to in Williams v. Roffey Bros, and it is in my judgment impossible, consistently with the doctrine of precedent, for this court to extend the principle of the Williams case to any circumstances governed by the principle of Foakes v. Beer. If that extension is to be made, it must be by the House of Lords, or, perhaps even more appropriately, by Parliament after consideration by the Law Commission.”

2.4.3.5　以承诺性禁反言回避约因/对价的 Collier v. P & MJ Wright (Holdings) Ltd.

这一问题还有下文，就是在另一个上诉庭的 Collier v. P & MJ Wright (Holdings) Ltd. (2008) 1 WLR 643 先例，案情涉及 Collier 先生、Broadfoot 先生与 Flute 先生成立一间合伙公司发展地产。期间公司向答辩人贷款 588414.32 英镑，由于这笔钱没有清还，答辩人起诉三位合伙人，大家在诉讼期间达成了和解协议。该和解协议也在 1999 年 4 月 21 日变为“和解判决”(consent judgment)，欠下的债务 46000 镑再加上利息由三位共同分期支付。理论上答辩人可以向三个合伙人中的任何一个取回债务，因为他们是共同与独自(jointly and severally)负责，这和解协议的做法也很常见。问题是不久后，Flute 先生与 Broadfoot 先生先后破产，也就停止了支付。可以说，只有 Collier 先生持续分期支付还债，在 5 年间总共支付了 15600 英镑，这看来也是 Collier 先生应占的份额。但答辩人由于无法向 Flute 先生与 Broadfoot 先生取回足够的金额，就转而向 Collier 先生追讨，并通过英国《Insolvency Rule》（SI 1986/1925）向 Collier 先生做出破产通知。Collier 先生向法院申请中止（stay）破产程序，因为他对这笔债务有争议，所以需要争议解决后才存在能否成功申请破产的问题。

这一争议根据 Collier 先生提供的证据就是在 2000 年年底，答辩人曾经口头告知 Collier 先生会想办法解决 Flute 先生与 Broadfoot 先生要支付的部分（当时这两位先生还没有破产，但显然支付已经有困难），并鼓励 Collier 先生按照较早的和解协议准时分期支付其债务。最后还加了一句说："Don't worry, I am happy to treat you separately."

显然这个口头协议没有约因/对价，但上诉庭没有像 In re Selectmove Ltd.（1995）1 WLR 474 先例一样在两个矛盾的先例中做出取舍，也没有跟从 Williams v. Roffey Bros. & Nicholls Ltd.（1991）1 QB 1 先例。上诉庭根据"承诺性禁反言"（promissory estoppel）认同 Collier 先生会有机会禁止答辩人（债权人）翻供，接受 Collier 先生的申请去中止答辩人的破产申请。其中 Arden 女法官说："... if (1) a debtor offers to pay part only of the amount he owes; (2) the creditor voluntarily accepts that offer, and (3) in reliance on the creditor's acceptance the debtor pays that part of the amount he owes in full, the creditor will, by virtue of the doctrine of promissory estoppel, be bound to accept that sum in full and final satisfaction of the whole debt. For him to resile will of itself be inequitable. In addition, in these circumstances, the promissory estoppel has the effect of extinguishing the creditor's right to the balance of the debt." Longmore 大法官虽然同意中止破产申请，让法院全面审理双方关于承诺性禁反言的争议，但也表示了初步看法，认为 Collier 先生这一争议不容易成功，说："The first question is: what was the oral promise or representation made by Mr Wright（答辩人）to Mr Collier? Mr Collier says that Mr Wright's promise was that if Mr Collier continued to pay £ 200 per month the company would look to Mr Broadfoot and Mr Flute for their share and not to Mr Collier... One would expect an agreement permanently to forgo one's rights (especially rights founded on a judgment) to be much clearer than the agreement evidenced in this case... The second question is whether, even if the promise or representation is to be regarded on a permanent surrender of the company's rights, Mr Collier has relied on it in any meaningful way. The judge could find no evidence that he had... There is then a third question, namely whether it would be inequitable for the company to resile from its promise. That cannot be inquired into on this appeal, but I agree that it is arguable that it would be inequitable. There might, however, be much to be said on the other side... it is perhaps all the more important that agreements which are said to forgo a creditor's rights on a permanent basis should not be too benevolently construed. "

这样看来，在现代的英国法律下，清还部分债务的和解协议是否可以超越没有约因/对价的问题仍待澄清。

总结而言，与更改合约有最密切关系的是履行现有的合约责任是否可以当做有价值的约因/对价，可以从两方面来看。反对的原因是：(1)要保护合约一方免受另一方在合约履行时做出勒索（extortion)（最常见的勒索就是要求提高或降低合约价格或费用)。虽然，被勒索一方会以"胁迫"(duress）为由推翻这种被迫做出的承诺，但这方面的保障可能不够与不容易证明。(2)一方既然要履行一个合约责任，再要求对方为了这同样的"回报"(return)做出另一个承诺，如何说得上是有"牺牲"或"损害"(detriment)？毕竟英国法律不承认虚拟的约因/对价(illusory consideration)：Wickham & Burton Coal Co. v. Farmer's Lumber Co.（1923）189 Iowa 1183 先例与 Arrale v. Coatain（1976）1 Lloyd's Rep. 98 先例。但赞成的原因是：(1)稍早已经提到尽快取回部分的债务，就可以避免对方在诉讼中倒闭等商业风险。在 Williams v. Roffey Bros. & Nicholls Ltd. 先例也提到，B 如果不顺利完成工作会令 A 被雇主罚款。也可以想到，如果 B 不能准时完成工作也可能会导致 A 的声誉受到影响等。可以说，这在各种商业交往中是经常发生，法律没有理由反对。(2)合约一方可以赔偿损失替代履行，因为这样做在经济上更划算，这也是本书第一章之 8.2 段提到"有效益违约"(efficient breach)理论。所以，Denning 大法官曾在 Ward v. Byham（1956）1 WLR 496 先例说过："... the performance of an existing duty, or the promise to perform it, was always good consideration. "对无辜方来讲，可能非常需要有效益违约的违约方履行这个合约，于是愿意减价，令实际履行合约变为更好或明智的选择。所以法律应该支持，让双方都各取所需。

2.4.3.6　约因/对价的利弊结论

在 14 或 15 世纪就已经开始有这种要求，对于是否应该全面取消要求一直有争议。例如，稍早提到的英国《The Statute of Frauds and the Doctrine of Consideration》的第六份报告(Cmnd 5449)就建议在许多类别的承诺取消约因/对价的要求，包括和解协议，虽然最终没有立法。另在关于《Contracts（Rights of Third Parties）Act 1999》的立法委员会报告中，建议第三人在合约下起诉的权利不受没有约因/对价的影响。但针对约因/对价这一大课题，立法委员会认为需要将来分开研究与做出针对性的立法建议。

建议全面取消约因/对价要求的原因有很多，如约因/对价不需要足够或相称，只要 1 元也可以，这看来约因/对价只是形式上的要求。但反对的声音也很多，如一个有效的合约最重要的就是双方要有订约意图(intention to contract)，但事后发生争议很难有证据证明订约双方在想什么。对法院或仲裁庭而言，客观来看是否有约因/对价就是最好的证明。即使只是 1 元作为约因/对价，也显示了双方有订约意图，而且是订立有法律约束力的合约,有意图受法律约束(intention to be legally bound)。实际上在现代社会,每个人每天做出的承诺不计其数,有很多涉及私人(private domain)的承诺没有法律效力。一直以来,英国法律是十分坚持约因/对价的要求,但通过 Williams v. Roffey Bros. & Nicholls Ltd. 等先例(虽然目前看来没有超越贵族院的 Foakes v. Beer 先例,但也只针对债务)也可以看出,个别英国法官试图逐步放松这个要求,但并不容易。

3. 弃权(waiver)

弃权的字面意思就是放弃已有的权利(right)或利益(benefit),现代关于弃权的法律是由 Panchaud Freres SA v. Etablissements General Grain Co. (1970) 1 Lloyd's Rep. 53 与 WJ Alan & Co. Ltd. v. El Nasr Export and Import Co. (1972) 1 Lloyd's Rep. 313 先例发展出来。在 WJ Alan & Co. Ltd. v. El Nasr Export and Import Co 先例中,Denning 勋爵说:"... If one party, by his conduct, leads another to believe that the strict rights arising under the contract will not be insisted upon, intending that the other should act on that belief, and he does act on it, then the first party will not afterwards be allowed to insist on the strict legal rights when it would be inequitable for him to do so..."

在 Oliver Ashworth (Holdings) Ltd. v. Ballard (Kent) Ltd. (2000) Ch. 12 先例中,说:"... the expression 'waiver' is often used in a wider sense of any deliberate decision by a party not to stand on his strict rights."

从这个角度看,弃权也可以包括有约因/对价的合约更改。但一般来说,弃权指没有约因/对价,与合约无关(non - contractual)地放弃已有的权利或利益。这会在接下来的段节介绍。

3.1 传统上弃权的两大类别

传统上在普通法下,"弃权"一词包括了两大类别:第一类是"因选择而弃权"(waiver by election),第二类是"因宽限而弃权"(waiver by forbearance)。

在 Kammins Ballrooms Co. Ltd. v. Zenith Investments (Torquay) Ltd. (1971) AC 850 先例中,Diplock 勋爵说:

"'Waiver' is a word which is sometimes used loosely to describe a number of different legal grounds on which a person may be debarred from asserting a substantive right which he once possessed or from raising a particular defence to a claim against him which would otherwise be available to him. We are not concerned in the instant appeal with **the first type of waiver**. This arises in a situation where a person is entitled to **alternative rights inconsistent with one another**. If he has **knowledge of the facts** which give rise in law to these alternative rights and **acts in a manner which is consistent only with his having chosen to rely on one of them**, **the law holds him to his choice** even though he was unaware that this would be the legal consequence of what he did.〔20〕He is sometimes said to have 'waived' the alternative right, as, for instance, a right to forfeit a lease or to rescind a contract of sale for wrongful repudiation or breach of condition, but this is better categorised as '**election**' rather than as 'waiver.'〔21〕It was this type of 'waiver' that Parker J. was discussing in Matthews v. Smallwood.

The second type of waiver which debars a person from raising a particular defence to a claim against him arises when he either agrees with the claimant not to raise that particular defence or so conducts himself as to be **estopped** from raising it.〔22〕This is the type of waiver which constitutes the exception to a prohibition such as that imposed by section 29 (3) of the Landlord and Tenant Act 1954 and other statutes of limitation. **The ordinary principles of estoppel apply to it.**〔23〕"（加黑部分是笔者的强调）

Diplock 勋爵将第一类弃权（选择）与第二类弃权（禁反言）进行了区分，选择是在两个不同与对立的权利中做出选择，而禁反言是失去了某种权利（法律或合约权利）或抗辩（如失去原本可以在法律或合约下作为有效抗辩的理由）。

另在更近期的 The "Happy Day" (2002) 2 Lloyd's Rep. 487 先例中，Potter 大法官说："Broadly speaking, there are two types of waiver strictly so – called: unilateral waiver and waiver by election. Unilateral waiver arises where X alone has the benefit of a particular clause in a contract and decides unilaterally not to exercise the right or to forego the benefit conferred by that particular clause. It has been described as: 'The abandonment of a right in such a way that the other party is entitled to plead the abandonment by way of confession and avoidance if the right is thereafter asserted.' . . . In such a case, X may expressly or by his conduct suggest that Y need not perform an obligation under the contract, no question of an election by X between two remedies or courses of action being involved. Waiver by election on the other hand is concerned with the reaction of X

---

〔20〕第一类弃权是一方有权在两个对立的权利中做出选择。如果他知道令他需要做出选择的相关事实，并且做出的行为只能解释为他已经选择了其中一个，法律会认定他已经做出了选择，即使他并不知道自己的行为的法律后果。

〔21〕弃权方有时被称为放弃了另一个权利，如房东终止租约的权利，或是货物买卖合约下因为对方的违约/毁约而终止合约的权利，但其实更应该被归为"选择"（election）。因此，这一类弃权也被称为"因选择而弃权"（waiver by election）。

〔22〕第二类弃权是如果弃权方通过语言或行动同意不以某个理由作为抗辩，他在之后的诉讼中就会被禁止以这个理由作为抗辩。

〔23〕准确地说，这类弃权应该属于"衡平法宽限"（equitable forbearance），更偏向于禁反言而不是弃权，因此适用禁反言的一般规则。

when faced with conduct by Y, or a particular factual situation which has arisen, which entitles X to exercise or refrain from exercising a particular right to the prejudice of Y. Both types of waiver may be distinguished from estoppel. The former looks principally to the position and conduct of the person who is said to have waived his rights. The latter looks chiefly at the position of the person relying on the estoppel. In waiver by election, unlike estoppel, it is not necessary to demonstrate that Y has acted in reliance upon X's representation. . . "

大致上 Potter 大法官是说第一类的弃权是单方面弃权，这是指一方在某些合约条文或法律规定下仅是受益方，则他单方面放弃合约条文或法律赋予他的权利或好处，并通过言行让对方知道与被对方依赖，所以，这种弃权也可被称为单方面弃权。第二类的弃权虽然也是属于单方面，但是与第一类不同的是在出现两个完全对立的合约与法律权利（inconsistent rights）时，一方要在规定或法律默示的合理时间内做出选择。而如果他不在规定或合理的时间内做出选择，法律就会剥夺这个选择权，这就会带来另一种因为没有及时做出选择而弃权的说法。在合约履行的过程中，经常会出现两个完全对立的合约与法律权利。举例说，合约给了其中一方“选择权”（option）在某些情况下可以延长合约期限或终止合约。另一个例子是本书第一章已经讲到的，合约的一方违约/毁约（repudiatory breach），另一方即无辜方在法律下有选择权去接受（accept）并终止合约或确认（affirm）而令合约继续存在与有效。因选择而弃权可以用在很多不同的情况，如一方在合约的履行过程中不按照合约规定履行，而另一方出于友好或无知没有反对或配合了对方，这是选择放弃了坚持对方按照合约履行的权利。Goff 勋爵在 The “Kanchenjunga”（1990）1 Lloyd's Rep. 391 先例举例说：“Election itself is a concept which may be relevant in more than one context. . . when a state of affairs comes into existence in which one party becomes entitled, **either under the terms of the contract or by the general law**, to exercise a right, and he has to decide whether or not to do so. His decision, being a matter of choice for him, is called in law an election. . . In all cases, he has in the end to make his election, not as a matter of obligation, but in the sense that, if he does not do so, the time may come when the law takes the decision out of his hands, either by holding him to have elected not to exercise the right which has become available to him, or sometimes by holding him to have elected to exercise it. . . ”（加黑部分是笔者的强调）

3.2 普通法下要求及时行使选择权

普通法默示在出现两个（或多个）完全对立的合约与法律权利时，有选择权的一方必须在合理时间内及时行使选择权（通常是取消或终止合约），否则就会导致失去权利，即一般所讲的弃权。最常见的例子就是如果有一方违约/毁约（repudiatory breach），无辜方可以行使选择权接受并终止合约，但如果无辜方没有选择终止合约，就是所谓对违约的弃权（waiver of breach），在本书第一章有介绍。另是在本书第五章之 1.1.1 段介绍的误述导致合约产生，在被陈述方（representee）发觉后，他就有普通法下的选择权去取消（rescind）该合约。这可节录 Goff 勋爵在 The "Kanchenjunga"（1990）1 Lloyd's Rep. 391（HL）先例中所说："... Characteristically, this state of affairs arises where the other party has **repudiated the contract or** has otherwise **committed a breach** of the contract which **entitles the innocent party to bring it to an end, or** has made **a tender of performance which does not conform to the terms of the contract**. But this is not necessarily so. An analogous situation arises where the innocent party becomes entitled to rescind the contract, i. e. to wipe it out altogether, for example because **the contract has been induced by a misrepresentation**; and **one or both parties may become entitled to determine a contract** ... Characteristically, the effect of the new situation is that a party becomes entitled to determine or to rescind the contract, or to reject an uncontractual tender of performance ..."（加黑部分是笔者的强调）

重点是有选择权的一方在两种完全对立的权利中做出选择，他必须做出通知或宣告他选择哪种：终止合约或不终止合约，接受不符合合约规定的履行或不接受等。有选择权的一方不能拖拖拉拉，犹疑不决。看市场好就不舍得取消或终止合约，但过了一段时间（如 3 个月或半年），市场有了逆转，就选择取消或终止合约。这显然不行，因为选择权已经失去或被放弃。

接下来笔者先介绍三种不同的选择权与相应的弃权中，涉及合约赋予的权利的两种。而普通法下默示权利，主要是违约/毁约（repudiatory breach）后，无辜方可选择接受（accept）或确认合约（affirm），或条件条文（condition）被违反后无辜方有权终止合约等。对该普通法默示权利的放弃，就是所谓的"waiver of breach"在本书第一章第 7 段有详细针对，这里不再重复，虽然本章接下来的内容仍会经常涉及这一课题。

3.3　合约条文下的选择

3.3.1　合约下两类不同的选择权

合约下的选择权可被分为两类，这与违约无关。第一类是"合约选择权"（contract option），即合约中规定了合约的不同履行方式。这种例子在不同类别的合约中都有很多。

可以一些比较古老的先例为例，如在 Reed v. The Kilburn Co – operative Society（1874 – 75）L. R. 10 Q. B. 264 先例中，相关的借贷合约规定说："We hereby agree to borrow from C. Reed the sum of 50l, at the rate of 6l. per annum; and the said C. Reed agrees to lend the said society the above sum for the term of **nine or six month**."（加黑部分是笔者的强调）

在 Christie v. Wilson（1915）S. C. 645 先例中，案情涉及一个农场的租赁合约，其中第 6 条文说："The proprietor agrees to supplement the present water supply so as to make it adequate **or** otherwise to lay a pipe from the well beside the steading, and if need be to provide a pump therefor so as to bring water up to the dwelling - house."（加黑部分是笔者的强调）

在国际商品买卖合约与航运合约中，这样的例子更是数不胜数。如在国际货物买卖中，付运期往往是几周甚至几个月的时间，如条文规定必须在2016年的10月至11月付运（Shipment period：October-November 2016）。这表示卖方可以选择这两个月中任何一天履行其在合约下付运的责任。

卖方在买卖合约也会被允许有提供不同种类货物的选择权，相应的航运合约或租约中承租人也有选择权去装运不同种类的货物。在Reardon Smith Line Ltd. v. Ministry of Agriculture, Fisheries and Food（also known as Vancouver Strike Cases）（1963）1 Lloyd's Rep. 12先例中，租约规定在温哥华装港提供的货物是大麦或小麦或面粉："... a full and complete cargo... of wheat in bulk... and/or barley in bulk, and/or flour in sacks..."

在租约中也有很多其他的例子。如在期租合约，一般都会约定租约期（如1年），这也是承租人在租约下使用船舶的首要合约责任。但与岸上的租约不同，船舶的营运会受很多无法人为控制的因素影响，如天气、海洋状况等，因此租约期往往会有一段明示或默示的宽限期（margin），如前后10天或15天。在The "Dione"（1975）1 Lloyd's Rep. 155先例中，相关租约规定租约期为："6 [six] months time charter 20 days more or less."由于合约双方有订约自由，这可以有各种写法，在The "Mareva A. S."（1977）1 Lloyd's Rep. 368先例中，租约规定租约期为："2 months minimum, 3 months maximum."

因此，在The "Mareva A. S."先例中，如果承租人在这段宽限期内还船，无论2个月、3个月或是2.5个月，承租人都履行了合约责任。但如果承租人在1个月29天就还船，承租人不足期（underlap）还船是违反了租约并要赔偿损失（如果存在损失）。类似的如果承租人3个月1天还船，承租人超期（overlap）还船也是违反租约并要赔偿损失。

在这类可选择的履行合约承诺下，没有任何一种履行方式是首要或基本合约责任（primary or basic obligation），它们加在一起是首要或基本合约责任。一方履行时无所谓是否曾经做出过选择或提前通知对方，在合约允许的范围内完全可以由自己决定如何履行或何时履行，并且可以任意改变主意。这些选择也谈不上是相对立的权利，如在以10月至11月为付运期的买卖合约，卖方在10月15日付运或选择在11月15日付运，根本没有任何对立之处。所以法律不要求卖方通知买方，更不会要求如果卖方原本在10月15日付运的计划有障碍，会因为已经做出了选择而无法改为10月17日。所以，合约选择权不要求有选择权的一方提前通知对方，并且即使曾经做出过选择也可以任意改变，除非：（1）合约另有明示规定，如租约约定承租人在还船前的3天做出确实通知（definite notice）；（2）合约默示要求或有默示责任通知另一方让其可以履行合约责任或合作的责任。[24] 如在 CIF 或 FOB 合约中，买方有选择权或裁量权（choice, discretion or option）在2个月的付运期内的任何时间付运。但在 FOB 合约中，由于买方必须提供船舶付运，他需要合理时间在市场上租船与让船舶开往装港。所以，虽然买卖合约没有明示说明，卖方也有默示责任做出合理通知向买方告知他意图的付运日期，买方才能及时租船并履行其合约责任。

第二类是“真正选择权”（true option）或“商业选择权”（business option）这一类选择权往往涉及对立的权利：取消合约或不取消合约，没收或不没收，延长时间或不延长等。这一类选择权必须与合约选择权进行区分，后者是允许合约方自由决定以何种方式履行合约的责任。但在真正选择权下，合约明示了唯一的履行方式或合约的首要责任（primary duty/obligation），但同时明示允许有真正选择权或商业选择权的一方可以选择另一种替代（alternative）的履行方式或合约首要责任，只要他及时与有效地行使了其选择权。一旦选择权被行使并向对方做出通知（notice）或宣告（declaration），原本的合约首要责任就被替代的合约责任取代，即替代的合约责任变为合约首要责任。因此，如果原本的合约首要责任在一方行使真正选择权之前就“受阻”（frustration），有选择权的一方没有权利或责任行使选择权令合约“复生”并重新以替代方式履行。[25] 简单来说，合约受阻无法以选择权挽救。

在订约自由下，合约双方使用的语言/文字可能不太明确。究竟是合约选择权还是真正选择权要根据对合约条文的解释，毕竟两者可能有很不同的结果。会有情况是在合约中甚至同一条文中这两者同时存在。如在 The “Aspa Maria”（1976）2 Lloyd’s Rep. 643 先例中，期租合约针对租约期规定说：“... the said Owners agree to let, and the said Charterers agree to hire the said vessel, from the time of delivery, for 6 months 30 days more or less at Charterers’ option... That the Charterers shall have the option of continuing this Charter for a further period of further 6 months 30 days more or less at Charterers’ option declarable at the end of the fourth month.”

因此，这里既有延长6个月租约期的真正或商业选择权（并且明示规定要在第四个月结束前行使这一对立的权利），也有前后30天的宽限期的合约选择权。

3.3.2 合约选择权

3.3.2.1 谁的选择权或谁的权利？

在 Christie v. Wilson（1915）S.C. 645 先例中，Dundas 勋爵说：“... I think article 6 of the lease... superadds a specific undertaking that the landlord should do one or other of two things—either supplement the existing water supply,— i.e. , by the intro-

---

〔24〕 杨良宜《合约的解释：规则与应用》一书第七章之 10.1 – 10.2 段。

〔25〕 参见 Denny, Mott and Dickson Ltd. v. James B. Fraser & Co. Ltd.（1944）AC 265；Blane Steamships Ltd. v. Minister of Transport（1951）2 Lloyd’s Rep. 155；Niarchos（London）Ltd. v. Shell Tankers Ltd.（1961）2 Lloyd’s Rep. 496；The “Badagry”（1985）1 Lloyd’s Rep. 395（CA）等先例。

duction of water from additional springs, if such could be found—or bring water to the dwelling – house from the well by a pipe and, if need be, a pump. The landlord would, in my opinion, have fulfilled her obligation under article 6 if she provided the tenant with either of the suggested modes of improvement... I do not agree with the Lord Ordinary when he says, ‘I think that the option is with the tenants and not with the landlord. That appears to me to be the natural effect of her agreeing to one or other of two alternatives.’ **Where a person undertakes to do one or other of two things, I consider that the option, as a general rule, lies with him as to the method of performing his obligation.** I see nothing in the language of article 6 which should take the case out of the general rule... therefore, I think the option plainly lay with the landlord, and not with the tenant."(加黑部分是笔者的强调)

在 Reed v. The Kilburn Co – operative Society (1874 – 75) L. R. 10 Q. B. 264 先例中,原告债主(lender)借给被告债务人(borrower)50 英镑为期 6 个月或 9 个月。在 6 到 9 个月之间,原告要求被告还钱并起诉。在一审中,法院判是 6 个月或 9 个月是原告的选择权,因此在原告开始诉讼时,债务已经到期。但这个决定在上诉庭被推翻,Blackburn 大法官认为合理看来将会走第一步的一方会有选择权,在本案就是债务人要走第一步去还债,说:"Where it is not said at whose option one of two alternatives is to take place the rule of law is, that the option is in the party who is to do the first act; here the borrower is to do the first act by paying."

Cockburn 大法官也说,如果债权人想要有选择权,大可以在合约内规定:"It is clear the alternative is put in for the benefit of the borrower. The lender is master of the situation, and could impose any terms in the first instance."

Quain 大法官同意其他两位大法官的观点,并多举了一个例子说:"A lease for seven, fourteen, or twenty – one years, without saying at whose option, is at the option of the lessee."

在近期的 Mora Shipping Inc. v. AXA Corporate Solution Assurance SA (2005) 2 Lloyd's Rep. 769 先例中,案情有关货方(cargo interests)或货物保险人(cargo insurers)在共同海损担保(general average guarantee)下支付共同海损分摊部分:"In consideration of the delivery in due course of the goods specified below to the consignees thereof without collection of a deposit, we, the undersigned insurers, hereby undertake **to pay to the shipowners or to the Average Adjusters, Richards Hogg Lindley Limited**, on behalf of the various parties to the adventure as their interests may appear, any contribution to General Average and/or Salvage and/or Special Charges which may hereafter be ascertained to be legally due in respect of the said goods."(加黑部分是笔者的强调)

双方对谁有选择权决定将共同海损分摊部分支付给谁存在争议。而在欧盟法律下支付给船东（船舶在利比里亚注册，但事实上船东位于挪威）或位于伦敦的海损精算师（average adjusters）对决定管辖权有很大影响。在 EC Council Regulation 44/2001 之 Article 5.1（a）说："A person domiciled in a Member State may, in another Member State, be sued: In matters relating to a contract in the courts for the place of performance of the obligation in question."

在共同海损担保下，很明显唯一需要履行的就是在海损精算师完成精算后，货方或保险人做出支付。因此，如果货方或保险人选择支付给伦敦的海损精算师，英国法院就有管辖权。但如果货方或保险人选择支付给船东，挪威或利比里亚（虽然会有争议性）法院会有管辖权。

高院与上诉庭都判是货方或保险人有选择权决定是支付给船东或海损精算师。因为共同海损但保中并没有规定货方或保险人只能支付给海损精算师，所以他们有权选择支付给船东。根据共同海损担保的措辞/用字，货方或保险人需要承担共同海损中的份额，但有权决定支付给谁，而收款的一方无权决定这笔钱要支付给谁。因此，英国法院没有管辖权处理船东告保险人没有或拒绝在共同海损担保下支付的争议。

即说，如果船东希望在发生保险人在共同海损担保下拒绝支付的争议时英国法院有管辖权（一般来说，船东都更偏向英国法院而不是利比里亚法院有管辖权），就需要在共同海损担保中加入一条明示的英国法院专属管辖权条文（exclusive English jurisdiction clause）。

3.3.2.2　有选择权的一方是否需要通知另一方？

简单而言，有选择权的一方在行使合约选择权时不需要通知另一方。他可以直接按照其选择的方式履行合约，并且可能有时进行改变或调整。如在期租合约中，租约期是"6 months 20 days more or less"。在航运市场高涨时，承租人可能一开始希望利用最长的租约期，即 6 个月 20 天。但在租约期即将届满时，航运市场突然急剧下跌，这时他就会转而希望履行最短的租约期，即 5 个月 10 天。但即使承租人的意图是只履行最短的租约期，他可能也找不到这么短的航次，最后真正履行的租约期是 5 个月 28 天。但承租人没有违反租约，因为这在租约允许的租约期内。

如果承租人违反了租约，也不是因为违反租约期的条文，而是可能违反了其他租约条文。例如，期租合约的另一条文规定要在还船前的 10 天、7 天、5 天、3 天与 1 天做出还船通知（redelivery notice）。其中 10 天与 7 天的是预计还船通知（expected/estimated redelivery notice），5 天、3 天与 1 天的是确实还船通知（actual/definite redelivery notice）。这是为了让船东掌握船舶动态以做出下一步的安排（入坞、出售、找下一个租约等），缩短或避免船舶在两个租约之间的空闲时间（idle time）。特别是在市场下跌时，出租非易事，而且谈判也需要时间。所以，如果承租人提前 5 天做出了确实还船通知，预计租约期是 5 个月 13 天，但之后因为天气原因造成了延误，导致 10 天后才真正还船。承租人可能违反了还船通知的条文，但没有违反租约期的条文。

"禁反言"(estoppel)在租约期的例子也可能适用。例如,如果船东想知道还船的准确时间并向承租人做出询问,承租人没有说清楚的责任,[26]可以无视船东的询问并保持沉默或说不肯定。如果承租人主动做出承诺说租约期是6个月20天,但在之后更接近的时间因为市场下跌改变主意,想在5个月10天就还船,这等于撤回了原本的承诺,可能会带来承诺性禁反言的问题。

这可见Devlin勋爵在Reardon Smith Line Ltd. v. Ministry of Agriculture, Fisheries and Food (also known as Vancouver Strike Cases) (1963) 1 Lloyd's Rep. 12先例中所说:"My Lords, 'option' in its widest interpretation means simply choice or freedom of choice. An obligation in a contract can frequently be performed in a large number of ways and the party under obligation can choose any one of the ways he likes. A contract may, for example, provide for September/October shipment and the shipper may then select any one of the 61 days which he likes. I doubt if in such a case the shipper would, in the ordinary use of language, be described as having 61 options. But when a contract itself limits and enumerates the obligations, as when it obliges the shipper to ship wheat or barley or flour, it is quite sensible and natural to talk of his having an option to ship any one of these three commodities. There is, however, a narrower sense in which the word can be used and that is to confer a right of choice specially granted to the holder of the option and to be used solely for his own benefit. It is in this sense, I think, that the word is generally used in the business world.[27]"

Devlin勋爵接着说:"At first sight this appears to be a distinction without a difference. When a party under obligation selects between various alternatives, is he not considering simply his own benefit and convenience? A shipper who ships on Sept. 4 and not on Sept. 5 has chosen that date because it suits him better than the other. The difference arises when for some reason or another the pursuit of one alternative is temporarily or permanently barred. Where there is no option in the business sense, the consequence of damming one channel is simply that the flow of duty is diverted into the others and the freedom of choice thus restricted. If then a shipper cannot ship wheat, he must ship either barley or flour. The width of the alternatives is in the contract for the benefit of both par-

---

[26] 关于有责任说清楚可见本书第四章之6.4段与第五章第10段。

[27] "合约选择权"一词可以被广义解释为做出选择的自由。合约中的责任可以很多不同方式被履行,合约方可以从中选择任何一种方式来履行。例如,买卖合约允许卖方/发货人在9/10月做出付运,这表示他可以在这两个月间的61天中的任何一天付运。但很难按照字面将其解释为卖方有61个选择权。又如果一个合约对合约承诺做出了局限与列举了不同的履行方式,如买卖合约要求卖方/发货人付运小麦或大麦或面粉,就表示卖方只要根据其自己的利益选择付运这三种商品的其中一种。

ties and it can be a liability as well as a benefit for the shipper.[28]"

在 The "Aspa Maria" (1976) 2 Lloyd's Rep. 643 先例，Denning 勋爵也说："There is another point I would mention. It seems to me that the phrase '30 days more or less at charaterers' option' was not a true option. It did not have to be exercised by express notice or declaration such as Lord Devlin said would be necessary for a true option: see the Reardon Smith case, (1963) 1 Lloyd's Rep. 12... The charterer could properly redeliver the vessel within the 30 days more or less so long as he gave the proper notice of redelivery, which would be 30 days in this case. It would not be necessary for him to do anything more by way of exercising an option."

3.3.2.3 合约选择权的总结

以上关于合约选择权的介绍可被总结如下：(1)这不是真正或商业选择权(不是商业意义上的选择权)，而只是一个可以多种方式履行的合约承诺。其中，任何一种方式都不属于首要合约责任(primary contract duty/obligation)，但加在一起是首要合约责任。(2)对有合约选择权的一方这有好处，也有坏处。好处很明显是其在履行时有一定的弹性，可以从双方同意的替代履行方式中自由选一种履行。但如果他原本希望的合约履行方式(如提供其中一种货物)"受阻"(frustrated)，合约选择权对其就不是好事。合约并不会因为其中一种履行方式受阻而自动终止，需要以其他的替代方式履行(提供另一种货物)，而如果做不到就是违约，要赔偿对方金钱上的损失。[29] (3)有合约选择权的一方行使选择权时不需要做出通知或宣告。选择以替代方式履行合约的权利不会受没有提前通知或宣告的影响。

3.3.3 商业(或真正)选择权

在 Reardon Smith Line Ltd. v. Ministry of Agriculture, Fisheries and Food (also known as Vancouver Strike Cases) (1963) 1 Lloyd's Rep. 12 先例，Devlin 勋爵说："... where there is a 'business option' the legal position is quite different. There is **not** then one contractual obligation to be performed in alternative ways, but one obligation to be performed in one way, unless the option holder chooses to substitute another way and does so by the effective exercise of his option. In exercising the option, which he has ac-

---

〔28〕 表面看来，上述不同写法的选择权没有实质区别，反正有权选择的一方总会根据他自己的利益或方便做出选择。卖方/发货人选择在9月4日而不是在9月5日付运，显然是他认为前者的时间更符合他的利益或方便。合约选择权与真正选择权的区别体现在当其中一个履行方式被暂时或永久禁止时，拥有合约选择权的一方就不得不选择其他履行方式履行，否则就会构成违约/毁约，这实际上令他失去了真正选择的自由。如卖方/发货人不能付运小麦，就必须付运大麦或面粉，否则就是违约/毁约。从这个角度看来，这种写法的合约选择权与其包括的各种替代选择履行方式是对双方都有利，而卖方/发货人既有在这三种商品中做出选择的好处，同时也有必须做出一种选择让合约获得履行的责任。

〔29〕 这可见本书第二章之7.5段介绍的 The "Super Servant Two" (1990) 1 Lloyd's Rep. 1 先例。

quired solely for his own advantage, the holder is not bound to consider the convenience or the interest of the other party. If the obligation is to ship a full and complete cargo of wheat with the option to change to barley or flour and the shipment of wheat is impeded, he is not obliged to change to barley or flour simply because that is the only way in which he could ship a full and complete cargo...[30]"

3.3.3.1 商业选择权与合约选择权的区别

商业(或真正)选择权与合约选择权的区别比较清楚:

1. 有商业(或真正)选择权的合约只有一个首要责任或履行方式。一旦被履行,合约就结束了。同样,如果合约首要责任或履行方式受阻,合约也自动终止,而有商业选择权的一方虽然可以选择以其他替代方式履行合约,但并非一定要行使选择权。

2. 因此,商业选择权是让有选择权的一方可以选择以替代方式履行合约。如果他通过宣告做出了选择,替代的履行方式就成为首要合约责任,原本约定的履行方式就消失了。但如果有选择权的一方没有做出选择,原本的首要合约责任就是合约唯一的履行方式,商业选择权消失。所以有说法是一旦商业选择权被行使,就是最终与不可撤销,不能回头:Scarf v. Jardine (1882) 7 App. Cas. 345 (HL)先例。Parker 大法官在 The "Trado" (1982) 1 Lloyd's Rep. 157 先例中说:"It is clear that if a charterer has an option as to port, berth method of loading and so on, that option, once exercised is binding and is as if written into the charter party as to the port, berth or means of loading, as the case may be."

3. 商业选择权只是有选择权的一方的单方面利益,而没有义务。如果商业选择权变为无用(如因为市场形势转变),有选择权的一方可以简单地不行使其选择权。这与合约选择权可能有时反而对有选择权的一方不利不同。在 Reardon Smith Line Ltd. v. Ministry of Agriculture, Fisheries and Food (also known as Vancouver Strike Cases) (1963) 1 Lloyd's Rep. 12 先例中,Devlin 勋爵说有选择权的一方在做出选择时纯粹是为了自己的利益,而不需要考虑对方的方便与利益:"In exercising the option, which he has acquired solely for his own advantage, the holder is not bound to consider the convenience or the interest of the other party."

4. 有商业选择权的一方在行使选择权时向对方做出通知或宣告至关重要。如果他没有正确与及时地做出通知或宣告,就会失去选择权或构成"弃权"(waiver)。

---

〔30〕 真正或商业选择权的法律地位就很不一样。这种选择权是没有责任以替代的选择履行合约,而只是根据一个约定的方式履行合约,直到享有商业(或真正)选择权的一方有效行使了选择权,令选择了替代方式取代了原来约定的方式,如替代方这就是合约原来约定的履行方式一样。而享有商业(或真正)选择权的一方这样做时,纯粹是为了自己的利益,根本不需要考虑对方的方便与利益。如果承租人在租约下的首要责任或履行方法只是满载一船的小麦,但同时有商业(或真正)选择权以大麦或面粉替代履行合约,他没有责任在无法满载一船小麦时选择以大麦或面粉替代履行合约,除非这样做对他有利。例如,大麦或面粉价格更便宜与马上有货供应可以装船。

3.3.3.2 行使商业选择权时做出通知或宣告

商业选择权常常涉及相互对立的权利或履行方式，以替代的合约责任取代原本的合约责任，这会影响合约的另一方。因此，如果一方要行使延期6个月的选择权，将合约从6个月变为1年，有选择权的一方必须向另一方做出通知。类似的，如果有商业选择权的一方决定行使选择权提前终止合约，如期租合约中著名的撤船条文（因为迟付租金，即使只迟了1分钟），或战争条文（War Cancellation Clause），[31]或房屋租赁合约中的终止条文（Break Clause）等，也必须向另一方做出通知。

通知或宣告必须清楚无误：Scarf v. Jardine (1882) 7 App. Cas. 345 (HL)；The "Mihalios Xilas" (1979) 2 Lloyd's Rep. 303；The "Kanchenjunga" (1990) 1 Lloyd's Rep. 391 (HL)等先例。正如 Parker 大法官在 The "Trado" (1982) 1 Lloyd's Rep. 157 先例中说："Those who have options in their favour must, if they wish to exercise them, exercise them in words which are not really capable of doubt."

如果合约明示要求了通知的形式或内容，有选择权的一方必须严格遵守。在 Hankey v. Clavering (1942) 2 K. B. 326 先例中，Greene 勋爵讲到了一个大原则，说："In an option clause the requirement is that a party must strictly comply with the condition for its exercise. If the condition includes the giving of a particular notice, it seems to me that the logical first approach is to interpret the notice, looking at the words and applying legal principles to their construction, and then ask whether it complying with the strict requirements as to exercise of the option.[32]"

另是 Hoffmann 勋爵在 Mannai Investments Co. Ltd. v. Eagle Star Life Assurance Co. Ltd. (1997) AC 749 先例中所说的，如果合约要求通知以蓝色纸张做出，就不能使用粉色纸张："If the clause had said that the notice had to be on blue paper, it would have been no good serving a notice on pink paper, however clear it might have been that the tenant wanted to terminate the lease."

在航运的期租合约，反技术取巧条文（anti – technicality clause）的要求必须被严格遵守，这可见杨大明《期租合同》一书第十八篇之18.6.2 – 18.6.5段。

至于什么才是向另一方做出通知或宣告的合适时间，绝大多数情况下合约都会有规定，必须严格遵守，早了不行，晚了也不行，即使只有1分钟的差别。如在 The "Aspa Maria" (1976) 2 Lloyd's Rep. 643 先例中，租约就规定了行使延期6个月的商业选择权的时间，说："... the Charterers shall have the option of continuing this Charter

---

〔31〕 可见近期著名的 The "Golden Victory" (2007) 2 Lloyd's Rep. 164 先例，该先例在杨良宜的《损失赔偿与救济》一书第十三章第6段有详细介绍。

〔32〕 合约中有选择权的一方在行使选择权时必须严格遵照合约条文规定的行使条件。如果这条件包括了要做出一个通知，合乎逻辑的做法就是解释该通知，看其在文字上可否被解释为完全遵照了行使选择权的严格要求。

for a further period of further 6 months 30 days more or less at Charterers' option **declarable at the end of the fourth month**."(加黑部分是笔者的强调)

即使没有像 The "Aspa Maria"先例一样规定第四个月月尾,法律也会默示做出通知或宣告的合理时间。正如 Bowen 大法官在 Tharsis Sulphur & Copper Co. Ltd. v. Morel Brother & Co. and others (1891) 2 QB 647 所说:"The option is given for the benefit of the person who has to exercise it. **He is bound to exercise it in a reasonable time**, but is not bound in exercising it to consider the benefit or otherwise of the other party."(加黑部分是笔者的强调)

什么才是合理时间,在不同的案件事实下会有不同的解释。如果合约涉及的标的物的市场波动很大或涉及一些可以营利的资产(船舶、飞机等),合理时间就会很短。针对租约中销约期条文(Cancelling Clause)下取消合约(船舶过了销约期)的商业选择权,或撤船条文(Withdrawal Clause)下撤船(承租人没有及时支付租金)的商业选择权,或国际货物买卖合约(市场波动很快与很大)中的商业选择权,有否在合理时间内行使,有很多著名先例。

Lloyd 大法官在涉及租约的 The "Scaptrade" (1981) 2 Lloyd's Rep. 425 (QB)先例中说:"... what is the shortest time reasonably necessary will still depend on all the circumstances of the case. In some cases it will be reasonable for owners to take time to consider their position, as withdrawal under a time charter is a serious step not lightly to be undertaken. In other cases it may be reasonable for owners to seek legal advice."

在 The "Great Marine" (No. 1) (1990) 2 Lloyd's Rep. 245 先例中,案情涉及二手船舶买卖,高院判是涉及像船舶或飞机这种可以营利的资产(in the context of a profit – earning chattel such as a ship or an aircraft),卖方没有在一周内行使取消合约的选择权是太迟,等于放弃了选择权。而放弃或弃权后再取消合约,就变成自己违约/毁约。

承租人根据租约的销约期条文取消租约的情况也是类似:Moel Tryvan Ship Co. Ltd. v. Andrew Weir & Co. (1910) 2 KB 844 先例。

但如果是在合约标的不存在买卖市场或不涉及营利的资产买卖的合约下终止合约的选择权,如建筑或工程合约中有权在一方出现经济问题时选择终止合约,合理时间就可能长得多。毕竟做出是否取消或终止合约的决定需要涉及大量的工作、调查、咨询与考虑,这可能需要一两个月的时间。

有商业选择权的一方如果没有及时(根据合约条文或默示的合理时间)向对方做出通知或宣告行使选择权,就会被认为失去或放弃了选择权,或当做他选择不行使选择权。

Goff 勋爵在 The "Kanchenjunga"先例中说:"In it a commonplace that the expression 'waiver' is one which may, in law, bear different meanings. In particular, it may refer to a forbearance from exercising a right or to an abandonment of a right. Here we are concerned with waiver in the sense of abandonment of a right which arises by virtue of a party making an election. Election itself is a concept which may be relevant in more than one context. In the present case, we are concerned with **an election which may arise in the context of a binding contract, when a state of affairs comes into existence in which one party becomes entitled, either under the terms of the contract or by the general law, to exercise a right, and he has to decide whether or not to do so.** His decision, being a matter of choice for him, is called in law an election... In all cases, **he has in the end to make his election**, not as a matter of obligation, but in the sense that, **if he does not do so, the time may come when the law takes the decision out of his hands**, either by holding him to have elected not to exercise the right which has become available to him..."（加黑部分是笔者的强调）

3.3.4　对合约将来权利或利益的提前放弃

这种弃权与本章之3.3.3段介绍的对商业（或真正）选择权的弃权（waiver of business/true option）与本书第一章第7段介绍的普通法下涉及违约/毁约的弃权（waiver by breach）不同，是一方提前放弃他在合约下单方面可以享有的权利或利益，不需要另一方同意。这可节录《Chitty on Contracts》（第32版，2015年）一书之22－046段，如下："**Waiver of condition for benefit of one party.** Where the terms of a contract include a provision which has been inserted solely for the benefit of one party, he may, without the assent of the other party, waive complicance with that provision and enforce the contract as if the provision had been omitted. He will not be permitted to do so where the provision has been inserted for the benefit of both parties or where there is in reality no concluded agreement."

3.3.4.1　有关先例

这种情况经常出现，可以通过介绍一些先例的案情帮助读者理解。首先是早期的Hawksley v. Outram（1892）3 Ch 359先例，案情涉及买卖纺织公司的交易。有关的合约中有条文允许买方以公司以前的名字Benjamin Outram & Co. 继续营运。另也有条文禁止卖方（这涉及好几个自然人的老板，包括Benjamin Outram先生）在该公司的50英里以内经营相同的业务。这种条文就是一条典型的限制商贸条文（restrain of trade clause/covenant），为了阻止卖方另外成立公司带来业务上的竞争，条文是否有效会有争议。[33] 但之后卖方拒绝履行合约，不肯将公司出售，背后的原因就

〔33〕 在Townend Group Ltd. v. Cobb（2004）EWHC 3432先例中，Briggs大法官说："The general principle is that all covenants in restraint of trade are void on public policy grounds, unless they are no more than reasonably necessary for the protection of the legitimate business interests of the employer. Prevention of competition, however desirable that is perceived to be, is not a legitimate business interest. Protection of goodwill, or of confidential information, is."

不得而知,可能是价钱问题或是卖方改变主意等,导致买方向法院申请“履约指令”(specific performance)。而卖方提出的抗辩是代表卖方进行谈判的代表超出了授权,因为涉及个人责任的问题,Benjamin Outram 先生不同意买方以公司以前的名字 Benjamin Outram & Co. 继续营运,另外卖方也不接受这条限制商贸条文的有效性。买方于是向法院保证放弃这两条条文的权利。法院认定这两条条文是买方单方面的权利,因此在买方同意弃权后,做出了履约指令。

另在 Heron Garage Properties Ltd. v. Moss (1974) 1 WLR 148 先例中,案情涉及土地的买卖。买方计划用购买的土地经营一个加油站以及相关业务,但这需要当地政府的批文。所以买卖合约的第 7 条是取得批文的后续条件(condition subsequent),[34]并说明如果在 6 个月内拿不到批文,双方都可以终止合约。而由于各种原因(可能是土地价格上涨,或是买方有信心最终拿到批文,或是即使拿不到批文买方也可以把这块土地用作其他用途等),买方事实上并不希望终止合约。由于没有在 6 个月内拿到批文,卖方做出通知终止合约,而买方赶紧通知卖方他放弃了这个后续条件,并要求卖方履行买卖合约。而在卖方拒绝后,买方向法院申请履约指令。高院驳回了买方的申请,因为合约第 7 条并非买方单方面的利益,买方不能单方面弃权,这方面的争议与原因在本章之 3.3.4.3.1 段会有详细介绍。另是合约规定了双方在拿到批文 1 个月后过户(closing),即合约第 7 条无法与合约其他条文分开(severable),而其他的合约条文是不存在可让买方单方面放弃。

但在更近期的 Irwin v. Wilson (2011) EWHC 326 (Ch)先例,案情不同,所以令判法看来有所不同。该先例的案情也是涉及土地/房屋的买卖,合约第 25.1 条文规定在卖方提供给买方律师一些关于房屋产权(title)的特定信息后 14 天,双方完成交易。而合约第 25.2 条文也规定如果卖方合理努力(reasonable endeavours)后仍无法在 2010 年 2 月 1 日前提供这些信息,双方都可以在做出通知的 5 个工作日后终止合约。卖方合理努力后,仍无法在 2 月 1 日前提供所有信息,于是在 2 月 2 日做出了终止合约的通知。买方律师在第 5 个工作日即 2 月 9 日,写信回复说第 25.1 条文是买方单方面的利益,买方弃权,卖方应继续完成合约。

之后双方开始诉讼,上诉庭推翻了一审判决,判是第 25.1 条文确实是买方单方面的利益,并且第 25.1 条文可以与合约其他条文分开,因此买方可以单方面弃权。如果买方弃权,就应该像卖方已经提供了相关信息,或是卖方从来不需要提供相关信息一样,法院可以决定完成交易的合理时间。但在该先例中,买方弃权是发生在合约已经被终止之后,这是太迟,当时买方已经没有合约权利可以被放弃,因此买方在另一方面败诉。[35]

相关的例子还有很多,显示了放弃合约单方面权利的课题的重要性。以笔者熟

---

〔34〕 见杨良宜《合约的解释:规则与应用》一书第七章。

〔35〕 见本章之 3.3.4.3.3 段。

悉的航运与国际贸易为例：

1. 在造船合约中，市场急升的时候，买方往往希望越早交船越好，因此会放弃船舶在交船前试航（sea trial）的权利。特别是如果买方并不是自己营运船舶而是在市场上转卖即时赚取利润，他根本不关心船舶的质量问题。

2. 同样是造船合约，如果买方知道或怀疑船厂无法在合约规定的时间内（如3个月），向银行（如进出口银行）取得还款担保（refund guarantee），就会提前通知船厂放弃这个买方单方面的利益，以防止造船合约自动终止。自然买方在做出这个决定时肯定将所有因素考虑在内，做出权衡。如市场急升，并且估计在船舶造出来之前市场的升势也不会改变等。当然，如果买方有向银行融资，还需要说服提供融资的银行同意放弃这个权利。

3. 二手船买卖合约国际上普遍使用的是挪威格式（Norwegian Sale Form）。该标准格式中有一个后续条件，是在合约订立并且买方支付了10%的订金到买方与卖方联名的银行账户（escrow account）或作为信托人（trustee）的卖方律师/经纪人账户后，买方可以派人上船检查船舶情况并对检查结果满意，才需要完成合约。往往在市场急升时，买方希望尽早进行检查（但可能由于船舶的航线不方便安排而快不了）并让卖方交船。而卖方则不着急，毕竟多营运一天就多赚一天的高运费或租金。如果买方对船舶的状况有一定把握（如卖方是一家管理好的船东），就可以考虑放弃这个单方面的权利，不要求检查而要求卖方交船。

4. 不止是造船合约或船舶买卖合约，事实上，大部分只对一方有利的后续条件都可以被单方面弃权。例如，在买卖房屋或其他财产时，合约中经常有条文规定“以银行融资为准”（subject finance）。[36] 如果买方没有成功向银行融资，但因为市场上涨或其他原因，买方决定自己全款买下房屋或其他相关财产。在这种情况下，他可以在合约自动终止或被卖方终止前，单方面放弃该后续条件。在英国枢密院的 Graham v. Pitkin (1992) 1 WLR 403 先例中，相关的房屋买卖合约中有条文写明“subject to the purchaser obtaining a mortgage from the Victoria Mutual Building Society of £ 19,000 for 10 years”。但买方并没有成功取得这笔抵押贷款，卖方想要以此终止合约。买方表示愿意以现金付清余款，但卖方拒绝。显然当时的房价涨了，所以卖方想脱身，但买方想履行。买方于是向法院申请履约指令强制卖方完成交易。枢密院判这个变数条件只是对买方单方面有利的后续条件而不是合约成立的先决条件，也不认为这一变数条件会令这个买卖合约不肯定而变成无效，因此买方可以单方面弃权。

5. 在国际货物买卖中，FOB 买方有时可能要求岸上交货，而不要求卖方将货物装船。其中的原因可能是航运市场高涨，买方租不到船而当时货物市场价格急升，买方也舍不得放弃这票货物。如果双方能达成一致在岸上交货，则没有问题，但如果卖方因为市场上涨想从合约中脱身拒绝，买方能否以货物装船是其单方面利益而他弃

---

〔36〕 参见杨良宜《合约的解释：规则与应用》一书第八章第7段。

权为由,要求卖方在岸上交货?卖方则可以争辩虽然从表面看来将货物装船属于买方单方面的利益,但如果把 FOB 合约改为岸上交货也影响卖方的利益。例如,在原买卖合约下这笔交易属于出口货物,如果在岸上交货则会变为属于本地买卖,无法享受一些政策优惠。总体来说,早前的先例显示了法院对买方企图单方面改变买卖合约的条文是抱有敌意,这方面的先例有:Waxckerbarth v. Mason (1812) 3 Camo 279; Maine Shipping Co. v. Scutcliffe & Co. (1917) 87 LJKB 382; Elton (John) & Co. Ltd. v. Page (Chas) & Co. Ltd. (1920) 4 Lloyd's Rep. 226; Societe Co - operative des Cereales v. La Plata Co. SA (1947) 80 Lloyd's Rep. 530 等。

3.3.4.2　该说法的合理性

这说法的合理性在早期的 Bennett v. Fowler (1840) 48 ER 1197 先例有说明,说是没有理由不允许有权与单方面好处或利益的一方向对方说:"我不要这一个好处,请你继续履行合约其他责任。"该先例的案情涉及土地买卖合约,卖方要证明他有合法的土地产权。因为卖方没有证明这一点,所以买方申请履约指令失败。在上诉到上诉庭时,买方放弃了对这点的要求,不再需要卖方证明产权,因此成功申请了履约指令。Langdale 勋爵说:"... it was the duty of the vendor to make out a good title, and the right of the other party to have it; but I do not know any reason why the purchaser who has that right may not, if he thinks fit, dispense with the performance by the other party of his duty, and waive carrying its objections to the title... The Plaintiff now says, I am willing to waive all the objections, and to accept the title which can be made: the question is, if he has not a right to say so, I am of opinion that the obligation to which a vendor is subject to make out a title is intended for the benefit of the purchaser only, and that if he thinks fit to waive it, he has a right to do so."

3.3.4.3　构成该说法的要件

一方要成功放弃单方面的权利或利益,必须满足三个要件。

3.3.4.3.1　有关条文必须是一方单方面的权利或利益

如果有关条文是一方单方面的权利或利益,完全可以单方面弃权。但如果有关的条文对双方都有利,就轮不到一方单方面放弃,而必须双方达成协议,更改(vary)合约。在 Heron Garage Properties Ltd. v. Moss (1974) 1 WLR 148 先例中,Brightman 大法官说到条文是否只是赋予一方单方面的权利或利益主要看条文的写法,而不必看文字以外的背景,而如果不明显是一方单方面的权利或利益,就不应该允许一方单方面放弃:"Without seeking to define the precise limits within which a contracting party seeking specific performance may waive a condition on the ground that it is intended only for his benefit, it seems to me that in general the proposition only applies where the stipulation is in terms for the exclusive benefit of the plaintiff because it is a power or right vested by the contract in him alone... or where the stipulation is by inevitable implication for the benefit of him alone... If it is not obvious on the face of the contract that the stipulation is for the exclusive benefit of the party seeking to eliminate it, then in my opinion it cannot be struck out unilaterally. I do not think that the court should conduct an enquiry outside the terms of the contract to ascertain where in all the circumstances the benefit lies if the parties have not concluded the matter on the face of the agreement they have signed."

在新西兰的 Globe Holdings Ltd. v. Floratos (1998) 3 NZLR 331 先例中,上诉庭也提到这方面的争议主要是根据合约的解释推断是否只是一方单方面的权利或利益,说:"A party may waive a condition or provision in a contract which is solely for that party's own benefit and is severable. In such a case the other party is denied the right to treat the condition as unsatisfied and is obliged to complete notwithstanding the loss of that advantage. The question is one of construction of the contract. It turns on whether the stipulation is in terms or by necessary implication for the exclusive benefit of the party, and the answer is derived from consideration of the contract as a whole in the light of the surrounding circumstances..."

在近期的 Irwin v. Wilson (2011) EWHC 326 (Ch) 先例中,[37] Blackburne 大法官提到了以上两个先例并总结说:"That seems to me, with respect, to be an entirely accurate summary of the relevant approach."

换言之,这方面的争议主要依靠对合约条文文字上的解释,除了有关的条文外,也要整体看合约来决定这个条文是否为一方单方面的权利或利益。如在稍早介绍的 Heron Garage Properties Ltd. v. Moss (1974) 1 WLR 148 先例中,法院判是合约的第 7 条文(取得经营一个加油站以及相关业务的政府批文的后续条件)不是买方单方面的利益。合约的其他条文显示卖方希望将其他没有出售的土地用作一个出售新车与二手车的展厅。因此,如果买方拿不到批文,显然会影响卖方对其他没有出售的土地的设想。所以,第 7 条文的后续条件对卖方也至关重要,不能让买方单方面放弃。Brightman 大法官说:"Looking at the matter broadly, even if I were allowed to travel outside the terms of the sale agreement, I would not conclude that the condition of town planning consent benefited the purchase alone. A vendor who retains land may be vitally affected by the grant of planning consent for the development of the adjoining land which he is selling off. Such consent may well be important to the maintenance of the value of the land retained. In the present case the redevelopment of the southern part of the site as a petrol filling and service station and car wash might attract motorists to the vicinity of the land upon which the vendors proposed to establish their showroom for the sale of cars. The possible advantage to the vendors of such redevelopment of the adjourning land is obvious ... (买方) could have made the contract unconditional the day after it was

---

〔37〕 该先例在本章之 3.3.4.1 段有介绍。

signed and, subject I suppose to planning consent, have erected a block of offices totally concealing the vendors proposed showroom from the road frontage..."

在 Irwin v. Wilson 先例中，相关合约中名为“递交文件条文”(documents service clause)的第25.1条文可节录如下：“The Completion Date shall be 14 days after the Seller's solicitors shall have served the Buyer's solicitors with copies of: (a) The Office copy entries relating to Title SGL32337, as amended by the Land Registry to show that the correct location Property on the Filed Plan; (b) A Deed of Variation to the Lease dated 21st April 1983, executed by the Freeholder and Seller to replace the existing Lease Plan with a plan showing the correct location and floor layout of the floor plan, drawn to scale and showing a north point and being fully Land Registry compliant..."

证明卖方产权(title)的租借土地保有权(leasehold)[38]文件附录中房屋的位置错误，该条文要求卖方向政府做出澄清与改正。卖方的争议是该条文并非只对买方单方面有利，也可以减少卖方将来因为文件错误面对争议与索赔的风险。卖方的争议被一审的 Madge 大法官接受，但上诉庭推翻了一审法院的判决，Blackburne 大法官判第25.1条文只对买方单方面有利，而卖方争辩的利益太空泛，说：“The nub of the matter... is whether the performance of the term is for the exclusive benefit of the buyer. If performed – and the transaction completes – the claimant(卖方) no longer has any interest in the property of which he was once but is no longer the owner. Defects in his former title cease to be of concern to him. It might have been otherwise if there was evidence that the claimant was the owner or had some interest in the adjoining flat (and was affected therefore by the defect because of the transposition of plans referred to earlier) and in consequence (in right of that other flat) interested in having the error corrected. There was no suggestion, however, that is this case. None of the other matters identified by Mr Carisle(卖方代表大律师) as constituting 'benefit' to the seller from the existence of the documents service term ...."

几年前，笔者(杨大明)曾处理过一个造船合约的争议，外国船东要放弃试航，让船厂尽早交船。笔者帮助船厂拒绝这一要求，争辩说试航并非只是船东单方面的利益。试航涉及船厂的调试，而且如果将来船舶营运时有问题，这对船厂的声誉有影响。这种争议(不论将来会否成立)最终令双方达成了相互妥协的和解协议。不过笔者也怀疑如果最后要通过诉讼解决，在双方提供了试航的有关工作与重要性的专家报告后，法院或仲裁庭是否会接受这是一个双方都有实质利益的条文，或是认为船厂所谓的利益太空泛。

---

〔38〕 这是有限地产权益，常见的有99年、999年、999999年。时限到之后，租权回归原地产所有权人(一般是政府)。

3.3.4.3.2　被弃权的条文必须能与其他合约条文分开

在 Heron Garage Properties Ltd. v. Moss（1974）1 WLR 148 先例中，Brightman 大法官说："There is an added difficulty in the way of Heron's(买方)case. The decision in Hawksley v. Outram（1892）3 Ch 359 suggests that a stipulation cannot be waived if it is inextricably mixed up with other parts of the transaction from which it cannot be severed. Clause 8 of the sale agreement specifies the date for completion. That date under clause 8 is dependent upon the date when Heron receives planning consent without conditions or when Heron is deemed to have approved conditions attached to the planning consent. Nothing is said about the date for completion if Heron waives the condition for planning consent. So it would seem that Heron's unilateral elimination of clause 7 of the sale agreement will also eliminate clause 8 and leave the date for completion in the air."

这一点在本章之 3.3.4.1 段介绍该先例时已经提到，合约第 8 条规定了双方在拿到批文 1 个月后完成交易。如果买方对合约第 7 条单方面弃权，合约第 8 条就无法运作以确定到底在哪天完成交易，即合约第 8 条与合约第 7 条分不开，买方不可以单方面弃权。但如果合约第 8 条换一种写法，如说明"当一切备妥后 1 个月完成交易"或是在考虑到取得批文需要的时间后直接规定了完成交易的具体日期，就不会存在这方面的问题。

3.3.4.3.3　一方弃权时合约必须仍然有效

一方弃权时合约必须仍然有效，因为合约被终止后任何一方都不再存在可以放弃的合约权利。这完全合理与可以理解，一旦合约被终止，就不再有任何权利可以被放弃。在 Irwin v. Wilson（2011）EWHC 326（Ch）先例中，根据合约规定，如果有关的后续条件没有被满足，任何一方可以做出 5 个工作日的通知终止合约。卖方在 2 月 2 日做出了终止合约的通知，而买方律师在第 5 个工作日即 2 月 9 日写信回复说第 25.1 条文是买方单方面的利益，买方弃权，卖方应继续完成合约。表面看来买方的弃权是及时的。之后双方开始诉讼，已经提到上诉庭判是第 25.1 条文确实是买方单方面的利益，并且第 25.1 条文可以与合约其他条文分开，因此买方可以单方面弃权。如果买方弃权，就应该像卖方已经提供了相关信息，或是卖方从来没有提供相关信息的责任一样，法院可以决定完成交易的合理时间。因此，争议的重点是在买方弃权时，买卖合约是否已经被终止，即合约是在一方做出有效的终止通知时就立即终止，还是要在 2 月 9 日后才终止。如果是后者，买方就及时放弃了第 25.1 条中的单方面权利。卖方的争辩是有关条文应解释为一方做出通知后立即终止，5 天的时间是为了让买方清空房屋（假设当时是买方占有房屋）与让卖方退回订金。

在稍早的 Akzo Nobel UK Ltd. v. Arista Tubes Ltd.（2010）EWCA Civ 28 先例中，上诉庭的 Mummery 大法官说："It is common ground that the notice provision must be construed as a whole, in its context and in its ordinary and natural meaning. As I read... the parties clearly agreed that, if the Property Consents had not been obtained by

12 months after the date of the agreement, they were entitled to serve notice in writing terminating the parties' pobligations in respect of the premises ... On service of the notice the position of the parties was that Arista(买方)would have to vacate the premises by the end of the notice period... The language of the paragraph does not allow Akzo(卖方)to reverse or vary that position... such as by obtaining the Property Consents at any point down to the expiration of the notice..."

虽然该先例中合约的写法与 Irwin v. Wilson 先例中合约的写法不同,Blackburne 大法官还是认为结论应该一样,所以判买方律师弃权的信件是太迟。因此,如果感觉需要弃权,一定要尽快,以免合约已经自动终止或被对方终止。

3.4 因选择而弃权

首先可节录一些权威说法,[39] 在澳大利亚的 Craine v. Colonial Mutual Fire Insurance Co. Ltd. (1920) 28 CLR 305 先例中,Isaacs 大法官针对因选择而弃权说:"A waiver must be intentional act with knowledge... **First**, 'some distinct act ought to be done to constitute a waiver' ... **next**, it must be 'intentional', that is, such as either expressly or by imputation of law indicates intention to treat the matter as if the condition did not exist or as if the forfeiture or breach of condition had not occurred; and **lastly**, it must be 'with knowledge', and essential supported by many authorities... 'Waiver' is a doctrine of some arbitrariness introduced by the law to prevent a man... taking up two inconsistent positions... it is a conclusion of law when the necessary facts are established. It looks chiefly to the conduct and position of the person who advantage to which he would not otherwise have been entitled, so as to deny to him a later election to the contrary... His knowledge is necessary, or he cannot be said to have... elected... estoppel is separated from waiver in point of principle by a very broad line of demarcation. First of all, the law of estoppel looks chiefly at the situation of the person relying on the estoppel, next, as a consequence of the first, the knowledge of the person sought to be estopped is immaterial; thirdly, as a further consequence, it is not essential that the person sought to be estopped should have acted with an intention to deceive; fourthly, conduct, short of positive acts, is sufficient... estoppel may be established where waiver cannot, and... waiver may be found where estoppel does not exist."

要构成因选择而弃权,首先,弃权方必须有一些明显的行动(或不行动)。其次,弃权方必须是有意识的行动。弃权方明示或默示其有意图当做合约条件条文不存在,或者没收或违约的行为没有发生。最后,弃权方必须知道自己的权利或相关的事实。弃权是用来防止一方可以同时保有两种相互对立的权利,但却迟迟不表态导致

---

〔39〕 主要是针对对违约的弃权(waiver of breach)与商业选择权的弃权。这与上一段针对的对合约单方面权利的放弃精神上一样。

另一方无所适从而带来的不公平。至于什么是相互对立的权利,大部分情况下是清楚的,如终止合约或是确认合约继续存在与有效。但也会有困难的情况,如在本书第一章之6.5段介绍的 Stocznia Gdynia SA v. Gearbulk Holdings Ltd.（2009）1 Lloyd's Rep. 461 先例,上诉庭推翻了一审法院的判决,判是在该先例中,根据合约明示条文终止合约与以普通法的违约/毁约终止合约,两者的救济没有矛盾与对立,而只是互补。原告终止合约的通知不视为做出任何选择,而被视为同时对违约/毁约的接受。如果能够满足构成弃权的要件,这就是法律上的结论。是否弃权主要看所谓弃权方的言行,如果其言行显示了他选择了其中一个权利,之后就不能再选择另一个对立的权利。

在近期的 The "Happy Day"（2002）2 Lloyd's Rep. 487 先例中,Potter 大法官针对因选择而弃权说:"So far as waiver by election is concerned, the basic proposition is that where two possible remedies or courses of action are to his knowledge open to X and he has communicated his intention to follow one course or remedy in such a manner as to lead Y to believe that his choice has been made, he will not later be permitted to resile from that position[40]: ... Waiver by election is essentially an illustration of the general principle that a party to a contract may not both approbate and reprobate[41]... In The Kanchenjunga [1990] 1 Lloyd's Rep. 391 at 397 – 399, Lord Goff of Chieveley dealt at some length with the principles underlying the doctrine of waiver by election in relation principally to the situation where: 'Characteristically, the effect of the new situation is that a party becomes entitled to determine or to rescind the contract, or to reject an uncontractual tender of performance; but, in theory at least, a less drastic course of action might become available to him under the terms of the contract. In all cases, he has in the end to make his election, not as a matter of obligation, but in the sense that, if he does not do so, the time may come when the law takes the decision out of his hands, either by holding him to have elected not to exercise the right which has become available to him, or sometimes by holding him to have elected to exercise it...'"

3.4.1　构成因选择而弃权的要件

早在 Scarf v. Jardine（1882）7 App. Cas. 345（HL）先例中,Blackburn 勋爵针对选择就说:"... a party **in his own mind** has thought that he would **choose one of two remedies**, even though he has written it down on a memorandum or has indicated it in some other way, that alone will not bind him; but so soon as he has not only determined

---

〔40〕 如果 X 知道他有两个对立的救济或诉因,并且做出的言行显示其意图是选择其中一种救济或诉因,令 Y 以为他已经做出了选择,那么 X 之后就不允许撤回这个选择。

〔41〕 因选择而弃权本质上是合约方不能"一脚踏两船",同时选择两个对立的权利,迟迟不表态,这显然对另一方不利与不公平。

to follow one of his remedies but has **communicated it to the other side** in such a way as to lead the opposite party to believe that he has made that choice, he has completed his election and can go no further; and whether he intended it or not, if he has done an **unequivocal act**—I mean an act which would be justifiable if he had elected one way and would not be justifiable if he had elected the other way—the fact of his having done that **unequivocal act to the knowledge of the persons concerned is an election.**"(加黑部分是笔者的强调)

分析构成"因选择而弃权"(waiver by election)要件的最重要的先例是 The "Kanchenjunga"(1990)1 Lloyd's Rep. 391 的贵族院先例。该先例涉及 8 个连续航次的油轮租约。相关的 Kanchenjunga 轮是一艘 20 万吨级油轮,属于印度船东。装港是承租人指定的波斯湾的一个安全港口。租约在 1978 年 8 月订立,当时伊朗与伊拉克虽然关系紧张但没有战事,所以租约允许去的装港包括个别伊朗港口,如 Kharg Island 港。到了最后一个航次,时为 1980 年 11 月 19 日,该船舶被分租的承租人下令前往 Kharg Island 港装货。但当时两伊战争已经开始,伊朗的 Kharg Island 港经常被伊拉克派出的飞机轰炸。在后来的仲裁中,仲裁庭认定承租人指定 Kharg Island 港时,该港口不安全,即承租人违反了租约中要指定安全港口的承诺。但印度船东并没有对承租人的违约做出抗拒或有所保留,而是要求船长把船舶开往 Kharg Island 港,并在 11 月 23 日抵达后递交了通知书,之后也多次做出要求承租人尽早安排靠泊装货等言行。船东在 11 月 25 日因被船长告知 Kharg Island 港不断有高射炮的射击,才首次在与承租人的通信中提出港口不安全。而到了 11 月 30 日,船舶才被告知可以靠泊装货,但由于坏天气的延误而靠不了泊。期间伊拉克飞机轰炸,船长与船员看来被吓坏,就起锚把船舶开走,并且没有再回到 Kharg Island 港装货。之后船东与承租人的通信往来中,船东要求承租人重新指定安全港口,而承租人坚持船舶返回 Kharg Island 港,并表示有其他船舶在 Kharg Island 港装货。12 月中,双方各自委任了律师,互相指称对方违约/毁约(repudiatory breach),自己接受违约/毁约并终止合约。

在之后的仲裁中,仲裁员判是 Kharg Island 港是不安全港口,承租人指定 Kharg Island 港并要求 Kanchenjunga 轮靠泊违反了租约。这就带来了另一个争议,即船东的言行有否构成对承租人违约的弃权或禁反言。仲裁庭认为船东的言行没有构成弃权或禁反言,这被承租人上诉,一直到贵族院。Goff 大法官认为,船东命令船舶开往 Kharg Island 港的言行构成了因选择(选择不抗拒承租人的违约)而弃权,而不是禁反言。Goff 大法官分析说:"'Waiver'... may refer to a forbearance from exercising a right or to an abandonment of a right. Here we are concerned with waiver in the sense of abandonment of a right which arises by virtue of the party making the election. Election itself is a concept which may be relevant in more than one context. **In the present case, we are concerned with an election** which may arise in the context of a binding contract, when a state of affairs comes into existence in which one party becomes entitled, either under the terms of the contract or by the general law, to exercise a right, and he has to decide whether or not to do so. His decision, being a matter of choice for him, is called in law an election... Characteristically, the effect of the new situation is that a party becomes entitled to determine or to rescind the contract, or **to reject an uncontractual tender of performance**; but, in theory at least, a less drastic course of action might become available to him, under the terms of the contract. In all cases, he has in the end to make his election, not as a matter of obligation, but in the sense that, if he does not do so, the time may come when the law takes the decision out of his hands, either by holding him to have elected not to exercise the right which has become available to him, or sometimes by holding him to have elected to exercise it... **In particular, where with knowledge of the relevant facts a party has acted in a manner which is consistent only with his having chosen one of the two alternative and inconsistent courses of action then open to him** – for example, to determine a contract or alternatively to affirm it – **he is held to have made his election accordingly**... **It can be communicated to the other party by words or conduct**; though, perhaps because a right, he will only be held to have done so if **he has so communicated his election to the other party in clear and unequivocal terms**... Once an election is made, however, it is final and binding... Moreover, it does not require consideration to support it, and so it is to be distinguished form an express or implied agreement, such as a variation of the relevant contract, which traditionally requires consideration to render it binding in English law."(加黑部分是笔者的强调)

根据Goff勋爵的判决,构成因选择而弃权要满足两个要件:弃权方知道令他要在两个对立的权利中做出选择的事实(knowledge of the facts which show that it has to choose between two inconsistent courses of conduct);弃权方通过明示或者默示的言行,让对方或者客观与合理的人士(实践中就是法官或仲裁员)看来选择放弃了其中一个权利。因选择而弃权不像"禁反言"(estoppel)需要看对方是否依赖有关言行并蒙受损害(detrimental reliance),而纯粹是看弃权方的言行。

一旦做出了选择,另一个对立的权利就被放弃。在The "Kanchenjunga"先例中,贵族院判是船东明知道相关的所有情况(如同一船东的姐妹船当时在Kharg Island港营运,所以知道该港的战争风险与程度),但通过其言行,让承租人看来选择跟从而不是拒绝承租人的指示,前往并在Kharg Island这个不安全港口停留。所以,船东不能之后在战争风险与危险程度没有改变的情况下再反悔,起锚把船舶开走。船东这样做属于违约/毁约。

3.4.2 因选择而弃权的形式

因选择而弃权可以是通过口头的(oral)或书面的(written)语言,也可以从行为推断(inference by conduct)。通常选择是以书面的形式做出,口头也有,但举证力弱了很多。尤其是在国际商务交往中,以口头形式构成的因选择而弃权不多,一般都是书面的,如发电传、传真给对方,讲明选择两个对立的权利中的一个,就是很明确的对另一个权利的弃权。

不过事实上,大部分的因选择而弃权都不是语言,特别是明确的语言构成,如说"我放弃我的某某权利"。而往往是通过行动或不行动。简单的例子就是选择方或弃权方在一个亏本合约的明示或默示条文下有终止合约的黄金机会,但弃权方竟然要求对方履行该合约的部分条文,显然这在任何客观与合理的人士看来都是选择方或弃权方选择不行使终止合约的权利或选择放弃终止合约的权利。至于不行动,就会是选择方或弃权方拖拖拉拉,犹豫不决,超过了合约规定或是法律默示的做出选择的合理时间,导致弃权。

例如,一份涉外合约中规定所有合约争议须提交北京仲裁,可一方/外方产生争议后却将案件拿到英国法院起诉。对此,英国法院有很明确的做法,就是被告可以要求法院中止(stay)原告提出的诉讼,因为有1958年《承认和执行外国仲裁裁决公约》(《纽约公约》)的规定。但中止申请必须在对方起诉后随即提出,若被告提出中止前在该诉讼中采取了进一步的行动(take further step in the proceeding),如收到原告的起诉书(points of claim)后提交了答辩书(points of defense),或者要求原告就官司费用提供担保(security for costs),就会构成放弃要求法院中止诉讼的弃权行为,被告事后再也不能向法院申请中止了。这种对中止申请的限制,正是基于因选择而弃权的理论。不难看出,如果没有弃权理论对上述中止申请的限制,会造成很多不公平的情况。

首先,被告进一步的诉讼行为已令原告相信,被告不会再坚持合约的仲裁条文去要求法院中止诉讼而将该案件转由北京仲裁,原告因此继续开展其在英国法院的诉讼,投入了相当的精力及律师费。如果半途被告才提出中止申请,而法院也允许的话,先前费时的诉讼将作废,所花的费用也白费了。其次,若允许先应诉,抗辩后中止,很可能给被告取巧的机会。如被告原本就认为争议去北京仲裁不见得有利,于是就在英国法院应诉抗辩。结果诉讼进行下来,被告发觉法官似乎更倾向原告的观点或对他有敌意,于是就根据《纽约公约》提出中止申请,要求把案子拿去北京仲裁。这显然是在取巧,法院不会容许的。所以,英美、新加坡以及中国香港特区的法院在对中止的弃权上都有很明确的时限规定,以防不公。因此,对要适用合约仲裁条文的被告而言,一旦被对方在英国、美国等外国法院起诉,最安全的做法就是马上向该法院申请中止诉讼,将案件转去北京仲裁。这是被告必须采取的第一步。若在1958年《纽约公约》缔约国的法院,只要仲裁条文符合公约规定,这种中止申请几乎一定能成功。否则,被告在应诉进行了一段时期后再提出中止,在英国等法院是行不通的,因为首先有立法的规定(如英国是1996年《仲裁法》),其次有弃权理论对这种迟到的中止权利的限制。

上述所举的被告进一步参与法院诉讼的行为是以行为构成弃权的典型例子。而有时当事人的不行动(negative act),即该方没有按合约或法律的要求做出某种行为,也同样会构成弃权。这较多表现在出现两个完全对立的权利(inconsistent right)时,当事人对合约或法律赋予的选择权(option)的行使上。如租约中著名的销约期条文,规定若租用的船舶过了销约期仍未备妥装货(或交船),承租人可以选择终止租约。但这种选择最迟必须在船舶备妥并递交准备就绪通知书(notice of readiness)之后的合理时间(或合约规定的时间)内做出,否则就属于弃权,之后不能再解约。又如期租规定租期1年,承租人有选择权续租1年,该选择必须在还船前1个月做出,如过了时间不做出选择,承租人选择续租的权利也就被放弃了。弃权理论之所以要针对这类情况,无非也是出于公平的考虑。如有关租约销约期的情况,船舶过了销约期才抵达装港并递交准备就绪通知书(notice of readiness),可承租人当时却没宣布解约,甚至还安排了装货。但装了两天以后,可能由于运费市场下降得很厉害,或者承租人备货出了问题,余货到不了,承租人就突然提出要把已装的货卸下,宣布船舶过了销约期,因此他要解约。这明显是承租人在取巧,若让其此时解约,显然对船东很不公平。所以,普通法上会视承租人先前不及时宣布解约并装货上船,均已构成弃权的言行,即放弃解约而选择将租约继续维持下去。

订约中出现“误述”(misrepresentation)情况时,也存在这类选择权行使的问题。如果一方知道对方在谈判中曾经有过重大甚至欺诈性误述令其有可使合约无效的权利,但他不迅速采取明确的行动取消(rescind)合约,就等于放弃了这种法定的权利。同样,对于在“胁迫”(duress)下订立的合约,被胁迫方也必须在合理时间内行使法律赋予的废约权(the right to rescind)。这是法律上的要求,被胁迫方下不了决心或水平低,不知道自己有这个权利将会构成对该废约权的放弃。因此,被威胁方要以胁迫为由废止合约,同样要做到迅速及时。在著名的 The “Atlantic Baron” (1979) 1 Lloyd’s Rep. 89 高院先例中,被告船厂签约以议定的价格(美元计价)为原告船东建造一艘油轮,原告分五期付款。第一期付款后,美元汇率下跌,贬值了10%,结果船厂在无正当理由的情况下威胁终止造船合约,除非余下的各期付款均追加10%。原告由于当时已将该船预早租出,并且是很赚钱的长期租约,船厂不交船,原告船东损失太大,对他来讲已无其他更合理的选择,于是只好同意船厂加价300万美元的要求。原告并无抗议地支付了加价后的各期付款,但却又在交船8个多月后不服气向法院起诉船厂胁迫,要求判对方退还那笔额外支付的10%的款项。最后法官认为,有关加价的协议虽是在胁迫下签订,但原告提出胁迫诉讼索回多付款额的行动实在太迟,已构成对有关加价的合约修改协议的确认(affirm a voidable contract),因而要受其约束。结果原告败诉,不能再依赖胁迫这一诉因废止修改协议,从而索回多付的价款。

同样的道理,期租中船东若遇到承租人不按时付租的情况,他依约撤船的权利(通常租约条文会有这样的权利)也必须在合理时间内及时行使,否则同样可能构成弃权。这里一样是出于公平合理以及防止取巧的目的。实际上,如果没有这种对船东撤船时间上的限制,船东很容易取巧。他可以在租金晚付时先不行动,而以后等到租金市场上涨后又提出撤船,而这样明显对承租人造成很大的不公。可见,有选择权的一方如果在一定时间内(合约规定或判定为合理的时间内)不行使选择权,实际上就等于选择了放弃这项选择权:The "Laconia" (1977) 1 Lloyd's Rep. 315;The "Scaptrade" (1981) 2 Lloyd's Rep. 425 等先例。

在涉及货物买卖的信用证合约方面,也存在一方不行动即构成弃权的例子。如根据国际商会制订的《跟单信用证统一惯例》1983 年修订本(UCP 400)第 16 条 c 款规定,银行必须在合理的时间内检查用以结汇的付运单证。而 1994 年修订本(UCP 500)第 13 条 b 款更是明确规定了 7 个银行工作日的检查期限。2007 年修订本(UCP 600)第 14 条 b 款进一步把检查期限缩短到 5 天。换言之,若银行未能在收到结汇的付运单证后一定时间内提出付运单证存在不符点并拒受该单证,即构成弃权,事后不能再以付运单证不符合信用证要求等理由退回付运单证并拒绝结汇,这在 Westminster Bank Ltd. v. Banco Nazionale di Credito (1928) 31 Lloyd's Rep. 306 先例中已经明确。此外,根据香港法院对 Hip Hing Hip Fat Co. Ltd. v. Daiwa Bank (1991) 2 HKLR35 先例的判决,若提交结汇信用证的付运单证有不符点(discrepancies),银行还必须在第一次给交单人(寄单行或受益人本身)的拒受单证通知(notice of refusal)上指出所有不符点。银行不能在给了第一份拒受通知之后发现有更多的不符点后,再给第二份通知。这样,等于银行在做出第一份指出结汇单证有某些不符信用证要求之处的拒受单证通知后,同样构成了对以其他未被提及的单证不符点为由拒受单证的权利的放弃,若交单人稍后在信用证规定期限前修正了银行第一次提出的不符点并重新提交了单证,银行不能再以单证尚有其他不符点为由拒受单证并拒绝结汇。之所以信用证有这些对银行验单、拒单的要求,银行违反了即构成弃权,也是出于公平的理由。因为银行只有及时、全面地通知了受益人银行拒受付运单证以及拒收的具体理由(单证不符点),信用证受益人才有机会在信用证交单结汇期限前及时充分的修正结汇单证。否则,若银行迟迟不做出拒受通知,或做出的拒受通知只提及单证的部分不符点,等到信用证交单结汇期快到甚至已过时才通知说,单证有不符或还有其他先前未提及的不符不能结汇,受益人根本就不能有合理的时间安排修正不符及重新交单,这对受益人是明显不公平的。所以,就需要有这种弃权的理论或规定约束银行检查、拒受单证的行为。

在解释有关的言行(无论是口头还是书面或是行为)时必须严格,不能轻易就解释为构成因选择而弃权。毕竟一个人也不会轻易放弃自己的权利,所以构成弃权的言行必须清楚无误并给予局限的解释。举一个国际货物买卖的例子,如果买方在卸港发现货不对版,他可以选择拒货。而如果买方选择了接受货物(可能是各种商业上的原因,如货物的市场上涨),这只应解释为他放弃了拒货的权利,而不能解释为他同时放弃了索赔损失的权利。但如果情况有所不同,卖方告知了买方有关货物的瑕疵(现实中更多是告知货物会延误付运),而买方回答说不要紧,这就可能被解释为同时放弃了拒货与索赔损失的权利。这种弃权经常被称为"完全弃权"(total waiver),往往会同时涉及"禁反言"(estoppel)的说法,因为被陈述方往往会对弃权方的言行做出依赖从而进行下一步的行动，并因此蒙受损害。这可部分节录《Chitty on Contracts》(第32版，2015年)一书之22-047段，如下："... It is however important to distinguish between the case in which a party waives his right to treat the contract as repudiated but does not abandon his right to claim damages for the loss suffered as a result of the breach and the case where the innocent party waives not only his right terminate performance of the contract but also his claim for damages for the breach. The former is an example of waiver by election, whereas the latter is more properly classified as a species of waiver by estoppel."

3.5 与弃权有关的合约明示条文

在《Chitty on Contracts》(第32版，2015年)一书之22-045段，说："**Contracting out of waiver.** It would appear that there is no general principle of law that parties to a contract cannot restrict the operation of the doctrine of waiver by the terms of their contract. In State Securities Plc. v. Initial Industry Ltd. (2004) EWHC 3482 (Ch.), Jonathan Gaunt QC sitting as a Deputy Judge of the High Court, stated: 'I can, however, see no reason in principle why the parties to an equipment lease... or other commercial contract, should not be free to stipulate that a particular act, such as payment of a rental instalment should not be taken to waive a right to terminate for an earlier breach. After all, such a provision may be very convenient and operate to the benefit of both parties. The finance compny may want to encourage the lessee to correct the breach but not want him to fall behind with his payments while he does so. It may be in the interests of the lessee that the finance company should not have to take an early decision whether to terminate.' However, it cannot be assumed that the courts in all cases will give effect to a term of the contract which purports to exclude or limit the operation of the doctrine of waiver; in some circumstances the term of the contract may not suffice to deny effect to a clear and unequivocal representation made by one party to the contract."

上述节录的说法完全可以理解，毕竟弃权是普通法原则，即默示地位，而合约方可以通过明示条文超越普通法的默示地位。[42] 这与一方违约后，另一方在通信往来中说明保留权利(reserve rights)等[43]一样，能否排除弃权(或禁反言)的适用还是要看措辞/用字是否足够清楚无误，与弃权方其他的言行是否一致等。正如上述节录的最后一句所说，明示条文在某些情况下不足以超越一个事后清楚无误的弃权言行。

接下来笔者对几种常见的明示条文进行介绍。

3.5.1 不弃权条文(non-waiver clause)

这种条文会在各种不同的合约中出现，如笔者近期在一个仲裁中所涉及的货物

---

〔42〕 参见杨良宜《合约的解释：规则与应用》一书第七章。

〔43〕 参见本书第四章之6.5段。

买卖合约中就见到不弃权条文,如下:"No relaxation, forbearance, delay, or indulgence by the Seller enforcing any of its rights, terms and conditions therein nor the granting of any time by the Seller to the Buyer shall prejudice, affect or restrict the Seller's rights and powers thereunder nor shall any waiver of any breach operate as a waiver of any further breaches."

这种条文的重要性与起到的作用可以保险合约为例。保险合约中经常出现弃权与禁反言的争议,如被保险人在投保时没有做出全面披露,本来保险人可以回避该保单,[44]但保险人仍然做出要求被保险人支付保费(premium)或签发保单(policy)等看来矛盾的言行。发生争议最多并有危险被视为构成弃权或禁反言(包括承诺性禁反言)的是在事故发生后,被保险人有明显违约的行为(最常见的是被保险人违反了保单明示规定的尽快通知保险人有关事故的先决条件[45]),但保险人在明知或应该知道有违反的情况下,没有马上或尽快拒绝赔付,[46]而是对有关事故进行调查[47]或向被保险人做出其他可以被解读为不拒绝赔付的言行。这些千变万化的言行可以包括双方谈判希望达成和解,[48]或向被保险人要求进一步的消息,或是对被保险人做出一些建议,[49]甚至将向第三人或被第三人索赔的诉讼接管过来[50]等。

---

〔44〕 1906年英国《海上保险法》之 section 18。

〔45〕 这种条文在许多保单,特别是责任保险或再保出现,如 Kosmar Villa Holidays Plc. v. Trustees of Syndicate 1243 (2008) EWCA Civ 147 等先例。

〔46〕 曾经有不少先例是保险人明知道被保险人违反了先决条件,但没有在合理时间内拒绝赔付,判是构成"因选择而弃权"(waiver by election)。但在 Kosmar Villa Holidays Plc. v. Trustees of Syndicate 1243(2008) EWCA Civ 147 先例中,上诉庭推翻了一审高院([2007] EWHC 458)的判决,澄清因选择而弃权不适用在这种情况,因为违反先决条件类似违反承诺性保证(promissory warranty),会即时在法律上自动免除保险人赔付的责任,这样就不再要求保险人做出选择。重要的还是看保险人的言行是否构成禁反言,包括言行是否是清楚无误,是否会被被保险人依赖等。这方面在本章之5.2.1段有进一步介绍,包括对 J. Kirkaldy & Sons Ltd. v. Walker (1999) 1 Lloyd's Rep. IR 410 等先例的介绍。

〔47〕 Donnison v. Employer's Accident and Life Stock Insurance (1897) 24 R 681; Sproul v. National Fire Insurance Co. (1925) 1 DLR 1152; King v. Commercial Union Insurance Company of New York 306 F Supp 9 (1969)等先例。

〔48〕 这一般不会被视为构成禁反言的言行,毕竟这种谈判通常会说明是无损害。另可见 Fortisbank SA v. Trenwick International Ltd. (2005) EWHC 399 先例(50段);Inframatrix Investments Ltd. v. Dean Construction (2011) EWHC 1947 先例(62段)等。

〔49〕 Kosmar Villa Holidays Plc. v. Trustees of Syndicate 1243 (2007) EWHC 458 先例(75-80段)等。

〔50〕 Soole v. Royal Insurance Co. Ltd. (1971) 2 Lloyd's Rep. 332;Kosmar Villa Holidays Plc. v. Trustees of Syndicate 1243 (2008) EWCA Civ 147 等先例。在英国法律中,如果保险人全数赔付了被保险人,可以根据代位求偿(subrogation)将被保险人可能已经开始的诉讼接管过来。但保险人如果还没有赔付,插手被保险人的诉讼就会面对两方面的问题。一是保险人法律上没有这一权利,二是有可能被视为弃权或禁反言的言行。所以像 Soole v. Royal Insurance Co. Ltd. 先例,保单中会有一条明示条文允许保险人接管有关的诉讼。

但被保险人延误通知保险人的事情经常发生，如在 Kosmar Villa Holidays Plc. v. Trustees of Syndicate 1243（2008）EWCA Civ 147 先例中，案情涉及旅游公司安排的责任保险。在该先例中，该旅游公司延误向保险人做出发生了承保事故的通知，同时在其他 16 个同类事故中，该旅游公司也延误向保险人做出通知，延误时间长短不一。但很多时候即使保险人知道这一赔付的先决条件有被违反（特别是延误时间不长），也不会马上拒绝赔付。因为如果一旦被保险人延迟通知保险人，保险人就马上拒绝赔付可能会对公司的声誉造成影响。发展下去，完全有可能是保险人调查后，发现有其他更加说得通的理由（如火灾是由于纵火造成）可以拒绝赔付，或是即使要赔付，金额也非常小等。没有必要一旦被保险人延误通知，保险人就马上拒付。但为了避免事后对事故进行调查等的言行构成弃权或禁反言，保险人往往需要在合约/保单中加入不弃权条文，以保护自己将来拒付的权利。

这种不弃权条文在海上保险合约是经常出现，如在海上货物运输保险的 Institute Cargo Clauses（A）的第 17 条文，Institute Cargo Clauses（C）的第 17 条文；在货物战争险与罢工险的 Institute War Clauses（Cargo）的第 12 条文，Institute Strikes Clauses 的第 12 条文；在船壳险的 Institute Time Clauses（Hull）的第 20 条文与 Institute Voyage Clauses（Hull）的第 20 条文等。船壳险的不弃权条文可节录如下："Measures taken by the Assured or the Underwriters with the object of saving, protecting or recovering the subject – matter insured shall not be considered as waiver or acceptance of abandonment or otherwise prejudice the right of either party."

此条文经常与施救条文（sue and labor clause）放在一起，因为在海上货物运输船舶出现了意外事件之后，保险人经常需要委任律师或其他专业人士对事故进行调查，看事故是否是由受保的风险导致。另保险人对事故的原因进行调查，如是否是船舶不适航所导致，以准备将来可能需要代位求偿向船东索赔货损货差。此外，保险人也会参与或协助很多急需处理的工作，如将货物转船付运，或是将易腐的货物立即拍卖等。至于船壳险的保险公司就会参与安排对事故船舶的救助，决定船舶损坏的情况下如何修理与在哪里进行修理等。为了避免这些言行会构成弃权或禁反言导致失去拒绝赔付的权利，货物或是船壳的保险人都需要这种不弃权条文的保护。

至于在岸上各种不同类别的保险，这种不弃权条文不像海上保险这样在标准格式保单普遍存在与使用，但仍然十分常见。如在 Yorkshire Insurance Co. , Ltd. v. Craine（1922）12 Lloyd's Rep. 399 先例中，相关条文可节录如下："19. – **Waiver.** No provision or requirement of this policy requiring any matter or thing to be done, or to be written or endorsed hereon, shall be deemed waived by reason of any alleged notice or waiver which has not been expressly written or endorsed hereon, nor shall the Company be deemed to have waived any provision or condition of this policy, or any forfeiture thereunder, by any requirement, act, or proceeding on its part relating to the appraisement of any alleged loss, unless such provision, condition or forfeiture, be expressly stated in writing to be waived by the Company."

这种条文显然对保险人有利,会起到一定的保护作用。法院承认这一类的条文(包括完整合约条文)可以排除弃权或禁反言:Lloyd v. MGL (Rugby) Ltd. (2007) EWCA Civ 153; Jet2. com Ltd. v. Blackpool Airport Ltd. (2010) EWHC 3166 (Comm)等先例。但由于这种条文被视为单方面保护保险人的利益,所以会针对保险人解释:[51] R v. Paulson (1921) 1 AC 271 先例。所以保险人必须注意如下方面:(1)像免责条文(exception clause)一样,不弃权条文必须写清楚包括哪些可能被视为弃权或禁反言的言行。如果保险人的言行没有被包括在相关的不弃权条文中,则该条文还是起不了保护的作用。(2)即使有不弃权条文,法院还是会全面解释保险人的所有言行,总体来看是否构成弃权或禁反言。不弃权条文只会作为部分的证据,而不是决定性。所以,如果涉及长时间的调查(因为通常也表示双方的交往繁多,容易被挑出有问题的言行),或在接手的诉讼中发现了与将来可能拒绝赔付有关的事实,保险人最好还是多向被保险人做出是在保留权利下继续调查或诉讼的特定声明。(3)这种条文(特别是印本条文)在一些针对消费者的岸上保险,考虑到《Unfair Contract Terms Directive》(93/13/EEC)与《The Unfair Terms in Consumer Contracts Regulations》(SI 1999/2083)等相关法律规定,不一定有效。

3.5.2 批准条文(approval clause)

很多类别的合约会涉及需要(或根据明示条文或行业习惯做法)让一方批准另一方的工作或备妥,如工程或建造合约的设计或图表需要在进行工程或生产前先让雇主批准,或是雇主或买方提供的设备要先让承建商或建造商检查与批准,或是船舶在装货前让承租人检查并批准是备妥与清洁才装货等。这种安排与做法通常对双方都有好处,毕竟雇主、买方或承租人(发货人)会对他的要求更熟悉,多一重检查与批准会减少出纰漏的机会。但之后如果不幸发生问题,如工程或产品有缺陷,需要负责的一方经常会以对方曾经检查与批准作为辩护。这等于是把检查与批准视为弃权或禁反言的言行。但有不少这方面的先例都不认同这钟抗辩,一方面是这一安排与做法对双方都有好处,不应该打击检查与批准的一方,令他一旦做出检查与批准就会把责任接过来。

另一方面是涉及弃权,在工程合约中,雇主通常委任一位建筑师或工程师进行检查与批准,这就带来这些专业人士是否有(真正授权或表面授权)代表雇主放弃对这些缺陷向承建商追责的权利。在 Sean Wilken QC 与 Karim Ghaly 先生所著的《The Law of Waiver, Variation, and Estoppel》(第 3 版,2012 年)一书之 19.13 段至 19.14 段说,这些专业人士不会有这种表见授权。毕竟这些专业人士被委任只是为了保护雇主的利益,即使这些专业人士有疏忽没有察觉明显的缺陷也是违反了与雇主之间的合约,是不会让犯错的承建商享有这个好处:East Ham Corporation Council v. Ber-

---

〔51〕 关于针对原则(*contra proferentem*),可见杨良宜的《合约的解释:规则与应用》一书第四章第 5 段。

nard Sunley (1966) AC 406 等先例。这些专业人士也没有责任指出与警告承建商工作的不足:AMF International Ltd. v. Magnet Bowling (1968) 1 WLR 1028 等先例。弃权不能成立的另一个原因是,弃权需要弃权方知道自己的权利与有关的事实,考虑到专业人士不会每天 24 小时在工地上检查与监督,这种检查与批准也通常只是表面与简略地检查,所以对缺陷的知情程度肯定有限。并且一些工程缺陷的性质属于潜在或隐藏的缺陷,从表面看不出来,而也有不少缺陷会随着工程每日进行而检查不出来,这样就不能说专业人士知道自己的权利与有关的事实。另是对于一些表面就能看出的明显缺陷,很难想象专业人士会不指出,而即使专业人士真的严重疏忽没有指出,并且这行为可以构成弃权,也只是针对这些表面就能看出的明显缺陷的弃权。

禁反言的适用也有两方面的困难,一是与上一段一样,在专业人士不知道有缺陷的情况下,无法对某些特定的缺陷做出清楚无误的陈述或承诺;二是依赖并蒙受损害(detrimental reliance)的要件无法满足。首先,承建商必须证明依赖了专业人士明确无误的陈述或承诺而改变了地位,即承建商原本想要修正这个缺陷,但在向专业人士指出或被专业人士发现该缺陷后,专业人士做出清楚无误的陈述或承诺不需要修正,而承建商因此没有做出修正。其次,承建商必须因为依赖而蒙受了损害,即事后再做出修正比当时修正要花费更多的时间与金钱。这样,可以说即使禁反言可以适用,适用范围也非常有限。但这种案例还是有,如在 Acme Investments v. York Structural Steel (1974) 9 NBR (2d) 699 先例中,雇主的代理人做出为了节省费用可以对屋顶做出改变的陈述,之后就不能再索赔屋顶改变导致的损失。另在 Update Construction Ltd. v. Rozelle Child Care Centre (1990) 9 ACLR 66 先例中,有关合约规定工程的更改必须以书面形式做出,但是雇主的代理人口头通知了有关更改并同意付钱,之后就被禁反言,不能拒绝承担对有关修改做出支付的责任。

在航运被最广泛使用的期租标准格式 NYPE 标准格式第 8 条文规定,装卸作业是承租人的责任,但要在船长监督下进行(under the supervision of the captain)。这就导致争议,如果发生货损货差,是承租人还是船东的责任。在贵族院的 Court Line v. Canadian Transport (1940) 67 Lloyd's Rep. 161 重要先例中,法院借鉴了建筑合约中的情况,即工程在专业人士监督下进行不代表责任有改变,除非在监督期间船长有过积极地干预,并被装卸工人依赖。如在 The "Ciechocinek" (1976) 1 Lloyd's Rep. 485 先例中,案情涉及程租合约,装卸作业由船东负责。承租人的代表在装货时坚持一种装法并向船东保证没有问题,但最后堆装出问题并导致货损,这样承租人与货方面对船东就被禁反言。

众所周知,在海上运输合约中,船东要负责船舶适航与适货。但有很多涉及清洁货物(特别是石油产品)的运输合约中规定或是行业的习惯做法上要求发货人在装货前上船检查船舱是否清洁与适货。这样如果之后发生货物污染,船东常常以发货人已经检查过为由拒绝承担责任。但法律不会支持船东的争议,毕竟已经在本段一开始提过这种安排与做法对双方都有好处。如果发货人上船检查时发现问题,船东可以补救,从而减少货损的发生。但如果发货人一旦上船检查并批准,就要承担船舶不适货的责任显然不是好的政策,也不公平。毕竟发货人上船检查的时间很有限,能看到的范围也有限。如发货人能看到船舱但检查不到输油管道是否清洁,货物污染的责任让发货人承担显然不公平。

为了避免这种争议,有些合约中会有明示条文说明,如在笔者(杨良宜)近期涉及的造船合约中有条文说:"The Buyer's approval of any plans and drawings shall not imply any alteration of the Builder's responsibilities referred to in the Specifications."

3.5.3 国际仲裁中委任仲裁员时的提前弃权

近年来,随着经济全球化的发展,跨国公司越来越多,大型的国际律师事务所也越来越多,这就给很多国际仲裁的仲裁员带来麻烦。例如,一个大型国际律师事务所可能在全球很多国家都有分所,有几千个律师。其中一位合伙人在某两个跨国公司的争议中担任仲裁员,他很难保证在仲裁进行的过程中,他所在的律师事务所中任何一个分所的任何一位律师不会接这两个跨国公司任何一间分公司或关联公司的业务。即使这笔生意与该合伙人作为仲裁员处理的案件无关,也有是否存在利益冲突的争议,难保被申请人以此拖延程序,甚至败诉后试图撤销裁决书。而要国际律师事务所对这些生意都以利益冲突为由不接显然也不现实,而只是合伙人之一的仲裁员也控制不了。因此,为了避免被委任为仲裁员后可能产生的利益冲突的争议,很多仲裁员在接受委任时会要求争议双方"提前弃权"(advanced waiver),措辞上可能是:"... in a global law firm of about 2000 lawyers... I cannot exclude that lawyers in this firm will act in the future for or against one of the parties or their affiliates. I will not act myself for or against any of the parties or their affiliates during the arbitration proceeding. At the same time, I will disclose any future act or circumstance that might, from the perspective of any of the parties, put my independence as an arbitrator into question."

甚至有些措辞会进一步要求争议双方明示同意仲裁员不需要披露将来产生的利益冲突,例如:"... accept that current or future member firms of(该仲裁员所在的律所)are free... to accept instructions from or against any of the parties to this arbitration... without any duty on my part to make any disclosure in connection with any such instructions."

国际律师协会新的《IBA Guidelines on Conflict of Interest in International Arbitration》(简称"IBA 利益冲突指引")(2014 版)针对国际仲裁利益冲突的规则,也注意到了这种越来越多的所谓提前弃权,在 General Standard (3)(b)说这种提前弃权不能取代仲裁员的披露责任:"An advance declaration or waiver in relation to possible conflicts of interest arising from facts and circumstances that may arise in the future does not discharge the arbitrator's ongoing duty of disclosure under General Standard (3)(a)."

虽然新的《IBA 利益冲突指引》对提前弃权的有效性并没有任何立场,但笔者认为如果仲裁员有责任披露，就很难说这个提前弃权有效。仲裁员要披露但争议双方不能反对可能存在的利益冲突没有理由，否则披露还有什么意义？尤其已经在本章之3.4.1段提到构成弃权的要件之一是弃权方知道令他在两个相对立的权利中做出选择的事实，而仲裁员要求所谓的提前弃权时，争议双方不可能知道这个事实（还没有发生），因此笔者倾向于这种提前弃权在英国法律下无效。

但也有说法是这种提前弃权并非一定无效，纽约律师公会国际商业争议委员的《Advance Waivers of Arbitrator Conflicts of Interest in International Commercial Arbitrations Seated in New York》（2016年3月）报告中就提到，如果这个提前弃权条文的范围相对狭窄并且足够清楚明确，争议双方有机会清楚了解提前弃权的后果（通过独立的律师意见），并在深思熟虑后做出决定，提前弃权就可能有效。该报告也建议仲裁员可以加上保证说如果他所在的律师事务所之后接受了争议双方其中一方的生意（虽然与该仲裁无关，但可以说有潜在的利益冲突），律师事务所内部会建立"长城"（Chinese wall）令他不会接触到任何相关信息，这样会增加被争议双方与仲裁机构或法院接受的可能性与提前弃权条文有效的可能性。

"长城"的正式叫法应该是"信息壁垒"（information barriers）。关于律所应该如何建立信息壁垒的结构，在英国《Solicitor's Code of Conduct》（2007）[52] Guidance to rule 4之44段有十分详尽的建议：

"(a) that the client who or which might be interested in the confidential information acknowledges in writing that the information held by the firm will not be given to them;

(b) that all members of the firm who hold the relevant confidential information ('the restricted group') are identified and have no involvement with or for the other client;

(c) that no member of the restricted group is managed or supervised in relation to that matter by someone from outside the restricted group;

(d) that all members of the restricted group confirm at the start of the engagement that they understand that they possess or might come to possess information which is confidential, and that they must not discuss it with any other member of the firm unless that person is, or becomes, a member of the restricted group, and that this obligation shall be regarded by everyone as an ongoing one;

(e) that each member of the restricted group confirms when the barrier is established that they have not done anything which would amount to a breach of the information barrier; and

(f) that only members of the restricted group have access to documents containing the confidential information.

---

[52] 这之后被《Solicitor's Code of Conduct》（2011）取代。

The following arrangements may also be appropriate, and might in particular be necessary where acting in circumstances set out in 4.05[53]:

(g) that the restricted group is physically separated from those acting for the other client, for example, by being in a separate building, on a separate floor or in a segregated part of the offices, and that some form of 'access restriction' be put in place to ensure physical segregation;

(h) that confidential information on computer systems is protected by use of separate computer networks or through use of password protection or similar means;

(i) that the firm issues a statement that it will treat any breach, even an inadvertent one, of the information barrier as a serious disciplinary offence;

(j) that each member of the restricted group gives a written statement at the start of the engagement that they understand the terms of the information barrier and will comply with them;

(k) that the firm undertakes that it will do nothing which would or might prevent or hinder any member of the restricted group from complying with the information barrier;

(l) that the firm identifies a specific partner or other appropriate person within the restricted group with overall responsibility for the information barrier;

(m) that the firm provides formal and regular training for members of the firm on duties of confidentiality and responsibility under information barriers or will ensure that such training is provided prior to the work being undertaken; and

(n) that the firm implements a system for the opening of post, receipt of faxes and distribution of e-mail which will ensure that confidential information is not disclosed to anyone outside the restricted group.

'Member', in the context of this note, applies to principals and all staff members including secretaries, but does not apply to any staff member (not having any involvement on behalf of any relevant client) whose duties include the maintenance of computer systems or conflict/compliance procedures and who is subject to a general obligation of confidentiality in relation to all information to which he or she may have access in the course of his or her duties."

在 Guidance to rule 4 之 43 段也提到在某些情况下,建立有效的信息壁垒是不可能:"It is unlikely that, for example, safeguards could ever be considered adequate where: (a) a firm has only one principal and no other qualified staff; (b) the solicitor possessing, or likely to possess, the confidential information is supervised by a solicitor who acts for, or supervises another solicitor in the firm who acts for a client to whom the

[53] Rule 4.05 针对的是无法获得客户同意的情况。

information is or may be relevant; or (c) the physical structure or layout of the firm is such that confidentiality would be difficult to preserve having regard to other safeguards which are in place."

这也配合 Bolkiah v. KPMG (1999) 2 AC 222 先例,Millet 勋爵说"长城"不能是临时(*ad hoc*)的安排,而必须是律师事务所结构性的安排:"In my opinion an effective Chinese wall needs to be an established part of the organisational structure of the firm, not created ad hoc and dependent on the acceptance of evidence sworn for the purpose by members of staff engaged on the relevant work."

这样看来,只有大型/国际律师事务所才有能力建立有效的信息壁垒。

3.5.4　造船合约中间接约定弃权不适用

在造船合约(日本造船标准格式)中的 Art. III(c)规定说,当船舶建造延误超过了死亡日期(drop - dead date),买方船东有权选择终止合约,除非船东通过言行放弃了这个权利:"... in such event, and after such period has expired, the BUYER may at its option rescind this Contract... The BUILDER may, at any time after the expiration of the aforementioned (period) of delay in delivery, if the BUYER has not served notice of rescission... demand in writing that the BUYER shall make an election, in which case the BUYER shall, within fifteen (15) days after such demand is received by the BUYER, notify the BUILDER of its intention either to rescind this Contract or to consent to the acceptance of the VESSEL at an agreed future date ..."

在 Simon Curtis 先生的《The Law of Shipbuilding Contracts》(第 4 版, 2012 年),第 71 页脚注 51,说:"... In The 'Great Marine' (No. 1) (1990) 2 Lloyd's Rep. 245, which concerned the sale of a second - hand vessel, the High Court held that 'in the context of a profit - earning chattel such as a ship or an aircraft' the seller's failure to exercise a cancellation right within one week of the date of its accrual was 'too long' and led to the waiver of such right. It is submitted, however, that this is inappropriately short in relation to a long - term newbuilding project and that **the existence of express provisions entitling the builder to require the buyer to elect whether or not to cancel the contract is likely in any event preclude the application of the doctrine of waiver.**"

以上加黑部分是指上述条文明示允许船厂可向买方船东询问是否选择终止造船合约,买方必须在 15 天内回复是否选择终止。这可以解释为买方不在死亡日期后的合理时间内做出选择并不会被视为弃权,因为合约已经明示约定买方行使选择权的做法与时间,即在船厂追问下,买方才需要做出选择。

在近期的一个伦敦仲裁中,造船合约规定的死亡日期是 2 月初,但买方船东直到 8 月末才做出了弃船通知(notice of cancellation)。期间市场有一些变动,买方延误了半年才终止造船合约,对船厂有很大影响。笔者所在的仲裁庭判是船东没有因为这漫长的延误而弃权,因为中国船厂从未做出通知要求船东在终止合约与继续合约中做出选择。

3.5.5 保险中的放弃代位求偿条文(waiver of subrogation clause)

损失计算的起点是不考虑无辜方有否购买保险:Bradburn v. Great Western Railway Co.(1874)LR 10 Ex 1; Parry v. Cleaver(1940)AC 1 等先例。这法律地位有若干方面的理由,其中重要的理由之一是让保险人享有代位求偿(subrogation)的权利,这可以提升保险行业的经济效益。而且无辜方是自己给保费以获得保险的保障,没理由让没有支付保费的过错方得到好处。

但在订约自由下,可能被保险人(assured)不希望保险人在赔付后向一些特定人士代位求偿,所以在保险合约或保单中加入放弃代位求偿条文(waiver of subrogation clause)。另一个普遍的做法是在保险合约或保单中将所有有关人士联名一并作为共同被保险人(co - assured or co - insured),即所谓的联合保险(joint insurance)。这在一些针对建筑或工程合约、光船租约等类别合约的保险合约中是惯常的做法。也会有情况是一方(通常根据有关合约条文的约定)承担了承保的保费,但被保险人是合约的另一方。一般来说,在这种情况下,保险人在赔付了被保险人之后,也被视为不能通过代位求偿向支付保费一方索赔,否则就等于支付保费的一方无法获得其在保单下期待的保障。但为了安全与肯定,直接或间接(如将保费加在相关合约的价款上)负责保费的一方要坚持联合保险。共同被保险人之间没有赔偿责任(即使其中一方向另一方违约)最早是美国法律的说法,后来也被英国法院接受:Petrofina(UK)Ltd. v. Magnaload Ltd.(1984)QB 127 先例与贵族院的 Co - operative Retail Services Ltd. v. Taylor Young Partnership Ltd.(2002)1 WLR 1419 先例。在 Petrofina(UK)Ltd. v. Magnaload Ltd. 先例中,法院的理由是为了避免"兜圈子诉讼"(circuity of action),即无辜方要求保险人赔付,保险人在赔付后代位求偿向违约方索赔损失,违约方在赔偿保险公司损失之后作为共同被保险人又要求保险公司做出赔付。而 Co - operative Retail Services Ltd. v. Taylor Young Partnership Ltd. 先例的理由看来更有说服力,在该先例中,贵族院认为在联合保险中有一条默示条文,说:"The implication is necessary because if the co-insureds are both insured against the relevant loss, the possibility of claims between them is financially irrelevant. It would be absurd for the insurer to bring a subrogated claim against a co-insured whom he would be liable to indemnify against having to meet it."

至于具体以哪种办法要求保险人放弃代位求偿权,要看具体情况。如在一个大公司投保的员工责任保险(受保的风险主要是员工疏忽导致公司蒙受损失)的保单中,就通常会有一条放弃代位求偿条文。因为大公司的员工众多且经常变动,把所有的员工作为共同被保险人显然不现实。但在建筑或工程合约的保险中,需要保险作为保障的人士可能只有几个,如雇主、总承建商、分承建商等,就可以把所有有关人士作为共同被保险人。

有关这方面的先例很多。首先在 Mark Rowlands Ltd. v. Berni Inns Ltd.(1986)

QB 211 先例中,案情涉及房屋租赁合约,租约要求租客支付租金与所谓的保险租金(insurance rent)。后者的金额就是房东为房屋购买的保险的保费。之后因为租客的疏忽,房屋被烧毁。保险人赔付了房东后,以房东的名义向租客索赔其疏忽导致的损失。上诉庭最后判是该保险事实上是为了保证房东与租客共同的利益。Kerr 大法官说:"... in my view this does not decide the real issue between the parties. This is whether the terms of the lease, and the full indemnification of the plaintiff by their receipt of the insurance monies, preclude them from recovering damages in negligence from the defendants, or whether the plaintiffs' right to recover such damages remains unaffected. In the former case the plaintiffs' insurer would obviously be equally precluded from bringing the present action in the name of the plaintiffs by virtue of its rights of subrogation. The only English authority cited to the judge in this connection was the decision of Lloyd J in Petrofina (U. K.) Ltd. v. Magnaload Ltd. [1984] QB 127. That decision is of considerable importance to insurances in the field of the construction industry, but for present purposes it is at most only of indirect relevance and distinguishable on its facts. In that case Lloyd J followed with approval a decision of the Supreme Court of Canada in Commonwealth Construction Co. Ltd. v. Imperial Oil Ltd. (1976) 69 DLR (3d) 558 which he regarded as indistinguishable. The feature which distinguishes those cases from the present case and from the Canadian and American cases mentioned below is that the defendants were co – insured with the plaintiffs under the same policy. They were accordingly not restricted to the contention that the insurance had been effected in part for their benefit, as the defendant is in the present case. **Being co – insured with the plaintiff under the same policy, it necessarily followed that the plaintiff's insurers in these two cases were unable to assert any right of subrogation.** "(加黑部分是笔者的强调)Kerr 大法官认为保险人不能向共同被保险人代位求偿,这应该被视为公理。

另一个例子是有关建筑合约的 Hopewell Project Management Ltd. v. Ewbank Preece Ltd. (1998) 1 Lloyd's Rep. 448 先例。该先例的原告承建一个在菲律宾的发电站的工程,而被告为原告提供工程服务。原告根据建筑合约的要求投保了建筑工程全险。问题是被告(与其他承包商或分承包商)是否属于共同被保险人?该先例判是被告不属于保单下的共同被保险人。但法院也说如果被告是共同被保险人,保险人就不能代位求偿,说:"... it would be nonsensical if those parties who were jointly insured under the CAR policy could make claims against one another in respect of damage to the contract works. Such a result could not possibly have been intended by those parties. I have little doubt that they would have said so to the officious by-stander. If, therefore, I were wrong on the co – insurance point, I would have held that there was an implied term ..."

之后贵族院在 Co – operative Retail Services v. Taylor Young Partnership 先例[54]也同意了这个说法,Hope 勋爵说:“Although your Lordships do not need to resolve the issue in this case, it seems to me that there is much force in the point that the rules about circuity of action do not provide the explanation. I would prefer to say that the true basis of the rule is to be found in the contract between the parties. In Hopewell Project Management Ltd. v. Ewbank Preece Ltd. [1998] 1 Lloyd's Rep. 448 , 458 Mr Recorder Jackson QC said that in his view it would be nonsensical if those parties who were jointly insured under a contractor's all risks policy could make claims against one another in respect of damage to the contract works, that such a result could not possibly have been intended by those parties and that had it been necessary for him to do so he would have held that there was an implied term to that effect. I would be content to accept that as a satisfactory basis for the rule on which, had it been necessary for them to do so, Wimpey and Hall would have been entitled to resist the claim.”

这个问题在航运也同样会发生。在 The “Evia” (1982) 2 Lloyd's Rep. 307 (HL)先例中,期租合约第 21 条战争条文(war risks clause)规定如果船舶被命令前往有战争风险的区域,船东有权购买战争险并从承租人那里取回保费。如果承租人命令船舶前往战争区域同时违反了租约中安全港口的规定,承租人支付了战争险保费后是否还需要承担违反租约的责任,并对损失做出赔偿(实际上是赔付给代位求偿的保险人)? 贵族院认为不需要,这个问题在《Time Charters》(第 6 版,2008 年)一书之 35.10 至 35.12 段与 37.109 段说:“A provision that the owners are to pay for the insurance of their ship does not usually imply that they may not claim against the charterers for damage to the ship caused by the charterers or their servants... Moreover, an agreement that the charterers may order the ship outside the charter trading limits in exchange for paying any extra premium required by the ship's underwriters does not relieve the charterers of their obligation as to the safety of the ports outside those limits to which they order the ship.[55] But in the ‘Evia’ ... the House of Lords held that the then war clause in the Baltime charter, which gave the owners the right to insure against certain war risks and charge the premium to the charterers, operate as a complete code and prevented the owners claiming under other provisions of the charter in respect of those described risks... one reason given by Lord Roskill in The ‘Evia’... why, in respect of

---

[54] 但在该先例中,相关的建筑合约明示排除了承建商与分承包商对火灾等保险风险的赔偿责任。雇主与承建商投保一份联合保险,投保风险发生后重建的费用由保险人承担。

[55] 在 The “Helen Miller” (1980) 2 Lloyd's Rep. 95 先例中,Mustill 大法官说:“by paying the premium the charterer does obtain a benefit-the benefit of being able to send the ship on a voyage which the owner would not otherwise allow her to perform. But this is not at all the same as saying that the charterer thereby obtains the right to send her on such a voyage risk – free.”

the war risks referred to... the charterers were relieved of their safe port obligation under Clause 2, was that, as the charterers were to refund the owners' war risk premium, it would be unjust that they should remain exposed to a subrogated claim by the war risk underwriters under clause 2."

在最近的 Pemberton Greenish LLP v. Henry (2017) EWHC 246 (QB)先例中,被告是一位律师,原告是他之前工作的律师事务所。原告声称被告在处理一宗抵押(mortgage)交易时疏忽,抵押人(mortgagee)事后被证实是个骗子。原告向抵押权人(mortgagor)赔偿了损失,并在专业疏忽保险下获得了保险人的补偿。之后保险人试图通过代位求偿以被告疏忽失职提出索赔,但被告争辩说根据保险中的放弃代位求偿条文(waiver of subrogation clause),[56]保险人放弃了向被告代位求偿的权利,除非损失是由于被告不诚实导致。这个说法得到了法院的支持,由于原告无法证明被告不诚实,原告的诉讼请求失败。

另一个重要先例是中租公司(Sinochart)作为租约链中的一个期租承租人的 The "Ocean Victory" (2017) UKSC 35 先例。有关租约链是原船东把船舶光租给光船承租人(光船船东),让后者拥有船舶并全权负责船舶的管理与营运。而后者以二船东的身份把船舶期租给 Sinochart,Sinochart 再转租给 Daiichi。[57] 该先例与上述介绍的先例有所不同,涉及的不是共同被保险人之间的索赔(或不能索赔),而是有关的联合保险下保险公司向第三方代位求偿的问题。简单而言,该先例的案情有关日本的鹿岛港(Kashima)是否为不安全港口。蒙受损失的船东从保险人/互保协会 Gard 处获得了补偿,并将向承租人 Sinochart 索赔的权利转让(assign)给了 Gard,而 Sinochart 向同是期租合约的分承租人 Daiichi 要求补偿。因此,该先例的原告是作为受让人(assignee)的 Gard,第一被告是承租人 Sinochart,第二被告是分承租人 Daiichi。

保险人行使代位求偿权的限制的争议在该先例也有涉及。船舶的光船承租人根据光租合约条文(BIMCO 的 BARECON 89 标准格式)为船舶购买了保险,并与注册船东共同作为保单下的被保险人。相关条文可节录如下:"12. **Insurance and Repairs** (a) During the Charter period the Vessel shall be kept insured by the Charterers at their expense against marine, war and Protection and Indemnity risks in such form as the Owners shall in writing approve, which approval shall not be unreasonably withheld. Such marine war and P. and I. insurances shall be arranged by the Charterers to protect the interests of both the Owners and the Charterers and mortgagees (if any), and the Charterers shall be at liberty to protect under such insurances the interests of any manag-

---

〔56〕 该放弃代位求偿条文的写法是:"The Insurer agrees not to exercise any such rights of recovery against any Employee, or former Employee, unless the claim is brought about or contributed to by the dishonest, fraudulent, intentional, criminal or malicious act or omission of such Employee..."

〔57〕 由于航运业的不景气,这家著名的日本船公司在 2015 年向东京法院申请破产。

ers they may appoint. **All insurance policies shall be in the joint names of the Owners and the Charterers as their interests may appear**..."

Sinochart 的争辩是在上述节录条文下，原船东（蒙受船舶全损的损失的一方）就相关的全损意外事故获得了保险人的赔付，所以保险人的代位求偿权来自原船东。由于原船东与光船承租人订立光船租约，而且该租约与保险合约中都将原船东与光船承租人作为共同被保险人，这表示光船承租人即使违约（去不安全港口），也没有对船东的赔偿责任。在这种情况下，即使鹿岛港确实构成不安全港口，Gard 在对原船东做出赔偿后，不能代位求偿向光船承租人索赔。而与 Sinochart 订立租约的光船承租人，因为不需要向原船东/Gard 赔偿船舶全损的损失，所以没有蒙受任何损失，也就不能向 Sinochart 索赔。而 Gard 作为受让人（assignee）的权利不会超过转让人（assignor）的权利，因此不能向 Sinochart 直接提出索赔，毕竟原船东与 Sinochart 之间没有合约关系，中间隔着光船承租人。上诉庭（[2015] 1 Lloyd's Rep. 381）支持了 Sinochart 的说法，Longmore 大法官说："We would accordingly hold that, even if the demise charterers had been in breach of the safe port obligation in the charter, they were under **no** liability to the owners for that breach because the owners had agreed to look to the insurance proceeds rather than to the demise charterers for compensation. The demise charterers cannot therefore show that they have suffered any loss as a result of the time charterers' breach of their safe port obligation in the time charter and the time charterers have no liability to the demise charterers which they can pass on the sub-time charterers, to whom we have more usually been referring as 'the charterers'."

该先例最后上诉到了最高院，针对这方面是以 3 比 2 的多数意见判 Gard 不能向 Sinochart 索赔，因为与 Sinochart 有合约关系的光船承租人作为共同被保险并没有责任与损失。这样，租约链下的分承租人 Daiichi 即使违约，也不需要承担赔偿责任。

这个多数意见的判法对将来的光船租约影响很大，因为光船租约的标准格式（BARECON）规定船东与光船承租人是共同被保险人，但正因如此，导致租约链下真正要负责任的承租人/分承租人却不需要承担违约责任（不论是去不安全港口还是装运危险品等的违约）。而万一保险公司破产或赔不足，蒙受损失的船东也无法向光船承租人索赔，再让光船承租人向承租人/分承租人要求补偿。看来 BIMCO 要重新考虑 BARECON 标准格式中的第 12 条文（尤其是上述加黑部分）的安排，防止将来面对这种索赔的"黑洞"。

但在该先例中，Gard 自己也存在一定的疏忽，最高院提到如果 Gard 以其他诉因，如托管（bailment）或代第三人索赔损失（transferred loss），而不是只以租约链中的合约责任索赔，可能有更好的机会。但因为 Gard 在一审时没有提出这些替代诉因，因此最高院无法再将这些诉因挖出来做出判决。Mance 勋爵说：

"... Gard's case before the Supreme Court has been put exclusively on the basis that charterers had a liability to owners, which in turn enables charterers to claim damages down the line. Mr Howard QC（Gard 在最高院新换的代表大律师）, who did not appear for Gard below, very frankly acknowledged that it had occurred to him, when he came into the case, that there could have been other bases on which the claim could have been presented, but that it had been concluded that Gard was confined to the way in which the case had been argued on its behalf below.

Those other bases are (i) that the charterers' possessory title gave them a sufficient interest to be able to maintain a claim for the hull loss: compare the principle in The Winkfield [1902] P 42, whereby a bailee can claim in tort in his own name, without showing that he has any liability to the head owner, but accounting to the head owner for any loss exceeding his own loss,[58] and/or (ii) that there are circumstances in contract where a contracting party can claim substantial damages for loss of or damage to property, when another person has actually borne such loss or damage[59]: Dunlop v. Lambert (1839) 6 Cl & F 600, The Albazero [1977] AC 774, 846G – 847F. More recently, this latter possibility has been more widely recognised, by giving special treatment to contracts relating to property where loss due to a breach of the contract will be suffered by a holder of the property other than the contracting party: see Linden Gardens Trust Ltd. v. Lenesta Sludge Disposals Ltd. and St Martins Property Corp Ltd. v. Sir Robert McAlpine Ltd. ("St Martins") [1994] 1 AC 85 where it was in the contemplation of the parties when the contract was made that the property, the subject of the contract and the breach, would be transferred to or occupied by a third party, who would in consequence suffer the loss arising from its breach...[60]

---

〔58〕 第一个替代争议是托管(bailment),因为光船租约中规定船长与船员都由光船承租人提供,等于是原船东将船舶交出给光船承租人以托管人(bailee)的身份占有(possession)该船舶。根据 The "Winkfield" (1902) P 42 先例,托管人可以自己的名字开始侵权的诉讼,并将索赔来的损失(超出他自己损失的部分)交给寄托人。这也是配合实际,毕竟以前通讯不便,运输中的货物在外国发生事故,让寄托人(如货物所有人)自己开始对第三人采取法律行动很可能不现实,更恰当的做法是让托管人(如外国仓库或船东)当场采取法律行动。关于托管,可见笔者《提单与其他付运单证》(2016年)一书第二章之1.5段。

〔59〕 第二个替代争议是代第三人索赔损失,这种情况经常会有,包括早期的提单合约。提单作为运输合约往往是卖方作为发货人与承运人订立,但提单作为物权凭证往往会转让给买方的收货人。而如果发生货损货差,损失是在买方,但由于合约关系(包括是否需要承担责任)是与卖方,买方就需要通过卖方向承运人索赔其所蒙受的损失。这些课题在笔者《提单与其他付运单证》(2016年)一书第三章之14.2段与杨良宜《损失赔偿与救济》一书第七章有详尽介绍。换言之,在该先例中,光船承租人有可能可以根据这个说法向 Sinochart 索赔不安全港口带来的损失,虽然真正蒙受损失的是船东或赔付之后代位求偿的 Gard。

〔60〕 对于一些由财产的拥有人而非合约方蒙受违约造成的损失的特殊案件,这个说法也越来越被接受。其中权威的 Linden Gardens Trust Ltd. v. Lenesta Sludge Disposals Ltd. and St Martins Property Corp Ltd. v. Sir Robert McAlpine Ltd. (1994) 1 AC 85 先例在杨良宜《损失赔偿与救济》一书第七章之5.2段。

In the absence of argument, it is not appropriate to reach any conclusion as to whether or how far either of these principles might have assisted Gard, had it been open to Gard to rely on them now... ”

Toulson 勋爵也说:“It does not follow that the demise charterers (or their insurers in their shoes) necessarily had no available remedy against the time charterers. The court was told that at one stage the insurers intimated a claim analogous to the claim which a bailee may bring under The Winkfield [1902] P 42. However, the matter was not pursued, and it would be inappropriate to express a positive view about the likelihood of success of such a claim (or any alternative), about which the court has heard no argument. ”

4. 禁反言的基本原则

“Estop”是古英语单词,原本的意思与“stop”一词相同。Coke 勋爵认为这一词来源于法语单词“estoupe”,说:“Estoppel cometh of the French word estoupe, from whence the English word stopped; and it is called an estoppel or conclusion because a man's own act or acceptance stoppeth or closeth up his mouth to allege or plead the truth. ”在现代社会,“stop”或“stoppage”被用在日常生活,而“estop”或“estoppel”只作为英国法律名词使用。

根据 Coke 勋爵[61]的分类,有三类禁反言:“estoppel by record”、“estoppel by deed”与“estoppel *in pais*”。

“estoppel by record”基本等同于现代的“estoppels *per rem judicatam*”或“*Res Judicata*”,[62]即一事不再审。这在现代已经不再被视为禁反言,只是因为历史原因,叫了“禁反言”的名字。

“estoppel by deed”与“estoppel *in pais*”(特别是后者)是现代“陈述性禁反言”(estoppels by representation)的起源,更准确地说,是陈述性禁反言中对事实的陈述。这可见澳大利亚高院的 Dixon 大法官在 Thompson v. Palmer (1933) HCA 61 先例中的说法:“The object of estoppels in pais is to prevent an unjust departure by one person from an assumption adopted by another as the basis of some act or omission which, unless the assumption be adhered to, would operate to that other's detriment... He may be required to abide by the assumption ... because he directly made representations upon

---

〔61〕 这是在早期的《Coke, A Commentary on Littleton》(第 11 版,1719 年)一书第 352 页。

〔62〕 可以再细分为“吸收原则”(merger)、“诉因的禁反言”(cause of action estoppel)、“争端的禁反言”(issue estoppel)、“滥用程序”(abuse of process)等,在本书第九章有详论。

which the other party founded the assumption ... "

"estoppel by deed"的名称显示了要有书面的责任或者盖章的文件。有说法是现代的"共识性禁反言"(estoppel by convention),包括双方在合约中达成的共识,即现代的"合约性禁反言"(estoppel by contract)也是源自"Estoppel by deed"。

4.1　禁反言的起源

禁反言的说法最初在衡平法提出是17世纪,并在Pickard v. Sears (1837) 6 Ad & El 469先例形成一套说法,被普通法院适用。这个被称为"普通法禁反言"(common law estoppel)的说法只适用在有限方面,如一方要受被郑重记录在契约上的陈述的约束(estoppel by deed),或受一些恶行的约束(estoppels *in pais*),后者主要涉及土地等不动产产权或货物。

一些早期的例子如Savage v. Foster (1723) 9 Mod. 35先例与Price v. Neault (1886) 12 App. Case 110先例等,涉及土地买卖。土地真正的所有人明知卖方不是土地所有人,但站在一边袖手旁观甚至鼓励买方向该卖方购买土地,令买方产生了该卖方就是土地所有人的错误印象,就会导致真正的土地所有人受该土地买卖合约的约束。

禁反言的说法是为了阻止一方曾做出事实的陈述,该陈述被另一方依赖并蒙受损害,但事后陈述方出尔反尔否认该陈述的真实性的情况发生。最初这适用在欺诈(fraud),但无辜的误述(innocent misrepresentation)导致禁反言也早在17世纪就有先例:Hobbs v. Norton (1683) 1 Vern 136先例(年金[annuity]买卖的无辜误述)与Hunsden v. Cheyney (1690) 2 Vern 150先例(在婚姻财产协议的谈判中的无辜误述)。

随着禁反言适用范围的拓展,Mansfield勋爵首先将禁反言的说法适用在商法,包括汇票等方面。

到了19世纪,普通法在禁反言有了新的发展,如果一方通过言行对已经存在的事实[63](而非法律[64])做出错误陈述并希望对方依赖,而另一方即被陈述方(representee)依赖了该陈述并蒙受损害,陈述方(representor)就会被禁反言。即陈述方在对被陈述方的诉讼中不允许声称事实与他做出的陈述不同。因此,传统上普通法的"陈述性禁反言"(common law estoppel by representation)一直被当做一种证据规则(rule of evidence),不允许陈述方在诉讼中举证以证明事实的真相是与其陈述不同。

在18世纪,衡平法将这个适用范围很狭窄的普通法说法引入了衡平法,并对适用范围进行了进一步拓展。"产权人禁反言"(proprietary estoppel)与"承诺性禁反言"(promissory estoppel)这两类禁反言的类别就主要是在衡平法院发展起来的。

---

〔63〕参见Jorden v. Money (1854) 5 H. L. C. 185先例。

〔64〕参见Territorial and Auxiliary Forces Assoc of the County of London v. Nichols (1949) 1 KB 35; Kai Nam v. Ma Kam Chan (1956) AC 358等先例。

在19世纪，产权人禁反言逐渐发展出了两个分支。[65] 如果土地/房屋所有人诱导另一方让其误以为自己对有关的土地/房屋有产权，而希望占有另一方在误解之后花钱对该土地/房屋进行改进与提升的好处，衡平法就会介入，阻止土地/房屋所有人不当得利（undue advantage or unjust enrichment）：East India Co. v. Vincent（1740）2 Atk. 83；Stiles v. Cooper（1748）3 Atk. 692等先例。另一个是如果一方想以没有满足程序/格式上的要求为由从土地/房屋的买卖合约中脱身，衡平法也会介入：Allen v. Bower（1790）3 Bro. C.C. 149；Gregory v. Mighell（1811）18 Ves. 328；Farrall v. Davenport（1861）3 Giff. 363等先例。

在差不多同一时间，承诺性禁反言的说法也逐渐形成，虽然在Hughes v. Metropolitan Railway Company（1877）2 App. Cas. 439先例中还没有使用禁反言这个说法，Cairns勋爵在该先例只是称为“first principle of equity”。

在Crabb v. Arun DC（1976）Ch 179先例，Denning勋爵说：“The basis of this proprietary estoppel – as indeed of promissory estoppel – is the interposition of equity. Equity comes in, true to form, to mitigate the rigours of strict law. The early cases did not speak of it as ‘estoppel.’ They spoke of it as ‘raising an equity.’ If I may expand what Lord Cairns L. C. said in Hughes v. Metropolitan Railway Co.（1877）2 App. Cas. 439, 448：‘it is the first principle upon which all courts of equity proceed,’ that it will prevent a person from insisting on his strict legal rights – whether arising under a contract, or on his title deeds, or by statute – when it would be inequitable for him to do so having regard to the dealings which have taken place between the parties.”

这两个类别的禁反言有两个共同的要件：（1）提出禁反言的一方（estoppel raiser）必须因为被禁反言的一方（estopped party）的行为而蒙受损害；（2）被禁反言的一方必须对对方蒙受损害有一定的责任，无论是诱导对方依赖他做出陈述或承诺或保证，或是没有及时纠正对方的错误理解或假设。

1875年11月1日《Judicature Act 1873》生效后，普通法法院与衡平法法院已经合并。法官在判决时会一并考虑，所以再也没有必要区分普通法与衡平法的区别。

4.2 禁反言的合理性

Steyn勋爵在《The Clifford Chance Millennium Lectures》（2000年）曾说大陆法的善意说法或原则，在英国就是通过默示条文、合约变更与禁反言体现，而其中最主要就是禁反言的说法：“Thus the continental systems recognize an overarching duty of good faith in the performance of contracts. The common law achieves similar results by a resort to implied terms, rectification and **estoppel**.”

在早期有很多先例对禁反言有敌意，甚至认为禁反言“面目可憎”（odious），因此

---

〔65〕 在当时的英国社会，商业尚不发达，活动不多，社会上的争议主要涉及在土地/房屋，如在邻居或家族之间。

只会在很有限的情况下适用。在 Baxendale v. Bennett (1878) 3 QBD 525 CA 先例中，Bramwell 说："estoppels are odious, and should never be applied without a necessity for it."在 Batten Pooll v. Kennedy (1907) 1 Ch. 256 先例中，Warrington 大法官说只有在迫不得已的情况下才会适用："(禁反言是)a doctrine to which it is not too much to say that the court will not resort except in the last extremity."

法院早期的这种敌意是因为禁反言的作用是排除真相，禁止被禁反言的一方事后举证证明事实(或法律)的真相，[66]而法律的大原则是追求真相。如甲方违约后，乙方对甲方说损失是 100 万美元，要求甲方赔偿，但甲方没有理会。之后乙方开始诉讼，提出 500 万美元的索赔。甲方能否以乙方曾经说过损失是 100 万美元为由，禁止乙方举证证明自己的损失是 500 万美元？如果乙方能证明 500 万美元的损失(或只能证明 400 万美元的损失)，这才是真相，而不会是较早前提到的 100 万美元。笔者看不出任何理由判如果乙方曾经做出过 100 万美元的陈述就要错到底，毕竟在英国，法律的大原则是一方以错误理由或不给理由拒绝履行合约可以事后才发现的合法理由进行补救。[67] 这也体现在诉讼或仲裁中，法院或仲裁庭在做出判决或裁决前，都尽量允许双方修改(amend)文书请求，以达到以双方最后认为是正确的地位做出审理的目的。

在 Spencer Bower 与 Turner 先生的《Estoppel by Representation》(第 3 版，1977 年)一书第 22 页提到早期其他对禁反言的批评，认为即使禁反言的说法不是"面目可憎"，也没有必要："If you are in a position to prove the falsity of your opponent's allegation, and if you object is not to shut out the truth, why do you object to prove such falsity by evidence in the ordinary way?[68]"

在 General Finance Mortgage & Discount Co. v. Liberator Permanent Benefit Building Society (1878) 10 Ch. D. 15 先例中，Jessel 大法官也说："the doctrine appears no longer necessary in law; it appears no longer useful, and in my opinion should not be carried further than a judge is obliged to carry."

但 Spencer Bower 与 Turner 先生认为禁反言说法的必要性显而易见，因为对方的陈述是虚假/错误的证据可能消失，或是不被法官接受，或是举证困难，说："the witnesses may be dead, documents may be lost, or for other reasons the necessary evidence may not be available except at a great expenditure of time and money; and in any event, there is the risk that it may not be accepted by an eccentric judge."

---

〔66〕 在 Coke 勋爵的《The First Part of the Institutes of the Laws of England or, A Commentary Upon Littleton》(第 1 版，1628 年)一书说明了这个作用："every estoppel concludeth a man to allege the truth."

〔67〕 参见本书第一章第 5 段。

〔68〕 早期陈述性禁反言的说法只适用于欺诈性误述，而如果提出禁反言的一方可以证明对方的陈述是虚假/错误，就可以欺诈性误述的说法要求陈述方承担责任，又何必禁止对方举证证明事实的真相，而要把虚假/错误的陈述作为正确的事实以适用相关的法律？

简单的例子就是提单(bills of lading),提单会在一连串的国际货物买卖合约中不断转让直到最后到真正买方的手上。如果没有禁反言的说法,真正买方发现提单上的陈述很可能是虚假,如提单的陈述是装载了 2 万吨食糖,但实际只交货了 1 万吨。买方作为提单的收货人,希望根据这个虚假陈述的理由向船东提出指控与索赔,在举证方面就会十分困难(甚至做不到)。而根据陈述性禁反言,只要船东在提单上做出了陈述,面对依赖陈述的收货人,无论该陈述虚假与否都会被视为真相,买方与船东之间的法律与合约关系就以提单上的陈述为准,可以要求船东赔偿短缺的 1 万吨。因此,Spencer Bower 与 Turner 先生认为禁反言的说法可以带给提出禁反言的一方极大的便利,并且避免可能会导致其立场无法被证明或不被支持的困难、危险与怀疑。

现在已经没有人说禁反言的说法"面目可憎",而认为如果没有这个说法,很多情况下法院就无法主持公道。而事实上,这些年来禁反言也有了很多改变与要件的限制,只在会造成不公平与不合情理的情况适用。正如 Blackburn 勋爵在 Burkinshaw v. Nicholls (1878) 3 App. Cas. 1004 HL 先例所说:"Now sometimes there is a degree of odium thrown upon the doctrine of estoppels, because the same word is used occasionally in a very technical sense, and the doctrine of estoppels in pais has even been thought to deserve some of the odium... But the moment the doctrine is looked at in its true light, it will be found to be a most equitable one, and one without which the law of this country could not be satisfactorily administered. When a person makes to another the representation, I take upon myself to say such and such things do exist, and you may act upon that basis, it seems to me of the very essence of justice that, between these two parties, their rights shall be regulated, not by the real state of facts, but by that conventional state of facts which the two parties agree to make the basis of their action; and that is what I apprehend is meant by estoppels in pais..."

Spencer Bower 与 Turner 先生的《Estoppel by Representation》(第 3 版,1977 年)一书第 21 页说陈述性禁反言适用的大多数案件(特别是早期)都涉及一些不诚实的言行,[69] 陈述性禁反言可以防止出现不公平与不合情理的情况:"A very cursory examination of the long series of decisions on the subject of estoppels by representation will convince any one that in practice the principle has always 'made for righteousness' and has in most cases operated to defeat some grossly dishonest claim or defence."

在 Barrow Mutual Ship Insurance Co. v. Ashburner (1885) 54 L. J. Q. B. 377 先例中,Brett 大法官在判决中说到一些看来振振有词与站得住脚的抗辩因为(且只因为)禁反言的适用而失败。这种例子很多,如被告的抗辩是根据合约的时效条文,但

---

〔69〕 但随着禁反言的发展,后期往往不会追究是否涉及不诚实的因素,即使陈述方是无辜,只要客观看来错误陈述被对方依赖并蒙受损害,就会构成禁反言。

原告指出被告曾经做出过清楚无误的承诺不会依赖时效，这构成承诺性禁反言。这样被告就可能因为禁反言的适用，而不能依赖时效。

而在现代，禁反言的说法被称为英国法律中保证公平的最有力与最有弹性的武器。Wright 勋爵在 Canada and Dominion Sugar Co. Ltd. v. Canadian National (West Indies) Steam Ships Ltd. (1946) 80 Lloyd's Rep. 13 (PC) 先例中说："There was, perhaps, a time when estoppels were described as odious and as such were viewed with suspicion and reluctance. Mr. Delvin has sought to apply the same test to a case where it is sought to qualify words which if unqualified would constitute an estoppels. But in more modern times the law of estoppel has developed and has become recognized as a beneficial branch of law. That great lawyer Sir Frederick Pollock has described the doctrine of estoppels as 'a simple flexible instrument to be found in any system of court jurisprudence.' How true that description is can be seen by looking to be found in Halsbury's Laws of England (Hailsham edition) Vol. Ⅷ, pp. 397 to 518."

4.3　禁反言说法适用范围的拓展

现在，禁反言说法的适用范围与最初相比有了很大拓展。上面已经提到在 18 世纪，衡平法引入了禁反言这个适用范围很狭窄的普通法原则，并对适用范围进行了拓展，发展出了"产权人禁反言"（proprietary estoppel）与"承诺性禁反言"（promissory estoppel）这两类禁反言。

之后，法院又将传统的"契约性禁反言"（estoppels by deed）的说法拓展到了其他文件（如一份简式合约）上的错误陈述：Carpenter v. Buller (1841) M & W 209; Ashpitel v. Bryan (1864) 5 B & S 723; McCance v. London & North Western Railway (1864) 159 E. R. 563 等先例。

陈述性禁反言的陈述原本只针对对过去或目前存在的事实的陈述。但在 Central London Property Trust Ltd. v. High Trees House Ltd. (1947) KB 130 先例[70]后，发展出了针对将来承诺的承诺性禁反言，这可以看做对陈述性禁反言的拓展。另是陈述不仅是对事实的陈述，对法律的陈述也可以构成陈述性禁反言，这方面可看本书第五章之 6.6 段。

另一个重要的拓展是共识性禁反言，从合约双方对事实的共同错误理解拓展到了对法律的共同错误理解：[71] Amalgamated v. Texas Bank (1982) 1 Lloyd's Rep. 27 先例。

4.4　将所有类别的禁反言统一？

近年来，有很多支持将所有类别的禁反言统一为一种更广泛的禁反言的说法。在 Amalgamated v. Texas Bank (1982) 1 Lloyd's Rep. 27 先例，Robert Goff 大法官

---

〔70〕 该先例在本书第四章之 2.3 段有详细介绍。

〔71〕 参见本书第六章之 2.2 段。

说："(a number of authorities) have supported a much wider jurisdiction to interfere in cases where the assertion of strict legal rights is found by the court to be unconscionable."

在 The "Indian Endurance" and The "Indian Grace" (No. 2) (1998) 1 Lloyd's Rep. 1 (HL)先例中，Steyn 勋爵提到一种包罗万象的原则(one overarching principle)，这比现有的禁反言更广泛，因为所有客观看来[72]不公平与不合情理的言行都可能构成禁反言，而不需要分辨到底是哪类禁反言与满足不同类别的禁反言的要件。

在澳大利亚最高院的 Waltons Stores (Interstate) Ltd. v. Maher (1988) 164 CLR 387 先例与 Commonwealth of Australia v. Verwayen (1990) 170 CLR 394 先例显示出了将不同类别的禁反言统一的趋势，但在之后的 Giumelli v. Giumelli (1999) 196 CLR 101 先例又拒绝将禁反言的说法统一。

目前英国法的法律地位还是将不同类别的禁反言进行区分，与必须满足不同类别的禁反言的不同要件，但英国最高院仍有可能进行改革。正如 Goff 勋爵在 Johnson v. Gore Wood & Co. (2002) 2 AC 1 先例中所说："In the end I am inclined to think that the many circumstances capable of giving rise to an estoppels cannot be accommodated within a single formula and that it is unconscionability which provides the link between them."

确实在现实中各种类别的禁反言互有重叠，针对个别的事实也常常很难确定到底会构成哪一类的禁反言。例如，现在共识性禁反言的说法与陈述性禁反言、承诺性禁反言与产权人禁反言就有很大重叠。双方不仅可能对一个事实或合约权利达成错误的共识，也可能对财产所有权产生错误的共识：Keen v. Holland (1984) 1 WLR 251 先例。另一个例子是陈述性禁反言与承诺性禁反言，虽然陈述性禁反言的陈述是针对过去或目前存在的事实，而承诺性禁反言的承诺是针对将来的事实，但在本书第五章之6.3 段的介绍可以看出，对过去或目前存在的事实的陈述与对将来的承诺很难区分。而产权人禁反言也涉及陈述或承诺，唯一的区别是产权人禁反言针对的是财产(主要是土地/房屋)。

但在有些情况下，有关的错误言行只能构成一类禁反言，不同类别的禁反言之间的差异还是存在。例如，共识性禁反言与陈述性禁反言或承诺性禁反言的最大差别在于双方必须有共同与分享的错误理解或共识(shared mutual agreement or understanding)。如果这个要件可以满足，就可能在无法构成陈述性禁反言与承诺性禁反言的情况下构成共识性禁反言。因为：(1)在共识性禁反言中，不需要被禁反言的一方做出清楚无误的陈述或承诺：[73] ING Bank NV v. Ros Roca SA (2011) EWCA Civ

〔72〕 事实上还是取决于法官或仲裁员的主观判断，虽然大多数情况下不会有传统意义上的偏见，但还是会受文化差异的影响而对亚洲或发展中国家十分危险。

〔73〕 参见本书第六章之3.1.4 段。

353 先例。(2)只要双方对这个共同的错误理解清楚无误地进行过沟通,谁先有这个错误的理解并不重要。[74]

4.5 不同类别的禁反言的共性

禁反言的类别很多,每一类都针对不同的法律认为不公平与不合情理的言行或情况。Denning 勋爵在 McIlkenny v. Chief Constable of the West Midlands (1980) 1 QB 283 先例中举了一个形象的例子,说英国法院在过去几百年通过无数的案例建立了一幢名为“禁反言”的大房子,里面有不同的房间。虽然不同的房间都在同一屋檐下,但每个房间有不同的告示说明是属于哪一类别的禁反言,而它们之间也有区别与重叠的构成要件,说:“... there has been built up over the centuries in our law a big house with many rooms. It is the house called Estoppel. ... By our time we have so many rooms that we are apt to get confused between them. Estoppel per rem judicatam, issue estoppel, estoppel by deed, estoppel by representation, estoppel by conduct, estoppel by acquiescence, estoppel by election or waiver, estoppel by negligence, promissory estoppel, proprietary estoppel, and goodness knows what else. These several rooms have this much in common: They are all under one roof. Someone is stopped from saying something or other, or doing something or other, or contesting something or other. But each room is used differently from the others. If you go into one room, you will find a notice saying, ‘Estoppel is only a rule of evidence.’ If you go into another room you will find a different notice, ‘Estoppel can give rise to a cause of action.’ Each room has its own separate notices. It is a mistake to suppose that what you find in one room, you will also find in the others.”

但除了“合约性禁反言”(contractual estoppel)[75]与“一事不再审”(*res judicata*)[76],构成其他类别的禁反言的要件大同小异,只是在重量上有所区别。

简言之,如果一方以言行对事实或法律向另一方做出了清楚无误的陈述或承诺或保证/鼓励,希望影响双方之间的法律关系(无论是合约或是其他法律关系),或另一方可以合理认为对方希望影响双方之间的法律关系,而另一方确实依赖该陈述或

---

〔74〕 参见本书第六章之3.1.2段。

〔75〕 这主要是在上诉庭的 Peekay Intermark v. Australia & New Zealand Banking Group (2006) 2 Lloyd's Rep. 511 先例与 Springwell Navigation v. JP Morgan Chase Bank (2010) EWCA Civ 1212 先例后,认定合约性禁反言纯粹是属于合约,与禁反言的普通法说法毫无关系,所以不存在依赖与蒙受损害或不公平与不合情理的要求。但这一判法被视为政策上的改变而受到批评,说这不仅偏离了之前上诉庭的 Lowe v. Lombank (1960) 1 WLR 196 先例,也偏离了合约性禁反言的根源“契约性禁反言”(estoppel by deed),特别是贵族院的 Greer v. Kettle (1938) AC 156 先例,需要最高院在适合的先例做出最后决定。关于这方面会在本书第八章介绍。

〔76〕 包括“吸收原则”(merger)、“诉因的禁反言”(cause of action estoppel)、“争端的禁反言”(issue estoppel)、“滥用程序”(abuse of process)等,将在本书第九章进行介绍。

承诺或保证/鼓励而改变地位与蒙受损害，让做出陈述或承诺或保证/鼓励的一方出尔反尔是不公平与不合情理，他就会被禁反言。如在本章之4.2段提到的甲方违约，乙方要求100万元赔偿，之后在诉讼中又改为500万元的例子。如果情况有所改变，乙方做出损失是100万元这个清楚无误的陈述或承诺[77]时，明知甲方与丙方有一个"背靠背"合约也涉及同样的争议，因此这个陈述或承诺会被甲方合理依赖。[78]之后甲方确实依赖[79]这个金额与丙方达成了和解，甚至在有关诉讼中取得了双方同意的判决书/裁决书(consent judgment/award)，再让乙方撤回陈述或承诺会不公平与不合情理，[80]会令甲方蒙受损害，乙方就会被禁反言，不能索赔500万元。

这里需要提出的是，虽然中国法下也有禁反言的说法，但不成体系，不需要满足明确的要件，所以在适用时很随意。笔者(杨良宜)近期在的一个仲裁涉及机械设备的买卖。之后设备出现问题，买方与作为卖方的中国公司联系，中国公司出于友好或希望打开市场的考虑，表示愿意去买方工厂修妥设备。但当中国公司到达工厂后，发现无法维修，并且设备出现问题主要因为买方自己在安装与日常使用维护中疏忽。但买方显然不接受这个说法，于是开始仲裁，向中国公司索赔设备质量问题造成的损失，而中国公司则向买方反索赔派人员修理的费用。在责任方面，到底设备有质量问题还是买方自己在安装与日常使用维护中严重疏忽，仲裁庭一致认为应该是中国公司胜诉。中国公司愿意去买方工厂维修只是为了友好，不是承认了责任。但在决定中国公司的反索赔金额时，一位仲裁员提出买方自己经济状况一般，现在败诉并且要赔一大笔钱已经很惨了，中国公司之前愿意去买方工厂维修构成禁反言，不能再向买方索赔这笔费用。这在笔者看来是不能接受，如果中国公司的言行构成禁反言，在责任方面就应该败诉。既然在决定责任时判只是为了友好，在决定买方是否应该支付这笔费用时就不该说构成了禁反言，这是自相矛盾。

4.5.1 宝剑与盾牌之争

关于禁反言的说法是否只能作为盾牌防守，不能作为宝剑进攻，在Spencer Bower与Turner先生的《Estoppel by Representation》(第4版，2004年)一书中将其称为"扫雷"(minesweeper)。禁反言不能作为诉因(cause of action)，但是可以毁掉原本可行的抗辩，或支持诉因(如欺诈或是取消合约，或是弥补原本有缺陷的诉因)。从这个角度看，禁反言可以是布雷，也可以是扫雷。

传统上，陈述性禁反言一直被视为证据规则(rule of evidence)，所以是程序性(procedural)而非实体性(substantive)，在普通法法院是不可能作为诉因开始诉讼。而承诺性禁反言也不可能作为诉因，因为承诺性禁反言中的承诺必须与有约因/对价

---

〔77〕 参见本章之4.5.2段。

〔78〕 参见本章之4.5.3段。

〔79〕 参见本章之4.5.3段。

〔80〕 参见本章之4.5.4段。

(consideration)的合约承诺进行区分,而只有合约承诺才可以作为诉因。共识性禁反言也是类似情况。所以在主要的禁反言类别中,只有产权人禁反言才能作为诉因,或产生新的权利(财产权):见 Ives v. High (1967) 2 QB 379 CA; Crabb v. Arun DC (1976) Ch 179 CA; Pascoe v. Turner (1979) 1 WLR 431 CA; Wayling v. Jones (1993) 69 P & CR 170 CA; Durant v. Heritage (1994) EGCS 134 等先例。

但澳大利亚的法律地位看来有所不同:Waltons Stores (Interstate) Ltd. v. Maher (1988) 164 CLR 387 先例与 Commonwealth of Australia v. Verwayen (1990) 170 CLR 394 先例。[81]

尽管目前英国法律针对宝剑与盾牌之争仍维持传统地位,有说法是英国关于禁反言的法律还在继续发展,最高院在适当的案件中仍有可能针对宝剑盾牌之争做出改革。[82]

4.5.2　陈述或承诺

构成陈述性禁反言或承诺性禁反言的要件之一,就是被禁反言的一方做出了一个清楚无误的陈述[83]或承诺。[84]

陈述性禁反言对于清楚无误的陈述的要求,[85]可见 Low v. Bouverie (1891) 3 Ch 82;Lowe v. Lombank (1960) 1 WLR 196;Woodhouse AC Israel Cocoa Ltd. SA v. Nigerian Produce Marketing Co. Ltd. (1972) 1 Lloyd's Rep. 439 (HL);Moorgate Mercantile Co. Ltd. v. Twitchings (1977) AC 890;The "Shackleford" (1978) 2 Lloyd's Rep. 154;Channel Island Ferries Ltd. v. Sealink UK Ltd. (1987) 1 Lloyd's Rep. 559 等先例。

承诺性禁反言对于清楚无误的承诺或保证的要求,[86]有无数的先例针对。其中在 Spence v. Shell UK Ltd. (1980) 256 E. G. 55 先例中,上诉庭的 Oliver 大法官说"some unambiguous promise or assurance"。在 Hillingdon London BC v. ARC Ltd. (No. 2) (2000) 3 E. G. L. R. 97 先例中,Arden 大法官说:"In our view ARC would have to satisfy the court that there was **some clear and unequivocal representation** by LBH to ARC that its claim was a valid one and in addition that LBH would not rely on any statutory limitation defence."(加黑部分是笔者的强调)

在 Emery v. UCB Corporate Services Ltd. (2001) EWCA Civ 675 先例中,Gibson 大法官说:"A promissory estoppels, in my judgment, arises where there is **a clear and unequivocal promise** that strict legal rights will not be insisted upon."(加黑部分是笔

〔81〕 在本书第四章第10段有详细介绍。
〔82〕 参见本书第四章第10段。
〔83〕 参见本书第五章第6段。
〔84〕 参见本书第四章第6段。
〔85〕 参见本书第五章之6.8段。
〔86〕 参见本书第四章之6.1段。

者的强调)

在 Seechurn v. ACE Insurance SA (2002) 2 Lloyd's Rep. 390 先例,Ward 大法官说其中要解决的一个争议是:"Is there **a clear**, **unequivocal**, **unambiguous and unconditional promise** by the insurers that they will not raise the defence that the action is statute barred. The focus has to be on whether or not they were giving up the right."(加黑部分是笔者的强调)

在 HIH Casualty & General Insurance Ltd. v. AXA Corporate Solutions (2002) EWCA Civ 1253 先例中,Tuckey 大法官说:"It is common ground that in order to establish waiver by estoppel HIH had to show (a) **a clear and unequivocal representation** by Axa that it would not insist on its right to treat the reinsurance cover as discharged because of the reduction in the number of films which were made ..."(加黑部分是笔者的强调)

是否足够清楚无误要从合理的被陈述方(representee)或被承诺方(promisee)的角度客观考虑。在 Seechurn v. ACE Insurance SA 先例中,Ward 大法官说:"The promise must be construed objectively, not subjectively. The question is whether the correspondence can reasonably be understood to contain that particular promise. It does not matter what Mr Seechurn(被承诺方)thought it meant nor does it matter what a layman might have thought ..."

产权人禁反言也有同样的要求,在 Thorner v. Major (2009) UKHL 18 先例中,Neuberger 勋爵说:"... that there must be some sort of an assurance which is '**clear and unequivocal**' before it can be relied on to found an estoppel."(加黑部分是笔者的强调)

在该先例中,Walker 勋爵也说:"that the doctrine [of proprietary estoppel] is based on three main elements... **a representation or assurance** made to the claimant; **reliance** on it by the claimant; and **detriment** to the claimant in consequence of his (reasonable) reliance."(加黑部分是笔者的强调)

在产权人禁反言中,被禁反言的一方(即产权人/业主)的陈述或承诺或保证可以有多种不同的形式:(1)书面承诺:Dillwyn v. Llewelyn (1862) 4 De G F & J 517 先例;(2)口头承诺:Gillett v. Holt (2001) Ch 210 先例;(3)对事实不准确的陈述:Pascoe v. Turner (1979) 1 WLR 431 先例;(4)向另一方提出要求:Plimmer v. Mayor of Wellington (1884) 9 App Cas 699 PC 先例;(5)无言的行为:Bibby v. Stirling (1998) EWCA Civ 994;(6)没有行动:Ramsden v. Dyson (1866) LR 1 HL 129; Fisher v. Brooker (2006) EWHC 3239 (Ch); Clark v. Clark (2006) EWHC 275 Ch); Lester v. Woogate (2010) EWCA Civ 199 等先例。

只有共识性禁反言,因为要求双方之间存在清楚无误的共同错误理解,所以不要求一方曾经做出过清楚无误的陈述或承诺。[87] 但双方对事实或法律的共同错误理解或共识必须曾经以语言或行动[88] 沟通过(crossed the line),被禁反言的一方必须共享或默认了这个错误理解(acquiesced with it),[89] 并根据这个错误理解进行交往与互动。

一般来说,沉默或不行动不足以构成清楚无误的陈述或承诺或保证,除非一方在这种情况下有责任说清楚(duty to speak)。[90] 如果一方有责任说清楚,他的沉默或不行动就会构成清楚无误的陈述。在 Youell v. Bland Welch & Co. Ltd.（the “Superhulls Cover” Case）（No. 2）（1990）2 Lloyd’s Rep. 431 先例中,Phillips 大法官说:“In the context of estoppels, silence differs from a positive representation in that its effect will not normally be to induce a misunderstanding but to permit a misunderstanding that has already been induced to persist. In such circumstances a party who has remained silent may be stopped from asserting that the facts are other than those which they were mistakenly assumed to be. But such an estoppel will only arise if the party stopped was under a legal duty to dispel the other party’s misunderstanding.”

“沉默性禁反言”(estoppel by silence or acquiescence)与共识性禁反言关系不大,因为共识性禁反言要求双方对错误的理解或共识沟通过(crossed the line)以达到共享(shared)的要求,这一般来说就要求双方有一些言行的互动。

但沉默性禁反言在产权人禁反言就特别重要。沉默性禁反言经常被视为“产权人禁反言”(proprietary estoppel)的分支。如果产权人/业主明知对方(如邻居)对财产(主要是土地/房屋)的所有权有误解但保持沉默,任由对方花钱对财产进行建设或提升,就会构成沉默性禁反言,令对方获得对财产的权利。而如果产权人/业主对对方的误解进行鼓励,就会构成另一个分支的“鼓励性禁反言”(estoppel by encouragement)。在早期的 Savage v. Foster（1723）9 Mod. 35 先例中,案情有关土地买卖,法院判是:“when anything in order to a purchase is publicly transacted, and a third person, knowing thereof, and of his own right to the lands intended to be purchased, doth not give the purchaser notice of that right, he shall never afterwards be admitted to set up such right to avoid the purchase.”

---

〔87〕 参见 Troop v. Gibson（1986）1 E. G. L. R. 1 先例(第 6 页)。

〔88〕 参见 The “August Leonhardt”（1985）2 Lloyd’s Rep. 28 先例(第 35 页)。

〔89〕 参见 The “August Leonhardt”（1985）2 Lloyd’s Rep. 28 at p. 35; The “Captain Gregos”（No. 2）（1990）2 Lloyd’s Rep. 395; The “Vistafjord”（1998）2 Lloyd’s Rep. 343; Hiscox v. Outhwaite（No. 3）（1991）2 Lloyd’s Rep. 524; The “Indian Endurance” and The “Indian Grace”（No. 2）（1998）1 Lloyd’s Rep. 1（HL）; Hillingdon London BC v. ARC Ltd.（No. 2）（2000）3 E. G. L. R. 97; British Glass Manufacturers’ Confederation v. University of Sheffield（2003）EWHC 3108（Ch）; Bridgestar Properties Ltd. v. London Underground Ltd.（2004）EWCA Cov 793 等先例。

〔90〕 参见本书第四章之 6.4 段与第五章第 10 段。

针对动产也是类似的法律地位：Pickard v. Sears（1837）6 Ad & El 469；Gregg v. Wells（1839）10 Ad. & El. 90 等先例。在 Gregg v. Wells 先例中，Littledale 大法官说："a party who culpably and negligently stands by, and allows another to contract on the faith or understanding of a fact which he can contradict, cannot afterwards dispute that fact in an action against the person whom he has himself assisted in deceiving."

例如，公司或其他利益相关人士没收或冲淡其中一位股东的股份时，该股东在知道的情况下，保持沉默而不提出抗议或投诉，他这种消极的行为就可能构成产权人禁反言：Prendergast v. Turton（1843）13 L. J. Ch. 73；Rule v. Jewell（1881）18 Ch. D. 660；Palmer v. Moore（1900）AC 317 等先例。

4.5.3　依赖

依赖（reliance）是构成所有禁反言的重要要件，也是弃权与禁反言最重要的区别：见 The "Kanchenjunga"（1990）1 Lloyd's Rep. 391 先例[91]中 Goff 勋爵的权威说法。

依赖可以从两个方面看待，第一个方面是做出会构成禁反言言行的一方希望他的陈述或承诺会影响双方之间的法律关系（无论是合约或是其他法律关系），或另一方可以合理认为对方希望影响双方之间的法律关系，即希望对方相信这一错误陈述或承诺或保证去行事。例如，提单（bill of lading）的陈述（如货物数量或表面状况良好）如果错误，签发提单的承运人或船东应该可以合理预计会被无辜的收货人相信与依赖。他应该知道货物的权利会通过提单这一物权凭证（document of title）经过背书与交出而转让。所以针对收货人或提单持有人，船东不能出尔反尔说提单的陈述错误并向其证明正确的事实（如准确的装船货量），因为他会被陈述性禁反言。当然有必要收窄禁反言的适用，限制一些随意或无意或不正式的错误陈述被第三人依赖，构成陈述性禁反言：Trane（UK）Ltd. v. Provident Mutual Life Assurance（1995）EGLR 33（Cooke 大法官在第 39 页所说）。再如，A 有内幕消息知道有某个股票会上涨，并想通过电邮通知 B，但错发给了 C。实际上这是个错误消息，依赖了该消息的 C 与他的大批亲友蒙受了损害。A 是不会因此被陈述性禁反言。[92]

第二个方面是提出禁反言的一方必须证明因为对方陈述或承诺或保证或双方的共识，他的确改变了原本的地位。不同的先例会使用一些不同的用字，但意思都相同。在 Central London Property Trust Ltd. v. High Trees House Ltd.（1947）KB 130 先例中，Denning 大法官说只有事实上被对方依照行事（was in fact so acted upon）的承诺才有约束力。在 Tool Metal Manufacturing Co. v. Tungsten Electric Co.（1955）1 WLR 761 先例中，Simonds 大法官说原告必须改变了地位（to alter his position）。这些不同用字的真正意思其实就是 Denning 勋爵在 WJ Alan & Co. Ltd. v. El Nasr Ex-

---

〔91〕　该先例在本章之 3.4.1 段与本书第四章之 11.3 段有详细介绍。

〔92〕　这方面在本书第五章第 7 段有详细介绍。

port and Import Co.（1972）1 Lloyd's Rep. 313 先例所说的对方做了一些他原本不会做的事："he must have been led to act differently from what he otherwise would have done."

在"陈述性禁反言"（estoppel by representation）中，如果被陈述方没有做出依赖或依赖不合理，就不能以禁反言为由禁止陈述方提供证据证明事实的真相。例如，被陈述方已经被警告过陈述不正确，但还是因为其他原因甚至因为自己没水平与不小心依照错误陈述行事，就会有可能被判是没有依赖或依赖不合理。再举提单为例，收货人做出的依赖就是接受这套付运单证并支付货款，进而改变了地位。但如果在收货人做出依赖前，已经被船东知会提单陈述不正确，但收货人因为当时货价高涨并且错误不严重，还是接受了这套付运单证，就可能不能依赖禁反言。

在很多"承诺性禁反言"（promissory estoppel）的先例种，提出禁反言的一方无法证明对方的言行影响了他自己的地位，因此不会构成承诺性禁反言：Central London Property Trust Ltd. v. High Trees House Ltd. ；Cerealmangimi Spa v. Alfred C Toepfer（1983）3 All ER 533；Southwark LBC v. Logan（1995）29 H. L. R. 40；The "Scaptrade"（1983）1 Lloyd's Rep. 146（CA）；The "Leonidas D"（1985）2 Lloyd's Rep. 18；The "Superhulls Cover" Case（No. 2）（1990）2 Lloyd's Rep. 431；Hiscox v. Outhwaite（No. 3）（1991）2 Lloyd's Rep. 524 等先例。这种情况千变万化，如承诺方在做出错误的承诺后很快纠正，令被承诺方来不及做出任何依赖。或是由于合约条文针对甲方要支付乙方的报酬不清楚，为甲方服务的乙方在一连串的交易成功后借机向甲方澄清，要求按照合约条文支付一笔钱，而甲方也承诺会支付并按照合约条文办事。但事后乙方再也没有为甲方带来成功的交易。这样如果双方有了争议，而最后法院对有关的合约条文解释是甲方不需要向乙方支付这笔报酬，乙方不能以事后甲方的承诺构成承诺性禁反言为由要求甲方支付。因为针对之前的成功交易，谈不上依赖事后的承诺，而在承诺后，乙方再也没有成功的交易。[93]

在 Transcatalana v. INCOBRASA（1995）1 Lloyd's Rep. 215 先例中，Mance 大法官说："... accepted that the buyers' telex of Feb 27, 1992 might be regarded as a representation... But .. cannot stand on the basis of estoppels since there is no suggestion that the sellers **acted or relied in any way on the faith of any representation** contained in the Feb 27, 1992 telex ..."（加黑部分是笔者的强调）

在 Towan v. VOF（1999）2 Lloyd's Rep. 443 先例，Steel 大法官说："Nor is there any basis（let alone evidential support）for inferring reliance upon the part of Rowan since the matter did not arise until after the time limit had expired."

依赖对"产权人禁反言"（proprietary estoppel）也很重要，即产权人/业主的保证

---

〔93〕　可见在本书第六章之 3.2 段介绍的有类似案情的 Wollenberg v. Casinos Austria International Holding GmbH（2011）EWHC 103（Ch）先例。

与提出禁反言的一方的损害之间的因果联系：Gillett v. Holt（2001）Ch 210 先例。

4.5.4 不公平与不合情理

不公平(unjust)与不合情理(unconscionable)[94]现在对所有类别的禁反言都至关重要。在将所有类别的禁反言统一到这个充满争议的说法下，不公平与不合情理可以说是唯一的共同要求。而要证明不公平与不合情理，最重要的考虑就是上一段介绍的是否依赖，并因此蒙受损害(detriment)。

承诺性禁反言是否一定需要蒙受损害才能适用有争议。如在追债的情况下，债权人承诺债务人偿还较少的金额，很明显债务人就算依赖了这个承诺偿还了较少的金额，也谈不上蒙受了任何损害：Collier v. P & MJ Wright（Holding）Ltd.（2007）EWCA Civ 1329 先例。比起损失(damage)的索赔，追偿债务(debt)下双方达成的和解协议就会存在一些问题。因为不存在约因/对价，所以无法构成合约，而能否构成承诺性禁反言也存在争议，这方面在本章之2.4.3.1 段与本书第四章之12.1 段有详细介绍。

在《Snell's Equity》(第32 版，2010 年)一书第12－012 段，说："Detriment (as opposed to reliance) has never been held to be a formal requirement of the doctrine. But even if detriment were a requirement of the doctrine the test might not be the same for promissory estoppels and proprietary estoppels. The term 'detriment' has never been used consistently and it can mean either expenditure incurred or loss suffered in a narrow sense..."

根据《Snell's Equity》(第32 版，2010 年)一书的说法，损害不像依赖，被认为是构成禁反言的要件之一，并且相比陈述性禁反言，承诺性禁反言接受的损害范围与类别更广。[95] 但近期的先例普遍认为是否蒙受损害是决定是否不公平与不合情理的重要考虑，因此必须被证明。如在 Collier v. P & MJ Wright（Holdings）Ltd. 先例中，Arden 女大法官说："... the requirement of detriment, and perhaps other requirements of the doctrine, have to be approached as part of a broader enquiry as to whether repudiation of an assurance is or is not unconscionable in all the circumstances..."

另在 Steria Ltd. v. Hutchison（2006）EWCA Civ 1551 先例中，上诉庭的 Mummery 大法官说："Detriment has to be established in the case of estoppel by representation... and, even if it is not a requirement of the doctrine of promissory estoppel, it is relevant to whether it is inequitable to act inconsistently with the promise."

4.5.5 禁反言的救济

陈述性禁反言的救济一般来说是根据陈述方维持自己的错误陈述来裁定双方的

[94] 参见本书第四章第8 段，第五章第9 段与第六章之3.3 段。

[95] 这可见 Mason 大法官在澳大利亚高院的 Commonwealth of Australia v. Verwayen（1990）170 CLR 394 先例所说。这方面在本书第四章之7.4 段有详细介绍。

合约或法律地位,避免被陈述方因为陈述方撤回自己的错误陈述而蒙受损害。所以,相对其他类别的禁反言来讲,陈述性的救济比较没有弹性(flexible)。

承诺性禁反言是衡平法救济,所以追求最低程度的救济,只要纠正不公平之处,尽量不影响原本的合约或法律地位,即所谓的"minimum equity"或"the mimimum equity to do justice":Pascoe v. Turner (1979) 1 WLR 431 等先例。在 Crabb v. Arun DC (1976) Ch 179 先例中,Scarman 大法官说:"I turn now to the... questions-the extent of the equity and the relief needed to satisfy it. There being... no enforceable contract ... I would analyse the minimum equity to do justice to the plaintiff... I do not think it is necessary to go further than that."

衡平法下的禁反言救济也很有弹性(flexible),如在 Roebuck v. Mungovin (1994) 1 Lloyd's Rep. 481 先例中,Browne – Wilkinson 勋爵就说:"when an equitable estoppel is raised is extremely flexible." 另在 Crabb v. Arun DC 先例中,Denning 勋爵也说:"Here equity is displayed at its most flexible, see Snell's Principles of Equity, 27th ed. (1973), p. 568, and the illustrations there given."即审理的法官或仲裁员如果对合约一方不满或看不惯一些言行,可以不管合约如何约定而通过这一说法做出救济,如暂时或永久禁止该方行使合约权利,以达到他希望的公平的结果。

在少数适合的案件中,救济的弹性也可以反映在改变合约条文。如在 Brikom Investments Ltd. v. Seaford (1981) 1 WLR 863 (CA)先例中,房东要求租务主任(rent officer)决定合理的租金,租务主任在当时的《Housing Act 1961》下,根据房东负责修理的默示基础计算出应支付的租金。但在该先例中,租约明示规定由租客负责修理,在此基础上计算出的租金显然比在房东负责修理的基础上计算出的要低。但房东接受了租客所支付的租务主任计算出的租金。法院最后判是房东可以通过合理通知行使租约中租客负责修理的条文,但必须先回复到正确计算与较低的租金,并将之前租客多支付部分的租金退回。即要先将租客回复到没有损害的地位,然后房东再通过做出合理通知回复到原本的合约地位。

另在 Baird Textile Holdings Ltd. v. Marks & Spencer Plc. (2001) EWCA Civ 274 先例中,[96] Mance 大法官提到败诉的原告代表律师曾经提出过一个非常有弹性的救济,说:

"Baird acknowledges that an estoppel precluding M & S from denying that the relationship with BTH could only be determined by the giving of reasonable notice would not assist, unless it also meant that **M & S (and presumably Baird) were precluded from ceasing to place and honour orders for a 'reasonable' or 'appropriate' share of whatever were M & S's requirements from time to time, so as to ensure, to that extent, that the production facilities that Baird had devoted to M & S's business to**

---

〔96〕 该先例在本书第四章之 5.1 段有介绍。

date were maintained, **or at least run down gradually**, during such period of notice. . . Baird's answer is that it **does not seek to protect its expectation interest**. That, it accepts, could only be done in contract. Rather it is **seeking to protect its reliance interest.**

In support of its claim based an estoppel protecting its reliance interest, Baird argues that estoppel is or should be viewed as a flexible doctrine, . . . and that it is open to English law to afford the protection proportionate to Baird's reliance for which Baird contends. . . "(加黑部分是笔者的强调)

在决定承诺性禁反言的救济时,法院或仲裁庭要考虑三个方面。第一,救济应该是暂时性的还是永久性的?如果暂时禁止承诺方行使合约或法律权利可以做到公平,就应该只是暂时性的救济,承诺方可以之后通过合理通知回复到原本的合约或法律地位,而不应该永远禁止承诺方行使合约或法律权利。第二,承诺性禁反言的救济(金钱或非金钱救济)应该根据预期利益(expectation interest)还是依赖利益(reliance interest)。在一个有效的合约中,绝大部分情况下都是根据预期利益进行赔偿,但是承诺性禁反言不是执行承诺,更恰当的救济是让因为依赖对方的承诺而蒙受损害的一方回复到原本的地位。[97] 第三,怎样弹性做出救济,令做出的救济与被承诺方的损害成比例。法院或仲裁庭需要考虑承诺方的行为(不诚实或疏忽做出承诺还是无辜或善意做出承诺)与双方相应的错误、[98] 被承诺方的损害、[99] 承诺或保证的范围等。[100]

法官或仲裁员在行使裁量权决定什么才是适合的救济时,要考虑与平衡双方的利益与损害。在 Roebuck v. Mungovin 先例中,被告被指称曾经向原告承诺不会以原告懈怠为由撤销诉讼请求, Browne-Wilkinson 勋爵说:" Assuming. . . that the defendant's conduct does raise such an equitable estoppel, such equitable estoppel would not impose an automatic legal bar to obtaining a striking – out order. The effect of such an estoppel is to give the court power to do what is equitable in all the circumstances. . . If an equitable estoppel is raised the Court's function is to determine what, if anything, is necessary to satisfy that equity in all the circumstances of the case. That is a far cry from

---

〔97〕 关于预期利益(expectation interest)与依赖利益(reliance interest),可参见杨良宜《损失赔偿与救济》一书第二章。

〔98〕 参见 D & C Builders Ltd. v. Rees (1966) 2 QB 617; Ogulvy v. Hope Davies (1976) 1 All ER 683 等先例。

〔99〕 参见 Emery v. UCB Corporate Services Ltd. (2001) EWCA Civ 675; Banner Industrial & Commercial Properties Ltd. v. Clark Paterson Ltd. (1990) 47 EG 64(损害太细微); Brown & Root Technology Ltd. v. Sun Alliance & London Insurance Co. Ltd. (1996) Ch. 51 等先例。

〔100〕 参见 Hillingdon London BC v. ARC Ltd. (No. 2) (2000) 3 E. G. L. R. 97; Civil Aviation Authority v. International Nederlanden Aviation Lease BV (1997) 1 Lloyd's Rep. 97 等先例。

saying that, where a defendant has led the claimant to some addition expense, he is therefore in all circumstances prevented from relying on inexcusable delay by the claimant which has seriously prejudiced him. If... the defendant is equitably estopped, then the effect of that estoppel would be to give the court a discretion whether or not to strike out the action (possibly on terms) depending upon the balance between the harm done to the defendant by the claimant's delay and the expense or other detriment incurred by the claimant by reason of the defendant's representation."

产权人禁反言的救济是所有禁反言中最有弹性的,也是法官最会按比例(proportionality)行使裁量权的,这也会带来一定的不可预测性。救济的最大程度当然就是令被禁反言的一方做出的承诺或鼓励变为现实,这会导致产权人/业主永久失去有关的财产(主要是土地/房屋):Dodsworth v. Dodsworth (1973) 228 E. G. 1115; Griffiths v. Williams (1978) 2 E. G. L. R. 121; Jones v. Jones (1977) 1 WLR 438; Baker v. Baker (1993) 25 H. L. R. 408; Sledmore v. Dalby (1996) 72 P & CR 196 CA 等先例。但显然这种救济在千变万化的情况下不一定都适合,也往往不成比例。例如,甲方曾经对乙方做出过陈述或承诺,说他可以在这房子永远住下去,而乙方也蒙受了一点损害,如花了小钱装修。如果因为这一点因依赖而蒙受的损害就永远剥夺甲方对这个可能价值几千万的房子的所有权,就很不成比例。要求甲方赔偿乙方这笔装修的钱或允许乙方多住半年是否为更恰当的救济?这千变万化的救济会在本书第七章进一步讨论。

5. 合约更改、弃权与禁反言的区别

5.1　弃权、禁反言与合约更改的区分

弃权、禁反言与合约更改(variation)的区别很明确,合约更改针对的是合约规定,而弃权与禁反言针对的是法律后果。在本章第2段一开始就提到,合约更改的要求与订立新合是一致。合约中也常常会有合约更改必须是书面的要求,如果不能满足书面与存在约因/对价的要求,就不能构成有效的合约更改,而需要弃权与禁反言的说法进行补充。在 Enrico Furst & Co. v. We Fischer Ltd. (1960) 2 Lloyd's Rep. 340 先例中,Devlin 大法官说:"Waiver〔101〕 does not vary the terms of the contract... Waiver is conduct on the part of a party to a contract which affects his remedies for a breach of contract by the other party."

然而在现实中,这三种说法的区分没有这么明确,很多情况下构成弃权或合约更改会带来一样的结果,即原本的合约条文暂时或永久性改变:Watson v. Healy Lands

〔101〕这里的弃权包括因选择而弃权与因宽限而弃权(即承诺性禁反言)。

Ltd.（1965）NZLR 511 先例。在很多案例中，被告往往也会将合约更改、弃权与禁反言作为替代争议一并提出，务求在原条文解释对他不利时，依赖这三种说法反败为胜。

以中国船厂这些年被外国船东大量弃船为例。在 2008“金融海啸”前与外国船东订立造船合约时，航运市场高涨，中国船厂的谈判力量很强，使用的日本造船标准格式（SAJ）对船厂是十分有利。但“金融海啸”后航运市场下跌，在船舶建造过程中，中国船厂的言行常常被外国船东抓住把柄，从而构成合约更改、弃权与禁反言，令中国船厂无法保住原本对自己十分有利的合约与法律地位。

5.2 弃权与禁反言的区分

区分弃权与禁反言就困难很多，Phillips 大法官在 The “Superhulls Cover” Case（No. 2）（1990）2 Lloyd’s Rep. 431 先例中说：“Mr Griffths（被告代表大律师）did not seek to distinguish between waiver at common law and equitable estoppel. This distinction is often elusive.”

但近年来有大量的先例对这两种说法做出区分，这会在稍后的小段做出详细介绍。

5.2.1 早期弃权与禁反言混为一谈

可以说，在很长一段时间内，弃权与禁反言混为一谈，毕竟两者之间的界限并不明确。一个简单的例子是 1979 年《货物销售法》之 section 11（2）规定：“Where a contract of sale is subject to a condition to be fulfilled by the seller, the buyer may waive the condition, **or** may elect to treat the breach of the condition as a breach of warranty and not as a ground for treating the contract as repudiated.”

即说在买方第一次有机会检查货物[102]后，如果发现货物描述或质量不符合合约规定或《货物销售法》之 section 13 与 section 14 的默示条件条文的要求，买方有权利取消买卖合约与拒绝这些劣质或有瑕疵的货物。当然买方也完全可以放弃取消买卖合约与拒绝货物的权利，只索赔货物劣质或有瑕疵所带来的损失。Michael Furmston 教授的《The Law of Contract》（第四版，2010 年）之 365 页认为 section 11（2）同时包含了两类弃权，说：“The first part of the section（‘the buyer may waive the condition’）refers to forbearance-waiver; the second to election.[103] Finally, a forbearance-waiver may be granted before or after the term waived falls due for performance, whereas an election waiver can only occur once a right, such as the right to terminate or to rescind, has arisen, and therefore in the context of breach an election can only be made

---

〔102〕 一般是在卸港，如果买方有机会检查货物而没有检查，就会被认为是放弃了检查货物的权利。

〔103〕 第一部分是“因宽限而弃权”（waiver by forbearance），这本质上是“承诺性禁反言”（promissory estoppel）。而第二部分是“因选择而弃权”（waiver by election）。

after the breach has occurred.[104]"

其他买方拒单/拒货的权利与弃权与禁反言说法的适用可见本章之6.2段与杨大明的《国际货物买卖》一书第四章。

根据1906年《Marine Insurance Act》之section 34(3)的规定,如果被保险人违反了保险合约的先决条件(如通知时效条文)或保单的保证(warranty,如船舶在开航前必须适航或雇用合资格的船员等),保险人可以通过言行向被保险人放弃不再需要理赔的权利。尽管使用了与1979年《货物销售法》类似的"may be waived by the insurer"的用字,这被判是属于"waiver by estoppel"或承诺性禁反言(或因宽限而弃权),而并非因选择而弃权:J. Kirkaldy & Sons Ltd. v. Walker (1999) 1 Lloyd's Rep. IR 410; The "Milasan" (2000) 2 Lloyd's Rep. 458; HIH Casualty & General Insurance Ltd. v. AXA Corporate Solutions (2002) EWCA Civ 1253等先例。在J. Kirkaldy & Sons Ltd. v. Walker先例中,Longmore大法官说:"Section 33 of the Marine Insurance Act provides for the insurer to be discharged from liability as from the date of breach of warranty.[105] It is therefore, apparent that no question of election arises although by s. 34 (3) the insurers may waive the breach. Since the breach of warranty does not give rise to any election by the insurer, e. g. to choose to keep the contract on foot, the doctrine of waiver by election has no application.[106] The owners must rely on the doctrine of waiver by estoppel.[107]"

在The "Milasan"先例中,案情有关一条游艇沉没,但保险人拒赔,理由是游艇的所有人违反了保单的保证,[108]没有雇佣一名专业船长。而游艇的所有人就抗辩说保险人在较早前知道他违反了保证的情况下仍然收取了第二期保费,属于弃权,但这最后没有被法院接受。从案情看,保险人在知道违反保证后仍然收取第二期保费,这言行明显是选择保单继续有效。但因为一旦被保险人(即游艇的所有人)违反了保证,保单自动终止,不存在保险人选择是否终止保单的问题,所以因选择而弃权不适用。可能适用的是因宽限而弃权,但被保险人在文书请求、证人证言与结案陈词中没有证

---

[104] 两者的重要区别之一是因宽限而弃权的言行可以发生在履约/违约之前或之后,但因选择而弃权只会发生在令弃权方有权做出选择的违约发生后。对买卖货物的货不对版,只有在买方有机会检查货物并知道货不对版后,才存在买方行使选择权决定是否拒货,而选择了其中一种就是对另一种权利的放弃。但因宽限而弃权可能会发生得更早(或更迟),如买方曾经被告知货物可能有瑕疵,但因为当时市场上涨,买方表示愿意接受,这可能就会构成因宽限而弃权。这样,如果之后市场情况逆转,买方就不能再以货物有瑕疵、货不对版为由拒货。

[105] 英国《海上保险法》规定被保险人破坏保证的一天,保单就自动终止。

[106] 一旦自动终止,就不再存在保险人有权做出是否终止保单的选择,所以因选择而弃权的说法不适用。

[107] 作为被保险人的船东面对保险人拒赔,想挑保险人的言行,就只能根据"waiver by estoppel"或衡平法宽限或承诺性禁反言的说法。这样,也就必须证明禁反言的所有要件都能被满足,如船东依赖了保险人的言行(明知保证被破坏后,仍追索保费或积极参与),没有另外投保而蒙受其他损失。

[108] 有关保证条文是:"Warranted professional skippers and crew in charge at all times."

明被保险人对保险人的言行有任何依赖并因此蒙受损害,没有满足因宽限而弃权或承诺性禁反言的要件,所以也不成功。Aikens 大法官说:"... the claimant's closing submissions, they accept that the doctrine of 'waiver by election' is not applicable to a breach of a warranty in a marine insurance contract. But they do argue that there has been a waiver by estoppels... Waiver by estoppels requires proof of a clear and unequivocal representation by the representor and reliance by the person to whom the representation was made. There is no plea of an express representation in the re-re-amended points of reply... The only points taken are that the insurers knew of the lack of the a professional skipper... yet they did not rely on the breach of warranty until five years later in their re-re-amended points of defence. No particular of reliance by the claimants are pleaded... "

在 Kosmar Villa Holidays Plc. v. Trustees of Syndicate 1243 (2008) EWCA Civ 147 先例中,Rix 大法官说到破坏先决条件与破坏保证是一回事,适用的是因宽限而弃权:"... the doctrine of election was unneeded in that context since, in a case where the handling of a claim by an insurer constituted an unequivocal representation that it accepted liability and/or would not rely on breach of some condition precedent as affording a defence, and there was detrimental reliance by the insured such as would make it inequitable for the insurer to go back on that representation, the doctrine of estoppel afforded sufficient protection; that, therefore, subject to any waiver by estoppel, breach by the insured of a procedural condition precedent, like breach of a promissory warranty in an insurance contract, automatically discharged the insurer from liability ... "

The "Copa Casino" (2012) 1 Lloyd's Rep. 129 先例也有类似说法,明确了英国《海上保险法》的"弃权"一词其实是禁反言。因此,如果被保险人要提出这方面的争议,要明白需要证明的要件有所不同。Aikens 大法官说:"In the leading case of The Good Luck (1991) 2 Lloyd's Rep. 191, the House of Lords confirmed that when an assured has been in breach of a warranty in a policy of marine insurance then the breach automatically discharges the insurer from further liability under the policy. No other positive action, whether described as avoidance or acceptance of repudiation or otherwise, is needed to make that discharge of liability effective. Because the discharge of the insurer's liability under the policy takes place automatically upon the breach of warranty and no further positive action is needed to bring about the discharge, the insurer therefore does not need to 'elect' whether to terminate the contract or its liability under it, or continue with the contract in being. Thus, logically, when it is alleged that an insurer has 'waived' a breach of warranty in a marine policy by an assured, this must mean that the insurer has waived the breach because the insurer is now estopped from relying upon it. So, where section 34(3) of the MIA 1906 states that 'a breach of warranty may be waived by the insurer'. This must refer to that type of 'waiver' which is concerned with the forbearance from exercising a legal right..."

在笔者(杨良宜)近期的一个有关造船合约的伦敦仲裁中,也涉及代表船厂的中国律师简单将弃权与禁反言这两个说法混为一谈。在该案件中,德国买方在超过死亡日期(drop-dead date)9个月后才终止合约,期间双方有很多互动,也有很多文件清楚证明了双方的言行。该案件没有开庭,而是让仲裁庭根据双方的文件审理。仲裁庭的首席是一位英国的造船设计师(naval architect),另一位共同仲裁员是英国律师。虽然首席与另一位共同仲裁员都认为德国买方胜诉,并在拟定的裁决书重点强调买方的一切言行都有十分合理的解释。笔者不认为可以通过内部讨论说服其他两位仲裁员,因此很快做出了不同意见。首先笔者认为该案件的争议分为弃权与禁反言两个方面。针对买方在死亡日期之后9个月才终止合约能否构成因选择而弃权(选择不终止造船合约),笔者不认为9个月的时间仍然合理,但什么是合理时间跨度可能会很广,笔者无意与其他两位仲裁员争论。但德国买方在死亡日期后的言行与弃权无关,而涉及能够构成禁反言的问题。构成禁反言的要件与弃权不同,要看船厂是否依赖并蒙受损害。有关的证据显示了德国买方向船厂提出很多要求,这在笔者看来是清楚无误的陈述或承诺。而船厂依赖了这些言行做了不少进一步的工作,这显然是蒙受了损害,因此笔者很明确这可以构成禁反言。至于买方的一切言行是否合理,与禁反言无关。在笔者做出这个不同意见后,首席没有警觉他拟定的裁决书需要修改,但另一位共同仲裁员意识到原本的裁决书的写法有严重的法律漏洞。为了防止裁决书被中国船厂上诉到英国法院后被撤销,两位仲裁员对原本的裁决书草稿进行了修改,加上一段说是德国买方的言行并非清楚无误(这与最开始的裁决书草稿中对事实的认定相反)。这属于对事实的认定,法院不会干涉,但笔者认为这种行为属于有理智的不诚实(intellectual dishonesty),但也无能为力。

5.2.2 近期先例关于两者区别的说法

随着弃权与禁反言理论的发展与完善,弃权与禁反言之间的区别也越来越明显。由于弃权的说法是由普通法发展而来,所以需要弃权方知道自己有怎样的权利,而不像主要由衡平法发展而来的禁反言,更强调对方有否依赖构成禁反言的言行并造成损害。所以,现在禁反言的说法不理会做出这种言行的合约方的想法,也不理会他是否知道自己有怎样的权利。特别是在 The "Kanchenjunga" (1990) 1 Lloyd's Rep. 391 先例中,Goff 勋爵明确弃权是基于弃权方知道相关的事实或自己权利(a prerequisite that the party making the election must be aware of the facts which have given rise to the existence of his new right),而禁反言是基于另一方依赖(reliance)了被禁反言一方的言行,但不追求被禁止一方是否知道相关的事实或自己的权利(no question arises of any particular knowledge on the part of the representor)。

这样,"因宽限而弃权"(waiver by forbearance)或"衡平法宽限"(equitable forbearance)已经比较明确是属于禁反言的一种,有说法是一直被称为弃权的衡平法宽限实是"承诺性禁反言"(promissory estoppel)的先驱。[109] 只有因"选择而弃权"(waiver by election)才属于真正的弃权,即在做出选择时,先决条件之一就是弃权方知道或应该知道相关的事实或自己权利。在 Elizabeth Cooke 女士的《The Modern Law of Estoppel》(2000 年)一书第 68 页,更是说可以放弃"弃权"一词,说:"In an ideal world we might abandon the word ' waiver ', splitting the cases to which it refers into election and estoppel. "

有关弃权与禁反言的区别,早在 Craine v. Colonial Mutual Fire Insurance Co. Ltd. (1920) 28 CLR 305 先例,Isaacs 大法官就总结如下:"When its true foundations are stated, it will be seen that estoppel is separated from waiver in point of principle by a very broad line of demarcation. **First** of all, the law of estoppel looks chiefly that the situation of the person relying on the estoppel; **next**, as a consequence of the first, the knowledge of the person sought to be estopped is immaterial; **thirdly** as a further consequence, it is not essential that the person sought to be estopped should have acted with any intention to deceive; **fourthly** conduct short of positive acts is sufficient. "

在 Kammins Ballrooms Co. Ltd. v. Zenith Investments (Torquay) Ltd. (1971) AC 850 先例中,Diplock 勋爵将第一类弃权(选择)与第二类弃权(禁反言)进行了区分。选择是在两个不同的权利中做出选择,而禁反言是失去了某种抗辩。

在对区分弃权与禁反言非常重要的 The "Kanchenjunga"先例中,Goff 勋爵依赖了 Kammins Ballrooms Co. Ltd. v. Zenith Investments (Torquay) Ltd. 先例中选择的说法(doctrine of election),说:"Election is to be contrasted with equitable estoppel... **There is an important similarity between the two principles, election and equitable estoppel, in that each requires an unequivocal representation**, perhaps because each may involve a loss, permanent or temporary, of the relevant party's rights. But there are important differences as well. In the context of a contract, the principle of election applies when a state of affairs comes into existence in which one party become entitled to exercise a right, and has to choose whether to exercise the right or not. His **election** has generally to be an informed choice, made **with the knowledge** of the facts giving rise to the right. His election once made is **final**; it is **not dependent upon reliance** on it by the other party. On the other hand, **equitable estoppel** requires an **unequivocal representation** by one party that he will not insist upon his legal rights against the other party, and such **reliance by the representee** as will render it **inequitable for the representor to go back upon his representation**. **No question arises of any particular knowledge** on the part of the representor, and the estoppel may be **suspensory** only. Furthermore, the representation itself is different in character in the two cases. The party making his **election**

[109] 这会在本书第四章介绍。

is **communicating his choice whether or not to exercise a right** which has become available to him. The party to an **equitable estoppel** is representing that **he will not in future enforce his legal rights**. His representation is therefore in the nature of a promise which, though unsupported by consideration, can have legal consequences; hence it is sometimes referred to as promissory estoppel."(加黑部分是两者的区别)

在 The "Superhulls Cover" Case (No. 2) (1990) 2 Lloyd's Rep. 431 先例中, Phillips 大法官认为分析与区分是属于弃权或禁反言,首先要看陈述方是否知道有关的事实与自己的权利。如果不知道,接下来就要看是否能满足构成衡平法宽限或承诺性禁反言的三个要件。[110]

更近期的 Kosmar Villa Holidays Plc. v. Trustees of Syndicate 1243 (2008) EWCA Civ 147 先例与 Persimmon Homes (South Coast) Ltd. v. Hall Aggregates (South Coast) Ltd. & Anor (2009) EWCA Civ 1108 先例对这方面也有针对。在 Kosmar Villa Holidays Plc. v. Trustees of Syndicate 1243 先例,Rix 大法官将因选择而弃权与禁反言(主要是承诺性禁反言)进行了区分,说:"In sum, therefore, election is the exercise of a right to choose between inconsistent remedies. It generally requires **knowledge** of the facts giving rise to the choice on the part of the party electing, and knowledge of the choice having been made on the part of the other party. Those are the conditions which make the doctrine mutually fair. It typically arises where the parties to a contract have to know where they stand. Thus the choice has either to be **communicated unequivocally** by the party electing to the other party or else the objective circumstances have to be such that the effluxion of time by itself constitutes that communication. Since the election is the choice of the party electing, it is his conduct which is decisive. Once made the **election is final and irrevocable**. **Estoppel, however, is a promise, supported not by consideration but by reliance.** It is a promise not to rely upon a defence (per Lord Diplock) or a right (per Lord Goff). It requires a representation, in words or conduct, which must be unequivocal and must have been relied upon in circumstances where it would be inequitable for the promise to be withdrawn. The need for such unfairness probably means that the reliance of the representee has to constitute a detriment, but even the detriment has, I would think, to be such as to make it inequitable for the promise to be withdrawn. For these reasons, the **estoppel may not be irrevocable, but may be suspensory only.** An unequivocal representation without the necessary reliance, and reliance without the necessary unequivocal representation, are each insufficient. It follows that, as concepts each in their own way designed to hold parties to fair dealings with one another, waiver by **estoppel is the more flexible doctrine.**"(加黑部分是 Rix 大法官认为

---

[110] 参见本书第四章之第 4-8 段与 11.5 段。

因选择而弃权与禁反言的区别。)

而在 Persimmon Homes (South Coast) Ltd. v. Hall Aggregates (South Coast) Ltd. & Anor 先例中,Rix 大法官也将因选择而弃权与"waiver by estoppel"或"衡平法禁反言"(equitable estoppel)进行了区分:

"A party to a contract (A) may waive the obligation of the other party to the contract (B) to perform a stipulation in the contract that is for the benefit of A. A may waive the obligation without any request by B that A do so. But A will only be taken to have waived the obligation of B to perform that stipulation of the contract if, (in the absence of a request to do so by B), A has made an unequivocal representation to B that A does waive the performance of the stipulation. That unequivocal representation can be by words or conduct, but does not have to be as blunt as 'I hereby waive' the other party's obligation to perform the stipulation. For the waiver to be effective, B must either act on the unequivocal representation of A to his detriment; or he must conduct his affairs on the basis of the waiver.

The doctrine of waiver, as summarised above, is similar to that of equitable estoppel, although in the case of the latter the effect of the equitable estoppel may only be temporary. Both doctrinesare to be contrasted with that of election, although all three have sometimes been called 'waiver'."

最后在 Westbrook Resources Ltd. v. Globe Metallurgical Inc. (2009) 2 Lloyd's Rep. 224 先例中,Moore-Bick 大法官将因选择而弃权与禁反言根据做出陈述的时间进行了有趣的区分。因选择而弃权的陈述是对过去有关的违约(past breach)弃权,而禁反言的陈述是对将来对合约的履行(future obligation)的弃权。该先例涉及 3 万吨锰矿砂的 CIF 买卖,所有矿砂必须在 2005 年 4 月 30 日前付运,其中第一批矿砂必须在 2005 年 1 月 28 日之前装船。因为矿砂存在大小不一的块与颗粒,所以根据买卖合约的要求矿砂在装船付运前必须进行筛选。但因为美国装港坏天气的影响,2005 年 1 月 28 日,矿砂的筛选还没有完成。尽管之后天气转好,第一批矿砂还是在 2005 年 4 月 12 日才全部装船。1 月 28 日后不久,双方持续了一段时间的通讯往来,同意等待天气好转。但之后买方(Globe)改变主意不想购买这批矿砂,于是故意不回复卖方(Westbrook)追问买方对于履行整个 CIF 买卖合约的意图与要求的信件。从卖方的信件中可以清楚看出卖方正在筛选矿砂与采取措施将第一批矿砂装船,即在履行合约的过程中。

一审法院的 Tomlinson 大法官判是 Globe 的行为属于放弃了因为第一批矿砂没有在 1 月 28 日付运而拒货的权利。上诉庭支持了 Tomlinson 大法官的判决,Moore-Bick 大法官解释因选择而弃权与承诺性禁反言或衡平法宽限的分别说:"Mr Mallin (买方的代表大律师)criticized the judge for failing to explain the legal basis on which he reached his conclusion, but in my view the conclusion itself was too obvious to call for detailed analysis of that kind. It is well established that if a party to a contract who is entitled to receive performance of an obligation by a stipulated date represents to the other that he is willing to accept performance out of time and the other relies on that representation, he cannot insist on performance by the date originally stipulated. If the representation is **made before the time of performance**[111] **has come**, the waiver will operate by way of equitable estoppels. If it is **made after the time for performance is past** it may also take effect as an election to affirm the contract."（加黑部分是笔者的强调）

6. 公平交易的 Panchaud 原则

除了上述所介绍的合约更改、弃权与禁反言，英国法下也有公平交易（fair dealing）的说法。这是来自非常有争议性的涉及 CIF 买卖的 Panchaud Freres SA v. Etablissements General Grain Co.（1970）1 Lloyd's Rep. 53 上诉庭先例。而由于这一先例没有被推翻或否定，有不少案件（不止是国际货物买卖类别的案件）会依赖这一所谓的 Panchaud 原则要求公平交易，特别是在案件本身的事实没办法满足合约更改、弃权与禁反言的要件时。正如 Sean Wilken QC 与 Karim Ghaly 先生所著的《The Law of Waiver, Variation, and Estoppel》（第 3 版，2012 年）一书之 13.02 段所说："... Where there is blatant inconsistency that cannot be categorized under either waiver or estoppels, a party may seek to rely on various statements made by the Court of Appeal in Panchaud Freres SA v. Etablissements General Grain Co."

以下笔者会对这一 Panchaud 原则做出详细的介绍。

6.1 Panchaud Freres SA v. Etablissements General Grain Co. 先例的案情

Panchaud Freres SA v. Etablissements General Grain Co.（1970）1 Lloyd's Rep. 53 先例的案情很简单，在 CIF/CFR 买卖经常发生。该先例的案情在杨大明的《国际货物买卖》一书第四章之 8.4.5.1 段有介绍。案情涉及巴西玉米 CIF 买卖，付运日期是 6 月/7 月。提单日期是 7 月 31 日，但与提单一起交出的付运单证中包括了一份检查证明，内容中显示了付运日期是在 8 月 10 至 12 日。显然针对检验人而言，他是不会有动机去隐瞒真正的付运日期，但这也显示了倒签提单的问题。买方却没有发觉这一点或并没有理会，就支付了货款以交换这套付运单证。在后来的实际交货中，买方拒绝接收该倒签提单的货物，仲裁是判买方由于时隔太久，不能再以这个理由拒绝货物。到了高院，Roskill 大法官认为买方没有弃权或严格说是禁反言。但到上诉庭，一审的判决被推翻。

已经提到买方如果看了整套的付运单证，就会发现检验报告中提到了巴西玉米

---

〔111〕 在该先例中，履行的时间就是 2005 年 1 月 28 日。

的样品是在8月份装货期间取得，装完货物是在8月12日、13日，付运日期根本不可能是提单的7月31日。但买方被认定没有注意这份检验报告而不知情，并接受了提单与支付了货款。[112] 但稍后买方在卸港以货不对版拒货，至于为什么这样做，可能是货物真的有瑕疵，也可能是玉米市场下跌。但后来买方因为担心这个理由站不住脚（事实上也是判货物的瑕疵与卖方无关），才在3年后的诉讼中第一次提出以卖方违反了付运日期为由合法拒货，[113] 并要求卖方退还已经支付的货款。这也没有被法院支持，上诉庭显然是考虑买方在3年后才提出这个争议对卖方很不公平，而如果买方在卖方递交付运单证时足够小心，早就可以发现倒签提单的问题，估计因此对买方有了一定的抗拒。

但该先例的案情导致了困难，买方虽然自己不小心接受了付运单证，但由于当时买方被认定确实不知道倒签提单的事实，无法构成因选择而弃权。而要构成禁反言，卖方必须证明他依赖了买方的陈述或承诺（不以违反了付运日期为由拒单）并蒙受损害（detrimental reliance）。但在该先例中，卖方并没有因为依赖买方的陈述或承诺而改变地位，也没有蒙受任何损害。因为当时货物已经装船开出，迟延付运的事实没有办法改变。另在该先例中，卖方涉及倒签提单，通常这是卖方自己的欺诈行为，不可能成功要求衡平法的救济。但在该先例中，卖方被认定对此恶行也不知情，这可能在一些案件发生，如卖方只是中间商，倒签提单的是分卖方/发货人。看来，由于弃权与禁反言的说法无法成立，导致上诉庭在不满意买方的情况下创立了这个公平交易的说法。

6.2 CIF/CFR 买卖中买方拒单/拒货的权利与弃权与禁反言说法的适用

首先，CIF/CFR 买卖这种单证买卖（documentary sale），买方有两种拒绝继续履行买卖合约的权利，一种是拒绝有瑕疵的付运单证，另一种是拒绝有瑕疵的货物。这两种权利不会同时发生，而是有先后顺序，虽然很多时候两者的瑕疵指的同一事实，

---

〔112〕 在国际货物买卖中，如果是以托收支付货款，买方可以检查一整套的付运单证，保证没有相互矛盾的问题后再做出支付。但买方不小心，如涉及的付运单证很多，或是当时货物市场高涨，或是时间仓促，买方只会关注最重要的付运单证，即装船提单。至于其他的付运单证，如检验报告，只会匆匆一瞥，只要有这份文件就可以，这也符合人性。而如果以信用证支付货款，银行审单时会小心一些。但检验报告内容中显示的不符点，银行也不容易发现，因为银行不在行，查看单证只是机械式而不警觉。另也通常不会太仔细看付运单证的内容，包括提单背后的条文。英国法律为了保证提单在国际货物买卖中的地位与保护无辜的买方，即使付运单证中的其他文件与提单有矛盾，英国的法院看来倾向支持提单持有人/买方还是可以合理依赖提单的错误陈述，除非提单持有人/买方可以通过明显矛盾之处即时肯定与明确提单陈述错误。这可见笔者的《提单及其他付运单证》（2016年）一书第六章之2.7.2.1段提到的 The "Johnstown" (1928) 32 Lloyd's Rep. 218 先例。另在 Aikens 大法官的《Bills of Lading》（第二版，2015年）一书，也说："... Fortunately, the courts have taken an extremely pragmatic line, holding that the contrary evidence must make the falsity of the statement in the bill absolutely clear to him 'and must be of absolutely conclusive and overwhelming importance."

〔113〕 英国法律允许以正确的终止合约的理由替代之前依赖的错误理由，这可见本书第一章第5段。

如货物表面有瑕疵导致船东签发了不清洁提单(unclean bills of lading)。

但如果买方在卖方交出付运单证托收(collection)或信用证结汇(negotiation)时,接受了不清洁提单(可能当时商品市场急升),买方之后能否改变主意并在卸港拒绝这批表面有瑕疵的货物(可能当时商品市场又骤降)?或是如果付运文件就显示了货物迟延付运,[114]买方虽然发现了这一点但还是接受了付运文件,即放弃了拒单的权利,买方之后能否在卸港以货物迟延付运为由行使拒货的权利?

这就涉及了弃权与禁反言的问题,可节录权威书籍《Benjamin's Sale of Goods》(第9版,2014年)一书之19-153段,如下:

"... A buyer who has knowingly accepted non-confirming documents cannot subsequently reject the goods where there is **either** a defect only in the documents (but none in the goods) **or** where the defect in the goods is apparent on the face of the documents and is known to the buyer.[115] In the latter case, the buyer will have waived his right to reject the goods by taking up the documents with knowledge of the defect in the goods. If he takes up the documents in ignorance of **facts** giving him the right to reject, he will not be taken to have waived his right to reject the documents or the goods, though he may have lost his right to reject by acceptance.[116]

Where a c. i. f. buyer, having taken up documents in ignorance of a**defect** giving him the right to reject either the documents or the goods or both, later discovers the defect and then takes delivery of the goods, he will be taken to have waived his right to reject, not only the goods, but also the documents, on account of that defect.[117] The position would be the same if the buyer learned of the facts giving rise to the right to reject after the goods have been delivered to him and with knowledge of those facts retained the goods.[118]

A number of dicta have cast some doubt on the requirement that the buyer must know of the defect before he can be said to have waived his right to reject. But if the basis of such waiver is that the buyer is 'taken to have affirmed' the contract, it would seem that knowledge of the defect (or at least 'obvious means of knowing it') and of

---

〔114〕付运期是货物买卖合约的重要条件条文。

〔115〕买方在知情的情况下接受了有瑕疵的付运文件,并且只是文件有瑕疵而货物没有,或是文件与货物的瑕疵一致,看到了文件也就知道货物有什么瑕疵,买方不能之后拒货。

〔116〕但如果买方在不知情的情况下接受了有瑕疵的付运文件,就不应被视为对拒单或拒货权利的弃权,虽然买方接受了文件的事实无法逆转。

〔117〕如果买方在不知情的情况下接受了有瑕疵的付运文件,但之后在货物抵达卸港前知悉有关瑕疵,仍可在卸港接受交货,这将被视为对拒单与拒货权利的弃权。

〔118〕如果买方在卸港交货后才知悉有关瑕疵,但买方保留货物而不马上通知卖方退回货物,也是同一弃权的地位。

the right to reject is essential before the buyer can be said to have waived the right〔119〕 to reject... Where the buyer has no such knowledge, he may, however, be precluded from rejecting on the different ground that he was estopped from denying that he had waived his right to do so〔120〕. Like waiver of the right to reject, such estoppel requires an unequivocal representation on the part of the buyer. But the two doctrines differ in that, while waiver of the right to reject requires such knowledge on the part of the buyer but no action in reliance on the part of the seller〔121〕, the converse is true of estoppel, i. e. it requires action in reliance by the seller but no such knowledge on the part of the buyer.〔122〕 The buyer's conduct in **taking up the shipping documents can account to the representation** required for the purpose of an estoppels if those documents on their face disclose the defect giving rise to the right to reject, even though the buyer has not actually become aware of the defect; and such conduct may similarly amount to such a representation even where the buyer does not have such means of discovering the defect. ... **coupled with the seller's detrimental reliance, may justify the view that it would have been 'unfair or unjust' to allow the buyer to object**〔123〕... In the absence of such special facts, it is submitted that the buyer should not have been prevented from relying on the defect if he neither knew of it nor could have discovered it〔124〕 ..."(加黑部分是笔者的强调)

6.3 Panchaud Freres SA v. Etablissements General Grain Co. 先例中关于公平交易的说法

回到 Panchaud Freres SA v. Etablissements General Grain Co. (1970) 1 Lloyd's Rep. 53 先例,Roskill 大法官在一审判是买方没有放弃以货物迟了付运(通过倒签提单伪装成在付运期内付运)为由拒货的权利,也没有被禁反言。但上诉庭推翻了 Roskill 大法官的判决,Denning 勋爵认定买方因为他的行为被禁反言,不能以货物迟了付运为由拒货,说:"... the basis of it is that a man has so conducted himself that it would be unfair or unjust to allow him to depart from a particular state of affairs which another has taken to be settled or correct... If a man, who is entitled to reject goods on a

〔119〕 这是指"因选择而弃权"(waiver by election)。

〔120〕 这是指"因宽限而弃权"(waiver by forbearance)或"衡平法禁反言"(equitable estoppel)或"waiver by estoppel"。

〔121〕 根据弃权说法,买方必须知情,但卖方有否依赖不必理会。

〔122〕 但根据禁反言的说法就是相反,卖方必须依赖并蒙受损害,而买方不必知情。

〔123〕 如果从付运单证的表面就可以看出货物的瑕疵,但买方还是接受了付运单证,这可以被视为清楚无误的陈述。如果再加上卖方依赖了该陈述并蒙受损害,就可能会被认为是让买方在卸港以同样的瑕疵拒货是不公平与不合情理,构成禁反言。

〔124〕 但如果没有这些特殊的事实,买方既不知道也不能发现货物的瑕疵,就不会被禁止以货物瑕疵为由拒货。

certain ground, so conducts himself as to lead the other to believe that he is not relying on that ground, then he cannot afterwards set it up as a ground of rejection, when it would be unfair or unjust to allow him to do so."

尽管买方对倒签提单不知情,但他本可以通过付运单证之一的检验报告发现真正的装船日期。因此 Denning 勋爵认为买方的不知情是他自己导致的,类似于他在卸港放弃了检查货物的权利,构成"waiver by estoppel"。Denning 勋爵说:"... It is a case of estoppels by conduct. The basis of it is that a man has so conducted himself that it would be unfair or unjust to allow him to depart from a particular state of affairs which another has taken to be settled or correct ... By taking up the documents and paying for them, they are precluded afterwards from complaining of the late shipment or of the defect in the bill of lading."

但正如 Michael Furmston 教授在《The Law of Contract》(第4版,2010年)一书第361页指出的,在该先例中,卖方没有依赖买方所谓的陈述(接受了倒签的提单),更不用说是因为依赖而蒙受损害,[125]因此无法满足构成衡平法宽限的要件。

在 Sean Wilken QC 与 Karim Ghaly 先生所著的《The Law of Waiver, Variation, and Estoppel》(第3版,2012年)一书之 13.11 段说:"It is clear that the case was not one of waiver in any form. The buyers did not have the appropriate knowledge of the defect.[126] **It follows that either the case was decided on the basis of estoppels or some other principle**. As far as estoppel is concerned, it is possible that the buyers were prevented from relying on a defect in the documents by reason of the explicit contradiction between the certificate of quality and the bill of lading. That contradiction was patent. The alternative view was that the buyers made some form of representation as to their future conduct which resulted in their losing their right to reject.[127] It is submitted that neither view is satisfactory especially as it is difficult to spell out any form of representation which would found an estoppel.[128] Further, in considering Panchaud the Courts have found it difficult to identify exactly what type of estoppels formed the basis of the decision.[129] Thus, Mr. Justice Goff, in BP Exploration Co. v. Hunt (1979) 1 WLR 783, was of the view that Panchaud did not raise any point of equitable estoppel and, in Avim-

〔125〕 该先例涉及的瑕疵是迟延付运,这是过去的事实,卖方无法扭转。

〔126〕 Panchaud Freres SA v. Etablissements General Grain Co 先例明显不属于任何形式的弃权,因为买方不知道这个瑕疵。

〔127〕 针对买方是否被禁反言,一种观点是提单与检验报告有明显冲突,因此买方不能在接受提单之后再依赖提单的瑕疵。另一种观点是买方接受付运单证构成了对将来的行为的陈述,因此失去了拒货的权利。

〔128〕 但这两种观点都不能成立,特别是根据该先例的案情,很难找出足以构成禁反言的陈述。

〔129〕 另是法院也认为很难确定究竟哪种类别的禁反言会适用。

ex SA v. Dewulf & Cie (1979) 2 Lloyd's Rep. 57, the Judge appeared to treat the case as one raising a common law estoppel. **The conclusion must therefore be that the better view is that Panchaud is not a case on estoppels in the proper sense of the word.**〔130〕"(加黑部分是笔者的强调)

上诉庭尽管与Denning勋爵一样做出了针对买方的判决,但Winn大法官提出了新的原则为理据,说:"In my own judgment it does not seem possible in this case to say affirmatively that there was here either a fresh agreement to rescind or vary the original contract, or anything which, within the scope of the doctrine as hitherto enunciated, could be described as an estoppel or a quasi estoppel.〔131〕 I respectfully agree with my Lord that what one has here is something perhaps in our law **not yet wholly developed as a separate doctrine** – which is more in the nature of **a requirement of fair conduct**〔132〕 – a criterion of what is fair conduct between the parties. There may be an inchoate doctrine stemming from the manifest convenience of consistency in pragmatic affairs, negativing any liberty to blow hot and cold in commercial conduct."(加黑部分是笔者的强调)

因此这个上诉庭先例涉及两种说法,第一种是Denning勋爵关于构成禁反言的要件的说法,他在之后的先例中也重申了这些要件。在Bremer v. Mackprang (1979) 1 Lloyd's Rep. 221先例中,Denning勋爵说:"I regard the decision of the House in Bremer v. Vanden (1978) 2 Lloyd's Rep. 109 as a most important decision on waiver〔133〕... it is the final step in the series of Central London Property Trust Ltd. v. High Trees House Ltd. (1947) KB 130; Ricksrds v. Oppenheim (1950) 1 KB 616; Panchaud Freres SA v. Etablissements General Grain Co. and W J Alan & Co. v. El Nasr Export & Import Co. Ltd. (1972) 1 Lloyd's Rep. 313. Applied to cases of waiver ... It may be stated thus: If a buyer, who is entitled to reject goods or documents on the ground of a defect in the notices or the timing of them, so conducts himself as to lead the seller reasonably to believe that he is not going to rely on any such defect – **whether he know of it or not** – then he cannot afterwards set up the defect as a ground for rejecting the goods or documents when it would be unfair or unjust to allow him to do so..."(加黑部分是笔者的强调)

第二种就是Winn大法官提到的有商业关系的双方有前后行事统一的责任,否则不是公平交易(fair dealing)。

---

〔130〕 因此更好的观点是禁反言在Panchaud Freres SA v. Etablissements General Grain Co先例并不适用。

〔131〕 Winn大法官认为该先例不存在有一个新合约取消或更改了原本的合约,禁反言或准禁反言(quasi estoppel)也不适用。

〔132〕 这是另一种还没有完全发展起来的说法,本质上属于对于公平交易的要求。

〔133〕 早期弃权与禁反言往往混为一谈。

这两种说法加起来可以说是法院会介入阻止一方采取一些不值得鼓励的与前后不统一的做法，即使从经济角度考虑完全合理（如因为市场变化），甚至是合法的。这在 Berg v. Vanden (1977) 1 Lloyd's Rep. 499 先例中，被 Lawton 大法官称为"公平交易的 Panchaud 原则"（Panchaud principle of fair dealing）。

6.4　适用公平交易的 Panchaud 原则的相互矛盾的先例

公平交易的 Panchaud 原则在之后的很多先例被考虑与适用，有些比较宽松适用，而有些比较严格：The "Astraea" (1971) 2 Lloyd's Rep. 494 at 502；The "Vladimir Illich" (1975) 1 Lloyd's Rep. 322；Alfred C Toepfer v. Peter Cremer (1975) 2 Lloyd's Rep. 118；The "Shackleford" (1978) 2 Lloyd's Rep. 154；Bunge v. Toepfer (1979) 1 Lloyd's Rep. 554；Avimex SA v. Dewulf & Cie (1979) 2 Lloyd's Rep. 57；Bunge v. Fuga AG (1980) 2 Lloyd's Rep. 516 等先例。

第一个宽松适用的例子是 Berg v. Vanden (1976) 1 Lloyd's Rep. 348 先例的一审。在该先例中，案情有关 GAFTA 格式的 CIF 买卖合约下的不可抗力通知（*force majeure* notice）是否有效。买卖合约的不可抗力条文规定想要依赖不可抗力的卖方（如遇上天灾令货物延误运到装港做出付运），在做出的通知中必须写明装港。真正的卖方是上海的一家进出口公司，它与 Berg 订立的合约中规定的装港是上海。因此该公司做出不可抗力通知，声称装港有坏天气要求延长付运期时，没有写明装港是上海，因为只会是上海。Berg 将这份不可抗力通知转发给了分买方 Vanden，说："... kindly note that we have received the following cable from Shanghai：'... owing to bad weather cannot load therefore please extend shipment to 31st March'."

这就产生了问题，因为 Berg 与 Vanden 之间的分买卖合约中并没有规定装港是中国哪个港口。Vanden 拒绝延长付运期与最终终止了合约，并索赔没有交付货物（土豆片）导致的损失。关于这份有瑕疵的不可抗力通知，[134] 有争议是 Vanden 在收到这份含糊的通知后，是否应该向 Berg 做出询问。如果 Vanden 做出了询问，这很容易澄清，也就不会存在通知有瑕疵的问题。

在高院，Donaldson 大法官认为公平交易的 Panchaud 原则适用，同意 Vanden 有责任要求 Berg 澄清含糊之处，而 Berg 可以马上回答说它与真正卖方的买卖合约的装港只是上海。Donaldson 大法官总结了双方的争辩说："Is the notice defective as failing to specify the port of shipment? This is a more difficult point. As between shipper and seller (Berg), there was only one possible port of shipment, namely, Shanghai. Accordingly, the shipper's notice impliedly referred to this port. But when the notice was passed on, this had to be expressed. This, Mr. Rokison (Berg 的代表大律师) claims that the sellers did by saying 'We have received the following cable from Shanghai'. Mr. Hallgarten (Vanden 的代表大律师), however says that this means no more than

[134]　有关通知必须清楚无误与严格符合合约要求可见本章之 3.3.3.2 段。

that the cable came from Shanghai... Mr Rokison submits that, at the worst, the cable was ambiguous and in such circumstances the buyers, Vanden, not having questioned it at a time when it could have been clarified, are not now free to do so. This submission he based upon the principle of commercial fair dealing enunciated in Panchaud Freres SA v. Etablissements General Grain Co. ... ”

最终 Donaldson 支持了 Berg 的观点,推翻了判 Vanden 胜诉的裁决书,说:“... The buyers (Vanden) by their failure to inquire whether the goods were to be shipped from Shanghai, in my view impliedly accepted the notice as having that meaning... The sellers (Berg) acted to their detriment in doing nothing to clarify the point, when they still had time to do so. It is now too late for the buyers to complain that the port of shipment was not specified. ”

看来 Donaldson 大法官是十分宽松地适用了公平交易的 Panchaud 原则。毕竟技术上来说,没有做出一份符合合约要求的准确的不可抗力通知是 Berg 的错误。但结果变成 Vanden 要承担没有警告与向 Berg 澄清以让 Berg 可以马上改正错误的责任。因此当这个先例上诉到上诉庭([1977] 1 Lloyd's Rep. 499),Donaldson 大法官的决定被推翻也不难理解。Lawton 大法官说:“I have never thought of the merchants and brokers in the international grain market as fragile characters wilting under the ups and downs of international trade. I can readily understand their being cross if there is unfairness or injustice, but I find it difficult to conceive of their so wilting when one merchant does not take a point about ambiguity in a commercial telex message. It seems to me that Mr. Justice Donaldson was expanding the Panchaud principle far beyond anything which Lord Denning had in mind in Panchaud and which the common law envisages in the doctrine of estoppels by conduct. There must be more robustness in the application of the Panchaud principle. ”

而 The “Shackleford”先例中,公平交易的 Panchaud 原则被更宽松的适用。一审([1978] 1 Lloyd's Rep. 191)的 Donaldson 大法官判是如果合约双方都很有经验与水平高,不需要满足依赖与蒙受损害的要件,也可以成立禁反言。该先例不涉及货物买卖合约,而涉及程租合约,案情在杨良宜的《装卸时间与滞期费》一书第九章第 9 段有详细介绍。简单而言,该先例涉及船长递交了一份有瑕疵或过早做出的不成熟的准备就绪通知书(notice of readiness),并被承租人的代理人没有保留地接受,之后承租人能否以通知书无效为由拒绝支付滞期费?即承租人因为没有立即警告与向船东澄清让船东对通知书的瑕疵进行补救,再做出另一个正确有效的通知书,所以要对船东递交了无效的通知书的错误负责?Donaldson 大法官适用了公平交易的 Panchaud 原则,判承租人败诉,说:“I my judgment, the acceptance of the notice creates an estoppels by conduct within the doctrine propounded in Panchaud Freres SA v. Etablissements General Grain Co, and the charterers cannot now be heard to allege that the notice was premature. . . . I do not understand these judgments（指 Denning 勋爵与 Winn 大法官的判决）as requiring any evidence of positive or active reliance. If a man so conducts himself that another could reasonably regard a particular state of affairs as existing or settled, the only question is whether or not in all the circumstances it would be just and fair to allow him to resile. It is in this context that the position of the other party has to be considered. Deliberate action or inaction in reliance upon the alleged estopping conduct will provide good, and probably overwhelming reason for holding that it would be unfair and unjust to allow any resilement. Evidence that the conduct was unnoticed or disregarded or treated as of no importance might well lead to the opposite conclusion."之后上诉庭也确认了 Donaldson 大法官的判决。

6.5　公平交易的 Panchaud 原则导致的问题

简单而言，公平交易的 Panchaud 原则过于含糊与不肯定。这说法与在本书第四章之 6.4 段与第五章第 10 段介绍的有责任说清楚（duty to speak）有冲突，如在商业合约没有善意（good faith）的要求，或买方自己小心（*caveat emptor*）的原则等。虽然有情况是法律上有说清楚的责任，但必须要满足一些要件，如不合情理（unconscionable）、涉及取巧（sharp practice）、故意不说清楚以误导另一方、设计陷阱等。

在 Panchaud Freres SA v. Etablissements General Grain Co. （1970） 1 Lloyd's Rep. 53 先例中，尽管 Denning 勋爵说构成了"行动性禁反言"（estoppel by conduct），但显然禁反言的几个要件都无法满足，如依赖与蒙受损害。而买方在不知道提单倒签时接受了提单（尽管如果买方仔细查看付运文件可以发现），很难说构成了清楚无误的行为。除了 3 年后才提出倒签提单的争议这一点（但没有过了法定时效），不合情理这个要件也很难满足。无论如何交出错误或倒签的提单是卖方的错误，买方没有发现或指出不能说是取巧或者设陷阱。因此，公平交易的 Panchaud 原则不可能属于禁反言。

公平交易的 Panchaud 原则也不可能属于因选择而弃权，因为根据上诉庭的判决，买方确实不知道倒签提单的事实。而在本章已经多次提到要构成因选择而弃权，弃权方必须知道令自己必须在两个相对立的权利中做出选择的事实与相关的权利。

这可节录权威书籍《Benjamin's Sale of Goods》（第 9 版，2014 年）之 19－162 段，如下：

"... In Panchaud Freres SA v. Etablissements General Grain Co, a c. i. f. contract for the sale of maize provided for shipment in June/July 1065. A shipment was made in August and the fact of late shipment should have been apparent to the buyers （even though the bill of lading was falsely dated July 31） since the shipping documents tendered by the sellers included a certificate of quality which referred to samples drawn in August as having been drawn 'concurrently with loading'. The buyers took up the documents and paid the price without actually becoming aware of this point, and when the goods arrived they rejected them on account of defects for which the sellers were not responsible. Three years later the buyers claimed the return of the price, now relying for the first time on the fact of late shipment as justifying their original rejection of the goods. Their claim was dismissed, the court being no doubt impressed by the possible harshness of allowing the buyers to rely, at such a late stage, on the originally unstated ground for rejection which they could have discovered by a careful inspection of the shipping documents when these documents were originally tendered. To allow the buyers to rely on that ground three years after it had arisen would, it was said, have been inconsistent with a 'requirement of fair conduct'.[135]

But the **vagueness** of this requirement makes it very hard to say which cases will be governed by it and which by the general rule that a buyer can rely on an originally unstated ground for rejection. Hence the Panchaud Freres case has in later cases been viewed with some skepticism.[136] It has been said that 'no distinctive principle of law can be distilled from the... case', and that no 'separate doctrine' can be derived from it; and various other explanations of it have been put forward. One suggestion is that the buyers had waived the right to reject; but in the actual judgments this suggestion was rightly rejected on the ground that the buyers did not know of the late shipment when they took up the documents.[137] Another suggestion is that the buyers' conduct gave rise to an estoppel or equitable estoppel; but it is hard to see that the buyers' taking up the documents amounted to an unequivocal representation that they would not reject the goods or that, if it did, the sellers had relied on it;[138] and in the absence of such a representation and such reliance there could be no scope for either waiver or estoppels. Certainly the sellers lost no chance of curing the defect in their tender, for when the tender was made such cure was no longer possible.[139] Probably the best explanation of the case is that the buyers lost their right to reject the documents by acceptance when they took up, and paid against, the documents, and that they at the same time lost their right to reject the goods as the fact of late shipment, which would have justified rejection of the goods, was ap-

---

〔135〕 这一段是有关案情与上诉庭判买方的言行不符合公平交易,不多重复。

〔136〕 但公平交易的说法十分含糊,所以在后来的案例中对此说法有所保留。

〔137〕 一种说法是买方对拒单/拒货弃权,但该先例的判决明确说买方对超过付运期付运不知情。

〔138〕 另一种说法是买方的行动构成禁反言,但买方接受了单证难以说是对卖方做出了清楚无误的陈述与承诺(将来在卸港不拒货)。毕竟不知情的买方在正常情况下接受倒签的提单是必需的事,不会是将来不拒货的陈述与承诺,更不会希望卖方依赖。

〔139〕 这样,既没有陈述或承诺,也没有依赖,更由于卖方无法补救或扭转这一迟了付运的瑕疵,所以没有损害,怎么会是禁反言?

parent on the face of the documents.[140]”

这个公平交易的 Panchaud 原则是否为比弃权与禁反言更广泛与更有弹性的原则，以保证有商业关系的双方间的公平交易？在笔者看来，这说法接近大陆法的善意（good faith）说法，虽然考虑的因素没有大陆法的善意广泛。如果这是至高无上，但也是无边无际，会带来极大的不肯定。好在根据之后的英国先例来看，答案是否定的，之后的先例一直在控制公平交易的 Panchaud 原则的适用。

在 BP v. Hunt (1979) 1 WLR 783 先例中，[141]案情不涉及货物买卖，而涉及有关在利比亚的石油开采权（oil concession）的合约。Goff 大法官确认公平交易的 Panchaud 原则只适用于货物买卖合约，因此在该先例不适用，说：

“Now it is well established in contracts for the sale of goods that, if a buyer accepts the goods (within the meaning of that expression as used in the Sale of Goods Act 1893), he cannot thereafter reject them: he has a choice, and if he chooses to accept the goods his decision in final. In a c. i. f. contract of sale, he has two opportunities of rejection — a right to reject the documents, and a right to reject the goods, if they are not in accordance with the contract. All that the Panchaud case decided was that if, in a c. i. f. contract, the documents show that the goods were shipped late, and the buyer nevertheless accepts the documents, then even if he has failed to notice the late shipment date when he took up the documents, he will be precluded from thereafter rejecting the goods for that reason. The decision stems from the need for finality in commercial transactions, as does the doctrine of acceptance in contracts for the sale of goods[142]... the Panchaud case does not depend in any way upon the representee having relied upon any representation by the buyer[143] — indeed, on the facts of the Panchaud case itself, the goods were (as is usually the case) on the high seas at the time when the documents were taken up by the buyer.

In a much - quoted passage in the Panchaud case, Winn L. J., having expressed the opinion that it was not possible to say that there was anything in the case which could be described as estoppel or quasi - estoppel[144], with on to say that he agreed with Lord Denning M. R. that

---

[140] 对该先例最好的解释是付运文件中的瑕疵可以从表面看到或察觉到，如果被买方接受，买方也就会失去以同样瑕疵拒货的权利。

[141] 案情在本书第二章之 10.3.1 段有介绍。

[142] Panchaud Freres SA v. Etablissements General Grain Co 先例的判法出于商业上的交往需要有终局性（finality），让双方当事人有肯定性，知道怎样做才在法律上正确，正如在货物买卖中，《货物销售法》之 section 35 就规定买方的一些言行会被视为接受了货物。

[143] 该先例不涉及买方有做出陈述与被陈述方的卖方有做出依赖。

[144] Winn 大法官在该先例经常被人引用的公平交易的说法中也说，在该先例不符合禁反言说法的要件。

'what one has here is something perhaps in our law not yet wholly developed as a separate doctrine — which is more in the nature of a requirement of fair conduct — a criterion of what is fair conduct between the parties. There may be an inchoate doctrine stemming from the manifest convenience of consistency in pragmatic affairs, negativing any liberty to blow hot and cold in commercial conduct.'

This passage is frequently invoked by parties, often as an argument of last resort, when they find it difficult to bring their case within the established principles of estoppel, waiver, or election.[145] But, as I read the words of Winn L. J., he was not attempting to state any principle of general application: he was simply expressing the principle of finality which underlies the doctrine of acceptance in contracts of sale of goods.[146]"

在 Glencore Grain Rotterdam BC v. Lebanese Organisation for International Commerce (1997) EWCA Civ 1958 先例,上诉庭总结了之前的相关先例,判是:(1)Panchaud Freres SA v. Etablissements General Grain Co 先例的唯一合法根据是防止买方太迟拒货的《货物销售法》之 section 35;[147](2)除此之外,没有任何说法要求有商业关系的双方要公平交易;(3)唯一可能有关系的说法是弃权与禁反言,但在该先例中争议双方没有提出、也没有证明满足这两个说法的成立要件;(4)因此,所谓的公平交易的 Panchaud 原则,或者是适用《货物销售法》之 section 35,或者是适用弃权与禁反言,而不是更宽松的新原则。

在 Sean Wilken QC 与 Karim Ghaly 先生所著的《The Law of Waiver, Variation, and Estoppel》(第 3 版,2012 年)一书之 13.15 段总结这个公平交易的 Panchaud 原则,如下:"... Panchaud is an unsatisfactory decision which accords neither with principle nor with logic. However, Panchaud has not been overruled and therefore must be treated as good law. It cannot therefore be baldly contended that Panchaud was wrongly decided. Accordingly, it is submitted that the proper view is that suggested in Glencore and in BP Exploration Co. , Panchaud is only authority for the proposition that in certain extreme circumstances a party to a shipping contract will be precluded from relying on an otherwise valid ground for repudiating the contract..."

---

〔145〕 在后来的案件中,如果案情不能满足禁反言、弃权或选择的要件,Winn 大法官的公平交易说法会被用来作为"最最后的防线"。

〔146〕 但在 Goff 大法官看来,Winn 大法官只是强调了货物买卖在买方是否接受货物的说法必须要有终局的结论。

〔147〕 这方面可见杨大明的《国际货物买卖》一书第四章之 8.4 段。

第四章　衡平法宽限与承诺性禁反言

1. 简　　介

因宽限而弃权(waiver by forbearance)就是弃权方单方面通过言行向对方做出陈述(representation)或承诺(promise),告知对方他放弃他合约或法律的权利。如,卖方对买方说我们合作愉快,下一票货你可以晚一点才付款,而有关的买卖合约是要求一手交钱一手交货。再如,A 对 B 说,你欠我 20 万,但我知道你经济不好,所以只要还 10 万就够了。很多情况是只要一方做出宽限,另一方也按照这宽限行事,最后事情也就过去了,不会产生什么争议。但也常常有情况是一方做出宽限的承诺并没有达到目的,如在上述的例子中,B 贪得无厌,到了应该还债的期限却要求 A 进一步宽限,从 10 万减到 5 万,否则不会还钱。这就可能逼得 A 忍无可忍,通过诉讼向 B 索赔他欠下的 20 万。这就涉及 A 曾经宽限 B 还 10 万就够了的承诺是否有法律效果?

另在国际货物买卖经常会出现的情况是,在订约后市场价格下跌,买方不按照合约准时开出信用证。这是买卖合约的条件条文,卖方可以终止合约并索赔损失。但卖方不想这样做,这会有很多原因,如不想再花费额外的时间与金钱处理手上已有的这批货物,或是想避免将来诉讼的费用与风险。于是卖方在买方没有准时开出信用证后,继续催促买方开出信用证,或是给出一个期限,要求买方在该期限内开出信用证。这种言行显然是一种弃权,既涉及"因选择而弃权"(waiver by election),因为他选择了不终止合约;也涉及因宽限而弃权,因为宽限买方准时开出信用证的合约责任或义务。如果在宽限期间,买方因为市场回升等原因回心转意,开出信用证,整件事情就不了了之。但如果市场继续疯狂下跌,买方坚持不开出信用证,逼得卖方在多次宽限后忍无可忍终止合约,并通过诉讼向买方索赔损失。可以肯定在这种情况下,宽限往往导致损失的扩大,难免在诉讼中带来很多方面复杂的争议。如在责任方面,会有危险是卖方之前的宽限构成确认(affirm)合约继续存在,[1]即做出了放弃终止合约的救济的选择。等到卖方忍无可忍终止合约,在严格的法律下反而变为违约/毁约方。至于损失方面,有争议的地方更多。

说到承诺,做出宽限的承诺只是其中一种。在当今社会,每个人每天都可能会随

---

〔1〕 见本书第一章第7段。

口做出很多陈述或承诺,必须能够区分其中哪些有法律后果,哪些没有法律后果。双方交换了有价的承诺,即有约因/对价(consideration),[2]显示双方有受法律约束的意图,就会构成合约,双方都受合约约束。对债务宽限的承诺也是,贵族院的 Foakes v. Beer (1882) 9 App Cas 605 先例明确必须要有对价,才会有法律效力。再一种是虽然不存在约因/对价,但对方知道了这个承诺,并有所依赖(reliance)甚至是改变自己的地位(change of position),也会带来法律后果。即本章会针对的衡平法宽限或承诺性禁反言。但也有一种情况是,向对方做出了宽限的承诺,可是因为公共政策或立法,对方被禁止依赖这个承诺,也就不会产生法律后果。[3]

一直以来,“宽限”(forbearance)的言行被视为弃权的一种,不仅是在很多早期的先例中是这样的叫法,甚至在严谨的立法如 1925 年《Law of Property》之 section 141 (3)中针对土地/屋宇的买方也说:“... does not render enforceable any condition of re-entry or other condition **waived or released** before such person becomes entitled as aforesaid.”(代表卖方对住客以前的承诺或宽限也约束买方。)另一种弃权是“选择”(election),在很多情况下,构成这两者的言行十分类似,甚至有重叠。近年来,才对这两者进行区分,将衡平法宽限归类为“禁反言”(estoppel),而弃权这一很广泛的称呼只是指因选择而弃权,这可见本书第三章的介绍。毕竟宽限与选择的要求还是有比较明显的区别,选择只是在出现了相对立的权利的情况下,看弃权方是否知道自己的权利与做出的言行,并不追究这个陈述或承诺是否被对方依赖。但宽限会出现在很多情况下,因此发生得更多,主要看对方的依赖,不追究宽限方是否知道自己会被暂时或永久禁止行使权利。在近期的 Kosmar Villa Holidays Plc. v. Trustees of Syndicate 1243 (2008) EWCA Civ 147 上诉庭先例中,Rix 大法官总结了选择与宽限的差异与重叠,如下:

“Election is to be contrasted with equitable estoppel, a principle associated with the leading case of Hughes v. Metropolitan Railway Co., (1877) 2 App. Cas. 439. Equitable estoppel occurs where a person, having legal rights against another, unequivocally represents (by words or conduct) that he does not intend to enforce those legal rights; if

---

[2] 约因/对价的重要性,可见本书第一章之 2.4.3 段与本章之 12.1.2 段。

[3] 在 Actionstrength Ltd. v. International Glass Engineering IN. GL. EN SpA (2003) 2 AC 541 先例,案情涉及口头保证(oral guarantee),根据英国 1677 年《Statute of Fraud》之 section 4,保证合约必须要是书面形式并有保证人的签名,因此,口头保证在普通法下无效。于是原告 Actionstrength 提出了被告的口头保证构成承诺性禁反言的争议,但这不被贵族院接受,Bingham 勋爵说:“... in seeking to show inducement or encouragement Actionstrength can rely on nothing beyond the oral agreement ... which, in the absence of writing, is rendered unenforceable by section 4. There was no representation ... that it would honour the agreement despite the absence of writing, or that it was not a contract of guarantee, or that it would confirm the agreement in writing.”看来如果做出口头保证的一方有其他的言行,就可能会满足承诺性禁反言的要求,Clyde 勋爵说:“In order to be estopped from invoking the Statute there must be something more, such as some additional encouragement, inducement or assurance.”

in such circumstances the other party acts, or desists from acting, in reliance upon that representation, with the effect that it would be inequitable for the representor thereafter to enforce his legal rights inconsistently with his representation, he will to that extent be precluded from doing so.〔4〕

There is an important similarity between the two principles, election and equitable estoppel, in that each requires an unequivocal representation, perhaps because each may involve a loss, permanent or temporary, of the relevant party's rights.〔5〕 But there are important differences as well. In the context of a contract, the principle of election applies when a state of affairs comes into existence in which one party becomes entitled to exercise a right, and has to choose whether to exercise the right or not. His election has generally to be an informed choice, made with facts giving rise to the right. His election once made is final; it is not dependent upon reliance on it by the other party. On the other hand, equitable estoppel requires an unequivocal representation by one party that he will not insist upon his legal rights against the other party, and such reliance by the representee as will render it inequitable for the representor to go back on his representation. No question arises of any particular knowledge on the part of the representor, and the estoppel may be suspensory only.〔6〕 Furthermore, the representation itself is different in character in the two cases. The party making his election is communicating his choice whether or not to exercise a right which has become available to him. The party to an equitable estoppel is representing that he will not in future enforce his legal rights. His representation is therefore in the nature of a promise which, though unsupported by consideration, can have legal consequences; hence it is sometimes referred to as promissory es-

---

〔4〕 选择与衡平法禁反言(衡平法宽限)不同。衡平法禁反言的说法来自 1877 年 Hughes v. Metropolitan Railway Company (1877) 2 App Cas 439 先例,针对的情况是如果一方有法律权利,但通过清楚无误的语言或行动做出他不会行使该权利的陈述或承诺,而另一方依赖了他的陈述或承诺行动(或不行动)。这时。如果再允许陈述方改变主意行使该权利会造成对另一方不公平,陈述方就被禁止行使自己的法律权利。

〔5〕 选择与衡平法禁反言有一个很重要的相似之处,就是都要求有清楚无误的陈述或承诺,这两个说法都会涉及令陈述方或承诺方永久或暂时性失去合约或法律权利。

〔6〕 但两者也有明显的区别。在合约下,选择是一方有权行使权利时,决定是否行使该权利。这个选择一般是在知道相关的事实与自己的权利后做出。一旦他做出选择就是最终,无论是否被另一方依赖。另一方面,衡平法禁反言要求的是被禁反言的一方有清楚无误的陈述或承诺他不会对另一方坚持自己的合约或法律权利,而这陈述或承诺被对方在履行中依赖,并导致让陈述方或承诺方撤回该陈述或承诺会造成不公平。被禁反言的一方是否知道自己会失去权利不重要。禁反言也可能只是暂时性的。

toppel.[7]

In sum, therefore, election is the exercise of a right to choose between inconsistent remedies. It generally requires knowledge of the facts giving rise to the choice on the part of the party electing, and knowledge of the choice having been made on the part of the other party. Those are the conditions which make the doctrine mutually fair. It typically arises where the parties to a contract have to know where they stand. Thus the choice has either to be communicated unequivocally by the party electing to the other party or else the objective circumstances have to be such that the effluxion of time by itself constitutes that communication. Since the election is the choice of the party electing, it is his conduct which is decisive. Once made the election is final and irrevocable.[8] Estoppel, however, is a promise, supported not by consideration but by reliance. It is a promise not to rely upon a defence (per Lord Diplock) or a right (per Lord Goff). It requires a representation, in words or conduct, which must be unequivocal and must have been relied upon in circumstances where it would be inequitable for the promise to be withdrawn. The need for such unfairness probably means that the reliance of the representee has to constitute a detriment, but even the detriment has, I would think, to be such as to make it inequitable for the promise to be withdrawn. For these reasons, the estoppel may not be irrevocable, but may be suspensory only. An unequivocal representation without the necessary reliance, and reliance without the necessary unequivocal representation, are each insufficient.[9] It follows that, as concepts each in their own way designed to hold parties to fair dealings with one another, waiver by estoppel is the more flexible doctrine.[10]"

---

〔7〕 这两种说法涉及的陈述在性质上不同。做出选择的一方是将他是否行使权利的选择告诉对方。而被衡平法禁反言的一方则是做出他将来不会行使他的法律权利的陈述。即说这陈述本质上是承诺，虽然没有约因/对价，但依然有法律后果。因此，衡平法禁反言有时也被称为承诺性禁反言。

〔8〕 总结而言，选择是行使在相互矛盾与对立的救济中做出选择的权利，如终止合约或确认合约继续存在与有效。一般来说，这要求选择方知道相关的事实与权利，而另一方也要能够知道选择方做出的选择。这对双方都公平，特别是在合约双方必须知道他们的法律地位才能有所应对的情况下。选择方做出的选择要清楚无误地及时告知对方，否则，随着时间推移，法律会代选择方做出选择。由于做出的选择是选择方自己的决定，所以选择方的言行才有决定性。而选择方一旦做出选择，就是最终与不能扭转的。

〔9〕 而禁反言是有关承诺虽然没有约因/对价，但被对方依赖。相关的承诺是将来不会以某个理由抗辩或是不会行使某种权利，而允许承诺方撤回相关的承诺会造成不公平。禁反言是暂时性的，而并非不能扭转的。清楚无误的陈述但没有被对方依赖，或是相关的陈述虽然被对方依赖但并非清楚无误都不足以构成禁反言。

〔10〕 虽然这两个说法都是为了保证双方的公平交易/交往，但禁反言的说法更有弹性(flexible)。一般的说法是，英国法律下禁反言是最有力与最有弹性的武器。

2. 历史与先例的发展

因宽限而弃权的说法来自普通法与衡平法。早在 Birmingham and District Land Company v. London & North Western Railway Company（1888）40 Ch. D. 268 先例中，Bowen 大法官就根据 Hughes v. Metropolitan Railway Company（1877）2 App. Cas. 439 先例的判法，说："It seems to me to amount to this, that if persons who have contractual rights against others induce by their conduct those against whom they have such rights to believe that such rights will either not be enforced or will be kept in suspense or abeyance for some particular time, those persons will not be allowed by a court of equity to enforce the rights until such time has elapsed, without at all events placing the parties in the same position as they were before. That is the principle to be applied. I will not say it is not **a principle that was recognised by courts of law as well as of equity.** It is not necessary to consider how far it was always a principle of common law."（加黑部分是笔者的强调）

针对普通法的说法，先节录《Chitty on Contracts》（第 32 版，2015 年）之 4 - 082 段如下："**Waiver or forbearance at common law.** A variation which is not contractually binding (e. g. for want of consideration) may nevertheless have certain limited legal effects. These are sometimes said to arise because the promise by a party to relinquish some or all of his rights under a contract amounts to a 'waiver' of those rights.[11] Unfortunately, however, 'the word waiver ... covers a variety of situations different in their legal nature ...' It is, for example, sometimes used to refer to the variation of a contract which is supported by consideration and therefore binding as a contract. To distinguish between such variations and those which are not supported by consideration, the latter will in the following discussion be referred to as 'forbearances.' A forbearance in this sense may in certain circumstances limit the right of the party granting it to enforce his rights under the contract[12] ..."

订立合约后双方达成的协议属于宽限或"合约更改"（variation），普通法下是取决于合约双方的意图：Stead v. Dawber（1839）10 Ad. & El. 57 先例。《Chitty on

---

〔11〕 一个没有合约效力的更改（如缺少约因/对价）也可能产生有一定局限的法律后果。这可以是合约一方向另一方承诺会放弃部分或全部的合约权利，属于对这些权利的弃权。

〔12〕 但"弃权"（waiver）这个词包括很多法律性质不同的情况。举例说，弃权有时被用来指有约因/对价并且有效的更改去放弃部分合约权利。为了区别有效的更改与没有约因/对价的更改，后者也被称为"宽限"（forbearance），宽限在一定的情况下可以限制做出宽限的一方行使他的合约权利。

Contracts》(第32版,2015年)之4－085段针对这会带来问题说:“**Basis of distinction between variation and forbearance.** The question whether a subsequent agreement amounted to a contractually binding variation or to a forbearance is sometimes said to depend on the intention of the parties. It seems that a statement should be a forbearance if the party making it intended to reserve a power to retract, and a variation if he intended it permanently to affect his rights. In practice, however, neither this nor any other explanation of the distinction provides any very sound basis for distinguishing between the authorities on this subject. The explanation is also open to the objection that it leads to the paradoxical result that, the more a party tried to bind himself by a subsequent agreement, the less he was likely to be so bound. An attempt to abandon a right altogether would be classified as a variation, and so be invalid without consideration; while an attempt merely to suspend a right would have at least a limited effect as waiver. The courts were, however, anxious to avoid the injustice which could result from holding that a variation was not binding for want of consideration. Accordingly, they were inclined to interpret the subsequent agreement as a forbearance, so as to give it at least some legal effects.〔13〕”

而在衡平法下的宽限,可节录《Chitty on Contracts》(第32版,2015年)之4－086段如下:“**Forbearance in equity.** Equity developed an approach more satisfactory than that taken by the common law to the problem discussed in para. 4－085 above by concentrating, not on the intention of the party granting the forbearance, but on the conduct of that party and on its effect on the position of the other party.〔14〕 The leading case is Hughes v. Metropolitan Ry ... This equitable doctrine can now be applied to arrangements which might formerly have been regarded as variations ineffective at common law for want of consideration.〔15〕 For reasons to be discussed in para. 4－104 below, the doctrine is often (if rather misleadingly) referred to as ‘promissory’ or ‘equitable’ estoppel.〔16〕”

稍早已经提到,普通法宽限显然不尽如人意,毕竟确定或找出双方的意图很困

---

〔13〕 订立合约后双方又达成协议,但没有约因/对价,这属于宽限或合约更改,有时被认为是取决于合约双方的意图。这看来是如果一方希望将来回复到原本的地位,则属于宽限,而如果一方打算永久放弃权利,则属于更改。但这会造成自相矛盾的结果,就是合约方越是希望被订立合约后双方达成的协议约束,越是可能不受约束。举例说,一方希望完全放弃某个权利,应该属于更改,但因为没有约因/对价而无效。但如果只是暂时中止行使权利,反而至少有一定的法律效力。而确定双方的真正意图很困难,因此在实践中,普通法法院一般都判是宽限而不是更改,防止因为缺乏约因/对价而无效。

〔14〕 衡平法宽限不重视做出宽限一方的意图,而关注他的言行与对另一方所造成的影响。

〔15〕 这个衡平法宽限可以适用在普通法下,因为没有约因/对价而无效的更改。

〔16〕 衡平法宽限有时也被称为承诺性禁反言或衡平法禁反言。

难,也因此在适用时会有一定的障碍。但在 1875 年 11 月 1 日《Judicature Act 1873》生效后,普通法法院与衡平法法院已经合并。法官在判决时会一并考虑,所以再也没有必要区分普通法与衡平法下宽限的区别。如在程序上,以前禁反言只能在衡平法院提出,但在《Judicature Act 1873》后,做法上就变为可以把禁反言作为抗辩(defence)或要求中止(stay),阻止对方行使他的合约或法律权利。

"宽限"(forbearance)有很多不同的称谓,包括"equitable forbearance"、"equitable estoppel"、"abandonment"、"waiver by estoppel"、"quasi estoppel"、"estoppel by encouragement"〔17〕等。由于宽限在合约的范畴通常发生在履行时,而且往往是通过言行向对方做出承诺不会行使权利,并被归类为禁反言,所以与"承诺性禁反言"(promissory estoppel)十分相似,甚至根本可以说是相同。正如在 Ajayi v. R. T. Briscoe (Nigeria) Ltd. (1964) 1 WLR 1326 先例中,Hodson 勋爵说:"The principle, which has been described as quasi estoppel and perhaps more aptly as promissory estoppel, is that when one party to a contract in the absence of fresh consideration agrees not to enforce his rights an equity will be raised in favour of the other party."

只是衡平法宽限的范围相对狭窄,只针对对合约权利的宽限,而承诺性禁反言可以针对合约权利外所有其他的承诺。

另是衡平法宽限与"因选择而弃权"(waiver by election)在很多先例中也常常被一并提及,虽然这两者的本质十分不同。前者强调对方要依赖宽限方的言行并蒙受损害,而后者强调弃权方知道自己的权利。如合约一方违反条件条文,如果无辜方选择要求对方继续履行合约,可以说是做出了选择,放弃了终止合约的权利。而如果违约方因为依赖无辜方要求继续履行合约的言行而蒙受损害,如没有将船舶分租给其他人,无辜方之后出尔反尔要终止合约就构成了衡平法宽限,带来与因选择而弃权同样的后果。

所以,本章就将承诺性禁反言与衡平法宽限一并介绍。

2.1 衡平法宽限先例之一:Hughes v. Metropolitan Railway Company

衡平法宽限(或承诺性禁反言,虽然当时还没有这说法)最早的先例是 Hughes v. Metropolitan Railway Company (1877) 2 App Cas 439,这也是《Judicature Act 1873》于 1875 年 11 月 1 日生效后的第一个案件。

在该先例中,房东根据租赁合约向租客发出通知,要求他在 6 个月内对房屋进行修理。发出通知后不久,双方开始谈判,让房东将这个租约买回,但最后无法达成协

---

〔17〕 "因鼓励被禁反言"(estoppel by encouragement)与承诺性禁反言有一定的区别。虽然两者都涉及一方做出了承诺,撤回承诺会对另一方造成不公平。但因鼓励被禁反言针对的是财产权(proprietary right),而承诺性禁反言针对的是个人的权利(personal right),包括合约的权利。另是因鼓励被禁反言是永久性的改变了双方的权利,而承诺性禁反言在很多情况下只是暂时性改变,被禁反言的一方可以通过合理通知回复到原本的合约或法律地位。

议。但在双方谈判期间,租客写信给房东说“... we propose to defer commencing the repairs until we hear from you as to the probability of an arrangement such as we suggest”,而房东也同意。在谈判破裂后,房东立即要求终止租约并收回房子,理由是租客没有按照租赁合约在,6 个月内进行修理。但房东的要求没有被法院支持,Cairns 勋爵说:“... it is the first principle upon which all Courts of Equity proceed, that if parties who have entered into definite and distinct terms involving certain legal results – certain penalties or legal forfeiture – afterwards by their own act or with their own consent enter upon a course of negotiation which has the effect of leading one of the parties to suppose that the strict rights arising under the contract will not be enforced, or will be kept in suspense, or held in abeyance, the person who otherwise might have enforced those rights will not be allowed to enforce them where it would be inequitable having regard to the dealings which have thus taken place between the parties.”

在该先例中,法院是做出了因延误被没收财产/丧失合约的衡平法救济(relief against forfeiture),判在房东与租客谈判的这段时间,6 个月内完成修理的时限暂停计算,谈判破裂后再开始继续计算。在该先例中,如果将谈判时间扣除,租客是有在 6 个月内完成修理。

2.2 衡平法宽限先例之二:Birmingham and District Land Company v. London and North Western Railway Company

在这个先例之后的 Birmingham and District Land Company v. London and North Western Railway Company (1888) 40 Ch. D. 268 先例中,原告根据合约可以在一块土地上建造房屋并长期租用该房屋。如果原告没有在某个日期前完成建造,土地所有人的被告可以终止合约。在该先例中,被告得知一个私人法案将会通过,并会影响他的土地,于是指示原告暂停建造等待结果。这被法院解释为向原告承诺如果他这么做,被告将不会行使时限的条文终止合约。之后法案果然通过,被告以原告没有按照合约在某个日期前完成建造为由而终止合约并收回了土地。原告向法院起诉,声称被告的言行是适用衡平法宽限,不能终止合约。三位大法官都认为 Hughes v. Metropolitan Railway Company (1877) 2 App Cas 439 先例适用,Cotton 大法官没有给任何理由。Lindley 大法官说:“(Hughes v. Metropolitan Railway Company 先例是)a general principle and ... it is plainly applicable.”Bowen 大法官说:“It seems to me to amount to this, that if persons who have contractual rights against others induce by their conduct those against whom they have such rights to believe that such rights will either not be enforced or will be kept in suspense or abeyance for some particular time, those persons will not be allowed by a Court of Equity to enforce the rights until such time has elapsed, without at all events placing the parties in the same position as they were before.”

2.3　承诺性禁反言先例之一：Central London Property Trust Ltd. v. High Trees House Ltd.

这种说法的案例沉静了约七十年后，Denning 大法官在 Central London Property Trust Ltd. v. High Trees House Ltd.（1947）KB 130 先例再把这个 Hughes v. Metropolitan Railway Company（1877）2 App Cas 439 先例挑出来，发展出了“承诺性禁反言”（promissory estoppel）的说法。该先例的案情涉及在 1937 年原告以每年 2500 英镑的租金将伦敦的一栋楼租给被告长达 99 年。1940 年，由于第二次世界大战爆发，伦敦被轰炸，很多人离开伦敦回到郊区，导致被告很难分租。经过双方谈判，原告同意租金减半。这个承诺显然只有单方面获利，没有约因/对价。到 1945 年第二次世界大战结束，租赁市场恢复，被告将整栋楼都分租了出去。原告要求被告支付合约规定的租金，但被拒绝。于是原告向法院提起诉讼，在一审，Denning 大法官就带出了承诺性禁反言的说法，并判原告在 1945 年可以恢复合约的租金，但在 1940 年至 1945 年之间收取合约规定的租金的权利已经被放弃。至于承诺性禁反言的说法或定义，Denning 大法官说：“Where, by words or conduct, a person makes an unambiguous representation as to his future conduct, intending the representation to be relied on and to affect the legal relations between the parties, and the representee alters his position in reliance on it, the representor will be unable to act inconsistently with the representation if by so doing the representee would be prejudiced.”

构成承诺性禁反言的要件会稍后针对。可以看到，承诺性禁反言与衡平法宽限之间的相似之处。在 Central London Property Trust Ltd. v. High Trees House Ltd. 先例中，房东承诺住客只需要支付一半的租金看来是普通法下的弃权或宽限。显然这会被租客依赖与照办，但后来情况有了变化与房东改变主意要行使他在租约下的权利，否则也不会出争议。

2.4　承诺性禁反言先例之二：Tool Metal Manufacturing Co. Ltd. v. Tungsten Electric Co. Ltd.

Central London Property Trust Ltd. v. High Trees House Ltd.（1947）KB 130 先例后，承诺性禁反言的说法在 Tool Metal Manufacturing Co. v. Tungsten Electric Co.（1955）1 WLR 761 先例有了进一步的发展。Tool Metal 作为专利所有人与 Tungsten 订立合约，授权 Tungsten 出售或使用专利下的材料。但超过一定数额之后，就要支付相等于超出部分价值 30% 的赔偿。1942 年，Tool Metal 同意暂停行使该赔偿条文，双方对新合约进行谈判。1945 年，Tungsten 声称 Tool Metal 欺诈性误述并索赔损失，而 Tool Metal 则在 1946 年 3 月 28 日向 Tungsten 反索赔 1942 年开始他没有根据合约支付的赔偿。这个反索赔没有被法院支持，因为在期间 Tool Metal 仍然属于弃权的状态。之后 Tool Metal 开始诉讼，要求 Tungsten 支付 1947 年 1 月之后根据合约应付的赔偿。

贵族院接受承诺性禁反言的说法（虽然贵族院使用的是“弃权”一词，这也是早期弃权与禁反言混为一谈的例子)是可以适用在减少支付应付款项的情况。在该先例中,贵族院主要针对了承诺性禁反言只是暂时性的,可以通过合理的通知回复到原本的合约地位。贵族院最终支持了 Tool Metal 的索赔,认为 Tool Metal 在 1946 年 3 月 28 日的反索赔已经是足够的通知,在合理时间(1947 年 1 月)后可以回复到合约规定的地位。Simonds 子爵说:"On my part I have, after some hesitation, formed the opinion that, as soon as the counterclaim was delivered, the respondents must be taken to know that the suspensory period was at an end and were bound to put their house in order... Equity demands that all the circumstances of the case should be regarded, and I think that the fair and reasonable view is that the respondents could not, after they had received the counterclaim, regard themselves as entitled to further indulgence."

Oaksey 勋爵也说:"In my view, the counterclaim of March 26, 1946, followed by a period of nine months to January 1, 1947, from which date compensation in the present action is claimed, is sufficient to satisfy the requirements of equity and entitle TMMC (appellants) to recover compensation under Clause 5 of the deed as from the latter date... Any other result would, I think, be highly inequitable."

2.5 承诺性禁反言说法的其他疑问与之后的发展

承诺性禁反言在 1946 年的 Central London Property Trust Ltd. v. High Trees House Ltd. (1947) KB 130 先例后有不断的发展,毕竟该先例的案情不能给这个说法全面的解释与适用范围。正如 Hailsham 勋爵在 Woodhouse AC Israel Cocoa Ltd. SA v. Nigerian Produce Marketing Co. Ltd. (1972) 1 Lloyd's Rep. 439 (HL)先例就提到:"... the time may soon come when the whole sequence of cases based on promissory estoppel since the war, beginning with [High Trees 先例] may need to be reviewed and reduced to a coherent body of doctrine... I do not mean to say that they are to be regarded with suspicion. But as is common with an expanding doctrine they do raise problems of coherent exposition which have never been systematically explored."

另在 Shelia Maharaj v. Chand (1986) AC 898 先例中,枢密院也说:"The doctrine of promissory estoppel is now firmly established although its frontiers are still being worked out."

例如,承诺性禁反言与合约的承诺究竟有何实际区别还是有一点模糊。当然可以说前者没有约因/对价,但后者就必须有,但如果两者都会带来法律后果就会导致有无约因/对价再没有实质意义与关系。因为如果做出承诺,有约因/对价,固然是受到合约的约束,但就算没有,也可以带来禁反言的后果。这样,岂非任何承诺都会导致法律后果,并导致坚持约因/对价的说法形同虚设?在 Central London Property Trust Ltd. v. High Trees House Ltd. 先例中,Denning 勋爵提到租客改变地位(led to act differently from what he would otherwise have done)与根据房东的承诺行事(conducted his affairs on the basis that he has that benefit),但没有进一步解释怎样改变地位与根据房东的承诺行事，毕竟有约因/对价的合约承诺也有这种情况出现。事实上 Denning 勋爵自己很快在 Combe v. Combe（1951）2 KB 215 先例就把没有约因的承诺加上了局限，说只能用在抗辩："... It only prevents a party from insisting upon his strict legal rights, when it would be unjust to allow him to enforce them, having regard to the dealings which have taken place between the parties..."

针对承诺性禁反言，Central London Property Trust Ltd. v. High Trees House Ltd. 先例也有其他方面的不明确。其中之一就是是否需要另一方因为依赖被禁反言方的陈述或承诺而蒙受损害(detriment)。这也导致在之后的先例中法院针对这点有不同的对待。其中一些先例要求另一方因为依赖被禁反言方的陈述或承诺而蒙受损害，但没有进一步的讨论：Augier v. Secretary of State for the Environment（1978）38 P. & C. R. 219；James v. Heim Gallery（London）Ltd.（1980）256 EG 819（CA）等先例。但在 The"Superhulls Cover"Case（No. 2）（1990）2 Lloyd's Rep. 431 先例中，Phillips 大法官明确认为不需要另一方因为依赖被禁反言方的陈述或承诺而蒙受损害。

另一个不明确的方面是，承诺性禁反言能否适用在合约关系外〔18〕的其他法律关系。这在之后的先例中应该比较明确可以适用在其他的法律关系，但模糊的地方在于究竟包括哪些法律关系或者说适用的范围究竟有多大。

在之后的先例中，针对衡平法宽限或承诺性禁反言逐渐发展出让承诺方撤回承诺会带来不公平，被承诺方依赖承诺并蒙受损害等条件或要求。这会在接下来的段节进一步讨论。

3. 是否要求衡平法宽限的承诺方知道自己的权利

Central London Property Trust Ltd. v. High Trees House Ltd.（1947）KB 130 先例没有针对承诺方是否需要知道自己会暂时或永久失去的权利这一重要问题，并带来了不明确之处。在该先例中，作为承诺方的房东知道自己在租约下的权利，所以承诺方知道自己的权利是否构成衡平法宽限或承诺性禁反言的要件在该先例没有针对，也无须针对。

3.1　不要求承诺方知道自己权利的先例：Bremer v. Vanden

在 Bremer v. Vanden（1978）2 Lloyd's Rep. 109 的贵族院先例中，案情涉及货物买卖合约下不可抗力条文中延期付运(extension of time)的通知。如果该通知有效，可以允许卖方延迟 1 个月付运有关货物。该先例中的延期付运通知有缺陷(没有明确装港)，但买方的言行令卖方相信该通知被买方接受。因此，卖方认为在延迟的 1

〔18〕 Hughes v. Metropolitan Railway Company（1877）2 App Cas 439 先例与 Central London Property Trust Ltd. v. High Trees House Ltd.（1947）KB 130 先例都涉及合约关系。

个月时间内做出付运就符合买卖合约的要求，并在后来做出了划归通知（appropriation notice）。但买方说是买卖合约规定的付运期已过（即买方不同意付运期被延长了1个月），所以拒绝接受这划归通知。贵族院判是即使该延期付运通知是有缺陷（装港没有明确与/或做出通知的时间太晚），买方接受了就构成弃权。Salmon勋爵说："... To make an unequivocal representation or waiver, it is not necessary for the buyers to say – 'We hereby waive it'. It is quite enough if they behave or write in such a way that reasonable sellers would be led to believe that the buyers were waiving any defect there might be in the notice and were accepting it as effectively extending the date for delivery... **If the buyers, by their telexes or by their conduct lead the sellers to believe that they accepted the notice as a good notice, they necessarily waived any defect it might contain, whether they were aware of it or not**..."（加黑的一句是说弃权不必理会弃权方是否知道他失去的权利。）[19]

Salmon勋爵这句话就带来了争议，就是看来弃权的说法再也不追究弃权方是否知道自己的权利。根据该先例的事实，同时涉及因选择而弃权（选择是否接受卖方有缺陷的通知）与衡平法宽限（宽限卖方做出有缺陷通知的违约）。因为该先例相对早期，Salmon大法官并没有进行区分，只是笼统地说是弃权，但从现在的角度来看也同时涉及禁反言的要素。

3.2 多数看法不要求承诺方知道自己权利的上诉庭先例：Bremer v. Mackprang

在接下来的上诉庭先例中，重要例外情况出现在Bremer v. Mackprang (1979) 1 Lloyd's Rep. 221先例中，它是无数的由于美国密西西比河发生大水泛滥，美国政府害怕出口太多导致美国本土牲畜粮食短缺，所以在1973年6月27日作出禁令禁止美国大豆出口所带来的案件之一。这事后被认为是美国政府过激的行动，而事实上美国也很快在1973年7月2日后放宽了禁令，允许已经订立了买卖合约的当事人去当局申请批准付运合约约定数量40%的大豆。也就是说，在1973年6月27日至1973年7月2日之间是完全禁止出口，除非已经在驳船上待装的大豆或已经装上船的大豆。该禁令最终在1973年10月1日全面取消。但期间，大豆市场价格狂升，导致大量的买卖合约（卖方主要是十几家世界出名的贸易商）无法被执行或执行要面临很大困难。而卖方即使执行，也会在绝大多数的合约中亏本。这些案件主要涉及GAFTA标准买卖合约格式中的条文，如"禁止出口免责条文"（prohibition clause）与

---

〔19〕 这里Salmon大法官用的虽然是弃权，但同样的事实下也可能构成禁反言。弃权是买方面对有缺陷的延期付运通知，选择不拒绝甚至放弃终止合约的权利，这要求买方知道他的权利才进行选择。同一事实下，如果要构成禁反言，就要求卖方依赖了买方通过无条件接受有缺陷通知做出的放弃权利的陈述，买方做出这样的陈述不需要知道他的权利。所以在较早的先例中，经常把弃权与禁反言一并提及。

不可抗力条文能否保障不愿意或无法提供货物的卖方，与卖方是否有责任购买“浮动货物”（floating cargo）以履行合约的问题。这在杨大明的《国际货物买卖》一书第六章有详细介绍，这里就不再赘述。

在 Bremer v. Mackprang 先例中，争议之一是针对对有缺陷通知的弃权，如 GAFTA 合约中的“延期付运通知”（extension of time notice）与未确定货物的买卖合约中的“划归通知”（appropriation notice）。后者主要是在 CIF 或 CFR 买卖中，卖方把货物装在他租用的船上，决定把装在某一艘船上的货物或部分货物划归给某个特定的买卖合约下的买方（因为一个业务量大的卖方往往手中有很多同类型的买卖合约）。这也表示该船上的货物风险转移到该特定的买方了。没有这个划归通知，如果某艘船舶半途沉没，风险恐怕就要卖方自己来承担，而不能从与他签订买卖合约的多位买方随便挑一个，并把风险推给该买方。Denning 勋爵在该先例也谈到同样的原则，即如果没有做出划归通知，则不可以依赖不可抗力条文。毕竟美国对大豆出口的禁令是有例外情况，如果没有做出划归通知就可以依赖不可抗力条文，并将符合禁令例外情况但还没有做出划归通知的货物再高价转售，这显然会造成不公平。Denning 勋爵说：“Once this embargo, with loopholes, was imposed, the sellers could cancel all their outstanding contracts in which they had not given notices of appropriation. They could cancel all those in which the goods had already been loaded or were already on lighters or in the process of being loaded[20]: but had not been appropriated. And they could resell those goods at the enhanced prices then ruling in the trade. That would be most unjust.”

以上的解释显示了划归通知的重要性，而与其他通知一样，划归通知必须完全正确与符合合约条文的要求，才会有效。正如 Hoffmann 勋爵在本书第一章之 6.3 段已经提到的 Mannai Investment Co. Ltd. v. Eagle Star Life Assurance Co. Ltd.（1997）AC 749 先例中说：“If the clause had said that the notice had to be on blue paper, it would be no good serving a notice on pink paper, however clear it might have been that the tenant wanted to terminate the lease.”

如果这些通知中有缺陷，但被对方（买卖合约中就是买方）所接受，这在英国法很明确会导致弃权或禁反言。在 Bremer v. Mackprang 先例中，上诉庭依赖了贵族院的 Bremer v. Vanden（1978）2 Lloyd's Rep. 109 先例中，并引用了 Salmon 勋爵的判决，如下：“To make an unequivocal representation or waiver, it is not necessary for the buyers to say – ‘We hereby waive it’. It is quite enough it they behave or write in such a way that reasonable sellers would be led to believe that the buyers were waiving any defect there might be in the notice and were accepting it as effectively extending the date for delivery ... If the buyers, by their telexes or by their conduct lead the sellers to believe

〔20〕 这是禁令的例外情况。

that they accepted the notice as a good notice, they necessarily waived any defect it might contain, whether they were aware of it or not."

这种涉及有缺陷通知的案例在程租合约中船东递交的"准备就绪通知书"(notice of readiness)上最为常见。发货人或收货人或其代理人在装港或卸港接受了船长递交的有缺陷的通知书(缺陷往往是船舶尚未满足租约条文中递交通知书的要求,但接受方并不知情)。这方面的问题不止在国际货物买卖或航运合约,在任何其他涉及通知的行业都会发生。无条件接受有缺陷通知的法律后果在本章之12.2段进一步探讨。

3.2.1 有关一连串买卖合约中下一手买方无法知道通知有缺陷的现实

在 Bremer v. Mackprang (1979) 1 Lloyd's Rep. 221 先例与有关的先例中,都涉及了一种"绕圈子"买卖(circle sales)或合约链(string contracts),即把有关的货物在付运前与付运后进行买卖,这种买卖或转卖会涉及几十甚至上百个不同贸易商,每个中间商都既是卖方也是买方,他们在同一票货物的买卖与转卖中纯粹是为了能赚取差价。这样,如果涉及通知,往往就是一手转给一手,即原卖方给的通知,第一手买方作为卖方给下一个合约的买方,下一个合约的买方再以卖方的身份转给下下合约的买方等。所以,有关的买卖合约标准格式是有条文针对这种转发的通知千万不要延误。如在 Bremer v. Mackprang 先例的 GAFTA 100 针对 CIF 买卖就有第 10 条文,要求如果在该天的下午 4 点之前收到划归通知(appropriation notice),就必须在当天转发。而如果是下午 4 点后才收到,就必须在第二天的早晨转发给下一手买方。而通常的做法中,每个合约中的买方都会接受并转发给下一手的买方,他们不会对有关的通知是否有缺陷提出质疑,也往往不会知道是否有缺陷。如在 Bremer v. Mackprang 先例中,其中一个中间商在收到通知后的 9 天后才转发给下一个买方,这显然是有严重缺陷的通知。但问题是除了延误的中间商(卖方/买方)知道外,接下来的买方没有人会知道。这样,如果接下来的买方都接受了该有缺陷的通知,会否是构成弃权,毕竟他们是无法知情。这带来上诉庭三位大法官之间的不同看法。

3.2.2 上诉庭多数看法与判决不要求买方的承诺方知道自己的权利

在 Bremer v. Mackprang (1979) 1 Lloyd's Rep. 221 先例中,多数意见的 Denning 勋爵与 Shaw 大法官是认为买方即使不知情也无法知情但还是弃权,所以接受了有缺陷的划归通知事后就无法在拒绝。Denning 勋爵说:

"The sellers claimed that the buyers had waived the defect – by accepting the notice of appropriation on Aug 14, 1973 without demur: and by treating the shipment as good all the time. On the face of it, the sellers held the shipping documents for the benefit of the ultimate receivers and presented them to them. They did not resell the goods at a profit, as they might have done, but tendered them at the contract price (the low price of \$135.25) to the buyers. They **thus changed their position** on the basis that the notice of appropriation was good.

This raises a **nice point on the law of waiver**.[21] It must be observed that as between these intermediate sellers and these intermediate buyers - **in the long string** - **no one had any knowledge of the nine day gap except the one who was responsible for it.** Everyone in the sting assumed that the notice of appropriation was passed down the line of communication in the time required by GAFTA 100. The only buyer who defaulted was the one who allowed nine days to elapse before serving it. Are all the others to suffer on that account? I do not think so. If the intermediate buyers down the line and ultimate receivers sought to challenge the notice of appropriation, they ought to have done so when they first received it. They ought to have made enquiries then of the buyers further up the string. They ought not to have treated it as good as they did - right up to the time when the shipping documents were presented.

It seems to me that the buyers right down the line by their conduct led the intermediate sellers to believe that the notice of appropriation was good...[22]

I regard the decision of the House in**Bremer** v. **Vanden as a most important decision on waiver**... Applied to cases of waiver in GAFTA cases, it may be stated thus: If a buyer, who is entitled to reject goods or documents on the ground of a defect in the notices or the timing of them, **so conducts himself as to lead the seller reasonably to believe that he is not going to rely on any such defect – whether he knows of it or not –**[23] then he cannot afterwards set up the defect as a ground for rejecting the goods or documents when it would be unfair or unjust to allow him to do so. It is unfair and unjust to allow it when the sellers all down the line have acted on the belief that the notices were good and have presented shipping documents accordingly. The sellers here allowed the buyers to have the goods at the very low contract price instead of the higher market price which they might otherwise have obtained. Fair dealing requires that the buyer should take them rather than seize upon some defect to reject them: simply to get more damages."(加黑部分是笔者的强调)

Shaw 大法官说:"**I see no reason... to limit the effect of waiver to rights known to exist.** It may be embracing enough, and so intended as to forego rights which might exist in regard to a particular contract or in a particular context."(加黑部分是笔者的强调)

3.2.3 少数意见的说法

但 Stephenson 大法官持不同意见,并对 Salmon 勋爵在 Bremer v. Vanden (1978)

---

〔21〕 虽然 Denning 勋爵使用的是"弃权"一词,但稍后节录的 Stephenson 勋爵的判决中使用的又是禁反言。这又是典型的早期先例中将两者混为一谈的例子。

〔22〕 虽然 Denning 勋爵使用的是"弃权"一词,但这实际上是禁反言要满足的要件。

〔23〕 同上。

2 Lloyd's Rep. 109 先例(贵族院先例中,针对性的决定对上诉庭有约束力)中的说法有不同的解读,说:"I do not understand Lord Salmon's reference to the buyers waiving any defect in the notice under cl. 22 'whether aware of it or not' as laying down any principle that **there can be waiver or equitable estoppel**〔24〕 **on the part of someone who does not know that his rights have been infringed or has not, at the least, such obvious means of knowing that his rights have been infringed that the other party can reasonably assume that the party waiving or estopped is acting with knowledge of their infringement.** Lord Salmon was, I think, referring to a patent defect which could only be missed by not reading the notice or not knowing the law. Here again what matters is the conduct of the 'waiving' or 'estopped' party, these buyers, and its effect on a reasonable seller, or a reasonable person in the position of the other party, these sellers. And if the buyer so acts as to lead a reasonable seller in these sellers' shoes to believe that he was waiving his right or accepting a non – contractual shipment as a fulfillment of their contract, and the seller does believe it, the buyer cannot be heard to say, 'I did not notice the obvious breach of contract on your part which gave me a right to complain or refuse'."(加黑部分是笔者的强调)

他也同意第一审的判决,即买方不知情也无法知情的情况下,并没有弃权。特别是在这个先例中的买方,即 Mackprang,在他与买方的大量通信往来中没有弃权,并在很多的文件中保留了他的权利。〔25〕 一审的 Robert Goff 大法官在分析了大量的通信往来文件之后针对买方的弃权争议是这样说:"I turn therefore to the first question, which is the question of waiver generally. On the whole question of waiver in the context of the GAFTA 100 Form, I have the guidance of the decision of the Court of Appeal in Finagrain S. A., Geneva v. P. Kruse, Hamburg (1976) 2 Lloyd's Rep. 508. Now, on this question of waiver, two subsidiary questions arise. The first is: Was there an unequivocal representation by the buyers that they would accept, in respect of the June shipment, post – June bills of lading? In the context of this case, that really means July bills of lading. The second subsidiary question is: If there was such unequivocal representation, was that relied on by the sellers?... Then the question arises whether there was any waiver ... In my judgment, there was no waiver.〔26〕 I can find in the messages no equivocal representation.〔27〕 All that happened was that there was a passing down of notices of appropriation without prejudice. In those circumstances, I do not think there can be read

〔24〕 在这个先例中,仍是把弃权与衡平法禁反言(即衡平法宽限)混为一谈。

〔25〕 这个课题可见本章之 6.5 段。

〔26〕 该先例的事实不涉及弃权。

〔27〕 Robert Goff 大法官也不认为有清楚无误的陈述。

into the telex messages any representation by the buyer that he was waiving his right to reject the documents even if it should be discovered later that the notices of appropriation were not correctly passed down the line in accordance with the time schedule.〔28〕 All he was doing was reserving the contractual position and trying to see whether the buyers further down the line – Messrs. Becher of Bremen – would be prepared to accept these particular bills of lading even though there was the break in the time schedule. In my judgment, there was no waiver in respect of the Pegasus shipment."

3.3　明确衡平法宽限不要求承诺方知道自己权利的贵族院先例：The "Kanchenjunga"

弃权方是否需要知道这个权利才能构成弃权的困惑，Goff 勋爵在 The "Kanchenjunga"（1990）1 Lloyd's Rep. 391（HL）先例〔29〕做出了权威性定论。Goff 勋爵认为"因选择而弃权"（waiver by election）需要承诺方知道自己有这个权利，而"因宽限而弃权"（waiver by forbearance）则不需要。可以说，这也是弃权与禁反言不同的地方，弃权针对的是弃权方，所以需要弃权方知道自己的权利，而禁反言针对的是要依赖禁反言的一方，因此不需要被禁反言的一方知道自己会暂时或永久失去的权利。因此，因选择而弃权属于典型的弃权，而因宽限而弃权则应该属于禁反言，而不再被归类于弃权。

这样看来像 Bremer v. Vanden（1978）2 Lloyd's Rep. 109 先例与 Bremer v. Mackprang（1979）1 Lloyd's Rep. 221 先例等涉及有缺陷通知被接受的先例中，弃权与禁反言还是应该作为替代抗辩同时提出。如果接受通知的一方知道或应该知道通知有缺陷的事实与自己可拒绝接受通知的权利，接受就属于弃权。而如果接受通知的一方不知道通知有缺陷的事实，则接受会属于禁反言（在其他要件也满足的情况下）。

在 HIH Casualty & General Insurance Ltd. v. AXA Corporate Solutions（2002）EWCA Civ 1253 先例中，一审的 Jules Sher QC 大法官根据 Goff 勋爵在 The "Kanchenjunga"（1990）1 Lloyd's Rep. 391（HL）先例的判决，说："... in the case of equitable estoppel what matters is how the representation appears to the representee, as opposed to election where the concentration is upon the knowledge of the representor."

衡平法宽限与承诺性禁反言通常不要求做出言行的一方知道自己的权利，这与因选择而弃权不同。衡平法宽限与承诺性禁反言重视的是做出的言行对对方的影响。但在上诉庭，Tuckey 大法官认为衡平法宽限与承诺性禁反言和做出言行的一方

---

〔28〕 所发生的只是一手手将有缺陷的通知转发下去。只是后来才发现该划归通知有时间上的缺陷，这不能被视为有清楚无误的陈述。

〔29〕 The "Kanchenjunga"（1990）1 Lloyd's Rep. 391（HL）先例的案情在本章稍后的 11.3 段与本书第一章之 3.4.1 段有介绍。

（承诺方）或多或少知道自己的权利还是有关，说：

“There is no dispute between the parties about the relevance of knowledge to waiver by estoppel and there was apparently no such dispute before the judge. Mr Hamblen Q. C. for Axa（做出承诺性保证言行的再保险人）does not and did not submit that the representor has to have knowledge of the legal right upon which he will not insist. This is clear from the passages in The Kanchenjunga and Superhulls cited by the judge. Mr Hamblen submits however that the representation must carry with it some apparent awareness of the right upon which the representor will not insist.〔30〕 Mr Flaux（保险人的代表大律师）did not dispute this and I do not think he could have done so because otherwise the representation would lack the necessary character to found the estoppel. As the judge put it ‘the essence of the plea must go to the willingness of the representor to forego its rights’. Unless the representation carries with it some apparent awareness of rights it goes nowhere: the representee will not understand the representation to mean that the representor is not going to insist upon his rights because he has said or done nothing to suggest that he has any.〔31〕

What I have said illustrates the difficulty in establishing this type of estoppel when neither party is aware of the right which is to be foregone. A representor who is unaware that he has rights is unlikely to make a representation which carries with it some apparent awareness that he has rights. Conversely arepresentee who is not aware that the representor has a particular right is unlikely to understand the representation to mean that the representor is not going to insist on that right or abandon any rights he might have unless he expressly says so.〔32〕

It follows I think that knowledge, or rather lack of it in this case is importantwhen one comes to consider whether the estoppel has been established. Nothing in the authorities or the texts to which we have been referred casts doubt on this conclusion.〔33〕”

---

〔30〕 承诺方不需要事实上知道他的合约或法律权利，但做出的陈述或承诺必须在表面看来承诺方是知道他的权利的。

〔31〕 构成衡平法宽限或承诺性禁反言的重要的一点是对方认为承诺方愿意放弃他的权利。因此，除非做出的陈述或承诺表面看来是承诺方知道自己的权利；否则，认为被承诺方会将这个陈述或承诺理解为承诺方将不再坚持他的权利说不通，也就无法构成衡平法宽限或承诺性禁反言。

〔32〕 这也显示了当双方都不知道承诺方有这样的权利时，要构成衡平法宽限或承诺性禁反言的困难。如果承诺方不知道自己有这样的权利，不太可能做出表面看来他知道自己有这样的权利但愿意放弃或宽限的言行。而被承诺方如果不知道承诺方有这样的权利，也不太可能将该陈述或承诺理解为承诺方不再坚持或放弃了他的权利。

〔33〕 因此，Tuckey 大法官认为承诺方是否知道自己的权利对能否构成衡平法宽限或承诺性禁反言是有关或重要。而双方当事人的代表大律师提供的先例与学术文章或书籍中也没有任何地方质疑这一点。

4. 衡平法宽限或承诺性禁反言的要件

构成衡平法宽限或承诺性禁反言的要件如下:(1)双方必须要有存在的合约关系或其他法律关系,毕竟如果没有这种关系,承诺方就不存在有合法权利可承诺放弃或宽限。(2)承诺方通过言行做出了陈述或承诺,表示他的合法权利将不会被执行,或会被暂时中止。(3)在承诺方知道的情况下,对方对该陈述或承诺做出依赖并改变了地位与/或造成损害。(4)承诺方事后试图撤回该陈述或承诺,并执行他的合约或法律权利,会对被承诺方不公平。

如果以上的要件都符合,法律就会以禁反言为由,暂时或甚至永久性的不允许承诺方出尔反尔,改变主意去执行原有的权利。以下会对这些要件进行进一步的分析。

5. 要件之一:双方有存在的合约关系或其他法律关系

首先可节录《Chitty on Contracts》(第32版,2015年)之4-089段,说:"**Requirement of pre-existing legal relationship**. It has, indeed, been suggested that the doctrine can apply where, before the making of the promise or representation, there is no legal relationship giving rise to rights and duties between the parties or where there is only a putative contract between them; e. g. where the promise is induced to believe that a contract into which he had undoubtedly entered was between him and the promisor, when in fact it was between the promise and another person.[34] But it is submitted that these suggestions mistake the nature of the doctrine, which is to restrict the enforcement by the promisor of previously existing rights against the promisee. Such rights can arise only out of a legal relationship existing between these parties before the making of the promise or representation. To apply doctrine where there was no such relationship would contravene the rule that the doctrine creates no new rights."

5.1 要求合约或法律关系的原因

先有有效的合约与相应的合约(或法律)权利存在,才会有宽限的问题。否则就会有逻辑上说不通的问题,如果原来没有合约(或其他法律关系下的)权利,何来承诺方向对方宽限权利一说?另是针对弃权与禁反言,一向有说法是只能作为盾牌防

---

〔34〕 这一点最主要是在笔者的《提单与其他付运单证》(2016年)一书第三章之9.9段介绍的The "Henrik Sif" (1982) 1 Lloyd's Rep. 456先例。

守而不能作为宝剑进攻,[35]即只可以作为抗辩,而不会产生新的权利,这是上述节录的《Chitty on Contracts》(第32版,2015年)之4-089段的最后一句。在本章第2段提到,在《Judicature Act 1873》前,被承诺方可以向独立的衡平法院以承诺方有过宽限的言行为由寻求救济。所以,宽限可以说在衡平法院是有诉因,可被称为"equitable cause of action"或"equitable right",是一把可在衡平法院进攻的宝剑。但在该立法生效后,衡平法院与普通法院合并,因宽限而弃权或多数其他类别的禁反言只能作为抗辩来防守。这与合约更改十分不同,合约更改完全可以令合约双方产生新的合约权利,并且可攻可守。上述节录的《Chitty on Contracts》(第32版,2015年)之4-089段中不认同稍后会在本章之5.2段介绍的The "Henrik Sif" (1982) 1 Lloyd's Rep. 456先例中,也主要是认为在这方面错判。

可以先举近期的例子来显示这方面的问题,该先例涉及著名的英国玛莎百货公司。在Baird Textile Holdings Ltd. v. Marks & Spencer Plc. (2001) EWCA Civ 274先例中,Baird向玛莎公司供应外衣,双方的业务关系长达30年之久。玛莎突然终止业务关系,这显然会给Baird带来很大困难,Baird要求玛莎至少做出3年的合理通知才能终止。可以想到这段时间是让Baird可以调整自己的生产与/或寻找其他的顾客。显然玛莎不答应,于是Baird采取法律行动。Baird的立场主要有两个方面:首先,双方虽然没有签订任何供应合约,但明显应有默示合约[36]存在;其次,双方30年的合作构成了禁反言,这包括承诺性禁反言与"共识性禁反言"(estoppel by convention)。[37] 针对默示合约,法院判是不会有默示合约,因为有证据显示双方知道玛莎刻意不肯签订任何合约约束自己,这显然无法满足默示的要求,说:"From this pleading, it appears that BTH(申请人Baird) are contending that notwithstanding the long and close business relationship with M & S(玛莎), it was perfectly well understood between them that M & S deliberately chose not to enter into an express contract to regulate the continuing, or future business relationship between them, or which would serve to impose any express contractual obligation to place orders in the future or give reasonable notice of termination. Given that the essential prerequisite of any contract is an 'agreement', it would seem rather surprising to hold that M & S was contractually bound by an implied agreement with BTH which it had deliberately, therefore intentionally, abstained from concluding expressly, or that an obligation in contract sounding in damages to give reasonable notice of termination, carrying with it a simultaneous obligation to place orders with BTH throughout the period of notice, was expressly rejected but impliedly accepted by M & S."

---

[35] 这在本章第10段会有详论。

[36] 关于默示合约,可见杨良宜的《合约的解释:规则与应用》一书第七章第11段。

[37] 这个课题可见本书第六章。

至于禁反言,不论是承诺性禁反言或是共识性禁反言,根本不会创造原本不存在的合约权利,让 Baird 可以向玛莎起诉:Combe v. Combe (1951) 2 KB 215 先例。

5.2　不严格存在合约或法律关系但构成禁反言的矛盾先例

这方面的困难之处不在合约的履行,毕竟可以通过解释合约找出双方的合约权利。但在合约谈判时,双方还没有存在合约权利,如果发生衡平法宽限或承诺性禁反言的争议又会怎样?[38]在 Brikom Investments Ltd. v. Carr (1979) QB 467 (CA)先例中,房屋租赁合约谈判时房东承诺会自行维修屋顶并承担所有费用,法院判是构成承诺性禁反言,原告不允许推翻承诺,虽然这个承诺是在双方还没有合约关系之前做出,并且也很难说双方的谈判就可以算是有了法律关系。如果说这个承诺是“附带协议”(collateral contract),也说不通,因为有所违反就大可以直接以违反合约(即使只是附带协议)提起诉讼,而无须依赖衡平法宽限了。虽然从案情看,这个判决公平合理,但与必须要有合约或法律关系才存在弃权或禁反言的说法看来是有所矛盾。

在 Bank Negara Indonesia v. Philip Hoalim (1973) 2 MLJ 3 (PC)先例中,案情将在本章之 7.4.4 段介绍,这里只说针对双方不严格存在法律关系,Wilberforce 勋爵说:“... the rights which the appellants had against the respondent, and whose enforcement is in question, were not strictly pre - existing rights... but... the same equitable principle applies. The fact that the respondent, as a result of the assurances given, entered into a legal situation which was less favourable than that which he previously enjoyed supports, rather than negatives, the equity of protecting him in the new position ...”

另一个带来同样困难的是上述节录的《Chitty on Contracts》(第 32 版,2015 年)之 4 - 089 段批评的 The “Henrik Sif” (1982) 1 Lloyd’s Rep. 456 先例中,这可参阅笔者的《提单与其他付运单证》(2016 年)一书第三章之 9.9 段有关部分。

合约一方没有指出另一方错误地认为他们之间存在法律关系,他就不能否认双方的法律关系。这个先例的判法也受到很多权威书籍的批评,因为收货人与承运人的代理人(实际上是承租人)Trade Line 没有任何提单合约的关系,[39]不能根据承诺性禁反言或衡平法宽限去建立新的权利。[40] 而 Webster 大法官根据双方的通讯往来说成他们之间有了法律关系,这就带来将法律关系定义得太广的危险,而令任何比较严肃的业务通讯往来中很多不正式的承诺,都有可能会构成衡平法宽限。即使根据 Webster 大法官把诉讼中或为了诉讼产生的通讯往来视为双方有法律关系,可以

---

〔38〕 这个课题在本章之 12.3 段有详论。

〔39〕 在提单合约中,收货人或提单持有人作为提单合约的一方要根据一份提单确定谁是“合约承运人”(contractual carrier),并向他提起诉讼(往往是为了货损货差或无单放货等索赔),经常是不容易。如“船东提单”(shipowner’s bill)或“承租人提单”(charterer’s bill)? 这复杂的问题在笔者的《提单与其他付运单证》(2016 年)一书第三章有详论。

〔40〕 这在本章第 10 段有进一步介绍。

适用承诺性禁反言或衡平法宽限,也是太广泛与危险。[41] 另在 The "Henrik Sif" 先例后不久的 The "Stolt Loyalty" (1993) 2 Lloyd's Rep. 281 先例中,也有大同小异的判法。但在 Shearson Lehman Hutton Inc. v. Maclaine Watson & Co. Ltd. (1989) 2 Lloyd's Rep. 570 先例中,Webster 大法官自己也对 The "Henrik Sif" 先例的正确性有一些疑问。在近期的 Baird Textile Holdings Ltd. v. Marks & Spencer Plc. (2001) EWCA Civ 274 先例中,上诉庭虽然同意 The "Henrik Sif" 先例的结果,但也对 Webster 大法官的理由提出了质疑。

从上述先例可以看出,什么属于法律关系与怎样的法律关系才适用衡平法宽限是不肯定与困难的。如针对土地所有人与非法侵入者(trespasser)之间的关系,Morris v. Tarrant (1971) 2 QB 143 先例与 Wallis Holiday Camp v. Shell-Mex (1974) 3 All ER 575 先例之间有不同的说法。虽然法律关系的定义在实践中重要性有限,但在 Methanex Motunui Ltd. v. Spellman (2004) 3 NZLR 454 先例也强调了双方必须存在最基本的关系,说:"... a defined legal relationship was a relationship which gave rise to the possibility that one party was entitled to some form of legal remedy against the other."

5.3 其他被视为有法律关系令言行可构成衡平法宽限/承诺性禁反言的先例

除了合约关系,以下可以节录一些被法律判是有法律关系与适用衡平法宽限的较近期先例:

1. 同居或夫妻关系:Maharaj v. Chand (1986) AC 898 (PC) 先例。案情涉及一对男女没有结婚,但以夫妻名义生活。斐济政府向已婚夫妻出租土地建造房屋,该先例中的男士向斐济政府申请土地,声称自己已经和该女士结婚,并保证租来的土地只为了建造房屋供他和家人居住。该女士在得到该男士建造的房屋会是她与她的孩子永远的家的承诺后,支持了这个申请,并在之后放弃了自己原来的住所,搬进了新造好的房屋。但后来两人分手,枢密院判是该男士不能撤回自己的承诺,将该女士与她的孩子赶走。

另在较早的 Vaughan v. Vaughan (1953) 1 QB 762 先例中,相关案情是丈夫在 1948 年离开了妻子从房子里搬出,搬走时承诺妻子可以永远在房子里住下去。1950 年,双方以丈夫通奸的理由正式离婚。之后男方希望收回房子,而女方则声称因为前夫的承诺,她拥有不可撤回的居住许可。并且在计算赡养费时,也将女方住在男方的房子里这点考虑进去。上诉庭判是女方作为合法妻子期间,可以无偿在房子里居住。但双方离婚后的关系就变为陌生人,男方可以通过合理通知撤回他的许可与承诺。在该先例中,上诉庭判是 6 个月的通知是合理时间,女方可以在期间向家事法庭申请提高赡养费。

2. 公司顾客与公司董事:Durham Fancy Goods Ltd. v. Michael Jackson (Fancy

---

[41] 见澳大利亚高院的 Waltons Stores (Interstate) Ltd. v. Maher (1988) 164 CLR 387 先例。

Goods) Ltd.（1968）2 Lloyd's Rep. 98 先例。原告开了一张自己是受益人的汇票并在上面写："Accepted payable... For and on behalf of M Jackson（Fancy Goods）Ltd. ..."但实际上，被告公司的正确的登记名字应该是 Michael Jackson（Fancy Goods）Ltd. 。被告公司的一名董事 Jackson 先生没有指出公司名称的错误，就在汇票上签了名，并交还给原告。之后汇票因为付款人名字不正确而被拒付，原告根据 1948 年《公司法》之 section 108，[42] 要求 Jackson 先生承担个人责任。法院认为虽然 section 108 在该案的情况适用，但原告因为承诺性禁反言不能从 Jackson 先生处拿回汇票的金额，因为原告在汇票上写的接受（accepted payable）一家名称不正确的公司的支付属于陈述或承诺。原告声称，承诺性禁反言不适用的理由是双方不存在合约关系，但 Donaldson 大法官说："This does not seem to me to be essential, provided that there is a pre – existing legal relationship which could in certain circumstances give rise to liabilities and penalties. Such a relationship is created by（a）s 108 of the Companies Act 1948,（b）the fact that Mr Jackson was a director of Jacksons and（c）whatever contractual arrangement existed between the plaintiffs and Jacksons which led to the plaintiffs drawing a 90 days bill on Jacksons."

有说法是承诺性禁反言也适用在双方不存在法律关系，或者只存在一个假定存在的合约的情况。[43] 在 Evenden v. Guildford City FC（1975）QB 917 先例中，Denning 勋爵引用了 Durham Fancy Goods Ltd. v. Michael Jackson（Fancy Goods）Ltd. 先例中，并更进一步认为，承诺性禁反言不需要双方已经存在法律关系，说："It applies whenever a representation is made, whether of fact or law, present or future, which is intended to be binding, intended to induce a person to act upon it and he does act upon it."

3. 规划局与申请人：Augier v. Secretary of State for the Environment（1979）38 P & CR 219 先例。案情涉及一家公司向规划局申请在自己的土地上挖砂石，但不被批准，主要原因是会影响交通。于是该公司承诺会增加辅助设施以保证交通，虽然该辅助设施是需要在他人的土地上设置，但该公司表示土地所有人愿意出售这块土地。规划局在该公司承诺会增加辅助设施的条件下，批准了该申请。法院判是该公司之后不能否定在他们承诺增加辅助设施的条件下，规划局才批准了申请。

---

〔42〕 1948 年《公司法》之 section 108 是说："（4）If an officer of a company or any person on its behalf—...（b）issues or authorises the issue of any business letter of the company or any notice or other official publication of the company, or signs or authorises to be signed on behalf of the company any bill of exchange, promissory note, endorsement, cheque or order for money or goods wherein its name is not mentioned in manner aforesaid; ... he shall be liable to a fine not exceeding fifty pounds, and shall further be personally liable to the holder of the bill of exchange, promissory note, cheque or order for money or goods for the amount thereof unless it is duly paid by the company."

〔43〕 这在本章之 12.3 段，针对合约谈判是否适用承诺性禁反言有详论。

4. 不正当影响的加害方与受害方：Goldsworthy v. Brickell (1987) Ch 378 (CA) 先例。在该先例中，原告（不正当影响的受害方）以很便宜的价格将农场租给被告（不正当影响的加害方）并让他可以很优惠的条件买下农场。法院判是在订立合约时，存在假设的不正当影响（presumed undue influence）。而如果要构成承诺性禁反言，令受害方不能再撤销合约，需要受害方明确的承诺（通过语言或行动），加害方依赖该陈述并蒙受损害。在该先例中，原告没有明确不会撤销合约的承诺，被告也没有依赖，因此不存在承诺性禁反言。

5. 房东与租客（即使他们之间不再存在合约关系）：Brikom Investments Ltd. v. Carr (1979) QB 467 (CA) 先例。〔44〕 但在 Fontana NV v. Mautner (1979) 254 EG 199 先例中，房东与租客之间租约已经到期，租客的妻子病重，如果搬家会造成严重影响。于是租客与房东会面，房东承诺他可以想住多久住多久。但不久之后，房东要求收回房屋，租客声称根据承诺性禁反言，房东不能将他们赶走。但法院判是租客没有依赖房东的承诺，并且没有蒙受损害，所以，承诺性禁反言不成立。

6. 讨论强制收购计划的当地政府与土地所有人：Co – operative Wholesale Society v. Chester le Street District Council (1997) 73 P & CR 111 先例。在该先例中，双方在索赔时效已过之后仍然进行谈判，法院判是当地政府放弃了以时效〔45〕已过进行抗辩的权利。

5.4 衡平法宽限或承诺性禁反言不适用的范畴：公法

政府当局会向公民做出承诺，但事后无法兑现。〔46〕 这可能有很多不同的原因，如立法禁止政府当局订立某些类别的合约，或是禁止政府放弃或宽限某些权利或做出相应的承诺。也可能是财政状况、政策改变、人事变动或是其他公众利益等原因，导致要撤回之前的陈述或承诺。这样，政府也要面对类似于私人之间出尔反尔的情况，这方面的法律有不少，但不在本书针对。只说政府官员没有实际或表面授权做出与法律规定不符的承诺或陈述，或者做出没有法律授权的行为：A – G for Ceylon v. De Silva (1953) AC 461 先例。禁反言的说法也不能作为政策实行或改变的阻碍：Laker Airways Ltd. v. Department of Trade (1977) QB 643 CA; Churchill Fisheries Export Pty Ltd. v. Director General of Conservation (1990) VR 968 等先例。如在 Maritime Electric Co. Ltd. v. General Dairies Ltd. (1937) AC 610 先例中，原告是一家提供电力的私营公司，但是根据当地法律属于“公共事业”（public utility）。根据相

---

〔44〕 该先例的案情在本章之 5.2 段有简单介绍。

〔45〕 有关时效的弃权与承诺性禁反言的案件很多，大多数涉及合约关系，这会在本书之第十章第 2 段有详述。

〔46〕 在现实中，公务员在做出对将来的承诺时往往会很谨慎。但公务员因为面对大众，常常要回应咨询、批准申请等，因此，会做出大量对过去或现在存在的事实的陈述，而这些陈述可能之后被认定是错误。所以，针对这方面的问题适用陈述性禁反言会比承诺性禁反言更多，虽然陈述与承诺经常很难区分。关于陈述性禁反言与公法的关系，将在本书第五章第 11 段介绍。

关法律，该公司要向公众提供合理足够的服务与设备，并且相关收费都有严格的限制，并要对公众公开。被告的乳制品公司使用的是旧式电表，表上的度数乘以十才是真正使用的电量，但原告公司直到28个月后才发现。即在这段时间内，被告只交了十分之一的电费，于是原告公司要求被告支付剩余的电费。最后，枢密院判是原告没有被禁反言，可以向被告追回少付的电费。根据相关的法律规定，原告有责任收取，被告有责任支付使用的所有电力的相应费用，这不会因为单纯的计算错误而改变。相关的法律规定是为了公共利益，被告不能以禁反言回避法律责任。

曾经有段时间，禁反言的说法是否能适用在公法（public law）并不明确。如在 Wells v. Minister of Housing and Local Government (1967) 1 WLR 1000 先例与 Lever (Finance) Ltd. v. Westminster Corp (1971) 1 QB 222 先例中，上诉庭的 Denning 勋爵都是以弃权与禁反言的说法阻止政府的出尔反尔（两个先例都涉及建筑是否需要申请批文，有关当局的代表曾经承诺过不需要申请批文）。在 Wells 先例中，上诉庭的 Russell 大法官有不同意见，认为有关当局并不能随意放弃立法的要求，说："The local planning authority is not a free agent to waive statutory requirements in favour of (so to speak) an adversary: it is the guardian of the planning system."

但在较近期的 Regina [Reprotech (Pebsham) Ltd.] v. East Sussex County Council (2002) UKHL 8 贵族院先例，已经明确了禁反言的说法不适用在公法。至于较早前带来不明确的 Wells v. Minister of Housing and Local Government 先例与 Lever (Finance) Ltd. v. Westminster Corp 先例是由于在那个年代，针对政府的出尔反尔，公法中政府滥用职权（abuse of power）和公民的合法期待（legitimate expectation）的说法与法院插手做出司法复核（judicial review）的制度还没有发展完善。Hoffmann 勋爵说："In any case, I think that it is unhelpful to introduce private law concepts of estoppel into planning law. As Lord Scarman pointed out in Newbury District Council v. Secretary of State for the Environment [1981] AC 578, 616, estoppels bind individuals on the ground that it would be unconscionable for them to deny what they have represented or agreed. But these concepts of private law should not be extended into 'the public law of planning control, which binds everyone'.[47] ... There is of course an analogy between a private law estoppel and the public law concept of a legitimate expectation created by a public authority, the denial of which may amount to an abuse of power...[48] But it is no more than an analogy because remedies against public authorities also have to

---

〔47〕 禁反言是私法中约束个人不能否认曾经同意或陈述过的事，否则会不合情理。但 Hoffmann 勋爵认为，禁反言不应该适用在《Town and Country Planning Act 1990》之类的公法，因为对城市规划的控制约束每个人。

〔48〕 私法中的禁反言与公法中的公民合法期待当然有相似之处，政府令公民产生的合法期待被否定会构成滥用职权。

take into account the interests of the general public which the authority exists to promote.[49]... public law has already absorbed whatever is useful from the moral values which underlie the private law concept of estoppel and the time has come for it to stand upon its own two feet.[50]"

现在,在公法中如果政府做出承诺令公民依赖并有了合法期待,法院就会通过司法复核禁止政府出尔反尔。在近期的 Regina v. North and East Devon Health Authority (2001) QB 213 上诉庭先例中,案情涉及申请司法复核的当事人在车祸中严重受伤并瘫痪。1993 年,在她与另外 7 位残疾病人的同意之下,他们从医院搬去一家疗养院,政府当局承诺他们可以在那里住一辈子。但在 1996 年,国家医疗服务政策发生变化。1998 年,政府当局决定关闭疗养院,并将申请人的看护服务转交给当地政府,但并没有指明要将申请人搬去哪里。申请人声称她因为政府在 1993 年的承诺产生了合法期待,而政府又举不出涉及哪些公共利益能令承诺被合法撤回,并且也没有指明要让申请人搬去哪里,因此不能关闭疗养院。上诉庭支持了申请人的申请,Woolf 大法官说:"That if a public body exercising a statutory function made a promise as to how it would behave in the future which induced a legitimate expectation of a benefit which was substantive, rather than merely procedural, to frustrate that expectation could be so unfair that it would amount to an abuse of power; that, in such circumstances, the court had to determine whether there was a sufficient overriding interest to justify a departure from what had previously been promised; that in view of the importance of the promise to the applicant, the fact that it was limited to a few individuals and that the consequences to the health authority of honouring it were likely to be financial only, the applicant had a legitimate expectation that the health authority would not resile from its promise unless there was an overreaching justification for doing so; and that, in the circumstances, including the fact that the quality of the alternative accommodation to be offered to the applicant was not known, the closure decision was an unjustified breach of that promise which constituted unfairness amounting to an abuse of power."

另在 In re Selectmove Ltd. (1995) 1 WLR 474 上诉庭先例中,案情涉及一家印刷行业的公司欠下了一大笔税金,税局威胁要把该公司清盘。之后在一个公司负责人与税局员工的会议中,该公司负责人声称说服了税局员工让他可以分期清还欠税,但事后税局否认有这样的约定,而且该公司负责人清楚税局员工没有同意这个安排的授权。之后税,局的确向法院申请要求把该公司清盘,但公司做出抗辩说双方有一个根据 Williams v. Roffey Bros. & Nicholls Ltd. (1991) 1 QB 1 先例存在约因/对价的协议,另一个抗辩是承诺性禁反言。前一个抗辩将会在本章之 12.1.4 段介绍,这

---

〔49〕 但两者之间不存在更多的相似之处,因为在针对政府当局的言行做出救济时,必须考虑公共利益。

〔50〕 禁反言的说法背后体现的是道德上的价值,公法已经吸收了这一点,需要与私法的禁反言分开。

里只针对承诺性禁反言的抗辩。税局的代表大律师不认为禁反言在该先例适用,但也承认如果撤回承诺会造成不公平,公法可以适用。但 Peter Gibson 大法官认为在该先例没有必要区分两者,因为在该先例中,该公司明知税局员工同意这个安排的授权,另外该公司也没有按照所谓的安排缴税,所以不接受这个抗辩不会造成任何的不公平,说:"It is unnecessary to consider the rival arguments in further detail as in my opinion Mr. Nugee's(公司的代表大律师)submission cannot succeed for at least two reasons. First, as Mr. Polland(税局员工)had no actual or ostensible authority to make the agreement claimed by the company, he had no authority to make the promise said to found the estoppel against the revenue. Second, because the company failed to honour its promise to pay the September P. A. Y. E. and N. I. C. as they fell due, it was not inequitable or unfair for the revenue on 9 October 1991 to demand payment of all the arrears, nor, in the light of the further late payments of the October and November P. A. Y. E. and N. I. C. and of various of the monthly instalments of £ 1,000, was it unfair or inequitable to serve a statutory demand and present a winding up petition to enforce the debt."

6. 要件之二:宽限方通过言行做出了陈述或承诺

在权威书籍《Chitty on Contracts》(第32版,2015年)之4-090段说:"**A promise or representation.** There must, next, be a promise (or an assurance or representation in the nature of a promise) which is intended to affect the legal relationship between the parties and which indicates that the promisor will not insist on his strict legal rights, arising out of that relationship, against the promisee.[51] Here, as elsewhere, the law applies an objective test. It is enough if the promise induces the promisee reasonably to believe that the other party will not insist on his strict legal right.[52] A mere threat to do something is not sufficient, nor, probably, is a reprcsentation or promise by a person that he will enforce a legal right: thus the doctrine does not apply where A tells B that he will exercise his right to cancel a contract between them unless by a specified date B has paid sums due

---

〔51〕 宽限方必须通过言行做出意图影响双方的法律关系的承诺(或保证或承诺性的陈述),显示他不会向对方行使他的严格法律权利。

〔52〕 承诺有否显示一方不会行使他的严格法律权利是客观的考验。如果宽限方的承诺使对方合理认为他不会行使他的严格法律权利就已经足够。

under the contract to A.〔53〕"

言行可能互补,也可能互相矛盾,要总体考虑是否属于清楚无误的陈述或承诺。如在 Jordan v. Money (1854) 5 HLC 185 先例中,宽限方或承诺方口头答应不执行债券,但拒绝将债券归还。法院判是这言行互相矛盾,不构成清楚无误的陈述或承诺。

什么是清楚无误的言行?这与本书第一章提到的接受违约/毁约与确认合约继续存在是一样的考验。只要是任何能显示一方的想法并令对方知道就足够,而没有任何形式上的要求。可以是口头表述、文字、没有文字的文件(如一张图表〔54〕),也可以是动作(如点头、眨眼、摇头、甚至微笑〔55〕)。正因为会有千变万化的语言与行动,再加上要考虑不同行业与交易习惯做法,言行是否清楚无误可以说每个不同案情的案件都会有不同,甚至在不同法官与仲裁员之间也有不同的认定。在近期的 Seechurn v. ACE Insurance SA (2002) 2 Lloyd's Rep. 390 先例中,涉及被保险人与保险公司之间多年来希望达成和解协议的谈判,双方的通信往来很多,对象也不一样。如被保险人写给保险公司的,被保险人写给律师的,保险公司内部员工之间的,保险公司写给律师的,写给保险业的申诉专员(insurance ombudsman)的。这些通信往来中语言/文字的风格都不同,必须要总体解释是否存在清楚无误的陈述或承诺,而高院与上诉庭得出了不同的结论。一审的 Previte 大法官说:"I find that Mr Seechurn(被保险人)was induced to believe, by the correspondence and statements therein, that the door would be kept open. In so finding, I bear in mind that the representation must be clear or unequivocal. I so find. I think, viewed objectively, a reasonable person reading the correspondence, especially with regard to the letters to which I have drawn attention, would conclude that the door was held open."

但上诉庭持不同看法,其中 Ward 大法官说:"The correspondence is typical of the attempts to negotiate a settlement of a claim with all the usual thrust and counter – thrust (or bluff or counter – bluff) of potential litigants striving to come to terms without losing too much face. That is not enough to found an estoppel."

类似解释合约,总体与全面解释双方的言行(往往涉及一连串的通信往来)是否清楚无误,也通常涉及审理的法官或仲裁员对整体文件证据与其他证据的印象。在澳大利亚上诉庭的 The "Zhi Jiang Kou" (1991) 1 Lloyd's Rep. 493 先例中,Kirby 大法官提到了这方面的不肯定或"诉讼风险",说:"The decision on whether an estoppel

---

〔53〕 仅仅是威胁要做某些事情是不足够(包括威胁要行使自己的法律权利):所以,如果 A 告诉 B 说除非 B 在某天前支付合约下要支付的金额给 A,否则 A 会行使权利终止合约,这言行不构成衡平法宽限或承诺性禁反言。A 的威胁也不是承诺,即使 A 没有按照威胁行使权利终止合约,并导致 B 蒙受更大的损失:Drexel Burnham Lambert International v. El Nasr (1986) 1 Lloyd's Rep. 356 先例。

〔54〕 可见 Espley v. Wilkes (1872) LR 7 Ex 298 先例与 Dabbs v. Seaman (1925) 36 CLR 538 先例。

〔55〕 可见 Walters v. Maorgan (1861) 3 De G F & J 718 先例中,Campbell 勋爵的说法。

is established in particular circumstances emerges from combing through the facts proved in the particular case and the inferences available from those facts. To this extent, the decision, being founded in an appeal to conscience, is partly impressionistic. It represents a reaction to the facts as elaborated. **The reaction to the same facts will necessarily differ from one judge to another, as the dissenting opinions in many cases of estoppel show. Such differences may reflect the different experiences of Judges, some of whom will evidence a conscience more tender than others.** "

6.1　言行总体来看必须清楚无误而非随意的陈述或承诺

由于衡平法宽限或承诺性禁反言针对将来的陈述或承诺，与合约更改(variation)的区别主要就是是否存在约因/对价。这表示两者所涉及的承诺在表达上基本要求一致，即能够构成衡平法宽限或承诺性禁反言的承诺，如果不是因为没有约因/对价，也可以构成合约的"更改"(variation)[56]。在 Woodhouse AC Israel Cocoa Ltd. SA v. Nigerian Produce Marketing Co. Ltd. (1972) 1 Lloyd's Rep. 439 (HL)先例中，Pearson 勋爵说："... the principle which is sometimes known as 'promissory estoppel,' ... **It may be that the 'representation' or promise or assurance has to have at least as much precision as would be needed for a variation of the contract.** "(加黑部分是笔者的强调)

在该先例中，被判是承诺不够清楚无误，Hailsham 勋爵询问了上诉方买方的代表大律师，是否曾有并非清楚无误的陈述或承诺也可以构成承诺性禁反言的先例。上诉方买方的代表大律师承认没有类似的先例。在 Hailsham 勋爵看来这也正常，毕竟如果并非清楚无误的陈述或承诺也可以构成承诺性禁反言，而一方错误理解了要约的意思，他就可以根据承诺性禁反言获得在常规的合约法下无法获得的利益是令人震惊的事。Hailsham 勋爵在之后节录了 Denning 勋爵在上诉庭([1971] 1 Lloyd's Rep. 25)的判决，说："Counsel for the appellants was asked whether he knew of any case in which an ambiguous statement had ever formed the basis of a purely promissory estoppel, as contended for here, as distinct from estoppel of a more familiar type based on factual misrepresentation. He candidly replied that he did not. I do not find this surprising, since it would really be an astonishing thing if, in the case of a genuine misunderstanding as to the meaning of an offer, the offeree could obtain by means of the doctrine of promissory estoppel something that he must fail to obtain under the conventional law of contract. I share the feeling of incredulity expressed by Lord Denning M. R. in the course of his judgment in the instant case when he said [1971] 2 Q. B. 23 , 59 – 60: If the judge be right, it leads to this extraordinary consequence: letter which is not sufficient to vary a contract is, nevertheless, sufficient to work an estoppel – which will have the same

---

〔56〕 关于合约更改的课题可见本书第三章第 2 段。

effect as a variation."

另在 The "Winson" (1980) 2 Lloyd's Rep. 213 先例中，上诉庭的 Megaw 大法官节录了 Spencer Bower 与 Turner 先生的《Estoppel by Representation》（第 3 版，1977 年）一书第 376 页，如下："When promissory estoppel is invoked, the promise or assurance necessary to support it is inevitably less than a promise binding upon the parties in contract – it would not be necessary to invoke the doctrine of promissory estoppel at all if the promise had contractual force. **But nevertheless the promise supporting a promissory estoppel is closely analogous in many respects to a promise having contractual effect.** One of its essential attributes is the same degree of unequivocality which, if the same assurance had been given full consideration, would have clothed it with contractual effect. This was the rock upon which the plea of promissory estoppel foundered, both in the Court of Appeal and in the House of Lords, in Wood – house A. C. Israel Cocoa Ltd. S. A. v. Nigerian Produce Marketing Ltd. [1972] A. C. 741. In his judgment in the Court of Appeal [1971] 2 Q. B. 23, 59, Lord Denning M. R. referred to **the 'extraordinary consequences' of holding that an assurance ineffectual (by reason of its indefiniteness) to vary a contract was yet definite enough to support a promissory estoppel bringing about the same result.**"（加黑部分是笔者的强调）

但由于衡平法宽限或承诺性禁反言是针对没有约因/对价的承诺，所以在解释言行是否构成衡平法宽限或承诺性禁反言时，必须小心区分是随意的退让（casual concession）或是会影响双方法律关系并导致其中一方失去（loss）或暂停（suspend）合约或法律权利的承诺，毕竟构成合约需要约因/对价就有这方面的考虑。因此，为了防止太轻易就会构成衡平法宽限或承诺性禁反言，双方之间必须先存在一定的合约或其他法律关系。

构成衡平法宽限或承诺性禁反言的言行必须清楚无误（clear and unequivocal），以显示做出言行的一方愿意或承诺放弃他的合约或法律权利。但由于言行的形式千变万化，判断是否属于清楚无误的陈述或承诺有困难，也有很强的主观性与不确定性，甚至会涉及文化差异。

如一方履行有瑕疵（不需要达到违约/毁约的严重程度），另一方没有提出抗议或索赔，而是看来满意地继续合作履行合约，这能否构成对履行有瑕疵所带来的损失索赔或是将来履行的合约责任的衡平法宽限或承诺性禁反言？或是被索赔方在索赔时效已过之后仍与索赔方进行或继续谈判，这能否构成对时效的衡平法宽限或承诺性禁反言?[57]又或是在保险合约中,事故发生后,保险公司进行调查或与被保险人合作参与了善后工作(如施救工作或对损坏的保险标的进行修理,如批准标书、指定修理厂等)。但之后却以一些与调查结果无关的理由(如被保险人没有满足及时通知保险公司的先决条件[58]或违反了承诺性保证[59])拒绝赔付,保险公司进行调查与参与善后工作的行为能否构成衡平法宽限或承诺性禁反言,以至于失去了本来可以拒赔的权利?

可以 The "Li Hai" (2005) 2 Lloyd's Rep. 389 先例为例,显示判断言行是否是清楚无误的困难。案情涉及期租合约下承租人没有准时与足数支付租金,而被船东趁机在市场高涨时撤船。在 2003 年 10 月,船东收到的租金被承租人扣减,包括 7 天的租金(估计船舶即将进船坞维修保养会需要停租的时间)与 500 美元在香港加油时产生的费用。船东对这两笔被扣减的钱都不接受与有争议,并写信给承租人,说:

"Re: Deduction for Estimate Drydocking

Sorry to find that charterershave deducted seven days for drydocking from hire payment, which is in breach of the charter - party dated 27 September 2002. In this respect, charterers are kindly requested to arrange same to our account as soon as possible... Please confirm by return...

Re: Debunker and cleaning of oil tanker No. 3 and No. 4

As we have stated, we fully reject charterers' claims of US $ 500 for cancellation of oil supply in Hong Kong, which results from inferior bunker supplied by charterers at Santo. We once again reject charterers to arrange the debunker and cleaning of the oil tanks no. 2 and no. 3. Please urgently confirm by return by 0800 GMT 14 October. Otherwise owners will arrange same during drydocking and all the time and costs involved to be for charterers' account."

当时航运市场高涨,为了保住租约,承租人在租约允许的 72 小时内对少付的租

---

〔57〕 在 Co - operative Wholesale Society v. Chester le Street District Council (1997) 73 P & CR 111 先例中,双方在索赔时效已过之后仍然进行谈判,并且当地政府曾经做出过陈述/承诺,法院判是当地政府放弃了以时效已过进行抗辩的权利。但如果双方纯粹在时效已过之后谈判,特别是被索赔方有说明是"无损害"(without prejudice),通常不构成对以时效已过作为抗辩的衡平法宽限或承诺性禁反言:Fortisbank SA v. Trenwick International Ltd. (2005) EWHC 399; Bridgestart Properties Ltd. v. London Underground Ltd. (2004) EWCA Civ 793; Super Chem Products Ltd. v. American Life & General Insurance Co. Ltd. (2004) UKPC 2; Hillingdon London BC v. ARC Ltd. (No. 2) (2000) 3 EGLR 97; Seechurn v. ACE Insurance SA (2002) 2 Lloyd's Rep. 390 等先例。这方面的课题在本书第十章第 2 段有详论。

〔58〕 这种先例数不胜数,较近期的有 Bolton Metropolitan Borough Council v. Municipal Mutual Insurance Ltd. & Anor (2006) EWCA Civ 50; Kosmar Villa Holidays Plc. v. Trustees of Syndicate 1243 (2008) EWCA Civ 147 等先例。

〔59〕 HIH Casualty & General Insurance Ltd. v. AXA Corporate Solutions (2002) EWCA Civ 1253 等先例。

金做出补救,将原本扣减的 7 天的租金支付给了船东,但没有支付香港加油期间产生争议的 500 美元。船东以承租人没有足数支付租金为由撤船。承租人声称船东错误撤船并索赔损失。在针对双方争议的其中一点,即上述节录的船东的电文是否构成衡平法宽限或承诺性禁反言,Jonathan Hirst QC 大法官认为是构成了衡平法宽限或承诺性禁反言,承租人理解为船东承诺承租人只要补足扣减的 7 天的租金而宽限了 500 美元是完全合理,从而在租约明示允许的 72 小时内没有补足这扣减的 500 美元,所以船东被禁反言不能撤船。Jonathan Hirst QC 大法官说:"This message led(承租人)to understand that, although the Owners(中国远洋散货公司/中散)were disputing the cross – claim for $500, the deduction from hire to which the Owners objected was that for anticipated off – hire. I think that understanding was entirely reasonable. It is how I understood the message when I first read it during my pre – reading for the trial... So they paid the sum deducted for anticipated off – hire, but not the $500. The Owners created this confusion... In my judgment the notice needed to state categorically that, unless the outstanding hire was paid in full without deduction, the vessel would be withdrawn... To create an estoppel, there needed to be an unequivocal representation that only the off – hire deductions need be paid. On the facts I have already found, I consider that the Owners' message of 14 October did make this representation... I am in no doubt that, as a result, the Charterers still believed that if they paid the off – hire deducted, that would avoid a withdrawal. So in my judgment... as a result of what they had said... the Owners were estopped from withdrawing the vessel."

这可以看出解释与认定言行是否清楚无误的危险性与不肯定性。虽然法律规定构成衡平法宽限或承诺性禁反言的陈述或承诺必须清楚无误,如果不是缺乏约因/对价是可以构成合约。但判断是否清楚无误很大程度是取决于一审法院或仲裁庭对事实的认定。在该先例中,如果换一位法官(或仲裁员)可能会判是既然对该 500 美金有争议,而在同一电文对同样有争议的 7 天的租金明示要求对方补足,上文下理来看应该不会是清楚无误陈述或承诺承租人不需要补足 500 美元。Jonathan Hirst QC 大法官的解读可能受中散只因为 500 美金的不足就撤船的影响,也可能有文化差异的影响。

6.2 总体言行可让对方有两个以上合理解释的情况

构成衡平法宽限或承诺性禁反言的言行不需要严格只能有一个解释,如绝对是清楚无误地说"我承诺放弃某合约或法律的权利"(I promise to give up my [specific] contractual/legal rights)。正如稍早节录的《Chitty on Contracts》(第 32 版,2015 年)之 4 – 090 段所说,只要整体的言行可让对方合理认为宽限方或被禁反言的一方不会行使他的严格法律权利就已经足够。在 Low v. Bouverie (1891) 3 Ch 82 先例中,Bowen 大法官说:"... an estoppel, that is to say, the language upon which the estoppel is founded, must be precise and unambiguous. That does not necessarily mean that the language must be such that it cannot possibly be open to different interpretations, but it must be such that it will be reasonably understood in a particular sense by the person to whom it is addressed."

在 Woodhouse AC Israel Cocoa Ltd. SA v. Nigerian Produce Marketing Co. Ltd.（1972）1 Lloyd's Rep. 439（HL）先例中，Hailsham 勋爵阐述了他对 Bowen 大法官上述节录所讲的理解，说："I am satisfied that, in the second sentence of the above quotation, the meaning is to exclude far – fetched or strained, but still possible, interpretations, whilst still insisting on a sufficient precision and freedom from ambiguity to ensure that the representation will（not may）be reasonably understood in the particular sense required."

事实上，很多宽限方或被禁反言一方的言行都可以有多过一个的合理解释，而不是 Hailsham 勋爵在上述所讲的牵强附会的解释。而这些合理解释中有个别可以构成衡平法宽限或承诺性禁反言，也有个别不会构成。这样，对方就有责任澄清，否则是不能成功依赖。这可以节录在 Kim v. Chasewood Park Residents Ltd.（2013）EWCA Civ 239 先例中，上诉庭的 Patten 大法官说："There is no doubt that in order to found a promissory estoppel（in the same way as any other estoppel based on a representation of fact）the representation or promise must be clear and unambiguous. But this principle raises a number of subsidiary questions. Does it mean that the estoppel cannot arise unless there is only one possible meaning of the words used or is the existence of other possible（but perhaps less probable）meanings not fatal to the creation of an estoppel where the Court can say that it was reasonable for the representee to have interpreted the words used in the way he did?〔60〕 There is also an issue about the test to be adopted by the Court. Few, if any, statements are not capable of being interpreted in more than one way.〔61〕 The Court's usual role in construing, for example, a contract is to arrive at the legally correct meaning of the words. Their construction is a matter of law and the Court's function is to resolve any ambiguities in reaching its conclusion.〔62〕 But it is arguable that in the case of estoppel it should not go any further than to identify the existence of any real ambiguities in the language.〔63〕 **If the statement is open to more than one reasonable interpretation（one of which is fatal to the estoppel defence）then the**

---

〔60〕 毫无疑问，承诺性禁反言与陈述性禁反言一样，相关的陈述或承诺必须清楚与不含糊。但这带来了进一步的问题，相关的陈述或承诺只能有一个解释才能构成禁反言，还是只要法院认为被陈述人的理解合理，即使存在其他可能的解释，也并不会影响构成禁反言？

〔61〕 法院应该采取怎样的考验也是一个问题，毕竟几乎没有一句话是只能有一种解释的。

〔62〕 法院在解释一份合约（或其他的任何文字或言行）时，是要找到用字在法律上的正确解释。解释合约是一个法律问题，法院在做出解释时，要解决任何语言上模糊的问题。

〔63〕 但针对禁反言，在指出存在其他可能的解释之后，是否应该进一步分析存在争议。

representee was not entitled to rely on what was said without further clarification and there is no basis for an estoppel.〔64〕"(加黑部分是笔者的强调)

6.3 沉默或不行动通常不是清楚无误的陈述或承诺

沉默(silence)或不行动(inactivity)通常不会被视为清楚无误的陈述或承诺。如果一方当事人对另一方的违约或试图违约保持沉默或不行动,可能是承诺不行使自己的权利,也可能只是犹疑不决导致延误行使自己的权利。中国公司/企业很喜欢争辩对方的沉默或不行动是默许,不能事后追究,但这在法律上往往站不住脚。〔65〕

有不少先例涉及双方发生争议与诉讼/仲裁时的沉默或不行动。如发生争议后双方进行谈判,在接近达成协议前,索赔方不再行动并保持沉默。其中的原因可能有很多,如索赔方有关人员发生变动,或公司/企业有其他突发事情导致注意力转移,或索赔方由于损失不大暂时放下案件等。而如果双方谈判并不友好,可能谈不拢,索赔方也会变得沉默或不行动,看来是放弃索赔。这种沉默或不行动通常都不被视为清楚无误的陈述或承诺放弃索赔。所以面对索赔,除非时效已过,或是对方确实承诺不会再推进索赔,否则,不可以依赖并销毁相关的证据,如档案或案卷。而如果重要证人要离职,离职前也要留下证人证言。千万不能以为对方态度放软,不再咄咄相逼,就不会有事。

在权威的《Chitty on Contracts》(第 32 版,2015 年)一书之 4 – 093 段,说:"**Conduct contrasted with inactivity.** Although a promise or representation may be made by conduct, mere inactivity will not normally suffice for the present purpose since 'it is difficult to imagine how silence and inaction can be anything but equivocal.' Unless the law took this view, mere failure to assert a contractual right could lead to its loss; and the courts have on a number of occasions rejected this clearly undesirable conclusion.〔66〕 Thus it has been held that there is 'no ground for saying that mere delay, however lengthy, destroys the contractual rights'〔67〕; that the mere failure to prosecute a claim regarded by both parties as hopeless did not amount to a promise to abandon it〔68〕; and that, because an insurer's failure for seven years to raise the defence that the insured was

---

〔64〕 如果有多于一种解释,并且其中的一种对构成禁反言可以说是致命(因为不够清楚无误),被陈述人在没有进一步澄清的情况下,就不能以依赖他对陈述的理解,也不构成禁反言。

〔65〕 这里指的是完全的沉默或不行动,而不是面对对方的违约/毁约忍气吞声时,往往会有其他的言行可以被一并解释为构成弃权或禁反言。

〔66〕 虽然可以通过行动做出陈述或承诺,仅仅是不行动一般不会构成衡平法宽限或承诺性禁反言,毕竟沉默或不行动说不上是清楚无误。仅仅是不主张合约权利就会导致一方失去这个合约权利的说法,法院已经在无数先例中拒绝采纳。

〔67〕 因此仅仅是延误行使权利,不论延误多久,都不会导致失去合约权利:Amherst v. James Walker Goldsmith & Silversmith Ltd. (1983) Ch 305 先例。

〔68〕 不提起一个双方都认为没有希望的索赔,也不代表放弃了索赔:Collin v. Duke of Westminster (1985) QB 581 先例。

guilty of a breach of warranty (discharging the insurer) amounted to mere 'silence and inaction', it did not give rise to an estoppel, and so did not prevent the insurer from relying on that defence[69]. The only circumstances in which mere 'silence and inaction' can have this effect are the exceptional ones ... in which the law imposes a duty to disclose facts or to clarify a legal relationship and the party under the duty fails to perform it.[70]"

在 MSC v. B. R. E（1985）2 Lloyd's Rep. 239 先例中，Saville 大法官说："As to estoppel, while it may be the case that one party could be prevented from pursuing his claim when he so conducted himself as to lead the other party to believe that the claim was abandoned and the other party acted on that belief to his detriment. I consider that the present case does not begin to fall within such a principle. Firstly, I cannot regard the conduct of the plaintiffs as amounting to a clear and unequivocal representation that the claim was or would be abandoned. As I said, it seems to me that its highest all that could be said was that at any particular time between 1978 and 1983 the plaintiffs were not pursuing the claim; not that they would not pursue it thereafter..."

另在 The "Leonidas D"（1985）2 Lloyd's Rep. 18 上诉庭先例中，Goff 大法官说："It is well settled that that principle requires that one party should have made an unequivocal representation that he does not intend to enforce his strict legal rights against the other; yet it is difficult to imagine how silence and inaction can be anything but equivocal...But silence and inaction are of their nature equivocal, for the simple reason that there can be more than one reason why the person concerned has been silent and inactive."

以上 Goff 大法官所讲的第二段是与本章之 6.2 段配合，即沉默或不行动是让对方可以有两个甚至更多的合理解释，谈不上是清楚无误的陈述或承诺。

另一个例子是在 20 世纪 80 年代曾经十分困扰英国仲裁的问题，即原告开始了仲裁，也保护了诉讼的时效，但没有推进仲裁。即原告保持沉默或不行动，可能拖延多年后才重新推进仲裁。但这样被告会受到影响（主要是证据的流失），并提出各种理由阻止原告重新推进仲裁。这种情况在法院的诉讼不是问题，因为高院的规则是允许法院撤销（strike out）原告延误或懈怠（want of prosecution）的诉讼。但在仲裁就带来很大问题，仲裁的存在完全来自双方当事人的仲裁协议。所以，能否让仲裁庭或法院撤销原告懈怠的诉讼请求，只能从合约法的角度分析，是否有明示或默示的条文

---

〔69〕 虽然保险人延误了 7 年才提出被保险人违反了保单中的保证，因此保险人不必赔付的抗辩，但仅仅属于沉默或不行动，不会构成禁反言令保险人之后不能再提出该抗辩：The "Copa Casino"（2012）1 Lloyd's Rep. 129 先例。

〔70〕 唯一的例外情况是法律规定有责任说清楚（duty to speak），这会在本章下一小段介绍。

可让法院或仲裁庭撤销原告懈怠的仲裁。在 Bremer Vulkan Schiffbau und Maschinenfabrik v. South India Shipping Corporation Ltd.（1981）1 Lloyd's Rep. 253 先例中，贵族院判是无论原告拖多久，有多严重的延误，仍不能被撤销。因为双方的仲裁协议没有这个权利，反而是双方有共同的默示责任以合理速度推进仲裁。即如果原告不推进仲裁，被告也应该推进。显然在现实中，被告不会这样做，除非他有更大的反索赔。这就带来了一连串的案件试图通过其他合约法说法阻止原告重新推进仲裁。包括说原告在仲裁协议中违约/毁约（repudiatory breach），没有以合理速度推进仲裁；或仲裁协议已经受阻（frustration）；或双方长期不推进仲裁，属于共同放弃（mutual abandonment）的协议，而如果没有有法律约束力的共同放弃的协议，也构成了衡平法宽限或承诺性禁反言，令原告不能重新推进仲裁。但这就免不了带来一个问题是原告的沉默或不行动是否构成清楚无误的陈述或承诺。这里只节录 CFID v. Deutsche Conti（1985）2 Lloyd's Rep. 592 先例的有关说法，Bingham 大法官说：

"We have here to consider an appeal from a decision that a binding agreement should be inferred from silence and inaction. Silence and inaction by both parties are apparently here considered to be capable of giving rise to an offer by one, and to an acceptance by the other communicated in response to that offer. **This is most surprising. We have all been brought up to believe it to be axiomatic that acceptance of an offer cannot be inferred from silence**, save in the most exceptional circumstances... In the absence of **special circumstances**, silence and inaction by a party to a reference are, objectively considered, just as consistent with his having inadvertently forgotten about the matter; with his simply hoping that the matter will die a natural death if he does not stir up the other party; or with his office staff, or his agents, or his insurers, or his solicitors, being appallingly slow. If so, there should, on ordinary principles, be no basis for the inference of an offer. Exactly the same comment can be made of the silence and inaction of the other party. For the same reasons, there appears to be no basis for drawing the inference of an acceptance in response to the supposed offer, still less of the communication of that acceptance to the offeror.

We should add that we see **the same difficulty in invoking the principle of equitable estoppel in such circumstances. It is well settled that that principle requires that one party should have made an unequivocal representation that he does not intend to enforce his strict legal rights against the other; yet it is difficult to imagine how silence and inaction can be anything but equivocal**."（加黑部分是笔者的强调）

由于很多先例〔71〕中得出的解释都表面上是该问题无法以合约法下的不同说法或原则解决，但原告严重延误或懈怠索赔也不能容忍，最后要解决该问题只能通过立

〔71〕 这些先例可见杨良宜的《国际商务仲裁》一书第八章之3.1段。

法。在英国 1996 年《仲裁法》之 section 41(3),就加上了以下的规定:"If the tribunal is satisfied that there has been inordinated and inexcusable delay in the part of the claimant in pursing his claim and that the delay . . . the tribunal may make an award dismissing the claim."在香港特区《仲裁条例》之 section 59 也有同样的规定。

上述 Bingham 大法官提到的特殊情况(special circumstances),就是法律要求不能保持沉默或不行动,这种所谓有责任说清楚(duty to speak)会在下一小段分析。

6.4　有责任说清楚/沉默性禁反言

有责任说清楚(duty to speak)的原则适用在各种不同类型的禁反言。如"沉默性禁反言"(estoppel by acquiescence)经常被视为"产权人禁反言"(proprietary estoppel)的分支之一。如果产权人/业主明知他人误解但保持沉默,就会构成沉默性禁反言。而如果产权人/业主对他人的误解进行鼓励,就会构成另一个分支的"鼓励性禁反言"(estoppel by encouragement)。沉默性禁反言在"陈述性禁反言"(estoppel by representation)这一类别中也非常重要,通常如果法律认为有责任说清楚,但一方沉默没有说清楚,就会被当做一种错误陈述并构成陈述性禁反言。这种情况适用陈述性禁反言比承诺性禁反言更多,如对于已经存在的事实,一方知道真相,并发现对方有了误解。由于让对方保持这个对事实的误解对自己是更有利,所以取巧不去指出。

由于有责任说清楚更多适用在陈述性禁反言的情况,因此将在本书第五章第 10 段详细介绍这一说法。在本章之 6.1 段已经提到,要构成承诺性禁反言言行,总体来看必须是清楚无误。如果合约一方做出的陈述不能被解释为清楚无误的承诺,但另一方误解为承诺并做出依赖。而做出陈述的一方知道自己无意做出承诺,也同时知道另一方有了误解,他就有责任向另一方说清楚,否则就有危险构成承诺性禁反言,虽然原先做出的陈述或承诺单独来看是不足以构成禁反言。

简单而言,法律上有责任说清楚的说法与道德或人际关系上的说法有重叠与相似的地方,只是法律上有明确的划分,而不仅是泛泛的要求。中国在道德、礼貌或人际关系上也一直有沉默是金(英文也有 silence is gold)的说法,在没有必要的情况下保持沉默,免得言多必失。但如何判断保持沉默是否有必要没有具体的标准,也因人而异。法律上也有这样的理念,但相比之下就规范得多。为了肯定性,英美甚至国际上的法律对是否有必要保持沉默是有明确的标准,也不能因人而异。英国法律是不愿意强加说清楚的责任在一方的身上,怕对方会误解或犯错。最典型的例子就是买卖合约中"caveat emptor"(英文是 let the buyer beware,即买方自己小心)的说法,卖方没有责任向买方说清楚,如同样的商品有其他地方售价更廉宜。当然这也有例外情况,如保护消费者的立法等,但这与一般的商业交往,特别是国际性的商业交往是不同的性质。

另是英国普通法与大陆法不同,没有善意(good faith)的要求,[72]不要求一方有

---

〔72〕　这可见杨良宜的《合约的解释:规则与应用》一书之第九章。

责任向另一方说明或提醒,以避免上当。正如 Hoffmann 勋爵在 BCCI v. Ali (2002) 1 AC 251 先例中说:"There is obviously room in the dealings of the market for legitimately taking advantage of the known ignorance of the other party."

以上所讲也可节录 Rix 大法官在 ING Bank NV v. Ros Roca SA (2011) EWCA Civ 353 先例中所说:"Outside the insurance context, there is no obligation in general to bring difficulties and defects to the attention of a contract partner or prospective contract partner. Caveat emptor reflects a basic facet of English commercial law (the growth of consumer law has been moving in a different direction). Nor is there any general notion, as there is in the civil law, of a duty of good faith in commercial affairs, however much individual concepts of English common law, such as that of the reasonable man, and of waiver and estoppel itself, may be said to reflect such a notion. In such circumstances, silence is golden, for where there is no obligation to speak, silence gives no hostages to fortune. If, however, the contractor speaks, then he may have to live up to what he says; so also where what is unsaid is sufficiently closely connected with what he has said to render what has been left unsaid misleading. In general, however, there is no duty of disclosure..."

上述节录的 Rix 大法官所说第一句就提到了保险合约有善意要求。这是因为 1906 年《海上保险法》的立法要求,包括被保险人必须披露所有情况,尤其是对保险公司不利的情况,否则会令保险合约无效与不能获得赔付。但在 2015 年《保险法》生效后,即使是保险合约,这方面的善意责任也有了改变和限制。其他有责任向对方说清楚的例外情况还有认购公司股份、[73]连带保证(surety)、[74]家庭和解协议[75]与合伙(partnership)[76]等。但这些涉及善意的例外情况与一般的商业活动所订立的简式合约有所不同,而商业合约在英国法下不存在善意的要求。英国法一直避免在商业合约中强加责任在合约方,不会默示要求一方披露、提醒、纠正对方的错误理解,而是让合约方自己小心。一般的原则是商业谈判或交易中的一方,只要不是通过自己的言行做出误述导致另一方产生错误理解,就没有向另一方说清楚的责任,即使他知道对方对交易有关键的错误理解:Smith v. Hughes (1871) LR 6 QB 597; Arkwright v. Newbold (1881) 17 Ch D 301; Coaks v. Boswell (1886) 11 App Cas 232; Marn-

〔73〕 Erlanger v. New Sombrero Phosphate Co. (1878) 3 App Cas 1218 等先例。

〔74〕 在 London General Omnibus Co. v. Holloway (1912) 2 KB 72 先例,Vaughan – Williams 大法官说:"A creditor must reveal to the surety every fact which under the circumstances the surety would expect not to exist, for the omission not to mention that such a fact does exist is an implied representation that it does not."更近期的先例有 Levett v. Barclays Bank Plc. (1995) 1 WLR 1260; Geest v. Fyffes Plc. (1999) 1 All ER (Comm) 672 等。

〔75〕 Gordon v. Gordon (1816 – 19) 3 Swans 400 等先例。

〔76〕 Conlon v. Simms (2006) EWCA Civ 1749 等先例。

ham v. Weaver (1899) 80 LT 412; Seddon v. North Eastern Salt Co. (1905) 1 Ch 326; Bell v. Lever Bros Ltd. (1932) AC 161; With v. O'Flanagan (1936) Ch 575; Banque Keyser Ullmann SA v. Skandia (UK) Insurance Co. Ltd. (1990) 1 QB 655, affirmed on other grounds (1991) 2 AC 249; Barton v. County NatWest (1999) Lloyd's Rep. Bank 408; BCCI v. Ali 等先例。

英国法律虽然对一般的商业合约与其他的交往不要求善意,但也不鼓励恶意(bad faith),因此就以有责任说清楚等衡平法原则来填补漏洞,防止一方恶意取巧(sharp practice)。Webster 大法官在 The "Henrik Sif" (1982) 1 Lloyd's Rep. 456 先例引述了 Wilberforce 勋爵在 Moorgate Mercantile Co. Ltd. v. Twitchings (1977) AC 890 先例的重要说法,说:"Nonetheless the dictum which I have cited seems to me to be most persuasive authority for the proposition that the duty necessary to found an estoppel by silence or acquiescence arises where 'a reasonable man would expect' the person against whom the estoppel is raised '**acting honestly and responsibly**' to bring the true facts to the attention of the other party known by him to be under a mistake as to their respective rights and obligations."(加黑部分是笔者的强调)

Wilberforce 勋爵"acting honestly and responsibly"的重要说法也在其他很多重要的先例中被提到,如 The "Lutetian" (1982) 2 Lloyd's Rep. 140 先例;The "Stolt Loyalty" (1993) 2 Lloyd's Rep. 281 先例;The "Indian Endurance" and The "Indian Grace" (No. 2) (1998) 1 Lloyd's Rep. 1 (HL)先例与 Thames Trains Ltd. v. Adams (2006) EWHC 3291 (QB)先例等。

即只有在一个合理人士会认为另一方如果诚实与负责任行事就会提醒他事实真相的情况下,另一方才会有说清楚的责任。但要注意的是,依赖禁反言的一方不需要证明另一方主观上不诚实(会有刑事欺诈的举证责任),只需要证明客观看来,另一方保持沉默是取巧。另一方保持沉默也是不公平(unfair)与不合情理繁荣(unconscionable),这显然是禁反言的要求。这一要求也在无数的先例中被提到,如近期的 MIOM 1 Ltd. v. Sea Echo ENE (No. 2) (2012) 1 Lloyd's Rep. 140 先例。

在 Riverlate Properties Ltd. v. Paul (1975) Ch. 133 先例中,针对有责任说清楚,Eveleigh 大法官明确说明这个说法或责任是根据禁反言,而 Buckley 大法官则没有特别指出根据禁反言或取巧,只是说根据公平的地位(equity of the position)。

总结而言,承诺性禁反言较少涉及有责任说清楚的情况,但并不是没有。也可以看出,虽然合约一方做出的陈述不能被解释为清楚无误的承诺,但另一方误解为承诺并做出依赖,为什么做出陈述的一方会有责任说清楚。毕竟做出陈述的一方知道自己无意做出承诺的真相,也同时知道另一方有误解,并且另一方的误解是由他的陈述(虽然不足以构成清楚无误的承诺)而导致。在这种情况下,一个合理的人士会认为如果做出陈述的一方诚实与负责任行事,是会指出真实的情况,说明不是承诺。如果做出陈述的一方保持沉默,特别是客观被认为取巧,是不公平与不合情理的。

但如果情况改变,一方做出的陈述与承诺没有关系,而另一方非要说他做出了承诺并且自己会依赖这个承诺行事。这样,很难说做出陈述的一方有责任说清楚,除了客观看和不公平与不合情理没有关系,而且做出陈述的一方根本不会认为对方有所误解,更有可能认为对方在耍赖而不想理睬。

6.5 以明示的语言/文字令言行不会构成清楚无误的陈述或承诺

为了保护自己的利益,一方可以对可能会被解释构成衡平法宽限或承诺性禁反言的言行做出限制,重要的做法之一是明确向对方说明"无损害"(without prejudice)[77]或"保留权利"(reservation of rights),这样相关的陈述或承诺也就变为不是清楚无误。

6.5.1 无损害(without prejudice)

《Black's Law Dictionary》对"without prejudice"的定义是:"Without loss of any rights; in a way that does not harm or cancel the legal rights or privileges."而《Oxford Companion to Law》对它的定义是:"A phrase used in offers, intended to guard against any inference of waiver of right."

这些表述在限制一些有危险被对方与法院/仲裁庭视为明确无误的陈述或承诺时特别重要。如在本书第一章之7.4.1段提到在一方拒绝履行合约(repudiation),另一方的无辜方如果接受违约/毁约并终止合约就很容易判断,但无辜方是否确认(affirm)合约继续存在则很难判断。因为当一方拒绝履行合约时,无辜方的自然反应往往是向对方施加压力,希望对方回心转意。直到发现没有希望后才会死心,接受对方的违约/毁约并终止合约。[78] 这自然反应的言行就可能被法院或仲裁庭认定为确认了合约,这样他之后终止合约的行为变为违约/毁约。但如果无辜方在向对方施加压力要求对方继续履行时,说明是"无损害",被法院或仲裁庭认定是确认合约的机会就大大减小了。

6.5.1.1 通过"无损害"保留了权利的先例

很多案件涉及在保险公司试图与被保险人或第三方达成和解的过程中,双方都会有言行可被视为清楚无误的陈述或承诺。如保险公司在谈判中将一张支票寄给被保险人或第三方,说明这是全部与最终解决款项。如果被保险人或第三方提现或收下支票,就可能被视为接受了这是全部与最终解决款项,或构成禁反言(令保险公司相信这笔钱已经令被保险人或第三方满意)。早在 Day v. McLea (1889) 22 QBD 613 先例中,Bowen 大法官就说:"If a person sends a sum of money on the terms that it

---

〔77〕"无损害"一词被用在很多不同的情况,甚至被滥用。其中在法律的范畴,该词是表示有关的文件或通讯往来享有特免权(privilege),可以被保障而不必披露,保持机密。在本段所介绍的无损害并非指这一方面。

〔78〕Moore-Bick 大法官在 Yukong Line Ltd. of Korea v. Rendsburg Investment Corporation (1996) 2 Lloyd's Rep. 604 先例的说法。

is to be taken, if at all, in satisfaction of a larger claim; and if the money is kept, it is a question of fact as to the terms upon which it is so kept. Accord and satisfaction imply an agreement to take the money in satisfaction of the claim in respect of which it I sent. If accord is a question of agreement, there must be either two minds agreeing[79] or one of the two persons acting in such a way as to induce the other to think that the money is taken in satisfaction of the claim, and to cause him to act upon that view...[80]”在Merkuria Foreign Trade Corp v. Dateline Electric Co. Ltd.（1979）CAT 413先例中，第一被告写信给原告说这是原告对第二被告所有索赔的全部与最终解决款项，并附上了6679英镑的支票。原告将支票兑现，但之后争辩说他只是接受支票的金额作为部分的赔偿。但这个说法不被法院接受，Stephenson大法官说：“They did not qualify or seek to qualify in any way, as they could have done, the terms under which they were accepting it. **They did not say ‘We are accepting it without prejudice to other claims’; they did not say ‘We are accepting it on account.’**”（加黑部分是笔者的强调，显示了说明无损害的重要性。）

Robert Goff大法官说：“By paying the cheque into their bank account without in any way objecting that they were not receiving it on those terms [i. e. in the covering letter] the plaintiffs clearly bound themselves by those terms.”

另在较近期的Stour Valley Builders v. Stuart（1992）CAT 1281先例中，Lloyd大法官也说：“Cashing the cheque is always strong evidence of acceptance, especially if it is not accompanied by immediate rejection of the offer. Retention of the cheque without rejection is also strong evidence of acceptance depending on the length of delay...”

保险公司在事故发生之后，委任理算师（loss adjustor）核算损失与委任专家或律师对事故做出调查的同时，为了避免无谓的诉讼与安抚被保险人，有时会做出中间支付（interim payment）。这可能会被认为承认了责任，即使之后发现有理由可以拒赔，也会因为承诺性禁反言而不能拒绝责任，只可以争议赔偿金额。因此，安全的做法是在做出中间支付时，明确说明无损害。这样，如果调查之后发现有理由可以拒赔，不仅不需要赔付，还可以将之前做出的中间支付根据复原原则（restitution）取回。在Callaghan v. Thompson（2000）CLC 360先例中，David Steel大法官说：“Against that background, the notation of ‘**WP**’ made by Mr James（劳合社保险人）whilst at Manson's（保险经纪）offices **must be construed as a complete reservation of rights.** Indeed, it must have been perceived as such given the absence of any suggestion in the correspondence thereafter or even in the pleadings that liability has been admitted at that stage.”（加黑部分是笔者的强调）

---

〔79〕 双方达成和解协议。

〔80〕 一方的言行令对方认为他接受这笔金钱已经满意，并依赖该言行采取行动。

在 The "Winson" (1980) 2 Lloyd's Rep. 213 先例中,也涉及"无损害"能否保护做出陈述或承诺的一方的争议。案情涉及双方在商谈救助成功的小麦的价值时,货方律师认为货方需要承担这笔争议的费用,并承诺会告知或建议给他的客户(货方),但在信件最后写明是无损害。双方的争议之一就是这是否构成承诺性禁反言,货方不能事后否认要承担这笔费用。信件的相关部分可节录如下:"As regards deductions, apart from the deduction of U. S. $272,410.65, we consider that the sum of U. S. $174,173.91 [– I pause to say that that is the figure with which we are concerned –] should also be deducted from the sound value of the cargo although this sum is to be claimed by your clients from our clients in the arbitration. **We have advised our clients that they are liable for the sum of $174,173.91. In this respect, we write without prejudice.**"(加黑部分是争议是否构成承诺性禁反言的文字)

但上诉庭判是上述加黑的文字只是意向(indication)并且明示了是无损害,显然不属于清楚无误的陈述或承诺,不能构成陈述性禁反言。Megaw 大法官说:"The reason is that what is said to be the promise is not unequivocal. At the best it was an indication by solicitors instructed on behalf of the cargo owners that they, the solicitors, had advised their clients that their clients were liable in law to the salvors in this claim for expenses. But that would not be enough, as I see it, to constitute either an offer which would give rise by acceptance to a contract to pay those sums; nor to a representation which could be treated as giving rise to a promissory estoppel. The matters put forward as constituting representation are not unequivocal."

在 The "Zenovia" (2009) 2 Lloyd's Rep. 139 先例中,[81] 承租人提前 30 天做出的预计还船日期通知中有无损害[82] 以及类似说法的不保证(without guarantee)一词,因此被判不属于明确无误的陈述或承诺,Tomlinson 大法官说:"Mr Priday(承租人代表大律师)for his part had not invited the arbitrators to go down this route. In his skeleton argument produced for the appeal Mr Priday observed that the arbitrators considered that the acronym 'wp' in the 30 day approximate notice meant 'without prejudice' and submitted 'if so, they ought to have held that a notice so qualified could not give rise to a promissory estoppel. Such an estoppel is tantamount to a contractual variation or waiver and cannot be based upon a statement made 'without prejudice'. I am inclined to agree. ... On the other hand even if not all who use the phrase understand its technical meaning, most in my view intend by its use to convey that what they say is not thereafter

[81] 案情会在本章之 11.8 段介绍。

[82] 通知中有"wp"字样,虽然懂航运的人(包括本案的法官)都会认为"wp"代表的是"weather permitting",但这被仲裁庭错误理解为"without prejudice"。因为这是对事实的认定,而且当事人也没有就这点提出异议,所以法官也没有做出改变。

something to which reference may be made, or to which they are to be held, in legal proceedings, should they eventuate. Putting it broadly, it is intended and, I think, generally understood, as indicating that what is said cannot usually be relied upon unless of course it leads to an agreement intended to be binding. I am reluctant to uphold a conclusion that a notice of approximate redelivery expressly given without prejudice can without leading to an agreement nonetheless give rise to a promissory estoppel binding the giver of the notice."

6.5.1.2　合约有争议下被终止,双方达成无损害协议的好处

在贵族院的 The "Scaptrade" (1983) 2 Lloyd's Rep. 253 先例中,涉及船东以承租人没有准时支付租金而撤船,具体的案情可见本章之6.5.2段。在该先例中,船东撤船后几天,双方达成一个无损害协议(without prejudice agreement),可部分节录如下:"... If within 60 days of the date of this agreement the discussions in Quito reach a conclusion mutually acceptable to both ... then the rate of hire under the re – charter will be US $4. 30. If the said discussions do not reach a mutually acceptable conclusion within 60 days then the rate of hire under the re – charter will be subject to the determination of the issue as to whether Owners were entitled to or were justified in withdrawing the vessel ... or would have been allowed to do so."

对于这种无损害协议的好处,Bridge 勋爵说:"In particular, when a shipowner becomes entitled, under the terms of his contract, to withdraw a time charterer, he may well wish to act swiftly and irrevocably. True, his problem may, in any particular case, prove to be capable of solution by entering into a without prejudice agreement with the original time charterer, under which the rate of hire payable in future will be made to depend upon a decision, by arbitrators or by a Court, whether he was in law entitled to determine the charter. But this is not always possible."

一般来说,这种无损害协议对双方都有益。对船东来说,首先是船上可能还存在货物,即使撤船,根据提单合约,他也需要开往卸港,将货物交给提单持有人。另是船东可以避免诉讼风险,否则万一他被判是错误撤船,就会面对可能昂贵的金钱损失索赔。而如果他被判是有合法理由可以撤船,根据该无损害协议,就可以赚取更高的租金。另一个对船东的好处是,如果承租人不接受该无损害协议,并且根据仲裁庭或法院的判决,船东是错误撤船,在决定损失金额时,船东就可以抗辩说承租人没有接受这个无损害协议,没有尽到减少损失的责任。而对承租人来说,省了再在市场上租船的麻烦,尤其是在有分租约的情况下。如果船东被判是错误撤船,仍是以原本的租金租船。而如果船东被判是有合法理由撤船,无损害协议中双方同意的租金,往往也较市场价格更低。同样的道理不止适用在期租合约,任何类别的合约终止后都可以考虑双方谈判达成这种无损害协议,然后双方通过诉讼/仲裁以决定较早的终止合约是否合法。

6.5.2 抗议(under protest)

有时一方在做出陈述或承诺的同时,也会向对方表示"抗议"(under protest),在《Black's Law Dictionary》,这被定义为:"A formal statement or action expressing dissent or disapproval . . . A formal statement, usually in writing, disputing a debt's legality or validity but agreeing to make payment while reserving the right to recover the amount at a later time . . . "

如在已经多次提到的贵族院的 The "Scaptrade"(1983) 2 Lloyd's Rep. 253 先例中,案情涉及航运中的期租合约准时支付租金的问题。期租合约的标准格式基本都有明示条文写明,如果承租人不准时支付租金,船东可以撤船。这导致船东经常试图在航运市场上涨时,借机撤船。由于航运市场经常大起大落,所以这方面的案件很多,可参见杨大明的《期租合约》第十八篇。这方面的案件很多涉及条文的解释,但也经常涉及弃权与禁反言。毕竟如果条文的解释明确支持船东可以撤船,承租人事实上支付租金的时间是晚了一天甚至一分钟,谈不上准时,承租人唯一能够胜诉的机会是依赖弃权与禁反言,作为最后防线。如指船东太晚才决定选择撤船,构成弃权,或是船东在撤船前做出的言行构成禁反言。[83] 贵族院虽然没有在 The "Scaptrade" 先例针对禁反言是否适用,但这点在上诉庭([1983] 1 Lloyd's Rep. 146)与高院([1981] 2 Lloyd's Rep. 425)都是主要的争议。而被用来支持禁反言的有关事实是,在交船后直到撤船前的 24 期的租金经常有迟付,但船东没有提出抗议或保留权利。在当时,还没有细分究竟这属于哪类禁反言,只是被法院称为"衡平法禁反言"(equitable estoppel)。但看来主要是根据相关的事实来决定是否构成衡平法宽限或承诺性禁反言,上诉庭的 Robert Goff 大法官说:"There was also no dispute that, in order to bring themselves within that principle, the charterers had to establish that two criteria had been fulfilled. First, they had to establish that the owners had represented unequivocally that they would not enforce their strict legal right, under the contract between the parties, to withdraw the vessel from the charterers' service in the event of a default in payment of an instalment of hire . . . Second, they had to establish that in the circumstances it would be inequitable to allow the owners to enforce their strict legal right, having regard to the dealings which had taken place between the parties: see Hughes v. Metropolitan Railway Co. (1877) 2 App. Cas. 439, 448, per Lord Cairns L. C."

在该先例中,高院与上诉庭都判是承租人败诉。船东过往对承租人迟付租金没有抗议的行为不影响承租人迟付租金并最终导致被撤船的决定。这也表示承租人没有依赖船东的行动与否。更重要的是,法院不认为船东没有抗议的行为不足以构成清楚无误的陈述或承诺,Robert Goff 大法官这样说:"Now it is not at all easy to infer, from **the mere fact that late payments had been accepted in the past by the owners**

[83] 如 The "Li Hai"(2005) 2 Lloyd's Rep. 389 先例,案情在本章之 6.1 段有介绍。

without protest, an unequivocal representation by them not to exercise their strict legal right of withdrawal in the event of late payment by the charterers of a subsequent instalment of hire – if only because the circumstances prevailing at the time when the earlier late payments were accepted may not be the same as those prevailing in the future."(加黑部分是笔者的强调)

但要小心在该先例的事实,看来有其他方面影响法院认为船东不抗议的行为不是会构成禁反言清楚无误的陈述或承诺,如:(1)在 24 期租金中,承租人有 6 期是准时支付,其余 18 期是迟付 1 到 3 天不等。针对这种不一致的过往事实,比较难说船东没有抗议接受迟付租金的行为是清楚无误的陈述或承诺令承租人可迟付租金。但如果交船后每一期的租金都迟付,法院的认定就可能会有不同。(2)过往的迟付中,曾经有一次船东向经纪人要求承租人支付迟付的利息。这表示船东已经意识到承租人的违约,并要求以利息的形式赔偿。总体来看,就不能说船东有清楚无误的陈述或承诺放弃他的合约权利。

所以根据整体的证据来看,高院与上诉庭都不认为船东被禁反言而不能行使撤船的权利。因为船东的言行远不足以构成清楚无误的陈述或承诺。但 Robert Goff 大法官也提到一个被法院视为足够的例子,说:"Of course, if for example the charterers chose regularly to use a particular route for payment which involved the consequence that payments were always received by the owners, say, two days late, and the owners knowingly acquiesced in this course of conduct, the court might be able (depending on the circumstances) to infer a sufficient representation from the owners' conduct."

总结而言,每个先例的案情都有不同,有时是否构成清楚无误的陈述或承诺像解释合约条文一样,取决于法官或仲裁员对言行的整体印象,而这印象会受文化背景、个人经历等的影响:The "Li Hai" (2005) 2 Lloyd's Rep. 389 先例。这样,最保险的做法就是一旦对方迟付租金,船东就明确是在抗议下接受。这样,无论法官或仲裁员是怎样的文化背景,都无法将这接受扭曲解释为清楚无误地放弃了撤船的权利的陈述或承诺。即使不是每次迟付租金都抗议,但只要抗议过,就还是有帮助。当然抗议的时间也会有影响,如果船东只在开始几次抗议,后来几次的迟付就不加理会(可能航运市场稳定),但在最后一次迟付后,突然决定撤船,也可能会不安全。时间上显然最好是在撤船前两三期迟付租金就表示抗议。如果要肯定,看来船东比较安全的做法是先向承租人做出通知,说明以后支付租金必须准时,以回复到原本的合约地位,[84]之后再找机会撤船。

以上虽然是以迟付租金为例,但在其他的同类情况,如支付房屋的租金、向银行分期还款、长期供应货物等,只要涉及持续的延误履行的违约,无辜方的言行是否构成禁反言,同样的理论与做法都适用。

---

〔84〕 见本章之 9.1 段。

6.5.3 保留权利(reserve rights)

在《Chitty on Contracts》(第32版,2015年)一书之4－092段,提到了若干同意不坚持原有的法律权利但同时写明保留权利而被判是不构成衡平法宽限或承诺性禁反言的案件。首先是 Finagrain SA Geneva v. P Kruse Hamburg (1976) 2 Lloyd's Rep. 508 先例中,该先例与在本章之3.2段介绍的 Bremer v. Mackprang (1979) 1 Lloyd's Rep. 221 先例一样,都是密西西比河泛滥,美国政府做出大豆出口禁令导致的无数案件之一。美国政府在1973年6月27日作出禁令,但在1973年7月2日后放宽,允许已经订立了的买卖合约申请当局的批准付运40%的大豆。该禁令最终在1973年10月1日全面取消。在该先例中,买卖双方在1973年1月22日根据 GAFTA 100 标准格式订立合约买卖1500吨的美国大豆,于5月到9月分5批付运。因为美国政府的禁令,卖方无法付运6月的300吨大豆,并在7月3日通过电传通知买方,对于无法在6月付运的部分,他们不得不依赖合约第21条的免责条文。7月4日,卖方通知买方说,虽然他们会依赖合约第21条的免责条文,但如果从上一手卖方收到了划归通知,会转给买方,说:"... in all cases where we received from our Sellers appropriations covering June shipment these appropriations will be passed on to our Buyers."

卖方认为这批本应在6月份付运的货物只要付运40%,即120吨。在8月6日,卖方向买方做出了第一份划归通知,作为对该120吨货物的部分履行:"...(i) We apply under usual reserves s. s. 'Kyravathia' ... destination Rotterdam b lading 8th July... U. S. S. soya meal... 30,430 Kilos part fulfilment of 40% ... June shipment... (ii) We apply under usual reserves s. s. 'Paul L. Russ' ... destination Rotterdam b lading 18th July... 32,749 kilos... June shipment."

但买方坚持要付运全部的300吨货物,并回复说:"... U. S. SBM per s. s. 'Kyravathia'... Please advise for which quantity of abt 40% this shall be valid. Independent of this I reserve all contractual rights, particularly I expect full delivery of the quantity for June...(针对 Paul L. Russ 轮上的货物)I accept only under reserve of all my contractual rights. I insist on full delivery of the quantity for June..."

8月7日,卖方又向买方做出了第二份划归通知,将 Pegasus 轮上的37748千克大豆作为对该120吨货物的部分履行。买方没有质疑划归通知的有效性,并在事实上接受了该划归通知。

9月4日,卖方向买方做出了第三份划归通知,将 Cape Palmas 轮上的29400千克大豆作为对该120吨货物的部分履行。说:"We apply under usual reserves... 'Cape Palmas'... bill of lading 16th August... 29,400 kilos balance 40% of... June shipment."

但买方拒绝接受该划归通知,说:"I hereby reject as uncontractual the appropriation which you gave me by your telex today for 29,400 kilos... per 'Cape Palmas' bill of lading 16th August. At the same time I hold the sellers in default for the deficit quantity of 204,073 kilos."

双方开始仲裁,GAFTA 的仲裁上诉庭判是卖方违约。被上诉到法院的相关法律问题之一是买方之前接受划归通知/7 月的提单的行为是否构成弃权或禁反言。高院的 Mocatta 大法官判是买方的行为构成弃权,但在上诉庭这一判决被推翻。上诉庭的三位大法官一致认为买方的行为不构成清楚无误的陈述或承诺。其中 Roskill 大法官说:"I unreservedly accept that the three small parcels which the buyers accepted and paid for at the contract price were accepted in pro tanto substitution for a like quantity of the contract goods though in law there was no obligation whatever on the buyers to accept those goods in such pro tanto performance. But that is a very different matter from saying that the buyers thereby waived - that is to say lost - all rights to claim damages for the non-shipment of the balance of the 300 tons, just over 204 tons, unless and until they gave notice to the contrary.... I see nothing in these telexes which does more than insist upon full delivery, to which the buyers were then entitled, and that under reiterated a phrase hardly consistent with an intention to waive their then existing right to claim damages.... In truth I do not think that the telexes and other matters to which I have referred come near to establishing waiver, or, ... a variation of the original contract provisions for June shipment, or waiver of the buyers' right to claim damages for the original default on July 10, 1973."

另在 Cook Industries Inc. v. Meunerie Liegeois SA (1981) 1 Lloyd's Rep. 359 先例中,案情与 Finagrain v. Kruse 先例十分相似,针对双方的通讯往来中买方的言行是否构成明确无误的陈述或承诺,Mustill 大法官说:"When one reads the message as a whole, including the reservation of the buyers' contractual rights, it cannot in my view be construed as sufficiently clear and unequivocal waiver of the buyers' rights to receive June shipments in fulfilment of the June instalment to satisfy the test laid down in the reported cases. I am fortified in this opinion by the findings in the award which indicate that these trade arbitrators have understood the telex in the same sense."

类似的先例还有 Peter Cremer v. Granaria B. V. (1981) 2 Lloyd's Rep. 583, Bremer Handels gesellschaft mbH v. Deutsche Conti - Handelsgesellschaft mbH (1983) 2 Lloyd's Rep. 476 等。

6.5.4 完整合约条文(entire agreement clause)

至于完整合约条文[85]对防止构成禁反言也会起到一定的作用。如在 Datec Electronic Holdings Ltd. v. United Parcels Service Ltd. (2005) 1 Lloyd's Rep. 470 先例中,案情涉及 UPS 在快递过程中遗失了昂贵的电脑,而被原告索赔一大笔损失。

---

〔85〕 杨良宜的《合约的解释:规则与应用》一书第十三章之第 2 段有介绍。

但 UPS 快递单中合并的运输合约条文有规定每次托运的赔偿不超过 5 万美金。原告提出各种理由否定这个条文的适用，争议之一涉及弃权与禁反言。这就是 UPS 已经为原告快递电脑与电脑配件一段时间，知道或应该知道这些货物价值昂贵与超出 5 万美金，所以这些行为就构成弃权与禁反言。但这被法院否定，认为这些行为不属于清楚无误。此外，UPS 快递单中合并的运输合约条文也包括一条完整合约条文，表示之前的行为不应该加以考虑，这也加强了法院的判决。Andrew Smith 大法官说："First, the Entire Agreement clause: I do not understand Mr Priday（UPS 的代表大律师）to argue that this provision would necessarily defeat the claimants' arguments however clearly the parties evinced an intention that the US $ 50,000 restriction should not apply, but that it was counter – indicative of such an intention. I accept that, and therefore accept that the clause does provide some further support to UPS's contentions."

但完整合约条文或其他类似条文只是可能而并非肯定可以排除衡平法宽限或承诺性禁反言。在 Jet2. com Ltd. v. Blackpool Airport Ltd. (2010) EWHC 3166 (Comm) 先例中，Beatson 大法官说："In Lloyd's case estoppel was held not to be inconsistent with the entire agreement clause because it only precluded reliance on pre – contractual representations and the representation relied on post – dated the contract. But the Court of Appeal recognised that a clause in suitable terms could preclude estoppel."

6.5.5 明示保留权利的例外情况

一般来说，一旦有这些明示的语言/文字的保护，就不会构成弃权或禁反言，但还是有两种情况要注意。首先，如果一方保留了一种权利，并不能保护另一种权利不被放弃。其次，在两类情况下，法院会认定即使一方保留了权利，依然会构成弃权或禁反言，以下会分段介绍。

6.5.5.1 例外之一：通过保留权利回避合约规定的明示或默示条文

第一类是一方试图通过保留权利回避合约规定的明示或默示条文，[86]这等于单方面改变合约条文，显然不能成功。道理很简单，要改变合约的明示或默示条文，必须双方同意，即"更改合约"（variation）。

在本章之 6.5.1.1 段提到的 The "Zenovia" (2009) 2 Lloyd's Rep. 139 先例[87]涉及了在期租合约到期需要还船时经常发生的情况，即承租人（因为他营运船舶，所以应该能够掌握船期）向船东做出还船通知，好让船东尽快尽早找下一票生意。从该先例可以看到，如果租约规定只需要给预计通知，承租人为了小心在预计通知中加上无损害，显然不是一个对有关通知中的还船日期的清楚无误的陈述或承诺。船东如果依赖该通知订立下一票生意或租约，需要自己承担风险。如果发生了 The "Ze-

---

〔86〕 关于合约默示条文（包括法律的默示与事实的默示），可见杨良宜的《合约的解释：规则与应用》一书第七章。

〔87〕 具体案情会在本章之 11.8 段介绍。

novia"的情况，船东必须证明承租人的通知是不小心与没有合理基础，才可以承租人违约[88]而索赔有关的损失。但不少条文，包括 BIMCO 的标准还船条文，会要求承租人给一个绝对的通知。BIMCO 标准还船条文可部分节录如下："The Charterers shall keep the Owners informed of the Vessel's itinerary and any changes thereto and in any event when requested by the Owners. In addition, the Charterers shall give the Owners the following notices of the Vessel's redelivery, unless otherwise agreed: Minimum 30 followed by 20, 15, 10, 7, 5 and 3 days' approximate notice and 2 days' definite notice of redelivery... The Charterers shall be entitled to qualify redelivery notices, save for the definite notice, with 'weather permitting' and/or 'unforeseen circumstances always excepted'; and all other qualifications shall be null and void.[89]"

显然，如果合约中有这样的明示条文，在最后两日内的还船通知中，即使承租人不确定能否在两日内还船而写了无损害，也起不了作用。因为承租人不能单方面改变合约条文。而一旦像 The "Zenovia"先例中，船东因为承租人没有准时还船而导致赶不及下一票生意，承租人要承担损失。

至于默示条文，可以货物买卖合约为例。如果订立合约后市场下跌，买方显然希望能有合法理由拒货，将市场风险或损失转移给卖方。但 1979 年《货物销售法》之 section 36 规定了一些针对不允许买方拒货的法律默示条文："The buyer is deemed to have accepted the goods subject to subsection (2) below—(a) when he intimates to the seller that he has accepted them, or (b) when the goods have been delivered to him and he does any act in relation to them which is inconsistent with the ownership of the seller...(4) The buyer is also deemed to have accepted the goods when after the lapse of a reasonable time he retains the goods without intimating to the seller that he has rejected them."

这样，买方如果做出了一些被上述立法(买卖合约的默示条文)视为接受货物的言行，就不能再通过无损害或抗议等的用字向卖方保留拒货的权利。如原本市场对买方有利，所以虽然货物迟了付运，但买方没有拒货，谁知之后在付运途中市场下跌，买方试图转卖却不成功，这时买方再向卖方拒货，理由是在之前接受货物时针对延误付运保留了权利，这不会被法院或仲裁庭支持。

但有些情况下，买方不得不采取一些可能事后被指称为构成放弃终止合约权利或衡平法宽限的行为，如买方为了避免损失扩大，向当地法院或仲裁庭申请并取得命令将卖方拒绝收回的货物(如香蕉)尽快处理掉(如出售)等。买方在采取这些行动时必须说明是"无损害"或"抗议"，或明确表示是作为托管人(bailee)或紧急代理人

---

〔88〕 这里是违反了双方必须给予协助/合作让对方顺利履行合约的默示条文，可见杨良宜《合约的解释：规则与应用》一书第七章之 10.2 段。

〔89〕 这应该包括"无损害"、"不保证"等。

(agent of necessity)来处理货物,就不会事后被卖方指称其言行构成弃权或禁反言。

另一个默示条文的例子是如果合约没有明示规定行使权利的具体时间,则法律会默示规定是在一个合理时间内。而什么是合理时间,则会根据不同案件的事实做出默示。合约一方不能犹疑不决以保留权利的形式延长行使权利的时间。以期租合约为例,如果承租人没有准时与足数支付运费,即使没有明示条文规定,船东也必须尽快在合理时间内做出选择是否撤船。[90] 不能在承租人没有准时与足数支付运费时,因为市场平稳没有选择撤船,只是对承租人保留了权利,而在3个月后市场猛涨时再选择撤船。在 The "Antaios" (1983) 2 Lloyd's Rep. 473 先例中,Donaldson 勋爵针对船东不能以保留权利的形式延迟做出是否撤船的决定,说:"I know of no authority for the proposition, and I do not think that I have ever heard it suggested before, that a shipowner can extend the time for reaching a decision whether or not to withdraw beyond what is reasonable in all the circumstances by the simple device of announcing that his failure to decide is without prejudice to his rights. He can certainly do so by reaching an agreement with the charterers either ad hoc or by including in the charterparty an anti – technicality clause. . . . If . . . the owner can extend his option to withdraw the vessel in this way, chaos would result. Ships would be have to at sea or tied up in port, no one knowing whether they were going to perform the chartered service."

Fox 大法官也说:"I cannot see how the mere unilateral assertion of the owners that delay after May 7 was to be without prejudice to their rights can affect the matter. If the owners can do that, the rule, whatever its basis, is largely useless. I can see that there might be circumstances in which the owners could not reasonably be expected to make up their mind at once and that if they bring that to the notice of the charterers (who might not otherwise be aware of it) they could reserve their position. That, however, is a quite different matter and goes generally to the question of reasonableness.[91] I would suppose that the question of reasonableness must be determined in the light of all the circumstances. One does not look at it exclusively from the point of view of either side. But, be that as it may, if the owners' right to withdraw must be exercised within a reasonable time I do not see how they can extend the 'reasonable time' simply by their own choice — though they could no doubt extinguish or reduce their rights by waiver."

---

[90] 关于撤船的合理时间,可见杨大明的《期租合同》一书第十八篇之18.4.2段。因为撤船是重大决定,所以船东需要合理时间向律师查问。另外,如果船东一直没有收到租金,船东因多次查询而拖延了2至3天,这种事实下也算是合理时间。用一些时间调查承租人是否作出合理的租金扣减,也应是同样道理。当然,每个案件的事实都会不同,但除非在非常特殊的情况下,一个星期应该是太长了。

[91] Fox 大法官说船东不可以通过保留权利单方面改变合约。但会有情况是船东无法马上做出决定,而在这种情况下,只要考虑的时间合理,船东可以在与承租人的通讯往来中保留权利。这涉及总体来看是否属于合理时间的问题,毕竟不同于明示条文,合理与否是要考虑所有的相关因素,有一定的弹性。

同样的道理,如果一方违约/毁约或合约明示在发生某些情况下可终止合约,无辜方或想终止合约的一方必须在合理时间或合约规定的时间内做出是否终止合约的选择。如果无辜方或想终止合约的一方犹疑不决,不能决定是否要终止合约,也不可以通过单方面保留权利延长这合理时间或合约规定的时间。在笔者曾经处理的一个造船合约的伦敦仲裁,船厂在过了造船合约中规定的死亡日期后仍然没有交船,即代表外国船东作为买方有权终止合约。但由于当时是在2008年“金融海啸”后船舶价格进一步下跌前的“小阳春”,中国船厂降价后的船舶价格相比市场价格与走势有一定的吸引力,因此船东没有立刻弃船,只是保留了权利。在之后的四十多天,船东也要求船厂做了很多工作,虽然部分电文中说明了是在抗议下或是无损害。之后市场再度下跌,船东向船厂弃船。笔者认为,虽然船东保留了权利(只针对部分的言行),但他让船厂继续工作的行为与保留权利明显不符。另是在这种标的物市场价格波动很大与很快的合约中,为了防止无辜方取巧,他必须做出选择的合理时间往往很短。虽然造船合约相比租约或商品买卖合约会有较长的合理时间或至少有可商榷的余地,但也不应是该仲裁中的四十多天,船东不能通过保留权利单方面延长造船合约默示的合理时间。但两位伦敦仲裁员看来并不愿意与笔者合议,笔者也只能做出不同意见。显然,中国船厂在该先例是因为延误过了“死亡日期”被船东弃船而败诉,裁决书的多数裁决针对弃权与禁反言的争议只是简单一句船东已经明示保留了权利。

再如,如双方同意香港仲裁,即双方有了一个仲裁协议。这样,即使没有明示规定,法律也默示规定香港特区《仲裁条例》适用。如果涉及对管辖权的质疑,根据香港特区《仲裁条例》,最迟要在递交抗辩书时提出。被申请人不能单方面在递交抗辩书时保留权利,而在之后才提出对管辖权的质疑。因为合约一方不能单方面改变双方在仲裁协议中的约定。

6.5.5.2 例外之二:总体看言行与保留权利不一致

第二类是违约方的行为与保留权利的立场完全不符,如虽然保留了终止合约的权利,但不断催促对方履行合约或做出其他与保留权利不一致的行为。已经在本章第6段提到,言行可能一致,也可能矛盾,要总体看待。法院是不会善待言行之间的矛盾,让泛泛保留权利的一方受到保护。在Bremer v. Mackprang (1979) 1 Lloyd's Rep. 221先例中,Shaw大法官说:“... I see no reason, however, to limit the effect of waiver to rights[92] known to exist. It may be embracing enough, and so intended, as to forego rights which might exist in regard to a particular contract or in a particular con-

[92] 已经多次提到,早期先例中弃权与禁反言往往混为一谈。虽然在这里用的是“弃权”一词,但实际上适用的是衡平法宽限或承诺性禁反言。这可见Denning勋爵在提到适用的法律时说:“The modern law as to waiver was stated by this Court in ... ‘If one party, by his conduct, leads another to believe that the strict rights arising under the contract will not be insisted upon, intending that the other should act on that belief, and he does act on it, then the first party will not afterwards by allowed to insist on the strict legal rights when it would be inequitable for him to do so’.”

text. . . . No tinge of ambivalence in this regard is introduced by such formulae as ‘without prejudice to our rights’ or ‘we reserve our contractual rights’. The implication of waiver survives such mild dilution where the surrounding circumstances are sufficiently cogent in themselves.”

Denning 勋爵也说:“The receivers seek to avoid this result by relying on the telexes in which the contractual rights were reserved. I do not think this was sufficient. If their conduct was **such as to constitute a waiver, they cannot by such a formula escape the consequences of it.**”(加黑部分是笔者的强调)

这与《Benjamen's Sale of Goods》(第 9 版,2014 年)一书之 8 – 030 段的说法是一致:“The mere reservation by the buyer of ‘his rights’ under the contract will not preclude a waiver or estoppels where the remaining circumstances justify a finding to that effect.”

6.5.5.2.1　先例之一:The “Libyaville”

在 The “Libyaville” (1975) 1 Lloyd's Rep. 537 先例中,案情涉及期租合约撤船。双方订立了 5 年的期租合约,但之后在装载货物时双方发生争议,船东认为可以装 17 辆拖车,而承租人认为只能装 16 辆。之后双方暂时达成和解,在租约中增加了一条条文说如果只能装 16 辆拖车,租金可以减少 1.5%。根据租约第 5 条文,如果承租人没有准时与足数支付租金,船东可以选择撤船。但根据第 44 条文,撤船前要先给承租人两天的通知,让承租人补救。

承租人在足数支付了 3 期的租金后,接下来支付的 3 期都扣减了 1.5% 的租金。前两期被扣减的租金,船东都在抗议下接受了。但在第 3 期租金被扣减后,船东以不足数支付租金为由撤船,并且没有根据第 44 条文做出通知。之后双方开始诉讼,针对船东在抗议下接受了两期被扣减的租金是否构成弃权或禁反言,Mocatta 大法官说:“The owners undoubtedly accepted these two payments, though they did so under strong protests, without prejudice to their rights and even purpoted to give the notice required unde cl. 44, though they failed to comply strictly with its terms. In my judgment, however, what they accepted was paid and received as hire and once having been accepted as such the right to withdraw the vessel under cl. 5 for short payment was lost.”

法院的判法也可以理解,毕竟在岸上的房屋租赁合约中,这个法律地位已经很明确。早在 Matthews v. Smallwood (1910) 1 Ch 777 先例中,Parker 大法官就说:“It is also, I think, reasonably clear upon the cases that whether the act, coupled with the knowledge, constitutes a waiver is a question which the law decides, and therefore it is not open to a lessor who has knowledge of the breach to say ‘I will treat the tenancy as existing, and I will receive the rent, or I will take advantage of my power as landlord to distrain; but I tell you that all I shall do will be without prejudice to my right to re – enter, which I intend to reserve.’ That is a position which he is not entitled to take up. If, knowing of the breach, he does distrain, or does receive the rent, then by law he waives the breach, and nothing which he can say by way of protest against the law will avail him anything."

在 Segal Securities Ltd. v. Thoseby (1963) 1 QB 887 先例中,房东在 1948 年将一套复式公寓以每年 300 英镑的价格出租给租客夫妇 21 年。租约中规定,租客只可以将该公寓用做自住,并且不能转租。丈夫在 1959 年去世后,妻子与其他两到三位女士共同居住在复式公寓里。1962 年 6 月,妻子是与她的朋友以及另一位通过招租广告招来的分租客住在一起。这违反了租约的约定,房东在 6 月 8 日发出通知,要求该女租客在 28 天内补救。期间在 6 月 25 日,由于租金到期,房东写了一封标题写着无损害的信给租客要求支付下一个季度的租金,并说:"... demand and any receipt for rent is made or given without prejudice to the service of the notice ... and to any breaches of covenant in respect of user."

租客写了一张支票支付租金,但房东没有接受,并将支票退还给她。8 月 27 日,房东出告票声称租客违约,要求收回复式公寓。而租客则否认自己违约,并声称房东之前要求支付房租的信件属于弃权或禁反言。Sachs 大法官认为要求支付租金与收取支付的租金本质是相同的,都会被租客认为是作出了不收回房子的选择,说:"It is thus a matter of law that once rent is accepted a waiver results... Where forfeiture is involved, in essence once the landlord has knowledge of a past breach, the law thus treats the rent as a piece of cake equivalent to the land out of which it derives: its nutritional qualities in the landlord's hands being unaffected by attaching to it the label 'without prejudice,' the law treats that attachment as having no effect... As both demand and acceptance respectively are in law merely different forms of a notification by a landlord of election not to avoid or forfeit the lease, to my mind no distinction can nowadays be drawn between them in relation to a question whether the label 'without prejudice' affects their quality as an election... It follows that the letter of June 25 is, to my mind, a demand of a type that waives forfeiture."

在航运与国际贸易中都十分重要的期租合约中,船东撤船也要小心。具体可看杨大明的《期租合同》一书第十八篇。

6.5.5.2.2 先例之二:Nichimen v. Gatoil

在 Nichimen v. Gatoil (1987) 2 Lloyd Rep. 46 先例中,根据合约,买方需要在 4 月 17 日开出信用证。4 月 18 日,买方仍没有开出信用证,卖方写信给买方说:"We are prepared to agree to extend period for your opening L/C in our favour to London noon... time next Monday 21st April 1986 ... All Nichiment's rights under the contract and generally are expressly reserved, including the right to claim from you damages and all other losses suffered by Nichimen as a result of you failure to perform."

到了 4 月 22 日,买方仍然没有开出信用证,于是卖方终止了合约。针对卖方是否放弃了终止合约的权利,上诉庭说:"All that the Sellers did in relation to the letter of credit after April 17 was to give the Buyers a number of fixed extensions of time; they never waived their right to continue to treat the time for opening of the letter of credit as of the essence and they never did anything whereby they implied agreed or represented that the Buyers' time for opening the letter of credit had become at large..."

针对保留权利,John Megaw 大法官说:"**I am unable to see by what process of logic a party to a contract can be said to waive his right to exercise a remedy when he expressly states, in the documents containing the alleged waiver, that he reserves his right to exercise that remedy if the party in breach does not fulfil his contractual obligation within a stated time.** Whether that stated time is not one which can reasonably be achieved by the party in breach in the circumstances which exist, as a result of the breach, at the time when the concession is offered, appears to me to be quite irrelevant. If, any authority were needed for that proposition, it is to be found in the decision of this Court in Buckland v. Farmer & Moody, [1979] 1 WLR 221."(加黑部分是笔者的强调)

但 Kee 大法官说:"I accept Mr. Pollock's(买方代表大律师)submission based on the decision of this Court in Bremer v. Mackprang per Lord Denning and Lord Justice Shaw that **a mere reservation of rights will not preclude a waiver if the remaining circumstances justify a finding to that effect.**"(加黑部分是笔者的强调)

6.5.5.2.3 先例之三:The "Fortune Plum"

在 The "Fortune Plum" (2013) 2 Lloyd's Rep. 618 先例中,案情涉及期租合约,无辜方的船东在承租人的违约/毁约(延误与没有支付租金)后,通知船长把货物卸下后撤船。承租人抗辩说船东卸货是确认了租约的存在,之后就不能再接受违约/毁约并撤船。仲裁庭支持了承租人的抗辩,但 Teare 大法官推翻了仲裁庭的裁决,说在认定无辜方确认了租约后,仍要看违约方之后的言行有否改变立场,如果没有,就可以当做持续性的违约/毁约,可以被无辜方接受。该先例的争议之一是仲裁庭做出裁决时,是否忽略了船东仍然保留权利的做法,针对这一点,Teare 大法官说:"The fourth argument was that the tribunal wrongly discounted the owners' repeated reservation of their rights. However, in my judgment **the tribunal did not 'wrongly' discount the owners' reservation of their rights. The tribunal held that in circumstances where, in the tribunal's view, the owners had acted in a manner which was inconsistent with withdrawing the vessel they had lost the right to do so because they had affirmed the charterparty.**"(加黑部分是笔者的强调)

7. 要件之三:对方对该陈述或承诺做出依赖并改变地位/做法

权威书籍《Chitty on Contracts》(第 32 版,2015 年)之 4－094 段说:“**Reliance.** The first requirement to be discussed under this heading is that the promise or representation must in some way have influenced the conduct of the party to whom it was made.[93] Although the promise need not form the sole inducement, it must (it is submitted) be some inducement. Hence the present requirement would not be satisfied if it could be shown that the other party's conduct was not influenced by the promise so that he was not in any way prejudiced by it. But if this is a matter of ' mere speculation, '[94] or if the promise or representation ' was one of the factors . . . relied upon, ' it would form a sufficient inducement. Where the promisee has, after the promise, conducted himself in the way intended by the promisor, it will be up to the promisor to establish that this conduct was not induced by the promise.[95]”

衡平法宽限或承诺性禁反言的说法是与其他类别的禁反言一样,都要求对方做出依赖。这在无数有关的先例中有明确:Wallis v. Semark (1951) 2 TLR 222 (CA); Morrow v. Carty (1957) NI 174; Tool Metal Manufacturing Co. v. Tungsten Electric Co. (1955) 1 WLR 761 (HL); Beesly v. Hallwood Estates Ltd. (1960) 2 All ER 314; Ajayi v. R. T. Briscoe (Nigeria) Ltd. (1964) 1 WLR 1326 (PC); WJ Alan & Co. Ltd. v. El Nasr Export and Import Co. (1972) 1 Lloyd's Rep. 313; Edm JM Mertens v. Veevoeder Import Export Vimex (1979) 2 Lloyd's Rep. 372; Avimex SA

---

〔93〕 针对这一要件,法院或仲裁庭通常是看被说成构成衡平法宽限或承诺性禁反言的有关陈述或承诺,是否是令对方做出与原本不同的行动或不行动的原因或部分原因,即是否如果没有该陈述或承诺,对方不会这样做。

〔94〕 这是 Denning 勋爵在 Brikom Investments Ltd. v. Carr (1979) QB 467 先例所说,因为有否依赖该陈述或承诺只能听被承诺方的一面之词或证人证言,不会有其他证据。

〔95〕 一旦可以假设被承诺方依赖了承诺方的言行改变了自己的行为,就需要承诺方证明被承诺方并没有依赖该陈述或承诺。这可以是证明如果没有该陈述或承诺,对方不可能(impossible)或不大可能(improbable)会有不同的做法。如本章之 7.4.3 段介绍的 The “Post Chaser” (1981) 2 Lloyd's Rep. 695 先例,案情涉及承诺很快被撤回,对方根本来不及依赖。即使技术上来说有依赖,也不可能因此蒙受任何损害。至于不大可能依赖的情况,可以是根据合约规定,买方要开出美元的信用证,但买方开出的是英镑的信用证。卖方将信用证兑现,并向买方索赔英镑贬值造成的损失。买方会以卖方兑现信用证的行为构成衡平法宽限或承诺性禁反言抗辩。而卖方如果可以证明买方开不出美元的信用证,或是通过其他渠道的安排在合约规定的时间内来不及,就可以证明买方不大可能依赖了相关的陈述或承诺,从而不会构成衡平法宽限或承诺性禁反言。

v. Dewulf & Cie (1979) 2 Lloyd's Rep. 57; Fontana NV v. Mautner (1980) 254 EG 199; Ets Soules & Cie v. International Trade Development Co. Ltd. (1980) 1 Lloyd's Rep. 129 (CA); Peter Cremer v. Granaria BV (1981) 2 Lloyd's Rep. 583; The "Athos" (1983) 1 Lloyd's Rep. 127; Amherst v. James Walker Goldsmith & Silversmith Ltd. (1983) Ch 305 (CA); Mebro Oil SA v. Gatoil International Inc. (1985) 2 Lloyd's Rep. 234; The "Leonidas D" (1985) 2 Lloyd's Rep. 18; Cie Francaise Importation et de Distribution SA v. Deutsche Continental Handelsgesellschaft (1985) 2 Lloyd's Rep. 592; The "Multitank Holsati" (1988) 2 Lloyd's Rep. 486; The "Kanchenjunga" (1990) 1 Lloyd's Rep. 391 等先例。

7.1 衡平法宽限或承诺性禁反言的陈述方或承诺方必须知道或希望有关陈述或承诺会被对方合理依赖

这是从陈述方或承诺方的角度来看依赖的问题,因为只是从被承诺方的角度看有否因为依赖而蒙受损害不足以满足这个要件。换言之,有关的陈述或承诺与依赖并蒙受损害之间必须有关联,才能满足这一要件。提出禁反言的一方,要证明两者之间有关联,最简单的就是证明陈述方或承诺方知道(know)或希望(intend)该陈述或承诺会被对方合理依赖。这与"因选择而弃权"(waiver by election)不同,弃权方要知道或应该知道自己的权利以及言行会构成弃权,并做出知情的选择(learned choice)。而要构成承诺性禁反言,陈述方或承诺方无需知道自己的权利,但需要知道或希望该陈述或承诺会被对方合理依赖。即希望对方会相信有关的陈述或承诺,并依照该陈述或承诺行事。

这在有关的重要先例都有提到,笔者只节录部分如下。首先是在确立承诺性禁反言说法的 Central London Property Trust Ltd. v. High Trees House Ltd. (1947) KB 130 先例中,Denning 大法官说:"I prefer to apply the principle that a promise intended to be binding, intended to be acted on and in fact acted on, is binding so far as its terms properly apply."

在接下来的 Brikom Investments Ltd. v. Carr (1979) QB 467 (CA)先例中,Denning 大法官也说:"To establish the defence of promissory estoppel the defendant must show an intention by the promsor that the promisee should act on the promise, that she did act on it in a way she would not have done but for the promise, and that she acted to her detriment."

该先例的案情在本章之 5.2 段已经简单介绍,房东承诺租客会自费修理屋顶,但房东争辩是他从未向租约的受让人(assignee)做出过任何承诺。这带来的争议就是构成承诺性禁反言的陈述或承诺所带来的法律救济是否能够被转让(assignable)?一审与上诉庭都说是可以,并认为房东做出有关的承诺时是知道或希望租客以及他的受让人会依赖。Denning 勋爵说:"It is plain ... that when the landlords made this promise they intended it to be for the benefit of all those from time to time holding the leases, realising that each in turn would tell his successor that the landlords were going to repair the roofs at their own expense. The landlords, having made a representation of that kind, knowing that it would be passed on, cannot escape from it by simply saying: 'These people are assignees.'"

另在 Goldsworthy v. Brickell (1987) Ch 378 先例中,Nourse 大法官说:"If the defence of promissory estoppel is to succeed in this case the defendant must establish the following: first, a clear and unequivocal representation, either by words or conduct, that the plaintiff would not enforce his right to set the tenancy agreement aside; **secondly, that the representation was made with the knowledge or intention that it would be acted upon by the defendant in the manner in which it was acted upon**; thirdly, that the defendant, in reliance on the representation, acted to his detriment, or in some other way which would make it inequitable to allow the plaintiff to go back on his representation."(加黑部分是笔者的强调)

而在 Morrow v. Carty 先例中,案情涉及一座平房的拍卖,根据规则要立即支付定金。原告是出价最高者,在订立了合约之后,原告表示他要回家取钱,被告同意多给他 1 个小时的时间。原告之后将他父亲的农场出售,声称是依赖了被告 1 个小时的宽限。然而事实上,他并没有在,1 个小时内交出这笔钱,因此被告不再等待,而将平房卖给了第三人。原告向法院要求履约指令,迫使被告把平房卖给他。法院判是即使他在 1 个小时内交出这笔钱,也不会获得衡平法救济。因为被告在做出 1 个小时的宽限时,以为他只是回家拿钱,而不知道他需要将父亲的农场卖掉而筹钱,所以被告的宽限或承诺与原告依赖并蒙受损害没有关联。法院说:"The acts in reliance were not ones which could reasonably have been contemplated as being done by(原告) on foot of the promise ... no vendor applying reasonable foresight would think a purchaser who asked for time to go home to get the deposit and who was to be back in a limited period such as an hour, was contemplating a sale of a property in order to obtain the deposit."

7.2　被陈述方或被承诺方依赖相关陈述或承诺改变原本的地位

从被陈述方或被承诺方的角度,证明有关的陈述或承诺被依赖(reliance)至关重要,否则陈述或承诺只会被视为无关紧要。依赖的重要性在重要的贵族院 The "Kanchenjunga" (1990) 1 Lloyd's Rep. 391 先例显示,禁反言(包括承诺性禁反言)与因选择而弃权最大的区别就是被陈述方或被承诺方的依赖。也有说法是依赖的地位相等于约因/对价,承诺如果有约因/对价就可以通过合约的形式被执行,而如果没有约因/对价但有被对方依赖,就可以通过禁反言被执行。

依赖是指被陈述方或被承诺方做了如果没有相关的陈述或承诺是不会做或有不同做法的事,所以有说法是"reliance take the form of change of position"。可以说,有否依赖是有两个层面,第一个层面是被陈述方或被承诺方心里怎样想,是否做出依赖。但这个层面往往只有被陈述方或被承诺方的口头证据,很难质疑。因此第二个层面就变得很重要,即被陈述方或被承诺方把心里的想法付诸行动,改变了原本的地位。这就需要被陈述方或被承诺方证明如果没有相关的陈述或承诺,他不会这样做。如果被陈述方或被承诺方没有因为依赖陈述方或承诺方的陈述或承诺而改变原本的地位,是不会构成衡平法宽限或承诺性禁反言。在 Tool Metal Manufacturing Co. v. Tungsten Electric Co.(1955)1 WLR 761 先例中,Simonds 大法官说:"... the gist of the equity lies in the fact that one party has by his conduct led the other to alter his position. I lay stress on this because I would not have it supposed, particularly in commercial transactions, that mere acts of indulgence are apt to create rights."

因为没有改变地位也可以推断是没有依赖陈述方或承诺方的陈述或承诺,而导致衡平法宽限或承诺性禁反言无法成立的先例有:The "Post Chaser"(1981)2 Lloyd's Rep. 695 先例,[96] The "Scaptrade"(1981)2 Lloyd's Rep. 425 先例,[97] North Down Hotels Ltd. v. Province - Wide Filling Stations Ltd.(1993)NI 261 先例中,Nationwide Building Society v. Lewis(1998)Ch 482 先例等。

可以 Nationwide Building Society v. Lewis 先例的案情为例。在该先例中,买方向原告(全英房屋贷款协会)贷款买房,并在申请上写明第一被告 Lewis 是他的代表律师。原告之后也聘用了 Lewis 作为合伙人的律师事务所为其处理这单交易。在依赖了 Lewis 出具的报告后,原告向买方提供了贷款。但事后证明 Lewis 的报告中有疏忽,买方在交易完成后拖欠还款,最后原告以低于贷款金额的价格将抵押的房屋出售。原告将 Lewis 与 Williams 作为共同被告索赔损失,因为在律师事务所的信纸上显示他们是合伙人。由于 Lewis 在期间破产,该律师事务所也已经结业,所以第二被告 Williams 是原告唯一能够追诉的对象。但 Williams 的抗辩他只是 Lewis 的雇员,并且完全没有参与相关交易的工作,所以不涉及职业上的疏忽。这样,原告要向 Williams 成功索赔损失,只能根据禁反言否定他提出的抗辩,即在 Williams 也知道与允许的情况下,在律师事务所的信纸上将两位都列为合伙人,这构成错误的陈述[98]并被原告依赖。所以 Williams 不能现在出尔反尔,试图反证他只是雇员而不是合伙人。

上诉庭判是在该先例没有任何证据显示或可以推断出原告依赖了 Williams 是共同合伙人的陈述。上诉庭认为不论该律师事务所只有 Lewis 作为唯一的合伙人或是多了一个 Williams 作为共同合伙人,对原告决定聘用律师事务所出具相关报告的行为是有影响。以下可以节录 Peter Gibson 大法官部分判决,如下:

"To my mind that is **not sufficient to establish the fact of reliance**. **There is no**

---

〔96〕 案情在本章之 7.4.3 段有介绍。

〔97〕 案情在本章之 6.5.2 段有介绍。

〔98〕 这先例涉及的应是"陈述性禁反言"(estoppel by representation),虽然报道中提的是"行动性禁反言"(estoppel by conduct)。但因为所有的禁反言都需要证明依赖,所以不影响本段所针对的内容。

evidence that anyone in the plaintiff noted from the letter that Mr. Williams's name appeared as a partner, still less that it was relied on by the plaintiff. It was not suggested that there was some personal characteristic of Mr. Williams that would bring him to the attention of the plaintiff.[99] It is merely the fact that Mr. Lewis had a partner that is said to be significant. I have to say that this seems to me unrealistic. It did not matter to the plaintiff whether or not Mr. Lewis was the sole principal when the plaintiff retained the firm. Why should it matter to the plaintiff whether or not Mr. Lewis was the sole principal less than a week later when it received the letter of 10 May and the report on title?

As is widely known, since 1987 there have been compulsory indemnity arrangements for solicitors. Solicitors in practice are covered by the Solicitors' Indemnity Fund(律师赔偿基金)subject only to limited exclusions, such as for fraud, which are specified in the Solicitors' Indemnity Rules 1987. It would require the attribution to the plaintiff of quite extraordinary foresight that it would actively have had in mind the possibility that it might not recover damages from the firm for negligence or breach of contract if the firm had a sole principal and he was fraudulent, but might recover if there were more than one partner, one of whom was not fraudulent.[100] It is certainly not obvious that the plaintiff would have noticed the name of Mr. Williams appearing in print alongside that of Mr. Lewis at the top of the letter of 10 May. Still less is it obvious that the plaintiff would have placed any reliance on the fact that Mr. Lewis had a partner... There is no evidence that Mr. Williams had ever done any work for the plaintiff. It would be astonishing if the significance of Mr. Lewis having a partner had ever crossed the mind of anyone in the plaintiff."(加黑部分是笔者的强调)

在举证责任(burden of proof)方面,究竟是由被陈述方或被承诺方证明存在依赖与改变地位,或是由陈述方或承诺方证明?如果是由陈述方或承诺方证明,这显然不容易,因为证明没有依赖与改变地位属于消极证明或证否(prove negative)。但在 Brikom Investments Ltd. v. Carr (1979) QB 467 (CA)先例中,Denning 勋爵说:"The

[99] 在该先例中,第二被告 Williams 并没有任何个人特征(如是一位著名的律师),也没有为原告在其他案件中服务过,是原告从来不认识/不知道的名字,所以 Williams 作为合伙人的陈述与原告委任 Lewis 的律师事务所的决定没有任何关系,更谈不上有依赖。

[100] 根据 1987 年的立法,英国律师协会成立了律师赔偿基金,律师疏忽造成的损失可以从该基金中获得赔付,除了针对一些特殊情况如欺诈,是无法获得赔付。因此,如果律师事务所只有唯一一个合伙人,并且该合伙人的行为不止是疏忽,也涉及欺诈,就无法获得赔付。但如果律师事务所多过一个合伙人,因为合伙人之间有共同与连带责任,客户可以通过向其他合伙人(不涉及欺诈行为)索赔,而从基金中获得赔付。但是上诉庭不认为在委任 Lewis 的律师事务所时,原告有考虑到这一点,不存在依赖。

principle extends to all cases where one party makes a promise or representation, intending that it should be binding, intending that the other should rely on it, and on which that other does in fact rely – by acting on it, by altering his position on the faith of it, by going ahead with a transaction then under discussion, or by any other way of reliance. It is no answer for the maker to say: 'You would have gone on with the transaction anyway.' That must be mere speculation. No one can be sure what he would, or would not, have done in a hypothetical state of affairs which never took place ... **Once it is shown that a representation was calculated to influence the judgment of a reasonable man, the presumption is that he was so influenced.**"(加黑部分是笔者的强调)

上述 Denning 勋爵的判决中强调的一句是说,如果被陈述方或被承诺方可以证明上一小段的要求,即陈述方或承诺方知道或希望该陈述或承诺会被对方依赖,就可以假设被陈述方或被承诺方有受到影响,即做出依赖。

因此在 Nationwide Building Society v. Lewis 先例中,一审法院判是有一个可反驳的假设(rebuttable presumption)是原告依赖了律所有两位合伙人才做出委任 Lewis 律师事务所的决定。显然 Williams 无法证否做出反驳,所以败诉。但这在上诉庭被推翻,上诉庭认为被陈述方或被承诺方更容易证明他依赖了相关的陈述或承诺而改变地位,除非是特殊的案件,否则不应该要求陈述方或承诺方证否。Peter Gibson 大法官说:"... It does not seem to me to be impractical or unjust for the law to require a person claiming an estoppel to have to prove ... Given that reliance is a necessary requirement, it is not obvious that there should be a presumption in favour of the person who claims reliance and is in a better position to know whether he did rely on the holding – out and who should thereby be able to prove it. The person held out, who is not in fact a partner(这是指第二被告 Williams), may well have difficulty in proving the negative, that the other person did not rely on the holding – out. Of course, there may be circumstances from which it would be appropriate for the court to infer that there was reliance on a holding-out. As is stated in Spencer Bower and Turner on Estoppel by Representation, 3rd edition (1977), pp. 114 – 115: 'Though on questions of fact the onus will be upon the representee, it may happen that the probability of inducement from a given set of facts is so great, or in other words the materiality is so plain and palpable, as to justify a finding of the inducement itself merely from the circumstantial context ... but it must be remembered that the inference so made is one of fact and not of law.'"

7.3 衡平法宽限或承诺性禁反言的依赖通常是给被承诺方带来好处而不是损害

相比其他类别的禁反言,如"陈述性禁反言"(estoppel by representation)或"产权人禁反言"(proprietary estoppel)明确要求对方因为依赖而蒙受损害,衡平法宽限或承诺性禁反言并没有太明确的要求,甚至有说法是没有这方面的要求。在 WJ Alan

& Co. Ltd. v. El Nasr Export and Import Co. (1972) 1 Lloyd's Rep. 313 先例中(详细的案情将在本章之7.4.1段介绍),涉及的争议是信用证以英镑而不是合约规定的肯尼亚先令开出,但卖方接受了该违反合约规定的信用证,并在信用证下获得支付。一审法院不接受买方的争辩说卖方的行为属于衡平法宽限,因为没有证据显示买方因为依赖而蒙受损害。但在上诉庭,Denning 勋爵认为无论是衡平法宽限还是承诺性禁反言,被承诺方受到了不利影响或损害都不是必须要满足的条件,说:"**I know that it has been suggested in some quarters that there must be detriment. But I can find no support for it in the authorities cited by the judge.** The nearest approach to it is the statement of Viscount Simonds in the Tool Metal case [1955] 1 W. L. R. 761, 764, that the other must have been led 'to alter his position', which was adopted by Lord Hodson in Ajayi v. R. T. Briscoe (Nigeria) Ltd. [1964] 1 W. L. R. 1326, 1330. But that only means that he must have been led to act differently from what he otherwise would have done. And if you study the cases in which the doctrine has been applied, you will see that all that is required is that the one should have 'acted on the belief induced by the other party'. That is how Lord Cohen put it in the Tool Metal case [1955] 1 W. L. R. 761, 799, and that is how I would put it myself."(加黑部分是笔者的强调)

这是因为衡平法宽限或承诺性禁反言属于做出放弃自己权利的言行,因此被承诺方依赖可能不仅不会有损害,还会带来好处。如在 Central London Property Trust Ltd. v. High Trees House Ltd. (1947) KB 130 先例中,租客依赖了房东的承诺,只需要支付部分房租。这只是好处,而不可能是损害,绝大部分同意对方少付钱或自己多付钱的承诺都会有这方面的问题。在 WJ Alan & Co. Ltd. v. El Nasr Export and Import Co 先例中,案情也涉及被承诺方依赖陈述或承诺获得了好处。Denning 勋爵在该先例提到了很多以前有关的先例(包括 Central London Property Trust Ltd. v. High Trees House Ltd. 先例)后,说:"In none of these cases does the party who acts on the belief suffer any detriment. It is not a detriment, but a benefit to him, to have an extension of time or to pay less, or as the case may be. Nevertheless, he has conducted his affairs on the basis that he has that benefit and it would not be equitable now to deprive him of it."

在其他很多后来关于衡平法宽限或承诺性禁反言的先例中,主要强调的是让承诺方撤回承诺会对被承诺方造成不公平。如 Goff 勋爵在 The "Kanchenjunga" (1990) 1 Lloyd's Rep. 391 先例中,说:"... such reliance by the representee as it will render it inequitable for the representor to go back on his representation."

在 Seechurn v. ACE Insurance SA (2002) 2 Lloyd's Rep. 390 先例中,Ward 大法官说:"**There is debate whether detriment is always required.** In Hughes v. Metropolitan Railway itself the promisee had forborne from taking steps that he would otherwise have taken to safeguard his legal position and it may be for the equitable doctrine to operate, **all that is required is that it should be inequitable for the promisor to go back on the promise**... as Mr Justice Oliver expressed it in Taylor Fashions Ltd. v. Liverpool Trustees Co.（1982）1 QB 133 at p. 155, **all that need be established is that it was unconscionable** for the defendant to seek to take advantage of the claimant's mistake. I am content to approach the case appeal on that basis."（加黑部分是笔者的强调）

7.4 衡平法宽限或承诺性禁反言下的依赖实际上是蒙受损害的近期说法

被承诺方需要因为依赖承诺而蒙受损害是较近期的说法。在 Collier v. P & MJ Wright（Holdings）Ltd.（2008）1 WLR 643 先例中，Arden 女大法官说："However... the requirement of detriment, and perhaps other requirements of the doctrine, have to be approached as part of a broader enquiry as to whether repudiation of an assurance is or is not unconscionable in all the circumstances [see generally per Robert Walker LJ (as he then was) in Gillett v. Holt（2001）Ch 210 at 232D.]"

Steria Ltd. v. Hutchison（2006）EWCA Civ 1551 先例又带来了另一个问题。在该先例中，声称依赖对方陈述或承诺的一方受到的损害不明显，而陈述性禁反言很明确依赖方必须蒙受损害。因此，依赖方同时提出了"陈述性禁反言"（estoppel by representation）与"承诺性禁反言"（promissory estoppel）作为替代争议，毕竟承诺性禁反言对蒙受损害的要求不明显。正如上诉庭的 Mummery 大法官说："Detriment has to be established in the case of estoppel by representation (see Tai Hing Cotton Mill Ltd. v. Liu Chong Hing Bank [1986] AC 80 at 110) and, even if it is not a requirement of the doctrine of promissory estoppel, it is relevant to whether it is inequitable to act inconsistently with the promise."

接下来 Neuberger 大法官也说道，陈述性禁反言或承诺性禁反言需要满足包括蒙受损害在内的三个要求（本章之 8.2 段有节录），才能满足连接所有禁反言类别的不合情理（unconscionability）的要件。在同样的案件事实下，Neuberger 大法官认为不论是在法理上还是实践操作上，承诺性禁反言都没有理由不需要依赖方蒙受损害，说："... The requirement for these three features, at least in relation to estoppels by representation, was very clearly put by the Privy Council in Tai Hing Cotton Mill Ltd. v. Liu Chong Hing Bank Ltd.（1986）AC 80, 110, in the following terms: 'the essence of estoppels is a representation (express or implied) intended to induce the person to whom it is made to adopt a course of conduct which results in detriment or loss'. I can see no reason, in theory or in practice, why this should not be equally true of promissory estoppel. In the present case, despite the argument on his behalf to the contrary, it seems to me that there is no reason for thinking that Mr Hutchison（提出禁反言的一方）should for some reason be excused from satisfying each of these three normal requirements of a claim of estoppel by representation (or promissory estoppel) if he is to make out his case."

在 Seechurn v. ACE Insurance SA（2002）2 Lloyd’s Rep. 390 先例中，案情在本章之 11.7 段有介绍。Ward 大法官指出针对承诺性禁反言是否需要被承诺方蒙受损害，英国法与澳大利亚法有不同之处，说：

“It is common ground that the promise or representation must be made intending to affect the legal relations between the parties and the promisee or representee must rely upon it and alter his position.

It is usually said that this must be an alteration to the detriment of the promisee or representee.〔101〕 Although the law in Australia and in this country may not have moved in exactly the same direction at all times,〔102〕 the decision of seven Judges of the High Court of Australia in Commonwealth of Australia v. Verwayen（1990）170 CLR 394 is interesting. Both before and after proceedings had been commenced by the plaintiff, the Commonwealth repeatedly represented that it would not rely on a limitation defence. Then it changed its mind and was granted leave to amend to plead that bar.〔103〕 Mason C. J. drew a distinction between two types of detriment：detriment which would flow from the denial of the assumption upon which a party had relied and detriment which the party had already suffered by relying on that assumption.〔104〕 In that case the first or the broader type of detriment would have been the plaintiff’s failure in his action for damages and the second would have been his costs incurred in mounting it up until the date when the defence was amended.〔105〕”

在该先例中，上诉庭认为 Seechurn 在时效已过之后不存在改变地位并蒙受损害，说：“After the limitation period had expired it is difficult to see how the claimant could have altered his position to his detriment. His claim was doomed. He could not be

---

〔101〕 一般来说，被陈述方或被承诺方需要因为该陈述或承诺改变了自己的地位并因此蒙受损害。

〔102〕 澳大利亚的法律与英国有所不同，这在本章之 12.3.2 段有详论。

〔103〕 关于澳大利亚高院的 Commonwealth of Australia v. Verwayen（1990）170 CLR 394 先例，案情可见本章之 11.6 段。该先例涉及澳大利亚政府作为被告，多次承诺原告 Verwayen 先生不会对他提出的疏忽导致伤害赔偿提出时效已过的抗辩。但后来政府想法有了改变，向法院申请修改抗辩，加入时效已过的抗辩。这带来原告在答辩中声称澳大利亚政府较早的言行构成衡平法宽限或承诺性禁反言。表面看来，原告应该蒙受了损害，因为修改抗辩显然会导致律师费用的增加与浪费。但由于修改请求（amendment of pleadings）通常都会有命令要求申请方支付所有相关浪费费用的命令，所以不严格对原告造成金钱上的损害。

〔104〕 Mason 大法官将损害分为两类：一类是如果允许承诺方撤回承诺，依赖了该承诺的被承诺方会蒙受的损害；另一类是被承诺方因为依赖该承诺已经蒙受的损害。

〔105〕 在上述的澳大利亚先例，原告被承诺不会以时效已过作为抗辩，第一类或更广泛的一类的损害是如果允许澳大利亚政府撤回承诺，原告的索赔就会因时效已过失败。第二类会是直到澳大利亚政府修改抗辩前原告的所有律师费用。根据前述，第二类损害不存在，因为法院会命令澳大利亚政府支付所有浪费的费用。这个先例也不存在如果不是因为澳大利亚政府的承诺，原告可以在时效届满前提起诉讼这一实质损害，因为原告知道他有权提起诉讼时，时效就已过。

worse off."

近期不断有人呼吁要将不同类别的禁反言统一,如在澳大利亚,[106]不少先例就已经统称"衡平法禁反言"(equitable estoppel)。事实上,确实也有个别案件在事实上很难区分究竟属于哪种禁反言与可以同时适用一种以上的禁反言,以及不少先例中,当事人是把很多不同类别的禁反言作为替代争议一并提出。这样,鉴于陈述性禁反言以及产权人禁反言,都要求因依赖而蒙受损害,就很难再坚持承诺性禁反言是不需要被承诺方依赖而蒙受损害。

至于在学术范畴,也有不少支持承诺性禁反言需要被承诺方蒙受损害。如在Michael Spence 律师所著的《Protecting Reliance: the emergent doctrine of equitable estoppel》(1999 年)一书,内容虽然是主要针对澳大利亚的法律,但也引述了英国法律的地位。在该书第 22 页,说:"There had been debate as to whether 'detriment' of the type necessary to found an estoppel by representation was also necessary to found a promissory estoppel. Spencer Bower and Turner claimed that this debate flowed from a misunderstanding of the term detriment in estoppel cases generally.[107] It was sometimes argued that estoppel by representation required proof of detriment in the very acts undertaken in reliance upon the representation, for example, proof of expenditure incurred.[108] Spencer Bower and Turner claimed that the detriment needed for both promissory estoppel and estoppel by representation consisted in any 'injustice to the promisee which would result if the promisor were allowed to recede from his promise'.[109] Detriment was therefore to be judged at the moment at which the promisor/representor proposed to resile from his promise/representation. Gauging detriment involved comparing the position of the promisee/representee before and after the proposed withdrawal by the promisor/representor and not before and after his reliance upon the promise/representation.[110]"

---

[106] 见本章之 12.3.2 段。

[107] Spencer Bower 与 Turner 的《The Law Relating to Estoppel by Representation》(第 3 版,1977 年)一书认为,之所以关于承诺性禁反言是否需要被承诺方蒙受损害存在争议,是因为大家对什么是禁反言案件中的损害存在误解。

[108] 有说法是陈述性禁反言必须证明因为依赖该陈述已经蒙受了损失,如花了钱。即在 Commonwealth of Australia v. Verwayen (1990) 170 CLR 394 先例,Mason 大法官提到的第二类也是较狭窄的一类损害。

[109] 但 Spencer Bower 与 Turner 的《The Law Relating to Estoppel by Representation》(第 3 版,1977 年)一书认为承诺性禁反言与陈述性禁反言所需要的损害一致,即让陈述方或承诺方撤回他的陈述或承诺会对被陈述方或被承诺方造成不公平。即在 Commonwealth of Australia v. Verwayen (1990) 170 CLR 394 先例中,Mason 大法官提到的第一类也是较广泛的一类损害。

[110] 因此,被陈述方或被承诺方是否蒙受损害是在陈述方或承诺方要撤回他的陈述或承诺时决定。衡量是否蒙受损害要对比陈述方或承诺方撤回他的陈述或承诺前后被陈述方或被承诺方的地位,而不是被陈述方或被承诺方依赖相关陈述或承诺后的地位。

另在 Sean Wilken QC 与 Karim Ghaly 先生更近期所著的有关英国法律的《The Law of Waiver, Variation, and Estoppel》(第 3 版,2012 年)一书,认为很多不同说法的先例只是语言上(semantic)的不同,但在本质上没有区别。在 7.49 段,说:"There is some doubt as to whether detriment is a necessary component of equitable forbearance. It is clear that it is essential to establish that resiling from the promise made would be inequitable having regard to the dealing between the parties. On balance, it is submitted that detriment is an essential prerequisite for establishing inequity. **Detriment is therefore required in all doctrines**. "(加黑部分是笔者的强调)

《The Law of Waiver, Variation, and Estoppel》一书显示了有三个要点:(1)被承诺方做出的依赖本身并不需要苛刻(onerous)、不愉快(unpleasant)或蒙受损失(damaging)。它不需要像其他类别的禁反言所要求的做出金钱的赔付或带来了新的责任,即通常所说的因依赖蒙受损害。如在陈述性禁反言,提单持有人因为依赖了提单上的错误陈述(如应是不清洁提单或是倒签提单)而支付了货款。(2)但在衡平法宽限或承诺性禁反言,被承诺方常常因为依赖承诺而带来利益。然而,考虑是否造成损害的时间是在承诺方试图撤回他的陈述或承诺而要坚持自己原本的合约或法律权利时。如在本章之 2.1 段介绍的 Hughes v. Metropolitan Railway Company (1877) 2 App Cas 439 先例中,房东同意租客推迟修理并参与将这个租约买回的谈判的言行是做出了默示的陈述或承诺,他不会以租客没有在 6 个月内完成修理为由终止租约或 6 个月以谈判破裂开始计算。这事实上是对租客有利,因为如果谈判成功,他无须进行修理。只是在谈判破裂后,房东撤回这个默示陈述或承诺时,立即要求终止租约并收回房子,这就对被承诺方造成了损害。(3)承诺方撤回对被承诺方有好处的承诺一定会对被承诺方造成损害,因为被承诺方无法继续享有这个好处。这看来是属于在 Commonwealth of Australia v. Verwayen 先例中,Mason 大法官提到的第一类也是较广泛的一类损害。但由于这一定会发生,一些先例认为仅仅是无法继续享有好处的损害是不足够,让承诺方撤回承诺必须是客观看来会带来一些不公平或不合情理的后果。

以下分析哪些类别的损害(部分是属于广泛与非金钱的类别)可以满足以上三点要求。

7.4.1　损害类别之一:被承诺方因为依赖相关的陈述或承诺,没有采取行动保障其法律或经济地位

在 Hughes v. Metropolitan Railway Company (1877) 2 App Cas 439 先例中,租客因为依赖房东的陈述或承诺没有修理房屋是典型的例子。其他例子还有很多,如被承诺方依赖了对方的陈述或承诺没有采取法律行动保护索赔的时效,或是向第三人(合约链下的分卖方或分买方)放弃了补偿等。

但如果没有损害或实质的损害,衡平法宽限或承诺性禁反言就不一定成立。如在 WJ Alan & Co. Ltd. v. El Nasr Export and Import Co. (1972) 1 Lloyd's Rep. 313

先例中,案情涉及一批咖啡豆的 FOB 买卖。合约规定货价是以先令支付,这表示可以解释为是英国先令或是肯尼亚先令,而当时这两种货币也是同等价值。FOB 买方的肯尼亚公司把这批咖啡豆转卖给西班牙的分买方,分买方开出了英镑的信用证,肯尼亚公司把信用证转给卖方,而卖方也接受了英镑的信用证。但这个接受的行为做出的陈述或承诺带来卖方的损失,因为不久后英镑大幅度贬值,导致卖方在信用证下少收了货款(法院判是买卖合约中写的先令应该解释为肯尼亚先令,这表示买方开出的信用证是违反合约规定的)。卖方之后向买方的肯尼亚公司索赔差价,争议之一就涉及衡平法宽限或承诺性禁反言。在该先例中,肯尼亚公司的买方究竟蒙受了什么损害不明确,案例报告中没有提到有任何关于买方的损害的争议,如买方在分合约下向西班牙分买方坚持要开出以肯尼亚先令作为支付币种的信用证,或可以在英镑大幅度贬值前去套汇。但由于当时法理上对构成衡平法宽限或承诺性禁反言是否需要蒙受损害不明确,所以 Denning 勋爵没有理会,判卖方接受英镑信用证的言行被禁反言,说:"The plaintiffs(卖方), by their conduct, waived[111] the right to have payment by means of a letter of credit in Kenyan currency and accepted instead a letter of credit in sterling, and accordingly had received all the money to which they were entitled."

但多数意见的 Megaw 大法官与 Stephenson 大法官避开了这个问题,判是构成了合约更改,仍是卖方败诉。Stephenson 大法官是这样说:"I would leave open the question whether the action of the other party induced by the party who 'waives' his contractual rights can be any alteration to his detriment, or for the worse, in some sense... so that I need not, and do not, express a concluded opinion on that controversial question."

在 Collier v. P & MJ Wright (Holdings) Ltd. (2008) 1 WLR 643 先例中,案情在本章之 12.1.5 段有介绍。Collier 先生争议说他因为答辩人的承诺没有向另外两位合伙人追讨他们应付部分的金额,但这不被一审法院的 HHJ Hodge QC 大法官接受。因为其他两位合伙人已经破产,而答辩人作为判决债务(judgment debt)的债权人,也没能从这两位合伙人处追回一分钱,所以 Collier 先生更不可能从另外两位合伙人处追讨到任何他们应付的部分。即对 Collier 先生来说,如果答辩人从未有这样的承诺他会面对的情况,与答辩人现在撤回承诺向他追讨全部欠款的情况相同,因此 Collier 先生没有蒙受任何损害。

7.4.2 损害类别之二:被承诺方依赖承诺方减少或放弃合约或法律权利的陈述或承诺,改变了预算或使费带来的损害

这种情况如果真的发生并有一定的证据支持,可以用来显示被承诺方蒙受了损害。如在 Central London Property Trust Ltd. v. High Trees House Ltd. (1947) KB 130 先例中,一样只需要租客支付部分租金。也可能是债权人同意或主动提出只要

---

[111] 这也是在较早期经常把弃权与衡平法宽限或禁反言混为一谈的例子。

支付部分债务,或是在 Williams v. Roffey Bros. & Nicholls Ltd. (1991) 1 QB 1 先例中,雇主愿意做出额外支付。

这里会有不同种类的损害。如 Hughes v. Metropolitan Railway Company (1877) 2 App Cas 439 先例如果不涉及修理,而是一方要支付一笔钱,否则另一方可以终止合约,或是合约规定了很高的利率。而承诺方主动提出可以只支付一半的金钱,在这种情况下,如果允许承诺方撤回承诺,岂不是可以终止合约或索赔高额利息?这显然会对被承诺方造成损害。

《The Law of Waiver, Variation, and Estoppel》(第3版,2012年)一书之8.61段也提到了一些其他接近或属于这类别的损害,说:"Thus, detriment if will be suffered the promisee has spent its money in a way it would not otherwise have done but for the reduced liability under the contract.[112] If, for example, it has spent its perceived windfall in a one - off dividend to its shareholders,[113] which it would not otherwise have made, withdrawal of the promise would leave it open to an onerous and unexpected liability. That may be sufficient to effect a permanent bar to resumption of the original contractual position. Similarly, and a more likely possibility, the promise may have rearranged its general day - to - day budget by, for example, committing itself to larger loan repayments or purchase contracts.[114] Here, peremptory withdrawal of the concession may cause prejudice in the short term only: income has been committed elsewhere and as a consequence there is insufficient cash flow to meet the demand. The previous contractual position may be reverted to, on giving the promise reasonable time to make the rearrangements to its budget. Put simply, it must be given time to revert to the position that it was in prior to the making of the promise in issue. This seems to be the explanation for the application of the equitable forbearance doctrine in the High Tree case[115]... It has been suggested that, given the realities of ordinary commercial practice, there will seldom be a case where a promise to accept partial payment will not lead to detriment in this latter sense, but such arguments have by no means always met with a favourable reception."

---

[112] 所以,如果被承诺方使用了一笔金钱(如借贷给第三人),而承诺方较早没有承诺减少或放弃权利,被承诺方就不会这样使用手中的钱,就可以说被承诺方蒙受了损害。

[113] 如被承诺方的公司法人将一笔意外之财给股东发了一次性红利,而如果不是承诺方少收或多给钱,它不会这样做。

[114] 更有可能的是,承诺方的承诺影响了被承诺方日常预算与做法,如被承诺方在另一个借贷合约中同意一笔更大的还款金额或订立了其他合约等。

[115] 这可解释在 Central London Property Trust Ltd. v. High Trees House Ltd. (1947) KB 130 先例中,原告(房东)要求被告(租客)支付合约规定的租金,而不是较早承诺的减半的租金,显然会影响被告的现金流。所以,Denning 大法官判原告在1945年第二次世界大战结束,租赁市场恢复后仍需要做出合理的通知才能回复到合约租金。这合理时间显然可解释为是让被告调整他的现金流与日常预算,之后就要回复到租约原本约定的租金。

7.4.3 损害类别之三:被承诺方依赖承诺方减少或放弃合约或法律权利的陈述或承诺,带来的其他实质损害

除了上述提到的预算或使费的损害,被承诺方也可能蒙受其他更实质的损害。如货物买卖合约中,卖方交付或告知买方会交付一批货不对板的货物。起初买方同意可以接受这批货物,但之后拒绝接受。这样,卖方很可能容易证明损失,如他本来可以不必花时间与金钱付运这批货物,但最终被买方在卸港或付运途中拒绝接受:Bremer v. Vanden (1978) 2 Lloyd's Rep. 109 (HL)先例。卖方也可能证明买方如果一开始就拒绝接受货不对板的货物,他可以更好地处理该批货物,如转售。卖方也会可以证明他可以取得其他符合买卖规格的货物交付。而期间如果货物的市场价格下跌,卖方更可以证明蒙受损害。

在 The "Post Chaser" (1981) 2 Lloyd's Rep. 695 先例中,双方以 CIF 买卖马来西亚棕榈油。卖方迟了做出划归通知(notice of appropriation),而买方既没有抗议,也没有表示接受这份迟交的划归通知,而只是将划归通知转给了分买方 Conti。Conti 要求买方提供单证,于是买方在 1975 年 1 月 20 日给卖方发电传,说:"We refer to our telephone conversations of Thursday last with your Mr. Van Pelt and just now with your Mr. Langhorst. Just now we received the following telex from our buyers: 'Present documents to Conti Rotterdam at Dollars 605.' We therefore request you to do this and to debit us in respect of the difference between our purchase price i. e. dollars 792. 50 and our sale price to Conti Grain Export dollars 605. - i. e. dollars 187. 50 Thanks in advance."

1 月 22 日,Conti 终止合约,于是作为中间商的买方也同样终止合约。事后双方的争议之一就是买方较早的言行是否构成衡平法宽限或承诺性禁反言。Goff 大法官判买方 1 月 20 日的电传属于清楚无误的承诺,并被卖方依赖。但由于买方很快撤回承诺终止合约,卖方没有蒙受实质损害,说:"This, in my judgment, is the principle which I have to apply in the present case. Here, all that happened was that the sellers, ... presented the documents on the same day as the buyers made their representation; and within two days the documents were rejected. Now on these simple facts, although it is plain that the sellers did actively rely on the buyers' representation, and did conduct their affairs in reliance on it, by presenting the documents, I cannot see anything which would render it inequitable for the buyers thereafter to enforce their legal right to reject the documents. In particular, having regard to the very short time which elapsed between the date of the representation and the date of presentation of the documents on the one hand, and the date of rejection on the other hand, I cannot see that, in the absence of any evidence that the sellers' position had been prejudiced by reason of their action in reliance on the representation, it is possible to infer that they suffered any such prejudice. In these circumstances, a necessary element for the application of the doctrine of equitable estoppel

is lacking; and I decide this point in favour of the buyer."

即如果做出承诺的一方很快撤回承诺,令对方来不及依赖,或即使技术上来说有所依赖,也不会因此蒙受损害,是不会构成衡平法宽限或承诺性禁反言。这也可以看出,衡平法宽限或承诺性禁反言与有约因/对价的合约或合约更改不同。一旦合约或合约更改成立,就再也不能单方撤回,无论两者之间相距的时间多短。

7.4.4　损害类别之四:被承诺方因为依赖相关的陈述或承诺,放弃了更佳选择或有价值的东西

这种例子很多,举例如下:

1. 继续营运与承担责任而非破产了事:Re William Porter & Co. (1937) 2 All ER 361 at 364; Ledingham v. Bermejo Estancia Co. Ltd. (1947) 1 All ER 749 等先例。

2. 继续对购买与推广专利进行谈判:Bruner v. Moore (1904) 1 Ch 305 先例。案情涉及原告向被告购买他的发明并在不同国家注册的专利,根据合约,原告在6个月内有是否全面购买的选择权。法院判是原告必须在3月16日前行使选择权。但双方在3月16日之后还是持续对专利的购买与推广工作有通讯往来。之后,被告以原告没有在规定时间内行使选择权为由,不再履行他与原告之间的合约。原告向法院要求履约指令,要求被告将其他国家的专利卖给他。法院判是被告在3月16日之后的通讯往来构成禁反言。

3. 允许承诺方占有被承诺方的部分建筑:在 JF Perrot v. Cohen (1951) 1 KB 705 (CA)先例中,租客占用了他租住的房屋旁的盥洗室,并声称这属于租住房屋的部分。租约结束后,房东要求租客根据租约修理好盥洗室,但租客拒绝并声称盥洗室不属于他租住房屋的部分。法院判是房东依赖租客的陈述让他继续占用盥洗室,而没有追究。所以,租客现在不能否定盥洗室属于他租住的房屋的部分,因此根据租约应该修理好盥洗室。

4. 放弃立法保护的租约:在 Bank Negara Indonesia v. Philip Hoalim (1973) 2 MLJ 3 (PC)先例中,租客是一名律师,租了房东的办公室作为办公地点。房东为了说服租客从一楼搬走,承诺如果租客搬到三楼,可以享受同样的立法保护,并且他可以租到他不再提供律师服务(即结业)为止。在这个承诺下,租客搬到了三楼。三年后,双方订立了一份新租约,提高了租金。在新租约结束后,租客仍以月租的形式占有该办公室,直到房东做出迁出通知书。双方的争议之一是,房东让租客可以租到他不再提供律师服务为止的承诺是否构成承诺性禁反言,而令他不能让租客迁出。一审的新加坡法院判是房东的承诺构成承诺性禁反言,但在双方订立新租约后,租客就不能再依赖。但新加坡上诉庭推翻了一审的判决,判是双方订立新租约唯一的目的就是提高租金,双方的谈判中也只讨论了这一点,不影响三年前租约会持续到租客不提供律师服务为止的承诺,因此租客仍然可以依赖承诺性禁反言。枢密院也支持了上诉庭的判法。

5. 支付以房东负责维修而非租客负责维修为基础计算出的租金(显然会多付一些):Brikom Investments Ltd. v. Seaford (1981) 1 WLR 863 (CA)先例(案情在本章稍后的9.1段有介绍)。

6. 延误转卖被拒货物,在卸港产生滞期费:在The"Eurometal"(1981) 1 Lloyd's Rep. 337先例。案情涉及大麦的CIF买卖,合约规定卖方递交提单时,买方支付现金。如果船到卸港时还没有递交提单,卖方就必须提供另外的文件(如保函),让买方可以提货。船舶抵达卸港时,提单还没有寄到。买方以大麦中有虫为由拒绝提货,坚持要先烟熏除虫。但双方对谁支付除虫的费用有争议,毕竟合约有一条装港检验为终条文。[116] 之后卖方递交提单,但买方拒绝接受。卖方将货物转卖,并向买方索赔转卖的损失与滞期费。法院判是根据合约,卖方需要提供提单或其他文件令买方可以提货,卖方没有这样做是构成违反条件条文。但买方以大麦有虫并要求烟熏除虫的理由拒货,这行为构成了弃权(可视为做出选择不以卖方违反递交提单或其他文件为由终止合约)与禁反言(可视为言行被卖方依赖导致船舶在卸港有了不必要的延误后,才被卖方转卖)。Lloyd大法官说:"In par. 6 of the award it is found that the sole reason for the buyers' refusal to take delivery of the cargo was infestation with weevils. They asked for the cargo to be fumigated at the sellers' expense. By making and maintaining that request, the buyers were conducting themselves in a way which was wholly inconsistent with an intention to exercise any present right to reject the documents. If the sellers had complied with the buyers' request, it would have been clear beyond argument that the buyers could not subsequently reject the document on the ground that they ought to have been tendered on arrival. Does it make any difference that the cargo was not in fact fumigated? I do not think it does, provided always the sellers can show that they relied on the buyers' request in some other respect. Fair dealing in commerce, though not in cards, requires that if a party has a trump in his hand, he should play it. In the present case the sellers incurred liability to demurrage in the belief, reasonably induced by the buyers, that the buyers were not insisting on the immediate provision of alternative documents. In so doing they relied on a representation to be inferred from the buyers' conduct."

7.4.5　损害类别之五:被承诺方因为依赖相关的陈述或承诺,继续履行亏本的合约

表面看来就算是亏本的合约,被承诺方还是要履行。所以,依赖对方的陈述或承诺(如多给一笔钱),不像是会带来任何损害。但是在本书第一章之8.2段提到过"有效益违约"(efficient breach)的说法,会有情况被承诺方宁可支付金钱的损失赔偿也比继续履行亏本合约好,更不用说被承诺方还有其他的选择。如是一个BVI公

---

[116] 关于装港检验为终条文,可见杨良宜的《合约的解释:规则与应用》一书第十四章之1.5段。

司,或可以随时清盘以逃避履行这个亏本合约的责任。但依赖了承诺方减少或放弃合约或法律权利的陈述或承诺,被承诺方就把一个亏本合约履行下去。因此在 Williams v. Roffey Bros. & Nicholls Ltd. (1991) 1 QB 1 的上诉庭先例中,承包商同意向分包商多支付一笔金钱,否则他在主合约下会有更大损失。而作为被承诺方的分包商,也因为依赖该承诺,没有倒闭而是完成了分包的工作。所以,虽然该先例判是构成合约更改,但看来针对带来损害这一要件,衡平法宽限或承诺性禁反言也可以有效。只是双方在高院没有提出这方面的争议,所以没有定论。这可以节录上诉庭 Glidewell 大法官所说:"It was suggested to us in argument that, since the development of the doctrine of promissory estoppel, it may well be possible for a person to whom a promise has been made, on which he has relied, to make an additional payment for services which he is in any event bound to render under an existing contract or by operation of law, to show that the promisor is estopped from claiming that there was no consideration for his promise. However, the application of the doctrine of promissory estoppel to facts such as those of the present case has not yet been fully developed: see e. g. the judgment of Lloyd J. in Syros Shipping Co. S. A v. Elaghill Trading Co. [1980] 2 Lloyd's Rep. 390, 392. Moreover, this point was not argued in the court below, nor was it more than adumbrated before us. Interesting though it is, no reliance can in my view be placed on this concept in the present case."

7.4.6 总结

总结而言,虽然比较明确 Mason 大法官在 Commonwealth of Australia v. Verwayen (1990) 170 CLR 394 先例中提到的第一类也是较广泛的一类损害是适用在衡平法宽限或承诺性禁反言,但如果类似本章之 7.4.2 段介绍的改变现金流或预算都可以被宽松地解释为损害,几乎只要宽限方承诺减少或放弃法律权利,就难免会带来这类损害。这也是在该段节录的《The Law of Waiver, Variation, and Estoppel》(第 3 版,2012 年)一书之 8.61 段最后一句提到的问题。

在澳大利亚的 Austral Standard Cables Pty Ltd. v. Walker Nominees Pty Ltd. (1992) 26 NSWLR 524 先例中,卖方没有在合约规定的日期将土地空置交出(vacant possession)给买方,但他声称买方令他产生假设不是在该天完成过户,因此买方被禁反言,从而不能终止土地买卖合约。一审法院认为,卖方无论如何都不可能在当天将土地空置交出给买方,所以不存在任何损害。但之后上诉庭将一审判决推翻,Handley 大法官认为卖方失去了避免损害(试图将土地空置)的机会,属于蒙受了损害。

这看来太宽松,并不是在所有的先例都能被接受。在英国的一些先例,如 James v. Heim Gallery (London) Ltd. (1980) 256 EG 819 (CA)先例中,案情涉及房屋租赁合约,合约规定租约每段时间后可以调整。房东迟延给调整租约通知,双方误以为该通知无效,于是房东没有继续要求调整租金。之后,房东发现 United Scientific Holding Ltd. v. Burnley Borough Council (1978) AC 904 先例说明延误的通知其实有效，于是要求租客补足应交的租金。租客则抗辩说房东承诺性禁反言，不能索赔这笔租金。租客声称房东承诺不再调整租金，而因为依赖房东的承诺，租客没有存钱、没有搬去租金更便宜的地方并且向慈善组织捐了一笔钱等。但上诉庭判是房东没有继续要求调整租金不等于清楚无误承诺不再调整租金。而房东不知道也不应该知道租客的财政状况，租客无法证明房东知道他的承诺会被租客依赖并改变地位。在 Amherst v. James Walker Goldsmith & Silversmith Ltd.（1983）Ch 305（CA）先例中，案情也与 James v. Heim Gallery（London）Ltd. 先例大同小异，法院判是租客没有任何损害，因为房东做出延误通知后才能调整租金，就多给了租客几个月可以较低租金使用房屋，这属于有好处而没有损害。另可见 Banner Industrial & Commercial Properties Ltd. v. Clark Patterson Ltd.（1990）47 EG 64 等先例。

看来在每个不同的案情，究竟什么属于可以构成禁反言的损害，什么属于极微小（de minimis）的损害，还是见仁见智。在这里不妨节录 Neuberger 大法官在 Steria Ltd. v. Hutchison（2006）EWCA Civ 1551 先例中的警告，说："If it were sufficient, the requirement for detriment in a claim for estoppel would be nugatory, because in every case where a claimant advances a claim based on estoppel, he will, virtually by definition, be better off if the estoppel is established than if it is not: otherwise he would not be raising an estoppel."

8. 要件之四：弃权方事后撤回该陈述或承诺会是不公平或不合情理

这个要件很容易理解，因为只有不公平与不合情理的情况下，法院才会考虑做出衡平法救济，在权威书籍《Chitty on Contracts》（第 32 版，2015 年）之 4－096 段说："**Inequitable.** It must be 'inequitable' for the promisor to go back on the promise. This requirement cannot be defined with anything approaching precision, but the underlying idea is that the promisee must have acted in reliance on the promise in one of the ways described in para. 4－095 above, so that he can no longer be restored to the position in which he was before he took such action. If the promisee can be restored to that position, it will not be inequitable for the promisor to go back on the promise.[117] In one case the promisor reasserted his strict legal rights only two days after the promise had been made. It was held that this was not 'inequitable' since the promisee had not, in this short peri-

〔117〕 这个要件是说让承诺方回复到原来的地位必须会造成不公平。这很难有准确的定义，重点是被承诺方必须依赖承诺方的承诺改变了自己的地位，并因此暂时或永久不能回复到原来的地位。而如果被承诺方完全可以回复到原本的地位，也就不会有任何不公平。

od, suffered any prejudice by acting in reliance on the promise: he could be, and was, restored to exactly the position in which he had been before the promise was made.[118] Sometimes, moreover, extraneous circumstances may justify the promisor in going back on the promise even without giving reasonable notice of his intention to do so. In Williams v. Stern the plaintiff gave the defendant a bill of sale of furniture as security for a loan; the bill entitled the defendant to seize the furniture if the plaintiff defaulted in making payments under it. When the fourteenth instalment became due, the plaintiff asked for extra time, and the defendant said that he 'would not look to a week.' Three days later he seized the furniture because he had heard that the plaintiff's landlord intended to distrain it for arrears of rent. It was held that the defendant's seizure was justified. The defendant's promise to give time was not binding contractually as the plaintiff had given no consideration for it; nor did it, in the circumstances, bring the equitable doctrine into operation. Brett L. J. said: 'Has there been any misconduct on the part of the defendant? I think not: it appears that a distress by the plaintiff's landlord has been threatened; and under these circumstances I do not blame the defendant for changing his mind.'[119] The conduct of the promisee in obtaining the promise may also be relevant to the issue whether the promisor has acted 'inequitable' in going back on it.[120]"

8.1 不公平

这个要件与上一个要件有关系。如果被承诺方没有蒙受任何损害(detriment),让承诺方回复到承诺之前的地位就不会造成不公平。相反,被承诺方如果蒙受损害,很难说不会造成不公平,虽然有说法是只有损害还不足够。但这个要件在很多先例

---

〔118〕 这是指 The "Post Chaser" (1981) 2 Lloyd's Rep. 695 先例,该先例的案情在本章之7.4.3段有介绍。

〔119〕 有时一些外来情况也可能令承诺方有合法理由不经通知就直接回复到原来的地位。如在 Williams v. Stern (1879) 5 QBD 409 先例中,原告向被告提供了一份家具的卖据(bill of sale)作为贷款的保证。在第十四期还款到期时,原告向被告要求延期还款,被告表示不能超过一个星期。但三天后,被告就扣押了原告的家具,因为他听说原告的房东将会为拖欠的房租扣押这些家具。法院判是被告有合法理由这样做,被告的承诺不构成合约(不存在约因/对价),而禁反言的说法也不成立,因为在原告的房东将会采取扣押行动的威胁之下,被告改变主意是无可指责的。

〔120〕 在 South Caribbean Trading Ltd. v. Trafigura Beheer BV (2005) 1 Lloyd's Rep. 128 先例中,Colman 大法官认为如果被承诺方威胁要违反合约,并以此获得或胁迫承诺方做出承诺,这本身是不合情理的。因此,即使之后被承诺方依赖了承诺方的承诺决定履行合约,也不能依赖承诺性禁反言。Colman 大法官说:"... unconscionability cannot normally be made out in a case where reliance consists of the promisee shifting his position from one of unjustifiably threatening to breach his contract with the promisor to one of performing that contract. If there were no contractual basis justifying the refusal, there would normally be a case of economic duress which is itself based in substance on principles of unconscionability. Accordingly, the balance of unconscionability as between the conduct of the promisor and that of the promisee would be left even to the effect that the court would not intervene to protect the promisee."

都有强调,而蒙受损害是否属于构成衡平法宽限或承诺性禁反言的要件曾不明确。在 The "Post Chaser" (1981) 2 Lloyd's Rep. 695 先例中,[121] Goff 大法官总结说:"I approach the matter as follows. The fundamental principle is that stated by Lord Cairns, viz. that the representor will not be allowed to enforce his rights 'where it would be inequitable having regard to the dealings which have thus taken place between the parties'. To establish such inequity, **it is not necessary to show detriment**; indeed, the representee may have benefited from the representation, and yet it may be inequitable, at least without reasonable notice, for the representor to enforce his legal rights. Take the facts of Central London Property Trust Ltd. v. High Trees House Ltd. , (1947) K. B. 130, the case in which lord Justice Denning, M. R. breathed new life into the doctrine of equitable estoppel. The representation was by a lessor to the effect that he would be content to accept a reduced rent. In such a case, although the lessee has benefited from the reduction in rent, because the lessee has conducted his affairs on the basis that he would only have to pay rent at the lower rate; and a Court might well think it right to concluded that only after reasonable notice could the lessor return to charging rent at the higher rate specified in the lease. Furthermore, it would be open to the Court, in any particular case, to infer from the circumstances of the case that the representee must have conducted his affairs in such a way that it would be inequitable for the representor to enforce his rights, or to do so without reasonable notice. But it does not follow that in every case in which the representee has acted, or failed to act, in reliance on the representation, it will be inequitable for the representor to enforce his rights; for the nature of the action, or inaction, may be insufficient to give rise to the equity in which event a necessary requirement stated by Lord Cairns for the application of the doctrine would not have been fulfilled."(加黑部分是笔者的强调)

只是被陈述方或被承诺方蒙受损害还不足以导致不公平的原因时,是否不公平要总体考虑双方的地位与相关事实,而被陈述方或被承诺方的损害只是从被陈述方或被承诺方的角度考虑。针对这一点在《The Law of Waiver, Variation, and Estoppel》(第 3 版,2012 年)一书之 8.50 段与 8.62 段,说:"There is one final theoretical point. A distinction may be analytically drawn between inequity and detriment with the former going to overall position of the parties and the latter to the impact on the promisee. The case law has not explicitly descended to this level of rigour. If, however, the distinction were to be maintained, the requirement of inequity should be satisfied in addition to the latter threshold test. Put simply, on this approach it may be that the existence of detriment is a necessary but by itself insufficient element of the doctrine... As set out

[121] 具体案情可见本章之 7.4.3 段。

above, the Courts have not explicitly stated (at least in relation to equitable forbearance) that inequity is required in addition to detriment. It is clear, however, that, in establishing whether it would be inequitable to permit the promise to be peremptorily withdrawn, the Courts are prepared to take into account a number of factors other than purely the detriment suffered by the promisee. Although the position is uncertain, it is submitted that at best the consideration of these factors amounting to inequitable conduct provides a superadded hurdle which must be satisfied in addition to the threshold detriment test. **On this analysis, detriment simpliciter is a necessary but not sufficient requirement for the doctrine to operate. Thus, the Courts may take into account all the circumstances in assessing whether to allow the promise in issue to be withdrawn.**"(加黑部分是笔者的强调)

8.2　不合情理

在早期的衡平法宽限或承诺性禁反言的先例中,法院的判决一般只会提到陈述或承诺被对方依赖与让承诺方撤回陈述或承诺会导致不公平这两个要件。直到 Goff 大法官在 Amalgamated v. Texas Bank (1982) 1 Lloyd's Rep. 27 先例与 Oliver 大法官在 Taylor Fashions Ltd. v. Liverpool Victoria Trustees Co. Ltd. (1982) 1 QB 133 先例中针对所有类别的禁反言(包括承诺性禁反言)引入了不合情理(unconscionable)的说法,之后有关衡平法宽限或承诺性禁反言的先例中,不合情理与不公平往往会一起出现。随着将不同类别的禁反言统一为一种禁反言的尝试,有说法是应用不合情理这一要件将不同类别的禁反言连接起来。但英国没有采纳这种将不同类别的禁反言统一的建议(这可见本章之 12.3.2 段),Goff 勋爵在 Johnson v. Gore Wood & Co. (2002) 2 AC 1 先例中说:"In the end, I am inclined to think that the many circumstances capable of giving rise to an estoppels cannot be accommodated within a single formula, and that it is unconscionability which provides the link between them."

关于不公平与不合情理之间的区别(或没有区别),可能是不公平相对来说更宽泛。而不合情理,因为英国法律一直以来有不少针对不合情理的合约[122]或合约条文[123]的判决,因此,相对来说有更加明确的判断标准。如在《Chitty on Contracts》(第 32 版,2015 年)一书之 8－133 段,针对不合情理交易(unconscionable bargain),

---

〔122〕 英国法院以前经常会对一些苛刻与不合情理的交易(harsh and unconscionable bargain)做出衡平法救济,以保护处于弱势的一方。1977 年《Unfair Contract Terms Act》保护消费者的立法后,在一些不受该立法管辖的商业合约中,英国法院看来会更加强调订约自由。而在国际商业合约中,更加是强调订约自由。但在社会上的交易中,还是会有情况需要英国法院保护有特殊弱势的一方。如有老年痴呆的老人以很低的价格将自己的房子出售。在《Chitty on Contracts》(第 32 版,2015 年)一书之 8－130 段,就提到了枢密院的 Borrelli v. Ting (2010) UKPC 21 先例,将有关的交易视为有经济上的胁迫(economic duress)。

〔123〕 包括惩罚性条文(penalty clause)与没收条文(forfeiture clause)等。

说："**Scope of the doctrine.** The doctrine of unconscionable bargains seems to be limited in three ways. The first is that the bargain must be oppressive to the complaint in overall terms; the second that it may only apply when the complainant was suffering from certain types of bargaining weakness; and the third that the other party must have acted unconscionable in the sense of having knowingly taken advantage of the complainant."

不合情理的说法适用在各种类别的禁反言（特别是承诺性禁反言）。在 Michael Spence 律师所著的《Protecting Reliance: the emergent doctrine of equitable estoppel》（1999 年）一书之第 59 至 66 页，根据澳大利亚的先例［特别是高院的 Waltons Stores (Interstate) Ltd. v. Maher (1988) 164 CLR 387 先例与 Commonwealth of Australia v. Verwayen (1990) 170 CLR 394 先例］总结了八个方面的考虑，可节录如下：

1. 一方怎样导致对方有一个假设（assumption）并依赖该假设的。尽管任何形式的陈述或承诺都可以构成禁反言，但陈述或承诺的形式还是会对法院或仲裁庭判断是否是不合情理造成影响。如法院或仲裁庭会倾向于认为让陈述方或承诺方撤回明示陈述或承诺，会比撤回以沉默或行为做出的陈述或承诺更不合情理。毕竟前者的表达方式更清楚无误，也更显示了被禁反言的一方的意图或知道会被对方依赖。

2. 有关陈述或承诺导致对方产生的错误假设的内容。相比对将来的承诺，法院或仲裁庭会认为让一方撤回一个对已经存在的事实的陈述更不合情理。在 Waltons Stores (Interstate) Ltd. v. Maher 先例中，澳大利亚高院的判决中说："failure to fulfil a promise does not of itself amount to unconscionable conduct."而即使该承诺被依赖，还需要满足其他的要件，才会被视为不合情理。这个说法也符合人性与常识，因为被承诺方通常不会完全安心依赖一个对将来的承诺（promisee may reasonably be expected to appreciate that he could not safely rely upon a voluntary promise）。例如，如果在提单中写上了 3 万吨食糖，这是针对事实的陈述，表示已经有了 3 万吨食糖装船。如果这套提单将来被善意的第三人依赖，并支付了货款以取得这套提单。但向船长提货时，被船东声称只有 1 万吨食糖装船，这显然极不合情理，法院不会允许船东撤回这种对事实的陈述。相反，如果一方向另一方承诺半年或一年后会运送 3 万吨食糖，不论这个承诺是否构成有法律约束力的合约，被承诺方也不会像前者这么肯定一定会有 3 万吨食糖到手。这样看来，在满足不合情理的要求方面，陈述性禁反言会比承诺性禁反言更容易成立。

3. 做出陈述或承诺的一方对对方情况的了解程度。如果做出陈述或承诺的一方知道对方会依赖并因此而蒙受损失，就很有可能被法院或仲裁庭认为让他撤回陈述或承诺是不合情理。如果陈述或承诺方明知对方会依赖，而且也知道自己的陈述或承诺不可靠，就更有可能被认为撤回该陈述或承诺是不合情理。相反，如果对自己做出的陈述或承诺中的问题不知情或不警觉，则被视为不合情理的机会较低。这可以本章之 7.4.3 段介绍的 The "Post Chaser" (1981) 2 Lloyd's Rep. 695 先例为例，一位中间商的言行被指称构成承诺性禁反言。而在国际货物买卖中，中间商一般不理会也不警觉有关的划归通知或付运单证是否有缺陷。一般的做法是将上一手卖方交给他的通知或单证直接转给下一手买方。提出通知或单证有缺陷的一般都是最终的买方,而如果最终的买方因为各种原因无条件接受,卖方的违约(不论是通知或单证有缺陷)也就不了了之。

4. 双方因为被陈述方或被承诺方的依赖而产生的利益或损害。这与法院或仲裁庭决定允许撤回陈述或承诺是否属于不合情理有关,因为陈述方或承诺方因对方的假设而能获得的好处越多,就越有可能是陈述方或承诺方做出的陈述或承诺导致对方做出这样的假设。另外,如果陈述方或承诺方因为被陈述方或被承诺方的依赖而获得了利益,就有责任避免对方蒙受本可避免的损失,即撤回陈述或承诺会对对方造成的损害。如将在本章之12.1.3段介绍的 Williams v. Roffey Bros. & Nicholls Ltd. (1991) 1 QB 1 先例中,虽然上诉庭判履行合约已经承诺了的责任,仍可以宽松地视为有约因/对价,但有说法是该先例适用衡平法宽限或承诺性禁反言的说法会更恰当。在该先例或类似的先例中,承建商在合约下同意只要分承建商完成合约,就会向分承建商多支付一笔金钱。因为承建商如果不能准时完成工程,需要支付很大的议定赔偿。这样就表示承建商事后撤回承诺会有更大程度的不合情理。

5. 双方关系的本质。一般来说在涉及消费者的合约中,法院或仲裁庭更愿意认定存在不合情理的地方,这是为了保护消费者作为弱势的一方的利益。而在商业合约尤其是国际商业合约中,不合情理就相对不容易成立。[124] 在后者,往往是合约一方自己依赖了错误的假设,而不是因对方的陈述或承诺而依赖了错误的假设。

6. 双方力量的强弱。这与上一点有一定的关系,也与判断是否属于不合情理的交易时的考虑一样。已经有澳大利亚先例将这两者混为一谈:Commercial Bank of Australia v. Amadio (1983) 151 CLR 447 先例与 Re Ferdinando, Ex p ANZ Banking Group Ltd. v. Official Trustee in Bankruptcy (1993) 42 FCR 243 先例等。在 Commonwealth of Australia v. Verwayen 先例中,Deane 大法官说:"The rationale of the doctrine of estoppel by conduct is that it is right and expedient to save people from being victimised by other people ... In this as in other areas of equity – related doctrine, conduct which is 'unconscionable' will commonly involve the use or insistence upon legal entitlement to take advantage of another's special vulnerability or misadventure."双方力量的强弱这点重要,是因为强势的一方很容易令对方依赖自己的言行并蒙受本可避免的损失。

7. 双方之间以往的交易。这显然与共识性禁反言关系最密切,双方在长期的交往中形成了错误的或与合约约定不同的共识或假设,之后令其中一方想回复到原本

〔124〕 在 V Berg and Son Ltd. v. Vanden Avennr – Izegem (1977) 1 Lloyd's Rep. 499 (CA)先例,上诉庭的 Lawton 大法官说:"I have never thought of the merchants and brokers in the international grain market as fragile characters wilting under the ups and downs of international trade..."

的合约地位会是不合情理。另也可能双方之间的长期关系会是一个影响法院或仲裁庭判断是否不合情理的因素：Hill v. A W J Moore and Co. Pty Ltd.（31 August 1991）Supreme Court of New South Wales, unreported 先例。

8. 陈述方或承诺方是否曾经采取任何行动来确保不会造成本可避免的损失。一方可以证明他已经在合理的能力范围内，尽力确保自己的陈述或承诺准确，或对方不会因为依赖而蒙受损失。如尽快向对方做出通知说不能依赖该陈述或承诺，只要通知是清楚无误并且当时对方还没有因为依赖而蒙受损失，事后对方就不能指称该陈述或承诺构成禁反言。或是在双方的谈判过程中，说明直到合约正式订立，谈判中的所有陈述或承诺都不会被依赖。在 Attorney General of Hong Kong v. Humphreys Estate（Queen's Gardens）Ltd.（1987）AC 114 先例中，枢密院说："It is possible but unlikely that in circumstances at present unforeseeable a party to negotiations set out in a document expressed to be 'subject to contract' would be able to satisfy the court that ... some form of estoppel had arisen to prevent the parties from refusing to proceed with the transaction envisaged in the document."

另一个类似的情况是合约中有一条完整合约条文（entire agreement clause）。[125] 在这种情况下，法院或仲裁庭一般不会接受一方指称另一方在谈判过程中做出过与合约规定的内容不同的陈述或承诺构成禁反言的说法。

英国法律下在 Steria Ltd. v. Hutchison（2006）EWCA Civ 1551 先例中，Neuberger 大法官提到不合情理的要求时说："When it comes to estoppels by representation or promissory estoppels, it seems to be very unlikely would be able to satisfy the test of unconscionability unless he could also satisfy the three basic requirements. They are（a）a clear representation or promise made by the defendant（陈述方或承诺方）upon which it is reasonably foreseeable that the claimant will act,（b）an act on the part of the claimant which was reasonably taken in reliance upon the representation or promise, and（c）after the act has been taken, the claimant being able to show that he will suffer detriment if the defendant is not held to the presentation or promise ...[126]"

8.3 不公平与不合情理的不肯定性与不可预测性

是否不公平或不合情理在现实中很大程度上取决于法官或仲裁员的主观"裁量权"（discretion）。而因为文化差异、个人经历等的不同，不同的法官或仲裁员可能对是否不公平或不合情理有不同判断，这就会带来不肯定与不可预测。正如英国法律对大陆法的"善意"的批评。这里可重复在本章第 6 段提到的 Kirby 大法官在澳大利亚上诉庭的 The "Zhi Jiang Kou"（1991）1 Lloyd's Rep. 493 先例的说法："The deci-

---

〔125〕 关于完整合约条文，可见本章之 6.5.4 段与杨良宜《合约的解释：规则与应用》一书第十三章之第 2 段。

〔126〕 这三个要求其实即构成陈述性禁反言或承诺性禁反言的要件。

sion on whether an estoppel is established . . . being founded in an appeal to conscience, is **partly impressionistic**. It represents **a reaction to the facts as elaborated. The reaction to the same facts will necessarily differ from one judge to another, as the dissenting opinions in many cases of estoppel show.** Such differences may reflect the different experiences of Judges, some of whom will evidence a conscience more tender than others."(加黑部分是笔者的强调)

但 Kirby 大法官接下来也说,禁反言并不是由法官或仲裁员任意(at large)决定,因为有规则做出指引,说:"However, the decision is not at large. There are rules to lay down the criteria and approach that must be taken by Judges in considering a claim to estoppel."

英国法律也试图控制这方面的不肯定性与不可预测性,在肯定性与公平之间做出平衡。在 Ward v. James (1966) 1 QB 273 先例中,Denning 勋爵认为只要有适当的指引,法官行使裁量权(包括决定是否是不公平或不合情理的裁量权)也可以做出可预测的决定,说:"It is an essential attribute of justice in a community that similar decisions should be given in similar cases, and this applies as much to mode of trial as anything else. The only way of achieving this is for the courts to set out the considerations which should guide the judges in the normal exercise of their discretion. And that is what has been done in scores of cases where a discretion has been entrusted to the judges."

Bingham 大法官在 1990 年的"The Royal Bank of Scotland Law Lecture"的演讲中说,给法官的裁量权做出指引就像将龙驯服并用短皮带拴住(a discretionay decision bound by guidelines is one in which the dragon of arbitrary discretion has been domesticated and put on a short leash)。

在 Steria Ltd. v. Hutchison (2006) EWCA Civ 1551 先例中,Neuberger 大法官说:"... **unconscionability can, be an issue upon which reasonable people can very easily differ** (in relation both in whether the claimant has a valid claim and as to how that claim should be satisfied). **Accordingly one can well see why it is appropriate to have some more specific principles.** The danger of having such principles, however, is that they can introduce an undue degree of rigidity into what is intended to be a flexible doctrine. The tension between asking whether it would be unconscionable in all the circumstances of a particular case to deprive a claimant of any relief, on the one hand, and, on the other hand, asking whether the claimant can satisfy the various requirements of a particular type of estoppels, will be apparent to anyone who has had to consider the law in this area, and it is easy to find cases to support either approach."(加黑部分是笔者的强调)

另在 The Parties named in Schedule A v. Dresdner Kleinwort Limited, Commerzbank AG (2010) EWHC 1249 (QB)先例中,Simon 大法官在引用了上述 Neuberger 大

法官的判决后,说:"... since unconscionability is the single factor that must be established for an estoppel and **views on unconscionability may vary**, it is necessary to have specific but flexible guiding principles."(加黑部分是笔者的强调)

即使有指引或特殊原则(如本书所介绍的构成不同类别禁反言的要件),笔者还是认为这方面是不可预测与危险。这里会有多方面的原因,如:

1. 本章多处都有显示,部分指引或特殊原则有很大的灰色地带,很容易带来不同的看法。如在 Commonwealth of Australia v. Verwayen (1990) 170 CLR 394 先例中,澳大利亚高院的不同大法官之间对于是否因依赖而蒙受损害与什么是最低程度的衡平法救济,就有十分不同的看法。[127]

2. 正如在本章之 8.1 段节录的《The Law of Waiver, Variation, and Estoppel》(第3版,2012年)一书之 8.62 段加黑的最后一句所说,针对不公平或不合情理,法院或仲裁庭在做出判断时可以将所有的情况(all the circumstances)考虑进去。而且这方面的决定一般都是对事实的认定,不存在可以上诉让其他法官重新考虑。正如上述节录的 Neuberger LJ 所说:"The tension between asking whether it would be unconscionable in all the circumstances of a particular case to deprive a claimant of any relief, on the one hand, and, on the other hand, asking whether the claimant can satisfy the various requirements of a particular type of estoppels, will be apparent to anyone who has had to consider the law in this area, and it is easy to find cases to support either approach."

3. 禁反言是英国法律中最有力的武器,也最有弹性(flexible)。如在 Roebuck v. Mungovin (1994) 1 Lloyd's Rep. 481 先例中,Browne - Wilkinson 勋爵就说:"when an equitable estoppel is raised is extremely flexible."审理的法官或仲裁员如果对合约一方不满或看不惯某些言行,可以不管合约如何约定,而通过这一说法禁止他行使合约权利,以达到希望的"公平"的结果。

4. 在国际仲裁中,部分外国人士会由于不了解或潜在偏见(imputed bias),而看不惯或不理解亚洲公司(或人士)的某些言行。这与上述的原因结合起来,会导致亚洲公司在仲裁案件中更容易被认定做出过不当的言行,构成禁反言(特别是衡平法宽限或承诺性禁反言)。

8.4 不公平或不合情理的先例介绍

由于衡平法宽限与承诺性禁反言是衡平法的救济,所以即使其他的要件都符合,但不存在不公平或不合情理,还是不会构成衡平法宽限或承诺性禁反言。不公平也包括希望依赖衡平法宽限与承诺性禁反言的一方自己不清白(unclean hands),正如衡平法的基本说法之一,寻求衡平救济的一方必须自己公平合理(he who seeks equity must do equity)。这方面可介绍一些先例。

---

[127] 该先例在本章之 11.6 段有具体介绍。

首先在 Combe v. Combe（1951）2 KB 215 先例中，案情涉及一对夫妻离婚时，丈夫同意每年给妻子 100 英镑。但丈夫从没给过钱，7 年后，前妻根据他的承诺提起诉讼。一审的 Byrne 法官认为尽管丈夫的承诺没有约因/对价，根据 Central London Property Trust Ltd. v. High Trees House Ltd.（1947）KB 130 先例，妻子依然可以拿到这笔钱。但这个判决被上诉庭推翻，原因之一是让前夫撤回承诺不会对前妻造成任何不公平，相反，如果让经济更富裕的前妻可以拿回这笔钱，会对前夫造成不公平。Denning 勋爵说："It may be that the wife has suffered some detriment because, after forbearing to apply to the court for seven years, she might not now be given leave to apply... Assuming, however, that she has suffered some detriment by her forbearance, nevertheless, as the forbearance was not at the husband's request, it is no consideration... The doctrine of consideration is sometimes said to work injustice, but I see none in this case... I do not think it would be right for this wife, who is better off than her husband, to take no action for six or seven years and then come down on him for the whole 600l."

另在 D & C Builders Ltd. v. Rees（1966）2 QB 617 先例中，被告雇主欠了原告的承建商近 500 英镑。原告在催促被告还钱一段时间后，同意被告可以只还 300 英镑了事。这是被告知道原告经济困难后，向他施压，说这 300 英镑是他全部能拿到的钱。尽管原告承诺过只收 300 英镑（这个承诺没有约因/对价），但之后向被告要求拿回剩下的钱，这等于撤回了承诺。Denning 勋爵认为，尽管原告的这个承诺可能会构成承诺性禁反言，但被告有意识地利用原告的经济状况来威胁原告的行为，意味着让原告撤回他的承诺没有不公平。

新西兰的 Re Goile（1963）NZLR 666 CA 先例也是类似的案情，判决债务的债务人（judgment debtor）与胜诉的债权人（creditor）达成协议，可以少付一点以解决这一笔败诉的判决债务。[128] 但债务人没有根据协议支付这笔钱，债权人申请将债务人破产，债务人以承诺性禁反言作为抗辩，但没有成功。

保险合约经常有弃权与禁反言的争议，包括承诺性禁反言的类别。有不少先例涉及事故发生之后，被保险人向保险公司要求赔偿，保险公司在委任理算师（loss adjustor）核算损失的同时，也会委任专家或律师对事故做出调查。期间与被保险人的交往中，保险公司会做出某些言行，事后被被保险人指称为承诺性禁反言，如做出中间支付（interim payment）或承诺会尽快赔付等。但如果被保险人不清白，如夸大了要求赔偿的金额或是有其他不诚实的行为，即使承诺性禁反言的要件能够成立，也不会获得法院的救济。这可简单节录《Colinvaux's Law of Insurance in Hong Kong》（2009 年）一书之 6.097 段，如下："However, it is to be borne in mind that the form of estoppel in question, promissory estoppel, based on the insurer's promise as to his future

---

〔128〕 这个课题可看本章之 12.1 段。

behaviour operates, only in equity. In accordance with the general principle applicable to equitable remedies, promissory estoppel can be relied upon only by an assured who has acted equitably."

接下来该书介绍了 Baghbadrani v. Commercial Union Assurance Co. Plc. (2000) Lloyd's Rep. IR 94 先例中,案情涉及房屋被第三人纵火而损坏,被保险人向保险公司索赔有关的损失,也威胁除非保险公司尽快赔付,否则会提起诉讼。而保险公司的回应是它无意拒绝责任(deny liability),这回应被被保险人在保险公司拒赔时指是承诺性禁反言。但这被英国高院否定,主要原因之一是被保险人要求的赔偿有虚假(fraudulent claim)。[129] 在《Colinvaux's Law of Insurance in Hong Kong》(2009 年)一书是简单介绍该先例说:"Accordingly, if the assured has sought to mislead the insurer; and in particular if there has been deliberate fraud in the presentation of the risk, a plea of equitable promissory estoppel against the insurer will not be available to him."

9. 衡平法宽限或承诺性禁反言的最低程度救济

由于衡平法宽限或承诺性禁反言都是衡平法的救济,所以追求最低程度的救济。只要纠正不公平之处,应尽量不影响原本的合约或法律地位。在 Crabb v. Arun DC (1976) Ch 179 先例中,Scarman 大法官就强调了要最低程度的衡平这一点,说:"the minimum equity to do justice to the plaintiff."

承诺性禁反言的救济不是执行承诺,因为执行承诺是合约法的范畴,当然承诺要有约因/对价。针对承诺性禁反言更恰当的救济是让因为依赖对方的承诺而蒙受损害的一方回复到原本的地位。[130] 正如 McHugh 大法官在 Commonwealth of Australia v. Verwayen (1990) 170 CLR 394 先例中说:"Once the detriment has ceased or been paid for, there is nothing unconscionable in a party insisting on reverting to his or her former relationship with the other party and enforcing his or her strict legal rights."

但在 Baird Textile Holdings Ltd. v. Marks & Spencer Plc. (2001) EWCA Civ 274 先例中,Mance 大法官对这种依赖利益与预期利益的区分持批判性态度,说:

"Baird acknowledges that an estoppel precluding M & S from denying that the relationship with BTH could only be determined by the giving of reasonable notice would not

---

[129] 由于保险合约要求善意,所以如果被保险人在要求赔偿时有虚假的行为(通常是以虚假文件或陈述来支持以多获得赔偿),会有特别严重与同一般合约不同的后果。有关欺诈性索赔的课题,在杨良宜《海上货物保险》(2010 年)一书第十二章第 10 段与《英国海上保险条款详论》(2009 年)一书之 413 - 419 页有详论。

[130] 关于预期利益(expectation interest)与依赖利益(reliance interest),可见杨良宜《损失赔偿与救济》一书第二章。

assist, unless it also meant that **M & S (and presumably Baird) were precluded from ceasing to place and honour orders for a 'reasonable' or 'appropriate' share of whatever were M & S's requirements from time to time, so as to ensure, to that extent, that the production facilities that Baird had devoted to M & S's business to date were maintained, or at least run down gradually**, during such period of notice.... Baird's answer is that it **does not seek to protect its expectation interest**. That, it accepts, could only be done in contract. Rather it is **seeking to protect its reliance interest.**

In support of its claim based an estoppel protecting its reliance interest, Baird argues that estoppel is or should be viewed as a flexible doctrine, ... and that it is open to English law to afford the protection proportionate to Baird's reliance for which Baird contends...

...In the present case, ... The suggested justification is the limitation of the relief claimed to reliance loss. On this submission, the requirements of contract (consideration, certainty and an intention to create legal relations) are irrelevant because no contract is asserted. The requirements of estoppel (e. g. that is an unequivocal promise to found a promissory estoppel or Conventional conduct of sufficient clarity to found an estoppel by Convention and, secondly, the objective intention to affect some actual or apparent pre-existing legal relationship) are by-passed by the limitation of relief. **But no authority in this jurisdiction supports the submission that estoppel can here achieve so expanded an application, simply by limiting recovery to reliance loss** (assuming that reliance loss could anyway be distinguished satisfactorily from expectation loss — an apparent difficulty which I have already mentioned). **Any development of English law in such a direction could and should, in my view, now take place in the highest court.**"(加黑部分是笔者的强调)

在追求最低程度的救济下,如在一个违反条件条文的违约/毁约案件中,无辜方做出放弃权利的言行,这言行除非是清楚无误,否则不会被解释为包括放弃将来针对该违约/毁约索赔金钱损失的权利,而只局限在放弃终止合约的权利。这在1996年英国《货物销售法》之 section 53 也有提到,说:"(1)... where the buyer elects (or compelled) to treat any breach of a condition on the part of the seller as a breach of warranty, the buyer is not by reason only of such breach of warranty entitled to reject the goods; but he may:...(b) maintain an action against the seller for damages for the breach of warranty...."

接下来的段节主要介绍两个方面。一是陈述方(representor)或承诺方(promisor)做出陈述或承诺愿意放弃或减轻合约或法律权利,可能是永久性的,也可能只是暂时性的。一般来说,如果可行,衡平法宽限或承诺性禁反言带来的后果是尽量让陈述方或承诺方可以通过合理通知(reasonable notice)回复到原本的合约或法律地位。二是做出的救济必须成比例(proportionate),即比较与平衡被陈述方或承诺方蒙受的损害,与如果被禁反言,陈述方或承诺方会蒙受的损害。

9.1 永久性或暂时性弃权/宽限

已经提到如果可行,衡平法宽限或承诺性禁反言都会是暂时性的,尽量让陈述方或承诺方可以通过合理通知回复到原本的合约或法律地位。毕竟构成衡平法宽限或承诺性禁反言的陈述或承诺不同于必须被严格执行的合约承诺,没有约因/对价。

在 Collier v. P & MJ Wright (Holdings) Ltd. (2008) 1 WLR 643 先例中,Arden 女大法官说:"The doctrine is generally suspensory because the courts do the minimum necessary to satisfy the equity."

另在 Ajayi v. R. T. Briscoe (Nigeria) Ltd. (1964) 1 WLR 1326 先例中,涉及卡车的租购合约(hire – purchase agreement),原告要求被告支付拖欠的分期付款。而被告指称原告的一封信中说,直到卡车修理完毕重新投入使用,被告不需要支付分期付款。被告的抗辩是他依赖了这封信而改变了自己的地位,所以原告不能要求他支付分期付款。但由于这封信是唯一证据,法院认为并不完整,不足以证明被告怎样改变了立场,因此不构成承诺性禁反言。关于构成承诺性禁反言的限制,枢密院说:"... when one party to a contract in the absence of fresh consideration agrees not to enforce his rights an equity will be raised in favour of the other party. This equity is, however, subject to the qualifications that (1) the other party has altered his position, (2) **that the promisor can resile from his promise on giving reasonable notice which need not be formal notice, giving the promisee reasonable opportunity of resuming his position**, (3) **the promise only becomes final and irrevocable if the promisee cannot resume his position**."(加黑部分是笔者的强调)

即被承诺方依赖承诺方的承诺改变自己的地位,如果被承诺方可以回复到原本的地位,承诺方就可以通过合理通知撤回承诺,而如果被承诺方无法回复到原本的地位,承诺方的承诺就变为是永久性的,不能撤销。

现实中这种例子很多,在 Clarke 教授的《The Law of Insurance Contract》(第 6 版,2009 年)一书举例说:"For example, if the claimant fails to produce the evidence of fire loss required by the contract[131] and the insurer does not insist on it until it is too late

〔131〕 火灾保险中,往往会约定被保险人要在规定时间内提供火灾损失的相关证据。如在涉及火灾保险的 Yorkshire Insurance Co. , Ltd. v. Craine (1922) 12 Lloyd's Rep. 399 先例中,相关条文规定:"The insured must within fifteen days after the loss or damage, or such further time as the Company may in writing allow in that behalf, deliver to the Company a claim in writing for the loss and damage, containing as particular an account as is reasonably practicable of all the articles or items of property damaged or destroyed, and of the amount of the loss or damage thereto respectively, and of any other insurances... No amount shall be payable under this policy unless the terms of this condition have been complied with."

for the claimant to obtain it, the insurer will not be allowed to refuse the claim on that ground. . . estoppel, although generally only suspensory, is also irrevocable, if the representee claimant cannot resume his former position, i. e. in this example, cannot obtain the evidence of the fire loss."

在本章稍早的7.4.2段提到的《The Law of Waiver, Variation, and Estoppel》(第3版,2012年)一书之8.61段中也举例说,如果被承诺方因将承诺方的承诺或宽限带来的意外之财当做一次性分红发给股东,这笔钱就永远也不可能再收回,承诺方也就不能再撤回承诺。而如果只是影响现金流或预算,通过合理通知,承诺方可以撤回承诺回复到原本的合约或法律地位。其他涉及承诺方通过合理通知撤回承诺回复到原本的合约地位的先例也很多,包括 Hughes v. Metropolitan Railway Company (1877) 2 App Cas 439 先例与 Central London Property Trust Ltd. v. High Trees House Ltd. (1947) KB 130 先例等。

在 Brikom Investments Ltd. v. Seaford (1981) 1 WLR 863 (CA)先例中,房东要求租务主任(rent officer)决定合理的租金,租务主任在当时的立法《Housing Act 1961》下,根据房东负责修理的默示基础计算出应支付的租金。但在该先例中,租约明示规定是由租客负责修理,在此基础上计算出的租金显然比在房东负责修理的基础上计算出的要低。但房东接受了租客所支付的租务主任计算出的租金。法院最后判是房东可以通过合理通知行使租约中租客负责修理的条文,但必须先回复到正确计算的较低租金,并将之前租客多支付的租金退回。即要先将租客回复到没有损害的地位,然后房东再通过做出合理通知回复到原本的合约地位。

法院要尽量避免判承诺方的承诺是最终与不能撤回的,并禁止承诺方回复到原本的合约或法律地位。因为这样就等于在衡平法宽限或承诺性禁反言中,将陈述或承诺作为约因/对价的替代。但实际上有不少先例确实造成了这种结果。如保险人陈述或承诺不会根据已经发生的违反保单中的前提条件或承诺性保证的事实拒赔,之后他就再也不能以此理由拒赔。这方面也有很多的先例,笔者可举若干例子介绍。

在 The "Ion" (1980) 2 Lloyd's Rep. 245 (CA)先例中,案情涉及货损索赔的时效问题。1978年7月4日,船东的互保协会在时效已过之后,向承租人的互保协会写信说:"We . . . would advise you that our Members are prepared to abide by the terms and conditions of the Inter – Club Agreement in so far as they are involved for any cargo claims which may have to be settled. . ."

之后双方仍然有信件往来,在1979年7月3日双方进行的会议上,船东的互保协会提出了时效问题,并在7月5日通过信件表示船东认为时效已过。双方之后开始仲裁,并且承租人根据1950年《仲裁法》向法院申请延长时效。Mocatta 大法官判是船东的互保协会在1978年7月4日的信件构成承诺性禁反言。而针对船东的抗辩说即使构成承诺性禁反言,根据船东的互保协会在1979年7月3日与5日的通知,可回复到了原本的地位,Mocatta 大法官说:"In my judgment, a promissory estoppel to the effect that a party will not take a time bar point that has already accrued in his favour at the time of his representation is not susceptible to lifting by notice enabling the promisor to raise afresh at a much later date the time bar in his favour."

另在 Bank Negara Indonesia v. Philip Hoalim (1973) 2 MLJ 3 PC 先例中,案情已经在本章稍早的 7.4.4 段提到。根据枢密院的判法,房东无法通过通知回复到原本的法律地位。

最后,在本章之 11.6 段介绍的 Commonwealth of Australia v. Verwayen (1990) 170 CLR 394 先例中,澳大利亚高院以四比三的多数意见判澳大利亚政府被永久性禁反言,不能回复到原本的法律地位(即依赖时效已过的抗辩)。而且该先例也涉及救济是否成比例的问题(在下一小段介绍),因此,大法官的合议(deliberation)与判决很有争议。

9.2 做出的救济必须成比例

首先可节录 Brennan 大法官在 Waltons Stores (Interstate) Ltd. v. Maher (1988) 164 CLR 387 先例中所说:"The element which both attracts the jurisdiction of a court of equity and shapes the remedy to be given is unconscionable conduct on the part of the person bound by the equity, and the remedy required to satisfy an equity varies according to the circumstances of the case. As Robert Goff J. said in Amalgamated Property Co. v. Texas Bank (1982) QB 84 at p 103: 'Of all doctrines, equitable estoppel is surely one of the most flexible.' Sometimes it is necessary to decree that a party's expectiation be specifically fulfilled by the party bound by the equity; sometimes it is necessary to an injunction to restrain the exercise of legal rights either absolutely or on condition; sometimes it is necessary to give an quitable lien on property for the expenditure which a party has made on it... However, in moulding its decree, the court, as a court of conscience, goes no further than is necessary to prevent unconscionable conduct."

Deane 大法官在澳大利亚高院的 Commonwealth of Australia v. Verwayen (1990) 170 CLR 394 先例中也说,如下:"There could be circumstances in which the potential damage to an allegedly estopped party was disproportionately greater than any detriment which would be sustained by the other party to an extent that good conscience could not reasonably be seen as precluding a departure from the assumed state of affairs if adequate compensation were made or offered by the allegedly estopped party for any detriment sustained by the other party.[132] An obvious example would be provided by a case in which the party claiming the benefit of an estoppel precluding a denial of his ownership of a

[132] 会有情况是如果判陈述方或承诺方被禁反言,他所蒙受的损害远远超出被陈述方或被承诺方因为依赖该陈述或承诺而蒙受的损害。这样,如果被陈述方或被承诺方因为依赖该陈述或承诺而蒙受的损害可以获得赔偿,不允许陈述方或承诺方回复到原本的地位会是不正确。

million dollar block of land owned by the allegedly estopped party would sustain no detriment beyond the loss of one hundred dollars spent on the erection of a shed if a departure from the assumed state of affairs were allowed [cf. , e. g. , Ramsden v. Dyson (1866) LR 1 HL 129, at pp 140 – 141];[133] . . . In other cases, particularly cases involving an assumption about a future state of affairs, the circumstances may be such that any significant detriment would be avoided altogether if the party affected were given reasonable notice of the intended departure. In such a case, the estoppel may only preclude departure from the assumed state of affairs otherwise than after such reasonable notice has been given[134] . . . Even in a case where an estoppel by conduct is established and would prima facie operate to preclude departure from the assumed state of affairs, the circumstances may be such that to grant unqualified relief on that basis would exceed any requirements of good conscience and be unduly oppressive of the other party.[135]"

Commonwealth of Australia v. Verwayen 先例就是典型的例子,这可见本章之 11.6 段。Verwayen 先生因为政府撤回承诺浪费的费用与禁止政府依赖时效已过的抗辩所带来的损失显然不成比例。这也是该先例如此富争议与高院三位少数意见的大法官坚持其观点的原因之一。

而案情性质相近的 Roebuck v. Mungovin (1994) 1 Lloyd's Rep. 481 英国先例中,显示了考虑救济时必须考虑被承诺方因为依赖了承诺方的承诺而带来损害的程度。显然,如果损害的程度很低,甚至实际上不存在,就根本无法构成衡平法宽限或承诺性禁反言。相反,如果有损害而做出救济也必须与被承诺方的损害成比例。在该先例中,涉及被告被指称曾经向原告陈述不会以原告懈怠为由申请撤销诉讼请求 (strike out claim for want of prosecution),[136] 原告依赖该陈述多花了律师费用,所以被告不能撤回原来的陈述。Browne – Wilkinson 勋爵说:"Assuming, for present purposes, that the defendant's conduct does raise such an equitable estoppel. . . such equitable estoppel would not impose an automatic legal bar to obtaining a striking – out order. The effect of such an estoppel is to give the court power to do what is equitable in the circumstances. . . the nature of the relief to be given when an equitable estoppel is raised is extremely flexible. If an equitable estoppel is raised the Court's function is to determine

---

〔133〕 典型的例子就是土地所有人允许对方在自己的土地上盖了一间小屋,如果法院判这构成产权人禁反言,土地所有人就会失去自己价值几百万英镑的土地。然而相比之下,如果允许土地所有人回复到原本的法律地位,对方除了盖小屋花的 100 英镑,是没有别的损失。

〔134〕 这是本章上一小段介绍的通过合理通知回复到原本的合约或法律地位。

〔135〕 会有情况是即使表面看构成禁反言的要件都可以成立,但如果不允许陈述方或承诺方回复到原本的合约或法律地位会是不正确,并给他带来过于沉重的负担。

〔136〕 这方面可见本章之 6.3 段介绍的 Bremer Vulkan Schiffbau und Maschinenfabrik v. South India Shipping Corporation Ltd. (1981) 1 Lloyd's Rep. 253 先例。

what, if anything, is necessary to satisfy that equity in all the circumstances of the case. This is a far cry from saying that, where a defendant has led the claimant to incur some additional expense, he is therefore in all circumstances prevented from relying on inexcusable delay by the [claimant] which has seriously prejudiced him. If on the assumption made, the defendant is equitably estopped, then the effect of that estoppel would be to give the court a discretion whether or not to strike out that action... depending upon the balance between the harm done to the defendant by the claimant's delay and the expense or other detriment incurred by the claimant by reason of the defendant's representation."

10. 衡平法宽限或承诺性禁反言是“盾牌”或“宝剑”之争

一直的说法是衡平法宽限与承诺性禁反言只能作为盾牌(shield)之用,即只能作为防御。典型的防御之一就是被告被原告指称违约,而被告虽然根据合约责任难逃,但他指原告曾经的言行可以构成衡平法宽限或承诺性禁反言,所以合约的约定不适用或被禁止适用。换言之,这种禁反言不会产生新的合约或法律权利,不能作为宝剑(sword)攻击对方,即不能以此作为诉因(cause of action)起诉与提出索赔。

这里除了有历史的原因(这在本章之5.1段有介绍),主要的原因是不能允许衡平法宽限与承诺性禁反言影响基本的合约法原则,即有约因/对价的合约承诺才能被执行。这可节录几个重要的先例中,首先是Combe v. Combe (1951) 2 KB 215 (CA)先例中,Denning大法官说:"... the principle(承诺性禁反言)never stands alone as giving a cause of action in itself, it can never do away with the necessity of consideration when that is an essential part of the cause of action. The doctrine of consideration is too firmly fixed to be overthrown by a side – wind. Its ill – effects have been largely mitigated of late, but it still remains a cardinal necessity of the formation of a contract, though not of its modification or discharge. I fear that it was my failure to make this clear which misled Byrne, J. in the present case. He held that the wife could sue on the husband's promise as a separate and independent cause of action by itself, although, as he held, there was no consideration for it. That is not correct. The wife can only enforce it if there was consideration for it."

另在Brikom Investments Ltd. v. Carr (1979) QB 467 (CA)先例中,Roskill大法官说:"... it would be wrong to extend the doctrine of promissory estoppel, whatever its precise limits at the present day, to the extent of abolishing in this backhanded way the doctrine of consideration."

这个大原则也适用在其他类别的禁反言,如“陈述性禁反言”(estoppel by representation),[137]但不适用在"产权人禁反言"(proprietary estoppel),[138]这在本书第七章第3段会进行解释。

进一步解释这个大原则首先要说明,虽然衡平法宽限与承诺性禁反言只能用作防御,但并非只能由被告提出。因为哪一方都可以先去法院要求解决争议而成为原告,原告或被告并非是决定性的。以 Central London Property Trust Ltd. v. High Trees House Ltd. (1947) KB 130 先例的案情为例,可以是房东作为原告起诉被告租客要求支付合约规定的租金,而租客以衡平法宽限或承诺性禁反言抗辩,这很好理解。但也可以是租客作为原告向法院申请宣告(declaration)被告的房东的言行构成衡平法宽限或承诺性禁反言,所以不可以要求租客支付合约规定的租金。这完全可以,现实中也在发生。

怎样可以构成诉因,在简式合约中,如果发生违约与需要提出索赔,原告就需要主张与证明以下几点:(1)被告曾经做出承诺(a promise was made to him);(2)这个承诺有约因/对价(the promise was backed by consideration);(3)双方有产生法律关系的意图(the promisor and the promisee intended that a legal obligation should flow from the promise);(4)承诺是肯定与可以被执行(the promise is sufficiently certain to be enforced);(5)对方违反了承诺(the promisor has broken the promise);(6)索赔的损失是由对方违反承诺导致与不遥远(the loss for which damages are claimed was caused by the breach of promise and is not too remote)。[139]

因此,衡平法宽限或承诺性禁反言无法满足上述六个要求,这也是较近期 Baird Textile Holdings Ltd. v. Marks & Spencer Plc. (2001) EWCA Civ 274 先例[140]的判法。

但衡平法宽限或承诺性禁反言也不纯粹是"盾牌",有说法是它也可以在一定程度上变为"宝剑"。毕竟有时这两者很难区分,正如 Ormrod 大法官在 Brikom Investments Ltd. v. Seaford (1981) 1 WLR 863 先例中说:"swords with a little ingenuity can be beaten into shields or shields into sword."另在 Amalgamated v. Texas Bank (1982) 1 Lloyd's Rep. 27 这个对"共识性禁反言"(estoppel by convention)的说法十分重要的先例中,上诉庭的 Brandon 大法官也说:[141]"In this way the bank, while still in form using the estoppel as a shield, would in substance be founding a cause of action on it. This illustrates what I regard as the true proposition of law, that, while a party cannot in

---

〔137〕 但这有不同看法,如 Colman 大法官在 Azov Shipping Co v. Baltic Shipping Co. (1999) 2 Lloyd's Rep. 159 先例认为宝剑与盾牌的说法只是为了保护约因/对价,所以只与承诺性禁反言有关。而其他类别的禁反言,包括陈述性禁反言、共识性禁反言与产权人禁反言,与约因/对价没有关系,不应该受到这个说法的影响。

〔138〕 Plimmer v. Mayor of Wellington (1884) 9 App Cas 699 先例。

〔139〕 这可见杨良宜的《损失赔偿与救济》一书第三章与第四章。

〔140〕 具体的案情请见本章之5.1段。

〔141〕 Amalgamated v. Texas Bank (1982) 1 Lloyd's Rep. 27 先例的案情,可见本书第六章之2.2.2段。

terms found a cause of action on an estoppel, he may, as a result of being able to rely on an estoppel, succeed on a cause of action on which, without being able to rely on that estoppel, he would necessarily have failed. That in my view is, in substance, the situation of the bank in the present case."

如果原告有其他诉因(如合约的违约),但这个诉因有缺陷(如合约更改没有足够法律承认的约因/对价),原告可以依赖禁反言进行补救。在这种情况下,可以说禁反言就在一定程度上变为"宝剑",因为如果不能依赖禁反言,原告的诉因不能成立。

的确在普通法国家,对于是否将禁反言(包括衡平法宽限或承诺性禁反言)严格视为只是盾牌有不同观点。毕竟,这个只能用作盾牌的说法并不是十分有说服力,根据 Denning 勋爵在 Combe v. Combe 先例所讲,做出这样的限制主要是因为害怕导致合约中约因/对价的基本要求会被禁反言的"边风"动摇(the doctrine of consideration is too firmly fixed to be overthrown by a side - wind)。但这会造成十分矛盾的后果,同样是没有约因/对价的陈述或承诺,部分可以因被陈述方或被承诺方依赖而有法律后果,[142]而另一部分则没有任何法律后果。[143]

尽管英国法律针对承诺性禁反言仍维持这一传统地位,[144]其他普通法国家(主要是澳大利亚[145])的地位已经有了改变并带来了不肯定。如在新加坡,虽然 Sea -

---

[142] 如对违约的宽限或承诺就不能撤回,因为在承诺方提起诉讼主张自己的合约或法律权利时,被承诺方可以此作为盾牌防守。

[143] 如一方承诺多给一笔钱,但之后出尔反尔,对方只能通过提起诉讼要求他履行承诺。但该承诺因为没有约因/对价,不构成合约,而承诺性禁反言又不能作为诉因进攻,等于该承诺没有法律后果。

[144] 但有说法是英国关于承诺性禁反言的法律还在继续发展,最高院仍有可能针对宝剑盾牌之争做出改革。在上诉庭的 Baird Textile Holdings Ltd. v. Marks & Spencer Plc. (2001) EWCA Civ 274 先例中,Andrew - Morritt VC 大法官说:"If I am right in believing that English law, as it now stands, does not permit the enforcement of an estoppel in the form alleged in this case then it is the duty of this court to apply it, notwithstanding that it may be developed by the House of Lords, who are not bound by any of the cases relied on, in the future."在该先例中,Judge 大法官也说:"It seems clear that the principles of the law of estoppel have not yet been fully developed... The second possible development, consigning to history the misleading aphorism that estoppel is a shield, not a sword. In reality that principle has no application to what is described as a proprietary estoppel. The cause of action founded on proprietary estoppel may, and should, so the argument runs, be extended generally in this jurisdiction, both in accordance with the recent decisions in the High Court of Australia ... and also on the basis that if the compartmentalisation of 'estoppel' were broken down, the remedies provided for one form of estoppel (proprietary estoppel) would then be extended to the others. These, very briefly summarised, were the considerations which led me to the preliminary view that although BTH's(原告) argument in contract was unsustainable, the possible development of the law in relation to estoppel might properly justify allowing the case to proceed to trial."

[145] 在本章之 7.4 段节录 Seechurn v. ACE Insurance SA (2002) 2 Lloyd's Rep. 390 先例时提到,针对承诺性禁反言,澳大利亚的法律地位已经与英国有所不同。另可见本章之 12.3.2 段。

Land Services Inc. v. Cheong Fook Chee Vincent (1994) 3 SLR(R) 250 等先例明确了承诺性禁反言只可以作为盾牌而非宝剑,但在近期的 Tee Soon Tay v. Attorney – General (2007) 3 SLR 133 先例中,上诉庭认为这点还是富有争议(shrouded in some controversy)。

可能是不同判法的新加坡先例是 Goh Swee Fang v. Tiah Juah Kim (1994) 3 SLR(R) 556,案情涉及一位母亲与她的儿子分权共有(tenants in common)一栋房屋。但由于婆媳关系不合,儿子同意将他持有的产权以 2 万新加坡币的价格转让给母亲。产权转移后,母亲并没有支付 2 万新加坡币给儿子。之后母亲承诺,她将来会把房子出售后的一半收益分给儿子。16 年后,母亲以低于市价的价格将房子卖给了她另一个儿子夫妇,但没有将收益的一半分给被承诺的儿子,于是儿子向法院起诉。上诉庭判是虽然儿子对房屋已经没有产权,但母亲对他的承诺构成"产权人禁反言"(proprietary estoppel),他可以获得一半的收益。但后来学者的评论,如 Sook Yee Tan 教授的《A Tale of the Tiahs and the Flexibility of Equity》(1995) 7 SALJ 195 一文,指出该先例中母亲承诺把出售房屋的一半收益分给儿子,并不涉及房屋的产权,因此不应适用产权人禁反言,而应该适用承诺性禁反言。但这样,承诺性禁反言(虽然伪装成或被错误认为是产权人禁反言)在该先例就被用作了宝剑,因为儿子唯一的诉因就是母亲承诺会将收益分他一半,但没有履行。

总体而言,新加坡法院目前还是跟从了英国的法律地位,衡平法宽限或承诺性禁反言只能用作盾牌而不能用作宝剑。

澳大利亚却越来越放宽甚至完全排除了这个盾牌与宝剑的区分与说法。

首先在 Stevens v. Standard Chartered Bank (1988) 53 SASR 323 先例中,Bollen 大法官比喻说在拿着他们的盾牌向前冲时,造成一些意外的冲击(thrusting forward with their shield handing out some incidental buffeting)。

在澳大利亚高院(这是最高院)的 Waltons Stores (Interstate) Ltd. v. Maher (1988) 164 CLR 387 先例中,Brennan 大法官说:"There is a logical difficulty in limiting the principle so that it applies only to promises to suspend or extinguish existing rights. If a promise by A not to enforce an existing right against B is to confer an equitable right on B to compel fulfilment of the promise, why should B be denied the same protection in similar circumstances if the promise is intended to create in B a new legal right against A? There is no logical distinction to be drawn between a change in legal relationships effected by a promise which extinguishes a right and a change in legal relationships effected by a promise which creates one. Why should an equity of the kind to which Combe v. Combe refers be regarded as a shield but not a sword?"

该先例的重要性在于澳大利亚高院允许因为依赖承诺方在双方谈判过程中的承诺而蒙受损害(detrimental reliance)的被承诺方,在最后没有达成有法律效力的合约的情况下,要求承诺方履行他的承诺。换言之,被承诺方除了承诺性禁反言是没有其他合约或法律关系与权利作为诉因。澳大利亚法院认为该先例没有否定约因/对价的要求,因为禁反言的说法只是用来纠正不合情理的行为,即使发生在双方的合约谈判中。Brennan 大法官说:"The unconscionable conduct which is the object of equity to prevent is the failure of a party, who has induced the adoption of the assumption or expectation and who knew or intended that it would be relied on, to fulfil the assumption or expectation or otherwise to avoid the detriment which that failure would occasion. The object of equity is not to compel the party bound to fulfil the assumption or expectation; it is to avoid the detriment which if the assumption or expectation goes unfulfilled, will be suffered by the party who has been induced to act or abstain from acting thereon."

另在 News Corporation Ltd. v. Lenfest Communications Inc. (1996) 21 ACSR 553 先例中,衡平法禁反言被明确归类为一种诉因。

在香港最高院的 Luo Xing Juan v. Estate of Hui Shui See (2009) 12 HKCFAR 1 先例中,案情涉及一位女士与男友同居并准备结婚,但男友不幸在婚前去世。双方生前同居的房屋属于男友控股的公司,男友承诺该女士会拥有该房屋 35% 的权利。男友去世后,他的姐姐作为该公司的董事,给了该女士一个月的时间要她搬走,而该女士则提出了承诺性禁反言的说法(因为在该先例中,房屋的所有权属于公司而非男友,所以不会是产权人禁反言)。法院最后判是承诺性禁反言成立,在该公司的清盘人(一审法院下令把该公司清盘)把房屋出售后,该女士可以获得售价的 35%。可以说,这是以承诺性禁反言获得了新的权利,即作为宝剑进攻,虽然香港最高院在判词中没有针对这一点。

针对这些普通法国家不同的看法,可节录新加坡潘文龙法官主编的《The Law of Contract in Singapore》(2012 年)一书之 4.096 段作为总结,如下:"In Waltons Stores, liability was imposed in circumstances where no legal relationship subsisted as between the disputing parties.〔146〕 In that context, the imposition of liability poses a real threat to the law of contract, for it has the effect of upholding a promise even if none of the rules on contractual formation have been satisfied.〔147〕 The same may not, however, be true if the doctrine is used as a sword for the limited purpose of validating contract modifications... the risk of undermining contractual principles is much reduced because a valid contract already subsists as between the parties and the only question is whether and to what extent the law should facilitate the adjustments of their mutual rights and obligations

---

〔146〕 在 Waltons Stores (Interstate) Ltd. v. Maher (1988) 164 CLR 387 先例,法院在争议双方没有法律关系的情况下,判承诺方的言行构成禁反言,有法律后果。

〔147〕 这对合约法是有真正的威胁,因为事实上法院支持了不满足合约成立条件的承诺有法律后果。

in the course of execution.[148] So in a case such as Williams v. Roffey Bros & Nicholls (Contractors) Ltd. (1991) 1 QB 1, it may be that it would have been defensible to allow the plaintiffs to rely on promissory estoppel as a cause of action.[149] Indeed, commentators have pointed out that the doctrine of promissory estoppel was developed specifically to address the problems arising from contract modifications and that being the case, a measured extension of this doctrine in this circumscribed context may be both logical and appropriate.[150]"

除了承诺性禁反言针对合约更改可以用作宝剑外,本章之 12.1.7 段也提到了解决这方面问题的其他办法,如美国《Uniform Commercial Code》已不再要求合约的更改要有约因/对价。

11. 衡平法宽限或承诺性禁反言的先例介绍

近年来涉及衡平法宽限或承诺性禁反言有无数的先例中,其中有:Auckland Harbour Board v. Kaihe (1962) NZLR 68; Woodhouse AC Israel Cocoa Ltd. SA v. Nigerian Produce Marketing Co. Ltd. (1972) 1 Lloyd's Rep. 439 (HL); Finagrain SA Geneva v. P Kruse Hamburg (1976) 2 Lloyd's Rep. 508 (CA); The "Shackleford" (1978) 2 Lloyd's Rep. 154; The "Winson" (1980) 2 Lloyd's Rep. 213; Fontana NV v. Mautner (1980) 254 EG 199; Spence v. Shell UK Ltd. (1980) 256 EG 55 (CA); James v. Heim Gallery (London) Ltd. (1980) 256 EG 819 (CA); Cook Industries Inc. v. Meunerie Liegeois SA (1981) 1 Lloyd's Rep. 359; The "Scaptrade" (1981) 2 Lloyd's Rep. 425; The "Post Chaser" (1981) 2 Lloyd's Rep. 695; The "Athos" (1983) 1 Lloyd's Rep. 127; The "Leonidas D" (1985) 2 Lloyd's Rep. 18 (CA); Mebro Oil SA v. Gatoil International Inc. (1985) 2 Lloyd's Rep. 234; Cie Francaise Importation et de Distribution SA v. Deutsche Continental Handelsgesellschaft (1985) 2 Lloyd's Rep. 592; Drexel Burnham Lambert International v. El Nasr (1986) 1 Lloyd's

---

〔148〕 但如果承诺性禁反言的说法针对更改合约时作为宝剑,并不会有这种威胁。毕竟双方已经存在有效的合约,法院要面对的唯一问题是是否要延伸承诺性禁反言的适用范围,令它可以作为诉因协助调整在合约履行过程中双方的权利责任,破坏合约法规则的风险被大大降低了。

〔149〕 所以在 Williams v. Roffey Bros & Nicholls Ltd. (1991) 1 QB 1 先例中,如果法院判是承诺性禁反言可以作为诉因,也可以理解与接受。但正如在本章之 7.4.5 段提到的,双方在高院没有提出这一争议,所以上诉庭没有针对。

〔150〕 正如学者指出的,承诺性禁反言说法的产生就是为了解决合约更改的问题(Central London Property Trust Ltd. v. High Trees House Ltd. [1947] KB 130 先例),在这种情况下,针对合约更改将承诺性禁反言的适用范围延伸到可以作为诉因,是符合逻辑与适当的。

Rep. 357；Goldsworthy v. Brickell（1987）Ch 378（CA）；The“Kanchenjunga”（1990）1 Lloyd's Rep. 391；The“Superhulls Cover”Case（No. 2）（1990）2 Lloyd's Rep. 431；London and Clydebank Properties v. HM Investment Co.（1993）EGCS 63；The“Chemical Venture”（1993）1 Lloyd's Rep. 508；Credit Suisse v. Allerdale BC（1995）1 Lloyd's Rep. 315；Marc Rich & Co. AG v. Portman（1996）1 Lloyd's Rep. 430；Dun & Bradstreet Software Services（England）Ltd. v. Provident Mutual Life Assurance Association（1997）EWCA Civ 1816；Thameside MBC v. Barlow Securities Group Services Ltd.（2001）EWCA Civ 1；Baird Textile Holdings Ltd. v. Marks & Spencer Plc.（2001）EWCA Civ 274；Soteriou v. Ultrachem Ltd. & Ors（2004）EWHC 983（QB）；Seechurn v. ACE Insurance SA（2002）2 Lloyd's Rep. 390；Thorner v. Major（2009）UKHL 18；The“Zenovia”（2009）2 Lloyd's Rep. 139；Prudential Assurance Co. Ltd. v. Exel UK Ltd. & Anor（2009）EWHC 1350（Ch）；Kim v. Chasewood Park Residents Ltd.（2013）EWCA Civ 239 等先例。笔者从中选择若干介绍，以帮助进一步理解。

11.1 先例之一：The“Winson”

在 The“Winson”（1980）2 Lloyd's Rep. 213 先例中，案情涉及 Lloyd's Open Form（LOF）的救助合约。有关船舶装了一船 37000 吨的小麦从美国运往印度。承租人与货主是印度政府，小麦显然是以 FOB 买入。在租约中，有关运费支付的规定在普遍以 CIF/CFR 进行买卖的今天比较少见，其中 50% 的运费是在签发提单后 7 天支付，40% 的运费在抵达卸港后支付，剩下的 10% 在结算滞期费或速遣费时一起支付。运费的风险由船东承担，显然船东需要对赚取运费的风险投保。1975 年 1 月 21 日，船舶在经过南海时，不幸发生严重的搁浅。于是船东与救助公司签订了 LOF 的救助合约。这个救助合约同时约束船东与货主，船长也有船东的授权与作为货方紧急代理的授权。根据 LOF 把船舶与货物救助到安全港口，救助人就已经履行了合约的责任。救助人并没有成功救起有关的船舶，船东在 1975 年 4 月 24 日通知承租人与货方他放弃（abandon）了这个航次，即租约与提单的运输合约因为这一事故受阻（frustration）。但救助人成功从搁浅的船舶卸下了 15500 吨货物，并用驳船运送到最近的安全港口马尼拉，之后有安排把货物卸下与储存在马尼拉的仓库。显然，救助人为这些安排花了一笔钱，而这笔钱也在事后带来争议，导致双方最后诉讼到了贵族院（[1982] 1 Lloyd's Rep. 117）。这笔钱有争议的原因是货物运到马尼拉后，根据 LOF 的约定以及货方提供的救助担保，救助工作已经告一段落。这笔事后的花费以什么理由向货方要回？

这里就涉及几个争议，包括在 LOF 下，应该是船东或是货方在马尼拉接收这些小麦，毕竟是在航次的半途，船东有将小麦转运到卸港以赚取运费的普通法权利。但在该先例中，船东已经在产生有争议的费用之前就放弃了租约，所以不存在转运赚取运费的问题。第二个争议是救助方有否积极通知船东或货方在马尼拉接收货物。第三个争议是救助方以什么身份花费这笔钱。如果是托管人（bailee）或分托管人（sub-bailee，假设船东才是托管人），这笔花费只要是合理，应该就可以向货方取回，但这个托管关系在小麦运到马尼拉与救助合约履行完毕时就同时终止。[151] 而如果救助方是以没有合约关系的货方紧急代理人身份，因为救助方没有积极通知货方在马尼拉接货，也不存在紧急与必须性，所以也不能成功。第四个也是重要的争议是，货方律师在船东放弃租约时发出的信件是否构成承诺性禁反言。信件的相关部分可节录如下："As regards deductions, apart from the deduction of U. S. $272,410.65, we consider that the sum of U. S. $174,173.91 [– I pause to say that that is the figure with which we are concerned –] should also be deducted from the sound value of the cargo although this sum is to be claimed by your clients from our clients in the arbitration. **We have advised our clients that they are liable for the sum of $174,173.91. In this respect, we write without prejudice.**"（加黑部分是争议是否构成承诺性禁反言的文字）

上述信件的背景是双方在商谈救助成功的小麦的价值（成功救助的15500吨小麦市值约二百多万美元），但救助的价值应该减去必须支付的费用（争议的这笔钱），仲裁庭也会根据这个救助价值裁定在LOF下货方应支付给救助方的奖金。上述加黑的文字显示了货方律师认为货方需要承担这笔争议的费用，并承诺会告知或建议给他的客户（货方）。这被救助方视为构成承诺性禁反言，但上诉庭判是上述加黑的文字只是一个意向（indication），并且明示了是无损害，显然不属于清楚无误的陈述或承诺，不能构成陈述性禁反言。Megaw大法官说："The reason is that what is said to be the promise is not unequivocal. At the best it was an indication by solicitors instructed on behalf of the cargo owners that they, the solicitors, had advised their clients that their clients were liable in law to the salvors in this claim for expenses. But that would not be enough, as I see it, to constitute either an offer which would give rise by acceptance to a contract to pay those sums; nor to a representation which could be treated as giving rise to a promissory estoppel. The matters put forward as constituting representation are not unequivocal."

11.2　先例之二：Drexel Burnham Lambert International v. El Nasr

Drexel Burnham Lambert International v. El Nasr (1986) 1 Lloyd's Rep. 357先例涉及黄金与白银的期货交易。原告Drexel是商品交易经纪人，被告Nasr是他的客户。1983年2月21日，Drexel要求Nasr支付70万美元保证金补仓，但Nasr没有支付。2月23日晚，Drexel与Nasr进行了通话。2月24日，由于市场持续下跌与期间

[151] 该争议上诉到了贵族院，贵族院判是小麦运到马尼拉后，救助方是以免费托管人（gratuitous bailee）的身份安排卸下小麦与储存在仓库，这笔钱可以向货方取回。贵族院没有针对承诺性禁反言，所以上诉庭的判决就是最终的。

进行的交易,Drexel 发电传要求 Nasr 在当天支付 150 万美元,否则就会强制平仓,Nasr 没有支付。双方之后另有一些通讯往来,3 月 4 日,Drexel 强制平仓,并向 Nasr 索赔约 300 万美元的损失。而 Nasr 就抗辩说 Drexel 没有遵守承诺在 2 月 24 日平仓,否则就不会有这 300 万美元的损失,甚至会有结余可以还给 Nasr。

在法院,第一个争议是 Drexel 与 Nasr 之间有否明确同意如果 Nasr 没有在当天支付 150 万美元,Drexel 就必须强制平仓。法院根据双方的口头与文书证据,判是 Nasr 没有给 Drexel 这样的指示,双方也没有明确达成一致。双方在 2 月 23 日的通话中同意的是,如果 Nasr 没有在当天支付 150 万美元,Drexel 可以选择强制平仓。

第二个争议是有否默示条文要求如果 Nasr 没有在当天支付 150 万美元,Drexel 就必须强制平仓。法院判是没有这样的默示条文,因为首先无法通过商业上有效力的考验(business efficacy)。[152] 即使没有这样的默示条文,双方之间的合约依然有效力与可行。如果 Nasr 想要在 2 月 24 日平仓,只需要做出指示。而对于是否有这样的交易习惯(custom),双方的专家证人同意没有交易习惯是如果经纪人威胁说要强制平仓,就必须这样做。毕竟市场变化很快,如果暴升,可能已经不再需要支付保证金补仓。

第三个争议是 Drexel 在 2 月 24 日的电传是否构成承诺性禁反言。在稍早已经提到,衡平法宽限或承诺性禁反言与合约更改的区别主要就是是否存在约因/对价,而两者对承诺基本要求一致。由于法院已经在第一个争议中判是不存在明确的陈述或承诺,因此只是根据这一点,就不会构成承诺性禁反言。Drexel 在 2 月 24 日的电传只是一个威胁(threat),而不是承诺(promise),并且双方都知道这一点。不构成承诺性禁反言的另一个原因是,根据权威的《Chitty on Contracts》一书,要构成承诺性禁反言,必须是承诺方承诺不会行使他的严格法律权利。而在该先例中,Drexel 并不是"承诺"不会行使他的权利,而是"承诺"会行使他强制平仓的权利,因此,不应该构成承诺性禁反言。

对该先例中,笔者想要强调的一点是有否默示条文的争议。双方提供了专家证据以争辩是否有这样的交易习惯,法院得出结论是没有。而如果涉及的是其他交易,根据专家证据,法院判是有交易习惯是如果一方做出威胁,另一方一旦不满足一定的条件,他就会行使权利,而在另一方确实没有满足这些条件时,他就必须行使权力,很有可能这个威胁也会被判是属于明确无误的陈述或承诺,并在满足其他要求的情况下,构成承诺性禁反言。

11.3 先例之三:The "Kanchenjunga"

The "Kanchenjunga" (1990) 1 Lloyd's Rep. 391 先例是针对弃权与禁反言的一个十分重要的贵族院先例。特别是针对"因选择而弃权"(waiver by election)与"因宽限而弃权"(waiver by forbearance)或承诺性禁反言之间的异同,该先例是主要权

---

[152] 可见杨良宜《合约的解释:规则与应用》一书第七章之 4.4.2 段。

威先例。该先例涉及8个连续航次的油轮租约。相关的Kanchenjunga轮是20万吨级油轮,属于印度船东。装港是承租人指定的波斯湾的一个安全港口。租约是在1978年8月订立,当时伊朗与伊拉克虽然关系紧张,但没有战事,所以租约允许去的装港包括个别伊朗港口,如Kharg Island港。到了最后一个航次,时为1980年11月19日,该船舶被分租的承租人下令前往Kharg Island港装货。但当时两伊战争已经开始,伊朗的Kharg Island港经常被伊拉克派出的飞机轰炸。在后来的仲裁中,仲裁庭认定承租人指定Kharg Island港时,该港口是不安全,即承租人违反了租约中要指定安全港口的承诺。但印度船东并没有对承租人的违约做出抗拒或有所保留,而是要求船长把船舶开往Kharg Island港,并在11月23日抵达后递交了通知书,之后也多次做出要求承租人尽早安排靠泊装船等言行。船东是在11月25日因为船长告知Kharg Island港不断有高射炮的射击,才首次在与承租人的通讯中提出港口不安全。而到了11月30日,船舶才被告知可以靠泊装货,但由于坏天气的延误而靠不了泊。期间,伊拉克飞机轰炸,船长起锚把船舶开走,之后也没有再回到Kharg Island港装货。之后船东与承租人之间的通讯往来中,船东要求承租人重新指定港口,而承租人坚持船舶返回Kharg Island港,并表示有其他船舶在Kharg Island港装货。到了12月中,双方各自委任了律师互相指称对方违约/毁约(repudiatory breach),接受并终止合约。

这个重要先例涉及很多其他方面的争议,已在本书多处有所分析。双方主要的争议是船东没有抗议地履行承租人的命令去一个不安全港口,构成弃权(放弃抗拒去该港装货)与/或禁反言(言行构成了去该港装货的承诺)。针对承诺性禁反言,主要是船长一连串的言行是否是清楚无误的陈述或承诺。

针对租约(不论是期租或程租)的安全港口问题,船东对承租人做出的命令是否需要尽快履行或拒绝履行,这在较早的The "Stork" (1955) 1 Lloyd's Rep. 349先例已经有针对。上诉庭是不认为船东履行承租人的命令去一个不安全的港口,而事后发觉危险才拒绝进港或离开会构成弃权或禁反言,否则就会导致船东在接到命令之后,要先派人去港口调查方方面面是否安全以确定承租人的命令是否是违约与不能遵从,而在调查期间船舶就需要等待,这会造成不必要的延误与影响航运操作。Morris大法官说:"It was submitted on behalf of the charterers that if they named a place to which the ship should go, there was no obligation on the ship to proceed thither until such time as those responsible for the ship decided that the place was safe. Alternatively stated, the argument was presented that a nomination by charterers must be either good or bad; that if bad it could be rejected; that if accepted there could not later be complaint made in regard to the place; and that shipowners would be estopped from making any such complaint. I am unable to accept this reasoning, which seems to me to give insufficient weight to the respective obligations undertaken by the parties to the contract. If the reasoning were sound the result would in practice be highly inconvenient to all con-

cerned. Indeed, it might involve that a ship should not obey an order to proceed to a place without sending an advance survey party and receiving a report from them."（加黑部分是笔者的强调）

仲裁庭判是船长与船东的言行不属于清楚无误的承诺，不会构成承诺性禁反言。但到了高院，Hobhouse 大法官有不同的看法，说："Owners contended, and the arbitrators implicitly found, that there was nothing unequivocal about owners' conduct. **I disagree**. In the context of what had passed between the parties previously, owners' communication to charterers on Nov. 21（这是承租人做出命令去 Kharg Island 港的一天）is correctly characterized as an acceptance of the order, not a mere compliance with it. But then owners went further. A notice of readiness was served. This must import that owners are saying that they are ready and willing to load at Kharg Island. Then again on Nov. 25, owners were still saying that the vessel was available to load and called upon charterers to arrange priority berthing. The next day owners referred to the running of lay – time. There was nothing equivocal about owners' conduct. They were dealing with charterers on the basis that the loading port nomination had been made and that Kharg Island was that port."

后来的上诉庭（[1989] 1 Lloyd's Rep. 354）与贵族院（[1990] 1 Lloyd's Rep. 391）也支持了这个看法。在该先例中，特殊的案情是在 11 月 21 日时，同一公司/船东还有其他船舶在 Kharg Island 港，对 Kharg Island 港的情况完全了解，所以船东无条件接受命令，让船舶前往 Kharg Island 港是在了解情况下的有意识决定。在笔者看来，法院判决带来的教训是如果船东怀疑对方有违约的可能，但不想也不敢马上做出决定拒绝履行，或需要调查或进一步明确等，最好在决定履行（或继续履行）时向承租人清楚说明保留合约权利（without prejudice），这至少可以显示并非无条件履行（或继续履行）。虽然这不是"万灵药"，[153]但只要船东不要太过犹豫不决与拖太长时间（时间拖得长通常也表示双方的交往变多，容易被挑出有问题的言行，说是前后言行完全不一致），还是可以保护船东。特别是如果船东不是非常了解当时的情况，成功保护船东的机会就更高。这个做法也适用在任何其他类别的合约，即无辜方对违约方也应该这样行事。

11.4 先例之四：The "Chemical Venture"

The "Chemical Venture"（1993）1 Lloyd's Rep. 508 先例的案情与上一小段介绍的 The "Kanchenjunga"（1990）1 Lloyd's Rep. 391 先例十分类似，所以一并介绍。在该先例中，承租人指示船东前往 Mina Al Ahmadi 港装货。当时正值两伊战争，伊朗频繁地轰炸前往 Mina Al Ahmadi 港必经的海峡区域，因此承租人在指示船舶前往 Mina Al Ahmadi 港时就应该知道该港是不安全，这是违反了租约规定。之后船舶被

[153] 这可见本章之 6.5.5 段。

伊朗的飞机轰炸受损,船东向承租人索赔这方面的损失。但承租人争辩说,船东清楚无误地陈述或承诺他不会将前往 Mina Al Ahmadi 港的指示视为违反租约,并因此构成了衡平法宽限或承诺性禁反言。法院最终支持了承租人的立场,根据 The "Kanchenjunga"(1990)1 Lloyd's Rep. 391 先例中,船东与船长都可以拒绝在他们认为有危险的港口装货。但在该先例中,船东的第一封电传说:"... crew members refused to go to Kuwait and in order to induce them to make the trip we are prepared to offer them war bonus in cash. . . which will be for your account. Please confirm your agreement by return telex enabling us to negotiate with officers/crew... for their agreement."

船东的第二封电传说:"Regret all crew refused to go to Kuwait in spite of our intervention and persuasions."

船东的第三封电传说:"... have further discussed with master and crew member and after long hard struggle we are pleased to be able to have at last convinced [them] to go to Kuwait in exchange for [a cash bonus]... Please confirm charterers agree to pay for such war bonus so that we can wrap up a deal with all serving on board."

船东的第四封电传说:"We leave the matter to you. Please contact master directly as this is a matter between you and the ship crew ... For your guidance. under clause 36 of the Charter – party, shipcrew have right to refuse to go to warlike area."

最终承租人同意支付船员奖金并确认了开往 Mina Al Ahmadi 港的指令。

Gatehouse 大法官认为,虽然船东没有直接说放弃船舶因轰炸而损坏索赔的权利,但总体解释船东说的话(或是没说的话,如说明抗议下或明示保留权利[154]),一个合理人士处于承租人的位置都会认为船东的言行是清楚无误的陈述或承诺,可以构成衡平法宽限或承诺性禁反言,说:

"It is self – evident that the owners did not say expressly that they would waive their right to claim damages should the vessel be attacked en route for the Kuwait terminal. But construing the telex exchanges objectively (as I think the Court is required to do) I conclude that a reasonable person in the charterers' position would understand the owners' various messages as conveying the following: — (i) That although cl. 36 conferred a right on either the master or owners or both to refuse to go to a port which they considered unsafe, only the master and his crew were so refusing: the owners were not; (ii) that the owners were taking the charterers' side in trying to persuade the crew to accept charterers' order. The charterers looked to the owners in the first place to persuade the crew to accept the order and, later, to try and renegotiate the claim downwards to minimize the bonus payment; (iii) that the owners eventually asked the charterers to deal di-

[154] 一有了这种明示的保留或抗议,通常就很难说船东的言行是清楚无误了,这可见本章之6.5段。

rectly with the master 'as this is a matter between you and the shipcrew.' (iv) The owners gave no hint that they themselves regarded a Kuwait terminal as unsafe and **they did not reserve their rights.**[155]

So it seems to me that by a combination of what they said, and more particularly what they did not say taken in context, **owners made an unequivocal representation**. They either waived their right to contend that charterers were in breach or they were estopped from so contending. Mr. Hallgarten QC(承租人的代表大律师) indeed argues that the exchanges of telexes amounted to an agreement that Mina Al Almadi was a port to which charterers might properly direct the vessel; an agreement supported by the consideration of some $34,000 – odd which charterers actually paid[156]....

I have hesitated in coming to this conclusion... But if I am right in construing the telex exchanges objectively... Lord Goff in The 'Kanchenjunga' had said this: 'Because the arbitrators did not approach the issue of election correctly they failed to consider the correct questions. In particular they did not ask themselves whether there had been the necessary unequivocal representation by the owners. It is true that they did ask themselves whether there had been the necessary 'clear and unequivocal promise' when considering the alternative principle of equitable estoppel. They held that there was not, on the basis that the mere acceptance of orders without protest does not amount to such a promise. As a general position this is no doubt correct.'

I respectfully adopt that.[157] It would seem to be objectively right that the mere acceptance of orders without more does not constitute an unequivocal representation. But here, of course, there is considerably more. In the circumstances, though with some hesitation, I think that the charterers' argument is right[158]..."(加黑部分是笔者的强调)

因此,Gatehouse 大法官判是船东的言行构成承诺性禁反言,不能索赔因轰炸而带来的损失。

11.5 先例之五:The "Superhulls Cover" Case (No.2)

在 The "Superhulls Cover" Case (No.2) (1990) 2 Lloyd's Rep. 431 先例中,案

---

[155] 这部分的判决是说总体与客观来看所有的电文来往,法院认定了船东向承租人做出了清楚无误的陈述或承诺。

[156] 承租人的替代争议之一是双方对于去这个不安全港口达成了新协议,承租人做出的约因/对价是支付34000 美元的船员奖金。这种协议也等于是"更改合约"(variation),经常会与弃权与禁反言一并提出,可见本书第三章第2段。

[157] Gatehouse 大法官在弃权与禁反言方面是跟从了 The "Kanchenjunga" (1990) 1 Lloyd's Rep. 391 先例的判法。

[158] Gatehouse 大法官同意如果只是保持沉默依照对方的命令进入不安全港口,这个行动不构成所要求的清楚无误的陈述或承诺。但在本先例中,船东做多了很多事情(与发出了很多电文),这样法院就有了不同的看法与判决。

情涉及船厂投保造船风险（builder's risks），有关的英国船厂与劳合社的一些保险人和英国保险公司有一个开口/预约保单（open cover）。但该船厂后来取得了三艘天然气（LNG）船舶的建造合约，而这些船舶非常昂贵，每一艘都价值上亿美元。这导致原来开口/预约保单的保险人无法接受承保所有的金额/风险，而需要被告的保险经纪人安排再保（excess loss policy）。这个再保的安排也被称为 Superhulls Cover。但再保的保单中有一条条文是保险人与船厂之间的保单没有的，这就是承保的期限是在船舶开始建造后的 48 个月。这在再保的保单中是写为："PERIOD Continuous open cover commencing 1st January 1974 and/or as original subject to 60 days cancellation clause to any anniversary date (not to apply to risks for which reinsureds are already committed or which are already ceded hereunder). **Risks attaching basis for period as original but not exceeding** 48 **months any one risk.**"（加黑部分就是 48 个月的承保期限。）

事后在建造的过程中船舶出事，导致整个造船工程被放弃，而出事时已经过了 48 个月。英国船厂向保险人提出索赔，而保险人根据他们之间的保单也做出了和解的赔偿（settlement payment）。但保险人向再保人索赔超出部分的损失（excess loss），再保人就以这 48 个月承保期限的条文做出抗拒。在这个诉讼中，Phillips 大法官针对这个争议先做出了判决，判是再保人胜诉。于是在该先例中，主要针对的是保险人指称保险经纪人没有按照保险合约进行再保，也没有向保险人指出这个多出来的条文，这是保险经纪人的疏忽。显然如果当时保险经纪人向保险人指出有这样的条文，保险人也可以做出应对以降低风险，如对于超出 48 个月的工程只承保份额较少的风险。

在这个先例中，弃权与禁反言是保险经纪人提出的主要抗辩。因为保险人与保险经纪人之间的很多文件往来，包括再保保单，都显示了有这 48 个月的承保期限的条文，但保险人接受并且没有提出异议。这个先例在两个方面做出了有趣的针对，第一个是根据 The "Kanchenjunga" (1990) 1 Lloyd's Rep. 391 先例中，如何将弃权与禁反言做出区分；第二个是保险人在双方的文件往来中对 48 个月的承保期限没有警惕甚至是默认的行为，能否构成弃权或禁反言。

针对第一个方面，由于 Goff 勋爵在 The "Kanchenjunga" 先例判是因选择而弃权需要弃权方知道自己的权利，因宽限而弃权则不需要，所以 Phillips 大法官首要的任务是要认定弃权方的保险人是否知道自己的权利去做出默认而构成弃权。根据双方的证人证言与反盘问，Phillips 大法官认定这个承保期限的条文，即使是保险人看到也不一定会了解该条文的正确解释与会带来的后果，说："I am not persuaded that ... each of the insured must have read the 48 month clause, duly considered its meaning and reached the conclusion... There are a number of different implications that might be drawn from the fact that each insurer signed the order letter and took no point on the 48 month clause. These include the following: (i) The insurer noticed the clause and correctly interpreted it as a cut – off, but did not think this was cause for concern because, for example, (a) he thought 48 months a sufficient protection against overrun; or (b) thought that if necessary the reinsurers would extend the period of cover; or (c) wrongly assumed that the original cover was subject to a similar clause. (ii) The insurer noticed the clause and, incorrectly interpreted it as a limitation on attachments, which was not of significance. (iii) The insurer noticed the clause, but did not apply his mind to what it meant – perhaps wrongly assuming that whatever it meant there was a similar clause in the original cover. (iv) The insurer did not notice the clause at all."

这样就表示保险人不一定知道这48个月的条文,而即使知道,也不一定知道它的正确解释或后果,所以不能构成弃权。Phillips大法官是这样说:"Mr. Griffiths(保险经纪人代表大律师)might have contended that the knowledge necessary to found a common law waiver was simply knowledge of the existence of the 48 month clause – not knowledge of its legal effect. He did not do so, perhaps because Mr. Sumption(保险人代表大律师)had preempted such an argument by referring me to Peyman v. Lanjani (1985) 1 Ch. 457. That was another case of election. The Court of Appeal held that, in the absence of estoppel, a waiver by election involved not merely knowledge of the facts giving rise to the right waived, but knowledge of the right to which those facts gave rise."

Phillips大法官在该先例接下来分析是否构成衡平法禁反言/衡平法宽限时说,必须要先满足三个要件:"(i) an unequivocal representation made by words or conduct that a party does not intend to enforce their strict legal rights; (ii) the other party has acted upon that representation; (iii) it would be inequitable in all the circumstances to permit the first party to re – assert their rights."

Phillips大法官逐个分析之后,发觉没有一个要件能满足,于是总结说:"In summary, I find that the brokers have failed to establish any one of the three elements that they set out to prove in order to make good their defence of equitable estoppel."

首先是第一个要件,这与稍早提到第二个方面保险人没有在双方的文件往来中对48个月的承保期限有所警惕甚至是默认有密切关系。保险经纪人声称保险人签署再保保单并对再保保单十分满意的言行是构成了明示的陈述,说:"In the present case the brokers can point to no express representation on the part of the insurers that they would not enforce their vested right to claim damages for the brokers' breach of duty. They rely on the insurers' conduct in signing and returning the order letters and accepting the cover notes and contract wording as conduct which implicitly indicated an abandonment of such right. The insurers' conduct, say the brokers, indicated that they were satisfied with the reinsurance cover that we had procured. The claim for damages that the insurers now pursue is irreconcilable with such satisfaction."

但这不被 Phillips 大法官接受,说:"The conduct of the insurers did not unequivocally represent, when viewed objectively, that they were aware of the existence and nature of the limitation of cover that had been inserted without their instructions and that the reinsurance was nonetheless satisfactory to them."

这里可以进一步解释,保险经纪人,尤其是有名气与有经验的保险经纪人,与代理人不同,雇用他的客户可以依赖经纪人的专业知识执行他的指令,而无须仔细检查自己的指令有否被全面执行。这也在该先例中被提到,说:"In my opinion, when a broker is employed to effect an insurance, especially when the broker employed is a person of repute and experience, the client is entitled to rely upon the broker carrying out his instructions, and is not bound to examine the documents drawn up in performance of those instructions and see whether his instructions have, in fact, been carried out by the broker."

在这样的背景之下,加上 48 个月的条文的法律后果不明确,Phillips 大法官判保险人的言行不属于明确无误的陈述。但如果案情稍加变化,是保险经纪人已经明示指出该条文,保险人的陈述就可能会变为明确无误,Phillips 大法官举例说:"It would have been open to the brokers to have written to the insurers saying, we regret that contrary to the information that we gave you and the instructions we received the cover that we have procured is subject to a 48 month cut – off. Is this satisfactory? Had they done so I have little doubt that they would have received replies that were unequivocal."

另在 General Accident Fire and Life Assurance Corporation Ltd. v. Minet (1942) 72 Lloyd's Rep. 48 先例中,案情与本案十分类似,Atkinson 大法官判是:"I think that, if I may so, with all respect, is very good law and very good sense. It may very well be that if the defect is so obvious that it springs to the eye and had been indeed observed by the employer, use might be made of the point ..."

所以在该先例中,Phillips 大法官根据 Atkinson 大法官的判决,说如果再保保单中有明显的错漏,是保险经纪人不提也可以马上看到(如三艘天然气船舶,只再保了两艘),同样的案情也会构成弃权或禁反言。Phillips 大法官的说法可节录如下:"If there is an obvious defect in the cover, as Mr. Justice Atkinson observed, a waiver or an estoppel may result. But I can see no justification for imposing on the client a duty owed to the broker to check the suitability of the cover obtained with a degree of care similar to that which the broker is paid to employ when obtaining it."

而如果双方的关系不涉及一方依赖另一方的专业知识,解释言行是否是清楚无误的陈述时,要求会更宽松。如在本章之 3.1 段提到的 Bremer v. Vanden (1978) 2 Lloyd's Rep. 109 先例中,贵族院判是即使卖方的延期付运通知有缺陷(装港没有明确与/或给出的时间太晚),买方接受与没有抗议就已经构成弃权,后来卖方做出划归通知时,买方就不能以合约规定的付运期已过为由拒绝。

由此看来，对一些重要的文件如合约或通知，还是要有警觉，不能不看，否则不小心就会构成弃权或禁反言，十分危险。

11.6　先例之六：Commonwealth of Australia v. Verwayen 澳大利亚先例

有关禁反言（特别是承诺性禁反言）在澳大利亚有一些与英国法律不同的发展，〔159〕主要涉及两个澳大利亚高院（即最高院）的先例。第一个是 Waltons Stores (Interstate) Ltd. v. Maher (1988) 164 CLR 387 先例中，案情会在本章之 12.3.1 段介绍。

另一个是 Commonwealth of Australia v. Verwayen (1990) 170 CLR 394 先例中，案情是在 1964 年 2 月 10 日晚，澳大利亚海军的两艘军舰相撞，Verwayen 先生与其他同袍在事故中受伤。事故的原因是其中一艘军舰或者两艘军舰上的操作人员的疏忽。根据当时 Windeyer 大法官在 Parker v. The Commonwealth (1965) 112 CLR 295 先例的附带意见（obiter），出于公共政策的考虑，武装部队中的一员不能因其他成员在执行任务时疏忽而给自己带来的伤害获得政府的侵权赔偿。这也解释了为什么 Verwayen 先生在当时没有采取任何法律行动。但在将近二十年后，法院在 Groves v. The Commonwealth (1982) 150 CLR 113 先例将侵权法律适用的范围扩展到武装部队成员执行任务时疏忽的情况。因此，Verwayen 先生（与他的同袍在其他案件）向政府提起索赔，并在 1984 年 11 月 2 日递交起诉书。在政府 1985 年 3 月 14 日递交的答辩书中，政府承认了责任，但不承认 Verwayen 先生因为事故受伤或蒙受损失。政府没有提出时效已过的抗辩，也没有抗辩说政府对 Verwayen 没有小心谨慎的责任（duty of care）。而在双方的通讯往来中，澳大利亚政府的律师曾在 1985 年 1 月 25 日提到政府会承认责任并放弃时效已过的抗辩，并在之后书面确认。在递交抗辩之后，在双方对责任没有争议的情况下，政府的律师也与 Verwayen 先生的律师多次一起申请，要求法院加快聆讯（an expedited hearing）损失赔偿的争议。政府也多次表示不会争辩责任与依赖时效已过的抗辩，虽然这些陈述很多并不是直接对 Verwayen 先生或他的律师说的。但在 1985 年 11 月 27 日，政府在律师的建议下写信给 Verwayen 先生寻求双方达成和解协议时，说："As you have pointed out, the Commonwealth has admitted negligence and is not pressing the statutory limitation period as a defence. Nevertheless, it still expects claimants to show that they have suffered injury ... and to prove the extent of their injuries and resultant loss, in order to justify an award of damages."

但事实上在 1985 年 11 月左右，政府已经决定改变在这起事故相关的诉讼中的立场，即提出时效已过与对 Verwayen 先生没有小心谨慎的责任的抗辩。因此，政府向法院申请修改（amend）答辩书，虽然当时距离开庭时间已经不多。法院同意了政府的申请，并命令政府负责 Verwayen 先生因为该修改答辩书的申请而产生与浪费的费用。1986 年 5 月 29 日，政府递交了修改后的答辩书。1986 年 6 月 5 日，Verwayen

〔159〕　这已经在本章之 7.4 段提到，并在本章稍后的 12.3.2 段有详论。

先生递交了回复书，声称政府放弃了时效已过的抗辩，或是政府被禁反言（应该是承诺性禁反言）而不能依赖时效已过的抗辩。

澳大利亚法院的不同法官之间对这个争议（主要是政府能否依赖时效已过的抗辩，因为时效已过是整个诉讼成败的决定性问题）的看法也有很大分歧。在一审，法院判是政府胜诉。但在上诉庭以二比一的多数判决被推翻，认为政府被禁反言不能依赖时效已过的抗辩。而到了高院，法院以四比三的多数判决驳回了上诉，但做出多数判决的四位大法官的观点也不一致。

首先笔者要指出，这个案件被法院搞得复杂了，因为原本可以是否允许修改文书请求的角度处理。一般来说，法院或仲裁庭允许诉讼方修改文书请求（amendment to pleadings），除非会对另一方造成不利（prejudice）。在 Ketteman v. Hansel Properties Ltd.（1987）AC 189 先例中，被告在开庭的总结陈词中要求修改文书请求，依赖时效已过的抗辩。但这不被法院接受，Griffiths 勋爵说："I have never in my experience at the Bar or on the Bench heard of an application to amend to plead a limitation defence during the course of the final speeches. Such an application would, in my view, inevitably have been rejected as far too late. A defence of limitation permits a defendant to raise a procedural bar which prevents the plaintiff from pursuing the action against him. It has nothing to do with the merits of the claim which may all lie with the plaintiff; but as a matter of public policy Parliament has provided that a defendant should have the opportunity to avoid meeting a stale claim. The choice lies with the defendant and if he wishes to avail himself of the statutory defence it must be pleaded. A defendant does not invariably wish to rely on a defence of limitation and may prefer to contest the issue on the merits. If, therefore, no plea of limitation is raised in the defence the plaintiff is entitled to assume that the defendant does not wish to rely upon a time bar but prefers the court to adjudicate on the issues raised in the dispute between the parties. If both parties on this assumption prepare their cases to contest the factual and legal issues arising in the dispute and they are litigated to the point of judgment, the issues will by this time have been fully investigated and a plea of limitation no longer serves its purpose as a procedural bar."

可以理解这种是否允许修改文书请求所针对的"不利"是指程序上，如开庭后才提出修改的申请，而这个申请原本可以更早提出。如果允许修改，就会令对方蒙受不利或损害，是申请方即使承担因修改而浪费的费用也不足以弥补的，如对整个诉讼的延误，而对方等不了这么久或案情本是要求尽快有决定（如工程进行了一半，有了决定才会进行下去）。但在该澳大利亚高院先例中，没有涉及程序上的不利，政府在开庭前提出修改，而修改主要是法律争议的问题，一般不影响开庭与开庭准备，Verwayen 先生也有足够时间递交回复书。所以，不得不搞得复杂要针对弃权与禁反言的问题，从而变为澳大利亚针对这方面最重要的先例之一，也可以理解。

以下会针对该先例是否满足弃权与禁反言（主要是承诺性禁反言）的要件，逐个进行讨论。首先是双方存在法律关系的要件,[160]一审法院的判法是与英国法律地位一致,认为诉讼双方不存在法律关系,所以承诺性禁反言不适用,政府胜诉。但这个判决是在 Waltons Stores (Interstate) Ltd. v. Maher 先例之前,而根据后者的判决,双方不需要存在法律关系,也可以适用承诺性禁反言。之后上诉庭与最高院都跟从了 Waltons Stores (Interstate) Ltd. v. Maher 先例,判是双方是否存在法律关系与承诺性禁反言适用不相关。

更为重要也最有争议的是,Verwayen 先生有否依赖政府的承诺并因此蒙受损害。上诉庭少数意见的 King 大法官认为,Verwayen 先生获得因为该修改答辩书(amendment to defence)的申请而产生与浪费的费用已经是足够的衡平法救济。高院的 Mason 大法官与 McHugh 大法官也同样认为,政府是在 Verwayen 先生递交起诉书之后才承诺不依赖时效已过的抗辩,所以,Verwayen 先生提起诉讼时没有依赖政府的承诺。而政府之后改变主意,撤回承诺并申请修改抗辩书后,Verwayen 先生获得因为该修改答辩书的申请而产生与浪费的费用已经是足够的衡平法救济。毕竟,衡平法是寻求最低程度的救济。[161] 此外,承诺性禁反言的救济不是执行承诺(针对构成合约承诺的救济),而是让因为依赖对方的承诺而蒙受损害的一方回复到原本的地位。所以,针对合约承诺与禁反言的承诺的损失,法律是有不同对待。

显然 Verwayen 先生提出了补偿费用不是足够的救济,因为还有其他方面的损害,包括丧失了胜诉与合理寻求庭外和解的机会、身体状况变差、诉讼的压力与不必要的期待等。在高院的多数意见中,有两位大法官根据弃权的说法认为不必针对有否损害。但另两位根据承诺性禁反言的说法的大法官,认为 Verwayen 确实有蒙受这些损害,其中 Dowson 大法官说:"There can be no question that the respondent (Verwayen 先生) acted upon the assumption that the appellant (政府) would not exercise its right to claim that the action was statute barred. No doubt the respondent was, or could be, compensated by an award of costs for any actual expense incurred as a result of the appellant's failure to plead the statute of limitations at the beginning. But the real detriment to the respondent was that he was induced by the assumption that the appellant would not insist upon the statute to allow the litigation to proceed for more than a year without taking any steps to bring it to a conclusion by way of settlement (较早的案情显示双方曾有过和解的谈判与尝试) or, if necessary, withdrawal. Furthermore, as Lord Griffiths observed in Ketteman v. Hansel Properties, at p 220, 'justice cannot always be measured in terms of money' and the strain of litigation, particularly where that litigation is between a natural person and a defendant with the resources of the Commonwealth, is not to be underestimated. By falsely raising his hopes, the appellant led the respondent to

---

[160] 这在本章第 5 段有介绍。

[161] 见本章第 9 段。

continue with the litigation and forgo any exploration of the possibility of settlement thereby subjecting himself to a prolonged period of stress in an action in which the damages claimed were for, amongst other things, a high level of anxiety and depression. I would hold that the appellant was estopped from insisting upon the statute of limitations, and would observe that the equity raised by the appellant's conduct was such, in my view, that it could only be accounted for by the fulfilment of the assumption upon which the respondent's actions were based."

但三位少数意见的大法官有不同看法。正如稍早提到衡平法救济是追求最低程度的救济,Brenna 大法官认为刚刚提到的这些损害是政府撤回承诺,坚持时效已过的抗辩而导致的损害,而不是 Verwayen 先生因为依赖政府一度做出的不会依赖时效已过的抗辩的承诺而导致的损害,因此不相关。并且在该先例中,禁止政府依赖时效已过的抗辩相对于 Verwayen 先生因依赖而蒙受的损害是不成比例的救济。Brenna 大法官说:

"Those 'detriments' flowed from the defendant's failure to fulfil its promise, but not from any act done or omission made by the plaintiff in reliance on the making of the promise. They are not relevant detriments.

The only relevant detriment which the plaintiff suffered, according to his pleadings and the argument of his counsel, was financial loss in continuing with the action until the defence was amended to deny negligence and to raise s. 5(6) of the Limitation Act. In these circumstances, to hold the Commonwealth to its promise to admit liability in negligence would be to go beyond the minimum equity."

McHugh 大法官认为 Verwayen 先生可能蒙受这方面非金钱的损害,但这可以通过要求政府赔偿来做出救济,[162] 而无须禁止政府依赖时效已过的抗辩,说:"It is possible that the plaintiff has suffered more worry and stress as the result of the assurance of the Commonwealth than he would otherwise have suffered if the Commonwealth had not given the assurance which it did. But the plaintiff led no evidence to this effect, and I do not think that it can be inferred. In any event, even if the plaintiff had sought to make out a case along these lines, his equity would be satisfied by an award of compensation for that additional worry and stress and would not require that the Commonwealth be estopped from relying on the Limitation Act."

而 Mason 大法官则认为这方面的损害属于臆猜(speculation),Verwayen 先生也没有提供任何证据,说:"However, as far as the respondent's emotional condition is concerned, it is sheer speculation to suggest that his reliance on the Commonwealth's actions after commencement of the action caused any deterioration of that condition. Evi-

[162] 这种非金钱(non-pecuniary)的赔偿在杨良宜的《损失赔偿与救济》一书第二章第 15 段有介绍。

dence of detriment must be affirmatively demonstrated..."

11.7 先例之七:Seechurn v. ACE Insurance SA

在 Seechurn v. ACE Insurance SA (2002) 2 Lloyd's Rep. 390 先例中,也可以显示现在的法院开始对不同类别的弃权或禁反言进行区分,并根据不同的要件,分析个别案情的言行是否构成禁反言与构成哪一类的禁反言。在该先例中,原告被保险人将所有弃权与禁反言的类别一并提出,但法院对这些弃权与禁反言的类别进行区分,认为在该先例中只可能适用承诺性禁反言,并进一步分析究竟能否满足构成承诺性禁反言的要件。这可以节录上诉庭 Ward 大法官的说法:"It is probably unnecessary for the purposes of this judgment to explore what differences, if any, there may be between estoppel by representation, promissory estoppel, estoppel by convention, waiver or what Chitty on Contract paragraph 3 - 080 calls 'forbearance in equity'. It may still be controversial whether or not 'all these can now be seen to merge into one general principle shorn of limitations'[163], as Lord Denning M. R. suggested in Amalgamated Investments and Property Co. Ltd. v. Texas Commerce International Bank [1982] Q. B. 84, 122 but counsel have not invited us to enter into that debate and I do not propose to do so. Since the essence of the claimant's case is that the course of correspondence contained some assurance by the defendant not to raise a limitation defence, it seems to me that it is most likely to be a case of promissory estoppel for there is no representation of existing fact and no shared assumption supporting an estoppel by representation or by convention respectively. Both counsel agree that the judge was correct to apply, as the locus classicus, the decision in Hughes v. Metropolitan Railway Co. (1877) 2 App. Cas. 439, and it is worth quoting fully from the speech of Lord Cairns at p. 488... Subsequent authorities serve to highlight some of the important elements. First, the promise (or representation) must be clear and unequivocal.... It is, in my judgment, important to emphasise that the unequivocal unambiguous promise or representation has to be that the party did not intend to enforce his strict legal rights. ... It is common ground that the promise or representation must be made intending to affect the legal relations between the parties and the promisee or representee must rely upon it and alter his position."

该先例的案情涉及原告被保险人在 1988 年 9 月 16 日乘坐巴士时发生意外,向被告保险公司索赔意外导致他无法继续工作造成的损失。这里涉及两个人身伤亡保单,一个价值 25 万英镑,另一个价值 15 万英镑。双方一直在进行谈判,希望达成和解。在谈判过程中,也因为各种原因延误,如被保险人委任的第一个律师死亡,需要更换律师。双方无法达成和解的主要原因是双方的医疗报告有分歧,被保险人的医疗报告说被保险人伤势很严重,而保险公司的医疗报告则说被保险人的伤势并不严

[163] 这方面,特别是有关澳大利亚法律的不同说法,可见本章之 12.3.2 段。

重。1995 年 4 月 13 日，保险公司要求被保险人以新仪器再做一次检查，说："In order to give your client the benefit of the doubt our client is prepared to go to the expense of carrying out further medical examination. To this effect therefore we would request that your client be examined by an orthopaedic consultant and also undergo examination with a Dynatron 2000 machine which will be able to confirm the level of his disability."

但被保险人拒绝接受检查。1995 年 5 月 9 日，距离时效还有 4 个月时，保险公司写信给被保险人，提出已支付的 2 万英镑就是最终的赔偿。而如果被保险人要求更多的赔偿，就必须接受新仪器的检查，说："On the basis of those reports your client was paid £ 20,000 which we considered to be a satisfactory settlement under the terms of his policy with our client. However, if it is your case that Mr Seechurn's physical disabilities will continue then before our clients are prepared to make any further payment they wish him to undergo the medical examination referred to in our letter of 13th April. Our client is not attempting to avoid their obligations under the policy but merely wish to determine that the amount they are required to pay is in accordance with the policy and is reasonable. As you will appreciate should Mr Seechurn decide to litigate then he will have to undergo further medical examinations in any event and if he does commence legal proceedings prematurely then we reserve the right to bring the contents of this letter to the attention of the court."

双方之后仍有通讯往来，1995 年 8 月 16 日，保险公司写信给被保险人再次表示现在双方的医疗报告有矛盾，如果被保险人接受新仪器的检查，双方根据新的医疗报告是很可能达成和解协议，说："... We would reiterate that neither we nor our clients wish to be difficult nor do we intend to cast any dispersions [sic] upon your own medical evidence save that we will say that the evidence is inconsistent and in part contradictory. If you submit to the further medical examinations that we have requested then we believe that it may well be possible for this matter to be concluded amicably once the results are known."

正如在本章第 6 段所讲，高院判是保险公司的上述言行构成清楚无误的陈述或承诺，表明其会继续谈判，而不会依赖时效已过的抗辩。但上诉庭认为上述言行不构成保险公司清楚无误放弃时效已过的抗辩的陈述或承诺，说：

"I do not disagree with the judge's conclusions that the defendant was intending to keep the door open and was promising that it would continue to look at and consider Mr Seechurn's claims over and above £ 20,000 that had already been paid. That, in my judgment, is not enough to enable the claimant to establish a promise of the kind which satisfies the first and second requirements I have outlined.[164]

The judge seems to me to have fallen into two errors. First, any promise to keep the door open was conditional upon the claimant submitting to the further medical examination. He refused to accept that condition.[165]...

Secondly, what the judge failed to consider, no doubt because his attention was not drawn to the need to do so, was whether or not there was a clear unequivocal promise or representation or common assumption, call it what you will, that the defendants would forgo their right to plead the Limitation Act 1980. I find nothing in the correspondence which justifies finding that there was any promise to that effect or anything at all like that effect.[166] To say that the door was open to further negotiations or even to point out that the proceedings could be stayed pending medical examination, did not in my judgment, carry any implication that a limitation defence would not be taken.[167]"

11.8 先例之八:The "Zenovia"

在 The "Zenovia"(2009)2 Lloyd's Rep. 139 先例中,承租人与船东(中间涉及了租约链)在 2006 年 7 月 28 日订立了期租合约,租期约为 13 个月,可以有 15 天加减。租约的条文要求承租人在还船前要提前 30 天做出预计还船日期通知,并在之后提前 20、15、10、7 天做出预计还船日期通知。在一连串的分租合约下,最后的承租人做出还船通知,说:"approximate notice of redelivery for the MV Zenovia at DLOSP[168] 1 sp China[169] on about 04 Nov 2007 basis agw[170], wp[171], wog[172], uce[173]..."该

[164] Ward 大法官同意保险公司承诺会继续谈判并考虑被保险人超过已支付的 20000 英镑的索赔,但这并不足以构成清楚无误的陈述或承诺。

[165] Ward 大法官认为高院的判决有两个错误。第一,承诺继续谈判是在被保险人同意接受新仪器检验的条件下,而被保险人拒绝接受这个条件。

[166] 第二,高院没有考虑保险公司的言行是否属于清楚无误的陈述或承诺会放弃时效已过的抗辩。Ward 大法官不认为在双方的通讯往来中,保险公司有任何言行属于清楚无误的陈述或承诺会放弃时效已过的抗辩。

[167] 仅仅表示仍可以继续谈判或指出索赔程序可以暂时停止以等待检验结果,并不代表不会依赖时效已过的抗辩。

[168] 这是最后领航员离船的缩写,即指这是双方同意还船的地点与时间,英文是 drop-off last out-bound sea pilot。

[169] "sp"是指 safe port,即还船的港口是中国的一个安全港口,即该航次的卸港。

[170] "all goes well"的缩写,是指预计 2007 年 11 月 4 日一切情况正常。

[171] "weather permitting"的缩写,指预计的还船时间是假设天气允许,即不会在海上遇到大风浪,或在卸港遇上大雨、大雪等导致延误。但该先例中,仲裁庭将该缩写错误理解为"without prejudice"。

[172] "without guarantee"的缩写,即说不保证预计的还船日期准确。有了这样的限制,通常做出的陈述就没有任何约束力。这方面的先例有 The "Lipa"(2001)2 Lloyd's Rep. 17,The "Lendoudis Evangelos II"(1997)1 Lloyd's Rep. 404 等。

[173] "unforeseen circumstances excepted"的缩写,即不可预见的情况被排除。

通知顺着租约链向上传,最后船东收到的通知是预计会在 2007 年 11 月 6 日还船。船东根据这个预计还船时间订立了新的租约。当时航运市场上涨,承租人发现在租约期内可以多行走一个短航次后还船,就乐得多赚点差价。承租人于是向船东做出通知更改还船时间,毕竟较早的通知只是预计。第二个通知是说:"Pls note that we hereby have to revise the date of redelivery to owners to about Nov 20th within the range of redelivery."这样,船东原先订立的新租约就赶不及销约期,并会蒙受损失。所以,船东认为承租人不能更改还船时间,而承租人则回复他们有权在租约允许的时间内使用船舶。船东最后在 11 月 2 日撤船,承租人声称船东错误撤船,双方之后开始仲裁。根据租约的有关条文解释,看来承租人并没有违约,因为第一个还船通知只要求预计,没有说不能修改。船东提出的争议是根据普通法下的承诺性禁反言,即通过做出第一个还船通知说明这是最后一个航次,承租人承诺会在中国还船,而放弃了在租约规定的最后一天才还船的权利。仲裁庭判是最初的通知构成承诺性禁反言,原因是第一个还船通知中虽然对预计还船日期有限制,但写明了是最后一个航次。承租人不能出尔反尔再主动多行走一个航次。但之后承租人上诉到法院,仲裁庭的决定被推翻。法院认为承租人的陈述不可以让船东合理推断承租人放弃了合约权利或影响了他们之间的合约关系。"without guarantee"一词已经显示了承租人没有清楚无误地承诺这会是最后一个航次或者会在 30 天内还船。即根据该先例中,承租人只要在预计还船日期通知中有清楚的文字上的限制,应该还是安全,不会构成承诺性禁反言。

这个判决也是配合航运实务,在租约中,这种预计还船通知经常不准确。如果船东通过合约条文坚持要承租人做出肯定的还船通知(definite redelivery notice),承租人即使愿意接受,也会把这种通知局限在还船前的一两天或三五天不等。承租人通常不会接受 30 天肯定的还船通知,因为这样的承诺违约的可能性很大。在此先例中,承租人的 30 天预计还船通知已经尽量使用一些文字加以限制,如"不保证"(without guarantee),但仍可以被船东断章取义说中间的某部分或某句属于承诺,并构成承诺性禁反言。如果判决禁反言成立,将会造成很大的影响。

11.9　先例之九:Kim v. Chasewood Park Residents Ltd.

在 Kim v. Chasewood Park Residents Ltd. (2013) EWCA Civ 239 先例中,案情涉及 Kim 夫妇有作为租客就一个住宅单位与房东签署了一份租期为 125 年的租约,根据租约规定,最开始的 33 年,Kim 夫妇要每年支付 100 英镑的地租;之后的 33 年,每年支付 200 英镑的地租;剩下的租约期,每年支付 400 英镑的地租。房东拥有这栋大厦 97 间单位的 999 年的主租约(head lease)。2006 年,房东希望将主租约转让,住户协会(residents' association)于是与房东开始谈判,希望接手主租约。8 月 24 日,住户协会给所有的租客写信询问是否会支持这个交易。该封信中错误将获得主租约写为成为产权所有人,其中列明的好处如下:

"The benefits of owning the freehold can be summarised as follows:

• Absolute control over the management of Chasewood Park including choosing the Managing Agents

• No ground rent to pay (currently £ 100 per annum per flat)

• No ongoing concern about diminishing leases. Once we own the freehold, whilst technically the leases will still be running, we can decide to extend these to say 999 years whenever we choose. There will be no additional cost for this apart from a small legal fee to amend our individual leases to reflect such a change.

• The immediate increase in the value of our properties by owning "A Share of Freehold" should at least cover the cost of the Freehold acquisition. In the future it will undoubtedly add value higher than this sum as the leases get shorter."

大部分租客包括 Kim 夫妇,支持了这个交易,并成立公司取得了主租约。2007年6月12日,该公司写信给支持了这个交易的租客说计划延长租期,并会继续收取地租以支付会计与法律费用。Kim 夫妇拒绝支付地租,理由是该公司2006年8月24日的信件中不必再交地租的承诺构成了承诺性禁反言。上诉庭判是2006年8月24日的信件不构成承诺性禁反言。该先例在一审法院被判是存在明确无误的陈述或承诺,但因为 Kim 夫妇没有依赖,所以不构成承诺性禁反言。之后,Kim 夫妇上诉到上诉庭。首先针对是否存在明确无误的陈述或承诺的争议,上诉庭判是这封信是在该公司成立并获得主租约之前一段时间写的,当时可以从租客获得多少支持与资金不明确,公司之后的财政状况如何也不明确,因此不属于明确无误的陈述,而只是列出了将来可能会有哪些好处。Patten 大法官说:"... It seems to me that the letter of 24th August did not promise anything. Even putting aside its obvious conditionality on the successful completion of the purchase, the fact that it was written well in advance of any possible acquisition and without the benefit of detailed knowledge of the financial position that would obtain once a purchase had taken place points overwhelmingly in my view to this being little more than a list of possible potential benefits rather than a guarantee or promise of what would be done. My view is not altered by the penultimate paragraph which does no more than to contrast the potential benefits to participators with the position of those tenants who remain outside the scheme."

而针对 Kim 夫妇是否依赖了该陈述,上诉庭同意一审法院的判决,认为 Kim 夫妇事实上没有依赖。[174]

---

〔174〕 见本章第7段。

12. 衡平法宽限或承诺性禁反言经常出现的情况

12.1 情况之一：双方达成和解协议同意少收债务或增加约因/对价

商业社会中的和解协议非常多，可探讨和解协议是否有约因/对价（consideration）。和解协议最通常要针对的是一方向另一方提出的索赔，索赔的一般是审理后才能确定金额（unliquidated damages）。但也有可能索赔一笔债务（debt）。也经常会有情况是同一诉讼中索赔的总金额部分是债务，部分是损失。如一个造船合约中，如果作为买家的船东没有支付一两期到期的预付船价，而令船厂终止合约。船厂向船东索赔的就是这到期没有支付的船价与因为市场下跌蒙受的损失。在诉讼中，处理债务与损失也很不一样，如船厂会先要求英国法院出"简易判决"（summary judgment），要求船东支付债务，而损失则留待之后的判决。仲裁也是同样，船厂会先要求仲裁庭就债务作出"中间裁决"（interim award），而损失则留待将来开庭后做出"最终裁决"（final award）。

由于损失的计算十分复杂，也极少有诉讼案件原告可以成功取回索赔中提出的所有损失（数字往往会被夸大，即所谓的"best possible case"），除非被告缺席。所以，如果和解协议针对的是损失，由被告支付部分损失，而原告放弃索赔所有损失的诉讼，不论协议有否说清楚这是约因/对价，都可以被视为法律可接受的约因/对价。有争议的是债务，因为债务在理论上没有争辩，通过法院或仲裁庭迟早可以连同利息将这笔钱取回。但在现实中，通过被告支付部分债务来达成和解协议也经常会有，但这就带来是否有约因/对价的问题。在笔者看来，这也是有约因/对价，如原告尽快取回部分债务，就可以避免被告在诉讼中倒闭等风险。另是对任何商业机构而言，早一点取回部分的债务可以帮助现金流，也可以比较安心。

12.1.1 普通法不认可债务减少的承诺，除非有约因/对价

但英国普通法的发展并不是这样解释，早在 Pinnel's Case (1603) 5 Coke's Rep. 117a 先例中，Edward Coke 大法官就已经说："payment of a lesser sum on the [due] day in the satisfaction of a greater cannot be any satisfaction of the whole."这所谓的 Pinnel's Case 规则在贵族院的 Foakes v. Beer (1882) 9 App Cas 605 先例被接受，并与约因/对价有关系，要求针对债务的和解协议，必须有约因/对价才有效。但在这个先例贵族院的法官们也有不同意见，Blackburn 勋爵是这样说："... conviction that all men of business, whether merchants or tradesmen, do every day recognize and act on the ground that prompt payment of part of their demand may be more beneficial to them than it would be to insist on their rights and enforce payment of the whole. Even there the debtor is perfectly solvent, and sure to pay at last, this is often so. Where the credit of the debtor is doubtful it must be more so."

在苏格兰,法律是认同 Blackburn 勋爵的不同意见,并早在 1937 年通过立法解决这个问题,废除了对约因/对价的要求。这在英国的《The Statute of Frauds and the Doctrine of Consideration》的第六份报告(Cmnd 5449)有提到,立法委员会建议取消约因/对价:"... we have no hesitation in recommending that legislation should be passed to give effect to it. This legislation would have the additional value of removing the logical difficulty involved in finding consideration for the creditors' promises in a composition with creditors when not under seal. It would be possible to enact only that actual payment of the lesser sum should discharge the obligation to pay the greater, but we consider that it is more logical and more convenient to recommend that the greater obligation can be discharged either by a promise to pay a lesser sum or by actual payment of it, but that if the new agreement is not performed then the original obligation shall revive."

但苏格兰没有相关的立法,普通法的地位不明确。在较近期的 Williams v. Roffey Bros. & Nicholls Ltd. (1991) 1 QB 1 上诉庭先例中(稍后会有详细介绍),更加被视为与 Foakes v. Beer 先例有直接冲突。Foakes v. Beer 是贵族院先例中应该约束 Williams v. Roffey Bros. & Nicholls Ltd. 的判决,但记录显示在后者的审理中,双方大律师没有提出这个先例中,所以法院也没有考虑。有关这方面的矛盾,稍后会进一步探讨。

12.1.2 英国法下对约因/对价的要求与坚持

一直以来,约因/对价(consideration)与合约的相对性(privity)都是英国合约法独有的。英国合约法坚持对价的理由可简单介绍如下。

没有任何法律体系会接受像合约法的严格/绝对责任一样去执行任何的承诺或言辞。因此,必须将没有法律后果的承诺或言辞与严肃的承诺或言辞区分开来。在英国普通法下,如果有盖章(sealing)的正式契约(deed),[175] 即使没有约因/对价的承诺,也可以执行。而如果是非正式的承诺或言辞,就必须依赖约因/对价的说法来区分是否为严肃的承诺或言辞。

在 Sharrington v. Stotton (1565) 75 ER 454 先例中,Wilmot 大法官说:"Because words are often spoke or uttered by a man without great advisement or deliberation, the law has provided that a contract by words shall not bind without consideration."

在 Brian Simpson 先生的《A History of the Common Law of Contract》(1975 年)一书之第 407 页,说:"In a sense Lord Mansfield's conception of consideration as 'evi-

---

〔175〕 1989 年有了《Law of Property (Miscellaneous Provisions) Act》,替代了普通法下盖章的要求。现在所需要的只是用清楚的文字表达该文件是一份契约,并公证(attestation)是由个人签字。如果是公司,除了对文件的盖章外,还可以用一个替代的方法是由董事与公司秘书或两个董事签字,并说明是代表公司签字。契约中也要有清楚的文字表明这是一份契约。这方面在《Chitty on Contracts》(第 32 版,2015 年)之 1 - 114 段有详细介绍。

dence' is historically correct[176], if the idea is given a somewhat extended sense along the following lines. The jury, before holding the defendant liable, need something more to go on to than merely a parole promise, inadequately perhaps proved, but if they can prove a good reason for the making of the promise which is also a good reason for holding the defendant liable then they can with more confidence award damages for breach, the consideration making it more plausible to say both that there was a promise and that it was seriously intended..."

在英国法律下,约因/对价只要存在而不必足够或相称(adequacy of consideration)。约因/对价不相称的情况经常发生,如船舶在当时市场出租得太便宜,或是国际货物买卖中买方支付的货价比当时市场价格高得多,造成这情况可能是有错误、误述、胁迫、欺诈行为或吃亏的一方无知。

针对错误、误述、胁迫、欺诈等行为,合约法有专门的机制否定这种订约时有缺陷的承诺或协议,所以不必以约因/对价是否相称来做出干预。而在现实中最常见的是,因无知而在国际商业活动中经常吃哑巴亏,英国法律是不加理会的。英国法律针对一方无知订下合约是有救济,可以撤销这个不合情理的交易(unconscionable bargain),这已经在本章之8.2段有所提及。衡平法法院在Fry v. Lane (1888) 49 CH. D. 312先例给予一个买了太过昂贵货物的人救济,法官指该人士年纪大且无知(a poor and ignorant man)。这衡平法做法也延展到岸上的房产买卖:Cresswell v. Potter (1978) 1 WLR 255; Blackhouse v. Blackhouse (1978) 1 WLR 243等先例。但在国际商贸与航运领域中的承诺与合约,不可能会接受有一方需要给予这种救济的。

由于约因/对价不必相称,只要存在即可,这就带来名义上的约因/对价的做法。这种"一元约因/对价"的合约,表面上有约因/对价,实质上是施予(gratuitous),但由于在形式上符合约因/对价的要求,法律将其视为有效并可以通过法院或仲裁庭执行。在个别商业活动中,会有立法禁止名义上的约因/对价,如为了防止公司负责人以名义上的约因/对价的承诺把公司资产出售,影响小股东的利益,《Law of Property Act 1926》之Section 205 (1) (xxi) 说:"valuable consideration does not include a nominal consideration in money."其他还有《Companies Act 1985》之ss. 103,320;《Insolvency Act 1986》之ss. 238,239,423等。

约因/对价不必是金钱或可以量化为金钱,只要有实质的利益或损害即可。如合约双方发生争议并导致损失的索赔时,在诉讼前或诉讼期间达成的和解协议,一般都是以一方放弃诉讼为约因/对价。英国法律接受原告放弃诉讼索赔是认可的约因/对价:The "Attika Hope" (1988) 1 Lloyd's Rep. 439等众多先例。

最后针对这个十分复杂的约因/对价问题,大陆法系没有约因/对价的要求,而在

---

[176] 这是Pillans v. Van Mierop (1765) 3 Burr 1663, 97 ER 1035先例中的说法,把约因/对价视为证据,证明是一个严肃的承诺。

英国法下,除非是“契约”(deed),否则一定要有约因/对价的存在。在中古时代的14或15世纪就已经开始有这种要求,对于是否应该把这个要求全面取消一直有争议。如稍早提到的英国《The Statute of Frauds and the Doctrine of Consideration》的第六份报告(Cmnd 5449)就建议在很多类别的承诺取消约因/对价的要求,包括和解协议,虽然最终没有立法。另在关于《Contracts (Rights of Third Parties) Act 1999》的立法委员会报告中,建议第三人在合约下起诉的权利不受没有约因/对价的影响。但针对约因/对价这一大课题,立法委员会认为需要将来分开研究与做出针对性的立法建议。

建议全面取消约因/对价要求的原因有很多,如约因/对价不需要足够或相称,只要一元也可以,看来约因/对价只是形式上的要求。但反对的声音也很多,如一个有效的合约最重要的就是双方有订约意图(intention to contract),但事后发生争议,很难有证据证明订约双方在想什么。对法院或仲裁庭而言,客观来看是否有约因/对价就是最好的证明。即使只是一元作为约因/对价,也显示了双方有订约意图,而且是订立有法律约束力的合约。所以一直以来,英国法律十分坚持约因/对价的要求,但通过 Williams v. Roffey Bros. & Nicholls Ltd. (1991) 1 QB 1 等先例(虽然目前看来没有超越贵族院的 Foakes v. Beer [1882] 9 App Cas 605 先例)也可以看出在英国法律下,这个要求在逐步放松。

加上在本章第10段与12.3段提到的,承诺性禁反言适用范围的不断扩展,根据澳大利亚高院的 Waltons Stores (Interstate) Ltd. v. Maher (1988) 164 CLR 387 先例中,即使双方不存在法律关系,谈判时的承诺或陈述仍然会构成禁反言。这在笔者看来是有危险,因为会导致大量的承诺都产生法律后果,这是任何法律系统都不想见到,这也是上一段提到的英国法律在最开始坚持约因/对价的原因。

12.1.3 放宽解释约因/对价的 Williams v. Roffey Bros. & Nicholls Ltd. 先例

传统上多支付一笔钱给对方,要求对方履行本应履行的现有合约责任,这属于没有有价值的约因/对价。直到 Williams v. Roffey Bros. & Nicholls Ltd. (1991) 1 QB 1 先例后,才有了重大改变。该先例中,A 向雇主总包了一座有27个单元的大楼翻新工程。A 把其中的木工部分分包给 B(分包商)进行,分包工程的费用为2万镑。开工后,A 发觉 B 陷入财政困难,而且2万镑的费用也确实太低,所以担心 B 不能按期完成工作。因为如果发生延误,A 是会在总包的工程合约下被雇主罚款。所以,A 主动向 B 承诺增加1万多镑的费用,鼓励与方便 B 继续工作。法院判这承诺有约因/对价,事后 A 必须支付这笔额外的1万多镑。

这个上诉庭的先例对“更改”(variation)这个课题很重要,因为之前的例子都涉及只有一方得益,而另一方为了大局或息事宁人而同意。之前一贯的说法是这被视为没有约因/对价。在这个先例之后,这个问题就可以大幅度减少。如较早前提到的针对债务的和解协议的问题,在贵族院的 Foakes v. Beer (1882) 9 App Cas 605 先例被判是没有约因/对价。但在 Williams v. Roffey Bros. & Nicholls Ltd. 的上诉庭先例后,支付部分债务也可以解释为有约因/对价。由于两个先例都是有效,关于部分支付债务的和解协议是否有效,就有了不肯定。这估计也导致 Williams v. Roffey Bros. & Nicholls Ltd. 先例做出后的二三十年中没有被太多先例跟从。

12.1.4　指出 Williams v. Roffey Bros. & Nicholls Ltd. 先例局限性的 In re Selectmove Ltd. 先例

在较近期的 In re Selectmove Ltd.（1995）1 WLR 474 上诉庭先例,更带出了 Williams v. Roffey Bros. & Nicholls Ltd.（1991）1 QB 1 先例的另一个不足之处。该先例涉及的法律关系与 Williams v. Roffey Bros. & Nicholls Ltd. 先例在本质上很不一样。案情是一家印刷行业的公司欠下了一大笔税金,税局就威胁要把该公司清盘。之后在一个公司负责人与一个税局员工的会议中,该公司负责人声称说服了税局员工让他可以分期清还欠税,毕竟该公司的业务在好转,清盘对大家都没有好处。但事后税局否认有这样的约定,而且该公司负责人清楚税局员工没有同意这个安排的授权。事情发展下去,税局的确向法院申请要求把公司清盘。但公司做出抗辩说,双方有一个约定,而该约定根据 Williams v. Roffey Bros. & Nicholls Ltd. 先例存在约因/对价,另一个抗辩是承诺性禁反言。上诉庭拒绝依照 Williams v. Roffey Bros. & Nicholls Ltd. 先例中,认为该先例只针对服务性的合约。Peter Gibson 大法官认为,如果 Williams v. Roffey Bros. & Nicholls Ltd. 先例不止适用在服务性合约而是可以适用在任何情况下的债务,Foakes v. Beer（1882）9 App Cas 605 先例就没有任何作用。而针对 Foakes v. Beer 先例与 Williams v. Roffey Bros. & Nicholls Ltd. 先例之间的矛盾,上诉庭看来是认为这个问题最终要由贵族院(现在是最高院)或通过立法才能解决。而在 In re Selectmove Ltd. 先例中,上诉庭选择依从贵族院的 Foakes v. Beer 先例中,Peter Gibson 大法官是这样说:"... if the principle of Williams v. Roffey Bros. & Nicholls（Contractors）Ltd.［1991］1 Q. B. 1 is to be extended to an obligation to make payment, it would in effect leave the principle in Foakes v. Beer, 9 App. Cas. 605 without any application. When a creditor and a debtor who are at arm's length reach agreement on the payment of the debt by instalments to accommodate the debtor, the creditor will no doubt always see a practical benefit to himself in so doing. In the absence of authority there would be much to be said for the enforceability of such a contract. But that was a matter expressly considered in Foakes v. Beer yet held not to constitute good consideration in law. Foakes v. Beer was not even referred to in Williams v. Roffey Bros. & Nicholls（Contractors）Ltd.［1991］1 Q. B. 1, and it is in my judgment impossible, consistently with the doctrine of precedent, for this court to extend the principle of Williams's case to any circumstances governed by the principle of Foakes v. Beer, 9 App. Cas. 605. If that extension is to be made, it must be by the House of Lords or, perhaps even more appropriately, by Parliament after consideration by the Law Commission."

12.1.5　较近期的相关先例:Collier v. P & MJ Wright（Holdings）Ltd.

这个问题还有下文,就是在上诉庭的另一个先例 Collier v. P & MJ Wright（Holdings）Ltd.（2008）1 WLR 643,案情涉及 Collier 先生、Broadfoot 先生与 Flute 先生成立一间合伙公司发展地产。期间公司向答辩人贷款 588414.32 英镑,由于这笔钱没有清还,答辩人向三位合伙人起诉,大家在诉讼期间达成了和解协议。该和解协议也在 1999 年 4 月 21 日变为"和解判决"(consent judgment),就是欠下的债务是 46000 镑再加上利息,由三位共同分期支付。理论上答辩人可以向三个合伙人中的任何一个取回债务,但和解协议中由三位分别做出支付的做法也是司空见惯的。但问题是不久后,Flute 先生与 Broadfoot 先生先后破产,也就停止了支付。可以说,只有 Collier 先生持续分期支付还债,5 年间总共支付了 15600 英镑,这看来也是 Collier 先生应占的份额。但答辩人由于无法向 Flute 先生与 Broadfoot 先生取回足够的金额,就转而向 Collier 先生追讨,并通过英国《Insolvency Rule》(SI 1986/1925)向 Collier 先生作出破产通知。Collier 先生向法院申请中止(stay)破产程序,因为他对这笔债务有争议,所以需要争议解决后才存在能否成功申请破产的问题。

这个争议根据 Collier 先生提供的证据就是在 2000 年年底,答辩人曾经口头告知 Collier 先生会想办法解决 Flute 先生与 Broadfoot 先生要支付的部分(当时这两位先生还没有破产,但显然支付有困难),并鼓励 Collier 先生按照较早的和解协议准时分期支付他的债务。最后还加了一句说:"Don't worry, I am happy to treat you separately."

显然这个口头协议没有约因/对价,但上诉庭没有像 In re Selectmove Ltd.（1995）1 WLR 474 先例一样在两个矛盾的先例中作出取舍,也没有跟从 Williams v. Roffey Bros. & Nicholls Ltd.（1991）1 QB 1 先例。上诉庭是根据"承诺性禁反言"(promissory estoppel)认同 Collier 先生会有机会禁止答辩人(即债权人)翻供,接受 Collier 先生的申请去中止答辩人的破产申请。其中 Arden 大法官说:"... if (1) a debtor offers to pay part only of the amount he owes; (2) the creditor voluntarily accepts that offer, and (3) in reliance on the creditor's acceptance the debtor pays that part of the amount he owes in full, the creditor will, by virtue of the doctrine of promissory estoppel, be bound to accept that sum in full and final satisfaction of the whole debt. For him to resile will of itself be inequitable. In addition, in these circumstances, the promissory estoppel has the effect of extinguishing the creditor's right to the balance of the debt."

另 Longmore 大法官虽然同意中止破产申请,让法院全面审理双方对承诺性禁反言的争议,但也表示了初步看法,认为 Collier 先生这个争议不容易成功,说:"The first question is: what was the oral promise or representation made by Mr Wright(答辩人)to Mr Collier? Mr Collier says that Mr Wright's promise was that if Mr Collier continued to pay £ 200 per month the company would look to Mr Broadfoot and Mr Flute for their share and not to Mr Collier. ... One would expect an agreement permanently to forgo one's rights (especially rights founded on a judgment) to be much clearer than the agreement evidenced in this case. ... The second question is whether, even if the promise or representation is to be regarded on a permanent surrender of the company's rights, Mr Collier has relied on it in any meaningful way. The judge could find no evidence that he had... There is then a third question, namely whether it would be inequitable for the company to resile from its promise. That cannot be inquired into on this appeal, but I agree that it is arguable that it would be inequitable. There might, however, be much to be said on the other side. ... it is perhaps all the more important that agreements which are said to forgo a creditor's rights on a permanent basis should not be too benevolently construed."

这样看来,在现代的英国法律下,清还部分债务的和解协议是否可以超越没有约因/对价的问题仍待澄清。

12.1.6 总结英国法下清还部分债务的和解协议是否有效

总结而言,与更改合约有最密切关系的是履行现有的合约责任是否可以当作有价值的约因/对价,这可以从两方面来看。

反对的原因是:(1)要保护合约一方免受另一方在合约履行时做出勒索(extortion),最常见的勒索就是要求提高或降低合约价格或费用。虽然,被勒索一方可以"胁迫"(duress)为由推翻这种承诺,但这方面的保障会不够与不容易证明。(2)一方既然要履行合约责任,再要求对方为了同样的"回报"(return)做出另一个承诺如何说得上有"牺牲"或"损害"(detriment)? 毕竟英国法律不承认虚拟的约因/对价(illusory consideration):Wickham & Burton Coal Co. v. Farmer's Lumber Co. (1923) 189 Iowa 1183 先例与 Arrale v. Coatain (1976) 1 Lloyd's Rep. 98 先例。

但赞成的原因是:(1)稍早已经提到尽快取回部分的债务,就可以避免对方在诉讼中倒闭等风险。另是对任何商业机构,早点取回部分的债务可以帮助现金流,也可以比较安心。另是在 Williams v. Roffey Bros. & Nicholls Ltd. (1991) 1 QB 1 先例也提到,B 如果不顺利完成工作会令 A 被雇主罚款,如果 B 不能顺利完成工作,也可能会导致 A 的声誉受到影响等。这在各种商业交往中经常发生,法律没有理由反对。(2)合约一方可以赔偿损失去替代履行,因为这样做在经济上更划算,这也是本书第一章之 8.2 段提到的"有效益违约"(efficient breach)理论。所以,Denning 大法官曾在 Ward v. Byham (1956) 1 WLR 496 先例说过:"... the performance of an existing duty, or the promise to perform it, was always good consideration."对无辜方来说,他可能非常需要有效益违约的违约方履行这个合约,于是愿意加价或减价,令实际履行合约变为更好或明智的选择。所以法律应该支持,让双方都各取所需。

12.1.7 可能令清偿部分债务的和解协议有效的办法

减低债务所达成的和解协议还是在英国法下有很大的问题,但偏偏这种和解协议经常发生。有效的办法可能如下:

1. 在和解协议中想办法制造有效与实质性的约因/对价,但这种约因/对价不容易。因为在债权人同意减低债务时,很难想象债务人可以做出何种回报作为约因/对价。毕竟债务人已经欠下债务,即使答应债权人在 1 个工作日内就会支付到他的账户,也谈不上是有效的约因/对价。在 Pinnel's Case (1603) 5 Coke's Rep. 117a 先例中,Coke 大法官虽然判债务不能扣减,但可以通过其他办法,说:"... the gift of a horse, hawk, robe etc. in satisfaction is good."这在后来的 Couldery v. Bartrum (1881) 19 Ch D 394 先例中,George Jessel 大法官说:"According to English common law a creditor might accept anything in satisfaction of his debt except a less amount of money. He might take a horse, or a canary, or tomtit if he chose, and that was accord and satisfaction; but, by a most extraordinary peculiarity of the English common law he could not take 19 shillings and sixpence in the pound; that was *nudum pactum*.[177]"但在现实中很难达成这种协议。

2. 在和解协议中写明适用的法律。这法律当然不能是英国法(包括香港特区、新加坡等国家与地区的法律),而是大陆法或苏格兰法(已经提到有立法解决这个问题),因为这些国家的法律不再要求约因/对价的存在。

3. 已经提到在英国法下,如果有盖章的正式契约(deed),即使没有约因/对价的承诺,也可以执行。因此,如果以契约的形式订立和解协议,和解协议的有效性是不受没有约因/对价的影响,但这不一定可行。

4. 最理想的办法就是最高院做出权威判决(要等机会),或是立法全面取消合约更改(包括双方同意减低债务所达成的和解协议)对约因/对价的要求。毕竟订立合约是令两个没有关系的人士产生法律关系,因此要保持约因/对价的要求。但更改合约时双方已经存在法律关系,严格执行对约因/对价的要求反而会导致无法达成双方的真正意图,因此应在这方面放宽要求。已经有普通法国家开始做出这方面的改变,如美国《Uniform Commercial Code》之 section 2 – 209 说:"(1) An agreement modifying a contractwithin this Article needs no consideration to be binding."另在《Uniform Commercial Code》之 section 2A – 208 说:"(1) An agreement modifying a lease contract needs no consideration to be binding."毕竟英国普通法下针对合约更改的格式要求看来也有所放松。[178]

但目前主要解决办法还是下一小段会介绍的衡平法宽限或承诺性禁反言,虽然这个办法不可靠与不肯定。

12.1.8 主要解决办法:衡平法宽限或承诺性禁反言

这是主要的解决办法,即通过衡平法宽限或承诺性禁反言的说法。毕竟针对没有约因/对价的承诺,要令其有效,就要通过衡平法宽限或承诺性禁反言。清偿部分

---

〔177〕 这拉丁文是指 bare or naked promise。

〔178〕 这可见本书第三章第 1 段。

债务的和解协议要有效,也是同样的道理。这可以节录 Arden 大法官在 Collier v. P & MJ Wright（Holdings）Ltd.（2008）1 WLR 643 先例的说法:"Denning J（as he then was）was the originator of another doctrine which was used to alleviate the effects of the rule in Pinnel's case, namely the doctrine of promissory estoppel. Mr Collier(三个合伙人中的一个)also relies on the doctrine and I shall have to explain it in more detail below. Suffice it to say at this stage that where there was a compromise agreement the doctrine of promissory estoppel meant that the agreement was binding if it was inequitable for the creditor to enforce his strict legal rights."

Arden 大法官说 Denning 大法官是承诺性禁反言说法的创始人(originator),她指的就是 Central London Property Trust Ltd. v. High Trees House Ltd.（1947）KB 130 先例。在之后的 Tool Metal Manufacturing Co. v. Tungsten Electric Co.（1955）1 WLR 761 先例中,法院判是承诺性禁反言适用在减少支付应付的款项的情况。在 D & C Builders Ltd. v. Rees（1966）2 QB 617 先例中,Denning 勋爵说:

"This principle(承诺性禁反言)has been applied to cases where a creditor agrees to accept a lesser sum in discharge of a greater. So much so that we can now say that, when a creditor and a debtor enter upon a course of negotiation, which leads the debtor to suppose that, on payment of the lesser sum, the creditor will not enforce payment of the balance, and on the faith thereof the debtor pays the lesser sum and the creditor accepts it as satisfaction: then the creditor will not be allowed to enforce payment of the balance when it would be inequitable to do so. This was well illustrated during the last war. Tenants went away to escape the bombs and left their houses unoccupied. The landlords accepted a reduced rent for the time they were empty. It was held that the landlords could not afterwards turn round and sue for the balance, see Central London Property Trust Ltd. v. High Trees House Ltd. This caused at the time some eyebrows to be raised in high places. But they have been lowered since. The solution was so obviously just that no one could well gainsay it.

In applying this principle, however, we must note the qualification: The creditor is only barred from his legal rights when it would be inequitable for him to insist upon them. Where there has been a true accord, under which the creditor voluntarily agrees to accept a lesser sum in satisfaction, and the debtor acts upon that accord by paying the lesser sum and the creditor accepts it, then it is inequitable for the creditor afterwards to insist on the balance. But he is not bound unless there has been truly an accord between them."

但承诺性禁反言也不容易成立,因为首先要证明有清楚无误的陈述或承诺,接着要证明这陈述或承诺被对方依赖并因此蒙受损失,最后要证明让陈述或承诺方撤销承诺会不公平与不合情理。在 Collier v. P & MJ Wright（Holdings）Ltd. 先例中,上诉庭最后就判是承诺性禁反言不能成立。

另在 In re Selectmove Ltd.（1995）1 WLR 474 上诉庭先例中，也判是禁反言不适用，因为该公司虽然声称税局员工做出了同意该公司分期支付欠下的税款的承诺，但依然迟交了 2 个月的税款，所以并没有依赖所谓的税局员工的承诺，就不能要求衡平法的救济。Peter Gibson 大法官说："... the company failed to honour its promise to pay the September P. A. Y. E. and N. I. C.（欠下的税款类别）as they fell due, it was not inequitable or unfair for the revenue on 9 October 1991 to demand payment of all the arrears, nor, in the light of the further late payments of the October and November P. A. Y. E. and N. I. C. and of various of the monthly instalments of £ 1,000, was it unfair or inequitable to serve a statutory demand and present a winding up petition to enforce the debt."

但在某些减少债务的和解协议的情况下，是会构成衡平法宽限或承诺性禁反言。如债务人对债权人说："如果你一定要我还这笔钱，我只能把公司清盘，大家都没有好处。但是如果你同意减少一部分债务，并同意我分期支付的话，我借钱也会把钱还给你。"而双方达成协议后，债务人也确实准时每期支付了双方同意的金额。并且债务人为了筹钱，曾经举债甚至做出个人担保。如果在这种情况下，债权人再反悔要求债务人支付剩余的债务，就有可能被禁反言。

12.1.9 单方面提高约因/对价以换取对方履行合约承诺的和解协议

虽然本质上大同小异，但与上述段节介绍的减少债务的情况相反，另一个经常出现的情况是类似 Williams v. Roffey Bros. & Nicholls Ltd.（1991）1 QB 1 先例中，因为担心对方不履行而单方面增加约因/对价。在该先例中，法院判是总包商为了让分包商准时完成合约，防止自己被雇主罚款，同意单方面增加约因/对价的行为构成了合约更改，即分包商也提供了约因/对价。明显这种多支付约因/对价以换取对方履行已经承诺且法律规定要履行的责任，算不上对方有提供相应的约因/对价。

虽然在 Williams v. Roffey Bros. & Nicholls Ltd. 先例中已经放宽了对约因/对价的要求，判总包商单方面增加约因/对价是有效的合约更改，但已经提到该先例很有争议性，在之后的二三十年并没有被跟从，另在 In re Selectmove Ltd.（1995）1 WLR 474 先例中 Williams v. Roffey Bros. & Nicholls Ltd. 先例被判是只适用在服务性合约。而且在不同的案例会有案情是即使宽松对待，也说不上存在有效的约因/对价。这样，在这种单方面增加约因/对价以换取对方履行合约承诺的情况下，又需要依赖承诺性禁反言的说法。但这也存在另一个困难，即已经在本章第 10 段提到的禁反言只能作为防守的盾牌，而不能作为进攻的宝剑。如果承诺单方面增加约因/对价的一方反悔，被承诺方事后无法以禁反言的说法要求承诺方履行他的承诺。

这可以看 The "Proodos C"（1980）2 Lloyd's Rep. 390 先例。该先例的案情涉及在 1976 年 10 月，Proodos C 轮装载 82 辆沃尔沃汽车从瑞典运往也门的 Hodeidah 港。相关的租约是期租合约，承租人签发了运费预付提单，但之后承租人破产。1976

年 11 月 9 日,船舶抵达 Hodeidah 港后,因为港口拥挤,就开往别的港口卸载船上的其他货物。1977 年 2 月 28 日,船东与这 82 辆汽车的收货人达成协议。1977 年 4 月 14 日,在收货人同意多支付 31000 美金的情况下,船舶回到 Hodeidah 港,将汽车卸下。但之后收货人拒绝支付 31000 美金,说双方的协议不存在约因/对价,或因为"胁迫"(duress)无效。船东根据协议中的仲裁条款开始仲裁,双方委任了 Donald Davies 先生作为独任仲裁员。Donald Davies 先生做出的裁决是该协议不存在约因/对价,不因为胁迫无效,但船东可以根据承诺性禁反言要求收货人支付 31000 美金。收货人向法院上诉,要求撤销该裁决书。法院不认为船东可以根据承诺性禁反言要求收货人支付 31000 美金,因为承诺性禁反言只能作为盾牌而不能作为剑进攻,说:

"In the present case the owners could have had no claim for the $31,000 which they are seeking to recover from the respondents in these proceedings if it were not for the 'agreement of Feb. 28, 1977. They have no independent cause of action: they are suing on the naked promise to pay the $31,000; they are using equitable estoppel as a sword and not as a shield; and that they cannot do.

Mr. Moore – Bick(船东代表大律师) tried to bring the case within the ordinary scope of equitable estoppel by arguing that the respondents had led the claimants to believe that they would not insist on their strict legal rights whereby they were entitled to have the cargo delivered at Hodeidah free of expense; and that they cannot now go back on that promise. But that is to stand equitable estoppel on its head. The reality is that the claimants are suing on the 'agreement' of Feb. 28, 1977. If, as the arbitrator has found, there was no consideration for that 'agreement' then it is unenforceable in law."

总结而言,英国法律看来要向澳大利亚法律靠拢或接纳在本章第 10 段节录的新加坡潘文龙法官的说法,即在双方已经存在法律关系的情况,承诺性禁反言可以作为诉因协助调整双方的权利与责任,而不追求约因/对价存在与否。另是像在本章之 12.1.7 段提到的通过立法做出改变,如美国《Uniform Commercial Code》之 section 2 – 209 与 section 2A – 208 规定合约更改不再需要约因/对价。

12.2　情况之二:有缺陷的通知书被无条件接受

在本章之 3.1 段介绍的 Bremer v. Vanden (1978) 2 Lloyd's Rep. 109 的贵族院先例与在本章之 3.2 段介绍的 Bremer v. Mackprang (1979) 1 Lloyd's Rep. 221 先例中,都涉及国际货物买卖合约中有缺陷的通知书(defective notice)被对方无条件接受而产生是否涉及衡平法宽限或承诺性禁反言的问题。有缺陷的通知在各种不同的行业都会发生,所产生的问题与争议也是大同小异。

在国际外贸与航运的实务中,最常涉及的课题是船长递交无效的准备就绪通知书(notice of readiness)。这个通知的重要性是在普通法或有关合约中通常都会明示或默示装卸时间的起算是取决于船长递交一份准确与有效的准备就绪通知书。众所周知,如果约定的装卸时间一结束,货方就会需要支付滞期费(demurrage)或滞期损失(damage for detention)。在航运市场高涨时,这会是一笔非常庞大的金额。而航运市场高涨时也往往是装卸港十分拥挤的时候,船舶滞留长达一两个月并不奇怪。高昂的滞期费或滞期损失加上长时间的滞留,就会带来一笔金额庞大的索赔。由于外贸与航运合约的数量非常庞大,并且每份合约都会涉及一个或多个装卸港,所以产生的争议非常多,其中不少一直上诉到贵族院(现在的最高院)。

经常会出现有缺陷通知书的原因是:(1)船长养成船舶一抵达装卸港的港内或者港外的锚地就马上/尽快递交通知书的习惯,显然这是为了保护船东的利益,可尽早起算装卸时间。(2)船长对每个不同的租约与航次约定的究竟怎样才算递交有效通知书通常一无所知。如第一个租约有"不论进港与否"(whether in port or not,简称WIPON)都可以递交通知书的条文,下一个租约就争取不到有 WIPON 条文。又如,有关租约的递交通知书条文中增加了一个先决条件,如清关之后才能递交。这在订约自由下是可以有各种约定。(3)船舶实质上无法递交有效的通知书,如船舱上下有两票不同的货物,直到上面的一票货物卸清后,压在下面的一票货物才能递交有效通知书。要了解会影响通知书是否有效的各种问题,需要了解与熟知日趋复杂的租船业务与相关法律方面的知识。

这种有缺陷与无效的通知书就像从来没有递交一样,这一点已经很明确,可参阅 The "Mexico 1" (1990) 1 Lloyd's Rep. 507 先例与很多其他的先例。如在 Christensen v. Hindustan Steel Ltd. (1971) 1 Lloyd's Rep. 395 先例中,Donaldson 大法官判:"... the general rule that a notice of readiness is wholly ineffective if ... the vessel is not ... ready when it is given."

但如果不成熟(premature)或有缺陷的准备就绪通知书已被承租人或其代理人(包括装港的发货人或卸港的收货人)无条件接受(通常就是在通知书上签署"接受"),就可能构成弃权或禁反言。构成弃权是在承租人或代理人知道通知书有缺陷的情况下,仍无条件接受。但更多的情况是承租人或其代理人不知道船舶有缺陷,但无条件地接受,这就会构成衡平法宽限或承诺性禁反言。原因是这个言行给了船东错误信号:这不成熟或有缺陷的通知书可算是有效。如果没有这错误信号,船东会进行弥补,对不成熟之处做出补救后,才另递交一份有效与正确的准备就绪通知书。这种无条件地接受在大量先例都被判是属于弃权或禁反言:The "North King" (1971) 2 Lloyd's Rep. 460; The "Helle Skou" (1976) 2 Lloyd's Rep. 205; The "Shackleford" (1978) 2 Lloyd's Rep. 154; The "Mexico 1"; The "Happy Day" (2002) 2 Lloyd's Rep. 487 等。

首先是 The "North King"先例中,案情是有关的准备就绪通知书没有在租约规定的时间内递交,等于无效。但这有缺陷的通知书被承租人代理无条件接受,于是船东就争辩说承租人接受了通知书,就要被禁反言不能去否定通知书的有效性与双方的代理人有了接受该通知书的协议。在仲裁中,公断人判是无效的通知书被接受,承租人不得事后否定,因为已经禁反言。之后在上诉庭,Mocatta 大法官也支持船东胜诉,因为公断人已经认定双方代理人达成协议的事实。而有关禁反言,他是这样说:"I have no doubt that the proper inference of fact is that a representation was made to the effect that if a proper notice, in the sense that the ship was then ready physically, was given on November 1, before noon, it would be treated as having the same effect as a similar notice given on any other Saturday. The question, however, whether the owners acted upon that representation in a way in which they would not otherwise have acted is, perhaps, more difficult. Accordingly, although it may be that on the point of estoppel, if it had stood alone, I would have reached the conclusion that the owners were entitled to succeed, I think it best not to base my judgment in the alternative upon that, but to restrict it to the firm ground with which I have already dealt, namely, that there was an agreement between the parties the effect of which was to treat Saturday, November 1, in the same way as other Saturday for the purpose of the giving of a notice of readiness."

在 The "Helle Skou"先例中,案情涉及的货物是袋装脱脂牛奶奶粉。租约规定船舶的船舱必须干净与没有味道,才可以递交准备就绪通知书。船长抵达装港后,诚实但错误地做出了准备就绪通知书,但事实上船舱被之前装载的鱼粉(fishmeal)的味道污染。承租人没有检查船舱情况就正式接受了这份准备就绪通知书,并立刻开始装货。一段时间之后问题被发现,装载作业停止并需要把已经装载的袋装脱脂牛奶奶粉卸下,以进一步清洁船舱。船东承认他要承担船舶不适航导致的损失,但既然承租人已经无条件接受了这份准备就绪通知书,就不能之后再认为其无效。Donaldson 大法官说:"... this is the first case in which charterers have accepted such a notice and later claimed to reject it. I do not think that they can do so. ... This notice is far from being a nullity. It was the key which unlocked the holds of the vessel and allowed loading to begin. And it was the charterers' act which created this position. **Whether it is labelled as waiver or estoppel or something else**, I do not consider that the charterers can resile from this position, save upon grounds of fraud."(加黑的一句显示在当时,法院仍没有细分各种类别的禁反言以及与弃权的区别。)

另在 The "Shackleford"先例中,租约有条文明示要求清关后才递交通知,然后起算卸货时间。Shackleford 轮去 Constanza 卸货,在 10 月 15 日的 8 时 26 分抵达。船长马上递交通知书,也被收货人接受。船舶在锚地待泊至 11 月 26 日才去靠泊加油,在泊位时清关才完成。之后船再待泊至 12 月 2 日才开卸。这一个多月的滞期费是否要支付的关键是看 10 月 15 日递交的通知书是否有效,该通知不成熟应无疑问,但它被收货人无条件接受。船东声称若非如此,他会马上安排靠泊加油,在泊位清了关才回锚地待泊,则不会有不成熟通知书的问题了。在高院,Donaldson 大法官判是代表承租人的收货人应该拒绝或者不理会无效的通知书,一旦接受了,就构成了"行动性禁反言"(estoppel by conduct),承租人不得事后否定该通知书。Donaldson 大法官是这样说:"The notice of readiness given on Oct. 15, 1976, was a good notice in that the vessel had arrived at Constanza and was ready to discharge but it was premature in that no customs entry had been obtained; under the terms of the charter, the receivers could have rejected or ignored the notice but they had accepted it and this created an estoppel by conduct so that the charterers could not allege that the notice was premature."

当这个先例到了上诉庭,高院的判决获得支持。上诉庭又提到几点可补充,首先是有关收货人是否知道船舶不能在外锚地取得清关与租约条文的先决条件。Sir David Cairns 大法官说:"There remains the question of what knowledge the receivers had and whether the state of their knowledge is relevant. Again we have no finding on the matter, but I think it is to be assumed that the receivers would know that customs entry could not be obtained at Constanza until after berthing. The second cable certainly shows that Navlomar had that knowledge on Oct. 28 and as an organization carrying on business connected with the reception of cargoes at Constanza it is a reasonable assumption that they would know the rules of the port. So far as knowledge of the contents of the charter-party is concerned, **the charterers themselves of course must have had or must be deemed to have had that knowledge and it was for them to impart to the receivers as much information as it was necessary for them to have when a notice of readiness was tendered to them. If notice of readiness was accepted with ignorance of what the effect would be under the charter-party I do not consider the charterers can take advantage of that ignorance.**[179]"

Sir David Cairns 大法官也有提及有关船东有否"依赖"(reliance)承租人无条件接受了无效通知书的事实。这在 Donald Davies 先生的裁决书也有提及并作出推断是有依赖,即不另作安排早日进港取得清关,说:"My note shows that it is correct that Mr. Rix(承租人代表大律师)first raised the question of reliance in his Reply to the Claimants' opening speech but, in dealing with that argument, Mr. Hunter(船东代表大律师), in his closing speech, invited me to infer that the Claimants had relied on the acceptance of the Notice of Readiness because, for example, they might have arranged for the vessel to securing a bunkering berth or by taking other steps and thereby obtaining custom's entry at an early stage."

Sir David Cairns 大法官是这样说:"An important issue at the arbitration and before the Judge was whether the acceptance was relied on by the shipowners. The arbitrator found that it was. The Judge held that he was bound by that finding and charterers have not challenged that part of the Judge's decision in this Court."

但弃权或禁反言对船东并非是万全的保障。一是因为更多情况下,通知书只会

---

〔179〕 承租人自己是一定知道这些通知书的先决条件,并应该告诉收货人。如果在这种情况下,收货人是无知接受了无效的通知书,Sir David Cairns 大法官不认为承租人可以以无知获利。

被有条件接受(如注明无损害),或干脆拒绝接受。二是要构成弃权或禁反言,除了不能存在欺诈(因为禁反言属于衡平法),还必须证明船东依赖了这"接受"的行为,并造成损失(detriment)。这在三个伦敦仲裁中可以显示:

1. 在 LMLN No. 180 报道的伦敦仲裁,The "Achillet"油轮在 3 月 21 日抵达装港并递交通知,通知在 3 月 22 日被承租人的代理人接受。约 8 个小时后,船舶的油柜被发现不清洁,在 3 月 25 日清洁完毕后,才可以开始装货。船东事后争议说通知书即使无效,但因为在 3 月 22 日被接受,所以装货时间应该起算。仲裁庭不同意有构成弃权与禁反言,认为在承租人接受通知后很快知悉船舶未曾备妥而推翻较早通知的情况下,船东不可能有依赖,也不会因此而产生本来可避免的损害,说:"The owners relied upon the Shackleford decision in support of their contention that the refinery, by way of the acceptance of the notice of readiness of March 22, estopped the charterers from denying the validity of the notice of readiness. The Shackleford case had its own special facts which supported an estoppel argument, further, there was no question of the Shackleford being rejected on account of the state of her cargo spaces after she had berthed, as in the present case. While we might well like to find a way to allow the owners the benefit of the time while the vessel was waiting off Aden(装港)we do not think that an estoppel can be established where mere acceptance of the notice of readiness on the evening of March 22 was followed by a rejection of the vessel not many hours later; further, there was no reliance by the owners on the acceptance of the notice. The mere acceptance of the notice of readiness could not, in the context of all the relevant circumstances, be considered as a surrender by the charterers of their fundamental right to reject the notice of readiness when it became clear that the vessel was not ready to load the intended cargo. Much more was required from the charterers' camp in order for an estoppel to be founded whereby there was a clear meaning that laytime would commence irrespective of the result of an inspection of the cargo tanks which was due to take place in the near future. It is worth mentioning that the notice of readiness which was passed to the refinery read 'please acknowledge receipt by signing and retaining to me the attached three copies' and was followed by the typed, 'accepted on'; we think that the refinery was making more of an acknowledgment of a receipt than a binding acceptance of a notice of readiness. The owners' estoppel argument fails."

2. 在 LMLN No. 206 报道的伦敦仲裁,有关航次是去美湾装粮至波斯湾,租约是要求通知书必须"附上船舱通过清洁检查的证明"(accompanied by pass of the Inspectors attesting to the fact that the vessel is clean - swept and ready in all compartments...)。但船舶一抵达美湾就递交通知书,承租人的代理人接受。而船舶是在第二天才取得该检查证明。船东依赖 The "Shackleford" (1978) 2 Lloyd's Rep. 154 先例中,指称该通知书已经被承租人的代理人接受,承租人构成弃权或/与禁反言。

仲裁庭区分了该仲裁与 The "Shackleford" 先例的不同之处,一是 Shackleford 轮的船东在当时很难知道真正的事实(the difficulty faced by the owner in establishing the true position)与前罗马尼亚的港口代理人是和承租人有密切关系(the closely connected identity of the charterers and their agents)更能代表承租人的立场。仲裁员认为在美湾这个港口,船东应该清楚了解美国农业部对船舱作出检查的要求,而且港口的代理人身份相对独立,不会与承租人有密切关系,这个就是和 The "Shackleford" 先例可区分之处。加上这个仲裁的情况是即使承租人的代理人一开始就拒绝接受通知书,并指出船舶尚没有检查证明,船东也没有办法提前安排做出检查。换言之,接受或者拒绝通知书都没有给船东带来任何后果/改变地位(change of position)或者损害。结果仲裁庭不接受船东的弃权或/与禁反言的说法。有关报道的裁决书内容如下:

"Such considerations might be very significant when one was considering a port in Eastern Europe. However, they could scarcely apply to a port in the United States. The owners could have been in no doubt about the fact that the US Department of Agriculture Inspection had not taken place at the time when the initial notice of readiness was tendered. Furthermore, although from a strict legal point of view an agent could act in such a way as to bind his principle, the owners would have had no reason to assume that the agents in question could be identified more closely with their principals than any other apparently independent port agent.

In addition, there was no evidence that the owners had in any way acted to their prejudice as a result of the charterers' agents having accepted the notice of readiness. Consequently, the arguments of waiver and/or estoppel would be rejected. Laytime commenced at 0800 on the day after the requisite pass had been issued."

3. 在 LMLN No. 266 报道的伦敦仲裁,案情是一艘油轮装一船原油从非洲去美国,租约有条文规定船舶必须符合所有美国海岸巡逻队的规定,并且船舶必须在所有有关时间拥有美国所要求的各种证书。美国法律是要求外国船舶有一份"符合证书"(certificate of compliance),才可以在美国水域航行或者在美国装卸石油产品。而该证书只会在船舶被详细检查并认为符合所有规定后,才会发出。当本案例中的船舶抵达美国,虽然船上并没有一份符合证书,但船东照样递交了通知书。收货人并不知道船舶没有这份证书,于是就接受并签署了通知书。船舶在第二天才取得这份符合证书。之后,双方就对通知书的有效性与什么时候起算卸货时间有了争议。承租人指称船舶没有这份符合证书,所以递交的通知书是无效的。

仲裁庭是判收货人在签署通知书时,并不知道船上缺少这份符合证书。收货人只是根据通知书上作出的陈述,以为船舶已真正备妥去卸货。但事实上这并不正确,因为船舶有一个重要的法律上的要求并未备妥,导致根本不可以开始卸货。船舶在通知书所说的备妥包括船舶"实质上备妥"(physical readiness),也包括"法律上备妥”(legal readiness)。结果是仲裁庭判船东提出与主张的弃权或/与禁反言不成立。

12.3 情况之三:合约谈判中的陈述或承诺

这个问题在本章第 10 段已经有所涉及。在澳大利亚高院的 Waltons Stores (Interstate) Ltd. v. Maher (1988) 164 CLR 387 先例中,即使双方之后没有订立有法律效力的合约,不存在任何法律关系,陈述方或承诺方在谈判时的陈述或承诺仍会构成承诺性禁反言,并令被陈述方或被承诺方可以此作为诉因提起诉讼。而英国虽然仍维持传统的地位,并且目前与澳大利亚法律在这方面有分歧。但在 Baird Textile Holdings Ltd. v. Marks & Spencer Plc. (2001) EWCA Civ 274 先例中,上诉庭认为英国关于承诺性禁反言的法律还在继续发展,最高院仍有可能针对宝剑盾牌之争做出改革。在新加坡近期的 Tee Soon Tay v. Attorney - General (2007) 3 SLR 133 先例中,上诉庭也认为这一点还是富有争议(shrouded in some controversy)。

这个法律地位在普通法的不同国家出现分歧在现实中的重要性是,普通法国家近年来都在追求判决的一致性,英国法院在做出判决时常常会参考或引用其他普通法国家的案例。因此,英国在这方面的法律地位很可能会受澳大利亚法律的影响,更不能排除不久的将来在适当的案件下,最高院做出改变,将承诺性禁反言的适用范围延伸。另是在国际仲裁中,会有不少仲裁员不警觉这个目前存在的微妙分歧,导致合约中虽然规定受英国法律管辖(毕竟很少跨国商业合约会明示适用澳大利亚法律),但仲裁员仍会接受当事人律师引用的澳大利亚先例[如 Waltons Stores (Interstate) Ltd. v. Maher 先例]做出裁决。因此,为了防止任何一方当事人的代表律师取巧或无知,导致仲裁员误判,笔者认为有必要针对这方面进行进一步介绍。

现实中的另一个重要性是一直以来,英国合约法的地位是只要双方还停留在谈判阶段,即使只有很琐碎的合约条文没有达成一致,任何一方都可以说走就走,不会产生法律后果。但一旦有合约存在,就再也不能反悔,如果无法履行合约承诺或责任,法律就会要求违约方承担“次要合约责任”(secondary obligation),就是对这个违约产生的损失向无辜方做出金钱上的赔偿。所以,订立合约的双方都会小心这个谈判阶段与订立了合约的分水线,在自己没有完全肯定可以履行前,不会轻易越过这个分水线而受到合约的约束。[180] 当然,双方在谈判过程中也可以达成初步协议(preliminary agreement)或附属协议(collateral contract),如过渡协议(bridging contract)等,以保护谈判会产生的费用,并通过这些中间协议约定如果最后的主合约谈不妥,这笔费用如何分摊。[181] 如果没有这种中间协议,就很难避免其中一方或双方浪费了大量时间、精力与金钱谈判但最后谈不妥,虽然这是商业社会(特别是国际商业社会)普遍接受的风险。在英国法律下,是不会想到在谈判中双方曾经做出的陈述与承诺会在合约谈不妥之后,其中一方以承诺性禁反言向对方寻求衡平法救济。重要

---

〔180〕 这在本书之第一章与杨良宜的《合约的解释:规则与应用》一书第二章有详论。

〔181〕 可见杨良宜的《合约的解释:规则与应用》一书第二章第 6 段。

原因之一是承诺性禁反言需要双方存在一定的法律关系,[182] 并且只能作为盾牌,而这两种要求实际上是有密切关系。所以,双方如果没有一个合约关系,只是在进行试图达成合约关系的谈判,这是完全不足以适用承诺性禁反言。

12.3.1 Waltons Stores (Interstate) Ltd. v. Maher 先例

在进一步介绍澳大利亚不同的法律地位之前,不妨先介绍 Waltons Stores (Interstate) Ltd. v. Maher (1988) 164 CLR 387 先例的简单案情。Waltons Stores 与土地所有人 Maher 谈判租用相关的土地与建筑。Maher 建议拆掉原有的建筑并新盖一栋 14000 平方英尺的建筑。Waltons Stores 也同意,但提出图纸与规格要符合该建筑用作超级市场的要求,并要在 1984 年 1 月 15 日完工。这个完工日期后来双方同意延迟到 1984 年 2 月 5 日。不久后,Maher 也开始动工,因为怕年底长假期的延误导致赶不及在要求的日期前完工。期间,双方已经就相关的租金与租约条文达成一致。但 Waltons Stores 保留了修改合约的权利,双方在之后也的确提出了一些小修改。1983 年 11 月 7 日, Waltons Stores 的代表律师写信给 Maher 的代表律师,附上了修改后的租约,并说:"You should note that we have not yet obtained our client's specific instructions to each amendment requested, but we believe that approval will be forthcoming. We will let you know tomorrow if any amendments are not agreed to."

Waltons Stores 的代表律师第二天没有做出进一步通知,于是 Maher 的代表律师认为 Waltons Stores 已经同意了相关修改。Maher 在 11 月 11 日签署了租约并交出给 Waltons Stores,虽然 Waltons Stores 签署后租约才会正式生效,但 Maher 认为这只是例行手续(formality)。然而在 1984 年 1 月 19 日,Waltons Stores 的代表律师回复说他的客户不接受有关修改,要从谈判中脱身。显然 Waltons Stores 是有其他的理由不想接受租约,这可能是经济或其他环境有了改变。但当时 Maher 已经花费了很多金钱将新建筑的工程完成了 40% 。

因此 Maher 以 Waltons Stores 被承诺性禁反言不能否认租约为由,向法院申请"履约指令"(specific performance)要求 Waltons Stores 履行租约,否则就要赔偿损失。Maher 的根据就是 1983 年 11 月 7 日 Waltons Stores 的代表律师的信件,以及从 1983 年 11 月 7 日到 1984 年 1 月 19 日之间的沉默与不行动。在该先例中,Waltons Stores 早就知道不会接受租约,也知道 Maher 有误解并在花钱进行工程,但没有提醒 Maher。[183] 看来法院十分同情 Maher,认为 Waltons Stores 的行为确实不合情理与恶劣,所以虽然存在双方之间没有合约关系这一障碍,仍然判 Maher 胜诉。

12.3.2 澳大利亚对禁反言的不同法律地位

澳大利亚的法律地位在高院(澳大利亚最高的法院)的 Waltons Stores (Interstate) Ltd. v. Maher (1988) 164 CLR 387 先例后有了重要改变,对构成禁反言双方

---

[182] 见本章第 5 段。

[183] 关于有责任说清楚(duty to speak),可见本章之 6.4 段与本书第五章第 10 段。

不再需要存在合约关系，承诺性禁反言可以作为宝剑，而不仅仅是盾牌。这与澳大利亚近年来试图将不同类别的禁反言统一为衡平法禁反言（equitable estoppel）以针对所有法院认为不合情理（unconscionable）的言行有密切关系。因为要同意不同类别的禁反言，对不同类别的禁反言的构成要件也必须一致。而"产权人禁反言"（proprietary estoppel）一直以来都可以作为衡平法诉因提起诉讼，[184]不要求双方存在一定的法律关系。这样，统一后其他类别的禁反言，尤其是本章介绍的承诺性禁反言，就可以作为宝剑，而不止是盾牌。

笔者可先节录 Michael Spence 律师所著的《Protecting Reliance：the emergent doctrine of equitable estoppel》（1999 年）一书有关澳大利亚法律的说法。该书根据 Commonwealth of Australia v. Verwayen（1990）170 CLR 394 与 Waltons Stores（Interstate）Ltd. v. Maher 等先例中，在第 30 页做出结论说："... the trend of Australian law towards a unified law of estoppel is to be welcomed and the first element of the doctrine of equitable estoppel is that it is 'One single doctrine of common law and equity ...'"

在 Commonwealth of Australia v. Verwayen 先例，[185] Mason 大法官说："... one doctrine of estoppel, which provides that a court of common law or equity can do what is required, but no more, to prevent a person who has relied upon an assumption as to present, past or future state of affairs（including a legal state of affairs）, which assumption the party estopped has induced him to hold, from suffering detriment in reliance upon the assumption as a result of the denial of its correctness."

在 Waltons Stores（Interstate）Ltd. v. Maher 先例中，Deane 大法官说："... unduly to preserve the importance of past separation and continuing distinctness as a barrier against the orderly development of a simplied and unified legal system which fusion was intended to advance.[186]"

《Protecting Reliance：the emergent doctrine of equitable estoppel》（1999 年）一书第 31 页，说："... pre – existing contractual relationship, this requirement is not a part of the new Australian doctrine. The plaintiff and defendant in Waltons were not in any kind of contractual relationship but were merely parties to unsuccessful contractual negotiations. Moreover, subsequent decisions have assumed that this possible limitation on the application of the doctrine no longer applies... The court in Waltons seemed to deny that any type of legal relationship was necessary. It was understood by both judges and academic commentators that the case had abolished this requirement ... However, in Ver-

---

[184] Plimmer v. Mayor of Wellington（1884）9 App Cas 699 先例。

[185] 见本章之 11.6 段。

[186] 这是说保留普通法法院与衡平法法院在针对不同类别的禁反言做出救济时的区分，反而会对达成两者合并时希望的简单与统一的法律系统造成阻碍。

wayen, the question of whether a pre – existing relationship was necessary was treated as still open by at least two of the judges, Mason CJ and Dawson J. Their judgements might be seen as raising a doubt that the requirement is not altogether abolished. The better view is that no pre – existing legal relationship should be required for the application of equitable estoppel. . . ”

在英国法中,近年来也有法官在先例中提到希望将不同类别的禁反言统一,毕竟在现实中,各个类别的禁反言互有重叠,在个别的事实下也常常很难区分究竟属于哪类的禁反言。如 Denning 勋爵在 Amalgamated v. Texas Bank (1982) 1 Lloyd's Rep. 27 先例中,就在提到产权人禁反言、陈述性禁反言、沉默性禁反言与承诺性禁反言后说:“All these can be seen to merge into one general principle shorn of limitations. When the parties to a transaction proceed on the basis of an underlying assumption – either of fact or of law, due to misrepresentation or mistake makes no difference – on which they have conducted the dealings between them – neither of them shall be allowed to go back on that assumption when it would be unfair or unjust to allow him to do so.”

另在 Taylor Fashions Ltd. v. Liverpool Victoria Trustees Co. Ltd. (1982) QB 133 先例中,Oliver 大法官也说:“Furthermore the more recent cases indicate, in my judgment, that the application of the Ramden v. Dyson L. R. 1 KL 129 principle – whether you call it proprietary estoppel, estoppel by acquiescence or estoppel by encouragement is reallt immaterial – requires a very much broader approach which is directed rather at ascertaining whether, in particular individual circumstances, it would be unconscionable for a party to deny that which, knowingly or unknowingly, he has allowed or encouraged another to assume to his detriment than to inquiring whether the circumstances can be fitted within the confines of some preconceived formula serving as a universal yardstick for every form of unconscionable behavior.”

但这些统一为一个禁反言的说法的建议在较近期的两个上诉庭先例被拒绝:Dun & Bradstreet Software Services (England) Ltd. v. Provident Mutual Life Assurance Association (1997) EWCA Civ 1816 先例与 Baird Textile Holdings Ltd. v. Marks & Spencer Plc. (2001) EWCA Civ 274 先例。

12.3.3　合约谈判适用禁反言带来的冲击

澳大利亚高院在 Waltons Stores (Interstate) Ltd. v. Maher (1988) 164 CLR 387 先例的判法也并非没有澳大利亚的法官与学者持异议。在 Handley 大法官所著的《Estoppel by Conduct and Election》(2006 年)一书中,就批评 Waltons Stores (Interstate) Ltd. v. Maher 先例令承诺性禁反言的适用范围延伸得太广。但这只是他个人的看法,而 Waltons Stores (Interstate) Ltd. v. Maher 先例作为一个生效的澳大利亚最高法院的判决是事实。这样,即使最终没有订立有法律效力的合约,但在谈判过程中的陈述或承诺也可能构成承诺性禁反言,这就会对英国一直以来的合约法地位与国际商业人士惯常的做法与认知产生冲击。

可以说在大部分情况下,双方都理解在谈判阶段,任何一方都可以随时脱身,因此,在订立合约前除了谈判所需要花费的时间、精力与金钱,是不会花钱做任何额外的事情。而如果最后合约谈不妥,双方也认为他们的花费是各自要承担的风险与成本。在这种情况下,由于没有不公平与不合情理的因素,双方也不会对谈判的陈述与承诺做出依赖,所以,承诺性禁反言或任何其他类别的禁反言不会适用。正如 Mason 大法官在 Waltons Stores (Interstate) Ltd. v. Maher 先例中说:"Parties who are negotiating a contract may proceed in the expectation that the terms will be agreed and a contract made out, so long as both parties recognize that either party is at liberty to withdraw from the negotiations at any time before the contract is made, it cannot be unconscionable for one party to do so"

Mason 大法官也引用了 Templeman 勋爵在 Attorney General of Hong Kong v. Humphreys Estate (Queen's Gardens) Ltd. (1987) AC 114 先例中,说:"It is possible but unlikely that in circumstances at present unforeseeable a party to negotiations set out in a document expressed to be 'subject to contract' would be able to satisfy the court that the parties had subsequently agreed to convert the document into a contract or that some form of estoppel had arisen to prevent both parties from refusing to proceed with the transactions envisaged by the document."

但在一些合约中,如工程合约或土地买卖合约,在双方达成有法律效力的合约前,确实有情况是谈判的其中一方需要做一些谈判以外的工作或事情。如由于时间紧,到合约成立后才开始工作会来不及,像 Waltons Stores (Interstate) Ltd. v. Maher 先例中的情况。这样,如果是他因为对最后可以订立合约过度有信心而自愿花费,这是他自己需要承担的风险。但也会是另一方要求他进行一些工作,而他为了巩固双方的关系等原因也花钱开始工作。或是另一方鼓励他进行一些工作或令他有了不切实际的期待而进行工作。在后两种情况之下,就可能涉及法律的救济。

通常这些合约的谈判分为三个阶段,首先是双方针对主要条文(main terms)进行谈判。谈妥之后,会进入第二阶段对一些细节进行谈判,包括等待满足合约的先决条件(condition precedent)[187]等。双方会在第二阶段签署一些没有法律效力的意向书(letter of intend):British Steel Corp. v. Cleveland Bridge & Engineering Co. Ltd. (1984) 1 All ER 504 先例等。第三阶段也是最后的阶段是正式订立合约,如双方交换并签署合约,而这也表示过了分水线,从谈判变为双方之间存在有法律效力的合约。其中一方甚至双方要提前做一些谈判以外的事情的情况一般发生在第二阶段,因为这时双方都比较确信最终会订立合约。如果最后无法订立合约,往往也不是因

---

〔187〕 如"subject finance"、"subject to board approval"等,关于合约的先决条件,可见杨良宜的《合约的解释:规则与应用》一书第八章。

为双方谈不妥,而是外部环境发生了改变。

在英国法下,因为对方的要求或鼓励而做了额外工作的一方,可能可以根据"复原原则"(restitution)/"不当得利"(unjust enrichment)从另一方取回这笔额外的花费。这复原原则可节录《McGregor on Damages》(第19版,2014年)一书之1-006段,如下:"Actions claiming monetary restitution in the law of unjust enrichment, actions introduced some centuries ago under the confusing title of quasi-contract, did not depend upon a wrong done to the claimant. Their introduction was indeed attributable to the fact that no wrong was available upon which the claimant might sue. Illustrations are provided by actions for money paid under a mistake of fact, actions for money paid under a contract which is in some way vitiated and actions to recover money paid to a third party for which the defendant is primarily liable. **Such claims depended not upon a loss to the claimant but upon a benefit to the defendant**..."(加黑部分是笔者的强调)

但复原原则针对一些客观看应该做出救济,也不是花钱的一方自愿承担谈判风险的情况,本身有一个大缺陷。这就是复原原则是追究另外一方所得到的好处(benefit)或不当得利。这样,复原原则所针对的如果是错给了对方一笔钱的情况,就清楚明了什么是要追讨的好处或得利(enrichment)。但在这种错误认为最终会订立合约而花费金钱与提供服务的情况,就会有困难是另一方不一定得利或有好处。正如Goff勋爵与G Jones大律师所著的权威书籍《The Law of Restitution》(第7版,2007年)一书所说:"the receipt of money always benefits the defendant. But services may not do so."

如在Waltons Stores (Interstate) Ltd. v. Maher先例中,就显然看不出Waltons Stores究竟有什么好处或得利,因为它最后没有租这个建筑,Maher拆掉旧的建筑所花的钱虽然是浪费,但对Waltons Stores并没有好处。这就是为什么Maher需要以承诺性禁反言作为诉因寻求救济。但如果承诺性禁反言的适用范围延伸到谈判阶段,对整个合约法的基础与惯常的商业做法都会造成冲击。而且在谈判阶段所用的惯常技巧也往往涉及很多陈述与承诺。即使如澳大利亚高院在Waltons Stores (Interstate) Ltd. v. Maher先例中所说,承诺性禁反言只会用来针对不合情理的言行,不会对合约法下谈判阶段任何一方都可以随时脱身的地位产生冲击。但在笔者看来,如果只有不公平或不合情理作为唯一的限制,仍是十分危险。因为虽然法律是要求客观看待个别案件的案情是否有不公平或不合情理,但现实中这很大程度取决于法官或仲裁庭的主观"裁量权"(discretion),这就会带来很大的不肯定,像英国法批评大陆法的善意。[188] 如在Brewer Street Investments Ltd. v. Barclays Woollen Co. Ltd. (1954) 1 QB 428的英国先例中,雇主在谈判中告诉对方他投的标是三个标书中价格最低的,就有可能被视为不公平或不合情理。

---

〔188〕 见本章之8.3段。

这也不止针对谈判中做了额外工作但结果没有订立合约的情况。如在建筑合约中,承建商在竞标前往往要先从他的供应商或分承建商得到报价,才能确定自己竞标的报价。而如果在竞标成功后,供应商或分承建商不肯按照之前的报价订立合约,承建商就会陷入十分被动的境地。一直以来,针对这种情况,英国法律采取的对策是承建商与供应商或分承建商先根据报价订立合约,但有一个后续条件(condition subsequent)[189]是承建商竞标成功,双方才需要履行。而如果承诺性禁反言可以适用在谈判阶段,承建商根本无需与供应商或分承建商提前订立任何合约。如果供应商或分承建商事后反悔,承建商可以根据承诺性禁反言,要求对方履行承诺。

12.3.4　英国法律针对在合约谈判中做了额外工作的一方的救济

英国这种先例也有很多,比较早期的有 Jenning and Chapman Ltd. v. Woodman Matthews & Co. (1952) 2 TLR 406, Brewer Street Investments Ltd. v. Barclays Woollen Co. Ltd. (1954) 1 QB 428, William Lacey (Hounslow) Ltd. v. Davis (1957) 1 WLR 932, British Steel Corp. v. Cleveland Bridge & Engineering Co. Ltd. (1984) 1 All ER 504 等先例。近期的先例包括 Countrywide Communications Limited v. ICL Pathway Ltd. (1996) C No 2446, MSM Consulting Ltd. v. United Republic of Tanzania (2009) EWHC 121 (QB), Whittle Movers Ltd. v. Hollywood Express Ltd. (2009) EWCA Civ 1189, Tahar Benourad v. Compass Group Plc. (2010) EWHC 1882 (QB), Killen v. Horseworld Ltd. (2011) EWHC 1600 (QB), Elek v. Bar – Tur (2013) EWHC 207 (Ch), Benedetti v. Sawiris (2013) UKSC 50 等先例。

英国目前的法律地位可节录 Nicholas Strauss Q. C. 大法官在 Countrywide Communications Limited v. ICL Pathway Ltd. 先例做出的总结,如下:

"I have found it impossible to formulate a clear general principle which satisfactorily governs the different factual situations which have arisen, let alone those which could easily arise in other cases.[190] Perhaps, in the absence of any recognition in English law of a general duty of good faith in contractual negotiations, this is not surprising.[191] Much of the difficulty is caused by attempting to categorise as an unjust enrichment of the defendant, for which an action in restitution is available, what is really a loss unfairly sustained by the plaintiff.[192] There is a lot to be said for a broad principle enabling either to be recompensed, but no such principle is clearly established in English Law.[193] Un-

[189] 见杨良宜《合约的解释:规则与应用》一书第八章第 3 段。

[190] 不可能有一个清楚的一般原则可以适用在所有在谈判过程中做了额外工作的情况。

[191] 考虑到英国法律一般来说不认为谈判的双方有善意的责任,这也不奇怪。

[192] 原告能够通过复原原则,以被告不当得利取回他的花费,但很多情况下其实只是让原告承担损害会造成不公平,而被告其实没有得利,将这种情况归类为不当得利有困难。

[193] 一直都有说法应该有更广泛的原则可以令原告在他蒙受损害与被告获益或不当得利的情况都可以获得赔偿,但英国法律没有明确建立这个原则。

doubtedly the court may impose an obligation to pay for benefits resulting from services performed in the course of a contract which is expected to, but does not, come into existence. This is so, even though, in all cases, the defendant is ex hypothesi free to withdraw from the proposed contract, whether the negotiations were expressly made 'subject to contract' or not. Undoubtedly, such an obligation will be imposed only if justice requires it or, which comes to much the same thing, if it would be unconscionable for the plaintiff not to be recompensed.[194]

Beyond that, I do not think that it is possible to go further than to say that, in deciding whether to impose an obligation and if so its extent, the court will take into account and give appropriate weight to a number of considerations which can be identified in the authorities. The first is whether the services were of a kind which would normally be given free of charge.[195] Secondly, the terms in which the request to perform the services was made may be important in establishing the extent of the risk (if any) which the plaintiffs may fairly be said to have taken that such services would in the end be unrecompensed. What may be important here is whether the parties are simply negotiating, expressly or impliedly 'subject to contract', or whether one party has given some kind of assurance or indication that he will not withdraw, or that he will not withdraw except in certain circumstances.[196] Thirdly, the nature of the benefit which has resulted to the defendants is important, and in particular whether such benefit is real (either 'realised' or 'realisable') or a fiction... Plainly, a court will at least be more inclined to impose an obligation to pay for a real benefit, since otherwise the abortive negotiations will leave the defendant with a windfall and the plaintiff out of pocket. However, the judgment of Denning L. J. in the Brewer Street case suggests that the performance of services requested may of itself suffice amount to a benefit or enrichment.[197] Fourthly what may often be decisive are the circumstances in which the anticipated contract does not materialise and in particular whether they can be said to involve 'fault' on the part of the defendant,

---

〔194〕 毫无疑问的是,如果双方都认为最终会订立合约,但最后没有订立,法院会判被告有责任为在这期间的服务的获益做出支付。虽然在当时还没有订立合约,双方还在谈判阶段都可以要走就走,无论谈判时是否明示说明"以订立合约为准"。当然,只有在不公平或不合情理的情况下,法律才会做出救济。

〔195〕 法院在做出判断时应考虑以下方面。第一,原告在谈判中提供的服务是否一般是免费的。

〔196〕 第二,原告提供服务时,是否接受了这服务最后可能无法获得回报的风险。这里需要考虑的是,原告提供服务时双方只是在谈判,并且明示或默示接受以订立合约为准,在这种情况下,就有很大可能原告要自己承担风险。或是被告向原告表示或做出保证,他不会从谈判中脱身或是除非特殊情况他才会从谈判中脱身,在这种情况下,被告就很有可能要对原告提供的服务做出支付。

〔197〕 第三,法院会考虑被告的获益的性质是真实的或只是虚构。法院会更愿意判事实上获益的被告做出支付,否则就会造成被告因为谈判不成发一笔横财,而原告要从口袋里冤枉掏钱出来的后果。

or (perhaps of more relevance) to be outside the scope of the risk undertaken by the plaintiff at the outset.[198] I agree with the view of Rattee J. that the law should be flexible in this area, and the weight to be given to each of the factors may vary from case to case."

在 MSM Consulting Ltd. v. United Republic of Tanzania 先例中, Clarke 大法官说:"(a) Although the older authorities use the language of implied contract the modern approach is to determine whether or not the circumstances are such that the law should, as a matter of justice, impose upon the defendant an obligation to make payment of an amount which he deserved to be paid (quantum meruit) . . . ;[199] (b) Generally speaking a person who seeks to enter into a contract with another cannot claim to be paid the cost of estimating what it will cost him, or of deciding on a price, or bidding for the contract. Nor can he claim the cost of showing the other party his capability or skills even though, if there was a contract or retainer, he would be paid for them. The solicitor who enters a 'beauty contest' in the course of which he expresses some preliminary views about the client's prospects cannot, ordinarily expect to charge for them. If another firm is retained; he runs the risk of being unrewarded if unsuccessful in his pitch;[200] (c) The court is likely to impose such an obligation where the defendant has received an incontrovertible benefit (e. g. an immediate financial gain or saving of expense) as a result of the claimant's services; or where the defendant has requested the claimant to provide services or accepted them (having the ability to refuse them) when offered, in the knowledge that the services were not intended to be given freely;[201] (d) But the court may not regard it as just to impose an obligation to make payment if the claimant took the risk that he or she would only be reimbursed for his expenditure if there was a concluded contract; or if the court concludes that, in all the circumstances the risk should fall on the claim-

---

[198] 第四,也通常是有决定性的考虑是什么原因导致最终合约没有订立,特别是是否涉及被告的错误,或是超出了开始谈判时原告愿意承担的风险。

[199] 尽管一些早期的先例会使用默示合约的说法,现代的说法是法院要看相关的事实是否需要法律从公众的角度来让被告承担支付他应支付的金钱的责任。

[200] 一般来说,合约一方不能取回谈判过程中的花费,如估计成本或价格的花费,或投标的花费等。同样,合约一方也不能取回显示自己能力或技术的花费,即使如果有合约关系,这些服务会获得报酬。如律师事务所为了抢生意,会对潜在客户的案件做出一些初步意见,而如果最后潜在客户委任了另一家律师事务所,他是不能获得这部分工作的报酬,而要自己承担无法获得委任的风险。

[201] 如果被告因为原告的服务无可争议地获益(如马上获得经济上的增长或节省了开支),或是被告要求原告提供服务,或是被告虽然知道原告并不是意图免费提供服务,但仍接受了原告提供服务的要约,法院会更愿意判被告有责任做出支付。

ant...;[202] (e) The court may well regard it as just to impose such an obligation if the defendant who has received the benefit has behaved unconscionably in declining to pay for it.[203]"

最后在《Chitty on Contracts》(第32版,2015年)之29－077段,对目前英国法律的地位做出结论,说:"... In MSM Consulting Ltd. v. United Republic of Tanzania, Clarke J. identified various principles relating to quantum meruit claims arising from work done in anticipation of a contract which did not materialise, including that it is not possible to claim for the cost of bidding for the contract; a remedy will not be available where the claimant took the risk of being reimbursed only if a contract was concluded; and the court might impose an obligation on the defendant who has received a benefit if they have behaved unconscionably in declining to pay for it."

上述节录的最后一句的法律地位与澳大利亚高院 Waltons Stores (Interstate) Ltd. v. Maher (1988) 164 CLR 387 先例的区别是,在该先例中,Waltons Stores 并没有获益。而针对被告没有获益只是原告有损失的情况,英国法律的地位还不明确。另是在该先例中,澳大利亚高院并不是判 Maher 可以取回40%工作的花费,而应是判 Waltons Stores 被禁反言,不能否认租约的存在。可以说,Waltons Stores (Interstate) Ltd. v. Maher 先例在这方面走得太远。

12.4 情况之四:合约履行中一方违约的情况下无辜方的应对

本章之11.3段介绍的 The "Kanchenjunga" (1990) 1 Lloyd's Rep. 391 先例与本章之11.4段介绍的 The "Chemical Venture" (1993) 1 Lloyd's Rep. 508 先例所涉及的不安全港口(unsafe port)问题是租船合约中经常会有的争议。显然,如果出事的港口的确是被事后认定为不安全,承租人就是违约,因为租船合约一般都会明示或默示承租人有这个合约责任或承诺只使用安全港口。但这只是租船合约中一种可能会出现的违约,还有其他数不胜数的违约。如承租人装载危险品/违禁品,没有准时支付租金或运费,下令船舶行走非法的最后航次(illegitimate last voyage),签发不合理或不正确的提单等;或船东交船或递交准备就绪通知书时船舶规格不符合租约描述,装货上船后船长不合理拒绝签发提单等。更不用说租船合约只是不同合约类别中的一种,每一类合约在履行过程中都会有各种违反合约责任或承诺的情况。"待履行合约"(executory contract)的履行中,一方违约要求或做一些看来是合约不允许的事,无辜方的应对就很重要与困难。最基本的就是抗拒与阻止对方这样做,或是听之任之。

---

〔202〕 但如果原告愿意承担一旦合约不能订立,他就无法获得支付的风险,或是法院认定无论如何都应该由原告承担这风险,法院就不会在被告身上强加要对原告提供的服务做出支付的责任。

〔203〕 如果法院认为因为原告提供的服务而获益的被告拒绝做出支付是不合情理,也会判被告有做出支付的责任。

如果无辜方马上抗拒对方的违约，拒绝履行，这除了不太友善外，潜在的危险是如果各走极端，但后来在仲裁被裁定[204]合约实际上允许对方这样做，即对方并没有违约，这就导致原本自以为是无辜方的一方其实是违约甚至严重至违约/毁约（repudiatory breach）而导致合约终止，并要面对可能是金额庞大的索赔。而如果无辜方想息事宁人，知道对方违约但还照样履行，但后来出现变数（如 The "Kanchenjunga" 先例中，船员抗拒停留在不安全港口）或后患（如 The "Chemical Venture" 先例中，船舶被炸受损），后果甚至可能比起初想象的严重得多。这时再想改变主意拒绝履行或索赔损失，就会面对弃权或禁反言（主要是衡平法宽限或承诺性禁反言）的争议。

如果对方的行为被判为违约的可能性较低，而且后果又不严重，或者会选择履行。但会有一些折中的做法，主要是在同意履行前明确表示抗议（under protest）或保留权利（reserve rights）。但正如本章之 6.5.5.2 段所介绍，如果无辜方在履行过程中有其他言行是与保留权利完全不符，还是起不到作用，法院或仲裁庭整体解释无辜方的言行，仍会构成弃权或禁反言。所以在履行的过程中要警觉性高，一旦发生变数，就要当机立断。履行的时间拖得越长，就会有更多的言行被对方指称构成禁反言。另一种折中的做法是双方针对这个可能是违约的履行达成合约更改（variation），如双方同意履行是在无损害（without prejudice）的地位下，也约定如果履行中途发生怎样的变数，无辜方可以中止履行，另是双方如何尽快确定是否有违约（如去法院或仲裁庭取得宣告判决/裁决）[205]等。

针对一方之前曾经违反合约条文，但无辜方因宽限而弃权的情况，无辜方之后不能坚持原本的合约条文。无辜方之前的宽限被视为以言行做出承诺，不会坚持原本的合约或法律权利。如租约中船东多次听从承租人的命令前往不安全港口，或是在租约不允许的地区营运，船东就不能突然以违反租约为由拒绝听从承租人前往不安全港口或在租约不允许的地区营运的命令。毕竟承租人会依赖无辜方的承诺做出安排，如订立分租约，而船东撤回承诺会造成损害。无辜方想要回复到原本的合约或法律地位，就必须做出合理通知，包括提前合理时间做出等：Hartley v. Hymans (1920) 3 KB 475 等先例。

可以上诉庭的 Charles Rickards Ltd. v. Oppenheim (1950) 1 KB 616 先例为例。该先例涉及货物买卖，有关的合约是 Oppenheim 向 Charles Rickards 订购了劳斯莱斯的底盘，并要求在底盘上建造房车车身。Charles Rickards 将建造房车车身的工程交给了一家第三方的大巴建造公司。该公司承诺在 6 个月，最多不超过 7 个月的时间内完成建造。合约中写明时间规定是重要（time of essence），房车应在 1948 年 3 月

---

〔204〕 要知道有诉讼风险，即仲裁庭会错判，更不用说合约是否允许对方这样做属于对合约的解释。由于订约自由，合约有千变万化的写法，所以即使自己认为合约已经足够清楚，一旦发生争议，还是会有灰色地带。

〔205〕 这种理智的做法在本书第一章之 3.6.4.3 段已有详尽介绍。

20 日之前交付。但在 3 月 20 日,房车建造工作没有完成,Oppenheim 并没有终止合约,而是不断催促 Charles Rickards(与大巴建造公司)完成建造并交付房车。但在 6 月 29 日,Oppenheim 写信给大巴建造公司,说明如果不能在 7 月 25 日之前交付,他会拒绝接受房车。房车最终在 10 月 18 日完成建造,但 Oppenheim 拒绝接受。Charles Rickards 于是开始诉讼,要求 Oppenheim 支付余款,而 Oppenheim 则反索赔已经支付的劳斯莱斯的底盘的费用。上诉庭判是 Oppenheim 在 3 月 20 日后没有终止合约并不断催促 Charles Rickards 完成建造的行为构成衡平法宽限或承诺性禁反言。但他在 6 月 29 日的通知,令他回复到原本的合约地位,即时间规定是重要,如果 Charles Rickards 无法在 7 月 25 日交付,他就可以终止合约。至于这个通知是否合理,包括是否有合理的时间让 Charles Rickards(与大巴建造公司)完成合约,Denning 大法官说:"So the next question is: was this a reasonable notice? Mr. Sachs(Charles Rickards 代表大律师)argued that it was not. He said that a reasonable notice must give sufficient time for the work, then outstanding, to be completed. He says that, on the evidence in this case, four weeks was not a reasonable time because it would, and did in fact, require three and a half months to complete it. In my opinion, however, the words of Lord Parker in Stickney v. Keeble (1915) AC 386 apply to such a case as the present just as much as they do to a contract for the sale of land. He said that 'in considering whether the time so limited is a reasonable time the court will consider all the circumstances of the case. No doubt what remains to be done at the date of the notice is of importance, but it is by no means the only relevant fact. The fact that the purchaser has continually been pressing for completion, or has before given similar notices which he has waived, or that it is specially important to him to obtain early completion, are equally relevant facts' – to which I would add, in the present case, the fact that the original contract made time of the essence of the contract. In this particular case, not only did the defendant press continually for delivery, not only was he given promises of speedy delivery, but on the very day before he gave this notice he was told by the works manager in charge of the work that it would be ready within two weeks. Then he gave a four weeks' notice. The judge found that it was a reasonable notice, and, in my judgment, there is no ground on which this court could in any way differ from that finding. The reasonableness of the time fixed by the notice must, of course, be judged at the time at which it is given. It cannot be held to be a bad notice because, after it is given, the suppliers find themselves in unanticipated difficulties in making delivery."

显然,这些做法能否取得满意的结果,很大程度还是取决于对手相对自己的强弱,特别是法律与业务水平的高低。

第五章　陈述性禁反言

1. 简　　介

1.1　误述

对事实做出错误陈述或“误述”(misrepresentation or misstatement)是经常会遇到的情况,本章所针对的“陈述性禁反言”(estoppel by representation)与其他方面的误述是两种不同的理论或说法。其他方面的误述在杨良宜《国际商务游戏规则——英国合约法》一书第五章有详论。其他方面的误述被分为三种:第一种也是最重要的一种是误述导致合约的产生;第二种是误述不导致合约产生,实际是侵权行为;第三种是履约中的错误陈述,虽然通常被称为误述,但实是违约的情况。

陈述性禁反言与其他方面的误述之间有很多相同或重叠之处,特别是针对什么才会构成错误陈述,这稍后会在本章第2段有详论。但两者所针对的情况以及会造成的后果或救济很不一样,陈述性禁反言只是不准陈述方事后针对正确的事实情况举证与推翻原来做出的错误陈述,而是根据错误的陈述确定双方的法律权利。错误陈述可以在任何时间做出,包括在合约履行的期间。严格来说,陈述性禁反言也无须与合约的成立有关系。

1.1.1　误述导致合约产生

导致合约产生的误述,普通法的救济主要是针对欺诈性误述(fraudulent misrepresentation),就是让被陈述方(representee)有权取消(rescind)[1]这一有缺陷的合约,即这种合约是可使无效的(voidable)。此外,被陈述方还可以欺骗的侵权行为(tortious action of deceit)作为诉因索赔蒙受的损失。到了19世纪,衡平法(equity law)允许由非欺诈性误述所导致的合约也可被取消,但被陈述方想再进一步索赔损失则不被允许。非欺诈性误述往往是指无辜的误述(innocent misrepresentation),即陈述方自己也不知道讲错了事实,如陈述方是从可靠的来源听到的所谓事实,但事实是错误的;也包括疏忽的误述(negligent misrepresentation),如没有合理小心谨慎(reasona-

---

〔1〕 在 Johnson v. Agnew (1980) A. C. 367 先例中,明确了取消与终止(terminate)合约的区别。因欺诈性误述而带来的取消是消除(wipe out)整个合约的存在,令双方回复到订约前各自的位置,所谓“rescission of a contract ab initio”。但终止合约,如履约时违反条件条文(condition),或违约/毁约(repudiation)被无辜方接受并终止合约,并不表示合约从不存在,不能回复到未订约前的位置。

ble care)地查清楚就陈述所谓的事实。1967 年《误述法》(Misrepresentation Act)生效后,疏忽的误述的被陈述方也可以获得损失赔偿。此外,该立法也给了法院或仲裁庭裁量权,即法官或仲裁员认为不公平的情况下(如有关误述只有微不足道的影响),可以不允许被陈述方以无辜或疏忽的误述取消合约,而改为以赔偿损失作为替代。导致合约产生的误述在做出的时间上显然必定是在合约产生之前,这才令合约的产生有了缺陷。与普通法下其他令合约无效(void)或可使无效的缺陷,如胁迫(duress)、错误(mistake)等相比,误述是发生得最多的情况。如在买卖合约中,双方谈判时,卖方常常会"卖花赞花香",一旦过分,就可能会构成误述。由于本章与本书都不会针对这一课题,所以只节录《Chitty on Contracts》(第 32 版,2015 年)一书之 7-001 段,如下:"**Preliminary.** The modern law relating to misrepresentation is a somewhat complex amalgam of rules of common law, equity and (since the coming into force of the Misrepresentation Act 1967) statute law. It is also complicated by the fact that misrepresentation may constitute an actionable tort in certain circumstances, as well as providing grounds for relief in the law of contract. Prior to the enactment of the Misrepresentation Act 1967, the position broadly speaking was that a misrepresentation which induced a person to enter into a contract gave the representee the right to rescind the contract, subject to certain conditions, but generally gave him no right to damages unless the misrepresentation was fraudulent, or, in some cases, negligent, or unless the representation amounted to a term of the contract. Since the coming into force of the Misrepresentation Act the representee who entered a contract as the result of a misrepresentation will always be able to claim damages for negligent misrepresentation in circumstances in which he could have recovered damages had the misrepresentation been fraudulent. In addition the Act gives the court a discretion to refuse to permit a representee to rescind a contract, but to award him damages in lieu of rescission, if the misrepresentation is negligent or wholly innocent; but it leaves the representee with an absolute right to rescind where the misrepresentation is fraudulent. The Act of 1967 does not, however, alter the rules as to what constitutes an effective misrepresentation..."

1.1.2 误述作为侵权行为

不导致合约产生,实际上是侵权[2]行为的误述,以前主要针对的只是双方有诚信关系(fiduciary relationship)的情况。这关系可能是父母与未成年子女、律师与客户、信托人与受托人、代理人与委托人、公司董事与股东等多种。基本上这关系是因为一方会受另一方的不当影响(undue influence),自己无法充分保障自己的利益而产生。在其他情况下的误述,即使有疏忽,但不至于是欺骗,只要不涉及合约的产生与

---

〔2〕 经济侵权(economic tort)的一种,其他还包括阴谋(conspiracy)、威胁(intimidation)、侵犯商标(infringement of trademarks)、骗卖(passing off)、侵犯版权(copyright)、专利(patent)等。

信托关系,法律一直以来对陈述方(representor)并不追究责任,直到贵族院的 Hedley Byrne v. Heller (1963) 1 Lloyd's Rep. 483 先例。在该先例中,案情关于银行提供客户资信的责任,银行在客户的要求下,给了原告一个对该客户资信满意的文件(原告与该客户有广告上的商业往来)。但事实上有错误,该客户欠银行不少钱。由于银行的疏忽与错误陈述,原告受损。在高院,McNair 大法官不认为银行有责任,因为双方没有诚信关系,说:"I am accordingly driven to the conclusion by authority binding upon me that no such action lies in the absence of contract or fiduciary relationship. On the facts before me there is clearly no contract, nor can I find a fiduciary relationship."

但在贵族院,法院认为如果一方有特别的技能(special skill)与知识,用来协助另一方并给予意见(advice)或资讯(information),他就有小心谨慎的责任(duty of care)。如果有疏忽或错误,破坏了这责任,他(如银行)应负上侵权的责任(liability in tort)。

这一重要的先例中,在《Chitty on Contracts》(第32版,2015年)一书多处都有提到,只节录7-089段部分内容如下:"Until the decision of the House of Lords in the Hedley Byrne case in 1964, it was thought that a duty of care in the making of statements could only arise in the case of fiduciary (or, of course, contractual) relationships, but that decision has shown that the law is, very much wider than this. Although the House made it clear that misrepresentations made in the course of a mere social relationship would not ground liability in tort, they also made it clear that many 'special relationships' would suffice. In particular, it is clear that professional relationships, even where there is no contract between the parties, will often give rise to a duty of care if it can be said that the representor knew or ought reasonably to have known that the representee was likely to act on the representation. So, for example, if a company's auditor gives negligent advice to a person who invests money in the company on the strength of the advice, and it can be shown that the auditor ought to have realized that the representee would act on the advice, an action for negligent representation will lie against the auditor.[3] Again advice given 'in a business connection' about the creditworthiness of a third party may give rise to a duty of care even where the adviser is not acting in a professional capacity, provided he has some financial interest in the transaction..."

疏忽的误述(相比疏忽的行为)的危险在于其无边无际,影响深远。如会计师做出的报告或者律师给出的意见可能被转发给其他人士,如果谁都可以对误述的侵权行为进行索赔,可能天下大乱,因此必须对可获得赔偿的被陈述方进行限制。一直以来侵权(主要是疏忽的行为)都有所谓的邻居原则(neighbour principle)的说法,即

[3] J. E. B. Fasteners Ltd. v. Marks, Bloom & Co. (1981) 3 All E. R. 289, (1983) 1 All E. R. 583 先例。

"persons so closely and directly affected by the defendant's(侵权方)act that they should be in his contemplation"。即侵权方只对其"邻居"有小心谨慎的责任,而一般社交层面(social relationship)不包括在内。

贵族院在 Hedley Byrne v. Heller 先例确立了以下三个要求:(1)陈述方可以合理预见被陈述方会依赖这陈述。例如,该案例的银行可以预见原告会依赖这份文件,但如果这份文件由原告给了其他不知名的朋友参考,就应不是银行可合理预见的了。(2)陈述方与被陈述方之间有足够的密切关系(necessary proximity),这应该就是上述节录的《Chitty on Contracts》(第 32 版,2015 年)一书之 7 - 089 段提到的特殊关系(special relationship)。(3)客观环境上看,要求陈述方向被陈述方尽小心谨慎的责任是公平与合理的(just and reasonable)。

关系要密切到何种程度的问题在 Caparo v. Dickman (1990) 2 WLR 358 先例中有详论。在该先例中,原告 Caparo 先生本来已是一家公司的小股东,他在看了 Dickman 先生(是该公司的审计师)对该公司做出的账目报告后,收购了公司其他股票而变为大股东。但报告有错,并引致 Caparo 先生投资损失。该案争议之一是双方是否有足够密切的关系?上诉庭说有,因为 Caparo 先生是股东之一,不是不知名的外来投资者,Dickman 先生应充分预见其报告会被 Caparo 先生参阅。但上诉到了贵族院,上诉庭判决被推翻,而这密切关系被进一步收紧。Oliver 勋爵说陈述方(Dickman 先生)在陈述时(给意见或做出报告时),必须知道依赖他的被陈述方(Caparo 先生)要此陈述的目的,而他也乐于被陈述方为此目的而依赖他的报告,甚至不会再另做调查。Jauncey 勋爵也说这依赖(即被陈述方依赖这报告或意见)达致某一目的必须是极有可能(highly probable)才可要误述方负责,而不能只是会有可能(possible)。

换言之,若要 Dickman 先生负责,情况应是 Caparo 先生想去收购公司的控股权而变为大股东,在进行收购前,先指示 Dickman 先生来评估公司的经济状况与前景。而如果 Dickman 先生在此报告有错,他对 Caparo 先生就有误述的责任。但如果 Dickman 先生只是例行公事的每年出一个账目报告,如给股东大会所用,他是不必对 Caparo 先生因这份报告而决定增持股份,而且并不另做调查的行为负任何责任。

如此看来,这种侵权下的误述的适用并不会无边无际。Millett 大法官在 Al Saudi Banquet v. Clark Pixel (1990) 2 WLR 344 先例中说:"In my judgment, Caparo marked the furthest limit to which the duty of care for negligent misstatement has so far been taken in England, and its reasoning does not encourage any further advance."

《Chitty on Contracts》(第 32 版,2015 年)一书之 7 - 090 段对 Caparo v. Dickman 先例总结说:"**Statement in connection with particular transaction.** In Caparo Industries Plc. v. Dickman it was held that there will be no liability in tort for negligent misrepresentation unless the maker of the statement knew that the statement would be communicated to the person relying on it specifically in connection with a particular transaction or a transaction of a particular kind. In relation to misrepresentation as between contracting parties, this appears to mean that the misrepresentation must have been made in connection with the contract in respect of which relief is sought, or at least that reliance on the representation in connection with the contract was likely."

1.1.3　误述实是违约行为

第三种是名为误述但实是违约的情况。这可分为两类，首先是在合约谈判时，一方做出了错误的陈述，导致或部分导致另一方订立合约。同时该错误陈述作为条文之一被写进了合约，并在履约中显示出来。如在买卖合约中，卖方在谈判中对货物的规格做出错误陈述，这可能是无辜，也可能是欺诈。前者可能是分卖方的错误陈述导致卖方在转告买方时也有了同样的错误陈述。而后者可能是卖方知道货物没有或很难有太高的规格，但为了做出交易，仍做出错误陈述。之后拟定买卖合约时，这货物规格也变为合约条文之一。但事后在履约中被买方发现卖方交付的货物货不对版。

这一类的情况带来的后果可节录《Chitty on Contracts》（第 32 版，2015 年）一书之 7 - 004 段，说："**Misrepresentation and contractual terms. . . .** there was also some authority for the proposition that if a misrepresentation was made before a contract was entered into, and the misrepresentation was subsequently incorporated into the contract as a contractual term, the law relating to misrepresentation was not applicable, and the case had to be dealt with as one involving a contractual term and nothing else.〔4〕 Since the passing of the Act of 1967 this is no longer the case, and it will often be necessary in any one situation to inquire carefully as to the effect of a misrepresentation both as a precontractual statement and as a contractual term. Where these effects differ (as they often do) it is in some cases a matter of considerable difficulty to determine with any certainty the effect of the Misrepresentation Act on the law relating to contractual misstatement.〔5〕"

另一类是在合约履行过程中做出的错误陈述，这明确属于违约。在《Chitty on Contracts》（第 32 版，2015 年）一书之 7 - 096 段，说："**Special relationship between parties already in contractual relationship.** It is now clear that one party to a contractu-

---

〔4〕 之前的说法是如果合约订立前对事实的错误陈述被写进了合约，则误述的相关法律不适用，只适用合约法。

〔5〕 但在 1967 年《误述法》生效后，就产生了困难，因为误述与违反合约会造成的法律后果不同，前者无辜方可以取消（rescind）合约，而后者无辜方只是终止（terminate）合约。如在上文举的买卖合约的例子，如果买方收货，只索赔货不对版的金钱损失，这问题不大。但在买方拒货的情况下，如果以误述取消合约，买方可向误述的卖方索赔侵权的损失。在《Benjamin's Sale of Goods》（第 9 版，2014 年）一书之 12 - 015 段，说："... may recover the loss he had suffered by entering into the contract, including consequential loss."如果涉及欺诈性误述，在近期的 Yam Seng Pte Ltd. v. International Trade Corporation Ltd. (2013) 1 Lloyd's Rep. 526 先例中，上诉庭认为不受损失的遥远性的合理预见（foreseeability）限制。而以合约条文终止合约，买方可索赔的损失在杨大明的《国际货物买卖》与杨良宜的《损失赔偿与救济》一书都有详论，不再重复。如果有关货物有市场，买方可以索赔的损失就是违约一天的市场价格与合约价格的差价。

al relationship may owe duties in tort to the other; these duties may overlap with contractual duties, and where this is the case the claimant may have alternative causes of action in contract and in tort.[6] It has also been held that damages may be obtainable for misrepresentations made in the course of renegotiating a contract already in existence, under the Misrepresentation Act, and there seems no reason to doubt that in an appropriate case liability could also arise under the Hedley Byrne principle in such a situation."

这种例子数不胜数,如在一个期租合约中,承租人询问船东可以装多少货,船东记错数,给了错误的答案,导致承租人准备的货物无法全部装上船而蒙受损失。这既属于违反期租合约的条文,也是错误的陈述。虽然这是同步责任(concurrent liability)的例子之一,但承租人提起的诉讼还是以合约条文为准。同样性质但千变万化的情况也会发生在其他类别的合约,这里不再举例。

至于《Chitty on Contracts》(第32版,2015年)一书之7-096段提到的1967年《误述法》也适用在合约"更改"(variation)[7]的谈判(renegotiation),可以笔者杨良宜曾经处理过一个案子为例。中方船东与南美承租人订立了包运合约,但是承租人声称没有货物付运,要求船东不执行其中一个航次。当时市场下跌,船东为了显示友好,保住这一赚钱的租约(其实没有关系,只是中方经常有一相情愿的让步),同意减少一个航次。但事后船东发现事实上承租人是在市场上另找了一艘运费较低的船舶进行同一航次的付运。笔者代表船东向承租人要求赔偿,而承租人则声称船东同意减少一个航次构成"合约更改"(variation)或"承诺性禁反言"(promissory estoppel)。但这两个说法显然不能成立,如果构成合约更改,双方重新谈判是基于承租人做出的错误陈述(没有货装),构成误述(应该是欺诈性误述),因此,船东可以根据普通法或1967年《误述法》取消合约更改,回复到原本的合约地位。至于承诺性禁反言,船东虽然做出了承诺,但承租人故意做出错误陈述,自己不干净(unclean hand),无法获得这一衡平法救济。

1.2 陈述性禁反言

"陈述性禁反言"(estoppel by representation)主要针对陈述方(representor)较早时做出了错误的陈述,而被陈述方(representee)依赖该陈述改变了地位并蒙受损害,陈述方就不能事后更正较早的错误陈述,而该错误的陈述也在考虑双方的法律关系时被视为事实(presumed fact)。这与上一段介绍的误述是不同的理论或说法。这种情况在复杂的社会可能经常出现,如在早期涉及欺诈性陈述的Montefiori v. Montefiori (1762) 1 Wm. Bl. 363先例中,案情是两兄弟试图怂恿一位女士嫁给他们其中一位,并让该女士相信他们其中一人交出的汇票真实、正确,以及是一位非常有钱的

---

[6] 合约履行过程中,一方可以同时有合约责任与侵权责任,并且两者会有重叠。关于这种同步/竞合责任(concurrent liability),可见杨良宜《损失赔偿与救济》一书第八章。

[7] 关于合约更改的课题可见本书第三章第2段。

人,但这并非事实。而在双方事后的诉讼中,Mansfield 勋爵就说到这一早在 17 世纪中衡平法院[8]就已经可以做出的救济,说:“Where, upon proposals of marriage, third persons represent anything material, in a light different from the truth... they shall be bound to make good the thing in the manner in which they represented it. It shall be as represented to be.”

这种例子也很多,典型的例子之一是提单上的陈述。提单上的错误陈述会被提单持有人(结汇的银行或买方)依赖并蒙受损害已经在无数的先例与权威书籍中明确,甚至被显示在相关的国际公约与立法中。这会在本章之 12.1 段介绍。

陈述性禁反言说法(doctrine)背后的原因完全合情合理,正如 Blackburn 勋爵早在 Burkinshaw v. Nicholls (1878) 3 App Cas 1004 先例中就解释说:“When a person makes to another the representation... that such and such things do exist, and you act upon that basis, it seems to me of the very essence of justice that, between these two parties, their rights shall be regulated, not by the real state of the facts, but by that conventional state of facts.[9]”

2. 陈述性禁反言考虑的是被陈述方的地位

陈述性禁反言是在 17 世纪英国的大法官法院(court of Chancery)发展起来的衡平法救济,正如 Macnaghten 勋爵在 George Whitechurch Ltd. v. Cavanagh (1902) AC 117 先例中说:“the doctrine... is a very old head of equity.”之后在 Montefiori v. Montefiori (1762) 1 Wm. Bl. 363 先例中,Mansfield 勋爵将这个说法引入了普通法。起初这种救济只是针对欺诈性误述,但不久后就延伸至无辜的误述(innocent misrepresentation):Hobbs v. Norton (1683) 1 Vern 136;Hunsden v. Cheyney (1690) 2 Vern 150;Low v. Bouverie (1891) 3 Ch 82 CA 等先例。延伸的原因是陈述性禁反言演变为主要考虑被错误陈述诱导并蒙受损害的被陈述方地位,而不理会陈述方是否知情。这变为陈述方是无辜或者是欺诈性做出陈述,在陈述性禁反言的说法下没有关系,因为被陈述方一样做出了依赖并蒙受损害。这方面可节录一些先例的权威说法,首先是 Shand 勋爵在 Sarat Chunder Dey v. Gopal Chunder Laha (1892) LR 19 Ind App 203 先例所说:“The law of this country gives no countenance to the doctrine that in order to

---

〔8〕 Hunt v. Carew (1649) 21 ER 786; Webb v. Borroughs (1676) SS vol 73 p 297; Bishop of Oxford v. Wise (1678) SS vol 79 p 669 等先例。

〔9〕 如果一方向另一方做出陈述说存在怎样怎样的事实,并导致对方在此基础上行事,则 Blackburn 勋爵认为从公正的角度,应该以陈述的事实,而不是真正的事实为基础调整双方之间的权利与义务关系。

create estoppel the person whose acts or declarations induced another to act in a particular way must have been under no mistake himself, or must have acted with an intention to mislead or deceive, [and] conduct short of positive acts is sufficient. What the law... mainly regard[s] is the position of the person who was induced to act."

在 Craine v. Colonial Mutual Fire Insurance Co. Ltd. (1920) 28 CLR 305 先例中, Isaacs大法官说:"... the law of estoppel looks chiefly at the situation of the person relying on the estoppel... the knowledge of the person sought to be estopped is immaterial... it is not essential that the person sought to be estopped should have acted with any intention to deceive."

Steyn 勋爵在 Super Chem Products Ltd. v. American Life & General Insurance Co. Ltd. (2004) UKPC 2 先例中,再次确认了这个说法:"Estoppel by representation is bilateral in character and focuses on the impact on the representee."

3. 陈述性禁反言本质上是证据规则

与上一小段密切相关的是陈述性禁反言本质上是证据规则(rule of evidence),而不是实体法律。这早在 19 世纪中的先例就已经显示,如 Jorden v. Money (1854) 5 HLC 185; Pickard v. Sears (1837) 6 Ad & El 469 等先例。陈述性禁反言的应用是禁止陈述方提出更正错误陈述的证据,而将错误的陈述视为事实,并在此基础上考虑双方的法律关系。[10]

以下可以节录少数早期与近期的权威说法。在 Coke 勋爵的《The First Part of the Institutes of the Laws of England or, A Commentary Upon Littleton》(第 18 版,1823 年)一书,说:"estoppel is called an estoppel or conclusion, because a man's owne act or acceptance stoppeth or closeth up his mouth to allege or plead the truth."

在 National Westminster Bank Plc. v. Somer International (UK) Ltd. (2001) EWCA Civ 970 先例中,上诉庭的 Potter 大法官说:

"There is no doubt that the preponderance of legal authority and judicial dicta at the highest level favours the view that estoppel by representation is **a rule of evidence rather**

---

[10] 有关的先例有 Low v. Bouverie (1891) 3 Ch 82 CA; Oliver v. Bank of England (1902) 1 Ch 610 CA; Bell v. Marsh (1903) 1 Ch 528 CA; London Joint Stock Bank Ltd. v. Macmillan (1918) AC 777; Greenwood v. Martins Bank Ltd. (1933) AC 51 (Tomlin 勋爵说这是"a procedural matter"); Nippon Menkwa Kabushiki Kaisha v. Dawsons Bank Ltd. (1935) 51 Lloyd's Rep. 147 (PC); Evans v. Bartlam (1937) AC 473; Hopgood v. Brown (1955) 1 WLR 213; Lyle - Meller v. A Lewis & Co. (Westminster) Ltd. (1956) 1 WLR 29 CA; Avon County Council v. Howlett (1983) 1 WLR 605 CA; Re Exchange Securities & Commodities Ltd. (1988) Ch 46 等。

than of substantive law: see Low v. Bouverie[1891] 3 Ch 82, 105 per Bowen LJ:

'**Estoppel is only a rule of evidence**; you cannot found an action upon estoppel. Estoppel is only important as being one step in the progress towards relief on the hypothesis that the defendant is estopped from denying the truth of something which he has said.'

And see to similar effect Nippon Menkwa Kabushiki Kaisha (Japan Cotton Trading Co) v. Dawsons Bank Ltd. (1935) 51 Ll L Rep. 147, 150 per Lord Russell of Killowen; see also London Joint Stock Bank Ltd. v. Macmillan [1918] AC 777, 818 per Viscount Haldane: 'it is hardly a rule of what is called substantive law in the sense of declaring an immediate right or claim. It is rather a rule of evidence, capable not the less on that account of affecting gravely substantive rights.' Finally Evans v. Bartlam [1937] AC 473, 484 per Lord Wright: 'estoppel is a rule of evidence which prevents the person estopped from denying the existence of a fact ...'"(加黑部分是笔者的强调)

陈述性禁反言既然只是证据规则,也就是程序法律(procedural law),而不是实体法律,所以和承诺性禁反言或共识性禁反言不同,不涉及实体法律。在后两者,被禁反言的一方可以通过通知回复到原本的合约或法律地位,依赖禁反言的一方蒙受的损害与救济必须成比例。但在陈述性禁反言,只涉及是否让陈述方提供证据更正错误陈述的问题。

而且陈述性禁反言的救济也没有弹性(flexibility),因为被禁反言的一方或者可以提供证据更正陈述,或者就不可以提供证据,即所谓的"all or nothing"。

因此有说法是陈述性禁反言比承诺性禁反言更明确是只能作为盾牌(shield)而不能作为宝剑(sword)。在近期的 Newport City Council v. Charles (2009) 1 WLR 1884 先例中,Laws 大法官说:"It is settled law that such an estoppel is a shield only and cannot found a cause of action."

在 SmithKline Beecham Plc. v. Apotex Europe Ltd. (2006) EWCA Civ 658 先例中,Jacob 大法官也说:

"(被告)contends that... An estoppel cannot be used as a key element of a claim (sword not shield) and particularly it cannot operate to create a legal relationship when there was none at the outset... I think he was right ...[11]

It is as well to remember here the fundamental nature of an estoppel. An estopped party is precluded from asserting that a particular fact or set of facts or state of affairs is

[11] Jacob 大法官同意被告的说法,禁反言(这里指陈述性禁反言与"共识性禁反言"[estoppel by convention])不能作为提起诉讼的关键要件,特别是不能在一开始不存在法律关系的情况下用来创造新的法律关系。

so. Thinking of it in procedural terms, an estoppel inherently must be raised by way of a riposte. The claimant pleads his case basing himself on alleged facts x, y, and z. The defendant then raises an estoppel saying: ‘you may not assert these facts by reason of an estoppel arising from representation, convention or whatever.’〔12〕

The pleaded case here does not fit that essential nature, as can be tested by the procedural model. If the Canadian companies(原告)applied to the court to enforce the existing undertakings without asserting the estoppel in their claim, the court would simply dismiss the application as bad on its face. There would be no need for GSK(被告)to assert that which they are alleged to be estopped from contending, namely that the Canadian companies are not to be treated as parties to the order. Even if GSK did not appear to argue the point, the claim would fail without the estoppel.

Thus it is essential to the Canadian companies' case that the estoppel be pleaded as part of the claim. The pleading is not a mere anticipation of a reply to a defence. This shows that what isrelied upon is not an estoppel at all — it is a naked attempt to create a legally binding agreement when there never was one and never any intention to create one. That an estoppel cannot do...〔13〕"

在 Haden Young Ltd. v. Laing O'Rourke Midlands Ltd. (2008) EWHC 1016 (TCC)先例中,Ramsey 大法官也做出了类似的判决,说:"Estoppel by representation cannot be used as a key element of a claim so as to create a legal relationship when there was none at the outset."

上述两个先例说的是陈述性禁反言不能作为提起诉讼的关键要件,但是否能成为一个支持性要件呢?确实在 Low v. Bouverie (1891) 3 Ch 82 CA(第 105 页);Canada and Dominion Sugar Co. Ltd. v. Canadian National (West Indies) Steam Ships Ltd. (1946) 80 Lloyd's Rep. 13 (PC)(第 56 页);Lyle - Meller v. A Lewis & Co. (Westminster) Ltd. (1956) 1 WLR 29 CA(第 40 页)等先例都提到陈述性禁反言的说法正逐步向可以被用作诉因扩展。

在 Nippon Menkwa Kabushiki Kaisha v. Dawsons Bank Ltd. (1935) 51 Lloyd's Rep. 147 (PC)先例中,Russell 勋爵说:"... in regard to estoppel in pais. Estoppel is not a cause of action. It may(if established) assist a plaintiff in enforcing a cause of action by preventing a defendant from denying the existence of some fact essential to estab-

〔12〕 陈述性禁反言的本质是被禁反言的一方被禁止指称某一事实或一系列事实或某个事件的情况是这样。因此从程序上考虑,陈述性禁反言一定只是作为反击。原告根据他声称的 x、y、z 的事实提起诉讼,被告则提出禁反言的抗辩。

〔13〕 在该先例中,禁反言是原告提起诉讼的关键要件,而不是对预期抗辩的回应。原告事实上不是依赖禁反言,而是希望在一开始不存在法律关系的情况下创造新的法律关系,这是禁反言做不到的。

lish the cause of action, or (to put it in another way) by preventing a defendant from asserting the existence of some fact the existence of which would destroy the cause of action. It is a rule of evidence which comes into operation if (a) a statement of the existence of a fact which has been made by the defendant or an authorized agent of his to the plaintiff or someone in his behalf, (b) with the intention that the plaintiff should act upon the faith of the statement, and (c) the plaintiff does act upon the faith of the statement."

在 Farrow v. Orttewell (1933) Ch 480 CA 先例中,农场的买方向佃户 Y 做出退佃通知。根据立法规定,在有效的退佃通知下离开的佃户可以获得赔偿。但事实上买方做出的该通知是无效的,因为当时他还没有获得农场的所有权。法院判是买方被禁止否定退佃通知的有效性,而在假设退佃通知有效的情况下,佃户有合法的诉因要求赔偿。

在 TCB Ltd. v. Gray (1986) Ch 621 先例中,案情有关担保合约的订立。担保人的律师在授权书(power of attorney)下删除了担保合约中的责任限制条文。之后担保人与银行发生争议,法院判是担保人被禁止以授权书没有盖章(seal)为由否认授权书的有效性。在假设授权书有效的情况下,银行可以追回所有的本金,而不受责任限制条文的约束。

在以上几个先例中,诉因都来自陈述性禁反言下假设的事实,而非真正的事实。因此有争议是陈述性禁反言可以作为宝剑而不止是盾牌。在 Canada and Dominion Sugar Co. Ltd. v. Canadian National (West Indies) Steam Ships Ltd 先例中,Wright 勋爵说:"the doctrine may be described as rule of evidence but is more properly viewed as substantive rule of law."

在 Moorgate Mercantile Co. Ltd. v. Twitchings (1976) QB 225 CA 先例中,Denning 勋爵也说:"Esoppel is a principle of justice and equity."但这在 National Westminster Bank Plc. v. Somer International (UK) Ltd 先例中受到了质疑,Potter 大法官说:"Thus, whether or not the dicta of Lord Denning MR in Moorgate Mercantile Co. Ltd. v. Twitchings be correct in terms of classification, it is clear that the doctrine of estoppel by representation stems from and is governed by considerations of justice and equity. That being so, it is difficult to see why equity should, as between the parties, be impotent in an appropriate case or category of case to require a person relying upon the defence of estoppel by representation to rely upon it only to the extent of any detriment suffered."

在更近期的 Azov Shipping Co. v. Baltic Shipping Co. (1999) 2 Lloyd's Rep. 159 先例中,Colman 大法官认为宝剑与盾牌的说法只是为了保护约因/对价,所以只与承诺性禁反言有关。而其他类别的禁反言,包括陈述性禁反言、共识性禁反言与产权人禁反言,与约因/对价没有关系,不应该受到这一说法的影响。Colman 大法官说:

"The sword/shield dichotomy appears to have originated in a phrase used in argument by counsel for the defendant husband and to have been adopted by Birkett LJ. at page 224[14].

This decision on analysis gives effect to the countervailing policy consideration that in English Law a bare promise cannot be sued upon without consideration moving from the promisee. In the field of estoppel the policy of protecting this principle displaces the policy of protecting the representee from the unfairness that would result from the promisor resiling from his position. Although this policy will obviously operate to limit the scope of promissory estoppel..., its applicability to other kinds of estoppel is not obviously required. Thus it is reasonably clear that, at least in cases of proprietary estoppel and estoppel by convention, the claimant may formulate his cause of action on the basis of a mutually - assumed factual or legal relationship which differs from that which truly exists. The estoppel is not in itself the cause of action but it prevents the party estopped from relying by way of defence on that factual and legal basis which truly exists...

It if is right that in cases of estoppel by convention and proprietary estoppel one party can found a cause of action on a basis which differs from the true legal basis, there can, in my judgment, logically be no reason in principle why the same approach should not apply in cases of estoppel by representation...

For these reasons I conclude that the sword/shield dichotomy represents a largely inaccurate description of the availability of remedies to a party who relies on an estoppel. It should be regarded as confined to the protection of consideration and as having no general application in the field of estoppel.

Accordingly... I am not satisfied that in the present case there is any reason in principle why Baltic(索赔方)should not rely on an estoppel by representation to found its claim ..."

之后在 BP Plc. v. Aon (2006) EWHC 424 (Comm)先例中,案情有关共识性禁反言,又是 Colman 大法官做出的判决,说:

"In my judgment in Azov Shipping Co. v. Baltic Shipping Co. [1999] 2 Lloyd's Rep. 159... I attempted to rationalise the objection to using an estoppel to found a cause of action as in Combe v. Combe [1951] 2 KB 215 and relying on an estoppel in support of a claim in the manner in which, albeit obiter, the Court of Appeal was prepared to allow it to be relied on in Amalgamated v. Texas, as explained by Brandon LJ... However, that judgment and that rationalisation was not cited or considered in Baird v. Marks & Spencer [2001] EWCA Civ 274, and as the authorities now stand, all that can be said is

[14] Combe v. Combe (1951) 2 KB 215 先例。

that there is much uncertainty as to the circumstances in which an estoppel by convention can be deployed as part of the necessary factual or legal background for founding a claim for breach of contract. Indeed, in Baird v. Marks & Spencer it was held that it was not even arguable that the lack of certainty of the assumed terms of an implied contract could be cured by the deployment of an estoppel by convention. Although this was a different case on its facts to Amalgamated v. Texas, it was said both in the judgments of Sir Andrew Morritt VC and Mance LJ. that the Court of Appeal was bound to adhere to the principle in Combe v. Combe, even in an estoppel by convention case, unless and until the House of Lords adopted a wider approach to the employment of an estoppel.

Therefore, as the law had developed up to the date of the settlement in July 2003, the authorities at Court of Appeal level contained no satisfactory explanation as to how the dictum of Brandon LJ. in Amalgamated v. Texas[15], with regard to the facts in that case could stand in relation to estoppel by convention consistently with the Court of Appeal's conclusion in Baird v. Marks & Spencer, that estoppel can only be used to provide a factual basis for a cause of action in cases of proprietary estoppel and not in cases of estoppel by convention: see also in this connection the valuable observations of Prof. Sir Gunter Treitel in Chitty on Contracts, 29 Edn, para 3 - 098 to 101. Whether conceptual consistency should be sacrificed on the altar of stare decisis remained then, as it does today, to be determined by the House of Lords."

在上面节录的判决中,Colman 大法官提到了上诉庭的 Baird v. Marks & Spencer (2001) EWCA Civ 274 先例,[16]在该先例被判是原告声称玛莎被禁反言不能否认合约的存在是没有希望的争议,因为共识性禁反言不能作为诉因。这显然否定了 Colman 大法官在 Azov Shipping Co. v. Baltic Shipping Co 先例中的说法,即宝剑与盾牌

〔15〕 Denning 勋爵在 Amalgamated v. Texas Bank (1982) 1 Lloyd's Rep. 27 先例的判决可节录如下:"The doctrine of estoppel is one of the most flexible and useful in the armoury of the law. But it has become overloaded with cases. That is why I have not gone through them all in this judgment. It has evolved during the last 150 years in a sequence of separate developments: proprietary estoppel, estoppel by representation of fact, estoppel by acquiescence, and promissory estoppel. At the same time it has been sought to be limited by a series of maxims: estoppel is only a rule of evidence, estoppel cannot give rise to a cause of action, estoppel cannot do away with the need for consideration, and so forth. All these can now be seen to merge into one general principle shorn of limitations. When the parties to a transaction proceed on the basis of an underlying assumption — either of fact or of law — whether due to misrepresentation or mistake makes no difference — on which they have conducted the dealings between them — neither of them will be allowed to go back on that assumption when it would be unfair or unjust to allow him to do so. If one of them does seek to go back on it, the courts will give the other such remedy as the equity of the case demands."

〔16〕 该先例的案情可见本书第四章之 5.1 段。

的说法只与承诺性禁反言有关,而陈述性禁反言、共识性禁反言与产权人禁反言不受影响。因此,在 Sean Wilken QC 与 Karim Ghaly 先生所著的《The Law of Waiver, Variation, and Estoppel》(第 3 版,2012 年)一书之 10.18 段说:"Thus, as the law currently stands, there are two school of thought – the historical expansive approach and the Baird approach. As Mr. Justice Colman recognized in BP Plc. v. AON Ltd, the result in Baird conflicts with the reasoning in Amalgamated Bank and the previously decided cases on estoppels by convention. . . . As (both cases) are Court of Appeal authorities, any resolution of the conflict must await the Supreme Court. Until then, considerable caution must be exercised in using an estoppels by convention where the pragmatic effect of so doing is to create a cause of action or, as it was put in the previous edition, the estoppel is acting as a sharp edged shield."

近期仍有先例坚持陈述性禁反言只能用作盾牌,不能用作宝剑。[17] 因此有人说,陈述性禁反言现在已经站在了十字路口,究竟是继续作为证据规则,还是变为像"承诺性禁反言"(promissory estoppel)与"产权人禁反言"(proprietary estoppel)等一样的实体法律。这也决定了陈述性禁反言究竟只是盾牌,还是也可以用作宝剑。这类的考虑或争论并非只有学术意义,这对解决复原请求中十分常见的问题也有实际意义(这会在本章下一小段介绍)。

4. 弄错事实下付钱的复原请求受到的影响

由于陈述性禁反言只是证据规则,这样是否能引入证据会令是否能够获得救济也变为"all or nothing"。受这种没有弹性的结果影响最大的也最有代表性的就是涉及弄错事实下付钱,事后要求"复原"(restitution)的例子。复原的救济与传统的合约与侵权的救济不同,如果 A 在弄错事实下将钱支付给了 B,通常 A 与 B 是没有合约关系,而 B 也没有因为天上掉下来这笔钱而对 A 有了侵权的行为。所以,A 如果想通过法律向 B 要回这笔钱,唯一就是靠复原的索赔(restitutionary claim)。复原的索赔通常要满足三个要件,一是被告的 B 必须得利(enrichment),二是 A 受损下(at the expense of the claimant)B 才得利(不论是钱或其他的利益),三是让 B 保留这笔钱或其他利益不公平。所以复原的法律现在被称为不当得利的法律(law of unjust enrichment)。在 Fibrosa Spolka Akcyjna v. Fairbairn Lawson Combe Barbour Ltd. (1943) AC 32 先例中,Wright 勋爵说:"It is clear that any civilized system of law is bound to provide remedies for cases of what has been called unjust enrichment or unjust benefit, that is to prevent a man from retaining the money of or some benefit derived from another

---

〔17〕 见本章之 11.1.2 段介绍的 Newport City Council v. Charles (2009) 1 WLR 1884 先例。

which it is against conscience that he should keep. Such remedies in English law are generically different from remedies in contract or in tort, and are now recognized to fall within a third category of the common law which has been called quasi – contract or restitution."

其中给错钱或多给钱的情况在商业社会与日常生活中都经常发生,所以这方面的先例不少。收钱的一方按照道理应该在给错钱的一方的要求下归还,但问题是经常会有情况是收钱的一方已经花了部分甚至是全部的钱。收钱的一方这样做也不一定有错,如他自己并不清楚这笔钱是错付的,而以为是自己应得的。而即使收钱的人收到一笔来历不明的钱,也不一定有渠道将钱退回,一段时间之后就当做是自己的钱使用,或是自己用觉得良心不安,于是将这笔意外之财捐给慈善机构。这样,如果给错钱的一方突然出现,根据复原要求收钱的一方归还这笔钱,收钱的一方就会有困难与失望。正如 Robert Walker 大法官在 Derby v. Scottish Equitable Plc.(2001)Pens. L. R. 163 先例中所说:"the claimant's demand for repayment 'must have come as a bitter disappointment'."Rimer 大法官在 Mahme Trust Reg v. Tayeb(2002)EWHC 1543(Ch)先例中也说:"... is a hardship which every defendant to a restitution claim has to face, and by itself it is no defence. Something rather more has to be shown."

面对这些困难,收钱的一方有两个可能的抗辩。一是较近期才发展起来的改变地位(change of position)。根据重要的 Lipkin Gorman v. Karpnale Ltd.(1991)2 AC 548 HL 先例,[18]针对弄错事实下给钱的一方要求复原的请求,如果让收钱的一方归还全部或部分会造成不公平,收钱的一方就可以改变地位作为抗辩。Goff 勋爵说:"Historically, despite broad statements of Lord Mansfield to the effect that an action for money had and received will only lie where it is inequitable for the defendant to retain the money (see in particular Moses v. Macferlan [1760] 2 Burr 1005), the defence was received at most only partial recognition in English law... Instead, where change of position has been relied upon by the defendant, it has been usual to approach the problem as one of estoppel.[19]... But it is difficult to see the justification for such a rationalization. First, estoppel normally depends upon the existence of a representation by one party, in reliance upon which the representee has so changed his position that it is inequitable for the representor to go back upon his representation. But in case of restitution, the require-

---

〔18〕 在该先例中,案情涉及一位律师非法挪用客户账户里的钱去俱乐部赌博,并在之后被判盗窃罪坐牢。他所在的律师事务所希望向俱乐部追回这笔钱。上诉庭判是俱乐部里的筹码只是娱乐活动的辅助,参与赌博的人士并没有购买筹码,俱乐部收到这笔钱的时候没有提供相应的对价,即这笔钱的所有权没有转移,俱乐部需要把钱归还给律师事务所。俱乐部提出传统的陈述性禁反言的抗辩显然会有困难,因为双方从来没有接触,律师事务所不可能做出过任何陈述让俱乐部依赖,因此俱乐部提出了改变地位的抗辩。

〔19〕 一直以来,针对弄错事实下付钱的复原请求,收钱的一方的抗辩是陈述性禁反言。

ment of a representation appears to be unnecessary.〔20〕 It is true that, in cases where the plaintiff has paid money directly to the defendant, it has been argued (though with difficulty) that the plaintiff has represented to the defendant that he is entitled to the money〔21〕; but in a case such as the present, in which was paid to an innocent done by a thief, the true owner has made no representation whatever to the defendant.〔22〕 Again, it was held by the Court of Appeal in Avon County Council v. Howlett that estoppel cannot operate pro tanto, with the effect that if, for example, the defendant has innocently changed his position by disposing of part of the money, a defence of estoppel would provide him with a defence to the whole of the claim.〔23〕 Considerations such as these provide a strong indication that, in many cases, estoppel is not an appropriate concept to deal with the problem.〔24〕"

二是有更长历史的抗辩是陈述性禁反言。在 Avon County Council v. Howlett (1983) 1 WLR 605 先例中,Slade 大法官根据 Goff 勋爵与 G Jones 大律师的《The Law of Restitution》一书,谈到满足陈述性禁反言的要求时说:"A plaintiff will be estopped from asserting his claim to restitution if the following conditions are satisfied: (a) the plaintiff must generally have made a representation of fact which led the defendant to believe that he was entitled to treat the money as his own; (b) the defendant must have, bona fide and without notice of the plaintiff's claim, consequently changed his position; (c) the payment must not have been primarily caused by the fault of the defendant."

在《Chitty on Contracts》(第 32 版,2015 年)一书之 29 - 183 段,针对以陈述性禁反言作为对复原的抗辩说:"**Nature of Estoppel.** In certain circumstances a person

〔20〕 但陈述性禁反言的适用存在一定困难。首先是陈述性禁反言一定要存在陈述,但在一方弄错事实付钱的情况,给错钱的一方不一定会对收钱的一方做出过任何陈述。

〔21〕 有说法是给错钱的一方直接将钱给收钱的一方,就是做出了收钱的一方有权拥有这笔钱的陈述。

〔22〕 但在类似 Lipkin Gorman v. Karpnale Ltd. (1991) 2 AC 548 HL 先例的情况,如果一方被偷走或骗走一笔钱,而这个贼或骗子又将钱给了无辜方第三方,如慈善组织。被偷走或骗走钱的一方显然找不到贼或骗子,不能向他追回这笔钱,所以只能要求最终收钱的无辜第三方慈善组织归还,而慈善组织确实已经将这笔钱全部或部分花掉了。在这种情况下,被偷走或骗走钱的一方显然不会有对慈善组织做出过任何陈述。这种情况也不需要涉及偷钱或骗钱,可以是 A 弄错事实付钱给 B,B 收了这笔意外之财将钱捐给了 C 慈善组织。A 发现真相后向 B 要求复原,但 B 因故身亡,而 A 向 C 寻求复原,C 就会因为双方从未有过任何陈述,面对无法以陈述性禁反言抗辩的困难。

〔23〕 另是根据上诉庭的 Avon County Council v. Howlett (1983) 1 WLR 605 先例,陈述性禁反言不可以被用来让收钱的一方只归还部分给错的钱。这就导致如果收钱的一方改变自己的地位,将这笔钱花了一部分,也就是因为依赖而蒙受损害。陈述性禁反言的抗辩如果成立,他一分钱都不用还,因为给错钱的一方被禁止提供任何他是错给了钱的证据,即"all or nothing"。

〔24〕 从上述困难可以看出陈述性禁反言在部分复原的案件中并不能令人满意地解决问题。

making a payment may be precluded from recovering it by an estoppel. He may, for instance, be estopped from subsequently alleging that he acted under a mistake. To raise an estoppel the payee must satisfy three conditions. First, he must show that either the payer was under a duty to give him accurate information and failed to do so, or that there was an unequivocal misrepresentation made to him for which the payer was responsible. Secondly, he must show that this inaccurate information led him to believe that he was entitled to treat the money as his own. Thirdly, he must show that because of his mistaken belief he changed his position in a way which would make it inequitable to require him to repay the money.[25]"

这两种抗辩相互重叠但也有很明确的不同,如改变地位的抗辩不需要给错钱的一方做出任何错误陈述,也不需要收钱的一方有任何依赖并蒙受损害。更明显的区别是后果不同,在还钱时因为改变地位是实质的抗辩(substantive defence),收钱的一方可以不用还钱(因为已经全部合理用掉)或只需要还一部分。但陈述性禁反言是程序上的抗辩(procedural defence),一旦成立,给错钱的一方就一分钱都拿不回来,没有中间地带,也不会考虑要求退还一部分没有合理用掉的钱是否公平。

当然,收钱的一方如果依赖改变地位的抗辩,就必须面对证明让他还钱是不公平(因为已经合理用掉)的困难。换句话说,就是要证明改变地位带来的损害。[26]如果被告无法证明改变地位或带来的损害到何种程度(合理花掉了多少钱),法院没有裁量权进行决定,正如 May 大法官在 Filby v. Mortgage Express (No. 2) (2004) EWCA Civ 759 先例中说:"... there is no residual general discretion to withhold the remedy nor to modify it simply to avoid harsh reality."

但被告要证明改变地位并导致损害并不容易,虽然《Chitty on Contracts》(第 32 版,2015 年)一书之 29-037 段说:"It appears that the burden of proving the causative effect of the mistake will not be heavy, at any rate if the mistake (by the payor) is serious."

在 Avon County Council v. Howlett 先例中,Slade 大法官说:"On further reflection, however, I think that references to broad concepts of justice or equity in a context such as the present may be somewhat misleading, as well as uncertain in their application. The conclusion of the judge in the present case really involves the proposition that, if the defendant is successfully to resist a claim for repayment of the entire sum of £ 1,007,

---

〔25〕 收钱的一方要依赖禁反言必须先满足三个要件。第一,他必须或者证明给错钱的一方有责任告诉他正确的信息但没有,或者证明给错钱的一方做出了清楚无误的错误陈述。第二,他必须证明错误陈述令其认为有权将钱视为自己的。第三,他必须证明因为这个错误的认为,改变了原本的地位,导致让他归还这笔钱不公平。

〔26〕 这一类改变地位造成的损害将在本章之 8.3.3 段有详细介绍。

the onus falls on him to prove specifically that the pecuniary amount of the prejudice suffered by him as a result of relying on the relevant representations made by the plaintiffs equals or exceeds that sum. For present purposes, however, one has to postulate a situation in which the defendant was perfectly entitled to conduct his business affairs on the assumption that the relevant representations were true, until he was told otherwise. Meantime, a defendant in the situation of the defendant in the present case may, in reliance on the representation, have either altered his general mode of living or undertaken commitments or incurred expenditure or entered into other transactions which it may be very difficult for him subsequently to recall and identify retrospectively in complete detail; he may even have done so, while leaving some of the particular moneys paid to him by the plaintiff untouched. If the pecuniary amount of his prejudice has to be precisely quantified by a defendant in such circumstances, he may be faced with obvious difficulties of proof."

正如Slade大法官所说,收钱的一方认为他完全有权拥有这笔钱,直到被告知事实并非如此。他收到钱后可能生活方式发生改变,做出了其他承诺或达成了其他交易。但要事后让他提供细节证明这些改变或交易是如果没有这笔钱就不会发生是很困难,尤其是生活方式的改变。从这个角度讲,陈述性禁反言对收钱的一方明显是更好的抗辩,当然前提是给错钱的一方曾经向他做出了清楚无误的陈述。

这两种不同的抗辩目前会保持区别,并且作为英国法律的一部分,直到英国最高院有了最终的说法。

在立法委员会的《Restitution: mistakes of law and ultra vires public authority receipts and payments》(Law Com No 227)(1994)报告中,考虑Lipkin Gorman v. Karpnale Ltd先例后这方面法律的发展。在该报告的5.14段建议不要立法进行干预,立法委员会咨询的人士大多数都认为应该同时保留陈述性禁反言的抗辩与改变地位的抗辩,但立法委员会认为关于两者之间的关系最好交给英国法院通过发展普通法来解决。该报告的5.17段说:"We believe that the importance of estoppel will diminish as a result of the introduction of a broad defence of change of position, but it is premature to regard it as redundant."

Jonathan Parker大法官在Philip Collins Ltd. v. Davis (2000) 3 All ER 808先例建议说如果改变地位的抗辩可以适用,就应该倾向于不提出陈述性禁反言的抗辩。

最后,在National Westminster Bank Plc. v. Somer International (UK) Ltd. (2001) EWCA Civ 970先例中,Peter Gibson大法官说:"... estoppel being a defence of general availability apt to be invoked against the assertion of any kind of right, whereas the defence of change of position may be available in circumstances where the defence of estoppel could not be established."

普通法在这一复杂的问题上的发展可看以下三个重要的上诉庭先例。首先是

Avon County Council v. Howlett 先例。在该先例中,案情涉及原告学校的 Howlett 老师在学校里受伤,不能工作。根据相关的规定,这期间他可以获得 6 个月的全额工资与 6 个月减半的工资,之后就没有工资了。但学校支付了他 9 个月的全额工资与 11 个月减半的工资。Howlett 老师曾经询问过学校有关支付是否正确,但被保证支付的工资是正确的。于是 Howlett 老师与他的妻子换了车子,买了新西装等,就是生活水平有了提高。之后学校要求归还错付的部分。毫无疑问 Howlett 老师蒙受了损害,但一审法官认定只限于 546.61 英镑,判学校有权取回剩下的 460.39 英镑。

但到了上诉庭,一审法院的判决被推翻。上诉庭判是陈述性禁反言的说法是证据规则,如果成立就是"all or nothing",因此学校的申请应全部被驳回,一分钱也取不回来。Slade 大法官说:"Estoppel by representation is a rule of evidence, the consequence of which is simply to preclude the representor from averring facts contrary to his own representation. It follows that a party who, as a result of being able to rely on an estoppel, succeeds on a cause of action on which, without being able to rely on it, he would necessarily have failed, may be able to recover more than the actual damage suffered by him as a result of the representation which gave rise to it... So far as they go, the authorities suggest that in cases where estoppel by representation is available as a defence to a claim for money had and received, the courts similarly do not treat the operation of the estoppel as being restricted to the precise amount of the detriment which the representee proves he has suffered in reliance on the representation."

但上诉庭的三位大法官都对特殊情况(是明显不公平的情况)有所保留,虽然认为该先例不属于特殊情况。Slade 大法官举例说,如果给错的金额与收钱的一方的损害完全不成比例,让给错钱的一方一分钱也取不回可能是明显不公平。Cumming-Bruce 大法官认为如果很明显收钱的一方会通过陈述性禁反言的抗辩获利并造成不公平,法院有权阻止。但该先例只是一个双方同意的测试案件(test case),一审法官认定的 546.61 英镑等数字都是假设的,[27] 所以不存在不公平或不合情理的争议。Eveleigh 大法官也说:"However I am far from saying that whenever the recipient of money paid under a mistake has been led to think that it is his, then he will be entitled to retain the whole by demonstrating that he has spent part of it.... there may be circumstances which would render it unconscionable for the defendant to retain a balance in his hands. There may also be circumstances which would make it unfair to allow the plaintiff to recover."

第二个是 Derby v. Scottish Equitable Plc. 先例。在该先例中,保险公司 Scottish

---

〔27〕 事实上有很多老师都被多给了钱,该先例是双方同意的测试案件,为了测试陈述性禁反言在复原请求中的法律地位。因此,在一审法院,虽然法官认为这笔多给的钱已经被全部花掉,但双方为了测试这方面的法律,并没有修改文书请求,而是假设有部分钱没有花掉。

Equitable 因为算错数而多付了一大笔钱给 Derby 先生,之后想取回这笔钱。一审的 Harrison 大法官支持了 Scottish Equitable 公司的请求,可以取回约 162000 英镑的本金加利息。Derby 先生上诉到上诉庭,但上诉庭支持了一审判决,认为该先例属于 Avon County Council v. Howlett 先例中提到的特殊情况或例外,Robert Walker 大法官说:"I would be content to follow the judge in refraining from attempting any general statement of principle and treating this case as comfortably within the exception recognized by all three member of this court in Avon County Council v. Howlett. We cannot overrule that case but we cannot that it was no seen, even by the court which decided it, as a wholly satisfactory authority, because of its fictional element. "

Robert Walker 大法官也对这方面法律的发展做出了预测,说:"Will estoppel by representation wither away as a defence to a claim for restitution of money paid under a mistake of fact?[28] It can be predicted with some confidence that with the emergence of the defence of change of position, the court will no longer feel constrained to find that a representation has been made, in a borderline case, in order to avoid an unjust result.[29] It can also be predicted, rather less confidently, that development of the law on a case by case basis will have the effect of enlarging rather than narrowing the exception recognized by this court in Avon County Council v. Howlett.[30] That process might be hastened (or simply overtaken) if the House of Lords were to move away from the evidential origin of estoppel by representation towards a more unified doctrine of estoppel[31]..."

最后是 National Westminster Bank Plc. v. Somer International (UK) Ltd 先例。在该先例中,Somer 是一家出口电脑设备的公司,并且是 National Westminster 银行的客户,在该银行有一个美元账户用来收取海外订单的付款。1997 年 4 月,Somer 通知银行会有一笔 70000 美元至 78000 美元的进项。在 4 月稍后的时间,银行收到一笔 76708.57 美元的款项,这是给银行另一位名字相近的客户,但银行错将这笔钱打进了 Somer 的账户。Somer 收到钱后认为已经获得了支付,将价值 13180.57 英镑的电脑设备发给了海外的买方,而事实上该买方并没有做出支付。1998 年 2 月,银行通

---

〔28〕 陈述性禁反言是否会不再成为弄错事实下付钱的复原请求的抗辩?Robert Walker 大法官提出这个疑问是因为针对复原已经有了改变地位这个新的抗辩,而这是实质性也是更适合的抗辩。

〔29〕 Robert Walker 大法官认为可以比较肯定预测的是随着改变地位的抗辩的出现,在一些临界的案件,法院不再拘泥于一定要找到所谓的陈述,令给错钱的一方被禁反言,以防止出现不公平的情况,而会更多适用改变地位的抗辩。

〔30〕 另一个相对不太肯定的预测是随着这方面法律在每个先例不同案情下的发展,Avon County Council v. Howlett (1983) 1 WLR 605 先例中例外的特殊情况只会增加不会减少。

〔31〕 如果贵族院将陈述性禁反言从证据规则变为与其他类别的禁反言更统一的实体法律,这方面的问题就可以更快解决。有关将不同类别的禁反言统一为一种禁反言,可看本书第四章之 12.3.2 段,但显然这在英国还没有发生。

知 Somer 这个错误并要求 Somer 归还这笔钱，但 Somer 拒绝，于是银行开始了诉讼。Somer 以陈述性禁反言作为抗辩，并希望保留错误打进其账户里的所有钱，虽然实质受到的损害是 13180.57 英镑。上诉庭判是："... that estoppel by representation was a rule of evidence which ordinarily required that where a recipient of a mistaken payment had suffered more than a de minimis degree of detriment he was entitled to retain the entirely of the payment.〔32〕 However, Avon County Council v. Howlett and Scottish Equitable Plc. v. Derby indicated there remained scope for the operation of equity to alleviate that position on grounds of unfairness or unconscionability.〔33〕 In cases of payment made under a mistake of fact it was difficult to see why such equitable principles should not apply to cover any case in which it appeared that a substantial windfall would otherwise be obtained by the transferee at the expense of the mistaken transferor.〔34〕 The defence of estoppel by representation and change of position under Lipkin Gorman v. Karpnale Ltd. (1991) 2 AC 548 remained distinct until the House of Lords decided otherwise.〔35〕 In the instant case, the judge had been entitled to hold that the repayment sought was of such a size that it bore no relation to the detriment which Somer could possibly have suffered and that it was unconscionable for Somer to retain the balance over and above the value of the goods shipped.〔36〕"

目前看来，Robert Walker 大法官的部分预测，如例外的特殊情况越来越多，获得了证实。而另一部分预测，如将陈述性禁反言与其他类别的禁反言统一，看来贵族院或最高院不会这么做。

最后节录《Chitty on Contracts》（第 32 版，2015 年）一书之 29 - 185 段总结说："**Inequitable to require restitution.** The third requirement of an estoppel that the payee has changed his position so as to make it inequitable to require him to repay the money, is clearly satisfied where he can established that a particular expenditure has been incurred

〔32〕 陈述性禁反言是证据规则，原本只要求收钱的一方蒙受一定的损害（只要不是极微小）就可以保留弄错事实支付的所有钱。

〔33〕 但 Avon County Council v. Howlett (1983) 1 WLR 605 先例与 Derby v. Scottish Equitable Plc. (2001) Pens. L. R. 163 先例显示衡平法可以做出调整以减轻不公平与不合情理的情况。

〔34〕 在弄错事实下做出支付的案件，法院看不出有何理由衡平法原则不适用在这种收钱的一方会发一大笔横财，而给错钱的一方要蒙受不成比例损失的情况。

〔35〕 直到贵族院的判决做出改变前，Lipkin Gorman v. Karpnale Ltd. (1991) 2 AC 548 HL 先例提到陈述性禁反言与改变地位仍然是两种不同的抗辩。

〔36〕 在 National Westminster Bank Plc. v. Somer International (UK) Ltd. (2001) EWCA Civ 970 先例中，上诉庭判是要求归还的金额与 Somer 蒙受的损害不成比例，Somer 保留多于付运了的电脑设备价值的金额不合情理。

as a result of the receipt of the money and he is no longer able to recover the money.〔37〕 Examples include investing the money in a company that has since failed, and irretrievably paying it over to a third party to whom the payee thought he was obliged to pay it. However, in certain circumstances, a sufficient change of position to found an estoppel may occur without any obvious exchange of position in the payee's style of living. In one case an employee who had been overpaid for a period of some eighteen months, and who had spent the money as part of his normal living expenses, successfully raised an estoppel.〔38〕 The test is whether, but for the payment, the expenditure would have been occurred. Thus, there may be circumstances in which, even after all the money has been spent, it would not be inequitable to require repayment.〔39〕 Conversely, in Avon CC v. Howlett it was stated that, while a plea of estoppel should not enable a profit to be made, a payee who has relied on a representation should not be subjected to the difficult task of having 'subsequently to recall and identify retrospectively in complete details' alterations to his general mode of living, commitments undertaken and other transactions entered into. The operation of estoppel might, therefore, result in the payee returning less than the difference between the amount paid and the precise amount he proved he had irretrievably spent.〔40〕 This was stated to follow from the fact that estoppel by representation is a rule of evidence and does not operate pro tanto. However, the finding that the whole of the overpayment had in fact been spent and the recognition by the court that injustice would result if the sum sought to be recovered were so large as to bear no relation to the payee's detriment and that recovery in such circumstances might be unconscionable, suggests that in an appropriate case estoppel may nevertheless operate pro tanto.〔41〕"

---

〔37〕 如果收钱的一方可以证明因为收到了这笔钱,他承受了一定的花销,不再可以归还这笔钱,他就满足了改变了原本的地位导致让他归还这笔钱不公平的要求。

〔38〕 如用这笔钱投资了一个公司,但是投资失败,或者将钱支付给了第三方。但在一定的情况下,即使收钱的一方的生活方式没有明显改变,也可以满足构成禁反言的改变原本的地位的要求。在 Avon County Council v. Howlett (1983) 1 WLR 605 先例中,一位雇员在 18 个月间都被多给了工资,虽然他只是用这笔钱支付了部分正常的日常开支,仍然成功依赖了禁反言的抗辩。

〔39〕 相关的考验是如果没有收到这笔钱,收钱的一方是否会有这样的花销。因此会有情况是,即使所有的钱都被花完了,让他归还这笔错给的钱也不会有不公平。

〔40〕 相反,在 Avon County Council v. Howlett (1983) 1 WLR 605 先例中,法院认为虽然收钱的一方不能通过禁反言获利,但作为依赖了错误陈述的一方,不应该需要完成回忆与追溯他究竟在日常的生活方式、做出的承诺或完成的其他交易中有怎样的改变这一困难的任务。因此,禁反言可能会导致收钱的一方归还比他依赖错误陈述而花费后剩下的钱少的金额。

〔41〕 陈述性禁反言是证据规则,不可以被用来让收钱的一方尽他所能归还部分给错的钱。但如果给错的钱确实已经被花掉,或是要归还的金额与收钱的一方的损害完全不成比例,或是让收钱的一方全部归还可能是不合情理与带来不公平,就有建议是陈述性禁反言可以做出归还部分的救济。

5. 构成陈述性禁反言的要件

5.1　权威说法

可先节录《Snell's Equity》(第32版,2010年)一书之12－002段有关历史与法院如果做出救济的说法:"**Estoppel by representation**... At common law, estoppel was at first narrowly confined to various formal matters. Thus, a party was bound by assertions which were solemnly recorded by deed (estoppels by deed) and by certain other limited acts of notoriety which were recognized as having the same effect such as livery (or delivery) or taking possession of land (estoppels in pais). The doctrine of estoppels by deed or estoppels in pais is the source of common law doctrine of estoppels by representation of fact whereby one party is prevented from denying the truth of a statement of fact if he or she has induced another party to rely on it to their detriment.〔42〕 Equity then extended the doctrine and in the eighteenth century the common law also began to adopt and to apply the equitable rules.〔43〕 By the nineteenth century the common law had developed a rule that there would be an estoppels where, by words or conduct, there had been a representation of existing fact (although not of law) which was intended to be acted upon and was in fact acted upon to his prejudice by the person to whom it was made. The maker of the representation was not allowed to allege in proceedings against the person to whom the representation was made that the facts were other than he or she had represented them to be.〔44〕"

至于构成陈述性禁反言的要件,可见《Hanbury & Martin Modern Equity》(第18版,2009年)一书之27－020段:"Estoppel by representation operates over a wide field of common law and equity. **The basic principle is that a person who makes an unambiguous representation**, by words, or conduct, or by silence, **of an existing fact**, and **causes another party to act to his detriment in reliance on the representation** will not

---

〔42〕 禁反言理论开始的说法是,一方做出对事实的陈述(representation of facts),诱导(induce)对方对此陈述依赖(reliance)并造成损害(detriment)。则陈述方不得在事后改变或否定该陈述的真实性。

〔43〕 这救济在18世纪开始也逐渐被普通法所吸收:见 Montefiori v. Montefiori (1762) 1 Wm. Bl. 363 先例。

〔44〕 19世纪普通法下的禁反言理论已经发展为,一方对过去或目前存在的事实(Jorden v. Money [1854] 5 HLC 185 贵族院先例的判法)做出陈述(无论是通过语言还是行为),希望能够被对方依赖,也确实被对方当事人依赖做出行为/决定并造成损害,陈述方就在诉讼程序中被禁反言,不可以举证试图改变或否定自己做出的陈述:见 Pickard v. Sears (1837) 6 Ad & El 469; Freeman v. Cooke (1848) ER 622; Canadian Pacific Ry v. R (1931) AC 414; Dean v. Bruce (1952) 1 KB 11 等先例。

be permitted subsequently to act inconsistently with that representation. The doctrine was originally applied only where there was **a representation of existing fact**, and not where the representation was one of law or of intention. **The representor could not subsequently allege, in dealing with the representee, that the facts were different from those represented.** Apart from a few long - established exceptions, such an estoppel works negatively. It is not capable of creating a cause of action. It works like a rule of evidence, a rule which excludes a particular defence or line of argument."（加黑部分是笔者的强调）

有关说法的先例很多，可先节录 Maclaine v. Gattey（1921）1 AC 376 先例中 Birkenhead 勋爵所说："Where A has by his words or conduct justified B in believing that a certain state of facts exists, and B has acted upon such belief to his detriment, A is not permitted to affirm against B that a different state of affairs existed at the time."

在近期的 Shah v. Shah（2002）QB 35 先例中，提出禁反言的被告的代表大律师根据《Halsbury's Law of England》（第 4 版，1992 年）第 16 卷，1039 - 1048 段，对构成陈述性禁反言的要件总结如下："To form the basis of estoppel a representation must be（1）of existing fact, not of intention or belief;（2）clear and unambiguous so as to be reasonably understood by the person to whom it is made in the sense contended for;（3）intended to be acted on in the manner in which it is acted on; or（4）made by a person who so conducts himself that a reasonable person would take the representation to be true and believe that it was meant that he should act on it in that manner. In acting on the representation the party to whom it was made must have altered his position to his prejudice."

5.2 总结构成陈述性禁反言的要件

总结而言，构成陈述性禁反言有四个要件：(1) 陈述方通过言行对过去或目前存在的事实做出了错误陈述；(2) 陈述方在做出陈述时知道（know）或希望（intend）被陈述方依赖；(3) 被陈述方有合理理由相信该对过去或目前存在的事实的陈述是真实的，并因此改变了他的地位与蒙受损害；(4) 允许陈述方更正之前对事实的陈述对被陈述方可能不公平或不合情理。

这些要件将在接下来的段节区别介绍，但可以看到这些要件与本书第四章介绍的构成"衡平法宽限"（equitable forbearance）或"承诺性禁反言"（promissory estoppel）的要件十分类似。如不能被用作诉因（盾牌与宝剑之争）、依赖与改变地位、蒙受损害等，都与承诺性禁反言十分类似。在本段会尽量避免重复，只针对与陈述性禁反言更相关之处与先例。

5.3 与衡平法宽限或承诺性禁反言的异同

这两种不同类别的禁反言都是针对出尔反尔的言行，即被禁反言的一方原来做出的对事实的陈述或承诺或宽限，在被对方依赖之后，又改变立场，希望更正陈述或撤回承诺或宽限。所以两者之间有很多共同点。

首先可节录 Sean Wilken QC 与 Karim Ghaly 先生更近期所著的《The Law of Waiver, Variation, and Estoppel》(第 3 版,2012 年)一书之 9.36 段,说:"**Analogy with equitable forbearance.** ... it appears that in this context estoppels by representation is governed by the same principles as equitable forbearance/ promissory estoppel."另在该书之 9.21 段,指出了陈述性禁反言与衡平法宽限或承诺性禁反言的区别。即前者的陈述针对已经存在的事实,而后者的陈述针对将来的意图或承诺。但自从有了承诺性禁反言的说法,这一区别再也不重要,反正两种陈述都会构成禁反言,说:"... The single distinction between the two is the nature of the representation: estoppel by representation requires a factual representation; equitable forbearance requires a promise or representation of future intention. The argument then is that this material distinction either does not exist or is unnecessary. Under either approach, the approach is to posit a single unified doctrine."

两个说法之间的另一个区别是在承诺性禁反言的救济是暂时或永久[45]不允许被禁反言的一方行使他的合约或法律权利,在可能的情况下也尽量允许通过合理通知回复到原本的合约或法律地位。但陈述性禁反言的救济是要求被禁反言的一方根据他所做出的错误陈述履行合约,通常就是通过第二种履行办法,即赔偿损失。这样也不存在可以通过提供证据在程序上回复到正确的事实地位。

笔者看到这两个说法之间还有一个区别,这就是在本书第四章第 5 段提到衡平法宽限或承诺性禁反言要求双方已经存在合约或法律关系,虽然澳大利亚有不同的说法。英国法律的考虑是不希望以衡平法宽限或承诺性禁反言的说法冲击约因/对价的要求。但陈述性禁反言没有这方面的考虑,所以陈述性禁反言没有双方已经存在合约或法律关系的要求。

对事实的陈述虽然通常只是向特定的被陈述方,但也经常有情况是向公众做出对事实的陈述。而且如果满足了陈述性禁反言的其他要件,如依赖并蒙受损害,一样可以构成陈述性禁反言。但显然陈述方不可能与公众已经存在合约或法律关系。向公众做出对事实的陈述并构成陈述性禁反言,最典型的例子就是提单(见本章之 12.1 段)、表见授权(见本章之 12.2 段)与股票买卖(见本章之 13.3 段)。

但表面看来陈述性禁反言如果不要求双方已经存在合约或法律关系,就与另一个大原则陈述性禁反言是证据规则且只能作为盾牌不能作为宝剑相矛盾。已经在本章第 3 段提到,虽然陈述性禁反言不能作为提起诉讼的关键要件,但可以作为支持性要件,即诉因来自陈述性禁反言下假设的事实,而非真正的事实。所以与衡平法宽限或承诺性禁反言对存在合约或法律关系的要求时间上有前后之分。

---

〔45〕 见本书第四章之 9.1 段。

6. 要件之一:通过言行对事实做出了错误陈述

6.1 事实必须是过去或目前存在

首先可分析“陈述”(representation)一词。在 Handley 大法官所著的《Estoppel by Conduct and Election》(2006 年)一书之 2 – 001 对陈述一词的字面解释是:“A statement made by, or on behalf of, one person to, or with the intention that it shall come to the notice of, another which relates, **by way of affirmation, denial, or description to an existing or past fact.** A representation is **a re – presentation of something, a repetition in words of a fact which has occurred or exists**.”(加黑部分是笔者的强调)

这与陈述性禁反言最开始属于证据规则匹配。一方只能提供证据过去或现在存在的事实,对所谓将来的“事实”,根本不可能存在证据。在本章之 1.1.1 段介绍的导致双方达成协议的“误述”(misrepresentation),要求引入证据证明陈述的事实是错误。但在陈述性禁反言是排除证据,被禁反言的一方不能证明真正的事实。

只有已经过去或目前存在的才可能是事实,将来的“事实”由于还没有发生,充其量只能是“预测”(prediction)或“意图”(intention)。Macnaghten 勋爵在 George Whitechurch Ltd. v. Cavanagh (1902) AC 117 先例中也强调说:“... a representation must be a representation of existing fact, or rather a representation as to some fact alleged to be in existence.”

对已经过去或目前存在的事实的陈述对构成陈述性禁反言的重要性可节录一些近期先例。首先是在 Midland Expressway Limited v. Carillion Construction Limited, Alfred McAlpine Construction Limited, Balfour Beatty Group Limited, AMEC Capital Projects Limited (2005) EWHC 2810 (TCC)先例中,Jackson 大法官说:

“In the course of his closing speech Mr Blackburn(原告代表大律师)candidly confessed his difficulty. **He could not support his plea of estoppel by representation because there was no representation of existing fact**. In his oral closing speech Mr Blackburn advanced a wholly new case on this issue, namely the contention that promissory estoppel debars CAMBBA(被告)from relying upon the strict requirements of clause 17.3.4. In support of this contention, Mr Blackburn produced a bundle of authorities relating to promissory estoppel.

Mr Streatfeild – James(被告代表大律师)objected to this approach. He submitted that MEL(原告)should not be allowed to advance a new case which had not been pleaded and which had not featured in the course of the trial. He further submitted that the afternoon of the day which had been allocated for oral closing speeches was not an appropriate occasion to introduce a bundle of authorities in support of novel legal arguments which had not previously been foreshadowed.

I accept Mr Streatfeild – James' submissions on this issue. In the exercise of my case management discretion I do not allow MEL at this late stage to advance a new case on estoppel which (a) has not been pleaded and (b) differs substantially from the case presented throughout the trial."(加黑部分是笔者的强调)

在 ING Lease (UK) Limited v. Mr Philip Ross Harwood (2007) EWHC 2292 (QB)先例中, Michael Harvey QC 大法官说:"Mr Harwood contends that ING are estopped from contending that the guarantee applies to the liability of HDUK in respect of the Coin TV debt. He relies upon both estoppel by representation and promissory estoppel. Miss Lucas, in her final address to me, did not seek to abandon her argument upon estoppel by representation but she accepted that her principal submissions were in respect of promissory estoppel. I think that she was right to concentrate upon promissory estoppel because it is **difficult to formulate any of the representations upon which she relied as being relevant representations of fact.**"(加黑部分是笔者的强调)

6.2 将来的事实

很多陈述有关将来的"事实",如陈述将来的意图(intention)、承诺(promise)、观点(opinion)或想法(belief)。在当时这些不是事实,因为可能会变为事实,也可能不会。正如 Saville 大法官在 Bank Leumi Le Israel BM v. British National Insurance Co. Ltd. (1988) 1 Lloyd's Rep. 71 先例中说:"A statement as to a future state of affairs can in itself neither be true nor false at the time it is made, since the future cannot be foretold."

这里的区分有公道之处,因为对一个存在或过去的事实,陈述方可以通过证据知道或明确真相。如果被挑战,陈述方也可以通过证据证明对事实的陈述的正确性。如果陈述方在做出陈述时不能完全确定真实性(如证据不完整或是来自二手传闻等),就应该加上限制(如说明"不保证"[without guarantee]),否则做出的陈述根据相关情况就会构成虚假、疏忽或是无辜的误述。但对将来的"事实"(不论是意图、承诺或是观点),陈述方都没有办法明确与肯定,因为将来的情况会变,陈述时的意图也会在将来做出改变等。另是逻辑上讲,对被陈述方来说,对于将来的陈述或承诺也应该有所保留,而不会像对已经存在的事实的陈述一样全心信任。所以针对后者,一般不会构成陈述性禁反言,即使被陈述方因为依赖而蒙受损害。Wilberforce 勋爵在 British Airways Board v. Taylor (1976) 1 WLR 13 先例说:"... the distinction is a real one and requires to be respected."

6.3 区分已经存在的事实与将来的事实的困难

但在现实中区分何为已经存在的事实与将来的事实不容易,特别是陈述方做出一个意见或是表达一个意图,但其中默示了以目前存在事实作为基础做出推算的情况。这种情况在澳大利亚高院的 Legione v. Hateley (1983) 152 CLR 406 先例中出现,有关的陈述是某人将会在几个月内死亡,这只是预测,但被法院视为默示某人目前有致命疾病的事实。

另在英国著名的 Jorden v. Money (1854) 5 HLC 185 先例中,Jorden 太太开始诉讼向 Money 先生追讨债券担保的债务。Money 先生则向衡平法院要求宣告 Jorden 太太已经放弃了债务与申请禁止她追讨债务的禁令。Jorden 太太向 Money 先生与他的父母做出的总重要的两个陈述是"I give you my word and honour that I will never use (the debt) against(Money 先生)"与"I will never make any claim on your son (Money 先生) in respect of that debt"。

Money 先生争辩说,Jorden 太太的陈述表示她已经放弃了债务,他依赖 Jorden 太太的陈述进行了婚姻财产契约(marriage settlement)的谈判。贵族院解释 Jorden 太太的陈述是承诺将来不会追讨债务,即陈述性禁反言不适用。虽然承诺性禁反言可能适用,但这个说法是在 Central London Property Trust Ltd. v. High Trees House Ltd. (1947) KB 130 先例后才发展起来,1854 年还不存在这个说法。但如果 Jorden 太太的陈述被法院解释为已经放弃了债务,或是她执行了免除债务契约(deed of release of debt),则陈述性禁反言就会适用。

在 Nippon Menkwa Kabushiki Kaisha v. Dawsons Bank Ltd. (1935) 51 Lloyd's Rep. 147 (PC)先例中,卖方将大米向银行质押(pledge),并由磨坊作为银行的代理人实际控制货物。之后卖方将大米卖给了买方,磨坊在交货单(delivery order)上写了"O. K."。买方根据交货单与发票支付了货价,但卖方并没有将这笔钱还给银行。买方在提货时被银行告知,因为卖方没有清偿债务,所以不能交货,而银行要将货物拍卖。双方的争议之一就是磨坊在交货单上写的"O. K."是否构成陈述性禁反言。Russell 大法官判这个陈述只针对交货单上有关货物的数量、唛头等信息,不属于对货物没有债务(unencumbered)的陈述,也不是银行将来不会执行货物担保的陈述或承诺。

在 Marquess of Salisbury v. Gilmore (1942) 2 KB 38 CA 先例中,案情涉及房东对租客表示租约结束后,他的意图是将房屋推倒。根据英国立法规定,如果房屋很快要被推倒,租客可以不用理会租约中要将房屋修好的规定。租客依赖了房东的陈述,在搬走时没有将房屋修好。之后房东改变主意,不将房屋推倒,于是向租客索赔他没有将房屋修好造成的损失。租客提出了陈述性禁反言的抗辩,但房东认为这属于对意图的陈述,不构成陈述性禁反言。但房东的争辩没有被上诉庭接受,Mackinnon 大法官说:"... the question must be what is the substance of the intimation by the man concerned, not what is the form or language of it. **A statement using the words 'intend' or 'intention' in form, may be, in substance, a representation of fact.** ... In substance the communication of November, 1937, stated facts... 'This house is... doomed to demolition in September, 1939.' That being the substance of the statement to the defendant, I do not think the rule in Jorden v. Money avails... merely because the words of the letter happen to use the word 'intention'."（加黑部分是笔者的强调）

这个房东意图将房屋推倒的陈述也不属于承诺，如果上诉庭判这不是对事实的陈述，即使在当时有承诺性禁反言的说法，也不会适用。

在 Sean Wilken QC 与 Karim Ghaly 先生所著的《The Law of Waiver, Variation, and Estoppel》（第 3 版，2012 年）一书之 9.25 段，介绍 Ismail v. Polish Ocean Lines (1976) QB 893 CA 先例说："In (this case) a cargo owner was stopped from denying that its goods had been improperly stowed during the shipment because it agent had insisted on the method used. This representation would seem to be capable of analysis either as a representation of fact, namely that the method of stowage used was the correct one or as a representation of intention, that the cargo owner would not insist on its right to demand proper stowage."

该书接着另举了一个例子，涉及的陈述是根据合约规定正确做出了通知，说："Similarly, a number of cases involve the representation of fact that notice required by a contract has been validly served. There would seem to be little to distinguish a representation that the notice was in fact validly served and a promise or representation of intention that the representee would not enforce its right to compliance with formalities required for notice."

最后可介绍 European Asian Bank AG v. Punjab & Sind Bank (No. 2) (1983) 1 WLR 642 CA 先例中，案情涉及一家印度公司向新加坡公司购买丁香，并约定以信用证付款。被告开证银行（issuing bank）通过原告议付银行（negotiating bank）通知新加坡公司信用证已经开出。之后新加坡公司交出提单等文件，原告将这些文件转交给被告，被告回复说文件被印度公司接受并且将会在到期日前做出支付。依赖被告的回复，原告向新加坡公司做出支付。但后来发现是诈骗，这批丁香根本没有付运，导致被告拒绝向原告做出支付。该先例的争议是被告的回复是对将来事实的陈述或是对过去或目前事实的陈述（或是将来会支付的承诺），能否构成禁反言。Robert Goff 大法官说："In all the circumstances, we have no doubt that, on a true construction of the relevant documents, the defendants did indeed unequivocally represent to the plaintiffs that they, the defendants recognised that the plaintiffs were entitled to act as negotiating bankers under the letter of credit and that the documents were in order so that there was, on the face of the documents, a liability upon the defendants to pay the plaintiffs the sum due under the letter of credit on the due date."

因为区分是事实还是意图十分困难，所以法院或仲裁庭在解释时有很大的裁量权（discretion），这也导致了不肯定（uncertainty），个别法官或仲裁员很容易操纵（manipulate）究竟是属于事实还是意图。针对这方面的问题也有不少批评，尤其是在对禁反言的说法更有弹性的澳大利亚。如在澳大利亚的 Legione v. Hateley 先例中，Mason 与 Deane 大法官说："a representation as to future conduct into a strait jacket of present descriptive fact... in our view nothing is to be gained... by such attempts at forced reconciliation..."在 Waltons Stores (Interstate) Ltd. v. Maher (1988) 164 CLR 387 先例中,Deane 大法官也说:"The distinction between a representation or assumption of existing fact and one of future action or inaction has always sat uncomfortably with the general notions of good conscience and fair dealing which underlay common law, as well as equitable doctrines of estoppel by conduct see, e. g., the dissenting speech of Lord St Leonards in Jorden v. Money and Marquess of Salisbury v. Gilmore."另在 Commonwealth of Australia v. Verwayen (1990) 170 CLR 394 先例中,Mason 大法官说:"the distinction between present and future fact is unsatisfactory and produces arbitrary results instead of serving [a] useful purpose. Indeed the difference between the majority and Lord St Leonards in Jorden v. Money was a striking illustration of the arbitrary nature of the distinction."

随着承诺性禁反言(promissory estoppel)的说法的发展,这个区分的重要性有所下降,因为在同样的事实下希望依赖禁反言的一方可以同时提出陈述性禁反言与承诺性禁反言作为替代争议。但问题是并不是所有对将来的"事实"的陈述都属于承诺。

6.4 对将来意图的表述

对将来的意图(future intention)或愿望,这不可能是事实,也不会将来一定变事实。所以,对将来的意图或是愿望会变事实的反而不多。同样因为将来环境的变化,陈述方的意图也会有相应改变,这也无可厚非。正如 Deane 大法官在 Waltons Stores (Interstate) Ltd. v. Maher (1988) 164 CLR 387 先例第 450 页说:"a representation or assumption which is confined to the existence of a present intention and does not exclude the possibility of a future change of mind will ordinarily be inadequate to found an effective estoppel... an estoppel denying departure of it would have nothing to say in relation to future conduct since it would not preclude any future change of mind."

在上一小段提到的著名的 Jorden v. Money (1954) 5 HLC185 先例中,法院也判是 Jorden 太太的陈述是对将来意图的表述,不能构成陈述性禁反言。陈述方之后改变主意不代表他/她在做出陈述时不是这么想的。

Russell 勋爵在 Evans v. Bartlam (1937) AC 473 先例也说:"A statement of intention... could ground no estoppels."另在 Kammins Ballrooms Co. Ltd. v. Zenith Investments (Torquay) Ltd. (1971) AC 850 先例中,Diplock 勋爵说:"... a statement of the landlord's present intention... would... estop them from denying that they had that intention at the time... but that would not help the tenants."

这样看来,对意图的表述实是空话一句,一般不构成陈述性禁反言。唯一例外是在 Edgington v. Fitzmaurice (1885) 29 Ch D. 459 先例的情况。在该先例中,某公司出了一份邀请认购债券的说明书声明公司意图将募得的金钱改建公司大楼,买马和车，以及发展公司业务。但实际上很快就将这些金钱用来还债。法院判是公司董事要负上"侵权的欺诈误述"（tort for deceit）的责任，上诉庭的 Bowen 大法官说："This is an action for deceit, in which the plaintiff complains that he was induced to take certain debentures by the misrepresentations of the defendants, and that he sustained damage thereby... A mere suggestion of possible purposes to which a portion of the money might be applied would not have formed a basis for an action of deceit. There must be a misstatement of an existing fact: **but the state of a man's mind is as much a fact as the state of his digestion.** It is true that it is very difficult to prove what the state of a man's mind at any particular time is, but, if it can be substantiated, it is as much fact as anything else... A misrepresentation as to the state of a man's mind is, therefore, a misstatement of fact. "（加黑部分是一句经常被引用的话）

换言之，在表述这意图或愿望时，陈述方或表述方已是在讲假话，他在当时根本已没有愿望（will）或能力（ability）把这意图将来转化为事实，这就是对事实的错误陈述。

《Chitty on Contracts》（第 32 版，2015 年）之 7 – 008 段总结这方面的先例中，说："**Statement of opinion amounts to statement of fact if not honestly held.** However, in certain circumstances a statement of opinion (or of intention) may be regarded as a statement of fact, and therefore as a ground for avoiding a contract if the statement is false. Thus, if it can be proved that the person who expressed the opinion did not hold it, or could not, as a reasonable man having his knowledge of the facts, honestly have held it, the statement may be regarded as a statement of fact. If a person states as his opinion something which he does not in fact believe, or which given the facts known to him, he could not honestly hold, he makes a false statement of fact. So where, at a sale of property, the vendor described the occupier as 'a most desirable tenant', while in fact he knew that the rent was considerably in arrear, this was held to entitle the purchaser to rescind the contract.〔46〕"

所以，在商业活动中，不要随便相信与依赖对方意图的表述。例如在租船，不要因承租人表述意图是装棉花或散粮而忽略了对租约条文的重视。如订明要禁止装废铁（scrap），因为本船是新造船，否则将来租船人装废铁，因为租约没有禁止，船东也就无话可说了。

笔者可以 1980 年 The "Kin Wai" (1980)的伦敦仲裁为例来说明这方面的危险，该仲裁案件在杨大明的《期租合同》一书第 11 页有详论。Kin Wai 轮被出租给一家美国承租人，订约前的谈判中，他多次说明这航次期租（Time – Charter – Trip, TCT）是意图自美湾装粮去意大利，租约订为："One time charter trip via safe port (s) berth

---

〔46〕 见 Smith v. Land and House Property Corp (1884) 28 Ch. D. 7 先例。

(s) always afloat and always within Institute Warranty Limits..."

而船东一向谨慎的航区范围(trading limit),如说明不准去战区,以及一些在当时受到船东排斥的以色列、伊拉克、古巴、朝鲜等国家,因为船东以为只是行走美湾去意大利,也就不多花时间谈判,没有在租约条文中将这些敏感区域排除。结果该承租人要用船装货去以色列,而不是意大利。船东知道时,货物已经几乎装完。当时阿拉伯国家严禁行走过以色列的船,所以一般船东不肯行走以色列。但仲裁结果是船东败诉,因为承租人只是意图而已。这样,租船人用很低廉的租金租一条船舶行走本来付出很高租金也不一定能租到船舶愿意行走的以色列航次。而船东事后损失惨重:包括之后被阿拉伯港口为难,因为船舶被阿拉伯国家列入黑名单只能以低价出售等。

如果 Kin Wai 轮的船东能证明租船人在表述他的意图是装粮去意大利时已经在说谎,根本没有愿望或能力转化为事实,便会胜诉。但这证明会非常困难,例如只能靠美国租船人文件的披露(discovery),而文件中显示在承租人向船东表述以及订约时,他正在洽谈去以色列的生意,或是早一天唯一在洽谈的去意大利的生意已告吹等。但精明的美国租船人怎会不小心披露不利的证据,他只要找一个经纪人给一份证供说明在他表述当天与订约一天市场上确有美湾去意大利装散粮的生意即可。

6.5 对观点或想法或理解的陈述

与上一小段介绍的性质类似的是对观点或想法或理解的陈述,上一小段节录的《Chitty on Contracts》(第32版,2015年)之7-008段也同时针对了本小段要介绍的这种陈述。在节录的7-008段最后一句提到的 Smith v. Land and House Property Corp (1884) 28 Ch. D. 7 先例中,涉及的陈述也并非是对未来意图的陈述,而是对观点的陈述。在该先例中,买方在出售他的一间酒店时,吹嘘说他的租客是一位称心如意的租客(a most desirable tenant),但事实上该租客从未按时交租,并且当时有债务未清。虽然表面看来这个陈述只是卖方的意见,但法院判这属于误述,买方可以取消(rescind)合约。因为只有卖方才了解他的租客,而买方不会了解,双方对事实的了解程度不同,知道得更多的一方的意见表达就通常会被认为是事实的陈述。

对观点或想法或理解的陈述代表的是陈述方当时(不是将来)的想法,一般来说不会构成禁反言,令陈述方不能事后否认他的观点或想法或理解的正确性。因为被陈述方很难证明陈述方在做出这样的陈述时,内心是知道自己的观点或想法或理解不正确。这一法律地位可见 Low v. Bouverie (1891) 3 Ch 82 CA 先例中,一位信托人在接受陌生人关于信托基金的询问时,提到了信托基金有用于支付保险等,但没有提到他不记得的其他抵押。陌生人依赖信托人的陈述借款给信托基金的受益人。事后受益人破产,因为其他抵押导致该陌生人无法收回全部借款,于是该陌生人要求信托人赔偿无法收回的部分。上诉庭判是信托人的陈述不构成禁反言,因为只是一个观点。Bowen 大法官说:"language would be reasonably understood as... an intimation of the state of his belief, without an assertion that the fact was so."

在《Chitty on Contracts》(第32版,2015年)一书,就谈到商贸交往中经常出现的吹牛(puff)与观点通常不属于对事实的陈述,不会有法律后果。这可节录该书之7-007段,如下:“**Puff and statement of opinion.** Mere ‘puffs’ do not amount to representations. A mere statement of opinion which proves to have been unfounded, will not be treated as a misrepresentation; for as a general rule these cannot be regarded as representations of fact, except in so far as they show that the opinion or intention is held by the person expressing it. The statement must be construed it would reasonably be understood by the recipient in the context in which the statement was made.”

但这也不绝对,会有例外情况是虽然表面看是对观点的陈述,但本质上属于对事实的陈述。这可节录 Mance 大法官在 Bankers Trust International Plc. v. PT Dharmala Sakti Sejahtera (1996) CLC 518 先例所说,如下:“The meaning and effect of words never fails to be viewed in a vacuum. It is shaped by the context of their communication, including the parties’ respective positions, knowledge and experience.〔47〕 A description or commendation which may obviously be irrelevant or may even serve as a warning to one recipient, because of its generality, superficiality or laudatory nature, or because of the recipient’s own knowledge and experience, may constitute a material representation if made to another less informed or sophisticated receiver... whether there was any and if so what particular representation must this depend an objective assessment of the likely effect of the proposal or presentation on the recipient. In making such an assessment, it is necessary to consider the recipient’s characteristics and knowledge as they appeared, or ought to have appeared, to the maker of the proposal or representation.〔48〕”

在 Cassa di Risparmio della Repubblica di San Marino SpA v. Barclays Bank Ltd. (2011) EWHC 484 (Comm)先例中,Hamblen 大法官总结区分对事实的陈述与对意见的陈述时要重点考虑的两点,说:“In order to determine whether any and if so what representation was made by a statement requires (1) construing the statement in the context in which it was made, and (2) interpreting the statement objectively according to the impact it might be expected to have on a reasonable representee in the position and with

---

〔47〕 解释有关的陈述与解释合约一样,不能脱离语境,包括双方相互之间的关系、知识水平与经验等。

〔48〕 判断是否本质属于对事实的陈述,必须客观评判在陈述方看来被陈述方的个性与知识水平。如果被陈述方知识水平不够或无法了解情况,而陈述方也明知这一点,则陈述方做出的表面看来是观点的陈述,也可能被认为属于对事实的陈述,如专业人士的专业意见,或是陈述方明知对方/被陈述方没有有关的知识只能依赖他的观点行事时做出的陈述。这也就是 Smith v. Land and House Property Corp (1884) 28 Ch. D. 7 先例的判法。另一个类似案情的近期先例是 Credit Lyonnais Bank Nederland v. Export Credit Guarantee Department (1996) 1 Lloyd’s Rep. 200,陈述方的银行指称公司管理层是受到尊敬(respectable)与可信赖的(trustworthy),但事实上银行知道公司的管理存在问题。

the known characteristics of the actual representee.〔49〕”

在《Chitty on Contracts》(第 32 版,2015 年)一书之 7 - 009 段,也总结说:“Statement of opinion may carry implication that grounds for belief. In Brown v. Raphael (1958) Ch 636... The Court of Appeal held that as the vendor was in a far stronger position than the purchaser to ascertain the facts, there must be implied a further representation that the former had reasonable grounds for his belief. If, on the other hand, it is clear that the person who expressed the opinion had no real way of knowing whether or not it was correct, no such implication can be made. In Economides v. Commercial Union Assurance Co. Plc. (1998) QB 587 it as held that a statement by an insured, a private person with no specialist knowledge... Thus a statement of the value which the insured made honestly was not a misrepresentation even though it was inaccurate. Equally, propositions out forward by parties engaged in negotiating the settlement of a dispute are likely to be treated as mere statements of opinion and, at least when the negotiations are conducted by experienced professionals in good faith, are unlikely to be treated as including a representation that they are based on reasonable grounds. ... Subject to the principles illustrated by Brown v. Raphael, an opinion expressed in good faith is not to be held to be a misrepresentation merely because it turns out to be incorrect. But a statement of opinion which is published as if it were a fact may be regarded as a statement of fact.”

在 2008 年发生“金融海啸”前后,很多金融产品的投资失利,导致产生大量投资者(包括个人、公司或其他银行)指银行在提供投资意见时有误述导致合约产生(或构成陈述性禁反言)的昂贵诉讼。如著名的 Peekay Intermark v. Australia & New Zealand Banking Group (2006) 2 Lloyd's Rep. 511; IFE Fund SA v. Goldman Sachs International (2007) 1 Lloyd's Rep. 264; Springwell Navigation v. JP Morgan Chase Bank (2010) EWCA Civ 1212; Raiffeisen Zentralbank Osterreich AG v. Royal Bank of Scotland Plc. (2011) 1 Lloyd's Rep. 123; Cassa di Risparmio della Repubblica di San Marino SpA v. Barclays Bank Ltd 等先例。这些案例都会涉及有关的投资意见究竟是对事实的陈述或是没有法律后果的意见。

即使做出了有法律后果的对事实的陈述,也可以明示条文逃避责任。如在贵族院的 Hedley Byrne v. Heller (1963) 1 Lloyd's Rep. 483 先例中,加上“without responsibility”的限定。或是在 Raiffeisen Zentralbank Osterreich AG v. Royal Bank of Scotland Plc. 先例所建议的把对事实的陈述向对方说明只是对意见的陈述:“In some cases the statement in question may have been accompanied by other statements by way of

〔49〕 决定是否构成对事实的陈述需要根据语境进行解释,或者客观看会对合理的被陈述方(与真正的被陈述方处于同样地位,有同样的知识水平、经验、个性、文化背景等)造成的影响。

qualification or explanation which would indicate to a reasonable person that the putative representor was not assuming a responsibility for the accuracy or completeness of the statement or was saying that no reliance can be placed upon it. Thus the representor may qualify what might otherwise have been an outright statement of fact by saying that it is only a statement of belief, that it may not be accurate, that he has not verified its accuracy or completeness, or that it is not to be relied on."

6.6　对法律的陈述

对法律的陈述〔50〕曾经被认为不能构成陈述性禁反言：Eaglesfield v. Marquis of Londonberry (1876) 4 Ch. D. 693 先例。关于对事实的陈述与对法律的陈述的区分的困难，正如上两个小段介绍的对过去或目前存在的事实的陈述与对将来意图或当时想法等的陈述区分的困难，导致了相当数量的诉讼与争议。这区分不仅对陈述性禁反言有重要性，对本章之 1.1 段介绍的"误述"(misrepresentation)也十分重要。

总体来说，纯法律(pure law)的陈述不会构成陈述性禁反言：Gresham Life Assurance Society v. Crowther (1914) 2 Ch 219；Lyle – Meller v. A Lewis & Co. (Westminster) Ltd. (1956) 1 WLR 29 CA；Kai Nam v. Ma Kam Chan (1956) AC 358 PC；Moorgate Mercantile Co. Ltd. v. Twitchings (1976) QB 225 CA 等先例。这个法律地位有两方面的原因：(1)对了解法律真正如何规定，双方都被假设是处于同样的地位，如可以咨询律师。正如 Hodson 大法官在 Lyle – Meller v. A Lewis & Co. (Westminster) Ltd 先例中说："If the representation had been a mere representation of law, I should find it difficult to get an estoppel out of it. There are, indeed, passages in various authorities to the effect that if you merely admit liability and say you are wrong in law, no estoppel arises. There may be an agreement for consideration which produces the same result, but in the absence of agreement the mere admission of liability standing by itself does not as a rule produce anything in the nature of an estoppel on the authorities because — as I think Lloyd – Jacob J. put it — it may be taken to be reasonable that each party is in as good a position as the other to satisfy himself on what the law is; and if one party admits he is wrong in law, he is not necessarily estopped from changing his mind hereafter."(2)有看法是对法律的陈述只属于对意见的陈述，因此不会构成陈述性禁反言。

这两方面的原因也带来了另一个有关依赖的问题，即被陈述方不能盲目与不合理〔51〕地依赖陈述方关于纯法律的陈述。这当然指一般的商贸关系，但即使是对方律师的陈述，也应该了解因为立场不同，不能盲目依赖，而应该咨询自己的律师。即只有自己律师的意见可以依赖，而如果律师给错意见，也不会构成禁反言，而涉及律师与客户之间的合约明示或默示责任，或如果律师提供的是免费的法律意见，就会涉

〔50〕 但要注意这里指的法律是英国法律，而不是外国法律，外国法律是事实问题，而不是法律问题。

〔51〕 关于依赖是否合理将会在本章之 8.1 段进一步介绍。

及本章之1.1.2段提到的侵权。

区分对事实的陈述与对法律的陈述有时会很困难,在很多情况下,这两者是混为一体(mixed law and facts)的。如对一份私人文件(如合约)的解释,传统上与程序上被认为是法律问题。但Diplock勋爵在The "Nema" (1981) 2 Lloyd's Rep. 239先例与The "Antaios" (1984) 2 Lloyd's Rep. 235先例中认为,解释一份私人文件虽然在程序上被视为是法律问题,但实际上是事实问题。

Reid勋爵在Brutus v. Cozens (1973) AC 854先例中说,解释立法中英文词语的一般意思是事实问题,说:"... The meaning of an ordinary word of the English language is not a question of law. The proper construction of a statute is a question of law. If the context shows that a word is used in an unusual sense the court will determine in other words what that unusual sense is. But here there is in my opinion no question of the word 'insulting'[52] being used in any unusual sense. It appears to me, ... to be intended to have its ordinary meaning. It is for the tribunal which decides the case to consider, not as law but as fact, whether in the whole circumstances the words of the statute do or do not as a matter of ordinary usage of the English language cover or apply to the facts which have been proved..."

Parker大法官在Commonwealth Smelting Ltd. & Another v. Guardian Royal Exchange Assurance Ltd. (1986) 1 Lloyd's Rep. 121先例中也有类似的说法,针对的是保险合约中的"爆炸"一词应该给一个广泛或是狭窄的解释,说:"It is of course trite law that the interpretation, whether it be of a statute or of a contract is a matter of law... If there is an ordinary English word used and it is not contended by either side that there is anything in the context which would result in it having a special meaning, then it is for the court to decide as a matter of fact. Whether the facts in the particular case are, or are not, within that ordinary meaning."

在Eaglesfield v. Marquis of Londonderry先例中,Jessel大法官举了不少例子说明不少对事实的陈述实际上涉及背后的法律,说:

"It was put to me that this was a misrepresentation of law and not of fact. It was said the company and the directors did not know their Acts of Parliament, and their solicitor had told them this, which they believed, that the new £ 15,000 Preference Stock would be and be treated as part of the Llanidloes No. 1 Preference Capital, and rank and stand upon the same footing in all respects as the £ 85,000 Llanidloes No. 1 Preference Stock.

Of course, solicitors can give wrong advice as well as other people, and I have no doubt he did think that this would rank as part of the Llanidloes No. 1 Preference Stock.

---

〔52〕 该先例涉及对1936年《Public Order Act》这一立法之section 5的"insulting behavior"一词的解释。

But does that make it a misrepresentation of law? A misrepresentation of law is this: when you state the facts, and state a conclusion of law, so as to distinguish between facts and law. The man who knows the facts is taken to know the law; but when you state that as a fact which no doubt involves, as most facts do, a conclusion of law, that is still a statement of fact and not a statement of law. Suppose a man is asked by a tradesman whether he can give credit to a lady, and the answer is, 'You may, she is a single woman of large fortune.' It turns out that the man who gave that answer knew thatthe lady had gone through the ceremony of marriage with a man who was believed to be a married man, and that she had been advised that that marriage ceremony was null and void, though it had not been declared so by any Court, and it afterwards turned out they were all mistaken, that the first marriage of the man was void, so that the lady was married. He does not tell the tradesman all these facts, but states that she is single. That is a statement of fact. If he had told him the whole story, and all the facts, and said, 'Now, you see, the lady is single,' that would have been a misrepresentation of law. But the single fact he states, that the lady is unmarried, is a statement of fact, neither more nor less; and it is not the less a statement of fact, that in order to arrive at it you must know more or less of the law.

There is not a single fact connected with personal status that does not, more or less, involve a question of law. If you state that a man is the eldest son of a marriage, you state a question of law, because you must know that there has been a valid marriage, and that that man was the first – born son after the marriage, or, in some countries, before. Therefore, to state it is not a representation of fact seems to arise from a confusion of ideas.

It is not the less a fact because that fact involves some knowledge or relation of law. There is hardly any fact which does not involve it. If you state that a man is in possession of an estate of £ 10,000 a year, the notion of possession is a legal notion, and involves knowledge of law; nor can any other fact in connection with property be stated which does not involve such knowledge of law. To state that a man is entitled to £ 10,000 Consols involves all sorts of law. Therefore this is a statement of fact, and nothing more; and I hold the argument to be wholly unfounded which maintained that it was a statement of law."

这样看来,多数表面看来的对法律的陈述(包括对合约与立法的解释)因为涉及事实,也可以构成陈述性禁反言。除非是对纯法律(pure law)的陈述,但这种情况不多。在 Central London Property Trust Ltd. v. High Trees House Ltd. (1947) KB 130 先例之后,禁反言的适用范围有了大幅度扩展,这也影响了陈述性禁反言。

在 Lyle-Meller v. A Lewis & Co. (Westminster) Ltd 先例中,案情涉及 Lyle-Meller 先生发明了一款充气式打火机(gas-filled lighters)替代原先的汽油打火机。Lyle-Meller 先生与 A Lewis 公司达成协议,Lyle-Meller 先生停止生产充气式打火机并将所有资料排他性提供给 A Lewis 公司。而作为回报,A Lewis 公司每生产一个根据 Lyle-Meller 先生的发明制造出的打火机(gas lighter embodying his inventions),就要支付他 6 便士。A Lewis 公司支付了前两年的费用,但拒绝支付之后的费用,理由是他们生产的打火机并不是根据 Lyle-Meller 先生的发明制造出的。事实上 A Lewis 公司在与 Lyle-Meller 先生订立合约之前就已经在生产充气式打火机,只是估计质量比不上 Lyle-Meller 先生的发明。Lyle-Meller 先生则提出了陈述性禁反言的抗辩,A Lewis 公司支付两年费用的行为属于对他保证,说:"we acknowledge that the lighters and refills which we are making embody your inventions and that we are liable to pay you royalties thereon. "

而 A Lewis 公司则回复说这个言行只属于对法律的陈述,不构成陈述性禁反言。毕竟 Lyle-Meller 先生完全知道这个充气式打火机的性质与生产工序,以及他自己的发明。所以事实方面没有什么陈述,A Lewis 公司的言行明确针对"embody your inventions"一词,要解释打火机是否是根据 Lyle-Meller 先生的发明制造,需要解释合约条文以及专利法,所以是对法律的陈述。

在上诉庭,Denning 勋爵说在 Central London Property Trust Ltd. v. High Trees House Ltd 先例之后,禁反言的适用范围有了大幅度的扩展。关于对法律的陈述能否构成禁反言,Denning 勋爵说:"This new estoppel also applies to representation about legal relations. This new estoppel also applies to representations about legal relations. Take the kind of assertion or assurance which was held binding in Robertson v. Minister of Pensions (1949) 1 K. B. 227, and in the decision of the Privy Council in Harnham Singh v. Jamal Pirbhai (1951) A. C. 688 to which Lord Hailsham drew our attention this morning. In each of those cases one party had made to the other a clear and explicit assertion of the legal relationship existing between them. In the Robertson case it was a statement by the Crown to an Army officer: 'Your disability has been accepted as attributable to military service.' In the Harnham case it was an unequivocal statement by a tenant that he 'will remain in occupation as a statutory tenant.' The statement was not in either case a contract, and not regarded as such, but it was an assurance as to the legal position — as to the legal consequences of the facts known to both — which was intended to be acted upon, it was acted upon, and it was held to be binding. It did not give rise to a cause of action in itself, but it did prevent the party making it from setting up a defence which would otherwise be open to him. In that sense it gave rise to an estoppel, but it was not the old kind of estoppel, which was only a rule of evidence. It was the new kind of estoppel which affects legal relations. "Hodson 大法官也说:"... That there may be a mixed question of law and fact does not destroy the estoppel. Nor does it matter that questions of patent law may be involved in considering whether or not there is an invention which is covered by a patent."

最后可节录近期的 Briggs v. Gleeds（Head Office）（2014）EWHC 1178 先例中，显示关于对法律的陈述的法律地位的进一步发展。在该先例中，Newey 大法官说：

"**To my mind, it is hard to see why the mere fact that a statement purely concerns law should invariably mean that it cannot give rise to an estoppel by representation.**[53] If, as appears to be the case, an estoppel by convention can relate to a legal assumption (see e. g. Republic of India v. India Steamship Co. Ltd. [1998] AC 878, at 913, and PW & Co. v. Milton Gate Investments Ltd. [2004] Ch 142, at paragraphs 171 – 173), there can be no rule of public policy to the effect that a person can never be estopped from asserting the true legal position. Further, there is force in Deane J's comment in Foran v. Wight (1989) 168 CLR 385 (at paragraph 5 of his judgment) that '**the distinction between a representation of fact and a representation of law is, in the context of the principles constituting the doctrine of estoppel by conduct, essentially illusory unless one subscribes... to the view that the law has no factual existence at all**'.

The key question, of course, is whether the rule that an estoppel by representation has to be founded on a statement of fact has survived the decision of the House of Lords in Kleinwort Benson Ltd. v. Lincoln City Council (1999) 2 AC 349[54] and the effects that case has already been recognised as having in contexts other than payment under mistake. I have concluded that the rule can no longer represent the law. In the past, commentary on whether a statement of law could give rise to an estoppel drew on cases dealing with misrepresentation: see e. g. the authorities cited in paragraph 42 of Spencer Bower and Turner, 'The Law Relating to Estoppel by Representation', 3rd ed. If the law now considers that a statement as to the law can constitute a representation for the purposes of the law relating to misrepresentation, such a statement must surely also be capable of constituting a representation in the context of estoppel by representation. Further, now that the Courts have retreated from the proposition that everybody should be taken to know the law, they must also, I think, recognise that it is not always the case

---

〔53〕 Newey 大法官认为仅仅是因为陈述针对的是纯法律就不能构成陈述性禁反言，没有道理。

〔54〕 在本章第 4 段提到，弄错事实下付钱可以根据"复原"（restitution）从收钱的一方追回这笔钱。但在弄错法律下付钱，一贯以来的说法是复原不适用。在 Kleinwort Benson Ltd. v. Lincoln City Council（1999）2 AC 349 先例中，贵族院拒绝对复原加以这样的限制，即弄错法律下付钱也可以根据复原追回。因此 Newey 大法官认为既然已经在复原中放宽，没有道理不在禁反言中放开。

that ' each party is in as good a position as the other to satisfy himself on what the law is'[55].

In short, I agree with Mr Newman that **it is now possible for an estoppel by representation to be based on a representation of law.** It will very often be the case that a statement about law will not be capable of giving rise to a relevant estoppel (because, say, it amounted to no more than an expression of opinion, the circumstances were such that the representee could not reasonably rely on it or allowing an estoppel would conflict with a statute), but **I do not think there is an absolute rule to that effect any more.** "(加黑部分是笔者的强调)

6.7 对将来的承诺

其中一种经常出现但属于将来意图的陈述,就是陈述方向被陈述方做出"承诺"(promise)。这可以是承诺将来会做一些事情或对一些权利做出宽限。但对将来意图的陈述并不一定会构成向被陈述方的承诺,正如 Carnwath 大法官在 ING Bank NV v. Ros Roca SA (2011) EWCA Civ 353 先例中说:"I find it difficult to see how the case can properly be based on promissory estoppels, in the absence of anything which could be categorized in ordinary language as a promise."

通常承诺可能是构成一个有约束力的合约,但由于有效的合约是需要各种先决条件才会被法律承认,如约因/对价、双方订约的意图、要约与接受等。这导致在一段很长的时间,陈述方做出承诺但事后没有兑现,只要没有构成合约,即使被承诺方或被陈述方因为依赖这个空的承诺而蒙受损害,也无法获得救济。这种情况直到 Central London Property Trust Ltd. v. High Trees House Ltd. (1947) KB 130 先例中,Denning 大法官创造性提出"承诺性禁反言"(promissory estoppels)才有所改变。关于承诺性禁反言在本书第四章有详述,这里只节录 Denning 大法官与对将来的意图的陈述有关的一段判决如下:"With regard to estoppel, the representation made in relation to reducing the rent, was not a representation of an existing fact. It was a representation, in effect, as to the future, namely, that payment of the rent would not be enforced at the full rate but only at the reduced rate. Such a representation would not give rise to an estoppel, because, as was said in Jorden v. Money, a representation as to the future must be embodied as a contract or be nothing."

涉及将来并属于承诺的陈述,在陈述性禁反言不能适用的情况下(如陈述方没有对过去或目前存在的事情进行任何陈述),也有了承诺性禁反言的救济。从这个角度看,禁反言的适用性有了大幅度的扩展,正如 Denning 勋爵在 Lyle - Meller v. A Lewis & Co. (Westminster) Ltd. (1956) 1 WLR 29 先例中所说:

---

[55] 法院也意识到并非所有人都知道法律如何规定,并且对于了解法律真正是如何规定,双方也并非处于同样的地位。

"I do not think it necessary to go into these refinements... no matter whether it concerns the present or the future. It may not be such as to give rise to an estoppel at common law, strictly so called, for that was confined to representations of existing fact: but we have got far beyond the old common law estoppel now. We have reached a new estoppel which affects legal relations.

This new estoppel applies to representations as to the future. Take the kind of assurance which was held binding in Central London Property Trust v. High Trees House Ltd. and in Tool Metal Manufacturing Co. Ltd. v. Tungsten Electric Co. Ltd. in the Court of Appeal (first action), and in the House of Lords (second action). In each of those cases a creditor during the war gave a promiseor assurance to the other party that he would for the time being forgo sums which were thereafter to become due to him. In the High Trees case it was rent. In the Tungsten case it was sums payable by way of compensation. The assurance was not a contract binding in law, but it was an assurance as to the future, it was intended to be acted upon, it was acted upon, and it was held binding on the party who gave it ..."

6.8 陈述必须清楚无误与不含糊

与承诺性禁反言一样,构成陈述性禁反言的陈述必须清楚无误(clear or unequivocal)与不含糊(unambiguous):见 Low v. Bouverie (1891) 3 Ch 82;Lowe v. Lombank (1960) 1 WLR 196 CA;Woodhouse AC Israel Cocoa Ltd. SA v. Nigerian Produce Marketing Co. Ltd. (1972) 1 Lloyd's Rep. 439 (HL);Moorgate Mercantile Co. Ltd. v. Twitchings (1977) AC 890;The "Shackleford" (1978) 2 Lloyd's Rep. 154;Channel Island Ferries Ltd. v. Sealink UK Ltd. (1987) 1 Lloyd's Rep. 559 等先例。由于这个要求已经在本书第四章第6段有所介绍,这里不再重复,只简单介绍两个关于陈述性禁反言的早期与近期的先例。

首先是在上诉庭的 Low v. Bouverie 先例中,Bowen 大法官说:"an estoppel, that is to say, the language upon which the estoppel is founded, must be precise and unambiguous. That does not necessarily mean that the language must be such that it cannot possibly be open to different constructions, but that it must be such as will be reasonably understood in a particular sense by the person to whom it is addressed."Kay 在该先例也说:"where no fraud is alleged, it is essential to shew that the statement was of such a nature that it would have misled any reasonable man, and that the Plaintiff was in fact misled by it."

在较近期的 Thor Navigation Inc. v. Ingosstrakh Insurance Company Ltd. (2005) 1 Lloyd's Rep. 547 先例中,案情涉及船舶保险。原告的船东所拥有的一条名为 Thor Ⅱ的船舶由于发生严重事故,被拖去希腊的 Piraeus 港。经过对损坏的检查与根据修理厂的报价,修理的费用远远高于船舶的价值,因此船东向被告的保险公司宣布推定全损(constructive total loss)。船舶是受保的风险导致全损没有什么争议,问题反而是保险公司在全损的情况下应该赔多少钱。在该保单中,有条文说明“SUM INSURED of US $1.5m”,而当时该全损船舶的市场价值只有 80 万美元。换言之,双方的争议是保险公司该赔的是 80 万美元或是 150 万美元。这个问题就涉及保险合约针对保险金额可以分为定值保险(valued policy)与不定值保险(unvalued policy)两大类。在前者的情况下,如果发生全损就要赔偿定值保险金额(一般保单用“value at”或“so value”或“agreed value”等文字表示)。至于后者的情况,显然不会有一个同意的定值保险金额,但往往还会有一个金额作为对保险公司的保障,赔偿不会超出这个金额。而发生全损时,有必要马上调查究竟有关的保险标的在当时的实际价值是多少,并按照这个价值进行赔付。针对船舶保险,一般都涉及懂业务的保险人,他应该知道投保船舶的市场价格,这种资料也很容易在市场上获得,因此一般来说,船舶保险都是定值保险的形式。这也可以理解,如船东购买船舶时向银行融资 5000 万美元,但是之后船舶市场价值下跌到 1000 万美元,如果发生全损保险公司只赔偿 1000 万美元,船东根本不够偿还银行的贷款。而针对海上货物保险,定值保险就普遍不被接受,因为有不少货物保险人无法从其他渠道知道投保货物的实际价值。毕竟有不少货物不会有市场,或是即使有也很狭窄。如果投保人夸大货物的价值,对一船垃圾投保了很高金额的定值保险,最后发生全损,保险公司还是要赔偿同意的定值保险金额,而不能只赔偿货物实际价值,这就不能接受了。这样,海上货物保险中不定值保险被普遍使用,一旦发生全损,就要马上调查有关货物的实际价值。

虽然“sum insured”与“agreed value”或“insured value”在文字上对外行人来说没有区别,但保险行业的人士(特别是海上保险)就很清楚他们之间的区别,而且有不少权威说法与先例的说明。在这里只节录在较近期的 Kyzuna Investments Ltd. v. Ocean Marine Mutual Insurance Assoc (Europe) (2000) 1 Lloyd's Rep. 505 先例中,Thomas 大法官说:“The use of the term ‘sum insured’ will normally indicate the amount for which the subject matter is insured and not as specifying the agreed value.”在 Quorum AS v. Schramm (2002) 1 Lloyd's Rep. 249 先例中,Thomas 大法官也说:“well known distinction between an insured value and a sum insured.”

所以在保单的解释上,船东明显是败诉,无法获得 150 万美元的赔偿。但合约解释的败诉方在许多案例中都会提出禁反言的替代争议,本先例也不例外。船东指称双方在投保的谈判时,船东曾经用上了“agreed value”或“insured value”的文字,虽然保险人的回复经常用的还是“sum insured”一词。船东认为这些通讯往来整体解释是属于清楚无误的陈述并构成陈述性禁反言。

但这不被法院接受,Gloster 大法官说:“In order to establish their case based upon estoppel by representation, Owners have to show that Insurers made a clear and unequivocal representation of fact to the effect that the words ‘sum insured’ meant ‘insured’ or ‘agreed value’, notwithstanding that, as I have held, the words did not bear that construction. In my judgment it is impossible to find any such representation in the correspondence. I accept Mr Davies'(保险公司代表大律师) submission that the fact that Mr Myrianthopoulos(船东) may have failed to appreciate the meaning of the words 'SUM INSURED' (when used on their own) is irrelevant when set against their well recognised meaning in the market and the fact that nowhere else in the Policies (or any of the quotes) was any reference made to 'values'. **There was no clear and unequivocal representation made by Insurers as contended for by Owners. Although valued cover may have been requested, Insurers stated on each occasion that that was not the type of cover they were prepared to offer and that they were only prepared to offer cover on an unvalued basis.** Nor, in my judgment, can the fact that Insurers did not spell out to Owners the difference between the two types of terms be said to amount to the type of clear and unequivocal representation of fact required to support an estoppel. Accordingly I reject Owners' claim based on estoppel."(加黑部分是笔者的强调)

在更近期的 Kim v. Chasewood Park Residents Ltd. (2013) EWCA Civ 239 先例[56], Patten 大法官说:"There is no doubt that **in order to found a promissory estoppel (in the same way as any other estoppel based on a representation of fact) the representation** or promise must be clear and unambiguous. But this principle raises a number of subsidiary questions. Does it mean that the estoppel cannot arise unless there is only one possible meaning of the words used or is the existence of other possible (but perhaps less probable) meanings not fatal to the creation of an estoppel where the Court can say that it was reasonable for the representee to have interpreted the words used in the way he did? There is also an issue about the test to be adopted by the Court. Few, if any, statements are not capable of being interpreted in more than one way. The Court's usual role in construing, for example, a contract is to arrive at the legally correct meaning of the words. Their construction is a matter of law and the Court's function is to resolve any ambiguities in reaching its conclusion. But it is arguable that in the case of estoppel it should not go any further than to identify the existence of any real ambiguities in the language. **If the statement is open to more than one reasonable interpretation (one of which is fatal to the estoppel defence) then the representee was not entitled to rely on what was said without further clarification and there is no basis for an estoppel.**"(加黑部分是笔者的强调)

沉默与不行动也可以算是一种陈述,只是通常不属于清楚无误与不含糊,不会构成陈述性禁反言。但如果一方在法律上有责任说清楚(duty to speak)却保持沉默,就可能构成陈述性禁反言或"沉默性禁反言"(estoppel by acquiescence)。由于有责任说清楚/沉默性禁反言的课题内容太多,将会在本章第 10 段单独介绍。

---

〔56〕 在本书第四章之 11.9 段有介绍。

7. 要件之二：陈述方在做出陈述时知道或希望被陈述方依赖

首先可节录《The Law of Contract》(第4版,2010年)一书之2.112段,如下:"It has been said that the misrepresentation must be 'wilful': Pickard v. Sears (1837) 6 Ad & El 469, but that this requires no more than that the representor should intend his representation to be acted upon, and this requirement will be satisfied if a reasonable person would believe the representation and would act on it, so that in this context, as elsewhere, 'intention' is assessed on an objective basis."即做出对事实的错误陈述的人,必须是从客观来看,希望或知道对方会依赖此陈述并做出相应的行为。

但陈述方无须是不诚实[57]或明知该陈述是虚假的,[58]正如Macnaghton勋爵在Jorden v. Money (1854) 5 HLC 185先例中说:"... I think it is not necessary that the party making the representation should know that it was false, no fraud need have been intended at the time. But if the party has unwittingly misled another you must add that he has misled another under such circumstances that he had reasonable ground for supposing that the person whom he was misleading was to act upon what he was saying."

陈述方的错误陈述也不需要是疏忽所导致:Moorgate Mercantile Co. Ltd. v. Twitchings (1977) AC 890先例。

换言之,在陈述性禁反言,陈述方不能以他完全不知道真正的事实,完全无辜地做出错误陈述作为抗辩:Low v. Bouverie (1891) 3 Ch 82 CA先例。

上述所讲可以举简单的例子,就是将在本章之12.1段介绍的提单上的错误陈述。无论是倒签提单、货物的数量或是表面状况记载错误等,船东常常以他是完全无辜,事实上提单是承租人(或分承租人)的代理人瞒着船东/船长签发作为抗辩,但这在英国法律下不管用,保护不了船东。

但被陈述方需要证明陈述方在做出陈述时的思想状态是希望或知道该陈述会被依赖。这个要件最开始是为了限制一些随意或无意或不正式的错误陈述被第三人依赖,构成陈述性禁反言:Trane (UK) Ltd. v. Provident Mutual Life Assurance (1995) EGLR 33(Cooke大法官在第39页所说)。如A有内幕消息知道有某个股票会上涨,并想通过电邮通知B,但错发给了C。但实际上这是个错误消息,依赖了该消息的C蒙受了损害。A不会因此被陈述性禁反言。

---

〔57〕见Roberts & Co. Ltd. v. Leicestershire County Council (1961) Ch 555等先例。

〔58〕见Jorden v. Money (1854) 5 HLC 185; Greenwood v. Martins Bank Ltd. (1933) AC 51; Farrow v. Orttewell (1933) Ch 480 CA; Spiro v. Lintern (1973) 1 WLR 1002 CA等先例。

在 Ing Re（UK）Ltd. v. R & v. Versicherung AG（2006）EWHC 1544（Comm）先例中,案情涉及份额风险分保条约(quota – share reinsurance treaty)。原告(一家英国保险公司)通过声称是被告(一家德国分保公司)委任的代理人的 Risks 公司与被告订立份额风险分保条约,在原告将保费汇到 Risks 公司的账户(这是伦敦保险业务的一般做法)中后不久,被告告知原告 Risks 已经被终止了承保的授权,并且不承认与原告之间的份额风险分保条约。原告指被告受到该条约的约束,并声称 Risks 作为代理人即使没有实际授权,也有表见授权。原告依赖的其中一份证据是被告的一位雇员曾经传真给 Risks 说让他订立这个份额风险分保条约,并接受相关的生意。原告也收到了这份传真,但同意是被告错发(misdirected/mis – sent)给他的。双方的争议之一是原告能否依赖这份传真,认为 Risks 有被告的表见授权。法院认为不可以,因为原告明知这份传真不是发给他的,即它不可能认为这是被告对他做出的陈述。Toulson 大法官说:"Since the doctrine of ostensible authority is founded on estoppel, I do not see in principle how a successful plea can be based on a document which the recipient believes that the supposed representor did not want the recipient to see. It is like listening to an eavesdropped conversation. The eavesdropper would not be entitled to treat what he heard, unintended by the speaker, as though it were a representation made to him by the speaker."

但在实践中,这个要件并不是十分重要与有争议。很多情况下,如果被陈述方确实依赖了该陈述,陈述方就会被假设有希望对方依赖的意图。如提单上的陈述,如果被银行或第三人的买方作为提单持有人依赖,船东根本无法争辩说他做出错误陈述时(签发提单时)不能合理知道会被一个不知名的第三人依赖。毕竟提单作为物权凭证(document of title)会通过转让与交出给第三人的情况是最基本与最普遍的国际商贸做法。这在本章之 12.1 段会有解释,只先节录 Scruton 大法官在 Brandit v. Liverpool Brazil & River Plate Steam Navigation Co. Ltd.（1924）1 KB 575 先例中所说:"The result was that the shipowner put into circulation a document which they knew might be passed on to other persons for value, and on the statements in which other persons might act, which contained the untrue and material statement that the goods had been shipped 'in apparent good order and condition'."

另是表见授权(apparent/ostensible authority),在本章之 12.2.4.4 段提到通常委托人做出的陈述是给予代理人一个职位,这是十分广泛的陈述,陈述方(公司法人)往往没有考虑到将来谁可能是依赖的第三人,更谈不上是希望某个特别的第三人依赖。

但在少数的案件中,会对这一要件有争议。如在 Re Exchange Securities & Commodities Ltd.（1988）Ch 46 先例中,案情就有一定的困难。该先例涉及两家公司分别在国际上的商品买卖与股票市场进行投机活动,而公司的资金来自公众的投资人。在起初 18 个月,该公司向投资者做出的报告是赚大钱,但实际上这些利润根本是虚假与不存在的。到了1984年,公司清盘,被告投资人显然拿不到投资的本金以及根本不存在的利润,并变成没有担保的一般债权人。这样,被告与被法院根据英国《公司法》委任的清盘人有了争议,导致清盘人向法院申请宣告判决。这一争议涉及破产的公司曾经通过虚报利润的账目与有关信件,向投资人做出了错误的事实陈述。这错误陈述显然被被告依赖,没有及时取回他的本金以及利润。事实上在该先例中,法院的宣告没有针对陈述性禁反言是否成立,而是针对破产公司的错误陈述造成的禁反言不能用来对抗清盘人,毕竟清盘人代表的是所有债权人的利益。这一判决也与本章第11段介绍的禁反言与立法之间的关系有关,稍后会进一步介绍。

这样的判法也带来陈述性禁反言并不是需要针对的重点,但法院也有谈到,特别是这一案件的案情在这个要件方面有一点困难。这就是破产公司向投资人做出的信件中,除了虚报了极高的利润外,也建议投资人将本金取回,只剩下利润继续投资,这就肯定保本。但显然大部分的投资人,包括被告都贪得无厌,看到这么高的利润就希望本金与利润可以一起像滚雪球一样越变越大。但这样,从一个角度看就是破产公司白纸黑字写明不希望被告投资人(至少在本金方面)依赖他信件中对利润的错误陈述。从另一个角度看,就是被告代表大律师的争辩,破产的公司是在说反话,明知道投资人在这么高的利润下不会将本金撤走。

Harman大法官说是这一方面是有点困难,但由于他已经做出了禁反言不能用来对抗清盘人的决定,所以不必再针对这一点,说:

"...(这个要件)... was also satisfied, because, on looking at the statements of account sent by the company to investors, it was inevitable that the court should conclude that the statement was made with intent and must have resulted in inducing the investor, who was the party raising the estoppel, to alter his position on the faith of that representation. The alteration of position that was suggested was that the investor in every case on seeing this handsome progression of profit ineluctably would be induced to leave his money with the company and thereby, since he had a right to recover it, and at earlier stages almost certainly could have recovered it, would have suffered a detriment if the company were now allowed to go back upon that representation.

The assertion that the company must have intended the investor to rely upon the representation was asserted as being a natural intent which the court inevitably would infer. I was shown, in fact, in Mr. Bainbridge's(被告投资人)case by way of example, a letter of, I think, February 1983 from the company to Mr. Bainbridge saying that his profits had now reached 100 per cent. of his original investment and that, as mentioned in the original literature inviting the investor to invest, **he would be well advised to withdraw his original investment of £ 4,000 leaving the alleged £ 4,000 of profit to support future dealings**, thus, in effect, allowing him to play entirely on the profits made and in no sense at risk for himself. Mr. Bainbridge's letter in answer to that was also shown to me and said that he had decided to leave the whole sum with the company upon the ground that he was very satisfied with the progress of his account.

I find it difficult in the absence of any actual evidence or any cross – examination to decide whether the company, which was urging investors in its original material and in its actual follow – up letters to withdraw their moneys, could be taken to have been so urging them with intent that they should do the opposite and not withdraw their moneys. It may be, as Mr. Stewart（被告代表大律师）suggested, that this was a cunning piece of marketing and a representation designed to produce the opposite effect which it was ostensibly intended to produce. I do not find it at all easy to decide whether that be right or wrong, but I do not think that that is a matter which need detain me further. It merely... is one which does raise some questions in the mind of a judge considering it."（加黑部分是笔者的强调）

8. 要件之三：被陈述方有合理理由相信该陈述真实，并因此改变地位与蒙受损害

关于依赖改变地位并蒙受损害这一要件，已经在本书第四章第7段有过介绍，这里不再重复。在陈述性禁反言中，虽然被陈述方没有需要自己调查有关对事实的陈述是否正确的一般责任，[59]但被陈述方不能盲目依赖陈述方的陈诉，必须有合理理由相信该陈述是真实的。虽然承诺性禁反言也有这个要件，但显然针对将来的承诺，因为还没有发生，相比过去或目前存在的事实，更容易被认为是可以被合理依赖。但对过去或目前存在的事实，因为已经发生，所以被陈述方可以根据从其他渠道获得的信息或常识做出自己的判断，因此依赖的合理性会更有争议性。

8.1 被陈述方的依赖必须合理

被陈述方必须证明他的依赖合理，即该对事实的错误陈述是可以误导合理人士，[60]被陈述方有合理理由相信该陈述是真实的，[61]并且因为依赖该陈述而改变的

〔59〕 见 Gresham Life Assurance Society v. Crowther（1914）2 Ch 219；Trane（UK）Ltd. v. Provident Mutual Life Assurance（1995）EGLR 33 等先例。

〔60〕 见 Low v. Bouverie（1891）3 Ch 82；Canada and Dominion Sugar Co. Ltd. v. Canadian National（West Indies）Steam Ships Ltd.（1946）80 Lloyd's Rep. 13（PC）等先例。

〔61〕 见 Canada and Dominion Sugar Co. Ltd. v. Canadian National（West Indies）Steam Ships Ltd.（1946）80 Lloyd's Rep. 13（PC）；Maclaine v. Gatty（1921）1 AC 376 HL；Hunter v. Senate Support Services Ltd.（2004）EWHC 1085 等先例。

地位是合理的。[62] 是否合理取决于相关的情况，Cooke 大法官在 Trane（UK）Ltd. v. Provident Mutual Life Assurance（1995）EGLR 33 先例举例说，如果一个跨国公司的小职员说公司有从月亮上取下的新鲜芝士（stocks of green cheese extracted from the moon），被陈述方就需要确认有关陈述的真实性或是小职员是否有授权。另如果有提单上写着船上装载着 1 万吨钻石，这明显不可能是事实，被陈述方（也就是提单持有人）的依赖可能是不合理。判断依赖是否合理时要考虑的重要因素之一是陈述涉及的主题是否属于陈述方（representor）的专业或有相关经验的领域，或是否是被陈述方（representee）在做出依赖的决定前通常会先进行确认的领域。

依赖必须合理与本章多处提到的被陈述方对可疑的陈述应进行调查是同样的道理，这可见本章之 12. 1. 1 段与本章之 12. 2. 4. 3 段。另也可见本章第 9 段介绍的 George Whitechurch Ltd. v. Cavanagh（1902）AC 117 先例与 National Westminster Bank Ltd. v. Barclays Bank International Ltd.（1974）2 Lloyd's Rep. 506 先例。另在 Sidney Bolsom Investment Trust Ltd. v. E. Karmios & Co.（London）Ltd.（1956）1 QB 529 CA 先例与 Trane（UK）Ltd. v. Provident Mutual Life Assurance 先例中，法院都认为需要判断被陈述方的依赖是否合理。

但在近期的 Downderry Construction Ltd. v. Secretary of State for Transport, Local Government and the Regions（2002）EWHC 2（Admin）先例中，法院判是被陈述方的依赖无须合理。在该先例中，在土地所有人（也是发展商）的要求下，政府在信中做出了土地规划状况的确认。但政府认为这封信有明显错误，因此被告作为很有经验的土地发展商，依赖这封信中的错误陈述不合理。但 Richards 大法官没有支持这个争辩，说："Apart from the absence of authority to support the proposition, it would in my view be surprising if, when a representor had made a false representation intending or knowing that it was likely to be acted upon and the representee, believing the representation, had in fact acted on it to his detriment, the representor could then defeat an estoppel on the basis that the representee's reliance on it was not reasonable."

显然 Richards 大法官没有考虑 Sidney Bolsom Investment Trust Ltd. v. E. Karmios & Co.（London）Ltd. 先例与 Trane（UK）Ltd. v. Provident Mutual Life Assurance 先例中，这通常是代表大律师的问题，没有将有关的先例挑出来争辩，并让法院一并考虑再做出判决。法官（或仲裁员）不是法律字典，双方没有提及的先例通常不会知道。即使个别法官（或仲裁员）知道也不愿意提，以免造成对一方当事人的偏袒。虽然根据该先例的案情，这个决定看来是正确，但是在法律上 Richards 大法官认为依赖不需要合理的说法是错误与不合逻辑的。按照 Richards 大法官的说法，即使是诚实但完全不理性地依赖了陈述方的陈述，也会构成禁反言。一般来说，如果有否定性宣

---

〔62〕 见 Freeman v. Cooke（1848）ER 622；Seton, Laing v. Lefone（1887）19 QBD 68 CA；Trane（UK）Ltd. v. Provident Mutual Life Assurance（1995）EGLR 33 等先例。

告(disclaimer),依赖该陈述会被认为不合理,但如果Richards大法官的说法正确,陈述方就再也不能通过否定性宣告来避免构成陈述性禁反言。这显然不能被接受,更不用说陈述性禁反言本质上是衡平法救济,将被陈述方完全不理性的依赖造成的损害转移到陈述方身上,这是不公平。

但在Downderry Construction Ltd. v. Secretary of State for Transport, Local Government and the Regions先例中,也提到了做出错误陈述的陈述方需要合理预见这陈述会被对方依赖(本章第7段介绍的第二个要件),在这种情况下,也很难争辩说被陈述方的依赖是不合理。

8.2　被陈述方因为依赖该错误陈述而改变地位

被陈述方如果想依赖陈述性禁反言,要证明相关的陈述与他改变地位有因果关系。在Sean Wilken QC与Karim Ghaly先生所著的《The Law of Waiver, Variation, and Estoppel》(第3版,2012年)一书之9.84段有简单介绍在以前的先例中,对因果关系是说错误陈述要被陈述方改变地位的真正原因或近因(proximate cause)[63]或是被陈述方改变地位是错误陈述直接导致。但该书的说法是这些早期的先例涉及的所谓的"疏忽性禁反言"(estoppel by negligence)说法。这种陈述方对被陈述方有小心谨慎的责任的案件被视为更适用侵权方面的法律,而不是禁反言。而近期的重要权威说法是Neuberger大法官在Steria Ltd. v. Hutchison (2006) EWCA Civ 1551先例所说,比合约与侵权方面对因果关系要求的"要不是"(but for)考验宽松。以下节录9.48段有关部分如下:"There must have been a causative link between the representee's belief that the representation was true and the acts which would give rise to detriment. This link has been described and analysed in various different ways. It has been averred that the representation must have been the real or proximate cause of the relevant conduct[64] or that the conduct must have resulted from the representation.[65] However the cases where such an approach has been adopted have tended to involve the so - called estoppel by negligence principle, to which different rule may apply. The better view is that it is unnecessary to show that the relevant actions were solely by the representation. As Neuberger LJ pointed out in Steria Ltd. v. Ronald Hutchison 'it is probably not necessary for a claimant to satisfy what is known in a some what different area of the law as the "but for" test... He merely has to show that the representation was a significant factor which he took into account'. It is sufficient if the representation influenced the representee's decision so as to act in the way that it did. It is necessary to establish that

---

〔63〕可参见杨良宜《损失赔偿与救济》一书第四章。

〔64〕见Seton, Laing v. Lefone (1887) 19 QBD 68 CA先例。

〔65〕见Greenwood v. Martins Bank Ltd. (1933) AC 51先例。

the representation encouraged or induced[66] the representee to act it the way it did. The fact that it was material to the decision so to act is probably insufficient.[67] The causative link may exist where a belief already held is strengthened or the representee is lulled into a false sense of security.[68]"

一般来说,错误陈述与改变地位的时间隔得越远,他们之间的关系链(causative link)就越遥远,需要更多与更明确的证明。但即使陈述之后马上改变地位,在 Lowe v. Lombank (1960) 1 WLR 196 CA 先例也被认为只靠这一点并不足够。而在一些明显的案件(如提单的转让),可以假设错误陈述与之后的行为与依赖有因果关系,从而不需要进一步的证据证明:Newbon v. City Mutual Life Insurance Society Ltd. (1935) 52 CLR 723 先例。

最后一提的是,通常被陈述方有举证的责任:Nippon Menkwa Kabushiki Kaisha v. Dawsons Bank Ltd. (1935) 51 Lloyd's Rep. 147 (PC); Lowe v. Lombank; Trane (UK) Ltd. v. Provident Mutual Life Assurance (1995) EGLR 33 等先例。

8.3 被陈述方因为依赖该错误陈述而蒙受损害

所有类别的禁反言(除了合约性禁反言)都要求被陈述方必须证明因为依赖该错误陈述而蒙受损害,这在陈述性禁反言也不例外。权威说法之一可见在 Tai Hing Cotton Mill Ltd. v. Liu Chong Hing Bank Ltd. (1986) AC 80 先例中,枢密院说:"the essence of estoppels is a representation (express or implied) intended to induce the person to whom it is made to adopt a course of conduct which results in detriment or loss."

正如本章已经多次提到的,构成陈述性禁反言与衡平法宽限或承诺性禁反言的要件有很多重叠,正如 Neuberger 大法官在 Steria Ltd. v. Hutchison (2006) EWCA Civ 1551 先例中说:"... When it comes to estoppels by representation or promissory estoppel, it seems to me very unlikely that a claimant would be able to satisfy the test of unconscionability unless he could also satisfy the three classic requirements... The claimant being able to show that he will suffer detriment if the defendant is not held to the representation or promise..."

在本书第四章之 7.4 段介绍了 5 类有关承诺性禁反言的不同类别的损害,本章接下来的段节也会节录 Sean Wilken QC 与 Karim Ghaly 先生所著的《The Law of Waiver, Variation, and Estoppel》(第 3 版,2012 年)一书第九章提到的关于陈述性禁反言的五类大同小异的损害与相关的先例。

---

[66] 见 Freeman v. Cooke (1848) ER 652; Re Bankruptcy Notice (1924) 2 Ch 76 CA; Farrow v. Orttewell (1933) Ch 480 CA; Hopgood v. Brown (1955) 1 WLR 213; Lowe v. Lombank (1960) 1 WLR 196 CA; Re Exchange Securities & Commodities Ltd. (1988) Ch 46 等先例。

[67] 见 Credit Suisse v. Allerdale BC (1995) 1 Lloyd's Rep. 315 先例(第 369 页)。

[68] 见 Dixon v. Kennaway & Co. (1900) 1 Ch 833 先例中,与涉及衡平法宽限的 Lark v. Outhwaite (1991) 2 Lloyd's Rep. 132 先例。

8.3.1 损害类别之一:被陈述方因为依赖相关陈述,放弃或失去有经济价值的东西

在《The Law of Waiver, Variation, and Estoppel》(第3版,2012年)一书之9.94段说:"**The representee forgoes something of value.** The detriment in this category results from the loss of money, labour or other assets of financial value.[69] Examples include advancing money by way of loan in reliance on the representation that the loan was supported by a valid unlimited personal guarantee by the managing director;[70] failing to withdraw funds from an investment scheme in reliance on the representation that large profits had been made and were being held by the scheme managers for the benefit of the representee;[71] giving up the tenancy of a farm, selling off neighbouring properties and entering the tenancy of new premises in reliance on the representation that a valid notice to quit had been served;[72] paying for extensive damp – proofing works to be carried out on a property in reliance on the representation that the representee had the benefit of a valid contract to purchase the premises;[73] purchase of goods in reliance on the representation by a warehouse owner that it was holding them for the seller;[74] building sea front houses in reliance on the representation that a neighbor was legally disabled from building so as to obstruct the view from them;[75] paying the purchase price for shares in reliance on the representation that the purported vendor was the owner of the shares;[76] failing to apply for social security payments in reliance on the representation that the representee was legally entitled to a specified level of pay from his employer;[77] failing to put oneself in a position to obtain a spouses' pension, by marrying, in reliance on a representation that unmarried partners were entitled to such a pension.[78]"

8.3.2 损害类别之二:被陈述方因为依赖相关陈述,没有采取行动保障其法律地位

在《The Law of Waiver, Variation, and Estoppel》(第3版,2012年)一书之9.96段说:

---

〔69〕 这一类损失是指被陈述方失去了金钱、工人或其他有经济价值的资产。

〔70〕 见 TCB Ltd. v. Gray (1986) Ch 621 先例。

〔71〕 见 Re Exchange Securities & Commodities Ltd. (1988) Ch 46 先例。

〔72〕 见 Farrow v. Orttewell (1933) Ch 480 CA 先例。

〔73〕 见 Spiro v. Lintern (1973) 1 WLR 1002 CA 先例。

〔74〕 见 Seton, Laing v. Lefone (1887) 19 QBD 68 CA 先例。

〔75〕 见 Piggot v. Stratton (1859) 45 ER 271 先例。

〔76〕 见 Re Bahia and San Francisco Railway Co. Ltd. (1867 – 68) LR 3 QB 584 先例与 In re Ottos Kopje Diamond Mines Ltd. (1893) 1 Ch 1892 CA 先例。

〔77〕 见 Avon County Council v. Howlett (1983) 1 WLR 605 CA 先例。

〔78〕 见 Catchpole v. Trustees of the Alitalia Airlines Pension Scheme (2010) EWHC 1809 (Ch)先例。

"**The representee fails to safeguard its legal position.** The detriment in this category results from positive acts (or more usually omissions) on the part of the representee which would make it vulnerable to legal proceedings in the event that the truth of the representation is denied.[79] For example, in Ismail v. Polish Ocean Lines (1976) 1 Lloyd's Rep. 489 CA, shippers stowed a cargo defectively in reliance on the representation by the cargo owner's agent that the method used was adequate. Had the cargo owner been permitted to deny the truth of his representation, he would have been able to claim damages for defective stowage against the shipowners (sic). In De Tchihatchef v. Salerni Coupling Ltd. (1932) 1 Ch 330, a company stated in a share prospectus that it had the benefit of a contract on lucrative terms, in reliance on the representation that the contract included the specified terms. Denial of the representation would have rendered the company vulnerable to legal proceedings by those who subscribed to the issue in reliance on the contents of the prospectus.

Further examples include contracting to sell shares to a third party in reliance on the representation that the representee was the owner of the shares. The denial of the representation leaves the representee vendor to an action for breach of contract by the person to whom it purported to sell the shares.[80] Failing to apply to the Family Court to have a maintenance agreement varied in reliance on the representation that maintenance was only payable for a limited period will suffice,[81] as will failing to serve notice to exercise a break clause within the time specified in the lease.[82]"

8.3.3 损害类别之三:被陈述方依赖陈述方的陈述,改变预算或使费

这一类损害与本书第四章之7.4.2段的损害十分接近。在《The Law of Waiver, Variation, and Estoppel》(第3版,2012年)一书,针对陈述性禁反言的这一类损害,作者主要引用了涉及在弄错事实下付钱的复原(restitution)请求[83]的先例。而有关的损害就是收钱的一方因为多了一笔钱而改变了预算或生活方式,但之后需要把这笔已经部分或全部花掉的钱还给给错钱的一方。这个损害并非将来的损害,因此即使很难证明(尤其是改变生活方式),也需要口头或书面证据支持。关于改变地位的抗辩中的损害,将在稍后分段介绍。

在该书之9.98段,说:

"**9.98 The representee alters its budget or expenditure.** The detriment in this

---

〔79〕 这一类损失是指被陈述方依赖相关的错误陈述而行动(不行动),导致如果相关陈述的正确性被否定,会让被陈述方在诉讼中处于不利地位。

〔80〕 见 Dixon v. Kennaway & Co. (1900) 1 Ch 833 先例。

〔81〕 见 Covell v. Sweetland (1968) 1 WLR 1466 先例。

〔82〕 见 Trane (UK) Ltd. v. Provident Mutual Life Assurance (1995) EGLR 33 先例。

〔83〕 见本章第4段。

category is relevant where the representor has led the representee to believe that the latter is legally entitled to some benefit received. The most usual example is where A makes a payment to B and represents that B is legally entitled to that payment and is thus free to spend the money as it wishes. B therefore needs to establish that it would suffer detriment if the representation is withdrawn, namely where A denies B's entitlement and asks for the return of the money. To establish detrimental reliance, the following three requirements must be satisfied.

First, B has spent money. There is no need to establish that the money spent was that actually received from the representor, nor is there any need to show that the money spent was the traceable proceeds of the money so received. **Second**, B has spent money in reliance on the representation. Put simply, the representee must have spent the money in a way it would not have done but for the representation. If the money has been spent on ordinary day – to – day expenses which the representee would have been obliged to meet anyway, the requirement of reliance has not been satisfied. The representee has done nothing which it would not have done in any event. **Third**, B has spent the money in a way which cannot be recouped. It is necessary to show that the money has been spent in a way which leaves the representee with no retained value. Examples might include spending the money on a holiday, paying it to charity or, in the case of a company, issuing a special one – off dividend to shareholders. If the money has been used to purchase a saleable asset which is retained by B, no detriment will result from its being asked to refund the money. B can sell the asset and return the money.

In Avon CC v. Howlett (1983) 1 WLR 605 CA, the defendant was overpaid by his former employer, who represented that the payments had been correctly made. The defendant and his wife altered their budget accordingly. It was found as a fact that they increased their spending in accordance with their perceived income. The money was thus spent on a number of small improvements to their daily life. Some goods bought with the money were retained but they were of minimal value. Although the defendant had received a benefit from the increased spending, to have required him to refund the overpayments would have been to impose an onerous and unexpected liability, which he would have been unable to meet."(加黑与下划线部分是笔者的强调,并会在稍后分段介绍。)

在本章第 4 段已经提到,在近期贵族院的 Lipkin Gorman v. Karpnale Ltd. (1991) 2 AC 548 先例中,面对给错钱的复原请求,改变地位的抗辩(实质的抗辩)取代了陈述性禁反言的抗辩(程序上的抗辩,会导致"all or nothing"的结果)。但即使是改变地位的抗辩,被告也必须证明改变地位是合理与蒙受的损害。

8.3.3.1　因果关系

在上述节录的《The Law of Waiver, Variation, and Estoppel》(第 3 版,2012 年)

一书之9.98段，首先就要满足因果关系。在给错钱的复原请求，被告首先必须证明他改变地位与原告给错钱有因果关系，即如果不是(but for)原告给错钱，他是不会改变地位的。但在 Corporate Management Services (Aust) Pty Ltd. v. Abi – Arraj (2000) NSWSC 361 先例中，澳大利亚法院判是："... it is not essential that the money expended... [was] identical with the money... received from the [claimant]."

在《Chitty on Contracts》(第32版，2015年)一书之29–189段，说："**Link between receipt and specific expenditure unnecessary**. The broad defence as formulated by the House of Lords does not appear to require a link between specific expenditure and specific receipts.[84] This means that deserving cases in which it would be difficult to show a specific link are not necessarily excluded. For instance, where a sick employee is erroneously paid his full salary instead of the reduced sick pay to which it is entitled and, as a consequence, the employee simply fails to adjust his outgoings in the light of his new income, or where it is difficult to characterize the expenditure as unusual, such as buying 'a better cut of meat, maybe, from time to time, or something extra from the grocer', or where a person with a complicated pattern of expenditure cannot attribute any particular items to the payment, provided that payee can satisfy the court that expenditure has increased in line with income, it may be possiuble to establish the defence[85]... The broad test of change of position may also be able to deal with situations where the payee's loss is not due to his reliance on the payment but to some other factor, such as where the money mistakenly paid has been stolen from him or where its loss is the result of a natural event, such as fire... It is submitted that the defence should be available.[86]"

8.3.3.2 额外开支的损害

在 Lipkin Gorman v. Karpnale Ltd. (1991) 2 AC 548 先例中，Goff 勋爵说："The mere fact that the defendant has spent the money, in whole or in part, does not of itself

---

[84] 见 Philip Collins Ltd. v. Davis (2000) 3 All ER 808 先例。

[85] 见 Home Office v. Ayres (1992) I. C. R. 175; Westdeutsche Landesbank Girozentrale v. Islington LBC (1996) AC 669; Philip Collins Ltd. v. Davis (2000) 3 All ER 808 等先例。

[86] 有许多先例的附带意见(*obiter dictums*)都提到这一点。在 Derby v. Scottish Equitable Plc. (2001) Pens. L. R. 163 先例中，Robert Walker 大法官说被告不需要证明他是因为原告给错了钱有意识地做出改变地位的决定，而只需要证明他确实改变了地位，而如果不是收到了这笔钱，这不会发生。Mance 大法官在 Cressman v. Coys of Kensington (Sales) Ltd. (2004) EWCA Civ 47 先例假设这是正确。在 Rose v. AIB Group (UK) Plc. (2003) EWHC 1737 (Ch)先例中，Nicholas Warren QC 大法官说："... the wide statement of the general principle of the change of position defence by Lord Goff includes a change brought about by the act of another (e. g. theft by a thief of the money paid)."其他普通法国家也有类似的先例中，在新西兰的 National Bank of New Zealand Ltd. v. Waitaki Internationmal Processing (NI) Ltd. (1999) 2 NZLR 211 先例中，被告将这笔钱交给了一家理财公司，之后理财公司破产，上诉庭最后支持了被告改变地位的抗辩。

render it inequitable that he should be called upon to repay, because the expenditure might in any event have been incurred by him in the ordinary course of things."

在 Dextra Bank & Trust Co. Ltd. v. Bank of Jamaica (2001) UKPC 50 先例中，Goff 勋爵再次提到被告要依赖改变地位的抗辩必须证明有额外开支(extraordinary expenditure)。如在澳大利亚的 Corporate Management Services (Aust) Pty Ltd. v. Abi – Arraj (2000) NSWSC 361 先例中，James 大法官对维修房产的费用(正常开支)与装修提升房产价值的费用(额外开支)进行了区分。在加拿大的 RBC Dominion Securities Inc. v. Dawson (1994) 111 DLR (4th) 230 先例中，纽芬兰上诉庭判是被告支付了如果不是这笔错给的钱是承担不起的花费去招待朋友，属于改变地位。在 Social Services Appeal Board (Nfld) v. Butler (1996) 139 Nfld & PEIR 282 先例中，Berry 大法官判是生活在贫穷线的被告在收到错给的这笔钱后生活水平提高属于改变地位(changed her position to enjoy a more relaxed and enriched standard of living during the period when she was receiving the overpayments by mistake)。

因为收到错给的钱偿还了债务一般不被视为损害，毕竟他的资产并没有任何减少。Robert Walker 大法官在 Derby v. Scottish Equitable Plc. (2001) Pens. L. R. 163 先例中说："in general it is not a detriment to pay off a debt which will have to be paid off sooner or later."这也被近期的 Credit Suisse (Monaco) SA v. Attar (2004) EWHC 374 (Comm)先例跟从。但在 Derby v. Scottish Equitable Plc. 先例中，Robert Walker 大法官也提到如果是提前偿还了长期债务，可能属于蒙受了损害。

8.3.3.3 金钱被不可恢复地花掉的损害

在本章之 8.3.3 段节录的《The Law of Waiver, Variation, and Estoppel》(第 3 版，2012 年)一书之 9.98 段举了一些例子，如度假花掉、捐给慈善组织、公司向股东发放一次性分红。除此之外还有很多其他例子，例如：(1)投资公司失败：Holt v. Markham (1923) 1 KB 504 先例；(2)不可恢复地支付了第三方：Deutsche Bank v. Beriro & Co. (1895) 1 Com. Cas. 123 先例等。

但如果这笔钱被用来购买资产，法院一般不愿意支持改变地位的抗辩，至少是针对被告因为拥有资产而获益的部分，因为被告可以将资产出售再获得花掉的这笔钱。

在 Lipkin Gorman v. Karpnale Ltd. (1991) 2 AC 548 先例中，Templeman 勋爵 认为用给错的钱买了一辆汽车的被告所蒙受的损害只是汽车从购买到诉讼期间的贬值。在 Credit Suisse (Monaco) SA v. Attar (2004) EWHC 374 (Comm)先例中，被告购买了公司股票，之后股票上涨，被告在原告开始诉讼前将股票出售，Gross 大法官判是被告不能依赖改变地位的抗辩。

但上述两个例子，汽车和股票都有市场，因此出售比较容易，如果有贬值确定金额也比较容易。但也有一些资产是无法出售或是不存在市场价值，因此在不同案件的不同案情下会有不同的判决，不能一概而论。

8.3.3.4 失去获利机会的损害

在National Westminster Bank Plc. v. Somer International (UK) Ltd. (2001) EWCA Civ 970先例中,上诉庭的Potter大法官说:"the defence of 'change of position' only protects the actual reduction of the transferee's assets...(and) a transferee who, in reliance upon a receipt, foregoes a realistic and quantifiable opportunity to increase his assets is not apparently protected."

但这个说法没有被之后的先例跟从,因此关于失去机会的损害是否能够构成改变地位的抗辩还没有确切答案。在Derby v. Scottish Equitable Plc. (2001) Pens. L. R. 163先例中,Robert Walker大法官认为如果被告因为这笔钱,在很难再找一份工作的年纪主动辞职,可能会构成改变地位。另在Commerzbank AG v. Price - Jones (2003) EWCA Civ 1664先例中,Mummery大法官对被告拒绝了一份报酬更高的工作也是一样的说法。

其他普通法国家也有类似的先例。如在澳大利亚,在Gertsch v. Atsas (1999) NSWSC 898先例中,被告没有找工作而用错给的钱去读大学,法院判是被告允许在归还给错的钱时,扣除她失去的工资部分。另在Palmer v. Blue Circle Southern Cement Ltd. (1999) NSWSC 697先例中,被告没有申请社会保险津贴被认为是属于改变地位。

这方面的法律地位不肯定是因为法院不愿意对假设的情况臆猜,尤其是这个假设的情况经常取决于不会出庭作证的第三方的行动。这可能是由于近期关于机会损失(loss of chance)的争议(在损失计算方面)[87]越来越多,法院传统抗拒臆猜的心态发生了改变。但无论如何,被告要证明因为获得这笔钱失去了获利的机会都可能有一定困难。

8.3.3.5 压力、焦虑、不便与其他非金钱方面的不幸的损害

在Derby v. Scottish Equitable Plc. (2001) Pens. L. R. 163先例中,Robert Walker大法官说:"The fact that the recipient may have suffered some misfortune ...; such as a breakdown in his health... is not a defence unless the misfortune is causally linked (with his enrichment)."

但在Commerzbank AG v. Price - Jones (2003) EWCA Civ 1664先例中,Munby大法官举了一些可能需要确定间接带来金钱损害的例子。例如,被告因为这笔钱决定结婚、离婚、开始家庭生活,这些决定都会有经济上的影响。但可以想得到,确定具体的金额可能十分困难。

8.3.4 损害类别之四:被陈述方因为依赖相关陈述,蒙受机会损失

有不少先例涉及被陈述方因为依赖相关的陈述,没有向第三人提起诉讼。从某种角度来说,这可以属于第一类与第二类损害的一种。但由于机会损失(loss of

---

〔87〕 参见杨良宜《损失赔偿与救济》一书第六章。

chance)在计算损失时是单独的类别,因此在禁反言将其视为单独的类别分开介绍,也是恰当。如在 ING Bank NV v. Ros Roca SA (2011) EWCA Civ 353 先例,[88]上诉庭同意失去重新谈判的机可能是足够的损害。Rix 大法官说:"That is demonstrated by ING's unwillingness to broach with Ros Roca the subject matter of its much larger fee, because of the danger of 'potential disruption' to the transaction. There would, in my judgment, undoubtedly have been a demand to renegotiate the contract; and I equally have no doubt that to a greater or lesser extent such a renegotiation would have borne fruit. In my judgment, Ros Roca relied on the implied representation and suffered detriment as a result."

《The Law of Waiver, Variation, and Estoppel》(第 3 版,2012 年)一书中提到早期的 Knights v. Wiffen (1869 – 70) L. R. 5 Q. B. 660 先例判错,因为在该先例贵族院不愿意臆猜究竟被陈述方是否值得提起诉讼,如果不值得,就没有真正的损害。但在近期的先例中,法院看来比较愿意做出这样的臆猜,如在本书第四章之 7.4.1 段介绍的 Collier v. P & MJ Wright (Holdings) Ltd. (2008) 1 WLR 643 先例。在该先例中,Collier 先生争议说他因为答辩人的承诺没有向另外两位合伙人追讨他们应付部分的金额,但这不被一审法院的 HHJ Hodge QC 大法官接受。因为其他两位合伙人已经破产,而答辩人作为判决债务(judgment debt)的债权人也没能从这两位合伙人处追回一分钱,所以 Collier 先生更不可能从另外两位合伙人处追讨到任何他们应付的部分。即对 Collier 先生来说,如果答辩人从未有这样的承诺他会面对的情况,与答辩人现在撤回承诺向他追讨全部欠款的情况相同,因此判 Collier 先生没有蒙受任何损害。

这可能是由于近期关于机会损失的争议(在损失计算方面)越来越多,法院传统抗拒臆猜的心态发生了改变。最后可节录《The Law of Waiver, Variation, and Estoppel》(第 3 版,2012 年)一书之 9.102 段,如下:

"**9.102 Loss of a chance: hypothetical loss.** . . . . The Court is required to compare what actually happened with what would have happened had the representation never been made. To establish detriment, the representee must show that it was worse off under the former situation than under the latter. This has sometimes given rise to difficulties, particularly where the representee's acts in reliance consist of foregoing some opportunity, such as a omitting to prosecute a cause of action. [89] In theory, it should be necessary to show that the opportunity foregone had some intrinsic value, that is,

---

[88] 案情在本章之 13.2 段有介绍。

[89] 法院要将真正发生的情况与如果没有相关错误陈述会发生的情况进行对比。被陈述方要证明有损害,就必须证明前者的情况比后者差。这不容易证明,尤其是在被陈述方依赖相关错误陈述放弃了一些机会(如没有对第三人开始诉讼)的情况。

that there was a chance of a successful outcome for the representee. If, for example, there was no chance that the representee would have obtained an enforceable judgment had it prosecuted the cause of action, it is difficult to aver that it suffered any detriment as a result of refraining from so doing. However, the Courts have sometimes seemed reluctant to investigate whether there was any chance of a successful outcome for the representee. [90]

For example, in Knights v. Wiffen, X sold some of the goods which he held in his warehouse to Y who sold them on to Z. X told Z that he had appropriated goods to the contract (which would have had the effect of passing title to the goods to Z). Y later became bankrupt. X had not in fact appropriated goods to Z's contract but was stopped from denying that he had. If Z had not received the assurance from X, he would have terminated the contract and asked for his moneyback, although 'very likely he might not have derived much benefit if he had done so. Their Lordships held that this conduct gave rise to detriment despite their doubts as to Z's chances of successful retrieving his money from Y.

Some doubt as to the correctness of the decision was expressed in Simm v. Anglo American Telegraph (1879) 5 QBD 188 CA, where the alleged detriment consisted of failing to pursue a third party who had executed a forged transfer of shares to the representee. The Court of Appeal emphasized that it was necessary to show not just that the representee had refrained from pursuing the wrong – doer but that it had been prejudiced by so doing. No such prejudice existed in Simms because the stock exchange rules gave the representee a watertight claim against the dealer through whom the forger had sold the shares.

There are four possible views on this issue. First, the rationale behind Knights rests simply on the Courts' reluctance to engage in speculation as to the outcome of hypothetical proceedings. Once the representor has allowed the opportunity to be lost to the representee, uncertainty should be resolved in the latter's favour and detriment is assumed. The result of Simms may be reconciled with such an approach because there was no such uncertainty in that case. The Court of Appeal was not required to assess what would have happened had the original claim been prosecuted, since it was clear that there was an al-

---

〔90〕 理论上讲,被陈述方必须证明被放弃的机会有真正价值,即被陈述方有机会成功。例如,如果被陈述方即使提起诉讼也不可能获得对他有利的可执行判决,则就很难说被陈述方有实质损害。但有时法院不愿意臆猜被陈述方是否真的有机会成功。

ternative and cogent remedy against a third party.[91] Second, the representee might be said to have suffered prejudice because it lost forever the opportunity to take a reasoned decision on the transaction, in the light of all the circumstances, unfettered by the misapprehension caused by the representation. The loss of a chance, in itself, might amount to detriment, regardless of the prospects of success.[92] Third, in Dixon v. Kennaway & Co. (1900) 1 Ch 833, Farwell J analysed the problem in terms of the onus of proof. The burden fell on the representee to prove that it had refrained from prosecuting its claim. Once it had done this, the onus shifted to the representor to prove that no prejudice or detriment resulted from the delay, ie that the wrongdoer had never been worth suing in the first place.[93] Fourth, Knights is wrongly decided.[94] On balance, the first view appears to be the most convincing explanation of the case law.[95]"

8.3.5　损害类别之五:被陈述方因为依赖相关陈述,订立了分租约

在《The Law of Waiver, Variation, and Estoppel》(第3版,2012年)一书之9.106段说:"9.106 **Granting or entering a sub – lease.** As a matter of basic analysis, there appear to be three circumstances where the grant of or entry into a sub – lease could amount to detriment. First, detriment would occur if the benefit gained from the arrangement was affected by the withdrawal of the representation. Take, for example, the case where a sub – lease is entered into in reliance on the representation that a neighbor had no power to build so as to obstruct the view from the sub – let property. If the representation is denied, detriment occurs in that the view expected is lost. The asset purchased is less valuable as a result of withdrawal of the representation.[96] Second, detriment would be

---

[91] 针对这个问题可以有四种看法。第一,Knights v. Wiffen (1869 – 70) L. R. 5 Q. B. 660 先例的判决原因是法院不愿意臆猜假设的诉讼结果。一旦陈述方的陈述导致被陈述方放弃机会,就应该将结果的不肯定性归利于后者,假设被陈述方有蒙受损害。而 Simm v. Anglo American Telegraph (1879) 5 QBD 188 CA 先例的判法也可以和这个看法做出协调,因为在该先例中没有不肯定性,因此,上诉庭不需要臆猜如果没有相关的陈述,被陈述方提起诉讼的结果。

[92] 第二,被陈述方可以说他蒙受损害,因为他永远失去了在不被错误陈述影响下,根据所有情况获得合理判决的机会。这本身就属于损害,而无须理可能是否有成功的前景。

[93] 第三,在 Dixon v. Kennaway & Co. (1900) 1 Ch 833 先例中,Farwell 大法官分析了举证责任的问题。被陈述方有责任证明他放弃了诉讼。一旦他证明了这一点,就变为陈述方有举证责任证明从他做出错误陈述到更正陈述期间的延误没有对被陈述方造成任何损害,因为被陈述方一开始就不值得对第三人开始诉讼。

[94] 第四,Knights v. Wiffen (1869 – 70) L. R. 5 Q. B. 660 先例是错判。

[95] 总的来说,第一种观点最有说服力。

[96] 这一类损害看来有三种情况。第一,如果错误的陈述被更正,分租约的好处会被影响。如类似 Piggot v. Stratton (1859) 45 ER 271 先例的情况,分租客依赖了邻居不可以建造影响其视野的房子的陈述,订立了海景房的分租合约。如果这个陈述可以被更正,则可以想到分租客的视野会被影响,海景房的价值也会因此下降,这显然有损害。

suffered if the sub – leasor and sub – leasee were restricted as to the terms on which they could transfer their interests.〔97〕Third, if denial of the representation means that the sub – lessor cannot give good title to the sub – leasee, the detriment suffered is clear. The lessor will be liable to the sub – leasee for breach of contract should the representation be denied.〔98〕Absent one of these factors, it is hard to see why the granting or entering of the sub – lease should necessarily give rise to detriment. If the representee was left with a valuable disposable asset, arguably no detriment is suffered: the representee has got what it paid for ... ”

9. 要件之四:允许陈述方推翻之前的陈述是不公平与不合情理的

这一要件与衡平法宽限或承诺性禁反言类似,这里不再重复。可以说,这是不同类别的禁反言作为衡平法救济的共同要求。〔99〕因此,如果陈述是在非法胁迫(duress)下做出,无论被陈述方或第三人的胁迫,都不会构成禁反言:见 Debs v. Sibec Developments Ltd.(1990)RTR 91 先例中 Simon Brown 大法官的说法。

Brampton 勋爵在 George Whitechurch Ltd. v. Cavanagh(1902)AC 117 先例中也说:“No representation can be relied on as estoppels if they have been induced by the concealment of any material fact on the part of those who seek to use them as such; and if the person to whom they are made knows something which, if revealed, would have been calculated to influence the other to hesitate or seek for further information before speaking positively, and that something has been withheld, the representation ought not be treated as an estoppels.”

在 National Westminster Bank Ltd. v. Barclays Bank International Ltd.(1974)2 Lloyd’s Rep. 506 先例中,Ismail 先生想将一笔钱从尼日利亚汇出来,但因为当时的外汇管制做不到。于是 Ismail 先生向第三人买了一张 8000 英镑的支票,从而可以在伦敦提现。事实上这张支票是第三人从原告 National Westminster Bank 的客户那里偷来的,上面的签名也是伪造的。Ismail 先生不知道支票是偷来的,但也对真实性有一定的怀疑。之后 Ismail 先生向被告 Barclays Bank 要求将支票兑现,再接下来是

---

〔97〕第二,因为房东的错误陈述,二房东与分租客之间的租约条文受到了限制。

〔98〕第三,如果允许陈述被更正,会导致二房东无法合法转移产权给分租客。二房东显然蒙受了损害,因为这样他就违反了分租约,要承担责任。

〔99〕只有“合约性禁反言”(contractual estoppel)没有不公平或不合情理的要求,也有说法是合约性禁反言并不属于真正意义上的禁反言。

Barclays Bank 向原告要求兑现支票。但原告没有发现签名是伪造的,将支票兑现。之后原告才发现签名是伪造的,向 Barclays Bank 和 Ismail 先生追回这笔钱。Barclays Bank 和 Ismail 先生作为共同被告的抗辩主要是原告疏忽没有发现签名是伪造的并将支票兑现,这构成了陈述性禁反言,不能之后再来否认支票签名的真实性。但 Kerr 大法官认为在没有专家帮助下,银行没有发现签名是伪造的不属于疏忽。而 Ismail 先生明知道情况很可疑(reeked of suspicion)但没有调查或提醒原告,不能依赖禁反言。

再举一个例子,如果一家公司 A 向 X 签发股票证书(share certificate),这就表示公司向全世界做出陈述,X 是股份所有人。之后如果 X 依赖这个股票证书认为自己是股份所有人而做出行动并蒙受损害,就可能构成陈述性禁反言。[100] 但根据 George Whitechurch Ltd. v. Cavanagh 先例的判决,如果在之前购买股份的交易时情况十分可疑,X 就有责任调查有关的情况并将信息告诉 A 公司。如果 X 没有这样做,就不会构成禁反言。这其实与本章之 8.1 段介绍的依赖必须合理是有关联,如果被陈述方依赖一个看来明显可疑的陈述是不合理。

更多关于有责任进行调查会在本章之 12.1.1 段与本章之 12.2.4.3 段介绍。

10. 有责任说清楚/沉默性禁反言

这一课题已经在本书第四章之 6.4 段有简单与原则性的介绍,但由于有责任说清楚(duty to speak)或"沉默性禁反言"(estoppel by acquiescence)与陈述性禁反言(以及产权人禁反言)的关系更密切,因此在本章进行进一步的详细分析。

在 Spencer Bower 的《Estoppel by Representation》(第 4 版,2004 年)一书第 46 - 47 页说:"It is well established that under certain conditions silence or inaction may constitute a representation, as much as positive language or conduct, for the purpose of an estoppel.[101] Silence or inaction will count as a representation if a legal (not a mere moral or social) duty shall have been owed by the representor to the representee to make a disclosure, or take steps, the omission of which is relied upon as creating the

[100] 在本章之 13.3 段有详细介绍。

[101] 在特定的情况下沉默或不行动与主动的言行一样,都属于可以构成陈述性禁反言的陈述:Freeman v. Cooke (1848) ER 622; Russell v. Thornton (1859) 4 H&N 788; Polak v. Everett (1876) 1 QBD 669; Greenwood v. Martins Bank Ltd. (1933) AC 51 等先例。在 Greenwood v. Martins Bank Ltd 先例中,Tomlin 勋爵说:"Mere silence cannot amount to representation but when there is a duty to disclose, deliberate silence may become significant and amount to a representation."

estoppel.[102] The theory is this. The parties to a transaction are entitled to assume, as against one another omnia rite esse acta[103]; each of them is entitled to suppose that the other has fully discharged all such obligations (if any) of disclosure or action towards himself as may have been created by the circumstances. If, therefore, he receives from that other no intimation, by language or conduct, of the existence of any fact which, if existing, it would have been the latter's duty, having regarded to the relationship between them, the nature of the transaction or the circumstance of the case, to reveal, he has legitimate ground for believing that no such fact exists, or that there is nothing so abnormal or peculiar in the nature of the transaction, or in the circumstances of the case as to give rise to any duty of disclosure, and to shape his course of action on that assumption.[104] In other words, he is entitled to treat the representor's silence or inaction as an implied representation of the non – existence of anything which would impose, or give rise to, such a duty, and if he alters his position to his detriment on the faith of that representation, the representor is estopped from afterwards setting up the existence of such suppressed or undisclosed fact.[105]"

在 Amalgamated v. Texas Bank (1982) 1 Lloyd's Rep. 27 先例的一审,Goff 大法官就以 Spiro v. Lintern (1973) 1 WLR 1002 先例[106]为例,指出沉默性禁反言与陈述性禁反言存在重叠说:"It is true that that case may be treated as a case of estoppel by acquiescence; but the Court of Appeal held that on the facts of the case the husband's failure to disclose to the purchaser that his wife had acted without his authority amounted to a representation by conduct that she had that authority."

---

[102] 如果一方在法律(而不止是在道德或人际交往)上有责任向另一方披露或采取行动,但他保持沉默或不行动就可能构成沉默性禁反言:Swan v. North British Australasian Co. (1863) 2 H & C 175; McKenzie v. British Linen Co. (1881) 6 App Cas 82; Mercantile Bank of India Ltd. v. Central Bank of India Ltd. (1938) AC 287; Tai Hing Cotton Mill Ltd. v. Liu Chong Hing Bank Ltd. (1986) AC 80; The "Tatra" (1990) 2 Lloyd's Rep. 51 等先例。

[103] 英文是 all things have been done correctly or in due form,即双方都有权假设另一方会正规行事,履行了披露对方应该合理知道的信息或有所行动的责任(如果有这种责任)。简单的例子是如果正规行事,则一方不会对另一方隐瞒(concealment),包括故意做出隐瞒的言行,或是单纯沉默或不行动。同样道理,一方如果正规行事,也不会存在不当影响(undue influence)或欺诈(fraud)与不诚实(dishonesty)这种刑事或准刑事(quasi criminal)的情况。

[104] 因此,如果根据双方的关系、交易的性质、相关的情况,A 有责任向 B 披露存在一些需要 B 知道,也是 B 肯定希望知道的事实。而如果 B 没有收到任何言行的暗示,则他就有权假设这个交易不存在任何不寻常或不常见的情况,并且根据这个假设行事。

[105] 换句话说,B 有权将 A 的沉默或不行动当做默示的陈述,即不存在任何令 A 有责任说清楚的不寻常或不常见的情况存在。如果 B 因为依赖这个无言的陈述(passive representation)而改变地位并蒙受损害,则 A 就会被禁反言,不能事后再提出这些没有披露的事实的存在。

[106] 案情将在本章之 10.1.2 段介绍。

换句话说,如果丈夫知道他的妻子没有他的授权,并且知道第三方即买方是依赖妻子有授权的错误行事,丈夫就有责任向买方说清楚。否则即使丈夫没有做出任何言行,也会被认作做出了妻子有授权的陈述。之后,如果买方向丈夫提起诉讼,丈夫被禁止以妻子没有他的授权因此他没有责任作为抗辩。

显然这种情况(包括但不限于商业关系与合约)很多,以下会分段介绍一些构成沉默性禁反言的一般情况。

10.1 有责任说清楚/沉默性禁反言的一般情况

10.1.1 一般情况之一:产权人知道另一方对所有权有错误理解

简单而言,有责任说清楚的情况存在在产权人/业主身上,否则会构成"沉默性禁反言"(equity by acquiescence)。在 Sir J. W. Ramsden, Bart v. Lee Dyson and Joseph Thornton (1866) LR 1 HL 129 先例中,Wensleydale 勋爵说:

"If a stranger begins to build on my land supposing it to be his own, and I, perceiving his mistake, abstain from setting him right, and leave him to persevere in his error, a Court of equity will not allow me afterwards to assert my title to the land on which he had expended money on the supposition that the land was his own.[107] It considers that, when I saw the mistake into which he had fallen, it was my duty to be active and to state my adverse title; and that it would be dishonest in me to remain wilfully passive on such an occasion, in order afterwards to profit by the mistake which I might have prevented.[108]

But it will be observed that to raise such an equity two things are required, first, that the person expending the money supposes himself to be building on his own land; and, secondly, that the real owner at the time of the expenditure knows that the land belongs to him and not to the person expending the money in the belief that he is the owner.[109] For if a stranger builds on my land knowing it to be mine, there is no principle of equity which would prevent my claiming the land with the benefit of all the expenditure made on it. There would be nothing in my conduct, active or passive, making it inequi-

---

[107] 如果一个陌生人(如邻居)误以为我的土地是他的,并在上面建造房屋或耕种,而我察觉他的错误但没有提醒他,任由他坚持自己的错误观点,则衡平法院不会允许我之后主张我对这块被陌生人误以为是自己的并在上面花了钱的土地的法律权利。

[108] 当我发现他的错误时,我有责任主动说清楚我对土地的权利;在这种情况下,如果我为了之后通过这个我本可以避免的错误获利而故意保持沉默,属于不诚实的行为。

[109] 但要衡平法介入必须满足两个要求,首先花钱的陌生人错误认为那是他自己的土地,其次在当时真正的土地所有人知道这块土地是属于他而不是花钱的人士。

table in me to assert my legal rights.〔110〕

It follows as a corollary from these rules, or, perhaps, it would be more accurate to say it forms part of them, that if my tenant builds on land which he holds under me, he does not thereby, in the absence of special circumstances, acquire any right to prevent me from taking possession of the land and buildings when the tenancy has determined.〔111〕 He knew the extent of his interest, and it was his folly to expend money upon a title which he knew would or might soon come to an end.〔112〕 The Appellant(原土地所有人 Sir John 的遗产继承人)contends that it is within this principle that Thornton(租客)is brought. He acquired, it is said, possession of the land in question as a mere tenant at will, or from year to year, to Sir John(原土地所有人), and if on that infirm title he thought fit to expend a large sum in building, there is no principle of equity which prevents Sir John, or his devisees, from asserting their legal rights by determining the tenancy, and so obtaining the benefit of his expenditure."

上述说法其实就是将在本书第七章介绍的"产权人禁反言"(proprietary estoppel)。所以不在此详论,只说这类的禁反言可能与有责任说清楚有最密切关系。

在有关产权人禁反言的 Moorgate Mercantile Co. Ltd. v. Twitchings (1977) AC 890 先例中,Wilberforce 勋爵针对有责任说清楚做出了附带意见(dictum),并被之后的许多著名先例引用,说:"... having regard to the situation in which the relevant transaction occurred, as known to both parties, a reasonable man, in the position of the 'acquirer' of the property, would expect the 'owner' **acting honestly and responsibly**, if he claimed any title in the property, to take steps to make that claim known to, and discoverable by, the 'acquirer' and whether, in the face of an omission to do so, the 'acquirer' could reasonably assume that no such title was claimed."(加黑部分是笔者的强调)

产权人禁反言主要涉及土地,但也会适用在其他英国法律认为属于不动产(real property)的财产所有权(title),因此与中国的公司/企业也会有一定的关系。例如:(1)保险合约或人寿保险下的利益:Strover v. Strover (2005) EWHC 860 (Ch)等先例;(2)以信托方式持股:Re Vandervelle dec'd (No. 2) (1974) 1 Ch 269; Murphy v. Rayner (2011) EWHC 1 等先例;(3)家具与其他个人资产:Re Basham dec'd (1986)

---

〔110〕 而如果在我土地上建造房屋的陌生人明知这块土地是属于我的,衡平法不会阻止我主张这块土地的所有权以及取得因为对方花钱而带来的好处。我的行为,无论是主动还是被动,都不会令我主张法律权利显得不公平。

〔111〕 因此,如果租客在我的土地上建造房屋(或涉及租房,租客在租约将届满前去大装修,自以为房东会续约),除非是特殊情况,他没有任何权利阻止我在租约结束后占有土地与房屋。

〔112〕 他知道他的权利范围,他明知对这块土地的占有权利可能很快会结束,但仍在上面花钱,属于自己做了蠢事。

1 WLR 1498; Yeoman's Row Management Ltd. v. Cobbe (2008) UKHL 55 等先例;(4)音乐作品的知识产权:Godfrey v. John Lees (1995) EMLR 307; Film Investors Overseas SA v. The Home Video Channel, The Times, 2 December 1996; Beckingham v. Hodgens (2003) EWCA Civ 143; Fisher v. Brooker (2008) FSR 26 等先例。在 Fisher v. Brooker 先例中,Mummery 大法官说:"This case is prima facie within the familiar territory of proprietary estoppel,(原告的) title to property in the form of a joint interest in the copyright in the Work."(5)整个商业企业:Wayling v. Jones (1993) 69 P & CR 170 CA(酒店生意); Thorner v. Major (2009) UKHL 18(农场生意的关联资产)等先例。

10.1.2　一般情况之二:委托人有责任说明代理人授权的局限

交易中如果明示或默示有授权或表见授权的代理人的授权有局限,或后来变为有局限(即收回了部分或全部的授权),委托人都有责任向另一方说明。如果委托人没有这样做,就等于做出了代理人有(或继续保有)他表面看起来有的授权而没有局限的陈述:Eastern Distributors Ltd. v. Goldring (1957) 2 QB 600 先例。

在 Spiro v. Lintern (1973) 1 WLR 1002 先例中,丈夫准备卖掉他名下的房产,虽然让他的妻子通过房产中介寻找卖方,他并没有授权妻子将房产卖掉。之后妻子与 Spiro 先生订立了书面买卖合约。丈夫知道后没有向 Spiro 先生提出妻子这样做没有他的授权,也没有表示不愿意继续房屋买卖程序。丈夫同意了 Spiro 先生聘请的建筑师对房屋进行维修,园艺师对花园进行修剪。之后丈夫在去印度之前,写了授权书授权妻子完成房产交易并签了一份给 Spiro 先生的房产转让书(transfer of house)。但之后妻子凭着该授权书,将房产转给了第三人。Spiro 先生向法院申请"履约指令"(specific performance)。双方的争议之一是丈夫是否因为他没有向 Spiro 先生讲清楚而被禁反言,即不能在 Spiro 先生因为依赖他的沉默或不行动而造成损害后,争辩妻子与 Spiro 先生订立买卖合约时没有授权。Buckley 大法官说:

"Where a man is under a duty — that is, a legal duty — to disclose some fact to another and he does not do so, the other is entitled to assume the non-existence of the fact. In such circumstances the conduct of the first man amounts to a representation by conduct to the second that the fact does not exist. In Bell v. Marsh [1903] 1 Ch. 528, 541, Sir Richard Henn Collins M. R. put the point in this way: 'He [the plaintiff] is entitled to say that the representation was made, not merely by language used, but by conduct, and conduct may include negligence. A man may act so negligently that he must be deemed to have made a representation, which in fact he did not make, but because he has acted negligently he is deemed to have made it.'

If A, having some right or title adverse to B, sees B in ignorance of that right or title acting in a manner inconsistent with it, which would be to B's disadvantage if the right or title were asserted against him thereafter, A is under a duty to B to disclose the existence of his right or title. If he stands by and allows B to continue in his course of action, A will not, if the other conditions of estoppel are satisfied, be allowed to assert his right or title against B... On similar grounds, in our judgment, if A sees B acting in the mistaken belief that A is under some binding obligation to him and in a manner consistent only with the existence of such an obligation, which would be to B's disadvantage if A were thereafter to deny the obligation, A is under a duty to B to disclose the non-existence of the supposed obligation."

10.1.3 一般情况之三:陈述方有责任通知原本的陈述已经改变

如果一方做出了正确的陈述(或有合理理由认为是正确的陈述,如信息是来自可靠来源),并希望另一方或任何人依赖该陈述行事,应该假设直到另一方依赖该陈述行事时,该陈述仍是正确,除非在此之前陈述方已经撤回或改变了陈述。所以,如果情况在半途发生改变,显示原来的陈述并不正确或不再正确,并且陈述方知道这个改变,显然他有责任通知被陈述方改变的性质与细节。这与"误述"(misrepresentation)的法律有关,[113]但也有可能会构成禁反言。如在合约履行过程中,一方从可靠来源获得信息并向另一方做出了陈述,[114]甚至特别小心说明了是不保证(without guarantee)。但几天后,他被可靠来源告知原本的陈述有错误,并做出更正。这样,虽然他本来只是做出了无辜的错误陈述,并说明了是不保证,应该不需要承担责任。但当他知道该陈述是错误的之后,他就有责任将更正后的信息告诉另一方。否则当另一方依赖错误陈述并蒙受损害向他索赔时,他就会被陈述性禁反言,不能以他是无辜误述与说明是不保证进行抗辩。

合伙人退休、共同担保人死亡、被担保的公司重组、代理人的授权范围是最常见的持续性陈述需要做出改变的情况:Goode & Bennion v. Harrison (1821) 5 B & Ald 147; Ashby v. Day (1886) 54 L.T. 408 CA; Willis Faber & Co. v. Joyce (1911) 104 L.T. 576; Leo Bridge District Gas Co. v. Malvern (1917) 1 KB 803 等先例。

10.1.4 一般情况之四:银行的客户有责任通知银行

原则上银行客户在两种情况下对银行有责任。第一种情况是不能签发可能会帮助欺诈或伪造行为的支票(refrain from drawing a cheque in such a manner as may facilitate fraud or forgery):London Joint Stock Bank Ltd. v. MacMillan (1918) AC 777; Welch v. Bank of England (1955) Ch 508 等先例。如是在签发支票时只写了数字而没有写文字,让第三人可以很容易改变支票的金额。这一责任不严格涉及有责任说清楚,但另一种情况就不一样。

这种情况就是在发现他的账户有支票被伪造的情况,要立即通知银行(a duty to

---

〔113〕 见本章之1.1段。

〔114〕 如国际货物买卖中,最早的卖方告知中间商一些有关货物的信息,中间商虽然没有合约责任,但好心转告了他的买方这些信息。

inform the bank of any forgery of a cheque purportedly drawn on the account as soon as he, the customer, becomes aware of it):Ogilvie v. West Australian Mortgage and Agency Corpn (1896) AC 257; Greenwood v. Martins Bank Ltd. (1933) AC 51; Fung Kai Sun v. Chan Fui Hing (1951) AC 489; Price Meats v. Barclays Bank Plc. (2000) 2 All ER (Comm) 346; Patel v. Standard Chartered Bank (2001) Lloyd's Rep. Bank 229 等先例。

在 Greenwood v. Martins Bank Ltd 先例中,案情涉及妻子一直假冒丈夫的支票签名,从丈夫的私人账户中取钱。丈夫发现了这一事实,但被妻子说服而没有通知银行。直到 8 个月后,丈夫终于决定通知银行,但他的妻子在通知银行之前自杀了。丈夫决定向银行追回妻子假冒签名取走的钱。贵族院最后判是丈夫在发现了妻子伪造他签名后有责任通知银行,让银行可以采取措施追回假支票付出的钱。Tomlin 勋爵说:"The appellant's(丈夫)silence, therefore, was deliberate and intended to produce the effect which it in fact produced – namely, the leaving of the respondents(银行)in ignorance of the true facts so that no action might be taken by them against the appellant's wife. The deliberate abstention from speaking in those circumstances seems to me to amount to a representation to the respondents that the forged cheques were in fact in order, and assuming that detriment to the respondents followed there were, it seems to me, present all the elements essential to estoppel."

10.1.5 其他情况

还有一些其他情况会令一方有责任说清楚,这在本章 10.3 段分别介绍的各个先例也可以看到。这里再举一个关于发生争议后的和解协议的例子。

BCCI v. Ali (2002) 1 AC 251 先例是有关合约解释的一个非常著名的先例中,具体的案情可看杨良宜《合约的解释:规则与应用》一书第一章之 8.4 段。这里只简单说涉及一个全面的和解协议,如果一方明知对方有其他方面的索赔在同意和解协议时没有考虑到,但为了自己的利益取巧保持沉默,法律就会介入做出救济。Nicholls 勋爵说:"... Materially different is the case where the party to whom the release was given knew that the other party had or might have a claim and knew also that the other party was ignorant of this. In some circumstances seeking and taking a general release in such a case, without disclosing the existence of the claim or possible claim, could be unacceptable sharp practice. When this is so, the law would be defective if it did not provide a remedy."

Hoffmann 勋爵虽然在该先例是少数意见,但关于这一点与其他法官的意见是一致,说:"A transaction in which one party agrees in general terms to release another from any claims upon him has special features. It is not difficult to imply an obligation upon the beneficiary of such a release to disclose the existence of claims of which he actually knows and which he also realises may not be known to the other party... On a principle of law like this, I think it is legitimate to go back to authority, to Lord Keeper Henley in Salkeld v. Vernon 1 Eden 64 , 69, where he said: ‘no rule is better established than that every deed obtained on suggestio falsi[115], or suppressio veri[116], is an imposition in a court of conscience.’ In principle, therefore, I agree... that a person cannot be allowed to rely upon a release in general terms if he knew that the other party had a claim and knew that the other party was not aware that he had a claim ...”

10.2 合约谈判或交易过程中

在商业合约订立前的谈判与交易过程中合约的履行,有责任说清楚的情况与中国公司/企业有最密切的关系。毕竟中国公司/企业在走出去的过程中,免不了要订立商业合约。所以,这种情况会在本段重点介绍。

首先是合约订立前的谈判过程,这就涉及本章之1.1段介绍的“误述”(misrepresentation)与“错误”(mistake)。而错误可分为双方共同错误(common mistake)与单方面错误(unilateral mistake)。共同错误与本章所针对的内容关系不大,因此不详细介绍。[117]

而单方面的错误,首先要明确,商业上做出错误决定没有任何救济。如在2008年“金融海啸”之前,中国有很多钢厂与西方公司订立长达10至20年的买卖合约(煤炭或矿砂),或海上运输合约。但在之后,商品与航运市场暴跌,中国公司作为买方或承租人根本无法履行下去,导致最终违约/毁约。这种错误根本没有任何救济可言。更常见的商业上的错误决定是本来以为肯定能赚钱的一宗业务,由于计算错误或计算不足而变为亏本,这也没有任何救济。

10.2.1 单方面错误之一:身份搞错

在法律上有救济的单方面错误主要有两类:一类是将对方的身份(identity)搞错,另一类是将合约条文搞错。绝大部分把对方身份搞错是来自对方的“欺诈性误述”(fraudulent misrepresentation),即对方冒名欺骗搞错的一方。如在Cundy v. Lindsay (1878) 3 App. Cas. 459先例中,涉及名为Blenkarn的骗子冒充一家著名公司Blenkiron & Co. 向原告订购一批货物。原告对这一Blenkiron & Co. 久闻大名,不以为意下把货物交给了骗子,以为交货给Blenkiron & Co. 大可以放心。骗子取得货物后转卖给被告(无辜第三人或善意买方)。显然骗子不会向原告支付货款并逃之夭夭,于是原告在知道真相后只能以“侵占”(conversion)作为诉因向无辜第三人要回这批货物。这是无辜的两方在斗,企图把损失转嫁给对方。

原告与被告之间的争议是原告与骗子所订立的买卖合约是否因为单方面的错误

---

[115] 英文是suggestion falsehood,即虚假的建议。

[116] 英文是suppression of the truth,即隐瞒真相。

[117] 有兴趣的读者可参见杨良宜《合约的解释:规则与应用》一书第三章之13.3段,杨良宜的《国际商务游戏规则——英国合约法》一书第八章与《Chitty on Contracts》(第32版,2015年)一书之第六章。

（对骗子的身份有单方面错误）而变为空与无效（null and void）。如果是，表示该批货物的所有权（title）没有从原告转移给骗子，因为没有过一份有效的合约。而骗子在没有所有权的情况下，当然也不能把该票货物的所有权再合法转移给被告。而被告作为善意与无辜的买方，反而变为侵占方，如果不马上把该票货物归还，就要承担在1977年《Torts（Interference with Goods）Act》立法下侵占的严格责任。但如果原告与骗子的合约并不是在订立时已经是空与无效，而只是因为欺诈性误述或后来骗子不付货款的违约可让原告令合约无效（voidable），[118]就表示只要骗子在合约被原告终止前把货物转卖了给被告，就是合法转移所有权，这批货物就属于善意的买方，即被告。最后法院判是原告与骗子的合约是空与无效。换言之，被告作为无辜与善意的买方可是冤枉，钱货两失。

搞错对方身份这种单方面错误与有责任说清楚/沉默性禁反言关系不大，因此在本章不再进一步介绍。[119]

10.2.2　单方面错误之二：合约内容或条文搞错

另一类单方面错误是一方对合约条文有错误理解，并且对方必须知道这个错误并知道正确答案。此外，这一错误也需要是严重与极端（serious and radical）或基本性（fundamental）。这些条件也可以理解，因为单方面错误理解（不论是法律方面如合约条文的解释，或是事实方面）实在发生得太多。如较早前谈到的订约一方从第三人处得来的消息有误甚至他理解错误，这与合约的另一方完全无关，另一方也不会知道，这就不可能让错误的一方从合约中脱身。再如在商业上经常发生向曾经与对方打过交道的朋友随口查问对方的商誉或财力，而朋友往往会说应该可以或没有不好的消息。这种随口查问很难得到准确、反映现况与全面的信息。但还是有很多人为了方便与省钱，在这样做之后就订立一个可能非常昂贵的长期合约。在订立的合约中，是没有针对对方的商誉或财力状况的条文，对方也不会知道他有错误理解（如对方自己知道财力不足，但另一方也没有向他查问或质疑，也就以为对方并不在乎）。所以这单方面的错误就不会有法律的救济。

针对可以获得救济的对合约条文的单方面错误，首先可节录《Chitty on Contracts》（第32版，2015年）一书之3-015段，说："**Known mistake may prevent party holding other to words used.**... normally a party is bound by what he said or wrote: he cannot escape by simply saying that he did not mean what the other reasonably understood, in the circumstances, by the words used. It may happen, however, that one party accepts a promise **knowing that the terms stated by the other differed from what the**

---

〔118〕这表示合约不是从一开始就空与无效，而是无辜的原告有选择权去令合约无效。毕竟有情况是虽然涉及欺诈性误述，但本质上不严重与当时市场高涨，原告（如买方）不选择令合约无效。

〔119〕有兴趣的读者可见杨良宜《合约的解释：规则与应用》一书第三章之13.3.7.1段与《Chitty on Contracts》（第32版，2015年）一书之第三章。

other party intended. In such circumstances, the mistake may prevent the party's acceptance being effective at face value: either the contract will be on the terms the other party actually intended or, possibly, **the 'mistake' will render the contract void**. This explains the cases on 'unilateral mistake as to the terms of the contract'."(加黑部分是笔者的强调)

另在《Chitty on Contracts》(第32版,2015年)一书之3-022段,说:"**Mistake known to the other party.** A mistake as to the terms of the contract, if known to the other party, **may affect the contract**. In this case, the normal rule of objective interpretation is displaced in favour of admitting evidence of subjective intention.[120]"(加黑部分是笔者的强调)

这种对合约条文的单方面错误不止发生在商业交易,在日常生活中也会发生。如海味店或药房的店员在某些海味或药材上只标明价格,但没有说明计量单位,而周围其他货品上写明是每斤的价格。顾客误以为该海味或药材的价格也是以斤计算。但当店员把海味或药材切片或磨粉后,则称标明的价格是一两甚至一钱的价格,同时以货品已切片或磨粉为由,拒绝取消交易。这就是典型的会涉及单方面错误的争议,并且法律会做出救济。这个例子中,店员知道真相,即该海味或药材的价格以两甚至钱计算,也知道顾客误以为以斤计算,甚至是在店员的诱导下才有了这个误解。在这种情况下,让店员对该海味或药材的价格以两甚至钱计算显然不公平与不合情理,店员也有责任向顾客说清楚。这与普通的买贵了东西不同,毕竟法律在这方面的大原则是让买方自己小心(*caveat emptor*, let the buyer beware)。如果某家海味店或药店只是东西特别贵,店员即使知道东西贵、顾客做了冤大头的真相,也不知道顾客有误解与错误是什么。因为可能有很多种解释,如附近的店缺货,只能来买贵的;这个店是大型连锁,虽然贵但顾客觉得更放心;或者顾客是大富豪,根本不在乎差价,只是店铺离酒店最近最方便,所以才在这家店买等。所以,无法证明店员在主观上知道顾客的错误。

上述两种不同事实的日常生活例子中,前者有法律上的救济而后者没有,在两种情况下店员知道真相(前者知道计量单位,后者知道自己的店铺价格很贵)没有区别,关键的区别就是在《Chitty on Contracts》(第32版,2015年)中所说的是否知道对方犯错但没有理会(turn a blind eye 或所谓的 Nelsonian knowledge[121]),并且知道错误是什么。另是前者是不公平(inequitable)与不合情理(unconscionable),但后者不

---

〔120〕 对合约条文的误解,如果另一方也知道对方有这样的误解,可能会影响合约的效力。即在这种情况下,可以允许法院或仲裁庭看一方主观意图的证据,找出一方是否错误理解与另一方是否知道,而不再是只能客观解释有关的合约。

〔121〕 Commission for the New Towns v. Cooper (Great Britain) Ltd. (1995) 2 All ER 929; Brown v. Westminster Bank Ltd. (1964) 2 Lloyd's Rep. 187 等先例。

存在不公平与不合情理的情况。关于这方面将在本章之10.2.3段进一步介绍。

10.2.3　法律的不同救济

对合约条文的单方面错误的救济可以是令合约空与无效(null and void)、或合约"变更"(rectification)与/或禁反言。而适用哪个救济更恰当,要根据不同的案情来看。

首先针对令合约空与无效的救济,这个救济的理论基础就是双方没有共同的订约意图。可在无数的有关先例中,节录Aikens大法官在The "Harriette N" (2008) 2 Lloyd's Rep. 685先例所说如下:"... **The general rule at common law is that if one party has made a mistake as to the terms of the contract and that mistake is known to the other party**, then the contract is not binding. The reasoning is that although the parties appear, objectively, to have agreed terms, it is **clear that they are not in agreement**. Therefore the normal rule of looking only at the objective agreement of the parties is displaced and the court admits evidence to show what each side subjectively intended to agree by way of terms. If it is clear from such evidence that there was not consensus, then **there can be no contract**, **because the parties have not truly agreed on the terms**. Some of the cases talk of such a contract being 'void', but I think it is clearer to say that there was never a contract at all."(加黑部分是笔者的强调)

合约变更的救济可节录《Chitty on Contracts》(第32版,2015年)一书之3-030段,说:"**Rectification cases.** The interpretation proposed in the previous paragraph is consistent with the cases granting rectification in cases of unilateral mistake. There it is said that if the party against whom rectification is sought knew that the documents did not represent the true intention of the party seeking relief, the documents will be rectified to show what the party seeking relief actually intended. This presupposes the existence of a valid contract despite the mistake, on the terms actually intended by the mistaken party and known by the other to be so intended."

而禁反言的救济可节录《Chitty on Contracts》(第32版,2015年)一书之3-031段,说:"**Estoppel.** To hold the party to the terms actually intended by the mistaken party is also consistent with cases on estoppel. There it has been said that if one party knows the other has made a mistake and fails to point it out when the reasonable person would expect him to do so were he acting honestly and reasonably, an estoppel by silence or acquiescence may arise and result in liability where there would otherwise be none."

针对如何适用不同的救济可以新加坡上诉庭的Chwee Kin Keong v. Digilandmall. com Pte Ltd. (2005) 1 SLR 502先例的案情为例。在该先例中,卖方在其网站上写错出售的激光打印机价格,从原来的3854新加坡币写为66新加坡币。原告的买方看到就趁机取巧,并马上接受这一要约。但被告发觉自己的错误后拒绝交付激光打印机。新加坡高院与上诉庭判有关的买卖合约由于单方面错误而空与无效。这显然正确,如果看双方提供的证据,卖方与买方都没有满足最基本的合约法要求,即对价格条文达成一致的订约意图(meeting of minds 或 *ad idem*)。

在该先例中,因为卖方拒绝交货,所以有关的救济是合约空与无效。但如果案情有所改变,买方只买了一台或有限的几台激光打印机,由于不是一手交钱一手交货,卖方在交货后才发现价格的错误,除了合约空与无效要求买方退还交付了的打印机之外,更可能是将合约价格从 66 新加坡币变更(rectify)为正确的 3854 新加坡币,或是禁止(estop)买方坚持合约规定的 66 新加坡币的价格而拒绝支付卖方要求收取的 3854 新加坡币。尤其是在买方已经开始使用或是将打印机转卖的情况下,法院就更可能认为合约空与无效的救济不适合,而变更与禁反言的救济可能更适合。但如果情况改变,有关的买卖不是一台或有限的几台打印机,而是买方看到有便宜可赚后太贪心,取巧订了一大批(该新加坡先例的案情),如 1000 台,变更的救济在这种情况下就不适合,因为买方根本不会有钱支付 1000 台单价 3854 新加坡币的打印机。这时,禁反言这种灵活的衡平法救济(equitable remedy)就最为合适。对于已经交付的激光打印机,可以禁止买方根据合约规定的价格是 66 新加坡币拒绝支付卖方要求收取的 3854 新加坡币。但对于还没有交付的激光打印机,卖方无须交货,买方也无须支付货价。

10.2.4 适用有责任说清楚的原则与要件

"合约变更"(rectification)的救济在杨良宜《合约的解释:规则与应用》一书第三章之 13.1 段已经有详细针对,这里不再重复。并且合约变更与禁反言的要件事实上有很大程度的重叠,有时也会混为一谈。但这里要指出,虽然不少先例中也提到了合约变更的救济,但也有说法是在很多情况下合约变更并不合适,陈述性禁反言或沉默性禁反言的救济更为常见,如本章上一小段提到的 1000 台激光打印机的例子。在 Commission for the New Towns v. Cooper (Great Britain) Ltd. (1995) 2 All ER 929 先例中,Stuart – Smith 大法官就合约变更是不合适的救济说:"The commonest circumstance in which rectification is granted is where the written contract does not accurately record the parties' joint agreement. In other words, there is a mistake common to both parties. In the case of unilateral mistake, that is to say where only one party is mistaken as to the meaning of the contract, rectification is not ordinarily appropriate. This follows from the ordinary rule that it is the objective intention of the parties which determines the construction of the contract and not the subjective intention of one of them. **Also, it would generally be inequitable to compel the other party to execute a contract, which he had no intention of making, simply to accord with the mistaken interpretation of the other party.**"(加黑部分是笔者的强调)

这里先节录一些权威说法介绍适用有责任说清楚的原则与要件,正如上一段提到的这些要件与适用合约变更的要件有很大程度的重叠。首先是 Oliver 大法官在 Taylor Fashions Ltd. v. Liverpool Victoria Trustees Co. Ltd. (1982) QB 133 先例的说法，说："... in a case of mere passivity, it is readily intelligible that there must be shown a duty to speak, protest or interfere which cannot normally arise in the absence of knowledge or at least a suspicion of the true position."

The "Nai Genova" (1984) 1 Lloyd's Rep. 353 (CA)〔122〕先例提到的权威书籍《Snell's Equity》(第25版，1960年)一书第569页有关单方面错误与有责任说清楚的部分，可节录如下："By what appears to be a species of equitable estoppel if one party to a transaction knows that the instrument contains a mistake in his favour but do nothing to correct it, he will be precluded from resisting rectification on the ground that the mistake is unilateral and not common."

在该先例中，Slade大法官也说："The general rule is that in the absence of a duty to speak, mere silence or inaction is not such conduct amounting to a representation which will give rise to an estoppel. The difficulty in any given case must lie in determining whether there are **special circumstances** such as **to give rise to a duty to speak**."(加黑部分是笔者的强调)

另也可记录Roberts & Co. Ltd. v. Leicestershire County Council (1961) Ch. 555先例所提到的产生说清楚的责任的四个要件："**first**, that one party A erroneously believed that the document sought to be rectified contained a particular term or provision, or possibly did not contain a particular term or provision which, mistakenly, it did contain; **secondly**, that the other party B was aware of the omission or the inclusion and that it was due to a mistake on the part of A; **thirdly**, that B has omitted to draw the mistake to the notice of A... **fourth**... that the mistake must be one calculated to benefit B. If these requirements are satisfied, the court may regard it as inequitable to allow B to resist rectification to give effect to A's intention on the ground that the mistake was not, at the time of execution of the document, a mutual mistake."

在Spencer Bower的《Estoppel by Representation》(第4版，2004年)一书第50页，说："Where the mistake is as to a term of a contract to be entered into between the parties. It has been held that it is necessary that the silent party actually know of the mistake rather than ought to know of the mistake. But actual knowledge includes Nelsonian knowledge, and mere silence must be distinguished from active concealment. Nothing... of substance is added to these criteria by requiring that the term be to the benefit of the silent party or detriment of the mistaken party or that reliance on the term 'be inequitable' or the silence unconscionable. **Whether the silence is unfair or unconscionable is the overall issue**..."(加黑部分是笔者的强调)

在澳大利亚的Taylor v. Johnson (1983) 151 CLR 422先例中，Mason大法官在

---

〔122〕 案情可见本章之10.3.3段。

参考了英国、美国与加拿大的先例后说："... a party who has entered into a written contract under a serious mistake about its contents in relation to **a fundamental term** will be entitled in equity to an order rescinding the contract if **the other party is aware** that circumstances exist which indicate that **the first party is entering the contract under some serious mistake or misapprehension** about either the content or subject matter of that term **and deliberately sets out to ensure that the first party does not become aware of the existence of his mistake or misapprehension.** What we have said is sufficient to demonstrate the broad basis of support which the authorities provide for that proposition. Moreover, and perhaps more importantly, it is a principle which is best calculated to do justice between the parties to a contract in the situation which it contemplates. In such a situation it is unfair that the mistaken party should be held to the written contract by the other party whose lack of precise knowledge of the first party's actual mistake proceeds from wilful ignorance because, **knowing or having reason to know that there is some mistake or misapprehension, he engages deliberately in a course of conduct which is designed to inhibit discovery of it.**"（加黑部分是笔者的强调）

总结而言，在双方进行商业或其他交易的案件，一般的原则是一方没有责任说清楚与指出对方的错误。要符合 The "Nai Genova"先例中 Slade 大法官说的特殊情况（special circumstances）或对一般原则的例外情况，必须满足以下条件：

1. 在双方的法律关系（如商业活动）中，对方对法律（主要是对合约条文的解释）或事实有重大的错误的理解。

2. 一方明知或有可信的怀疑对方有错误的理解，并知道正确的答案。这通常是一回事，毕竟只有知道正确的答案，才会知道对方错误。但只满足这两点并不足够，否则会产生无数禁反言的情况。已经提到过，在商业活动中没有善意的要求，唯一的要求是本章第 10 段一开始提到的双方都可以假设对方会正规行事，即在法官或仲裁员客观看来是诚实与负责任。如果只要满足这两个要求就有说清楚的责任，公司/企业根本没有必要了解市场行情或可以疏忽行事，毕竟如果自己错误理解，对方有责任进行提醒，否则就会构成禁反言。而产生了争议并需要诉讼，也无须找好的律师，反正如果有遗漏的或有误解，对方与对方律师有责任提醒，如清楚时效将近必须要尽快开始诉讼等，否则会构成禁反言。

3. 让一方事后指出对方的理解是错误的可能不公平（inequitable）与不合情理（unconscionable）。这是所有的禁反言的共同要求，而这个要求在有责任说清楚也是重要，毕竟已经提到知道对方犯错并知道正确答案的情况太多，必须以这个要求对有责任说清楚的情况做出区分。

4. 最后一点也是判断是否不合情理时需要考虑的，因为在有责任说清楚特别重要，这里单独列出来。这就是对方的错误理解与合约一方的沉默与不行动有一定关系，客观来看，一方的沉默与不行动被对方以为是对这个错误理解的认同或默许

（silence can be taken to have indicated an endorsement of a particular and erroneous assumption）。

10.2.4.1 要件之一：知道另一方有错误理解并知道正确答案

这也就是上一段提到的第一点和第二点，即一方有错误理解，另一方知道这个错误理解并知道正确答案。知道另一方有错误理解可以有不同的程度。Millet 大法官在 Agip（Africa）Ltd. v. Jackson（1990）Ch. 265 先例引用了 Peter Gibson 大法官在 Baden v. Societe General pour Favoriser le Development du Commercice et de I？ ndustrie en France SA（Note）（1993）1 WLR 509 先例中的说法："Knowledge may be provided affirmatively or inferred from circumstances. The various mental states which may be involved were analysed by Peter Gibson J in Baden case as comprising：（i）actual knowledge；（ii）wilfully shutting one's eyes to the obvious；（iii）wilfully and recklessly failing to make such inquiries as an honest and reasonable man should make；and（iv）knowledge of circumstances which would indicate the facts to an honest and reasonable man；and（v）knowledge of circumstances which would put an honest and reasonable man on inquiry. According to Peter Gibson J.，a person in category（ii）or（iii）will be taken to have actual knowledge[123]，while a person in categories（iv）or（v）has constructive notice only[124]. I gratefully adopt the classification but would warn against over refinement or a too ready assumption that categories（iv）or（v）are necessarily cases of constructive notice only. The true distinction is between honesty and dishonesty.[125] It is essentially a jury question. If a man does not draw the obvious inferences or make the obvious inquiries, the question is：why not? If it is because, however foolishly, he did not suspect wrongdoing or, having suspected it, had his suspicions allayed, however unreasonably, that is one thing.[126] But he did suspect wrongdoing yet failed to make inquiries because 'he did not want to know'（category［ii］）or because he regarded it as 'none of his business'（category［iii］），that is quite another.[127] Such conduct is dishonest, and those who are guilty of it cannot complain if, for the purpose of civil liability, they are treated as if they had actually knowledge.[128]"

---

〔123〕 上述五个程度的知道中的第二个故意对明显的事情视而不见，与第三个故意与疏忽不对诚实与合理人士会做出调查的情况做出调查，属于真正知道。

〔124〕 而第四个知道会对诚实与合理人士显示真相的情况，与第五个知道会令诚实与合理人士进行调查的情况，属于推定知道。

〔125〕 但这也不能一概而论，两者真正的区别是诚实与否。

〔126〕 如果一位人士没有做出明显的推断或进行调查，则接下来的问题就是，他为什么这样做？如果只是因为他没有产生怀疑或他的怀疑消除了，无论多不合理，这是一回事。

〔127〕 但如果他确实产生了怀疑，没有调查是因为他不想知道或决定不关他事，这是另一回事。

〔128〕 这样的行为是不诚实的，在民事索赔中会被当做真正知道对待。

因此,只有当一方真正知道[这包括(i)与(ii)、(iii)的所谓 Nelsonian knowledge]对方犯错时,才有责任说清楚:Thomas Bates & Son Ltd. v. Wyndham's (Lingerie) Ltd. (1981) 1 WLR 505 等先例。

推定知道(constructive knowledge)一般来说不足够:Price Meats v. Barclays Bank Plc. (2000) 2 All ER (Comm) 346; Patel v. Standard Chartered Bank (2001) Lloyd's Rep. Bank 229 等先例。

10.2.4.2 要件之二:不公平与不合情理

这个题目在第四章第8段与本章第9段介绍,这里不会重复。针对单方面错误导致另一方有责任说清楚,否则就会构成陈述性禁反言或沉默性禁反言,有一些特殊的要求。

1. 沉默的一方必须是有意识(deliberately)不说清楚,并往往涉及取巧(但不需要到欺骗或隐瞒的程度)。这取巧可以是不同形式,如知道对方的错误并不代表双方的订约意图,但为了占便宜不说清楚。在 Riverlate Properties Ltd. v. Paul (1975) Ch. 133 先例中,Russell 大法官说:"Whether there was in any particular case knowledge of the intention and mistake of the other party must be a question of fact to be decided upon the evidence. Basically it appears to us that it must be such as to involve the lessee (沉默方) in **a degree of sharp practice**."(加黑部分是笔者的强调)

另在 Thomas Bates & Son Ltd. v. Wyndham's (Lingerie) Ltd. (1981) 1 WLR 505 先例中,Buckley 大法官说:"Undoubtedly I think in any such case the conduct of the defendant must be such as to make it inequitable that he should be allowed to object to the rectification of the document. If **this necessarily implies some measure of 'sharp practice'**, so be it; but for my party I think that the doctrine is one which depends more upon the equity of the position... in my view, the conduct must be such as to **affect the conscience of the party who has suppressed the fact that he has recognised the presence of a mistake.**"(加黑部分是笔者的强调)

2. 保持沉默对沉默的一方有利,或对有错误理解的一方有损害。这很明显,因为如果对沉默的一方不利,他又知道真相,肯定不会保持沉默。而在合约关系中,一般来说对沉默的一方有利,肯定就会对有错误理解的一方有损害。因为依赖而蒙受损害(*detrimental reliance*)是所有禁反言的共同要求,这在有责任说清楚的情况也不例外。

在上述介绍的 Thomas Bates & Son Ltd. v. Wyndham's (Lingerie) Ltd 先例中,案情涉及房屋租赁合约。发生争议的双方原本有一个旧的租赁合约,租约中规定租约到期前6个月,租客有选择权选择延长7或14年租约。新的租金由双方同意,如果不能同意,由独任仲裁员决定。租客行使了选择权延长了14年租约。租约规定租金在第五年与第十年末调整,但房东在起草新租约时只写了租金要由双方同意,而没有写如果双方不能同意要怎么办。租客注意到了这个问题,但没有提醒房东。在新租约第五年末,双方无法对新租约达成一致,房东向法院要求合约变更的救济(在条文中加上,如果双方不能同意,就由独任仲裁员决定)。上诉庭最终支持了房东的申请,除了上述节录的 Buckley 大法官提到的取巧,明知道房东的错误但为了占便宜故意不说清楚,还有对租客自己有利,或对房东有损害的考虑。相关判决可总结如下:"... *where one party to a document was aware that it did not give effect to the common intention of the parties due to* **a mistake** on the part of the other party and executed the document **without telling the other party** and where (per Buckley L. J.) the **mistake was one calculated to benefit him**, or (per Eveleigh L. J.) the **mistake was detrimental to the other party**, he was precluded from resisting rectification on the ground that the mistake was not, at the time of execution of the document, mutual..."(加黑部分是笔者的强调)

3. 在本章之 10.2.4 段已经提到,如果对方的错误理解与合约一方的沉默有一定的关系,客观来看被对方以为是对这个错误理解的认同或默许,就更有可能满足不公平与不合情理的要求。

在 Sean Wilken QC 与 Karim Ghaly 先生所著的《The Law of Waiver, Variation, and Estoppel》(第 3 版,2012 年)一书之 11.36 段,关于"产权人禁反言"(proprietary estoppel)的章节,就提到沉默的一方除非对对方的错误理解扮演了一定的角色,否则没有理由要他承担责任,说:"... The underlying basis of the doctrine is unconscionability or unfairness: P〔129〕 will be prevented from taking unfair advantage of C's〔130〕 belief. There seems little warrant for making P bear the consequences of his belief unless he played some part in its formation or continuance..."

这也就是 Mason 大法官在澳大利亚的 Taylor v. Johnson (1983) 151 CLR 422 先例中说的沉默一方故意不说话,让对方踩入陷阱:"he engages deliberately in a course of conduct which is designed to inhibit discovery of it."

Kerr 大法官在 The "August Leonhardt" (1985) 1 Lloyd's Rep. 28 先例中说:"The applicability of the doctrine of estoppel in any given case can also be tested in another way. There cannot be any estoppel unless the alleged representor has said or done something, or failed to do something, with the result that – across the line between the parties-**his action or indication has produced some belief or expectation in the mind of the alleged representee**, so that, depending on the circumstances, it would thereafter no longer be right to allow the alleged representor to resile by challenging the belief or expectation **which he has engendered**. To that extent at least, therefore the alleged representor must be open to criticism."(加黑部分是笔者的强调)

---

〔129〕 土地或财产的产权人,即沉默的一方。

〔130〕 原告,有错误理解的一方。

在 S & E Promotions v. Tobin Brothers Pty Ltd. (1994) 122 ALR 637 先例中,澳大利亚法院判是如果因为一方的沉默令对方错误认为自己的地位有了保障(lulled the other into a false sense of security),就会构成衡平法禁反言。

4. 客观来看,沉默的一方保持沉默没有履行他诚实与负责任行事(acting honestly and responsibly)的责任。

这一说法最早是 Wilberforce 勋爵在 Moorgate Mercantile Co. Ltd. v. Twitchings (1977) AC 890 先例提出,之后被不少先例引用。如 Webster 大法官在 The "Henrik Sif" (1982) 1 Lloyd's Rep. 456 先例说:"Nonetheless the dictum which I have cited seems to me to be most persuasive authority for the proposition that the duty necessary to found an estoppel by silence or acquiescence arises where 'a reasonable man would expect' the person against whom the estoppel is raised '**acting honestly and responsibly**' to bring the true facts to the attention of the other party known by him to be under a mistake as to their respective rights and obligations."

另是涉及期租合约的 The "Lutetian" (1982) 2 Lloyd's Rep. 140 先例也跟从了这个说法。案情涉及承租人没有准时与足数支付租金而在市场高涨时,被船东趁机撤船。在该先例中,根据租约在第二年的租约期每天的租金应该提高 100 美元至 5200 美元,但承租人还是依照第一年租金的 5100 美元来计算与支付,这明显是错误与造成少付。法院认为虽然船东没有责任向承租人指出如果收不足数的租金就会撤船(虽然这是正常做法),但船东不能试图阻止承租人发现支付的租金不足的事实或制造假象误导承租人以求出现撤船的好机会。在实践操作中,这分水线比较难掌握,船东对承租人少支付租金的反应往往是马上提出抗议或拒绝接受这笔钱,会马上让承租人知道少付的租金。这样,由于租约有明示条文允许承租人在船东的通知后 3 天内补救不足部分,不想被撤船的承租人肯定会这样做。但在该先例中,法院认为船东千方百计隐瞒实情与制造假象,希望承租人不在 3 天内做出补救,以获得撤船的机会。如船东私下通知他的银行拒收承租人准时但不足数支付的 86000 美元租金,但告诉银行不要告知对方银行原因是不足数。这不是对承租人做出的言行,但显然是不合情理与不公平的做法。当承租人在 3 天内追加支付 3000 美元的时候,船东也不告诉承租人有关早付的一笔租金已经被拒收,再也不是支付 3000 美元可以足数。而承租人向船东经理人(应与船东是一家人)追问并要求确认已经收到租金时,经理人回复是仍在等船东的确认,虽然在那个时候他是完全应该知道两笔钱都被拒收。在这样的事实背景下,法院认为船东有责任说清楚,否则会构成禁反言。Bingham 大法官说:"The relationship of owner and charterer is not one of the utmost good faith. One must be careful not to impute unrealistically onerous obligations to those who may choose to conduct their relations in a tough and uncompromising way. There is nonetheless a duty not to conduct oneself in such a way as to mislead. I have no doubt that the owners knew that the charterers believed they had paid the right amount. **It was their duty, act-**

ing honestly and responsibly, to disclose their own view to the charterers. They did not do so and indeed thwarted the charterers' attempts to discover their views. Their omission to disclose their own calculation led the charterers to think, until a very late stage, that no objection was taken to the calculation. It would in my view be unjust in the circumstances if the owners could rely on the incorrectness of a deduction which they had every opportunity to point out at an earlier stage and which their failure to point out caused the charterers to overlook."(加黑部分就是上述 Wilberforce 勋爵在 Moorgate Mercantile Co. Ltd. v. Twitchings 先例提到的说法。)

除此之外,"acting honestly and responsibly" 的重要说法也在其他很多重要的先例中被提到,如本章之 10.3.4 段介绍的 The "Stolt Loyalty" (1993) 2 Lloyd's Rep. 281 先例;The "Indian Endurance" and The "Indian Grace" (No. 2) (1998) 1 Lloyd's Rep. 1 (HL)先例与本章之 10.3.6 段介绍的 Thames Trains Ltd. v. Adams (2006) EWHC 3291 (QB)先例等。

10.3 关于有责任说清楚的权威先例

涉及有责任说清楚的争议的先例很多,本章只介绍一些主要的商业领域或笔者认为比较有趣的先例。

10.3.1 先例之一:Mangles v. Dixon

在 Mangles v. Dixon (1852) 3 HL Cas 702 先例中,原告是承租人,他与船东订立了租约付运一票货物。双方在另一份文件约定在扣除租金之后,平摊承租人这票生意的亏损与利润。之后船东将租约转让(assign)给了被告,被告与船东也将转让通知了原告。在通知中,被告没有向原告做出任何询问。之后这票生意被证明是亏损,于是原告要求被告作为受让人(assignee)承担一半的亏损。因为如果租约没有被转让,他有权要求船东承担这一半的亏损。而被告则认为原告在收到转让通知时没有提醒他存在这一安排,不能事后再要求他承担一半的亏损。

转让是受到衡平法权利的影响(subject to equity),即如果追回债务的时效已过,或是债务人(debtor)对债权人(creditor)的债务有衡平法抵销(equitable set - off)的权利,或其他合约权利,同样会影响受让人。在该先例中,贵族院最后判是原告在收到转让通知后没有责任通知被告受让人有关的衡平法权利,毕竟做出询问保证自己的转让利益是受让人的责任,没理由让原告来照看被告的利益。并且原告在收到通知时也不会知道被告是否知道相关的衡平法权利或影响。但如果情况有所改变,原告收到的通知显示了被告是明显不知道相关的衡平法权利或影响,他就有责任向被告说清楚。判决的相关部分可节录如下:

"The assignee of a chose in action, or security of any kind, where there has been no fraud, stands in exactly the same situation as the assignor as to the equities arising upon it. He must be taken to be cognisant of them. It is his duty to make inquiries, and, as a general rule, the creator of the security thus assigned is not bound, on receiving a simple notice of the assignment, to volunteer information. If a loss arises, it falls upon him whose duty it is to make the inquiries and who has not made them.

But if the notice given by the assignee discloses, on the face of it, that which induces the belief that he has been deceived in accepting the assignment, the creator of the security is bound to inform the assignee of the real circumstances, and if he should not do so, he will be bound to perform the stipulations of the security, and cannot be allowed to take advantage of the equities existing as between the assignor and himself."

10.3.2　先例之二：Hartog v. Colin and Shields

这与本章之10.2.3段介绍的Chwee Kin Keong v. Digilandmall. com Pte Ltd. (2005) 1 SLR 502先例的案情类似。在Hartog v. Colin and Shields (1939) 3 All ER 566先例中，案情涉及被告卖给原告3000块兔皮。谈判期间双方谈到的价格是指一块多少钱，这也是该行业订兔皮价格的一贯做法，但在做出要约时，被告错误地写了价格是10元一磅，虽然他的主观想法是10元一块。原告估计也看到这个被告的错误，马上接受了这个要约，希望捡个大便宜。当被告发觉并拒绝履行时，原告提起索赔。法院判是原告一定知道这个要约不代表原告的真正意图，所以谈不上订约时双方想法一致(meeting of minds)，合约空与无效。虽然判决中没有针对，但显然原告在知道被告的错误时，有责任说清楚。

10.3.3　先例之三：The "Nai Genova"

在The "Nai Genova" (1984) 1 Lloyd's Rep. 353先例中，案情涉及两艘意大利新造超级油轮的7年多的长期运输合约(contract of affreightment)。在当时高通胀的年代，很多长期的合约中都会有一条通货膨胀条文(Escalation Clause)，写明按照通货膨胀来调整将来的运费或租金的公式。至于怎样订立可以准确反应实际的通货膨胀的公式并不容易，曾有过案件涉及几艘船舶的长期期租合约，有关的通货膨胀以黄金价格为准。在订约时，黄金的市场价格还是在1945年的布雷顿森林体系(Bretton Woods Regime)制定的35美元/盎司。但在该长期期租合约履行的后期，由于在1971年8月美国单方面宣布美元与黄金脱钩，导致黄金的市场价格以数十倍的速度猛涨。这意味着该长期租约的租金需要调整至一个不可思议的金额，最后令一家著名的日本承租人要抛开面子向香港船东哀求，说是如果强制执行，它就只能倒闭。最后这个案件也是以友好的和解而告终。

回到The "Nai Genova"先例的案情，在70年代末到80年代初，通货膨胀十分严重。运输合约中的通货膨胀条文，是以1974年4月1日的船员与维修保养费用作为基数，而之后如果上涨，也就在每年要支付的运费中作出同样百分比的调整。在签署的合约中，这基数的费用是写下美元的数字，但后来承租人向仲裁庭申请合约变更，指双方在谈判中达成的订约意图是以意大利里拉为准，所以需要把合约中的美元改为里拉。这里所造成巨大的差别显然是因为两种货币之间的汇率有了很大波动，意大利从70年代开始就出现了很严重的通货膨胀问题，意大利里拉对美元出现大幅贬值。

承租人申请合约变更的理据是有关的运输合约错误记录了他们在签约前的谈判会议中共同/分享的持续订约意图,船东当然否认有此共同意图。而另一个替代争议是即使船东的意图是以美元为准,他也知道或应该知道承租人在订立合约时单方面错误认为是以里拉为准,所以有责任说清楚。

针对有关谈判会议,参与的双方证人都做出了证人证言与出庭接受了盘问,最后在一审法院认定事实是双方曾经在会议中提到了以里拉作为基准,但是没有进一步讨论并同意,说:"On 29th November 1974 the base figure in the escalation clause of 700,000,000 lire for repairs and maintenance was only mentioned without being discussed. It was not expected to constitute an impediment to a concluded agreement. Nor, on the other hand, was it so firmly established as a term of the clause that either party was justified in assuming, without confirming, that the escalation clause in any subsequent draft of the charter – party would be in a form which was not open to argument, or that the base figure included in it would necessarily remain the same."

而针对单方面错误的替代争议,上诉庭认为合约要根据单方面错误变更,一方必须真正知道另一方犯错。而在该先例中,根据相关的证据,上诉庭认为船东并不知道。并且船东没有取巧,承租人的错误主要是他自己不小心,而船东在其中没有扮演角色。Slade 大法官说:"... in the absence of estoppel, fraud, undue influence or a fiduciary relationship between the parties, the authorities do not in any circumstances permit the rectification of a contract on the grounds of unilateral mistake, unless the defendant had actual knowledge of the existence of the relevant mistaken belief at the time when the mistaken plaintiff signed the contract. ... The loss which the plaintiffs have sustained in this case, though most unfortunate for them, is in my opinion not attributable to the defendants. It is attributable solely to the plaintiffs' own carelessness in failing properly to read the provisions of the charter – party, coupled with adverse supervening circumstances consisting in the fall in the Italian lira, in relation to the U. S. dollar. If the lira had risen, the clause might have operated to their advantage."

10.3.4 先例之四:The "Stolt Loyalty"

在 The "Stolt Loyalty" (1993) 2 Lloyd's Rep. 281 先例中,Stolt Loyalty 轮的注册船东(registered owner) Soframar 将船舶光租给了 Stolt Loyalty Inc. ,并完全由 Stolt Loyalty Inc. 营运。并且尽管 Soframar 才是真正的注册船东,在 1987 至 1988 年的《Lloyd's Shipping Register》上 Stolt Loyalty 轮的注册船东是 Stolt Loyalty Inc. 。Soframar与 Stolt Loyalty Inc. 都在 Gard 互保协会购买了责任险,包括货损货差的责任。该先例涉及的问题,首先是在提单合约下是谁作为合约承运人(contractual carrier)负责货损货差。[131] Stolt Loyalty 轮完全由 Stolt Loyalty Inc. 营运,包括雇佣船长

〔131〕 参见笔者的《提单与其他付运单证》(2016 年)一书第二章第 4 段。

等,因此很明显由船长签发的提单合约下的承运人应是 Stolt Loyalty Inc. 。另一个争议是根据 1924 年《海牙规则》或英国的相关立法,货损货差的索赔必须在 1 年内提出。双方谈判过程中货方要求延长时效与 Gard 回复的同意的信件中都只提到了“船东”(owners)一词,但没有提到光船承租人(demise charterer)或也可被称为光船船东。但已经提到,光船承租人要负责货损货差。这就带来一个争议,“船东”一词只是指注册船东 Soframar,还是也包括光船承租人 Stolt Loyalty Inc. 。如果不包括后者,这一货损货差的索赔就时效已过。Clarke 大法官认为,“船东”一词应该也包括光船承租人。即使“船东”只是指 Soframar, Gard 与 Stolt Loyalty Inc. 没有说清楚也构成禁反言,说:“In my judgment Gard were under a duty to inform Clyde & Co. (货方代表律师) of the true position here if they were going to reply to that part of the telex of Mar. 3 which asked for an extension of time. It seems to me that a reasonable man would expect someone in the position of Gard, knowing or even suspecting that Clyde & Co. had mistakenly failed to refer expressly to the demise charterers, **acting honestly and responsibly** to have drawn that mistake to their attention in any reply to the relevant part of the telex . . . Gard took advantage of a mistake which at the very least they suspected had been made. In my judgment if they were going to send a reply they owed a duty to send a full reply. Instead, they deliberately allowed Clyde & Co. to continue in their mistaken belief that they had asked for all relevant extensions of time. They encouraged them to continue to make the same mistake.”(加黑部分是笔者的强调)

10.3.5 先例之五:OT Africa Line Ltd. v. Vickers Plc.

这种类似的情况也在其他很多先例出现,较近期的有 OT Africa Line Ltd. v. Vickers Plc. (1996) 1 Lloyd's Rep. 700 先例中,案情涉及的索赔金额是 70 万美元。在法院的审理中途,被告支付法院(payment into court)103000 美元作为和解金额。原告反要约的金额是 185000 美元加上 280000 美元的诉讼费用。双方持续的谈判后被告律师作出 150000 英镑的要约,这包括已经支付法院的一笔钱。但这里被告律师犯错,实际上被告愿意作出和解的是美元而不是英镑,但发传真的时候把“ $ ”写成了“£ ”,要约也被原告接受。被告试图以单方面错误与禁反言从和解协议中脱身,但 Mance 大法官不认为原告知道被告的错误,所以就不存在上述所讲的想法不一致的情况,也不应该存在禁反言。

但如果事实稍一变动,就可能有很不同的结果。如原告提出和解的金额是 30 万美元,被告的反要约是 29 万英镑,折算为美元比 30 万更多。这样,原告不可能不知道被告单方面的错误,如果取巧接受并坚持这一 29 万英镑的和解协议,法律很有可能做出救济,判原告有责任说清楚,向被告指出他的错误。

10.3.6 先例之六:Thames Trains Ltd. v. Adams

在 Thames Trains Ltd. v. Adams (2006) EWHC 3291 (QB)先例中,案情也涉及和解协议。法院最后判是在诉讼中即使明知对方律师有了错误理解,律师也没有责任要向对方说清楚。该先例的案情涉及 Adams 先生在火车碰撞中受到严重的伤害，于是起诉 Thames 火车公司。2003 年 2 月，法院判是 Thames 火车公司的责任成立，只剩下 Adams 先生的损失要核算，并安排了在 2005 年 2 月 28 日针对损失金额开庭。期间双方一直进行谈判，而保险公司知道责任已定，只是赔多赔少的问题，所以也向 Adams 先生做出了多次中间支付（interim payment）。在开庭前不久，保险公司向 Adams 先生做出支付 930 万美元的要约。2 月 25 日，Adams 先生的律师打电话给 Thames 火车公司的律师要求 Thames 火车公司提高 930 万美元的赔偿，原因是他需要一笔 1000 万美元进行长期投资，以对他的将来做出保障。但 Thames 火车公司的律师则回复说不会再提高金额，如果 Adams 先生不接受，就必须由法院进行核算。之后，Adams 先生的律师在内部讨论并获得 Adams 先生的太太的同意后，在 2 月 25 日向 Thames 火车公司的律师发出传真确认接受 930 万美元的赔偿，但有条件是要 Thames 火车公司承担已产生的诉讼费用，并且之前保险公司做出的中间支付不计算在内。严格来说，这属于反要约（counter-offer），而非接受保险公司的原要约。但同时（可能因为很快要开庭，所以双方都很快做出行动），Thames 火车公司的律师也在与 Thames 火车公司内部讨论后，同意增加 50 万美元的赔偿。之后 Thames 火车公司的律师就打电话给 Adams 先生的律师提出新的要约（980 万美元），Adams 先生的律师马上接受了这个要约。毫无疑问，Adams 先生的律师在电话中知道对方律师不知道之前的传真，但不确定是自己律师事务所的通讯部门延误导致传真尚未发出，还是 Thames 火车公司的律师还没有看到。后来律师事务所内部人员向 Adams 先生的律师确认传真已经发出，他立即写邮件说明撤回之前的传真并再次确认接受电话中的新要约。Thames 火车公司的律师在看到传真之后，坚持新要约作废，以之前传真中接受的 930 万美金的赔偿金额为准。这显然不被 Adams 先生接受，双方开始诉讼。Thames 火车公司的主张主要根据两个理由：一是错误（mistake）导致合约无效，二是 Adams 先生的律师有责任说清楚，但没有提醒 Thames 火车公司的律师之前的传真，构成禁反言。

在该先例中，Adams 先生的律师没有做出任何陈述会诱导 Thames 火车公司的律师，唯一可能涉及诱导的是他没有提醒 Thames 火车公司的律师之前已经通过传真接受了 930 万美元的金额，虽然有其他附带的次要条件。因此，错误导致合约无效要成立，必须要求 Adams 先生的律师有向 Thames 火车公司的律师说清楚的责任。禁反言也是同样的道理，因为除非 Adams 先生的律师做出明确无误的陈述或承诺，否则无法构成禁反言。而除非 Adams 先生的律师有责任说清楚，否则他的沉默不构成明确无误的陈述或承诺。因此，最关键的争议就是 Adams 先生的律师是否有责任说清楚。

并且在 Thames Trains Ltd. v. Adams 先例中，不能说 Adams 先生的律师在电话中接受 Thames 火车公司的要约时，双方想法不一致。毕竟 Thames 火车公司的律师在电话中做出的要约确实是 980 万美元，只是当时不知道 Adams 先生的律师通过传真做出的反要约。而 Adams 先生的律师在反要约被接受之前就将它撤回,转而接受了新要约。

针对 Adams 先生的律师是否有责任说清楚,高院的 Nelson 大法官并不认为有,说:"There is however no general duty upon one party to litigation or potential litigation to point out the mistakes of another party or his legal advisors. . . . In the Court of Appeal decision in The "Indian Grace" (No. 2) (1996) 2 Lloyd's Rep. 12, Lord Justice Staughton said:'As Mr Rokison(船东代表大律师)put it, a party to litigation is not obliged to be the nursemaid of his opponent, at any rate if the opponent is not an untutored individual but as well acquainted with commercial litigation as the Government of India(货方). The law does sometimes impose a burden on solicitors and counsel to help their opponent's case, but the burden should only be imposed when it is truly necessary as otherwise... the client will be tempted to ask "Whose side are you on?".'[132]. . . In these circumstances I do not consider that a reasonable man would expect Ms Christian (Adams 先生的律师), **acting honestly and responsibly**, to have informed Mr Rae - Reeves(Thames 火车公司的律师)of her earlier offer. Her conduct was not unconscionable, nor deceitful[133], nor sharp practice, nor was she taking unfair advantage of Mr Rae - Reeves' ignorance of her offer, given, in particular, that it had only been made as a result of him inaccurately informing her that no further monies were available, and that he had failed to receive it because of systems failures within his own office.[134] She was not therefore, in my judgment, on the particular facts of this case under any duty to speak. She was entitled to stay silent, act in her client's best interests and accept the increased offer. . . "(加黑部分是笔者的强调)

10.3.7 先例之七:MIOM 1 Ltd. v. Sea Echo ENE

最后介绍的是比较近期的 MIOM 1 Ltd. v. Sea Echo ENE (No. 2) (2012) 1 Lloyd's Rep. 140 先例。该先例案情涉及船舶碰撞,即双方是侵权关系而非合约关系,该先例与英国海事法院(admiralty court)的规则与做法有密切关系。简单来说,

---

〔132〕 根据英国律师的执业操守规则,在合法的情况下,客户的利益超越一切。所以法律不可能要求律师有责任提醒对方或对方律师,否则正如上诉庭的 Staughton 大法官在 The "Indian Endurance" and The "Indian Grace" (No.2) (1996) 2 Lloyd's Rep. 12 先例中说的,客户会问:"你究竟是帮哪一边的?"

〔133〕 这一方面就是针对英国律师的职业操守规则,律师不可以欺骗另一位律师。即如果 Thames 火车公司的律师在做出新要约之前问过 Adams 先生的律师是否接受 930 万美元的要约,而 Adams 先生的律师说不接受,之后 Thames 火车公司的律师才提出新要约,则 Adams 先生的律师就涉及欺骗对方或不诚实。

〔134〕 这是说 Thames 火车公司的律师的单方面错误是因为他给出了不准确的信息(不会再增加赔偿金额),并且他自己的律师事务所的延误或效率不高导致不能及时看到传真,而不是因为 Adams 先生的律师的诱导。

根据规则与做法，即使双方对船舶碰撞各负一半责任，如果只有一方有损失（会有情况是碰撞事故中只有一方船舶损坏），另一方就要负责全部的诉讼费用。但如果在各负一半责任的情况下，双方都有损失（主要是船舶损坏），则双方各负责一半的费用。在该先例中，双方被判是对船舶碰撞各负一半的责任，但原告的损失远大于被告，加上被告认为可以把他的损失用来抵销原告的损失，因此，被告没有在2年时效内（根据英国的《商船法》）提出反索赔。而原告根据英国海事法院的规则与做法需要尽早提出依赖时效已过的抗辩，这样被告就可以申请延长时效并提出反索赔。但原告没有这样做，而只是在后来费用分摊时以这一理由要求被告承担所有诉讼费用。被告则声称原告之前的沉默或不行动构成禁反言，不能现在才提出反索赔的时效已过，这是不公平与不合情理的。Teare 大法官支持了原告被禁反言的说法。在2年时效已过之后，双方的案件管理会议（case management conference 或 CMC）中，原告就应该向被告提出他会依赖反索赔时效已过的抗辩。在 Teare 大法官看来，原告有责任向被告说清楚，而这沉默的行为是清楚无误的陈述或承诺原告不准备依赖被告反索赔时效已过的抗辩，说：

"The Claimant's conduct in failing to inform the Defendant at the time of the CMC that it was intending to rely on the time bar was, in my judgment, a clear and unequivocal representation that the Claimant was not relying upon the time bar. If the Claimant had been intending to rely upon the time bar the Claimant ought to have informed the Defendant (and the Court) of that by the time of the CMC at the latest. Its failure to take the point by that time was, in one sense, **silent conduct**, but it was silent conduct at a time when the Claimant had a duty to take the point if it wished to rely upon it. Silence in that context is a clear statement that the time bar point is not to be relied upon. It is inconsistent with an intention to rely upon the point.

The evidence of Mr. Leonard of Wikborg Rein（被告代表律师）was that if the limitation issue had been raised the Defendant would have made an application for an extension of time. There is no reason to doubt that. For the reasons explained below such application would have succeeded and so it would be **unfair or unconscionable to permit the Claimant to rely upon the time bar**."（加黑部分是笔者的强调）

11. 陈述性禁反言与公法/立法的关系

针对这一方面，笔者会节录 Sean Wilken QC 与 Karim Ghaly 先生所著的《The Law of Waiver, Variation, and Estoppel》（第3版，2012年）一书。这一课题与本书第四章之5.4段有类似重叠，这里尽量不再重复，而主要从陈述性禁反言角度进行探讨。

在本章接下来的11.1段,笔者会介绍一般情况下禁反言的说法不适用在公法,因为会影响立法的效力。而11.2段会介绍越权(ultra vires)的问题。

11.1 影响立法效力

一般来说,禁反言是私法/普通法,因为政策原因不能被用来超越立法,影响立法效力。禁反言也通常不能被依赖去干预或改变政府的政策:Maritime Electric Co. Ltd. v. General Dairies Ltd. (1937) AC 610; Laker Airways Ltd. v. Department of Trade (1977) QB 643 CA;Churchill Fisheries Export Pty Ltd. v. Director General of Conservation (1990) VR 968 等先例。

但就像合约双方有订约自由一样,禁反言的说法能否超越或改变立法规定还是要看立法的目的、背后的公共政策与每个案件不同的事实,如有关立法的规定是否是强制适用的。在 Yaxley v. Gotts (2000) Ch 162 先例中,Beldam 大法官说:"The general principle that a party cannot rely on an estoppels in the face of a statute depends on the nature of enactment, the purpose of the provision and the social policy behind it."

11.1.1 强制适用的立法

合约需要书面记录并有双方签字才有效是典型的立法强制适用的例子。这表示如果双方没有签署合约,合约就被视为无效。但如果合约一方依赖了另一方确认双方有合约关系的言行并蒙受损害,能否构成禁反言不让另一方否认有合约存在?如果可以,这显然与立法的强制规定有冲突。

英国1677年《Statute of Frauds》之 section 4 规定了五类合约/文件必须是书面并且有双方签署才有效,分别是:土地买卖合约、遗产执行人自己掏钱支付遗产债务的承诺、婚约、担保与1年内无法履行完毕的合约。之后土地买卖合约的书面与签署的要求被1989年《Law of Property (Miscellaneous Provisions) Act》之 section 2 替代。[135]而在1954年《Law Reform (Enforcement of Contracts) Act》之 section 1,删除了除担保以外的另外三类合约的书面与签署要求。

针对这两类仍有书面与签署要求的合约有很多争议。如果卖方或担保人(guarantor)在订立土地买卖合约或担保合约前口头或书面做出陈述(或承诺),之后希望更正或撤回,但另一方已经做出依赖并蒙受损害,卖方或担保人是否会被禁反言?如果禁反言因为合约没有满足立法要求而不能成立,会对依赖了口头陈述或承诺并蒙受损害的一方太苛刻。但如果禁反言可以成立,可能会影响1989年《Law of Property (Miscellaneous Provisions) Act》与1954年《Law Reform (Enforcement of Contracts) Act》的效力与立法目的。

看来法院会根据每个案件不同的事实、相关立法的用字与目的做出判断。如果适用禁反言的说法会影响立法的法律效力,甚至令它变为空的(null)与无效(void),显然不会被允许。但如果适用禁反言的说法与立法的目的(通常在法律委员会的有

[135] 这方面会在本书第七章"产权人禁反言"(proprietary estoppel)段之4.1段谈及。

关报告上清楚说明)不冲突,甚至可以加强立法目的,法院就没理由判禁反言不能适用。这在下一小段的例子中会进一步说明。

11.1.2　相关先例

笔者接下来介绍几个先例,对上一小段的内容做进一步说明。

1. 在 Re Exchange Securities & Commodities Ltd.（1988）Ch 46 先例中,案情在本章第7段有介绍。该先例涉及1985年《公司法》之 section 540(4),有关公司破产、债权人与公司清盘人的关系的规定。法院最后判是禁反言不能被用来对抗清盘人,因为与立法规定的清盘人必须将公司的财产在真正的债权人之间分配不符。

2. 在 Shah v. Shah（2002）QB 35 先例中,案情涉及原告投资失利,被告做出个人担保会退回原告投资的这笔钱。但原告在法院执行个人担保时,被告提出抗辩说担保合约的格式不符合立法规定,因此无效。1989年《Law of Property（Miscellaneous Provisions）Act》之 Section 1(3)规定担保人要在见证人面前签署,说:"An instrument is validly executed as a deed by an individual; if, and only if –（a）it is signed;（i）by him in the presence of a witness who attested the signature ..."

但在该先例是被告签署之后再将文件寄给见证人补签,而不是在见证人面前签署。上诉庭节录了法律委员会的报告《Report of the Law Commission, Deeds and Escrows》(Law Com No. 163)(1987)中针对不符合立法要求的格式,说:"It would be undesirable if failure to have just one signature witnessed, perhaps on a deed which had many, were to render the whole deed invalid. We therefore recommend that failure to have a signature witnessed and attested should have the effect that the signatory would not prima facie be bound but that the deed, if capable of operating without that signature, would still be valid. The signatory should still be bound if he took the benefit of the deed... or through estoppels if someone else had acted on the assumption that the deed was properly executed."

上诉庭判原告可以根据陈述性禁反言执行这份担保,相关的判决被总结如下:"... general social policy did not require the exclusion of estoppels in all circumstances when the validity of a deed was in issue either before or after the enactment of the Law of Properties（Miscellaneous Provisions）Act 1989; that what was fundamental to the public interest for the perceived need for formality in section 1 was in the requirement for a signature and not that the person attesting the signature should be present when the document was signed, since attestation was at one stage removed from the imperative out of which the need for formality arose; that failure to comply with the additional formality of attestation should not permit a party to escape the consequences of an apparently valid deed by claiming that the attesting witness was not present at the time of signature; that, since the lack of proper attestation would be peculiarly within the knowledge of the signatory and would often not be within the knowledge of the other parties, there were sound policy reasons for not permitting a party to escape his obligations under a deed by reason of a defect in attestation; that, in the circumstances, the delivery of the document was a clear representation that the defendants had signed it in the presence of the witness, and that they had validly executed it as a deed; that, therefore, the defendants had to have known that the plaintiff would assume that it was so signed, that the statutory requirements had been complied with to render it a valid deed and that they intended it to be relied on as such; and that, accordingly,... was correct to allow the plaintiff to raise an estoppels and to conclude he could bring proceedings on the document as a deed."

3. 在 Actionstrength Ltd. v. International Glass Engineering IN. GL. EN SpA(2003)2 AC 541 贵族院先例中,案情涉及担保合约。在该先例中,原告与第一被告订立劳务合约,为第二被告建造工厂。第一被告一直延误支付,原告威胁会停止工作。于是第二被告介入并与原告达成口头协议,承诺会说服第一被告付款,如果不成功会扣下要支付给第一被告的钱直接支付原告。在第二被告的保证之下,原告继续工作了 1 个月。但之后第一被告破产,很明显给不出这笔钱,第二被告也拒绝支付(估计没有扣下支付给第一被告的钱)。于是原告从工厂撤走,并开始诉讼索赔延误支付的工钱。第二被告的抗辩是这个口头协议本质是担保合约,而根据 1677 年《Statute of Frauds》之 section 4,担保合约必须是书面并且有担保人签署,否则无效。因此原告不可以根据口头担保要求第二被告做出支付。而原告的回复是第二被告明知原告依赖了他的陈述(或承诺)并蒙受损害,被禁反言,不能否认担保合约的有效性。

上诉庭判是第二被告没有被禁反言,可以依赖《Statute of Frauds》之 section 4 的规定,这也被贵族院支持。该先例与 Shah v. Shah and Others 先例的区别可节录 Walker 大法官的说法,如下:"The other case is Shah v. Shah... There the Court of Appeal was concerned with section 1 of the Law of Properties (Miscellaneous Provisions) Act 1989... The deed in question appeared on its face to comply with these requirements, but the evidence was that the witness to the signatures of two of the defendants had not signed in their presence (but shortly afterwards, not in their presence) Pill LJ said: 'The delivery of the document constituted an unambiguous representation of fact that it was a deed.' .... In the present case, by contract, what passed between the parties did not amount to an unambiguous representation that there was an enforceable contract, or that St – Gobain(第二被告)would not take any point on section 4 of the Statute of Frauds."

换言之,要构成禁反言不让担保人依赖 1677 年《Statute of Frauds》之 section 4,担保人必须做出其他的鼓励或诱导或保证,令被担保人相信口头陈述(或承诺)会被履行。单纯的口头/文书保证不足以构成禁反言与令担保人不能依赖 1677 年《Statute of Frauds》之 section 4 的格式要求。因为要订立有效的担保合约,第一步一定是担保人做出口头/文书保证,第二步才是满足立法规定的格式要求。如果只是完成第一步就可以构成禁反言，等于根本不需要第二步，而立法规定也就毫无意义。至于1677年《Statute of Frauds》之 section 4 的格式要求的目的或背后的政策原因可见 Walker 勋爵的说法："... a clear public policy underlying a statute (for instance, the need to protect vulnerable persons dealing with moneylenders or landlords) prevents an estoppels arising... no English case in which an oral contract of guarantee has been enforced through the medium of an estoppels ..."

4. 在 Newport City Council v. Charles (2009) 1 WLR 1884 先例中，案情涉及公屋(public housing)租赁。儿子与母亲一起租住政府提供的三室的公屋。2003年1月，母亲去世，儿子知道一旦告知政府，他就必须搬去小一点的公屋，于是就没有注册他母亲死亡并一直以她的名义交租。政府直到2006年3月才发现儿子的欺瞒行为，向法院申请重新占有公屋。但当时已经超过了1985年《Housing Act》规定的时效，即政府没有在母亲去世12个月内向儿子发出通知搬出并开始诉讼程序重新占有房屋。政府声称儿子隐瞒母亲死亡的行为构成陈述性禁反言或"产权人禁反言"(proprietary estoppels)。

一审法院的法官同意重新占有的申请，理由是儿子被禁反言，不能否认12个月的时效是从2006年3月而不是母亲真正去世的时间开始计算。但这在上诉庭被推翻。上诉庭判是政府要求重新占有的申请完全是根据1985年《Housing Act》的立法，但陈述性禁反言是不能作为诉因(或宝剑)。[136] 至于产权人禁反言虽然是可以作为诉因，但因为该先例不涉及财产权，所以不适用。Law 大法官说：

"In truth the defendant's acts in this case all bear the marks of an estoppel by representation; and that is what it was. **However, as I have sought to indicate, it is settled law that such an estoppels is a shield only and cannot found a cause of action.** If that is right the housing authority cannot in my view maintain the possession claim because it is outwith the time limit, which is a constituent element of ground 16 (order for possession), and there is no legal mechanism by way of estoppels such as might avoid its operation.

---

[136] 关于这一点可见本章第3段。根据 Farrow v. Orttewell (1933) Ch 480 CA 先例，Nippon Menkwa Kabushiki Kaisha v. Dawsons Bank Ltd. (1935) 51 Lloyd's Rep. 147 (PC)先例与 TCB Ltd. v. Gray (1986) Ch 621 先例中，陈述性禁反言虽然不可以作为诉因的关键要件，但可以作为支持性要件。即诉因可以来自陈述性禁反言下假设的事实，而非真正的事实。在 Azov Shipping Co. v. Baltic Shipping Co. (1999) 2 Lloyd's Rep. 159 先例中，Colman 大法官更是认为宝剑与盾牌的说法只是为了保护约因/对价，所以只与承诺性禁反言有关。而其他类别的禁反言，包括陈述性禁反言、共识性禁反言与产权人禁反言，与约因/对价没有关系，不应该受这一说法的影响。这样看来在 Newport City Council v. Charles (2009) 1 WLR 1884 先例中，上诉庭以陈述性禁反言不能作为诉因为由拒绝政府重新占有的申请是有一定的问题。从另一个方面也可以看出，陈述性禁反言在这方面法律的不肯定。

I should say that I reach this conclusion with very consideration regret. I think it is unjust in the circumstances. It frustrates the statutory purpose of ground 16. It means that this family house cannot, at any rate for the present, be released for use by a family who need it. **I share the unease expressed by Sir Peter Gibson as to the limitations the law places on estoppels as shields only and not as swords** (see Riverside Housing Association Ltd. v. White [2006] HLR 282, para. 70); an unease shared by other members of the court. If I may say so I hope that... the legislation may find an early opportunity to alleviate the difficulty if not by altering the law of estoppels then perhaps by amending the 1985 Act."(加黑部分是笔者的强调)

Longmore 大法官也说:"... speaking for myself, that if a party cannot contract out of the statute, he can no more be estopped from relying on any rights arising out of the statute... The argument that this principle only applies where the reliance on the estoppel promotes the policy of a statute such as the Housing Act 1985 rather than frustrates it is I fear an argument that may be too uncertain a statement of law to be useful in future cases."

11.2 政府机构与越权

越权(ultra vires)在私法范畴(private sector)的说法可节录《Bowstead on Agency》(第 19 版,2010 年)一书之 8 - 033 段:"... that a company was not bound by a contract or (in some cases) other act into which by virtue of the objects clause in its memorandum it had no capacity to enter, or which it similarly had no capacity to perform. This doctrine as sometimes interpreted rather widely so as to cover situations where the activity was authorized but the move for doing of it was improper, or where the exercise of a power was in the circumstances illegal, or where delegation to particular offers was not authorized by the memorandum or articles. More recent case law, however, confined the ultra vires doctrine to strict questions of capacity - that is to say, to matters outside the actual objects clause in the company's memorandum [137]; the other matters go rather to questions of authority of an agent and notice to the third party. Nevertheless, even in a limited form it remained a trap in respect of the apparent authority of a company's agent: the activity in which he was engaged might be ultra vires in the narrower sense and hence his act simply void against the company, whatever the appearance of authority to the third party. [138] The EC First Directive on Company Law required member states to abolish this doctrine in order to ensure security of transactions between companies and those with

---

〔137〕 在近期的先例中,越权的说法只针对超出了公司章程的规定,即公司没有能力履行的情况。

〔138〕 如果公司职员的言行越权,无论他的表见授权如何明显,都不会约束公司。

whom they deal[139]...."

另可节录《Bowstead on Agency》(第19版,2010年)一书之8-036段:"**Statutory reforms: ultra vires.** Limited provisions protecting third parties dealing with companies in s.9(1) of the European Communities Act 1972, later re-enacted as s.35 of the Companies Act 1985, proved inadequate to abolish the ultra vires doctrine completely, particularly in that they failed to distinguish between issues of corporate capacity and directors' authority. Further reform in 1989 has not been carried through into the Companies Act 2006. Section 39 of the 2006 Act provides that 'the validity of an act done by a company shall not be called in question on the ground of lack of capacity by reason of anything in the company's constitution'.[140] This provision effectively removes ultra vires as a relevant factor in the company's external relations in this context, and hence from questions of apparent authority... To preclude the ultra vires doctrine being reintroduced by the back door, the 2006 Act provides that 'the power of the directors to bind the company, or authorise others to do so, is deemed to be free of any limitation under the company's constitution'..."

在公法中,也有越权的说法。不同的立法往往会规定公共机构(public authority)与其职员的权责。如果政府职员向一方(个人或公司)做出陈述,而之后被认定是错误,会否构成陈述性禁反言,令政府要履行该错误陈述,即使这意味着根据相关法律规定政府是越权?根据本章之11.1段的介绍,这种情况下是不会构成禁反言。

在本书第四章之5.4段提到并将在本章接下来的11.3段介绍的Regina [Reprotech (Pebsham) Ltd] v. East Sussex County Council (2002) UKHL 8先例中,贵族院决定总体来说,禁反言(主要是陈述性禁反言与承诺性禁反言)这个私法的说法,再不能适用在公法。针对政府做出的错误陈述(或承诺),[141]只能适用合法利益(legitimate interests)与滥用职权(abuse of powers)的说法,而这些说法近年来也有了充分地发展。正如Sullivan大法官在R (Wandsworth) v. Secretary of State for Transportation Local Government and the Region (2003) EWHC 622 (Admin)先例中所说:"...In my judgment the House of Lords could not have made it more plain that estoppel no longer has any place in planning law. The observations of Lord Hoffmann and Lord Mackay apply with equal force to a 'kind of estoppels [that] is akin to res judicata'. If a

[139] 欧盟Directive 68/151/EEC之Article 9要求成员国的立法取消越权的说法,以保护商业上的肯定性与第三人的利益。即在本章之12.2.1段提到的,法院在保护股东的利益与保护商业上的肯定性与第三人的利益的两难局面中选择了后者。

[140] 英国2006年《公司法》之section 39取消了越权的说法。

[141] 在现实中,公务员在做出对将来的承诺时往往很谨慎,但队伍庞大的公务员因为面对大众,常常要回应咨询、批准申请等,因此会做出大量对过去或现在存在的事实的陈述,而这些陈述可能之后被认定是错误。

matter is res judicata there is no need for an estoppel, if it is not there is no longer any scope for estoppels which are akin to res judicata."

但禁反言的说法比合法利益更广泛适用去保护被陈述方,因为后者必须考虑公共利益(public interests),可能会对依赖政府的错误陈述而蒙受重大损害的被陈述方十分苛刻。因此在 Eastbourne Borough Council v. James Foster (2001) LGR 529 先例中,又令改变地位(change of position)[142] 的说法回归。但改变地位也不属于禁反言的说法。

《The Law of Waiver, Variation, and Estoppel》(第3版,2012年)一书之9.134段说:"9.134 An important example of the principle that estoppels may not be used to nullify the effect of a statute concerns public authorities. Estoppel by representation cannot be used where its effect would be to force a public authority to do that which is beyond its powers.[143] No authority can be estopped from denying that which it could not lawfully have agreed. An ultra vires agreement cannot become ultra vires by estoppels, lapse of time, acquiescence or delay[144]: if an authority had no power to enter a particular agreement or give an undertaking, it cannot give itself the power through estoppel.[145] Estoppel cannot be raised to prevent the exercise of a statutory discretion or excuse the failure to perform a statutory duty.[146] This strict approach may lead to some harsh results[147], where members of the public have relied to their detriment on ultra vires representations. It has been held, however, that the duty of an authority to obey the law and stay within the limits of its statutory powers is more important than any duty not to cause injury by inadvertent representations.[148] The damage to the general public, which would result from permitting an authority to go beyond the powers granted by Parliament, is deemed to outweigh the damage to individual representees.[149]"

---

[142] 见本章第4段介绍的 Lipkin Gorman v. Karpnale Ltd. (1991) 2 AC 548 HL 先例。

[143] 陈述性禁反言不能被用来迫使政府做越权的事情:Islington Vestry v. Hornsey UDC (1900) 1 Ch 695 CA 先例。

[144] 见 York Corpn v. Henry Lethal & Sons (1924) 1 Ch 557 先例。

[145] 见 Minister of Agriculture Fisheries and Food v. Matthews (1950) 1 KB 148 先例。

[146] 见 Customs & Excise Commissioners v. Hebson Ltd. (1953) 2 Lloyd's Rep. 382; Western Fish Products v. Penwith DC (1981) 2 All ER 204 CA; Graham v. Secretary of State for the Environment and Anor (1993) JPL 353 等先例。

[147] 见 Rowland v. Environment Agency (2003) EWCA Civ 1885 先例。

[148] 见 Maritime Electric Co. Ltd. v. General Dairies Ltd. (1937) AC 610 PC Canada 先例。

[149] 见 Western Fish Products v. Penwith DC (1981) 2 All ER 204 CA 先例。在该先例中,政府发展局的职员做出陈述是预定发展计划被包括在设施的现有用途,不需要额外审批。Megaw 大法官说如果政府被职员的陈述约束,就要在不考虑公众对发展计划反对的情况下做出决定。另外,他认为政府应该被允许与受到鼓励自由地向公众做出建议,而不用担心所有疏忽的陈述都会构成禁反言。

11.3 贵族院的 Regina [Reprotech (Pebsham) Ltd] v. East Sussex County Council 先例

《The Law of Waiver, Variation, and Estoppel》(第3版,2012年)一书之9.135至9.137段针对贵族院的 Regina [Reprotech (Pebsham) Ltd] v. East Sussex County Council (2002) UKHL 8 先例介绍说:

"The House of Lords case of R v. East Sussex CC, ex p Reprotech (Pebsham) Ltd. (2002) UKHL 8 appears to have put an end to the previously widespread use of estoppels against public authorities exercising statutory powers. Dealing with a claim that a local authority was estopped by its representation that no planning permission was required, Lord Hoffmann expressed the opinion that '**it is unhelpful to introduce private law concepts of estoppels into planning law... public law has already absorbed whatever is useful from the moral values which underlie the private law concept of estoppel and the time has come for it to stand upon its own two feet**'. In Flanagan v. South Bucks DC (2002) EWCA Civ 690, the Court of Appeal was concerned with a first instance decision that a local authority was estopped from enforcing certain planning notices that purported to restrict the use of land. Keene LJ considered the effect of Reprotech and the relationship between estoppel and the public law concepts of legitimate expectation and abuse of power: 'it is clear that the House saw the earlier cases where estoppel had been applied in planning law as an attempt to achieve justice at a time when the concepts of legitimate expectation and abuse of power had scarcely made their appearance in public law. Now that those concepts are recognized, there is no longer a place for the private law doctrine of estoppel in public law or for the attendant problems which it brings with it.'

In case where estoppel would have arisen but for the ultra vires principle, the authority may have breached a public law duty such as the duty to act fairly or the duty not to undermine legitimate expectation. As suggested by Lord Hoffmann in Reprotech, some claims which would previously have succeeded by virtue of an estoppel may now be brought in reliance on public law principles. However, it appears that the scope of doctrine of legitimate expectation in public law is somewhat narrower than the scope of estoppel by representation as it operates in private law cases. Remedies against public authorities must take into account the interests of the general public.[150] In R (Wandsworth) v. Secretary of State for Transportation Local Government and the Region

---

[150] 见 Regina [Reprotech (Pebsham) Ltd] v. East Sussex County Council (2002) UKHL 8 先例(第34段);Association of British Civilian Internees Far East Region v. Secretary of State for Defence (2002) EWHC 2119 (Admin) 先例(第37段)。

(2003) EWHC 622 (Admin), Sullivan J rejected the argument that a local authority could be estopped from pursing enforcement action, having wrongly approved the installation of a telecommunications mast, and then went on to consider: 'the proposition that the same decision could be reached by applying public law principles of legitimate expectation, I accept it is entirely possible that the same decision might be reached. But it is plain... that the circumstances in which it will be appropriate to find a legitimate expectation in the planning field are limited, and the decision taker is engaged in a task that is very different from an attempt to decide whether or not there is an estoppel in private law.'

The potential hardship created by Reprotech may, however, be mitigated by the availability of a change of position defence to a local authority's claim. For example, the Court of Appeal has held that a local authority employee, having received redundancy payments in excess of powers, was not to be obliged to repay moneys spent in reliance upon a series of payments received prior to discovery of ultra vires.[151]"(加黑部分是笔者的强调)

12. 适用陈述性禁反言的典型例子

12.1 提单上的陈述

作为物权凭证的装船提单,通过背书(endorsement)与交出(delivery)给无辜第三人(往往作为质押人的银行与支付货款的买方/收货人)后,在对提单上的陈述有争议时,会由于此时通常满足了英国法下构成陈述性禁反言的要件,导致船东/承运人被禁反言,不得改变或否定提单上对货物与其他内容(如运费预付)的陈述。

对于船东/承运人来说,船长或船东/承运人对记载了有关货物内容的大副收据与/或提单的签字确认可以被视为做出了陈述。如提单中对装港、运费预付(在 CIF/CFR 买卖中通常需要有的陈述)、货物的装船日期、唛头/标记、数量/重量、表面状况等事实内容的描述或记载。而在提单正面填写或记载的卸港,虽然货方也为此承诺而付出了作为对价的运费,但只是提单作为海上运输合约的合约承诺(contractual promise)之一。这与提单记载的装港不同,并非已经发生的事实,因此并不属于陈述

---

[151] 见 Eastbourne Borough Council v. James Foster (2001) LGR 529 先例。在该先例中,案情涉及政府多付了钱给雇员(公务员),之后向他追回,但这时雇员已经将这笔钱用了一部分。在该先例中,上诉庭用的是"改变地位导致禁反言"(estoppel by change of position),这就令人产生困惑与容易混淆,因为改变地位不属于禁反言,而禁反言也不再适用在公法。上诉庭判是要依赖这个改变地位的救济的前提条件是雇员自己清白(with clean hands)。

性禁反言的范畴。如果船东/承运人违反承诺,如没有前往提单记载的卸港,货方(收货人)可以有违约上的救济,包括索赔金钱赔偿。如果卸港的承诺与禁反言有关系,也只可能是构成"承诺性禁反言"(promissory estoppel),但由于这是有效的合约承诺,没有这个必要。

另是由于陈述必须是清楚无误与不含糊,如果提单上写明了有"否定性条文"(disclaimer),船东/承运人明确指出自己对确切装载了多少货物数量或重量并不清楚(weigh quantity quality unknown 或 said to contain),英国法下就很难说会构成禁反言了。[152]

而提单的错误陈述,往往会被以提单作为质押(pledge)的银行或买方/收货人依赖。做出了清楚无误陈述的船东/承运人显然清楚知道在国际外贸与航运中,提单这份重要的付运文件会通过背书与交出在不同的人士之间流转,而且合法持有提单的人士往往会依赖这份提单上的对货物与其他内容的陈述而相应改变地位。如银行在收到一份与信用证要求一致的提单时,会做出付款。也可见 Compania Naviera Vasconzada v. Churchill & Sim (1906) 1 KB 237 先例中 Channell 大法官所说:"Bills of lading are transferable, and the object of the shipper in asking for the insertion of the statement that the goods are in good condition at the time of shipment is clearly rather to have evidence to offer to his transferee than for his own direct benefit. The advantage of what is known as a clean bill of lading is obvious, and I think it would be idle for a master of a ship to say that he did not contemplate a purchaser of the goods acting on the statement that the goods were shipped in good condition."

也可见 Brandit v. Liverpool Brazil & River Plate Steam Navigation Co. Ltd. (1924) 1 KB 575 先例中,上诉庭的 Atkin 大法官说:"This is a representation which, as the learned judge says, the shipowner must contemplate will be made and repeated to and acted upon by every successive holder of the bill of lading, and each indorsee who takes delivery under the bill of lading."

另 Scrutton 大法官也说:"The result was that the shipowner put into circulation a document which they knew might be passed on to other persons for value, and on the statements in which other persons might act, which contained the untrue and material statement that the goods had been shipped 'in apparent good order and condition'."

在已有悠久的历史与已经成熟的国际货物买卖做法中,提单持有人也就是被陈述方有对提单错误陈述的依赖,并会因此蒙受损害是简单易明的道理。在提单下,如作为被陈述方的银行根据提单陈述是否与信用证要求一致而决定结汇或拒单,CIF/CFR 买方根据提单陈述决定是否支付货款或拒单等。有关国际货物买卖与贸易融资中提单持有人会依赖提单的陈述已经有许多先例重复强调,如 Compania Naviera

---

[152] 关于否定性条文的问题,笔者的《提单与其他付运单证》(2016 年)一书第六章之§6 段有详细介绍。

Vasconzada v. Churchill & Sim 先例与 Brandit v. Liverpool Brazil & River Plate Steam Navigation Co. Ltd 先例等。

这也可以节录一些有关提单权威书籍，首先是《Voyage Charters》(第 4 版，2014 年)一书之 18.12－18.13 段：

"The contents of a bill of lading may also become conclusive as against the carrier as a result of an estoppel, which will arise when the holder of the bill of lading has relied to his detriment upon the statement in the bill of lading, and it would be inequitable to allow the carrier to resile from the statement. In the case of a person who (or whose bank) has given value for the bill of lading these requirements will normally be assumed to be satisfied, at any rate where the statement in question relates to quantity, or apparent good order and condition.[153]

The bill of lading holder will not be entitled to take advantage of an estoppel if he knew that the statement was untrue, but the mere fact that he had some grounds for suspecting its truth is immaterial; there must be 'evidence of conclusive importance'.[154]"

另是在 Aikens 大法官等的《Bills of Lading》(第 2 版，2015 年)一书之 4.42 段，说："Theoretically, at least, in order to estop the carrier, the transferee must not only prove the unambiguous representation by the carrier, but also that he relied upon it to his detriment. This requirement has not, however, been applied in its full rigour by the courts. Uncontroversially, where the transferee would have had a right to reject the documents had they been accurate, and he has accepted them, and paid for the documents in full or in part,[155] he has acted to his detriment, being deprived for his right of rejection.[156] Even where the transferee has a right to the return of the money paid, the fact of payment is itself sufficient detriment.[157] Given the importance of bills of lading remaining tradable documents, Scrutton L. J. said that merely taking up the bill of lading without objection raises a presumption of sufficient detrimental reliance.[158] This presumption is, however, rebuttable; once it is established the burden of proving that the transferee

---

〔153〕 在提单被转让给第三人(如银行等人士)后，也会因禁反言，船东/承运人不得再否定提单内容中的陈述(如货物数量、表面状况等)。

〔154〕 但如果提单持有人获得提单转让时，明知提单陈述错误或不真实，则不得以禁反言对抗船东/承运人。但仅仅是有理由怀疑陈述错误或不真实并不足够，而必须是证据确凿的情况：见 The "Johnstown" (1928) 32 Lloyd's Rep. 218 先例。

〔155〕 见 Martineaus Ltd. v. Royal Mail Steam Packet Co. Ltd. (1912) 106 LT 638 先例。

〔156〕 见 Dent v. Glen Line (1940) 45 Com Cas 244；Amis Swain & Co. v. Nippon Yusen Kabushki Kaisha (1919) 1 Lloyd's Rep. 51 等先例。

〔157〕 见 Compania Naviera Vasconzada v. Churchill & Sim (1906) 1 KB 237 先例。

〔158〕 见 Silver v. Ocean SS Co. Ltd. (1930) 1 KB 416；The "Saga Explorer" (2013) 1 Lloyd's Rep. 401 等先例。

did not rely upon the representation falls upon the carrier, who can, for example, rebut the presumption of reliance by showing that the transferee was contractually bound to take up the bill. This, however, will only raise a further presumption that in taking it up the transferee suffered no detriment,[159] and the burden of showing detriment then passes back to the transferee who may then show that, on the balance of probabilities, he would, had the bill been accurate, have broken his contract and rejected it.[160] Consequently, it will be very difficult for a carrier to rebut the presumption that the transferee did rely on the bill to his detriment."

12.1.1 不合理的依赖

上述节录的 Aikens 大法官等的《Bills of Lading》(第 2 版,2015 年)一书的内容中介绍了,在船东/承运人对禁反言的抗拒中,最常用的辩解是提单持有人没有依赖(reliance)该错误陈述或依赖是不合理(unreasonable)的,与/或提单持有人并没有因为依赖而蒙受损害(detriment)。这方面也有少数的先例,如 Simmonds v. Rose (1893) 10 TLR 125 先例中,提单上记载了装载的货物有多少"袋"(bag)与有多少"总重量"(total weight)。虽然并没有否定性条文,Wills 大法官判定此先例中的船东/承运人没有任何办法检查货物的重量,提单持有人也知道这一点,因此不应该依赖[161]提单上记载的货物重量,而只有可以点算的袋数是船东/承运人被禁反言。显然这种例子很少,也不会与现实中海上货物运输很有关系。付运一台几百吨重的设备/机械,即使提单上记载了这个重量,也应可以争辩说提单持有人应该合理知道船东/承运人无法检查重量,货物重量的数据肯定是由发货人提供。但即使机器的重量有误差,也不可能是货损货差,因此对这记载船东/承运人是否被禁反言实际意义不大。

另一个例子也可见 Canada and Dominion Sugar Co. Ltd. v. Canadian National (West Indies) Steam Ships Ltd. (1946) 80 Lloyd's Rep. 13 (PC)先例。该先例是以 CIF 买卖一票袋装食糖,在装港货物被寄存在仓库中待装已经有一段时间(因此有损坏),装港装载的理货单也记录了是"many bags stained, torn and resewn",但付运后仍然签发了一份写有"received in apparent good order and condition"的提单,同时加上印章说"Signed under guarantee to produce ship's clean receipt"。船舶的航行途中也显示天气良好,没有遇到会造成货损货差的事故。在加拿大蒙特利尔港卸货时发现有货损,这就涉及船东是否可以通过证据(如装载货物的理货单)证明货物装船时已经损坏,面对无辜收货人时不会因签发了有上述写法提单而被禁反言。主要争议就是上述写法的提单是否为清洁提单,另一方面的争议是收货人是否可以合理依赖这些

[159] 见 The "Skarp" (1935) P 134 先例。

[160] 见 Cremer v. General Carriers SA (1974) 1 WLR 331 等先例。

[161] 有关合理依赖有关陈述可看本章之 8.1 段。

陈述。上诉到英国上议院,最后判不构成禁反言,Wright 勋爵说:“Their Lordships in so deciding are not in any way weakening the rule that a shipowner who issues a clean bill of lading is bound by the statement in it that the goods are shipped in good or in apparent good order and condition: **if the statement turns out to be untrue the shipowner is estopped from alleging its falsity as against a purchaser who relies on the statement at its face value and acts upon it to his detriment. This is a rule which may be applied any day in the case of c. i. f. contracts.** To cast doubts upon it would be to weaken the whole course of dealing between business men in regard to bills of lading in their character of documents of title used in connection with overseas shipments of goods. It is true that the unqualified statement is only one step in the establishment of the estoppel. Estoppel is a complex legal notion involving a combination of several essential elements: the statement to be acted upon, action on the faith of it, resulting detriment to the actor. Estoppel is often described as a rule of evidence, as indeed it may be so described. But the whole concept is more correctly viewed as a substantive rule of law. The purchaser or other transferee must have acted upon it to his detriment, as for instance he did in this case when he took up the documents and paid for them. It is also true that he cannot be said to rely on the statement if he knew that it was false: **he must reasonably believe it to be true and therefore act upon it.** Estoppel is different from contract both in its nature and consequences. But the relationship between the parties must also be such that the imputed truth of the statement is a necessary step in the constitution of the cause of action. **But the whole case of estoppel fails if the statement is not sufficiently clear and unqualified.** That in their Lordships' judgment is the position in this case.”(加黑部分是笔者的强调)

以上 Wright 勋爵所说已经将提单中的陈述性禁反言问题总结得非常清楚。此先例中的情况被判是没有构成禁反言对抗船东。毕竟涉及提单上的陈述并非是清楚无误、不模糊,加上的印章中的措辞/文字显示了船东是在有保证的前提下[162]才签发了清洁提单。同时这也导致法院判收货人在合理的情况下不应该依赖这陈述。

但在本章之 12.1.2.1 段会介绍的 The “Johnstown”(1928) 32 Lloyd's Rep. 218 先例中,买方同时有一份清洁提单与一份内容相矛盾的船长书面抗议,法院判是买方对清洁提单的依赖合理。可见根据不同先例的事实会有不同的判决,不能一概而论。笔者觉得近期的先例会更加保护无辜收货人的利益,除非是案情显示依赖有关的提单陈述极不合理,否则都不会判收货人不应该/不合理依赖。

---

〔162〕 在租约中,承租人会要求船东保证会签发清洁提单,否则不会租该船。这样,船东在后来签发的提单上加上的印章上的措辞/文字等于向依赖的提单持有人说明,此清洁提单是因为有了保证不得不签。

12.1.2 船东/承运人在提单持有人依赖陈述前通知提单陈述错误

船东/承运人一旦发觉承租人(或代理人)背后代船长签发的一套提单上的陈述与事实不符,一般的做法是尽快联系船东互保协会,在互保协会的帮助下通知所有会受到提单错误陈述影响的有关人士。如果提单持有人及时收到这个通知,之后看来就不能再依赖提单上的记载了,船东/承运人也就不会对提单上的错误陈述被禁反言了。这可节录 Aikens 大法官等的《Bills of Lading》(第 2 版,2015 年)一书之 4.44 段:"Finally, even where the bill makes an unambiguous representation, if the transferee receives information from another source that contradicts the bill, it might be argued that he cannot be said to have reasonably relied upon the statement in the bill..."

向提单持有人发出的通知必须非常及时,以及清楚与肯定指出提单上陈述的问题,使提单持有人可以绝对明确提单陈述错误而不能依赖。而一般能够通知到的可能是买方,在记名提单(named 或 straight B/L)中,买方会被记载为收货人肯定没有问题。而在指示提单(order B/L)中,也往往是在通知人(notify party)一栏填上买方(或买方的代理人或与买方有密切关系的人士)的名字。但通知有关银行对船东/承运人而言就比较困难,毕竟难以知道买卖合约下信用证(如果这是支付货款的办法)的细节,真正支付货款给卖方的银行可以是不知名的议付(negotiation)、保兑(confirming)或是贴现(discount)银行。但即使船东/承运人及其互保协会能够及时通知有关人士,这是否可以阻止提单持有人的依赖还有两方面的问题。

12.1.2.1 提单持有人必须绝对明确提单陈述错误

在 The "Johnstown" (1928) 32 Lloyd's Rep. 218 先例中,运输的是木材,装载作业中,船长曾书面抗议装载的木材受污染与有污泥,并且部分掉下水被冲走。但之后船长仍然签发了清洁提单。此先例中的支付是通过托收(collection)进行,而事实上在托收时,买方手中同时有一份清洁提单与一份内容相矛盾的船长书面抗议。所以船东争辩说,买方托收时已知真相,所以并没有真正依赖提单上的错误陈述或依赖是不合理,不得指称船东被禁反言。

要求提单持有人(买方)能绝对明确提单陈述错误也完全合理公平,因为如果买方只是通过其他渠道知道或怀疑提单有错误的陈述,就不能再依赖陈述性禁反言以对抗船东/承运人,这会对买方不公平。毕竟如果要求买方依赖可能是错误的陈述采取行动,这行动就可能是要终止合约(如买卖合约),拒绝支付货款(如 The "Johnstown"先例中拒绝在托收时支付货款)或是设法(甚至包括向法院申请止付禁令)在信用证下拒绝支付货款,这都会带来非常严重的后果,也会要衡量孰轻孰重的问题。而且在针对提单中的错误陈述是否被依赖时要有局限,如果动辄就可以质疑收货人/提单持有人已经通过其他渠道知悉货物装船的准确情况,就会影响商业社会对提单这份重要付运单证与物权凭证的信心。所以 Wright 大法官在此先例中警告说:"I do not say that there may not be cases where an indorsee for value of a bill of lading may be estopped from saying that he took the bill of lading according to its apparent tenor and its face value; there may be such cases. There may be cases where the independent knowledge possessed by the indorsee, to whom the bill of lading is presented, is **of such a character as to make it absolutely clear to him that the bill of lading statement is not accurate**, but such cases, in my judgment, must be very rare indeed. In my judgment, in business the persons to whom the bills of lading are tendered to implement a contract like the present ought to be entitled as against the shipowner to take the bill of lading at its face value unless, as I have said, the contrary evidence and the contrary circumstances are of absolutely conclusive and overwhelming importance. **Any other view would, I think, tend to diminish the value of bills of lading in commerce and would also tend to promote carelessness, if not fraud, on the part of a ship's master in a foreign port when duly clausing them, if the statement of condition and quality is not precisely accurate...**"(加黑部分是笔者的强调)

Wright 大法官接下来指出每个案件中都要严格分析后,才能下结论说提单持有人没有真正或不合理依赖提单上的陈述:

" It is said that there could be no estoppel where the truth of the matter was known to both parties, and that a false representation made to a person who knew it to be false was not capable of being relied upon as constituting an estoppel.

As to the soundness of that as a general principle there can, of course, be no question, but it is necessary in my judgment to consider very carefully the precise circumstances of the case in order to see whether there was such information before the bill of lading holder in a case like the present as to debar him from acting upon the statement in the bill of lading."

而回到 The "Johnstown"先例中,Wright 大法官说针对这两份都是出自船长、但内容相异的文件来说,即使船长的抗议书写得明明白白,但相对来说提单的地位要高得多,所以半信半疑的货方(收货人)完全可以依赖提单上对货物表面状况的描述(清洁提单):"In the present case I do not think the information before(买方/收货人) was of such a character as to justify them in rejecting the bills of lading as not representing the true facts. I assume that the date I to take into account for this purpose is Aug. 17, 1927, that is, the date of the acceptance of the bills of exchange. That, of course, beyond question was an act done to their prejudice in relying on the terms of the bills of lading. They had in their possession the clean bills of lading before them; on the other hand, they had the protests... taking the master's protest their position was that they had on the one side a bill of lading signed by the master, an authoritative document under his signature, and on the other hand they had his protest. Even if the protest is treated as of equal value to the bill of lading, and it cannot be regarded as of superior value, they had in their hands two documents each from the master contradicting each other. With that contradiction it seems to me they would be entitled to treat the statement in the bill of lading as one on which they were justified and bound to act, even if there were no ambiguity in the protest."

不妨节录 Aikens 大法官等的《Bills of Lading》(第 2 版,2015 年)一书之 4.44 段对此先例的说法:"... Fortunately, the courts have taken an extremely pragmatic line, holding that the contrary evidence must make the falsity of the statement in the bill 'absolutely clear to him' and must be of 'absolutely conclusive and overwhelming importance'."

这样,要指称收货人/提单持有人应该知道真相,故此没有真正依赖提单内容与错误陈述或依赖是不合理,可能绝不容易。毕竟什么文件地位会比一份清洁提单高呢?岂非买方/收货人通过船长在装港抗议或检验报告与提单陈述不符,或代理人告知了货物装载有不妥或短装,都可以不予理睬(特别是在货物市场价格高涨时),而继续依赖一份清洁提单?至于对一些可能有争议性的陈述(如货物的重量或表面状况)来说,本来在发货人与船东/承运人之间就有争议,看来买方/收货人即使知道,也很难说是绝对明确知道提单的有关陈述错误。只有少数可以使得买方/收货人绝对明确提单陈述错误的情况,如提单记载的货物装船日期不正确,特别是船东发出的通知还加上了其他证明,如航海日志的复印件显示了货物在不同的日期装船,收货人此时不予理睬并继续依赖倒签的提单就有危险。

12.1.2.2 提单持有人完全可以不依赖提单错误陈述的情况

第二个方面的问题可见 Aikens 大法官等的《Bills of Lading》(第 2 版,2015 年)一书之 4.42 段:"This presumption is, however, rebuttable; once it is established the burden of proving that the transferee did not rely upon the representation falls upon the carrier, who can, for example, rebut the presumption of reliance by showing that the transferee was contractually bound to take up the bill."

也就是说,提单持有人知道提单陈述错误也非要接受提单不可。这种情况经常出现在信用证下支付货款时。因为只要付运单证与信用证下的要求相符合,即使买方已经收到船东通知提单陈述错误,买方作为开证人仍必须向银行赎单并支付货款,毕竟信用证合并的 UCP 600 清楚说明银行对提单的错误(即使是虚假)没有责任。

但如果是付运单证还存在其他不符点(如缺少一份装港的调查报告),此时买方本可以合法拒绝接受这一套付运单证。收到通知获悉提单陈述错误的买方,可能会通知开证银行放弃不符点并仍然接受这套提单。买方这样做的原因可能很多,如货物的市场价格不断上涨,或买方急需货物,提单陈述中的"轻微"错误不会严重影响买方的使用。此时,提单持有人(买方)有没有依赖提单中错误陈述并蒙受损害呢?这很有争议性,英国法院在目前的心态还是会尽量宽松对待提单持有人,以保护商业社会对提单这份文件的信心。

最后不妨节录 Aikens 大法官等的《Bills of Lading》(第 2 版,2015 年)一书之

4.45段作为总结："Despite paying lip service to the requirement that the transferee show reliance, it is very seldom shown to be absent. The transferee who takes up a bill without protest can surely be said to have relied upon the accuracy of the bill. To inquire into whether or not he would have been able and willing to reject the bill under his contract of purchase ignores the fact that, even if he would not have been able to reject the document had the details of the goods been accurately stated and even if he would not have breached his contract, he is likely still to have been disadvantaged by the inaccuracies in the bill if only by being deprived of his best source of evidence of a non – conforming shipment against his seller. It is, therefore, right to be wary about an over – formalistic application of the requirement of reliance."

12.1.3 面对发货人时，船东/承运人是否会被禁反言提单中的错误陈述

禁反言的说法通常只适用在无辜提单持有人，通常为买方，不适用在作为发货人的卖方。因为提单陈述错误，即使发货人是无辜的，也不会因为依赖而改变地位并蒙受损害。但会有罕见的情况，发货人也需要依赖禁反言。如在 Heskell v. Continental Express Ltd. (1950) 1 All ER 1033 先例中，卖方以 CIF 方式出售一票捆装的全棉织物(poplin)，寄存在仓库并指示仓库保管人之后，将货物送去码头以装载上船。仓库保管人疏忽并未将货物送出，导致货物一直滞留在仓库中。但承运人的代理人［实际上是装载代理人(loading broker)］也同时有疏忽，错误地签发了一套货物装船提单给卖方。在结汇后才发现船舶上根本没有装载这票货物，导致卖方在买卖合约下违约与要向买方赔偿损失。卖方之后向承运人(船舶的承租人)索赔这笔损失(没有针对仓库保管人可能是因为仓库保管人没有资产等原因)，诉因就是发货人依赖了提单的错误陈述。但在该先例中 Devlin 大法官判发货人不能同时没有交出货物装船但又依赖禁反言："A man cannot in one breath invoke both the truth and an estoppels... He cannot... mix fact and fiction in the proportions which suit him best."

《Carver on Bills of Lading》(第 3 版，2011 年)一书之 2 – 011 段对此先例进一步解释说："... however, questionable since ‘the reason why [a contract of carriage] was not made was because of a fault or breakdown on the plaintiff's side’: the goods were not shipped because they were not delivered to the ship or to the loading broker by the warehouseman, who were the prospective shipper's agents.[163] In such circumstances, a court would be justifiably reluctant to hold the carrier liable to the shipper, whether on the basis of an estoppels or otherwise.[164] But there would probably be no such reluctance if the fact of non – shipment had been due to the fault of the carrier or of his agent: e. g.

---

〔163〕 此先例中海上运输合约(提单合约)并未真正订立的原因，是作为发货人的代理人的仓库保管人由于疏忽/过错没有将货物交出付运，没有交出给承运人的装载代理人。

〔164〕 这种情况下看来法院不会愿意让发货人依赖陈述性禁反言，毕竟禁反言是衡平法救济。

if the goods had been delivered by the shipper's forwarding agent to the loading broker and the latter had failed to get them on board the ship but had nevertheless issued a bill of lading (on behalf of the carrier) stating that the goods had been shipped.[165] Even in such a case, however, a claim by the shipper based on estoppels would face the difficulty that, as a general rule, estoppels does not give rise to a cause of action;[166] this is certainly true of the type of estoppels whith which we are here concerned, i. e. of estoppels by representation. Where the cause of action on which the putative shipper relies is the contract of carriage, and where the fact of shipment is necessary to establish the contract, then it would appear that the shipper who seeks to invoke the estoppels (or fiction of shipment) is attempting to do so in order to give rise to his cause of action. His claim based on estoppels would therefore succeed only if the contract could be established aliunde: e. g. by evidence of an antecedent contract between himself and the carrier.[167]"

12.2 表见授权

12.2.1 代理在现代商业与日常生活中的重要性

任何人士多了解一些有关代理的法律都会有帮助,因为生活中常常涉及代理人的问题。这既是为了方便、现实的需要,也能更有效地使用时间与资源。对国际业务而言,了解国际上适用的关于代理的法律更加重要。如航运/外贸业务因为其国际性与复杂性,对船东/承运人或货方等而言,业务上有很多实际执行必须通过代理人完成。往往一个海上运输合约(租约或提单)的订立与履行会涉及多达几十个不同的代理人,如租船合约就涉及租船经纪人、船舶管理人、每一个不同港口的港口代理人、保险经纪人、船长船员等。提单(特别是租约提单)与租船业务紧密联系,提单的签发也通常是通过船长或装港代理人签发,而委托人是谁,可能明确,但也经常没有在提单中明确。多式联运提单则可能会有货代作为代理人,或在部分运输方式中作为承运人而其他部分作为代理人的各种做法[货代在多式联运中的身份可见笔者《提单与其他付运单证》(2016 年)第二章之 3.5.2.3 段]。

同样为了方便、现实的需要,以及有效地使用时间与资源,船东/承租人在海上运输合约的履行也涉及了几十个不同的承包商(contractor),如装卸港码头公司、货物装卸作业公司、拖轮船东、中流作业公司、货代、二船东、分承租人等。必须一提的是船东/承运人的雇员(employee)或仆人(servant),其中最重要的是船长,也是履行海

〔165〕 但如果情况稍作变化,如仓库保管人没有任何疏忽/过错,确实将货物送去码头并交给了装载代理人,只是装载代理人的疏忽/过错导致货物未被装船,却代表承运人签发了装船提单。此时法院就有可能判陈述性禁反言适用。

〔166〕 但无论如何,正如本章第 3 段提到,一般情况下大部分禁反言都不能作为单独的诉因要求索赔损失,这包括此先例中的陈述性禁反言。

〔167〕 但如果发货人是以其他的诉因起诉,如以海上运输合约(早已订立的租约或是订舱单等)起诉,禁反言就很重要。而正如本章第 3 段中提到的,此时是可以依赖禁反言的说法/原则。

上运输合约必须要的一环。现今的船东再也不可能像数百年前一样亲力亲为履行海上运输的责任。这些不同的代理人都是为了方便、现实的需要，帮助船东/承运人履行运输合约的承诺。

对代理人的授权通常可以分为"实际授权"（actual authority）与"表见授权"（ostensible/apparent authority）两种。在著名的 Freemen & Lockyer v. Buckhurst Park Properties（Mangal）Ltd.（1964）2 QB 480 先例中，案情涉及发展商 K 先生与另一位 H 先生共同成立一家公司去收购与转售一个地产项目，K 先生自己找了承建商，为地产项目做了一些工作，并同意费用从出售地产项目所获款项中支付。期间这家公司没有根据公司章程委任董事总经理，所以 K 先生作为新公司的董事之一是否有实际或表见授权做出承诺并约束这家公司向承建商支付费用就有了争议。Diplock 大法官针对实际授权和表见授权做出明确与权威的解释说："An 'actual' authority is a legal relationship between principal and agent created by a consensual agreement to which they alone are parties. Its scope is to be ascertained by applying ordinary principles of construction of contracts, including any proper implications from the express words used, the usages of the trade, or the course of business between the parties. To this agreement the contractor is a stranger: he may be totally ignorant of the existence of any authority on the part of the agent. Nevertheless, if the agent does enter into a contract pursuant to the 'actual' authority, it does create contractual rights and liabilities between the principal and the contractor...[168] An 'apparent' or 'ostensible' authority, on the other hand, is a legal relationship between the principal and the contractor created by a representation, made by the principal to the contractor, intended to be and in fact acted upon by the contractor, that the agent has authority to enter on behalf of the principal into a contract of a kind within the scope of the 'apparent' authority, so as to render the principal liable to perform any obligations imposed upon him by such contract. To the relationship so created the agent is a stranger. He need not be (although he generally is) aware of the existence of the representation but he must not purport to make the agreement as principal himself. The representation, when acted upon by the contractor by entering into a contract with the agent, operates as an estoppel, preventing the principal from asserting that he is not bound by the contract. It is irrelevant whether the agent had actual authority to

---

〔168〕 实际授权是根据委托人（公司）与代理人（K 先生）的协议产生的法律关系。实际授权的范围由一般的合约解释的规则确定，包括双方协议中的明示条文与必要的默示条文、贸易习惯、双方曾经的交往等。从这个合约来看，与第三人（承建商）无关，他甚至可能完全不知道委托人与代理人之间有代理关系的存在或授权范围。无论如何，如果代理人在实际授权下订立合约，委托人与第三人之间就存在合约权利与义务。

enter into the contract.[169]"

在大部分争议中涉及的都是表见授权，而涉及实际授权的情况比较少。表见授权的说法来自陈述性禁反言，是十分困难与富争议性，每个争议都会涉及不同的案情。正如在 First Energy v. HIB (1993) 2 Lloyd's Rep. 194 先例中，Nourse 大法官所说："A question of ostensible authority is primarily one of fact. Did the principal hold out the agent as having the authority to make the representation ort do the act on which the other relies?"

一般来说，第三人不关心究竟代理人的授权是实际授权或是表见授权。在很多案件中，他也不会知道委托人与代理人之间授权书的内容。只有当产生争议，如委托人否认代理人订立的合约的有效性时，第三人才需要在文书请求中指称代理人有委托人的实际授权与/或有表见授权：The "Suwalki" (1989) 1 Lloyd's Rep. 511 先例。如果涉及法院的诉讼，第三人也会把代理人作为第二被告，如果代理人有委托人的实际授权与/或表见授权的诉求都不成功，就诉代理人缺乏授权（want of warrant of authority）而要承担严格责任并赔偿损失。

涉及表见授权，法院会面对两难的局面，正如 Steyn 在 First Energy v. HIB 先例所说："... a tension between two conflicting principles. The first is that the shareholders of a company should be protected against hasty and ill considered transactions entered into by the company. The second is that third parties who deal with companies in good faith ought to be protected."

但看来为了商业上的肯定性与保护无辜第三人，[170]法院更倾向于认为如果委托人（公司法人或自然人）因为疏忽违反了小心谨慎的责任，帮助或没有采取合理行动防止第三人被误导以为代理人有授权代表委托人订立合约或做出陈述的情况发生，委托人就会被禁反言，不能否认代理人的授权，即使事实上所谓的代理人没有实际授权。

12.2.2　实际授权

"实际授权"（actual authority）或"真正授权"（real authority）可以分为两种，"明示授权"（express authority）与"默示授权"（implied authority）。一般实际授权可以通过文书或口头。但与其他合约关系一样，通过文书达成的代理合约会有更明确的授

---

〔169〕 另一方面，表见授权则是委托人与第三人之间，由于委托人对第三人通过言行做出的代理人有权以委托人的名义订立合约的陈述而产生的法律关系。委托人在做出陈述时希望第三人依赖，而该陈述也确实被第三人依赖。这样，委托人就需要承担代理人在表见授权下订立的合约责任。在表见授权的法律关系中，代理人是无关人士。他无须知道委托人有这样的陈述（虽然一般他是知道），但他必须并非想自己与第三人订立合约。在与代理人订立合约时被第三人依赖的陈述，构成了陈述性禁反言，禁止委托人后来声称他不受合约约束，因为他没有授权代理人这样做。在表见授权下，代理人是否有实际授权订立合约是无关。

〔170〕 见 First Energy v. HIB (1993) 2 Lloyd's Rep. 194 先例中，Steyn 大法官所说。

权范围以及在有争议时可以提供更加肯定的证据。在国际业务之中,代理合约的达成通常就是委托人与代理人之间的电文往来满足了构成合约的要件,包括要约、接受、约因/对价等。商业活动中经常涉及有限公司,在重要的交易中,第三人往往会要求披露授权书(power of attorney),这是明示授权最有代表性的证据。如重大买卖或并购交易中的一方会要求对方公司的董事局通过决议,出具授权书。而如果是上市公司,更会根据公司章程要求通过股东大会的决议授权。

正如本章上一小段提到的 Freeman & Lockyer v. Buckhurst Park Properties (Mangal) Ltd. (1964) 2 QB 480 先例中 Diplock 大法官所说,如果对授权的范围有了争议,解释书面的代理合约与解释其他合约的做法基本一样。

有先例提到对一份授权书需要严格解释,毕竟这是正规的实际授权。如 Bryant, Powis and Bryant Ltd. v. La Banque Du Peuple (1893) AC 170 先例中,MacNaghten 勋爵说:"Nor was it disputed that powers of attorney are to be construed strictly — that is to say, that where an act purporting to be done under a power of attorney is challenged as being in excess of the authority conferred by the power, it is necessary to shew that on a fair construction of the whole instrument the authority in question is to be found within the four corners of the instrument, either in express terms or by necessary implication."

在《Bowstead & Reynolds on Agency》(第 20 版,2014 年)一书之 3-011 段针对授权书说:"Powers of attorney are strictly construed and are interpreted as giving only such authority as they confer expressly or by necessary implication. The following are the most important rules of construction: (1) The operative part of a deed is controlled by the recitals where there is ambiguity. (2) Where authority is given to do particular acts, followed by general words, the general words are restricted to what is necessary for the proper performance of the particular acts. (3) General words do not confer general powers, but are limited to the purpose for which the authority is given, and are construed as enlarging the special powers only when necessary for that purpose. (4) A deed must be construed so as to include all incidental powers necessary for the effective execution of the power it confers."

如果是以一般文书或口头做出的实际授权,通常可能是代理合约中的部分内容,对授权范围的解释会比较宽松,并会考虑双方以往交往与有关的行业做法。如在 Boden v. French (1851) 10 CB 886 先例中,代理人被授权以特定价格出售煤炭,该代理人成功以较高价格出售,但允许买方 2 个月后付款(煤炭买卖中的惯常做法),这被判在实际授权范围内。另在 Ireland v. Livingston (1872) LR 5 HL 395 先例中,委托人要求代理人代为购买 500 吨食糖,代理人也被告知数量上下 50 吨不重要,只要价格合理。结果代理人买了 400 吨,法院判委托人要受代理人所订立的买卖合约的约束。原因是委托人的指示或授权可以有两个不同解释,代理人是根据自己所理解的授权范围做出合理与诚实的解释。在近期的 Glencore International AG v. Metro

Trading Inc.（1 August 2001）（unreported）先例中，Moore - Bick 大法官提到了 Ireland v. Livingston 先例中，并指出大部分代理合约的授权都可以明确授权范围。即使有含糊之处，在今天通讯十分发达的情况下，代理人会有责任向委托人问清楚。

12.2.3 默示授权

默示授权也属于实际授权，所以有时被称为"默示实际授权"（implied actual authority）。与解释一般合约条文的道理一样，对合约的解释不能只看明示条文，往往需要有默示条文[不论是法律默示（implied by law）、事实默示（implied by fact）还是习惯默示（implied by custom）]以针对明示条文没有包括的问题。在普通法下很多合约的漏洞与问题可以通过这种方式做出满意与完整的解释，这方面可以看杨良宜的《合约的解释：规则与应用》一书之第七章。

代理合约下的实际授权也是同样的道理，代理人在履行时的所作所为不可能全部在代理合约中明示列明。如作为委托人的卖方授权代理人出售一批或多批货物，授权范围会明示针对出售价格或价格上下的幅度。但不可能明示出售过程中千变万化的安排，如代理人需要向买方做出承诺、如交货时间或多批货物更会有长短不一的交货时间、付款的期限等。这样，如果不允许代理人做任何不在明示授权范围内的事情，即使完全是为了委托人的利益，该代理人也无法当场做出合理与诚实的陈述或承诺。因为代理人这样做会有危险，作为委托人的卖方面对买方可能会在市场逆转时拒绝承认代理人曾做出过的承诺，进而导致代理人面对作为第三人的买方指控其缺乏授权（want of warrant of authority）。也会有危险是作为委托人的卖方指控代理人在代理合约下违反授权与诚信责任。这个问题在早期通讯不发达的时期更严重。所以在合理与习惯做法的情况下，有了默示授权填补明示授权的不足，实在有必要。

有了上述的解释，可以说默示授权主要是指代理人为了履行委托人明示授权的任务时，往往需要根据当时的需要（incidental）、一般做法（usual）、习惯做法（customary）与环境需要（circumstances of the case）同时做一些相关与辅助的事情。法律会默示这种事情也是有委托人的实际授权，即使没有任何明示。笔者可以节录一些权威的说法，首先可以介绍是 Pole v. Leask（1860）28 Beav 562 先例中，上诉庭说："An agent has implied authority to do whatever is necessary for, or ordinarily incidental to, the effective execution of his express authority in the usual way."

在更早的 Howard v. Baillie（1796）2 H Bl 618 先例中也有类似的说法："An authority of this nature necessarily includes medium powers, which are not expressed. By medium powers I mean all the means necessary to be used in order to obtain the accomplishment of the object of the principal power..."在较近期的 Hely - Hutchinson v. Brayhead Ltd.（1968）1 QB 549 先例中法院说："Implied authority is that inferred from the conduct of the parties and the circumstances of the case."另在 Targe Towing Ltd. v. Marine Blast Ltd.（2004）1 Lloyd's Rep. 721 先例中，上诉庭说："The correct test was that agreement between principal and agent might be implied in a case where one party had conducted himself towards another in such a way that it was reasonable for that other to infer from that conduct consent to the agency relationship."

关于默示授权的范围已有很多先例的明确判法。可以说在普通法下,已有一套针对不同业务的委托人与代理人之间的法律默示地位。这表示代理人了解这些法律的默示地位,加上明示的授权,就可以知道自己什么可以做、什么不可以做。

12.2.4 表见授权

"表见授权"(ostensible/apparent authority)是指委托人虽然没有对另一人(被第三人视为代理人)的授权,但委托人对第三人的陈述或行为被法律视为导致了第三人合理认为另一人有委托人的授权代为订立合约或做出陈述或承诺,第三人依赖另一人在其表见授权范围内行事的行为得以约束委托人:Inland Revenue Commissioners v. Ufitec Group (1977) 3 All ER 924;British Bank of the Middle East v. Sun Life Assurance Co. of Canada (UK) Ltd. (1983) 2 Lloyd's Rep. 9;The "Rhodian River" (1984) 1 Lloyd's Rep. 373 等先例。在 Hely – Hutchinson v. Brayhead Ltd. (1968) 1 QB 549 先例中,Denning 勋爵是这样描述:"Ostensible or apparent authority is the authority of an agent as it appears to others. It often coincides with actual authority. Thus, when the board appoint one of their number to be managing director, they invest him not only with implied authority, but also with ostensible authority to do all such things as fall within the usual scope of that office. Other people who see him acting as managing director are entitled to assume that he has the usual authority of a managing director. But sometimes ostensible authority exceeds actual authority. For instance, when the board appoint the managing director, they may expressly limit his authority by saying he is not to order goods worth more than £ 500 without the sanction of the board. In that case his actual authority is subject to the £ 500 limitation, but his ostensible authority includes all the usual authority of a managing director. The company is bound by his ostensible authority in his dealings with those who do not know of the limitation. He may himself do the 'holding – out.' Thus, if he orders goods worth £ 1,000 and signs himself 'Managing Director for and on behalf of the company,' the company is bound to the other party who does not know of the £ 500 limitation."

《Bowstead & Reynolds on Agency》(第 20 版,2014 年)一书之 8 – 013 段中说:"Where a person, by words or conduct, represents or permits it to be represented that another person has authority to act on his behalf, he is bound by the facts of that other person with respect to anyone dealing with him as an agent on the faith of any such representation, to the same extent as if such other person had the authority that he was represented to have, even though he had no such actual authority.[171]"

表见授权与默示授权其实是两回事,虽然在早期先例中并没有做出这样的区分。因为刚刚已经提到,表见授权其实是以表见代理人实际上没有委托人的实际授权为前提的。有说法是这两种授权的范围都属于"一般授权"(usual authority),即"the authority which a person normally possess in certain circumstances to act on behalf of another person, whether or not he is actually authorized so to act"。

在 First Energy v. HIB (1993) 2 Lloyd's Rep. 194 先例中,Steyn 大法官有说到一般授权的两种方式说:"... it is important to remember that the idea of usual authority is used in two senses. First, it sometimes means that the agent had implied actual authority to perform acts necessarily incidental to the performance of the agency. Secondly, it sometimes means that the principal's conduct in clothing the agent with trappings of authority was such as to induce a third party to rely on the existence of the agency."

实际授权(包括默示授权)与表见授权常常在诉讼中被作为替代争议一并提及。代理人即使没有实际授权(第三人除非已经取得一份委托人做出的授权书,否则通常不知道或不肯定授权范围,实际授权范围在委托人与代理人之间也可能时常变化),如超出了实际授权的范围,或超过了有实际授权的期限,也会有表见授权。这可见 Hambro v. Burnand & Ors (1904) 2 K. B. 10; The "Raffaella" (1985) 2 Lloyd's Rep. 36; The "Suwalki" (1989) 1 Lloyd's Rep. 511; AMB Generali Holding AG v. SEB Trygg Liv Holding (2006) 1 Lloyd's Rep. 318 等先例。

常见情况之一可能是委托人曾经向第三人做出过清楚与无可置疑的陈述(representation),表示代理人/经纪人可以代表自己,即 Steyn 大法官所说的让他穿上了有授权的服饰。这样第三人就可以依赖表见授权的说法以合约关系或错误的陈述或承诺约束委托人了。这些情况会发生在经纪人受委托人委托后,与第三人进行了一段时期的谈判。[172] 如果委托人在过程中向第三人做出了经纪人有授权的言行,更是很难否认经纪人有他的实质或表面授权。即使后来发生了经纪人无权或越权的情况,如委托人没有确认但经纪人(可能是心急赚取佣金或以为有把握事后说服委托人)已经向对方确认合约的订立,委托人也难辞其咎。这样,第三人就会依赖表见授权的

---

〔171〕 如果 A 以语言或行动做出 B 有他的授权的陈述或允许 B 被陈述为有他的授权,并且 C 依赖该陈述与他以为代理人的 B 在该陈述的授权范围内订立合约,则 A 就会受到该合约的约束,即使 B 并没有实际授权。

〔172〕 在 The "Wave" (1981) 1 Lloyd's Rep. 521 先例中,案情涉及租船合约,Mustill 大法官说:"Throughout the transaction(船东经纪人)was the chosen method of communication of negotiation on behalf of the owners(船东). There was nothing in the conduct of (船东) to lead(作为第三人的承租人) to suppose that there was any limitation on the authority of(船东经纪人) to agree the terms which he did agree. (船东经纪人) was, with the knowledge and consent of(船东) presenting himself to(承租人) as someone empowered to contract on their behalf."

说法要求委托人受约束了,毕竟向没有实际授权的经纪人索赔损失不一定行得通或值得做。

但如果从一开始纯粹是经纪人自称代表委托人(如某家著名的公司)前来谈判,而所谓的委托人也从来没有与受影响的第三人接触过,这时就不存在有表见代理的说法,因为从来没有做出过相应的陈述,自然也不会受该经纪人自说自话与之行为的约束了。英国法律不接受这种自我授权代理(self-authorizing agent)的说法,但这是十分复杂的问题,将会在本章之12.2.4.2.1.2段详细介绍。

12.2.4.1　表见授权的说法是基于陈述性禁反言的说法

表见代理的说法是来自禁反言。首先可节录《Bowstead & Reynolds on Agency》(第20版,2014年)一书之2-005段对表见授权与禁反言的关系的解释:"**Apparent authority and estoppels** There is also a way in which some of the consequences of agency can arise, under the doctrine of apparent authority. Under this, the principal may as against a third party be unable to deny that a person is or was his agent. The principal is here bound by the acts of his apparent agent: but the full relationship of principal and agent does not arise between him and such person, the legal position between them being governed by rules which start from the assumption that there is no agreement between them, at least in respect of the transaction in question. Apparent authority is therefore referred to above as a way in which a person not already an agent can bind a principal. ..."

至于先例可节录Buxtron大法官在AMB Generali Holding AG v. SEB Trygg Liv Holding (2006) 1 Lloyd's Rep. 318先例中所说,如下:"Recognition that ostensible authority operates as a form of estoppels goes back at least as far as the speech of Lord Selborne LC in Scarf v. Jardine (1882) 7 App Cas 345."

在近期的Lloyd's Bank Plc. v. Independent Insurance Co. Ltd. (2000) QB 147 CA先例中,Waller大法官说:"... the weight of authority is to the effect that the doctrine of apparent authority is based on estoppel: see Bowstead & Reynolds on Agency, 16th ed. (1996), article 73, p. 365, para. 8-009."

更准确地说,表见授权的说法来源于"陈述性禁反言"(estoppel by representation),即第三人依赖(reliance)委托人所做出的语言或行为,以为另一人有实际授权代委托人行事与订立合约,从而改变自己的法律地位(通常就是愿意订立合约并受到约束)。此时,如果允许委托人争辩事实真相,说另一人并非是其代理人并否定合约的存在,就会给第三人带来损害(prejudice)。所以,即使委托人事实上没有对另一人的授权,法律也不允许委托人以此为由进行抗辩与提供证据证明事实真相。因此,也有把这个说法叫做"证据性禁反言"(evidential estoppel),这是因为陈述性禁反言本质上是证据规则,这可见本章第3段。

以下可节录部分英国先例的权威说法。在Rama Corp v. Proved Tin and General Investments (1952) 2 QB 147先例中,Slade大法官说:"Ostensible or apparent authority which negatives the existence of actual authority is merely a form of estoppel, indeed, it has been termed agency by estoppel, and you cannot call in aid an estoppel unless you have three ingredients: (i) a representation, (ii) a reliance on the representation, and (iii) an alteration of your position resulting from such reliance."

在 Freemen & Lockyer v. Buckhurst Park Properties (Mangal) Ltd. (1964) 2 QB 480 先例中,Diplock 大法官是如此描述表见授权的:"An 'apparent' or 'ostensible' authority, on the other hand, is a legal relationship between the principal and the contractor created by a representation, made by the principal to the contractor, intended to be and in fact acted upon[173] by the contractor, that the agent has authority to enter on behalf of the principal into a contract of a kind within the scope of the 'apparent' authority, so as to render the principal liable to perform any obligations imposed upon him by such contract. To the relationship so created the agent is a stranger. He need not be (although he generally is) aware of the existence of the representation but he must not purport to make the agreement as principal himself. The representation, when acted upon by the contractor by entering into a contract with the agent, operates as an estoppel, preventing the principal from asserting that he is not bound by the contract. It is irrelevant whether the agent had actual authority to enter into the contract."

另在 The "Suwalki" (1989) 1 Lloyd's Rep. 511 先例中,Steyn 大法官也提到了满足表见授权的两个条件:"For present purposes it is unnecessary to enter into the academic debate whether in relation to ostensible authority one is dealing with a 'true' estoppel. What is clear is that the doctrine can only apply if it be shown (a) that a relevant representation was made by the principal, and (b) that the plaintiff(第三人) entered into the contract on the faith of the representation."

上诉庭 Goff 大法官在 The "Ocean Frost" (1985) 1 Lloyd's Rep. 1 先例中也对表见授权做出了解释说:"It appears... that ostensible authority is created by a representation by the principal to the third party that the agent has the relevant authority[174]; and that the representation, when acted upon by the third party, operates as an estoppel, precluding the principal from asserting that he is not bound.[175] The representation which creates ostensible authority may take a variety of forms; but the most common is a representation by conduct, by permitting the agent to act in some way in the conduct of the

---

〔173〕 这在《Bowstead & Reynolds on Agency》(第 20 版,2014 年)一书之 8－020 段被批评是太狭窄,说:"**Representation need not be deliberate**. This general analysis suggests that the words of Diplock L. J., which appear to require that the representation be deliberate, and certainly say that it must be actually intended to be acted on, are too narrow. This wording does not appear elsewhere in the judgment."

〔174〕 表见授权是由委托人向第三人做出陈述而产生的。

〔175〕 对第三人而言,这个陈述就会对委托人构成禁反言。

principal's business with other persons, and thereby representing that that agent has the authority which an agent so acting in the conduct of his principal's business usually has.[176]"

就第三人而言,只要代理人有授权,至于该授权是实际授权还是表见授权其实并不十分重要。然而在实践中,因实际授权产生的争议显然要远远少于因表见授权产生的争议。表见授权也是十分困难与不稳定的,正如 Steyn 大法官在 The "Suwalki" 先例中所说:"Ostensible authority is a notoriously difficult branch of the law."常见的情形是一方当事人以被告的雇员、经纪人、中间人或代理人存在表见授权为由主张与委托人订立合约。这种案件特别多,包括所谓的代理人或雇员越权以公司的名义行事,甚至涉及欺诈。

12.2.4.2 陈述或显示

委托人必须曾经以语言或行动向第三人做出陈述或有显示(holding out)代理人有授权。在 Attorney – General for Ceylon v. Silva (1953) AC 461 先例中,枢密院(privy council)说:"All 'ostensible' authority involves a representation by the principal as to the extent of the agent's authority. No representation by the agent as to the extent of his authority can amount to a 'holding out' by the principal'."

《Bowstead & Reynolds on Agency》(第 20 版,2014 年)一书之 8 – 021 段 也说:"The representation as to the authority need not be made by the principal himself: it may obviously be made by an intermediate agent with actual authority to do so. More difficulties arise if the authority is apparent. It seems correct in principle to say that an agent can have apparent authority to make representations as to the authority of other agents, provided that his own authority can finally be traced back to a representation by the principal or to a person with actual authority from the principal to make it..."

除了委托人本人外,代理人在很多情况下有委任分代理人的"一般授权"(usual authority)。例如公司总经理,他自己本身是公司法人的代理人,有实际授权任命公司的其他职员,或是委任专业代理人(如律师事务所、会计师事务所等),并约束公司。

在《Bowstead & Reynolds on Agency》(第 20 版,2014 年)一书之 8 – 018 段,提到了两类主要的做法或陈述,会导致在第三人看来,代理人有委托人的授权:"If the doctrine is based on the idea of representation, it may be suggested that the cases can be divided into two types. First, cases where there is something that can be said to some-

---

[176] 这个陈述可以是千变万化的形式。如委任一位总经理,这对第三人而言,可能是表达了该总经理有实际(明示或默示)授权为公司签订商业合约。又如委托人与第三人的业务会议中与代理人一同参加。而最常见的就是委托人的行为是允许代理人参与委托人与第三人之间的事务(如参与交易中的谈判,甚至表示可以与代理人谈),从而向第三人显示该代理人有委托人的授权。

thing like a genuine representation (orally, in writing, by course of dealing or by allowing the agent to act in certain ways, e. g. entrusting him with the conduct of particular negotiations[177] or allowing him to run a business that appears to be the principal's business[178]) by the principal of the agent's authority, on which the third party relies: such as cases could be called cases of 'genuine apparent authority' and more easily (but not always perfectly) based on estoppels. Secondly, cases where the representation is only of a very general nature, and arises only from the principal's putting the agent in a specific position carrying with it a usual authority, e. g. making him a partner[179] or appointing him managing director,[180] or using the services of a professional agent, viz., someone whose occupation normally gives him a usual authority to do things of a certain type, e. g. a solicitor.[181] It is said that: 'by so doing the principal represents to anyone who becomes aware that the agent is so acting that the agent has authority to enter on behalf of the principal into contracts with other persons of the kind which an agent so acting in the course of his principal's business has usually 'actual' authority to enter into'..."

这两类做法或陈述也在 AMB Generali Holding AG v. SEB Trygg Liv Holding (2006) 1 Lloyd's Rep. 318 先例提及,Buxton 大法官在第 32 段说:"Bowstead points out that ostensible authority covers two types of case: where the agent has been permitted to assume a particular position that carriers a usual authority; and where a specific representation is made as to the agent's authority. If either type of conduct on the part of the principal gives rise to an estoppel, that is because of the understanding that it creates in the mind of the third party representee. An alteration on the principal's part of the relationship between himself and the agent cannot, once the estoppel has been created, alter or withdraw the representation if the alteration of the relationship is not communicated to the representee."

上述 Buxton 大法官的判决与《Bowstead & Reynolds on Agency》(第 20 版,2014 年)一书之 8-018 段提到的两类做法或陈述,第一类也是最常见的一类是令代理人位于可假设有一般授权的职务,第二类是对代理人的授权做出了特定陈述。这两类做法或陈述会对委托人构成禁反言,因为该做法或陈述令第三人产生代理人有授权的理解。如果在构成了陈述性禁反言之后,委托人与代理人的关系发生改变(如双

---

〔177〕 委托他参与相关的谈判:Crabb v. Arun D. C. (1976) Ch. 179; Inland Revenue Commissioners v. Ufitec Group (1977) 3 All ER 924; The "Raffaella" (1985) 2 Lloyd's Rep. 36 等先例。

〔178〕 允许他营运表面看来属于委托人的生意:Gurtner v. Beaton (1993) 2 Lloyd's Rep. 369; Lease Management Services Ltd. v. Purnell Secretarial Services Ltd. (1994) CCLR 127 等先例。

〔179〕 见 1890 年《Partnership Act》之 sections 5 与 section 14。

〔180〕 见 Hely-Hutchinson v. Brayhead Ltd. (1968) 1 QB 549 等先例。

〔181〕 见 Waugh v. H. B. Clifford & Sons Ltd. (1982) Ch. 374 等先例。

方关系中断),委托人必须通知第三人。

12.2.4.2.1 第一类陈述:代理人位于可假设有一般授权的职务

这是最常见的一种情况,正如 Keith 勋爵在 The“Ocean Frost”(1986)2 Lloyd's Rep. 109 先例中,针对一位副总裁与租船部经理是否有表见授权说:“... In the commonly encountered case, the ostensible authority is general in character, arising when the principal has placed the agent in a position which in the outside world is generally regarded as carrying authority to enter into transactions of the kind in question.”

概括而言,公司法人是依靠代理人运作的,包括公司职员(总经理、分公司经理、业务员等),或者代理人/专业代理人(如地产中介、港口代理、律师事务所等)。当另一方与一位应当是公司代理人的人士交往时,知道他是否有做这些事的实际授权十分困难,总不能动辄就向该公司的董事局或负责人查询。因此公司代理人的表见授权的问题十分重要。同样,公司法人在任命可以代表公司行事的职员时也必须小心,一旦他们被任命,就会成为有“一般授权”(usual authority)的代理人,其言行也会约束作为委托人的公司法人。

关于一般授权,可再次节录 Steyn 大法官在 First Energy v. HIB(1993)2 Lloyd's Rep. 194 先例中所说:“This type of ostensible authority is often described as the usual authority of an agent. But it is important to remember that the idea of usual authority is used on two senses. First, it sometimes means that the agent had implied actual authority to perform acts necessarily incidental to the performance of the agency. Secondly, it sometimes means that the principal's conduct in clothing the agent with the trappings of authority was such as to induce a third party to rely on the existence of the agency.”

在早期的 Hambro v. Burnand & Ors(1904)2 K. B. 10 先例中,案情涉及劳合社承保的做法。Burnand 先生与其他四位共同被告都是劳合社的会员,但只是 Burnand 先生被书面委任为负责承保与决定保费的承保会员(underwriting member),其他的共同被告也有书面授权让 Burnand 作为代理人为他们承保。根据劳合社的惯常做法,Burnand 先生在劳合社可以经营十分广泛的承保业务。虽然书面的委任对 Burnand 先生的承保范围有一定限制,但这不是一般人士(包括劳合社的经纪人)所知道的。后来,Burnand 先生为了自己的利益为原告(一家银行)承保还款风险,有关风险就是原告贷款给一家公司,而 Burnand 先生是该公司的董事之一。看来这样古怪的合约/业务关系涉及利益冲突。该公司事后倒闭,显然没有清还原告的贷款。而 Burnand 先生以他自己以及其他共同被告的名义承保原告没有获得还款的风险,但 Burnand 先生一直向其他被告隐瞒了这个安排与有关的保单。后来东窗事发,Burnand 先生也没有出庭,估计已经破产。问题是其他共同被告是否要作为保险人向原告银行做出赔付?这里就涉及 Burnand 先生为了自己的利益而越权(abuse of authority),而其他共同被告的抗辩包括原告应该要求 Burnand 披露书面授权,如果原告这样做,就会知道 Burnand 先生是越权。但上诉庭认为一般来说,要求作为代理人的承保会员披露书面授权可能是一种冒犯,因此原告不需要这样做。其他共同被告的另一个抗辩是原告在中期已经知道 Burnand 先生是该公司董事,这是有利益冲突,原告应该对 Burnand 先生是否有授权承保产生怀疑,并有责任向其他共同被告进行确认。但上诉庭认为,原告只是知道 Burnand 先生是公司董事,但并不足以警觉 Burnand 先生是超越了他的一般授权。上诉庭最后推翻了一审的判决,判原告是善意与合理,其他四位共同被告受 Burnand 先生承保的保单约束。

另在 The "Raffaella" (1985) 2 Lloyd's Rep. 36 先例中,又是一宗涉及欺诈的不幸交易。案情是原告的埃及贸易公司作为买方希望购买水泥,第一被告 Spolex 向原告做出了要约,双方最后也达成协议。Spolex 的银行 Refson(一家小型商业银行)为卖方履行这笔交易提供担保,包括付运的船舶会在 1979 年 8 月 8 日前抵达卸港与付运的水泥是符合埃及政府要求的规格,说:"We are pleased to guarantee irrevocable payment of... to you on first demand and without any condition in the event, (1) The vessel not arriving by 8th August 1979 at Port Said or (2) The cement not being in accordance with quality BSS 12/58/71 and being unacceptable to the Egyptian authorities..."

这份担保上有一位 Booth 先生的签名与 Refson 银行的印章。Booth 事实上只是跟单信用证部门的经理,没有签署这份担保的实际授权。根据 Refson 银行的内部规定,这种担保只有当时银行的四位董事才可以签署。

在合约的谈判与履行中,Soplex 作为卖方向埃及买方做出了很多欺诈性或至少是错误的陈述,并在提单上重复。如提单上写着是在 Constanza 装货的新鲜水泥,但事实上是水泥已经在 1 年前装上 Sea Tiger 轮(当时改名为 Raffaella 轮),估计有关的买卖出了问题导致该船舶滞留在 Limassol 港。水泥只有 3 个月的保质期,因此这整船水泥事实上只是一堆垃圾。显然这堆垃圾运到埃及卸港,被埃及买方与政府当局拒绝。已经支付了货款的埃及买方事后不得不向 Soplex 与 Refson 银行提起诉讼。可以想到,做出欺诈的 Soplex 是不会出庭,只有 Refson 银行在高院与上诉庭出现并抗辩。双方的主要争议是 Booth 先生(骗局曝光后也消失了)是否有表见授权约束 Refson 银行。高院与上诉庭都判是 Refson 银行败诉,其中显示怎样决定这种职员越权行事案件的相关判决可节录如下:

"It is important to bear in mind that the doctrine of holding out is a form of estoppel. As such, the starting point is that the principal must be shown to have made a representation, which the third party could and did reasonably rely on, that the agent had the necessary authority. The relevant enquiry, therefore, in all cases is whether the acts of the principal constitute a representation that the agent had a particular authority and were reasonably so understood by the third party. This requires the court to consider the principal's conduct as a whole. **In many cases, the holding out or representation by the company consists solely of the fact that the company has invested the agent with a**

particular office, e. g., 'managing director' or 'secretary'. For example, in a case such as British Bank of the Middle East v. Sun Life Assurance of Canada Ltd. (1983) 2 Lloyd's Rep. 9, the only holding out by the defendants to the third party was to invest someone with the title 'Branch Manager', which enabled him so to describe himself in correspondence relied upon by the third party: in such a case, the only representation which the third party can reasonably rely upon is the representation that that person has the powers normally or usually enjoyed by a branch manager. Therefore, **in such a case, the only relevant enquiry is as to the powers normally enjoyed by branch managers in general.** But where, as in the present case, the holding out is alleged to consist of a course of conduct wider than merely describing the agent as holding a particular office, although the authority normally found in the holder of such an office is very material, it must be looked at as part and parcel of the whole course of the principal's conduct in order to decide **whether the totality of the principal's actions constitute a holding out of the agent as possessing the necessary authority**.

I therefore cannot accept either of the ways in which Mr. Stamler(Refson银行代表大律师)put his case. It is not right in this case simply to enquire what is the normal authority of Documentary Credit Managers(Booth先生)in general. Nor is it right to start by seeking to establish the normal authority of Documentary Credit Managers in general and then looking to see whether there are any additional factors which alter the position. **The only correct approach is** the one adopted by the judge (一审的Leggatt大法官), which is **to consider the whole of Refson's**(第二被告)**conduct to determine whether it amounted to a holding out by Refson of Mr. Booth as having the necessary authority.**

The expert evidence accepted by the judge shows that Documentary Credit Managers are to be found in three different types of bank: clearing banks, merchant banks and trading banks. The working methods of clearing banks are different from those of the other two and, as Mr. Stamler accepted, can be ignored. Normal practice in merchant and trading banks is that they have two categories of authorised signatories, category A (who can bind on their sole signatures) and category B (who cannot). Lists of category A and B signatories are confidential and could not have been known to anyone in the position of the plaintiffs. In merchant and trading banks some (but not all) managers are category A signatories. In such banks, it is common for there to be a particularly close relationship between a particular senior manager and one particular customer.[182] Mr. Spiers(原告埃

---

[182] 这一段是说专家证据显示不同类型的银行(结算银行、商业银行、贸易银行)针对跟单信用证部门经理通常有否授权代银行单独签发担保有不同做法。

及买方的专家证人之一）gave evidence that, in this type of bank, it is not unusual for a manager to concentrate on, and look after, one customer: in such a case, he said that the manager has 'complete authority, within the banking parameters to do what is required'. Mr. Stamler suggested that the evidence of the other expert witness for the plaintiffs, Mr. Stephens, did not justify the judge's view that he supported Mr. Spiers' evidence, since it did not indicate that Documentary Credit Managers in general enjoyed this 'general authority'. Mr. Stephens（Kleinwort 的跟单信用证部门经理）said in his original report that, as such manager, he had not had authority to bind on his sole signature but, when made a 'full' or "senior" manager, he was given such authority. In my judgment, when Mr. Stephens' evidence is read as a whole, it is clear that he remained Documentary Credit Manager throughout: in the earlier stages he did not have authority to commit on his sole signature, but in the later stages (when he was given wider functions in addition to that of Documentary Credit Manager) he did. I do not find this in any way inconsistent with the evidence of Mr. Spiers. The picture which emerges is that a Documentary Credit Manager may or may not be a sole signatory: if he in fact looks after a client's affairs generally (as opposed to being limited to documentary credits alone) he would be expected by those who know the practices of such banks to have general authority to bind the bank and to be an A signatory (as Mr. Stephens himself became in his later days as Documentary Credit Manager).

If the plaintiffs were suing on a letter signed by Mr. Booth as Documentary Credit Manager and had known nothing more about Refson's mode of operating, it may be that this expert evidence would not have been sufficient to show a representation by Refson that Mr. Booth had authority to commit them on his sole signature. But the facts of this case are quite different. Mr. Booth had been acting for Refson in relation to Soplex's（欺诈的卖方）business over a wide field, far outside that of documentary credits. He was the representative of Refson who dealt generally with Soplex's affairs and not only in relation to this particular transaction. There is no suggestion that, save in giving the undertaking, Mr. Booth was acting outside his authority or that his superiors were not aware of what he was doing. Indeed, Mr. Waters, the managing director of Refson, accepted that it was entirely natural that the plaintiffs should approach Refson through Mr. Booth for the undertaking. Mr. Booth is a senior manager, answerable directly to the Board. Therefore, to the knowledge of the Board, Mr. Booth had been acting outside this strict area of documentary credits as the representative of Refson in their dealings with Soplex; i.e., he appeared to fall into the category of manager whom Mr. Spiers and Mr. Stephens would expect to have a general authority. Although the plaintiffs（埃及买方）were not aware of the full range of Mr. Booth's activities, they did know that he had a wide knowledge of Soplex's affairs: indeed, in their presence, Mr. Booth telephoned Cyprus to make enquiries about the progress of the vessel and, on Soplex's behalf, reassured the plaintiffs about the performance of the commercial contract. **In my judgment, on those facts alone Refson held out Mr. Booth as being a manager of the kind who dealt with his clients' affairs generally and who could, therefore, reasonably be expected to have a general authority.** "(加黑部分是笔者的强调)

接下来笔者会对这类做法或陈述经常带来的问题进行分析。

12.2.4.2.1.1 以公司名片、信纸抬头等显示代理人的职位

在 Martin v. Britannia Life Ltd. (2000) Lloyd's Rep. P. N. 412 先例中,案情涉及保险公司职员疏忽向 Martin 先生做出了投资建议。法院相关判决可节录如下:

"In my judgment the business card which Mr Sherman(保险公司派去见客户 Martin 先生的职员)proffered at the outset of the meeting on 9 May 1991 was the clearest representation that he was authorised by LAS(合并后变为被告 Britannia Life Ltd.)to give such financial advice. It may well be the case that, as Mr Burrell(被告保险公司代表大律师)submitted, the unqualified use of the expression 'Financial Adviser'(名片上的职位)on the business card would not have led a reasonable person to believe that Mr Sherman was authorised to give financial advice on matters wholly unconnected with the sale of insurance, but that is nothing to the point. It plainly did represent, in my judgment, that Mr Sherman was authorised to give advice in relation to the sale of insurance, including advice concerning associated or ancillary transactions: in other words, to give 'investment advice' in the sense in which that term is used in the 1986 Act (Financial Services Act 1986). In particular, it represented that Mr Sherman was authorised by LAS to advise on the package of transactions which, in the event, he recommended.

...In the instant case, however, it is common ground that LAS supplied Mr Sherman with the business card, and the fact (to be assumed for present purposes) that Mr Sherman did not have actual authority to advise about the remortgage does not lead to the conclusion that the representation that he had such authority could not have been made by LAS: it merely sets the scene for consideration of the question whether ostensible authority existed. In any event, it follows from my conclusion as to the width of the concept of 'investment advice' in the 1986 Act that such a representation could properly have been made by LAS.

As to the further requirements for establishing ostensible authority, the inference is overwhelming that the representation in the business card was intended by LAS to be acted on by clients to whom it was presented, in the sense that the clients would be reassured that the salesman who presented the card was backed by a responsible insurance company: that, presumably, was the primary, if not the whole, purpose of the card.[183] Further, I find that the representation was in fact acted on by Mr and Mrs Martin in that each of them proceeded throughout on the footing that in giving advice Mr Sherman was acting in every respect as the agent of LAS, with authority from LAS so to act.[184]

Accordingly, had Mr Sherman lacked actual authority to advise Mr and Mrs Martin concerning the remortgage, I would have held that he had ostensible authority to do so.[185]"

其他类似性质的先例还有 Pilot v. Craze (1888) 52 J. P. 311; Royal Albert Hall Corp v. Winchilsea (1891) 7 T. L. R. 362; F. Mildner & Sons v. Noble (1956) C. L. Y. 32; Povery v. Taylor (1966) 116 New L. J. 1656; Derham v. Amev Life Insurance Co. Ltd. (1981) 56 F. L. R. 34 等。

但名片或信纸抬头属于比较弱的证据,因为太容易被伪造:Kooragang Investments Pty Ltd. v. Richardson & Wrench Ltd. (1982) 1 AC 462. 等先例。曾有两名持印有职务为一家跨国石油公司亚洲区总经理的名片的外国人,拜访了一家中国企业并希望以跨国石油公司的名义订立合约。估计如果石油市场上涨,这两个骗子可以将合约转让(assign)或更替(novate)给另一家公司(如他们控制下的 BVI 公司)履行并赚取利润。而如果市场下跌,他们就会消失。换言之,这两个骗子只是冒用跨国石油公司的名义以取得中国企业的信任与取得这票生意。但问题是如果骗子消失,中国企业不能拿着合约让跨国石油公司履行或赔偿市场下跌的损失,因为表见授权不成立。

但如果案情有改变,如这两个骗子向中国国企递出名片时,有该跨国石油公司的职员(如副总裁)陪同在场,并且应该看到这一切发生,情况就会很不同。正如在 Spiro v. Lintern (1973) 1 WLR 1002 先例中,法院判是:"If an agent enters into a contract outside the scope of his authority, and the principal, knowing this, stands by while the contracting party alters his position to his detriment in reliance on the contract, the principal will be estopped from denying the agent's authority."

12.2.4.2.1.2　自我授权代理

已经在稍早提到,一般来说英国法律是不接受自我授权代理(self - authorizing agent)的说法。这道理完全说得通,如在本章上一小段举的骗子冒充跨国石油公司职员的例子,如果他在出示名片时同时做出他有跨国石油公司的授权订立合约的陈述,而该陈述可以导致他变为自我授权代理约束跨国石油公司,就会天下大乱,对任

[183] 名片的作用就是 LAS 作为雇主希望被出示名片的客户依赖与信任该名片,客户可以被保证出示名片的销售员背后是有保险公司支持。

[184] 并且 Martin 夫妇也确实依赖了这个陈述,在认为 Sherman 先生是 LAS 的代理人并有 LAS 的授权做出投资建议的情况下,他们根据 Sherman 先生的建议进行了投资。

[185] 因此即使 Sherman 先生没有做出相关投资建议的实际授权,也会有表见授权。

何公司来说都是十分危险。但如果代理人真的是公司的职员，对第三人自说自话已经获得了公司的实际授权，问题就变了十分复杂，会根据不同的案情有不同的判决。

首先是在 The "Ocean Frost"（1986）2 Lloyd's Rep. 109 先例（案情会在本章之 12.2.4.3 段介绍），承租人的副总裁和租船经理（Magelssen 先生）在上诉庭与贵族院都被判是没有实质与表见授权订立一个 3 年的期租合约，但 Magelssen 先生曾经告诉船东，承租人的董事局特别批准他订立这一 3 年的租约。这就带来一个微妙的争议，Magelssen 先生虽然没有授权订立 3 年的租约，但他被承租人委以副总裁与租船权力，是否有表见授权做出自己已经获得董事局的批准的错误陈述？上诉庭的 Goff 大法官说："the effect of the judge's conclusion was that, although Mr. Magelssen did not have ostensible authority to enter into the contract, he did have ostensible authority to tell... that he had obtained actual authority to do so. This is, on its face, a most surprising conclusion. It results in an extraordinary distinction between (1) a case where an agent, having no ostensible authority to enter into the relevant contract, wrongly asserts that he is invested with actual authority to do so, in which event the principal is not bound; and (2) a case where an agent, having no ostensible authority, wrongly asserts after negotiations that he has gone back to his principal and obtained actual authority, in which event the principal is bound. As a matter of common sense, this is most unlikely to be the law."

但这个说法不能一概而论，在 The "Raffaella"（1985）2 Lloyd's Rep. 36 先例（案情在本章之 12.2.4.2.1 段有介绍），上诉庭的 Browne – Wilkinson 大法官判是即使 Booth 先生没有签署担保并约束银行的表见授权，也有做出他一个人的签名就足够的陈述的表见授权，说："I have so far ignored the representation made by Mr. Booth that 'in London one signature is sufficient'. Mr. Stamler（银行代表大律师）submitted that a principal cannot be held liable as a result of the agent holding himself out as possessing an authority he does not in fact possess... As at present advised, I am not satisfied that the principle to be derived from those cases is as wide as Mr. Stamler suggests; they were all cases or dicta dealing with the position where the agent had neither authority to enter into the transaction nor authority to make representations on behalf of the principal. It is obviously correct that an agent who has no actual or apparent authority either (a) to enter into a transaction or (b) to make representations as to the transaction cannot hold himself out as having authority to enter into the transaction so as to effect the principal's position. But, suppose a company confers actual or apparent authority on X to make representations and X erroneously represents to a third party that Y has authority to enter into a transaction; why should not such a representation be relied upon as part of the holding out of Y by the company? By parity of reasoning, if a company confers actual or apparent authority on A to make representations on the company's behalf but no actual authority on A to enter into the specific transaction, why should a representation made by A as to his authority not be capable of being relied on as one of the acts of holding out?... If, as I am inclined to think an agent with authority to make representations can make a representation that he has authority to enter into a transaction, then the Judge was entitled to hold, as he did, that Mr. Booth, as the representative of Refson in charge of the transaction, had implied or apparent authority to make the representation that only one signature was required and that this representation was a relevant consideration in deciding whether Refson had held out Mr. Booth as having authority to sign the undertaking. However, since it is not necessary to decide this point for the purposes of this appeal, I express no concluded view on it."

另在 First Energy v. HIB (1993) 2 Lloyd's Rep. 194 先例中,被告(银行)的曼彻斯特分行经理 Jamison 先生虽然在谈判中明确表示他没有批准贷款(200 万英镑的信用额)的授权,但是他在 8 月 2 日做出总部已经批准了贷款的陈述属于一个要约,并且他有做出总部已经批准的陈述的表见授权,原告无需向被告的伦敦总行确认其对 Jamison 先生的授权。Steyn 大法官说:"Miss Arden accepted that if the managing director of HIB had confirmed that the transaction had been approved by HIB a case of ostensible authority could be made out... Miss Arden was prepared to accept that the same would generally be true of a general manager. Confining myself strictly to a situation of a merchant bank or a trading bank, such as HIB, I take the view that I would be unrealistic to assert the contrary. And the reason is that in accordance with the general understanding in commerce the manager director and general manager of such a bank is clothed with a general actual or apparent authority to convey such information. It would be absurd to suggest that the third party should seek information from the board of directors as a whole. But Miss Arden submitted that as senior manager in Manchester Mr. Jamison was in a different position.... I have come to the conclusion, on the particular facts of this case, that Mr Jamison's position as senior manager in Manchester was such that he was clothed with ostensible authority to communicate that head office approval had been given... Although his status was below that of a managing director or general manager, it was nevertheless considerable. And, in the circumstances of this case, the idea that First Energy should have checked with the managing director in London whether HIB had approved the transaction seems unreal."

Evans 大法官也说:"... the present case is one where Mr Jamison by virtue of his position necessarily had some authority to communicate with third parties dealing with the bank. The judge found that this included communications .... If the defendants (HIB) were correct, it would mean that the plaintiffs (First Energy) were bound to seek confirmation from the defendant's head office in London of what Mr. Jamison said on their behalf, which would defeat the apparent objection of appointing a senior manager in charge of office in Manchester so that local businessmen could deal with him there."

由此可见,这方面的法律取决于每个先例的不同事实,分水线在哪里不清楚。单从职位上看,The "Ocean Frost"先例中 Magelssen 先生副总裁和租船部经理与 The "Raffaella"先例中 Booth 先生的跟单信用证经理、First Energy v. HIB 先例中 Jamison 先生的分行经理并没有实质性差别。

12.2.4.2.1.3 委托人要为代理人表见授权范围内的疏忽负责

很明显英国法律地位是只要职员在表见授权/一般授权的范围内行事,公司要承担职员错误或疏忽行为的"替代责任"(vicariously liability)。早在 Barwick v. English Joint Stock Bank (1867) L. R. 2 Ex. 259 先例中,Willes 大法官就说:"In all these cases it may be said... that the master has not authorised the act. It is true, he has not authorised the particular act, but he has put the agent in his place to do that class of acts, and he must be answerable for the manner in which the agent has conducted himself in doing the business which it was the act of his master to place him in."

12.2.4.2.1.4 委托人要为代理人表见授权范围内的欺诈负责

在《Bowstead & Reynolds on Agency》(第 20 版,2014 年)一书之 8-063-8-064 段说:

"An act of an agent within the scope of his apparent authority does not cease to bind his principal merely because the agent was acting fraudulently and in furtherance of his own interests.

This principle is applicable to cases of contract[186], tort[187], in the disposition of property,[188]... but for the principal to be responsible under agency principles the agent must normally have been acting within the scope of his actual or apparent authority. It is a well-known proposition that the mere fact that the principal by appointing an agent gives that agent the opportunity to steal or otherwise to behave fraudulently does not without more make him liable."

典型的例子是国际外贸与航运中经常出现的假提单问题,包括倒签提单、对不清

[186] 见 Bryant, Powis and Bryant Ltd. v. La Banque Du Peuple (1893) AC 170; Hambro v. Burnand & Ors (1904) 2 K. B. 10; A. L. Underwood Ltd. v. Bank of Liverpool (1924) 1 KB 775; Lloyd's Bank v. Chartered Bank (1939) 2 KB 248; Uxbridge Permanent Benefit Building Society v. Pickard (1939) 2 KB 248; Alliance and Leicester B. S. v. Edgestop Ltd. (1993) 1 WLR 1462 等先例。

[187] 见 Lloyd v. Grace, Smoth & Co. (1912) AC 716; Uxbridge Permanent Benefit Building Society v. Pickard (1939) 2 KB 248; Morris v. C. W. Martin & Sons Ltd. (1966) 1 QB 716 等先例。

[188] 见 Oppenheimer v. Attenborough & Son (1908) 1 KB 221; Sorrell v. Finch (1977) AC 728 (HL); Canadian Laboratory Supplies Ltd. v. Engelhard Industries of Canada Ltd. (1979) 2 S. C. R. 787; Lexi Holdings Plc. v. Pannone & Partners (2009) EWHC 2590 (Ch)等先例。

洁货物做出的清洁提单、数量不符的提单等。这种欺诈性的行为通常是船东作为提单承运人自己也不知道的，往往是承租人或分承租人以及其代理人在背后所做的恶行。但显然在法律上，船东作为委托人是要为这些人士的恶行向第三人的货方负责。具体可见笔者的《提单与其他付运单证》(2016 年)一书第三章之 2.5.4.2 段部分内容。

12.2.4.2.2　第二类陈述：对代理人的授权做出了特定陈述

这与上一类的区别是没有令代理人位于任何有“一般授权”(usual authority)的职务，而是通过语言、行动或之前的交往做出了关于代理人获得授权的特定陈述。例如，一位男士经常给他妻子订立的合约支付账单，之后因为双方关系变化，该男士不再愿意授权妻子使用他的信用订立合约。但他的妻子仍向不知情的供应商订货，该男士在表见授权下仍需要负责：Debenham v. Mellon (1880) 16 App. Cas. 24; Drew v. Nunn (1879) 4 QBD 661; Hawthorne Bros. v. Reilly (1949) VLR 137 先例。即使只是同居关系而非夫妻关系的情况也适用：Ryan v. Sams (1848) 12 QB 460 先例。但如果该男士只支付过一张账单，不足以构成表见授权要对以后的账单负责：Durrant v. Holdsworth (1886) 2 TLR 763 先例。或该男士是陪同一起购物，也不会构成表见授权要对账单的支付负责：Seymour v. Kingscote (1922) 38 TLR 586 先例。

以下可介绍两个针对其他方面的英国先例。

12.2.4.2.2.1　先例之一：Trickett v. Tomlinson

在 Trickett v. Tomlinson (1863) 12 C. B. (N. S.) 663A 先例中，原告是采石场主，被告是 Merthyr Tydfil 镇上水源供应基础设施建设的承包商。Evans, Brothers 作为前承包商(之后破产)曾经同意从原告处购买一批花岗岩盖顶石用在工程上。被告后来替代 Evans, Brothers 继续进行工程，显然被告也需要这批花岗岩。之后被告、Evans, Brothers 与原告有通讯往来讨论被告从原告处购买花岗岩盖顶石的事宜，并最终对价格达成一致。但是当花岗岩盖顶石送到时，被告发现规格与之前的模型与说明不符，拒绝接受。之后三方进行了长时间的通讯往来，试图解决这一困境。1861 年 3 月 12 日，原告写信给被告说他委任了 Joseph Evans 先生(前承包商的老板)见被告希望达成和解协议，以解决被拒花岗岩的困境：“I have seen Mr. Joseph Evans, of the late firm of Evans, Brothers, and he has kindly consented to see you on the subject of the granite for Merthyr Tydfil; and I have authorized him to do so, and if possible come to some amicable arrangement in the matter. As there is plenty of stone, a slight alteration of joints and face is all that is required.”

3 月 18 日，Joseph Evans 先生前往 Merthyr Tydfil 镇与被告达成协议，同意这批花岗岩盖顶石的价格减为 50 英镑，并准备与签署备忘录如下：“It is hereby agreed between us, the undersigned, Joseph Evans, on behalf of Mr. Trickett, and Samuel Harper, on behalf of Tomlinson, Harper, & Harper, that, on payment of 50l. by the said Tomlinson, Harper, & Harper to the said Samuel Trickett, the granite now lying upon the

premises of Mr. Young at Briton Ferry, as delivered in November last by the ship 'Telegraph,' shall be the absolute property of the said Tomlinson, Harper, & Harper, and no further claim on account thereof shall be made by Mr. Trickett: in consideration whereof, Samuel Harper agrees to pay Mr. Trickett the sum of 50l."

3 月 24 日，原告在得知 Joseph Evans 先生与被告达成的协议后，估计不满意，也认为 Joseph Evans 先生越权。于是写信给被告说 Joseph Evans 先生没有授权，不承认他与被告订立的合约："I have just seen Mr. Evans, and I hasten to state that he had no authority from me to make any such arrangement as he says you proposed to him. I hereby repudiate any agreement he may have made, for which he had not my authority."

Joseph Evans 先生在同一封信里也承认他之前没有原告的授权，所以希望被告把该协议视为无效："I have seen Mr. Trickett, and he declines to accept the terms offered by you to me. He also denies having given me his authority to accept any such terms,—which is perfectly true. I must therefore ask you to destroy the memorandum given by me to you, such being now null and void."

估计协议对被告有利，所以被告不接受，于是导致了之后的诉讼。原告在诉讼中说，在 Joseph Evans 先生见被告之前，他做出的指示是可以从原价减少 20 英镑，但总价无论如何不能低于 100 英镑。Joseph Evans 先生也同意这一点，但没有证据显示被告知道 Joseph Evans 先生的授权有这个最低金额的局限。而被告则坚持原告 3 月 12 日的信函是明确告知了他们 Joseph Evans 先生有代表原告达成协议的授权，也没有提到授权有任何的局限。

法院判是被告不知道 Joseph Evans 先生的授权有局限，认为 Joseph Evans 先生有表见授权达成 50 英镑的协议完全合理，所以原告必须接受该协议的约束。Erle 大法官说："In pursuance of that very general authority (in letter of 12 March 1861), Evans went down to Merthyr Tydfil and arranged with the defendants that they should have the stone for 50l. The plaintiff now claims to repudiate the act of Evans, on the ground that he had given him secret instructions not to take less than 100l. As, however, those instructions were never communicated to the defendants, they were perfectly justified in treating Evans as a person duly authorized to make such agreement with them as he might think proper. Having held out Evans to the defendants as a person having authority to settle the matter in dispute with them at his discretion, it is not competent to the plaintiff now to turn round and repudiate that authority."

12.2.4.2.2.2 先例之二：The "Suwalki"

在 The "Suwalki" (1989) 1 Lloyd's Rep. 511 先例中，案情涉及国际贸易与航运中一种十分常见的不幸情况。在真正的船东与最终的承租人或货方之间往往有一连串的租约。如果最终的承租人或货方根据租约关系支付了运费给二船东或三船东（反正是与承租人订约的一方），但二船东没有将钱支付给真正的船东（这可能是欺诈,也可能是三船东没有支付给二船东,或是因为二船东收到运费后破产等),真正的船东就必须在收不到运费的情况下提供“免费服务”,把货物运到提单上约定的卸港。真正的船东或许可以向货方取回这笔运费,但这取决于提单上的写法是运费预付(freight prepaid)或运费到付(freight to collect)等,毕竟提单是他们之间的海上运输合约。

在该先例中,一票煤炭被卖给了一家名为 Anker Kolen 的荷兰公司。Anker Kolen 与一家名为 Anro 的小型航运公司订立了包运合约,Anro 为了履行包运合约向原告程租了 Suwalki 轮。航次被履行并且 Anker Kolen 支付了运费给 Anro,但 Anro 没有将运费支付给原告并宣布破产。原告开始希望向 Anker Kolen 取回运费,声称虽然 Anro 是以自己的名字订立租约,但曾经向原告披露背后的委托人是 Anker Kolen,因此 Anker Kolen 才是租约的承租人。但 Anker Kolen 否认是承租人,并且 Anro 也没有授权代为订立租约。于是原告转而起诉被告(可以粗略地说是 Anro 的关联公司),指 Anro 是被告的代理人,被告才是真正承租人,因为 Anro 的最大股东是被告的实益所有人(beneficial owner),并且被告为这个航次提供了装货与平舱的服务。

该先例的争议是:(1)Anro 是否是以被告代理人的身份订立的租约?(2)如果是,Anro 是否有实际授权?(3)如果没有实际授权,是否有表见授权?

Steyn 大法官判是被告在该航次只涉及装卸小工部分的服务,Anro 没有代被告订立租约的实际授权。

所以要看在原告船东与被告的交往中,被告是否做出了可以构成表见授权的陈述。相关的事实有:(1)Anro 是被告的专属经纪人(exclusive broker);(2)Anro 曾经作为被告的代理人向原告船东租船;(3)Anro 在市场上被视为被告的经纪人;(4)Anro与被告的商业地址是一样的;(5)该先例涉及的航次,被告提供了装货与平舱的服务;(6)货物是在被告的私人码头上装载上船舶;(7)有关货物、装港、租约条文与发货人代理人都与之前的租约相同。

但 Steyn 大法官不认为这些属于足够构成表见授权的陈述,针对上述(1)与(3),Anro 作为被告的专属经纪人(被告的租船业务都是通过 Anro)的事实在航运的租船市场并不足以构成 Anro 可以代其订立租约并约束被告的陈述。Steyn 大法官说:“A broker, or even an exclusive broker, is not in the shipping trade regarded as having authority to commit his principals without reference back to them. In other words, there is no usual authority vesting in a broker to commit his principals to a contract.”

针对(2)与(7),曾经有过的交往确实能构成表见授权,如本章之 12.2.4.2.2 段提到的丈夫一直帮妻子支付账单的情况。另在 The “Ocean Frost”(1986)2 Lloyd's Rep. 109 先例中,Keith 大法官说:“Ostensible general authority may also arise where the agent has had a course of dealing with a particular contractor and the principal has acquiesced in this course of dealing and honoured transactions arising out of it.”

但在 The “Suwalki”先例中,证据显示了有争议的租约与以前的租约在做法上有很大不同,如以前的租约是由被告签署,但争议的租约只是由 Anro 签署。

而针对(4)、(5)、(6),法院认为这只是泛泛的陈述。在商业社会(特别是在历史悠久的国际航运),设立独立公司法人局限商业风险与针对不同的业务是常见的做法。而这些联营公司相互帮助的情况很常见。究竟它们之间是否是代理关系,要看具体的案情。但法院不会轻易认定联营公司之间有代理关系,,这可节录《Time Charters》(第 6 版,2008 年)一书之 2. 21 段,如下:"Businesses are often carried on through groups of companies. In such cases, it is common to find that a contract is made by one company in order to serve the interests of a business carried on by another company in the group. In such cases, it is sometimes suggested that the contracting company must be taken to have had implied authority to contract as an agent on behalf of the company taking the benefit of the contract. Whether that is so will depend on the facts of the case. However the courts are slow to infer a relationship of agency in such circumstances: see The 'Coral Rose' (1991) 1 Lloyd's Rep. 563 (CA)... and The 'Rialto' (No. 2) (1998) 1 Lloyd's Rep. 322."

总结下,Steyn 大法官说:"These points must be put in context. A. J. Williams Fuels(被告,Anro 的关联公司)were fulfilling the commercial role of stevedores in relation to the cargo in question. When A. J. Williams Fuels had in the past chartered from the owners, somebody on behalf of A. J. Williams Fuels signed the charter – parties. More importantly, during the course of previous dealings it became clear to (shipowner) that, on the main terms of negotiations, Anro had to refer back to A. J. Williams Fuels for instructions. This point is clearly established by the evidence... Having regard to these circumstances, I make the following findings of fact: (a) That the prior transactions between the parties ought to have alerted the owners to the fact that Anro did not have authority to commit A. J. Williams Fuels, and (b) that the specific circumstances of the transaction of May 7, 1982 are equally reconcilable with A. J. Williams Fuels playing the limited commercial role which I have already set out. Looking at the totality of the evidence, I find as a matter of fact that A. J. Williams Fuels made no relevant representation. That is, of course, the end of the matter on ostensible authority."

12.2.4.3 被陈述方进行调查的责任

在本章之 8.1 段已经提到要构成陈述性禁反言,被陈述方的依赖必须合理。因此如果公司职员或代理人越权行事,被陈述方在知道或有怀疑的情况下有责任向陈述方或委托人求证。在《Bowstead & Reynolds on Agency》(第 20 版,2014 年)一书之 8 – 055 段说:"An agent acting outside such authority (e. g. usual authority)... is acting abnormally, and in the absence of other indications of authority there may well be a duty to inquire..."

简单地说,对于特定代理人在一般授权内的行为不需要向委托人求证或要求代理人提供实际授权的证明。正如本章之 12. 2. 4. 2. 1 段介绍的 Hambro v. Burnand &

Ors（1904）2 K. B. 10 先例提到的，这两种做法会导致代理人感觉被冒犯。但如果相关的交易有不同寻常之处，或是出现了一些情况显示有可疑之处，被陈述方可能会有责任向委托人进行询问，否则不能依赖表见授权约束委托人。至于这种不同寻常或可疑之处，在现实中可能千变万化。根据代理人的不同身份，如律师、财务人员、总经理或是刚入职的文员，都会有不同的一般授权。这可能是某个行业的惯常做法，也可能是先例中曾经有说明，某个职务可以做什么，除非有实际授权，否则不能做什么。显然，如果有关的代理人所做出的行为超出了一般授权，依赖表见授权的第三人就应该有所警惕。例如，代理人做了看来与委托人的利益相违背的事情，明显不会包括在一般授权的范围内。

在 Midland Bank Ltd. v. Reckitt（1933）AC 1 先例中，案情涉及一位律师获得其客户（一位大部分时间住在英国以外的大富豪）的授权，管理他的账户，包括签发支票支付他在英国的一些固定支出。该律师作为代理人在客户的支票上签字，其中有总数很大的 15 张支票是用来偿还律师自己在被告银行的个人账户的欠债。法院判是被告银行在看到明显不是律师自己的钱被用来还他的欠债时，不能依赖表见授权，而需要律师提供他有实际授权的证据，如授权书。

即使同样是律师作为代理人，但如果涉及诉讼，代表的律师事务所是有表见授权可以代客户收钱，如诉讼对方败诉或和解下支付的赔偿、退回的预付款等。而律师事务所也常常会扣除自己被欠下的律师费后，再将剩下的钱退还给客户。这都属于表见授权的范围，第三人或诉讼对方无须确认律师事务所是否有真正的授权。

即使知道对方的代理人有表见授权收取一笔钱，但如果有会造成疑问的情况，就有调查的责任。如代表的律师要求第三人或诉讼对方将钱汇入他的个人账户（不是律师事务所的账户），或是一间与客户毫无关联的 BVI 公司等，第三人或诉讼对方就应该警觉，需要向客户确认律师的真正授权。曾有一家著名的律师事务所要求香港国际仲裁中心将剩余的预付款退给律师事务所的账户，但不久后客户就通过电邮要求香港国际仲裁中心将剩余的预付款退给客户在外国的账户。很明显，客户与代表律师之间存在争议，估计代表律师希望用这笔剩余的预付款支付被欠下的律师费，但客户不同意这样做，甚至对律师费有异议。在这种情况下，显然香港国际仲裁中心就不能依赖律师的表见授权，将剩余的预付款退给律师事务所，而是希望双方达成协议。而如果双方不能很快达成协议，香港国际仲裁中心的决定也可能是将钱退给客户，因为授权是来自客户，根据当时的情况已经不存在表见授权。但该律师事务所很快就向香港法院申请了冻结令（freezing injunction），要求冻结这笔仍在香港国际仲裁中心手中的钱，以保护自己被欠下的律师费。最后显然是通过法院对费用的核算，拿到判决并执行，才能把这笔剩余的预付款取走。

至于委托人在面对第三人对代理人的表见授权的调查与咨询的恰当回应，在《Bowstead & Reynolds on Agency》（第 20 版，2014 年）一书之 8－061 段说："Sometimes the response to an inquiry may be indecisive. For example, the person of whom the inquiry as to the authority of an agent is made may, if he is not himself the principal (as in the case of a company), say that he will investigate and make further contact but may not do so. In such a case there may be apparent authority if his conduct is such as to give the impression that the authority questioned exists.[189] Any response, whether indirect in this way or direct, will however only bind the principal if given by the principal himself or by an agent with authority to make it. Such authority will normally only be attributed to a person authorized to act in connection with the particular business in question[190]: it is difficult to believe that authority to give answers to inquiries which bind the employer will easily be inferred. Where apparent authority is otherwise established, the mere fact that the third party seeks unsuccessfully to get confirmation from the principal of the agent's authority, and does not renew its efforts, will not remove its ability to rely on the apparent authority.[191]"

接下来可介绍重要的 The "Ocean Frost"(1986) 2 Lloyd's Rep. 109 先例。在该先例中,原船东(Mundogas)同意将船舶出售给经纪人指定的买方(Armagas),并之后作为承租人将船舶租回,租约为期 1 年。但事后 Mundogas 的副总裁和租船经理(Magelssen 先生)代表 Mundogas(以承租人的身份)与 Armagas 在谈判后先后签署了两份租约,一份为期 1 年,另一份为期 3 年。另外又口头约定要对这份 3 年期的租约保密,甚至不告诉 Mundogas 的租船和营运部门,双方的履行与操作以 1 年的期租合约为依据。[192] 这

〔189〕 如果委托人犹疑不决,只是泛泛说会调查并回应,但最后没有回应,这可能会令原本有怀疑的第三人认为有实际授权,从而构成表见授权:Canadian Laboratory Supplies Ltd. v. Engelhard Industries of Canada Ltd. (1979) 2 SCR 787 先例。

〔190〕 见 British Bank of the Middle East v. Sun Life Assurance Co. of Canada (UK) Ltd. (1983) 2 Lloyd's Rep. 9 先例。

〔191〕 见 Flexirent Capital Pty Ltd. v. EBS Consulting Pty Ltd. (2007) VAC 158 先例第 219 段。

〔192〕 这种做法显然是 Magelssen 先生作为 Mundogas 的雇员在搞鬼。对 Mundogas 来说,在这个出售与租回(sale and charter back)的交易中只是想租 1 年,也可能是对 1 年后的市场并不看好。但 Magelssen 先生估计看好航运市场,尤其认为 1 年期后市场仍然上涨,其中有机可乘。即使 Magelssen 先生能够说服公司董事会租 3 年,并且市场的确上涨,由于是 Mundogas 租用船舶,利润也不可能属于 Magelssen 先生自己,但 Magelssen 先生作为雇员,即使以自己的名义成立公司作为承租人,Armagas 也不会愿意将船舶租用给这家名不见经传的新公司,而只有 Mundogas 这种大公司作为承租人才会令他安心。于是 Magelssen 先生就暗自以 Mundogas 的名义,自己作为副总裁与租船部经理与 Armagas 签署这份 3 年期的租约。希望是在 1 年期满之后,如果市场继续上涨,Magelssen 先生就可以从中图利。一种做法是私下与 Armagas 谈判,要求 Armagas 支付一笔金钱以交换提早还船,让 Armagas 可以在高涨的市场中赚取更高的利润。另一种可能是另行成立公司(因为显然不能让 Mundogas 知道有这个以 Mundogas 为名义订立的合约的存在)作为分承租人营运与转租这艘租用的船舶,以继续履行这个租约。这样,Magelssen 先生就会凭空赚一笔大钱,可能从雇员晋变成自己是老板。

显然很不正常,Armagas 应该对此交易有疑问。[193] 1981 年 4 月,Mundogas 在船舶买卖合约下向 Armagas 交船,并作为承租人随即接受船舶并开始 1 年期的租约。1982 年 4 月,1 年期的租约届满时,Mundogas 作为承租人向 Armagas 还船。但 Armagas 提出根据 3 年期的租约,租期未满,Mundogas 不能提早还船。显然,在当时租船市场下跌,Armagas 希望 Mundogas 继续按 3 年期的租约租用船舶,以继续享有较高的租金。但 Mundogas 主张双方租约的租期只是 1 年(签订于 1980 年 11 月),并表示从不知晓那份 3 年的租约。Armagas 认为 Mundogas 因此构成违约/毁约,表示接受违约/毁约,并索赔 800 万美金的利润损失。

经纪人与 Magelssen 先生之间的电传往来显示在 1980 年 11 月,Magelssen 先生曾代表 Mundogas 与 Armagas 谈判签订 1 年的租约。而事实上 Mundogas 的租船和营运部门的其他人士均不知道有另一份 3 年的租约存在。在谈判初期,Armagas 已经明确知道 Mundogas 想订立的是 1 年期租约,因为 Armagas 要求的 3 年期租约曾被 Mundogas 坚决拒绝。但 Magelssen 先生后来告诉 Armagas 自己虽然没有租用 3 年船舶的"一般授权"(usual authority),但是已经取得 Mundogas 最高管理层的批准获得签订 3 年期租约的"特别授权"(specific authority)。Mundogas 在诉讼中否认给过不诚实雇员的 Magelssen 先生任何特别授权,因此 Magelssen 先生签署该租约时既没有实际授权,也没有表见授权,3 年的租约对 Mundogas 没有约束力。

一审法院判决 Magelssen 先生享有表见授权,Staughton 大法官认为虽然表见授权的范围只是一般授权,但判 Mundogas 委任 Magelssen 先生为副总裁以及租船部经理的职务,是向经纪人(与其他相关的人士)显示 Magelssen 先生有权代表 Mundogas 做出陈述。在这个先例中,Magelssen 先生做出的陈述就是通知 Armagas 说自己已经获得最高管理层的批准特别授权去订立 3 年期租约。所以 Mundogas 应该受到 3 年期租的约束。至于代理人订立合约约束委托人的表见授权与做出他已经获得委托人的实际授权的陈述的表见授权的微妙区别,可见本章之 12.2.4.2.1.2 段。

Mundogas 对一审判决不服而提起了上诉,上诉审理问题包括 Magelssen 先生订立为期 3 年的租约是否在表见授权的范围内。上诉庭([1985] 1 Lloyd's Rep. 1)认为 Armagas 在谈判早期就知道 Magelssen 先生没有一般授权,Mundogas 也从来没有与 Armagas 直接接触过,也没有做出明示或默示的有关 Magelssen 先生有权代表订立 3 年期租约的陈述,因此 Mundogas 不受 3 年期租约的约束。而关键之处之一是 Magelssen 先生被 Mundogas 委以副总裁与租船部经理的职务,是否令他有表见授权做

---

[193] 这里涉及的问题是,陈述性禁反言需要这个陈述必须清楚无误(clear and unequivocal),这主要是不要让被禁反言的被告太轻易失去了法律的权利,如被告可能只是讲了一句客气话或稍作让步。在本先例中,就存在很多疑点,从整个事件经过来看,有太多不合情理之处,这就会导致 Armagas 不能依赖这些不清楚与并非无可置疑的陈述,而是需要向 Mundogas 问清楚 Magelssen 先生是否有订立 3 年期租约的授权。

出自己已经获得 Mundogas 最高管理层的批准的错误陈述？上诉庭在这点的看法与一审法院并不一样。上诉庭认为根据该先例的案情并不可以，Goff 大法官说："No doubt, by appointing Mr. Magelssen to his position and allowing him to act as such, they did represent that he had authority to bind his principals to those contracts which an agent in his position ordinarily has authority to make; and no doubt that ostensible authority would embrace the making of such representations concerning the subject matter of any such contract as might reasonably be understood to fall within such usual authority. But that does not, in my judgment, embrace authority by Mr. Magelssen to communicate approval by his superiors to his making contracts which, to the knowledge of the third party, he had no authority to enter into without such approval, with the effect that Mundogas would be bound by such communication... The representation by Mundogas which was to be derived from the fact that they appointed Mr. Magelssen as chartering manager and vice-president, and allowed him to act as such in the conduct of its business, was simply that Mr. Magelssen had that authority to bind his principal to contracts which a person in his position usually had. No representation can be derived from Mr. Magelssen's appointment, or his being allowed to act in that capacity, that he would be given specific authority to enter into any contract which he stated that he had received authority to enter into. Indeed, any other conclusion could lead to principals being bound to the most extravagant transactions, which they had never authorized and which were far beyond the usual authority of a person in the agent's position."

这方面需要在不同事实的案件中做出判断与区分。如在 First Energy v. HIB (1993) 2 Lloyd's Rep. 194 先例中，就得出不同的判决，法院认为被告（银行）的曼彻斯特分行经理 Jamison 先生有表见授权，原告可以依赖 Jamison 先生在 8 月 2 日做出的融资要约与陈述，而无需向被告的伦敦总行确认其对 Jamison 先生的特别授权。

看来，在 The "Ocean Frost" 先例会有不同的判法主要是因为 Magelssen 先生要求将 3 年期租约对 Mundogas 的租船和营运部门保密的做法十分不正常，这导致第三人想依赖表见授权就有了调查责任，因为整件事件全面来看，谈不上 Mundogas 有清楚无误的陈述。即依赖表见授权的第三人如果在有合理怀疑的情况下就不能继续依赖表见授权，而应该进行调查并确认是否有实际授权，这也是配合陈述性禁反言来源的衡平法精神。对这一点上诉庭说："What Mr. Magelssen did was so clearly and extravagantly unusual for a man in his position that it should not only **have put Armagas on inquiry** but it fell right outside the scope of his authority or employment; authority to sell the ship did not give him authority to back the sale with the charter; **Armagas took the risk of Mr. Magelssen's representation of authority being untrue and could not hold Mundogas responsible for this fraudulent misrepresentation either in contract or tort.**"（加黑部分是笔者的强调）

之后贵族院也支持了上诉庭的判决，即 Armagas 向 Mundogas 索赔提早还船后剩余 2 年租期损失的诉讼失败。

12.2.4.4 表见授权与禁反言的关系

有说法是表见授权与禁反言之间的关系很薄弱与不稳固。首先，在表见授权中的陈述可以十分宽泛，如在 Freeman & Lockyer v. Buckhurst Park Properties (Mangal) Ltd. (1964) 2 QB 480 与 Pharmed Medicare Privte Ltd. v. Univar Ltd. (2003) 1 All ER (Comm) 321 等先例中的"by permitting the agent to act in some way in the conduct of the principal's business with other persons"；或是如 Debenham v. Mellon (1880) 16 App. Cas. 24 与 Todd v. Robinson (1825) 1 Ry & M 217 等先例根据以往的做法默示。而其他所有类别的禁反言，包括陈述性禁反言都要求存在清楚无误的陈述或承诺：Low v. Bouverie (1891) 3 Ch. 82 等先例。相比之下，构成表见授权的陈述解释起来比较宽松。

其次，构成表见授权的陈述做出的时间与希望会做出依赖的第三人[194]十分广泛，特别是在本章之 12.2.4.2.1 段介绍的第一类陈述。在很古老的 Whitehead v. Tuckett (1812) 15 East 400 先例中，说是可以对全世界显示(holding out)。会有争议是委托人在以语言或文字做出陈述时，并没有考虑到特定的第三人，因此很难说他在做出陈述时希望被第三人依赖。很多情况下，第三人只是简单依赖了在代理人的位置或职位上的人会有的"一般授权"(usual authority)。但陈述性禁反言的要求必须是相互关系(mutuality)，即该陈述必须是陈述方向希望依赖禁反言的一方做出的：Jordan v. Money (1854) 5 HLC 185(第 212 页)；Gresham Life Assurance Society v. Crowther (1914) 2 Ch 219(第 227 页)；Jones Bros v. Holloway Ltd. (1923) 2 KB 117 DC(第 124 页)等先例。但陈述性禁反言的陈述也可以向一群人或大众或全世界做出：Bell v. Marsh (1903) 1 Ch 528(第 541 页)；Hammersmith and Fulham BC v. Top Shop Centres Ltd. (1990) Ch 237(第 257 页 c–d)等先例。另在本章之 12.1 段介绍的提单的转让与将在本章之 13.3 段介绍的股票买卖，都是向大众或全世界做出陈述的例子。在 Sean Wilken QC 与 Karim Ghaly 先生近期所著的《The Law of Waiver, Variation, and Estoppel》(第 3 版，2012 年)一书之 9.39 段认为，这部分取决于陈述方的意图，如果陈述方希望大众依赖他的陈述，即使是向大众做出的陈述，也可能是足够。

《Bowstead & Reynolds on Agency》(第 20 版，2014 年)一书之 8-029 段在探讨了与其他可能的说法(如弃权)的关系之后，总结说："It seems preferable therefore, and in accordance with English authority, to retain the estoppels justification; but to treat it as invoking a special (and weak) type of estoppels relevant only in the agency context."

在笔者看来，由于构成表见授权的陈述解释起来比较宽松，并且会做出依赖的第三人十分广泛，因此公司在这方面要特别小心。否则一位职员不论是由于不诚实或疏忽，与一个不知道哪里冒出来的第三人订立了很不利的合约，而在表见授权的说法下，公司

[194] 见本章第 7 段。

也要受到约束,可能十分危险。面对 Steyn 大法官在 First Energy v. HIB (1993) 2 Lloyd's Rep. 194 先例所说的两难局面,法院还是倾向于保护商业的肯定性与无辜的第三人。如果公司职员在表见授权的说法讲得通的情况下订立合约,公司要受到约束。

13. 中国公司/企业需要注意的方面与有关先例

本章已经对陈述性禁反言在各种不同的范畴举了很多先例帮助读者了解这一重要的课题,以下只选与中国的公司/企业关系密切的先例做出较全面的介绍。

13.1 派遣职员或代理人拜访对方公司

涉及涉外的业务,中国公司/企业在年来喜欢在谈判过程中,派遣公司职员(通常是高管)拜访外国公司。这可能是为了进一步协商消除分歧,或是表示友好,或是作为尽职调查的一部分,或是探讨技术方面的问题。这个做法本身没有问题,外国公司也有类似的做法,特别是在一些涉及漫长谈判的大项目。

但要注意公司派遣这些职员出去,如果事前不说清楚授权的局限,就很容易被解释为这些职员有广泛的实际授权或表见授权。如果在拜访过程中,他们做出了陈述、承诺或保证(并有书面或录音记录作为证据),或是签了文件,中国公司很难不承认。对中国公司来说,这种做法特别危险,因为被派遣出去的职员往往不知道国际上构成合约与表见授权的法律,外国公司一方面盛情接待,同时引诱或鼓励被派遣的职员做出陈述、承诺或保证,或是让他们签署文件,将来可以被说成是一份合约。

被中国公司/企业派遣出去的职员被视为有表见授权是很容易理解,首先已经在本章之 12.2.4.2.1 段提到,委任员工有一般授权的职务本身已经是足够的陈述。更不用说派遣他们去拜访对方公司也属于清楚无误的陈述,甚至被派遣的不是自己公司的职员,而是有实际授权或表见授权的代理人,他做出的陈述、承诺或保证或是签署的文件,一样会约束中国公司/企业:The "Samah" and The "Lina V" (1981) 1 Lloyd's Rep. 40 先例。

因此,如果中国公司/企业还没有做好订立合约的准备,也不想被派遣出去的职员(或代理人)为了特定原因做出合约承诺,最安全的做法是:(1)在谈判过程中明确最后与有约束力(final and binding)的合约是有前提条件(condition precedent),如"以签署合约为准"(subject contract),"以董事会批准为准"(subject board approval of the deal),"以……机构批准为准"(subject [name of the relevant authority] approval of the deal)等;(2)在派职员拜访对方公司之前先以文书向对方说明这次拜访的目的,并清楚表明[195]该职员没有订立合约(无论最后或中间合约)或做出陈述或承诺的授权。

---

[195] 在本章之 10.1.2 段已经介绍过,如果代理人的授权有局限,委托人即中国公司有法律责任向对方说清楚。

在 The “Samah” and The “Lina V”先例中,案情是在70年代后期,尼日利亚因为石油价格暴涨而大兴土木,带来了一些著名的国际事件。如上百条船舶装的水泥卸不下来,造成长达两三年的滞留,部分船舶与水泥报废。该先例也是有关的事件,有一个集团想到办法可以帮助尼日利亚(特别是 Bonny 河上游港口)尽快卸下水泥。具体做法是租两艘滚装船做出改装,用来替代驳船在尼日利亚营运。该集团于是与滚装船船东进行谈判,谈判过程相对漫长,因为还涉及改装的费用与怎样改装的技术问题。双方谈判的后期,还有些细节没有谈拢,其中最重要的就是船舶的改装还需要进一步达成协议。此时,代表船东的经纪人(England 先生)在船东的批准下,连同工程顾问(Norman 先生)前往希腊承租人所在地就船舶改装的问题与承租人进行谈判。船东也打了一份电文给他的经纪人,说:“Authorise you to fly to Greece accompanied by Mr Harry Norman, for discussing terms of charterparty, but not to sign C/P unless/until you send us the modifications required by the Charterers with the comments of Mr Norman for our study and we advise you our approval.”

这个授权的电文其实写得很清楚,他被派遣去希腊承租人所在地只是谈判船舶改装的问题。但这一有局限的授权并没有告知希腊承租人。

到希腊后,在承租人的大力怂恿与诱导下,England 先生签署了租约。法院认定 England 先生以为签署的租约对船东有利,估计当时的情况是 England 先生对船舶改装的谈判结果很满意,担心如果不早点签订租约会有变数,而令之前谈判的花费(包括他自己会赚取的佣金)都打水漂。并且 England 先生估计如果将租约向船东汇报,船东也会追认(ratify)。谁知后来船东并不同意,并且拒绝履行。在诉讼过程中,双方都提供了口头证据,并且很多是相互矛盾。如 England 先生说他曾经将船东对他签署租约的权利有所局限的电文给承租人看过,但这被承租人否认。England 先生还说他在签署前曾经表示是以船东批准该租约为准(subject to shipowners’ approval),但这也被承租人否认。法院最后判是船东要受 England 先生签署的租约的约束,船东拒绝履行是违约/毁约,要赔偿承租人的损失。

由此可见,口头证据的分量十分有限与不肯定。[196] 为了保证安全,还是要像笔者提到的,在派职员拜访对方公司之前,先以文书向对方说明职员授权的局限。

---

〔196〕 国际仲裁最热门的话题之一就是仲裁员是否有利益冲突,是否公平与独立。包括很多仲裁机构在委任仲裁员时都需要仲裁员做出越来越多的声明与披露。但笔者(杨良宜)认为普遍被关注的都是细枝末节的问题,除了 IBA 规则中红灯的关系(直系亲属、在公司工作等),一位有地位的仲裁员会对几年前工作过的公司有偏袒之类的情况发生的可能性不大。普遍被仲裁机构关注的国籍问题也不见得重要,如很多海外华人虽然是外国国籍,但不会被当地人信任。而真正重要的文化差异带来的潜在偏见(imputed bias)反而讨论的人不多,这在本书第一章之 8.4.2.4 段已经提到。无论是违约/毁约的争议,还是是否存在弃权或禁反言,很大程度都取决于仲裁员对事实的认定。这样,因为文化差异的影响,中国(包括其他亚洲国家)的证人证词往往不会被外国仲裁员取信,从而导致大量败诉。

另一个有关的先例是 Azov Shipping Co. v. Baltic Shipping Co. (1999) 2 Lloyd's Rep. 159。根据争议双方的名字可推断案情涉及航运,但其实该先例最重要的争议是签署相关的文件(主要是一份合约的附录)有否实际授权或表见授权以及一些言行是否构成陈述性禁反言。该先例的案情与前苏联解体有关。前苏联解体后,原本控制所有船队(包括集装箱船)的 Morflot 不再存在,而拆分成 9 个(或更多)国营的船公司。但这些船公司之间,船公司与铁路、码头之间集装箱的交接(interchange)必须继续,才能持续提供"门到门"的货物运输服务。以前因为都由 Morflot 控制,所以是总的账目。而在拆分之后,它们之间集装箱的交接、租赁与为其他公司提供运输服务,就存在账目结算的问题。因此几次会议探讨有关操作与结账等问题后,1992 年 12 月,达成了一份名为"General Use of Containers International Standard ISC"(简称 GUCA)的协议。GUCA 建立了一个系统或规划,向集装箱交接的各公司之间提供账目结算,由 Transglobe Container Services(简称 TCS)组织负责。

在 GUCA 协议的谈判过程中,Azov 一直明确表示它不接受,主要是各公司之间以美元结算这一点。这导致 GUCA 的第一部分有如下说明:

"As from 1. 10. 92 Transglobe shall carry out control and estimation of debts of shipping for utilization of containers with payment in USD under new balance which accounts all the containers taken for utilization,

Accounting position of Azov Shipping Company about refusal to accept payment in USD for container utilization, TCS shall effect container I/C balance with ZSCO as from 1. 10. 92 by separate 'null' line."

在一连串的会议中,其中一个是在 1992 年 10 月 20 日至 22 日于圣彼得堡召开。在会议上,各个船公司、铁路公司与 TCS 通过了 GUCA 协议的草案。Azov 的一位集装箱部门的分部经理 Chigareva 女士参加了会议,并在草案上签字。但根据 Chigareva 女士的说法,她参加会议只是作为见证,并保证 Azov 关于以美金结算的抗议被记录在会议纪要上。

1993 年 6 月 15 日至 17 日,另一个会议在莫斯科召开。除了 Chigareva 女士,还有一位更高职位的 Ushkalov 先生(集装箱部分的老总)代表 Azov 参加了会议。Ushkalov 先生签署了名为"The technical conditions of interchange procedure"的附录四,内容有关技术操作上的安排。

之后,Baltic 要求 Azov 支付 667 – 679 个集装箱的租金,并以美元结算。但 Azov 否认它受 GUCA 约束,于是 Baltic 根据 GUCA 协议中的仲裁条文开始伦敦仲裁。由于 Azov 否认受 GUCA 约束,因此仲裁庭需要首先针对管辖权争议。仲裁庭(Donald Davis 先生作为独任仲裁员)判 Azov 受 GUCA 协议约束,即仲裁庭有管辖权。Azov 根据 1996 年英国《仲裁法》之 section 67 上诉英国高院要求重审并撤销管辖权的裁决书。

这就带来很多在仲裁庭已经有过的争议(包括法律与事实方面)要被重审,而其中与本小段内容有关的是参加会议的代表是否有代 Azov 签署 GUCA 协议的实际授权或表见授权。首先是 Chigareva 女士，她没有实际授权是没有争议。至于她是否有表见授权，Colman 大法官根据整体的言行，包括职位的高低、在会议上的表现以及其他参与会议船公司代表的理解，判是 Chigareva 女士没有表见授权代 Azov 接受 GUCA 协议。这个会议对该先例的争议也不是非常重要，因为 GUCA 协议的第一部分已经记录下了 Azov 对以美元结算的反对。

但另一个 Ushkalov 先生签署了附录四的莫斯科会议，Colman 大法官就有不同看法，判根据 Ushkalov 先生的职务、在会议上的表现等，他有表见授权，他的签字也约束 Azov。Colman 大法官的判决可部分节录如下：

"As to whether there was ostensible authority in this case, it is necessary to show that the company held out Mrs. Chigareva, who attended a meeting which, as I have held, was not designed to arrive at a binding agreement. As regards Mr. Ushkalov, he went to a meeting designed to conclude amendments to the GUCA. He was head of the container department. . . . I infer that this was the kind of function that people in such positions of management could normally be expected to perform by people in executive position working in the shipping industry of the former Soviet Union. This inference is further supported by the fact that the GUCA itself was signed by Mr. Antonov of Baltic.

In these circumstances, if the effect of Mr. Ushkalov's signature of Addendum No. 4 and his other personal conduct was in all the circumstances sufficient to indicate assent by Azov to be bound by the GUCA, he did have ostensible authority so as to bind Azov."

虽然 Colman 大法官认为 Ushkalov 先生有签署附录四的表见授权，他的签字也约束 Azov。但根据其他的事实，包括 Azov 虽然反对以美元结算，但与其他船公司、铁路公司的集装箱交接仍然存在，所以对针对技术操作的附录四有兴趣并签署也不奇怪，但这不代表 Azov 同意了以美元结算。另是会议的主席的笔记中没有 Ushkalov 先生代表 Azov 同意了以美元结算或同意受 GUCA 约束。如果 Ushkalov 先生代表 Azov 同意了以美元结算或同意受 GUCA 约束，针对这么重要的改变，没有理由不另签一份附录或至少在附录四中记录，改变 GUCA 第一部分的说明。因此综合考虑，Colman 大法官认为 Azov 签署了附录四并不代表已经接受 GUCA 与以美元结算，可以说他对这部分事实的认定是与 Donald Davis 先生很不一样，推翻了 Donald Davis 先生的裁决书。

从该先例也可以看出公司代表签署文件的危险，即使只签署了一份附录，也有被认为受整份协议约束的危险，这也是 Donald Davis 先生的裁决。虽然在该先例最后裁决书被推翻，但毕竟还是不肯定与不安全，如拿到上诉的批准（该先例并没有发生），其他的上诉庭法官也可能支持 Donald Davis 先生的观点等。

13.2　专业人士的收费

中国公司在走出去的过程中，免不了要接受不同专业人士（如律师、财务顾问、专家等)的高端服务。但不少中国公司/企业不知道判断与珍视这些高端服务之间的差异与相应的价值。

近期的例子之一就是很多中国公司/企业会邀请几家律师事务所竞标,然后选择报价最便宜的一家。这在有些法律服务中问题不大,如公司收购或安排上市,因为大部分工作量是可预测的。但在法院诉讼或仲裁,报价是很困难与不可靠。诉讼如战场,工作量与花费是未知的,很大程度上取决于对手的强弱、案情的复杂性、证据的完整性等。

在本小段,笔者会针对的是陈述性禁反言对专业人士收费的影响。在 ING Bank NV v. Ros Roca SA (2011) EWCA Civ 353 先例中,案情涉及 ING 作为被告 Ros Rosa 的财务顾问向被告提供财务方面的服务,包括但不限于寻找适合的投资者。服务顺利完成,但双方对收费金额产生争议。律师有这种争议的可能性就相对较少,因为他们普遍更谨慎,不会做出之后可能构成禁反言的陈述。

在该先例中,根据双方的合约,ING 可以收取的额外报酬是根据"the Enterprise Value/EBITDA 2006 entry multiple implicit in the Transaction"公式计算,但最后双方按照合约规定的公式计算出来的数字有很大差异,ING 计算出的收费比 Ros Rosa 计算的多 570 万欧元。在第一审,判是 ING 对有关合约公式的计算不正确,所有没有深入针对 Ros Rosa 提出的禁反言的替代争议。但在上诉庭,一审判决被推翻,判是 ING 的解释与计算正确,这样 Ros Rosa 避免败诉的唯一机会就是根据禁反言。会构成禁反言的言行是双方在履行合约时的有关事实。这主要是指在 2007 年 11 月,ING 已经有足够资料可以根据合约公式计算出正确的收费,并且 ING 的内部文件显示 ING 已经知道这一事实(显然是通过披露找出的内部文件),但在给 Ros Rosa 的信中还是说估计总共的收费应该是在 400 万欧元左右,估计是过早提出会被 Ros Rosa 施加压力,要求减低这高昂的收费。Ros Rosa 认为这构成了禁反言,包括陈述性禁反言、[197] 承诺性禁反言[198] 与共识性禁反言。[199]

在上诉庭,三位大法官都认为 ING 的言行构成了禁反言,但他们之间对究竟构成哪种禁反言有不同的看法。Carnwath 大法官认为构成共识性禁反言。Stanley Burnton 大法官看来是不肯定,但倾向是共识性禁反言,说:"In relation to the estoppels issues, I have been less certain as to whether the requirements of a binding estoppels were established by Ros Rosa, but I have been convined by my Lords' cogent judgments. I incline to the view that this is not a case of promissory estoppels, but of estop-

〔197〕 这是指 ING 在 2007 年 11 月给 Ros Rosa 的信件中做出的收费应该在 400 万欧元左右的陈述,这显然是一个错误陈述。此外这个先例也涉及本章第 10 段介绍的有责任说清楚。

〔198〕 这是将 ING 在 2007 年 11 月给 Ros Rosa 的信件中做出的收费应该在 400 万欧元左右的陈述解释为一个承诺。

〔199〕 这是指表面看来双方对合约中的公式有共同的错误解释,认为总共的收费可能是在 400 万欧元左右,并在这个共识下合作与履行。

pels by convention, but I think it unnecessary for me to decide this question, which is largely one of terminology."

至于 Rix 大法官,则认为有关的案情所构成的禁反言属于陈述性禁反言,说:"I am more than content to adopt Lord Justice Carnwath's solution in terms of estoppel by convention. However, I also consider that the same solution can be found in the doctrine of promissory estoppel, and is supported by a duty to speak. This should not perhaps come as a surprise since what we are concerned with is an estoppel which alters the effect of a contract by preventing a party from making an assertion or claim contrary to a position adopted mutually between its parties. Although a shared assumption may be lacking from many situations, a representation which is relied upon to the detriment of the representee includes many of the critical aspects of the doctrine of estoppel by convention. Moreover, in a situation in which it is plain that, internally, ING did not share the assumption concerning transaction costs [200] which externally and objectively, it affected and purported to share, there is, to my mind, good sense in considering the matter through the eyes of an estoppel by representation."

Rix 大法官接下来判这是陈述性禁反言下的分类——"沉默性禁反言"(estoppel by silence),[201] 并引用了 The "Lutetian" (1982) 2 Lloyd's Rep. 140 先例作为比较与依赖,说:"In my judgment, the facts of our case are relevantly analogous, but ours is an a fortiori case. The relationship between an advising bank and its client is closer, and more professional, than that between an owner and a charterer of a vessel.[202] Although such an owner and his charterer co – operate on what is hoped to be the success of their maritime adventure, that is commerce in the raw. In our case, the bank is advising its client on its potential transaction, and is earning its fee for doing so and for a successful outcome. Moreover, the contract required the parties to co – ordinate their estimates of the transaction costs, and that is what ING outwardly purported to do, while internally intending to charge a fee which was totally inconsistent with its outward show of agreement with its client.[203] It was not honest and responsible for ING, but unconscionable as Mr Phillips(ING 的代表大律师)had in effect to accept, to fail to disclose to Ros Rosa, in the run – up to the closing of its transaction, that Ros Roca and ING differed on the

---

[200] Rix 大法官认为虽然表面看来是双方的共识,但从 ING 的内部文件看,ING 并没有这一共识,所以不属于共识性禁反言。

[201] 关于有责任说清楚/沉默性禁反言,可见本章第 10 段。

[202] 相比 The "Lutetian" (1982) 2 Lloyd's Rep. 140 先例中,该先例双方的关系更密切与涉及一定程度上的专业性依赖。

[203] 合约中规定了双方要合作,而 ING 虽然表面看来如此,但事实上在内部文件显示准备收不一样的费用。

calculation of ING's fee.[204] Just as the owner in The Lutetian was estopped from denying the accuracy of the charterer's calculation of hire for the purpose of its monthly payment and thus for the purpose of preventing the owner's right to withdraw, because it had represented by its silence that the charterer's calculation was correct, so in my judgment ING is estopped from saying that its calculation based on EBITDA 2006 is the correct calculation. In both cases, one party has represented by his silence (in truth on the facts of this case by more than silence) that the other party's understanding of the situation is correct.[205] ING sought its own advantage in keeping quiet, when it knew that speaking out would lead to a dispute and to a renegotiation.[206] Ultimately, the dispute could not be avoided, and has occurred, but ING considered that its position would be strengthened if the dispute only took place after the event.[207]"

总之,结果就是判 ING 的索赔因为禁反言而败诉。

13.3 股票证书(share certificate)

股票是公司股份的表现形式,股份则是代表对一家公司的所有权份额,所以股票买卖实质上是对公司所有权的拥有与出让。这种交易不止涉及上市的股份有限公司,在私人的有限责任公司中也会有很多股份买卖的活动。如想买一家公司的全部资产,通常有两种做法。一种做法是通过资产本身的买卖,而公司出售了资产后,就变为一家空壳公司。另一种做法就是干脆将公司股份买下,买方也就可以通过控制公司而实际拥有公司资产。如买方想买一艘船舶,而该船舶名义上是一家单船公司所拥有。买方可以通过实体的船舶买卖获得这艘船舶的所有权,但也可以通过卖方将单船公司的股份转让给他实现。两种做法中通常是后者简单与快捷得多。至于能否这样做,要看每个案件不同的环境。不论是 20 年前外国公司大量进入中国投资,或是现在中国公司/企业走出去投资,很多都是通过收购公司股份(无论是上市的股份有限公司或是私人的有限责任公司)的形式。而这些股份收购协议(share purchase agreement,简称 SPA)与其他的商业合约/买卖合约本质上没有差异,有特定的针对性条文,如要求卖方做出各种保证。股份收购协议内往往也有一条仲裁条文,其中不少是香港仲裁或新加坡仲裁,笔者也经常有涉及这方面争议的案件。

至于股票转让的实际法定操作,在英国是卖方填写股票买卖格式(stock transfer form),在香港特区是填写买卖单据(bought and sold note),写明公司名称、卖方名称、

---

[204] ING 没有向 Ros Rosa 披露计算出的费用不同的行为是不诚实、不负责任与不合情理的。

[205] 正如在 The "Lutetian" (1982) 2 Lloyd's Rep. 140 先例中,船东被禁止撤船,在该先例中,ING 也被禁止根据合约公式计算收费。在两个先例中,都涉及一方的沉默构成另一方对事实的理解是正确的陈述。

[206] ING 为了自身利益保持沉默,因为它知道如果当时提出会引起争议与需要再次谈判。而 Rix 大法官认为如果当时再次谈判,收费降低的可能性是很大。

[207] 虽然最后无法避免争议,但 ING 认为在提供服务之后,他收费的立场会更强。

买方名称、股票的数量、每一股的价格。一旦股票买卖被批准，公司需要更新注册股东名册，取消卖方的股票证书（share certificate），并签发新股东的股票证书。在今天，由于证券交易市场（二级市场）的交易频密，已经放弃了书面股票凭证。

一旦公司签发了股票证书，就等于向全世界做出了重要的陈述，也显然会被将来的股票买方依赖。所以，如果公司 A 在 X 先生的申请之下签发了股票证书，公司 A 就做出了 X 先生是公司股份的所有人的陈述。而如果 Y 先生依赖股票证书而蒙受损害（一般来说，就是向 X 先生支付了购买股票的费用），A 公司就会被禁反言，不能否认 X 先生的所有权。以上所说可节录 Cockburn 勋爵在 Re Bahia and San Francisco Railway Co. Ltd.（1867－68）LR 3 QB 584 先例所说，如下："This power of granting certificates is to give the shareholders the opportunity of more easily dealing with their shares in the market, and to afford facilities to them of selling their shares by at once showing a marketable title, and the effect of this facility is to make the shares of greater value. The power of giving certificates is, therefore, for the benefit of the company in general; and it is **a declaration by the company to all the world** that the person in whose name the certificate is made out, and to whom it is given, is a shareholder in the company, and it is given by the company with the intention that it shall be so used by the person to whom it is given, and acted upon in the sale and transfer of shares. It is stated in this case that the claimants acted bona fide, and did all that is required of purchasers of shares; they paid the value of the shares in money on having a transfer of the shares executed to them, and on the production of the certificates which were handed to them. It turned out that the transferors had in fact no shares, and that the company ought not to have registered them as shareholders or given them certificates, the transfer to them being a forgery. That brings the case within the principle of the decision in Pickard-v-Sears [6 AD & E 469] as explained by the case of Freeman-v-Cooke [2 Ex 654] that **if you make a representation with the intention that it shall be acted upon by another, and he does so, you are estopped from denying the truth of what you represent to be the fact.**"（加黑部分是笔者的强调）

因为股票证书在股票买卖的重要性，所以相关的先例很多。[208] 再加上它是一份文件，就难免出现很多涉及伪造（forgery）的案件。这种骗局已经有上百年的历史，直到现在仍在发生。如在 Re Bahia and San Francisco Railway Co. Ltd 先例中，Trittin 小姐将她的股票证书交给了一个经纪人保管。之后有人制造了 Trittin 小姐将公司股票转卖给两个骗子的虚假交易，公司将 Trittin 小姐的名字从公司股东名册上删除，并

---

[208] 如 Simm v. Anglo American Telegraph（1879）5 QBD 188 CA; In re Ottos Kopje Diamond Mines Ltd.（1893）1 Ch 1892 CA; Dixon v. Kennaway & Co.（1900）1 Ch 833; Cadbury Schweppes Plc. v. Halifax Share Dealing Ltd.（2006）EWHC 1184（Ch）等先例。

向骗子签发新的股票证书。这些股票之后被卖给了无辜的买方,买方向公司递交了相关的买卖文件与骗子交给他们的股票证书,被注册为新的股东。之后骗子的骗局在 Trittin 小姐查询时被发现,公司被法院命令将 Trittin 小姐重新注册为股东,毕竟 Trittin 小姐是股票的合法所有人,不会因为骗子而被剥夺法律权利或财产权利。这导致公司拒绝承认无辜的买方是公司的股东,但法院判是公司向骗子签发股票证书的行为构成陈述性禁反言,因为这错误的陈述被无辜买方所依赖,公司不能之后否认骗子对相关股票的所有权,必须向无辜的买方做出赔偿。Lush 大法官说:"And the claimants having acted on this statement by the company, there arises an estoppel as against the company, prohibiting them from denying that what it states is true. And the question then is, what does the certificate mean? Does it mean merely, that [the fraudsters' names] are on the register, and the company have done their best to ascertain that they are entitled to the shares, but cannot say whether they are so entitled? Or does it amount to a statement that the company take upon themselves the responsibility of asserting that they are the registered shareholders entitled to the specific shares? I think the certificate must amount to the latter assertion. It is the company who are to keep and look after the register, and they are the only persons who have control over it, and they can refuse to register a person until he shews that he is legally entitled. Having, therefore, put the names of [the fraudsters] upon the register, and granted them a certificate, the company are estopped after that statement has been acted upon and cannot deny that those persons were the legal holders of the particular shares which have been transferred to the claimants. The claimants, therefore, are entitled to recover from the company the value of the shares at the time when they were deprived of them."

另一个近期的先例是 Cadbury Schweppes Plc. v. Halifax Share Dealing Ltd. (2006) EWHC 1184 (Ch)。案情涉及两家著名上市公司 Cadbury Schweppes 与 Unilever 的股票。案情可节录案例的有关报道:

"The story that emerges is this. A number of shareholders (whom I shall call 'the Original Shareholders') in one or other of the Companies became the objects of attention by fraudsters who, by communication with the Registrars, procured first that there should be a false change of address on the members' register of the Company in respect of the holdings of the Original Shareholders concerned.[209] The new addresses were chosen by the fraudsters and it will be convenient to call them 'the fraudsters' addresses'. Next the fraudsters, in further communication with Registrars and as if they were and in the respective names of the Original Shareholders, falsely (and unknown to the Original Share-

[209] 骗子看定了目标,首先是向公司注册处更改地址,将原本股票合法持有人的地址改为骗子控制的地址。

holders) claimed that the Original Shareholders' certificates had been lost and asked for duplicate certificates (still in the names of the Original Shareholders) to be issued and to be sent, as they then were, to the fraudsters' addresses.[210]

At the next stage there were forged transfers of shares purporting to be by the Original Shareholders respectively by way of gift to new names (the fraudsters' names or names used by the fraudsters and which I will call 'the fraudsters' names'). The forged transfers were sent with the duplicate certificates to the Registrars together with express or implied requests for the transfer of the holdings into the fraudsters' names and the issue of fresh share certificates in the names of the fraudsters. Fresh certificates under the common or securities seals of the Company concerned and in the fraudsters' names (which I shall call 'the false certificates') were thus procured from the Registrars and were sent to the fraudsters' addresses.[211] The false certificates were false in the sense that they misrepresented who at the time should truly have been in the register of members as holders of those particular shares and where the legal title in the shares they described should then truly have lain.[212]

Finally (although the mechanisms used varied a little from one case to another and in some cases involved the Crest system and a move to a certificate – less holding and in other cases did not) a sale would be procured by the fraudsters by way of their lodging the false certificate and a transfer executed in the fraudster's name with the Stockbrokers.[213] The transfer so lodged with the Stockbrokers was, of course, fraudulent as devised as part of a fraud but was regular on its face in that the identity of the transferor and of the registered holder of the shares as indicated on the share certificate accorded with each other. The shares in question were then sold in the market and the Stockbrokers lodged the fraudulent transfers and the false certificates with the Registrars for the transfers to be registered and (generally) for fresh certificates to be issued to those who had purchased the shares in the market.[214]"

事后原本股票合法持有人出现,这时骗子已经逃之夭夭,剩下的只有原本股票合法持有人、公司与买方这三个无辜方。已经明确在这种情况下,公司必须将原本股票

[210] 第二步就是报失原本的股票证书,要求公司向原本股票合法持有人补发新的股票证书,寄去骗子控制的地址。

[211] 第三步是伪造原本股票合法持有人将股票以低价卖给或作为礼物送给骗子的交易,并将相关文件与补发的股票证书交给公司,要求公司签发骗子名字的新股票证书,并寄去骗子控制的地址。公司也就照做了。

[212] 这些本质是虚假的股票证书对谁拥有这些股票的事实做出了错误陈述。

[213] 最后,骗子将这些虚假的股票证书交给股票经纪人,在股票市场买卖。

[214] 无辜的买方买入股票并在公司注册处注册为新的股东。骗子收到钱后就逃之夭夭。

合法持有人重新登记为公司股东,因为根据英美法,个人财产权至高无上,不会因为骗子的骗局就被剥夺。而无辜的买方因为依赖了公司签发的股票证书,根据陈述性禁反言,公司必须赔偿买方损失,即从买方手中将这些虚无的股票买回来。而蒙受损失的公司就希望找到另一个"替罪羊",将损失转嫁出去,这就是股票经纪人。

这里涉及一个很早期先例就确立的说法,如果股票经纪人将虚假的股票转让交给公司注册,并要求公司签发股票证书给新的股票持有人,令公司蒙受损失,是有承担赔偿的默示责任(implied indemnity)。这个说法最早是在 Sheffield Corp v. Barclay (1905) AC 392 确立,在该先例中,贵族院的 Halsbury 勋爵根据 30 年前的 Dugdale v. Lovering (1874 – 75) LR 10 CP 196 先例中,说:"It is a general principle of law when an act is done by one person at the request of another which act is not in itself manifestly tortious to the knowledge of the person doing it, and such act turns out to be injurious to the rights of a third party, the person doing it is entitled to an indemnity from him who requested that it should be done ....."

这也是很基本的法律原则,即 A 在 B 的要求下做出一些本来不会做的行动,而该行动造成对第三人的损害,提出要求的 B 就有默示责任补偿 A 的损失。无论是否有合约关系,这个法律原则都适用。

另在该先例中,Davey 勋爵也说:"I think that the appellants [Sheffield Corporation] have a statutory duty to register all valid transfers, and on the demand of the transferee to issue to him a fresh certificate of title to the stock comprised therein. But, of course, it is a breach of their duty and a wrong to the existing holders of stock for the appellants to remove their names and register the stock in the name of the proposed transferee if the latter has, in fact, no title to require the appellants to do so. I am further of opinion that **where a person invested with a statutory or common law duty** of a ministerial character **is called upon to exercise that duty on the request, direction, or demand of another** (it does not seem to me to matter which word you use), **and without any default on his own part acts in a manner which is apparently legal but is, in fact, illegal and a breach of the duty, and thereby incurs liability to third parties, there is implied by law a contract by the person making the request to keep indemnified the person** having the duty against any liability which may result from such exercise of the supposed duty. And **it makes no difference that the person making the request is not aware of the invalidity in his title to make the request, or could not with reasonable diligence have discovered it.**"(加黑部分是笔者的强调)

这个法律原则在之后的很多先例中被跟从,包括涉及香港特区的 Stanley Yeung Kai Yung and another v. Hong Kong and Shanghai Banking Corporation (1981) AC 787 枢密院先例。该枢密院先例谈到了为什么要无辜的股票经纪人负责,说:"The true principle of the law is that a person is liable for his engagements (as for his torts) even though he is acting for another, unless he can show that by the law of agency he is to be held to have expressly or impliedly negatived his personal liability. But, upon the view of the letters, which the Courts below accepted and this Board believes to be correct, the brokers cannot avoid personal responsibility for whatever consequences the law attaches to the making of the request and the bank's compliance with it. It was their request — even though made on Mr Wong's [the transferee's] behalf."

但也有一个历史悠久的说法是一家有限公司根据《公司法》等法律规定,必须签发新的股票证书让股票可以正常交易,新的股票证书会对公司构成禁反言,公司不能对第三人否认股票证书持有人对股票的所有权。这除了稍早介绍的 Re Bahia and San Francisco Railway Co. Ltd 先例中,在 The Balkis Consolidated Co. Ltd. v. Tomkinson and Others (1893) AC 396 先例中,Herschell 勋爵也说:"The Court held that the giving of the certificate amounted to a statement by the company, intended by them to be acted upon by the purchasers of shares in the market, that the persons certified as the holders were entitled to the shares; and that the purchasers having acted on the statement by the company, they were estopped from denying its truth and liable to pay as damages the value of the shares."

Cadbury Schweppes Plc. v. Halifax Share Dealing Ltd 先例是第一个涉及这两个历史悠久的原则在有关案情中都适用而起了直接冲突的先例。股票经纪人依赖陈述性禁反言的说法作为抗辩,认为公司签发虚假的股票证书是错误的陈述,股票经纪人依赖该陈述并蒙受损害(面对补偿的默示责任)。高院判是在这种情况下,禁反言的说法优先。Lindsay 大法官说:"The old maxim that 'All estoppels are odious' — see e. g. Baxendale-v-Bennett (1878) 3 QBD 525 at 529 CA — never uniformly respected, no longer represents modern practice, at any rate as to estoppels by representation. Undeterred by the maxim and for the reasons I have given, I hold the Stockbrokers to have satisfied the conditions required if an estoppel by representation is here to be asserted and I find no reason why it should not be deployed. The Claimants' claim, for the expense involved in their reinstating the Original Shareholders, was on the basis that all along such Original Shareholders were the persons who alone were to be recognised as the true shareholders. However, the onus is on the Companies to displace the prima facie title which their own share certificates conferred — see Dixon -v- Kennaway supra at p. 837 per Farwell J — and thus the Claimants, being, by reason of the estoppel, unable in these proceedings to deny the truth of their own share certificates naming others, the fraudsters, as the shareholders at the only time at which the Stockbrokers did anything of relevance, find themselves unable to assert or prove that the persons they reinstated were, indeed, the true shareholders. Their claims thus end up as if the Claimants had reinstated strangers, persons who had no right to be shareholders, a claim against which they received no Barclay implied indemnity from the Stockbrokers. The Companies have no right against the Stockbrokers other than by way of that indemnity and, that being denied them, their claims against the Stockbrokers thus fail."

13.4 总结

陈述性禁反言与承诺性禁反言一样,在日常生活与商业交易中都十分危险。

在本书第四章与本章早前介绍的先例中可以看出,无论合约订得多好,措辞/文字多么清楚无误,都可能因为禁反言而被暂停、更改或失去权利:Thor Navigation Inc. v. Ingosstrakh Insurance Company Ltd.(2005)1 Lloyd's Rep. 547 先例与 ING Bank NV v. Ros Roca SA(2011)EWCA Civ 353 先例。甚至可能因为陈述性禁反言导致要受原本不存在的合约约束:Azov Shipping Co. v. Baltic Shipping Co.(1999)2 Lloyd's Rep. 159 先例。

所以,如果双方在对一个很赚钱的合约进行谈判,但不谨慎与水平低的一方犹疑不决,谨慎与水平高的一方可以主动提议做一些事,并口头保证这只是为了显示友好,即使双方还没有达成合约。但这种诱导的做法不会留下证据,将来如果发生争议,也会被否认。如果不谨慎与水平低的一方不承认双方订立了合约,谨慎与水平高的一方就会说之前做的事显示他已经开始履行或准备履行,指不谨慎与水平低的一方接纳或认同是构成禁反言等。类似的,如果合约中的规定对谨慎与水平高的一方不利,他可以在合约履行中诱导不谨慎与水平低的一方做出可以构成禁反言的言行,包括陈述性禁反言。

对合约方来说,相比担心合约条文对自己不利,更应该担心对方比自己水平高并且比自己谨慎。

第六章　共识性禁反言

1. 共识性禁反言（estoppel by convention）的定义

这种形式的禁反言历史悠久，早在 McCance v. London & North Western Railway（1864）159 E. R. 563 先例中，法院就提到双方对一个事实的共识对双方有约束力。该先例涉及原告通过火车付运一匹马匹，运费收得比较低，因为原告向铁路公司告知马匹的价值不超过 10 英镑。马匹在运输途中受伤，原告提出索赔，但被判是赔偿金额受到他向铁路公司告知的马匹价值的约束。虽然这一先例中，也不严格是共识性禁反言的案情，但 William 大法官就说双方对合约的事实有了解，并根据这一共识的事实处理，双方就受到这一"事实"（错误）的约束，即使它并非正确（... the contract declared on was to be governed and regulated by **a state of facts** understood by the parties... when parties have agreed to act upon an assumed state of facts their rights between themselves are justly made to depend on the conventional state of facts and not on the truth... we think that both parties are bound by the conventional state of facts agreed upon between them）。

共识性禁反言的说法早期比较技术性，所以被引用的并不太多。但近年来，特别是从 1980 年开始，贵族院在 Amalgamated v. Texas Bank（1982）1 Lloyd's Rep. 27 先例将共识性禁反言的适用范围扩大到对法律（特别是对合约解释）的共识后，出现了大量的且案情各异的先例中，形成了一种相对重要的禁反言的类别。

以下首先对共识性禁反言的一些权威定义做介绍：

1. 在 Burkinshaw v. Nicholls（1878）3 App Cas 1004 先例中，Blackburn 勋爵说："their rights shall be regulated, not by the real state of facts, but by that conventional state of facts which the two parties agree to make the basis of their action.[1]"

2. 在澳大利亚的 Grundt v. Great Boulder Proprietary Gold Mines Ltd.（1938）59 CLR 641 先例中，Dixon 大法官认为如果一方当事人想偏离双方的共识，而这被视为不公道或不允许，他就必须受到这一共识的约束，说："Whether a departure by a party

---

〔1〕 双方的权利将会受到双方对某些"事实"的共识的约束，因为双方是基于这种共识去行动，而不是另外存在的真实或正确的事实。

from the assumption should be considered **unjust or inadmissible** depends on the part taken by him in occasioning its adoption... He may be required to **abide by the assumption because it formed the conventional** basis upon which the parties entered into contractual or other mutual relations... **or** because he has exercised against the other party rights which would exist only if the assumption were correct... **Or** because knowing the mistake the other laboured under, he refrained from correcting him when it was his duty to do so[2]; **or** because his imprudence, where care was required of him, was a proximate cause of the other party's adopting and acting upon the faith of the assumption; or because he directly made representations upon which the other party founded the assumption[3].... **belief in the correctness of the facts or state of affairs assumed is not always necessary**. Parties may adopt as the conventional basis of the transaction between them an assumption which they know to be contrary to the actual state of affairs. A tenant may know that his landlord's title is defective, but by accepting the tenancy he adopts an assumption which precludes him from relying on the defect."（加黑部分是笔者的强调）

3. 在 Taylor Fashions Ltd. v. Liverpool Victoria Trustees Co. Ltd.（1982）QB 133 先例中，Oliver 大法官说："The inquiry which I have to make therefore, as it seems to me, is simply whether, in all the circumstances of this case, it was unconscionable for the defendants to seek to take advantage of the mistake which, at the material time, everybody shared...[4]"

4. 之后在 Habib Bank v. Habib Bank AG（1981）2 All ER 650 先例中，上诉庭确认了 Spencer Bower 与 Turner 所著的《Estoppel by Representation》（第 3 版，1977 年）一书[5]第 157 页的英国法律地位："This form of estoppel is founded, not on a representation of fact made by a representor and believed by a representee, but **on an agreed statement of facts the truth of which has been assumed by the convention of the parties**, as the basis of a transaction into which they are about to enter. When the parties have acted in their transaction upon the agreed assumption that a given state of facts is to be accepted between them as true, then as regards that transaction each will be estopped

---

〔2〕 在这种情况下，特别是有一方不诚实，也会涉及本书第四章之 6.4 段与第五章第 10 段介绍的有责任说清楚（duty to speak），而不说明会构成陈述性禁反言。

〔3〕 这是在 The "Indian Endurance" and The "Indian Grace"（No. 2）（1998）1 Lloyd's Rep. 1（HL）先例与很多其他先例提到的一种共识："assumption made by one and acquiesced in by the other."

〔4〕 判断是否构成共识性禁反言的考验十分简单，就是被告是否不合情理（unconscionable）与想从双方的错误共识中获利。

〔5〕 该权威书籍在 2004 年已有第 4 版。

as against the other from questioning the truth of the statement of facts so assumed.[6]"（加黑部分是笔者的强调）

5. 在 Amalgamated v. Texas Bank 先例中，Denning 勋爵说："when **the parties to a contract are both under a common mistake as to the meaning or effect of it** – and embark on a course of dealing on the footing of that mistake... then the original contract is replaced by the conventional basis.[7]"Denning 勋爵也说："... **There is no need to inquire whether their particular interpretation is correct or not – or whether they were mistaken or not – or whether they had in mind the original terms or not.** Suffice it that they have, by the course of dealing, put their own interpretation on their contract, and cannot be allowed to go back on it."（加黑部分是笔者的强调，这个先例后共识性禁反言也包括了合约的解释，这是法律问题。）

6. 在 Shearson Lehman Hutton Inc. v. Maclaine Watson & Co. Ltd.（1989）2 Lloyd's Rep. 570 先例中，Webster 大法官说："I take the requirements of an estoppel by convention to be：（i）An assumption of **fact or law shared between both parties**；（ii）which is mistaken；（iii）which is acted upon by the party against whom the estoppel is alleged in the sense that he has taken some action which affects the particular relationship between the parties；（iv）... in a way which would make it unfair for the first party to resile from the common assumption.[8]"（加黑部分是笔者的强调）

7. 在 The "Indian Endurance" and The "Indian Grace"（No. 2）（1998）1 Lloyd's Rep. 1（HL）先例中，Steyn 勋爵说："It is settled that an estoppel by convention may arise where parties to a transaction act on **an assumed state of facts or law, the assumption being either shared by them both or made by one and acquiesced in by the other**.[9]

---

[6] 这种形式的禁反言并非是根据陈述方向被陈述方做出错误的陈述并被后者所依赖，而是根据双方对错误事实的认同，认为它是真实，并作为依据进行交易。如果双方根据这种共识去行动，并接受该事实为真实，双方的任何一方都会被禁反言去对该事实的真实性事后做出质疑。

[7] 双方当事人之间对合约的解释或者其效力有了共同错误的理解，并根据这种共识进行交往与互动，这样原来合约的本意就被双方的共识所替代。

[8] 共识性禁反言的要求是：(1)双方对事实或者法律有一个共同的假设；(2)这假设是错误的；(3)双方根据这一错误的假设或共识行动并影响了他们之间的关系；(4)其中一方如果想从这一共同的假设脱身会造成不公平。

[9] 在一方做出法律或事实的错误陈述（不论他是否知道这是错误），而另一方也认同与做出相应行动，并且双方进一步交往与互动，这也是共识的一种。这可能会导致做出错误陈述的一方被禁反言，不论是因为陈述性禁反言或是共识性禁反言。而另一方如果在双方交往与互动后反悔，只要是不公平与不合情理，也会因为共识性禁反言被禁止这样做。在 ING Bank NV v. Ros Rosa SA（2011）EWCA Civ 353 先例中，Rix 大法官说："... a shared assumption may be lacking from many situations, ... In a situation in which it is plain that, internally, ING did not share the assumption concerning transaction costs which externally and objectively, it affected and purported to share ..."

The effect of an estoppel by convention is to preclude a party from denying the assumed fact or law if it would be unjust to allow him to go back on the assumption: The 'August Leonhardt' (1985) 2 Lloyd's Rep. 28; The 'Vistafjord' (1988) 2 Lloyd's Rep. 343... It is not enough that each of the two parties acts on an assumption not communicated to the other. But it was rightly accepted by counsel for both parties that a concluded agreement is not a requirement for an estoppel by convention."(加黑部分是笔者的强调)

8. 与陈述性禁反言只针对做出陈述的一方不同,共识性禁反言对双方都有约束(mutuality)。正如Carnwath大法官在ING Bank NV v. Ros Rosa SA (2012) 1 WLR 472先例中说:"... the only distinction between an estoppel by convention and other forms of estoppel now lies in the manner in which the party to be estopped assumes responsibility for the proposition from which he is to be estopped from departing, namely by mutual assent rather than unilateral assertion."

当事人过往的一些习惯上的错误做法,看来是双方已经达成不会坚持原有权利的共识,其中一方如果改变主意想主张原有的权利,就会被禁反言,暂时甚至永远失去其原有的权利。如一个两年的期租租约规定,每30天预付一期租金,若不按时按数支付,船东有权立即撤船并解除租约。结果起租后的半年、一年,每期租金支付都晚了两、三天甚至更长,船东也从来没提出过异议,等于习惯上接受了承租人晚付租金。到了第13个月,租金市场往上涨了,船东就马上打了份电传给承租人称:"你这期租金没按时付,我现在依租约撤船。"承租人一看就急了,说:"过去12个月的租金都是晚付的,你也没提出什么,一直高高兴兴,现在突然就要撤船,怎么行啊?"这个案子如果拿到法院按普通法判,法院还是会说:"既然合约清楚订明了不按时付租金可以撤船,那么船东什么时候都有这种权利,现在承租人晚付了租金,船东当然有权撤船了。至于他先前一贯接受晚付租金的做法并不相干,不可能令合约写清楚了的条文有不同解释。"但案子如果结合衡平法去判,判法就完全不同了。因为有禁反言的理论,法院会说:"既然船东过往一直对租金晚付没有异议,表示他习惯上已接受了这种晚付的做法,也与承租人达成了这个共识,因此现在就不能在毫无通知的情况下突然采取撤船行动,否则会造成不公平。"实际上船东先前的习惯做法已构成禁反言(共识性禁反言或承诺性禁反言):The "Petrofina" (1948) 82 Lloyd's Rep. 43先例。站在船东的立场,遇有这类屡屡晚付租金的情况,怎样才可能确保撤船的权利呢?通常,在市场租金水平更低时,即使租金晚付,船东也不会撤船,承租人这时也不怕撤船,甚至希望以此来刺激船东撤船,反正晚付租金并不等于承租人声明不付租金而违约/毁约(repudiation),充其量晚付也只是违反保证条文(breach of warranty),撤船解约仅仅是船东行使租约赋予的选择权(exercise option)所致,船东日后若索赔解约造成的损失亦不大可行。[10] 因此承租人在租金市场下跌时，更希望船东撤船以甩掉这个不很有利的租约，所以很多时候都会有意无意地晚付租金。这时船东若想不撤船而又要保有租约中撤船的权利，就必须在每次租金到期未付时向承租人提出抗议，抗议其晚付租金。虽然这种抗议承租人很可能置之不理，但却在法律上保证了船东日后依约撤船解约的权利。等到以后租金市场上涨了，高于租约水平时，若承租人未有警觉而仍然晚付租金，船东就可以候机撤船了。这样，承租人就不能说船东被"共识性禁反言"（estoppel by convention），因为船东对每次租金晚付都提出了抗议，表明他并没有与承租人达成接受晚付租金的共识，因而不构成禁反言。这样承租人就只能看着船东撤船了。

不难看出，上述禁反言（特别是承诺性禁反言）的情形实际上与弃权极为相似，船东接受晚付租金的行为也可解释为船东放弃了在租金晚付时撤船的合约权利。事实上，已经在本书多次提到禁反言与弃权的理论常常被一并提出。但上例中船东无论是弃权还是禁反言，都不必是永久性的（final），即船东租期内依约撤船的合约权利只是暂时（suspensive）地失去了，船东尚可以通过提前给承租人适当通知来恢复原有租约下的撤船权利。如以前 12 个月租金都是晚付了，船东也没抗议过，现在租金市场涨了，船东就可以提前给承租人通知说：过去 12 个月你都晚付租金，从现在开始不行了，第 13 个月起租金一定要按时付。这样一通知，下次承租人如果再晚付租金，船东就可以撤船了。因为有了船东的这种合理的提前通知，日后再依约撤船对承租人就不存在不公平了。

再举一个近期涉及造船合约仲裁的例子。案情也是航运市场低迷，外国船东作为买方以造船延误，过了合约规定的死亡日期或销约期为由终止合约。但在该仲裁案件中，双方有一个争议是正确的死亡日期到底是哪一天。因为根据合约规定，这日期是从中国船厂收到第一期分期付款（船价）的一天开始计算。在买方终止合约后，双方有争议是船厂在哪天才收到支付。船厂声称（并提供证据）是买方以为到期的一天之后的 3 天。换言之，终止合约的死亡日期应是在买方终止合约后 3 天才届临，买方提早行动等于违约/毁约。但问题是双方在第一期支付后的交往与互动，包括第二期与第三期分期付款，都是以买方以为的一天为准，船厂也完全接受与没有异议。结果在开庭前，船厂的代表律师撤销了这一争议，估计知道难逃被仲裁庭判是共识性禁反言成立的命运。

---

〔10〕 详见杨良宜《合约的解释：规则与应用》一书第十章 3.2.3.6 段。在本书第一章之 6.2 段也提到近期的 Spar Shipping AS v. Grand China Logistics Holding（Group）Co. Ltd.（2016）EWCA Civ 982 先例也确认了这一法律地位。

2. 共识性禁反言的改变与放宽

在本章第 1 段曾经提到过,这种形式的禁反言一开始非常技术性,但后来不断有改变与放宽,这里介绍两个重要的改变。

2.1 改变之一:从契约延伸到简式合约

"共识性禁反言"(estoppel by convention)源自普通法发展起来的"契约性禁反言"(estoppel by deed),契约就是指有盖章与签署的合约。主要是在这种合约中,如果在序言或者在合约条文中有说明一些特定的事实作为双方交易的依据,这就对双方当事人有约束,不允许事后以其他事实才是真实去推翻。这种形式的禁反言可节录 Greer v. Kettle (1938) AC 156 先例中,Maugham 勋爵说:"... the recital must relate to specific facts... be certain, clear, and unambiguous... Estoppel by deed is a rule of evidence founded on the principle that a solemn and unambiguous statement... in a deed must be taken as binding between parties and privies, and therefore as not admitting any contradictory proof... this is a rule of common law."

第一个改变与放宽是在 Carpenter v. Buller (1841) 8 M & W 209 先例。该先例将这种形式的禁反言放宽适用在一般的简式合约(simple contract),令简式合约中的一些特定事实,也对双方当事人产生同样的禁反言后果。Parke B 大法官是这样说:"If a distinct statement of **a particular fact** is made in the recital of a bond or other instrument under seal, and a contract is made with reference to that recital, it is unquestionably true that, as between the parties to that instrument, and in an action upon it, it is not competent for the party bound to deny the recital... and **a recital in instruments not under seal may be... conclusive to the same extent**."(加黑部分是笔者的强调)

2.2 改变之二:从事实的错误假设延伸到法律

这一十分重要的改变与放宽在近三十年来带来大量涉及共识性禁反言的案件。这一变就是来自英国上诉庭的 Amalgamated v. Texas Bank (1982) 1 Lloyd's Rep. 27 重要先例。

可以注意的是,所有早期有关这种形式的禁反言都只是局限在事实方面。如在澳大利亚高院的 Con - Stan Industries of Australia Pty Ltd. v. Norwich Winterthur Insurance (Australia) Ltd. (1986) 160 CLR 226 先例中,就有说明共识性禁反言只是局限在对事实的错误共识。另在 Burkinshaw v. Nicholls (1878) 3 App Cas 1004 先例中,Blackburn 勋爵说:"... their rights shall be regulated, not by the real state of facts, but by that **conventional state of facts** which the two parties agree to make the basis of their action."(加黑部分是笔者的强调)

2.2.1　双方订约后的行为不能解释合约的大原则

共识性禁反言只局限在对事实的理解的部分原因是合约法解释合约条文的重要大原则之一，即不能根据双方订约后的所作所为去协助合约的解释。[11] 这一大原则在贵族院的 Whitworth Street Estates (Manchester) Ltd. v. James Miller & Partners Ltd. (1970) 1 Lloyd's Rep. 269 先例中明确下来，Reid 勋爵说："... it is not legitimate to use as an aid in the construction of the contract anything which the parties said and did after it was made. Otherwise one might have the result that a contract meant one thing the day it was signed, but by reason of subsequent events meant something different a month or a year later."

在同一个先例中，Wilberforce 勋爵也说除非是为了寻找是否有禁反言，或者另有新协议，订约后的行为与合约的解释没有任何关系："Unless it were found an estoppel or a subsequent agreement, I do not think that subsequent conduct can be relevant to this question." Viscount Dilhorne 也说一方当事人的事后行为会带来禁反言："... subsequent conduct by one party may give rise to an estoppel."

这表示对双方订立的合约的解释只会在两种情况下被一方当事人或者双方当事人事后的行为改变，一是事后的另一个新的协议，也通常被称为合约更改（variation）[12]；二是禁反言。

首先更改合约，众所周知是需要满足与订立有效合约同样的条件，其中主要的条件是要有约因/对价。第二种会改变对原来合约解释的情况就是禁反言，这主要是本书第四章介绍的承诺性禁反言与本章介绍的共识性禁反言。这种禁反言会令原来合约的解释有了改变，像更改合约的后果一样，但不涉及双方同意更改与有约因/对价。正如 Denning 勋爵在 Amalgamated v. Texas Bank (1982) 1 Lloyd's Rep. 27 先例中说："If parties to a contract, by their course of dealing, put a particular interpretation on the terms of it - on the faith of which each of them - to the knowledge of the other - acts and conducts their mutual affairs - they are bound by that interpretation just as much as if they had written it down as being a variation of the contract.[13]"

从 Denning 勋爵的判决可以看到，共识性禁反言延伸到对合约解释的错误理解，再也不是只局限在事实方面的错误理解。这是非常重要的改变，而且是经常会发生的情况。换言之，双方在订约后的行为不会影响对原合约的解释，但可能会构成共识性禁反言，而带来的后果实际上也等同于影响对原合约的正确解释。

---

〔11〕见杨良宜《合约的解释：规则与应用》一书第六章之 2.5.2 段。

〔12〕见本书第三章第 2 段。

〔13〕如果合约方在交易过程中给了一条条文特定的解释，并且根据这一解释去行动与处理他们共同的事情，他们就会受这一解释的约束（即使这一解释并非是该合约条文正确的解释），如同双方更改原合约的条文一样。

2.2.2 Amalgamated v. Texas Bank 先例的案情

Amalgamated v. Texas Bank (1982) 1 Lloyd's Rep. 27 先例是针对"共识性禁反言"(estoppel by convention)的发展与普及的主要先例。首先可简单介绍该先例的案情。Amalgamated 是一家英国的地产公司,它想要借钱让其子公司 ANPP 在巴哈马建一栋大厦。英国的一家商业银行 Texas Bank 同意借钱,但作为担保,除了之后将建成的大厦抵押,Amalgamated 还向 Texas Bank 签发了一份对全部 325 万美元贷款的见索即付保函(demand guarantee)。[14]

之后,因为巴哈马金融管制的原因,Texas Bank 需要通过一家名为 Portsoken 的巴哈马子公司将这笔钱借给 ANPP。具体做法如下:(1)Portsoken 从 Texas Bank 得到美元的款项,然后将美元直接借给 ANPP,而无需将钱转为巴哈马元。(2)Portsoken 将取得该大厦的美元抵押。(3)Portsoken 保留一个美元账户,用来收取与支持这个背靠背贷款的本金与利息。

但由于 Texas Bank 的疏忽,Amalgamated 的见索即付保函的受益人没有更改为或加上 Portsoken。可以说在有关的时间,如果 Texas Bank 向 Amalgamated 要求一份新的保函或是要求在原来的保函上加上 Portsoken 作为受益人,Amalgamated 是不会拒绝的。接下来双方在一连串的交往与互动中,都当做钱是由 Texas Bank 借给 ANPP,Amalgamated 做出的保函是有效。这一系列的交往与互动包括放款给 ANPP,推迟支付利息的协议,对大厦进行估价,之后在 Amalgamated 经济发生困难时推迟还款的讨论等。

这栋在巴哈马的大厦建成后,只卖了 250 万美元,即还欠了 Texas Bank 75 万美元。Amalgamated 签发的见索即付保函就成了 Texas Bank 剩下的唯一担保。除了这笔巴哈马的贷款,Texas Bank 与 Amalgamated 之间还有一笔针对伦敦地产/房屋的贷款。Amalgamated 经济出现问题后,它在伦敦的地产/房屋被卖掉以偿还 Texas Bank 这笔伦敦的贷款。在扣除相关的费用后,Texas Bank 发现卖出房屋的钱还剩下超过 75 万美元。Texas Bank 可以也确实从中拿了 75 万美元来抵销(set off)这一笔巴哈马贷款的欠款。但 Amalgamated 申请破产,清盘人质疑了这份见索即付保函,认为这份保函的受益人只是 Texas Bank,不包括真正对 ANPP 提供贷款的 Portsoken。而鉴于 Texas Bank 从来没有向 ANPP 提供贷款,这一份文件只是废纸一张。为此,Amalgamated 的清盘人向法院提起诉讼,申请宣告判决 Amalgamated 在见索即付保函下对 Texas Bank 没有责任。

在解释这份见索即付保函时,一审的 Goff 大法官做出了不利于 Texas Bank 的判决,毕竟文件上没有包括 Portsoken。Goff 大法官也不接受 Portsoken 可以被解释为

〔14〕 有关担保会涉及弃权与禁反言的各种不同情况,将在本书第十一章详论。

Texas Bank 的代理人[15]的主张。这样,Texas Bank 就要依赖另一个重要的替代争议,即在 Amalgamated 与 Texas Bank 的交往与互动过程中是否构成共识性禁反言。在这一替代争议,Goff 大法官与上诉庭的判决基本上一致,即 Amalgamated 败诉。

Goff 大法官根据"衡平法禁反言"(equitable estoppel)判 Texas Bank 胜诉,因为 Amalgamated 没有向 Texas Bank 指出保函没有加上 Portsoken 的错误,也以行动鼓励并加强了 Texas Bank 的错误理解,认为保函还是可以保障它自己。Goff 大法官跟从了 Taylor Fashions Ltd. v. Liverpool Victoria Trustees Co. Ltd.(1982) QB 133 先例说:"... that a representation by a party as to the legal effect of an agreement can give rise to an estoppel."Goff 大法官接着说:"... I am satisfied that Mr. Foster's(Amalgamated 的代表)conduct, though, of course, completely innocent, so influenced Mr. Oldfield's(Texas Bank 的代表)conduct, as to render it unconscionable on the part of the plaintiffs(Amalgamated)now to take advantage of the bank's error."

Goff 大法官也强调了陈述方推翻他曾经做出的陈述不合情理(it was unconscionable for the representor to go back on his representation)。

但根据"陈述性禁反言"(estoppel by representation)有一点牵强,因为没有证据显示了 Amalgamated 曾经对 Texas Bank 做出一些足以被认为是禁反言的陈述。Amalgamated也谈不上有责任提醒 Texas Bank 犯了错,[16]因为它自己也不知道有这一错误。事实上,证据显示 Texas Bank 的错误完全是自己疏忽,与 Amalgamated 无关,这在上诉庭被指出,Denning 勋爵是这样说:"The mistake by the bank was self-induced. They had overlooked the wording of the guarantee. They thought it applied to moneys owing to Portsoken as well as moneys owing to the bank. This was the bank's own mistake. It was not induced by the plaintiffs. Nor did the plaintiffs do anything to contribute to it, or to reinforce it - except this: that they did not contradict it. They did not tell the bank that it was mistaken. But then, it is said, how could the plaintiffs be expected to contradict it, when they were under the same mistake? So runs the argument on behalf of the plaintiffs. The bank made a mistake of its own - everything it did followed

---

〔15〕 在上诉庭,Denning 勋爵说 Texas Bank 是 Portsoken 的分身(alter ego)。但在跨国企业中,出于商业考虑,总公司往往会成立一些分公司。虽然这些分公司是由总公司完全控制,但如果可以轻易说总公司是分公司的分身,就会造成混乱与不肯定。一般来说,总公司与分公司之间不属于分身或有关系方(privity),只有在涉及欺诈需要刺破公司面纱(piercing the corporate veil)时,才会将两者视为分身关系。因此在该先例中,上诉庭的其他两位大法官支持了 Denning 勋爵对共识性禁反言的判决,但对 Denning 勋爵说 Texas Bank 是 Portsoken 的分身的说法,没有支持或有所针对。

〔16〕 见本书第四章之 6.4 段与第五章第 10 段。

from its own mistake. So it should put up with the consequences.[17]"

这就带来了该先例最重要的问题,如果 Amalgamated 知道 Texas Bank 犯错但为了自己的利益没有提醒 Texas Bank,Amalgamated 事后不能利用 Texas Bank 的错误获利是很清楚。Texas Bank 可以依赖陈述性禁反言或"沉默性禁反言"(estoppel by acquiescence),甚至双方事后的交往会构成"鼓励性禁反言"(estoppel by encouragement)。但如果 Amalgamated 不知道 Texas Bank 犯错,它是否可以因为 Texas Bank 的错误获利,Texas Bank 是否有类似的救济?如果没有类似的救济,法院做出判决前必须先分辨 Amalgamated 主观上是否知道 Texas Bank 犯错,这显然很困难。在一审,Goff 大法官不认为 Amalgamated 是否知道 Texas Bank 犯错会带来不同的结果。

原告 Amalgamated 的清盘人上诉,在上诉庭有两个主要的争议。一是 Texas Bank 自己有了错误理解,原告 Amalgamated 最多只是无辜地沉默(innocently acquiesced),没有任何陈述,能否构成禁反言。二是 Texas Bank 是将禁反言用作宝剑而不是盾牌。

针对第一个争议,上诉庭的三位大法官都认为这种情况可以构成共识性禁反言。Denning 勋爵总结说:"So I come to this conclusion: When the parties to a contract are both under a common mistake as to the meaning or effect of it – and thereafter embark on a course of dealing on the footing of that mistake – thereby replacing the original terms of the contract by a conventional basis on which they both conduct their affairs, then the original contract is replaced by the conventional basis. The parties are bound by the conventional basis. Either party can sue or be sued upon it just as if it had been expressly agreed between them....[18] The general principle applies to this case. Both Amalgamated and the bank proceeded for years on the basis of the underlying assumption that the guarantee of Amalgamated applied to the US $ 3,250,000 advanced by the bank for the Nassau building. Their dealings in rearranging the portfolio, in releasing properties and moneys, were all conducted on that basis. On that basis, the bank applied the surplus of US $ 750,000 (on English properties) in discharge of the obligations of Amalgamated under the guarantee. It would be most unfair and unjust to allow the liquidator to

---

〔17〕 在见索即付保函上犯的错是 Texas Bank 自己的疏忽。Amalgamated 自己也不知道有这一错误,更不用说会向 Texas Bank 做出任何陈述诱导 Texas Bank 做出错误假设,或是提醒 Texas Bank 犯错。这就带来一个疑问是,在这种情况下会有什么后果。这方面对显示不公平与不合情理这一要件的重要性在本章之 3.3.1 段会进一步讨论,并介绍一些后来针对性的先例中,如 The "August Leonhardt" (1985) 2 Lloyd's Rep. 28 先例与 Credit Suisse v. Allerdale BC (1995) 1 Lloyd's Rep. 315 先例等。

〔18〕 当合约双方对合约的意思或后果有共同的错误理解,并根据该错误的理解进行了一连串的交往与互动,这一共识/错误理解就替代了原来合约的解释。双方也受到这一共识的约束,任何一方可以依据这一共识提出起诉或被诉,好像双方明示同意了合约更改一样。

depart from that basis and to claim back now the US $750,000.[19]"

Eveleigh 大法官也同意,说:"... the parties negotiated upon the agreed assumption that the plaintiff guaranteed the Nassau loan... Estoppel operates... to prevent a party from denying a representation or an assumed state of facts in relation to the transaction supported by that representation or assumed state of facts. The estoppel does not go beyond the transaction in which it arose."

Brandon 大法官认为双方事后的交往与互动显示出对这一担保是针对巴哈马这笔贷款的共识,而这属于典型的共识性禁反言,说:"... for the purposes of those transactions both the bank and the plaintiffs assumed the truth of a certain state of affairs, namely that the guarantee given in relation to the Nassau loan effectively bound the plaintiffs to discharge any indebtedness of (the subsidiary) to (the bank's subsidiary). The transactions took place on the basis of that assumption, and their course was influenced by it in the sense that, if the assumption had not been made, the course of the transactions would without doubt have been different. These facts produce... a classic example of... estoppel by convention."

虽然这一重要的先例没有说清楚共识性禁反言是适用在对事实还是法律方面的错误理解,[20]但显然对合约或协议的解释属于法律问题。如果双方对合约条文有共同的错误理解,就可以构成共识性禁反言,这就令共识性禁反言的适用范围有了很大延伸。在这个重要先例后的很多案件中,笔者只挑一个对 Amalgamated v. Texas Bank 先例的总结,就是在 Hamel – Smith v. Pycroft & Jetsave Ltd. (unreported, 5 February 1987)先例中 Peter Gibson 大法官所说:"I do not propose to essay a definition of estoppel by convention. It is sufficient for the purposes of this case to adopt the description given by the Court of Appeal in Keen v. Holland, of the essential nature of the

---

〔19〕 这一案件的大原则就是 Amalgamated 与 Texas Bank 为了这笔贷款交往了几年,双方都理解为 Amalgamated 做出的担保就是为了 Texas Bank 提供这笔贷款建造巴哈马的大厦。双方的安排,包括把大厦抵押以及提供这笔贷款,都是根据这一理解与共识。如果允许 Amalgamated 的清盘人撤回这一理解与共识,并要求银行交出用来抵销这笔贷款的 75 万美元会是十分不公平与不合情理。

〔20〕 对一份私人文件或是针对私人权利的立法所做出的陈述在很多先例被视为事实的陈述(虽然与法律有混合):Reynell v. Sprye (1852) 1 De G M & G 660; Cooper v. Phibbs (1867) LR 2 HK 149; West London Commercial Bank v. Kitson (1884) 13 QBD 360 CA; Derry v. Peek (1889) 14 App Cas 337 HL; Sarat Chunder Dey v. Gopal Chunder Laha (1892) LR 19 Ind App 203; Burrows v. Rhodes (1899) 1 QB 816; de Tchihatchef v. Salerni Coupling Ltd. (1932) 1 Ch 330; Farrow v. Orttewell (1933) Ch 480 CA; Algar v. Middlesex CC (1945) 2 All ER 243; Lyle – Meller v. A Lewis & Co. (Westminster) Ltd. (1956) 1 WLR 29 CA; Kai Nam v. Ma Kam Chan (1956) AC 358; Sidney Bolsom Investment Trust Ltd. v. E. Karmios & Co. (London) Ltd. (1956) 1 QB 529 CA; Taylor Fashions Ltd. v. Liverpool Victoria Trustees Co. Ltd. (1982) QB 133; Amalgamated v. Texas Bank (1982) 1 Lloyd's Rep. 27 等先例。

Amalgamated case, and to say that it applies where (1) parties have established by their construction of their agreement or their apprehension of its legal effect a conventional basis, (2) on that basis they have regulated their subsequent dealings, to which I would add (3) it would be unjust or unconscionable if one of the parties resiled from that convention.〔21〕"

针对第二个争议,即宝剑与盾牌之争,不同类型的禁反言针对这方面的法律地位都不稳定。〔22〕 在该先例中,Brandon 大法官说:

"In my view much of the language used in connection with these concepts is no more than a matter of semantics. Let me consider the present case and suppose that the bank had brought an action against the plaintiffs before they went into liquidation to recover moneys owed by A. N. P. P. to Portsoken. In the statement of claim in such an action the bank would have pleaded the contract of loan incorporating the guarantee, and averred that, on the true construction of the guarantee, the plaintiffs were bound to discharge the debt owed by A. N. P. P. to Portsoken.〔23〕 By their defence the plaintiffs would have pleaded that, on the true construction of the guarantee, the plaintiffs were only bound to discharge debts owed by A. N. P. P. to the bank, and not debts owed by A. N. P. P. to Portsoken.〔24〕 Then in their reply the bank would have pleaded that, by reason of an estoppel arising from the matters discussed above, the plaintiffs were precluded from questioning the interpretation of the guarantee which both parties had, for the purpose of the transactions between them, assumed to be true.〔25〕

In this way the bank, while still in form using the estoppel as a shield, would in substance be founding a cause of action on it. This illustrates what I would regard as the true proposition of law, that, while a party cannot in terms found a cause of action on an estoppel, he may, as a result of being able to rely on an estoppel, succeed on a cause of action on which, without being able to rely on that estoppel, he would necessarily have

---

〔21〕 Amalgamated v. Texas Bank 先例本质上最重要的地方是可以适用在:(1)双方对协议有共同的错误解释或对其法律后果有共同的错误理解;(2)他们在这个基础上交往与互动;(3)其中一方事后想从这一共识中脱身是不公平与不合情理——加起来就构成共识性禁反言。

〔22〕 见本章第 5 段,本书第四章第 10 段与本书第五章第 3 段。

〔23〕 如果不是 Texas Bank 将 75 万美元用来抵销 ANPP 向 Portsoken 欠下的贷款,Texas Bank 就会在 Amalgamated破产前开始诉讼,要求它在见索即付保函下承担责任。

〔24〕 而 Amalgamated 在答辩书中就会抗辩说根据保函的解释,Amalgamated 只对 ANPP 向 Texas Bank 欠下的贷款要承担责任,而对 ANPP 向 Portsoken 欠下的贷款没有责任。

〔25〕 而之后 Texas Bank 在回复书中就会说根据共识性禁反言,Amalgamated 被禁止撤回双方对这一担保是针对巴哈马的这笔贷款的共同理解。

failed.[26] That, in my view, is, in substance, the situation of the bank in the present case."

2.2.3　Amalgamated v. Texas Bank 先例后的蓬勃发展

Amalgamated v. Texas Bank（1982）1 Lloyd's Rep. 27 先例大受欢迎，因为经常会发生双方订约后基于对合约的共同错误理解而有一系列履行合约的交往与互动的情况，如果这可以构成禁反言并超越合约条文，将会对已经按照错误理解做出履行的双方更为合理。众所周知，除了一些例外情况，[27] 解释合约条文时不可以考虑双方订约后的行为。[28] 但这个问题也颇有争议，一个说法是双方的订约意图只有他们最清楚，因此应该考虑双方订约后的行为以帮助解释合约条文，尤其是含糊的合约条文。但也有说法是解释合约应该是客观来看合约条文的意思，而不应考虑双方各自存在理解错误的情况，所以也就不应该考虑双方订约后的行为。这在 Whitworth Street Estates（Manchester）Ltd. v. James Miller & Partners Ltd.（1970）1 Lloyd's Rep. 269 先例中，Reid 勋爵已经一锤定音，判是英国法律不可以考虑双方订约后的行为以帮助解释合约条文，说："... it is not legitimate to use as an aid in the construction of the contract anything which the parties said or did after it was made. Otherwise one might have the result that a contract meant one thing the day it was signed, but by reason of subsequent events meant something different a month or a year later."

在同一个先例中，Dilhorne 勋爵说虽然双方订约后的行为不能帮助解释合约，但可能会构成禁反言（subsequent conduct by one party may give rise to an estoppel）。这表示双方后来的交往与互动并非不重要，反而可能十分关键。这些交往与互动可能会构成承诺性禁反言，还有可能构成共识性禁反言。在合约尤其是商业合约的履行过程中，双方总要有一定的交往与互动，很容易就可以从中挑出一些言行说是双方之间存在错误的共识或有共同的错误理解才会这样互动。尤其对合约的解释有共同的错误理解的情况经常发生，毕竟解释合约本来就不肯定，经常带来争议，即使是法院的判决，也常常发生上诉后被推翻的情况。合约双方在之前的履行中对合约的理解很可能与发生争议后法官的解释不一致，即使咨询过称职律师，也无法避免。

因此在这一 Amalgamated v. Texas Bank 的上诉庭先例开了方便之门令共识性禁反言的说法适用在双方对合约的条文或法律后果有共同错误理解的情况之后，笔

---

〔26〕这样，显然 Texas Bank 将共识性禁反言用作了盾牌，但实际上是根据禁反言成立了诉因。因此，Brandon 大法官认为真正的法律地位是如果原告有其他诉因（在该先例就是 Texas Bank 要求 Amalgamated 在保函下承担责任），但这个诉因有缺陷（保函的受益人没有加上 Portsoken），原告可以依赖禁反言进行补救。在这种情况下，可以说禁反言就在一定程度上变为宝剑，因为如果不能依赖禁反言，原告的诉因不能成立。

〔27〕如果合约不是全部都是书面形式，或干脆是口头合约：Carmichael v. National Power Plc.（1999）1 WLR 2042；Maggs v. Marsh（2006）BLR 395 等先例。

〔28〕见杨良宜的《合约的解释：规则与应用》一书第六章之 2.5.2 段。

者经常见到共识性禁反言作为替代争议被提出。如果不对是否满足共识性禁反言的构成要件严格把关,就有令合约条文如何规定变得不再重要的潜在危险,要改变原本的合约地位也比需要约因/对价的合约更改(variation)容易得多。本章接下来的段节会逐一介绍构成共识性禁反言的要件。

3. 构成共识性禁反言的要件

在 Commissioners for Her Majesty's Revenue and Customs v. Benchdollar Limited and Others (2009) EWHC 1310 (Ch)先例中,Briggs 大法官针对构成共识性禁反言的要件总结说:"In my judgment, the principles applicable to the assertion of an estoppel by convention arising out of non – contractual dealings, to be derived from Keen v. Holland, and the cases which comment upon it, are as follows: i) It is not enough that the common assumption upon which the estoppel is based is merely understood by the parties in the same way. It must be expressly shared between them.[29] ii) The expression of the common assumption by the party alleged to be estopped must be such that he may properly be said to have assumed some element of responsibility for it, in the sense of conveying to the other party an understanding that he expected the other party to rely upon it.[30] iii) The person alleging the estoppel must in fact have relied upon the common assumption, to a sufficient extent, rather than merely upon his own independent view of the matter.[31] iv) That reliance must have occurred in connection with some subsequent mutual dealing between the parties.[32] v) Some detriment must thereby have been suffered by the person alleging the estoppel, or benefit thereby have been conferred upon the person alleged to be estopped, sufficient to make it unjust or unconscionable for the latter to assert the true legal (or factual) position.[33]"

在之后的 Anthony Stephen Wollenberg v. Casinos Austria International Holding GMBH (2011) EWHC 103 (Ch)先例中,Preedy v. Dunne (2016) EWCA Civ 805 先例与 Sean Wilken QC 与 Karim Ghaly 先生所著的《The Law of Waiver, Variation, and Estoppel》(第 3 版,2012 年)一书之 10.01 段,也都直接或间接引用了 Briggs 大法官

---

〔29〕 双方不仅需要知道有共同的错误假设,并且需要明示沟通过有这样的共识。

〔30〕 被禁反言的一方在与对方沟通自己做出的假设时,必须希望对方依赖这个假设,即对双方达成共识或共同假设有一定的责任。

〔31〕 声称存在共识性禁反言的一方必须依赖共同假设,而不只是他单方面的观点行事。

〔32〕 对共同假设的依赖体现在双方随后的交往中。

〔33〕 声称存在禁反言的一方必须蒙受了一定的损害或是声称被禁反言的一方必须获得好处,从而导致允许后者偏离双方的共识是不公平与不合情理。

在 Commissioners for Her Majesty's Revenue and Customs v. Benchdollar Limited and Others 先例的判决。

接下来会对这些要件逐一分析。

3.1　要件之一:共同的假设

3.1.1　双方必须有共同的假设

要构成共识性禁反言,合约双方必须有共同的假设(shared common assumption),而不能只是自己一方的错误理解。这在很多先例都有提到,如在近期的 Wilson v. Truelove (2003) EWHC 750 (Ch)先例中,Simon Berry QC 大法官说:"In my judgment,... that the parties must be jointly proceeding on the basis of a **shared common assumption**... In the instant case the parties did not jointly proceed on the basis of a shared common assumption. They did no more than both enter into an agreement in circumstances in which they individually misunderstood the legal effect of one of its terms. They did not thereafter proceed jointly on the basis of that misunderstanding: things were done or not done individually... on the basis of their own misunderstanding, and not on the basis of any encouragement, still less representations on the part of the Wilsons."(加黑部分是笔者的强调)

在 Durbam v. BAI (Run Off) Ltd. (2008) EWHC 2692 (QB)先例中,Burton 大法官说:"... it seems to me, by reference to the passage in Spencer Bower to which I have referred in paragraph 206 above, that it can be said, by adapting the words of Mr Simon Berry QC, sitting as a Deputy Judge of the Chancery Division in Wilson v. Truelove [2003] EWHC 750 Ch, that, if there was a misunderstanding as to the effect of that wording, [MMI and Zurich] did not... **proceed jointly on the basis of that misunderstanding**: things were done or not done individually [by Zurich] on the basis of their own misunderstanding and not on the basis of any encouragement, still less representations on the part of [MMI]."(加黑部分是笔者的强调)

至于这个错误的假设是何原因造成并不重要,如记错或错误解释合约。在 Dixon & Anor v. Blindley Heath Investments Ltd. & Anor (2015) EWCA Civ 1023 先例中,Hildyard 大法官说:"It may be that most cases of estoppel by convention arise from a mistake made by the parties or a mistake made by one party and acquiesced in by the other. But the authorities do not suggest that the principle is confined to cases of mistake. Moreover, a mistaken recollection is not, to our minds, legally different from a state of forgetfulness. The essence of the principle is that the parties have conducted themselves on a conventional basis which is, wittingly or unwittingly, different from the true basis. Whether the true state of things has been misappreciated, misremembered or forgotten should make no difference to whether the parties have in the event mutually adopted a common assumption."

Gloster 大法官在 Centrica Plc. & British Gas Trading Limited v. Premier Power Limited (2006) EWHC 3068 (Comm)先例中说,共同的假设必须双方沟通过(crossing the line),说:"It was common ground that **a common assumption must be based on conduct 'crossing the line'**; The August Leonhardt [1985] 2 Ll Rep. 28 at 34 ; The Indian Endurance (No 2) [1998] AC 878 at 913, HL (Lord Steyn); Philip Collins Ltd. v. Davis (supra) at 823 (Jonathan Parker J)."(加黑部分是笔者的强调)

在 ING Bank NV v. Ros Roca SA (2011) EWCA Civ 353 先例中,Carnwath 大法官认为构成共识性禁反言最重要的就是所谓的共同假设,并引用了 Spencer Bower 与 Turner 的《Estoppel by Representation》(第 4 版,2004 年)一书 之Ⅶ2.3 段,说:"that the only distinction between an estoppels by convention and other forms of estoppels... namely by **mutual assent** rather than unilateral assertion."(加黑部分是笔者的强调)

该先例的案情已经在本书第五章之 13.2 段有介绍,有关的争议是 ING 作为财务顾问的收费如何计算。虽然从双方的互动(interaction)与通信往来(correspondence)看 ING 与 Ros Roca 有收费约为 400 万欧元的共同假设,但实际上 ING 内部已经知道根据合约的计算公式,他们可以获得的收费会大大超过这个数字,即不存在错误的假设。但 ING 没有向 Ros Roca 说明,希望履行后再根据合约计算正确的收费。之后 ING 提起诉讼,要求 Ros Roca 支付根据合约的计算公式计算出的收费,而 Ros Roca 的抗辩之一就是共识性禁反言。在上诉庭,Rix 大法官认为共识性禁反言在该先例不适用,因为双方之间事实上不存在共同假设,适用的反而是陈述性禁反言,说:"... in a situation in which it is plain that, **internally**, ING did not share the assumption concerning transaction costs which **externally and objectively**, it affected and purported to share, there is, to my mind, good sense in considering the matter through the eyes of an estoppel by representation..."

在 The "Indian Endurance" and The "Indian Grace" (No. 2) (1998) 1 Lloyd's Rep. 1 (HL)先例中,一艘前往印度柯枝市(Cochin)给印度政府运输军火的 Indian Grace 轮起火。起火的船舱货物全损,另有部分货物被丢弃/投弃(jettison)。印度政府在柯枝法院向船东索赔被投弃货物的损失,另在英国法院对 Indian Grace 轮的姐妹船 Indian Endurance 轮提起诉讼,索赔起火船舱货物的全损。双方同意英国法适用,被告船东根据 1982 年《Civil Jurisdiction and Judgments Act》之 section 34(一事不再审)声称印度政府应该在柯枝法院的诉讼中一并提出货物全损的索赔并要求撤销诉讼,毕竟涉及的是同一个事故。[34] 在贵族院([1993] AC 10),法院判是不应撤销诉讼,而应由海事法院重审以决定船东在程序上的抗辩是否被禁反言。在重审([1994] 2 Lloyd's Rep. 331)中,Clarke 大法官判是柯枝法院的诉讼是在双方对有关全损的争议会在英国法院诉讼的共同假设上进行的,因此,被告的船东被禁止提出一

---

〔34〕 关于一事不再审的课题,可见本书第九章。

事不再审的抗辩。但这被上诉庭与贵族院推翻,法院判是双方的通讯往来中只是提到了在英国诉讼的意向与可能性,证据显示事实上双方没有共同的假设。

双方没有共同的假设而只是双方之间存在相互误解的例子可见本章之7.1段介绍的The "August Leonhardt" (1985) 2 Lloyd's Rep. 28 CA先例。

3.1.2　双方必须明示沟通过这一共同假设或共识

这方面可节录一些权威说法。首先在Spencer Bower与Turner的《The Law Relating to Estoppel by Representation》(第4版,2004年)一书第184页之Ⅷ.3.2段,说:"It is not enough that each of the two parties acts on an assumption not communicated to the other.[35] It is not, however, necessary that the assumption by the estoppel raiser be created or encouraged by the party to be estopped:[36] but if not, it must be shared in the sense that each is aware of the assumption of the other.[37] – the party of be estopped must have at the very least communicated to the other that he is indeed sharing his ex hypothesi mistaken assumption.[38] Further, if the convention does not bind by contract, the party to be estopped must be unfair for the former to resile from the convention.[39]"

在The "August Leonhardt" (1985) 2 Lloyd's Rep. 28 CA先例中,[40]一票食糖发生货损,相关的提单受1924年《海牙规则》约束,货方必须在卸货后的1年内提起诉讼。原告货方向船东的互保协会要求3个月的延期,这也是惯常的做法。互保协会同意3个月的延期,但加上了无损害与承租人也要同意这3个月延期的限制条件(on a without prejudice basis and provided charterers agree likewise)。而承租人与船东加入同一个互保协会的事实令原告货方产生错觉是,互保协会会在内部获得承租人同意,或者这个限制根本不重要。但一两个月之后,互保协会告知原告货方因为承租人不同意延期,诉讼时效已过。

在一审,Bingham大法官支持原告货方的观点,说:"In the circumstance it was not fair to permit the owners to challenge the assumption made by the plaintiffs that the club would obtain the consent of the charterers to the extension of time."

但这在上诉庭被推翻,因为双方之间没有对这个错误假设(双方都假设对方会取得承租人的同意)沟通过,也谈不上有共识。这是双方之间的误解。互保协会没有可指责的,因为互保协会没有做出任何言行令货方产生这样的误解。Kerr大法官

---

〔35〕 双方即使有同样的错误假设,但没有与对方沟通过就不足够。

〔36〕 这个错误的共识不一定需要是被禁反言的一方造成或鼓动的,这方面在本章之3.3.1段有略有不同的说法。

〔37〕 双方必须都知道对方也有这个错误的假设,即共享这个错误的假设。

〔38〕 被禁反言的一方至少曾经与对方沟通过他也有这个错误的假设。

〔39〕 如果这个错误假设没有被写进双方的合约,要依赖禁反言的一方必须证明另一方从这个错误假设中脱身是不公平与不合情理。

〔40〕 在本章之7.1段有具体介绍。

说："All estoppels must involve some statement or conduct by the party alleged to be estopped on which the alleged representee was entitled to rely and did rely. In this sense all estoppels may be regarded as **requiring some manifest representation which crosses the line between representor and representee, either by statement or conduct**. It may be an express statement or it may be implied from conduct... in cases of so – called estoppels by convention, there must be some mutually manifest conduct by the parties... in the present case... each acted – or failed to act – independently from the other on the basis of a mutual mistake which remained uncommunicated between them. There cannot be any estoppel unless the alleged representor has said or done something, or failed to do something, with the result that – across the line between the parties – his action or inaction has produced some belief or expectation ion the mind of the alleged representee."（加黑部分是笔者的强调）

在 The "Captain Gregos"（No. 2）（1990）2 Lloyd's Rep. 395 先例中，Bingham 大法官说："It is, however, now clear that an estoppel by convention **requires communications to pass across the line between the parties**. It is not enough that each of the two parties acts on an assumption not communicated to the other：The "August Leonhardt"；The "Vistafjord"（1988）2 Lloyd's Rep. 343. In our judgment an estoppel by convention fails here for much the same reasons as made it impossible to imply a contract or find evidence of attornment：nothing whatever passed between PEAG and the shipowners until after the cargo had been delivered to BP."（加黑部分是笔者的强调）

在 The "Indian Endurance" and The "Indian Grace"（No. 2）（1998）1 Lloyd's Rep. 1（HL）先例中，Steyn 勋爵说："It is settled that an estoppels by convention may arise where parties to a transaction act on an assumed state of fact or law, the assumption being either shared by them both or made by one and acquiesced in by the other... **It is not enough that each of the two parties acts on an assumption not communicated to the other.**"（加黑部分是笔者的强调）

Lawrence Collins 大法官在 T& N Ltd.（In Administration）v. Royal & Sun Alliance Plc.（2003）EWHC 1016（Ch）先例说到共识性禁反言不是看双方主观对合约解释的看法或理解，而是重视双方通讯往来的沟通中的共识与共同理解："... estoppel by convention is not... a vehicle to admit evidence of the parties'... subjective intentions or understanding as to the meaning of contractual documents."

在本章第 3 段提到的 Commissioners for Her Majesty's Revenue and Customs v. Benchdollar Limited and Others（2009）EWHC 1310（Ch）先例中，Briggs 大法官说："In my judgment, the principles applicable to the assertion of an estoppel by convention arising out of non – contractual dealings, to be derived from Keen v. Holland, and the cases which comment upon it, are as follows：i）It is not enough that the common assumption upon which the estoppel is based is merely understood by the parties in the same way. **It must be expressly shared between them.** ..."（加黑部分是笔者的强调）

这给中国公司/企业与律师带来的启示是，如果遇到要证明双方是否存在共识的争议，要非常小心处理与重视利用诉讼程序中的盘问环节。因为在盘问中，精明的律师很可能会设计一些陷阱，如针对在文书请求中对方提出的用以证明存在共识的书信往来、电话沟通或口头证据等，律师就会逐一询问对方证人在当时是怎样看待或理解这些往来？得出的假设是什么？根据双方交往的背景是否其他的解释与假设也说得通？对方会否也有同样的理解或假设？证人稍有不慎，就会被带入其实双方并不存在共识的结果。

3.1.3　沉默或不行动通常不代表双方有沟通

在 HIH Casualty & General Insurance Ltd. v. AXA Corporate Solutions (2002) EWCA Civ 1253 先例中，Tuckey 大法官说："Thus formulated it seems to me that the argument based on the estoppel by convention runs into the same difficulties as waiver. **Mere silence, inactivity or failure to take a point cannot be enough to found an estoppel by convention.** Furthermore I am attracted by the way in which the judge dealt with this point. In other words if estoppel by convention works in this situation at all the common assumption must relate to Axa's non – assertion of its right to treat itself as discharged from cover. As neither party was aware of this right there was no such assumption."（加黑部分是笔者的强调）

Gloster 大法官在 Fortisbank SA v. Trenwick International Ltd. & Others (2005) EWHC 399 (Comm)先例引用了上述 Tuckey 大法官的说法，说："In my judgment, Mr Bhalla's（原告代表大律师）argument based on estoppel by convention fails for similar reasons to those which I have already articulated in relation to his arguments based on waiver and promissory estoppel. In my judgment it cannot be said here that Fortis and underwriters proceeded on the basis of an underlying assumption that the contractual limitation provision would not be relied upon. As Tuckey LJ said in HIH Casualty and General Insurance Limited (supra): '**Mere silence, inactivity, or failure to take a point cannot be enough to found an estoppel by convention.**' There was no common assumption that underwriters would not rely on the limitation provision and indeed, as I have already said, Fortis was not aware of this right."（加黑部分是笔者的强调）

即双方仅仅有共同的假设还不够，还需要明示（express）沟通过这一共同分享（shared）的假设，因此沉默或不行动通常无法构成共识性禁反言。在 Spencer Bower 与 Turner 的《The Law Relating to Estoppel by Representation》（第 4 版，2004 年）一书第 187 页脚注 6，说："Assent to a convention by silence will be found only where there is a duty expressly to deny[41] such assent if it is not given. If the court has found there to be such a duty the question of unequivocality will not arise. The question of unequivocality may not, therefore, arise in terms in relation to assent by silence."

在 The "Indian Endurance" and The "Indian Grace" (No. 2) (1998) 1 Lloyd's Rep. 1 (HL)先例中,Steyn 勋爵说除了双方共享,也可以是"made by one and acquiesced in by the other"。但这看来很危险,如 A 向 B 收取一笔账目,但做出的发票(invoice)在金额上明显有错,如少了一个零。B 按照发票上的金额支付后,双方同意结账(close book)。之后 A 发觉错误,要求 B 另做出支付,B 能否以共识性禁反言作为抗辩?答案看来是不能,沉默也可被视为有过沟通的例外情况的要求看来是与有责任说清楚(duty to speak)相同。在 Spencer Bower 与 Turner 的《The Law Relating to Estoppel by Representation》(第 4 版,2004 年)一书第 185 页之Ⅷ.3.3 段说:"It may be sufficient that one party communicates his assumption to the other and the other acquiesces in it: whether the latter has thereby impliedly communicated that he shares the assumption will depend on whether such assent is, in the circumstances, to be inferred from his conduct, or, alternatively, is to be inferred from his silence. It is submitted that the question whether the former is entitled to infer assent to the relevant proposition from the latter failure to correct it, or from the latter's conduct, should be determined on the same principles as the question whether one party has made to another a representation by silence or conduct."

3.1.4 共识性禁反言不要求清楚无误的陈述?

已经在本书第四章与第五章多处提到,"陈述性禁反言"(estoppel by representation)与"承诺性禁反言"(estoppel by promise)需要清楚无误的陈述或承诺,但有说法是共识性禁反言没有这方面的要求。在 Troop v. Gibson (1986) 1 EGLR 1 先例中,John Arnold P. 大法官说清楚无误的要求不适用在共识性禁反言:"... Since this(共识性禁反言)is of a consensual character and the terms of the convention, just as those of a contract once the language is established by the evidence, must be interpreted by the Court and the only true meaning is that decided upon by the Court."

在 ING Bank NV v. Ros Roca SA (2011) EWCA Civ 353 先例中,Carnwath 大法官说:"Mr Phillips(原告代表大律师)provided an apparently straightforward summary of 'the relevant principles'... (ii) The shared common assumption must be sufficiently certain: see Troop v. Gibson [1986] 1 EGLR 1, 6d - f. (iii) ... On examination, none in my view can stand without qualification: ... (ii) **Sufficiently certain**. The proposition refers to a comment in the concurring judgment... in Troop v. Gibson... on

[41] 即在本书第四章之 6.4 段与第五章第 10 段介绍的有责任说清楚(duty to speak)。这是唯一的例外,令在一方沉默的情况下也可被视为有对错误的假设有过沟通。

a point which he acknowledged was unnecessary for the decision. With respect, I find more persuasive the way in which the point was expressed in the leading judgment of Sir John Arnold P. After referring to the extensive argument on the need for a ‘representation’ to be clear and unequivocal to found an estoppel, he said that the same question did not arise in relation to estoppel by convention...:‘Since this is of a consensual character and the terms of the convention, just as those of a contract once the language is established by the evidence, must be interpreted by the court and the only true meaning is that decided upon by the court’.”

根据上述判决,看来 Carnwath 大法官不接受双方的共识必须要向对方做出清楚无误(clear and unequivocal)的陈述或承诺的说法。事实上,在 Spliethoff's Bevrachtingskantoor BV v. Bank of China Ltd. (2015) 2 Lloyd's Rep. 123 先例,〔42〕Carr 女大法官在面对陈述性禁反言与共识性禁反言的争议是判陈述性禁反言的抗辩不成立,因为被告中国银行没有做出过清楚无误的陈述,但共识性禁反言的抗辩成立。

看来在上述的先例是把共识性禁反言与合约的解释视为一回事。针对双方同意的合约条文,即使有含糊之处,法院或仲裁庭也可以通过相关的证据与解释合约的规则找出正确的解释,〔43〕不会否定一条含糊的条文。但笔者认为共识性禁反言与解释合约不同,在前者,如果双方的言行有两种可能的解释,如一方的解释是 A,另一方的言行可以合理解释为 A,也可以合理解释为 B,就很难说双方之间有共同的假设或共识。毕竟在这种情况下,一方应向另一方澄清,如果另一方确认也同意 A,才可以说是双方存在共识。在 Spencer Bower 与 Turner 的《The Law Relating to Estoppel by Representation》(第 4 版,2004 年)一书第 187 页之Ⅷ.4.1 段说:“The certainty of terms necessary for a consensus is, nonetheless, required. A requirement of unequivocality, it might be argued, is, therefore, implicit in the requirement of communication of the shared assumption between the parties: if the estoppel raiser is to succeed in establishing that the language or conduct of the party to be estopped communicated to the estoppel raiser assent to proposition ‘A’, then the language or conduct must be reasonably so understood by him, and the estoppel raiser will not be able to establish that to be the case if the relevant language or conduct could also be reasonably understood as entailing assent to proposition ‘Not A’, and it was unreasonable that the estoppel raiser did not seek clarification. Thus, where the assent of either or both parties to the relevant convention is to be inferred unequivocally convey the consent. While a consensus will be established in accordance with an acceptor's reasonable interpretation of the offer made to him, the question is whether, if there was an ambiguity in the offer, such an interpretation (with-

〔42〕 案情将在本章之 7.16 段介绍。

〔43〕 参见杨良宜《合约的解释:规则与应用》一书第三章第 11 段。

out seeking clarification) was reasonable."

另是双方必须清楚无误地同意他们之间的共同假设,Colman 大法官在 BP Plc. v. Aon (2006) EWHC 424 (Comm)先例中说:"... **unequivocal assent** to the common understanding required for an operative estoppel by convention."(加黑部分是笔者的强调)

在更近期的 Preedy v. Dunne (2016) EWCA Civ 805 先例中,简单介绍案情是一位名叫 Jeannie 的老妇人生前与她的丈夫 Bruce 合伙经营一家酒吧,酒吧所在的物业属于 Jeannie。Jeannie 后来去世,不过她生前在遗嘱中设立了信托,信托的受益人是她与前夫的 3 个孩子——Sarah、Peter 与 Jonathan。但在 Bruce 在世时,如果 Bruce 不愿意继续经营酒吧,物业的收益归 Bruce 所有,如果愿意继续经营酒吧生意,所有收益都可以保留。如果 Bruce 继续经营酒吧生意,Jeannie 希望能让 Jonathan 参与并获得一定的报酬。2001 年 8 月左右,Bruce 以 5 万至 6 万英镑的价格将酒吧一半的生意卖给了 Jonathan。之后,Bruce 因为酗酒与其他身体原因,对酒吧生意的参与越来越少。2013 年 2 月 1 日,Bruce 去世。1999 年至 2003 年,Jonathan 期间花费了超过 30 万英镑对酒吧所在的物业进行了翻新,这无疑提升了物业的价值。信托人后来开始诉讼程序要求 Jonathan 将酒吧交出。

Jonathan 在一审声称,信托人(trustee)的言行令他认为可以想占有这个物业多久就多久,因此他才会出钱进行翻新,即构成了"产权人禁反言"(proprietary estoppel),但这被一审法院拒绝。Jonathan 上诉时提出了共识性禁反言的争议,指 Jeannie 的遗嘱只涉及酒吧所在的物业,在她去世之后,酒吧生意就只属于 Bruce 所有。但 Jonathan 与信托人存在共同错误假设,认为信托人也是酒吧生意的合伙人,因此要承担一半的翻新费用。上诉庭判是双方从来没有这样的共同假设,即使有,也是在 2003 年翻新之后,因此 Jonathan 没有依赖该共同假设并蒙受损害,无法构成共识性禁反言。

而 Jonathan 另一个争议是受益人都因为翻新工程而获益,让他承担所有的翻新费用不公平。但这也不被上诉庭接受,因为其他两位受益人(或信托人)从来没有做出任何承诺或与 Jonathan 有共同理解会共同承担翻新费用。

总结而言,共识性禁反言虽然不需要双方做出清楚无误的陈述或承诺,但通过双方的言行必须能够对共同的假设或共识的具体内容做出清楚无误的解释,否则无法满足双方之间对这点有共同的假设或共识这一要件。另是双方在对这个共同假设或共识表示同意时,必须清楚无误。如果一方没有清楚无误地同意这个假设,就称不上是明示沟通过的共同的假设。

3.2 要件之二:共识或共同假设被依赖

正如在本章其他章节多次提到的,依赖、[44]不公平与不合情理[45]是所有禁反

〔44〕 见 Goff 勋爵在 The "Kanchenjunga" (1990) 1 Lloyd's Rep. 391 (HL)先例所说。

〔45〕 如 Goff 勋爵在 Johnson v. Gore Wood & Co. (2002) 2 AC 1 先例中说:"In the end, I am inclined to think that the many circumstances capable of giving rise to an estoppel cannot be accommodated within a single formula, and that it is unconscionability which provides the link between them."

言(除了合约性禁反言)的共同要件。这里会先针对共识性禁反言对依赖的要件进行介绍。

在 Commissioners for Her Majesty's Revenue and Customs v. Benchdollar Limited and Others (2009) EWHC 1310 (Ch)先例中,Brigg 根据之前的先例总结说:"... (iii) The person alleging the estoppel must in fact have relied upon the common assumption, **to a sufficient extent**, rather than merely upon his own independent view of the matter. (iv) **That reliance must have occurred in connection with some subsequent mutual dealing between the parties.**"(加黑部分是笔者的强调)

如在 Wollenberg v. Casinos Austria International Holding GmbH (2011) EWHC 103 (Ch)先例中,原告 Wollengberg 先生是一位熟悉赌场业务的律师,而被告赌场背后的老板本身没有涉足过赌场业务,但因为觉得赌场业务赚钱,所以想涉足。因此,赌场背后的老板在 2005 年聘用 Wollengberg 先生作为顾问,双方在 2008 年 6 月拓展了聘用合约。新的聘用合约规定了 Wollengberg 先生的工作范围与获得的报酬,除了每年的聘用费,在特定的情况(引进业务)下他还可以获得一定的成功费(success fee)。看来业务发展顺利,赌场在英国的 Glasgow、Milton Keynes 与 Bath 都有了项目,并在意大利政府开放赌业后,试图在意大利发展赌场业务。Wollengberg 先生认为他可以获得英国与意大利赌场 4% 的股票权益(equity)作为成功费。但估计他不肯定聘用合约的有关条文对这一点是十分明确,所以在 2009 年,就开始试图通过双方的会议建立共识,并秘密录音。在会议上,Wollengberg 先生一直试图让赌场高层确认这 4% 的股票权益作为项目的成功费,但估计高层自己也不确定合约是否应该这样解释,所以只是说了一些模棱两可的话,没有说给,也没有说不给。之后 Wollengberg 先生威胁赌场他会将这些秘密录音作为呈堂证供,以显示双方存在共识要将 4% 的股票权益作为成功费。而赌场则以 Wollengberg 先生秘密录音是恶意行为,违反了聘用合约善意的要求为由终止了聘用合约。

于是 Wollengberg 先生开始诉讼,双方最重要的争议是根据聘用合约的解释,Wollengberg 先生能否获得这 4% 的股票权益。Lewison 大法官认为不能,聘用合约中引进(introduce)业务的解释应该是由 Wollengberg 先生自己引进或是与 Wollengberg 先生有直接关系的业务。赌场聘用或雇佣的其他人士(Nuttell 先生)引进的业务,即使该人士是由 Wollengberg 先生向赌场介绍,Wollengberg 先生也不能获得成功费。Wollengberg 先生另一个替代争议是双方在 2009 年的会议中达成一个新的合约。但这也不被 Lewison 大法官接受,因为会议上赌场高层讲的话都是模棱两可的,不会构成新的合约。因此,Wollengberg 先生只能依赖共识性禁反言的替代争议。但 Lewison 大法官判是 Wollengberg 先生在声称双方达成共识或共同假设的会议后,没有再继续为赌场引进新的项目。因此即使双方存在共识或共同的假设,Wollengberg 先生也没有在事后交往(subsequent mutual dealing)中依赖。Lewison 大法官说:"The convention said to be established by the exchange of e-mails arose, at the earliest, on 2

February 2009. By then the Glasgow project had already been introduced by Mr Nuttell. So also had the projects at Milton Keynes and Bath. No further project has since been introduced. So that the introduction of projects (which forms the basis of Wollenberg's claim) cannot be referable to the convention. The pleaded case is a bare assertion of reliance, with no further details..."

另在 Ease Faith Ltd. v. Leonis Marine Management Ltd. & Anor. (2006) EWHC 232 (Comm)先例中,案情将会在本章稍后的7.15段介绍。在该先例中,Andrew Smith 大法官认为提出共识性禁反言的一方必须以为假设是正确的,并依赖该假设行事。而如果他知道这个所谓的共同假设是错误的,但没有向对方指出,如让步或是想息事宁人,他就谈不上是依赖了这个共同的错误假设,不会构成共识性禁反言。Andrew Smith 大法官说:"Mr Holmes(被告代表大律师) accepted that, in order to demonstrate that it would be unjust or unconscionable to allow Leonis to resile from the common assumption (or the assumption in which Leonis acquiesced), they must show that Cloudfree acted on the basis that the assumption was correct: see Wilken & Villiers, The Law of Waiver, Variation and Estoppel, para 10.10, p.228..."

3.3 要件之三:让其中一方否认会导致不公平与不合情理

3.3.1 不公平(unjust or inequitable)

因为合约双方(尤其是商业合约)在履行合约时总会有互动与交往,除非每一份通讯往来都是针锋相对,否则很容易就能从中挑出一些表面是看来双方达成的共识或共同假设。如果只要存在共识或共同的假设就能成立共识性禁反言,就有危险是带来太多涉及共识性禁反言的争议。所以,加入不公平与不合情理这一要件作为把关就显得十分重要。在判断共识性禁反言是否成立以及它的救济时都需要考虑公平原则。Peter Gibson 大法官在 Hamel - Smith v. Pycroft & Jetsave Ltd. (unreported, 5 February 1987)先例提到一个局限,说:"Thus the court is not so rigid and inflexible as to insist on the parties being held to an assumed and incorrect state of fact or law **when there is no injustice in allowing a party to resile therefrom** [see, for example, Multon v. Cordell (1988) 277 Estates Gazette 198]. Further, if the estoppel applies it will do so only '**for the period of time and to the extent required by the equity which the estoppel has raised**' (per Ralph Gibson LJ in Troop v. Gibson at p. 1144). Thus, once a common assumption is revealed to be erroneous the estoppel would not apply to future dealings between the parties (per Purchas LJ in the same case at p. 1144)."(加黑部分是笔者的强调)

上述 Peter Gibson 大法官所讲,就是共识性禁反言只会在为了公平需要时才做出的救济,所以适用的时间是有局限的。一旦共识或共同假设被发现是错误,禁反言在将来的交往中就不适用。典型的例子之一就是在本章第1段提到的期租合约承租人持续迟付租金,而船东没有反对,这可能会构成共识性禁反言。但一旦船东做出通知,要求承租人准时支付租金,承租人仍然延误支付,船东就可以马上撤船,而承租人不能以共识性禁反言作为抗辩。这方面的公平原则是涉及最低程度的衡平法救济(minimum equity remedy)的说法,这在本书第三章之4.5.5段与第四章第9段也提到过。这里只节录Purchas大法官在Troop v. Gibson (1986) 1 EGLR 1先例中所说:"... the equitable relief afforded (by the estoppel by convention as to contractual rights) will persist only so long as it is necessary to protect the tenant who has altered his position on the basis of the common mistake or common misrepresentation – however it may be put."

公平原则的要求也体现在其他方面,如共识性禁反言能否成立。一般来说在共识性禁反言,谁先提出错误的假设或对事实或法律有错误理解并不重要。[46] 在The "Leila" (1985) 2 Lloyd's Rep. 172先例中,Mustill大法官说:"In my judgment, these authorities lend no support to the argument that the party who asserts an estoppel by convention must show that the other party has made some representation as to the legal position, or that the other party must at least have been the source of the mistake, if any equity is to arise. Indeed, the whole tenor of the judgments in the Amalgamated Property case is to the effect that the estoppel is not so confined."

另在John v. George (1996) 1 EGLR 7先例中,Morritt大法官说:"It would, in my judgment, be quite inconsistent with that decision to conclude that it was a necessary ingredient in the case for(依赖禁反言的一方) that the assumption was created or encouraged by(被禁反言的一方). No doubt the assumption if not created or encouraged by one party must be shared in the sense that each is aware of the assumption of the other for otherwise there may be nothing which crosses the line as explained by Kerr L. J. in The August Leonhardt."

但在公平原则的要求下,通常会是被禁反言的一方先提出错误的假设,并希望对方依赖这个假设,即他对双方达成的错误共识或共同假设有一定的责任。[47] 正如Kerr大法官在The "August Leonhardt" (1985) 2 Lloyd's Rep. 28先例中所说:"There cannot be any estoppel unless the alleged representor has said or done something, or failed to do something, with the result that – across the line between the parties – **his action or inaction has produced some belief or expectation in the mind of the alleged representee**, so that, depending on the circumstances, it would thereafter no longer be right to allow the alleged representor to resile by challenging the belief or expectation

---

〔46〕 这在本章之3.1.2段也有提到。

〔47〕 这一点在本章之2.2.2段介绍的Amalgamated v. Texas Bank (1982) 1 Lloyd's Rep. 27先例的案情中表现得并不明显,虽然高院的Goff大法官有认定Amalgamated的言行鼓励并加强了Texas Bank的误解,但上诉庭也没有针对或提出此要求。

which he has engendered. To that extent at least, therefore, the alleged representor must be open to criticism."（加黑部分是笔者的强调）

另是 Briggs 大法官在 Commissioners for Her Majesty's Revenue and Customs v. Benchdollar Limited and Others（2009）EWHC 1310（Ch）先例中所说："The expression of the common assumption **by the party alleged to be estopped** must be such that he **may properly be said to have assumed some element of responsibility** for it, in the sense of conveying to the other party an understanding that he expected the other party to rely upon it . . ."（加黑部分是笔者的强调）

提出禁反言的一方（estoppel raiser）是否是被被禁反言的一方（estopped party）诱导（induce）是判决是否有不公平的重要考虑，Spencer Bower 与 Turner 的《The Law Relating to Estoppel by Representation》（第 4 版，2004 年）一书第 189 页之 VIII. 5. 3 段，说："As to the requirement of unfairness, whether unfairness would result depends（as in relation to the other estoppels）on whether the party seeking to raise the estoppel by convention has been induced by the convention understanding so to act that he will be worse off if the other party is allowed to resile from the convention, then he（the estoppel raiser）would be if he had not been induced to act or refrain from acting by the convention. The test whether the relevant conduct of the estoppel raiser was induced by the convention should, it is submitted, be the same test of causation as applies to an estoppel by representation, promissory or proprietary estoppel. Thus, in Credit Suisse v. Allerdale BC, Colman J rejected a plea of estoppel by convention on the ground（inter alia）that he was not satisfied that the estoppel raiser had been induced to act to its detriment by the convention."

在 Credit Suisse v. Allerdale BC（1995）1 Lloyd's Rep. 315 先例中，Colman 大法官把这个道理讲得很清楚，可节录如下："That the mere existence of a common assumption as to the legal rights of one party to the transaction is insufficient to give rise to an estoppel by convention is clear from the decision of the Court of Appeal in The 'August Leonhardt'. **There must be conduct on the part of the party said to be estopped which represents that that party holds the assumption in question and it must further be established that the conduct of that party at least influenced the mind of the representee by reinforcing that assumption...** It is indeed fundamental to the availability of estoppel by convention that it would be unconscionable for the party said to be estopped to rely upon a legal relationship with the other party other than that which the other party had represented to be commonly assumed. **The basis for that unconscionability is that the party said to be estopped would otherwise be allowed to adopt a position which was inconsistent with that which he had previously led the other party to believe was common ground.** There would therefore be both inconsistency of conduct and potential prejudice from that inconsistency which is the essence of estoppel by whatever name it is known. . . ”

换一种情况,如果一方发现另一方有了对他自己不利的事实或法律上的错误理解(如错误解释合约条文或计错数),但取巧(sharp practice)保持沉默(acquiesce),配合对方按照这个错误理解履行下去,之后以共识性禁反言要求另一方不能偏离这个对他不利的错误理解,就很可能会有问题。如在本章之 3.1.3 段提到发票金额少写了一个零的例子,B 以共识性禁反言作为抗辩就会有问题。这里会涉及 B 取巧或没有合理依赖与很可能没有任何损害等难以满足公平原则要件的事实。

这除了涉及上述所讲的诱导以及依赖并蒙受损害,和本书第四章之 6.4 段与本书第五章第 10 段介绍的有责任说清楚(duty to speak)也有关系。在本章之 3.1.1 段介绍的 ING Bank NV v. Ros Roca SA (2011) EWCA Civ 353 先例就是这样的情况。在该先例中,ING 披露的文件显示了他知道正确的合约地位,但是取巧没有提醒 Ros Roca。但在实践中,很难证明一方取巧。如合约条文有终止条文,但一方没有注意继续履行合约,另一方(通常是对合约与法律了解更多的一方)发现继续履行合约对他来说更有利,于是保持沉默,并配合去继续履行合约。表面看来,这属于双方共同错误假设合约继续存在并继续履行,法官或仲裁员在没有证据的情况下很难证明另一方私下有这方面的正确理解,或是有取巧的动机,或不公平与不合情理的情况存在。

3.3.2　不合情理(unconscionable)

3.3.2.1　共识性禁反言对不合情理的要求

不合情理这个课题在本书第四章第 8 段与第五章第 9 段都有详细介绍,也提到不合情理一般显示在对方因为依赖而改变地位(change of position)并蒙受损害(detriment),这与上一小段介绍的不公平(unfair 或 inequitable)也有很大重叠。在 PW & Co. v. Milton Gate Investments Ltd. (2003) EWHC 1994 (Ch)先例中,Neuberger 大法官将共识性禁反言对不合情理同样的要求总结如下:“In almost all cases, such unconscionability must be based on the prejudice which would be caused to the claimant if the strict legal position applied. As I see it, **the claimant must also establish that that prejudice arises from its reliance upon the convention**. In other words, the Court generally must be satisfied that (a) the claimant will suffer real prejudice, and (b) the prejudice arises from its reliance upon the convention. It should be emphasised that, even if the claimant satisfies these criteria, there may still be no estoppel, because there may be other, more powerful, factors pointing the other way. ”(加黑部分是笔者的强调)

在 Commissioners for Her Majesty’s Revenue and Customs v. Benchdollar Limited and Others (2009) EWHC 1310 (Ch)先例中, Briggs 大法官也有同样说法:“**Some detriment must thereby have been suffered** by the person alleging the estoppel, or benefit thereby have been conferred upon the person alleged to be estopped, **sufficient to make it unjust or unconscionable** for the latter to assert the true legal (or factual) position.”（加黑部分是笔者的强调）

也就是说，即使双方有一个错误共识或共同的错误假设，但如果一方要撤回这个错误共识或共同的错误假设以回复到事实或法律上正确的地位，只要不是不合情理，仍然不会构成共识性禁反言。例如，如果一方还没有因为依赖该共识而蒙受损害，[48]或是损害是极轻微，另一方就已经撤回这个错误共识，是不会被共识性禁反言。如在 Edward Michael Gloyne v. Linda Rosemary Richardson, Barber Young Burton & Rind（A Firm）（2001）EWCA Civ 716 先例中，[49]上诉庭 Aldous，Laws 与 Blackburne 大法官一致判虽然双方是有共同的错误理解，但原告（EMG）事后反悔并非是不合情理（unconscionable）。Laws 大法官说：

“The doctrine of estoppel by convention was explained in this court in The ‘Vistafjord’［1988］2 Ll LR 343. Bingham LJ... said this ...：

It is sufficient... to say that it（the doctrine of estoppel by convention）applies where（1）parties have established by their construction of their agreement or their apprehension of its legal effect a conventional basis,（2）on that basis they have regulated their subsequent dealings, to which I would add（3）it would be unjust or unconscionable if one of the parties resiled from that convention.

I accept without demur that conditions（1）and（2）in this formulation are established on the facts of this case. My difficulty is with（3）. At the very least, once R had resiled from the terms of the letter agreement by asserting a claim based on option rights covering 38,085 shares（see the letters of 28 August 1996 and 18 October 1996, to which I have referred）it cannot be said that it was unconscionable for EMG thereafter himself to depart from the ‘convention’ constituted by the letter agreement, and to seek to stand on the original terms of OA88/92. In these circumstances, in my judgment there is no estoppel by convention either so as to bind the parties to a basis of 22,018 shares as the subject of R’s option rights, or so as to bind the parties to an acceptance（contrary to the fact）that the option had been exercised.”

在该先例中，双方的错误共识是被告 Richardson 太太已经行使了购买 22018 股公司股票的选择权。Richardson 太太首先希望撤回这个错误共识，回复到她认为的正确的合约地位，即她有购买 38085 股而不是 22018 股公司股票的选择权。在这种 Richardson 太太先撤回共识的情况下，EMG 再撤回所谓的共识，回复到双方原本的

---

[48] 在 Hillingdon London BC v. ARC Ltd.（No.2）（2000）3 EGLR 97 先例中，双方在时效过去前后都有进行谈判。原告 ARC 声称被告弃权或被禁反言（包括承诺性禁反言与共识性禁反言），不能以时效作为抗辩。但上诉庭判是在该先例中，原告的损害（错过时效）是自己的错误理解造成的，而并非是依赖了任何被告的言行，因此不会是不合情理。

[49] 案情将在本章之 7.12 段介绍。

合约条文的地位不是不合情理。而如果案情稍有变化，如 Richardson 太太没有首先撤回错误共识，而是因为股票价格上涨，EMG 声称 Richardson 太太没有做出有效的通知，所以没有在规定时间内行使选择权，就会是不合情理并被判是共识性禁反言。或是相反，股票价格下跌，Richardson 太太反悔不想购买这 22018 股，说她原本就没有做出有效通知，因此还没有行使选择权，即想撤回这个错误共识，也会是不合情理。

3.3.2.2　涉及多方的利益

在考虑是否是不合情理时，对第三方的影响也要考虑在内。在 Steria Ltd. v. Hutchison（2006）EWCA Civ 1551 先例中，案情有关一个涉及多方的退休金计划。Hutchison 先生通过他的雇主参加了一个退休金计划，该计划的信托人对他做出陈述是只要工作了 20 年以上，他可以在 62 岁提前退休，而不会扣减退休金。Hutchison 先生之后换到 Steria 公司工作，Steria 公司也参加了该退休金计划。Hutchison 先生之后被 Steria 公司告知他的退休年龄是 65 岁，提前退休不扣减退休金是他前雇主的裁量权。Hutchison 先生则认为，他依赖了信托人的陈述或承诺或双方的共识是他可以提前退休而不扣减退休金，并蒙受损害，可以构成陈述性禁反言或承诺性禁反言或共识性禁反言。上诉庭认为禁反言不成立，因为根据该先例的案情，Hutchison 先生没有蒙受损害。另针对退休金这种涉及多方人士的安排，法院倾向于不支持只针对个别人士的言行构成禁反言，即使被这个别人士依赖。因为如果禁反言成立，这个别人士得利，而蒙受损害的不是信托人而是其他参与该退休金计划的成员。Neuberger 大法官说："An additional reason why the court should lean against an estoppel in favour of one, or only some, of the members of a pension scheme, is that it involves favouring only one or some of the members of the scheme over the other members of the scheme. As was pointed out by Lewison J in the Trustee Solutions case [2007] ICR 412 , para 51, this could in some cases put the trustees of the scheme in a position where they might be in breach of their statutory duties (in that case, which would not apply in this case, the duty in question would have been that contained in section 62 of the Pensions Act 1995). ..."

而且如果能够成立禁反言，对所有退休金计划的其他成员也应该一视同仁。这样，就会带来荒谬的后果，即因为信托人曾经对 Hutchison 先生做出他可以在 62 岁提前退休而退休金不会被扣减的错误陈述，为了补救就将同样的错误陈述延伸适用到退休金计划的所有成员。在 Foster Wheeler Ltd. v. Hanley（2008）EWHC 2926（Ch）先例中，Patten 大法官说：

"... This passage was quoted and applied by Lewison J. in Trustee Solutions (at [50]) and was referred to with approval by the Court of Appeal in Steria Ltd. v. Hutchison [2006] EWCA Civ 1551 at [109]. When applied to the facts of this case, it gives rise to obvious difficulties.

In essence, for the estoppel to apply, it has to be shown that the members as a class agreed to the provision in question as governing their relationship with the trustees and their entitlement under the scheme."

在 Catchpole v. Trustees of the Alitalia Airlines Pension Scheme (2010) EWHC 1809 (Ch)先例中,Warren 大法官说:"A number of authorities have considered the difficulties facing estoppel claims in the context of pension schemes. These have been addressed mainly in the context of estoppel by convention and what have been termed 'group estoppels'. Some of the problems in that context were identified by Sir Andrew Morritt V-C in Redrow Plc. v. Pedley [2002] Pen LR 339, paras 60-64. Lewison J noted those difficulties in his judgment in Trustee Solutions Ltd. v. Dubery [2007] ICR 412 adding some more difficulties of his own. Thus, although the courts have recognised the possibility of establishing estoppels binding trustees of pension schemes, they are to be approached with caution..."

另一个涉及第三人的问题的是什么样的第三人会受到禁反言的约束。已经有明确的先例显示受让人(assignee)[50]与继承人(successor)[51]都会受禁反言的约束。这也是理所当然,否则就会导致合约一方被禁反言,为了脱身就安排一个转让或继承,而他的受让人或继承人不必受到约束。

PW & Co. v. Milton Gate Investments Ltd. (2003) EWHC 1994 (Ch)先例是涉及另一类的第三人,即分租客(sub-tenant)。该先例的案情涉及房屋租赁合约,房东 Milton Gate 与租客 PWC 就 7 层办公楼订立了一份 25 年的租约。双方约定 PWC 可以在 2002 年 6 月 24 日选择终止租约,但如果 PWC 终止租约时,没有将 7 层办公楼的 75% 分租出去并且分租约有效期还剩至少 5 年,就要支付罚金。但根据上诉庭的 Pennell v. Payne (1995) QB 192 先例,新的法律地位变为主租约终止后,分租约也变为无效。这样该条款就变为是基于双方的共同错误(以为主租约终止之后,分租约依然有效)而订立。PWC 将办公楼分租给了 BT 与 Merrill Lynch (Europe) Limited (之后将租约转让给了 BT)。PWC 在 2002 年 6 月 24 日选择终止租约,Milton Gate 要求 PWC 支付罚金,因为根据上诉庭的 Pennell v. Payne 先例,主租约终止后,分租约不再有效,即 PWC 没有满足合约规定的将 7 层办公楼的 75% 分租出去并且分租约有效期还剩至少 5 年的要求。双方的争议之一就是 PWC 与 Milton Gate 之间是否存在主租约终止之后分租约依然有效的共识,如果存在共识,这个共识是否也约束分租客 BT,即三方是否存在共识。

在高院,Neuberger 大法官根据 PWC 与 Milton Gate 之间的主租约与 PWC 订立

---

[50] Cuthbertson v. Irvin (1860) 6 H & N 135 先例与 Brikom Investments Ltd. v. Carr (1979) QB 467 等先例。

[51] Hopgood v. Brown (1955) 1 WLR 213 先例与 Valentine v. Ash (2003) EWCA Civ 915 (unreported) 等先例。

分租约时 PWC 与 Milton Gate 之间的言行，判 PWC 与 Milton Gate 存在主租约终止之后分租约依然有效的共识。而关于这个共识是否也约束分租客没有相关的先例，Neuberger 大法官引用了涉及受让人（assignee）与继承人（successor）的先例中，认为分租约的租客也应该受主租约中房东与租客的共识的约束，说："The general thrust of the authorities to which I have referred tends to support the proposition that, once an estoppel（perhaps other than estoppel by representation）is established as between a landlord and a tenant, then it would normally bind their respective successors in title. As a matter of logic the same conclusion must apply to a convention which in due course may give rise to such an estoppel. If that is correct, then it appears to support the conclusion that a subtenant would also be normally bound, at least provided his subtenancy does not predate the coming into being of the convention. In my judgment, such an estoppel, and therefore such a convention, which unambiguously relates to the relationship of landlord and tenant, and can only fairly work if it extends to the subtenant, will generally do so, particularly if the subtenant had prior notice of it. In such a case, unconscionability would normally, I would have thought, work in favour of the estoppel binding the subtenant rather than not."

该先例 Neuberger 大法官最后判是虽然存在共识，但 PWC 并没有依赖并蒙受损害，所以 Milton Gate 与 BT 想从这个共识中脱身并不是不合情理，共识性禁反言不成立。

3.4　要件之四：相互性

相互性（mutuality or reciprocity）的要求在其他衡平法救济中也存在，如"履约指令"（specific performance）。这背后的原因是一句衡平法格言："he who seeks equity must do equity."

虽然履约指令不是本书针对的内容，但为了读者能够更好地理解相互性这一要件，关于履约指令对相互性的要求简单介绍如下。相互性曾经是履约指令做出时要考虑的非常重要的原则之一，就是说在双方都遵守履约指令的前提下，法院才会给予该救济。判断是否符合相互性原则的时间点是法院做出判决的时候。因为被告在法院的履约指令下，战战兢兢的"重新做人"，不敢在履约中有任何差错。但反过来，原告不受法院任何指令/禁令约束，在履约中乱来或不配合，这对被告并不公平。如租约的原告/承租人不支付租金，但被告的船东因有法院的履约指令在身，只能继续履约，这显然不公平。所以，法院想通过这个原则为被告争取一些保障，防止将来原告会违约/毁约。Buckley 大法官在 Price v. Strange（1978）Ch. 337 先例中说："The court will not compel a defendant to perform his obligation specifically, if it cannot at the same time ensure that any unperformed obligations of the plaintiff will be perfectly performed, unless, perhaps, damages would be adequate remedy to the defendant for any default on the plaintiffs part."

在这种说法下,原告是未成年人的不能成功申请履约指令,因为被告将来无法向原告获得同样保障:Flight v. Bolland (1828) 4 Russ. 298;Lumley v. Ravenscroft (1895) 1 Q. B. 683 等先例。但如果原告申请时已是成年,则合约虽在他还未成年时订立,是一个可使无效(voidable)的合约,法院仍会做出履约指令(稍早已经提到相互性原则是在做出判决时考虑):Clayton v. Ashdown (1714) 9 Vin. Abr. 393 (G. 4) 1 先例。另是,一般来说,在一个由自然人和公司法人签订的合约下是不可以做出履约指令的。因为通常公司法人不能以履约指令强迫自然人提供个人服务:Stocker v. Wedderburn (1867) 3 K & J 393 先例。又或者原告自己的经济情况不稳(plaintiff was doubtful solvency),将来会对被告违约/毁约并赔不出钱。这样,如 Burrows QC 在《Remedies for Torts and Breach of Contract》(第 3 版,2004 年)一书所说,法院可要求原告提供一定数额的金钱上的担保,以交换做出履约指令(... The court could grant it on terms that insure adequate monetary security to the defendant or otherwise provide an incentive for the plaintiff to perform)。

总体来说,禁反言也要求相互性,这包括起源于普通法与衡平法的"陈述性禁反言"(estoppel by representation)。但由于陈述性禁反言涉及陈述方(representor)有意或无意做出了错误的陈述,不需要被陈述方(representee)的互动或和陈述方合作,所以,相比共识性禁反言对相互性的要求就完全不明显,因此本书第五章没有针对这个课题。但陈述性禁反言有两个方面也会涉及相互性,一是依赖错误陈述的只能是被陈述方,而不能是第三人;[52] 二是被陈述方不能同时依赖错误的陈述与正确的陈述。在 Scarf v. Jardine (1882) 7 App. Cas. 345 HL 先例中,A 与 B 是事务所合伙人,但之后合作关系解除,B 退休,而 A 又找了 C 作为新的合伙人加入事务所,从事原来的生意。该先例的原告曾经与原来的事务所做过生意,他并不知道合伙人的改变,而将一票货卖给了新的事务所。之后新的事务所没有支付货款,于是原告开始诉讼向新的事务所追讨货款,并加上了 B 作为被告。贵族院判是原告可以在错误的事实下,让 B 因为禁反言而承担责任,或是在正确的事实下,让 A 与 C 承担责任,但不能同时告他们三位,让他们共同承担责任。

共识性禁反言对相互性的要求,在 Spencer Bower 与 Turner 的《The Law Relating to Estoppel by Representation》(第 3 版,1977 年)一书第 175 页[53],说:"**Mutuality**. It has been said ever since the days of Coke that estoppels by deed must be mutual - i. e., that both parties must be estopped by the recital; ... In the case of estoppels by convention the requirement of mutuality, for long the subject of criticism, may in special circumstances be relaxed, at least since the decision of the Lords in Greer v. Kettle (1938) AC 156 HL ..."

---

[52] 本书第五章第 7 段。

[53] 在该书的最新版(第 4 版,2004 年)中,这一段被删除了,但这方面的法律没有变化。

这一要求也可以想到,因为共识性禁反言是双方共同的错误理解(shared common assumption)。要依赖共识性禁反言的一方禁止另一方撤回错误理解,必须自己也要受这个错误理解约束。例如,原告不能在责任方面用共识性禁反言作为对被告抗辩的回复,但在损失方面却根据真正的法律或合约地位进行计算。涉及这方面的争议不会太多,但也存在,如在 Amalgamated v. Texas Bank (1982) 1 Lloyd's Rep. 27 先例就有针对。一审的 Goff 大法官说:"There remains, however, one further argument advanced on behalf of the plaintiffs, with which I must deal. Mr. Morritt(原告 Amalgamated代表大律师)submitted on the basis of dicta of Lord Cranworth L. C. in Ramsden v. Dyson, L. R. 1 H. L. 129, 152, and of Bramwell L. J. in Simm v. Anglo – American Telegraph Co. (1879) 5 Q. B. D. 188, 203, that an estoppel will not be enforced unless there is reciprocity. Here, he said, there was none, because if the plaintiffs were estopped from asserting the invalidity of the guarantee, the bank would obtain the benefit of the guarantee but the plaintiffs would not get the benefit of subrogation rights which they would have had if the money had in fact been advanced by the bank and the guarantee had been binding.〔54〕 Now I can understand the force of such an argument in certain cases. No doubt, he who comes to equity must do equity; and it might well be contrary to principle that a party should, by virtue of the doctrine of equitable estoppel, obtain the benefit of rights without incurring the burden of corresponding obligations which he would have incurred if the rights had been enforceable without the aid of the doctrine of estoppel.〔55〕 But I cannot see that this is so in the present case. If the guarantee had been binding, then any right of subrogation would have been to securities enforceable against the principal debtor, that is, against A. N. P. P. which could only have been the mortgage over the Harrison Building. But that security was in fact realised and the proceeds paid in partial discharge of the debt; so that no further benefit would have accrued to the plaintiffs by virtue of such right of subrogation, and I cannot therefore see that the lack of any such right on the part of the plaintiffs should preclude the bank from

〔54〕 Amalgamated 的争辩是除非是有相互性,否则禁反言不能成立。而在该先例是没有相互性,因为如果 Amalgamated 被禁止声称该保函是无效的,Texas Bank 就会获得保函下的好处,即从 Amalgamated 处取回 ANPP 的欠款。但同时 Amalgamated 无法获得如果贷款事实上是由 Texas Bank 做出并且保函有效,它应该可以获得的代位权(本段稍后有详解)。因为巴拿马的大厦是抵押给了 Portsoken,而不是 Texas Bank。

〔55〕 Goff 大法官同意如果一方只获得权利,而不用承担如果这权利不需要禁反言的帮助就可以行使时要承担的责任,就可能与衡平法禁反言的原则有冲突。

relying upon the estoppel against them.[56]"

4. 订约前的谈判能否构成共识性禁反言?

4.1 双方在"以订立合约为准"的限制下谈判

在合约谈判中,双方常常会加上"以订立合约为准"(subject to contract)[57]的明示说明。一般来说,一旦有这样的明示说明,就代表直到签署正式的书面合约,双方都还停留在谈判阶段,双方都可以说走就走。但谈判的一方能否以双方在签署合约之前的谈判交往中有了最终会订立合约的共识为由,禁止另一方在签署合约之前脱身?

在 London & Regional Investments Limited v. TBI Plc. , Belfast International Airport Limited (2002) EWCA Civ 355 先例中,Mummery 大法官说:"The 'subject to contract' state of the joint venture negotiations at the date of the Sale Agreement indicates that there is nothing unconscionable in TBI's subsequent refusal to proceed with the joint venture after the Sale Agreement was completed.[58] The validity of this conclusion can be tested by asking this question: when did... the estoppel take effect? It is accepted that no... estoppel could have arisen after 13 May 1999 when the parties expressly agreed in the Sale Agreement that the joint venture was 'subject to contract'.[59] In general, it is not unconscionable for a party to negotiations, which are expressly stated to be 'subject to contract,' to exercise a reserved right to withdraw from the negotiations before a final agreement has been concluded. If that was the effect of the agreement between the parties on 13 May 1999 I do not see how the conduct of TBI before that date can now be relied on to establish unconscionable conduct giving rise to... an estoppel. For the court to hold that a constructive trust existed in those circumstances would be contrary to what

---

[56] 但在该先例并不是这样的情况。如果保函有效, Amalgamated 就可以代位取得执行主债务人 ANPP 提供担保的权利,在该先例中,这担保就是巴拿马的大厦。但这担保事实上已经被执行(即大厦已经被收回与拍卖)并用作归还部分贷款。因此,即使 Amalgamated 获得代位权也不会获得任何的好处,即不涉及相互性的问题。因此,Goff 大法官不认为在该先例 Amalgamated 无法获得代位权会阻止 Texas Bank 依赖禁反言。

[57] 参见杨良宜《合约的解释:规则与应用》一书第八章第 4 段。

[58] 在双方订立的出售协议中,明示了合资公司的谈判是以订立合约为准,因此 TBI(被禁反言的一方)在履行完出售协议后,拒绝继续进行合资公司的谈判没有不合情理的地方。

[59] 合约双方在 1999 年 5 月 13 日订立的出售协议中写明合资公司的谈判是以订立合约为准后,不存在禁反言。

the parties had expressly agreed was to be subject to the making of a future agreement.[60] In Derby & Co. Limited v. ITC Pension Trust Limited [1977] 2 All ER 850 at p. 896 (a case concerning 'subject to contract' negotiations for a new business tenancy), Oliver J said: '... where parties negotiate on a basis "subject to contract" everybody knows that there is a risk that, at the end of the day, either side may back out of the negotiations, up to the point where leases are exchanged. I do not think that a party who relies on the other side not to back out can be said to have estopped that party from backing out simply because he has not done something which he might have done in the intervening period'.[61]"

看来,如果在谈判中说明了是以订立合约为准,很难说双方会存在一个双方之间有或将会有合约的共同假设。毕竟这与下一段所讲的宝剑与盾牌之争有密切关系,即以禁反言为由产生原本不存在的合约关系。但在 Spring Finance Ltd. v. HS Real Company LLC (2011) EWHC 57 (Comm)先例中,Mackie QC 大法官引用了 Gonthier v. Orange Contract Scaffolding Limited (2003) EWCA Civ 873 先例的判决,说并不是完全不可能:"After the hearing Counsel for the Defendant sent me a helpful note after they had found the decision of the Court of Appeal in a case called Gonthier v. Orange Contract Scaffolding Limited [2003] EWCA Civ 873 . In that case Lindsay J, in a judgment with which his colleagues agreed and after a review of the authorities including Gillett v. Holt [2001] Ch 210 , said this about the application of estoppel in the context of a 'subject to contract' arrangement: 'Unless there is some principle by reason of which, in relation to its effect on the parties and the consciences of either of them, "subject to contract" revocability is invariably to be treated differently to the revocability of wills during a testator's lifetime, I see Gillett opening up a possibility which Attorney – General of Hong Kong had seemed to deny. **The possibility**, after Gillett, **at any rate where a very strong case can be made on the facts as to the obviousness and duration of reliance on a "subject to contract" dealing nonetheless being implemented**, is that notwithstanding the Privy Council case, **the right to withdraw from the dealing may be lost**, as the earlier Salvation Army and Island Holdings cases had suggested could be the case.' "(加黑部分是笔者的强调)

---

〔60〕 一般来说,谈判的一方在明示谈判是以订立合约为准的情况下,从谈判中抽身不会是不合情理。因此,Mummery 大法官不认为在出售协议中明示写明合资公司的谈判是以订立合约为准的情况下,TBI 在 1999 年 5 月 13 日之前的言行可以被合理依赖并构成禁反言,否则就是与双方明示约定的以订立合约为准有冲突。

〔61〕 如果双方明示谈判是在以订立合约为准的基础上,他们都应该清楚会有合约任何一方最后从谈判中脱身的风险。Oliver 大法官认为仅仅是一方依赖另一方不会从谈判中脱身的陈述,从而一厢情愿的没有做一些原本该做的事,不会构成禁反言。

4.2　共识性禁反言可以被完整合约条文否定

合约中"完整合约条文"(Entire Agreement Clause)[62]的本意是订约双方想排除合约明示条文/文字以外的争议,如附带保证/协议(collateral warranty/contract)、默示条文(implied terms)、误述(misrepresentation)、引导(inducement)、商业习惯做法/惯例(custom/usage)、侵权的共同责任(concurrent liability in tort)等。换言之,如果合约中的完整合约条文被法院/仲裁庭接受是有效,就表示解释合约就只能看有关合约文件之内的明示条文/文字。法院/仲裁庭不能或不该看在谈判中与订约过程中的口头证据(parole evidence)或外来证据(extrinsic evidence)。因此,如果合约中有一条完整合约条文,即使双方在谈判中曾经有某些共同的理解,但如果这共同的理解与后来订立的合约条文不一致,共识性禁反言也不能适用。因为这种可以构成共识性禁反言的共同理解被后来合约中的完整合约条文超越或排除:Sere Holdings Ltd. v. Volkswagon Group United Kingdom Ltd.(2004)EWHC 1551; Lloyd v. MGL(Rugby)Ltd.(2007)EWCA Civ 153 等先例。

在 Jet2. com Ltd. v. Blackpool Airport Ltd.(2010)EWHC 3166(Comm)先例中,Beatson 大法官说:"It is therefore not necessary to decide whether the ground based on estoppel by convention gives rise to a serious issue to be tried. In the light of the evidence as to the mutual dealings I am not able to conclude that there is no serious issue to be tried on the matter of those dealings. But the variation part of the entire agreement provision in clause 4 of the Letter Agreement makes the prospect of a claim that the defendant is estopped fragile: see Sere Holdings Ltd. v. Volkswagon Group United Kingdom Ltd. [2004] EWHC 1551(Ch) and Lloyd v. MGL(Rugby)Ltd. [2007] EWCA Civ 153. In Lloyd's case estoppel was held not to be inconsistent with the entire agreement clause because it only precluded reliance on pre – contractual representations and the representation relied on post – dated the contract. But the Court of Appeal recognised that **a clause in suitable terms could preclude estoppel**."(加黑部分是笔者的强调)

4.3　共识性禁反言与合约变更的异同

针对在谈判中双方达成了共同假设但没有体现在之后订立的合约,共识性禁反言与"合约变更"(rectification)[63]有很大相似性。两者都是以谈判中双方达成的共同假设,去改变合约明示条文应有的客观解释。有说法是共识性禁反言也可以作为合约变更的替代争议,如 Hoffmann 勋爵在 Chartbrook Ltd. v. Persimmon Homes Ltd.

---

〔62〕 在杨良宜《合约的解释:规则与应用》一书第十三章第 2 段有详细解释。该条文适用合约解释原则而无需像禁反言要满足一些要件。这可参阅本书第八章有关"合约性禁反言"(contractual estoppel)的介绍。

〔63〕 针对合约变更,在杨良宜《合约的解释:规则与应用》一书第三章第 13 段有详细介绍。

（2009）UKHL 38 先例中说："If the parties have negotiated an agreement upon some common assumption, which may include an assumption that certain words will bear a certain meaning, they may be estopped from contending that the words should be given a different meaning."

既然两者的效果相同,逻辑上讲共识性禁反言的举证责任与合约变更也应该相同。在 T&N Ltd.（In Administration）v. Royal & Sun Alliance Plc.（2003）EWHC 1016（Ch）先例中,Lawrence Collins 大法官就说:"... since the effect of any estoppel by convention will be the same as the rectification of the exclusion wording (i. e. to change and contradict the true meaning of the written contract), the court should require the same standard of proof from the Royal as it would for rectification; i. e. convincing proof of the allegedly shared or common assumption to the same effect."

但事实上,虽然两者的举证责任都在提出禁反言或合约变更的一方,但在程度上有很大差异。在本章之 3.1.4 段已经提到,构成共识性禁反言不需要一个清楚无误的陈述或承诺。双方达成的错误共识只需要与合约的客观解释不同,不需要相反。但在《Chitty on Contracts》(第 32 版,2015 年)一书之 3－089 段针对合约变更的举证责任时说,不仅要有令人信服的证据,变更的具体内容必须清楚,并且合约记录的内容必须与双方的共同意图相反:"The burden of proof is on the party seeking rectification. He must produce '**convincing proof**' not only that the document to be rectified was not in accordance with the parties' true intentions at the time of its execution, but also that the document in its proposed form does accord with their intention. It is essential that **the extent of the rectification should be clearly ascertained** and defined by evidence contemporaneous with or anterior to the contract. ... Indeed, it has been said that it is not sufficient that the written contract does not represent the true intention of the parties; it must be shown that the written contract was **actually contrary to the intention of the parties.**"(加黑部分是笔者的强调)

因此,合约变更要成功是很不容易。虽然共识性禁反言也要满足在本章第 3 段介绍的各个要件,但相对容易。

共识性禁反言与合约变更另一个区别是会否被"完整合约条文"(entire agreement clause)否定。已经在上一段提到共识性禁反言可以被完整合约条文否定,而合约变更不受影响。在 JJ Huber（Investment）Ltd. v. The Private DIY Co. Ltd.（1995）NPC 102 先例中,Roger Cooke 大法官判是完整合约条文的作用是说明合约有哪些有效条文并在哪里(就是只在双方签署合约中)找得到。所以,这种条文并不能用来抗拒合约变更的申请。合约变更并非针对去哪里找到双方同意了的有效条文,而是针对双方签署的合约准确的内容应该是什么。在澳大利亚也有先例判完整合约条文不能用来抗拒合约变更的申请。在 Macdonald v. Shinki Australia Pty Ltd.（1998）QCA 53 先例中,McPherson J. A. 大法官判是合约变更是无法通过合约条文回避的救济,说:“... well be impossible for the parties by means of any contractual provision, however artfully drawn, to escape the court's jurisdiction to order rectification in a matter calling for its exercise.”

5. 宝剑与盾牌之争

这一课题在本书第四章第10段与第五章第3段已经有过介绍。传统上共识性禁反言可以用来禁止另一方否认他是担保的一方[64]或是否认双方订立的合约有效[65]等,这样看来共识性禁反言只能作为盾牌抗辩。

但宝剑与盾牌之争仍然不肯定,正如Andrew Smith大法官在Ease Faith Ltd. v. Leonis Marine Management Ltd. & Anor.(2006)EWHC 232先例[66]中说:“I should mention that Leonis also dispute that Cloudfree would be entitled to deploy an estoppel to assert a positive claim for ‘sea demurrage’ or payment in respect of the delay. I see force in their argument, but **the question when an estoppel can operate only as a shield and not as a sword is not straightforward, particularly in respect of estoppel by convention.** Since the question does not arise in view of my other conclusions, I do not express any concluded view about this.”(加黑部分是笔者的强调)

一个富争议性的例子是共识性禁反言能否被用来支持有一个本来不存在的合约?这种禁反言通常发生在双方的谈判过程中,如双方谈判的合约是“以订立合约为准”(subject to contract),但A在一切条文都谈妥只等待签署时向B保证合约一定会订立,只是有权签署合约的人士出差,半个月后才会回来,并鼓励B立即开始工作。B依赖了A的承诺开始工作,双方也互相配合。谁知道之后因为市场变化或其他原因,最终合约没有被A签署。这种情况经常会发生,特别是在建筑/工程合约。这个行业中经常会发生主合约或分包合约还不是最终与有约束力时,双方或其中一方已经做了一些工作的情况。这些工作能否被说成是依赖了对方的承诺并蒙受损害,因此构成承诺性禁反言?[67]或是双方有一个合约最终会订立的错误共同假设,并进行互动,虽然最终合约没有订立,但构成共识性禁反言?如果可以,就说明共识性禁反言可以被用作宝剑,即允许共识性禁反言替代一个有约束力的合约作为诉因。

贵族院的Amalgamated v. Texas Bank(1982)1 Lloyd's Rep. 27先例大篇幅地针对这个宝剑与盾牌之争,这里就不再重复。以下只介绍一些近期先例中针对共识

---

〔64〕 Amalgamated v. Texas Bank(1982)1 Lloyd's Rep. 27先例。

〔65〕 Mitsui Babcock Energy Ltd. v. John Brown Engineering Ltd.(1997)41 Con LR 129先例。

〔66〕 案情将在本章之7.15段介绍。

〔67〕 见本书第四章之12.3段。

性禁反言在这一方面的说法。在 Baird Textile Holdings Ltd. v. Marks & Spencer Plc. (2001) EWCA Civ 274 先例,[68] Mance 大法官说:

"In the present case, what is submitted is that the law ought to attach legal consequences to a bare assurance or conventional understanding (falling short of contract) between two parties, without any actual contract or third party being involved or affected. The suggested justification is the limitation of the relief claimed to reliance loss. On this submission, the requirements of contract (consideration, certainty and an intention to create legal relations) are irrelevant because no contract is asserted. The requirements of estoppel (e. g. that is an unequivocal promise to found a promissory estoppel or conventional conduct of sufficient clarity to found an estoppel by convention and, secondly, the objective intention to affect some actual or apparent pre – existing legal relationship) are by – passed by the limitation of relief. But no authority in this jurisdiction supports the submission that estoppel can here achieve so expanded an application,... Any development of English law in such a direction could and should, in my view, now take place in the highest court.

It is also, on authority, an established feature of both promissory and conventional estoppel that the parties should have had the objective intention to make, affect or confirm a legal relationship..."

在 Baird Textile Holdings Ltd. v. Marks & Spencer Plc. 上诉庭先例后,有不少高院先例都跟从了该先例的判法,包括 Haden Young Ltd. v. Laing O'Rourke Midlands Ltd. (2008) EWHC 1016 (TCC)先例(该先例的案情请见脚注)。其中 Ramsey 大法官说:"H[69] was not estopped from contending that no sub – contract was concluded between the parties. **Estoppel could not be used as a key element of a claim so as to create a legal relationship when there was no such legal relationship at the outset**, SmithKline Beecham Plc. v. Apotex Europe Ltd. [2006] EWCA Civ 658... applied. There was no difference between a party that sought to bring a claim by way of a contract

---

〔68〕 该先例的案情在本书第四章之 5.1 段有介绍。Baird 向玛莎公司供应外衣,双方的业务关系长达 30 年之久。玛莎突然终止业务关系,这显然会给 Baird 带来很大困难,Baird 要求玛莎至少做出 3 年的合理通知才能终止。显然玛莎不答应,于是 Baird 采取法律行动。Baird 的立场主要有两个方面:首先,双方虽然没有签订任何供应合约,但明显应有默示合约存在;其次,双方 30 年的合作构成了禁反言,这包括承诺性禁反言与共识性禁反言。上诉庭判是有证据显示双方知道玛莎是刻意不肯签订任何合约约束自己,即不会满足默示合约的要求。而针对禁反言,上诉庭判是毫无希望,因为无论是承诺性禁反言还是共识性禁反言都不能作为诉因。

〔69〕 H 是原告分承包商,为足球场的建造进行机电工程。双方还没有就责任限制条文与保证达成协议,不存在已经签订的分包合约。H 完成工程后向法院起诉主承包商 L,要求支付合理费用(*quantum meruit*)。关于在这种情况下索取合理费用,可见本书第四章之 12.3.4 段。

based on estoppel or one that sought to defend a claim by asserting a contract based on estoppel.[70] In the instant case, L had sought to rely on estoppel so as to create a contract which it then sought to rely on to assert those rights and liabilities that would exist under the contract. That was to use estoppel to assert an obligation equivalent to a cause of action and was prohibited, Baird Textile Holdings Ltd. v. Marks & Spencer Plc. ... applied.[71] Moreover, for there to be a sub – contract based on estoppel, there had to be a sub – contract incorporating all terms, including the limitation of liability under the warranties and the sub – contract. **In thc absence of agreement by the parties on those essential terms it was unclear how the parties could be estopped to particular limits, and it was not for the court to bridge the lacuna by an estoppel.**"(加黑部分是笔者的强调)

另一个跟从 Baird Textile Holdings Ltd. v. Marks & Spencer Plc. 上诉庭先例的是 Tesco Stores Limited v. Costain Construction Limited (2003) EWHC 1487 (TCC)先例。在该先例中,Richard Seymour QC 大法官提出了共识性禁反言不能被用来支持双方存在合约的另一个原因。根据普通法,要订立一个有效的合约,双方必须有订约意图。但如果双方在谈判中没有明确的要约与接受,或是明示是"以订立合约为准",这说明双方在当时不存在订约意图。这样就无法由于双方有过互动,就认定双方之间存在他们已经达成有效合约的错误共识,以共识性禁反言令一个不存在的合约成立。Richard Seymour QC 大法官说:

"Leaving aside for a moment the question whether it is possible to found a cause of action upon an estoppel by convention,... the recent decision of the Court of Appeal in Baird Textile Holdings Ltd. v. Marks & Spencer Plc. [2001] EWCA Civ 274, there is, as it seems to me, an obvious conceptual problem to be faced in relation to a submission that a party is estopped by convention from denying the existence of a contract which a fortiori has not actually been made. That is that it is plain from the authorities to which I have been referred that the essence of an estoppel by convention, if it is to exist, is an agreement between the relevant parties as to the state of affairs upon the assumption as to which they will conduct their dealings. At the same time it is fundamental to the making of a contract in English law that the parties to it should have reached agreement, quite apart from the necessity for other elements, such as consideration, in a binding con-

---

〔70〕 禁反言不能被用来作为诉讼的关键要件,即不能产生一个原本没有的法律关系。依赖禁反言建立合约关系开始诉讼,与依赖禁反言建立合约关系进行抗辩没有区别。

〔71〕 在本先例中,L 依赖禁反言产生一个合约,然后依赖该合约如果存在双方应该有的权利与责任向 H 反索赔,指称工程没有做好。利用禁反言主张原本不存在的法律责任等同于提供一个诉因,是不被允许的。

tract... If, for whatever reason, the correct conclusion in a particular case is that parties have not made a binding contract — and unless that is the conclusion the issue of whether there was an estoppel by convention in relation to a contract cannot arise — then **it is logically impossible to see how there could nonetheless be agreement between them sufficient to give rise to an estoppel by convention that they have made the contract which actually they have not made**.

The point which I have made in the preceding paragraph does not seem ever to have been considered in any of the decisions to which my attention was drawn. That is probably because it seems only in relation to construction cases that it has ever occurred to anyone to seek to establish an estoppel by convention that a contract which had not in fact been made had been agreed to have been made."（加黑部分是笔者的强调）

最后可节录 Sean Wilken QC 与 Karim Ghaly 先生所著的《The Law of Waiver, Variation, and Estoppel》（第 3 版，2012 年）一书之 10.17 - 10.18 段对这方面的总结，如下：

"The approach in Baird has been reflected in three cases where the Court has been considering whether or not the parties had, contrary to the case now advanced by one party. Entered into a concluded contract – Tesco Stores Limited v. Costain Construction Limited, Investments Ltd. v. Development Ventures Ltd. and Haden Young Ltd. v. Laing O'Rourke Midlands Ltd. In each case the Court held that an estoppel by convention could not be relied on in support of the case that there was a concluded contract – either because of Baird or because of a finding that a state of affairs which has not sufficiently clear to create a contract could not be sufficiently clear to generate the necessary convention.

Thus, as the law currently stands, there are two schools of thought – the historical expansive approach and the Baird approach. As Justice Colman recognized in BP Plc. v. AON Ltd, the result in Baird conflicts with the reasoning in Almalgamated Bank and the previously decided cases onestoppel by convention.〔72〕 Further, it is difficult to see, if Baird is right, what role – if any – remains for estoppel by convention or indeed how the doctrine continues to be used to modify contractual obligations... As Amalgamated Bank and Baird are both Court of Appeal authorities, any resolution of the conflict must

---

〔72〕 已经在本章之 2.2.2 段提到，在 Amalgamated v. Texas Bank（1982）1 Lloyd's Rep. 27 先例中，Branson 大法官认为真正的法律地位是如果原告有其他诉因，但这个诉因有缺陷，原告可以依赖共识性禁反言进行补救，即作为诉因的支持性（supportive）要件。但在 Baird Textile Holdings Ltd. v. Marks & Spencer Plc.（2001）EWCA Civ 274 先例中，法院认为利用共识性禁反言补救一个不存在的合约的争辩是毫无希望。所以 Colman 大法官认为这两个上诉庭先例有冲突。

await the Supreme Court. Until then, considerable caution must be exercised in using an estoppel by convention where the pragmatic effect of so doing is to create a cause of action or, as it was put in the the previous edition, the estoppel is acting as a sharp edged shield."

6. 共识性禁反言的局限:强制性立法与/或普通法大原则

一般人士不能漠视或者超越一个立法或者普通法所强加的大原则。在一般情况下,双方的协议也做不到这一点,更不用说是通过禁反言的说法。所以禁反言只能说是属于私法,而在公法没有立足点。

虽然早期的 Wells v. Minister of Housing and Local Government (1967) 1 WLR 1000 先例与 Lever (Finance) Ltd. v. Westminster Corp (1971) 1 QB 222 先例的判决带来了一定的不肯定,但现在法律已经很清楚明确,禁反言不适用在公法。这已经在本书第四章之5.4 段与第五章第11 段有过介绍,这里尽量不重复。只节录 Hoffmann 勋爵在 Regina [Reprotech (Pebsham) Ltd] v. East Sussex County Council (2002) UKHL 8 先例中所说:"... it is unhelpful to introduce private law concepts of estoppel into planning law. As Lord Scarman pointed out in Newbury DC v. Secretary of State for the Environment (1981) AC 578, estoppels bind individuals on the ground that it would be unconscionable for them to deny what they have represented or agreed. But these concepts of private law should not be extended into 'the public law of planning control, which binds everyone'... There is of course an analogy between a private law estoppel and the public law concept of a legitimate expectation created by a public authority, the denial of which may amount to an abuse of power... But it is no more than an analogy because remedies against public authorities also have to take into account the interests of the general public which the authority exists to promote... public law has already absorbed whatever is useful from the moral values which underlie the private law concept of estoppel and the time has come for it to stand upon its own two feet."

简单的例子就是普通法对一个有效合约(契约除外)的基本要求是要约、接受、订约意图与约因/对价,因此,如果一个合约没有这些要件,就是无效的。而双方之后的共同的假设(convention)可以令一个无效的合约因禁反言而变为有效的说法显然不符合逻辑。这在本章第5 段介绍宝剑与盾牌之争时有提到。

在 Keen v. Holland (1984) 1 WLR 251 CA 先例中,为了避免 1948 年《Agricultural Holdings Act》立法适用,双方在租约到期前几周补签了农地租约(agricultural tenancy),即在 1979 年 10 月 19 日签订了租约期为 1978 年 9 月 1 日到 1979 年 10 月

31 日的租约。但根据立法规定,租约不允许有这种回溯效力(retrospective effect)。法院判是共识性禁反言不能取代立法规定。Oliver 大法官说:"... what (counsel) appears... to be contending for is... that where parties... had a common view about the legal effect of a contract into which they have entered and it is established that one of them would not, to the other's knowledge have entered into it if he had appreciated its true legal effect, they are, without more, estopped from asserting that the effect is otherwise than they originally supposed. So broad a proposition... cannot... be right."

但 Hiscox v. Outhwaite (No. 1) (1991) 2 Lloyd's Rep. 1 (CA)先例看来有不同的判法。上诉庭判共识性禁反言超越了英国 1975 年《仲裁法》(这立法承认了 1958 年有关签约国之间裁决书的相互承认与执行的《纽约公约》)并导致了一个有趣的结果。[73]

在英国法下,虽然共识性禁反言与其他类别的禁反言通常不可以用来超越本国的立法,但可以用来超越外国的立法。这与英国法律与实践中将外国法律视为事实问题(issue of fact)一致。在 The "Amazonia" (1990) 1 Lloyd's Rep. 236 CA 先例中,[74]虽然租约中的仲裁条文在澳大利亚法律下是非法(illegal)与无效(void),但上诉庭判共识性禁反言适用,船东不能在一连串的互动(包括委任一个伦敦仲裁的独任仲裁员)后反悔,以非法与无效否认伦敦仲裁条文的有效性。Dillon 大法官说:"It is urged for the disponent owners that there can be no estoppel, since **it is established law that there can be no estoppel in the face of a statute**; it is said that the estoppel if allowed, would defeat the Australian Act. I can well see that there may be many cases in which an estoppel would not be allowed because to allow it would defeat a statute. In the present context, however, the Australian Act is, in my judgment, irrelevant. If I am right, for the reasons given above, that the ad hoc contract, as a contract to be performed in England and governed by English law, is valid and enforceable in England despite the Australian Act, it must follow that the Australian Act cannot prevent a party to the ad hoc contract being precluded, by a principle of English law, from resiling from the ad hoc contract. It may well be correct that parties cannot achieve, by estoppel by convention, a result which they would not achieve by a direct contract because it is prohibited by statute. But in the circumstances of the present case, the parties can achieve by direct ad hoc contract in England the object of commencing or continuing the English arbitration, without regard to the Australian Act."(加黑部分是笔者的强调)

---

〔73〕 这将在本章之 7.9 段有详细介绍

〔74〕 该先例的案情可见本章之 7.5 段。

7. 权威先例与笔者涉及的仲裁案件

Amalgamated v. Texas Bank (1982) 1 Lloyd's Rep. 27 先例之后带来了很多有关共识性禁反言的先例中,这里只对部分做出介绍,让读者可以看到禁反言能够适用的多元化情况。如合约履行中双方的安排〔75〕,一方在合约下的权利〔76〕,有缺陷的通知〔77〕,担保的有效性〔78〕,诉讼程序中的告票送达〔79〕、时效〔80〕、管辖权〔81〕,文书请求的修改〔82〕,滥用司法程序〔83〕等。

7.1　先例之一:The "August Leonhardt"

The"August Leonhardt" (1985) 2 Lloyd's Rep. 28 CA 先例涉及提单下的货损货差索赔,众所周知 1924 年的《海牙规则》,其中是规定了很短的 1 年索赔时效。由于诉讼十分昂贵,所以代表货方的律师与代表船东的互保协会通常先通过谈判试图达成和解,诉讼只是作为最后的解决争议办法。而针对索赔时效,通常双方会达成协议去延长以让大家有更多的时间可以继续谈判。

在该先例中,货方的代表律师(伦敦一家著名律师行)与船东互保协会(西英)谈判并同意延长 3 个月的时效。西英的电传是说:"... our members are prepared to extend time to your clients for a period of three months beyond 26. 1. 82 on a without prejudice basis and provided charterers agree likewise."

显然,这项时效延长有一个先决条件,就是要求承租人也同意该时效的延长。该先例中,西英的做法也是所有船东互保协会的惯常做法,即只要知悉有租约存在,它们在同意延长时效时即会多加一句话"provided charterers agree likewise"。这样做要

---

〔75〕　本章之 7.3 段介绍的 The "Vistafjord" (1988) 2 Lloyd's Rep. 343 先例中,本章 7.4 段介绍的 Shearson Lehman Hutton Inc. v. Maclaine Watson & Co. Ltd. (1989) 2 Lloyd's Rep. 570 先例。

〔76〕　本章之 7.15 段介绍的 Ease Faith Ltd. v. Leonis Marine Management Ltd. & Anor. (2006) EWHC 232 (Comm)先例。

〔77〕　本章之 7.8 段介绍的 Mannai Investment Co. Ltd. v. Eagle Star Life Assurance Co. Ltd. (1997) A. C. 749 先例中,本章之 7.12 段介绍的 Edward Michael Gloyne v. Linda Rosemary Richardson, Barber Young Burton & Rind (A Firm) (2001) EWCA Civ 716 先例中,本章之 7.13 段介绍的 Riverside Housing Association v. White (2005) EWCA Civ 1385 先例。

〔78〕　本章之 7.14 段介绍的 Triodosbank NV v. Dobbs (2005) 2 Lloyd's Rep. 588 先例中,本章之 7.16 段介绍的 Spliethoff's Bevrachtingskantoor BV v. Bank of China Ltd. (2015) 2 Lloyd's Rep. 123 先例。

〔79〕　本章之 7.6 段介绍的 Allison v. Limehouse & Co. (1992) 2 A. C. 105 先例。

〔80〕　本章之 7.1 段介绍的 The "August Leonhardt" (1985) 2 Lloyd's Rep. 28 CA 先例。

〔81〕　本章之 7.2 段介绍的 The "Lelia" (1985) 2 Lloyd's Rep. 172 先例中,本章之 7.5 段 The "Amazonia" (1990) 1 Lloyd's Rep. 236 CA 先例。

〔82〕　本章之 7.7 段介绍的 G S Fashions Ltd. v. B & Q Plc. (1995) 1 WLR 1088 先例。

〔83〕　本章之 7.11 段介绍的 Johnson v. Gore Wood & Co. (2002) 2 AC 1 先例。

起到什么作用,笔者也不太清楚。或许是先取得承租人同意延长时效,将来船东赔付了货方之后(被判败诉或庭外和解),再以租约条款的规定(如会有条文针对承租人要承担装卸作业造成的货损货差)要求承租人做出"补偿"(indemnity)时,承租人难以再指称较早的延长时效有不合理之处。但照理说,只要做法合理,船东不必事事都要先取得承租人的同意,因为这并不会影响后来的补偿行动。从另一角度看,若承租人什么都不同意,如延长时效、庭外和解等,船东也不见得就会什么都不做,只要这明确是合理的做法。

且不论这起到什么作用,对货方而言,取得船东这样一个有先决条件的对延长时效的同意毫无用处。因为直到先决条件获得满足,即承租人也同意,否则根本就没有过有效的协议。

在该先例中,承租人也在西英投保了货损货差责任险。这给货方律师一个借口说他收到了西英的电传后,以为西英会直接向承租人要求授权延长时效,毕竟大家都在同一个互保协会。之后货方没再听到异议,也就以为先决条件已经被满足了。但船东或是西英的立场是以为货方会接触承租人并取得延长时效的同意,以令船东的延长时效协议生效。虽然承租人会把这方面的事务交给他的互保协会处理,整件事会回到西英的同一个负责人,但在程序上还是需要货方接触承租人取得对时效延长的同意。看来,如果接受双方的说法,就表示了他们之间有了真正的误解,即大家假设对方会向承租人取得延长时效的同意。

在一审,Bingham 大法官根据共识性禁反言与衡平法禁反言判货方胜诉,说:"... The present case does accordingly present itself to me as one in which the **inaction** of both parties... was attributable to a common but mistaken assumption that the agreement of the charterers had been or certainly would be obtained... it is a requirement of ANY estoppel that the circumstances should be such as to make it unfair or unjust or unconscionable to permit any change of position by the party said to be estopped... Mr. O'Donovan's(西英的有关人士)conduct was both reasonable and morally irreproachable. It is nonetheless the case that the owners now seek to profit from an adventitious advantage which, but for the parties' common mistaken assumption, they never would have enjoyed..."(加黑部分是笔者的强调)

但去了上诉庭,Bingham 大法官的判决被推翻,货方被判索赔已经过了时效。而上诉庭的原因主要就是针对 Bingham 大法官判决中所讲的"双方没有行动"(inaction),的确在相关的时间直到时效届满,货方和西英之间没有任何接触。上诉庭认为双方没有沟通过的共同假设并不能构成禁反言,[84]而仅仅是双方都不知道的误解,这误解令他们独立决定不再采取进一步行动。其中 Kerr 大法官是这样说:"There cannot be any estoppel unless the alleged representor has said or done something,

〔84〕 见本章之3.1.2段。

or failed to do something, with the result that-across the line between the parties-his action or inaction has produced some belief or expectation in the mind of the alleged representee, so that, depending on the circumstances, it would thereafter no longer be right to allow the alleged representor to resile by challenging the belief or expectation which he has engendered. To that extent at least, therefore, the alleged representor must be open to any criticism... But in the present case there was nothing in Mr. O'Donovan's conduct after 12 Jan 1982 which passed across the line so as to enable the cargo owners to contend... a common assumption. Each acted-or failed to act-independently from the other on the basis of a mutual mistake which remained uncommunicated between them... **The position would have been crucially different if, after the letter of 12 Jan, Mr. O'Donovan did in some way manifested to (cargo owners) his acceptance that the extension was in force between the parties**..."(加黑部分是笔者的强调)

上诉庭的 Kerr 大法官也指出该先例不存在依赖,货方任由 1 年索赔时效逝去而没有做出告票是出于他的误解,而并非依赖西英有关人士的言行,而依赖是构成禁反言的重要条件。Kerr 大法官说:"Mr Short (cargo owner) understandably relied on the assumption by not issuing a writ (to protect time bar). But he did not do so in reliance on anything said or done by Mr. O'Donovan which might have been capable of giving rise to an estoppel. All estoppels must involve some statement of conduct by the party alleged to be estopped on which the alleged representee was entitled to rely and did rely."

这一先例在稍后的 The "Vistafjord" (1988) 2 Lloyd's Rep. 343 先例被 Bingham 大法官提到,并说是完全接受该先例的原则:"I, with respect, entirely accept that statement of principle and have no doubt as to the correctness of the Court of Appeal's decision in that case. It was a case in which each party thought something had been done but each party though the other had done it. There was, therefore, no true coincidence between the states of minds of the two parties."

7.2 先例之二:The "Lelia"

The"Lelia" (1985) 2 Lloyd's Rep. 172 先例涉及一个 CIF 买卖与在海上运输过程中发生货损,但案情本身非常独特与罕见。相关 CIF 买卖针对的是 20 辆汽车与相关零件,由于不是大宗货,所以 CIF 卖方就委托了名为 Lampke 的货代安排运输。Lampke 在 Lelia 轮订了仓位,而该船舶的经理人与光船承租人是一家名为 MSC 的德国船公司。MSC 的揽货代理人名为 Bertling,它已经与 Lampke 有过很多的业务往来,包括这次的付运。因为这一长期业务的关系,Bertling 给了 Lampke 大量的空白提单(MSC 的班轮提单),方便后者在货物付运后填写,然后交给 Bertling,让 Bertling 代 MSC 签署。原来的 MSC 的班轮提单格式中有一条英国法院的专属管辖权条文,这表示有争议的话,去英国法院诉讼。但后来 MSC 有了改变,希望去它的所在地即汉堡仲裁,而新版本的班轮提单也做出了这一改变。换言之,新版与原版针对争议处理的管辖权/仲裁条文并不一致。

在该先例中,很巧的是 Lampke 在货物装船后准备填写提单时,发觉正本提单已经用完,而剩下的只是副本提单。于是 Lampke 向 Bertling 要求进一步提交正本提单,而 Bertling 也的确这样做了。但 Bertling 提供的正本提单是新的格式,即有汉堡仲裁的条文。而 Lampke 就把新的正本提单加上旧的副本提单作为一套填写,并取得 Bertling 代 MSC 或承运人的签字。

这一套提单通过转让到了买方的手中,并在卸货时发觉货损,这就带来了常见的货损货差索赔。适用的相关的法律通常即《海牙规则》,其中有很短的 1 年索赔时效。这是 CIF 的买卖,所以涉及德国的保险人,他们在赔偿买方后,代位向船东或 MSC 作为承运人索赔,并委任了一位名为 Dr. Schackow 的德国律师与船东互保协会在德国的代表 Klaas W. Brons 进行接触与谈判。Dr. Schackow 只被提供了一份副本提单,所以他认为如果谈不拢,就需要到英国法院提起诉讼。而 Klaas W. Brons 也是只有一份由 Dr. Schackow 提供的副本提单。所以他们两位都假设是英国法院的管辖,但这显然是错误,因为正本提单才能作准,而正本提单说明是汉堡仲裁。由于他们无法达成和解,所以各自委任了英国律师在英国法院提起法院诉讼。直到文书请求的阶段,双方才发觉正本提单与副本的不一致。这令双方陷入了僵局,之后 MSC 根据 1958 年《纽约公约》向英国法院申请终止法院程序,并强制双方去汉堡仲裁。代表货方或代位求偿保险人的律师显然大力抗拒,毕竟如果要去汉堡重新开始仲裁,劳民伤财不说,1 年的索赔时效也早已过去。

主要反对终止法院程序的理由就是双方一直以来共同假设(shared/mutual assumption)是英国法院有管辖权,双方的行为也是基于该假设,虽然这是错误的理解,但共识性禁反言完全适用。这表示 MSC 不能从这一错误理解中脱身,因为是不公平与不合情理的。

Mustill 大法官把有关的时间分四个时段:(1)签发了正本与副本不一致的提单;(2)订立提单合约的时间,而对买方来说这合约订立的时间往往就是提单背书与交出给买方的时间,如果涉及信用证,即结汇时;(3)Dr. Schackow 与 Klaas W. Brons 在德国交涉与谈判的时段;(4)双方英国律师在法院诉讼的时段。

Mustill 大法官判前两个时段无关,因为双方当事人(即 MSC 与货方的买方)还没有接触,谈不上他们之间有错误的共识与根据这个共识所做出的行为。至于第四时段,由于当时货损索赔的 1 年时效已经过去,所以双方的共识也没有影响〔85〕,说:"The fact that the London solicitors were each proceeding on the footing that the contract contained an English jurisdiction clause, needs no argument... Nevertheless, all this

〔85〕 注意是在 The "Amazonia" (1990) 1 Lloyd's Rep. 236 先例中,Staughton 大法官对 Mustill 大法官针对这点的判法是有保留说:"Presently, I have some hesitation in following the reasoning of Mr Justice Mustill in ... (The 'Leila')."

happened after the expiry of the time limit and the extensions to it... I do not see how the subsequent events could create an equity, the effect of which would be to resurrect a claim which had already become defunct."

而针对第三时段,Mustill 大法官判是构成了共识性禁反言。而错误的共识就是 Dr. Schackow 与 Klaas W. Brons 认为要去英国法院诉讼。

MSC 争辩说不应该对它做出禁反言,因为整个事件的错误是来自货方的买方,因为他提供了一份副本的提单,并且没有提到正本提单会有不同的规定。而 MSC 没有任何错误,它从来没有表示原来的提单格式适用。但 Mustill 大法官认为这种解释不现实,因为作为货代,Lampke 代表货方不可能详细阅读一份班轮提单背后密密麻麻上百条的条文,然后与之前的提单格式比较看有否更改或不同之处。所以,Mustill 大法官认为这一错误的共识实际上是双方的,因为他们都没有提供给其法律代理人一份正本提单。根据过往的先例中,Mustill 大法官认为在共识性禁反言没有必要认定是谁的错导致的错误的共同假设,说:"In my judgment, these authorities lend no support to the argument that the party who asserts an estoppel by convention must show that the other party has made some representation as to the legal position, or that the other party must at least have been the source of the mistake, if any equity is to arise. Indeed, the whole tenor of the judgements in the Amalgamated Property case[86] is to the effect that the estoppel is not so confine.[87]"

Mustill 大法官认为重要的还是看被告即 MSC 是否不合情理,说:"Considering the matter in this way I have come to the conclusion that it would not in all the circumstances be conscionable to allow the defendants to insist on the arbitration clause in preference to the English jurisdiction clause.[88]"Mustill 大法官最终驳回了 MSC 要求终止英国法院程序的申请。

7.3 先例之三:The "Vistafjord"

The"Vistafjord"(1988) 2 Lloyd's Rep. 343 先例也是涉及航运的租船业务,但租用的船舶是一艘旅游船。而船东就是著名的 Norwegian American Cruises A/S(简称 NAC)。而承租人是一个名为 British Leyland 的英国汽车制造商。它想租用 NAC 旗下的一艘最大的旅游船 Vistafjord 轮招待它的零售商或代理人并推广一个新型号的车。British Leyland 想租用的时间是在 1980 年 9 月,交船与还船的地点是汉堡,而双方在谈的租金是 130 万英镑/月。NAC 是通过它在伦敦的专属代理人 Paul Mundy

---

〔86〕 关于 Amalgamated v. Texas Bank (1982) 1 Lloyd's Rep. 27 先例的案情请见本章之 2.2.2 段。

〔87〕 过往的先例没有支持这一争辩,实际上在这一主要的 Amalgamated v. Texas Bank (1982) 1 Lloyd's Rep. 27 先例中,上诉庭的判决更是明确了这一点,因为在该先例错误理解见索即付保函的一方是 Texas Bank,而不是 Amalgamated。但被禁反言的是 Amalgamated 或它的清盘人。

〔88〕 Mustill 大法官得出的结论就是,在本案件中不能让被告坚持汉堡仲裁条文,因为这样不公平。

Ltd（简称 Mundy）和 NAC 派驻在该代理人公司的长期代表 Atkins 先生与 British Leyland 谈判这一租约。

这一租约如果成事，会给 NAC 带来很大收益，特别是 9 月份本来是旅游淡季。但在谈判中，British Leyland 嫌租金太高并希望减轻这部分的经济负担，Atkins 先生因此设计了一个做法，就是 British Leyland 把英国港口（估计旅客上船/下船地点）与汉堡（交船/还船地点）之间的来回空放航程分租给 Mundy，让 Mundy 在这一段时间（大概一周内）自负盈亏进行短航次的营运，而期间 British Leyland 就可以通过收取分租金减少经济负担。这种做法在笔者看来是十分古怪与带来不必要的复杂性，简单与正规的做法就是 British Leyland 在谈判中要求 NAC 减租金，如从 130 万英镑变为 100 万英镑。另一个更加古怪之处是 Atkins 先生没有把这件事情向 NAC 总部报告。而在这一分租的 6 天左右的时间，Mundy 是用该旅游船走了从利物浦到马恩岛的 9 个短航次，但案例没有报道这方面到底是盈或是亏。反正这整个分租约的做法一审的 Hobhouse 大法官是说："Mr Atkin's idea, as he developed it between April and July, was that there should be a sub – charter back to the defendant company. This would be a sub – charter for the two legs amounting, as it turned out, to about six days in all, and it would involve, as it turned out, a time charter hire of GBP106,400... Mr Mundy was naturally involved in this, but it does appear from the evidence that the prime mover was Mr Atkins and he did most of the work on it. Mr. Atkins was fully aware of what it involved. The evidence before me is that, notwithstanding all this, it was accepted that the sub – charter was for the account of the defendants and, therefore, they took the risk of profit or loss."

在 1 个月的租期届满时，British Leyland 支付了 130 万英镑的租金给 Mundy，而 Mundy 则扣除了 13 万英镑作为佣金。而 NAC 在发觉有这一分租约的安排后看来十分不满意，并最终开始这一场诉讼向 Mundy 取回 13 万英镑的佣金。

该先例的报告说是没有证据显示 Mundy 是否知道 Atkins 先生有否向 NAC 报告，反正是认定 Atkins 先生有权代表 NAC。对这一古怪的情况，上诉庭的 Bingham 大法官是这样说："If Mr Mundy knew that Mr. Atkins was practising some fraud on the plaintiffs（原告是指 NAC）, the situation might, of course, be entirely different... In this case, it is not suggested that Mr. Atkins was guilty of fraud or any breach of fiduciary duty. He was, at worst, a careless servant. In my judgment it was not for Mr Mundy to judge what Mr Atkins should pass on, and it is in my view plain that the knowledge of Mr Atkins as the plaintiffs' servant is, on the present facts, correctly to be treated as the knowledge of the plaintiffs."

而上诉庭的判决是 Atkins 先生代表 NAC 与 Mundy 之间的交往与共同假设（shared/mutual assumption）是希望通过这一分租约让 British Leyland 的租约能够成事，而不答应支付这笔佣金给 Mundy，Mundy 就不会肯承租这一盈亏不明朗的分租约。而双方也是基于这种共识行事，导致 NAC 因为共识性禁反言而不得向 Mundy 取回 13 万英镑。Bingham 大法官说："... it was Mr Atkins who devised the sub-charter scheme encouraging the defendants（被告是 Mundy）to participate and knew that the defendants would not commit themselves without the expectation of the commission as a cushion against the loss; the defendants know that Mr Atkins appreciated their expectation of commission and that he appreciated that the defendants would not incur this liability without that expectation; and the parties entered into the transaction between themselves on the basis of the agreed assumption. It would not be fair to allow the plaintiff to repudiate the assumption which enabled them to obtain the business in the first place."

7.4 先例之四：Shearson Lehman Hutton Inc. v. Maclaine Watson & Co. Ltd.

Shearson Lehman Hutton Inc. v. Maclaine Watson & Co. Ltd.（1989）2 Lloyd's Rep. 570 先例的简单案情是，1985 年，金属锡的价格暴涨暴跌是当时的国际大新闻。当时专门有一个名为 International Tin Council（简称 ITC）的国际机构去保持锡的价格平稳。其工作就是在锡的价格上升时，通过出口国家与 ITC 的储存，多放一些锡到市场，让价格不再上升；如果价格下跌，则 ITC 会在市场收购，以让价格不再下跌。ITC 的财政来源主要是出口与进口的国家政府资助，如马来西亚就是十分重要的出口国家之一。ITC 的财政来源也有部分是通过银行的融资，作为担保的就是其储存的锡。1985 年下半年，由于锡价暴跌，ITC 在财政上最后还是撑不住，并宣布无法进行业务。这令进行锡买卖最主要的交易所即最近被香港证券交易所收购的 London Metal Exchange（简称 LME）采取紧急措施，引进了一个名为 M 的规则，暂停已经存在的合约的履行，并确定了一个锡价要求交易双方和解。

这一先例的案情十分复杂，在这里只做简单介绍。原告 Shearsons 与被告 Maclaines互相之间进行锡的买卖，主要是 Shearsons 卖给 Maclaines，但也有小部分是 Shearsons 向 Maclaines 买。但他们之间的身份不一样，Maclaines 是 LME 的会员，所谓的"ring dealing members"（简称 RDMs），它显然是要受 LME 规则的约束，包括该 M 规则改变进行时交易的游戏规则。但 Shearsons 不是 LME 的会员，LME 改变游戏规则能否约束 Shearsons 并导致 Shearsons 蒙受庞大损失就是该先例的主要争议。显然，Shearsons 如果通过合约接受 LME 的规则，包括 LME 改变游戏规则的权利，Shearsons 即使不是会员，也受到合约的约束。但 Shearsons 并没有订立这种合约，不论是与 LME 或是与 Maclaines。这样，就只能通过共识性禁反言，从双方的交往中看看有否适用 LME 规则的共识，并根据这一共识行事。

这方面在 Webster 大法官的判决中有解释，如下：

"Shearsons are not members of the LME; therefore they can only be bound in principle by the rules in force on Oct. 24, if by their contracts with Maclaines they agreed to be bound by the rules in force at the date of the contracts and if those rules were still in force on Oct. 24; and they can only be bound by a rule which came into force after the date of those contracts if by those contracts they agreed to be bound by such rules as might come into effect from time to time between the dates upon which the contracts were made and the time when they were performed.

Therefore Shearsons can only be bound by the suspension if the rules in force at the dates when the contracts were made and still in force on Oct. 24, enabled the LME to suspend the performance of contracts between 'ring dealing members'（RDMs）and non – members who had agreed to be bound by the rules..."

针对共识性禁反言,双方的交往有以下的通信往来,如早在1月10日Shearsons给Maclaines的信函中说要依据LME规则来买卖这批锡:"We and all other parties who have entered into contracts subject to LME rules for the sale of tin ..."

之后Shearsons的律师给Maclaines的律师的信函中也说到双方的合约是依据LME规则以及有争议时,以LME仲裁解决,说:"We appreciate that our client's contracts with your clients referred to in the writ are subject to the rules and regulations of the London Metal Exchange which provides for disputes to be resolved by LME arbitration."

Webster大法官是这样判:"This evidence fully substantiates the allegation that the parties shared a common assumption that the contracts were contracts known colloquially as B contracts[89] and that they were subject to all the applicable rules. If, contrary to my previous decision, either of those assumptions were wrong, they were mistaken. The correspondence, in particular the correspondence passing between Shearsons or their solicitors and Maclaines or their solicitors, and the plaintiff' original points of claim, constitute evidence of action taken by Shearsons upon those assumptions, and it was action which 'crossed the line' from their side of the relationship to the other... and that it was action which at least related to and, it can be inferred, affected the particular relationship between the parties. Although there was no evidence to the effect that Maclaines had conducted the proceedings in any way in reliance upon the belief that there was a common assumption between themselves and Shearsons that the contracts were B contracts, it is an inevitable inference that they early conduct of the proceedings and preparation for trial will have proceeded upon that basis; and they were entitled to assume, at any rate until Mar 5, that it was common ground that the contracts were subject to all the applicable rules."

7.5　先例之五:The "Amazonia"

The"Amazonia"（1990）1 Lloyd's Rep. 236 CA先例涉及了一个航次租约,航次是从澳大利亚运锌精矿去印度。租约的第34条文是伦敦仲裁,而第33条文是合并了澳大利亚1924年《海上运输法》(类似1924年《海牙规则》),并强调适用在澳大利

---

〔89〕 A合约一般是指两个LME会员之间的合约,B合约一般是指LME会员与其客户之间的合约。

亚签发的提单，其中立法的 section 9 规定如下："（1） All parties to any... document relating to the carriage of goods from any place in Australia to any place outside Australia shall be deemed to have intended to contract according to the laws in force at the place of shipment, and any stipulation or agreement to the contrary, or purporting to oust... the jurisdiction of the Courts of the Commonwealth or of a State in respect of the... document shall be illegal, null and void and of no effect ..."〔90〕

从这个租约的条文来看，仅是解释上述有关的条文，会得出伦敦仲裁的条文实际上是非法与无效的结论。根据之后法律的发展，这个先例不会这样解释，这是因为在独立原则（separation principle）下，把合约内的仲裁条文视为与主合约分离的另一个协议。加上有 XL Insurance v. Owens Corning（2000）2 Lloyd's Rep. 500 等先例判是主合约的适用法条文只是针对主合约，而针对独立的仲裁协议，在没有明示规定下，就要看与之最密切关系的法律，伦敦仲裁显然最密切关系就是英国法，针对这方面在《仲裁法——从 1996 年英国仲裁法到国际商务仲裁》一书第二章有详论。此外，也有 OT Africa Line Ltd. v. Magic Sportswear & Ors（2005）2 Lloyd's Rep. 170 先例说明英国法院不承认加拿大的同类立法，并做出"止诉禁令"（anti - suit injunction）以保护伦敦仲裁。

但在本先例中，大概是发生的时间还早，大家是接受第 34 条的伦敦仲裁如果与第 33 条一并解释，第 34 条就会是非法与无效。但起初，双方当事人都没有觉察到这一点，包括澳大利亚立法之 section 9。在时效即将届满前，承租人为了保护时效与船东（实际上是二船东），同意去伦敦仲裁，并委任 Donald Davies 为独任仲裁员。直到 4 年后（估计在这段时间，双方也没有努力推进仲裁，只是在拖拖拉拉地谈判），这一点才被原船东发觉，并向二船东提出伦敦仲裁无效。这也导致夹在两份租约当中的二船东采取同样的行动，并向英国法院要求一个宣誓判决，说明双方同意 Donald Davies先生作为独任仲裁员的协议是无效。但二船东败诉，原因是根据共识性禁反言，因为二船东与承租人之间的交往与互动，令双方产生一个租约中的伦敦仲裁条文是有效的共同错误理解，并最终同意 Donald Davies 先生作为独任仲裁员。其中 Staughton 大法官是这样说：

"There was little or no dispute that the first requirement of an estoppel by convention was satisfied. The evidence plainly shows a common shared assumption - in this case that there was a valid arbitration agreement between the parties. The argument has been as to when that common shared assumption came into being, and whether it would be unconscionable for the owners to depart from it...

As to unconscionability, it does not seem to me significant who first made the mis-

〔90〕 从澳大利亚出口货物的运输文件中涉及的所有当事人应被视为有意图约定装货地点的法律为实体法，任何排除澳大利亚法院管辖权的规定或协议将被视为非法与无效。

take, or who had the better opportunity to ascertain the true position. It was a shared mistake, which could easily be made. There is some force in... that the owners, if they are now held liable, may have lost their right to indemnity from the registered owners. I am by no means persuaded that they had lost it. It is a nice point... Mr. Gilman(二船东的代表大律师) says that it is a disadvantage to the owners to have to overcome a nice point.

I would give far more weight to the disadvantage to the claimants(原告是承租人)if they lose altogether their right to pursue their claim, and the costs that they have already incurred in the arbitration. It would in my view be monstrous if the owners were allowed to retreat from the position which they had taken for over four years."

7.6　先例之六:Allison v. Limehouse & Co.

Allison v. Limehouse & Co. (1992) 2 A. C. 105 先例涉及是否妥当与有效的送达告票(writ)。原告(在清盘中的 Allison)声称被告(Limehouse,一间合伙制的会计师事务所)在较早前对其公司的财务进行审计时存在疏忽,并向被告索赔损失。告票在 1987 年 10 月 5 日做出。1988 年 10 月 4 日,即该告人告票一年有效期的最后一日,该告票才被送达(serve)到被告的办公室,Hall 先生作为被告的合伙人之一,让他的秘书或者私人助理 Morgan 女士接受了告票。后来,被告向法院申请确认该告票无效送达的命令。如果该送达被否定,原告将没有机会再重新送达该告票,因为该告人告票的有效期为 1 年,该告票已经于 1988 年 10 月 5 日失效,且原告再要重新申请另一张告票的时效已过。同时,该失效告票也无法被延期,原因有二:第一,因其已经失效而无法向法院申请延长;第二,原告在整个告票 1 年的有效期内有充分的机会向被告送达,却非要等到有效期的最后一天才做出一个被指是不适当的送达。

告票的有效送达对于被告来说非常重要,因为他要知道对他的指控以及要如何做出应对,包括聘请律师在时限内出庭抗辩。如果告票被适当的送达至被告,但被告选择漠视告票,原告的律师在提交了诉讼申请书之后,就可以做出告票已经被适当送达但被漠视的宣誓书(affidavit)。法院根据该宣誓书就会只是根据诉讼申请书而做出缺席判决(default judgment)。

为了保证告票的适当送达与正当程序,最高院的程序规则(Rules of Supreme Court 简称 R. S. C.)中对告票的送达有详细的规定。其中与本案有关的规定是 R. S. C. Order10, r. 1 与 Order 81, r. 3。在 Order10, r. 1,说:"A writ **must be served personally on each defendant** by the plaintiff or his agent."(加黑部分是笔者的强调)

Order 81, r. 3 是有关被告是合伙人的情况,说:"Where... partners are sued in the name of a firm, the writ may,... be served – (a) on any one or more of the partners, or (b) at the principal place of business of the partnership within the jurisdiction, on any person having at the time of service the control or management of the partnership business there; or (c) by sending a copy of the writ by ordinary first – class post (as defined in

Ord. 10, r. 1(2)) to the firm at the principal place of business of the partnership within the jurisdiction and ... the writ shall be deemed to have been duly served on the firm, whether or not any member of the firm is out of the jurisdiction ..."

RSC 中还有其他的条文针对其他方法的送达,包括 Order 10, r.1(2) & (3)针对的用一等邮件(first class mail)送达至被告通常或者最后知悉的住址与将告票放入该住址的信箱内;Order 10, r.1(4)针对的被告律师接受告票而完成送达;Order 10, r.3(1)针对的按照合约规定的方式完成送达,该方式中,外国公司同意在伦敦指定一个代理(通常是律师所)来接受送达的做法很常见。在 Order 65, r.4 中,法院也可以在其认为正规送达方式是不切实际时(如找不到被告或者不知道被告的住址等)做出替代送达的命令。

回到本案,主要的争议点是 RSC 中对于送达本人的规定是否是强制性(mandatory)规定告票一定要送达 Hall 先生本人。虽然 RSC 中还规定了其他的送达方式,但却从没有提到告票由被告的秘书或者私人助理接受也可以视为可接受的送达方式。

在一审的地区法院,被告要求撤销告票送达的申请被否决。但在上诉法院,这个结果被推翻,上诉庭的多数法官(Donaldson 大法官持不同意见)认为告票并没有被适当的送达给被告。最后本案上诉到当时的最高院即贵族院,贵族院又将上诉庭的多数意见推翻。贵族院认为根据立法的历史来看,R. S. C. 的 Order 10 中没有禁止当事人之间同意一种在此条文规定之外的送达方式。所以,相应的,在有 Hall 先生明示授权的情况下,其秘书或私人助理对于告票的接受应该构成告票的有效送达。

但在贵族院,Goff 勋爵不太同意其他勋爵对于 R. S. C. 的 Order 10 的宽松解释,他说:

"... It is important that those concerned at court offices, and especially those who have to deal with applications for judgment in default, should know precisely what mode of service has been adopted, and therefore be able to know (by reference to the relevant rules of court) the precise date upon which the proceedings are treated as having been served. In these circumstances, it is suggested, it is not surprising that the rules should provide for a mandatory method of service, subject to specified exceptions.

I approach the matter as follows. First of all, as it seems to me, effect must be given to the rules of court in accordance with their terms. Here, the rules of court do indeed provide a comprehensive code, with a mandatory rule of personal service subject to certain specified exceptions. Such service alone constitutes good and effective service for the purpose of the rules of court. With all respect, I feel unable to accept earlier authority in so far as it suggests that any different form of service, for example such service in accordance with an agreement between theparties (otherwise than as permitted by the Rules), can constitute good and effective service."

在本案的事实中,没有任何的合约规定显示双方同意 Morgan 女士作为 Hall 先生的代理人去接受告票就应被视为告票是有效送达。所以,R. S. C. 的 Order 10, r. 3(1)不适用。

Goff 勋爵继续提到了禁反言。在上诉庭,双方曾经有关于"承诺性禁反言"(promissory estoppel)的争议,但上诉庭驳回了该争议,其认为 Hall 先生根本没有对原告做出任何的陈述或承诺,他们之间甚至没有任何的沟通,除了通过 Morgan 女士接受告票,Goff 勋爵说:"In the Court of Appeal, it was argued that what happened gave rise to a promissory estoppel on the part of Mr. Hall, binding the defendants, precluding them from asserting that the service was ineffective in law. This argument was rejected, expressly by Lord Donaldson of Lymington M. R. and by Farquharson L. J., and implicitly by Russell L. J., because no representation was made as to the validity of the service. This conclusion was, in my opinion, plainly right; and the argument was not pursued by the plaintiffs before your Lordships' House..."

Goff 勋爵在双方当事人没有提出的情况下,根据自己的想法提出共识性禁反言(estoppel by convention)在这里应该适用,说:

"But, as it seems to me, the matter does not stop there. For what in reality happened was that both Mr. Hall and the plaintiffs... proceeded on the common but mistaken assumption that service of the writ upon the duly authorised agent of Mr. Hall would constitute good and effective service upon the defendants. Furthermore it is legitimate to infer that the course of action of Mr. Swann(原告送达告票的律师)was influenced by the adoption by both parties of that common mistaken assumption in that, if they had not proceeded on the basis of it, Mr. Swann would in all probability not have been content with service upon Mrs. Morgan but would have asked to serve the writ upon Mr. Hall personally, and there is no reason to suppose that that request would have been refused. On these facts, in my opinion, **the defendants will be estopped by convention from thereafter contending that there was not good and effective service of the writ upon them**, on the principle established in Amalgamated Investment & Property Co. Ltd. v. Texas Commerce International Bank Ltd. [1982] Q. B. 84.... where both parties proceed on the basis of a common, but mistaken, assumption as to the legal effect of a certain transaction between them, and in consequence one party is so influenced by the conduct of the other that it would be unconscionable for the latter to take advantage of the former's error... It is the principle of estoppel by convention in this sense that can, in my opinion, be invoked by the plaintiffs in the present case.

I must confess to being troubled by the fact that no argument was addressed to your Lordships upon this point, and I naturally hesitate to reach a conclusion upon a point which has not been argued. However since, as I understand the position, the remainder of your Lordships have reached the same conclusion by a rather different route, I am content in the circumstances to state that I agree that the appeal should be allowed."(加黑部分是笔者的强调)

7.7 先例之七:G S Fashions Ltd. v. B & Q Plc.

G S Fashions Ltd. v. B & Q Plc.(1995)1 WLR 1088 先例涉及一个在诉讼程序(本案是针对法院诉讼,但也可以发生在仲裁中)中有趣的问题,就是双方在诉讼开始后,通常第一个步骤是双方交换文书请求,即先要提交索赔请求与答辩。但在诉讼程序进行中,由于各种原因(如看到新的证据、换了律师等),会令原告或被告对原来的文书请求有了不同看法(甚至是本来有争议的事项变为没有争议,或本来同意的对方的指控变为有争议)而需要改变立场,就会需要申请把索赔请求与答辩进行修改。这看来在英国诉讼的做法下是十分明确的,即是可以自由修改。英国法是把索赔请求与答辩内提到的内容视为原告与被告对自己案件的说明,以供对方同意或否认而并非是对于事实的陈述。

这可节录 Parke B 大法官在 Boileau v. Rutin(1848)2 Exch 665 先例中所说:"... pleadings... are not to be treated as positive allegations of the truth of the facts... for all purposes, but only as statements of the case of the party, to be admitted or denied by the opposite party, and if denied to be proved, and ultimately submitted for judicial decision."

另 Viscount Simon LC in 大法官在 United Australia Ltd. v. Barclays Bank Ltd.(1941)AC 1 先例中说原告可以随时在判决之前对他在告票或索赔请求中做出的指控进行修改:"There is nothing conclusive about the form in which the writ is issued, or about the claims made in the statement of claim. A plaintiff may at any time before judgment be permitted to amend."

Mason 大法官在澳大利亚的 Laws v. Australian Broadcasting Tribunal(1990)170 CLR 70 先例中说:"The suggestion that unverified pleadings should be treated in the same way as any other form of admission fails... to take account of the function and object of pleadings, when they are not required to be verified, in outlining the party's case and defining the issue to be tried. Especially is this so in the case of... defences. A defendant is entitled to put a plaintiff to proof his or her cause of action and to raise alternative matters of defence which may possibly answer the plaintiff's claim, without asserting in an absolute sense the truth or correctness of the particular matters pleaded."

所以,文书请求总是可以在判决做出之前申请对文书请求进行修改,做出与之前不一致的指控或抗辩,现实中经常会有在开庭审理的途中才修改的情况。显然提出修改的一方要承担因修改而浪费的费用,毕竟另一方针对之前的指控已经花费了费用准备,而这个费用因为修改而被浪费。只有在修改会给对方带来不公平或金钱无法弥补的损失的情况下,法院才会不允许修改。如申请修改的一方早就可以提出却留待最后的一刻(如开庭审理后),而如果允许修改会带来诉讼的严重延误。这方面的简单道理在 Clarapede & Co. v. Commercial Union Association (1883) 32 WR 262 CA 上诉庭先例中,Brett 大法官说:"The rule of conduct of the court in such a case is that, however negligent or careless may have been the first omission, and however late the proposed amendment, the amendment should be allowed if it can be made without injustice to the other side. There is no injustice if the other side can be compensated by costs, but if the amendment will put them into such a position that they must be injured, it ought not to be made."

这样看来,文书请求的做出是不存在禁反言的说法。诉讼双方对对方的指控不能视为对事实的陈述,所以不存在陈述性禁反言。而即使在双方的文书请求中同意了某些重要事实,因为将来被对方修改的可能,这种同意或理解不会构成共识性禁反言。

但是如果诉讼中有一方合理依赖了另一方文书请求中的立场而做出相应的行动,但另一方事后反悔(即申请修改),是否可以共识性禁反言为由而禁止一方修改其诉讼请求呢?

G S Fashions Ltd. v. B & Q Plc. 先例涉及房屋租赁的合约。房东因租客违约转租给第三人(本案是第四被告)而在告票与索赔请求中要求收回房产。租客在答辩中承认了责任并且终止了与分租客之间订立的许可使用房产的协议,但对赔偿中间收益(Mesne profit[91])有争议,这看来是唯一的抗辩。不过,随后房东改变主意而修改请求将收回房产这一项删除。法院认为房东不可以这样做,因为他之前的诉讼请求被租客依赖并产生了终止与分租客之间的许可使用房产的协议的损失,所以适用共识性禁反言的理论。

Lightman 大法官说:"If I am wrong and the pleadings do not constitute the necessary mutual confirmation of the forfeiture. I think that on the facts of this case the landlord was estopped on 27 January 1994 from resiling from its claim to a valid forfeiture, for it had acquiesced in the tenant's acceptance of the validity of the forfeiture since 23 December 1993 and... It should have anticipated that the tenant would act on the basis of common agreement between the parties that the leases had been forfeited, and the tenant did so act in the interim, and accordingly the landlord is debarred by application of the doctrine of estoppel by convention."

7.8　先例之八:Mannai Investment Co. Ltd. v. Eagle Star Life Assurance Co. Ltd.

Mannai Investment Co. Ltd. v. Eagle Star Life Assurance Co. Ltd. (1997) A. C.

---

〔91〕这是一个土地法术语,指租客在租期届满后还继续占用租赁产业,出租人可向他索取的赔偿,赔偿数额是根据租金的市价来计算。

749 贵族院先例是一个较近期的针对解释合约的重要先例中，案情在杨良宜《合约的解释：规则与应用》一书第一章之8.2段有详细的介绍，在此不重复。该先例涉及房屋租赁。在英国经常会有时间较长的房屋租赁合约，如15年或20年，而在这种长期的租约中经常会见到一种名为终止条文（break clause）的条文，该条文允许租客在一定时间（5年或7年不等）之后，提前给房东通知而终止租赁合约。英国法一直以来对此类通知的要求都非常严格，做出通知的一方一定要非常精确地遵守条文中对通知的规定，正如Hoffmann勋爵所说："If the clause had said that the notice had to be on blue paper, it would have no good serving a notice on pink paper, however clear it might have been that the tenant wanted to terminate the lease."

在本先例中，贵族院是以3比2的多数意见判虽然该通知的内容有错误，但有关的通知有效。租客在通知中把终止租约的日期算错了，终止条文中要求租客在终止租约6个月前给通知，租客做出通知后的6个月是1月13日，而租客却在通知中写成了1月12日。要注意的是，该有关的终止条文中只规定需要至少给出6个月的通知，而没有要求在通知中写明6个月后是哪一天。

贵族院多数意见的决定即在解释终止条文与有关的通知时是根据完全客观的考验，而不考虑主观的想法。正如Clyde勋爵所说："The standard of reference is that of the reasonable man exercising his common sense in the context and in the circumstances of the particular case... To demand a perfect precision in matters which are not within the formal requirements of the relevant power would in my view impose an unduly high standard in the framing of notices ... While careless drafting is certainly to be discouraged the evident intention of a notice should not in matters of this kind be rejected in preference of a technical precision... The test is an objective one. **In circumstances where an estoppel might arise the actual understanding of the recipient may be relevant, but in general the actual understanding of the parties is beside the point**..."

在以上最后加黑的一句中，Clyde勋爵提到如果涉及禁反言的法律理论，解释合约的客观考验就不适用，反而要看接收通知一方的主观理解（针对承诺性或陈述性禁反言）或是双方的主观理解（针对共识性禁反言）。在本先例中，虽然是多数意见，但由于决定是支持通知的有效，所以就不需要理会禁反言的理论。而如果是判有关的通知无效，就可能会涉及禁反言的争议。如终止条文中写明要注明具体的终止租约的日期，但在通知中对此有了错误。或是通知中的错误是双方都不会警觉的，否则就不会事后才有争议，因为一有警觉的话，马上就可以提出而做出新的正确的通知。但现实往往是双方把有缺陷的通知当做有效，并进行一连串的交往与互动。之后，由于市场发生变化或者其他的变数，令一方的立场有变化，等到有律师介入，通知中存在的错误才被找出来。在这种情况下，有关通知究竟是否有效，往往会作为主要争议，而双方事后的交往与互动会构成禁反言（特别是共识性禁反言），就会被双方作为一个替代争议。例如，房东在收到通知后，没有觉察到有错就登广告招租，而租客在做出通知之后又改变主意想继续租约，并以通知不符合终止条文的规定而无效作为理由，房东就会以禁反言作为对抗。这样，双方在其后的交往与互动中的主观想法（即双方是否有该通知有效的共同与分享的假设）就会变得很重要。

在该先例中，Steyn 勋爵说："Depending on the circumstances a party may be precluded by an estoppels by convention from raising a contention contrary to a common assumption of fact or law (which could include the validity of a notice) upon which they have acted... Such an issue may involve subjective questions. That is however, a different issue and not one relevant to this appeal（只是针对解释合约的问题）. I proceed therefore to examine the matter objectively."

7.9 先例之九：Hiscox v. Outhwaite (No.1)

Hiscox v. Outhwaite (No.1) (1991) 2 Lloyd's Rep. 1 (CA)先例[92]的案情涉及仲裁中一个非常有趣的问题。在当时，因为美国石棉中毒事件导致了大规模的索赔，很多劳合社的保险人破产。该先例涉及一个再保合约，保险人与再保人根据再保合约开始伦敦仲裁，并委任了 MacCrindle QC 作为独任仲裁员。MacCrindle QC 频繁往返伦敦与巴黎，并在两地都有办公室。该仲裁虽然是在伦敦开庭并且草拟了大部分的裁决书，但他将裁决书带到了巴黎签字，并有一栏说明是在巴黎签字（signed in Paris）。在英国法院与部分的伦敦仲裁中，有一个习惯做法是在双方的英国律师保证不会泄露给客户的情况下，法官或仲裁员先将拟定的判决或裁决书发给他们，让双方检查有否明显的文书错误，之后才正式签署与做出判决或裁决书。在该先例中，双方的代表律师检查后，在大家的文书交往中没有对 MacCrindle QC 在巴黎签字一栏有任何异议。之后，败诉的 Hiscox 根据 1979 年《仲裁法》向法院上诉，另也根据 1950 年《仲裁法》要求法院把裁决书发还给仲裁员。Outhwaite 则以裁决书在巴黎签字，是法国的裁决书，根据 1975 年《仲裁法》与《纽约公约》，英国法院只能执行（或拒绝执行），不存在可以处理上诉或发还裁决书的管辖权。后者的管辖权只是针对英国作为仲裁地点的裁决书。

上诉庭的一致意见推翻了高院的一审判决，认为该先例的裁决书确实是一个《纽约公约》裁决书，因为写明是在巴黎签署。[93] 这样，英国法院应该没有管辖权，但上诉庭的多数意见（Leggatt 大法官不同意，认为双方在互动中没有想到这个问题，也就说不上有共识）判共识性禁反言成立，Outhwaite 被禁止反对英国法院的管辖权。因为双方一直都共同假设在巴黎签字不会影响英国法院的管辖权。直到 Hiscox 开

---

〔92〕 该先例虽然上诉到了贵族院（[1991] 2 Lloyd's Rep. 435），但不涉及禁反言的争议。

〔93〕 这一先例所带来的问题也导致了英国《仲裁法》需要做出针对，这在 1996 年《仲裁法》之 section 53 加上了以下的条文："Unless otherwise agreed by the parties, where the seat of the arbitration is in England and Wales or Northern Ireland, any award in the proceedings shall be treated as made there, regardless of where it was signed, despatched or delivered to any of the parties."

始向法院做出申请与上诉,看来 Outhwaite 才警觉这一技术性漏洞,Hiscox 也才知道自己的权利被挑战。针对这个漏洞,Hiscox 提出了共识性禁反言,双方在整个仲裁的互动(尤其是检查拟定的裁决书后双方的文书交往)中都假设这是一个英国仲裁的裁决书。如果让 Outhwaite 撤回这个假设,会不合情理。毕竟如果 Outhwaite 的律师在检查拟定的裁决书时就提出,在巴黎签字会令一个英国本地仲裁的裁决书变为一个《纽约公约》裁决书,MacCrindle QC 可以很方便地改为在伦敦签字。

Donaldson 勋爵说:“It was quite clearly the assumption of the parties that either this was not in fact or law a Convention award or that, if it was, there was no impediment under the Act of 1975 or otherwise to the exercise of the court's jurisdiction under the Act of 1950 and 1979.”

上诉庭的多数意见在笔者看来是十分现实与有可操作性。这表示将来在双方履行或诉讼的互动中对总体的大方向有共识,但中间有一些技术性的纰漏,就可以共识性禁反言作为抗辩。

7.10 先例之十:Thornton Springer v. NEM Insurance Co. Ltd. & Ors

Thornton Springer v. NEM Insurance Co. Ltd. & Ors (2000) CLC 975 先例的案情涉及专业责任保险(professional liability insurance)。该先例再次显示了一种对保险人十分危险的情况,即根据保险合约的解释(根据后来的判决)保险人可以不用赔偿,但因为他的言行造成弃权或禁反言而导致最后需要赔偿。这种危险也并非仅限于保险合约,而是存在于任何类别的合约关系。

在该先例中,第三人 Roscoe 先生向原告会计事务所与其中的一个合伙人 Kaye 先生索赔,指称 Kaye 先生对一宗股票转让交易与相关事宜做出财务建议时疏忽,另也有其他方面的违约,例如有利益冲突违反了诚信责任(fiduciary duty)等。在 Roscoe 先生对原告与 Kaye 先生的诉讼中,法院最后判是 Kaye 先生从未以会计的专业身份做出建议,Roscoe 先生没有雇佣原告,原告对 Roscoe 先生没有责任。

虽然原告会计事务所最后从诉讼中脱身,但无论如何还是花费了一定的律师费,所以向被告(专业责任保险的保险人)要求补偿。事实上,被告已经在无损害(without prejudice)的前提下支付了部分抗辩费用,于是反索赔要求原告返还这笔钱。

相关的保单针对保险范围说:“Now we the Underwriters to the extent and in the manner hereinafter provided hereby agree: To indemnify the Assured against any claim first made against the Assured during the period of insurance... of any civil liability whatsoever or whensoever arising (including liability for claimants' costs) **incurred** in connection with the conduct of any professional business carried on by or on behalf of the Assured.”

法院判是上述加黑的“incurred”一词应被解释为被保险人(assured)即原告真正有责任,而不是被声称有责任。在该先例中,因为原告被判是对 Roscoe 先生没有责任,所以不在保单第 1 条的范围之内。

但该保单还有一条特殊条文名为“Special Condition 1”说:“Underwriters shall in addition indemnify the Assured in respect of all costs and expenses incurred with their written consent in the defence or settlement of any claim made against the Assured which falls to be dealt with under this Certificate .... ”

法院判这个特殊条文的作用之一是:“The condition is concerned with costs and expenses incurred in two eventualities — (i) the defence of a relevant claim and (ii) the settlement of a relevant claim. Expenditure of costs or expenses on defence may occur in relation to a claim which is subsequently successful, but also to a claim which is subsequently unsuccessful. Equally, costs or expenditure incurred in the settlement of a claim may be paid to settle a claim which may or may not have succeeded. In the context of this state of uncertainty as to whether the claim is well – founded or not, **the written consent of the underwriters is an agreed control mechanism.** Decisions on expenditure have to be taken by the assured before the determination of the claim or ascertainment of liability. If underwriters withhold consent, the assured is entitled not to defend or settle the claim. ”(加黑部分是笔者的强调)

其中 Colman 大法官也说:“In my judgment, special condition I does not require that the costs must have been incurred in defence of a successful as distinct from an unsuccessful claim against the assured. It is significant that the condition is concerned not only with the costs of defence but with the expense and cost of settlement of any such claim. If there were to be super – added to the requirement that the underwriters should have consented to the costs or expenses being incurred also the requirement that there should be actual liability to the claimant, that requirement must apply equally to the expenses of settlement. However, the assured is not permitted to enter into a settlement unless the underwriters have consented to it. A construction which left it open to underwriters to decline indemnity in respect of such costs or expenses, when they had already consented to the settlement being entered into, on the grounds that there had in truth been no liability of the assured to the claimant would, I have to say, be quite absurd. ”

有这个特殊条文针对诉讼费用完全可以理解。根据保单的保险范围,被保险人真正有责任才可以获得保险人赔偿,如果没有责任,就不会获得赔偿。但是否真正有责任往往需要经过长时间的诉讼才能最后决定,即使最后判是没有责任,也会产生一大笔律师费。如果这笔律师费无法获得赔偿,岂不是鼓励被保险人在诉讼中投降?另是双方达成和解的情况(通常包括已经产生的律师费),这种情况下很难说是否真正有责任,如果保险公司拒绝赔偿就会很不合理。例如,专业疏忽诉讼的原告因为自己的原因向被保险人提出终止诉讼,各自承担律师费。这种情况下如果保险公司不愿意赔偿,被保险人就可能选择不和解继续诉讼。专业疏忽诉讼的原告被迫要将诉讼进行下去,因为诉讼风险的存在,绝对有可能是最后被保险人败诉,保险人不仅要承担被保险人被判要赔偿的金额还要承担双方的律师费，这明显不符合保险人的利益。同时为了保障自己的利益，保险人即使不将诉讼或和解谈判接手过来，也希望通过书面同意这个要求，对被保险人自己进行的诉讼与和解协议有一定的控制，没有保险人的书面同意，被保险人不可以达成和解协议，也没有办法取回已经花费的律师费。

因此，被告1997年6月5日的信件是否能被解释为一份书面同意就变得至关重要。而如果该信件不能被解释为书面同意，能否被解释为对书面同意要求的弃权或共识性禁反言或"承诺性禁反言"（promissory estoppel）？首先可节录Colman大法官对该信件中部分内容的解释：

"It is to be observed that the letter（即被告1997年6月5日的信件）is careful both to distinguish any liability in damages arising out of Kaye's private business transactions from liability arising out of the conduct of the practice's professional business and to reserve the position on costs awarded in favour of Roscoe.

The letter thus far reflects the effect of insuring cl. 1 of the policy.

（3）The third paragraph deals exclusively with defence costs incurred or to be incurred by the practice. The statement that 'it follows from the above that our clients **are prepared to indemnify** your clients for both the costs which have been incurred to date and future costs, save for those which are attributable to the investigation and defence of the allegations made against Mr Kaye acting in his personal capacity' set out two material commitments on the part of the insurers：

（a）they were in principle prepared to provide indemnity in respect of costs already incurred and in respect of future costs subject to the following qualification；

（b）by parity of reasoning with their approach to indemnification for damages and costs liabilities their indemnity in respect of costs would not extend to those attributable to investigation and defence of allegations against Kaye in his personal capacity."（加黑部分是笔者的强调）

被告争辩上述加黑的"are prepared to indemnify"一句只表示保险人愿意解决这个专业疏忽的争议导致的问题，但要以保单的保险范围为准，没有进一步的意思。

但Colman大法官不同意被告的争辩，认为加黑的一句属于书面同意，或对书面同意要求的弃权，说："I am not able to accept this analysis of the letter. That is because it has to be read against the background of a policy which contains not only the insuring clause but also special condition 1 which has the meaning which I have already determined. I have no doubt whatever that this letter would have been read by any reader ... against the background of both the policy and the previous correspondence, as having the effect of a consent by insurers to the practice（原告）having already incurred the costs in respect of the preparation of the defence of the claim in so far as that preparation was directed to the claim for breach of professional duty as distinct from the claim based on allegations against Kaye acting in his personal capacity and to the incurring of such defence costs and expenses in future. The statement that the insurers were prepared to indemnify the practice in respect of such costs would be understood as meaning that they would pay such costs in such circumstances as defence costs and expenses would be payable under special condition 1 if such costs had been incurred with the underwriters' consent, subject always to apportionment and, if the defence were successful, to rights of subrogation in respect of costs orders against Roscoe.

It follows that this letter did operate as a consent to the practice having incurred and incurring in future defence costs and expenditure to the extent specified.

... If the letter of 5 June 1997 did not contain a consent for the purposes of special condition 1, it is submitted that the effect of that letter and of subsequent letters, in particular that of 15 August 1997, was to waive the requirement for consent under that special condition."

虽然在该先例中,没有必要再决定是否构成共识性禁反言,但 Colman 大法官还是进行了简单的针对如下:"As indicated above, the practice(原告)ceased to concern itself with legal costs insurance once it had received the 5 June letter, for it then believed that, apart from quantification by apportionment, there was no risk that the insurers would decline to pay defence costs if the defence claim succeeded.〔94〕 Having regard to what I have held to be the proper construction of that letter, this was an entirely understandable and reasonable course. In the event, the practice did not re – investigate such insurance until after it had received Cameron's(被告的律师事务所)letter of 26 July 1998 which told them that insurers would make no further contribution to defence costs beyond the two payments of £ 75,000 and £ 50,000 already made〔95〕. By then the legal costs insurers were quoting significantly higher premiums than had been offered in early June. Indeed, the decision was then taken that the cost of cover was so great that the practice could not afford it. It is on that basis that it is submitted that it would suffer irremedia-

〔94〕 笔者认为该先例显示了共识性禁反言的危险性。如果单纯是一个合约规定下的书面同意带来共识让诉讼继续,属于合约性质,与 Kaye 先生分摊费用的保留就可能导致根本没有书面同意存在。对于信件后产生的费用,即使双方对分摊的比例有争议,也可以通过默示让第三人(通常是法院或仲裁庭)决定,不会对书面同意的存在产生障碍。但是对在信件前已经产生的费用,如果双方没有对分摊的比例达成一致,就说明双方在当时没有真正同意(meeting of minds),也就不存在真正意义上的书面同意。但在共识性禁反言(或承诺性禁反言),只需要提出禁反言的一方(estoppel raiser),在该先例即原告,合理依赖对方泛泛的承诺或共识。因此原告将禁反言作为替代,如果法院认为不存在书面同意,也可以通过不同考验的共识性禁反言获得律师费用的赔偿。

〔95〕 被告从共同假设中脱身。

ble prejudice if the insurers were permitted to go back on the terms of the letter of 5 June for by resiling from their position as to defence costs indemnity defined by the letter the insurers had effectively deprived the practice of legal costs insurance at an affordable premium.[96] I interpose that this would represent a typical estoppel by convention scenario, in accordance with the principles approved in 'The Vistafjord' [1988] 2 Lloyd's Rep. 343."

7.11 先例之十一:Johnson v. Gore Wood & Co.

可先介绍 Johnson v. Gore Wood & Co. (2002) 2 AC 1 先例的简单案情。1991 年 1 月 8 日,一家由原告 Johnson 先生控制的 WWH 公司以专业疏忽起诉被告 GW 律师行。WWH 之前曾聘任该律师行为其土地买卖的交易提供法律服务,不过因 GW 没有将行使选择权的通知送达给卖方本人,而是送达给他的代表律师而令卖方有借口不履行合约并带来诉讼。显然在当时土地价格上涨而导致卖方以该借口扯皮,而法院最后的判决也是判卖方履行有关的土地转让合约。但诉讼的延误令土地直到行使选择权的通知送达的 4 年后才转让给 WWH 公司,4 年后的土地市场价格大跌,令 WWH 蒙受巨大的经济损失,从而开始对 GW 的诉讼索赔该损失。1992 年 11 月,WWH 与 GW 在和解谈判之后达成和解协议。该和解协议中也提到 Johnson 先生的个人诉讼,并有一条条文针对,说:"Mr Johnson undertakes that the amount of any claim made by him personally in any action against [GW] in respect of any losses suffered by him by reason of loss of income, dividends or capital distribution in respect of his position as a shareholder of [WWH] will not exceed Pds. 250,000 not including interest accruing in respect of any period after the date of this agreement nor costs. **This undertaking does not limit any other of Mr Johnson's rights against [GW].**"(加黑部分是笔者的强调)

也另有一条机密条文(即对和解协议要保持机密,估计是为了 GW 律师行的信誉不会受影响)提到 Johnson 先生将来会提起的诉讼会成为机密性的例外说:"Exception... In connection with any action which Mr Johnson may bring gainst [GW]."

Johnson 先生作为 WWH 的控制人,也以个人名义在 1993 年 4 月另外提出对 GW 的诉讼,索赔一些他本人蒙受的经济损失,包括影响了他其他的生意。诉讼开始 4 年半后,GW 向法院申请以"滥用司法程序"(abuse of process)[97] 为由,将 Johnson 的诉

---

[96] 这是原告蒙受的损害,即因为依赖双方的共同假设,原告没有及时对律师费用投保。

[97] 滥用司法程序是一个非常困难的课题,这是针对本来可以在同一诉讼中解决的问题但当事人却开始开启不同的诉讼程序,导致滥用法律资源与劳民伤财。如在一个诉讼中针对合约的索赔败诉,原告败诉后又改以侵权提出另一个诉讼,这就会导致第二个诉讼因滥用司法程序被撤销。这将在本书第九章有详细介绍,包括最近期针对这一课题的 Teekay Tankers Ltd. v. STX Offshore & Shipbuilding Co. Ltd. (No.2) (2017) 1 Lloyd's Rep. 387 先例。本案中如果 Johnson 先生只是 WWH 公司股东之一,他完全可以以自己的名义索赔个人的损失。但是 Johnson 先生对 WWH 公司的绝对控制会被视为该公司的分身(alter ego),这就带来滥用司法程序的说法。

讼取消。一审法院驳回了该申请，认为 GW 签署和解协议时有一个与 WWH 的共同假设，就是 Johnson 先生可以再向 GW 提起个人的诉讼已经构成禁反言，从而不能以滥用司法程序为由申请取消 Johnson 提起的诉讼。GW 上诉去上诉庭，上诉庭认为不存在共识性禁反言，所以根据 Henderson v. Henderson（1843 – 60）All E. R. Rep. 378 先例的原则，判 Johnson 先生存在滥用司法程序的行为。这导致 Johnson 先生上诉去了贵族院。

贵族院认为允许 Johnson 先生提出个人诉讼并不能构成滥用司法程序，上诉庭的判决太过僵化，没有充分考虑 Johnson 先生提出的多个不参与 WWH 对 GW 的诉讼的原因包括受财务之限、加入个人的索赔会增加复杂性从而延误程序等。在考虑当事人是否应该参与之前的法律程序一并解决争议而不再开始一个新的程序去解决基于同一事件而产生的争议，法院应该持更加宽松的态度对待与更看重不同的案件事实。[98] 关于禁反言的问题，贵族院给出了与上诉庭不同但支持一审法院的意见。Bingham 勋爵认为 Denning 勋爵在 Amalgamated v. Texas Bank（1982）1 Lloyd's Rep. 27 先例中确立的构成共识性禁反言的条件在本案中得到满足，和解协议是在双方都有一个共同分享的假设，即 Johnson 先生有将来以个人名义提起诉讼的可能性，这显然是在不会构成滥用司法程序的基础上达成的，允许 GW 偏离这一假设是不公平的。就本案来说，允许 GW 声称 Johnson 先生在和解协议达成后再提起个人诉讼是滥用司法程序是不合情理的。

其中 Bingham 勋爵说："On the estoppel by convention issue, Mr. Steinfeld Q. C.（GW 的代表大律师）submitted that the Court of Appeal had been right and the judge wrong. There had been no common understanding between the parties on the issue of abuse, a topic which had never been raised. There was nothing to suggest that GW had tacitly agreed to forgo any defence properly open to it. Mr. Steinfeld further submitted that the present proceedings did amount to an abuse, as the Court of Appeal had rightly held. Mr. Johnson could have advanced his personal claim at the same time as the company's claim and therefore should have done so. The consequence of his not doing so was to expose GW to the harassment of further proceedings canvassing many of the same issues as had been canvassed in the earlier action, with consequential waste of time and money and detriment to other court users. The facts relied on to excuse his earlier inaction were not accepted.... The question is whether the parties to the settlement of WWH's action（relevantly, Mr. Johnson and GW）proceeded on the basis of an underly-

---

〔98〕这看每一个案件的情况是指法院要充分考虑原告没有在之前诉讼一并解决所有争议的原因。如果原告有一个很合理的原因，如当时不知道有这样的替代争议，是审理后法律的改变，才有了这个争议。这样原告在第一个诉讼败诉后，以新的争议作为诉因提出另一个诉讼，就变得合理与可以被接受了。

ing assumption that a further proceeding by Mr. Johnson would not be an abuse of process and whether, if they did, it would be unfair or unjust to allow GW to go back on that assumption. In my judgment both these conditions were met on the present facts. Mr. Johnson was willing in principle to try to negotiate an overall settlement of his and the company's claims but this was not possible in the time available and it was GW's solicitor who said that the personal claim 'would be a separate claim and it would really be a matter for separate negotiation in due course.' It is noteworthy that Mr. Johnson personally was party to the settlement agreement, and that the agreement contained terms designed to preclude (in one instance) and limit (in another) personal claims by him. Those provisions only made sense on the assumption that Mr. Johnson was likely to make a personal claim. GW did not, of course, agree to forgo any defence the firm might have to Mr. Johnson's claim if brought, and the documents show that GW's solicitor was alert to issues of remoteness and duplication.... The terms of the settlement agreement and the exchanges which preceded it in my view point strongly towards acceptance by both parties that it was open to Mr. Johnson to issue proceedings to enforce a personal claim, which could then be tried or settled on its merits, and I consider that it would be unjust to permit GW to resile from that assumption."

7.12 先例之十二：Edward Michael Gloyne v. Linda Rosemary Richardson, Barber Young Burton & Rind (A Firm)

Edward Michael Gloyne v. Linda Rosemary Richardson, Barber Young Burton & Rind (A Firm) (2001) EWCA Civ 716 先例是另一个关于没有递交通知与通知无效的上诉庭先例中，但被双方错误当做是已经有有效通知而进行一系列互动后才发生争议，进而将通知是否递交与有效的问题提出来，并把共识性禁反言作为一个替代争议。

该先例是关于一个股票买卖与期权的协议。在 1988 年 Richardson 先生（其死后，由其遗产继承人——他的妻子 Richardson 太太来执行）与 Gloyne 先生（以下称"EMG"）与 Gardiner 女士（以下称"HG"）签订了一份 OA88 的期权协议。该协议给与 Richardson 先生一个购买一间英国公司 UIS (Holdings) Ltd.（以下称"UIS"）股份的权利。UIS 随后被一间美国公司 Raxco 收购。1992 年 11 月 30 日，Richardson 先生又与上述人士签订了 OA92 协议，其中 UIS 公司的股份被 Raxco 公司的股份所替代。其他的协议条文都与 OA88 协议一样。

其中 OA92 协议的操作条文针对期权的份额有如下规定："The option to acquire from EMG and HG such number of shares in Raxco Inc. as is equal to 3.498% (in the case of EMG) and 1.344% (in the case of HG) of their respective beneficial shareholdings in Raxco Inc. pursuant to completion of the said Share Exchange Agreement scheduled for 30 November 1992, that is to say 38,085 Raxco Common Stock in the case of

EMG and 5,776 for Raxco Common Stock in the case of HG.〔99〕"

期权的股票价格定为9.12美元每股。触发期权行使的条件之一是公司上市。这在两份协议中可见第4.1与第4.4条 。第4.1条规定Richardson先生在公司上市之前最后一个工作日或尽量接近该日的时间给出书面通知以行使期权。另是第4.4条要求EMG在Raxco上市之前30日要给Richardson先生一份书面的通知,并且第4.1条规定Richardson先生可以行使他的期权去购买EMG在Raxco公司所占股份的3.498%。

相关条文可节录如下:"4.1 AFR(Richardson先生)shall be entitled to exercise either or both of the options granted under Clause 3 by written notice to each of EMG and HG given on or as near as possible to the last business day prior to the Company going public or being acquired or on the 31 day of December 2008 whichever is the sooner against payment by AFR of $400,000 in aggregate payable to EMG and HG pro rata to the number of Option Shares the subject of each option....4.4 EMG and HG shall ensure that AFR is given not less than 30 days prior notice of the intended date for the Company going public or being acquired."

1993年4月,EMG给Richardson一份要约,要求后者购买其股票,而当时股票的市场价格在3美元/股。Richardson先生并不奇怪的没有接受该要约。Raxco公司后来改名为Axent Technologies Incorporated。EMG将其在公司的股票卖出42.2%,剩余629312股Axent公司的股票。1995年3月,Richardson先生去世,遗产继承人是他的太太Richardson夫人。1996年3月,EMG的律师根据两份协议中的第4.4条文通知Richardson太太的律师Barber Young Burton & Rind(以下称"BY",也是本案的第二被告),Axent公司将在1996年4月上市,并且Axent公司也确实在1996年4月24日 在纳斯达克(NASDAQ)挂牌上市。该通知是在1996年3月26日做出,如下:

"... to notify you pursuant to that agreement... that it is proposed that Axent Technologies Inc. will be floated on NASDAQ in the USA some time in the second part of April this year.

The Option Agreement now applies in respect of the remaining shares held by... (EMG)... I believe it is 629,441 shares.

That means that the estate has an option to buy... (I believe) 21,986 from (EMG) ..."

上述通知有缺陷也被法院判是无效。第一个原因是该通知中没有写明预计上市的日期,而只是说大概在四月下半个月。更重要的缺陷是该通知也没有满足第4.4条明确规定的在上市前30天做出的要求,因此通知无效。同时法院也判无需将第4.4条与第4.1条联系在一起,而将EMG必须做出有效的上市通知作为Richardson先生行使期权的先决条件。这也表示Richardson先生或太太根据第4.1条还是必须

〔99〕 Richardson先生可以行使的期权为EMG在Raxco公司所占股份的3.498%,即当时等于38085股。

在 Axent 公司上市前最后一个工作日或尽量接近该日的时间通过文书通知行使期权。

Richardson 太太指示她的律师所 BY 以遗产执行人的身份行使该期权，但是该律师所的合伙人之一 Burton 先生并没有按照第 4.1 条的规定在行使期权的时候给出通知。

尽管如此，EMG 错误假设 Richardson 太太已经行使了期权，购买其当时持股 629312 股的 3.498%，即约 22018 股。这种错误解释是对法律不熟悉的商人经常会有的问题，因为双方一路都在交谈与互动，EMG 是知道 Richardson 太太是要行使期权，但没有留意第 4.1 条中对书面通知规定（包括时间上与文书的要求）。1996 年 10 月，Burton 先生首次提出质疑，行使的期权应该为 38085 股而非 EMG 卖出 42.2% 股票之后的份额。1997 年 1 月，EMG 先生的律师声称 Richardson 太太并没有按照协议以书面通知行使期权。正如上一个案例中所讲，通知的问题往往是在双方互动出争议之时才被提出来。虽然 EMG 仍然向 Richardson 太太做出有效行使约 22018 股期权的要约，但 Richardson 太太拒绝了该要约。1997 年 4 月，Richardson 太太停止雇佣 BY，而换了新律师。

1998 年，EMG 开始法院程序，申请宣示判决认定 Richardson 太太没有行使期权，Richardson 太太也将她以前委任并漏了做出通知的 BY 一并加入，希望一次过解决所有争议。而 Richardson 太太在抗辩中主张她有权行使期权 38085 股与 22018 股的差别。

一审高院的 Hart 大法官对 OA92 协议解释，他认为 3.498% 的比例针对的是在期权被行使之时 EMG 所持有的股份。1995 年，Richardson 先生拒绝在股价为 3 美元/股行使期权之时，42.2% 的股份被售出后也相应地从期权中脱离。所以，正确的股份份额为 22018 股。这一判决也得到上诉庭的支持。但 Hart 大法官判双方在后来的互动中已经达成了一个协议（agreement or accord）。

这一判决结果对 Richardson 太太很不利，所以她提出上诉，而其中协议与共识性禁反言的替代争议也变得重要。为了更好地理解这两个替代性争议，相关的事实背景（双方按照书面通知被正确递交与 EMG 的股份份额为 22018 股）讲述如下。

1996 年 4 月 24 日 EMG 的律师写信给当时 Richardson 太太的前律师 BY 如下：

"Confirming our conversation yesterday, when I had already spoken to (EMG), (EMG) would be happy for the option rate that applies to his shareholding (3.498%) to apply to the 100,000 shares he hopes to sell fairly shortly in the after – market of the US public offering of Axent Technologies Inc. ...

Linda Richardson would receive from the sale proceeds of the 3,498 option shares, 75% of the excess over and above the \$9.12 per share exercise price (see Clause 5.2.1. of the Option Agreement). According to my calculations, this is subject to an ultimate cap at a price of \$27.36 ...

In your fax of 19 April . . . you ask about changes in shares during 1992 and 1993. If you refer to the Supplemental Option Agreement of 30 November 1992. . . Recital C and Clause 1 make the position at that time clear. The sales in 1993 reduced the shareholdings of (EMG). . . to their present levels. . . That is to say 629,441 for (EMG). . . This produces 22,018 Option Shares at (EMG)'s rate of 3.498% (reduced to 18,520 to take account of the 3,498 that will shortly be sold). . .

Perhaps you could confirm that the above is the way to proceed, and we can then deal with the necessary documentation."

BY 在 1996 年 4 月 26 日回复如下:"... I have spoken to Linda Richardson and I am pleased to confirm that she agrees to the proposals contained in your letter. . . Please let me know whether you wish to draft the document (which I think should be between just(EMG) and Linda with a separate agreement being entered into between Linda and Helen [HG]) or whether you would like me to do so."

根据以上的往来互动,可以看出双方之间有一个共同的错误假设,就是 EMG 的股票份额数量(22018 股)以及期权被有效行使。

双方还在 1996 年 5 月 21 日签订了一份信函协议(letter agreement),并且也做出了支付与接受了付款。

Richardson 太太在几个月后才反悔,这也不难想到,因为在当时科技股的股票大涨,几十倍甚至上百倍的上升,当中涉及的金额也十分巨大。1996 年 8 月 28 日,BY 向 EMG 的律师写信说:"Further to my fax of 23 instant my client has raised several queries concerning the price of shares sold and at this stage I am not prepared to accept that payment is in full final settlement of monies due to her. I will write to you again shortly with my calculations."

1996 年 10 月 18 日,BY 又写信给 EMG 的律师,辩称 Richardson 太太行使的期权是针对 EMG 未出售 42.2% 股份前的全部股权。该信最后一句如下:"My client therefore requires that your client transfer with immediate effect a share certificate for 38,085 shares and upon receipt of the same my client will account to your client under the provisions of Clause 5.2.1."

在一审,Hart 大法官判双方在 1996 年 5 月 21 日签订了一份信函协议是具体并且可以执行的协议。所以在 Hart 大法官的判决书中,EMG 在合约(OA92)的解释方面胜诉,但由于在互动中达成的协议却要向 Richardson 太太履行 22018 股的期权责任。

在上诉庭 Aldous,Laws 与 Blackburne 大法官一致判决信函协议不能被认定为是一份协议,因为在签署时,双方认定已经按照 OA88/92 协议的第 4.1 条做出了有效行使期权的通知,但其实并没有该有效的通知,所以,该信函协议因为共同错误(common mistake)而无效。至于共识性禁反言,Laws 大法官(其他大法官也同意)认为也不能成立。虽然双方是有一个共同分享的错误理解,但 EMG 事后反悔并不能满足不合情理(unconscionable)的要求,说:

"The doctrine of estoppel by convention was explained in this court in The 'Vistafjord' [1988] 2 Lloyd's Rep. 343. Bingham LJ (as he then was) said this at 352:

It is sufficient... to say that it (the doctrine of estoppel by convention) applies where (1) parties have established by their construction of their agreement or their apprehension of its legal effect a conventional basis, (2) on that basis they have regulated their subsequent dealings, to which I would add (3) it would be unjust or unconscionable if one of the parties resiled from that convention.

I accept without demur that conditions (1) and (2) in this formulation are established on the facts of this case. My difficulty is with (3). At the very least, once (Mrs. Richardson) had resiled from the terms of the letter agreement by asserting a claim based on option rights covering 38,085 shares... it cannot be said that it was unconscionable for EMG thereafter himself to depart from the 'convention' constituted by the letter agreement, and to seek to stand on the original terms of OA88/92. In these circumstances, in my judgment there is no estoppel by convention either so as to bind the parties to a basis of 22,018 shares as the subject of R's option rights, or so as to bind the parties to an acceptance (contrary to the fact) that the option had been exercised.[100]"

上诉法院的判决令 Richardson 太太的地位变得更加糟糕,不仅失去了一个有效协议的一审判决,也不能依赖共识性禁反言,连在一审法院得到的 22018 股好处也失去。

7.13 先例之十三:Riverside Housing Association v. White

Riverside Housing Association v. White (2005) EWCA Civ 1385 先例涉及的争议是,有关的合约明示要求一方向对方做出明示通知才能主张权利,但该通知并不正确而无效。这样法律的地位是好像他从来没有做出过通知一样,所以他不能根据该错误的通知主张权利。但问题是对方会不警觉通知的错误之处而将其视为有效并遵守或者有一系列的互动。如果双方事后有争议,主张权利的一方虽然没有根据合约的要求做出有效的通知,能否根据共识性禁反言而被法院支持?这种情况在不同领域的商业活动都经常在发生,如涉及外贸与航运的准备就绪通知书(notice of readi-

---

[100] 在该先例中,Richardson 太太先从双方共同的错误理解中偏离,回复到她认为的原本的合约地位,即她拥有购买 38085 股公司股票的选择权,而不是信函协议中双方错误理解的 22018 股。在这种情况下,原告从所谓的共识中偏离,回复到双方原本的合约条文的解释没有不合情理。因此,Law 大法官认为信函协议既不会构成 Richardson 太太有购买 22018 股选择权的共识性禁反言,也不会构成双方接受 Richardson 太太已经行使了选择权的共识性禁反言。

ness)的做出就经常是不正确而无效,要不是没有按照法律的默示要求,或更多的是没有按照合约的明示要求。[101] 但通常会是被通知的货方(发货人或收货人)不警觉而与船长进行一连串的互动,客观来看,是有共同假设这通知书是有效,如安排船舶靠泊与准备装卸货等。这样,如果船东向货方索赔根据不正确与无效的通知书计算出来的滞期费,遇上货方攻击通知书无效时,船东是否可以共识性禁反言作为索赔理由或答辩?看来这里最重要的争议就是共识性禁反言能否作为索赔的诉因,即十分令人困扰的宝剑与盾牌的说法。

这一先例涉及房租租赁合约,原告的房东根据合约的规定通知租客提高租金,但这个通知看来因与合约规定的时间不一致而不正确。但双方客观看来是假设该通知有效而进行互动,包括租客也在没有反对的情况下,按照通知上的时间开始支付新的租金金额。这些事后互动的事实被判是构成共识性禁反言,但上诉庭认为共识性禁反言不能作为房东的宝剑索赔租金。

虽然房东的代表大律师声称他的诉因只是针对欠下的租金,这是独立的诉因,共识性禁反言充其量只是对其诉因的扩张或者说是对租客否认的抗辩。但上诉庭不同意,认为索赔欠下的租金就是需要以共识性禁反言作为基础。[102]

Peter Gibson 大法官说:

"The Judge (of first instance) found all the necessary ingredients for an estoppel by convention to be present: the parties had a common assumption about the validity of the rent increase notices; on that basis they had regulated their subsequent dealings; Riverside(房东) would suffer detriment if the Whites(租客) were to be permitted to resile from that convention. However, he held that Riverside wished to use the estoppel as a sword and not a shield and that this was not permitted ...

Mr Arden(房东的代表大律师) suggested that the Judge had misunderstood the facts. He submitted that the cause of action was arrears of rent... He argued that the cause of action existed independently of the estoppel ... that accordingly Riverside can succeed in its claim in reliance on the estoppel, even if the effect is to grant it greater rights than existed under the contract; that the estoppel is not being used as a sword but as a sharp-edged shield... to the Whites' defence denying the amount of Riverside's claim for arrears.

---

[101] 这方面的课题可以参阅杨良宜所著的《装卸时间与滞期费》一书之第九章与本书第四章之12.2段,其中提到的重要先例包括:The "North King" (1971) 2 Lloyd's Rep. 460; The "Helle Skou" (1976) 2 Lloyd's Rep. 205; The "Shackleford" (1978) 2 Lloyd's Rep. 154; The "Mexico 1" (1990) 1 Lloyd's Rep. 507; The "Happy Day" (2002) 2 Lloyd's Rep. 487 等。

[102] 这用滞期费的例子来解释更加容易明白。如果准备就绪通知书无效,装卸时间不会起算,就更不需要支付任何的滞期费。这样,共识性禁反言根本就是作为宝剑的诉因,因为没有共识性禁反言,根本不存在有诉因索赔滞期费。

Mr Luba(租客的代表大律师)submitted that in the existing state of English law it is not open to this court to accede to the submissions of Mr Arden as that would be to allow the use of estoppel by convention as a sword rather than a shield ...

... True it is that Riverside has a cause of action for some arrears and possession which is not dependent on the validity of the rent increase notices, but it must rely on the estoppel in claiming that the other arrears are lawfully due. Its cause of action ... is that the claimed factual situation giving rise to the remedy is that the Whites are in arrears of rent lawfully due not only in respect of the rent not dependent on the validity of the rent increase notices but also inrespect of the rent so dependent. I cannot see how Riverside can be said not to be using the estoppel as a sword to create a cause of action in relation to the bulk of those arrears.

... English law can only permit an estoppel by convention to be relied on to give rise to a cause of action... only if the House of Lords so decides, as this court in Baird Textile Holdings Ltd. v. Marks & Spencer Plc. [2001] EWCA Civ 274 made clear. The existing state of English law on estoppel does not seem to me entirely satisfactory (see for example, the critique in Anson's Law of Contract 28th ed. pp. 122 ff) and, for my part, I regret that on estoppel by convention Riverside's arguments must fail on the ground identified by the Judge."

作为本案例的结论,Peter Gibson 大法官提到这个不令人满意的结果,毕竟原告是地方的机构,这一先例影响很多其他的租客。如果通知不正确就无法主张权利。反过来,只有租客想要回多支付的租金,房东才可以提出共识性禁反言作为抗辩。这看来是有点可笑,Peter Gibson 大法官并提到期待最高院就宝剑与盾牌的说法给出最后的定论,说:"We are told that there are only a small handful of cases where Riverside has sought possession for arrears of rent in circumstances similar to those of the Whites. If other tenants sought recovery of rents by reason of the invalidity of the rent increase notices, it is possible that an estoppel by convention could be raised by way of defence. However, there is a danger that tenants may withhold rent and leave it to Riverside to sue, in which case the same difficulty over the use of the estoppel may arise as in this case. I regret this result, but for the reasons which I have given I am compelled to the conclusion that the Whites succeed on this appeal."

7.14 先例之十四:Triodosbank NV v. Dobbs

Triodosbank NV v. Dobbs (2005) 2 Lloyd's Rep. 588 先例是关于在没有取得担保人同意或明示许可下,双方对主合同内容做出实质变更之后,针对主合约的担保是否仍然有效的案件。这里的逻辑很简单,如果第三方担保人同意为建造一架飞机提供担保,而主合同后来被双方变更为建造一艘轮船,就不能假设担保人仍然愿意为交易提供担保。

这可节录 Longmore 大法官在该先例的权威说法如下：

"It is, of course, the law that a material variation in the contract between the creditor and the principal debtor will discharge the guarantor, unless the variation is one to which he assented or which is provided for in the contract of guarantee. In his book (1898) on the Law of Principal and Surety, Mr. Sidney Rowlatt (as he then was) said this:... it is apprehended that assent, whether previous or subsequent to a variation, only renders the surety liable for the contract as varied, where it remains a contract within the general purview of the original guarantee... If a new contract is to be secured there must be a new guarantee.

This passage was retained in the second edition of the book (1926) edited by the son of (the by then) Rowlatt J with his father's encouragement and was adopted by Lord Atkin in his speech in Trade Indemnity Co. Ltd. v. Workington Harbour and Dock Board (1937) AC 1, 21 with whom the other members of their Lordships' House concurred...

Lord Atkin's approval has been followed in the later cases of The 'Nefeli' (1986) 1 Lloyd's Rep. 339, 345 per Bingham J and Melvin International SA v. Poseidon Schiffahrt GmbH (The 'Kalma') (1999) 2 Lloyd's Rep. 374, at page 378 per Cresswell J."

在本先例中,(涉及的交易本质上与 Amalgamated v. Texas Bank [1982] 1 Lloyd's Rep. 27 先例类似)被告 Dobbs 先生对一间名为 Acorn Televillages Ltd 的公司享有控制权,该公司向原告银行借贷并签署了两份贷款协议,涉及金额为 90 万英镑。1996 年 4 月 26 日,Dobbs 先生给本案的原告即贷款银行签发了一份 5 万英镑的个人担保,用以担保偿还上述两笔贷款。贷款的款项主要用于在英格兰的房地产发展项目。

1998 年 11 月 4 日,银行又与 Acorn Televillages Ltd 公司进一步签署了两份贷款协议,总额为 198 万英镑。这两份贷款协议中明确写明,之前的两份贷款协议被取代。1999 年 9 月 10 日,双方又进一步同意了一份贷款总额达 260 万英镑的贷款协议,该 1999 年协议进而又取代了 1998 年签订的两份贷款协议。作为对贷款的担保,银行共取得建筑土地的抵押、对借款公司财产的浮动押记、Dobbs 先生人寿保险金的转让权以及 Dobbs 先生个人担保的 5 万英镑。2000 年 8 月 7 日,银行不看好该地产发展项目,所以向该公司发出正式的还款要求(demand),并在 2000 年 10 月 20 日委任了清盘人(liquidator)对公司的资产进行清盘。地产项目被出售之后仍然有 80622.79 英镑的欠款无法还清,于是银行决定要 Dobbs 先生履行他的个人担保。

本案有两个争议:(1)Dobbs 先生 1996 年 4 月 26 日做出的个人担保是否应被延伸适用在 1999 年的贷款协议?(2)如果不能被延伸适用,根据共识性禁反言,Dobbs 先生是否不能否认该担保已经被延伸适用了?

针对第一个争议，上诉庭认为并不能仅仅因为后来的 1998 年甚至更有关系的 1999 年协议，在文字上写明替代（replace）了 1996 年协议就视为结论性，毕竟英国法律更重视实质内容。因为这种变更可以是前者的协议中已经考虑将来会发生的（如前者的协议中说明有些事项有待将来同意），或者替代的协议与被替代的协议内容非常相似，根本不是新的合约。但想要担保协议延伸适用的话，任何对于前协议的变更都必须是在个人担保协议考虑到的范围内（within general purview）。在本先例中，Dobbs 先生提供的个人担保不适用在 1999 年贷款协议，因为 1999 年协议相比于 1996 年协议有了重大改变，即使认为 1999 年协议只是针对 1996 年协议的变更或修改，合约的本质没有改变，但该修改与变更也不是在 Dobbs 先生个人担保协议考虑到的范围之内的。

这样，作为替代争议的共识性禁反言就变得对银行非常关键。在决定该替代争议时，首先涉及本案是否能够以简易判决（summary judgment）的形式处理争议。第一审判是可以，并通过客观的考验判银行胜诉。但这一判决被上诉庭推翻。正如 Amalgamated v. Texas Bank 先例判共识性禁反言是否成立要看具体的事实，所以需要全面的审讯而并非简易判决能够决定。而且看双方是否有共同分享的错误理解是主观的考验，所以一审法院运用的客观考验是错误的。在本案，Longmore 大法官说：

"This is a difficult area of the law and a claimant who relies on the doctrine will be fortunate to obtain summary judgment. The judge has dealt with this aspect of the case in meticulous detail but, on balance, I do not feel that the Bank's claim is capable of being dealt with in a summary way. I would not quarrel with the statement of the law on the topic agreed by the parties and accepted by the judge. He expressed the first requirement of the doctrine as being that 'the parties have made a common but mistaken assumption as to the meaning of an agreement or something very similar to such a mistaken assumption' save to observe that the words 'very similar to such a mistaken assumption' show the uncertain ambit of the doctrine. The essential matter, however, is that there should be a common assumption. This necessarily requires a finding of fact that each party made that assumption. It is also necessary to be clear what the assumption is. It is insufficient to say, as Mr Levy does say, that both parties assumed, in a general sense, that the guarantee continued to apply. What he has to show is that both parties assumed that the 1996 guarantee applied to the 1999 facility.

As to this, even if one takes it as clear that the Bank did so assume, Mr Dobbs' evidence is to thecontrary. He accepts... his witness statement of 4 March 2002 that he thought he remained liable under the guarantee but he goes on to say in paragraph 14: 'However I can say that I did not understand or believe that, in so signing the loan agreements on behalf of the company, I was thereby guaranteeing or even expressing any agreement or intention to guarantee the £ 2m 1998 loan or, subsequently, the £ 2.6m

1999 loan. The 1998 and 1999 facilities were very much larger than the 1996 facility of £ 900,000. I never agreed to nor did I understand or believe that I remained liable for anything other than £ 50,000 of £ 900,000.'

Mr Dobbs is there saying in express terms that he did not himself believe (or assume) that his guarantee applied to the 1999 facility. For judgment to be given on the basis of an estoppel by convention, the court would have to disbelieve this assertion and find that Mr Dobbs did, in fact, assume that the guarantee applied to the 1999 facility and thus that the Company's indebtedness under that facility was an indebtedness under or pursuant to the 1996 agreement. It may very well be that he did so assume but it is not appropriate to make such a finding in summary proceedings when he himself says the precise opposite.

The judge (first instance) approached Mr Dobbs' evidence with caution and then made his own objective assessment, which led him to the conclusion that Mr Dobbs thought the guarantee was a continuing security for the Company's borrowing after it had been rescheduled in 1998 and 1999. Quite apart from the fact that the 1998 agreements and the 1999 facility were much more than a mere rescheduling of early borrowing, it was with respect not right to make an objective assessment of the evidence without a trial if Mr Dobbs' assertion as to his state of mind was not to be believed."

7.15 先例之十五:Ease Faith Ltd. v. Leonis Marine Management Ltd. & Anor.

Ease Faith Ltd. v. Leonis Marine Management Ltd. & Anor. (2006) EWHC 232 (Comm)先例的原告 Ease Faith 经营拆旧船的生意,是旧船的买主。一艘名为 Kent Reliant 的船舶因为搁浅而船底严重损坏,停泊在波多黎各的圣胡安港。原告从该船舶的船东处以“as is where is”的条件购买了该船舶并转售给中国买方作为拆船之用。原告随后与被告 Leonis 签订了拖带协议,将该旧船拖带至位于中国张家口的拆船厂。履行拖带协议的拖船名为 Naporistyi,有两个引擎,真正船东是俄罗斯公司 Inspectors & Marine Surveyors Corp,但将该拖船光船租给 Cloudfree 公司营运。Leonis 与光船船东 Cloudfree 公司签订了该拖带协议。Naporistyi 轮是在 2004 年 1 月 27 日从巴拿马的 Balboa 开始履行拖带协议,但是直到 2004 年 5 月 2 日才将 Kent Reliant 拖带至目的地交船,这比拖带协议中规定的日期晚了 3 至 4 个星期。因为废钢市场价格的下跌,Ease Faith 在其中国买方的要求下,被迫降低船价而蒙受了损失。Ease Faith 因此根据拖带协议起诉 Leonis(后者将 Cloudfree 也一并加入程序)违反了合理速遣(due dispatch)的责任。造成拖带延误有很多原因,其中主要的有两个:一是拖船只使用了一个引擎而不是两个;二是 Leonis 与 Cloudfree 因为 Ease Faith 没有支付拖带的费用而在半途中暂停航程。

这两个主要的原因中,只有第二个原因涉及共识性禁反言的问题,并且只存在于两个被告 Leonis 和 Cloudfree 之间，不涉及 Ease Faith。由于延误主要发生在二月份，所以被称为“February delay”。

共识性禁反言争议产生的事实背景可以引述如下：

首先，Leonis 与 Cloudfree 之间的主拖带协议和 Leonis 与 Ease Faith 分拖带协议[103]由于都是以 BIMCO 的标准拖带协议 TOWCON 为准，所以有很多相同的条文，其中第 16 条名为“销约与撤船”（Cancellation and Withdrawal）条文。该条文允许拖船的船东在拖带协议中规定的拖带费用在到期 7 天后仍然没有得到支付时，结束拖带协议并且在特定的情况下将 Kent Reliant 轮停在航程中留给其船东（即指 Ease Faith）处置。第 21 条是名为“留置”（Lien）条文，该条文允许拖船船东在任何拖带费用没有得到支付时对 Kent Reliant 享有留置权，并且可以因为延迟支付而收取 3500 美金每日的延误费。

在分拖带协议的履行过程中，第二期分期付款的 20% 的拖带费用为 108000 美金，在拖带离开 Balboa 港时就应该支付，但 Ease Faith 因为当时现金紧张，所以晚了支付，在 2004 年 2 月 5 日与 2 月 12 日分两次付清了该 20% 的拖带费用。

同时，Leonis 在主拖带协议下也没有按时做出支付，所以 Cloudfree 没有收到应在拖带离开 Balboa 港时支付的第三期分期付款，即 25% 的拖带费用 122500 美金（主拖带协议与分拖带协议在如何支付拖带费用的条款上存在不同）。Leonis 声称是由于 Ease Faith 晚了支付，所以导致他也无法在主拖带协议下做出支付，当然这在法律上也不是合法不履行的理由。其中 Leonis 并没有向 Cloudfree 披露 2004 年 2 月 5 日 Ease Faith 支付了 50000 美金的事实，看来如果披露的话，Leonis 至少道德上应该先支付这笔费用给 Cloudfree。

2004 年 2 月 5 日，Cloudfree 通知 Leonis 由于没有按照主拖带协议支付拖带费用，所以根据主拖带协议的第 21 条，除非 Leonis 支付 122500 美元，加上从 2004 年 1 月 28 日驶离 Balboa 港开始计起每日 3500 美元的延误费共 31500 美元，否则拖船将会停止拖带。

2004 年 2 月 6 日，Leonis 做出回复声称并不认同 Cloudfree 对于主拖带协议的解释，并提出自己对该协议的理解。在笔者看来，Leonis 的理解也有问题与不清楚。但重要的是，Leonis 提到只有第 16c(iii)条中允许 Cloudfree 在航次途中停止拖带以及收取海上滞期费，并询问 Cloudfree 是否有意停止拖带，说：“We do not agree with your interpretation of the Contract. Towcon never mentions that there will be ‘sea demurrage’ for delay payment. As per Clause 16c(iii) you are free to stop and charge sea demurrage. Please advise if you intend to do so.”

2004 年 2 月 7 日，Cloudfree 就是否会停止拖带以及收取海上滞期费回复说，已

---

[103] 这是从拖带船舶船东的角度来看，所以 Leonis 与光船船东 Cloudfree 订立的拖带协议是主拖带协议，Leonis 与 Ease Faith 订立的拖带协议是分拖带协议。

经向 Naporistyi 船长发出指示停止拖带直至拖带费用被支付，且承租人需要承担延误支付带来的 3500 美元每日的延误费，说："Owners gave instructions for Master of Naporistyi to stop towage till freight is paid. Time spend for delay of payment to be for Charterers account USD 3,500 pdpr ..."

2004 年 2 月 10 日，Leonis 发出一份电邮给 Cloudfree，声称 Leonis 与 Cloudfree 是站在同一立场。如果被拖带船舶的船东（Ease Faith）不支付给他，他也无法支付给 Cloudfree，他们目前能做的只是以停止拖带与收取海上滞期费向 Ease Faith 施压要求支付，说："At the outset, you must understand that we are 'on your side'. Let there be no misunderstanding on this. We are well aware of the fact that 'Leonis' has a Contract with you. However, if Tow owners do not pay us, it is difficult for us to cough up so much funds. You, as Tug Owners, have the tow with you. And we can only pressurize Tow Owners to pay us by stopping the convoy and charging sea demurrage. The Tow Owners are very well known to us, though not for the right reasons. In the circumstances, since he has advised that he has 'cash flow problems and cannot pay until Feb 17 – 18' we would request you to advise Tug Master to hold on to tow and drift with the tow until receipt of funds. We intend to advise Tow Owners accordingly. Sea demurrage will continue to incur. If and when funds are received, we will resume towage. Then, we will raise out Invoice for sea demurrage. If that is not paid within 7 days, we once again stop the convoy. This Tow Owner only understands tough measures! Thanking you for your continued co – operation."

2004 年 2 月 11 日，Cloudfree 要求 Leonis 传递消息给 Ease Faith 即宣称 Cloudfree 行使留置的权利，并停止拖带活动直到第三期分期付款，每日 3500 美元的延误费以及因超重而收取的 100000 美元的额外拖带费用被付清。2004 年 2 月 13 日，Leonis 给 Cloudfree 通知他支付的情况，并要求拖带继续进行如下："Please be advised that we have today remitted instalment of lump sum due on sailing from Panama in full to your account from Barclay's Bank. We will fax you copy of bank swift copy on receipt today. Also, be advised that Tow Owners have promised to remit funds today and we are sending you funds in good faith in order not to lose weekend idling and increasing liability for Tow Owners and adding to existing disputes. We will be sending to Tow Owners 'demurrage incurred due to waiting for funds' after we receive Tug Master's report of resuming voyage. We will be requesting Tow Owners to remit sea demurrage within 7 days on receipt of invoice failing which we will once again stop the convoy."

Cloudfree 给 Leonis 的回复是直到 Leonis 将上述 2 月 11 日通信中提到的三笔款项被付清，Cloudfree 才会给 Naporistyi 轮的船长做出指示开船。

2004 年 2 月 13 日，Leonis 回应表达失望，并说 Cloudfree 再继续延误航程非常不必要，并要求马上开航。Leonis 也提到，Cloudfree 因额外拖带重量而要求的额外

100000 美元是胁迫赎金(ransom in midsea)。

Cloudfree 终于指示 Naporistyi 轮的船长在 2 月 18 日重新开始拖带,但是仍然坚持要收取共 48750 美元的海上滞期费。

在高院,Andrew Smith 大法官支持了 Ease Faith 关于没有合理速遣的指控,认为针对拖带中产生的延误 Cloudfree 要对 Leonis 负责,Leonis 要进一步对 Ease Faith 负责。就"February delay",Cloudfree 针对 Leonis 提出了共识性禁反言的抗辩,指称暂停拖带航程是双方共同认可的。

Andrew Smith 大法官认为根据上述援引的双方电邮往来,大家的错误理解并不相同。其中 Cloudfree 是根据第 21 条,但是留置只可以在抵达目的地港张家口或附近海域才能行使,在航程中途行使是错误的。此外,额外拖带重量而要求的额外 100000 美元的费用作为另一个争议,也被法官驳回。

而 Leonis 对于 16 条文的理解也是错误的,该条文针对的是拖带协议的完全终止与废除,而非暂时性的中止航程。而且也没有证据显示 Cloudfree 依赖了双方的共同错误理解去暂停航程。Leonis 在 2 月 13 日要求 Cloudfree 重新开始拖带航程时,Cloudfree 并没有照做,而是直到 2 月 18 日第三期拖带费用被支付但海上滞期费仍然没有支付时,才重新开始拖带。

笔者相信 Andrew Smith 大法官还有考虑其他的因素,包括 Cloudfree(也包括 Leonis)试图以暂停航程作为胁迫 Ease Faith 提供赎金。

Andrew Smith 大法官判没有共识性禁反言存在的判决内容如下:

"Cloudfree contend that Leonis are precluded from disputing that they were entitled to have the convoy stop or slow steam from 7 February 2004 until payment of the outstanding hire, and that therefore they are not entitled to complain about this period of delay, or to dispute Cloudfree's claim for payment for this period. They argue that the facts give rise to an estoppel by convention. Such an estoppel will arise where the parties to a transaction act on an assumed factual or legal basis, that assumption either being shared by the parties or being made by one and acquiesced in by the other. If there is such an assumption, then a party is not permitted to deny what was assumed if it would be unjust to allow him to do so . . .

Captain Krishna(Leonis 的证人)explained why he sent the communications that he did on and after 5 February 2004. He said that it became clear to him that Cloudfree had made up their mind not to continue with the voyage because the instalment of hire had not been paid and that he would not be able to dissuade them from this course. He was anxious that the claim in respect of the displacement of the Kent Reliant should not aggravate the dispute. He was therefore, he said, trying to placate Cloudfree and press Ease Faith to pay the hire due from them. I regard this evidence with some scepticism in view of the fact that he did not let Cloudfree know that Leonis had received part of the instalment of hire, but I do not need to reach a concluded view about Leonis' intentions. **Captain Krishna's reasons for sending his e-mails are irrelevant to the question whether there is an estoppel by convention.**

Captain Aliev's（Cloudfree 的证人）evidence was that, after Captain Krishna sent his e-mails of 6 February 2004, his clear impression was that he and Captain Krishna had a common understanding that Cloudfree had the right to stop the convoy because of Leonis' failure to pay hire and the right to charge for any resultant delay, and that he proceeded on that basis. He gave the order to stop only on 7 February 2004, after these e-mails had been sent. However, Captain Aliev did not state that, but for what Captain Krishna wrote in his e-mails, Cloudfree would not have ordered the convoy to stop. There is no evidence that Cloudfree were influenced in any way by Leonis' apparent understanding of what they were entitled to do or what they should do, and no evidence that Cloudfree would have acted differently had Leonis adopted a different position.

Cloudfree's pleaded case is that 'there were conventional understandings and/or assumptions among Cloudfree and Leonis... that Cloudfree were entitled to stop the Tug and Tow at sea pending payment of sums outstanding under the Head Towcon and to recover Delay Payments for delay to the towage during such stoppage or slow steaming'. To establish this contention, Cloudfree must show that there were such understandings or assumptions evinced in communications between Cloudfree and Leonis: the internal understanding of the parties about their rights and obligations is not in point, nor do their communications with third parties（including Leonis' e-mails to NWSS［拖带协议中的经纪人 Northwest Ship Services of California Inc.］, since there is no evidence that NWSS conveyed any relevant communications to Cloudfree）assist Cloudfree. In this case Cloudfree and Leonis both accept that all their relevant exchanges were written, and neither relies upon any oral exchanges.

The only communications before the order to stop was given on 7 February 2004 upon which Cloudfree rely are Cloudfree's e-mail of 5 February 2004 and Leonis' response of 6 February 2004. Leonis submit that those communications do not show any common understanding or assumption between them and Cloudfree. Cloudfree asserted on 5 February 2004 that they were entitled under clause 21 of part II of the Head Towcon to stop towage until payment was received, and had put forward a claim for 'sea demurrage'. Leonis' response was to dispute Cloudfree's understanding of the towcon but to acknowledge that under clause 16 Cloudfree were 'free to stop and charge sea demurrage'. Miss Jones（Leonis 的代表律师）pointed out that clause 16 did not allow Cloudfree to stop them temporarily as they proposed, but allowed them to abandon the tow altogether, leaving the hirer to repossess her.

Mr Holmes(Cloudfree 的代表律师) submitted that it is irrelevant that Cloudfree based their understanding of the towcon on clause 21 whereas Leonis considered that clause 16 defined Cloudfree's rights, arguing that what matters is the parties' understanding of the position under the towcon to be, and not how they reached that understanding. I accept this submission as far as it goes, but it does not engage with Leonis' point. It is not that Cloudfree were relying upon different contractual provisions for their understanding that Cloudfree were entitled to halt the tow and charge for the delay, but that the nature of the right that Cloudfree asserted, a right temporarily to stop the tow, was quite different from that which Leonis acknowledged, a right to elect to abandon the tow once and for all. I accept Miss Jones'(Leonis 的代表律师) submission that the exchanges of 5 and 6 February 2004 do not show a common understanding or a common assumption, nor that Leonis were acquiescing in Cloudfree's understanding of the position.

Accordingly, Cloudfree's case that there was an estoppel by convention depends upon the exchanges after the order to stop had been given. (It is not entirely clear whether any of the communications on 7 February 2004 to which I have referred were sent before the order was given, but Cloudfree do not plead, and Mr Holmes does not argue, that they are relevant to Cloudfree's case that there was an estoppel by convention.) The first communication after the order upon which Cloudfree rely is Captain Krishna's e-mail to them of 10 February 2004. In it, (i) he stated that pressure could be put upon Ease Faith only by 'stopping the convoy and charging sea demurrage'; (ii) he requested Cloudfree to instruct the Master to 'hold on to the tow and drift with the tow until receipt of funds'; (iii) he said that Leonis would raise an invoice for sea demurrage; and (iv) he contemplated again stopping the convoy if the sea demurrage was not paid within seven days.

The e-mail did not indicate a view whether this conduct was in accordance with the towcons, and was not, on its face, concerned with the parties' contractual rights. It did not directly express a view about the matter that, as Cloudfree plead their case, was then the subject of the alleged conventional understandings and assumptions, namely that Cloudfree were entitled under the head towcon to stop the tug and tow pending payment of the outstanding sums and to charge 'sea demurrage'. However, in my judgment, in this e-mail Leonis acquiesced in Cloudfree's claim that they were so entitled. This leads to the question whether it is unjust to allow Leonis to deny this.

The following considerations seem to me particularly relevant to this question: (i) Cloudfree were not, as I conclude, influenced by Leonis' views about what they were entitled to do or what they should do when they took their decision to delay the convoy and to make a claim for sea demurrage. (ii) Cloudfree took that decision before Leonis sent the e-mail of 10 February 2004 and so before they had acquiesced in Cloudfree's views about their rights under the head towcon. (iii) Despite Leonis' request on 13 February 2004 that the convoy should resume its progress, Cloudfree insisted upon waiting until 18 February 2004 when they had received into their bank the instalment of hire. They did so although (Leonis) told (Cloudfree) could not 'support your stand since it does not comply with Towcon Contract'.

Mr Holmes accepted that, in order to demonstrate that it would be unjust or unconscionable to allow Leonis to resile from the common assumption (or the assumption in which Leonis acquiesced), they must show that Cloudfree acted on the basis that the assumption was correct... It is not necessary for Cloudfree to show that they have suffered 'detriment' by acting in reliance on the position that Leonis adopted, but generally, I think, 'It is necessary... to establish that [the person asserting an estoppel by convention] was induced to act in reliance on the shared convention so that it would be unjust to permit [the other party] to depart from it': Snell's Equity (31st ed, 2005) para 10 - 06. I do not say that this is an invariable rule limiting what view the court can properly take about what might be unjust or unconscionable on the facts of the particular case. However, I do conclude that it would be neither unjust nor unconscionable to allow Leonis to dispute Cloudfree's claim that they were entitled to delay the convoy in February 2004 and to claim payment for the delay when the position adopted by Leonis in their communication of 10 February 2004, and indeed before and after that e-mail, did not, as I conclude, in any way affect or influence the course adopted by Cloudfree.

I therefore conclude that Leonis are entitled to complain that the delay between 7 and 18 February 2004 was in breach of the towcon. I also reject Cloudfree's claim for sea demurrage."

7.16 先例之十六：Spliethoff's Bevrachtingskantoor BV v. Bank of China Ltd.

Spliethoff's Bevrachtingskantoor BV v. Bank of China Ltd. (2015) 2 Lloyd's Rep. 123 先例的案情如下:2006 年 6 月 30 日,原告(丹麦的船公司,以下简称 SBV)与山东省荣城西霞口船厂(以下简称 XXK)和山东电机出口公司签订了两份造船合约,分别是“38 号船壳”与“39 号船壳”合约,交船日期为 2008 年 9 月 30 日与 2008 年 1 月 31 日。在建造两艘船舶期间,SBV 在 2006 年 10 月与 2011 年 7 月之间共支付预付分期付款 2868 万美元。中国银行为全部预付款以及合约中规定的利息提供了还款担保(Refund Guarantee)。这两艘船舶都迟延交船,由于航运市场在 2008 年大跌,SBV 也相应取消了该 38 号船壳造船合约。为了阻止 SBV 在 38 号船壳造船合约向中国银行要求履行还款担保,XXK 和山东电机出口公司在 2009 年 9 月 9 日开始了伦敦仲裁,指称 SBV 无权取消造船合约,这样做构成违约/毁约(repudiation)。

由于39号船壳的在建船舶没有在2009年8月28日的“死亡日期”(drop-dead/cancellation date)前交船,SBV相信他有权取消造船合约,但是他怕这么做不安全,因为在38号船壳进行的伦敦仲裁下他被指称违约/毁约。SBV曾经想要以同意延长39号船壳的造船合约的交船期而换取38号船壳造船合约的和解。但是XXK没有做出任何明确的答复。SBV在2009年11月11日开始了伦敦仲裁,要求仲裁庭做出宣示裁决书(declaratory award),宣告他有权取消39号船壳的造船合约与可以取回之前预付的1650万美金的预付款。

SBV在两个伦敦仲裁中均胜诉,先是38号船壳的伦敦仲裁判SBV胜诉。2012年2月9日,伦敦仲裁的仲裁庭做出了宣示裁决,支持了SBV的请求。

与本案相关的事实背景的复杂之处是在2011年7月,XXK在青岛海事法院开始了针对主机制造商Wartsila与SBV的诉讼,XXK诉称SBV与Wartsila存在欺诈,因其二者合谋提供二手与有缺陷的船舶主机而令主机无法安装在船舶内,进而导致无法及时交船。青岛海事法院判XXK胜诉,也做出命令禁止SBV向中国银行要求履行还款担保。SBV参与了青岛海事法院的诉讼程序,后又将该判决上诉至上海高级人民法院(以下简称上海高院)。该判决被上海高院支持后,SBV又将判决进一步上诉至最高人民法院,在英国法院程序进行时,最高人民法院仍未做出判决。于是在相关时间内,存在两个同步的诉讼(concurrent litigation):伦敦的仲裁与中国法院的程序,这两个程序中的当事人都是一样,除了在中国法院程序中的Wartsila。而在伦敦仲裁完结后,SBV在英国法院向中国银行提起诉讼,虽然并不完全是同步诉讼,但都是针对一回事。

本案就是SBV在英国高院以还款担保为标的合约而起诉中国银行,其中存在多项争议,包括对还款担保性质如何认定、欺诈的存在也令还款担保无效、青岛海事法院做出的命令和判决的性质和效果如何、对中国法院命令与判决的承认、国际友好、公共政策等。英国法院拒绝了中国银行的所有抗辩,并做出中国银行在还款担保下要做出支付的判决。

针对以上中国银行的抗辩,其中针对39号船壳的造船协议有多一个独特的争议,即禁反言。SBV指称中国银行的言行构成陈述性禁反言和共识性禁反言。

针对这个禁反言争议的事实背景是在2010年12月23日,SBV的律师通知中国银行39号船壳的造船合约的伦敦仲裁以及仲裁的原因,并要求中国银行确认根据针对该造船合约的还款担保的第8条将有效期延长至仲裁裁决书做出后的45日,该信引述如下:

“By this letter, we inform you that there now exists an arbitration between the Buyer and the Seller. By way of summary, the dispute submitted to arbitration relates to the Delivery Date under the Shipbuilding Contract referred to in the Guarantee; whether the Buyer is entitled to terminate the Contract forthwith (if it has not already done so by the date of the Award); whether upon the exercise [of] that right, the Seller shall be liable to repay any instalments paid by the Buyer; and consequently whether, should the Seller fail to make such repayment to the Buyer, the Buyer shall have the right to demand payment from you under the Guarantee, together with interest, pursuant to the terms of the Guarantee. The Buyer also seeks from the Tribunal an order that [the Sellers] must jointly and severally make repayment of the above – mentioned instalments upon notice from the Buyer that it has exercised its rights to terminate the Shipbuilding Contract, as aforesaid. We would accordingly be grateful for your confirmation that the validity of the guarantee has been automatically extended until the date falling on the fourth – fifth... day after the arbitration award has been published.

We look forward to receiving the requested confirmation by return."

中国银行在2011年1月24日以SWIFT信息的形式做出确认延长有效期如下："We confirm that the validity of a/m guarantee is extended until the date falling on the forty-fifth calendar days after the arbitration award or court order is published."

SBV认为以上的书信往来中，国银行构成了禁反言，即中国银行既然确认还款担保在仲裁裁决书做出后的45日仍然有效，就不能在事后再批评和质疑该宣示裁决书对引发履行还款担保的有效性与相关性。否则，SBV完全可以在当时做出改变（如终止合约并在仲裁中改为申请金钱赔偿的裁决书）或者开始一个新的仲裁。

Carr女大法官在主要争议判中国银行败诉，即判宣示裁决书也是能够令还款担保要被履行的裁决书。这导致没有必要针对SBV的替代争议如禁反言，但Carr女大法官也在判决中有涉及。Carr女大法官认为这是共识性禁反言而不是陈述性禁反言，因为中国银行没有做出任何清楚无误的陈述。其上述引述的信件只不过是一个确认，而没有任何关于仲裁裁决书性质的评论。Carr大法官是这样说："SBV's case for estoppel by convention is a more promising one. Estoppel by convention may arise where both parties to a transaction act on an assumed state of facts or law, the assumption being either shared by both or made by one and acquiesced in by the other. The parties are then precluded from denying the truth of that assumption, if it would be unjust or unconscionable to allow them (or one of them) to go back on it. The assumption must be unambiguous and unequivocal; the mistaken assumption of the party claiming the benefit of the estoppel must have been shared or acquiesced in by the party alleged to be estopped; both parties must have conducted themselves on the basis of such a shared assumption: the estoppel requires communications to pass across the line between the parties".

Carr女大法官针对中国银行构成共识性禁反言，不能在事后再批评和质疑该宣示裁决书对引发履行还款担保的有效性与相关性，是这样说：

"At the outset I reject the submission for BOC that SBV was acting in an underhand manner by choosing 'not to be transparent' in its dealings with BOC. SBV (and its lawyers) may at times have presented the situation to BOC in a manner designed to minimise the risks to SBV, but it did not set out to mislead BOC. So, for example, whilst the letter of 23rd December 2010 from SBV's solicitors to BOC was designed to maximise the chances of procuring BOC's consent, the scope of the dispute being referred was not inaccurately stated in any way. It was made clear that SBV had yet to cancel the Hull 39 Contract. And whilst the letter did not spell out SBV's concerns as to whether or not the dispute fell within the scope of the Proviso, the existence of such a concern was implicit in the request for what was an automatic extension. In any event, there was no obligation on SBV to inform BOC of its concerns.

As to whether BOC was misled in any way, as set out below, there is no evidence that it was. BOC was at all times a large commercial organisation with unrestricted access to both Chinese and UK lawyers and in possession of the Hull 39 award itself from 14th March 2012 onwards . . .

It is difficult to imagine that the sealed letter from BOC's International Settlements Department to Electronics sent out on the same day, 14th March 2012, was written without careful consideration on the part of BOC. It stated: 'Following verification by our bank, there are no material discrepancies in the claim documents. In accordance to the terms of the guarantee, our bank shall make the payout prior to April 10, 2012. . . The full amount of the monies claimed must be deposited into your company's bank guarantee account no later than April 9 2012. . . '

Turning to the witness and other documentary evidence, I am satisfied that at all material times both SBV and BOC were proceeding (both before but more importantly for present purposes after) the Hull 39 award on the basis that the award fell within the terms of the Proviso.

This is the evidence of Mr Nietzman for SBV, which I accept, and which is wholly consistent with SBV's conduct. There is nothing in the evidence for BOC, namely the witness statement of Mr Sheng, to suggest that BOC was not proceeding on the same assumption both before and after the Hull 39 award was issued. Indeed all the contemporaneous material from BOC suggests that it was - see for example its submissions to the QMC of 26th September 2011, 18th November 2011, 12th March 2012, 21st March 2012 and 21st May 2012, and its letter to the Sellers of 14th March 2012 already referred to above.

More importantly, in terms of 'crossing the line', BOC was also clearly acting on this assumption in its dealings direct with SBV. In particular, on 23rd March 2012 BOC wrote to SBV as follows: 'Re your demand under our advance payment guarantee. . . we regret to inform you that your demand for payment has not been honored by us, because there are court injunction orders . . . prohibiting us. . . at home and abroad from paying you under this guarantee. we, as the guarantor. . . applied to the domestic competent court [QMC] for lifting the payment injunction, however, the application was rejected by the court on 120306, so all payment under the a/m guarantee shall not be effected by us without lifting the injunction. ' . . .

For BOC it is said that, whilst it may have been proceeding on that assumption, it was simply doing so on the basis of what it had been told by SBV, namely that the Hull 39 award was as required by the Hull 39 Guarantee and had ordered (immediate) repayment. First, there is no evidence to support this assertion. Secondly, the assertion is inconsistent with the involvement of lawyers for BOC. [Mr Sheng gave no evidence as to the involvement of lawyers for BOC, but it is apparent that UK lawyers were involved by 21st May 2012 at the latest and not credible that at least in-house legal advice was not taken before 26th March 2012. It is clear from Mr Sheng's evidence that BOC's legal and compliance department was involved in the applications to theQMC to lift the XXK orders, including at a hearing before the QMC on 12th March 2012. There is no evidence that BOC (and/or its lawyers) did not look at the form of the Hull 39 award upon receipt because, for example, it was simply relying on SBV's representations.] Thirdly, in any event, SBV did not represent to BOC that the content of the Hull 39 award was for an immediate monetary award (as opposed to a conditional one) that met the requirements of the Proviso. None of the communications relied on by BOC (including the SWIFT messages of 20th February and 12th March 2012) went that far. Finally, even if SBV did represent to BOC that the Hull 39 award was sufficient to trigger the Proviso, that is because that is what it believed at the time and what it believed had been agreed with BOC (as set out in the evidence of Mr Nietzman). . .

Thus, but for my primary conclusion on the validity of the demand of 12th March 2012, I would have found it to be unconscionable for BOC to be allowed after expiry of the Hull 39 Guarantee to resile from the parties' shared assumption that the Hull 39 award was an award for the purpose of the Proviso. "

7.17　笔者涉及的仲裁案件与做出合理通知回复到原本的法律地位

不久前,笔者曾经涉及一个金额很大的香港仲裁,败诉方后来试图在香港法院撤销(set aside)笔者作为首席仲裁员做出的裁决书,但不成功。该香港法院的判决也是近年来一个为撤销裁决书确立指引的十分重要的先例,但由于仲裁的机密,笔者不能提该先例的名字。

该仲裁案件的案情涉及2006年年初中国一个城市的土地转让,双方当事人一方是土地所有人,另外一方即买方是香港地产商。双方通过转让拥有该土地的公司股份来进行土地买卖。但由于这块土地转让仍然需要完成一些手续,包括政府批准、发展批文等，于是双方先订立了意向书（letter of intent）。该意向书中包括香港法律适用条文与香港仲裁条文，被笔者所在的仲裁庭判有关文件虽然名为意向书，但事实上属于有效的合约。[104]

根据该意向书，香港地产商要付1亿多港币给土地所有人（或公司背后的老板）。在该意向书中，另有一条条文约定如果土地所有人在签订意向书后1年内无法完成手续，意向书就自动终止，[105]土地所有人要将1亿多港币还给香港地产商，除非双方通过书面形式延期。结果是相关手续在1年内没有完成，双方通过书面形式延期两次，每次3个月，这等于是对意向书的更改（variation）。之后手续依然没有完成，双方虽然没有再通过书面形式延期，但仍在不断会面与密切互动，并且香港地产商做了不少发展土地的前期工作。根据双方提供的证据，当时地价还相对稳定。2008年，该城市地价开始猛涨，土地所有人突然以意向书终止为由，通过一间香港律师事务所将1亿多港币还给了香港地产商。香港地产商开始香港仲裁，在仲裁中，双方的主要争议之一就是两次延期后，虽然没有继续延期，但双方的互动与土地所有人做出陈述或承诺的言行，构成各种禁反言。

在最后的审理中，包括笔者在内的仲裁庭判土地所有人败诉，笔者与另一位仲裁员的多数裁决判共识性禁反言成立。双方的争辩根据的有关先例中，主要是香港终审法院的Siegfried Adalbert Unruh v. Hans – Joerg Seeberger and Company（2007）2 HKC 609先例中，Ribeiro大法官说：

"131. By 1998, in the 'Indian Endurance', Lord Steyn was able to state that the doctrine was well-settled: 'It is settled that an estoppel by convention may arise where parties to a transaction act on an assumed state of facts or law, the assumption being either shared by them both or made by one and acquiesced in by the other. The effect of an estoppel by convention is to preclude a party from denying the assumed facts or law if it would be unjust to allow him to go back on the assumption. It is not enough that each of the two parties acts on an assumption not communicated to the other. But it was rightly accepted by counsel for both parties that a concluded agreement is not a requirement for an estoppel by convention.'

135. It must, however, be shown that the assumption was communicated between the parties and acted upon. There must be some 'mutually manifest conduct of the parties'...

136. But, there is no necessity for the parties or either of them to believe that the assumed state of affairs is true. Nor is it necessary for them... to have been mistaken

---

〔104〕 这方面可见杨良宜《合约的解释：规则与应用》一书第二章之6.1段。

〔105〕 这类似于一个后续条件，可见杨良宜《合约的解释：规则与应用》一书第八章第3段。所以即使这一份名为"意向书"的文件是存在后续条件，双方也已经有合约约束。

about the matters assumed.

137. What is important is for them to act in the belief, manifested by words or conduct, that they are both proceedings with the transaction on the basis of the same shared assumption...

150. Two further elements must be established for constituting an estoppel by convention. First, there must be an attempt by one party to depart from the common assumption which departure would be unjust because of 'the part taken by him in occasioning its adoption by the other party'. Secondly, the other party would suffer detriment arising out of his having entered into the relevant transaction on the basis of the common assumption 'if the opposite party were afterwards allowed to set up rights against him inconsistent with the assumption' when abandoning the common assumption."

该仲裁的事实很明显能满足共识性禁反言的所有要求。从双方频繁开会与密切地互动可以看出,双方有意向书继续存在的共识并沟通过。否则,香港地产商不会做发展土地的前期工作,土地所有人也不会积极完成手续并与香港地产商沟通,包括不时要求香港地产商提供资料。至于依赖这一共识并蒙受损害也是很明显,除了发展的前期工作的花费外,如果土地所有人没有将这1亿多港币扣了这么久,并在地价上涨时突然决定终止意向书,香港地产商完全可以在地价还没有大幅上涨时,用这笔钱买别的土地。因此,土地所有人之后反悔与撤回共识不合情理。仲裁庭的多数裁决判是构成共识性禁反言。

而不同意见的仲裁员认为,香港地产商是一个大公司,对这方面的法律知识比土地所有人多,它知道意向书的正确地位,不存在误解,只是取巧保持沉默。但笔者与另一位仲裁员认为没有证据能显示这一点,毕竟仲裁员要客观对待有关的事实,不能因为其中一方水平稍高但却认同错误的共识,就认为是取巧。

因为土地所有人在事实上并没有做出合理通知,所以这个共识性禁反言是永久性还是暂时性对最后的结果没有影响,双方的代表大律师也没有提出与争辩这一点。只是在仲裁庭内部合议时,笔者与另一位仲裁员都倾向这个禁反言应该是暂时性。如果土地所有人做出合理通知,在接下来的合理时间(3个月或半年不等)仍然无法完成手续,意向书就会自动终止,并且通过保留的证据显示在接下来的合理时间曾经试图完成手续,最后终止意向书并退回1亿多港元就不会是不合情理。毕竟即使双方曾经对意向书有过错误的共识,也不应该是永久性。总不能因为始终拿不到批文,香港地产商就必须一直等下去,既拿不到地,也拿不回钱,这显然也不是双方可以接受的结果。而卖方也会受到损害,因为如果不是受到合约约束,它可以将这块地用作别的用途,而不需要政府的批文。这也是本章之3.3.1段提到的最低程度的衡平法救济(minimum equity remedy)。这可以以一个没有报道的英国土地审判庭先例作为支持,案情有关双方对诉讼时效有共同的错误理解,之后其中一方(被告)如果想做出时效已过的抗辩而不会被共识性禁反言,就需要先向原告做出通知纠正这一错误理解。审判庭认为2个月时间让原告可以提起诉讼是合理时间。这在《Limitation Periods》(第6版,2010年)一书之21.021段说:"Where an estoppel by convention can be established, it is apparently possible for the defendant to give notice that it will take the limitation point if proceedings are not commenced promptly. Thereafter the claimant must commence proceedings within a reasonable time. In The Executors of the Estate of the Right Honourable Herbert Robert Cayzer Baron Rotherwick v. Oxfordshire CC (March 21, 2000, Lands Tribunal, Unreported), it was held that a reasonable time was two months after the giving of the notice by the defendant."

第七章　产权人禁反言

1. 简　　介

英国物权法的主要特色是衡平法(rules of equity)的干预,用酌情裁量原则(discretionary system of jurisprudence)补充和更正普通法(common law)的严格规定。基本上每个土地权均有两类权益,即普通法的法定产业权(legal estate)和衡平法权益(equitable interest)。在大多数情况下,这两类权益都是由同一人[即一般所说的法定产业权人(legal owner),以下称为业主]拥有。但也经常会有由业主以外的衡平法权益人(equitable owner)在同一时间分别拥有的。例如,受益人(beneficiary)拥有衡平法权益,而业主拥有普通法的法定产业权。

普通法权益必须遵守法律规定建立并要符合正确的法定手续要求。土地/房屋的买卖即产权的转让与让与(conveyance)主要是基于法律的规定完成。但衡平法权益也一样重要,它们之间的根本区别是优先权规则(priority rule)。业主的产权是专有权,可以约束全世界。衡平法的产权也有专有权的特点与功能,如可以转让、破产清算、继承等,但不是完全的专有权。基本上优先权规则是业主的产权可以约束世界,而衡平法权益人的产权也可以约束世界,除了付钱购买了某些土地/房屋,并且没有意识到存在该土地/房屋的衡平法权益的善意买方(the bona fide purchaser for value of a legal estate without notice of the equitable interest)。例如,某个房屋的业主拥有房屋的普通法的法定产业权,而B作为受益人拥有该房屋的衡平法权益。如果业主将房屋送给第三方X,X受衡平法权益的约束(理由是X没有付钱,不是付钱购买房屋的善意买方)。如果业主把将房屋卖给Y,并告诉Y该B的衡平法权益,Y受到约束(理由是Y知道该衡平法权益,并不是没有意识到存在该衡平法权益)。如果业主把房屋卖给Z,但Z懒得查看。而如果一旦Z查看了该房屋,就应当可以发现是B住在里面,这可构成B是受益人的推定通知,在这种情况下,Z会受该衡平法权益的约束(理由是Z可以推断知道B在该房屋衡平法权益)。但如果某君付了钱购买该房屋,并勤勉诚实行事,符合善意买方的要求,他会不受到B在该房屋的衡平法权益约束(理由是他是付钱购买,并且没有意识到存在该房屋的衡平法权益的善意买方)。因此稍早提到在某程度上,衡平法的产权不是完全专有。衡平法针对的是有违良心(conscience)的行为,一般情况下是用来让拥有衡平法权益的一方可以向第三方主张他在产业享有的权益。

信托(将在下一小段介绍)与产权人禁反言是衡平法干预土地/房屋的两种最主要形式。产权人禁反言(proprietary estoppel)主要涉及土地,但也会适用在其他英国法律认为属于不动产(real property)的产权(title)。[1] 这方面的法律非常复杂[2]与历史悠久,有关产权人禁反言的先例很多都远远早于其他商业活动中常见的禁反言。这也不难理解,当时商业活动不多,对于很多人来说,最值钱与重要的财产就是土地/房屋(,现在也是如此)。因此,也只会对土地/房屋的相关权益产生争议。

首先,笔者可以节录权威的《Chitty on Contracts》(第32版,2015年)一书之5–044段,如下:"**Proprietary estoppel.** In its work towards the 1989 Act[3] the Law Commission saw proprietary estoppels as a particularly attractive technique for the avoidance of injustice caused by a rigid adherence to the new formality rules because, unlike the doctrine of part performance, it does not simply enforce the underlying agreement but allows a flexible remedy which can vary according to the particular circumstances.[4] . . . there are three main elements of proprietary estoppels: **a representation made or assurance given to the claimant, reliance by the claimant on that representation or assurance and detriment suffered by the claimant in consequence on such reliance.** It is to be noted, however, that the representation or assurance must have encouraged the claimant to believe that he has or will in the future enjoy some right or benefit over the owner's

[1] 见本书第五章之10.1.1段。在Yeoman's Row Management Ltd. v. Cobbe (2008) UKHL 55先例中,Scott勋爵说:"An 'estoppel' bars the object of it from asserting some fact or facts, or, sometimes, something that is a mixture of fact and law, that stands in the way of some right claimed by the person entitled to the benefit of the estoppel. The estoppel becomes a 'proprietary' estoppel—a sub–species of a 'promissory' estoppel—if the right claimed is a proprietary right, usually a right to or over land but, in principle, equally available in relation to chattels or choses in action."

[2] 在Sean Wilken QC与Karim Ghaly先生近期所著的《The Law of Waiver, Variation, and Estoppel》(第3版,2012年)一书之11.01段说是过于复杂与理念上相互矛盾。

[3] 这是指1989年的《The Law of Property (Miscellaneous Provisions) Act》,其中section 2要求土地买卖合约必须是书面形式并有双方的签字,否则土地买卖合约无效。

[4] "部分履行"(part performance)的说法是在18世纪到19世纪衡平法院发展出来的,主要是为了减轻1677年《Statute of Frauds Act》之section 4的效力:Lester v. Foxcroft (1701) Colles PC 108; Maddison v. Alderson (1883) 8 App Cas 467等先例。这个说法与产权人禁反言的说法十分类似,法院不允许一方保持沉默或不行动,任由对方履行口头合约中他需要履行的责任,但之后以不符合立法要求为由拒绝执行合约。在Steadman v. Steadman (1976) AC 536先例中,Steadman夫妻离婚后前妻向法院申请婚房是两人共同所有的宣告,而前夫申请更改需要支付的赡养费命令。双方之后进行了谈判,前妻同意以1500英镑的价格将婚房的产权转让给前夫,而前夫支付100英镑之前拖欠的赡养费。前夫支付了100英镑并让律师准备了转移婚房产权的契约,但前妻拒绝在契约上签字,理由是之前双方的协议只是口头协议,没有满足书面的要求。贵族院判是前夫支付100英镑与让律师准备契约的行为属于部分履行,前妻受口头协议约束。

property[5] and so, even if adopted by a court in a case where an agreement for the sale of land did not satisfy the formal requirements of s. 2[6], it would apply only so as to give a remedy to a would – be purchaser: any claim by a would – be vendor would not be for a right to land nor indeed for a specific asset, but for a sum of money, a simple claim for a debt..."(加黑部分是笔者的强调)

产权人禁反言的说法来自衡平法,早期是用来阻止涉及不诚实的一方主张其法律权益或产权。即产权人禁反言如果成立,会禁止产权人主张他对财产的严格法律权益。

产权人禁反言的说法现在是被用来阻止一些产权人主张财产权益是不合情理(unconscionable)的情况。不合情理有三个要件:(1)陈述(representation)或保证(assurance)/承诺(promise);(2)依赖(reliance);(3)蒙受损害(detriment)。换句话说,原告只有证明他依赖了产权人说他有或将获得有关财产权益的陈述或保证并因此蒙受损害,产权人禁反言才能成立。除了涉及的是财产权益而不是其他方面如合约权益外,产权人禁反言与陈述性禁反言与/或承诺性禁反言本质上一样。

在 Taylor Fashions Ltd. v. Liverpool Victoria Trustees Co. Ltd. (1982) QB 133 先例中,Oliver 大法官说:"if A, under an expectation created or encouraged by B that A shall have a certain interest in land, thereafter, on the faith of such expectation and with the knowledge of B and without objection from him, acts to his detriment in connection with such land, a Court of Equity will compel B to give effect to such expectation."

在 Thorner v. Major (2009) UKHL 18 先例中,Scott 勋爵也提到了类似的构成产权人禁反言的要件并说明陈述或保证/承诺要求明确无误,主张产权人禁反言的原告做出的依赖必须合理并且蒙受的损害足够严重,才能要求衡平法的救济,说:"Lord Walker, in...his opinion, identified the three main elements requisite for a claim based on proprietary estoppel as, first, a representation made or assurance given to the claimant; second, reliance by the claimant on the representation or assurance; and, third, some detriment incurred by the claimant as a consequence of that reliance. These elements would, I think, always be necessary but might, in a particular case, not be sufficient. Thus, for example, the representation or assurance would need to have been sufficiently clear and unequivocal; the reliance by the claimant would need to have been reasonable in all the circumstances; and the detriment would need to have been sufficiently substantial to justify the intervention of equity."

一旦满足了这三个要件,法院就会考虑所有的情况(all the circumstances of the

[5] 在 Capron v. Government of Turks and Caicos Islands (2010) UKPC 2 先例中,枢密院强调构成产权人禁反言的陈述必须是原告将获得一定的土地权利。

[6] 1989 年《The Law of Property (Miscellaneous Provisions) Act》之 section 2。

case),以决定不让原告有任何救济是否不合情理。因为所有案件的事实都不完全相同,所以法院为了平衡不合情理的行为,会做出不同的救济。除了最低程度的衡平法救济(minimum remedy in equity)的要求之外,法院做出救济以防止不合情理的情况的裁量权十分广泛与有弹性。包括但并不是每次都有必要给予原告财产的产权。也正是因为法院的裁量权过于广泛,[7]会导致这方面法律的不肯定与不可预测,这将在本章稍后的第5段有详论。

2. 默示或推定信托

默示或推定信托(implied or constructive trust)的说法与产权人禁反言的说法有密切关系。前者显然是来自信托法(trust law),这涉及一种持有与管理财产的协议。一般上指财产所有权人把财产委托他人信托保管,以利第三者,即受益人(beneficiary)。调整信托关系的法律主要是衡平法。受委托人即信托人的责任重大,权力也大,其任务在于尽忠职守,为受益人的利益服务。所以,信托人不准依靠信托产业为自己谋利。一般资产的信托可以通过签订信托契约(deed of trust)成立,由遗嘱设立,或由法律本身的实施推定信托的存在。在信托中,信托人是财产的合法所有人(legal owner),而受益人是获得信托真正利益的衡平法所有人(equitable owner)。本章所针对的财产是土地/房屋,这类信托必须以书面契约成立,但在特别的案情中,法庭可推定口头的信托有效。

在 Yeoman's Row Management Ltd. v. Cobbe (2008) UKHL 55 先例中,Scott 勋爵通过典型的双方或多方合资购买土地/房屋的例子解释推定信托说:"It is impossible to prescribe exhaustively the circumstances sufficient to create a constructive trust but it is possible to recognize particular factual circumstances that will do so and also to recognize other factual circumstances that will not. A particular factual situation where a constructive trust has been held to have been created arises out of joint ventures relating to property, typically land. If two or more persons agree to embark on a joint venture which involves the acquisition of an identified piece of land and a subsequent exploitation of, or dealing with, the land for the purposes of the joint venture, and one of the joint venturers, with the agreement of the others who believe him to be acting for their joint purposes, makes the acquisition in his own name but subsequently seeks to retain the land for his own benefit, the court will regard him as holding the land on trust for the joint ventures. This would be either an implied trust or a constructive trust arising from the

---

[7] 见 Burrows v. Sharpe (1898) 23 HLR 82 等先例。

circumstances...[8]"

在《Chitty on Contracts》(第32版,2015年)一书之5－040段,说:"... In Yaxley v. Gotts (2000) Ch. 162, Robert Walker LJ considered that the relevant 'species of constructive' trust for this purpose is one based on '**common intention**' and is to be found where, in the words of Lord Bridge in Lloyd's Bank Plc. v. Rosset (1991) 1 AC 107 there ... '**agreement, arrangement or understanding**' actually reached between the parties and relied on and acted on by the claimant ... Equity enforces it because it would be unconscionable for the other party to disregard the claimant's rights."(加黑部分是笔者的强调)

针对推定信托与产权人禁反言这两种说法相互重叠,Robert Walker 大法官在 Yaxley v. Gotts (2000) Ch 162 先例说:"(constructive trust is) closely akin to, if not indistinguishable from, proprietary estoppel."

但除了产权人禁反言属于禁反言的类别而非信托之外,这两种说法也有其他很重要的区别。

1. 1989年《The Law of Property (Miscellaneous Provisions) Act》之 section 2(5) 明确规定了书面的要求不影响构成默示或推定信托,说:"... nothing in this section affects the creation or operation of resulting, implied or constructive trusts."但该立法并没有提到产权人禁反言可以是书面与签署要求的例外,因此在 Yeoman's Row Management Ltd. v. Cobbe 先例中,Scott 勋爵说:"Section 2 of the 1989 Act declares to be void any agreement for the acquisition of an interest in land that does not comply with the requisite formalities prescribed by the section. Subsection (5) expressly makes an exception for resulting, implied or constructive trusts. These may validly come into existence without compliance with the prescribed formalities. Proprietary estoppel does not have the benefit of this exception. The question arises, therefore, whether a complete agreement for the acquisition of an interest in land that does not comply with the section 2 prescribed formalities, but would be specifically enforceable if it did can become enforceable via the route of proprietary estoppel[9] ... My present view, however, is that proprietary estoppel cannot be prayed in aid in order to render enforceable an agreement that statute has declared to be void. The proposition that an owner of land can be estopped from asserting that an agreement is void for want of compliance with the requirements of section 2 is, in

---

[8] 典型的例子是几个人打算开一家联营公司并合伙买下一块土地让其联营公司使用。但出于种种原因(如避税),所有人同意虽然是由他们共同买下土地,但所有人只写其中一个合伙人的名字。之后该合伙人出尔反尔,声称他拥有土地的所有权利。法院就会判该合伙人是联营公司的信托人,至于是默示信托还是推定信托,要根据具体的事实情况决定。

[9] 问题是完整但因为没有满足立法的书面与签署的要求而不能执行的合约,能否通过产权人禁反言执行?

my opinion, unacceptable.[10] The assertion is no more than the statute provides. Equity can surely not contradict the statute.[11] As I have said, however, statute provides an express exception for constructive trusts."

2. 在《Chitty on Contracts》(第32版,2015年)一书之5－049段,说产权人禁反言对救济的弹性更大,说:"One important aspect of the difference between proprietary estoppels and constructive trust lies in the former's greater flexibility of remedial response, although sometimes, the effect of the application of the two doctrines will be the same. For:'... if there is a constructive trust the court must naturally give effect to it, often by ordering a transfer of the relevant proprietary interest[12], whereas if there is an estoppel the court will give a remedy that reflects the value of the equity in question'."

3. 在Thorner v. Major (2009) UKHL 18先例中,Scott勋爵认为最好还是将产权人禁反言与推定信托两种说法分开。Scott勋爵说:"... **the relationship between proprietary estoppel and constructive trust and their respective roles in providing remedies where representations about future property interests have been made and relied on**. There are many cases in which **the representations relied on relate to** the acquisition by the representee of **an immediate, or more or less immediate, interest in the property in question**.[13] In these cases a proprietary estoppel is the obvious remedy. The representor is estopped from denying that the representee has the proprietary interest that was promised by the representation in question. Crabb v. Arun District Council (1976) Ch 179 seems to me a clear example of such a case. The council had represented that Mr Crabb would be entitled to have access to the private road at gateway B and had

〔10〕 Scott勋爵的看法是不能。毕竟从立法与/或合约解释的角度看,1989年立法明示把默示或推定信托作为书面与签署要求的例外,但没有针对产权人禁反言,立法的意图应该明了。这可参见笔者(杨良宜)《合约的解释:规则与应用》一书第四章第7段。

〔11〕 衡平法肯定不能超越立法。

〔12〕 在Yeoman's Row Management Ltd. v. Cobbe (2008) UKHL 55先例中,在Scott勋爵所举的联营公司的例子中也提到了这一点,说:"(if) the joint venturers have not agreed or cannot agree about what is to be done with the land, the land would have to be resold and, after discharging the expenses of its purchase and any other necessary expensive of the abortive joint venture, the net proceeds of sale divided equally between the joint venturers."

〔13〕 Hoffmann大法官在Walton v. Walton (unreported) 14 April 1994先例中说:"... in many cases of promises made in a family or social context, there is no intention to create an immediately binding contract. There are several reasons why the law is reluctant to assume that there was. One ... is that such promises are often subject to unspoken and ill－defined qualifications... But a contract, subject to the narrow doctrine of frustration, must be performed come what may ... But none of this reasoning applies to equitable estoppel, because it does not look forward into the future and guess what might happen. It looks backwards from the moment when the promise falls due to be performed and asks whether, in the circumstances which have actually happened, it would be unconscionable for the promise not to be kept."

confirmed that representation by erecting gateposts and a gate across the gateway. Once Mr Crabb, in reliance on that representation, had acted to his detriment in selling off a portion of his land so that his only means of access to and egress from his retained land was via gateway B, it was too late for the council to change its mind. The council was estopped from denying that Mr Crabb had the necessary access rights.〔14〕 Ramsden v. Dyson (1866) LR 1 HL 129 is another case, straightforward if viewed through the spectacles of the jurisprudence that has emerged since, of proprietary estoppel. In cases where the owner of land stands by and allows a neighbour to build over the mutual boundary, representing either expressly or impliedly that the building owner is entitled to do so, the owner may be estopped from subsequently asserting his title to the encroached upon land. This, too, seems to me straightforward proprietary estoppel.〔15〕 There are many other examples of decided cases where representations acted on by the representee have led to the representor being estopped from denying that the representee had the proprietary interest in the representor's land that the representation had suggested. Constructive trust, in my opinion, has nothing to offer to cases of this sort.〔16〕 But cases where the relevant representation has related to inheritance prospects seem to me difficult, for the reasons I have given, to square with the principles of proprietary estoppel established by the Ramsden v. Dyson and Crabb v. Arun District Council line of cases and, for my part, I find them made easier to understand as constructive trust cases.〔17〕 **The possibility of a remedial constructive trust over property, created by the common intention or understanding of the parties regarding the property on the basis of which the claimant has acted to his detriment**, has been recognised at least since Gissing v. Gissing (1971) AC 886〔18〕: see particularly Lord Diplock, at p 905. The 'inheritance' cases, of which Gillett v. Holt (2001) Ch 210; In re Basham, decd (1986) 1 WLR 1498 and Walton v. Walton

〔14〕 Crabb v. Arun District Council (1976) Ch 179 先例是一个明确的产权人禁反言的例子，该先例中，Arun 区政府向 Crabb 先生做出陈述或保证，他可以 B 闸作为出入通道。Crabb 先生依赖了这个陈述或保证将他的部分土地出售，只保留了必须以 B 闸出入的部分土地。所以 Arun 区政府被禁反言，不能不让 Crabb 先生使用 B 闸。

〔15〕 Ramsden v. Dyson (1866) LR 1 HL 129 先例是另一个好例子。如果土地所有人对邻居在共同边界建筑视而不见，会被禁反言将来不能再主张土地的产权。

〔16〕 但推定信托与这类案件无关。

〔17〕 但涉及将来继承财产的陈述或保证/承诺，Scott 勋爵认为以推定信托的说法比较容易理解。

〔18〕 如果双方对财产/土地权利有共同的期待或理解，而原告因此而蒙受损害，可能可以推定信托作为救济。接下来 Scott 勋爵提到的例子都是家庭之间对财产/土地的继承权利或将来的权利，虽然这几个先例都是以产权人禁反言做出判决，只有 In re Basham, decd (1986) 1 WLR 1498 先例一并提到推定信托。

(unreported) 14 April 1994 and, of course, the present case are good examples[19], are, to my mind, more comfortably viewed as constructive trust cases ... For my part **I would prefer to keep proprietary estoppel and constructive trust as distinct and separate remedies, to confine proprietary estoppel to cases where the representation, whether express or implied, on which the claimant has acted is unconditional and to address the cases where the representations are of future benefits, and subject to qualification on account of unforeseen future events, via the principles of remedial constructive trusts.**[20]"(加黑部分是笔者的强调)

3. 宝剑盾牌之争

传统上,禁反言只能用作盾牌防守,而不能作为宝剑进攻,虽然近年来随着禁反言适用范围的拓展,这方面的法律地位有了一些不肯定。[21] 但与其他类别的禁反言不同,产权人禁反言一直以来都被认为可以用作宝剑,即可以作为诉因向产权人提起诉讼:见 Crabb v. Arun DC (1976) Ch 179 等先例。

3.1 Plimmer v. Mayor of Wellington 先例:确定产权人禁反言可以作为宝剑

这方面最早的先例是在 Plimmer v. Mayor of Wellington (1884) 9 App Cas 699 枢密院先例中,简单的案情是 Plimmer 先生在政府批准下在相关土地上建立了码头。1856 年,新西兰政府为了帮助接收英国(新西兰当时是殖民地)的移民,鼓励 Plimmer

〔19〕 在 Thorner v. Major (2009) UKHL 18 先例中(案情将在本章之 3.3 段介绍),Scott 勋爵认为适用推定信托的说法更为合适。因为在该先例中,不仅 David Thorner 先生与 Peter Thorner 先生之间存在共同意图或理解(shared common intention or understanding),Peter Thorner 先生向 David Thorner 先生做出的陈述也是将来的利益与有条件。Scott 举例说:"If, for example, Peter had become, before his death, in need of full time nursing care, so that he could not continue to live at Steart Farm or continue as a farmer and needed to sell Steart Farm or some part of it in order to fund the costs of necessary medical treatment and care, it seems to me questionable whether David's equity in Steart Farm, bred from the representations and conduct in evidence in this case, would have been held by a court to bar the realisation of Steart Farm, or some sufficient part of it, for those purposes. I do not, of course, imagine for a moment that, in the circumstances I am postulating, David would have raised any objection. However, the conceptual possibility of a dispute arising in the circumstances postulated has to be borne in mind. Would it really be the case that the representations made by Peter, relied on and acted on by David as they were, would have barred the use of Steart Farm as a source of funding for the needs of Peter in a decrepit old age? For my part, I doubt it. But it is an odd sort of estoppel that is produced by representations that are, in a sense, conditional."

〔20〕 Scott 勋爵认为如果原告依赖的陈述是无条件的,产权人禁反言适用。而如果陈述是针对将来的权利,并且取决于一些将来的不可预见的变数,推定信托的说法更合适。

〔21〕 见本书第四章第 10 段,第五章第 3 段与第六章第 5 段。

先生花了大量金钱扩建码头与新建了仓库。政府使用 Plimmer 先生的码头与仓库，并支付费用。双方维持这种互利关系超过 16 年，但之后政府希望回收土地与码头。枢密院判是虽然没有证据显示双方曾经探讨更不用说同意 Plimmer 先生对码头与仓库的使用许可，双方的交往清楚地显示了双方的意图都是 Plimmer 先生对码头与仓库有无确定限期与不可撤销的使用许可。也就等于 Plimmer 先生有永久性的使用码头与仓库的权利，因此根据 1882 年《Public Works Act》之 section 4，Plimmer 先生作为原告可以因政府收回土地而获得赔偿。

在该先例 Plimmer 先生作为原告除了产权人禁反言外没有任何诉因支持他对该土地的权益，因此枢密院的判决等于确认了产权人禁反言可用作宝剑。枢密院判决可部分节录如下："In the present case, the equity is not claimed because the landowner has stood by in silence while his tenant has spent money on his land. This is a case in which the landowner has, for his own purposes, requested the tenant to make the improvements. The Government were engaged in the important work of introducing immigrants into the colony. For some reason, not now apparent, they were not prepared to make landing - places of their own, and in fact they did not do so until the year 1863. So they applied to John Plimmer to make his landing - place more commodious by substantial extension of his jetty and the erection of a warehouse for baggage. Is it to be said that, when had had incurred the expense of doing the work asked for, the Government could turn round and revoke his licence at their will? Could they in July, 1856, have deprived him summarily of the use of the jetty? It would be in a high degree unjust that they should do so, and that the parties should have intended such a result is, in the absence of evidence, incredible."

3.2　Yeoman's Row Management Ltd. v. Cobbe 先例：产权人禁反言之死？

但在 Yeoman's Row Management Ltd. v. Cobbe (2008) UKHL 55 先例中，贵族院严重扭曲或重新解释了产权人禁反言的说法，以至于一些学者称之为产权人禁反言之死。[22]

该先例的案情是 Yeoman 公司是伦敦骑士桥（伦敦市中心十分昂贵的区域）一块有重新开发价值的土地的注册产权人。Cobbe 作为很有经验的开发商，与 Lisle-Mainwaring太太（Yeoman 的实际老板，即这块土地的实际产权人）进行了长时间的谈判。双方达成了一个口头协议，包括：(1) Cobbe 去申请拆除与重建的规划许可；(2)在获得规划许可与将现有租客赶走之后，土地会被卖给 Cobbe 或指定公司，而 Cobbe 或指定公司要预先支付 1200 万英镑；(3) Cobbe 在重新开发土地之后将房屋出售，并将出售金额超出 2400 万英镑的部分的一半支付给 Yeoman。

---

〔22〕 如 Ben McFarlane 教授与 Andrew Robertson 教授就在《Lloyd's Maritime and Commercial Law Quarterly》(2009 年 11 月)发表了一篇名为"The Death of Proprietary Estoppel"的文章。

这份口头协议没有写成书面形式与签署,即没有满足 1989 年《The Law of Property (Miscellaneous Provisions) Act》之 section 2 的要求。并且因为双方都希望进一步谈判合约中的其他条文,所以这份口头协议还不完整,双方只对一些核心条文达成了一致想法或共识。例如,Lisle-Mainwaring 太太希望在最终的正式合约中加入一些条文针对开发开始与进行过程中 Yeoman 的合理使费,超出 2400 万英镑的部分支付给 Cobbe 的时间表与担保[毕竟这个交易的性质令 Yeoman 无法行使卖方留置权(vendor's lien)]。同样,Cobbe 希望正式合约中 Yeoman 对将现有租客赶走的时间表有所保证。

但在 Cobbe 花了大量的时间与金钱取得规划许可后,Yeoman 改变了口头协议的立场,试图重新谈判更高的预付费用。Lisle-Mainwaring 太太之后要求预付 2000 万英镑,并且 Cobbe 将重新开发的房屋出售后要支付给 Yeoman 的金额也要改变。但 Cobbe 坚持要 Yeoman 履行口头协议,甚至在一开始向法院申请"履约指令"(specific performance)的救济。但显然因为这个口头协议看来并不完整,Cobbe 之后将该申请撤销,并开始寻求非合约性的救济,而本章相关的就是产权人禁反言或"推定信托"(constructive trust)。

高院的 Etherton 大法官以产权人禁反言支持了 Cobbe 的请求,因为口头协议包括了所有商业交易中的核心条文(all points of principle which were at the core of the commercial deal),Yeoman 之后出尔反尔显然不合情理。上诉庭也支持了高院的判决,但贵族院推翻了上诉庭与高院的判决。Cobbe 只在按劳计酬(quantum meruit)的说法下可以拿回为了取得规划批准花费的 15 万镑。

贵族院推翻判决的原因(最主要的就是合约不完整)可简单介绍如下:

1. 正如在本章第 2 段已经提到的,Scott 勋爵将推定信托与产权人禁反言进行了区分。1989 年《The Law of Property (Miscellaneous Provisions) Act》之 section 2(5) 已经明确书面与签署的要求不影响推定信托的说法。因此,Scott 勋爵认为衡平法救济不能与该立法条文有冲突(equity can surely not contradict the statute)。在权威的《Chitty on Contracts》(第 32 版,2015 年)一书之 5-046 段最后总结了 Scott 勋爵的判决说:"Unlike resulting, implied or constructive trusts, the statute does not recognize any exception from the formal requirements for proprietary estoppel."

2. 正如在本章第 1 段节录的 Oliver 大法官在 Taylor Fashions Ltd. v. Liverpool Victoria Trustees Co. Ltd. (1982) QB 133 先例中所说,产权人禁反言是被禁反言的一方的鼓励或保证令另一方对获得土地权益有所期待。但在该先例中,合约并不完整,Lisle-Mainwaring 太太令 Cobbe 产生的期待并不是土地权益,而是取得规划批准后会对将土地转让合约的其他条文谈判达成共识(upon the grant of planning permission there would be a successful negotiation of the outstanding terms of a contract for the sale of property to Cobbe)。这只是对谈判成功的期待而非对土地权益的期待,因此不会构成产权人禁反言。Scott 勋爵说:"The problem is that when he (Cobbe) made

the planning application his expectation was, for proprietary estoppel purposes, the wrong sort of expectation. It was not an expectation that he would, if the planning application succeeded, become entitled to ‘a certain interest in land’. His expectation was that he and Mrs Lisle - Mainwaring, or their respective legal advisers, would sit down and agree the outstanding contractual terms to be incorporated into the formal written agreement, which he justifiably believed would include the already agreed core financial terms, and that his purchase, and subsequently his development of the property, in accordance with that written agreement would follow. This is not, in my opinion, the sort of expectation of ‘a certain interest in land’ that Oliver J in the Taylor Fashions case or Lord Kingsdown in Ramsden v. Dyson (1866) LR 1 HL 129 had in mind."

3. Scott 勋爵接着说如果提出禁反言的一方获得财产权益取决于完全可以由对方控制的变数条件,一般来说不会构成产权人禁反言:"... a proprietary estoppel cannot ordinarily arise is that the would - be purchaser's expectation of acquiring an interest in the property in question is subject to a contingency that is entirely under the control of the other party to the negotiations."

Scott 勋爵引用了一些之前先例的判决,如 Templeman 勋爵在 Attorney General of Hong Kong v. Humphreys Estate (Queen's Gardens) Ltd. (1987) AC 114 先例判一个以签署合约为准(subject to contract)的房屋买卖不能构成产权人禁反言,说:"It is possible but unlikely that in circumstances at present unforeseeable a party to negotiations expressed to be ‘subject to contract’ would be able to satisfy the court that the parties had subsequently agreed to convert the document into a contract or that some form of estoppel had arisen to prevent both parties from refusing to proceed with the transaction envisaged by the document. But in the present case the Government chose to begin and elected to continue on terms that either party might suffer a change of mind and withdraw."

4. Cobbe 最多只能证明存在一个没有约束力的合约,而产权人禁反言作为承诺性禁反言的分支(Scott 勋爵的说法),不能给予 Cobbe 新的权益。[23] Lisle-Mainwaring 太太的言行虽然不合情理,但在该先例的情况下并不足以令 Cobbe 获得土地权益。

5. 贵族院也拒绝了 Cobbe 推定信托的请求。毕竟这块土地从来都不是联营公司财产。该先例显著的特征之一就是 Yeoman 或者说 Lisle-Mainwaring 太太在 Cobbe 出现前就一直是这块土地的所有人。另外,虽然推定信托是 1989 年《The Law of Property (Miscellaneous Provisions) Act》之 section 2(5)规定的例外情况,但该先例涉及的是不完整的协议,而不仅仅是没有写成书面形式与签署。

---

〔23〕 即不能用作宝剑。

在笔者看来,该先例可以简单以 Cobbe 对该口头协议的依赖是不成熟与主观臆猜,即 Cobbe 的依赖不合理来解释,不存在产权人禁反言已死的严重性。

3.3 Thorner v. Major 先例:产权人禁反言的复生?

不到一年后,贵族院在 Thorner v. Major (2009) UKHL 18 先例看来得出了与 Yeoman's Row Management Ltd. v. Cobbe (2008) UKHL 55 先例相反的结论。该先例的案情是 David Thorner 先生从 1976 年起在他堂叔 Peter Thorner 先生的农场里工作。Peter 没有孩子,也没有其他关系密切的亲人。他不爱说话,也不会跟人谈论自己的财务状况。David 开始是兼职为 Peter 工作,但从 1986 年开始直到 2005 年 Peter 去世之前,David 基本就全职为 Peter 工作,但没有获得报酬。Peter 在 1990 年的言行令 David 对继承农场与 Peter 的遗产有期待(expectation),如向 David 暗示他将会长期介入农场生意等。事实上在 1997 年,Peter 曾经立过一份遗嘱,其中包括一部分金钱上的遗赠(pecuniary legacies),而他所有剩余的遗产(包括农场)都将留给 David,并且 David 是唯一的遗嘱执行人(executor)。但之后 Peter 与一位金钱上的受遗赠人(pecuniary legatee)闹翻,单纯因为这个与 David 无关的原因,Peter 将遗嘱销毁了(所以并没有找到这份遗嘱)。直到 Peter 在 2005 年去世前,他都没有再立新的遗嘱。因此,David 没有继承到任何财产,于是以产权人禁反言为由向法院请求救济。

贵族院推翻了上诉庭的判决,判产权人禁反言成立。笔者可节录《Chitty on Contracts》(第 32 版,2015 年)一书之 5-047 段对该先例的介绍如下:

"In Thorner v. Major a somewhat differently constituted House of Lords ... took a more positive view of the role of proprietary estoppels in relation to the requirements of the 1989 Act, although, as has been explained its context was domestic rather than commercial. In relation to the 1989 Act Lord Neuberger observed that: 'The notion that much of the reasoning in Cobbe's case(即 Yeoman's Row Management Ltd. v. Cobbe [2008] UKHL 55 先例)... was directed to the unusual facts of that case is supported by the discussion ... relating to section 2 of the Law of Property (Miscellaneous Provisions) Act 1989. Section 2 may have presented Mr Cobbe (the developer) with a problem, as he was seeking to invoke an estoppels to protect a right which was, in a sense, contractual in nature ... and section 2 lays down formalities which are required for a valid 'agreement' relating to land. However, at least as at present advised, **I do not consider that section 2 has any impact on a claim such as the present, which is a straightforward estoppels claim without any contractual connection.** It was no doubt for that reason that the defendants, rightly in my view, eschewed any argument based on section 2'.

This observation therefore suggests **a distinction between claims for proprietary estoppels based on an assurance reasonably relied on and made in a family or domestic context** (where s. 2's requirements of formality are not relevant) **and those based on an agreement** which would (otherwise) qualify as a contract (where s. 2's requirements of formality are relevant and arguably, should not be circumvented)."(加黑部分是笔者的强调)

3.4　商业上与家庭成员之间的产权人禁反言说法的区别

上述节录的《Chitty on Contracts》(第32版,2015年)一书之5－047段中加黑部分显示了商业上与家庭成员之间的产权人禁反言说法的区别。Walker勋爵在Yeoman's Row Management Ltd. v. Cobbe (2008) UKHL 55先例就强调了这一点,说:"In the commercial context, the claimant is typically a business person with access to legal advice and what he or she is expecting to get is a contract. In the domestic or family context, the typical claimant is not a business person and is not receiving legal advice. What he or she wants and expects to get is an interest in immovable property, often for long－term occupation as a home. The focus is not on intangible legal rights but on the tangible property which he or she expects to get. The typical domestic claimant does not stop to reflect (until disappointed expectations lead to litigation) whether some further legal transaction (such as a grant by deed, or the making of a will or codicil) is necessary to complete the promised title... they stretched the boundaries of the doctrine of equitable estoppel too far in granting relief going well beyond the restitutionary relief to which I would hold Mr Cobbe to be entitled. In my opinion the Court of Appeal's decision, if it were to stand, would tend to introduce considerable uncertainty into commercial negotiations, and not only in the field of property development [compare Baird Textile Holdings Ltd. v. Marks & Spencer Plc. (2002) 1 All ER (Comm) 737...]. Equity has some important functions in regulating commercial life, but those functions must be kept within proper bounds..."

因此在商业交易中,有水平与相同谈判力量的合约方在明知双方只存在没有法律效力的君子协定时,不能依赖禁反言执行一个不能执行的协议。毕竟在商业社会,法律的肯定性至关重要。正如Walker勋爵在Yeoman's Row Management Ltd. v. Cobbe先例中所说:"...Mr Cobbe's case seems to me to fail on the simple but fundamental point that, as persons experienced in the property world, both parties knew that there was no legally binding contract, and that either was therefore free to discontinue the negotiations without legal liability—that is, liability in equity as well as at law ... Mr Cobbe was therefore running a risk, but he stood to make a handsome profit if the deal went ahead, and the market stayed favourable.[24] He may have thought that any attempt to get Mrs Lisle-Mainwaring to enter into a written contract before the grant of planning permission would be counter-productive. Whatever his reasons for doing so, the fact is

〔24〕 Cobbe作为有经验的开发商,是清楚知道他在冒险(花钱取得规划批准),但只要一切顺利,包括地产市场好,就有机会赚取高利润。

that he ran a commercial risk, with his eyes open, and the outcome has proved unfortunate for him ... ”

因此在涉及土地买卖的商业交易中，双方不能通过产权人禁反言绕过1989年《The Law of Property (Miscellaneous Provisions) Act》之section 2对于土地买卖合约的书面与签字要求。

但在家庭成员之间，很多案件都涉及对将来特定财产权益的陈述或承诺/保证存在一定的变数，也通常不存在书面与签署的财产/土地转让合约，就会获得产权人禁反言（或推定信托）的救济。Hoffmann大法官在Walton v. Walton (unreported) 14 April 1994先例中举的例子可见本章第2段之脚注13，这里不再重复。另在Gillett v. Holt (2001) Ch 210先例中，Walker大法官说：“Mr Gillett was cross - examined at length about some increasingly improbable eventualities: that Mr Holt would marry his housekeeper, that he would have children, that his elderly sister would suddenly lose all her investments and turn to him for help. Mr Gillett naturally enough conceded that in those circumstances Mr Holt could or would have made some provision for these moral obligations. But, in giving evidence, he stuck resolutely to the promises made to him ... Mr Gillett was not in the witness box to take part in a seminar on the elements of proprietary estoppel (although parts of his cross - examination suggest otherwise). He was there to give evidence, which was largely unchallenged and which the judge accepted, about the assurances made to him and his detrimental reliance on them.”

因此，在家庭案件中能否构成产权人禁反言的考验是依赖禁反言的一方/原告是否合理依赖相关的陈述或保证/承诺，并认为该陈述或保证/承诺是有约束力与不可撤销的。与商业交易不同，在家庭成员之间的产权人禁反言中，原告期待的是财产/土地的权益，获得救济没有问题。但在商业交易中，如果还不存在有约束力的合约，原告的期望是谈判能够成功与/或能有约束力的完整合约。

3.5 Herbert v. Doyle先例：商业交易要依赖推定信托或产权人禁反言，必须有完整与肯定的合约

之后在Herbert v. Doyle (2010) EWCA Civ 1095先例中，上诉庭参考了贵族院在Yeoman's Row Management Ltd. v. Cobbe (2008) UKHL 55先例与Thorner v. Major (2009) UKHL 18先例的判决，认为在商业交易中要依赖推定信托或产权人禁反言，必须先有一个完整与肯定的合约，只是尚未写成书面形式与签署。Arden大法官（Morgan大法官与Jackson大法官也同意）说：“It appears from Cobbe that, in some situations at least, both doctrines have a requirement for completeness of agreement with respect to an interest in property. Certainty as to the interest in those situations is a common component. **A relevant situation would be where the transaction is commercial in nature.**”（加黑部分是笔者的强调）

在《Chitty on Contracts》（第32版，2015年）一书之5-048段，针对Herbert v.

Doyle 先例说："... For Arden LJ, on the facts before her, the relevant question was 'whether, subject to section 2 of the 1989 Act, there was a valid contract' and for this purpose Arden LJ agreed with the finding of the trial judge below that the agreement of the parties was sufficiently certain. **This suggests that where the agreement is sufficiently certain (notably, where it is not made subject to contract nor is merely 'an agreement to agree'), then this agreement may provide the basis for the recognition of a constructive trust or for proprietary estoppel.** "（加黑部分是笔者的强调）

4. 适用产权人禁反言的情况

产权人禁反言说法适用的情况大致可以分为三种。在 Yeoman's Row Management Ltd. v. Cobbe (2008) UKHL 55 先例中，Walker 勋爵有提到这三种情况并强调了构成产权人禁反言的要件，说："The authors of Gray & Gray, at para 10.189, propose a classification which Mr Ivory（Cobbe 先生代表大律师）adopted in his printed case: 'The concatenation of ideas underlying proprietary estoppel emerges from three broad, and not entirely distinct, categories of circumstance. These categories comprise (1) the 'imperfect gift' cases, (2) the 'common expectation' cases, and (3) the 'unilateral mistake' cases. These cases alike present the essential characteristics of proprietary estoppel, but each class of case in its turn gives a heightened emphasis to one or other of the constituent elements of representation, reliance and unconscionable disadvantage. The tendency in the modern case law is to synthesise the jurisprudence of proprietary estoppel in a more unified doctrine of 'detrimental reliance'."

4.1　情况之一：不完善的赠与

第一种产权人禁反言适用的情况是不完善的赠与（imperfect gift）。在这类产权人禁反言的先例中，产权人向原告（提出禁反言的一方）做出陈述或保证/承诺，他将财产送给他或她（如夫妻或同居的情侣之间）作为礼物，但之后没有完成必要的手续，将产权转移。手续一般就是指 1989 年《The Law of Property (Miscellaneous Provisions) Act》之 section 2 的书面与签署的要求，买卖土地的口头合约（oral contract）无效。[25]

---

〔25〕 英国 1677 年《Statute of Frauds》之 section 4 规定了五类合约/文件必须是书面并且有双方签署才有效，分别是：土地买卖合约、遗产执行人自己掏钱支付遗产债务的承诺、婚约、担保与 1 年内无法履行完毕的合约。之后土地买卖合约的书面与签署的要求被 1925 年《Law of Property Act》之 section 40 替代，接着又被 1989 年《Law of Property (Miscellaneous Provisions) Act》之 section 2 替代。这在本书第五章之 11.1.1 段有简单介绍。

在权威的 Dillwyn v. Llewelyn (1862) 4 De G F & J 517 先例中,父亲想将土地送给其儿子之一(即该先例的原告),并让他建造房屋,签了一份土地转让的备忘录(memorandum)。但备忘录并非契约,不符合土地转让的要求。原告在该土地上花了 14000 英镑建造房屋,但在父亲死后,原告的兄弟质疑原告对土地的产权。Westbury 勋爵说:"About the rules of the Court there can be no controversy. A voluntary agreement will not be completed or assisted by a Court of Equity, in cases of mere gift. If anything be wanting to complete the title of the donee, a Court of Equity will not assist him in obtaining it; for a mere donee can have no right to claim more than he has received. But the subsequent acts of the donor may give the donee that right or ground of claim which he did not acquire from the original gift[26] . . . so if A puts B in possession of a piece of land, and tells him, 'I give it to you that you may build a house on it', and B on the strength of that promise, with the knowledge of A, expends a large sum of money in building a house accordingly, I cannot doubt that the donee acquires a right from the subsequent transaction to call on the donor to perform that contract and complete the imperfect donation which was made. The case is somewhat analogous to that of verbal agreement not binding originally for the want of the memorandum in writing signed by the party to be charged, but which becomes binding by virtue of the subsequent part performance."

在更近期的 Pascoe v. Turner (1979) 1 WLR 43 先例中,产权人与原告同居了一段时间之后分手,产权人离开并说:"这房子和里面的一切都是你的了。"房屋的产权没有正式转移,但产权人鼓励被告在认为房屋已经属于她的情况下,花了 230 镑进行修整与重新装修。上诉庭的 Cumming - Bruce 大法官说:"This court concludes that the equity to which the facts in this case give rise can only be satisfied by compelling the appellants(产权人)to give effect to his promise and her(原告)expectations. He has so acted that he must now perfect the gift."

4.2 情况之二:共同期待

第二种产权人禁反言适用的情况是共同期待(common expectation)。在这类先例中,原告(提出禁反言的一方)在与产权人的交往中,合理相信他会被给予或赠与财产权益。

在 Ramsden v. Dyson (1866) LR 1 HL 129 先例中,Ramsden 是一大片土地的所有人,Thornton 先生是其中一小块土地的不定期租客(tenant at will)。Ramsden 先生(通过他的代理人)做出承诺说,Thornton 先生永远不会被赶走,Thornton 先生依赖了

---

〔26〕 如果捐赠的不是不动产,而是金钱,产权人禁反言就不适用,但承诺性禁反言可能适用:见本书第四章。但承诺性禁反言的要件,如已经存在法律关系、依赖并蒙受损害、不公平与不合情理等,不一定能够满足。即如果捐赠人做出捐赠金钱的承诺之后,又出尔反尔撤回承诺,只能从道德层面谴责。

该承诺,花钱在土地上建造了房屋。Kingsdown 勋爵针对了 Ramsden 先生对 Thornton 先生期待的鼓励说:“If a man, under a verbal agreement within landlord for a certain interest in land, or, what amounts to the same thing, under an expectation, created or encouraged by the landlord, that he shall have a certain interest, takes possession of such land with the consent of the landlord, and upon the faith of such promise or expectation, with the knowledge of the landlord and without objection by him, lays out money on the land, a Court of equity will compel the landlord to give effort to such a promise or expectation. ”

在这些涉及共同期待的产权人禁反言的先例中,其他可以通过两种稍有不同的方式产生。一种是通过产权人将会给予财产/土地权益的明确承诺产生:见 ER Ives Investment Ltd. v. High (1967) 2 QB 379; Crabb v. Arun DC (1976) Ch 179 等先例。另一种是在双方的交往过程中产生,Scarman 大法官在 Crabb v. Arun DC 先例中说:“Short of an actual promise, if(产权人), by his words or conduct so behaves as to lead another to believe that he will not insist on his strict legal rights - knowing or intending that the other will act on that belief - and he does so act, that again will raise an enquiry in favour of the other. ”

从这个角度来说,涉及共同期待的产权人禁反言的说法与“共识性禁反言”(estoppel by convention)十分类似。

涉及共同期待的产权人禁反言的还有已经在本章之 3.1 段介绍的 Plimmer v. Mayor of Wellington (1884) 9 App Cas 699 先例。在较近期的 Inwards v. Baker (1965) 2 QB 29 CA 先例中,儿子考虑建造一栋房屋,父亲说:“你为什么不在我的土地上建并且建大一点呢?”法院判是父亲的言行令儿子产生了期待,虽然父亲没有说是赠与该土地,但儿子可以合理认为,他可以想占有父亲的土地多久就占有多久。

在 Gillett v. Holt (2001) Ch 210 先例中,Gillett 先生从青少年时期开始,为 Holt 先生工作了四十多年。在这期间,Holt 先生多次保证在他死后 Gillett 先生会继承他的农场和相关生意,并且立了一份继承人是 Gillett 先生的遗嘱。但之后 Holt 先生与 Gillett 先生关系破裂,Holt 先生将遗嘱中的继承人改为另一个人。这构成了产权人禁反言,Holt 先生改变遗嘱并不能阻止 Gillett 先生依赖之前的保证申诉土地权益。

共同期待与上一小段介绍的不完善的赠与的区别不大,部分取决于产权人做出的陈述的性质与所讲的话,部分取决于提出禁反言的一方因为依赖陈述而产生的想法。将来会转移财产的承诺应该属于共同期待,而“这房子和里面的一切都是你的了”的陈述既可以属于共同期待,也可以属于不完善的赠与。最后,如果提出禁反言的一方在法律(相信赠与形式就已经足够的陈述)或是事实(知道有法律上的要求,但认为要求已经被满足)方面弄错,以为是完善的赠与,就应该属于涉及不完善的赠与的产权人禁反言。

4.3 情况之三:单方面错误

第三种产权人禁反言适用的情况是单方面错误(unilateral mistake)。[27] 在这类案件中,原告(提出禁反言的一方)错误认为他或她有财产的产权,然而事实上产权人另有其人。这类产权人禁反言与稍早介绍的另外两类的不同之处在于,产权人从来没有做出过引导或鼓励令原告产生误解。这个错误完全是原告自己单方面犯错,所以这种情况与"推定信托"(constructive trust)完全无关。

构成这类产权人禁反言的不合情理之处在于,产权人明知原告犯错并因为依赖这个错误而蒙受损失,但选择保持沉默与不行动。即本书第五章之10.1.1段介绍的产权人有责任说清楚(duty to speak)的情况。一般来说,产权人的鼓励是需要一些主动的言行,但这种明知对方犯错但保持沉默或不行动的情况有时会被称为消极的鼓励(passive encouragement),从而被禁反言。

这类产权人禁反言的先例在19世纪经常发生,当时英国大面积修建运河与铁路系统,加上大量没有登记的产权转让或让与(conveyance),经常会没有获得土地所有人的同意,就在土地上进行了工程。之后真正土地所有人出现申诉他的土地权益,趁机要求过度赔偿等,双方产生争议。一个早期这种说法的例子是 Rochdale Canal Company v. King (No. 2) (1853) 16 Beav 630 先例中,John Romilly 大法官说:"The principle... is one often recognized by the Court, namely, that if one man stand by and encourage[28] another, though but passively, to lay out money, under an erroneous opinion of title, or under the obvious expectation that no obstacle will afterwards be interposed in the way of his enjoyment, the Court will not permit any subsequent interference with it, by him who formally promoted and encouraged those acts of which he now either complains or seeks to take advantage."

在 Ramsden v. Dyson (1866) LR 1 HL 129 先例中,Cranworth 勋爵针对这类单方面错误的产权人禁反言的说法,说:"If a stranger builds on my land supposing it to be his own, and I, perceiving his mistake, abstain from setting him right, and leave him to persevere in his error, a court of equity will not allow me afterwards to assert my title to the land on which he had expended money on the supposition that the land was his own. It considers that, when I saw the mistake into which he had fallen, it was my duty to be active and to state my adverse title; and that it would be dishonest of me to remain willfully passive on such an occasion, in order, afterwards to profit by the mistake which I might have prevented."

---

[27] 这与本书第五章之10.2段介绍的合约的单方面错误类似,后者会令合约空与无效(null and void),或合约变更(rectification)或构成禁反言。

[28] 包括消极鼓励与保持沉默。

5. 产权人禁反言的救济十分有弹性与需要成比例

一旦构成产权人禁反言的要件(陈述或保证/承诺,依赖并蒙受损害)被满足,法院就要考虑是否给予救济与适当的救济。已经在本章第1段提到,法院在这方面有非常广泛的裁量权。救济的范围可以从法院认为原告(提出禁反言的一方)蒙受的损害太少,不值得获得赔偿:Burrows v. Sharpe (1989) 23 HLR 82 先例;到满足原告的期待,即令他获得新的财产权益。

满足原告的期待或假设令他获得新的财产权益反映了传统上对所有类别的禁反言的理解,即出的事不能出尔反尔(established a state of facts which the estopped party could not then deny)。但产权人禁反言涉及土地或其他不动产,满足原告(提出禁反言的一方)的期待或假设很可能是过度赔偿了原告。澳大利亚的 Commonwealth of Australia v. Verwayen (1990) 170 CLR 394 先例举例说,如果 A 因为依赖 B 的承诺(或其他类型的鼓励,或 B 只是沉默),花了 100 镑在 B 的土地上建造了一间小屋,他就可以获得 B 这块价值 100 万英镑的土地的产权,这显然就是过度赔偿了 A。

构成其他类别的禁反言的要件与产权人禁反言的类似,都包括陈述或承诺或行动、依赖并蒙受损害、不公平与不合情理等。然而,不同类别的禁反言的侧重点与结果不同。在"陈述性禁反言"(estoppel by representation)或"承诺性禁反言"(promissory estoppel)中,强调有清楚无误的陈述或承诺并被对方依赖,对被陈述方或被承诺方蒙受的损害的要求比较宽松。但产权人禁反言的侧重点则相反,原告蒙受的损害必须是显著与实质性,产权人的言行很可能只是保持沉默。也有说法是产权人禁反言的救济是永久性(permanent),而陈述性禁反言(或承诺性禁反言)的救济只是暂时性(temporary)。

因此,为了避免过度赔偿原告而造成对产权人不公平,传统的满足提出禁反言的一方的期待或假设的救济逐渐被考虑每个不同事实的案件中的公平而做出的救济取代。法院会考虑原告的期待与他蒙受的损失,做出成比例(proportional)的适当救济。

这个成比例的说法来自澳大利亚高院的 Commonwealth of Australia v. Verwayen 先例中,Dixon 大法官说:"... a court of Common Law or Equity may do what is required, but not more, to prevent a person who has relied upon an assumption as to a present, past or future state of affairs, which assumption the party estopped has induced him to hold, from suffering detriment in reliance upon the assumption as a result of the denial of its correctness. **A central element of that doctrine is that there must be a proportionality between the remedy and the detriment which is its purpose to avoid. It would be wholly inequitable and unjust to insist upon a disproportionate making good of the relevant assumption.**"(加黑部分是笔者的强调)

这被之后的 Sledmore v. Dalby（1996）72 P & CR 196 CA 先例与近期重要的 Jennings v. Rice（2003）1 P & CR 8 先例的多数意见引用。在 Sledmore v. Dalby 先例中，上诉庭推翻了一审法院的判决。Hobhouse 大法官总结了该先例的案情，认为原告的期待与蒙受的损害要成比例（proportionality），说：

"In 1962 the freehold title of number 15A was purchased jointly by Mr and Mrs Sledmore.[29] In 1965 their daughter Jacqueline married Richard Dalby and they moved into the occupation of number 15A as joint tenants of Mr and Mrs Sledmore. There was no formal lease but Mr and Mrs Dalby paid a weekly rent[30] ... In 1966 and 1969 the two children of the Dalby marriage were born. In 1973 the Dalbys were offered an opportunity to purchase number 15A for £ 6,000 but declined the offer. In 1976, Mr Sledmore discussed with his bank manager the idea that the title to number 15A might be transferred to the Dalbys for a payment of £ 2,000 but it was not followed up.[31] In 1976, at about the time that Mrs Dalby first fell ill, the Dalbys were allowed to stop paying rent on the basis that they pay the outgoings—the council and water rates and maintain the property.[32] At about the same time Mr Sledmore, to the knowledge of Mrs Sledmore, was in the habit of making observations to the Dalbys along the lines that number 15A 'is going to be yours some day'—'will be yours one day'.[33] ... Between 1976 and 1978, with the encouragement of Mr Sledmore, various improvements were made to number 15A. A bathroom was converted to a bedroom. A store was converted into a bathroom. Central heating was installed. The kitchen was modernised. The making of these improvements was ... something of a co – operative family exercise in which Mr Sledmore certainly played a part and bore some of the expense ... the evidence was not precise. Mr Dalby's circumstances would not have permitted a large outlay. It must have been between about £ 700 and double that sum.[34] The improvements were undoubtedly carried out to improve number 15A as a family home, and in the expectation that the Dalbys would be bringing up their young family there ... The position in 1979 was therefore that the Dalbys had a tenancy. They had incurred expenditure improving

〔29〕 Seldmore 夫妇在 1962 年合资买入了 15A 的房屋，但他们自己住在 15 号。

〔30〕 他们的女儿与她的新婚丈夫（Dalby 先生）在 1965 年搬进了 15A，并每周支付租金。

〔31〕 之后 Sledmore 夫妇数次试图将该房屋转卖给女儿（Dalby 太太）与 Dalby 先生，但不成功。

〔32〕 之后 Dalby 太太生病，Sledmore 夫妇允许他们免费住在 15A，但要负担一些日常的支出。

〔33〕 同时，Sledmore 先生也常常对 Dalby 夫妇说类似于"这房子早晚是你们的"的话，而 Sledmore 太太也知道这一点。

〔34〕 在 Sledmore 先生的鼓励之下，15A 在 1976 年到 1978 年间进行了许多装修与提升的工程。这是全家共同参与的工程，Sledmore 先生也参与并承担了部分费用，但没有证据显示准确的金额。而 Dalby 先生的经济状况不允许他有大笔的支出，他承担的费用大概在 700 至 1400 镑。

the house. They had done so with the encouragement of the Sledmores and in the belief and expectation, derived from the Sledmores, that the freehold title would, if not transferred to them earlier, be left to Jacqueline Dalby by will.〔35〕 The expectation was not falsified. Mrs Sledmore had left the freehold title in the property to Jacqueline Dalby in her will.

In 1980 Mr Sledmore died and in 1983 Jacqueline Dalby died.〔36〕 Between that time and the date of the issue of the County Court Summons, there were mutual acknowledgements from time to time of Mr Dalby's status as tenant but requests to Mr Dalby that he should pay rent were refused by him. The Sledmores had throughout been paying the insurance on number 15A and in 1989 and 1990 they also at their own expense carried out substantial repairs to it. In 1990 Mr Dalby was given notice to quit and the proceedings for possession were instituted.〔37〕 He defended the claim to possession on two bases. He said that by reason of what had occurred between 1975 and 1979, he had acquired an equitable right to have transferred to him the freehold title to the property or at the least the interest of a life tenant. Alternatively, he said that he was a protected tenant and the statutory grounds for his eviction had not been made out.〔38〕

It was Mrs Sledmore's case that she would be caused hardship if she was not allowed to move into number 15A and that number 15 where she was living was too large and no longer suitable for her. Also, she was in financial difficulties if she was not able to dispose of number 15. She could not keep up the mortgage payments; she was on income support.〔39〕 At the commencement of the trial the defendant, Mr Dalby, abandoned the defence that he was a protected tenant who could resist Mrs Sledmore's application. He asserted that he was a bare licensee but with an equity based upon a proprietary estoppel. He did not allege any promissory estoppel. At the time of the trial, number 15A was be-

---

〔35〕 1979 年,Dalby 夫妇以租客的身份住在 15A,但没有支付租金。而在 Sledmore 夫妇的鼓励下,Dalby 夫妇认为 15A 的产权要么之前被转移,要么会在遗嘱中被留给 Dalby 太太,因此他们花钱对 15A 进行了进一步的提升。

〔36〕 Sledmore 先生在 1980 年去世,Dalby 太太(女儿)在 1983 年去世。

〔37〕 之后 Dalby 先生仍然以租客的身份住在 15A,期间 Sledmore 太太数次让他支付租金,但被他拒绝。1990 年,Dalby 先生收到通知,要求他搬出 15A,并且 Sledmore 太太开始了重新占有的程序(proceedings for possession)。

〔38〕 Dalby 先生的抗辩主要有两点:一是他在 Sledmore 夫妇的鼓励下,在 1975 年与 1979 年花钱提升了 15A,所以他应该有 15A 的衡平法权益,或者至少应该可以有一辈子免费住在 15A 的利益。二是他是受保护的租客(protected tenant),让他搬出去的立法要求没有满足(这点开庭前被放弃,显然是因为站不住脚)。

〔39〕 Sledmore 太太的主要争辩是,她现在经济状况不好,在领收入保障金。如果不让她搬进 15A,令她可以把更大的 15 号房屋出售,会对她造成很大困难。

ing occupied by one of his daughters as his sub – licensee with the defendant only spending one or at the most two nights a week there. The daughter is in her mid – twenties; she is employed and able to provide for herself.

The judge decided that there was an equitable proprietary estoppel and that Mrs Sledmore was not entitled to the possession of number 15A and that the defendant should have the right to occupy it for the remainder of his life, apparently free of any payment.〔40〕

The disproportion of this result is obvious as, in my judgment, is its injustice.〔41〕 The defendant by virtue of carrying out very limited improvements to number 15A between 1976 and 1978 and incurring an expenditure which was likewise limited, has been held to have acquired a right to occupy number 15A for the remainder of his natural life rent free to the exclusion of Mrs Sledmore, although his tenancy has been lawfully terminated and he has no right to an extension of that tenancy.〔42〕 Further, he has, since 1976, had the benefit of the occupation of number 15A, together with such members of the family as were living there from time to time, without paying any rent for such occupation.〔43〕 The primary case which he has been presenting to the courts, right up to the time that he abandoned it before this Court, was that his expenditure in 1976 to 1978 entitled him without more to have transferred to him the freehold title."

在相对近期的 Jennings v. Rice 先例中,Jennings 先生在 Rice 女士的家里兼职做帮佣,帮 Rice 女士做园艺、购物、办事等,超过 30 年。大概在 Jennings 先生做了 20 年后,Rice 女士停止支付他工资。当 Jennings 先生向 Rice 女士要工资时,Rice 女士就会说:"别担心,这些最后都会是你的。"Rice 女士去世前最后几年,她病得很严重,生活十分依赖 Jennings 先生。Jennings 先生会在 Rice 女士家里过夜,防止出事,帮她购物、穿衣服、洗澡、去洗手间。Rice 女士去世后,Jennings 先生认为他应该有权拥有她超过 100 万英镑的所有财产,或者至少是价值 43.5 万英镑的房产。上诉庭支持了一审法院的判法,判是 Jennings 先生有权获得 20 万镑,这个数字是根据如果在市场上需要提供类似 Jennings 先生的服务的佣人所需要的花费计算出来。上诉庭的多数意见强调法院在决定适合的救济时,必须考虑提出禁反言一方的期待与他因为依赖而蒙受的损害,并做出平衡。

〔40〕 一审的救济就是让 Dalby 先生一辈子都可以免费占有 15A 的住所。

〔41〕 在上诉庭看来,这个救济是不公平与不成比例。

〔42〕 Dalby 先生只花了非常有限的钱对房屋进行了提升,其他方面的花销也同样有限,一审的判决令他有权免费一辈子占有 15A 的住所,并且可以不让 Sledmore 太太住进去。

〔43〕 尤其是考虑到从 1976 年起,Dalby 先生已经免费住在 15A。

第八章　合约性禁反言

1. 合约性禁反言(contractual estoppel)的本质

首先可以节录权威的《Chitty on Contracts》(第 32 版,2015 年)一书之 4 - 116 段,说:"**Contractual Estoppel**. This form of 'estoppel' is said to arise when contracting parties have, in their contract, agreed that a specified state of affairs is to form the basis on which they are contracting or is to be taken, for the purpose of the contract, to exist.[1] The effect of such 'contractual estoppel' is that it precludes a party to the contract from alleging that the actual facts are inconsistent with the state of affairs so specified in the contract.[2] Three points must here be made about this concept. The first is that the answer to the question when the contract term alleged to be of the kind described above in fact has this effect turns on the construction of the contract; and once the court has decided that, as a matter of construction that term is held to preclude one of the parties from denying the existence of a specified state of affairs, then nothing of substance is gained by classifying this conclusion under the rubric of 'contractual estoppel'.[3] The second is that, even if that phrase is used, such an 'estoppel' would differ from estoppels by convention in that 'contractual estoppel' gives effect to a term of a contract which, on its true construction, prevents a party from denying facts specified in that term and in the circumstances (if any) specified in it; while estoppel by convention invoke factors extrinsic to the contract as grounds for precluding the estopped party from denying facts such as the existence of a promise **not** included in the contract on its true construc-

---

〔1〕 如果合约双方在合约中同意了某种特定情况构成合约的基础,或在该合约下接受存在某种特定情况,就会构成合约性禁反言。

〔2〕 合约性禁反言的作用是禁止合约任何一方引入证据证明实际情况与合约中的特定情况不符。

〔3〕 关于合约性禁反言有三点需要注意。第一,合约条文能否构成合约性禁反言,取决于对条文的解释。一旦法院认定该条文可以禁止合约任何一方引入证据证明实际情况与合约中约定的特定情况不符,也就无需与禁反言的说法挂钩了。

tion and holding him bound by that promise[4] ... The third is that 'contractual estoppel' does not give rise to any of the problems of consideration ... ; the term alleged to give rise to such an estoppel derives its binding force from the fact of being part of a legally binding contract, it being simply assumed that the requirement of consideration is satisfied[5] ..."

近年来所发展的合约性禁反言的说法在本质上并不是禁反言,纯粹是合约条文的解释。事实上使用"禁反言"一词反而会带来困惑,被称为禁反言主要是因为这个说法是由"契约性禁反言"(estoppel by deed)演变而来。简单而言,契约性禁反言是指契约的双方,包括他们的继承人(successor),都要受契约上的陈述的约束。如在有关契约性禁反言的 Greer v. Kettle (1938) AC 156 重要先例中,Russel 勋爵总结 Stroughill v. Buck (1850) 14 QB 781 先例的判法,说:"Where a recital is intended to be an agreement of both parties to admit a fact, it estops both parties, but it is a question of construction whether the recital is so intended."

Pollock 大法官在更早的 Ashpitel v. Bryan (1864) 5 B & S 723 先例说:"Estoppel may arise without any mistake or misleading, as by matter of recital in a deed executed by two parties. So here, for the purpose of the transaction in question, the parties agreed that certain facts should be admitted to be facts on the basis of which they would contract, and they cannot recede from that."

众所周知,契约(deed)与简式合约(simple contract)不同,即使不存在约因/对价,也会约束契约的双方。因此,合约性禁反言的存在令达成协议的双方无需存在契约,只要存在令合约有效与可执行的约因/对价(consideration),[6]双方就会受合约条文中对事实的陈述的约束。

合约性禁反言的说法与"共识性禁反言"(estoppel by convention)也有很多相似之处,即合约双方存在共同错误假设。唯一的区别是合约性禁反言中双方的共同错误假设是来自合约条文中对事实的陈述,而共识性禁反言的共同错误假设或共识虽然双方通过言行沟通过,但并没有合约性质,如不存在约因/对价。有时两者会在类似的事实情况下(存在可以构成共识性禁反言的共同假设或合约条文中可以构成合约性禁反言的陈述),作为替代争议被一并提出,如 Nram Plc. v. Jeffrey Patrick McAdam, Ann Hartley (2014) EWHC 4174 (Comm)先例。

简单总结以上所讲,契约性禁反言与共识性禁反言本质上属于禁反言的不同类

---

[4] 第二,即使使用了合约性禁反言的说法,这种所谓的禁反言也与共识性禁反言不同。合约性禁反言是通过解释合约条文禁止合约任何一方否认合约中的特定情况。而共识性禁反言是禁止合约任何一方否认双方之间存在没有在合约中记载的共识并受该非合约性的共识约束。

[5] 第三,合约性禁反言不会有任何约因/对价的问题。构成合约性禁反言的条文有约束力是因为它是一个有约束力的合约的一部分,可以假设已经满足了约因/对价的要求。

[6] 约因/对价在英国合约法的重要性,可参阅本书第三章之 2.4.3 段与第四章之 12.1.2 段。

别,需要满足所有禁反言的要件,包括依赖并蒙受损害(detrimental reliance)、不公平与不合情理(unjust and unconscionable)等。但现代的合约性禁反言已经变质,再也不能说属于禁反言,而只是合约的解释。

2. 曾经的合约性禁反言说法与近年政策性的改变

合约性禁反言曾经也要求满足禁反言的要件,不承认可以将合约中的条文作为"保护伞",完全无须理会真实情况。重要先例之一就是上诉庭的 Lowe v. Lombank (1960) 1 WLR 196 先例。[7] 案情涉及一个 65 岁的老妇人通过租购合约(hire - purchase agreement)向一家车行租了一辆汽车。在该合约中,有条文说明老妇人已经检查过车辆并确认状况良好,但其实老妇人根本没有检查过该汽车。同样的条文也出现在交车的收据(delivery receipt)中,但该老妇人依然没有检查过该车辆。反正给她什么文件,她就在上面签字。事实上,该汽车是不能安全使用,并且即使检查过,像老妇人这样的外行人也看不出这种潜在瑕疵。上诉庭认为"检查过车辆并确认状况良好"属于对现在或已经存在的事实的陈述(representation of fact),条文是否有效要看能否满足构成"陈述性禁反言"(estoppel by representation)的要件。[8] Diplock 大法官说:"no doubt for the very good reason that there was no evidence (and it is difficult to see how there could be any truthful evidence) that the defendants believed in the truth of the representation. To call it an agreement as well as an acknowledgement by the plaintiff cannot convert a statement as to past facts, known to both parties to be untrue, into a contractual obligation, which is essentially a promise by the promisor to the promisee that acts will be done in the future or that facts exist at the time of the promise or will exist in the future."

Diplock 大法官在判决中也说明了这种确认事实的合约条文要有效,第一,要清楚无误。第二,被禁反言的一方希望该条文中的陈述被依赖,而提出禁反言的一方可以合理依赖该陈述。第三,提出禁反言的一方确实认为该陈述是正确,并依赖该陈述行事。显然在 Lowe v. Lombank 先例中,车行作为提出禁反言的一方,无法满足这些要件。Diplock 大法官说:"In order to found an estoppel on this statement in the delivery receipt... the defendants must show... (1) that it is clear and unambiguous; (2) that the plaintiff meant it to be acted on by the defendants or at any rate so conducted herself that a reasonable man in the position of the defendants would take the representations to be true and believe that it was meant that he should act upon it... (3) that the defendants

[7] 该先例的详细介绍,可见杨良宜《合约的解释:规则与应用》第十三章之 2.4.9 段。

[8] 见本书第五章第 5 - 9 段。

in fact believed it to be true and were induced by such belief to act upon it."

但这说法或法律地位在 Peekay Intermark v. Australia & New Zealand Banking Group（2006）2 Lloyd's Rep. 511（CA）与 Springwell Navigation v. JP Morgan Chase Bank（2010）EWCA Civ 1212 这两个近年的上诉庭先例后有了重大改变，即现代合约性禁反言的说法不再要求提出/需要依赖禁反言的一方依赖并蒙受损害，虽然这仍是其他类别的禁反言都需要满足的要件：The "Kanchenjunga"（1990）1 Lloyd's Rep. 391（HL）先例。另是提出禁反言的一方也无须证明不公平与不合情理这一其他类别的禁反言都需要满足的要件。在上诉庭的 Springwell Navigation v. JP Morgan Chase Bank 先例中，[9] Aikens 大法官在参考了之前的权威先例中，包括 Lowe v. Lombank 先例后，说：

"To my mind, once it is accepted that there is a separate doctrine of 'contractual estoppel' then there is **no room for a requirement** that the party which wishes to rely on that estoppel **must demonstrate that it would be unconscionable** for the other party to resile from the conventional state of affairs that the parties have assumed.[10] The reason why that is a requirement in the case of 'estoppel by convention' is precisely because there is no contract between the parties. Therefore some other mechanism has to come into play to make the non-contractual 'convention' enforceable.[11]

Mr Brindle（Springwell 代表大律师）relied on the statement of Peter Gibson J in Hamel-Smith v. Pycroft and Jetsave（unreported, 5 February 1987）that the ability to rely on an estoppel by convention is governed by 'considerations of justice and equity'. Therefore, **before an estoppel by convention can be enforced it is necessary to demonstrate that it would be unjust or unconscionable for one of the parties（against whom it is sought to enforce the convention）to resile from it.** That statement was part of a long passage of Peter Gibson J's judgment that was approved by the Court of Appeal in The Vistafjord（1988）2 Lloyd's Rep. 343. **But, in my view, it is irrelevant to the doctrine of 'contractual estoppel' for the reasons that I have given.**"（加黑部分是笔者的强调）

以上所讲可节录权威的《Chitty on Contracts》（第 32 版，2015 年）一书之 15-147 段，如下：

"Clauses are often inserted in standard form agreements whereby one party 'ac-

---

[9] 该先例的案情在杨良宜《合约的解释：规则与应用》第十三章之 2.4.9 段有详细介绍。

[10] Aikens 大法官认为，如果接受合约性禁反言是不同与独立的说法，就没有理由要求希望依赖合约性禁反言的一方必须证明另一方反悔，想从合约性共识中脱身是不合情理的。

[11] 共识性禁反言要满足不合情理的要件正是因为双方没有合约关系的约束。因此需要有另一种说法（即共识性禁反言）令双方受这一非合约性的共识约束。

knowledges and agrees that he has not been induced to enter into contract by any representation of the other party', or that he has 'examined the goods', or that he has 'not made known to the other party expressly or by implication the purpose for which the goods are required'. In Lowe v. Lombank Ltd, the Court of Appeal held that such a clause can only give rise to an estoppel, preventing the party making the acknowledgement from asserting the contrary, and cannot operate as a positive contractual obligation〔12〕...

In the particular case, which concerned an acknowledgement by a hirer under a hire-purchase agreement, the court found that none of the requirements for an estoppel by representation was satisfied, and so no estoppel arose.〔13〕

It has, however, more recently been said that〔14〕: '.. there is no reason in principle why parties should not agree that a certain state of affairs, should form the basis for the transaction whether it be the case or not.'

And that, in such an event: '.. neither can subsequently deny the existence of the facts and matters upon which they have agreed, at least so far as those aspects of the relationship to which their agreement was directed.'

The contract itself then gives rise to an estoppel. This analysis was followed in a number of cases at first instance〔15〕 and it has subsequently been endorsed by the Court of Appeal in Springwell Navigation v. JP Morgan Chase Bank (2010) EWCA Civ 1212. As a result, provided that an acknowledgement clause is appropriately drafted as an agreement or contract, it can be effective by virtue of a contractual estoppel and it is unnecessary to show, as suggested in Lowe v. Lombank, that the requirements for estoppel by representation have been satisfied.〔16〕 Further, the Court of Appeal stated that the

---

〔12〕 在标准格式合约中，常常会有条文说明“一方确认与同意没有受另一方的陈述诱导订立合约”(这是一个典型的完整合约条文或没有依赖条文)，或是“买方检查了货物”，或是“没有明示或默示告知卖方货物的用途”，以免将来对这些事实有争议。在 Lowe v. Lombank (1960) 1 WLR 196 先例中，上诉庭判是这样的条文如果能满足有关要件，可以构成陈述性禁反言以禁止做出确认的一方声称事实并非如此，而不能将其作为合约承诺文字，怎样写就怎样解释。

〔13〕 在 Lowe v. Lombank (1960) 1 WLR 196 先例中，案情涉及租购合约，法院判是老妇人作为租购方做出的确认，双方都明知不是事实也不存在依赖，无法满足陈述性禁反言的要件，因此不存在禁反言。

〔14〕 Moore-Bick 大法官在 Peekay Intermark v. Australia & New Zealand Banking Group (2006) 2 Lloyd's Rep. 511 (CA)先例第 56 段所说。

〔15〕 这些一审法院的先例包括 Donegal International Ltd. v. Zambia (2007) 1 Lloyd's Rep. 397; Trident Turboprop (Dublin) Ltd. v. First Flight Couriers Ltd. (2008) 2 Lloyd's Rep. 581; Titan Steel Wheels Ltd. v. Royal Bank of Scotland Plc. (2010) 2 Lloyd's Rep. 92; Raiffeisen Zentralbank Osterreich AG v. Royal Bank of Scotland Plc. (2011) 1 Lloyd's Rep. 123 等。

〔16〕 因此，只要确认事实(即使双方明知道事实并非如此)的合约条文的措辞/用字恰当，就会因为合约性禁反言的说法而有效，而无须像 Lowe v. Lombank (1960) 1 WLR 196 先例中所说要满足陈述性禁反言的要件。

words of Diplock J quoted above：'... are not binding authority for the far – reaching proposition that there can never be an agreement in a contract that the parties are conducting their dealings on the basis that a past event had not occurred or that a particular fact was the case, even if it was not the case and both parties knew it was not'〔17〕"

最后，现代合约性禁反言的说法除了适用在对过去或已经存在的事实的陈述，已经拓展到了对未来的承诺。在 Credit Suisse International v. Stichting Vestia Groep（2014）EWHC 3103（Comm）先例中，Andrew Smith 大法官说：

"In his formulation of the doctrine of contractual estoppel in Peekay Moore – Bick LJ said that parties are able to agree upon 'a state of affairs [that] should form the basis for the transaction'. In most of the subsequent cases that have considered the doctrine, the parties had agreed about a present or past state of affairs and made their contract on the deemed basis that that state of affairs obtained or had obtained. **But I can see no reason of authority, principle or policy that the doctrine should be confined to agreements of that kind, or that the law should adopt a different approach where parties have made an agreement about a state of affairs in the future**, whether or not the label contractual estoppel should be attached in those circumstances. Indeed, all three considerations seem to me to indicate that the doctrine should not be so confined.

As for authority, I know of no case in which the point has been expressly considered in theseterms, but in two first instance decisions in this court it was apparently assumed that an agreement about the future engaged the doctrine. In Titan Steel Wheels v. RBS, [2010] EWHC 211 (Comm) David Steel J applied the doctrine in a case in which one of the relevant terms was an agreement about the future: Titan were to seek independent advice if required: see paragraph 82 of the judgment. In Bank Leumi (UK) Plc. v. Wachner, [2011] EWHC 656 (Comm) Flaux J applied the doctrine to a term, 'You agree that you will rely on your own judgment for all trading decisions': at paragraphs 183, 184."（加黑部分是笔者的强调）

3. 现代合约性禁反言的说法带来的问题

商业上需要合约性禁反言的说法的原因很容易理解。对于商业人士来说，很多时候终局性（finality）与肯定性（certainty）比绝对的公正更重要。毕竟要找出合约条文以外的事实真相（更不用说是完全的真相）可能十分困难与昂贵，所谓的事实也可

〔17〕 Diplock 大法官的判决不能被解释为合约双方永远不能在合约中约定双方以某个事实情况（虽然他们知道事实并非如此）为基础进行交易。

能很有争议性,必须通过诉讼或仲裁这种对抗性的程序才能确定。只有法律有肯定性,商业人士才能计划未来的经营与发展,能做什么与避免做什么。

一些涉及合约性禁反言的常见例子在杨良宜的《合约的解释:规则与应用》一书有介绍,如第十三章第2段介绍的完整合约条文(entire agreement clause),第十四章第1段介绍的最终与有约束力条文(final and binding clause),第十四章第2段介绍的专家决定条文(expert determination clause),第十四章第3段介绍的视为条文(deeming clause)等。而现代合约性禁反言政策性的改变主要是来自完整合约条文,因此下一小段会先简单介绍完整合约条文。

3.1 完整合约条文与类似条文

3.1.1 类似条文的本意

完整合约条文在英文中有好几种叫法,除了 entire agreement clause 外,也被称为 merger clause 或 integration clause。该条文内的部分内容会专门针对谈判时的陈述或误述,也被称为没有陈述条文(no representation clause)或没有依赖条文(non – reliance clause)。这是近年来十分重要的一条惯用条文(boiler – plate clause),在金融服务、合资、合并/收购、技术转让、保险、造船、货物买卖、和解协议等合约都可以见到。这些合约涉及的金额往往很大,也导致了很多昂贵的争议与先例。

一个完整合约条文中包括了没有依赖条文的例子可见上诉庭的 Watford Electronices Ltd. v. Sanderson CFL Ltd. (2001) EWCA Civ 317 先例:"[1] The parties agree that these terms and conditions... represent the entire agreement between the parties... and [2] that no statement or representations made by either party have been relied upon by the other in agreeing to enter into the Contract."

另外的写法也可以是"一方没有做出过任何陈述",即使这不是事实情况,只是以合约条文否定这个事实的存在。如在 Trident Turboprop (Dublin) Ltd. v. First Flight Couriers Ltd. (2008) 2 Lloyd's Rep. 581 先例中,相关条文的写法是:"(飞机供应商)has not and shall not be deemed to have made any warranties or representations, express or implied, about the Aircraft (在合约谈判中)."又或是以条文说明以前所有的承诺与约定全部作废,如 Fontana GB Ltd. v. Fabio (unreported, 4 July 2002)先例中的条文说:"This Agreement shall be in substitution for any previous letters of appointment, agreements or arrangements, whether written, oral or implied."

简单而言,完整合约条文与类似条文的本意都是订约双方想局限或排除对合约内明示条文/文字的解释以外的争议,如附带保证/协议(collateral warranty/contract)、默示条文(implied terms)、误述(misrepresentation)、引导(inducement)、商业习惯做法/惯例(custom/usage)、侵权的共同责任(concurrent liability in tort)等。而没有依赖条文主要是为了确认双方没有依赖任何对方的陈述(representation)而订立这份合约,因为误述的争议可能带来的后果是最严重。

这种条文的好处显而易见。在英国法下,双方同意了合约内容的最好证明就是在合约上的签字。如果双方签了一个合约，除非是由欺诈或是误述所导致，否则就代表双方对责任、承诺与权利有了终局性的同意。这所谓的签字规则（signature rule）与禁反言的说法有相似之处，虽然在适用签字规则时，没有人说过这属于禁反言的说法。在重要的 L'Erstrange v. F Graucob Ltd.（1934）2 KB394（DC）先例中，Scrutton 大法官说："When a document containing contractual terms is signed, then, in the absence of **fraud**, or, I will add, **misrepresentation**, the party signing it is bound, and it is wholly immaterial whether he has read the document or not."（加黑部分是笔者的强调）

3.1.2 谈判时的误述可能导致的严重后果

经常有情况是，一旦相关的交易进行不顺利，一方想从合约中脱身，就会提出在合约谈判期间另一方曾经有过误述（通常是口头的陈述或保证），导致合约可使无效（voidable）。除非这种指称完全站不住脚，否则唯一能确定是否存在误述的方法就是进行全面的诉讼程序，包括文件披露、证人证言、开庭交叉盘问等。这无疑很昂贵，也并不科学。但这往往是一方在合约解释对自己不利时会用的方法，因为他只能指称对方在谈判时曾经误述才能扭转败局，正如 Lightman 大法官在 Inntrepreneur Pub Co. v. East Crown Ltd.（2000）2 Lloyd's Rep. 611 先例所说："a party to a written agreement... threshing through the undergrowth and finding in the course of negotiations some（chance）remark or statement（often long forgotten or difficult to recall or explain）on which to found a claim ..."

3.1.3 现代合约性禁反言说法的上诉庭先例：Springwell Navigation v. JP Morgan Chase Bank

在 Springwell Navigation v. JP Morgan Chase Bank（2010）EWCA Civ 1212 先例中，案情涉及 20 世纪 90 年代，专业投资者在新兴市场（涉及发展中国家）的投资因为债务危机而蒙受严重损失，他们试图向提供投资意见的私人银行提起诉讼并索赔损失。在该先例中，原告是专业投资者，他的钱来自一个希腊的著名船东（Polemis 家族）。该船东在航运赚了大钱，并希望在航运以外找其他的投资。本先例就涉及投资 7 亿美元在新兴市场的债券，其中最重要的新兴市场就是俄罗斯。1998 年，俄罗斯发生经济危机，8 月份对部分债券违约，这导致希腊船东蒙受严重损失，并在英国法院向投资银行摩根大通提出诉讼与索赔损失。在诉讼中，关键争议之一是摩根大通能否依赖他们之间的协议中的一条十分详尽的完整合约条文与不依赖条文。诉讼的一审持续了 68 天，有 390 个开庭文件案卷，另有 22 个其他权威性先例的案卷。Springwell 声称，从双方在订约前的谈判过程中的通讯往来（书面与口头）中找出了摩根大通 149 个误述，包括这个衍生品交易对 Springwell 是很适合的投资、有合理理由认为会获利而不会存在太大风险、对俄罗斯经济状况的正面陈述、对衍生品的正面陈述等。而摩根大通也需要披露 1000 个磁带与 1500 个电话交谈的录音。

如果一条写得完善的完整合约条文被法院或仲裁庭判为有效,双方会被禁止声称与引入证据证明在订立合约前,一方曾经做出过误述(misrepresentation)或引导(inducement),或附带保证/协议(collateral warranty),或存在默示条文(implied term)等,即使这些确实存在。换句话说,完整合约条文表示双方明示同意了合约中的条文/文字就是双方合约的全部内容,双方都会被禁反言,不能证明可能存在的误述(或者附带保证/协议等,取决于完整合约条文的写法)。这表示上述先例中的希腊船东会被禁止提出这 149 个误述与引入相应的大量证据。

完整合约条文构成合约性禁反言的说法可见 Moore – Bick 大法官在上诉庭的 Peekay Intermark v. Australia & New Zealand Banking Group (2006) 2 Lloyd's Rep. 511 (CA)先例〔18〕所说,如下:"**There is no reason in principle why parties to a contract should not agree that a certain state of affairs should form the basis for the transaction, whether it be the case or not.** For example, it may be desirable to settle a disagreement as to an existing state of affairs in order to establish a clear basis for the contract itself and its subsequent performance. Where parties express an agreement of that kind in a contractual document neither can subsequently deny the existence of the facts and matters upon which they have agreed, at least so far as concerns those aspects of their relationship to which the agreement was directed. **The contract itself gives rise to an estoppel**: see Colchester Borough Council v. Smith [1991] Ch 448, affirmed on appeal [1992] Ch 421 ."(加黑部分是笔者的强调)

3.2 对现代合约性禁反言说法的批评

已经提到在 Peekay Intermark v. Australia & New Zealand Banking Group (2006) 2 Lloyd's Rep. 511 (CA)先例中,首先对合约性禁反言进行了政策性的改变后,高院的法官在很多重要先例中毫无异议地接受了这个改变。之后,上诉庭的 Springwell Navigation v. JP Morgan Chase Bank (2010) EWCA Civ 1212 先例在参考了之前的先例中,包括 Lowe v. Lombank (1960) 1 WLR 196 先例与 Peekay Intermark v. Australia & New Zealand Banking Group 先例后,确认了现代合约性禁反言的说法,而令依赖并蒙受损害(detrimental reliance)与不合情理(unconscionable)不再是必须满足的要件。现代合约性禁反言的说法受到了批评,如在 Gerard McMeel 教授 2011 年的《Documentary fundamentalism in the Senior Courts: the myth of contractual estoppel》一文中就说,这是一类非法的禁反言(illegitimate species of estoppels)。

Gerard McMeel 教授的批评也可以理解,现在完整合约条文(包括没有依赖条文与没有陈述条文)在几乎所有的商业交易合约,尤其是涉及金融交易的合约中都会存在。但如果只要有一条完整合约条文就可以完全排除谈判过程中虚假〔19〕或错误

〔18〕 该先例的案情在杨良宜《合约的解释:规则与应用》第十三章之 2.4.8 段有详细介绍。

〔19〕 涉及虚假陈述的情况比较特殊,会在本章稍后的第 4 段详论。

的陈述构成误述的争议,即使事实上确实存在严重的误述,这种法律发展是很不合理的。McMeel 教授也提到在 Peekay Intermark Ltd. v. Australia & New Zealand Banking Group Ltd 先例与 Springwell Navigation v. JP Morgan Chase Bank 先例后,已经有些案例涉及因为这类条文的存在而令误述导致的合约无法获得救济。虽然这种条文有可能受到相关保护消费者的立法〔20〕限制,但还是无法保护商业活动中的弱方。因为在国际商贸中,即使双方强弱分明,弱方也不会被认定为消费者,而是会被视为像 Springwell Navigation v. JP Morgan Chase Bank 先例中一样,双方有相同的谈判力量与高水平,所以这种完整合约条文会被宽松对待。

Gerard McMeel 教授在该 2011 年的文章中总结说:“... such clauses are endemic in commercial transactions more generally; and where they constitute the standard terms of one party, and where one party is a substantial concern and the other a small or medium - sized enterprise, the courts are still required to investigate the substance of claims of pre - contractual representations either at common law or pursuant to the statutory controls... The myth of contractual estoppel must be exploded, but only the Supreme Court can now light the fuse.”

McMeel 教授对这两个上诉庭先例的批评可以总结为两点。

3.2.1 忽略了合约性禁反言起源——契约性禁反言

尽管相对后期才产生的合约性禁反言与历史悠久的“契约性禁反言”(estoppel by deed)之间的密切关系很明显,更有说法是十分狭窄的契约性禁反言已经被合约性禁反言吸收(absorb)了,但近期有关合约性禁反言的先例都没有提到契约性禁反言的本质与要件。契约性禁反言的本质可节录澳大利亚的 TV Shopping Network Ltd. v. Scutt & Anor (1998) NSWSC 705 先例中 Young 大法官所说:“Deeds are the most solemn formal act that parties can enter into and the law is that they meant what they say. Should this action have been an action on the deed, no - one would have allowed to deny any statement of fact in it.”

构成契约性禁反言要满足五个要件:(1)双方之间存在有效的契约;(2)契约中

---

〔20〕《Chitty on Contracts》(第 32 版,2015 年)一书之 13 - 107 段的脚注 499 在介绍了有关完整合约条文的先例后,说:“It has been suggested that the clause may in any event be ineffective under s. 3 of the Misrepresentation Act 1967 (as amended by s. 8 of the Unfair Contract Terms Act 1977) or under s. 3(2)(b)(ii) of the 1977 Act.”

有关于事实的陈述是来自(attributable)一方或双方契约方;[21](3)这个对事实的陈述属于合约的基础;(4)一方出尔反尔,否认该陈述来自他;(5)不存在契约是无效(void)或可使无效(voidable)或需要变更(rectifiable)等其他方面的抗辩。要满足这五个要件,看来是十分合乎逻辑。但现代的合约性禁反言的说法看来是与早期贵族院的 Greer v. Kettle (1938) AC 156 先例对契约性禁反言的权威说法格格不入。在该先例中,Maugham 勋爵分析说:"It is at least equally clear that in equity a party to a deed could not set up an estoppel in reliance on a deed. . . in reliance on an untrue statement or an untrue recital induced by his own representation, whether innocent or otherwise, to the other party."

Maugham 勋爵以上所讲是说从衡平法角度考虑,契约一方不能因为依赖来自(attribute)他的错误陈述(无论是无辜的误述或是疏忽的误述)而构成契约性禁反言。但在上诉庭的 Peekay Intermark v. Australia & New Zealand Banking Group (2006) 2 Lloyd's Rep. 511 (CA)先例与 Springwell Navigation v. JP Morgan Chase Bank (2010) EWCA Civ 1212 先例后,现代合约性禁反言的说法只考虑合约条文的措辞/用字,而不考虑是谁做出的错误陈述。实际上,往往是一方在合约谈判时做出了错误陈述后,以完整合约条文构成合约性禁反言为由禁止另一方引入证据证明存在该错误陈述,可以说与上述 Maugham 勋爵所讲完全相反。

3.2.2　偏离了上诉庭的 Lowe v. Lombank 先例

Lowe v. Lombank (1960) 1 WLR 196 先例在很长一段时间都被用来支持合约中对事实的确认只有在构成陈述性禁反言时才有效的说法。但现代合约性禁反言的说法可以说完全偏离与改写了该上诉庭先例的判法。因此,McMeel 教授把现代合约性禁反言称为"文件基要主义"(documentary fundamentalism),即合约文件的写法至高无上。

在英国法下,法院或仲裁庭十分重视记载双方商业交易的合约文件与双方选择的措辞/用字,不存在法院以善意(good faith)或公平合理等原则或说法改写商业交易的双方通过艰难的谈判才确定的合约的危险。这可见 Steyn 勋爵在 Society of

---

〔21〕 Sean Wilken QC 与 Karim Ghaly 先生更近期所著的《The Law of Waiver, Variation, and Estoppel》(第3版,2012年)一书之12.04段与12.08段针对这一点说:"There is no term which accurately describes the parties to an estoppel by deed. Representor and representee are not quite accurate because of the mutuality of many of the statements which give rise to an estoppel by deed. . . . Superficially it has more in common with the mutual assumption that triggers the operation of estoppel by convention. However, in reality, neither estoppel by deed nor estoppel by representation will operate unless the statement is attributable to(被禁反言的一方). As far as estoppel by deed is concerned, in many cases that attribution will flow from the fact that (被禁反言的一方)has executed the deed in which the statement was contained. However, this is not invariably the case. If it can be shown that the parties intended the statement to be attributable to a person other than(被禁反言的一方), no estoppel by deed will arise."

Lloyd's v. Robinson (1999) 1 All ER (Comm) 545 先例所说:"Loyalty to the text of a commercial contract, instrument or document read in its contextual setting is the paramount principle of interpretation."

另在 2005 年 10 月 18 日的"The Commercial Bar Association Lecture", Falconer 勋爵说:"English law is respected by the commercial community – our common law of contract is now a world – wide commodity. It has become so because it is a system that people like. In ever more complex, sophisticated and inter – related markets, English commercial law provides predictability of outcome, legal certainty, and fairness. It is clear and built upon well – founded principles, such as the ability to require exact performance and the absence of any general duty of good faith."

但 McMeel 教授认为现代合约性禁反言走得太远,完全忽视了商业上的现实与公正[22]说:"... over the last five years a sequence of decisions of the High Court and Court of Appeal have embraced virtues of English law to excess, tipping the commercial approach over into a philosophy which can be described as documentary fundamentalism. Applied mechanically, this approach will often require judges to abdicate responsibility for determining whether or not the contract before them was procured by false statements during the negotiation process, however fundamental or negligent those misrepresentation may have been."

McMeel 教授希望最高院能在适当的先例中,将合约性禁反言的说法重新收紧。在后来的先如 AXA Sun Life Services Plc. v. Campbell Martin Ltd. (2011) 2 Lloyd's Rep. 1 先例中,也说到被告认为 Springwell Navigation v. JP Morgan Chase Bank (2010) EWCA Civ 1212 先例是错判,并保留上诉到最高院的权利,希望最高院能改过来。

4. 完整合约条文或类似条文能否排除误述

但笔者认为 McMeel 教授对误述(欺诈、疏忽或无辜)无法获得救济的担心有点过度,尤其是考虑上诉庭的 Peekay Intermark v. Australia & New Zealand Banking Group (2006) 2 Lloyd's Rep. 511 (CA)先例与 Springwell Navigation v. JP Morgan Chase Bank (2010) EWCA Civ 1212 先例后的判决。

4.1 普通法地位

首先,笔者可节录《Chitty on Contracts》(第 32 版,2015 年)一书之 13 – 115 段所说的普通法地位,即合约一方永远可以引入外来证据(extrinsic evidence)证明存在欺

[22] 现实谈判中连哄带骗,严重误述令对方订立商业合约的例子很多。

诈、非法或误述,以推翻契约或合约条文:"**Fraud**, **illegality**, **etc**. Extrinsic evidence will always be admitted to defeat a deed or written contract on the ground of fraud〔23〕, illegality〔24〕, misrepresentation〔25〕 . . . "

在本章稍后的第6段与第7段会介绍,因为公共政策(public policy)的原因,任何合约条文都不能超越普通法对欺诈与非法的规定。而针对误述,普通法地位可以通过清楚的合约条文改变,这显然也就是完整合约条文(包括没有依赖条文与没有陈述条文)希望达到的效果。

但即使是根据合约性禁反言,完整合约条文能否排除谈判时所做出的错误陈述(即使是非欺诈性,更不用说是欺诈性)的普通法地位,也要看条文的措辞/用字。而法律在这方面很清楚,任何人想依赖排除误述的条文都会被严格解释。

4.2　有关先例介绍

在 Alman and Benson v. Associated Newspapers Group Ltd. (20 June 1980, unreported)先例中,相关条文的措辞/用字是"the entire agreement and understanding",这被法院判是不能排除误述的责任。Browne - Wilkins 大法官说,"understanding"一词指双方共同的理解与用来排除附带保证/协议(collateral warranty),要排除误述的责任需要更进一步的说法,如"acknowledging that the parties had not relied on any representations in entering into the contract"(一条没有依赖条文)。

在 Thomas Witter Ltd. v. TBP Industries Ltd. (1996) 2 All ER 573 先例中,Jacob 大法官判是条文说明合约一方没有被所列陈述外的陈述引导(induce)订立合约,并不足以排除所列陈述外的误述责任。Jacob 大法官说:"if a clause is to have the effect of excluding or reducing remedies for damaging untrue statements then the party seeking that protection cannot be mealy - mouthed in his clause. He must bring it home that he is limiting liability for falsehoods he may have told."

在之后的 Deepak Fertilisers and Petrochemicals Corp v. ICI Chemicals and Polymers Ltd. (1999) 1 Lloyd's Rep. 387 先例中,相关的完整合约条文没有提到任何陈述或误述,只是说:"This CONTRACT comprises the entire agreement between the PARTIES. . . and there are not any agreements, oral or written, expressed or implied, concerning the subject matter which are not merged into this CONTRACT and superseded hereby."

一审([1998] 2 Lloyd's Rep. 139)的 Rix 大法官判是该条文只能排除附带保证,而不能排除误述的责任。上诉庭在这点支持了 Rix 大法官的判决,不支持被告上诉时将同样的陈述分为附带保证与误述这一十分技术性(highly technical to draw a dis-

---

〔23〕 见 Pickering v. Doowson (1813) 4 Taunt. 779 等先例。

〔24〕 见 Collins v. Blantern (1787) 2 Wils. 347 等先例。

〔25〕 见 Pennsylvania Shipping Co. v. Compagnie Nationale de Navigation (1936) 2 All ER 1167 等先例。

tinction between misrepresentations and collateral warranties based on the selfsame representations)的争议。

在 Inntrepreneur Pub Co. v. East Crown Ltd.（2000）2 Lloyd's Rep. 611 先例中，有关的完整合约条文只是简单而言："this Agreement... constitutes the entire Agreement between the parties."

Lightman 大法官首先说明了这类完整合约条文的目的，说："The purpose of an entire agreement clause is to preclude a party to a written agreement threshing the undergrowth and finding in the course of negotiations some (chance) remark or statement (often long forgotten or difficult to recall or explain) on which to found a claim such as the present to the existence of a collateral warranty... For such a clause constitutes a binding agreement between the parties that the full contractual terms are to be found in the document containing the clause and not elsewhere."

Lightman 大法官接着对排除附带保证与排除误述进行了区分，也提到完整合约条文一般不能排除误述，所以会加上一条没有陈述条文(no representation clause)，说："An entire agreement provision does not preclude a claim in misrepresentation, for the denial of contractual force to a statement cannot affect the status of the statement as a misrepresentation. The same clause in an agreement may contain both an entire agreement provision and a further provision designed to exclude liability for misrepresentation and breach of duty."

在 Man Nutzfahrzeuge AG v. Freightliner Ltd.（2005）EWHC 2347（Comm）先例中，相关条文可节录如下："This Agreement together with the Ancillary Agreements constitutes the entire agreement between the Parties and supersedes all prior agreements, understandings, negotiations and discussions, whether oral or written, of the Parties. **There are no representations**, warranties, covenants, conditions or other agreements, express or implied, collateral, statutory or otherwise, **between the Parties in connection with the subject matter of this Agreement** except as specifically set forth herein and none of the Parties has relied or is relying on any other information, discussion or understanding in entering into and completing the transactions contemplated in this Agreement and the Ancillary Agreements... **Nothing in this Section** 14.10 **shall affect any Party's liability for fraud or fraudulent misrepresentation**."(加黑部分是笔者的强调)

Moore－Bick 大法官分析了这条复杂与全面的完整合约条文与没有陈述条文(第二句)，认为可以排除误述的责任，但是因为最后一句明确写明不影响欺诈或欺诈性误述，所以只能排除无辜或疏忽的误述责任。Moore－Bick 大法官说：

"While recognising that this clause specifically excludes fraud from the scope of its operation, Mr. Vos(被告代表大律师)submitted that it clearly was intended to prevent the purchaser from seeking relief of any kind based on innocent or negligent misrepresentations. He argued that either MN(原告)relied on representations or it did not. It made no sense to say that MN did not rely on representations if they were made innocently or negligently, but did rely on representations if they were made fraudulently.

I can see the logic of that submission, but in my view it fails to have sufficient regard to the parties' intentions in including this provision in the agreement. The first two sentences are in my view intended to make it clear that the agreement contains the definitive statement of the parties' rights and liabilities arising out of the negotiations. Although the second sentence is worded in terms of an absence of any representations etc. outside the agreement itself, it does in fact operate as a contractual renunciation of the right to rely on anything said or done in the course of the negotiations as giving rise to a ground of complaint, or indeed for any other purpose. To that extent the clause does alter the parties' positions, but it is subject to the exception in the final sentence which makes it clear that they did not intend to give up the right to hold each other liable for fraud or fraudulent misrepresentations made before entering into the agreement. For these reasons I am satisfied that Section 14.10 does not prevent MN(原告) from holding Freightliner (被告)liable for the fraud of Mr. Ellis."

在 Trident Turboprop (Dublin) Ltd. v. First Flight Couriers Ltd. (2008) 2 Lloyd's Rep. 581 先例中，相关条文的措辞/用字是："The Lessee(FFCL)also agrees and acknowledges that save as expressly stated in this Agreement and the other Transaction Documents to which the Lessor(Trident) is a party, **the Lessor has not and shall not be deemed to have made any** warranties or **representations**, express or implied, about the Aircraft, including but not limited to the matters referred to above."(加黑部分是笔者的强调)

Aikens 大法官认为该没有陈述条文(no representation clause)足够排除无辜与疏忽的误述的责任，说："Here the parties agree that no representation was made at all. FFCL has agreed with Trident that a state of affairs is the case, ie. that there were no pre - contract (non - fraudulent) representations by Trident. More importantly, the parties agree that this state of affairs is to form the basis of the transaction. Even if it was not in fact the case that there had been no representations, the parties are free to agree that it was so and base their contractual relations on that state of affairs... Therefore... I conclude that Trident can rely on that clause to defeat the misrepresentation defence."

该租约另有一条条文说："The Lessee gives up any rights against the Lessor regarding any warranty or representation, except in respect of any warranty or representation expressly made in this Agreement or the other Transaction Documents to which Lessor is a party. The Lessee cannot make any claim against the Lessor at any time after Delivery relation to the condition of the aircraft."

针对这条条文,Aikens 大法官认为不能排除欺诈与欺诈性误述,说:"This conclusion is reinforced when the position in respect of fraudulent misrepresentations... They will not be excluded because of the law's attitude to fraud, particularly in a commercial context. **Fraud is 'a thing apart', proof of which unravels all. On public policy grounds the law does not permit a party to exclude liability for its own fraud.**〔26〕 Liability for the fraudulent acts of a party's agents will only be excluded if the language of the contract is in clear and unmistakable terms: see the HIH case at paragraphs 15 – 16 per Lord Bingham of Cornhill.〔27〕 Rights in respect of fraudulent misrepresentations, whether by Trident or its agent, are therefore not waived by clause 19.2. However, given that rights in respect of all types of fraudulent misrepresentation claims are not given up, it is necessary to ask: what rights are covered by the clause? In my view, the comprehensive wording of the clause indicates clearly that it was the parties' intention and agreement that FFCL agreed to give up all its rights based on all other types of misrepresentation by Trident."(加黑部分是笔者的强调)

在 BSkyB Ltd. v. HP Enterprise Services UK Ltd.（2010）EWHC 86（TCC）先例中,相关条文的措辞/用字是:"this Agreement and the Schedules shall together represent the entire understanding and constitute the whole agreement between the parties in relation to its subject matter and supersede any previous discussions, correspondence, representations or agreement between the parties with respect thereto notwithstanding the existence of any provision of any such prior agreement that any rights or provisions of such prior agreement shall survive its termination... This clause does not exclude liability of either party for fraudulent mis-representation."

Ramsey 大法官考虑了上述介绍的先例后,认为该条文的措辞/用字不足以排除无辜与疏忽的欺诈性误述的责任。Ramsey 大法官判决的主要部分可节录如下:"Those words **do not, in my judgment, amount to an agreement that representations are withdrawn, overridden or of no legal effect so far as any liability for misrepresentation may be concerned.** It provides that the Agreement represents the entire understanding and constitutes the whole agreement. It is in that context that the Agreement supersedes any previous representations. That is, representations are superseded and do not become terms of the Agreement unless they are included in the Agreement. If it had intended to withdraw representations for all purposes then the language would, in my judg-

〔26〕 欺诈是异类,因为公共政策是不允许一方合约方排除欺诈的责任。

〔27〕 而只有在合约条文完全清楚无误的情况下,法律才允许一方合约方排除他的代理人欺诈的责任:见 HIH Casualty and General Insurance Ltd. and Ors v. Chase Manhattan Bank and Ors（2003）2 Lloyd's Rep. 61 先例(将在本章之 4.5 段详细介绍)。

ment, have had to go further ... In this case the statement that the Agreement superseded any previous discussions, correspondence, representations or agreement between the parties with respect to the subject matter of the agreement prevented other terms of the agreement or collateral agreement from having contractual effect. It did not supersede those matters so far as there might be any liability for misrepresentation based on them ... Secondly, while there is a reference to representations, there is **nothing in the clause that indicates that it is intended to take away a right to rely on misrepresentations... I consider that clear words are needed to exclude a liability for negligent misrepresentation** and that this clause does not include any such wording."（加黑部分是笔者的强调）

在 Springwell Navigation v. JP Morgan Chase Bank（2010）EWCA Civ 1212 先例中，上诉庭确认了 Peekay Intermark v. Australia & New Zealand Banking Group（2006）2 Lloyd's Rep. 511（CA）先例的判决，判一条没有陈述条文可以有效排除误述责任，而不需要像 Lowe v. Lombank（1960）1 WLR 196（CA）先例一样要求满足陈述性禁反言的要件。

4.3　AXA Sun Life Services Plc. v. Campbell Martin Ltd. 先例

在 AXA Sun Life Services Plc. v. Campbell Martin Ltd.（2011）2 Lloyd's Rep. 1 先例中，案情涉及 AXA 保险公司授权 Campbell Martin 作为代表销售保险产品，双方的合约有一条完整合约条文（第 24 条）说："This Agreement and the Schedules and documents referred to herein constitute the entire agreement and understanding between you and us in relation to the subject matter thereof. Without prejudice to any variation as provided in clause 1.1, **this Agreement shall supersede any prior** promises, agreements, **representations**, undertakings or implications **whether made orally or in writing** between you and us relating to the subject matter of this Agreement but this will not affect any obligations in any such prior agreement which are expressed to continue after termination."（加黑部分显示了这条完整合约条文所用的文字是"本文书合约超越了以前不论是口头或文书所做出的陈述"。）

在该先例中，Campbell Martin 指 AXA 曾经作出误述，但 AXA 以上述完整合约条文作为抗辩之一。上诉庭在这一点是判 AXA 败诉，其中 Stanley Burnton 大法官说：

"I have no doubt that **clause** 24 **does not exclude or supersede misrepresentations as to matters that are not the subject of the term of the agreement.** Notwithstanding the words of... 'this Agreement shall supersede any prior... representations... I have difficulty in seeing how a written agreement can 'supersede' a representation that does not relate to the terms of the agreement. Thus, I think that a representation by AXA such as 'We are the largest insurance company in the country', if false and relied upon, is not superseded by the clause.

In an effort to give some effect to the inclusion of the word ‘representations’, I initially considered that a representation that relates to the terms of the agreement could be excluded or superseded. However, having read and been convinced by Rix LJ's compelling judgment, I have resiled from this position. In summary, in addition to the difficulty of reading ‘representations’ as including ‘misrepresentations’, as Rix LJ points out, such representations do not relate to ‘the subject matter’ of the agreement, but to the terms of the agreement. The context too points away from the interpretation contended by AXA."(加黑部分是笔者的强调)

Rix 大法官说：

"... Given that the clause as a whole is concerned with agreements rather than misrepresentations, and that the word ‘misrepresentations’ does not appear in it, it is not to my mind fertile ground for AXA's submission. Nevertheless, the word ‘representations’ does appear, albeit it will be seen that it is completely sand – wiched between words of contractual import, namely prior ‘promises, agreements,... undertakings or implications’.[28] It will also be observed that... does not in terms state either that no representations have been made, or that no reliance has been placed on any representations, or that liability for (mis)representations is excluded: each of which is a traditional way in which potential liability for misrepresentations has been sought to be avoided.

In these circumstances, I would be inclined, subject to authority, to regard clause 24 as being concerned only with matters of agreement, and not with misrepresentation at all. The essence of agreement is that it is concerned with matters which the parties have agreed. The essence of misrepresentation, however,, is that it is not concerned with what the parties have agreed, butrather with inaccurate statement (innocently, negligently or fraudulently inaccurate statements) which have been made by one party to the other, have been relied on by the representee in entering into their agreement... In a clause therefore... in which all the other sibling words in the critical part are words of agreement, and where the critical single word ‘representations’ (not [mis]representations) is likely in context to refer to representations which might be argued, but for the clause, to have been **terms** of the agreement... I would thus provisionally conclude that misrepresentation and the exclusion of misrepresentation or liability for it are simply not the business of the clause at all ...

---

〔28〕 第24条文虽然没有“误述”一词，但毕竟有提到“陈述”一词。这词是夹在其他合约性质的文字，如订约前谈判中曾做出的承诺(promise)、协议(agreement)、保证(undertaking)等。所以，“陈述”一词应是针对同样合约性质的事实，不会是针对性质完全不同的误述。

（在参考了一些之前的先例后，Rix 大法官总结说）No doubt all such cases are only authority for each clause's particular wording：nevertheless it seems to me that there are certain themes which deserve recognition. Among them is that the exclusion of liability for misrepresentation has to be clearly stated. It can be done by clauses which state the parties' agreement that there have been no representations made；or that there has been no reliance on any representations；or by an express exclusion of liability for misrepresentation. However，save in such contexts，and particularly where the word 'representations' takes its place alongside other words expressive of contractual obligation，talk of the parties' contract superseding such prior agreement will not by itself absolve a party of misrepresentation where its ingredients can be proved.〔29〕"

4.4　谈判时做出的欺诈性误述能否在现代合约性禁反言说法下被排除？

以上的先例可以看到与排除附带保证/协议（collateral warranty/contract）不同，要通过条文排除误述的责任十分困难，这要求条文的措辞/用字十分清楚。普通的完整合约条文一般达不到这个要求，必须包括没有依赖条文或没有陈述条文，才会有机会。但即使条文的措辞/用字再清楚，也不能排除欺诈（deceit）。上述介绍的先例中往往明示相关条文不能排除欺诈性误述（fraudulent misrepresentation）的责任，但如果没有明示针对欺诈性误述，一方能否利用相关条文排除责任？

首先，民事法律中对欺诈的定义相对广泛，这可见在著名的 Derry v. Peek（1889）14 App. Case. 337 先例中，Herschell 勋爵所说："... fraud is proved when it is shown that a false representation has been made：（1）knowingly；or（2）without belief in its truth；or（3）recklessly，careless whether it be true or false."因此，民事法律的欺诈与刑事法律的欺诈（2006 年《The Fraud Act》的立法中有定义〔30〕）不同，不必证明被告的动机是不诚实（dishonesty）：Polhill v. Walter（1832）3 B & Ad 114；Denton v. G. N. Ry（1856）5 E & B 860；Brown Jenkinson & Co. Ltd. v. Percy Dalton（London）Ltd.（1957）2 QB 621（涉及发货人做出保函以交换船东签发虚假清洁提单）；

---

〔29〕虽然每个先例只是针对有关完整合约条文特定文字的权威先例中，但还是可以看到一些解释这种条文的共同认知。其中之一就是排除误述的责任需要明确写明。写法上可以是说明双方同意在谈判中没有做出过任何陈述，或是对这些陈述没有任何依赖，或明示排除误述的责任。但在本先例中，只把以前的陈述与其他合约的承诺（以前的承诺、协议、承担与默示）一并说是被文书合约超越并不足够。

〔30〕有关定义是 Section 2："**Fraud by false representation**（1）A person is in breach of this section if he—（a）dishonestly makes a false representation，and（b）intends，by making the representation—（i）to make a gain for himself or another，or（ii）to cause loss to another or to expose another to a risk of loss.（2）A representation is false if—（a）it is untrue or misleading，and（b）the person making it knows that it is，or might be，untrue or misleading.（3）"Representation" means any representation as to fact or law，including a representation as to the state of mind of—（a）the person making the representation，or（b）any other person."

Standard Chartered Bank v. Pakistan National Shipping Corp（No. 2）（2002）UKHL 43（同样涉及虚假提单）；Gabriel v. Little（2013）EWCA Civ 1513；Morrell v. Stewart（2015）EWHC 962（Ch）（如果卖方明知房子做了一些修缮工程，但以为问题已经解决，就声称没有做过工程属于欺诈）等先例。

"欺诈超越一切"（fraud unravels all）的说法一定可以适用在刑事欺诈。欺诈性误述也可能会构成刑事欺诈，如故意欺骗（deceit）另一方。显然，无论完整合约条文或没有依赖条文或类似的条文的措辞/文字写得多清楚，双方都不能通过合约条文排除这种故意与不诚实的欺诈性误述的责任。但同样也是欺诈性误述的鲁莽（reckless）不理会陈述是真或假，看来本质上与疏忽（negligence）或严重疏忽（gross negligence）一样，只是程度上有区别，不会是刑事欺诈，就不应阻止合约方通过条文排除责任。毕竟，明示排除疏忽责任在商业活动中经常发生。在 Sabah Shipyard（Pakistan）Ltd. v. Pakistan（2008）1 Lloyd's Rep. 210 先例中，Christopher Clarke 大法官说："The guarantee（issued by the defendant, Government of Pakistan）has an entire agreement clause. But **such a clause cannot**, as Sabah accepts, **exclude liability in the case of deceit** unless the guarantee is very clearly worded **and the deceit is not that of a party to the contract itself**."（加黑部分是笔者的强调）

这又涉及另一方面的问题，合约一方不能通过合约条文明示排除自己做出欺诈性陈述的责任，这是公共政策，应该没有疑问。但如果不诚实的欺诈不是出自合约一方，而是第三人（但该合约方在合约下要为他负责），合约方能否明示排除责任？Christopher Clarke 大法官说的不涉及合约一方自己欺诈的情况，可以举两个简单的例子。一是代理人做出欺诈性误述，但委托人自己不知情。当然委托人也可能是自己鲁莽或不小心（careless），没有理会代理人的陈述，但也可能是委托人自己根本无法控制的情况，像稍后会介绍的 HIH Casualty and General Insurance Ltd. and Ors v. Chase Manhattan Bank and Ors（2003）2 Lloyd's Rep. 61 先例。二是做出误述的一方自己也被第三方欺骗（如合约链中的上一手卖家）。但他没有求证，而是很鲁莽与不小心地将这个欺诈性误述转给了无辜方，当然也有可能是他根本无法求证。如一份倒签的提单（back - dated bills of lading），中间商可能是鲁莽与不小心，没有调查，也可能是根本没法知道，就通过背书与交出这份倒签的提单，将货物转卖给最后的买方/收货人。但本质上对无辜方来说，这些错误陈述还是欺诈性，区别只是陈述方（较早的例子就是中间商）自己有没有参与欺诈。而如果没有，看来就可能可以通过措辞/用字必须十分清楚的条文排除这种误述责任。

4.5 可以排除代理人（不涉及委托人）的欺诈性误述责任的 HIH Casualty and General Insurance Ltd. and Ors v. Chase Manhattan Bank and Ors 先例

在贵族院的 HIH Casualty and General Insurance Ltd. and Ors v. Chase Manhattan Bank and Ors（2003）2 Lloyd's Rep. 61 先例中，案情涉及 90 年代发展起来的一种名为"time variable contingency"或简称"TVC facility"的保险。这种保险的对象是电影

项目,显然主要来自好莱坞。摄制电影是一种高风险、高利润的商业活动或项目,其中的风险包括拍摄超过预算、中途演员出现意外或丑闻而不得不替换演员重拍、与几部大片撞期导致排片与票房受到影响等。而现在一部电影,尤其是好莱坞大片的投资常常是上亿美元,如此巨额的投资,必然需要向银行融资,而银行为了尽量规避风险,就会要求借款人购买保险。这种保险可能是电影公司或者投资方/制片人作为被保险人(assured),但需要把保险赔付的利益转让(assign)给银行。也可能像 HIH Casualty and General Insurance Ltd. and Ors v. Chase Manhattan Bank and Ors 先例一样,是融资的银行作为被保险人。但银行作为被保险人就会面临一个问题,通常保险公司需要知道很多细节才能决定是否承保与保费多少,而银行不清楚这些细节,只能依靠电影公司或者投资方/制片人的陈述,如主演与导演是谁、拍摄地点在哪儿、拍摄时间的长度与预算是多少等。所以在该先例中,由于融资银行[美国大通银行作为银团(syndicate)的带头人]作为被保险人,所以在 TVC facility 的保单中有一条名为"Statement of Truth"的条文,明示免除或放弃(waive)大通银行对错误陈述的责任,[31]因为有关的陈述(并以明示条文的形式在保单内说明)是保险人(HIH)通过经纪人(Heaths)向电影公司(Elmwood Films)取得的事实陈述。相关条文可节录如下:

"It is a condition precedent to this Policy that:

Truth of Statement Elmwood Films Inc. has truthfully completed Section I of the Questionnaire to the best of its knowledge. Any reference in the Questionnaire to the Revenue Participation Agreement is qualified by reference to the copy thereof attached to the Questionnaire or the Declaration. In completing the Questionnaire, Elmwood may rely on certificates of third parties to the extent such reliance is disclosed on the Questionnaire.

Provided that Elmwood films Inc. completes the sections of the Questionnaire required to be completed by it and delivers the same to the Lead Insurers (**it being acknowledged that any misstatement in any part of the questionnaire** (other than Section 1 thereof) **shall not be the responsibility of the Insured or constituted a ground for avoidance of the insurers' obligations under the Policy or the cancellation thereof**). In addition, the failure of Elmwood Films Inc. , to update Section I of the Questionnaire for a film Production **shall not be the responsibility of the Insured or constitute a ground for avoidance of the insurers' obligation under the Policy or the cancel-**

---

〔31〕 1906 年《海上保险法》要求,被保险人必须准确陈述与披露所有情况,尤其是对保险人不利的情况,否则会导致保险合约无效与不能获得赔付。但在 2015 年《保险法》生效后,即使是保险合约,在这方面的善意责任也有了改变和限制。这条"Statement of Truth"条文一直以来主要目的就是防止保险人以被保险人没有准确陈述与披露所有情况为由逃避保险合约的赔付,做法通常是把无边无际的陈述与披露责任(两者有时也很难区分)界定在一份详细与有针对性的问卷中,而受保人只要准确回答了这些问题,保险人/保险公司明示承诺不得以普通法下要求的准确陈述与完全披露被违反为由,逃避保险合约。

lation thereof. Subject to the obligations of the Insured under 'General Conditions – Due Diligence Clause' after acceptance by the Lead Insurers of the Declaration with regard to the Film Production, **the Insured will not have any duty or obligation to make any representation**, warranty or disclosure of any nature, **express or implied** (**such duty and obligation being expressly waived by the insurers**) **and shall have no liability of any nature** of the insurers for any information provided by or nondisclosure by other parties including, but not limited to, Heath North America & Special Risks Ltd. (other than section 1 of the Questionnaire) shall not be a ground or grounds for avoidance of the insurers' obligations under the Policy or the cancellation thereof."(加黑部分是笔者的强调)

该保险涉及5部好莱坞电影,显然后来发生严重亏损,才有了这个争议。作为被保险人,大通银行向HIH索赔损失。但HIH拒赔并指控投保时Heaths曾经对HIH做出过多个欺诈性误述。如说该保险涉及的电影公司与几年前的另一个保险所涉及的电影公司基本一样,但事实却上有重大不同。而Heaths在做出陈述时,知道陈述不正确,所以构成欺诈性误述。

在该贵族院先例中,针对的并非对事实的认定(即是否有发生过HIH指称的误述),而是该"Statement of Truth"广泛的措辞/用字能够在何种程度保护大通银行。贵族院的判决是如果Heaths做出的误述是疏忽(negligent)或无辜(innocent),该条文足够保护大通银行。但如果Heaths做出的是欺诈性误述,该条文则不足够。有关的理由可以节录Bingham勋爵所说如下:

"Lord Grabiner QC(大通银行代表大律师)for Chase emphasised the comprehensive language already noted, 'no liability of any nature'. Read literally, those words would cover liability for fraudulent misrepresentation, or deceit. If Chase's security for its loan is to be cast-iron, the policy must stand even if induced by the deceit of Heaths.

This is not a negligible argument. But neither the judge nor the Court of Appeal accepted it and I am satisfied that they were right not to do so. For, as Rix LJ observed more than once in his judgment (paragraphs 160, 169), **fraud is a thing apart. This is not a mere slogan. It reflects an old legal rule that fraud unravels all: fraus omnia corrumpit. It also reflects the practical basis of commercial intercourse.** Once fraud is proved, 'it vitiates judgments, contracts and all transactions whatsoever': Lazarus Estates Ltd. v. Beasley [1956] 1 QB 702 at 712, per Denning LJ. **Parties entering into a commercial contract will no doubt recognise and accept the risk of errors and omissions in the preceding negotiations, even negligent errors and omissions. But each party will assume the honesty and good faith of the other; absent such an assumption they would not deal. What is true of the principal is true of the agent**, not least in a situation where, as here, the agent, if not the sire of the transaction, plays the role of a very active midwife...

It is clear that the law, on public policy grounds, does not permit a contracting party to exclude liability for his own fraud in inducing the making of the contract. The insurers have throughout contended for a similar rule in relation to the fraud of agents acting as such. After a very detailed examination of such authority as there is, **both the judge... and the Court of Appeal... decided against the existence of such a rule**... I do not however think that the question need be finally resolved in this case. For it is in my opinion plain beyond argument that if **a party** to a written contract **seeks to exclude the ordinary consequences of fraudulent or dishonest misrepresentation or deceit by his agent**, acting as such, inducing the making of the contract, such intention **must be expressed in clear and unmistakable terms on the face of the contract... General words, however comprehensive the legal analyst might find them to be, will not serve: the language used must be such as will alert a commercial party to the extraordinary bargain he is invited to make.** It is no doubt unattractive for a contracting party to propose a term clearly having such effect, because of its predictable effect on the mind of the other contracting party ..."(加黑部分是笔者的强调)

上述所讲主要是大通银行认为该"Statement of Truth"条文的措辞/文字十分广泛,完全可以排除大通银行的所有误述责任(no liability of any nature),包括欺诈性误述。但无论上诉庭或Bingham大法官都认为欺诈超越一切。这是一切商业活动的基础,双方在交易时毫无疑问都知道谈判过程中有风险,双方可能对某些事实搞错或是看漏或是疏忽,但都可以假设对方不会欺诈,否则他们根本不会进行这个交易。涉及代理人时也如此,毕竟委托人要为代理人负责,现实中委托人在绝大多数情况下,也对代理人的欺诈知情或可以知情。法律是很清楚,因为公共政策的原因,一方不能以合约排除欺诈的责任。因此,保险公司认为委托人同样不能以合约排除他的代理人欺诈导致他要承担的责任。但在一审法院与上诉庭,都判是并没有这样的肯定说法。[32] 而Bingham勋爵认为,无需决定是否存在这样的说法,可以通过解释合约的一般规则与精神做出判决,即无论合约条文写得多清楚与完整,一般被广泛使用的用字无法排除欺诈性误述的责任。要排除欺诈性误述,相关的措辞/用字必须足够让一位商业人士警惕他在谈判的是一单非同寻常的交易,即对方可能是在欺骗自己,以达成这个交易。这样,几乎可以说所有被广泛使用的完整合约条文,包括没有依赖条文、没有陈述条文等都无法满足可以排除代理人做出的欺诈性误述的要求。因为这些在商业活动(不会假设对方欺诈)中广泛使用的条文不足以令对方警惕交易会涉及欺诈。而在该先例中,贵族院也就判大通银行败诉,因为TVC facility保单的"Statement of Truth"条文不足以令保险公司HIH警惕大通银行的代理人Heaths会涉

〔32〕 这代表英国法律在这点是被上诉庭确立。

及欺诈。

另在 Trident Turboprop (Dublin) Ltd. v. First Flight Couriers Ltd. (2008) 2 Lloyd's Rep. 581 先例中，Aikens 大法官说："This conclusion (the Defendant, FFCL, agreed to give up all rights in respect of all types of representation, other than fraudulent ones) is reinforced when the position in respect of fraudulent misrepresentations by either Trident or BAE acting as its agent are considered. They will not be excluded because of the law's attitude to fraud, particularly in a commercial context. Fraud is 'a thing apart', proof of which unravels all. **On public policy grounds the law does not permit a party to exclude liability for its own fraud. Liability for the fraudulent acts of a party's agents will only be excluded if the language of the contract is in clear and unambiguous terms...** Rights in respect of fraudulent misrepresentations, whether by Trident or its agent, are therefore not waived by clause 19.2. However misrepresentation claims are not given upon, it is necessary to ask: what rights are covered by the clause? In my view, the comprehensive wording of the clause indicates clearly that it was the parties' intention and agreement that FFCL agreed to give upon all the rights based on all other types of misrepresentation by Trident."(加黑部分是笔者的强调)

而在本章之4.4段所节录的 Christopher Clarke 大法官在 Sabah Shipyard (Pakistan) Ltd. v. Pakistan (2008) 1 Lloyd's Rep. 210 先例的判词也是同样的道理。

5. 其他可能构成合约性禁反言的条文

在很多其他的商业活动中，经常会有条文构成合约性禁反言，这在它们的语境(context)下是完全合理与可以接受，但却与本章较早介绍的会带来批评与对抗的完整合约条文或类似条文，或是 Lowe v. Lombank (1960) 1 WLR 196 先例的确认(不正确)事实条文(但该先例涉及消费者，已有立法保护)是两回事。本段以下举一些常见的例子并进行简单介绍。这些例子或条文已经被使用了几十年，都是以合约基础进行解释，不需要满足禁反言说法的要件才有效。

5.1 专家决定条文

专家决定条文的介绍可见杨良宜《合约的解释：规则与应用》的第十四章第2段。简单而言，一些商业合约中会约定针对一些专业或技术方面的问题或争议，由一位个人(通常是双方都可以接受的有名专家)做出决定，而该决定就是终局、结论性与对双方有约束力，从而提供一种相对快捷与便宜的非正式争议解决方式，或者防止争议的发生。这条文通常会在商品买卖合约与建筑合约中决定货物或工程质量是否符合要求、股份买卖合约决定股价、租约的租金调整条文决定新的租金、期租合约中决定调整的租金等情况出现。

大宗商品买卖合约(包括石油等湿货)普遍会有货物数量(如20万吨原油)或是质量很难确定的问题,在装港与卸港做出的检验结果一定会不同。为了防止最后需要通过昂贵与费时的谈判甚至诉讼解决争议,买卖双方(货物的价格取决于货物的数量或质量)会在合约中加上一条专家决定条文,约定在装港(如装船前24小时)做出的检验报告的结果就是最终与有约束力的。当然,双方也完全可以约定以卸港的结果为准,这完全是订约自由。这样,买卖合约本身构成了禁反言,禁止任何一方引入证据显示真正的事实与质疑约定为最终与有约束力的装港(或卸港)的检验结果的准确性。以石油产品的买卖合约为例,为防止货物在卸港被买方以质量不符合合约约定为由拒货,常常会有一条条文说:"Quality and quantity, basis shoretank, to be determined by a mutually agreed independent inspector at the loading installation, in the manner customary at such installation. **Such determination shall be final and binding for both parties, except in case of fraud or manifest error.**"(加黑部分是笔者的强调)

在股权转让协议(share transfer contract),相关的条文可以是:"The price of a share sale should be determined by the auditors for the time being of the company whose valuation acting as experts and not as arbitrators **shall be final and binding on all parties.**"(加黑部分是笔者的强调)

在合伙协议(partnership agreement),相关条文的例子是:"(A) In the event of any dispute regarding (i) the amount of any profit or loss allocations due to a Member pursuant to Clause 9 or (ii) any payment due to an Outgoing Member under Clause 17, ... any affected party **may refer the matter or matters in dispute to a partner in an independent firm of internationally recognised chartered accountants agreed upon between them, or failing such agreement within 7 days to be selected at the instance of any party by the President for the time being of the Institute of Chartered Accountants of England and Wales**. ... (B) Such accountant shall act as an expert and not as arbitrator and shall determine the matter or matters in dispute (which may include any dispute concerning the interpretation of any provision of this Agreement or his jurisdiction to determine the dispute or the content or interpretation of his terms of reference) and his decision **shall be final and binding on the parties hereto**."(加黑部分是笔者的强调)

而在造船合约(ship-building contract)也会有一条标准条文,说:

"The VESSEL, including its machinery and equipment, shall be designed and constructed in accordance with the rules and regulations of the Classification Society issued and having become effective up to an on the date of signing this Contract.

Decision of the Classification Society as to the compliance or noncompliance with the classification rules and regulations including those statutory rules and regulations which the Classification Society is authorized to act on behalf of the relevant authorities

shall be final and binding upon the Parties hereto."(加黑部分是笔者的强调)

在 Campbell v. Edwards (1976) 1 Lloyd's Rep. 522 先例中,Denning 勋爵认为这种条文会构成合约性禁反言:"It is simply the law of contract. If two persons agree that the price of property should be fixed by a valuer on whom they agree, and he gives that valuation honestly and in good faith, they are bound by it. Even if he has made a mistake they are still bound by it. The reason is because they have agreed to be bound by it. If there were fraud or collusion, of course, it would be different. Fraud or collusion unravels everything."

另在 Bernhard Schulte v. Nile Holdings (2004) 2 Lloyd's Rep. 352 先例中,Cooke 大法官也说:"The determination will be binding between them unless it can be challenged on the basis of fraud, collusion, bias[33] or material departure from instruction[34], but if there has been negligence on the part of the expert, the damaged party may sue the expert in respect of any loss suffered."

5.2 提单上记载的数量

针对提单上对货物的描述,国际公约(1968 年《海牙—维斯比规则》)与立法(如英国 1992 年《海上货物运输法》)规定:"... proof to the contrary shall not be admissible when the Bill of Lading has been transferred to a third party acting in good faith."

这样,根据公约与立法规定,提单上的陈述就会构成"陈述性禁反言"(estoppel by representation),保护无辜的提单持有人(bills of lading holder)。但有一种情况是善意的无辜买方(根据提单支付了货款)无法获得这个立法的陈述性禁反言的保护。这就是 FOB 买方租船去装港装货,之后他的银行根据这套付运单证(尤其是提单)支付货价。但这套提单对作为承租人(charterer)的买方来说,只是货物收据。[35]《海牙—维斯比规则》(与相关的立法)的规定不适用于买方与船东之间的租约。因此为了享受同样的保护,FOB 买方通常会坚持在租约中加上一条条文从而构成"合约性禁反言"(contractual estoppel)。如在 The "Herroe" and "Askoe" (1986) 2 Lloyd's Rep. 281 先例中,相关的条文是:"The vessel owners are to be responsible for the number of bags/packages as signed for in the bills of lading. These bills of lading to be **conclusive evidence of the quantity of cargo shipped.**"(加黑部分是笔者的强调)

5.3 除非在特定时间内提出异议,否则就是最终

这种条文在各种不同类别的合约中都会出现。如在 Burroughs Adding Machine Ltd. v. Aspinall (1925) 41 TLR 276 (CA)先例中,双方的代理协议中明确规定除非经销商在公司发出对账单的 30 天内提出异议,否则该对账单就会被视为被经销商接

---

〔33〕 这例外将在本章之 7.1 段介绍。

〔34〕 这例外将在本章之 7.2 段介绍。

〔35〕 有关上述提单方面的问题,可参阅笔者的《提单与其他付运单证》(2016 年)一书。

受。经销商在收到对账单后，没有在规定时间内提出异议，因此被判不能之后再提出异议。

在国际货物买卖合约与程租合约中，滞期费（如装卸货延误超出了买卖合约或租约规定的装货时间，负责付运的 FOB 买方或 CIF/CFR 卖方或船东就有权向对方索赔滞期费）的计算总是十分困难与有争议性。这甚至可能涉及去装港或卸港对事实进行调查，如当时是否确实因为下雨等坏天气无法装卸货物，而根据滞期费条文的规定这段时间不应该计入装卸时间。所以，近来越来越多的条文会试图通过合约性禁反言令滞期费的计数尽量快捷与顺利，如果需要对事实进行调查，也能在证人的记忆还新鲜时进行。

这可以是对 FOB 卖方或 CIF/CFR 买方（买卖合约）或承租人（租约）有利的时效条文，即如果对方没有在很短的时间内提出滞期费的索赔，并附上详细的计算与支持的证据，就会被视为不存在滞期费的索赔。也可以是对 FOB 买方或 CIF/CFR 卖方（买卖合约）或船东（租约）有利的形式，即如果对方没有在收到滞期费索赔的一段时间内提出异议，FOB 买方或 CIF/CFR 卖方或船东对滞期费的计算就会被视为最终。

5.4　仲裁条文

仲裁条文也会构成合约性禁反言。在机构仲裁中，常常需要仲裁机构根据仲裁规则做出一些决定。如在《香港国际仲裁中心机构仲裁规则》（2013 版）之第 7 条与第 8 条规定了香港国际仲裁中心有权委任独任或首席仲裁员。《中国国际经济贸易仲裁委员会仲裁规则》（2015 版）之第 27 条与第 28 条也有类似规定。

有疑问的是，如果仲裁机构根据仲裁规则做出了决定，争议方对结果不满，是否可以提出上诉？一般来说，除非双方同意改变（这变为合约更改），答案是不可以。争议双方在仲裁条文中同意了在某个仲裁机构仲裁与受该机构仲裁规则约束，构成了合约性禁反言。而机构仲裁规则往往会规定它做出的决定是最终与有约束力的。如《香港国际仲裁中心机构仲裁规则》（2013 版）之第 3.2 条就说："香港国际仲裁中心依本规则作出的任何决定都是终局的，且在任何适用法律允许的范围内不得上诉。"

因此，即使其中一方争议方对结果不满意，也会因为禁反言，不能提起上诉。

5.5　和解协议

在涉及土地的 Colchester BC v. Tillson & Others（1992）Ch 421 先例中，一位土地占用者（occupier of land）在和解协议中确认他对土地的占有不构成逆权侵占（adverse possession）。这就构成了合约性禁反言，他不能事后出尔反尔再在诉讼中说自己根据逆权侵占获得了土地的所有权。

在该先例中，在 1983 年 11 月的 12 年之前，Tillson 先生就侵占了政府拥有的土地。在 1983 年 11 月开始的通讯往来中，政府试图通过有偿给予他使用土地的许可（license）来规范他对土地的占有。但 Tillson 先生的律师在一开始坚持 Tillson 先生通过逆权侵占获得了土地的所有权。而在政府威胁要开始重新占有的程序后，1983

年11月3日，双方订立了一个租约，Tillson先生在租约中确认了政府对土地的所有权与他没有通过逆权侵占获得任何土地的权利（right）、所有权（title）或利益（interest）。在之后的诉讼中，政府希望法院宣告它才是土地的所有人，而Tillson先生只拥有租约中作为租客的权利。一审法院判Tillson先生被禁反言，不能声称他有任何所有权。之后Tillson先生上诉到了上诉庭，理由是他逆权侵占土地超过12年，根据《Limitation Act》，他获得了土地的所有权，而政府失去了的所有权是不能"复生"的。

上诉庭驳回了Tillson先生的上诉，判是1983年11月3日的租约是防止需要通过诉讼解决争议的善意的妥协。Tillson先生有自己的律师给予了法律建议，因此被合约性禁反言，不能再在诉讼中声称他通过逆权侵占获得了土地的所有权。笔者看来这先例也可以"承诺性禁反言"（promissory estoppel）或"陈述性禁反言"（estoppel by representation）解释。但这样，政府要证明满足禁反言的要件，如依赖并蒙受损害（detrimental reliance）。而这不一定存在，也就是可能无法满足要件。但有了清楚无误的和解协议，根据合约基础的合约性禁反言就简单得多。

6. 双方完全可以同意明知是错误的事实或法律地位

正如已经在本章第2段介绍的，在现代禁反言与订约自由的说法下，合约双方完全可以同意明知是错误的事实或法律地位，并构成合约性禁反言。Aikens大法官在Springwell Navigation v. JP Morgan Chase Bank（2010）EWCA Civ 1212先例中说："... I would say that A and B can agree that A has made no pre – contract representations to B about the quality or nature of a financial instrument that A is selling to B. Should it make any difference that both A and B know at and before making the contract, that A did, in fact, make representations, so that the statement that A had not is contrary to what each side knows is the case?... **Mr Brindle**（Springwell代表大律师）**did not show us any case that might support the proposition that parties cannot agree that X is the case even if both know that is not so. I am unaware of any legal principle to that effect**..."（加黑部分是笔者的强调）

另在Standard Chartered Bank v. Ceylon Petroleum Corporation（2011）EWHC 1785（Comm）先例中，Hamblen大法官说：

"I recently reviewed the recent authorities on contractual estoppel in Cassa di Risparmio della Repubblica di San Marino SpA v. Barclays Bank Plc.［2011］EWHC 484 at［492 – 508］.

Those authorities show that:... **parties to a contract may agree that a particular state of affairs is to be the basis upon which they are contracting, regardless of whether or not that state of affairs is true**, and that such an agreement may give rise to a ‘contractual estoppel’, precluding the assertion of facts inconsistent with those which have been agreed to form the basis of the contract.

Further：(1) If a term is to be construed as having this effect (and thereby prevent from arising the ordinary consequences which would otherwise follow as a matter of law) clear words are necessary...(2) Whether or not a clause or collection of clauses has this effect is a matter of construction of the contract. (3) The principle may not apply where there has been a misrepresentation as to the effect of the contractual documents which give rise to the estoppels...”(加黑部分是笔者的强调)

只有一种情况合约性禁反言不能成立,即违反公共政策(public policy),毕竟任何合约条文都不能超越公共政策。例如,如果一位仲裁员因为违反自然公正(natural justice)被质疑,根据《香港国际仲裁中心机构仲裁规则》(2013 版)之第 11 条或《国际商会国际仲裁院仲裁规则》(2017 版)第 14 条与第 15 条,仲裁机构可以做出决定是否要求仲裁员回避与替换仲裁员。但这并非最终与有决定性的,即使仲裁条文或仲裁规则里明确写明了这一点。对结果不满意的一方永远可以向仲裁所在地的监督法院(supervising court)上诉,因为自然公正属于公共政策,不可以通过合约排除。

7. 合约性禁反言的例外

现代合约性禁反言的说法是只要双方在合约中同意过以某些事实情况为准(如以专家决定为准),这就对双方是最终与有约束力的。在这种情况下,除非该专家决定涉及欺诈(fraud)、共谋(collusion)或偏见(bias),或者完全偏离了合约中的明示规定(如用了另一种检验方式),该专家的决定就对双方都有约束力。这两个例外情况在很多有关先例都提到,如在 5.1 段节录的 Bernhard Schulte v. Nile Holdings (2004) 2 Lloyd’s Rep. 352 先例。否则任何一方对结果不满意都不能引入证据证明真正或至少更正确的事实情况应该是怎样。事实上,如果一方否定该专家决定属于违约,但很多时候都会被说是被“禁反言”(estoppel)。

7.1　欺诈、共谋或偏见

第一个例外十分合乎逻辑与容易理解。已经多次提到,欺诈超越一切(Fraud Unravels All)。这属于公共政策(public policy)超越所有合约方的协议。一旦欺诈被证明,整个合约或合约有关部分就会变为无效。因此从逻辑上讲,如果欺诈或共谋被证明存在,合约性禁反言(如一条专家决定条文)就无效。欺诈的极端例子是专家受贿,也有可能是一方提供了假的材料让专家检验做出决定。

至于偏见(bias),看来是与自然公正(natural justice)或正当程序(due process)有关。自然公正有两条规则,针对仲裁第一条是仲裁员必须独立与不能有利益冲突,毕竟仲裁是司法程序/诉讼。但针对专家决定条文,如果买卖合约中约定的专家是卖方的专家(而不是双方共同委任的专家),该条文依然有约束力。如果不能证明欺诈或共谋的存在,买方不能以专家有利益冲突或缺乏独立性为由质疑结果。因此,为了保证能委任一位更中立与独立的专家,双方需要在谈判时同意一条更平衡的专家决定条文,特别是针对专家的资格与委任流程。简单而言,自然公正的第一条规则不适用在专家决定条文,毕竟这不是一个诉讼。但一般来说,合约方不会同意一条对其有损害的很不平衡的专家决定条文。另外,由于自然公正的第一条规则只适用在仲裁员而不适用在专家,因此,很多专家决定条文中会再次强调是专家而非仲裁员。

自然公正的第二条规则是:

1. 仲裁员必须让双方(尤其是利益受影响的一方)有足够的机会争辩其立场。但这在专家决定条文中也不适用,因为专家在做出决定时常常会私下调查,而他或她不需要在做出决定前再让双方对该调查做出回应:Bernhard Schulte v. Nile Holdings (2004) 2 Lloyd's Rep. 352; Owen Pel Limited v. Bindi (London) Limited (2008) EWHC 1420 (TCC)等先例。

2. 仲裁员与需要决定的争议必须没有利益关系(disinterested)与不存在偏见(unbiased)。因为这可能也会影响专家做出的决定的最终性与约束力。首先可将偏见分为两种:表面偏见与实际偏见。在 Porter v. Magill (2002) 2 AC 357 先例中,贵族院的 Hope 勋爵针对表面偏见说:"where the fair - minded and informed observer, having considered the facts, would conclude that there was a real possibility that the tribunal was biased."

在 Director General of Fair Trading v. Proprietary Association of Great Britain (2001) 1 WLR 700 先例中,上诉庭的 Phillips 勋爵针对实际偏见说:"where a judge had been influenced by partiality or prejudice in reaching his decision, and where it had been demonstrated that a judge is actually prejudiced in favour of or against the party."

像法官一样,仲裁员只要被证明存在偏见(无论是表面偏见或是实际偏见),他的裁决就会被撤销。毕竟仲裁与诉讼一样,必须严格遵守自然公正。但专家决定并非司法程序,所以在 Bernhard Schulte v. Nile Holdings 先例中,Cooke 大法官提到的欺诈、共谋与偏见的例外中的偏见,指的是实际偏见。即只有当专家被证明有实际偏见时,他的决定才会变为无效。

7.2 完全偏离了合约中的明示规定

第二个例外也很容易理解,实际上就是对合约的解释。如果合约中双方同意专家通过 A + B + C 的程序做出决定,而专家实际上通过 X + Y + Z 的程序做出决定,除非双方达成新的协议,否则专家做出的决定就不符合合约规定,不会在合约下有约束力。任何一方都有权说"这不是我在订立本合约时所同意的"。即使 X + Y + Z 的程序更新、更好与更准确,也是毫无意义与没有任何帮助的:Veba v. Petrotrade (2002) 1 Lloyd's Rep. 295 先例。

在 Kollerich v. The State Trading Corporation of India (1980) 2 Lloyd's Rep. 32

先例中,案情有关袋装水泥的买卖。相关合约中有条文规定卖方有权选择 A 或 B 两间检验机构中的一间在装港做检验,并以该机构做出的检验证书为终局。但卖方选择了 A 后,A 没有做任何检验,而是将检验的工作授权给了 C。之后在卸港,买方发现很多袋子已经开口,或在正常卸货过程中开口,于是向卖方提出索赔,而卖方依赖这一条专家决定条文与装港检验证书,认为无需负责。高院与上诉庭都判是根据相关专家决定条文的解释,应该只有 A 或 B 做出的检验证书才符合合约要求与有约束力,而并非任何一间其他检验机构。在该先例中,A 根本没有做出检验,而 C 做出的检验报告不符合合约规定,因此没有约束力。

在 Nikko Hotels (UK) Ltd. v. MEPC Plc. (1991) 2 EGLR 103 先例中,Knox 大法官说:"If he has answered the right question in the wrong way, his decision will be binding. If he has answered the wrong question, his decision will be a nullity."

在 Ackerman v. Ackerman and others (2011) EWHC 3428 (Ch)先例中, Vos 大法官说:"... a departure from substantive instructions would be material and would automatically invalidate a decision unless it was trivial whereas a departure from express or implied procedural instructions or unfairness will not always do so."

8. 合约性弃权

在订约自由下,合约双方也完全有权同意合约性弃权(无论是因选择而弃权还是因宽限而弃权)的自由。一般来说,合约性弃权会通过三种形式。

8.1　合约条文

通过合约条文构成合约性弃权(contractual waiver)的例子很多。如在 The "Pera" (1985) 2 Lloyd's Rep. 103 先例中,相关的仲裁与时效条文说:"Arbitration. Any claim must be made in writing and claimant's arbitrator appointed within 12 months of final discharge and where this provision is not complied with, the claim shall be deemed to be **waived** and absolutely barred."

这种时效条文因为写法的不同,可能是排除/放弃诉讼的权利(action barred),也可以是排除/放弃救济(remedy barred)。关于这两者的区别,在笔者的《提单与其他付运单证》(2016 年)一书第五章之 17.2.4 段有详论。

8.2　合约合并了有弃权规定的规则与条例

合约双方也可以同意适用一些规则与条例,而其中如果包括一些弃权的规定,就会构成合约性弃权。如信用证(letter of credit)一般会合并国际商会的 UCP 600,其第 16 条规定针对受益人递交议付信用证的付运文件有不符点时,银行可以自行决定联系申请人放弃(waive)不符点(一般是轻微的不符点)。如果银行决定拒付,必须在交单后 5 天内做出拒付通知,如果没有及时发出拒付通知,或是通知受益人有关的不符合要求,银行就等于放弃了以单证不符为由拒付的权利。

仲裁条文中合并了机构仲裁规则也是一样。如《中国国际经济贸易仲裁委员会仲裁规则》(2015 版)第 10 条提到了放弃异议的权利(Waiver of Right to Object),说:"一方当事人知道或理应知道本规则或仲裁协议中规定的任何条款或情事未被遵守,仍参加仲裁程序或继续进行仲裁程序而且不对此不遵守情况及时地、明示地提出书面异议的,视为放弃其提出异议的权利。"

在《香港国际仲裁中心机构仲裁规则》(2013 版)有不少条文都涉及弃权,如第 19.3 条针对提起管辖权争议的时间,如果没有在答辩书中提出就会被视为弃权:"对仲裁庭管辖权的抗辩,如可能,应在对仲裁通知的答复中提出,最晚应在第 17 条所述的答辩书中提出,或就反诉而言,最晚应在对反诉的答复中提出。当事人提名或参与提名仲裁员的事实不妨害其提出此抗辩。[36]"

而第 31 条与《中国国际经济贸易仲裁委员会仲裁规则》(2015 版)第 10 条十分相似,说:"当事人知道或理应知道未按本规则(包括一个或多个仲裁协议)的规定或其引发的要求行事,但仍继续参与仲裁而未立即提出异议的,应视为已放弃提出异议的权利。"

8.3　合约规定了适用法

合约规定了适用法(governing law,无论是程序法或是实体法),也会导致构成合约性弃权。典型例子就是根据《货物销售法》之 section 11(2),买方的言行构成对拒货的权利的弃权。[37]

而因为规定了适用的程序法而导致合约性弃权,可以仲裁为例。如果双方在仲裁条文中规定在伦敦仲裁,英国 1996 年《仲裁法》就会强制适用。其中 section 73 规定了争议方弃权或失去反对的权利(Loss of right to object)的情况,如下:"**Loss of right to object** (1) If a party to arbitral proceedings takes part, or continues to take part, in the proceedings without making, either forthwith or within such time as is allowed by the arbitration agreement or the tribunal or by any provision of this Part, any objection—(a) that the tribunal lacks substantive jurisdiction, (b) that the proceedings have been improperly conducted, (c) that there has been a failure to comply with the arbitration agreement or with any provision of this Part, or (d) that there has been any other irregularity affecting the tribunal or the proceedings, he may not raise that objection later, before the tribunal or the court, unless he shows that, at the time he took part or continued to take part in the proceedings, he did not know and could not with reasonable diligence have

---

〔36〕 这主要是为了让被申请人配合指定仲裁员,而不用担心这样做会构成弃权。因为根据独立原则(separation principle)与仲裁庭管辖权自治原则(competence - competence),应尽快成立仲裁庭,让仲裁庭先自己决定有否管辖权。

〔37〕 这在本书第三章之 6.2 段有详细介绍。

discovered the grounds for the objection. (2) Where the arbitral tribunal rules that it has substantive jurisdiction and a party to arbitral proceedings who could have questioned that ruling—(a) by any available arbitral process of appeal or review, or (b) by challenging the award, does not do so, or does not do so within the time allowed by the arbitration agreement or any provision of this Part, he may not object later to the tribunal's substantive jurisdiction on any ground which was the subject of that ruling."

第九章　一事不再审

“一事不再审”(*res judicata*)的起源是“estoppel by record”，其中“诉因的禁反言”(cause of action estoppel)与“争端的禁反言”(issue estoppel)的分支与最开始的“estoppel by record”有一定的类似之处，都是因为之前记录在案的判决而被禁反言。但“滥用司法程序”(abuse of process)的分支是与法院的固有管辖权(inherent jurisdiction)有关。虽然一事不再审在现代已经不再被视为禁反言的类别之一，只是因为历史原因叫了禁反言的名字，但因为它的起源与相似性，笔者仍会在本书进行简单介绍。因为笔者在《仲裁法——从开庭审理到裁决书的作出与执行》一书第十章已经对这个课题有所针对，本章尽量减少重复，只进行一些补充与更新。

“*res judicata*”是拉丁文，翻译过来就是“已经被判决的事”(a matter adjudged)。这句准则的完整版应是“*res judicata pro veritate accipitur*”，翻译过来就是“已经被判决的事即被当做事实”(a matter adjudged is taken as truth)。英国普通法下也被称为“Rules of Preclusion”。从这个方面看，一事不再审与禁反言的说法类似。在适格(competent)法院或仲裁庭(一般是指有管辖权)做出最终判决书或裁决书后，即使因为出现了新证据，或是因为上一级法院之后的不同判决导致法律地位有了改变，或是下级法院因为管辖权有限，对认定的损失金额只能部分赔偿等各种其他原因，显示原本的判决或裁决很有可能是错误或不符合事实，诉讼的一方(一般来说是败诉方，但也有可能是没有获得足够赔偿的胜诉方)也被禁止对已经解决的争议(或应该在该诉讼中解决的争议)再次开始诉讼。换句话说，一事不再审是诉讼的终局性(finality to litigation)的基础。

一事不再审是历史十分悠久的说法，在罗马法学家的著作、希腊社会习俗与印度教典籍中都被承认。这个说法体现了“一种永恒的智慧”(a wisdom that is for all time)。《Statute of the International Court of Justice》之 Article 38(1)被认为是国际法来源的最权威说法。一事不再审应属于 Article 38(1)(c)规定的国际法院(International Court of Justice)在行使管辖权时适用的为文明国家所承认的一般法律原则。

1. 诉讼结果终局性的重要性

诉讼结果终局性的重要性(无论是从公共利益还是个人利益的角度考虑)很早

就被意识到并一直被不断强调,这在商业活动尤其重要。诉讼结果没有终局性会根本性破坏法治,对个人(自然人或公司)造成不公平。这也是拉丁文准则"*interest rei publicae ut finis sit litium*"(英文是 it is in the public interest that there be an end to litigation,即公众利益要求所有的诉讼必须要有尽头,而非漫无止境的纠缠下去)与"*nemo debet bis vexari pro una et eadem causa*"(英文是 a person should not be troubled twice for the same reason,即一个人不应该因为同样的原因被骚扰两次)所说。

关于这方面有许多权威说法,笔者可先节录 Neil Andrews 教授的《English Civil Procedure》(2003 年)一书之 942 页,如下:"Without finality of decision, litigants and indeed the legal system as a whole would be exposed to many hazards: that is a dispute might continue to drag on; greater legal expense and delay might result; scarce judge - time might be spent re - hearing the matter; inconsistent decisions might follow; litigation would cease to be a credible means of settling disputes; the victorious party in the first case would be deprived of the legitimate expectation that the first action would not be merely a dress rehearsal for further contests."

在 Davidson's Settlement Trusts, Re (1872 - 73) L. R. 15 Eq. 383 先例中,James 大法官说如果法院之间不互相承认对方的判决,文明世界的秩序就无法维持:"... it would be impossible to carry on the business of the world if Courts refused to act upon what had been done by other Courts of competent jurisdiction."

在 Thrasyvoulou v. Secretary of State for the Environment (1990) 2 A. C. 273 先例中,Simon 勋爵说:"As a means of resolution of civil contention litigation is certainly preferable to personal violence. But it is not intrinsically a desirable activity〔1〕... The law itself is fully conscious of the evil of protracted litigation. Our forensic system, with its machinery of cross - examination of witnesses and forced disclosure of documents, is characterised by a ruthless investigation of truth. Nevertheless the law recognises that the process cannot go on indefinitely.〔2〕... the fundamental principle that it is in society's interest that there should be some end to litigation is seen most characteristically in the recognition by our law - by every system of law - of the finality of a judgment.〔3〕If the judgment has been obtained by fraud or collusion it is considered as a nullity and the law provides machinery whereby its nullity can be so established. If the judgment has been

---

〔1〕作为解决争议的手段,民事诉讼显然比个人暴力好。但这并不是说诉讼本质上令人满意,如果诉讼没完没了进行下去,可能让人不得不以个人暴力作为解决争议的手段。

〔2〕法律完全意识到诉讼拖延的弊端。通过盘问与反盘问证人与强制披露文件等机制,整个诉讼程序以尽量不带感情因素地找出真相,但法律也意识到这个程序不能无限制地持续下去。

〔3〕而为了整个社会的公共利益考虑,诉讼必须有尽头这一点,在法律中最典型的体现就是诉讼结果的终局性。

obtained in consequence of some procedural irregularity, it may sometimes be set aside.[4] But such exceptional cases apart, the judgment must be allowed to conclude the matter. That, indeed, is one of society's purposes in substituting the lawsuit for the vendetta.[5]"

Bridge 勋爵在该先例也说:"The doctrine of res judicata rests on the twin principles which cannot be better expressed than in terms of the two Latin maxims 'interest reipublicae ut sit finis litium' and 'nemo debet bis vexari pro una et eadem causa.' These principles are of such fundamental importance that they cannot be confined in their application to litigation in the private law field. They certainly have their place in criminal law. In principle they must apply equally to adjudications in the field of public law."

在 Fraser v. HLMAD Ltd. (2006) EWCA Civ 738 先例中,Moore – Bick 大法官说:"It has been recognised for centuries that it is neither just nor in the public interest that a person should be allowed to litigate the same issue more than once. The principle is encapsulated in the well known maxims nemo debet bis vexari pro una et eadem causa and interest reipublicae ut sit finis litium. Out of these broad principles of justice and policy, however, there have developed three distinct principles of law usually referred to as 'cause of action estoppel', 'issue estoppel' and 'abuse of process'. The first two are aspects of estoppel by record since they both depend on a prior decision by a court or tribunal of competent jurisdiction on matters before it. The third involves the exercise of the court's inherent jurisdiction to prevent abuse of its process. This appeal is concerned with cause of action estoppel."

在更近期的 Sans Souci Limited v. VRL Services Limited (2012) UKPC 6 先例中,Sumption 勋爵说:"The importance of finality in litigation has been emphasised by generations of common lawyers. Ultimately there must come an end to the parties' opportunities for reopening matters procedural or substantive which have been judicially decided. This principle is, however, founded **on an assumption that they were decided in accordance with the rules of natural justice.**[6]"

总结而言,一事不再审的说法既符合公共利益,也符合个人利益。其中公众利益包括但不限于:(1)为了法治社会的健康与安全,诉讼必须有终局而不能没完没了;(2)法院必须以经济与有效率的方式运作,应避免让法院负担过重;(3)矛盾的判决会影响法院的公信力,令民众对法院判决的尊敬与遵从减少;(4)引起不肯定,影响社会和谐等。

---

〔4〕 如果是通过欺诈或贪污受贿的手段获得判决,法律应有机制令判决书无效,这在本章之 3.3.2.3 段有解释。而如果有程序不当(procedure irregularity),判决书也可能被撤销。

〔5〕 但除了这些特殊情况,诉讼结果即判决书就代表争议走到尽头。

〔6〕 一事不再审的说法是基于判决是符合自然公正原则的假设。也就是说,如果判决是违反自然公正的原则做出的,原本的判决书可能无效或被撤销,一事不再审的说法就不再适用。

2. 一审判决或决定导致一事不再审的说法适用

2.1　司法决定

构成一事不再审的司法决定可以是对事实问题的认定或是对法律问题的判决，或是既有事实也有法律(mixture of law and facts)的问题。这可以是任何司法审裁处(judicial tribunal)做出的决定,包括判决书(judgment)、命令(order)、法令(decree)、判刑(sentence)、裁定破产(bankruptcy adjudication)、宣告(judicial declaration)、执行令状(writ of execution)、仲裁的裁决书(arbitral award)等。

在澳大利亚的 Blair v. Curren (1939) 62 CLR 464 先例中,Dixon 大法官说只有在较早的司法决定中作为基础或是解释所必需的事实或法律问题才能构成禁反言,约束双方当事人或有利害关系人士:"A judicial determination directly involving an issue of fact or law disposes once and for all the issue so that it cannot afterwards be raised between the **same parties or their privies**. The estoppel covers **only those matters** which the prior judgment, decree or order **necessarily established** as the **legal foundation** or **justification of its conclusion** . . . Nothing but what is legally indispensable to the conclusion is thus closed or precluded."(加黑部分是笔者的强调)

显然这个司法决定要针对实体的争议,这在本章稍后的 3.3.3 段会有进一步介绍。另是这个司法决定必须是最终与结论性的,这在本章之 3.3.4 段有进一步介绍。最后做出司法决定并能导致一事不再审的说法适用的司法审裁庭必须针对有关的当事人与有关争议有管辖权,这在本章之 3.3.1 段有进一步介绍。英国的上级法院(包括高院与上诉庭)由于享有一般性与广泛的管辖权(所谓的剩余管辖权,即对所有法律没有规定/针对管辖权的争议都有管辖权),所以上级法院的决定都会被假设有管辖权。这可节录 Strachan v. The Gleaner Co. Ltd. and Another (2005) UKPC 33 PC 先例判决,如下:"An order of a judge without jurisdiction was obviously vulnerable but it was not wholly without effect. It has to be obeyed unless and until it was set aside. The Supreme Court of Jamaica, like the High Court in England, was a superior court of unlimited jurisdiction, namely it had jurisdiction to determine the limits of its own jurisdiction. Whenever a judge made an order he must be taken implicitly to have decided that he had jurisdiction to make it. If he was wrong, his error could be corrected by the Court of Appeal. . . However, unless and until reversed, his decision was res judicata."

相对来说,下级法院或审裁庭往往被立法限制管辖权,如可以做成决定的赔偿金额方面,或只能针对某些特定的争议:Christopher Brown Ltd. v. Genossenschaft Oesterreichischer Waldbesitzer Holzwirtschaftsbetriebe Registrierte GmbH (1954) 1 QB 8 先

例。而众所周知,仲裁庭的管辖权来自受制于争议双方的仲裁协议以及他们的委任。

2.2 符合自然公正原则的公平审讯

《欧洲人权公约》(European Convention on Human Rights)保证了每个人对他拥有的民事权利与主张要有符合自然公正原则的公平审讯的权利。在欧洲人权法院的 Ferencikova v. Slovakia, Application No 39912/09 (ECtHR, 25 September 2012)先例中,说:"the right to **a fair hearing**, as guaranteed by Article 6 § 1 of the Convention, must be construed in the light of the principle of the rule of law, which requires that all litigants should have an effective judicial remedy enabling them to assert their civil right... In this was the right to **a fair hearing** embodies the 'right to court', one aspects of which is the right of access, that is the right to institute proceedings before courts in civil matters... In other words, everyone has the right to have any claim relating to his civil rights and obligations brought before a court or tribunal..."(加黑部分是笔者的强调)

自然公正(natural justice)与公平审讯(fair trial)是十分重要的大课题,一审判决不符合这方面的要求,一事不再审也就无从说起。这重要课题在本章之 3.3.2 段简单针对,不进一步详细介绍。针对外国法院的判决,英国法院适用"一事不再审"(res judicata)与"滥用司法程序"(abuse of process)的说法会更加谨慎。

2.3 判决结果的正确性不重要

没有人能保证任何一审判决对事实的认定与对法律的决定是绝对正确的,只能根据平衡的可能性(balance of probability)做出决定。这只是在正确性与终局性之间做出平衡。

Wilberforce 勋爵在 Committee for Privileges the Ampthill Peerage (1977) AC 547 先例中,说:"Any determination of disputable fact may, the law recognises, be imperfect: the law aims at providing the best and safest solution compatible with human fallibility and having reached that solution it closes the book.〔7〕The law knows, and we all know, that sometimes fresh material may be found, which perhaps might lead to a different result, but, in the interest of peace, certainty and security it prevents further inquiry.〔8〕It is said that in doing this, the law is preferring justice to truth. That may be so: these values cannot always coincide. The law does its best to reduce the gap.〔9〕But there are

〔7〕任何一个对有争议的事实的认定都可能不完美,而法律是在这个基础上提供能力范围内能做到的最好与最安全的解决争议方式。一旦通过这个方式解决,就是终局。

〔8〕确实有时可能会找到新的证据令整个案件可以有不同结果,但为了和平、肯定与有保证(终局性),法律禁止做出进一步的调查。

〔9〕有说法是这显示了相比于找出争议背后的事实真相,法律更倾向于保证公正。换言之,只要程序公正,最后判决的对错就不必理会,毕竟谁也无法做出绝对正确的判断。有时确实两者不可得兼,而法律只能尽量两者兼顾。

cases where the certainty of justice prevails over the possibility of truth (I do not say that this is such a case), and these are cases where the law insists on finality. For a policy of closure to be compatible with justice, it must be attended with safeguards: so the law allows appeals; so the law, exceptionally, allows appeals out of time; so the law still more exceptionally allows judgments to be attacked on the ground of fraud; so limitation periods may, exceptionally, be extended.〔10〕 But these are exceptions to a general rule of high public importance, and as all the cases show, they are reserved for rare and limited cases, where the facts justifying them can be strictly proved.〔11〕"

Simon 勋爵在该先例也说:"A line can thus be drawn closing the account between the contestants. Important though the issues may be, how extensive soever the evidence, whatever the eagerness for further fray, society says, 'We have provided courts in which your rival contentions have been heard. We have provided a code of law by which they have been adjudged. Since judges and juries are fallible human beings, we have provided appellate courts which do their own fallible best to correct error. But in the end you must accept what has been decided. Enough is enough.'〔12〕 and the law echoes: 'res judicata, the matter is adjudged.' The judgment creates an estoppels — which merely means that what has been decided must be taken to be established as a fact, that the decided issue cannot be reopened by those who are bound by the judgment, that the clamouring voices must be stilled, that the bitter waters of civil contention (even though channelled into litigation) must be allowed to subside.〔13〕"

特别是在民事诉讼,法院或仲裁庭根据平衡的可能性做出判决或裁决,因此无论哪一方是败诉方,都会对法院或仲裁庭的裁决(无论是对事实的认定还是对法律的判决/裁决)有不满与抱怨,并且表面上看来很合理。民事诉讼中做出的判决或裁决对每一方都很公平且让每一方都满意,几乎不可能。因此,不论一审的决定是正确或错误,一事不再审的说法都适用。〔14〕 在 Diag Human SE v. The Czech Republic

---

〔10〕 当法律坚持诉讼的终局性时,可以说是司法的肯定性超越了找出真相的可能性。但为了保证公正,法律也必须设置一些防护与保障:允许上诉;在特殊情况下允许逾时上诉;在更特殊的情况下允许败诉方以欺诈攻击判决的有效性;在特殊的情况下延长时效等。

〔11〕 但一些对公众十分重要的极其特殊与有限的案件属于例外情况,有关的事实有合理理由需要被严格证明。

〔12〕 不论有关争议多么重要、有多少证据、败诉方多么渴望继续争论,法律提供了公平审讯的机会,有法律原则规定怎样对有关争议做出判决,有上诉机制尽量纠正错误,因此,败诉方必须接受最终的结果。

〔13〕 法律规定了一事不再审,即判决结果即被视为事实,败诉方被禁反言,不能再继续争论。

〔14〕 见 The "Good Challenger" (2004) 1 Lloyd's Rep. 67; Watt (formerly Cater) v. Raghib Ahsan (2007) UKHL 51; Smith & Anor v. QBE Insurance (Europe) Ltd. & Ors (2010) EWHC 3172 (Ch); Diag Human SE v. The Czech Republic (2014) 2 Lloyd's Rep. 283 等先例。

(2014) 2 Lloyd's Rep. 283 先例中,Eder 大法官说:"... it is immaterial that an English court would regard the reasoning of the foreign court[15] as open to criticism. Indeed, it is irrelevant that an English court subsequently faced with the same issue might take the view that the decision of the foreign court was wrong either on the facts or as a matter of English law. This proposition was affirmed by the Court of Appeal in The Good Challenger (2004) 1 Lloyd's Rep. 67 a case in which the authorities on issue estoppel[16] were reviewed and the following principles set out: 'The authorities show that in order to establish an issue estoppel four conditions must be satisfied, namely (1) that the judgment must be given by a foreign court of competent jurisdiction;[17] (2) that the judgment must be final and conclusive and on the merits;[18] (3) that there must be identity of parties;[19] and (4) that there must be identity of subject matter, which means that the issue decided by the foreign court must be the same as that arising in the English proceedings[20]...'"

2.4 英国确保判决正确的保障与防护:上诉到上一级法院

诉讼的终局性或者一事不再审的前提是一审经过了公平审讯。这在英国问题不大与可以改正与控制(至少英国自己这样觉得),其中尽量确保判决正确的最重要的保障与防护就是可以上诉到上一级法院。

根据《Civil Procedure Rules》(CPR) r 52.3(1),一方(上诉方)必须获得许可才能上诉高等法院做出的判决。上诉许可可以向做出判决的法院申请,也可以向上诉的上一级法院申请:CPR r 52.3(2)。只有当法院认为上诉方有成功的机会,或有其他令人信服的理由时,才会做出上诉许可:CPR r 52.6(1)(a)-(b)。

上诉许可中可以限制上诉的争议并有条件:CPR r 52.6(2)(a)-(b)。但重要的是,这个条件不能扼杀上诉的权利。在近期英国最高院的 Goldtrail Travel Ltd. (In Liquidation) v. Onur Air Tasimacilik AS (2017) UKSC 57 先例中,案情涉及一审法院判申请人 Goldtrail Travel 败诉,要赔偿 364 万英镑的赔偿。Goldtrail Travel 提出上诉,但上诉许可中要求将这笔判决债务先存入法院。这是胜诉方的请求下,英国法院常会对一些败诉后经济有问题并好像以上诉拖延的当事人使用的手段,理念上类似以费用担保(security for costs)对付经济有问题的原告。虽然 Goldtrail Travel 背后有

---

[15] 该先例与外国法院做出的判决有关。

[16] "争端的禁反言"(issue estoppel)是一事不再审的说法的一个分支,将在本章 7.2 段介绍。

[17] 称职外国法院的判决将在本章之 3.3.1 段介绍。

[18] 这将在本章之 3.3.3 段与 3.3.4 段介绍。

[19] 注意"吸收原则"(doctrine of merger)的适用不需要满足这个前提条件,这将在本章之 7.1 段介绍。

[20] 关于同一标的(subject matter)如果指的是同一诉因(cause of action)会适用吸收原则与诉因的禁反言,什么是诉因将在本章之 6.2 段介绍;如果指的是同一争端(issue in dispute)会适用争端的禁反言,什么是争端将在本章之 7.2.2 段介绍。

个有钱的老板/大股东,但证据显示他已经不愿意再对 Goldtrail Travel 进行资助。看来一审法院与上诉庭是想用这个条件逼 Goldtrail Travel 背后的老板掏钱以博取上诉的机会。但这被最高院的多数意见推翻,认为如果有证据显示当事人无法满足上诉许可的条件,就不应该做出这样的要求,否则就是扼杀了他上诉的权利。

上诉法院的管辖权仅限于上诉的理由,因此,上诉方在做出申请时应写明一审法院判决的错误之处,或程序或其他不当导致的不公平:CPR Practice Direction 52C 5(1)段。

正如 Laws 大法官在 Subesh v. Secretary of State for the Home Department (2004) EWCA Civ 56 先例所说:"... the appeal process is not merely a re – run second time around of the first instance trial. It is because of the law's acknowledgement of an important public interest, namely that of finality in litigation. The would – be appellant does not approach the appeal court as if there had been no first decision; as if, so to speak, he and his opponent were to meet on virgin territory. The first instance decision is taken to be correct until the contrary is shown. ... The true distinction is between the case where the appeal court might prefer a different view (perhaps on marginal grounds) and one where it concludes that the process of reasoning, and the application of the relevant law, require it to adopt a different view. The burden which an appellant assumes is to show that the case falls within this latter category."

如果上诉法院在管辖权内认为一审法院的判决错误,或是有严重的程序或其他不当并造成不公平,可以判上诉得直:CPR r 52.21(3)。

上诉法院有一审法院的所有权力,包括:(1)确认(affirm)、撤销(set aside)或更改(vary)一审法院的命令或判决;(2)将任何诉讼请求或争议发回一审法院重审;(3)进行新的审讯或开庭;(4)做出支付利息的命令;(5)做出关于费用的命令:CPR r 52.20(1)-(2)。

CPR 没有列举上诉法院在何种情况下可以撤销一审法院对事实的认定。但因为上诉法院有一审法院的所有权力,所以理论上是在适合的案件中,上诉法院有权撤销一审法院对事实的认定,并做出自己对事实的认定。在 Floyd v. John Fairhurst & Co. (2004) EWCA Civ 604 先例中,Arden 大法官说:"The CPR do not, therefore, purport to set out the circumstances in which an appellate court can set aside findings of fact made by a trial judge. However, the CPR equip the appellate court with all the powers to enable it to do so, and to substitute its own findings, in an appropriate case."

但在决定什么才是合适的案件时,上诉法院会很谨慎,不会轻易推翻一审法院对事实的认定。Steyn 勋爵在 Smith New Court Securities Ltd. v. Citibank N. A. (1997) AC 254 先例中说:"if the Court of Appeal is left in doubt as to the correctness of the conclusion, it will not disturb it."

一般来说,上诉法院不会再次开庭:CPR r 52.21(1)。除非上诉法院做出命令,否则法院不会接受口头证据或一审中没有的新证据:CPR r 52.21(2)。上诉法院可以在有关证据下,对事实做出任何合理推断:CPR r 52.21(4)。除非经上诉法庭许可,否则上诉人无权在上诉开庭时,依赖任何没有上诉通知书中指明的上诉理由:CPR r 52.21(5)。上诉法院只能检查一审法院的决定/判决是否正确。

但也有特殊情况,在 Preedy v. Dunne (2016) EWCA Civ 805 先例中,[21]原告一审时提出了"产权人禁反言"(proprietary estoppel)[22]的说法,但没有被一审法院接受。原告提起上诉,并根据一审法官对事实的认定提出了"共识性禁反言"(estoppel by convention)的说法。Vos 大法官做出了上诉许可说:"I agree with (the Defendants) that the case now being advanced by the appellants (Claimants) is not what was alleged before the trial now what was advanced at the trial. It could be said, uncharitably, to be somewhat opportunistic attempt, to spell an arguable case out of the facts found by way of background by the judge. That said, the important elements of the case were pleaded by the appellants, albeit not fully... Since the appellants are not suggesting that this court should decide additional facts ... I do not see why we should not fairly be able to decide the issues now raised by the newly devised case."

2.5 仲裁

仲裁也一样,一事不再审的说法适用的前提是经过了公平审讯。与法院系统一样,无法保证仲裁裁决绝对正确。而与法院不同,仲裁主要是通过当事人的控制以减轻仲裁庭做出不准确裁决书的危险。首先,仲裁的当事人在订立仲裁协议时可以写明对仲裁员的专业资格与经验的要求,在发生争议后,也可以挑选他们认为合适的仲裁员组成仲裁庭解决争议。毫无疑问,精通法律与专业知识、有经验与没有偏见的仲裁庭出错的机会小得多。

而如果仲裁庭真的做出错误裁决,或是有严重的程序问题或其他不当并造成不公平,在英国法律下也有类似的上诉与监督机制。但伦敦仲裁的机制并不受 CPR 管辖,而是受 1996 年《仲裁法》之 section 68 与 section 69 管辖。Section 68 的立法条文允许仲裁的当事人以严重不当(serious irregularity)[23]向伦敦仲裁的监督法院(supervisory court),即英国高院请求撤销(set aside)裁决书。而 section 69 则允许仲裁的当事人在获得批准(leave)的情况下,将法律问题向法院上诉,法院有权确认(affirm)、撤销或更改(vary)仲裁的裁决书。法院也可以将裁决书发还(remit)给仲裁庭重审,而不是撤销整个裁决书。[24]

2.6 上诉过程中的判决书或裁决书与一事不再审的说法

开始上诉(或有可能上诉)本身不会影响一事不再审的说法。在 Niru Battery

---

〔21〕 有关的案情可见本书第六章之 3.1.4 段。

〔22〕 见本书第七章。

〔23〕 见笔者《仲裁法——从 1996 年英国仲裁法到国际商务仲裁》一书第七章之 3.7.3 段。

〔24〕 见笔者《仲裁法——从 1996 年英国仲裁法到国际商务仲裁》一书第七章之 2.3.5 段。

Manufacturing Co. v. Milestone Trading Ltd.（No. 2）（2004）EWCA Civ 487（CA）先例中，一审法院的 Moore – Bick 大法官说："The fact that the judgment is under appeal is in my view irrelevant to the question now under consideration. Unless and until it is set aside or varied by the Court of Appeal it establishes with complete finality the parties' respective positions in law. This is an elementary principle that provides the foundation for the rule of estoppel by record."

但法院在执行判决书或裁决书时会加上考虑了上诉方利益的条件，因此在适当的案件中，实质执行的程序可能会被中止（无条件或有如败诉方要提供担保等的条件），等待可能的上诉结果：Scott v. Pilkington（1862）2 B & S 11；Colt Industries Inc. v. Sarlie（No. 2）（1966）1 WLR 1287；Four Embarcadero Center Venture v. Mr Greenjeans（1988）65 O. R.（2d）160（CA）；Arrowmaster Inc. v. Unique Farming Ltd.（1993）17 O. R.（3d）407；The "Varna"（No. 2）（1994）2 Lloyd's Rep. 41 等先例。

3. 外国法院的判决或仲裁裁决

对待外国法院的判决，英国法院早期的做法是被当做证据。一份外国法院的判决只是判决债权人（judgment creditor）的诉因的表面证据（prima facie evidence），并不绝对。判决债务人（judgment debtor）仍可以在英国法院做出抗辩与证明该债务不存在。这样，表示虽然有一份外国法院的最终判决，英国法院仍然是重审了这个案件。在早期的 Houlditch v. Donegal（1834）2 Cl. & F. 470 先例中，贵族院的 Brougham 勋爵说："a foreign judgment is only prima facie, not conclusive, evidence of a debt."

Wilberforce 勋爵在 Carl Zeiss Stiftung v. Rayner & Keeler Ltd.（No. 2）（1967）1 AC 853 先例提到这个先例与这段历史说："Unlike English judgments, they were not considered to be judgments of a court of record so that the simplest form of estoppel-by record-could not be applied to them. They were, in the early stages of private international law, considered only to be prima facie evidence of the rights of the parties and were examinable on the merits. This attitude can be found as late as 1834 in the Irish appeal of Houlditch v. Donegal 8 Bligh（N. S.）301..."

但也有一些古老的先例中说道，如果外国法院在英国冲突法规则（rules of conflict of laws）下有管辖权，英国法院不能重审案件的实质争议：Henderson v. Henderson（1843）3 Hare 100；Bank of Australasia v. Harding（1850）9 C. B. 661；Bank of Australasia v. Nias（1851）16 QB 717；De Cosse Brissac v. Rathbone（1861）6 H & N 301 等先例。

最后在 Godard v. Gray (1870) LR 6 QB 139 先例中,判是即使外国法院的判决很明显搞错了,英国法律也是如此。自该先例之后,如果适格外国法院做出了最终判决就不能再在英国法院对实质争议(无论是事实问题还是法律问题)提出质疑。这与诉讼的终局性与同一个人不应该因为同样的原因被骚扰两次的说法一致。

3.1 现在承认外国判决的做法

相对现代对待外国判决的做法是承认外国判决,适格外国法院做出的判决会产生法律责任。Parker B 大法官在 Russell v. Smyth (1842) 152 E. R. 343 先例中引入了法律责任的说法:"Where the Court of a foreign country(苏格兰)imposes a duty to pay a sum certain, there arises an obligation to pay, which may be enforced in this country."

在 Nouvion v. Freeman (1887) 37 Ch. D. 244 先例中,Lindley 大法官说:"In an action on a foreign judgment not impeached for fraud, the original cause of action is not re-investigated here, if the judgment was pronounced by a competent tribunal having jurisdiction over the litigating parties ... The judgment is treated as res judicata, and as giving rise to a new and independent obligation which it is just and expedient to recognise and enforce."

承认外国判决的理由主要是两点:(1)适格法院做出的判决就是最终保障了私人利益与公正,即一个人不应该因为同样的原因被骚扰两次,一次是外国法院,再一次是英国法院;(2)从国与国互相尊重的角度考虑,英国法院的判决也是能被外国法院执行的公共利益。关于第二点,Greer 大法官在 Yukon Consolidated Gold Corp Ltd. v. Clark (1938) 2 KB 241 先例中说:"It was however fully appreciated by those who thought about foreign judgments, that British judgments were never enforced as of right in foreign countries, and that was believed, and rightly believed, to operate as an injustice to this country."

而第二点的公共利益也促使英国颁布了 1933 年《Foreign Judgments (Reciprocal Enforcement) Act》的立法,并与其他国家谈判与达成框架协议相互承认与执行法院判决。

而不承认外国法院的判决对诉讼方造成的困境也可以从两个方面考虑。第一,拒绝执行外国法院的判决会对令判决债权人(judgment creditor)无法向资产在外国或被转移到外国的判决债务人(judgment debtor)获得赔偿,造成很大的不公平。第二,尽管外国法院已经做出了判决,但是不满意的一方(一般是败诉方)仍然有无限机会在其他国家获得不同判决。

3.2 现在的法律框架

现在承认与执行外国法院判决的法律框架大致如下:

1. 1920 年《The Administration of Justice Act》之 section 9(1),说:"Where a judgment has been obtained in a superior court in any part of His Majesty's dominions outside

the United Kingdom to which this Part of this Act extends, the judgment creditor may apply to the High Court in England or or to the Court of Session in Scotland, at any time within twelve months after the date of the judgment, or such longer period as may be allowed by the court, to have the judgment registered in the court, and on any such application the court may, if in all the circumstances of the case they think it just and convenient that the judgment should be enforced in the United Kingdom, and subject to the provisions of this section, order the judgment to be registered accordingly."至于程序方面，可见 CPR Part 74 section I 与 PD 74A section I。

2. 1933 年《The Foreign Judgment Judgments（Reciprocal Enforcement）Act》之 section 2(1),说:"A person, being a judgment creditor under a judgment to which this Part of this Act applies, may apply to the High Court at any time within six years after the date of the judgment, or, where there have been proceedings by way of appeal against the judgment, after the date of the last judgment given in those proceedings, to have the judgment registered in the High Court, and on any such application the court shall, subject to proof of the prescribed matters and to the other provisions of this Act, order the judgment to be registered: Provided that a judgment shall not be registered if at the date of the application—（a）it has been wholly satisfied; or（b）it could not be enforced by execution in the country of the original court."

3. 1982 年《The Civil Jurisdiction and Judgments Act》之 section 4(1),说:"A judgment, other than a maintenance order, which is the subject of an application under Article 31 of the 1968 Convention for its enforcement in any part of the United Kingdom shall, to the extent that its enforcement is authorised by the appropriate court, be registered in the prescribed manner in that court. In this subsection "the appropriate court" means the court to which the application is made in pursuance of Article 32（that is to say, the High Court or the Court of Session)."

4. 2015 年《The Brussels I Recast Regulation》。

5. 2004 年《The European Enforcement Order for uncontested claims Regulation》。

6. 2007 年《The European Small Claims Procedure Regulation》。

7. 1965 年《Carriage of Goods by Road Act》与其他针对特定事项的公约。

8. 在普通法下,判决债权人必须向其他要求债务人支付债务一样开始诉讼要求判决债务人支付外国判决中要求支付的债务。如果债务的有效性被质疑,英国法院就会以一般的诉讼程序解决争议并做出有效判决。判决债权人也可以判决债务人没有真正可能会成功的抗辩为由,根据 CPR Part 24 的规定,要求英国法院做出简易判决(summary judgment)。[25] 因为程序简单快速,而且英国法官倾向于限制外国判决下的判决债务人的抗辩,所以在英国普通法下执行外国法院判决比在很多国家容易得多。如在 Owens Bank Ltd. v. Etoile Commerciale SA (1995) 1 WLR 44 先例中,就提到针对没有互惠安排的国家,普通法就会介入执行外国法院的判决。

3.3 承认外国判决的前提条件

3.3.1 适格法院

司法审裁庭(judicial tribunal)是根据所在国家的有关法律行使司法职能的审裁庭,无论它是上级法院(superior courts)、[26] 民事或刑事法院,甚至是否被称为法院或审裁庭,都不是关键。司法审裁庭适格(competent)是指它对诉讼方与有关争议有管辖权。如果审裁庭超出了自己的管辖权,无论是决定了不在管辖权内的争议,还是做出了没有权力做出的命令,有关的决定(部分或全部)不会构成一事不再审。

英国法院不会直接适用外国法律,而是会适用英国的冲突法规则(rules of the conflict of laws)。Buckley 大法官在 Emanuel v. Symon (1908) 1 KB 302 重申了这些在 19 世纪发展起来的冲突法规则,并在之后不断被引用:"In actions in personam there are five cases in which the courts of this country will enforce a foreign judgment: (1) where the defendant is a subject of the foreign country in which the judgment has been obtained; (2) where he was resident in the foreign country when the action began; (3) where the defendant in the character of plaintiff has selected the foreign in which he is afterwards sued; (4) where he has voluntarily appeared, and (5) where he has contracted to submit himself to the forum in which the judgment was obtained."

在英国,上级法院的管辖权与权力来自立法。正如 Diplock 勋爵在 Bremer Vulkan Schiffbau und Maschinenfabrik v. South India Shipping Corporation Ltd. (1981) 1 Lloyd's Rep. 253 先例[27] 所说:"... True it is that, in typical English fashion, the supervisory jurisdiction over inferior tribunals that is vested in the High Court by statute is that which was vested in or capable of being exercised by the superior courts of common law, principally the Court of Queen's Bench, before the Supreme Court of Judicature Act 1873; so one must look to see over what inferior courts or tribunals the Court of Queen's Bench did assert a supervisory jurisdiction. The procedure by which it exercised this jurisdiction until the very recent change in the Rules of the Supreme Court was by the issue of the prerogative writs (certiorari, prohibition, mandamus, etc.) or the making of orders of the like nature, although there existed too at common law the confessedly anoma-

---

[25] 见 Grant v. Easton (1883) 13 QBD 302 (CA); Colt Industries Inc. v. Sarlie (No. 2) (1966) 1 WLR 1287 (CA)等先例。

[26] 英国的上级法院是上诉庭(Court of Appeal)与高院(High Court)。

[27] 该先例有关法院以原告懈怠推进诉讼(want of prosecution)为由撤销(strike out)仲裁索赔的权利。

lous jurisdiction to set aside an award of private arbitrators for error of law upon its face..."

法律赋予上级法院的管辖权很广泛，除非法律明示规定不属于法院的管辖权（如为了确保仲裁裁决的终局性，英国1996年《仲裁法》中就严重削减了监督法院的管辖权）。上级法院无法扭转的判决中，对所有有关争议的决定是最终与结论性的。

在Strachan v. The Gleaner Co. Ltd. and Another（2005）UKPC 33 PC先例中，原告起诉被告诽谤并在1992年4月9日获得了牙买加高院（虽然叫做Supreme Court，但类似英国高院，判决可以上诉到牙买加上诉庭）在责任方面的缺席判决（default judgment），赔偿金额待定。之后，被告才参加了计算赔偿金额的诉讼程序，双方在Bingham大法官与陪审团面前进行了为期6天的庭审，最后法院在1995年5月16日做出判决，判被告要赔偿原告2300万美元。被告在1996年4月4日向高院申请撤销（set aside）责任方面的缺席判决，并让被告引入新的证据进行责任的抗辩。Walker大法官在1996年9月20日驳回了原告认为他没有管辖权的初步反对意见（preliminary objection），撤销了最初的缺席判决，并在被告支付浪费的费用的前提下同意被告递交答辩书。之后，被告向上诉庭申请中间程序命令，上诉庭独任法官Downer大法官拒绝做出命令并撤销了Walker大法官的命令，认为Walker大法官无权做出实际上是重审的命令。被告上诉，上诉庭的三位大法官撤销了Downer大法官的命令，因为原告并没有对Walker大法官的命令上诉，双方也没有在Downer大法官争辩这一点，Downer大法官没有管辖权撤销Walker大法官的命令。

当时已经超过了上诉的时效，原告向上诉庭申请对Walker大法官的命令上诉的批文，理由是缺席判决已经是最终的，被告只能选择向上诉庭上诉，Walker大法官没有撤销判决的管辖权。但这个申请之后被原告撤回，并在1997年3月4日转而向高院申请撤销Walker大法官的命令，声称Walker大法官没有管辖权因此该命令无效，高院的另一位大法官可以且应该撤销该命令。但高院与上诉庭都没有驳回原告的申请，于是原告上诉到了英国枢密院。

诉讼双方的争议之一是在被告参与了赔偿计算的诉讼程序的情况下，Walker大法官有无撤销责任方面的缺席判决的管辖权。大部分类似的先例责任方面与赔偿方面都是缺席审判，而被告之后申请撤销判决。枢密院的Millet勋爵说："The Supreme Court of Jamaica, like the High Court in England, is a superior court or court of unlimited jurisdiction, that is to say, it has jurisdiction to determine the limits of its own jurisdiction. From time to time a judge of the Supreme Court will make an error as to the extent of his jurisdiction. Occasionally (as in the present case) his jurisdiction will have been challenged and he will have decided after argument that he has jurisdiction; more often he will have exceeded his jurisdiction inadvertently, its absence having passed unnoticed. But whenever a judge makes an order he must be taken implicitly to have decided that he has jurisdiction to make it. If he is wrong, he makes an error whether of law or fact which can be corrected by the Court of Appeal. But he does not exceed his jurisdiction by making the error; . . . In the present case Walker J held that he had jurisdiction to make the order he did. If wrong, his decision could be reversed by the Court of Appeal which would be bound without going into the merits to set aside his substantive order as a nullity. As between the parties, however, and unless and until reversed by the Court of Appeal, his decision (both as to jurisdiction and on the merits) was res judicata."

3.3.2 英国法律下的公平审讯

如果会对判决债务人(judgment debtor,即败诉方)造成严重的不公平,英国法院不会承认与执行外国法院的判决或仲裁庭的裁决书。Lindley 勋爵在 Pemberton v. Hughes (1899) 1 Ch 781 先例中说:"If a judgment is pronounced by a foreign court over persons within its jurisdiction and in a matter with which it is competent to deal, English courts never investigate the propriety of the proceedings in the foreign court, **unless they offend against English views of substantial justice.**"(加黑部分是笔者的强调)

《Dicey, Morris & Collins on The Conflict of Laws》(第 15 版,2012 年)之 14R-162 段与 14-163 段总结说:

"**A foreign judgment may be impeached if the proceedings in which the judgment was obtained were opposed to natural justice.**[28]

In a celebrated passage in his judgment in Pemberton v. Hughes (1899) 1 Ch 781 (CA) . . . Lord Lindley observed: 'If a judgment is pronounced by a foreign court over persons within its jurisdiction and in a matter with which it is competent to deal, English courts never investigate the propriety of the proceedings in the foreign court, unless they offend against English views of substantial justice.' This passage refers to irregularity in the proceedings, for it is clear that a foreign judgment, which is manifestly wrong on the merits or has misapplied English law or foreign law, is not impeachable on that ground.[29] Nor is it impeachable because the court admitted evidence which is inadmissi-

---

[28] 如果做出外国判决的程序违反了自然公正,该外国判决就可以被挑战:Buchanan v. Rucker (1808) 9 East 192; Crawwley v. Isaacs (1867) 16 L. T. 529; Perberton v. Hughes; Richardson v. Army, Navy and General Assurance Association Ltd. (1925) 21 Lloyd's Rep. 345; Adams v. Cape Industries Plc. (1990) Ch. 433 (CA); Masters v. Leaver (2000) I. L. Pr. 387; Beals v. Saldanha (2003) 3 SCR 416 等先例。

[29] 这里指的是做出外国判决的程序不当,而不是对实质争议做出判决或适用英国法/外国法时有错误:Jacobson v. Frachon (1927) 138 L. T. 386 (CA); Adams v. Cape Industries Plc. (1990) Ch. 433 (CA)等先例。

ble in England,[30] or did not admit evidence which is admissible in England,[31] or otherwise followed a practice different from English law[32]...

A mere procedural irregularity would not offend English concepts of substantial justice[33]..."

笔者只选其中三个方面进一步介绍。

3.3.2.1 如果外国法院有违反自然公正的救济,败诉方还能否在英国法院以违反自然公正为由要求拒绝执行?

英国法院在承认与执行外国法院判决(或外国仲裁裁决)时常常会面对这方面的问题:如果外国法院有违反自然公正的救济,只是败诉方没有在外国法院寻求救济,英国法院应如何反应?或是败诉方在外国法院寻求救济失败,英国法院还能否对违反自然公正的争议重审?

针对这个问题,笔者可节录《Dicey, Morris & Collins on The Conflict of Laws》(第15版,2012年)之14-167段如下:"May the defence of breach of natural justice be raised before the English court if the objection could have been taken before the foreign court? In Jet Holdings Inc. v. Patel (1990) 1 QB 335 (CA), Staughton LJ said, obiter, that logically the foreign court's view should be neither conclusive nor relevant as to the propriety of its own proceedings.[34] In Adams v. Cape Industries Plc. (1990) Ch 433, the evidence was that the judgment debtors had the right to apply in the United States to set aside the default judgment on the ground that the assessment of damages was irregular, and it was recognized that such an application would have been allowed if made in due time. The Court of Appeal thought that where the objection came within the two categories mentioned by Atkins L. J., want of notice or lack of opportunity to be heard, the judgment debtor may raise the objection even if there is a remedy in the foreign country. But in other categories (as in the one under consideration in that case) **the existence of a remedy in the foreign court is not wholly irrelevant in determination whether the proceedings in the foreign court, viewed as a whole, offend against English views of substantial justice**: it would be anomalous if the English court were obliged to disregard

---

〔30〕 也不是外国法院接受了英国法院不会接受的证据:De Cosse Brissac v. Rathbone (1861) 6 H & N 301 等先例。

〔31〕 或是相反的不接受英国法院会接受的证据:Scarpetta v. Lowenfeld (1911) 27 TLR 509; Robinson v. Fenner (1913) 3 KB 835 等先例。

〔32〕 又或是在做法上与英国法不同:Boissiere v. Brockner (1899) 6 TLR 85 等先例。

〔33〕 仅仅是程序不当也不一定会违反到英国法下自然公正说法:Adams v. Cape Industries Plc. (1990) Ch 433 等先例。

〔34〕 在 Jet Holdings Inc. v. Patel (1990) 1 QB 335 (CA)先例中,Staughton 大法官随口说外国法院对自己程序是否正当的决定既不是结论性,也与在败诉方英国法院提出违反自然公正的争议无关。

the existence of a remedy under a foreign system of procedure in considering whether the defective operation of that procedure had led to a breach of natural justice. The judgment debtor cannot justify a failure to avail himself of the remedy by reference to his unwillingness to submit to the jurisdiction of a foreign court.〔35〕... In Masters v. Leaver (2000) I. L. Pr. 387, the Court of Appeal held that, on the evidence before it, it was not incumbent on the judgment debtor to have pursued his complaint before the foreign court. **It appears that there is no general answer**, and that in each case the plea that the judgment debtor should have complained to the foreign court will be assessed in the context of the broader merits. But **where the issue or procedural error has been raised before the foreign court and rejected, it is less likely that an English court will entertain arguments** concerning natural or substantial justice which are based on it.〔36〕"(加黑部分是笔者的强调)

英国(或香港)法院在承认与执行外国裁决书时也是同样的逻辑: Minmetals Germany GmbH v. Ferco Steel Ltd. (1999) CLC 647; Gao Haiyan v. Keeneye Holdings Ltd. (2012) 1 HKLRD 627 等先例。

国际商业纠纷往往涉及国际仲裁,在《纽约公约》下承认与执行裁决书导致的问题中,近期相当热门的课题之一就是已经被仲裁地的监督法院撤销(set aside)的裁决书能否在其他国家法院执行。这种先例已有不少,有不少对仲裁友好的国家(如法国〔37〕与美国〔38〕)愿意执行已经在仲裁地的监督法院被撤销了的裁决书。至于英国的地位可先节录《Russell on Arbitration》(第 24 版,2015 年)一书之 8-047 段说:

---

〔35〕 在 Adams v. Cape Industries Plc. (1990) Ch 433 先例中,败诉方有权在美国法院以损失计算不当为由要求撤销缺席判决,并且如果败诉方及时提出,应该是以获得批准。英国上诉庭认为,如果涉及没有得到通知或没有机会争辩这两类情况,即使可以在外国法院获得救济,败诉方仍可以在英国法院要求拒绝执行。但如果涉及其他情况,英国法院在决定外国法院的程序瑕疵是否违反英国自然公正的大原则时,就必须考虑外国法院存在救济这一点。毕竟败诉方不愿意在外国法院上诉,才导致无法获得救济。

〔36〕 在 Masters v. Leaver (2000) I. L. Pr. 387 先例中,上诉庭判是败诉方没有在外国法院上诉寻求救济的义务。败诉方是否应该在外国法院上诉寻求救济,应该根据所有的事实情况整体判断,而不存在一般性的答案。但如果有关的争议/程序错误已经在外国法院提出并被拒绝,英国法院就不太可能会接受有关外国判决的程序违反自然公正的争辩。

〔37〕 原因见 Gary Born 的《International Commercial Arbitration》(2009 年)一书第 2566 页:"Under French law, an arbitral award is presumptively valid and enjoys immediate res judicata effect once it has been made. Article 1504 of the French New Code of Civil Procedure provides that the same grounds exist for annulling an international arbitrational arbitral award made in France as for denying recognition of an award made abroad. These grounds are 'exhaustive' and set forth bases for annulment that are more limited than those contained in Article v. of the New York Convention for non-recognition."

〔38〕 见 Chromalloy Gas Turbine Corporation v. Arab Republic of Egypot, 939 F. Supp. 907 (DDC 1996); Commisa v. Pemex No 13-4022 (2d Cir Aug 2, 2016)等先例。

"... where the court at the seat has made an order setting aside the award, the English court will usually, but not invariably, recognise that order and decline to enforce the award. It has a narrow discretion to allow enforcement notwithstanding the setting aside of the award as a result of the discretion which the word 'may' in s. 103(2) confers."

该书稍早的8－035段也说:"... The court will usually give effect to a decision of the court of the seat to set aside an award unless the decision of the court offended basic principle of honesty, natural justice and domestic concepts of public policy.〔39〕A successful challenge at the court of the seat has may give rise to an issue estoppel.〔40〕Equally, where the court at the seat has considered and rejected an application to set aside the award that will be persuasive but not conclusive evidence in favour of enforcement.〔41〕However, a simple failure to challenge at the court of the seat cannot set up an issue estoppel〔42〕..."

简单而言,英国法律一般会尊重仲裁地监督法院的判决,不会执行一个已经被仲裁地法院撤销的判决。但因为《纽约公约》之 Article V 与 1996 年《仲裁法》之 section 103 (2)用的是"可以"(may),而不是"必须"(shall)拒绝执行,所以,英国法院还是有有限的裁量权可以决定是否仍然执行已经被仲裁地监督法院撤销的裁决书。但英国法院会很狭窄地行使这个裁量权,并且也会受到仲裁地监督法院撤销裁决书的命令的影响。即如果英国法院认为仲裁地监督法院是在被欺诈或贪污受贿等违反了公共政策与自然公正的情况下撤销裁决书,就有裁量权决定仍然执行裁决书。也就是说,如果英国法院经过审理认为仲裁地的监督法院撤销裁决书的命令违反自然公正与公共政策,就可以拒绝承认该撤销裁决书的命令,即承认裁决书依然有效与可以执行。这种情况与本章之3.3.2.2段介绍的 Merchant International Co. Ltd. v. Natsionalna Aktsionerna Kompaniya "Naftogaz Ukrayiny" (2011) EWHC 1820 (Comm)先例类似。

而这种情况在国际仲裁中也不少见,因为很多商业合约中有一方会坚持在自己的所在地仲裁。之后,双方各退一步同意在该地仲裁,但要由一个国际仲裁机构(如 ICC 或 LCIA)管辖。国际仲裁机构委任的仲裁员(特别是首席)一般会来自不同国家,不会受仲裁地影响。而仲裁庭做出的裁决可能判仲裁地的公司败诉,于是仲裁地的公司希望在仲裁地监督法院撤销裁决书。而仲裁地监督法院出于地方保护主义或

---

〔39〕 见 Yukos Capital Sarl v. OJSC Rosneft Oil Co. (2012) 2 Lloyd's Rep. 208(第20段); Malicorp v. Egypt (2015) EWHC 361 (Comm)等先例。

〔40〕 见 Diag Human SE v. The Czech Republic (2014)2 Lloyd's Rep. 283 先例(第58－63段)。

〔41〕 见 Minmetals Germany GmbH v. Ferco Steel Ltd. (1999) CLC 647; Gao Haiyan v. Keeneye Holdings Ltd. (2012) 1 HKLRD 627 等先例。

〔42〕 见 Dallah Co. v. Ministry of Religious Affairs of Pakistan (2009) EWCA Civ 755 先例(第61段与第90段)。

法官被买通或完全合情合理地撤销裁决书。这样,仲裁的胜诉方在其他国家(如英国)执行裁决书时,败诉方就会以裁决书已经被法院撤销为由抗辩。执行地法院的主要考虑之一就是胜诉方能否证明仲裁地监督法院撤销裁决书的命令违反自然公正与公共政策,因为这是不承认外国法院判决的主要理由。而如果不承认,就会令该裁决书获得执行。

这种情况可以 Yukos Capital Sarl v. OJSC Rosneft Oil Co. (2012) 2 Lloyd's Rep. 208 先例为例。案情涉及 Yukos Capital Sarl 借给 OJSC Rosneft Oil Co 的前身一笔巨款,但后者没有归还,导致 Yukos Capital Sarl 开始了 ICC 仲裁。最后仲裁庭做出了四个裁决,判 OJSC Rosneft Oil Co(在做出裁决书前不久,OJSC Rosneft Oil Co 的前身被俄罗斯政府收归国有,成为 OJSC Rosneft Oil Co)要归还 4.5 亿美元。但 OJSC Rosneft Oil Co 在俄罗斯法院成功撤销了裁决书。Yukos Capital Sarl 在荷兰开始执行裁决书,OJSC Rosneft Oil Co 就提出裁决书已经在俄罗斯的法院被撤销,Yukos Capital Sarl 根本没有裁决书可以执行。荷兰的阿姆斯特丹法院判俄罗斯法院是有偏见与不独立(partial and depend),判决是受到俄罗斯政府的压力,不承认该判决并执行 ICC 仲裁裁决书。虽然收到了裁决书金额的 4.5 亿美元,但仍有高达 1.6 亿美元的利息,于是 Yukos Capital Sarl 在英国法院要求执行裁决书。一审的 Hamblen 大法官认为荷兰法院对俄罗斯法院是有偏见与不独立的判决构成争端的禁反言,约束英国法院。但这在上诉庭被推翻,上诉庭认为每个国家的公共政策都不同,俄罗斯法院是否在英国法下有偏见与不独立与是否在荷兰法下有偏见与不独立,并非相同的争端。Rix 大法官说:"'public order' or 'public policy' is inevitably different in each country. The standards by which any particular country resolves the question whether the courts of another country are 'partial and dependent' may vary considerably and it is also a matter of high policy to determine the circumstances in which this country should recognise the judgments of a state where the interests of that very state are at stake. Normally such recognition will be given and, if it is to be refused, cogent evidence of partiality and dependency will be required. Our own law is (or may be) that considerations of comity necessitate specific examples of partiality and dependency before any decision is made not to recognise the judgments of a foreign state. It is our own public order which defines the framework of any assessment of this difficult question; whether such decisions are truly to be regarded as dependent and partial as a matter of English law is not the same question as whether such decisions are to be regarded as dependent and partial in the view of some other court according to that court's notions of what is acceptable or otherwise according to its law."

3.3.2.2 妥当通知诉讼程序和送达告票与缺席判决

妥当通知诉讼程序对确保自然公正(natural justice)与公平审讯(fair trial)十分重要,被告必须有充分的时间准备与进行抗辩。如果这方面做不到,诉讼程序是否符合自然公正就根本无从谈起,因为被告没有参与的机会。而涉及外国的判决,是否妥当通知取决于英国法院的标准而不是管辖的外国法院。看来英国法院对外国法院的判决也不是一视同仁,对某些国家法院的做法实在放心不下,需要这个说法把关。如在 Buchanan v. Rucker (1809) 9 East 192 先例中,多巴哥岛(Island of Tobago)法院在被告没有出现的情况下做出了判决。但被告从来没有到过多巴哥岛,也没有同意接受多巴哥岛法院的管辖。有关告票是以多巴哥法律下将告票钉在法院门口的替代方式方式送达,因此被告从来都不知道有这个诉讼程序。英国 1933 年《Foreign Judgments (Reciprocal Enforcement) Act》之 section 4(1)(a)(iii)规定判决债务人作为外国法院法律程序中的被告,在接获有关该等诉讼程序的通知后(即使有关法律程序文件可能已按照外国法律妥当向他送达)没有充分时间进行抗辩,该判决要求执行的登记须予作废:"... that the judgment debtor, being the defendant in the proceedings in the original court, did not (notwithstanding that process may have been duly served on him in accordance with the law of the country of the original court) receive notice of those proceedings in sufficient time to enable him to defend the proceedings and did not appear; or..."

但如果告票根据英国法律的标准已经妥当送达,是被告自己选择不进行抗辩令法院最终做出了缺席判决(default judgment),这又是另一回事。《Dicey, Morris & Collins on The Conflict of Laws》(第 15 版,2012 年)之 14-022 段说:"... a default judgment may, in this sense, be final and conclusive, even though it is liable to be set aside in the very court which rendered it.[43] Otherwise, the clearer the claimant's case, the more useless his judgment would be..."

该书在 14-169 段也说:"The effect of Art. 34(2) of the Brussels I Regulation and the Lugano Convention is that judgments in default of appearance, falling within their scope, will not be entitled to recognition, and may not be enforced, in the United Kingdom... But if he had the opportunity of instituting proceedings to challenge the judgment when he learned of it, yet failed to do so, he forfeits the protection of Art. 34(2) and the judgment will be liable to be recognized after all..."

如果外国法院的缺席判决被撤销,就不再可以被承认与执行,一事不再审与滥用司法程序的说法也不会适用:Benefit Strategies Group Ltd. v. Prider (2007) 211 F. L. R. 113 (SASC)等先例。在 Merchant International Co. Ltd. v. Natsionalna Aktsioner-

---

〔43〕 缺席审判被视为最终与结论性的,虽然法院有可能会接受被告对缺席的解释,撤销判决并允许被告做出实质的抗辩:Vanquelin v. Bouard (1863) 15 CB (NS) 341; Boyle v. Victoria Yukon Trading Co. (1902) 9 BCR 213; Barclays Bank Ltd. v. Piacun (1984) 2 Qd. R. 476; Minkler and Kirschbaum Center Venture v. Mr Greenjeans (1988) 64 O. R. (2d) 746, app. Dismissed (1988) 65 O. R. (2d) 160 (CA); Schnabel v. Lui (2002) NSWSC 15; CLE Owners Inc. v. Wanlass (2005) 8 WWR 559 (Man. CA)等先例。

na Kompaniya "Naftogaz Ukrayiny" (2011) EWHC 1820 (Comm)先例中，原告获得乌克兰法院的判决(第一份乌克兰法院判决)并在英国执行(第一份英国法院判决)，之后被告在乌克兰法院获得了撤销原判决的判决(第二份乌克兰法院判决)，并要求英国法院撤销第一份承认乌克兰法院原判决的判决。这被 David Steel 大法官以第二份乌克兰法院判决违反《欧洲人权公约》为由拒绝，说："(被告) threshold submission that, since the Ukrainian courts have set aside the lower court's judgment, there is no judgment to enforce and the English default judgment must by definition be set aside. This, to my mind, simply begs the question. The issue is not so much the enforcement of the original judgment but the recognition of the judgment setting it aside. If the judgment setting aside the judgment of the lower court lacked due process then the default judgment will stand. . . . It is well established that a foreign judgment is impeachable on the ground that its recognition would be contrary to public policy: Dicey & Morris: The Conflict of Laws, 14 Ed. Rule 44. Accordingly, if the recognition of a foreign judgment would be contrary to the Convention, recognition will in principle be refused. Indeed this outcome is not so much driven by consideration of public policy as by the terms of Section 6 of the HRA."

遗憾的是，很多中国公司/企业不熟悉规则，收到告票或程序通知也不参加法院或仲裁的诉讼程序，这导致大量对中国公司/企业的缺席法院判决或仲裁裁决。因为这些判决已经根据英国法律的标准妥当送达，中国公司/企业自己选择不进行抗辩，将来也不能抗拒执行，因为这些缺席判决或裁决也适用一事不再审的说法。

3.3.2.3　外国法院判决涉及欺诈

在普通法下，如果胜诉方是通过欺诈获得之前的判决，而败诉方在事后才发现与能够证明欺诈，就可以否定之前的判决：Boswell v. Coaks (No. 2) (1894) 86 L. T. 365n 先例。显然，如果之前的判决中已经涉及欺诈的争议，但法院判不成立，依然构成一事不再审。但这一普通法的地位只适用于英国的判决，对于外国的判决就没有这个说法。在 Abouloff v. Oppenheimer & Co. (1882 - 83) LR 10 QBD 295 先例中，Coleridge 勋爵说："where a judgment has been obtained by the fraud of a party to a suit in a foreign country, he cannot prevent the question of fraud from being litigated in the courts of this country, when he seeks to enforce the judgment so obtained. The justice of that proposition is obvious: if it were not so, we should have to disregard a well - established rule of law that no man shall take advantage of his own wrong. . ."

另在 Vadala v. Lawes (1890) 25 QBD 310 先例中，Lindley 勋爵说得更直白："if the fraud upon the foreign court consists in the fact that the plaintiff has induced that court by fraud to come to a wrong conclusion, you can reopen the whole case even although you will have in this court to go into the very facts which were investigated, and which were in issue in the foreign court."

英国法院当时有这种态度也可以理解,因为当时的大英帝国并不是十分尊重外国法院的判决。但之后有立法针对这种情况,首先是 1920 年《Administration of Justice Act》section 9(2)规定:“No judgment shall be ordered to be registered under this section if — . . . (d) the judgment was obtained by fraud;. . . ”

该立法只针对英联邦国家,之后在针对其他外国法院的 1933 年《Foreign Judgments (Reciprocal Enforcement) Act》之 section 4(1)(a)(iv)也有类似规定。但这些立法与之后一段时间的先例并没有澄清这些外国法院判决是否应与英国法院判决有同样对待的问题。

在 Owens Bank Ltd. v. Etoile Commerciale SA (1995) 1 WLR 44 先例中,案情涉及 Owens Bank Ltd 向 Etoile Commerciale SA 对第三人的债务做出担保。之后,Etoile Commerciale SA 要求 Owens Bank Ltd 在担保下承担责任,并在法国开始诉讼。法国法院判 Owens Bank Ltd 要承担责任,但 Owens Bank Ltd 提起上诉并首次提出担保倒签即涉及虚假文件的争议。法国上诉庭审理之后,判欺诈不成立。Etoile Commerciale SA 在圣文森特和格林纳丁斯(Saint Vincent and the Grenadines)执行法国判决时,Owens Bank Ltd 则以欺诈作为抗辩,并向法院申请检查正本文件的命令。一审法院支持了 Owens Bank Ltd 并做出命令,但这被上诉庭推翻,接着,Owens Bank Ltd 又上诉到了枢密院。枢密院则认为没有必要对这个立法做出解释或推翻 Abouloff v. Oppenheimer & Co 先例的判决,而可以通过“滥用司法程序”(abuse of process)的说法撤销 Owens Bank Ltd 的请求。Templeman 勋爵说:“There is nothing in the authorities which precludes a party from obtaining summary judgment or an order striking out a pleading on the grounds of abuse of process where a fraud is alleged. It is axiomatic that where fraud is alleged full particulars should be given. Where allegations of fraud have been made and determined abroad, summary judgment or striking out in subsequent proceedings are appropriate remedies in the absence of plausible evidence disclosing at least a prima facie case of fraud. No strict rule can be laid down; in every case the court must decide whether justice requires the further investigation of alleged fraud or requires that the plaintiff, having obtained a foreign judgment, shall no longer be frustrated in enforcing that judgment.”

另可节录 Rix 大法官在 Yukos Capital Sarl v. OJSC Rosneft Oil Co. (2012) 2 Lloyd’s Rep. 208 先例中针对通过欺诈获得的外国判决说:“The English rules about foreign judgments procured by fraud provide a possible analogy with the present case. English law is that a foreign judgment may be impeached for fraud in an English court whether by original action or in defence to an action for enforcement of that judgment, see Abouloff v. Oppenheimer & Co. (1882) 10 QBD 295 approved by the House of Lords in Owens Bank v. Bracco [1992] 2 AC 443. English law could, of course, be different and say that a foreign judgment is to be recognised unless it is set aside for fraud in the country where it is given. (Lord Templeman thought that should indeed be the law in relation, at least, to those countries whose judgments the United Kingdom had agreed to register and enforce, see Owens Bank v. Etoile Commerciale [1995] 1 WLR 44, 50). If the judgment creditor went first of all to a third country where the law was that a foreign judgment must be recognised even if arguably obtained by fraud, an English court would presumably neither recognise that judgment nor regard it as giving rise to an issue estoppel, simply because English public policy in this case is different from the third country's public policy. Lord Collins also touched on this point in AK Investment v. Kyrgyz Mobil [2011] 4 All ER 1027 in relation to an argument that the English (and Isle of Man) law on this point should be changed to accord with Lord Templeman's view in the Privy Council precisely because (inter alia) the current law ignored the doctrine of issue estoppel. He said (para 116) that, on any view, the question whether the law should be altered might require a nuanced approach depending on the 'reliability of the foreign legal system' as well as the scope for challenge in the foreign court and the type of fraud alleged."

通过欺诈获得的外国判决或是仲裁裁决通常会在事后被败诉方知悉,如通过告密者。这种情况可以是胜诉方以伪造的文件证据或虚假的证人证言,甚至是向法官或仲裁员行贿而胜诉。但希望以欺诈拒绝判决或裁决的执行要求的标准很高,针对仲裁(与外国法院判决的道理一致)的法律地位可以节录 Double K Oil Products 1996 Ltd. v. Neste Oil Oyj (2010) 1 Lloyd's Rep. 141 先例中 Blair 大法官所说:"The authorities show that the applicable principles are as follows. In accordance with the high threshold applicable to s. 68 Arbitration Act 1996 (Lesotho Highlands Development Authority v. Impregilo SpA [2006] 1 AC 221 at 235H, Lord Steyn), **it is not enough in an application under s.** 68(2)(g) **to show that one party inadvertently misled the other**, however carelessly (Cuflet Chartering v. Carousel Shipping Co. Ltd. [2001] 1 Lloyd's Rep. 707 , Moore – Bick J, at [12]). It will normally be necessary to satisfy the court that **some form of reprehensible or unconscionable conduct has contributed in a substantial way to the obtaining of the award**. A challenge to an award cannot, therefore, be made on the grounds of an **innocent failure to give proper disclosure** (Profilati Italia SRL v. PaineWebber Inc. [2001] 1 ArbLR 51, [2001] All ER (Comm) 1065, Moore – Bick J at [17] and [22]), or the **innocent production of false evidence** (Elektrim SA v. Vivendi Universal SA [2007] All ER (Comm) 365, Aikens J at [80] – [81]). Where, as in the present case, the allegation is fraud in the production of evidence, the onus is on the applicant to make good the allegation by cogent evidence (Cuflet at [12], Elektrim at [81]). The applicant must show **that the new evidence relied upon to demonstrate the fraud was not available at the time of**

the arbitration and would have had an important influence on the result（Westacre Investments Inc. v. Jugoimport – SDPR Holding Co. Ltd. ［1999］2 Lloyd's Rep. 65 at 76 – 77, Waller LJ, applied by Cooke J in Thyssen Canada Ltd. v. Mariana Maritime SA［2005］ArbLR 62 at［60］–［66］and in DDT Trucks of North America Ltd. v. DDT Holdings Ltd. ［2007］2 Lloyd's Rep. 213 at［22］–［23］). The latter point（important influence on the result）takes effect within the statutory requirement that the irregularity has caused or will cause substantial injustice to the applicant（Thyssen at［65］). "(加黑部分是笔者的强调)

以上加黑部分的标准可总结如下:(1)胜诉方不经意的误导仲裁庭是不足够;(2)胜诉方为了取得胜诉的裁决书做出了一些应受谴责的行为;(3)无辜地(或无法证明有意地)没有披露对胜诉方不利的文件或提供伪造的文件是不足够;(4)败诉方有责任证明可以证明欺诈的新证据在仲裁时无法合理取得,并且如果新证据在仲裁中拿出来,会对仲裁结果有重要影响。

这一先例的标准也在之后的Chantiers de L'Atlantique SA v. Gaztransport & Technigaz SAS（2011）EWHC 3383（Comm)先例被适用。

但可能有情况是外国法院/仲裁庭已经针对欺诈的问题做出实质性判决/裁决,就会构成一事不再审。在 Westacre Investments Inc. v. Jugoimport – SDPR Holding Co. Ltd.（1999）2 Lloyd's Rep. 65 先例中,案情有关南斯拉夫向科威特出售军火。负责牵线的 Westacre 在有关合约下要求南斯拉夫公司支付报酬,而南斯拉夫公司就以 Westacre 是通过行贿/个人影响而取得军火合约为由抗辩。在 ICC 仲裁中,仲裁庭判有关合约有效,南斯拉夫公司要向 Westacre 支付报酬。南斯拉夫公司向监督法院上诉,申请撤销裁决书,但被监督法院拒绝。之后 Westacre 在英国法院执行裁决书时,南斯拉夫法院再次提出了行贿/利用个人影响违反英国公共政策,应该拒绝执行的抗辩。但英国法院认为,仲裁庭已经针对这个问题做出了实质裁决,构成一事不再审。Mantell 大法官说:"It is of crucial importance to evaluate both the majority decision in the arbitration and the ruling of the Swiss Federal Court, Swiss Law being both the proper law of the contract and the curial law of the arbitration and Switzerland, like the United Kingdom, being a party to the 1958 New York Convention. **From the award itself it is clear that bribery was a central issue. The allegation was made, entertained and rejected.** Had it not been rejected the claim would have failed, Swiss and English public policy being indistinguishable in this respect. Authority apart, in those circumstances and **without fresh evidence I would have thought that there could be no justification for refusing to enforce the award.** ... First, there was evidence before the Tribunal that this was a straightforward, commercial contract. Secondly, the arbitrators specifically found that the underlying contract was not illegal. Thirdly, there is nothing to suggest incompetence on the part of the arbitrators. Finally, there is no reason to suspect collusion or bad faith in the obtaining of the award."(加黑部分是笔者的强调)

3.3.3 对实质争议的判决

外国法院的判决必须针对实质性(on the merits)的争议,而不是纯粹针对程序方面。这表示外国法院的判决通常要涉及对双方争议的事实做出认定(finding of facts)或/与对法律做出判定(holding of law)。在 The "Sennar"(No. 2)(1985)1 Lloyd's Rep. 521 先例中,原告货方主要的争议是荷兰法院做出的在提单下苏丹法院有专属管辖权(exclusive jurisdiction)只是程序上的决定,但贵族院不同意,认为荷兰法院的判决是针对实质性问题,Diplock 勋爵说:"It is often said that the final judgment of the foreign court must be 'on the merits'. The moral overtones which this expression tends to conjure up may make it misleading. What it means in the context of judgments delivered by courts of justice is that the court has held that it has jurisdiction to **adjudicate upon an issue raised in the cause of action to which the particular set of facts give rise; and that its judgment on that cause of action is one that cannot be varied, re – opened or set aside by the court that delivered it or any other court of co – ordinate Jurisdiction although it may be subject to appeal to a court of higher Jurisdiction**."(加黑部分是笔者的强调)

Brandon 勋爵也说:"The argument in relation to the first contention was that the judgment of the Dutch Court of Appeal was procedural in nature, in that it consisted only of a decision that a Dutch court had no jurisdiction to entertain and adjudicate upon the appellants' claim, and did not pronounce in any way on the question whether the claim itself, or any substantive issue in it, if it were to be entertained and adjudicated on, would succeed or fail. In my opinion, this argument is based on a misconception with regard to the meaning of the expression 'on the merits' as used in the context of the doctrine of issue estoppel. **Looking at the matter negatively a decision on procedure alone is not a decision on the merits. Looking at the matter positively a decision on the merits is a decision which establishes certain facts as proved or not in dispute; states what are the relevant principles of law applicable to such facts; and expresses a conclusion with regard to the effect of applying those principles to the factual situation concerned. If the expression 'on the merits' is interpreted in this way, as I am clearly of opinion that it should be, there can be no doubt whatever that the decision of the Dutch Court of Appeal in the present case was a decision on the merits for the purposes of the application of the doctrine of issue estoppel.** In my view, therefore, the argument for the appellants on this point is misconceived and should be rejected."(加黑部分是笔者的强调)

上述加黑部分是说,要构成争端的禁反言(或诉因的禁反言)的要件之一是实质性(on the merits)司法决定/法院(英国或外国)判决。从字面上与否定的角度看,程序方面的决定不是实质性决定。但从积极与肯定的角度看,只要是对有争议需要证明的事实做出认定,并根据适用的法律决定这些认定的事实会有何法律后果,即可被视为实质性决定,而无须计较是程序方面的决定或是实体方面的决定,均可使用争端的禁反言的说法。毕竟区分程序方面的决定和实体方面的决定也并不容易,如时效问题算是程序还是实质性问题?可以说,英国自从 1984 年的《Foreign Limitation Act》立法后,已经明确把外国法院对时效的判决当作实质性问题。因此对时效(如已经过去或受到保护)的决定或判决,一事不再审的说法适用。这是在 Section 3 所说的,如下:"Where a court in any country outside England and Wales has determined any matter wholly or partly by reference to the law of that or any other country (including England and Wales) relating to limitation, then, for the purposes of the law relating to the effect to be given in England and Wales to that determination, that court shall, to the extent that it has so determined the matter, be deemed to have determined it on its merits."

这一个问题与下一小段要介绍的内容有很强的关联性,将在下一小段介绍。

3.3.4　最终与结论性

被承认与执行的外国法院判决必须是最终与结论性的。上诉庭的 Lindley 大法官在 Nouvion v. Freeman (1887) 37 Ch. D. 244 先例中说:"The test of finality and conclusiveness of any judgment is to be found in the view taken of it by the tribunals of the country in which it is pronounced, and if a judgment leaves the rights of the parties uninvestigated and undetermined, and avowedly leaves those rights to be determined in some other proceeding, the judgment cannot be treated here as imposing an obligation which our tribunals ought to enforce."

因此必须要对最终判决与中间决定、实质性判决与程序性决定(后者通常可以申请做出更改)进行区分。Black Clawson Ltd. v. Papierwerke AG (1975) AC 591 先例中说:"a final judgment on the merits cannot apply when there was no more than an interlocutory decision on a procedural and non – substantive issue."

这个区分在仲裁中也导致了很多问题出现。如 1958 年《纽约公约》只能用来执行对实质内容的最终裁决书,而不能用来执行中间程序命令。在新加坡的 PT Asuransi Jasa Indonesia (Persero) v. Dexia Bank SA (2007) 1 SLR 602 先例中,法院判仲裁庭对管辖权的决定不能被称为裁决书。在英国的 Svenska Petroleum Exploration AB v. Lithuania & Anor (2006) 1 Lloyd's Rep. 181 先例中,Teare 大法官判仲裁庭针对管辖权的中间裁决(interim award)不是最终的。在 Australian Resort Condominiums International Inc. v. Ray Bolwell and Resort Condominiums (Australiasia) Pty Ltd. (1993) 118 ALR 655 先例中,澳大利亚法院拒绝执行一份名为"Interim Arbitration Order and Award"的美国裁决书。

程序命令与裁决有很多明显区别,程序命令通常不是最终可以更改,甚至仲裁庭可以不经双方申请自行更改。而裁决书一旦做出，仲裁庭就不能再更改，除非被监督法院发回重新考虑（reconsideration）。区分程序命令与判决（或裁决）并非看起来那么简单。大部分的程序命令都不会是最终与结论性的命令与决定，如是完成某个中间程序的时限或披露等命令，就经常在后来情况有变化而有所改变。但在笔者的《仲裁法——从开庭审理到裁决书的作出与执行》一书第六章第1段也提到一些程序命令本质上不能再更改，做出了决定就是最终与结论性的，包括：原告懈怠诉讼（want of prosecution）而被撤销（The "Smaro" [1999] 1 Lloyd's Rep. 225）；允许检查船舶（The "Vasso" [1983] 2 Lloyd's Rep. 346）；拒绝做出中间裁决书（The "Trade Fortutude" [1992] 1 Lloyd's Rep. 169）；原告的索赔已经过期、被撤回或放弃（Cargill v. Kadinopoulos [1992] 1 Lloyd's Rep. 1）等。

中间程序的禁令（interim injunction），如冻结令（freezing injunction）就显然是暂时性的，即使做出该命令时涉及一些事实与法律的实质争议。但止诉禁令（anti – suit injunction）本质上是最终与结论性的，是最终禁令（final injunction）。

英国1996年《仲裁法》允许两类"程序性裁决书"（procedural award）。第一类是在 section 41(3)下以原告懈怠诉讼为由撤销仲裁申请。第二类是在 section 41(6)下以原告没有提供费用担保（security for costs）为由撤销仲裁请求。这两类裁决书都不能说是对实质争议的裁决书，但都显然是最终与结论性的。

也就是说，在诉讼与仲裁中，并非所有的中间程序命令都是暂时性的，有一些是最终与结论性的。这些决定可能涉及法律，因此，在仲裁中做出可能会导致不利的一方获得批文上诉到法院。Evans 大法官在 Desert Sun Loan Corp. v. Hill (1996) 2 All ER 847 CA 先例中说外国法院做出的决定即使是非实质性，只是程序方面，在满足一些条件的情况下也可以适用一事不再审的说法："On balance, and regarding the question entirely as one of principle, I would be prepared to hold that an issue estoppel could arise from an interlocutory judgment of a foreign court on a procedural i. e. non – substantive issue, where the following conditions were fulfilled: (1) there was express submission of the procedural or jurisdictional issue to the foreign court; (2) the specific issue of fact was raised before and decided by the court; and (3) the need for 'caution' recognised by Lord Reid in Carl Zeiss is carefully borne in mind. Practical considerations such as whether the issue was or should have been fully ventilated are likely to be especially relevant in relation to procedural, as distinct from substantive issues, and for this reason I would hesitate long before including issues which might have been, but were not in fact raised or decided by the foreign court [cf. (2) above]. Moreover, as Mr Semken（被告代表大律师）submitted, there is some danger of injustice if an issue estoppel is based, not upon the foreign court's adjudication on a claim or cause of action which is sought to be raised for a second time here, but upon a specific issue which can only be identified within it by a process of 'refining down' or, as he put it, of salami –

slicing. As he might have said, Occam's razor can be taken too far."

简单而言,一个对于中间程序(即不涉及实质争议)与/或管辖权的决定可以被认为属于实质性决定,如果:(1)双方明确对有关的中间程序或管辖权向法院/仲裁庭向递交了申请与陈述;(2)法院/仲裁庭做出了决定;(3)从实务方面考虑,有关的争端已在或应在法院/仲裁庭前充分争论。

Evans 大法官注意到,在实践中,仅针对程序而不涉及实质争议的决定很少被认为是实质性决定并构成一事不再审。根据 The "Sennar" (No. 2) (1985) 1 Lloyd's Rep. 521 先例与 Desert Sun Loan Corp. v. Hill 先例的判决,是否构成"争端的禁反言"(issue estoppel)主要取决于之前的法院是否对双方递交的有关的争议做出了最终与结论性的决定。至于该决定是程序性还是实质性的并不重要。[44]

但也有权威先例认为法院或仲裁庭认定自己没有管辖权而撤销诉讼请求并非实质性决定(on the merits)。如仲裁庭就经常要决定自己是否有管辖权的争议。如果最后的决定是没有管辖权,该仲裁庭就不是适格(competent)的审裁庭,理论上它的决定就不会构成一事不再审。在 Upendra Nath Bose v. Lall (1940) AIR (PC) 222 先例中,枢密院说:"The res judicata here was the lack of jurisdiction ... not the reason for that decision. A Court which declines jurisdiction cannot bind parties by its reasons for declining jurisdiction: such reasons are not decisions, and are certainly not decisions by a court of competent jurisdiction. It would indeed be strange if on a dispute as to the jurisdiction of a Court to try an issue, that Court by its reasons for holding that it had no jurisdiction, could, on the principle of res judicata decide and bind the parties upon the very issue it was incompetent to try."

4. 确保诉讼终局性的体系

在英国法下,有一套复杂的体系确保诉讼的终局性,包括各种不同的说法与规则。其中,限制法院对之后的案件的管辖权的说法与规则有:(1)限制法院对已经做出最终判决的案件重审的管辖权,即认为法院职责已履行完毕(*functus officio*),不再拥有管辖权;(2)一事不再审(*res judicata*)[45]的说法,包括"吸收原则"(doctrine of merger 或拉丁文的 *transit in rem judicatam*)、"诉因的禁反言"(cause of action estoppel)与"争端的禁反言"(issue estoppel),后两类也可被统称为"*estoppel per rem judicatam*";(3)禁止"滥用司法程序"(abuse of process),包括与重新诉讼有关的滥用

---

〔44〕 见《Dicey, Morris & Collins on The Conflict of Laws》(第 15 版,2012 年)之 14 – 035 段。

〔45〕 *Res Judicata* 是很大的课题,在美国 Robert C Casad 与 Kevin M. Clermont 的《Res Judicata》(2001 年)一书中说:"in general it is just too complex a subject for successful codification."

(relitigation - abuse)、间接攻击做出的最终判决的滥用(collateral attack - abuse)与"Henderson v. Henderson Rule"。

Millett 勋爵在 Johnson v. Gore Wood & Co. (2002) 2 A. C. 1 先例说到这些抗辩都是为了同一个目的,就是确保诉讼的终局性与不让被告不必要的面对持续被起诉的情况:"... these various defences are all designed to serve the same purpose: to bring finality to litigation and avoid the oppression of subjecting a defendant unnecessarily to successive actions."

在近期的 Virgin Atlantic Airways Ltd. v. Zodiac Seats UK Ltd. (formerly Contour Aerospace Ltd) (2013) UKSC 46 先例中,Sumption 勋爵说一事不再审(res judicata) 可被细分为若干分支(Sumption 勋爵看来是将滥用司法程序也归为一事不再审的说法),说:"Res judicata is a portmanteau term which is used to describe a number of different legal principles with different juridical origins. As with other such expressions, the label tends to distract attention from the contents of the bottle. The **first** principle is that once a cause of action has been held to exist or not to exist, that outcome may not be challenged by either party in subsequent proceedings. This is 'cause of action estoppel'. It is properly described as a form of estoppel precluding a party from challenging the same cause of action in subsequent proceedings. **Secondly**, there is the principle, which is not easily described as a species of estoppel, that where the claimant succeeded in the first action and does not challenge the outcome, he may not bring a second action on the same cause of action, for example to recover further damages: see Conquer v. Boot [1928] 2 KB 336 .[46] **Third**, there is the doctrine of merger, which treats a cause of action as extinguished once judgment has been given on it, and the claimant's sole right as being a right on the judgment. Although this produces the same effect as the second principle, it is in reality a substantive rule about the legal effect of an English judgment, which is regarded as "of a higher nature" and therefore as superseding the underlying cause of action: see King v. Hoare (1844) 13 M & W 494 , 504 (Parke B). At common law, it did not apply to foreign judgments, although every other principle of res judicata does. However, a corresponding rule has applied by statute to foreign judgments since 1982: see section 34 of the Civil Jurisdiction and Judgments Act 1982. **Fourth**, there is the principle that even where the cause of action is not the same in the later action as it was in the earlier one, some issue which is necessarily common to both was decided on the earlier occasion and is binding on the parties: Duchess of Kingston's Case (1776)

---

[46] Sumption 勋爵所提的第二种可以称为"former recovery",即在第一个判决已经成功索赔部分的损失,但又开始第二个诉讼想获得进一步的赔偿,这和吸收原则与"Henderson v. Henderson Rule"会有重叠。

20 State Tr 355 . "Issue estoppel" was the expression devised to describe this principle by Higgins J in Hoysted v. Federal Commissioner of Taxation (1921) 29 CLR 537 , 561 and adopted by Diplock LJ in Thoday v. Thoday [1964] P 181 , 197 - 198. **Fifth**, there is the principle first formulated by Wigram V - C in Henderson v. Henderson (1843) 3 Hare 100, 115, which precludes a party from raising in subsequent proceedings matters which were not, but could and should have been raised in the earlier ones. **Finally**, there is the more general procedural rule against abusive proceedings, which may be regarded as the policy underlying all of the above principles with the possible exception of the doctrine of merger."

5. 职责已履行完毕(*functus officio*)

法官在做出最终判决后,职责已履行完毕(*functus officio*),不再拥有管辖权,即法官无权重审或改变已经决定的争议并做出不同或矛盾的判决,这是判决的终局性的基础。如果败诉方希望引入新的证据(经常发生),可以通过上诉提出重审或做出改变,即使成功机会不大。但如果已经不可以继续上诉,找到了可能令原来的判决有不同结果的新证据也没有意义了。

仲裁也有这个说法,所以仲裁庭在做出裁决书后,职责已履行完毕(*functus officio*),即使事后他自己也理解是错判,也不能与没有权利做出改变。如有经验的仲裁员都可能经历过仲裁庭已经在中间裁决书(interim/partial award)中对责任方面做出了裁决,但在决定损失时,败诉方找到了新的证据,希望仲裁庭对责任方面重新做出判决。虽然仲裁庭可能也在新证据的影响下,对中间裁决书的正确性有所怀疑,但仍没有权利改变中间裁决书中的裁决。现在连英国法院在1996年《仲裁法》下也无权以发现新证据为由撤销裁决书或将裁决书发回仲裁庭重审。

在 Profilati Italia Srl v. Painewebber Inc. (2001) 1 Lloyd's Rep. 715 先例中,Moore - Bick 大法官说:"The court has no general jurisdiction to interfere with the working of the arbitral process . . . the court no longer has the power to remit an award simply on the grounds that new evidence has come to light."

在 Elektrim SA v. Vivendi Universal SA (2007) 1 Lloyd's Rep. 693 先例中,Aikens 大法官说:"In my view it is important to recall, in this regard, that under the Arbitration Act 1950 (and its predecessors going back to the 1889 Act), the court had frequently held that it had power to remit an award in cases where fresh evidence came to light after the award, if the new evidence might have affected the decision of the arbitrator if it had been adduced at the hearing. The 1996 Act gives the court no such power. . ."

诉讼方不能说服已经做出判决的法院改变主意，而只能在可能是局限的情况下，通过上诉去试图改变判决书。Russell 大法官在 Re Barrell Enterprises（1973）1 WLR 19（CA）先例中说："... it is clearly not permissible for a party to ask for a further hearing merely because he has thought of a possible ground of appeal that he originally overlooked.〔47〕 The discovery of fresh evidence has never been suggested as a ground for reopening the argument before the Court of Appeal.〔48〕 If fresh evidence comes to light, of such a character as to call for further consideration of the issues, the right way to deal with the situation is by applying for leave to appeal to the House of Lords〔49〕..."

在 Taylor v. Lawrence（2002）EWCA Civ 90 先例中，Woolf 勋爵依据 Re Barrell Enterprises 先例说："It is not uncommon for fresh evidence to come to light after a judgment has been perfected which puts that judgment in doubt. In such circumstances the unsuccessful litigant may be able to invoke that evidence in order to challenge the judgment by an appeal. Once the judgment is perfected, however, the court that has delivered the judgment, be it a court of first instance or the Court of Appeal, would not entertain an application to reopen the judgment in order to consider the effect of the fresh evidence.〔50〕 This is not because of any express statutory prohibition. In considering the extent of their jurisdiction the courts have ruled that a perfected judgment exhausts their jurisdiction because this accords with the fundamental principle that the outcome of litigation should be final.〔51〕 This can be demonstrated by reference to the judgment of Russell LJ in In re Barrell Enterprises [1973] 1 WLR 19..."

但在十分特殊的情况下，法院有固有管辖权（inherent jurisdiction）改变自己的命令或判决令法院的意图或意思更明确：CPR Part 40 PD（Judgments and Orders）4.5。正如 Russell 大法官在 In Re Barrell Enterprises（1973）1 WLR 19 先例说："When oral judgment has been given, either in a court of first instance or on appeal, the successful party ought save in most exceptional circumstances to be able to assume that the judgment is a valid and effective one."

被更改的判决往往涉及一些极不常见的情况（most unusual element），Russell 大法官在 In Re Barrell Enterprises 先例也说："The cases to which we were referred in which judgments in civil courts have been varied after delivery (apart from the correction

〔47〕 一方当事人不能在看了判决发现他原来看漏了一个可能改变判决结果的理由后，上诉要求重审。

〔48〕 发现了新证据从来不是可以要求上诉庭重审的理由。

〔49〕 如果发现的新证据是极不常见的情况（如显示原来的判决是通过欺诈/伪证获得，为避免真正不公平需要重审），可以向上一级法院上诉要求重新考虑。在该先例是上诉庭判决，上一级就是贵族院。

〔50〕 经常会有情况是在一审或上诉庭做出判决后，发现新证据令该判决有疑问。但这种情况法院不会允许重审，看新证据会带来何种后果。

〔51〕 这也不是根据立法的明示规定，而是基于确保诉讼终局性的大原则。

of slips) were all cases in which some most unusual element was present...(Russell 大法官引用了几个先例)... In all these cases there were circumstances of a wholly exceptional character."

关于高院或上诉庭可以对已经是最终的上诉判决(包括是否允许上诉的判决)重启上诉,可见标题是"Reopening of final appeals"的 CPR r 52.30,除非同时满足以下三个条件,高院或上诉庭才会重审已经是最终的判决:(1)为了避免真正导致不公平,有必要重审;(2)属于适合重启上诉的特殊情况;(3)没有其他的补救方式。

例如,如果之前的判决是通过欺诈获得,高院或上诉庭可能会决定重启上诉程序:见 Wood v. Gahlings, The Times, 29 November 1996, Court of Appeal (Civil Division); Taylor v. Lawrence; Jaffray and others v. Society of Lloyd's (2007) EWCA Civ 586 等先例。

5.1　更正判决书

英国法院为了保证在正式做出书面判决书前就能及时发现错误并改正,会在机密的基础上,将终稿发给双方的代表大律师做最后检查。往往双方的代表律师对案情与双方在法院争辩过的要点最清楚,他们可向法院指出草拟的判决书终稿有否在案情的事实(如发生某件事的日期或地点)记录错或漏了针对某个争端(issue)。但在国际仲裁中,显然不能这样做,英国法院可以控制或惩戒英国律师(包括事务律师与大律师),而仲裁庭是无法做到这一点(特别是在国际仲裁中,有时是当事人自己参与,没有代表律师)。

即使已经法院正式做出了判决书或命令,仍可以根据 CPR r 40.12 与 PD (Judgments and Orders)下的所谓"文书修改规则"(slip rules)修改判决书或命令中一些文书上意外疏忽与错漏,如拼错字或计算有误。仲裁庭也可以根据 1996 年《仲裁法》之 section 57 做出类似的修改。

5.2　近期有关仲裁的 *functus officio* 先例

笔者可简单介绍如下近期有关仲裁的 *functus officio* 先例:

1. 在 NYK Bulkship (Atlantic) NV v. Cargill International SA (2016) 1 Lloyd's Rep. 629 先例中,高院([2013] 1 Lloyd's Rep. 455)与上诉庭([2014] 2 Lloyd's Rep. 103)都认为仲裁庭没有对双方提出的争端(issue)之一做出决定,因此根据 1996 年《仲裁法》之 section 69(7)(c),将裁决书发还给仲裁庭。但最高院(Clarke 勋爵做出了不同意见)判无须将裁决书发还给仲裁庭,因为裁决书做出了正确裁决。

2. 在 Hussmann (Europe) Ltd. v. Ahmed Pharaon (2003) EWCA Civ 266 先例中,Ahmed Pharaon 先生以 Al Ameen Development and Trade Establishment 公司(简称 Establishment)的名义与 Hussmann 订立合约。之后 Ahmed Pharaon 先生成立了一个新的公司,并将原本以 Establishment 的名义营运的生意转移到该新公司。接着 Establishment 被注销,根据沙特阿拉伯的法律,Hussmann 相当于与 Ahmed Pharaon 先生个人订立了合约。Hussmann 在 1997 年开始仲裁,仲裁庭做出了对新公司有利的第

一份裁决书。但法院认为新公司不是合约方，仲裁庭对新公司没有管辖权，第一份裁决书无效。之后同一仲裁庭做出了第二份对 Ahmed Pharaon 先生有利的裁决书。Hussmann 根据 1996 年《仲裁法》之 section 67 向法院要求撤销该裁决书，理由是：(1) 虽然 Ahmed Pharaon 先生是合约方，但他并非该仲裁的诉讼方，他在诉讼一开始选择了新公司作为诉讼方；(2) 仲裁庭在做出第一份裁决书后职责已履行完毕，无权做出第二份裁决书。但这两点都不被法院接受，高院与上诉庭都判：(1) Ahmed Pharaon 先生一直是仲裁的诉讼方；(2) 只有一份有效的裁决书才会令仲裁庭 *functus officio*，第一份裁决书被法院判无效，不影响仲裁庭做出第二份判决书。

3. 在 Dawes v. Treasure & Son Ltd. (2010) EWHC 3218 (TCC) 先例中，Dawes 与 Treasure & Son 订立了工程合约。Treasure & Son 以 Dawes 拖欠款项为由开始仲裁，而 Dawes 则反索赔 Treasure & Son 的工程缺陷造成的损失。之后，双方达成除了费用外的和解。在仲裁庭做出了费用裁决书（costs award）后，Dawes 以 Treasure & Son 工程有缺陷，需要补救与造成损失为由开始了新的诉讼。Treasure & Son 请求原仲裁庭做出 Dawes 的索赔已经包括在双方的和解协议中的裁决。原仲裁庭支持了 Treasure & Son 的请求，并做出裁决书。Dawes 向法院要求撤销裁决书，但被法院拒绝，不认为仲裁庭在双方达成和解后（不论是全面或部分和解）就变为职责已履行完毕，判决有关部分可节录如下："The following conclusions can be drawn from the law and practice relating to arbitrations in relation to the point at which an arbitrator may become functus officio: (a) Primarily, as arbitration is, usually, a consensual process, one must look to the contract between the parties pursuant to which the arbitrator has been appointed to determine what the parties have agreed, expressly or by implication, about when an arbitrator's jurisdiction becomes exhausted. (b) The settlement of a dispute after it has been referred to arbitration but before any final award does not generally, and certainly does not necessarily, bring to an end to the jurisdiction. Section 51 suggests that even if the dispute is settled there remains a jurisdiction to terminate the substantive proceedings and to resolve issues of costs or indeed any other matters remaining in dispute at that time. That jurisdiction is not expressed to be statutorily limited."

4. 在 Sun United Maritime Ltd. v. Kasteli Marine Inc. (2014) EWHC 1476 (Comm) 先例中，作为原告的 Sun United Maritime Ltd 向被告 Kasteli Marine Inc. 做出了费用担保（该仲裁中有索赔与反索赔，但总之最终是 Sun United Maritime Ltd 向第三方账户支付了一笔钱作为担保），最后仲裁庭判 Kasteli Marine Inc. 胜诉。双方律师对费用达成口头和解，但取决于（subject to）一份书面和解协议（主要是为了从第三方账户中取钱）。双方一直没有签署书面和解协议，Kasteli Marine Inc. 请求仲裁庭做出费用裁决书。相比口头和解协议，仲裁庭做出的费用裁决书对 Kasteli Marine Inc. 更有利，于是 Sun United Maritime Ltd 根据 1996 年《仲裁法》之 section 67 向法院申请撤销裁决书，因为双方已经达成和解协议，仲裁庭就变为职责已履行完毕

(*functus officio*),不再有管辖权。但法院没有支持该申请,认为仲裁庭仍有管辖权决定双方是否存在有效的和解协议的争议,说:

"In my judgment, where there is a dispute as to whether the claim (or a claim) which has been referred to arbitration has been settled that will generally fall within the reference made to the arbitral tribunal. The alleged fact of settlement will be a defence to the continuing claim and, like any other defence, a matter for the arbitral tribunal to determine. The same applies where the only remaining claim in the arbitration is one for costs. The alleged settlement is a defence to the claim for a costs order and within the reference made. An arbitration reference generally includes the power to make an award on costs, as the Act makes clear (see sections 59 to 65). Even where there is an agreed settlement that does not generally of itself bring the reference to an end (see section 51).

Theissue between the parties in a case such as the present is not as to 'whether matters have been submitted to arbitration in accordance with the arbitration agreement', but whether matters which have been so submitted has been resolved by agreement.

I therefore agree with Kasteli that the application does not fall within s. 67."

6. 吸 收 原 则

英国的民事司法制度(civil justice system)是建立在"有权利就有救济"(*ubi jus ibi remedium*,英文是 where there is a right, there is a remedy)这一原则的基础上。换句话说,如果一方声称他有诉因,他就有诉权。Diplock 勋爵在 Bremer Vulkan Schiffbau und Maschinenfabrik v. South India Shipping Corporation Ltd. (1981) 1 Lloyd's Rep. 253 先例中说:"The means provided are courts of justice to which every citizen has a constitutional right of access in the role of plaintiff to obtain the remedy to which he claims to be entitled in consequence of an alleged breach of his legal or equitable rights by some other citizen, the defendant. Whether or not to avail himself of this right of access to the court lies exclusively within the plaintiff's choice; if he chooses to do so, the defendant has no option in the matter; his subjection to the jurisdiction of the court is compulsory."

在近期的 Technotrade Ltd. v. Larkstore Ltd. (2006) EWCA Civ 1079 先例中,Mummery 大法官也说:"Underlying all these cases can be heard the drumbeat of a constant theme, which could possibly be described as ubi ius ibi remedium, the maxim that where there is a right there is a remedy; but it could also be said that the courts are anxious to see, if possible, that where a real loss has been caused by a real breach of contract, then there should if at all possible be a real remedy which directs recovery from the defendant towards the party which has suffered the loss."

但如果原告在民事司法系统下,已经胜诉并获得赔偿,就不允许对同一被告开始同一"诉因"的新诉讼,以获取更多的赔偿:见本章第1段节录的 Fraser v. HLMAD Ltd.(2006) EWCA Civ 738 先例。理由是原有的诉因已被胜诉的判决吸收(merger)而不再存在。

在 Redcar and Cleveland BC v. Bainbridge Surtees v. Middlesbrough BC(2008) EWCA Civ 885 先例中,Mummery 大法官说:"The doctrines of res judicata and merger are rooted in the need for finality in litigation, both in the public interest and in the interests of the litigants themselves. Whether he has won a case or lost a case, a litigant is not normally entitled to reactivate the same case against the same party in another action. Subject to a right of appeal, a litigant is entitled to one go at his claim, but no more ... **Merger is a defence where the litigant has won his case and obtained a final judgment on a particular cause of action. In general, he is not entitled to bring another case against the same party seeking a greater remedy for the same cause of action, because it has 'merged in the judgment' and been extinguished.**"(加黑部分是笔者的强调)

这个所谓的"单一诉讼规则"(single action rule)在英国普通法下根深蒂固, Hoffman 勋爵在 Grieves v. FT Everard & Sons Ltd.(2007) UKHL 39 先例也说:"This 'single action rule' is very old and for the protection of defendants. Coke[52] said that it was based upon the maxim interest rei publicae ut sit finis litium, 'otherwise great oppression might be done under colour and pretence of law': see Bowen LJ, at p 147. A defendant should not have to answer more than once for the consequences of the same act. A corollary of the rule is that if a claimant does have a cause of action, he may recover damages for the risk that he may suffer further injury in consequence of the same act of negligence, even though (under the principle in Gregg v. Scott [2005] 2 AC 176), such risk would not be independently actionable. There are also cases which suggest that he may be able to recover damages for anxiety consequent upon an actionable injury. But recovery is predicated upon the existence of actionable injury. There is nothing to suggest that a claimant can rely upon the single action rule to sue in circumstances in which he does not have a cause of action in the first place."

但吸收原则或单一诉讼规则在普通法下不适用在:(1)海事的对物诉讼(*in rem proceedings*),这将在本章之6.2.4段有进一步的介绍。(2)外国(非英国)法院。但这方面的普通法地位之后被立法改变,1982年《The Civil Jurisdiction and Judgments

---

[52] 这是指 Coke 勋爵的《The First Part of the Institutes of the Laws of England or, A Commentary Upon Littleton》(第18版,1823年)一书。

Act》之 section 34，说："No proceedings may be brought by a person in England and Wales or Northern Ireland on a cause of action in respect of which a judgment has been given in his favour in proceedings between the same parties, or their privies, in a court in another part of the United Kingdom or in a court of an overseas country, unless that judgment is not enforceable or entitled to recognition in England and Wales or, as the case may be, in Northern Ireland."

Goff 勋爵在 The "Indian Endurance" and The "Indian Grace" (No. 1) (1993) 1 Lloyd's Rep. 387 先例解释说，该条文并非排除吸收原则，而只是提供防止诉讼再来一次(second bite at the cherry)的抗辩："the words of section 34 can appropriately be read as providing no more than a bar against proceedings by the plaintiff rather than excluding the jurisdiction of the court."

6.1　吸收原则的效果

类似时效(time bar)，[53]吸收原则会影响诉因的可诉讼性(actionability)，即法律否定了诉因的诉权。时效与吸收原则都属于对原告的索赔做出的抗辩，唯一的区别是，时效已过的抗辩令原告不能主张他的诉因，而吸收原则令原告不能再次主张他的诉因。

如果被告没有提出吸收原则的抗辩，法院必须对有关的诉讼请求做出决定，即使这个诉讼请求涉及的是已经获得赔偿的诉因。法院不能自己主动适用吸收原则，说自己缺乏管辖权(want of jurisdiction)，诉讼的终局性的公共利益要为这种诉讼双方都希望法院对同一诉因重审的情况让路。但这种情况极少发生，因此也没有什么先例。现实中，法院通常也不会知道外国法院曾经对同样的事实做出过判决，当事人自己对此才更清楚。

另一方面，被告以吸收原则抗辩成功，就意味着原告对他主张的诉因没有诉权，法院可以做出不审讯实质争议就撤销诉讼请求的简易判决(summary judgment)：见 CPR r 24.2(a)(i)、CPR r 24.3 (1)、CPR r 24.3 (2) (a)(i) – (ii)与 CPR r 24.3 (2) (b)。原因很简单，既然诉讼的结果已经确定，为了诉讼方、法院与公共利益考虑，就应该尽快结束，而不应该在花费时间、精力与金钱准备开庭与争辩实质争议。

6.2　什么是诉因？

吸收原则(诉因的禁反言也一样)特别困难很大程度在于"诉因"(cause of action)这个概念的复杂性。每次决定吸收原则能否适用，都要看新诉讼的诉因与之前诉讼的诉因的大致相似程度：Drake v. Mitchell (1803) 102 E. R. 594 先例。

在 Coburn v. Colledge (1897) 1 QB 702 先例中，Esher 勋爵对诉因的定义是："every fact which it would be necessary for the plaintiff to prove, if traversed, in order to support their right to the judgment of the court."

---

〔53〕 见本书第十章第 2 段。

Diplock 勋爵在 Letang v. Cooper (1965) 1 QB 232 先例对诉因的定义是:"a factual situation, the existence of which entitles one person to obtain from the court a remedy against another person."

Millet 大法官在 Paragon Finance Plc. v. D B Thakerar & Co. (1998) EWCA Civ 1249 先例中说:"a cause of action is defined by its factual ingredients, not by the name ascribed to it. As Juliet observed of the rose, its essential character is not dependent on the name by which it is called."

在国际法协会(International Law Association)的《Interim Report on Res Judicata and Arbitration, Berlin Conference (2004)》与《Final Report on Res Judicata and Arbitration and Resolution No. 1/2006, Toronto Conference (2006)》[54] 中对诉因的定义是:"all the facts and circumstances necessary to give rise to a right to relief... all claims which arise from the same event and rely on the same evidence make up one cause of action."

因此,复合型违约(composite breach of contract)只属于一个诉因,Goff 勋爵在 The "Indian Endurance" and The "Indian Grace" (No. 1) (1993) 1 Lloyd's Rep. 387 先例中举例说:"the failure to construct a building in accordance with a certain specification, which can result in a whole series of defects which may nevertheless lead to a single breach of contract, i. e., the failure to hand over the building constructed in accordance with the terms of the contract.[55]"

6.2.1 情况之一:同样的违约造成了多种损失

一般来说,一个诉讼请求中包含不同的损失,即使性质与金额不同,也不代表就一定有不同的诉因。正如 Longmore 大法官在 Berezovsky v. Abramovich (2011) EWCA Civ 153 先例[该先例的诉因不是合约,而是经济侵权行为的恐吓(economic tort of intimidation)]中说:"the additional or substitution of a new loss is by no means necessarily the addition or substitution of a new cause of action."

Longmore 大法官举例说,如果被告疏忽导致原告人身伤害,无法赚钱(loss of earning)是人身伤害的间接损失,所以,人身伤害与无法赚钱是同一个诉因。

违约就更明显,原告必须将所有的真正损失(actual damages)加在一起一次过起诉。这些损失的名称、性质与金额可能不同,原告必须证明(民事诉讼是根据平衡的可能性)他确实蒙受了这些损失,这也是为什么原告要花大量的时间与金钱收集证据,以支持他对真正损失的索赔。而针对将来的预期损失(expectation damages),特别在诉讼时知道或应该知道会有这样的损失,就必须在该诉讼中一并提出。这无可

---

〔54〕 可在 http://www.ila-hq.org 下载。

〔55〕 房屋建造合约下会有很多不同的缺陷,但这只是违约,即承建商没有按照合约要求把房屋建,好并按时交出给雇主。不会窗子漏水是一个违约或诉因,另屋顶漏水有时是另一个独立的违约或诉因。

避免地会导致法院通过专家证人(如人身伤害就是医生)做出的估计,而认定的预期损失在事后被证实有偏差或遗漏或医学知识在当时尚未知道会有此后果的情况经常发生。但原告(受害方)仍受到一事不再审的约束,不能再提出新诉讼要求额外的损失。

在人身伤亡的案件,早在涉及疏忽驾驶的 Brunsden v. Humphrey (1884 – 85) LR 14 QBD 141 先例中,上诉庭的 Bowen 大法官就明确说:"It is a well settled rule of-law that damages resulting from one and the same cause of action must be assessed and recovered once for all."

在 Curwen v. James (1963) 1 W. L. R. 748 先例中,Pearson 勋爵说到对将来的预期损失(特别是人身伤害)做出臆猜的困难,但法院又不得不做:"... the normal rule in accident cases is that the sum of damages falls to be assessed once for all at the time of the hearing. When the assessment is made, the court has to make the best estimate it can as to events that may happen in the future. If further evidence as to new events were too easily admitted, there would be no finality in such litigation. There are quite often uncertain matters which have to be estimated and taken into account to the best of the ability of the judge trying the action. For instance, to give an obvious example, the court often has to consider whether an operation on the patient is likely to be successful or not and, if so, how successful, and what result it is likely to achieve, and therefore whether the plaintiff is likely to suffer from a continuing disability or not. That is a very important matter in the assessment of damages, and quite often the continuing disability is foreseen merely as an uncertain future possibility or as a future probability at most. Another question which very frequently has to be taken into account in assessing damages in accident cases is whether and when osteo – arthritis is likely to supervene."

另在 Conquer v. Boot (1928) 2 KB 336 先例中,案情涉及一间平房的建造合约。原告以被告违反合约没有以优良与精湛工艺完成工程(breach of contract to complete in a good and workmanlike manner)为由起诉,并获得赔偿。之后原告又以违反同一合约为由,提出了另一些索赔。被告以一事不再审为由,要求法院撤销诉讼请求,上诉庭的 Sankey 大法官与 Talbot 大法官支持被告的请求。Sankey 大法官说:

"The plaintiff in the first action gave particulars of a number of matters which he stated constituted a breach of contract to build in a good and workmanlike manner. These particulars are fairly numerous and are set out with great particularity. In the second action the particulars are of similar character; they also are fairly numerous and are set out with great particularity. But so far as the claim is concerned it appears to me to be identical in both cases-namely, a claim for breach of contract to complete the bungalow in a good and workmanlike manner. That was a matter which obviously struck the learned county court judge, for he says in his judgment: 'As to the plea of res judicata, I allowed this so far as the claim in respect of the manhole and air bricks were concerned because these defects were obvious at the time of an earlier action in August, 1926, between the same parties. So far as the bulk of the claim is concerned I disallowed it, as the state of dampness and rottenness of the premises and particularly of the flooring, was not apparent at the time of the earlier action.' The question remains whether this is a correct determination in point of law.

With regard to the plea of res judicata a great number of cases have been cited to us, the most informative of which is that of Brunsden v. Humphrey.... **One knows that in personal injury cases damages are assessed once for all ... In the present case, adopting the same analogy, it seems to be quite impossible to say that in the first month of the year the plaintiff could have brought his action for failure to complete the dining room in a proper and workmanlike manner and next month for failure to complete the drawing room and so forth**..."(加黑部分是笔者的强调)

Talbot 大法官也说:"There are many authorities on this subject or connected with it, but they all come back to the same test, is the cause of action in the second action the same as that for which the plaintiff had judgment in the first? If it is, the second action cannot be maintained, and (speaking generally) **it is immaterial whether the plaintiff knew or might have known, when he brought the first action, the facts on which he relies in the second**..."(加黑部分是笔者的强调,即只要之后的诉讼是同一诉因,原告在第一个诉讼是否知道或应该知道第二个诉讼中依赖的事实并不重要。)

Talbot 大法官认为在 Conquer v. Boot 先例中,之后的诉讼的诉因与之前的诉讼无论形式还是实质内容上都是一样的,说:"there is one contract and one promise to be performed at one time, although no doubt the defendant may have failed to perform it in one or in many respect."

但 Talbot 大法官也强调说,如果合约中有不同的承诺(通常针对不同方面的不同条文),违反每个承诺都会构成不同的诉因:"there may of course be many promises in one contract, the breach of each of which is a separate cause of action."

在 Purser & Co. (Hillingdon) Ltd. v. Jackson (1977) Q. B. 166 先例中,原告买了一栋新的平房,被告承建商保证房屋满足政府的所有要求。合约中还规定了原告在发现缺陷后,应尽快告知承建商,承建商在被告知后,应在合理时间内修正。如果双方对缺陷有争议,应通过仲裁解决。1970 年 8 月,原告针对主卧天花板的缺陷开始仲裁。1972 年 6 月,一位测量师代表原告写信给仲裁员,提到了屋顶的缺陷,并估计修正缺陷需要 800 英镑。1972 年 8 月,仲裁员判被告要向原告做出 105 英镑的赔偿。原告声称仲裁员在做出裁决时没有考虑屋顶的缺陷,因此要求委任第二位仲裁员裁决屋顶缺陷的争议。而承建商认为根据一事不再审的说法,原告不能再提起针对屋顶缺陷的索赔,因为第一位仲裁员已经做出了判决,所有的缺陷都已经或应该在第一次仲裁中提出。关于原告是否因为1972年8月的裁决书而不能再提起针对屋顶的缺陷的索赔，Forbe大法官说："（1） that in arbitration proceedings the matters which determined the issues to be decided by the arbitrator were those matters which had been included in the terms of reference and it was only if a matter had been before the arbitrator that there was an estoppel per rem judicatam. （2） Further that, by providing in the contract for disputes to be settled by arbitration, the parties intended serial arbitration as they envisaged that disputes about building defects would arise from time to time; consequently there could not be a bar by estoppel per rem judicatam to the raising on a subsequent occasion of a defect which was not covered by a first arbitration.[56]"

在Steamship Mutual Underwriting Association Ltd. v. Trollope & Colls（City）Ltd.（1986）2 Const. L. J. 75先例中，May大法官也警告说，如果原告成功向建筑师索赔了中央温控系统的缺陷后，对泥瓦工作的缺陷或地基缺陷开始新的诉讼以索赔损失，很难想象一事不再审的抗辩会成功（it is inconceivable that they could have been met with a successful plea of res judicata）。因此，仅仅是一栋建筑里的不同缺陷的事实并不代表就一定构成同一诉因（constituents of one and the same cause of action）。May大法官总结说，是否为新的诉因混合了事实问题与法律问题（whether there is a new cause of action in any circumstances is a mixed question of law and fact）。在近期的Cleveland BC v. Bainbridge Surtees v. Middlesbrough BC（2008）EWCA Civ 885先例中，上诉庭在应用吸收原则时支持了May大法官的总结。

6.2.2　情况之二：一个疏忽行为侵犯了两种权利

侵权诉讼与违反合约的诉讼不同，诉因更局限。一般侵权的行为就是疏忽（negligence），但疏忽经常发生，不能让疏忽单独成为诉因令无关人士也可以起诉疏忽方，疏忽加上损失才能构成诉因。如一宗疏忽导致的车祸，并非所有看见或在附近的人士都有诉因可以起诉疏忽的驾驶员。只有真正受伤的路人才有诉因可起诉驾驶员，也就是侵权方。相比之下，违反合约本身就是诉因，不需要加上损失，合约方可以向违约方起诉，或要求一个宣告判决（declaratory judgment），或只能获得名义损失（nominal damage）的赔偿。所以说，侵权的诉因更为局限。Goff勋爵在The "Indian Endurance" and The "Indian Grace"（No.1）（1993）1 Lloyd's Rep. 387先例中说："a simple action in negligence, . . . where damage is of the essence of the claim in the sense that damage must be proved to establish the cause of action. In that case, **it is theoretically possible to segregate different causes of action by reference to different causes of**

---

〔56〕 仲裁庭只有权对他被委任的争议做出裁决，而且在建筑合约中经常会有建筑的缺陷不断出现，导致同一建筑合约下有一连串的仲裁。所以，在第一个仲裁时尚未发觉的缺陷不会受一事不再审的约束，可在另一个新的仲裁提出。从另一角度分析，在第一个仲裁没有出现或/与发觉的缺陷也就是没有争议。而有了争议是提起仲裁的先决条件，所以一事不再审不应适用。

action to different heads of damages. Thus in Brunsden v. Humphrey (1884 – 85) LR 14 QBD 141 . . . but so narrow an approach is not in any event possible in a contractual context, where proof of damage is not necessary to establish the cause of action. . . "(加黑部分是笔者的强调)

Hoffmann 勋爵在 Grieves v. FT Everard & Sons Ltd. (2007) UKHL 39 先例针对疏忽的侵权也有同样的说法:"Some causes of action arise without proof of damage. Trespass and breach of contract are examples. Proof of the trespass or breach of contract is enough to found a cause of action. If no actual damage is proved, the claimant is entitled to nominal damages. **But a claim in tort based on negligence is incomplete without proof of damage.** Damage in this sense is an abstract concept of being worse off, physically or economically, so that compensation is an appropriate remedy. It does not mean simply a physical change, which is consistent with making one better, as in the case of a successful operation, or with being neutral, having no perceptible effect upon one's health or capability. "(加黑部分是笔者的强调)

因此,正如 Goff 勋爵所说,理论上在同一个疏忽行为导致两种不同损失的情况(如人身伤害与财产受损),会有两个不同的诉因。但如果是两种不同的人身伤害,如腿摔断了与大脑受损,属于同一诉因,吸收原则仍适用。在 Serrao v. Noel (1884 – 85) LR 15 QBD 549 先例中,Brett 大法官说:"Where separate rights have been infringed, separate actions may be maintained, because the infringement of separate rights gives rise to separate causes of action: this was elaborately shown in Brunsden v. Humphrey. . . "

Goff 勋爵与 Brett 大法官都提到的 Brunsden v. Humphrey (1884 – 85) LR 14 QBD 141 先例,案情涉及被告疏忽导致原告人身伤害与马车受损。原告先开始第一个诉讼索赔对马车造成的损失,之后又开始了新的诉讼索赔人身伤害的损失。Bowen 大法官先强调了如果原告先索赔人身伤害的损失,之后又发现新的人身伤害损失(隐藏的伤害),[57] 仍属于同一诉因,在吸收原则与一事不再审的说法下,不能开始新的诉讼,说:"if the plaintiff had recovered any damages for injury to his person, he could not have maintained a further action for fresh bodily injuries caused by the same act of negligence, merely because they had been discovered or developed subsequently. "

而针对对马车造成的损失与人身伤害的损失,上诉庭的多数判决是虽然是由同一疏忽行为导致但属于不同类别或性质的诉因,因此,原告可以进行另一个新的诉讼。

但这个多数判决并非没有争议,做出不同意见的 Coleridge 勋爵就说一个手臂或大腿受伤的人士不能因为裤子或衬衣也破了而变为有两个诉因:"[because] it seems

〔57〕 受害方应如何应对这种危险,在本章之 6.4 段有介绍。

to me a subtlety not warranted by law to hold that a man cannot bring two actions, if he is injured in his arm and in his leg, but can bring two, if besides his arm and leg being injured his trousers which contain his leg, and his coat – sleeve which contains his arm, have been torn."

也不必对这种微妙的情况过分担心,因为"滥用司法程序"(abuse)的说法可以针对这种情况。Smith 大法官 Talbot v. Berkshire County Council (1994) Q. B. 290 先例就说,上诉庭在 Brunsden v. Humphrey 先例本可以以滥用司法程序或违反"Henderson v. Henderson Rule"[58]为由撤销原告对人身伤害的诉讼请求。

6.2.3　情况之三:故意与非故意的错误行为

在 Paragon Finance Plc. v. D B Thakerar & Co. (1998) EWCA Civ 1249 先例中,原告 Paragon Finance 原本以违反合约与疏忽违反诚信责任(fiduciary duty)开始诉讼,但之后原告希望修改诉讼请求(amendment to pleadings),增加对被告欺诈的指控。这时诉讼时效(time bar)已过,法院拒绝做出批文。该先例涉及典型的非故意的错误行为(unintentional wrongdoing,疏忽或违反了合约中的严格责任)与故意的错误行为(intentional wrongdoing,欺诈),显示了对两者做出区分的必要性。上诉庭驳回了原告的上诉,认为这是两个不同的诉因,原告不能通过修改诉讼请求而加入一个时效已过的独立诉因,因此拒绝做出批文。Millet 大法官说:"In my judgment, it is incontrovertible that an amendment to make a new obligation of intentional wrongdoing by pleading fraud, conspiracy to defraud, fraudulent breach of trust or intentional breach of fiduciary duty where previously no intentional wrongdoing has been alleged constitutes the introduction of a new cause of action."

Millet 大法官解释说,对于故意的错误行为的诉因,原告必须证明被告故意(intention),这与非故意的错误行为的诉因不同。因此,如果原告成功证明了被告疏忽,吸收原则或一事不再审是不会排除原告再次以欺诈的诉因开始另一个新诉讼以获得更多的赔偿,即使欺诈的诉讼针对的是一回事。

Paragon Finance Plc. v. D B Thakerar & Co. 先例并非针对一事不再审,而是针对时效,但道理相通。如果是同一个诉因,只要提起诉讼及时,后来提出修改请求(如增加索赔损失的金额或项目)是不会面对时效已过的困境。而不是同一个诉因,没有人反对放在同一个诉讼一并处理,但如果时效已过后,原告或被告想通过修改请求加上一个不同诉因的争议,就会面对时效已过的困境。航运就有不少这种案件,船东在时效内(6 年)内向承租人提起诉讼(或仲裁)索赔运费、租金等,而承租人以货损货差的损失作为"抗辩",而提出时,《海牙规则》的 1 年时效已过。由于运费或租金的诉因与货损货差的诉因不同,承租人的"抗辩"其实是独立的反索赔,会面对时效已过的困境。这在杨良宜的《程租合约》一书第九章之 4.2 段,杨大明的《期租合同》

---

〔58〕 在本章稍后的第 8 段有详论。

一书第五十篇之 50.3 段，笔者的《提单与其他付运单证》(2016 年)一书第五章之 5.9.1段与 17.2.4 段有介绍：The “Aries”（1977）1 Lloyd’s Rep. 334；The “Standard Ardour”（1988）2 Lloyd’s Rep. 159；Wholecrop Marketing Ltd. v. Wolds Produce Ltd.（2013）EWHC 2079(Ch)等先例。

6.2.4 情况之四：对人诉讼与对物诉讼

这种情况涉及复杂的海事法，简单而言，关于对物诉讼(action in rem)可节录 George Jessel 大法官在 The “City of Mecca”（1881）5 PD 106 先例的说法：“You may in England and in most countries proceed against the ship. The writ may be issued against the owner of such a ship, and the owner may never appear, and you get your judgment against the ship without a single person being named from beginning to end. This is an action in rem, and it is perfectly well understood that the judgment is against the ship.”

如果船舶被扣押并被送达了对物诉讼的告票，船东可以选择出面抗辩，也可以选择无视这个对物诉讼。这样，法院会做出缺席判决，被扣押的船舶在败诉后会被实质执行(一般来说是通过海事法院拍卖)。正如 Fletcher Moulton 大法官在 The “Burns”（1907）P. 137（CA)先例中说：“...[an action in rem] is an action in which the owners may take part, if they think proper, in defence of their property, but whether or not they will do so is a matter for them to decide, and if they do not decide to make themselves parties to the suit in order to defend their property, no personal liability can be established against them in that action.”

Denning 勋爵在 The “Banco”（1971）1 Lloyd’s Rep. 49 先例也说：“If the defendant enters an appearance, the action in rem proceeds just as an action in personam. If judgment is entered against the defendant, it can be executed against any of his property within the jurisdiction, be it his other ships or any other goods... If no appearance is entered, however, the action remains, as it began, an action in rem only, operating only against the ship arrested. If judgment is entered in default of appearance it can be enforced by sale of the ship, but not against the defendant personally...”

因此在普通法下，对物诉讼与对人诉讼是有实质区别，而并非只是形式不同。也就是说，对物诉讼的判决并不会吸收对人诉讼的诉因：The “Bengal”（1859）Swab. 468；The “John and Mary”（1859）Swab. 471；The “Sylph”（1867）LR 2 A & E 24；Nelson v. Couch（1863）15 C. B.（N. S.）99；The “Cella”（1888）13 P. D. 82；The “Joannis Vatis”（No. 2)（1922）P. 213；The “Rena K”（1978）1 Lloyd’s Rep. 545；The “Nordglimt”（1987）2 Lloyd’s Rep. 470；香港的 The “Alas”（2014）6 HKC 239 等先例。

但英国这方面的普通法地位在欧共体法院判例的影响下有了改变，可见笔者《仲裁法——从开庭审理到裁决书的作出与执行》一书第十章之 4.1 段。

6.3 在唯一的诉讼中提出所有救济的重要性

保险起见，原告最好与必须在诉讼中将所有可能的救济或赔偿一并提出，因为在同一诉因（cause of action）下，只有一次获得赔偿的机会（a single bite at the cherry）。

在 Serrao v. Noel（1884－85）LR 15 QBD 549 先例中，原告将公司股票交给一个经纪人协助出售。经纪人死后，原告才发现经纪人在没有授权的情况下，将他的股票作为担保存放在被告处。在收到公司将把被告登记为股东的通知后，原告向高院的衡平法院（Chancery Division）申请禁令（injunction）禁止被告与公司这样做，并要求将股票归还给他。衡平法院做出命令说："upon delivery of the deed or form of transfer and the securities representing the same, and upon payment of costs to the plaintiff... all proceedings in the said Chancery action should be stayed."

但股票直到命令后 4 个月才被交还原告，原告之后又在高院的皇家法院（Queen's Bench Division）开始了新的诉讼程序，索赔被告错误扣押（detention）股票期间的损失。但法院判损失与禁令是同一诉因下的不同救济，原告原本可以在第一个诉讼中就提出索赔损失的请求，现在不能在新诉讼中再获得赔偿。Brett 大法官说："Even before the Supreme Court of Judicature Acts, 1873, 1875, and still more now [i.e. after the merger of law and equity], no more actions than can be brought for the same cause of action."

这个精神也显示在了普通法院与衡平法院合并后的 1981 年《Senior Courts Act》立法之 section 49："（英格兰与威尔士的所有法院）shall give the same effect as hitherto－（a）to all equitable estates, titles, rights, reliefs, defences and counterclaims, and to all equitable duties and liabilities; and（b）subject thereto, to all legal claims and demands and all estates, titles, rights, duties, obligations and liabilities existing by the common law or by any custom or created by statute, ... shall so exercise its jurisdiction in every cause or matter before it as **to secure that, as far as possible, all matters in dispute between the parties are completely and finally determined, and all multiplicity of legal proceedings with respect to any of those matters is avoided.**"（加黑部分是笔者的强调）

6.4 吸收原则导致的严苛后果

吸收原则在许多先例中也会导致严苛后果，可以说，一事不再审的说法要很好地平衡诉讼的终局性与保证公平这两个公共政策是不容易。以 Fraser v. HLMAD Ltd.（2006）EWCA Civ 738 先例为例，在该先例中，原告在劳资审裁处（employment tribunal）起诉被告（雇主）不公平解雇（unfair dismissal）与错误解雇（wrongful dismissal）。不公平解雇涉及雇员在 1996 年《Employment Rights Act》立法下的权利，根据该立法，被不公平解雇的雇员有权在劳资审裁处起诉索赔损失。错误解雇涉及雇主违反雇佣合约，雇员作为无辜方在合约下有权在劳资审裁处或高院起诉。劳资审裁处根据立法能做出的最高裁决是 25000 英镑，因此，原告在诉讼中保留了如果损失超出

25000英镑在高院诉讼的权利。劳资审裁处最后认定损失是80000英镑,但因为立法限制只能做出25000英镑的裁决,原告在高院开始另一个新诉讼,索赔剩下的部分,即55000英镑。被告则以一事不再审与滥用司法程序为由向高院申请撤销这个诉讼请求,并被高院支持。之后上诉庭也驳回了原告的上诉,认为虽然原告明示保留了权利,劳资审裁处的裁决仍然吸收(merger)了错误解雇的诉因,该诉因不再存在,原告无法再在高院开始诉讼。

Mummery大法官建议原告本应只在劳资审裁处起诉不公平解雇,而不起诉错误解雇:"In future claimants and their legal advisers would be well advised to confine claims in employment tribunal proceedings to unfair dismissal, unless they are sure that the claimant is willing to limit the total damages claimed for wrongful dismissal to £ 25,000 or less. If the claimant wishes to recover over £ 25,000, the wrongful dismissal claim should only be made in High Court proceedings. The findings of the employment tribunal in its judgment on the unfair dismissal claim will assist, as they will give rise to an issue estoppel in any subsequent High Court proceedings for wrongful dismissal, but there will be no merger of causes of action and the claimant will not be prevented by success in the employment tribunal claim for unfair dismissal from pursuing an action for wrongful dismissal. An application for summary judgment in the High Court for the wrongful dismissal claim will be appropriate in straightforward cases."

在更近期的Redcar and Cleveland BC v. Bainbridge Surtees v. Middlesbrough BC (2008) EWCA Civ 885先例中,Mummery大法官再次提到吸收原则会带来严苛后果。

但Mummery大法官在Fraser v. HLMAD Ltd做出的建议有问题,如果原告采取了这种策略,之后在高院的诉讼也会面对滥用司法程序或违反了"Henderson v. Henderson Rule"的抗辩。Jacob V. Van de Velden的《Finality in Litigation》一书第40页质疑Mummery大法官的判决与建议说:"The correctness of His Lordship's decisions is questionable. The merger doctrine applies only if the claimant had the opportunity to recover in the former case the remedy claimed in the subsequent case; in this case, however, though damages were available in the employment tribunal, the claimant had no opportunity to recover the whole remedy to which they were by law entitled for their cause of action, because the employment tribunal's jurisdiction was limited to GBP 25,000. On these facts, the defendant cannot show that the claimant had in the prior case an opportunity of claiming the whole remedy, and but for their own fault might have recovered, what they sought to recover in the new case. Consequently, the claim should have been allowed."

这也导致了隐藏的损失(hidden damage)无法获得赔偿(如对人身或财产伤害)的问题。在本章之6.2.1段提到的Curwen v. James (1963) 1 W. L. R. 748先例中,

Talbot 大法官说无论原告在之前的诉讼中是否知道或应该知道有关的损失，吸收原则都适用，原告都不能再提起诉讼："... it is immaterial whether the plaintiff knew or might have known."

这方面的问题在《McGregor on Damages》（第19版，2014年）第十一章有十分详尽针对。笔者只节录部分内容，首先是11－030段针对只有一个诉因（cause of action）的情况："The corollary of the proposition that damages for prospective loss resulting from a single cause of action may be recovered in one action is the proposition that such damages must be recovered in one action once and for all. If the claimant fails to secure recovery for all his damage in one action he cannot bring another action to repair the omission. This principle applies equally to cases where the damage is or ought to be evident to the claimant before trial of the first action, where there is no real hardship in refusing a second action, and to cases where the damnage does not become evident until after trial of the first action and is sufficiently unanticipated as not to be claimed as prospective damage, in which case refusal a second action will cause hardship where the unanticuipated loss was great."

接下来的11－031段介绍了几个案例，包括 Clarke v. Yorke（1882）47 L. T. 381；Conquer v. Boot（1928）2 KB 336；[59] Furness Withy & Co. v. Hall（1909）25 T. L. R. 233 与 Rowntree v. Allen（1936）41 Com. Cas. 90 先例。在 Furness Withy & Co. v. Hall 先例中，案情涉及修船合约，原告将修理船舶冷藏设备的修理工作分包给了被告。被告没有及时完成工作，导致原告对船东违约。船东成功向原告索赔了损失，原告则向被告索赔赔给船东的这笔钱。之后，原告开始第二个诉讼向被告索赔在第一个与船东的诉讼中做出抗辩的诉讼费用。但原告第二个诉讼因为一事不再审或吸收原则的说法败诉。在 Rowntree v. Allen 先例中，案情涉及一个公司将生意包括当时的所有合约转让给原告。合约中有一份是由被告供应的烧碱（caustic soda）。在转让前，该公司已经因为烧碱的质量问题蒙受损失。转让后，原告在不知道烧碱质量有问题的情况下继续使用，导致自己也蒙受了损失。原告之后开始第一个诉讼，成功索赔了该公司在转让前蒙受的损失。之后又开始第二个诉讼，索赔自己蒙受的损失，但这个诉讼请求也是因为一事不再审或吸收原则的说法败诉。

这些先例虽然可以说原告都有合理的理由开始第二次诉讼，但也可以说在进行第一次诉讼时应该知道或估计到会有这样的损失，最多是金额多少还不能确定。但有些情况是原告在第一个诉讼完全无法知道会有这样的损失，在这种情况下，吸收原则会对原告带来十分严苛的后果。特别是侵权造成的人身伤亡，但也可能是合约下（如雇佣合约），有关的损失在之前的诉讼中完全无法合理被发现的情况并非罕见。在早期的 Fitter v. Veal（1701）12 Mod. 542 先例与 Fetter v. Beale（1701）1 Ld.

---

〔59〕 案情已经在本章之6.2.1段介绍。

Raym. 339 先例中,原告已经获得了被告“袭击”(assault)与“殴打”(battery)下造成的伤害的赔偿。之后,原告因为被告的袭击与殴打导致的伤口引起了进一步的伤害,但法院判原告不能再次提起索赔。另在 Derrick v. Williams (1939) 2 All ER 559 CA 先例中,死者的继承人对死者的死亡向被告索赔损失,但不包括死者如果没有死亡,可以赚取的预期损失,因为在当时的法律下,不允许死者的继承人索赔这种损失。但之后贵族院改变了原本的法律地位,原告仍不被允许开始第二个诉讼索赔预期损失。

所以针对这种严苛的情况,现在针对人身伤亡损失赔偿的法律已经稍有改变。这可节录《McGregor on Damages》(第 19 版,2014 年)一书之 11－033 段,如下:“Certain inroads have indeed been made upon the universality of the requirement that all of a claimant's damages must be awarded at the hearing on damages. Concentration has been on the difficulties encountered by the victims of personal injury. Interim awards were introduced for them in 1970, followed by provisional awards in 1985. Now and most dramatically of all, with the availability of awards of periodical payments from April 2005 the door has been opened to awards stretching into the future which may later be varied should the injured party's condition seriously deteriorate or significantly improve... And quite apart from the statutory provisions designed for personal injury cases, there is a general greater preparedness today, though it is still exceptional, to postpone the assessment of items of loss which at the time of trial are still in the future and cannot be readily quantified.[60]”

至于不涉及人身伤亡的案件,如果原告知道将来会有一些类别的损失,只是不清楚具体的金额,怕将来再次提出索赔会面对一事不再审或吸收原则的抗辩,可能可以要求法院或仲裁庭做出宣告(declaration)或保留计算损失的权利。在 Trans Trust S. P. R. L. v. Danubian Trading Co. Ltd. (1952) 2 Q. B. 297 先例中,买方错误拒货,卖方索赔他的损失,但同时考虑到他的供应商将来会提出其他损失,这要将来向买方要求补偿。所以,他在一审法院要求对将来的损失(但这时根本没办法核算金额)做出宣告,McNair 大法官支持了卖方的要求。之后买方上诉到上诉庭,上诉庭认为宣告可能并不适合。因为如果将来卖方真正提出这个额外的损失,买方应有权做出抗辩,包括损失的遥远性或没有减少损失,因此更合适的方法是保留计算损失的权利。Denning 大法官说:“If the liability of the sellers to a third party were within the contemplation of the parties, but had not yet been assessed, then the proper course for the judge was to reserve that head of damages. Judgment could be entered for the damages already ascertained, leaving the rest to be ascertained later by the same or another judge.”

在近期的 Deeny v. Gooda Walker (1995) 1 WLR 1206 先例中,案情与本章 8.6.3

---

〔60〕 见 Deeny v. Gooda Walker (1995) 1 WLR 1206; A v. National Blood Authority (2002) Lloyd's Rep. Med. 487; Cook v. Cook (2011) EWHC 1638 等先例。

段介绍的 Barrow v. Bankside Members Agency Ltd.（1996）1 WLR 257 先例类似。法院针对劳合社(Lloyd's)的受保代理人或管理代理人或成员代理人在受保时是否对保险人有合理具有专业知识与小心谨慎的责任与有否违反这个责任(如果有)这两个特定争议,判原告保险人胜诉与可以获得赔偿。Deeny 先生作为保险人的损失可以分为两部分,一部分是已经蒙受的损失,另一部分是将来的损失。已经蒙受的损失没有太大争议,因此法院做出了简易判决(summary judgment)。困难的是将来的损失,因为 Deeny 先生完全无法知道将来会有多少被保险人向他索赔,于是向法院申请可以向被告获得补偿的宣告,而被告申请推迟对将来的损失金额的核算。高院的 Phillips 大法官支持了被告推迟对将来的损失金额的核算的申请,说:"In my judgment these provisions enable the court to make an award of damages in relation to part of a claim while deferring for adjudication another part . . . I have concluded that I have jurisdiction to make an award in respect of claims that have been paid while reserving for future determination that part of the Names' claim that relates to anticipated claims. A similar, although not identical, effect could be achieved by ordering an interim payment to reflect the paid claims . . . **The desirability of bringing an end to litigation will normally make it appropriate for the court to make a single award of damages which includes the best assessment possible of future loss. This will not always be the case. . .**"(加黑部分是笔者的强调)

7. Estoppel *per rem judicatam*

这个说法包括"诉因的禁反言"(cause of action estoppel)与"争端的禁反言"(issue estoppel)两个分支。传统的定义可节录 Diplock 大法官在 Thoday v. Thoday (1964) P. 181 (CA)先例中的说法:"The first species, which I will call 'cause of action estoppel', is that which prevents a party to an action from asserting or denying, as against the other party, the existence of a particular cause of action, the non – existence or existence of which has been determined by a court of competent jurisdiction in previous litigation between the same parties. **If the cause of action was determined to exist, i. e., judgment was given upon it, it is said to be merged in the judgment, or, for those who prefer Latin, transit in rem judicatam.** If it was determined not to exist, the unsuccessful plaintiff can no longer assert that it does; **he is estopped per rem judicatam.** This is simply an application of the rule of public policy expressed in the Latin maxim. 'Nemo debet bis vexari pro una et eadem causa'. In this application of the maxim 'causa' bears its literal Latin meaning."(加黑部分是笔者的强调,并且可以看出 Diplock 大法官是把吸收原则与诉因的禁反言视为一回事。)

7.1 诉因的禁反言

吸收原则、诉因的禁反言与争端的禁反言的说法都属于一事不再审下的分支（特别是诉因的禁反言）。Jacob V. Van de Velden 的《Finality in Litigation》一书中第45页提到了诉因的禁反言与吸收原则的区别之一是后者影响更大，因为诉因不再存在后，原告不能向其他人士寻求额外的救济或赔偿，说："Apart from the general requirements that the judgment relied upon must stem from a court of competent jurisdiction and must remain in force, and that the defendant must duly invoke the doctrine, the only condition for application is that the new claim is based on a case of action for which judgment was previously recovered. In addition to this ' identity of cause of action ' – requirement, and in contract to the doctrine of estoppel per rem judicatam, the merger doctrine does not require that the same parties are involved in the new and in the prior case; no ' identity of parties ' – requirement applies. "

要构成诉因的禁反言，必须是适格法院对同样诉讼方同样诉因的诉讼做出了最终与结论性的判决。但吸收原则的适用不需要诉讼方一致。Parke B 在 King v. Hoare（1844）13 M & W 494 先例解释了为什么吸收原则不需要诉讼方一致，说："There is but one cause of action, whether it be against a single person or many.[61]"

因为原告获得判决赔偿后，原本的诉因就被吸收，不再存在。无论原告最开始起诉的是谁，他都已经获得了赔偿并且也只能获得一次赔偿，双重赔偿（double recovery）是不被允许的，并会涉及滥用司法程序。在很多案件中，一个诉因（无论违约或侵权）可以有几个潜在的被告，如多方商业合约（multiparty contract）并不罕见；在弃权案件中，共同侵权人（joint or concurrent tortfeasors）也很常见。

原告选择其中一个作为被告，而不是将所有人都加入作为被告的原因有很多，如被告之一是有钱的大公司。这导致原告只选择把这家大公司作为被告，并不理会有其他潜在的被告，这样也可以节省诉讼时间与费用。但不幸的是，在诉讼期间或之后该大公司倒闭，而在法院做出原告获得赔偿的判决（而不是庭外和解）后，即使无法实质执行，原告也不能再以同样的诉因起诉其他被告（如另一个共同侵权人）是很合理，因为诉因不存在了。

当然不同诉因的诉讼即使针对的是同一件事也不受影响，如之前的诉讼中的被告可以向另一个共同侵权人要求补偿或分摊（根据 1978 年《Civil Liability [Contribution] Act》立法[62]）等救济。

---

〔61〕 不论是针对一位或多位人士，都只有一个诉因。

〔62〕 该立法之 section 3 规定："Judgment recovered against any person liable in respect of any debt or damage shall not be a bar to an action... against any other person who is (apart from any such bar) jointly liable with him in respect of the same debt or damage. "关于这个课题可见笔者《提单与其他付运单证》一书第五章之 17.2.9.4 段。

Goff 勋爵在 The “Indian Endurance” and The “Indian Grace”（No. 1）（1993）1 Lloyd’s Rep. 387 先例中说：“... it is perhaps more difficult for a plea of waiver or estoppel to be effective in a case where the doctrine of merger in judgment applies, since the effect of the merger is that the cause of action ceases to exist; and indeed in Spencer Bower and Turner it is pointed out, at pp. 398 – 399, that the only instances of estoppel as an affirmative answer to a case of this kind are to be found in cases of waiver or estoppel by omission to plead the former recovery. Even so, I hesitate to conclude that estoppel or waiver can otherwise have no application in such a case. However once again your Lordships did not have the benefit of argument on the point; and I will assume, in favour of the defendants that generally a plea of estoppel or waiver will not be effective where the doctrine of merger in judgment applies at common law.”

典型的例子之一是对间皮瘤（mesothelioma）的人身伤害索赔。间皮瘤是一种潜伏期长达 40 年的致命癌症，通常会在发现后的两年内死亡。虽然这种癌症的病原还没有科学上的定论，但绝大部分的例子显示是由于病人曾经接触石棉（asbestos）。这种癌症不像另一种涉及石棉的肺尘症（pneumoconiosis），是一种累积性的疾病，所以没有办法科学地说明患者是哪次接触石棉才引发了间皮瘤。也就是说，如果患者曾经多次在为不同的雇主服务的时候接触过石棉，就没有办法较科学地证明哪位雇主应该为他的患病或死亡负责。而且很有可能患上间皮瘤的人士二三十年前服务过的雇主大部分已经破产/结束营业，只有一两家大公司还存在。如果该患上间皮瘤的人士向大公司索赔，该公司就会以无法证明因果关系（causation）抗辩。

因此，英国 2006 年《The Compensation Act》之 section 3 规定曾经在工作中导致或者允许原告接触石棉的被告就要负责，并对原告的全部损失承担共同与连带责任（the responsible person shall be liable in respect of the whole of the damage caused to the victim by the disease... jointly and severally with any other responsible person）。但这不影响做出赔偿的被告起诉其他应承担责任的雇主根据 1978 年《Civil Liability（Contribution）Act》立法分摊责任（does not prevent one responsible person from claiming a contribution from another）。关于这个课题，杨良宜的《损失赔偿与救济》一书第四章之 4.3.3 段有详细介绍。

在这种情况下，患上间皮瘤的人士在向前雇主 A 索赔了所有损失之后，再次对前雇主 A 开始诉讼，这就涉及诉因的禁反言。但如果他又开始对前雇主 B 的索赔，诉因的禁反言就不适用，因为他们之间不存在任何适格法院做出的判决。但为了防止他双重赔偿（甚至多重赔偿），吸收原则的说法就会适用。

7.2　争端的禁反言

7.2.1　与诉因的禁反言的区别

诉因的禁反言与争端的禁反言的区别可见 Keith 勋爵在 Arnold v. National Westminster Bank Plc.（1991）2 AC 93 先例中所说：“Cause of action estoppel arises where the cause of action in the later proceedings is identical to that in the earlier proceedings, the latter having been between the same parties or their privies and having involved the same subject matter. In such a case the bar is absolute in relation to all points decided unless fraud or collusion is alleged, such as to justify setting aside the earlier judgment. The discovery of new factual matter which could not have been found out by reasonable diligence for use in the earlier proceedings does not, according to the law of England, permit the latter to be reopened... **Issue estoppel may arise where a particular issue forming a necessary ingredient in a cause of action has been litigated and decided and in subsequent proceedings between the same parties involving a different cause of action to which the same issue is relevant one of the parties seeks to reopen that issue.**"(加黑部分是笔者的强调)

也就是说,在同一个诉因下的诉讼会有多个替代(alternative)的争端(issue)。该诉讼的判决会对提出的多个争端逐一做出决定。在之后双方不同诉因的诉讼中如果涉及个别同样的争端(无论是对合约条文的解释、对事实的认定及其法律后果、时效的计算、管辖权等),之前双方的诉讼中的决定仍有约束力,不能重新争议并试图否定。

在美国的 San Remo Hotel, LP v. City and Countty of San Fransco, Cal, 545 US 323, 336 (2005)先例中,将争端的禁反言称为"附带的禁反言"(collateral estoppel),说:"Under res judicata, a final judgment on the merits of an action precludes the parties or their privies from relitigating issues that were or could have been raised in that action. Under collateral estoppels, once a court has decided an issue of fact or law necessary to its judgment that decision, may preclude relitigation decided in a suit on a different cause of action involving a party to the first case."(第一句针对滥用司法程序,第二句针对争端的禁反言)

7.2.2 什么是争端

对于"争端"(issue)的传统定义可见 Diplock 大法官在 Fidelitas Shipping Co. Ltd. v. V/O Exportchleb (1965) 1 Lloyd's Rep. 223 先例中所说:"The final resolution of a dispute between parties as to their respective legal rights or duties may involve the determination of a number of different 'issues', that is to say, a number of decisions as to the legal consequences of particular facts, each of which decisions constitutes a necessary step in determining what are the legal rights and duties of the parties resulting from the totality of the facts... To determine an 'issue' in this sense, which is that in which I shall use the word 'issue' throughout this judgment, it is necessary for the person adjudicating upon the issue first to find out what are the facts, and there may be a dispute between the parties as to this. But while an issue may thus involve a dispute about facts, a mere dispute about facts divorced from their legal consequences is not an 'issue'."

7.2.3　争端的禁反言带来的问题

争端的禁反言相比诉因的禁反言有更多与不同的问题,特别是外国法院判决或裁决是否构成争端的禁反言。

如果由于第一个诉讼金额不大并且某个争端不重要,所以该争端的败诉方没有进行昂贵的调查取证与花费太多时间精力做出争辩。而如果将来在另一个涉及金额庞大与不同诉因的诉讼中,该争端变为重要,但该诉讼方因为争端的禁反言而受到第一个不同诉因的判决中对该争端的决定的约束,就会造成不公平。正如 Reid 勋爵在 Carl Zeiss Stiftung v. Rayner & Keeler Ltd.（No.2）（1967）1 AC 853 先例中所说:"Suppose the first case is one of trifling importance but it involves for one party proof of facts which would be expensive and troublesome; and that party can see the possibility that the same point may raise if his opponent later raises a much more important claim. What is he to do? The second case may never be brought. Must he go to great trouble and expense to forestall a possible plea of issue estoppel if the second case is brought? This does not arise in cause of action estoppel: if the cause of action is important, he will incur the expense; if it is not, he will take the chance of winning on some other point."

所以,Reid 勋爵针对外国法院判决能否构成争端的禁反言有两个方面要特别注意:(1)英国因为对陌生的外国法院程序不熟悉,不少外国法院的判决也不会写得十分完整、分析全面与有条例,所以有时很难肯定该外国法院是否已经针对某个争端做出了最终决定,或该决定是否只是附带的或随口说说,因此要特别小心(the English courts are not familiar with modes of procedure in many foreign countries, and it may not be easy to be sure that a particular issue has been decided or that its decision was a basis of the foreign judgment and not merely collateral or obiter)。(2)也会有情况是该争端的败诉方在原来的判决中是因为做出全面的争辩不现实而导致获得对他不利的判决,这样,在后来的英国诉讼中对该争端被禁反言也不公平(it might be unjust to hold that a litigant here should be estopped from putting forward his case because it was impracticable for him to do so in an earlier case of trivial character abroad, with the result that the decision in that case went against him)。

在 Diag Human SE v. The Czech Republic（2014）2 Lloyd's Rep. 283 先例中,Eder 大法官针对外国法院的判决构成争端的禁反言说:"The authorities establish that there must be 'a full contestation and a clear decision' on the issue in question. ... The cases also underline four further important features of the approach of the courts to issue estoppel[63], which I will consider in turn. They are as follows: i) It is irrelevant that the English court may form the view that the decision of the foreign court was wrong either

〔63〕 有不少先例说让如果一个争端已经有了全面争辩与清楚的司法决定就会构成争端的禁反言,而其中四个方面尤其重要。

on the facts or as a matter of English law.[64] ii) The courts must be cautious before concluding that the foreign court made a clear decision on the relevant issue because the procedures of the court may be different and it may not be easy to determine the precise identity of the issues being determined.[65] iii) The decision of the court must be necessary for its decision.[66] iv) The application of the principles of issue estoppel is subject to the overriding consideration that it must work justice and not injustice'.[67]"

7.2.4 争端的禁反言对长期合约的影响

"争端的禁反言"(issue estoppel)除了适用在法院(包括本土与外国)的判决,也适用在仲裁裁决[68]甚至是专家的决定(expert determination),[69]这对一些长期的商业合约会有重大影响。这些长期的合约经常会有一些条文针对将来会不断与重复出现的争议,如通货膨胀条文(escalation clause)、价格调整条文(price review clause)或查账条文(account inspection clause)等。这种条文(特别是草拟得不好的条文)会带来争议,这样第一次出现争议时的判决或裁决或决定就尤为重要。因为一旦对条文做出了解释或对事实做出了认定,就会对之后履行合约时再次出现的同样的争议产生影响。即使几年后又出现同样的争议,也因为这个争端的禁反言(或滥用司法程序)的说法,而无法再重新解释该条文或对同样的事实做出认定,只能根据第一次出现争议时对该条文的解释做出判决或裁决或决定。

例如,中国现在大量进口天然气(LNG),为了保证货源稳定,供应这些合约的合约期往往很长,可能会超过25年甚至30年。这样,无论是确定合约价格或是将来根据某个价格指数(index)做出调整都不足以令人安心,因为都受限于订约时的想法对将来做出估计,而在这么长的合约期内,情况会发生订约时根本想不到的重大改变。因此在合约中加入一条价格调整条文就尤为重要,如双方约定每3年或5年(看双方的约定)在满足一定的条件的情况下,任何一方都可以开始价格调整机制。如果双方无法达成一致,则交由法院或仲裁庭或专家决定。有关的写法可以是:"(a) If the circumstances beyond the control of the Parties change significantly compared to the un-

---

〔64〕 第一方面是外国法院对某个争端(如是对合约条文的解释,如提单是否合并了租约的仲裁条文)有了决定,无论英国法律是否认同这个决定,都会构成禁反言。

〔65〕 第二方面是稍早提到的由于对外国法院的程序不了解,不容易判断对某个争端是否已经有了最后决定。

〔66〕 第三方面是该外国法院做出判决时必须对该争端做出决定。

〔67〕 第四方面是争端的禁反言毕竟涉及衡平法,必须符合公平合理的大原则。所以,如果涉及任何的不公平(特别在某些外国法院),英国法院就会不愿意适用这个说法。

〔68〕 见 Fidelitas Shipping Co. Ltd. v. V/O Exportchleb (1965) 1 Lloyd's Rep. 223 (CA)先例与 Associated Electric and Gas Insurance Services Ltd. v. European Reinsurance Co. of Zurich (2003) 1 WLR 1041 (PC)先例等。

〔69〕 见《Kendall on Expert Determination》(第5版,2015年)一书第12.9-3段与13.3-3段所说。另可见本书第八章之5.1段。

derlying assumptions in the prevailing price provisions, each Party is entitled to an adjustment of the price provisions reflecting such changes. The price provisions shall in any case allow the gas(也可以是任何其他商品/标的) to be economically marketed based on sound marketing operation. (b) Either Party shall be entitled to request a review of the price provisions for the first time with effect of dd/mm/yyyy and thereafter every three years. (c) Each Party shall provide the necessary information to substantiate its claim. (d) Following a request for a price review the Parties shall meet to examine whether an adjustment of the price provisions is justified. Failing an agreement within 120 days either Party may refer the matter to arbitration in line with the provisions on arbitration of the Contract. (e) As long as no agreement has been reached or no arbitration award has been rendered all rights and obligations under the agreement - including the price provisions - shall remain applicable unchanged. Unless otherwise agreed or decided by the arbitral award, differences to the newly established price shall be retroactively compensated inclusive of interest on the difference calculated at a rate reflecting the conditions on the international financing market."

即使是上述拟定得十分完整的价格调整条文,也免不了有争议,因为要调整价格,除了要满足时间要求,还要满足在市场因不受合约双方控制的情况发生重大改变的要求。有关情况是否不受合约双方控制(beyond the control of the parties)、什么才叫做重大改变(significant/material change)、怎样定义市场(market)都需要仲裁庭对事实做出认定与对合约条文做出解释。一旦仲裁庭做出裁决,第一个仲裁庭对价格调整条文的解释就会对以后的诉讼构成争端的禁反言。即双方第二次无法对调整的价格达成一致时,第二个仲裁庭必须跟从第一个仲裁庭做出的解释。[70] 而第一个仲裁庭对事实的认定是否构成争端的禁反言,取决于这个事实是否在第一个仲裁的争议中重要与必要,正如 Dixon 大法官在澳大利亚的 Blair v. Curren (1939) 62 CLR 464 先例中说:"a state of fact or law which is necessarily decided by the prior judgment, decree or order."也就是说,如果与第一次争议是同样的原因造成市场发生重大改变,第一次仲裁庭对事实的认定(是否不受合约双方控制)就构成了争端的禁反言。

但如果第二次争议涉及的合约与第一次争议不同,即使涉及相同的合约方与有关的文字完全相同,第一个仲裁庭对事实的认定与对条文的解释也不会构成争端的

---

〔70〕 有关一事不再审或争端的禁反言在仲裁中是否像英国法院判决一样严格适用,在本章第 9 段有介绍。

禁反言。这里不同的合约是指不同时间、情况或/与标的(subject matter)[71]的合约,如同样是天然气的长期供应合约,但订立时间与情况不同,价格与天然气的供应量也不同,这两个合约之间就不存在争端的禁反言。而如果是可分开(severable/divisible)合约,[72]只是涉及多个不同的独立任务(adventure),仍受到争端的禁反言的说法约束。

因此,从仲裁员的角度,第二个仲裁庭必须小心是否曾有裁决可以构成争端的禁反言。而从合约方的角度,应该对第一个仲裁更加小心对待,全面针对与不能掉以轻心。如果第一个仲裁庭做出的裁决对自己不利,如对什么才叫重大改变的要求太高,受影响的一方(如卖方/供应方)就不能自认倒霉,在有可能的情况下,要向英国法院上诉(如果是伦敦仲裁)或希望能有关的裁决书。否则有关的裁决一旦对后来同样的争议构成争端的禁反言,合约剩下的十几年甚至二十几年都有可能难以调整合约价格。

7.2.5 仲裁的机密性对争端的禁反言的影响

在商业活动中经常会出现合约链,在这种情况下,一旦发生争议也经常会带来一连串有相同争议的仲裁。在真正的无辜方 A 向与他订立合约的中间商 B 索赔成功后,中间商 B 就会根据合约(通常是有关条文相同的背靠背合约)向上一手中间商 C 要求补偿。而 B 向 C 索赔时,要证明他的损失,往往只能依赖并披露他在与 A 的仲裁中所获得的文件与裁决书。但根据仲裁的机密性(confidentiality),如果 B 没有获得 A 的同意,不能自己单方面向 C 与新的仲裁庭披露有关的裁决书。

在 Hassneh Insurance Co. of Israel and others v. Stuart J. Mew (1993) 2 Lloyd's Rep. 243 先例中,Colman 大法官判如果仲裁当事人为了保护他对第三人的权利,合理地有需要(reasonably necessary)披露仲裁裁决书及其理由,不会违反仲裁保密的责任,说:"... Accordingly, I conclude that the exception to the duty of confidentiality which I have held to apply by implication to arbitration awards applies equally to the reasons. If it is reasonably necessary for the protection of an arbitrating party's rights vis – à – vis a third party that the award should be disclosed to that third party, so to disclose it, including its reasons, would not be a breach of the duty of confidence. That Counsel has advised the arbitrating party of such reasonable necessity should in practice normally

---

〔71〕 Clarke 大法官在 The "Good Challenger" (2004) 1 Lloyd's Rep. 67 先例中说,要构成争端的禁反言必须满足四个条文:"The authorities show that in order to establish an issue estoppel four conditions must be satisfied, namely (1) that the judgment must be given by a foreign court of competent jurisdiction; (2) that the judgment must be final and conclusive and on the merits; (3) that there must be identity of parties; and (4) that there must be **identity of subject matter**, which means that the issue decided by the foreign court must be the same as that arising in the English proceedings..."(加黑是笔者的强调)

〔72〕 见本书第二章第 8 段。

be conclusive of the matter."

本段主要针对的是即使B可以披露他与A的仲裁裁决,这个裁决也不会对他与C之间的仲裁构成争端的禁反言,毕竟两个仲裁的当事人不同。即有关的仲裁裁决对新的仲裁庭只有说服性(persuasive),并可能影响仲裁庭。如果两个仲裁庭有至少一位仲裁员相同(一般都会是这种情况),有较大可能新的仲裁庭也会与第一个仲裁庭做出同样或尽量不矛盾的裁决,但第二个仲裁庭在法律上是不受第一个仲裁庭的裁决的约束。

但在上一小段已经提到,如果涉及的是可分开(severable/divisible)合约,在对履行不同的任务时发生的同样争议进行裁决时,争端的禁反言的说法就可能会适用。同一个造船合约下经常会涉及多艘船舶的建造,这属于可分开合约,每艘船舶的建造都是不同的任务。本段会介绍两个涉及造船合约下仲裁机密性与争端的禁反言之间的冲突的近期先例。

首先是Ali Shipping Corporation v. Shipyard Trogir(1998)1 Lloyd's Rep. 643先例,该先例是英国仲裁法在机密性方面的重要先例,在笔者《仲裁法——从1996年英国仲裁法到国际商务仲裁》一书第十三章之2.4.4段有介绍。在该先例中,合约的关系是同一个航运集团向船厂订立合约建造六艘船舶。第一个合约是在1988年4月29日订立,涉及Hull No. 200与Hull No. 201两艘船舶。1988年12月12日,双方另外订立了第三艘船舶Hull No. 202的建造合约。1990年3月30日,双方又签订了附件一,多建造Hull No. 204、Hull No. 205、Hull No. 206这三艘船舶。附件一针对的三艘船舶也稍后在3月15日各自签订了新的造船合约,该航运集团指定了三个不同的船公司(Lavender,Leeward与Leman)来拥有船舶。由于Hull No. 202没有及时交船,该船舶的船东(Ali)取消合约并向船厂索赔损失。船厂的抗辩是该航运集团没有支付Hull No. 204、Hull No. 205、Hull No. 206三艘船舶的预付款,因此船厂拒绝履行Hull No. 202的造船合约与交船。于是双方在伦敦开始仲裁,并委任Bruce Harris先生作为独任仲裁员。Bruce Harris先生在裁决书中判Ali胜诉,并获得加上利息高达3400万美元的赔偿。Bruce Harris先生大致上是说这些合约是独立的任务,而Hull No. 202在合约与法律上并不取决于后来的造船合约的履行。但Bruce Harris先生也在裁决书中简单提到船东没有支付Hull No. 204、Hull No. 205、Hull No. 206三艘船舶的预付款是违约,说:"49. ... I should perhaps deal briefly with the failure to pay the relevant instalments. On the evidence before me it appeared clear that those representing the buyers of Hulls 204 to 206 clearly considered that the contracts for those ships had become fully binding and indeed I consider that they had. It also appeared clear that the excuses raised on behalf of those buyers for not paying the first instalments under those contracts were bad and that the failures to pay those instalments amounted to breaches of contract. If—contrary to my view (paragraph 32 above)—it is necessary for the purpose of this case that I make findings in respect of these matters, I should be taken as having reached conclusions according with the indications given in the previous two sentences. I appreciate, of course, that nothing I say can bind the parties to those contracts."

船厂没有支付3400万美元的判决债务(judgment debt),而是马上开始对Hull No. 204、Hull No. 205、Hull No. 206三艘船舶提起仲裁。显然,船厂是希望尽快拿到胜诉的裁决书与Hull No. 202的判决债务对冲(set – off)。因此,船厂声称Bruce Harris先生已经裁决船东没有支付预付款属于违约,这构成争端的禁反言,要求第二个仲裁庭做出简易裁决或中间裁决书。这就带来两个问题:一是在仲裁的机密性下,船厂能否向第二个仲裁庭披露Bruce Harris先生的裁决书以及在第一个仲裁中取得的文件;二是Bruce Harris先生的裁决能否构成争端的禁反言。

针对第一个问题,本段就不详细针对,只说Potter大法官判还是要看能否满足合理地需要的考验。而针对第二个问题,看来双方没有争议是否属于不同的合约,毕竟Hull No. 204、Hull No. 205、Hull No. 206是Hull No. 202造船合约下的附件一。而主要的争议是当事人(identity of parties)是否相同,毕竟买方是四家不同的单船公司(虽然属于一个航运集团),仲裁庭能否刺破公司面纱(piercing the corporate veil),将它们当做同一个当事人对待?

英国上诉庭认为船厂没有希望依赖争端的禁反言,因为指定单船公司拥有个别船舶是国际航运上的惯常做法。在这种不涉及欺诈或其他不寻常因素的情况下,英国法律不会允许刺破公司面纱。此外,Bruce Harris先生在裁决书的第32段已经说道,没有必要认定有关没有支付预付款的违约,另在上述节录的第49段也只是泛泛的一句并说明是观察,不约束这三艘船舶的船东。这样根本没有办法满足争端的禁反言的要件,特别在第二个仲裁船东提出实质性的抗辩。上诉庭判是第二个仲裁庭(三个仲裁中的仲裁庭成员相同)完全可以根据双方提供的证据,独立决定船东没有支付预付款是否构成违约/毁约。Potter大法官说:"Whether or not Mr. Harris was right in his decision that the case was **not one in which it was appropriate to pierce the corporate veil**, . . . it is quite plain that his view that **the parties must be treated as separate legal entities**, albeit acting through the same, or largely the same, personnel, conditioned his whole approach to any findings which he made on the question of the excuses advanced by Lavender, Leeward, or Leman for non – payment. In paragraph 32 of his award, **Mr. Harris appears to have regarded it as unnecessary to make any findings in that respect**; moreover, in paragraph 49, **his findings that the excuses were bad were made in very general terms** and subject to his express observation that nothing he said could bind Lavender, Leeward and Leman. **It does not seem to me that findings of that kind, in the context in which they were made, can be said to satisfy the requirements of issue estoppel** in respect of the detailed defences raised in the second arbitrations. . . That is plainly so in respect of the award in the first arbitration which, absent any viable plea of res judicata, is strictly irrelevant to the task of the **Hull 204 to 206 arbitrators, which is to come to their own decision on the factual evidence placed before them**."(加黑部分是笔者的强调)

第二个是近期的 Teekay Tankers Ltd. v. STX Offshore & Shipbuilding Co. Ltd. (No.2)(2017) 1 Lloyd's Rep. 387 先例。该先例也涉及造船合约,作为买方的航运集团(简称为 TT)原本是在香港,后来搬到加拿大温哥华并在纽约上市。船厂(简称 STX)是一家韩国的大型船厂,但因为 2008 年"金融海啸"后航运市场低迷,首尔法院在 2016 年向该经济困难的船厂做出保护令并接管。2013 年 4 月 5 日,TT 以四家独立船公司作为船东与 STX 订立四艘油轮的造船合约,每艘油轮的造价为 4250 万美元。同一日,TT 与 STX 订立了名为"Option Agreement"的合约,令 TT 有选择权建造更多的船舶。该选择权涉及三组,每组 4 艘船舶的建造,加上独立的造船合约的 4 艘船舶,总共涉及 16 艘船舶。后来 STX 因为自身经济状况严峻,无法提供造船合约要求的还款担保(refund guarantee)。TT 或其属下的四个单船公司接受了 STX 对独立造船合约下的四艘船舶的违约/毁约(repudiatory breach),并根据仲裁条文开始伦敦仲裁,向 STX 索赔损失。四个同样成员的仲裁庭判 TT 胜诉,STX 的违约/毁约在每艘船舶下造成的损失约 800 万美元,即 STX 要赔偿 TT 约 3300 万美元。

同样在 Option Agreement,因为 STX 无法或拒绝提供还款担保,TT 终止了合约并索赔 12 艘船舶总共约为 1.79 亿美元的损失。估计因为 Option Agreement 没有仲裁条文,所以 STX 于 2014 年 3 月 20 日在首尔地方法院开始诉讼,要求法院做出它在 Option Agreement 下没有责任的宣示判决(declaration)。TT 做出反击,于 2014 年 4 月 11 日在伦敦法院开始诉讼,起诉 STX 违约/毁约。TT 在首尔地方法院与伦敦法院都披露了伦敦仲裁的胜诉裁决并希望依赖争端的禁反言的说法。显然伦敦法院要做出的对事实的认定与对法律的判决有部分已经在伦敦仲裁中有所针对,所以产生了 TT 是否可以依赖争端的禁反言(或滥用司法程序)的争议。

在这个很长的判决书中,Walker 大法官针对了很多方面复杂的问题。首先在责任方面,由于 Option Agreement 中说明如果 TT 行使选择权,双方需要继续商讨这些船舶的交船日期,Walker 大法官判 Option Agreement 只是属于协议将来达成协议(agreement to agree),[73] 太不肯定(uncertain),无法构成在法律上有约束力的合约。即 TT 在责任方面败诉,法院无须继续针对争端的禁反言的争议。但 Walker 大法官还是针对假如有必要 TT 能否依赖争端的禁反言(或滥用司法程序)做出了判决。与 Ali Shipping Corporation v. Shipyard Trogir 先例类似,TT 要依赖争端的禁反言首先要面对的障碍就是仲裁与诉讼涉及不同的当事人。TT 试图依赖四个单船公司与其有利益相互性(privity of interest)原则克服不同当事人的障碍,但这不被 Walker 大法官接受。Walker 大法官最终判 TT 无法依赖争端的禁反言(或滥用司法程序)。

---

〔73〕 见杨良宜的《合约的解释:规则与应用》一书第三章之 12.1.3 段。

Walker 大法官说："... The answer, it submitted, to my concern was that if TT was not a privy, the views of the arbitrators, however distinguished those arbitrators may be, were in no different position from the views of an eminent QC. They were simply irrelevant to the point that the court had to decide."

另外 Walker 大法官也针对了 STX 对 TT 违反了仲裁机密性（在首尔地方法院与伦敦法院披露伦敦仲裁的胜诉裁决）的反索赔。Walker 大法官驳回这个反索赔并确立了一个重要的大原则，节录如下："... importantly, there are wider considerations. In order to obtain justice a litigant may well conclude in good faith that it is necessary to disclose confidential information to the court in support of a particular argument. It would be inimical to the doing of justice if the litigant were liable for breach of confidence merely because an argument advanced in good faith had not been successful. Predictions as to whether an argument will be successful can rarely be certain. Such a rigid approach could well deter those who fear that by disclosing material to the court, no matter how carefully they go about it, they could incur a substantial liability."但 Walker 大法官也说，要构成善意披露涉及仲裁的机密文件，通常应该预先向对方做出恰当通知。如果对方反对，就有必要向法院申请允许披露的批准，如证明是合理的需要，毕竟在法院审理是公开程序。

8. 滥用司法程序

在 CPR r 3.4(2)(b)下，法院有权撤销"滥用司法程序"（abuse of process）的案件陈述（statement of case）。Diplock 勋爵在 Hunter v. Chief Constable of the West Midlands Police（1982）AC 529（HL）先例中说："It concerns the inherent power which any court of justice must possess to prevent misuse of its procedure in a way which, although not inconsistent with the literal application of its procedural rules, would nevertheless be manifestly unfair to a party to litigation before it, or would otherwise bring the administration of justice into disrepute among right – thinking people."

这是一种法院可以在多种不同情况下行使的广泛与有力的权力，如法院可以滥用司法程序为由撤销时效已过的诉讼请求：[74] Ronex Properties Ltd. v. John Laing Construction Ltd.（1983）QB 398 等先例。在 Barton Henderson Rasen v. Merrett（1993）1 Lloyd's Rep. 540 先例中，Saville 大法官说开始一个不会继续推进的诉讼属于滥用司法程序。另在 McDonald's Corporation v. Steel（1995）3 All ER 615 先例中，法院判做出完全无法证明的案件陈述属于滥用司法程序。但只有在十分不同寻

---

〔74〕 在本书第十章第 2 段有详细介绍。

常与少见的先例中，才有足够清楚与明显的情况令法院做出撤销该案件陈述的严苛措施。Rattee 大法官在 Re Bank of Credit and Commerce International SA（1994）The Times, 5 May 1994 先例中重申，法院是抗拒撤销表面看来是没有实质内容的诉讼请求。

最后笔者可节录 Terence Etherton 大法官在近期的 Price v. Nunn（2013）EWCA Civ 1002 先例做出的简明定义："Res judicata operates as a substantive rule of law. It is to be distinguished from the court's exercise of its procedural powers to control the court's processes from being abused. They are juridically very different even though there are overlapping legal principles with the common underlying purpose of limiting abusive and duplicative litigation. In the case of the exercise of the court's procedural powers to prevent abuse the court should take a broad, merits - based judgment taking account of the public and private interests involved and all the facts of the case, focusing on the crucial question whether, in all the circumstances, a party is misusing or abusing the process of the court by seeking to raise before it the issue which could have been raised before."

8.1　与重新诉讼有关的滥用司法程序

本段会介绍与重新诉讼（relitigation）有关的滥用司法程序。第一类可被称为"间接攻击的滥用"（collateral attack - abuse），即别有用心地开始新诉讼以直接或间接推翻之前的判决。如在 Smith v. Linskills（1996）1 WLR 763 先例中，Smith 先生被判犯严重入屋犯法罪（aggravated burglary），被监禁 7 年。Smith 先生出狱后，起诉他的代表律师专业疏忽并索赔损失。Smith 先生声称，如果他的代表律师没有专业疏忽，就可以引入新的证据，他就不会被定罪。法院最后判虽然 Smith 先生是通过民事诉讼间接攻击刑事判决，属于滥用司法程序。在该先例中，Smith 先生已经出狱，如果他是在入狱之前，希望通过民事诉讼攻击刑事判决以避免入狱，显然也会属于滥用司法程序。其他类似的先例还有 Saif Ali v. Sydney Mitchell & Co.（1980）AC 198；Arthur JS Hall & Co. v. Simons（1999）3 WLR 873 等。

在一些涉及间接攻击的滥用的案件中，会将第二类（与本章稍早介绍的诉因的禁反言和争端的禁反言类似但不同）的说法作为替代争议一并提出。这个说法最早是来自 Henderson v. Henderson（1843）3 Hare 100 先例中，所以有"Henderson v. Henderson Rule"这一名称。

在该先例中，Bethel Henderson 先生与 Jordan Henderson 先生两兄弟合伙经营生意。Jordan Henderson 先生去世后，他的遗孀在纽芬兰法院起诉 Bethel Henderson 先生欠下的债务。之后，Jordan Henderson 先生的遗孀试图在英国执行该判决债务，但 Bethel Henderson 先生开始诉讼，并首次提出 Jordan Henderson 先生去世前从两人合伙的生意中多拿了钱，所以 Jordan Henderson 先生的遗孀作为 Jordan Henderson 先生的遗产执行人，事实上是欠他钱。双方的争议之一是 Bethel Henderson 先生没有在纽芬兰法院审理合伙生意的财务关系时提出的债务能否在英国法院提出并证明？

James Wigram 大法官认为不行,说有关的新争议应在纽芬兰法院的诉讼中一并提出,不应让 Jordan Henderson 先生的遗孀在英国法院第二次面对本质上同样的争议:"... where a given matter becomes the subject of litigation in, and of adjudication by, a Court of competent jurisdiction, the Court requires the parties to that litigation to bring forward their whole case, and will not (except under special circumstances) permit the same parties to open the same subject of litigation in respect of matter which might have been brought forward as part of the subject in contest, but which was not brought forward, only because they have, from negligence, inadvertence, or even accident, omitted part of their case. The plea of res judicata applies, except in special cases, not only to points upon which the Court was actually required by the parties to form an opinion and pronounce a judgment, but to every point which properly belonged to the subject of litigation, and which the parties, exercising reasonable diligence, might have brought forward at the time."

本来这一说法也是有很强的"禁反言"(estoppel)意味,但在贵族院 Johnson v. Gore Wood & Co. (2002) 2 AC 1 先例中,这一说法被视为滥用司法程序,而不再是禁反言理论的延伸。Bingham 勋爵在 Johnson v. Gore Wood & Co. 先例说:"But Henderson v. Henderson abuse of process, as now understood, although separate and distinct from cause of action estoppel and issue estoppel, has much in common with them. The underlying public interest is the same: that there should be finality in litigation and that a party should not be twice vexed in the same matter. The public interest is reinforced by the current emphasis on efficiency and economy in the conduct of litigation, in the interests of the parties and the public as a whole.[75] The bringing of a claim or the raising of a defence in later proceeding may, without more, amount to abuse if the court is satisfied (the onus being on the party alleging abuse) that the claim or defence should have been raised in the earlier proceedings if it was to be raised at all. I would not accept that it is necessary, before abuse may be found, to identify any additional element such as a collateral attack on a previous decision or some dishonesty, but where those elements are present the later proceedings well be much more obviously abusive, and there will rarely be a finding of abuse unless the later proceeding involves what the court regards as

---

〔75〕 滥用司法程序和诉因的禁反言与争端的禁反言虽然是独立与不同的说法,但也有很多相同之处。这几种说法下考虑的根本公共政策是相同的,即诉讼应该有终局性以及同一个人不应该因为同样原因被骚扰两次,特别是现在十分强调为了诉讼方与整个社会的利益,应该加强诉讼的效率与经济性。

unjust harassment of a party.[76] It is, however, wrong to hold that because a matter could have been raised in earlier proceedings it should have been, so as to render the raising of it in later proceedings necessarily abusive. That is to adopt too dogmatic an approach to what should in my opinion be a broad, merits – based judgment which takes account of the public and private interests involved and also takes account of all the facts of the case, focusing attention on the crucial question whether, in all the circumstances, a party is misusing or abusing the process of the court by seeking to raise before it the issue which could have been raised before.[77] As one cannot comprehensively list all possible forms of abuse, so one cannot formulate any hard and fast rule to determine whether, on given facts, abuse is to be found or not . . . While the result may often be the same, it is in my view preferable to ask whether in all the circumstances a party's conduct is an abuse than to ask whether the conduct is an abuse and then, if it is, to ask whether the abuse is excused or justified by special circumstances. Properly applied, and whatever the legitimacy of its descent, the rule has in my view a valuable part to play in protecting the interests of justice."

总结而言,可以看出根据这个著名的"Henderson v. Henderson Rule",双方在适格法院(无论是英国法院或是外国诉讼)开始诉讼时,应该提出所有可能的争议或争端,无论是对责任的认定或是损失的计算,让法院可以一次过审理做出决定。除非有特殊的情况,否则诉讼的任何一方都不能要求重新审理之前的判决遗留的争端(甚至希望新争端会有不同的判法以否定较早的法院判决)。例如,可以是责任方面没有提出弃权与禁反言的争议,或是没有依赖合约另一条有关条文,或是没有提出对自己有利的先例等;而在损失方面,可能是原本的损失计算有遗漏或错误等。这些被遗漏的争端由于没有被决定过,所以不会构成争端的禁反言。但这些争端应该在之前的诉讼中一并提出与被审理,而不应遗漏,所以,开始新的诉讼会构成滥用司法程序,带来同样的后果。

但这个"Henderson v. Henderson Rule"带来了千变万化的先例中,在适用时需要

---

〔76〕 如果提出滥用司法程序的一方可以向法院证明对方在之前的诉讼程序中就应该提出某个索赔或抗辩,另一方在之后的程序再提出这个索赔或抗辩本身就会是滥用司法程序,而不需要存在额外的因素,如是对之前诉讼结果的间接攻击或不诚实。当然如果这些额外的因素确实存在,就更容易证明之后的诉讼是滥用司法程序。但要注意的是,除非之后的诉讼程序会对一方造成不公平与困扰,否则法院很少会认定另一方滥用司法程序。

〔77〕 但并不能教条地说只要在之前的诉讼程序中就可以提出某个索赔或抗辩,之后的诉讼就是滥用司法程序。法院要根据不同先例的事实在公共和私人利益之间做出平衡,在考虑了所有情况之后,决定一方在之后的诉讼中提出一个之前的诉讼程序中就可以提出的索赔或抗辩,是否属于滥用司法程序。如果有关的当事人对为何不在之前的诉讼中提出有合情合理的解释,就不会是"滥用"。这种特殊情况会在本章之8.3段介绍。

进一步的澄清。

8.2 "Henderson v. Henderson Rule"与诉因的禁反言和争端的禁反言的异同

已经提到"Henderson v. Henderson Rule"与"诉因的禁反言"(cause of action estoppel)和"争端的禁反言"(issue estoppel)虽然有类似之处,但也有很大区别,即双方在之前的诉讼中从未提出有关的争议,所以适格法院从未做出判决。另一个重要区别是诉因的禁反言与争端的禁反言都是实体法(substantive law),而滥用司法程序是程序法(procedural law),是法院为了整体的公正与合理分配有限的司法资源进行的行政性管理。

在实践中,诉讼方常常将争端的禁反言与滥用司法程序作为替代争议(alternative argument)一并提出。也就是说,有关的争议已经在之前的判决中有所针对,所以构成争端的禁反言;而即使因为争端并非完全相同而令争端的禁反言无法成立,也应该在之前的诉讼中提出,现在再提出,就构成了滥用司法程序。如在本章之7.2.5段介绍的 Teekay Tankers Ltd. v. STX Offshore & Shipbuilding Co. Ltd. (No. 2) (2017) 1 Lloyd's Rep. 387 先例中,就是将争端的禁反言与滥用司法程序作为替代争议一并提出。法院有时也会做出三种说法全部成立的判决,即使是错判了诉因的禁反言与争端的禁反言可以成立(如诉因/争端并非完全相同),原告的行为也会构成作为撤销诉讼请求的替代理由的滥用司法程序。如上诉庭在 House of Spring Gardens Ltd. v. Waite and Others (1991) 1 QB 241 先例就判:"... it was not now possible for any of the defendants to reopen the matter. Each defendant was estopped by cause of action or issue estoppel. Alternatively, it would be an abuse of the process of the court for the defendants to re – run the same claim of fraud which had already been determined..."

在 Aldi Stores Ltd. v. WSP Group Plc. (2008) 1 WLR 748 先例中,上诉庭判之前的诉讼中是诉讼双方达成和解还是法院做出判决没有区别。如果诉讼方没有在之前的诉讼中提出有关的争议,就不能在之后的诉讼中提出,否则就会构成滥用司法程序。Thomas 大法官说:"It seems to me clear that no distinction should be drawn as a matter of law between cases where the original action concludes by settlement and where it concludes by judgment."

已经提到"Henderson v. Henderson Rule"或滥用司法程序与诉因的禁反言和争端的禁反言考虑的公共政策是相同的,因此也有人将诉因的禁反言与争端的禁反言称为"狭窄的一事不再审说法"(restricted/narrow doctrine of res judicata),而将"Henderson v. Henderson Rule"或滥用司法程序称为"广泛的一事不再审说法"(broad doctrine of res judicata)。如在 Barrow v. Bankside Members Agency Ltd. (1996) 1 WLR 257 先例中,上诉庭的 Bingham 大法官说:"The rule in Henderson v. Henderson is very well known. It requires the parties, when a matter becomes the subject of litigation between them in a court of competent jurisdiction, to bring their whole case before the court so that all aspects of it may be finally decided (subject, of course, to any appeal) once and for all. **In the absence of special circumstances**, the parties cannot return to the court to advance arguments, claims or defences which they could have put forward for decision on the first occasion but failed to raise. **The rule is not based on the doctrine of res judicata in a narrow sense, nor even on any strict doctrine of issue or cause of action estoppel.** It is a rule of public policy... that litigation should not drag on for ever and that a defendant should not be oppressed by successive suits..."(加黑部分是笔者的强调)

因此,一旦"Henderson v. Henderson Rule"适用,法院有固有管辖权(inherent jurisdiction)撤销原告的诉讼请求并要求原告承担费用,除非有特殊情况。正如May大法官在Manson v. Vooght and others (1999) BPIR 376先例中说:"... If in all the circumstances the bringing of the claim in the succeeding action is an abuse, the court will strike it out unless there are special circumstances."

8.3　什么属于特殊情况?

那么什么才属于特殊情况(special circumstance)?显然在之前的诉讼中疏忽或是其他个人原因导致有所遗漏是无法排除"Henderson v. Henderson Rule"的适用。如果一个争议或争端虽然没有出现在之前的诉讼的文书请求中,但在披露的过程中显现出来,也不能排除"Henderson v. Henderson Rule"的适用,因为原告完全可以通过修改文书请求(amendment of pleadings)将漏掉的争议或争端加上。同样,如果因为意外而漏掉了争议/争端也不足以排除"Henderson v. Henderson Rule"的适用。正如Bingham大法官在Barrow v. Bankside Members Agency Ltd. (1996) 1 WLR 257先例中说:"It is plain... that negligence, inadvertence and even accident will not excuse non - compliance with the rule."

May大法官在Manson v. Vooght and others (1999) BPIR 376先例中认为,决定是否存在特殊情况其实就是决定是否存在滥用司法程序的情况,在某些先例中分开进行诉讼是明智与合理的:"... To find that there are **special circumstances may**, for practical purposes, be **the same thing as deciding that there is no abuse**... It may in particular cases be sensible to advance cases separately. It depends on all the circumstances of each case... Special circumstances may negative or excuse what would otherwise by an abuse."

典型的特殊情况之一是原告因为种种原因,无法在之前的诉讼中提出某个争议(或争端),之后原告在不同诉因的诉讼中再提出某个争议时,就不属于滥用司法程序,被告不能争辩说原告应该在之前的诉讼中就提出这个争议:Yat Tung Investment Co. Ltd. v. Dao Heng Bank Ltd. (1975) AC 581; Arnold v. National Westminster Bank Plc. (1991) 2 AC 93; Barrow v. Bankside Members Agency Ltd等先例。

因为先例的事实千变万化,所以Bingham大法官在Barrow v. Bankside Members

Agency Ltd 先例中说,要定义什么属于特殊情况很不明智(it is plainly unwise to attempt to define what may amount to a special circumstance)。

是否存在特殊情况其实就是决定是否存在滥用司法程序的情况,只有有关的案件属于滥用司法程序的情况下,“Henderson v. Henderson Rule”才会适用。在 Brisbane City Council v. Attorney – General for Queensland (1979) AC 411 先例中,枢密院说:“This reference to ‘abuse of process’ had previously been made in Greenhalgh v. Mallard [1947] 2 All ER 255 per Somervell LJ . . . the true basis of the doctrine and it ought only to be applied when the facts are such as to amount to an abuse; otherwise there is a danger of a party being shut out from bringing forward a genuine subject of litigation.”

May 大法官在 Manson v. Vooght and others 先例也警告说:“It is of course axiomatic that the court will only strike out a claim as an abuse after most careful consideration. But the court has to balance a plaintiff's right to bring before the court genuine and legitimate claims with a defendant's right to be protected from being harassed by multiple proceedings where one should sufficed. Abuse of process is a concept which defies precise definition in the abstract. In particular cases, the court has to decide whether there is abuse sufficiently serious to justify preventing the offending litigant from proceeding. . . .”

因此在每个不同的案件中,法院必须在全面考虑所有有关情况之后才决定是否存在滥用司法程序的情况(broad merits approach):见 Johnson v. Gore Wood & Co. (2002) 2 AC 1; Aldi Stores Ltd. v. WSP Group Plc. (2008) 1 WLR 748; Dickinson v. UK Acorn Finance Ltd. (2015) EWCA Civ 1194 等先例。因此有说法是上诉庭不应该改变一审法院的认定与判决,除非一审法院考虑了不应考虑的情况或没有考虑应该考虑的情况。在近期的 Dickinson v. UK Acorn Finance Ltd 先例中, Longmore 大法官说:“The abuse of process relied on by the lender is of the Henderson v. Henderson (1843) 3 Hare 100) variety (the fifth variety of res judicata identified by Lord Sumption in Virgin Atlantic Airways v. Zodiac Seats UK Ltd. [2014] A. C. 160 at [17]). This is the principle that **a litigant should in general bring forward all his claims in one proceeding rather than successively, otherwise a defendant will be doubly harassed by the litigation.** . . . That broad merits – based judgment is, of course, that of the judge at first instance (here Judge Smith). It is not an exercise of discretion but a multi-factorial evaluation. In Aldi Stores Ltd. v. WSP Group Plc. [2008] 1 W. L. R. 748 this court held that **it would be reluctant to interfere with a judge's decision, reached by balancing relevant factors, unless he or she had taken into account immaterial factors, omitted to take account of material factors, erred in principle or had come to a conclusion that was impermissible or not open to him.**”(加黑部分是

笔者的强调）

8.4　在之后的诉讼中提出怎样的新争端会属于滥用司法程序？

如果是全新与真正的争端是不应被禁止，只有所谓的"新争端"实际上在之前的诉讼中应该被提出，才会构成滥用司法程序。在 Aldi Stores Ltd. v. WSP Group Plc.（2008）1 WLR 748 先例中，上诉庭判是要以滥用司法程序为由撤销诉讼必须满足一定的要求，即之后的诉讼必须与之前的诉讼有一定程度的同一性。

仅仅是这一争端可以（could）在之前的诉讼中提出并不足够，必须客观来看这一争端应该（should）在之前的诉讼中提出。在 Greenhalgh v. Mallard（1947）2 All ER 255 先例中，Somervell 大法官说："... issues or facts which are so clearly part of the subject - matter of the litigation and so clearly could have been raised that it would be an abuse of process of the Court to allow a new proceeding to be started in respect of them."

例如，一个完全独立的反索赔（counterclaim 或 cross - claim）可以在之前的诉讼中提出，这样比较方便与/或可以节省时间、金钱，但被告没有提出，而是之后开始了针对该反索赔的新诉讼，这不属于滥用司法程序。被告也可以有很多正当理由解释他为什么不在之前的诉讼中提出反索赔，如希望由不同的法院或另一个仲裁庭来审理，证据还没有准备充分，因为各种原因无法同时准备抗辩与一个完全独立的反索赔等。但如果所谓的反索赔实际上是一个抗辩，就会构成滥用司法程序。如货物或服务有缺陷是可以减低价格或费用，如果买方或接受服务的一方不在卖方或提供服务的一方开始的诉讼中提出货物或服务有缺陷，而是之后另外开始新的诉讼，就会构成滥用司法程序。

8.5　谁会受到约束？

在诉因的禁反言或争端的禁反言以及滥用司法程序，明确谁会受到约束很重要。毕竟虽然诉讼可以加入第三人，原告提出诉讼时也不可能将所有有关人士都列为被告。而对原告有合约与侵权责任的往往不止一个，所以在诉讼中原告可能留下几个对象，不予起诉。至于选谁作为主要诉讼对象的原因有很多，如诉讼对象之一经济状况最好，或是将所有被告加入，费用会大大增加。所以如果原告在第一个诉讼败诉只能约束被告，就表示原告可以用同样事实、同样的证据、同样的诉因选择另一个被告开始第二个新诉讼，这等于诉讼还是没有终局性。因此，法院做出第一个判决后，不止约束被告而是约束原告、被告与有利害关系人士（privy 或 privity）。即 A 起诉 X 并败诉后，不能再以同样的事实与诉因起诉与 X 有利害关系的 Y 或 Z，与 A 有利害关系的 B 或 C 也不能以同样的事实与诉因起诉 X 或 Y 或 Z。Spencer Bower 的《Estoppel by Representation》（第 4 版，2004 年）一书在引用了 Issacs & Sons & Salbstein and Another（1916）2 KB 139（CA）先例的判决后，说："there can be no bar by former recovery unless the parties in the second action are **the same or privies** of those in the first."

诉讼的当事人记录在案，所以不存在争议，但谁是与诉讼当事人有利害关系的人士就经常会产生争议。因为很少会有人以同样当事人的名义开始新一轮诉讼。所以，判断谁是有利害关系人士必须看法院记录以外的情况，这就涉及大量对事实的认定与审理法官的裁量权。因为一旦被认定为是有利害关系人士，就会失去起诉与抗辩的权利，所以法院在做出认定时一定要谨慎与要有一定的弹性。美国的 Akhenaten v. Najee, LLC, 544F. Supp. 2d 320 (S. D. N. Y. 2008)先例说："The doctrine of privity ... is to be applied with flexibility ... There is no bright line rule as to whether privity exists for res judicata purposes. Rather, a finding of privity ... depends on whether, under the circumstances, the interest of the [被告] were adequately represented [in the earlier action]."

在英国的 Johnson v. Gore Wood & Co. (2002) 2 AC 1 先例中，Bingham 大法官引用了 Megarry 大法官在 Glesson v. J Wippell & Co. Ltd. Ltd. (1977) 1 WLR 510 先例的说法："... I cannot see that this provides any basis for a successful defendant to say that the successful defence is a bar to the plaintiff suing some third party, or for that third party to say that the successful defence prevents the plaintiff from suing him, unless there is a **sufficient degree of identity between the successful defendant and the third party**. I do not say that one must be the alter ego of the other: but it does seem to me that, having due regard to the subject matter of the dispute, there must be **a sufficient degree of identification between the two to make it just** to hold that the decision to which one was party should be binding in proceedings to which the other is party. It is in that sense that I would regard the phrase 'privity of interest'."(加黑部分是笔者的强调)

在近期的 Secretary of State for Business, Innovation and Skills v. Potiwal (2012) EWHC 3723 (Ch)先例也有同样的说法。另在 Littlewoods v. The Commissioners for HMRC (2014) EWHC 868 (Ch)先例中，Henderson 大法官说："An issue estoppel binds not only the parties to the earlier determination but also their **privies in blood, title or interest.**"(加黑部分是笔者的强调)

Silja Schaffstein 博士的《The Doctrine of Res Judicata Before International Commercial Arbitral Tribunals》(2016 年)一书之 1.44 段提到英国法下有 3 种类别的有利害关系人士："There are three categories of privy: privy in blood, title or interest. **Privy in blood** include ancestors and heirs. **Privies in title** include any person who succeeds to the rights or liabilities of a party upon death or insolvency. **A privy in interest** has some kind of interest, legal or beneficial, in the previous or other litigation or its subject matter. The requirements of privity in interest are highly fact - dependent. They have been succinctly expressed in the following terms: 'There must be an examination of the **parties' interests**, as well as the **existence of a sufficient degree of identification between**

the parties, before it is just to hold that a decision in respect of one party should be binding in proceedings to which another is party. Moreover, the interest in the previous litigation or its subject matter must be legal or beneficial: a mere curiosity or concern in the litigation or some interest in the outcome is not sufficient.[78]'."(加黑部分是笔者的强调)

该书之1.42段也提到除了有利害关系人士,英国法下还有"假设当事人"(deem party)的说法,这种假设当事人与有利害关系人士稍有不同,但也受到约束,说:"While deemed parties are parties in their own right, privies acquire privity through the right, title, or interest of another party. Deemed parties include those who intervene and take an active part in the proceedings, third and subsequent parties who become parties to the proceedings between the prior parties, and those who insist on being added as a party and obtain an order to that effect. Furthermore, a court can look behind the record to identify the 'real' party. Accordingly, those who direct another person to pursue litigation on their behalf may also be deemed parties."

英国法对诉因的禁反言与争端的禁反言也有相互性(mutuality)的要求:见 Hunter v. Chief Constable of the West Midlands Police (1982) AC 529 (HL)先例。即禁反言对诉讼双方(包括与他们有利害关系的人士)都有约束力,即在之前的诉讼中的一方(或与他有利害关系的人士)不能在之后的诉讼中对另一方(或与他有利害关系的人士)提出同样的索赔或抗辩。

在美国法下,什么叫有利害关系人士有一定程度的模糊,每个不同州份的法院也会有不同说法。笔者可简单节录两个不同的定义。《BLACK's Law Dictionary》对"有利害关系人士"定义是:"A person having a legal interest of privity in any action, matter, or property; a person who is in privity with another. Traditionally, there were six types of privies: (1) **privies in blood**, such as an heir and an ancestor; (2) **privies in representation**, such as an executor and a testator or an administrator and an intestate person; (3) **privies in estate**, such as grantor and grantee or lessor and lessee; (4) **privies in respect to a contract** – the parties to a contract; (5) **privies in respect of estate and contract**, such as a lessor and lessee where the lessee assigns an interest, but the contract between lessor and lessee continues because the lessor does not accept the assignee; and (6) **privies in law**, such as husband and wife."

Silja Schaffstein 博士的《The Doctrine of Res Judicata Before International Commercial Arbitral Tribunals》(2016年)一书之1.77段提到美国《Restatement (First) of Judgments》对"有利害关系人士"定义如下:"The term 'privity' expresses the general

---

〔78〕 美国《Restatement (Second) of Judgments》提到仅仅是对诉讼程序提供经济或其他帮助,或是提供建议,或是作为法院之友(*amicus curie*)出现向法院做出意见,都不足以成为有利害关系人士。

idea that persons who are not parties to proceedings, but who are connected with the proceedings in their interests, may be bound by or benefit from a judgment as if they were parties. Under the first Restatement of Judgments the word ‘privy’ included non – party: (i) who control the proceedings, (ii) whose interests are represented by a party to the proceedings, and (iii) successors in interest to those having derivative claims.”

笔者可列举若干有利害关系人士的例子:

1. 在一个多方合约(multi – party contract)中,可能有个别合约方没有参与之前的诉讼,但仍会作为有利害关系的人士受到约束。

2. 在之前的诉讼中就可以加入作为共同原告或共同被告的一方,如共同侵权人(tortfeasors)。但如果第三人知道这个诉讼,而原告有合理理由不将他加入诉讼,他在之后的诉讼中就不能以原告原本可以将他加入作为共同被告(co – defendant)为由要求法院撤销诉讼,因为他完全可以自己申请加入之前的诉讼作为共同被告。在House of Spring Gardens Ltd. v. Waite and others (1991) 1 QB 241 (CA)先例中,原告在爱尔兰法院起诉三位被告侵权并胜诉。而第一被告与第二被告以原告是通过欺诈获得胜诉判决为由,向爱尔兰法院要求撤销判决,但最后败诉。原告在英国法院向三位被告执行爱尔兰法院的判决书,第一被告与第二被告被禁反言不能再争辩说原告是通过欺诈获得胜诉判决应是没有疑问。针对没有在爱尔兰法院起诉原告是通过欺诈获得胜诉判决的第三被告能否在英国法院提出这个争议,Stuart – Smith 大法官认为从公正与常识的角度看,第三被告作为有利害关系人士也同样被禁反言,说:“All three defendants were joint tortfeasors ... The judgment against them was joint and several. If the... action to set aside [the] judgment had succeeded, [it] would have been set aside in to... he was content to sit back and leave others to fight the battle, at no expense to himself. In my judgment that is sufficient to make him privy to the estoppels...”该先例的判决被 Latham 大法官在 Powell v. Wilshire (2004) EWCA Civ 534 先例与 Lewison 大法官在 Thomas and Agnes Carvel Foundation v. Carvel (2007) WHC 1314 (Ch)先例确认。

3. 诉讼方只是名义上的诉讼方,实际上被另一方完全控制或是另一方实质参加了诉讼。如一个 BVI 公司或巴拿马公司背后实质控制的管理代理人(managing agent)。

4. 诉讼方的分身(alter ego)。在 Johnson v. Gore Wood & Co. 先例中,[79] 法院判 Johnson 先生作为 WWH 有限公司的完全股权所有人,是 WWH 的分身(alter ego),WWH 与 Gore Wood & Co. 的和解协议应该约束作为有利害关系人的 Johnson 先生(但在该先例因为共识性禁反言的存在,最后 Johnson 先生可以起诉)。而如果 Johnson 先生只是 WWH 公司股东之一(特别是只是个小股东),他完全可以以自己

〔79〕 在本章之 8.6.4 段与本书第六章之 7.11 段有所介绍。

的名义索赔他个人损失。

当然也有特殊的例外情况,如在 C（A Minor）v. Hackney LBC（1996）1 WLR 789 先例中,原告是一名唐氏综合征儿童,与她的母亲一起住在被告的政府租给她母亲的房屋中。原告的母亲之前开始诉讼向政府索赔因房屋状况不好与潮湿而导致的损失,并最终获得 15000 英镑的赔偿。之后原告又开始诉讼起诉政府疏忽与违反 1972 年《Defective Premises Act》导致人身伤害的赔偿。政府没有出庭抗辩,所以原告获得缺席判决。但之后政府以双重赔偿(double recovery)与一事不再审(res judicata)为由,向法院要求撤销判决。一审法院支持了政府的申请,但上诉庭推翻了一审法院的判决。如果没有根据 1981 年《County Court Rules》立法中保护残疾人利益的 Order 10 获得批准,残疾儿童的母亲获得的赔偿不能约束该残疾儿童。

8.6　有关先例介绍

8.6.1　先例之一:Yat Tung Investment Co. Ltd. v. Dao Heng Bank Ltd.

Yat Tung Investment Co. Ltd. v. Dao Heng Bank Ltd.（1975）AC 581 先例是上诉到英国枢密院的先例,案情涉及产权人获得银行(香港的道亨银行,该银行在 2001 年以 55 亿港元的价格被新加坡 DBS 银行收购)140 万港元的贷款并将建造中的大厦作为抵押。该产权人与承建商背后的老板都是一位黎先生(Mr. Lai),不久之后,黎先生出现经济问题,没有及时还款给银行,银行就行使其权利,将该建造中的大厦公开拍卖给 Yat Tung Investment Co. Ltd(之后简称 Yat Tung),作价 88 万港元。银行根据买卖合约,将大厦转让给 Yat Tung,并在同时向 Yat Tung 做出 100 万港元的贷款用以购买大厦,抵押物仍是该大厦。但实际上 Yat Tung 背后的老板还是这位黎先生,因为判决中没有提,所以也不知道银行是否知道有关情况。之后再次发生没有及时还款的情况,于是银行再次行使其权利,将大厦公开拍卖,最后以更便宜的价格卖给了作为第二被告的 Choi Kee Ltd. 。

这一系列的交易带来的第一个诉讼是 Yat Tung 与承建商(背后都是黎先生)要求法院做出 Yat Tung 只是银行的信托人而不是产权人的宣告(declaration)。黎先生声称银行将大厦出售给 Yat Tung 是一个骗局(sham),银行与 Yat Tung 之前谈好了价格不是正常的公开拍卖。但法院最后宣告银行与 Yat Tung 之间的交易是正常与有效,不存在骗局。而银行的反索赔(贷款还剩下 45000 港元没还清)胜诉。

在这个判决做出之后约一个月,黎先生以 Yat Tung 作为申请人,在香港法院开始了另一个诉讼程序,告银行(第一被告)以比市场低得多的价格将大厦卖给 Choi Kee Ltd.(第二被告)是骗局与违反了抵押权人的责任,并要求法院将这个买卖撤销(set aside as fraudulent and/or in breach of the 1st defendant's duty as mortgagee and/or was otherwise improper)。这在 Marriott v. The Anchor Reversionary（Limited）（1860）66 ER 191 先例说:"Where a mortgagee enters into possession of the mortgaged estate, with a view to sale, he is bound to act with the same care and the same prudence, and to use every effort, which a prudent proprietor would use, to have the sale conducted to the greatest advantage."

另在加拿大的 Wood v. Bank of Nova Scotia (1980) 10 RPR 156 (Ont. H. C.) 先例中,一审的 Cromarty 大法官说:"If the mortgage debt is very small in relation to the value of the property, the mortgagee is not entitled to sell the property at a price sufficient to pay off his mortgage debt. The general principle requires him to go further, and to take reasonable care to get a proper price; otherwise he would simply be sacrificing the rights of the mortgagor."

而银行根据滥用司法程序要求香港法院将原告的诉讼请求撤销,双方一路上诉到枢密院,最后银行胜诉,第二个诉讼请求被撤销。枢密院同意香港法院的判决,在第一个诉讼中,Yat Tung 面对银行的反索赔是没有理由不可以提出银行第二次拍卖给 Chai Kee Ltd. 有违反债权人责任与造成损失,并将 Choi Kee Ltd. 加入(如有必要)作为第二被告一起审理。

枢密院同意香港上诉庭的判决,可节录如下:"As it seems to me the root of the matter is concerned with **the vital issue of the counterclaim in 969**(第一个诉讼)... That counterclaim... **squarely put before the court the correctness of the defendant bank's manner of accounting for the sum which it said was owed to it by the plaintiff**... That being the case... it was necessary to plead that the defendant's manner of accounting, which left the plaintiff owing a sum of $45,000, was, aside from all the other complaints concerning the bogus nature of the mortgage between the bank and the plaintiff, itself wholly erroneous. **It should not have been difficult to plead that at current market prices, if the sale to Choi Kee Ltd. had been a valid sale, a sum would have been realised** which would not only obliterate the debt owing to the defendant (even accepting the defendant's account of the facts) but which would, in addition, leave the defendant in possession of a balance in favour of the plaintiff. **No compelling reason has been advanced to show that this matter could not have been pleaded by way of defence to the counterclaim.** It would not have been a question of the plaintiff company taking up contradictory postures in relation to its own cause of action but simply of meeting the defendant upon his own ground in the event that the court disbelieved the plaintiff on the substance of its claim. But whether pleaded by way of defence to counterclaim or by way of defence and counterclaim to counterclaim (and no especial difficulty in the way of such a pleading has been shown) it was, to my mind, **so clearly a matter necessary and proper to be litigated at the same time with all the other issues between the parties** that it would have been wholly wrong for the judge in chambers to have permitted the amendment."(加黑部分是笔者的强调)

8.6.2 先例之二:House of Spring Gardens Ltd. v. Waite and Others

House of Spring Gardens Ltd. v. Waite and Others (1991) 1 QB 241 先例涉及一

个典型的商业上的尔虞我诈、欺瞒背叛。在该先例中,原告公司的老板 Sacks 先生发明了技术含量很高的防弹衣,因此获得有关怎样生产的信息将带来一笔很大的财富。1978 年末,Sacks 先生与 Waite 先生见面讨论成立合资公司的事宜,主要由 Sacks 先生负责提供技术与信息,而 Waite 先生负责生产与市场营销。Waite 先生在北非特别是利比亚有关系,Waite 先生的儿子与女婿 McLeod 先生(第二与第三被告)也参与他的生意。Sacks 先生在 Waite 先生的诱导下,相信了双方将来会成立合资公司在利比亚出售防弹衣并平分利润的口头协议,提供了技术与怎样生产的信息。双方合作的早期阶段,Waite 先生告诉 Sacks 先生有可能以 2000 万美元的价格出售 5 万件防弹衣给利比亚军方。Sacks 先生还专门前往利比亚展示了他的防弹衣,并给利比亚军方留下了很深的印象。但 Waite 先生欺骗了利比亚方面,让对方以为是他自己的公司 Molex 发明了防弹衣并已经开始生产。

1979 年 8 月 11 日,Waite 先生通过一间皮包公司与利比亚军方订立了价值 500 万英镑的合约,并偷偷成立工厂生产。1980 年 2 月,Waite 先生骗 Sacks 先生说是与利比亚的谈判破裂,生意谈不成。但 Sacks 先生之后发现了这个谎言,并在英国与爱尔兰开始了第一轮诉讼。第一轮诉讼以双方达成和解协议告终,和解协议的主要内容是 Waite 先生与他的公司要为出售给利比亚军方的防弹衣支付 11.58% 的特许权使用费(royalty fee),并且将来任何与利比亚军方的合约都要通知 Sacks 先生。

Waite 先生与他的公司支付了第一个合约下的特许权使用费,但隐瞒了与利比亚军方第二个价值 500 万英镑的合约。该合约在 1981 年 1 月 22 日订立,但直到 1982 年年初才被 Sacks 先生发现。于是,Sacks 先生在英国与爱尔兰开始了第二轮诉讼。爱尔兰的 Costello 大法官判 Waite 先生败诉,Waite 先生提起上诉,并在之后引入新的证据说,Sacks 先生欺骗了 Costello 大法官他在发明防弹衣过程中起到的作用。爱尔兰最高院同意开始新的审讯,但前提是 Waite 先生先将 375 万英镑放到法院。Waite 先生没有将这笔钱放到法院,法院在不会再开始新的审讯的基础上做出判决,驳回上诉。

1985 年 1 月 28 日,Waite 先生与儿子(McLeod 先生没有参与)在爱尔兰法院对 Sacks 先生开始诉讼,理由与在最高院上诉时提到的完全一样。1987 年 10 月 9 日,Egan 大法官判 Waite 先生败诉,Sacks 先生没有作伪证。[80] Waite 先生继续上诉,但在 1988 年 6 月 10 日被驳回。

1985 年 3 月 21 日,Sacks 先生在英国要求执行爱尔兰的 Costello 大法官的判决,Waite 先生、他的儿子与 McLeod 先生的抗辩都是 Sacks 先生作伪证才拿到 Costello 大法官的判决,所以不应该执行,也提到了在爱尔兰要求撤销 Costello 大法官的判决的诉讼。直到 1987 年 10 月 27 日,即 Waite 先生与儿子在爱尔兰的上诉被驳回后,

---

〔80〕 如果可以证明一方作伪证才取得法院判决,一事不再审的说法就不再适用:D. P. P v. Humphrys (1977) AC 1 先例。另可见本章之 3.3.2.3 段。

Sacks 先生才进一步推动要求执行 Costello 大法官的判决的程序。

Sacks 先生认为 Egan 大法官已经对 Sacks 先生是否作伪证才拿到 Costello 大法官的判决做出了决定，构成“诉因的禁反言”(cause of action estoppel)或“争端的禁反言”(issue estoppel)。即使没有，重新再审也会构成滥用司法程序。一审 Peter Pain 大法官支持了 Sacks 先生，McLeod 先生提起上诉(Waite 先生与儿子没有上诉)。上诉庭驳回了 McLeod 先生的上诉，Stuart – Smith 大法官说：“The question is whether it would be in the interests of justice and public policy to allow the issue of fraud to be litigated again in this court, it having been tried and determined by Egan J. in Ireland. In my judgment it would not; indeed, I think it would be a travesty of justice. Not only would the plaintiffs be required to re – litigate matters which have twice been extensively investigated and decided in their favour in the natural forum, but it would run the risk of inconsistent verdicts being reached, not only as between the English and Irish courts, but as between the defendants themselves. The Waites have not appealed Sir Peter Pain's judgment, and they were quite right not to do so. The plaintiffs will no doubt proceed to execute their judgment against them. **What could be a greater source of injustice, if in years to come**, when the issue is finally decided, a different decision is in Mr. McLeod's case reached? Public policy requires that there should be an end of litigation and that a litigant should **not be vexed more than once in the same cause.**”(加黑部分是笔者的强调)

8.6.3　先例之三：Barrow v. Bankside Members Agency Ltd.

20 世纪 90 年代中期，英国法院就涉及大量的有关劳合社的重要先例。80 年代，英国劳合社的保险人因为大量来自美国的石棉污染的再保赔付而严重亏损，几乎没有能力赔付，以至于要破产。在短短的 3 年期间，劳合社保险人亏损了 60 亿英镑，其中 1990 年的亏损就高达 29 亿英镑，这是劳合社从来没有过的亏损。英国 1720 年的《Bubble Act》只允许个人的保险人经营业务，所以劳合社的做法是以个人名义(name)参与各种保险小组(syndicate)。而由于这些保险人都是自然人以个人名义承保，所以要承担无限责任，而不像有限公司可以法人局限损失。当年的亏损导致几个保险人自杀与/或破产，这种恶劣情况到 1993 年劳合社委任了新的主席与首席执行官并做出了基本性的改革，成功吸收了有限公司的大量资本(corporate capital)后，才慢慢恢复元气。

自然人加入保险小组是需要通过劳合社的成员代理人(member agent)的介绍与安排(不同小组会针对不同的险种，也有不同的业绩)，但该成员代理事后并不一定参与受保或管理的工作。这些作为保险人的自然人往往只是希望获得可观回报的投资者，并不一定懂得保险，所以只是依赖劳合社代理人(Lloyd's agent)的受保代理人(underwriting agent)或管理代理人(managing agent)的专业技能与小心谨慎去接受投保。

面对大量的索赔与严重亏损，显然有不少劳合社的保险人希望转嫁损失，诉讼对象包括受保代理人或管理代理人、成员代理人、经纪人、劳合社等。让英国法院分别处理每个案件显然不现实，因此法院将案件分组，并在每组中挑出几个涉及共同争议的案件先行审理，希望对这些共同争议的决定可以帮助部分其他案件和解，进而减少在法院的争议案件的数量。

Barrow v. Bankside Members Agency Ltd. (1996) 1 WLR 257 先例与其中一组"The Gooda Walker group action"有关。Barrow 先生与其他 3000 位保险人作为共同原告向 71 位被告(包括 Bankside Members Agency Ltd)索赔违反合约与在受保或管理时疏忽导致的损失。1993 年夏天，Saville 大法官组织了所有诉讼方的代表律师召开案件管理会议，并在 7 月底做出了时间表。法院首先针对受保代理人或管理代理人或成员代理人在受保时是否对保险人有合理具有专业知识与小心谨慎的责任与有否违反这个责任(如果有)这两个特定争议做出了判决，判原告保险人胜诉与可以获得赔偿。在该判决下，Barrow 先生可以获得约 60% 的损失的赔偿。

之后，法院又针对成员代理人在介绍与安排保险人加入不同的保险小组时的责任做出了判决，保险人(Sword - Daniels 先生与 Brown 先生被选为原告代表)再次胜诉。Barrow 先生在之前的诉讼中没有起诉他的成员代理人疏忽或违反了有关责任并索赔损失。但在法院做出该判决后，Barrow 马上开始新的诉讼，显然是企图转移他另外 40% 的损失。

作为被告的成员代理人就提出了 Barrow 先生滥用司法程序的抗辩，即 Barrow 应该在之前的诉讼就一并起诉他的成员代理人疏忽或违反了在介绍与安排保险人加入不同的保险小组时的责任，要求法院撤销 Barrow 先生现在的诉讼请求。

针对这种涉及类似争议的大规模诉讼，英国法院常常会先对典型案件(sample case)做出判决。如果没有其他的不同证据或可显示与典型案例不同的情况，在法院对典型案件做出判决后继续推进自己的诉讼属于滥用司法程序。在 Ashmore v. British Coal Corp (1990) 2 QB 338 先例中，Ashmore 与其他 1500 名煤矿食堂女性员工起诉其雇主违反了 1979 年《Equal Pay Act》，她们受雇的条件低于男性员工。法院在典型案件中判原告败诉，但这个判决不约束其他原告。Ashmore 继续推进与她的雇主的诉讼程序，但是雇主以滥用司法程序为由申请撤销诉讼请求。上诉庭最后判是虽然典型案件的判决不约束其他原告，但如果没有其他不同证据或不同情况，继续推进自己的诉讼属于滥用司法程序。

但在 Barrow v. Bankside Members Agency Ltd 先例中，上诉庭认为 Ashmore v. British Coal Corp 先例的判决不适用。因为诉讼双方都同意根据法院的程序安排，即使 Barrow 先生在之前的诉讼中就提出了有关争议或争端，也不会在开庭时被处理。所以，Barrow 先生现在再开始新的诉讼不属于滥用，"Henderson v. Henderson Rule"不适用。另外，即使"Henderson v. Henderson Rule"可以适用，法院在涉及劳合社的大量先例的特殊管理安排也属于特殊情况(special circumstances)，令 Barrow 先生有合法理由不遵守"Henderson v. Henderson Rule"。而且虽然被告不会愿意被 Barrow 先生索赔,但新的诉讼没有造成任何实质损害。所以,上诉庭不同意撤销 Barrow 先生的诉讼请求。

Bingham 大法官说:

"So it seems right to begin by asking whether the procedure adopted by Mr. Barrow is an abuse of the process of the court. I do not think it is. Since his portfolio selection claim would not have been decided before now anyway, he is not causing there to be two trials where there would have been one. He is not exposing the defendant to an unnecessary series of trials. The defendant is not, in truth, any worse off as matters now stand than if Mr. Barrow had made and pleaded this new claim at the outset. One can, of course, understand the defendant's dismay at the emergence of this new claim, and Mr. Barrow's may not be the only claim of its kind; but the claim would not have been other than unwelcome whenever presented.

I do not therefore think that this unusual case falls within the mischief at which Henderson v. Henderson was directed. But if that conclusion is wrong, and the case does fall within that mischief, one must consider whether Mr. Barrow can plead special circumstances excusing him from compliance with the duty to bring forward his whole case at the outset. . . . It is plain from both cases that negligence, inadvertence and even accident will not excuse non – compliance with the rule, but it is plainly unwise to attempt to define what may amount to a special circumstance. In this case, the same considerations which lead me to conclude that the rule does not apply also seem to me, if that first conclusion is wrong, to amount to special circumstances in the special setting of the Lloyd's litigation. If the defendant could point to any prejudice it had suffered as a result of Mr. Barrow's course of conduct which it would not have suffered anyway, my view would probably be different. But the defendant can point to none. If Mr. Barrow is in breach of the rule, the present facts in the context of the Lloyd's litigation do, in my judgment, provide a special circumstance."

8.6.4 先例之四:Johnson v. Gore Wood & Co.

Johnson v. Gore Wood & Co. (2002) 2 AC 1 先例的案情在本书第六章之 7.11 段有所介绍,这里不再重复。该先例中,Johnson 先生对 WWH 公司的绝对控制会被视为该公司的分身(alter ego),这就带来滥用司法程序的说法。而如果 Johnson 先生只是 WWH 公司股东之一,他完全可以以自己的名义索赔他个人的损失。Bingham 勋爵在考虑了所有事实情况(包括是否存在共识性禁反言)后认为 Johnson 先生再次提起诉讼不属于滥用法律程序,并做出了被之后众多先例引用的判决:

"Lord Diplock said at the outset of his speech in Hunter v. Chief Constable of the West Midlands Police [1982] AC 529 , 536, an 'inherent power which any court of justice must possess to prevent misuse of its procedure in a way which, although not inconsistent with the literal application of its procedural rules, would nevertheless be manifestly unfair to a party to litigation before it, or would otherwise bring the administration of justice into disrepute among right – thinking people. **The circumstances in which abuse of process can arise are very varied; those which give rise to the instant appeal must surely be unique. It would, in my view, be most unwise if this House were to use this occasion to say anything that might be taken as limiting to fixed categories the kinds of circumstances in which the court has a duty (I disavow the word discretion) to exercise this salutary power.'**

One manifestation of this power was to be found in RSC Ord 18, r 19[81] which empowered the court, at any stage of the proceedings, to strike out any pleading which disclosed no reasonable cause of action or defence, or which was scandalous, frivolous or vexatious, or which was otherwise an abuse of the process of the court. A similar power is now to be found in CPR r 3.4.

GW(被告) contends that Mr Johnson(原告) has abused the process of the court by bringing an action against it in his own name and for his own benefit when such an action could and should have been brought, if at all, as part of or at the same time as the action brought against the firm by WWH. The allegations of negligence and breach of duty made against the firm by WWH in that action were, it is argued, essentially those upon which Mr Johnson now relies. The oral and documentary evidence relating to each action is substantially the same. To litigate these matters in separate actions on different occasions is, GW contends, to duplicate the cost and use of court time involved, to prolong the time before the matter is finally resolved, to subject GW to avoidable harassment and to mount a collateral attack on the outcome of the earlier action, settled by GW on the basis that liability was not admitted...

In my opinion, **based on the facts of this case, the bringing of this action was not an abuse of process. The Court of Appeal adopted too mechanical an approach, giving little or no weight to the considerations which led Mr Johnson to act as he did and failing to weigh the overall balance of justice.** I would allow Mr Johnson's appeal."(加黑部分是笔者的强调)

8.6.5　先例之五:Dexter Ltd. (In Administrative Receivership) v. Vlieland-Boddy

滥用司法程序的说法现在除了适用在应该但没有在之前的诉讼中提出的争议或争端不能在之后的诉讼中提出的情况,还拓展到在之前的诉讼中应该加入但没有加

---

〔81〕 RSC(《Rules of Supreme Court》)是英国在民事诉讼改革(1999年)前的高院诉讼规则。这条规定是授权法院在原告滥用司法程序时撤销索赔请求。

入第三人的情况：Yat Tung Investment Co. Ltd. v. Dao Heng Bank Ltd.（1975）AC 581；Dexter Ltd.（In Administrative Receivership）v. Vlieland-Boddy（2003）EWCA Civ 14 等先例。这也就是为什么现在滥用司法程序不再被视为一类禁反言的说法，而被视为对司法资源的行政性管理。当然，相比之下没有在之前的诉讼中将对某个被告的所有争议或争端一并提出比没有在之前的诉讼中将对所有被告的所有争议一并提出更容易构成滥用司法程序。

Dexter Ltd.（In Administrative Receivership）v. Vlieland-Boddy 先例的案情是 Wensley Haydon-Baillie 在 1997 年 5 月 20 日成立了 Dexter 公司。当时 Wensley Haydon-Baillie 是唯一的公司董事，而 Martin Vlieland-Boddy（之后简称 MVB）是公司秘书。1997 年 9 月 30 日，MVB 升为公司董事，而在此之前他就已经实质上执行董事业务（de facto director）。1997 年 10 月 1 日，第一被告 Vlieland-Boddy（VB）与他的孪生兄弟 MVB 伪造了一单虚假交易（其他被告也有参与），以骗取银行的 200 万美元贷款。

1998 年 4 月 23 日，Dexter 被破产行政接管（administrative receivership）。1999 年 8 月 24 日，行政接管人开始对 MVB 提起诉讼，声称 MVB、Wensley Haydon-Baillie 与/或 VB 伪造虚假交易从银行骗取 200 万美元，而这笔钱并没有用在 Dexter，而是被他们私吞。MVB 与 Wensley Haydon-Baillie 违反了他们作为公司董事对 Dexter 的诚信责任（fiduciary duty），MVB、Wensley Haydon-Baillie 与/或 VB 属于共谋（conspiracy），MVB 作为推定信托人（constructive trustee）要承担责任。在这个诉讼中，VB 递交了证人证言，但并没有被盘问，因为 MVB 在诉讼半途就放弃了抗辩，逃到了西班牙。2000 年 12 月 11 日，法院做出了缺席判决。

但显然因为 MVB 已经逃到了西班牙，所以，虽然 Dexter 获得了胜诉的判决，仍无法追回 200 万美元。于是，Dexter 在 2002 年 2 月 7 日开始新的诉讼，起诉 VB 协助 MVB 与 Wensley Haydon-Baillie 伪造虚假交易，并在明知这笔钱的性质的情况下接收了部分。VB 以滥用司法程序为由，向法院申请撤销 Dexter 的诉讼请求，指称 Dexter在第一次诉讼时就可以并应该将他列为共同被告一并审理，现在再开始诉讼会对 VB 造成不公平，包括额外的花费、Dexter 的一位证人去世而另一位证人很难被找到等。

一审法院在考虑所有事实情况后判 Dexter 没有滥用司法程序，包括 Dexter 在之前的诉讼中不知道 VB 到底参与了多少、当时的证据还不够提出欺诈这一严重指控、来不及将 VB 加入作为第二被告、在之前的诉讼开庭前曾经告诉过 VB 会起诉他（这表示 VB 自己也可以向法院申请加入作为第二被告）等。上诉庭支持了一审法院的判决，Gibson 大法官认为如果一审法院正确适用了有关的法律（即 broad merits approach），上诉庭就不应该干涉一审法院对事实的认定，[82]说：

---

〔82〕 这在本章之 8.3 段也有提到。

"The judge rightly approached the applications before him on the basis of the broad merits-based assessment which Lord Bingham had advocated. The judge considered whether Dexter in all the circumstances was abusing the process of the court by the current proceedings. He had recognised... that the First Defendant could have been sued in the First Action, but the judge concluded that there was nothing in the facts relied on by the First Defendant to show that the bringing of the current proceedings was abusive. Those facts include that the First Defendant had been told before the trial of the First Action that Dexter would proceed against him but chose not to do so until the present action. The judge held that the First Defendant was not being vexed a second time even though involved in the First Action as the provider of a witness statement. The judge clearly thought that there was no unjust harassment of the First Defendant by the present action. I respectfully agree. It is only in this action that for the first time the First Defendant is sought to be made liable.

In these circumstances, where the judge, in whom the discretion to strike out a claim is vested, has correctly directed himself as to the law, this court cannot properly interfere with that exercise of discretion unless the applicant shows that the judge, in making his assessment, omitted to take account of material facts or took account of immaterial facts or was otherwise plainly wrong....

For my part I am prepared to accept that, so far as the First Defendant was concerned, the general and largely unparticularised statement of Mr. Shierson (Dexter 证人)... provides little justification for Dexter not joining the First Defendant as a defendant to the First Action. But the judge does not treat it as justification. As I read the judgment, the judge was saying two things. First, he said it was for the First Defendant to establish that it was an abuse of process for a claimant to bring an action against a defendant who could have been joined in earlier proceedings[83], and the facts relied on by the First Defendant (VB), such as the mere fact of the bringing of the later action, were not sufficient to show abuse. Second, the judge pointed to the fact that MVB was the obvious prime target for Dexter. That in itself was an important consideration for a claimant like Dexter in administrative receivership and therefore likely to have limited funds at its disposal for litigation.... the judge had well in mind all the facts and I am unable to say that his assessment was not one properly open to him. The judge considered the prejudice said to have been suffered by the First Defendant in consequence of being sued in the present action rather than in the First Action, but was unimpressed by that point. Before us Mr. Taylor (VB 代表大律师) sought to establish detriment to the First Defendant resulting

[83]　见本章之 8.5 段。

from the death of Mr. Trubshaw(Dexter 的证人)after the First Action; but I was not persuaded that the unavailability of Mr. Trubshaw, who had been called by Dexter as a witness in the First Action, constituted real prejudice to the First Defendant in his defence in the present proceedings."

Clarke 大法官总结了 Bingham 勋爵在 Johnson v. Gore Wood & Co. (2002) 2 AC 1 先例的判决,并重点针对了 A 在针对 B 的诉讼中没有将 C 作为共同被告(co-defendant)的情况做出了指引,说:

"The principles to be derived from the authorities, of which by far the most important is Johnson v. Gore Wood & Co. [2002] 2 AC 1, can be summarised as follows: i) Where A has brought an action against B, a later action against B or C may be struck out where the second action is an abuse of process.[84] ii) A later action against B is much more likely to be held to be an abuse of process than a later action against C. iii) The burden of establishing abuse of process is on B or C or as the case may be. iv) It is wrong to hold that because a matter could have been raised in earlier proceedings it should have been, so as to render the raising of it in later proceedings necessarily abusive.[85] v) The question in every case is whether, applying a broad merits based approach, A's conduct is in all the circumstances an abuse of process.[86] vi) The court will rarely find that the later action is an abuse of process unless the later action involves unjust harassment or oppression of B or C.

Proposition ii) above seems to me to be of importance because it is one thing to say that A should bring all his claims against B in one action, whereas it is quite another thing to say that he should bring all his claims against B and C (let alone against B, C, D, E, F and G) in one action.[87]

There may be many entirely legitimate reasons for a claimant deciding to bring an action against B first and, only later (and if necessary) against others.

Those reasons include, for example, the cost of proceeding against more than one defendant, especially where B is apparently solvent and the case against B seems stronger than against others. More defendants mean more lawyers, more time and more expense. This is especially so in large commercial disputes. It by no means follows that either the

---

〔84〕 A 在第一个诉讼中起诉 B,后来以同样的事实与证据再次起诉 B 与 C。相比 C,B 成功以 A 滥用司法程序抗辩的可能性大得多。

〔85〕 不能简单而言,可以在第一次审理提出就不能有第二个诉讼,因为不一定涉及滥用。

〔86〕 要根据所有的情况全面看 A 的做法是否涉及滥用。

〔87〕 除非 A 的第二次诉讼对 B 或 C 带来不公平的干扰或压迫,否则法院通常不会认为 A 滥用司法程序。毕竟在一个诉讼中提出所有对 B 的索赔是一回事,在一个诉讼中将对所有可能的被告(B、C 甚至 D、E、F 等)的索赔一并提出是另一回事。

public interest in efficiency and economy in litigation or the interests of the parties, including in particular the interests of C, D and E, is or are best served by one action against them all.[88]

It seems to me that the courts should be astute to ensure that it is only in a case where C can establish oppression or an abuse of process that a later action against C should be struck out. I could not help wondering whether the defendants in this case would have given their lawyers the same instructions on the question whether they should have been sued in the first action if they had been asked before that action began as they have given now that a later action has been begun.[89]

It is clear from the speeches of both Lord Bingham and Lord Millett that all depends upon the circumstances of the particular case and that the court should adopt a broad merits based approach, but it is likely that**the most important question in any case will be whether C, D, E or any other new defendant in a later action can persuade the court that the action against him is oppressive. It seems to me to be likely to be a rare case in which he will succeed in doing so.**[90]"

当事人(如是原告)不在较早的时候把所有合理应该针对的争端或救济都一并提出可以由许多原因造成,如疏忽、看漏了或是意外,正如 Kilbrandon 勋爵在 Yat Tung Investment Co. Ltd. v. Dao Heng Bank Ltd 先例中所说:"The shutting out of a 'subject of litigation' – a power which no court should exercise but after a scrupulous examination of all the circumstances – is limited to cases where reasonable diligence would have caused a matter to be inadvertence or even accident will not suffice to excuse, nevertheless 'special circumstances' are reserved in case justice should be found to require the non – application of the rule. . . . "

例如,A、B、C 三家公司从欧洲或者南美以 FOB 购买并且需要运输一批大宗货物(如 40000 吨玉米或 30000 吨化肥)回中国,其中三家公司同意由 A 出面租船。但这三家公司都没有一份针对将来如果有诉讼或运输途中出事之后大家的权利义务如

---

[88] A 单独对 B 提起诉讼的合法原因可能有很多,如对 B 的诉因相对独立并且比对其他被告的更有利,同时对多个被告提起诉讼意味着更多的律师,诉讼要花费的时间与金钱更多(即使最后胜诉可以从被告方取回,一开始还是要自己承担)等。特别是在一些争议金额巨大的商业争议案件,无论是从诉讼经济与有效率的公共利益还是从诉讼方(尤其是 C、D、E 等)的私人利益考虑,都不能说 A 一次过向所有可能的被告索赔是最好的选择。

[89] 因此,除非 C 可以说服法院 A 开始对 C 的诉讼对 C 是严苛或是滥用司法程序,否则法院不会撤销(strike out)A 对 C 的诉讼请求。如果 C 在第一个诉讼前就被问是否应该在对 B 的诉讼中作为共同被告一并被起诉,C 会否向律师做出与现在(即 A 开始了对 C 的诉讼)同样的指示?

[90] 法院在决定是否是滥用程序时要全面考虑所有的情况,特别是 C、D、E 或任何新诉讼中的被告能否说服法院 A 的新诉讼对他来说是严苛。Clarke 大法官认为只有在少数案件,被告才能成功说服法院。

何分摊的详细协议,而仅仅是很简单的一句"同意由 A 租船"了事。如果在运输途中遇到事故而使船货全损, A、B、C 就要向船东提出索赔。A 是承租人,所以即使另有提单的签发,也是根据租约向船东索赔。而 B 与 C 公司如果想就货损向船东提出索赔,有可能必须通过 A 向船东提出诉讼索赔全部的货物。这种情况会是:(1)船东只签发一套提单,而没有针对三个不同的公司分别签发不同的提单;(2)即使有不同的提单并由 B 与 C 公司持有,但想向船东提出索赔时,《海牙规则》的 1 年时效已过,但租约下的 6 年时效还有很长可以开始诉讼;(3)B 与 C 不愿意自己打官司。

合理的做法就是由 A 代表三家公司向船东索赔损失,毕竟 A 本来也是代表三家公司与船东订立租约而将一整票货物运回中国。但这样做,就有可能这三家公司先产生争议,而非是一致对外。如 B 与 C 不愿意按比例与 A 分摊诉讼费用,或各自找不同的律师,又或不合理要求 A 对诉讼的结果做出担保等。这样 A 就可能只自己为他 10000 吨化肥的损失向船东索赔并成功将损失取回,而不顾 B 与 C 公司 20000 吨化肥的损失。之后,B 与 C 公司受到鼓舞,也想以侵权作为诉因或要求 A 把租约索赔的利益转让(assign)给他们而对船东采取索赔的法律行动。但在这种做法下,都会面对船东提出的一事不再审的抗辩。

8.6.6 先例之六:Angeli Luki Kotonou v. National Westminster Bank Plc.

在 Angeli Luki Kotonou v. National Westminster Bank Plc. (2015) EWCA Civ 1106 先例中,Kotonou 先生是 ORS 的董事与主要股东。ORS 为了获得 National Westminster Bank 的 50 万英镑贷款与 Theodossiades 夫妇达成协议,由 Theodossiades 夫妇做出还款担保。这个担保到 2001 年 3 月 16 日到期,National Westminster Bank 没有在此之前提现。2001 年 3 月 16 日,Theodossiades 夫妇向银行要求延期到 3 月 31 日,但被银行拒绝。之后 Theodossiades 夫妇拒绝做出新的还款担保。这样等于 National Westminster Bank 的 50 万英镑贷款就没有了保障,于是 Kotonou 先生在 2001 年 7 月 12 日对 ORS 尚未还清的 42.5 万英镑做出了个人担保。ORS 没有继续还款,并在 2005 年 2 月 2 日破产。ORS 在破产前于 2004 年 3 月 5 日将诉权转让给了 Kotonou 先生。

2004 年 4 月 2 日,National Westminster Bank 开始诉讼,要求 Kotonou 先生在个人担保下还款。在开庭前两个星期,Kotonou 先生要求修改答辩书,在一开始的修改草稿中包括增加还款担保的历史与过期的情况,并提出反索赔声称 National Westminster Bank 是以信托(trust)的形式为 ORS 持有还款担保,任由还款担保过期是违反了合约/法律/信托责任。这个没有推进的反索赔理由与之后的诉讼中的理由几乎相同,但在最后的答辩书终稿中没有直接提到 National Westminster Bank 对 ORS 与 Kotonou 先生有这个责任,只说还款担保的历史与过期的情况是理解 Kotonou 先生对银行误述的指称的重要事实背景。Kotonou 先生在修改的抗辩与反索赔草稿中也提到 ORS 将诉权转让给了自己,但因为这样就要引入大量涉及转让是否有效的事实证据,会导致原本订下的开庭延期。Kotonou 先生不希望承担这笔浪费的费用,所以放弃了在抗辩与反索赔中通过修改加入与转让有关的争议。

Sher 大法官判 National Westminster Bank 员工有责任保护银行的利益,不让还款担保过期,但对 ORS 或任何其他人(即 Kotonou 先生)没有责任不让还款担保过期。另判 Kotonou 先生对 National Westminster Bank 做出的个人担保也因为 National Westminster Bank 存在误述而无效。

之后,Kotonou 先生马上以 ORS(作为受让人)与他自己的名义开始新的诉讼,起诉 National Westminster Bank 是以信托(trust)的形式为 ORS 持有还款担保,任由还款担保过期是违反了合约/法律/信托责任。National Westminster Bank 则以滥用司法程序为由,要求法院撤销诉讼请求。一审的 Mogan 大法官和上诉庭都支持了 National Westminster Bank 的请求,认为 Kotonou 先生现在的诉讼请求不仅让 National Westminster Bank 要就同样的事实问题诉讼两次,而且属于对 Sher 大法官的判决的攻击。上诉庭的 Gloster 女大法官说:"I am satisfied that the Bank has discharged the burden imposed upon it of demonstrating that this is a case which clearly, in the circumstances outlined above above, engages both limbs of the abuse of process principle referred to in Hunter and the rule in Henderson v. Henderson[91]. **It is a case where not only would it be unfair to the Bank to have to relitigate these factual issues, but also would bring the administration of justice into disrepute if a second court, years after the event, were obliged to examine the same substratum of fact which gave rise to the subject of litigation in the proceedings before the deputy judge(Sher 大法官):** see Potter LJ in Divine – Bortey v. Brent LBC supra at 898. . . . I reject his submissions that there had been no detailed, or adequate, evidential investigation at the trial in front of the deputy judge into the issues as to whether the Bank owed ORS or Mr Kotonou a duty of care. Not only was Mr Sears(Kotonou 先生代表大律师)unable to identify any such further evidence which could have been relied upon by Mr Kotonou, but it is also clear from the transcript of the proceedings before the deputy judge, and his judgment itself, that the relevant factual matters were investigated in considerable detail and at considerable length during the course of the twelve day trial. As Morgan J held at [96] of the Morgan judgment, the state of the pleadings in the earlier action did not in any real way curtail the extent to which those matters of fact were investigated. The deputy judge would not have ventured to make findings of fact, having been asked to do so, if he had not had sufficient basis upon which to do so. Morgan J held at [96] that nothing which happened in the earlier trial 'caused there to be any concern about the way in which the Deputy Judge investigated the matters of fact and made his findings on them'. The depu-

---

〔91〕 这是指针对滥用司法程序的说法的两个重要先例:Hunter v. Chief Constable of the West Midlands Police (1982) AC 529 与 Henderson v. Henderson (1844) 6 QB 288。

ty judge's conclusion, after having carefully considered the evidence from both sides, was that many of Mr Kotonou's allegations of fact fell to be rejected, not least because of Mr Kotonou's lack of credibility as a witness. . . . It follows that, having concluded that any departure in Mr Kotonou's pleading from the facts as found by the deputy judge would amount to an abuse of process, I would also maintain paragraph (3) of Morgan J's order that there should be summary judgment in favour of the Bank on the basis of the findings of fact made by the deputy judge (as opposed to on the basis of the facts as alleged by Mr Kotonou in the present proceedings). On the basis of those former findings, I agree with Morgan J's analysis of the law. Indeed there was no argument presented to this court on behalf of Mr Kotonou that, if it were necessary to proceed on the basis of the facts as found by the deputy judge, Morgan J had reached the wrong conclusion as a matter of law."(加黑部分是笔者的强调)

9. 仲裁中的一事不再审与滥用司法程序

9.1 普通法国家的仲裁

普通法国家(包括英国、美国、新加坡等)的仲裁中也有类似一事不再审与滥用司法程序的说法。Denning 勋爵在 Fidelitas Shipping Co. Ltd. v. V/O Exportchleb (1965) 1 Lloyd's Rep. 223 先例中说:"Like principles(这里指的是诉因的禁反言与争端的禁反言)apply to arbitration."

在 Nomihold Securities Inc. v. Mobile Telesystems Finance SA (No. 2) (2012) EWHC 130 (Comm)先例中,也明确滥用司法程序的说法适用在仲裁,只是因为仲裁要求双方同意的性质,仲裁裁决书也不能约束第三人,所以,滥用司法程序的说法只约束仲裁双方,而不能约束没有参与仲裁的与他们有利害关系的人士(privies)。Andrew Smith 大法官说:"However, where the previous dispute was determined in arbitration, the **principle of Henderson v. Henderson has a narrower application than where it was determined in court proceedings**: Mustill & Boyd, Commercial Arbitration (1989) 2nd Ed. p. 412. The consensual nature of arbitration means that a tribunal determines disputes referred to it by the parties. It is because of this, as Mance LJ explained in Sun Life Assurance Co. of Canada v. Lincoln National Life Insurance Co, [2004] EWCA Civ 1660, that the principle of Henderson v. Henderson applies in relation to previous arbitrations only if all parties to subsequent litigation (or their privies) have also been parties to the earlier reference (whereas the principle of Henderson v. Henderson can apply where the parties to the earlier and subsequent litigation are different: see Dexter v. Vieland - Boddy; [2003] EWCA Civ 14 at para 49)."(加黑部分是

笔者的强调）

在 Sun Life Assurance Co. of Canada v. Lincoln National Life Insurance Co.（2005）1 Lloyd's Rep. 606 先例中，上诉庭确认了相互性（mutuality）的要求，即因为有关裁决书与滥用司法程序的说法不约束第三人，第三人也不可以依赖之前的裁决书。

对一事不再审的说法的适用，笔者可简单[92]节录《Russell on Arbitration》（第 24 版，2015 年）之 6 - 176 段作为对英国法下地位的总结："A valid award will create an estoppel with regard to the matters with which it deals, preventing either party from pursuing these matters in a later stage of the arbitration[93] or in subsequent proceedings.[94] To the extent that a cause of action has been decided by the award, a party will be prevented from asserting or denying, as against the other party, its existence or non - existence in subsequent proceedings. Any attempt to do so may be met by a plea of res judicata and abuse of process[95], both of which can apply to the decisions of arbitration tribunals.[96] Similarly where one or more issues have previously been determined[97], even if the cause of action is different, a party will again be prevented from seeking to contradict the earlier findings on those issues on the basis of 'issue estoppel'.[98] In an appropriate case, the court can issue an anti - suit injunction to restrain a party from pursuing proceedings which amount to a collateral attack on a binding award.[99] Indeed issues which have been referred to arbitration, even if not actually determined in the award, will be subject to an estoppel in the event no challenge is made to the award on the basis of a

---

〔92〕 此课题将在《仲裁法》的更新版（估计将在 2019 年出版）有更详细的针对。

〔93〕 见 Westland Helicopters Ltd. v. Al - Hejailan（2004）2 Lloyd's Rep. 523 等先例。

〔94〕 见 Fidelitas Shipping Co. Ltd. v. V/O Exportchleb（1965）1 Lloyd's Rep. 223（CA）; Siporex Trade SA v. Comdel Commodities Ltd.（1986）2 Lloyd's Rep. 428; Noble Assurance Co. v. Gerling - Konzern General Insurance Co.（2007）EWHC 253 等先例。

〔95〕 见 Price v. Nunn（2013）EWCA Civ 1002; Johnson v. Gore Wood & Co.（2002）2 AC 1 等先例。

〔96〕 见 Michael Wilson v. Thomas Sinclair（2012）EWHC 2560; Injazat Technology Capital Limited v. Dr Hamid Najafi（2012）EWHC 4171; Arts & Antiques Ltd. v. Richards（2013）EWHC 3361; Swallowfalls Ltd. v. Monaco Yachting &Technologies SAM（2015）EWHC 2013 等先例。

〔97〕 见 Sun Life Assurance Co. of Canada v. Lincoln National Life Insurance Co.（2005）1 Lloyd's Rep. 606 等先例。

〔98〕 见 Associated Electric and Gas Insurance Services Ltd. v. European Reinsurance Co. of Zurich（2003）1 WLR 1041; Arts & Antiques Ltd. v. Richards（2013）EWHC 3361 等先例。

〔99〕 见 C v. D（2007）2 Lloyd's Rep. 367 and（2008）1 Lloyd's Rep. 239; Injazat Technology Capital Limited v. Dr Hamid Najafi（2012）EWHC 4171; Noble Assurance Co. v. Gerling - Konzern General Insurance Co.（2007）EWHC 253 等先例。

failure to deal with them.〔100〕 It may even be possible to prevent issues being raised in subsequent proceedings which could and should have been raised in the earlier proceedings, i.e. those issues which properly belong to the subject of the earlier proceedings.〔101〕 The principle has been specifically applied to arbitrations.〔102〕"

为了帮助读者理解,笔者选择若干近期案例进行介绍。

9.1.1 先例之一:The "Jonna V"

The "Jonna V"(2003) 2 Lloyd's Rep. 617 先例的案情涉及约3万吨的豆粕从阿根廷运到中国。船舶在离开装港后不久就发生搁浅并需要救助(salvage),船东宣告共同海损(general average)。救助成功之后救助人要求船东与货方各自提供救助担保,货方的担保是由人保(PICC)提供。船舶后来抵达宁波卸货,但收货人扣船,要求船东赔偿他要支付的救助奖金与其他损失。

收货人在宁波海事法院开始诉讼,声称船舶不适航,所以救助费用与共同海损要船东承担。有关货物的租约提单中有合并一条伦敦仲裁条文,〔103〕船东就在宁波海事法院申请中止法院程序,但不成功。宁波海事法院认为这个共同海损的争议只与租约有关,但不是租约仲裁条文包括的争议。船东同时在伦敦开始仲裁,伦敦仲裁庭认为根据仲裁条文,仲裁庭是有管辖权。这导致宁波海事法院与伦敦仲裁在同步推进诉讼(concurrent litigation),宁波海事法院最后在2001年9月28日针对实体争议判船东败诉。而伦敦仲裁庭在2001年3月14日做出第一份裁决书,判船东有恪尽职责令船舶适航,所以收货人要分摊共同海损与承担在宁波扣船带来的延误。

2002年3月,人保与收货人在英国法院申请宁波海事法院的判决是可执行(enforceable)的宣告(declaration),并申请禁止船东执行伦敦裁决的禁令(injunction)。但这个申请不成功,原因是伦敦裁决书比宁波海事法院的判决早,而根据一事不再审的说法,时间较早的判决/裁决才有约束力。Thomas大法官说:"In Showlag v. Mansour [1995] 1 AC 431, the Privy Council held that where there are conflicting final decisions each pronounced by a court of competent jurisdiction **the earlier in time is to be recognised and given effect**. Assuming for these purposes that the decision in the Ningbo Maritime Court should be one recognised as one made with jurisdiction, it is clear that

〔100〕 见 Lidl GmbJ v. Just Fitness Ltd. (2010) EWHC 39; Purser and Co. (Hillingdon) Ltd. v. Jackson (1971) 1 QB 166 等先例。

〔101〕 见 Henderson v. Henderson (1843) 3 Hare 100; Yat Tung Investment Co. Ltd. v. Dao Heng Bank Ltd. (1975) AC 581; Johnson v. Gore Wood & Co. (2002) 2 AC 1 等先例。

〔102〕 见 Fidelitas Shipping Co. Ltd. v. V/O Exportchleb (1965) 1 Lloyd's Rep. 223 (CA); Siporex Trade SA v. Comdel Commodities Ltd. (1986) 2 Lloyd's Rep. 428; Arnold v. National Westminster Bank Plc. (1991) 2 AC 93; Nomihold Securities Inc. v. Mobile Telesystems Finance SA (No. 2) (2012) EWHC 130 (Comm)等先例。

〔103〕 这方面的课题在《提单及其他付运单证》(2016年)第四章之2.4段有详论。

the award of Mr Donald Davies on the merits was given earlier and should therefore be recognised in preference to the judgment of the Ningbo Maritime Court. Similarly, in Vervaeke v. Smith [1983] 1 AC 145, Lord Diplock in the House of Lords observed that **an earlier judgment which was previous in date to a second judgment made the matters in issue res judicata.**"(加黑部分是笔者的强调)

9.1.2　先例之二:C v. D

在 C v. D (2008) 1 Lloyd's Rep. 239 先例中,美国被保险人 C 向英国法院申请禁令与宣告禁止美国保险人 D 在纽约法院挑战伦敦裁决书。C 与 D 之间的保险是 Bermuda Form,[104] 在该保单下,D 对 C 与它的子公司、附属公司与联营公司的人身伤害赔偿承保。保单中规定了伦敦仲裁与受纽约州法律管辖。

之后,C 要求 D 根据保单做出赔付,但被 D 拒绝。于是双方开始伦敦仲裁,仲裁庭在 2007 年 3 月 13 日做出了裁决判 C 胜诉,并命令 D 做出高达 1 亿美元(保单下的最高限额)的赔偿。败诉的 D 向美国法院要求以明显漠视纽约法律(manifest disregard of New York Law)[105] 为由撤销裁决书。这导致 C 在 2007 年 4 月 27 日向英国法院做出申请并成功取得了对 D 的止诉禁令(anti – suit injunction)。D 提起上诉,认为第一审的法院错判,但这不被上诉庭接受。上诉庭认为双方选择了仲裁地点也就是选择了只能向该地点的国家法院而不是任何其他国家的法院寻求对裁决书的救济,

---

〔104〕 20 世纪 80 年代,由于美国法院解释保单覆盖的责任范围超出保险人预期,令保险人蒙受了巨额损失(尤其是石棉与污染导致的人身伤害,这在本章之 8.6.3 段介绍的 Barrow v. Bankside Members Agency Ltd. [1996] 1 WLR 257 先例有提到),因此,美国保险公司在伦敦再保意外责任保险(casualty [liability] insurance)越来越困难。为了满足美国公司的需求,保险公司在百慕大成立了新的保险公司与使用特殊的标准格式保单,这些标准格式保单被统称为"Bermuda Form"。关于 Bermuda Form 的更多介绍,可见 Richard Jacobs QC, Lorelie S. Masters, Paul Stanley 的《Liability insurance in international arbitration: the Bermuda Form》(第 2 版,2011 年)一书。

〔105〕 在 Gary Born 的《International Commercial Arbitration》(2009 年)第二卷第 2639 页名为"Annulment of International Arbitral Awards"的章节中说:"Under the FAA (Federal Arbitration Act), in the United States, courts have for a number of decades applied a 'manifest disregard of law' standard of review, including to applications to vacate international arbitral awards made in the United States. There is a substantial body of U.S. authority on the 'manifest disregard' standard, much of which is not completely clear or consistent; nonetheless, the overwhelming weight of this authority recognizes a very narrow, seldom – exercised power of judicial review of the arbitrators' substantive legal rulings. More recently, however, the U.S. Supreme Court suggested that the FAA's statutory grounds for vacatur of an award are exclusive, arguably leaving no room for the manifest disregard doctrine: Hall Street Assoc., LLC v. Mattel, Inc., 128 S. Ct. 1396 (U.S. S. Ct. 2008)."简单而言,在美国的《联邦仲裁法》下,只有仲裁庭对实质争议的错判属于"明显对法律漠视"这种情况,才会导致裁决书被撤销。但在其他国家(包括以《联合国示范法》立法的国家或地区)仲裁庭对事实的认定或对法律的裁定就是最终的,仲裁地的监督法院不得干预。监督法院只能在仲裁程序上有错,违反自然公正或正当程序时才能干预。但美国这个"明显对法律漠视"的说法一直十分局限地在部分州份适用,有美国律师说几乎要在裁决书说"仲裁庭知道什么才是美国法律,但我们就不理会"的情况才会适用,并非错判这么简单。

D 向美国法院寻求救济违反了仲裁协议。

9.1.3 先例之三：Parakou Shipping Pte Ltd. v. Jinhui Shipping and Transportation Ltd.

在 Parakou Shipping Pte Ltd. v. Jinhui Shipping and Transportation Ltd.（2011）2 HKLRD 1 先例中，案情涉及香港金辉船务通过附属公司 Galsworthy 将船舶期租给 Parakou，但之后市场大跌，导致 Parakou 不愿意接船，并声称与二船东 Galsworthy 没有合约关系。双方开始伦敦仲裁，仲裁庭判 Galsworthy 胜诉。但在仲裁庭做出裁决书前，Parakou 在香港法院另外开始了针对金辉船务的诉讼，声称如果它在伦敦仲裁败诉，是金辉船务的误述所导致。伦敦仲裁的仲裁庭在香港法院的诉讼开庭前 1 个月做出了裁决书。香港法院以"滥用司法程序"（abuse of process）为由，撤销了 Parakou 的诉讼请求。Reyes 大法官说："It may be an abuse of process for a plaintiff, P, to initiate proceedings in court for the purposes of mounting a collateral attack upon an adverse final decision against P made by another court or tribunal of competent jurisdiction in previous proceedings. This is especially so where P has had a full opportunity of contesting the decision in the court by which it was made. Abuse arises because it would be 'a scandal to the administration of justice if, the same question having been disposed of by one case, the litigant were to be permitted by changing the form of the proceedings to set up the same case again'. See Hunter v. Chief Constable of the West Midlands Police [1982] AC 529 [Lord Diplock at pp. 541B, 542C citing from Lord Halsbury LC in Reichel v. Magrath (1889) LR 14 App Cas 665, 668)]. ... the abuse of process jurisdiction was available to prevent Parakou from relitigating fundamental findings in the Arbitration which were binding on Parakou, Galsworthy and (as Galsworthy's privies in interest) the defendants. Following the release of the Award, the Court came under a duty upon the defendants' application to refuse to allow the Hong Kong action to proceed and, by such refusal, to prevent manifest unfairness to the defendants and the bringing of disrepute to the administration of justice."

9.1.4 先例之四：Injazat Technology Capital Limited v. Dr. Hamid Najafi

Injazat Technology Capital Limited v. Dr. Hamid Najafi（2012）EWHC 4171（Comm）先例与第一原告 Injazat Technology Capital Limited 和 Broadlink 公司在 2006 年 9 月 22 日订立的股份认购协议（Share Subscription Agreement）有关。Broadlink 公司是被告 Hamid Najafi 博士与 Comisky 先生为了商业化其开发的一款手机而成立。在 SSA 中，Hamid Najafi 博士与 Comisky 先生被称为是担保人（guarantors）。第一原告以 300 万美元的价格购买 Broadlink 35% 的股份，并分 3 期支付。Broadlink 与两位担保人在 SSA 中做出了一系列的保证。双方在 SSA 中约定伦敦仲裁并受 ICC 仲裁规则管辖，独任仲裁员应是一名英国律师。

第一原告与 Broadlink 公司在同一天也订立了股东协议（Shareholders Agreement,简称"SHA")。SHA 中规定了双方在管理与营运 Broadlink 时的权利与义务,包括在没有董事局(其中至少要包括一名由第一原告委任的董事)的批准下,不可以对一些事情做出决定(certain matters should not be undertaken without prior approval of the board of directors)。SHA 中也包括一条伦敦仲裁条文,内容与 SSA 大致相同。

在订立 SSA 与 SHA 之前,Broadlink 与第二原告(第一原告的经理)在 2006 年 7 月 23 日订立了募资代理协议(Placement Agency Agreement,简称"PAA")。Broadlink 委任第二原告作为其募资代理,为它筹集不超过 300 万美元的资金。PAA 中有一条 Dubai International Financial Centre(简称 DIFC)仲裁条文。

在第一原告做出共 200 万美元的两期分期付款后,Broadlink 停止交易并破产,即第一原告损失了 200 万美元的投资。于是,第一原告在 SSA 与 SHA 下开始伦敦仲裁,以原告是因为对 Broadlink 的盈利情况的误述(misrepresentation)[106] 才订立合约等原因起诉两位担保人并索赔损失。两位担保人在伦敦仲裁抗辩,但没有提出反索赔。最终,伦敦仲裁庭判两位担保人做出了误述,认定 Broadlink 在订立合约时已经破产,这等于骗了第一原告 300 万美元。但两位担保人没有支付裁决书下的 3426533.45 美元的赔偿。于是第一原告在 Hamid Najafi 博士居住的加州执行裁决书。

这促使 Hamid Najafi 博士在 ICC 仲裁规则与 DIFC 仲裁规则下对第一原告与第二原告开始仲裁,索赔的理由(诉因)包括第一原告没有支付第三期分期付款、第二原告没有尽最大的努力筹集资金违反了 PAA、承诺性禁反言、违反信托责任与侵权干扰(tortious interference)、非法监禁(false imprisonment)等。

第一原告在英国法院申请针对 Hamid Najafi 博士的禁令,Flaux 大法官说:"... the claims for breach of the SSA ... are concerned, they are clearly an attempt to re – open matters decided against the defendant(Hamid Najafi 博士)in the final award. Alternatively, they are entirely spurious claims ... Similarly, the claims for tortuous interefer-ence and breach of fiduciary duty are all attempts to re – open matters decided against the defendant by the final award, or matters matters which could and should have been raised by the defendants(Hamid Najafi 博士与 Comisky 先生)in the first arbitration... Accordingly, in my judgment, those are all claims either precluded by res judicata or claims which are an abuse of process."

Flaux 大法官因此对 Hamid Najafi 博士做出了禁令,禁止他开始或继续推进第二个伦敦仲裁与 DIFC 仲裁(第三个仲裁),说:"... although the jurisdiction to grant an anti – arbitration injunction will be exercised sparingly, I propose to grant the order ... which is clearly appropriate in the circumstances of this case."

针对 PAA 下的 DIFC 仲裁,Flaux 大法官也说 PAA 是以 Broadlink 的名义订立,

[106] 这个课题可见本书第五章之 1.1 段。

但该公司已经被当局除名，根本不能再以此名义开始 DIFC 的仲裁，这明显是乱来："The claim for breach of the PAA is not one of the defendant can bring since he was not party to the PAA... third arbitration in the name of Broadlink against the second claimants under the PAA in Dubai claiming damages for the second claimant's alleged breach of the PAA... The commencement of that arbitration was allegedly authorised by shareholder's resolutions... Broadlink is insolvent and in fact no longer licensed in Dubai, the resolution is invalid and, in any event, Broadlink has no standing to pursue that arbitration."

9.1.5 先例之五：Nomihold Securities Inc. v. Mobile Telesystems Finance SA (No. 2)

Nomihold Securities Inc. v. Mobile Telesystems Finance SA (No. 2) (2012) EWHC 130 (Comm)先例有关被告（Mobile Telesystems Finance SA，简称 MTSF）在股份买卖合约（简称 SPA）下同意从原告 Nomihold（一家 BVI 公司）处购买 Tarino（一家在塞舌尔共和国注册的公司）51% 的股份。Tarino 间接拥有 Bitel（一家吉尔吉斯斯坦的移动通信公司），而 Bitel 拥有十分值钱的吉尔吉斯斯坦 GSM 900/1800 频段全国通信许可。这笔交易涉及的金额庞大，除了 SPA 下以 1.5 亿美元购买 51% 的股份外，双方还有涉及剩下的 49% 股份的期权协议（Option Agreement）。在该期权协议下，MTSF 在一定时间内可以行使认购期权（call option），以 1.7 亿美元买入 49% 的股份；Nomihold 也可以在一定时间内行使认沽期权（put option），以 1.7 亿美元卖出 49% 的股份。

但不久后，Bitel 的办公室被第三方查封，根据吉尔吉斯斯坦最高院的判决，Bitel 实际上已经毫无价值。也就是说，MTSF 投资的 1.5 亿美元都打了水漂。而 Nomihold 行使了认沽期权，要求 MTSF 支付 1.7 亿美元。MTSF 拒绝支付，于是 Nomihold 在期权协议下开始了第一个 LCIA 伦敦仲裁院仲裁。MTSF 的抗辩主要是 Nomihold 无法满足期权协议下的责任，所以不能行使认沽期权（Nomihold was not in a position to satisfy the obligations under the option agreement and therefore could not make its put option rights）。笔者从表面看来，MTSF 这抗辩十分无力，更完整与有力的抗辩是在第二个 LCIA 仲裁首次提出。

之后，MTSF 在 SPA 下开始了第二个 LCIA 仲裁，声称 SPA 因为误述或错误无效或 Nomihold 违反了 SPA 条文，要求 Nomihold 返还已经支付的 1.5 亿美元与赔偿损失。这个新的争议包括 Tarino 对 Bitel 的控制是不完整与有误导性，Tarino 并非 Bitel 在法律上的所有人。

但 MTSF 没有推进第二个 LCIA 仲裁，只是通知了 Nomihold 与第一个 LCIA 仲裁的仲裁庭，要求将两个仲裁合并，但 Nomihold 不同意。MTSF 也要求仲裁庭中止仲裁程序等待第二个 LCIA 仲裁结果，理由是 MTSF 认为期权协议的有效性取决于 SPA 的有效性，但 Nomihold 也不同意这一点。

接下来第一个 LCIA 仲裁的仲裁庭做出裁决,认为 SPA 的有效性应在该仲裁中决定,说:"For the avoidance of doubt, the 'SPA issue' is whether the option agreement is predicated upon a valid PA and the valid performance thereof and, if it is, whether the SPA was invalid and not performed, thus amounting to a defence to Nomihold's claims in these proceedings under the option agreement."

于是 MTSF 修改了第一个 LCIA 仲裁的答辩书,加入了在第二个 LCIA 仲裁中提出的抗辩。最后,仲裁庭没有支持 MTSF 针对不能行使认沽期权的抗辩,判 SPA 有效,MTSF 要支付 1.79 亿美元,裁决书可部分节录如下:"[MTSF] has failed to establish that the SPA or the Option Agreement are void or unenforceable for misrepresentation or mistake or that there was any breach of warranty in relation to either."

之后 MTSF 修改了第二个 LCIA 仲裁的仲裁申请(SPA 下)并开始了第三个 LCIA 仲裁(期权合约下),提出 Nomihold 涉及洗钱。Nomihold 声称这两个新仲裁是滥用程序,因为洗钱的争议应在第一个 LCIA 仲裁中提出,并且这两个新仲裁属于对第一个 LCIA 仲裁的裁决书的间接攻击,向高院申请止诉禁令(这里是 anti-arbitration injunction)。

但 MTSF 的代表大律师(估计是面对 Nomihold 在英国法院申请止诉禁令时才被委任)警觉地在诉讼中向法院做出了如下保证:"MTSF undertakes not to advance in [the new arbitrations] (a) any claim for a declaration (i) that MTSF is not obliged to carry out [the award] and (ii) that so far as the award is concerned MTSF is not bound by LCIA rule 26.9 or (b) a claim for an order that MTSF be released from any obligation to pay the purchase price of US $179m to be paid under the Option Agreement."

在该保证的基础上加上涉及金额巨大等因素,Andrew Smith 大法官没有做出针对 MTSF 的止诉禁令,而是认为应该交由新的仲裁庭处理这个是否再次仲裁(re-arbitration)的争端,说:

"I must ask myself whether in these circumstances it would be right to restrain MTSF from pursuing the New Arbitrations. They raise the money laundering complaint that was not considered in the Award because it was not an issue presented to the Tribunal. On its face it is a complaint of the kind that the parties agreed should be determined by LCIA arbitration. If the New Arbitrations proceed, the tribunals appointed to them will have adequate powers to determine the re-arbitration complaints. I say no more about the complaints themselves other than that they do not seem to me as straightforward as Mr Beltrami(Nomihold 代表大律师)submitted, but the tribunals could adopt procedures to deal with the re-arbitration complaint as a preliminary issue. It is for them to decide whether to do so.

I consider that the undertaking offered by MTSF will go a long way to answer Nomihold's submission that MTSF will be able effectively to deploy the New Arbitrations to prevent enforcement of the Award. As Mr Flynn（MTSF 代表大律师） submitted, Nomihold will still have available to it all the usual means of enforcement."

在笔者看来,MTSF 处理这个金额庞大的案件是十分差劲与不专业。

9.1.6 先例之六:Shanghai Fusheng Soya – Food Co. Ltd. v. Pulmuone Holdings Co. Ltd.

Shanghai Fusheng Soya – Food Co. Ltd. v. Pulmuone Holdings Co. Ltd. (2014) HKCFI 894 先例是笔者（杨大明）处理的案件。两家上海企业（上海福生豆制食品有限公司与上海张小宝绿色食品发展有限公司）与一家韩国企业在一份合资协议下发生了争议,根据仲裁协议是通过香港仲裁解决。韩国公司除了在香港启动仲裁之外,同时在上海法院启动了法院程序,指控上海公司与公司高层人员非法挪用合资公司资金等不当行为。这些指控也作为韩国公司在香港仲裁并向上海公司提出金额巨大的索赔的理据之一。

在香港仲裁庭做出裁决的前夕,上海法院做出判决,判韩国公司的大部分指控不成立,上海公司与公司高层人员的行为不像韩国公司指控的那么严重。中国公司马上把判决内容提供给仲裁庭,要求仲裁庭的裁决不得与上海法院的裁决有出入,否则违反一事不再审的原则。但结果仲裁庭以仲裁程序已经完毕为由不理会这个判决,仲裁裁决的结果是韩国公司完全胜诉。

上海公司向香港法院申请撤销仲裁裁决,理由是仲裁庭违反了一事不再审的原则,不理会上海法院较早前的判决结果。这是违反公共政策,因此裁决应该被撤销。但最终香港法院没有接纳这观点,认为就算违反了一事不再审的说法,也不足以构成违反公共政策（public policy）并以此撤销仲裁裁决。Mimmie Chan 大法官说:

"The Applicants（上海公司）complain that it is contrary to public policy to allow the Respondent（韩国公司）to re – litigate and reopen the issue of the alleged misappropriation of RMB 19.4 million decided in the Shanghai Action. As mentioned in paragraph 19 above, the Applicants had been aware of the commencement and conduct of Action No 80（上海法院诉讼）and the issues raised therein. They had participated in both Action No 80 and the Arbitration with such knowledge. They had been given the opportunity to make submissions in the Arbitration on Action No 80, any duplication of issues raised in the Arbitration and Action No 80, and the effect which Action No 80 (and any judgment which may be made in Action No 80) may have on the Arbitration, and they did make such submissions. They applied for a striking out in the Arbitration, which was determined by the Tribunal (rightly or wrongly). The Tribunal was aware of the issues raised in Action No 80, and decided that they had no relevance to or effect on their award in the Arbitration. The issues decided in the Arbitration and the findings made in the Award in relation to the Applicants' breach of the JV Agreement, its termination and the dissolution of the JV Company, are distinct from the issues of the Applicants' misappropriation of the funds of the JV Company, as decided in Action No 80.

In my view, this is not a case which cries out for setting aside the Award on the ground that it is an affront to the administration of justice, or that to enforce the Award would be to violate the most basic notions of morality and justice of the Hong Kong Court. There is no serious breach which has undermined due process, the Applicants had a fair opportunity to present their case on all the issues raised in the Arbitration, and I can find no injustice caused to the Applicants as a result of the existence or effect of the Judgment."

已经在本章一开始提到,一事不再审的说法是诉讼终局性的基础,而诉讼如果没有终局性会根本性地破坏法治,因此一事不再审明显属于公共政策。香港法院将违反一事不再审的说法只作为法律上的错误(error in law),显然与这个说法的重要性不相称。虽然这可能导致将来很多裁决书因此被撤销或被拒绝承认与执行,与现在国际上支持仲裁的趋势不符。这或许就需要法院像程序中违反自然公正一样,对每个案件的事实与违反的严重性进行考虑。即使在一些不太重要的违反,如"争端的禁反言"(issue estoppel)的情况下可以放宽要求,也应该避免 Shanghai Fusheng Soya – Food Co. Ltd. v. Pulmuone Holdings Co. Ltd 先例这种造成双重赔偿(double recovery)的情况。甚至可以想得到会有更严重违反一事不再审的情况,这也是下一个要介绍的先例中, Bernard Eder 大法官担心会出现的取巧的情况。

9.1.7 先例之七:Diag Human SE v. The Czech Republic

在本章之 3.3.2.1 段与 7.2.3 段已经提到的 Diag Human SE v. The Czech Republic (2014) 2 Lloyd's Rep. 283 先例中,案情涉及 Diag Human 与捷克政府约定了在捷克仲裁,解决有关捷克政府一位官员无理错误的破坏了 Diag Human 的企业声誉及带来巨额损失的争议。Diag Human 最终胜诉,但捷克政府声称按照有关仲裁条文规定,任何一方可以有复审 (review)的过程,因此不能马上执行。Diag Human 不同意,并尝试在不同地方执行裁决。其在奥地利与法国的申请被驳回,而在美国与卢森堡的程序还在进行中。

但在英国的程序,Bernard Eder 大法官认为不能执行仲裁裁决,原因是奥地利法院已经判该捷克仲裁裁决书由于还没有复审,所以并非最终与有约束力的而不能执行,即已经对这个问题做出了决定。因此,英国法院不应该把这个问题再审,否则就违反一事不再审的说法,并鼓励像 Diag Human 的原告在不同管辖地的法院不停尝试执行一个有问题的裁决书,直到有一天获得对他有利的判决为止。

这个著名与富争议性的英国先例的判法看来与 Shanghai Fusheng Soya – Food Co. Ltd. v. Pulmuone Holdings Co. Ltd. (2014) HKCFI 894 先例相反,虽然案情的本质也不尽相同。这个先例对中国公司/企业的重要之处在于,如果取得了金额较大的胜诉裁决书(如贸仲仲裁的裁决书),可以先在香港(一般支持仲裁的执行)要求承认与执行裁决书(即使败诉方在香港没有或只有很少的财产可供执行)。稍后去败诉方有财产的地方根据 1958 年《纽约公约》要求承认与执行裁决书时,即使当地法院相对不那么支持,或是裁决书的理由不充分导致法院有敌意,至少在获得了香港承认与执行裁决书的判决后,就多了一个一事不再审的争辩。

9.2 国际仲裁

这里的国际仲裁包括仲裁地(seat)并非是普通法国家/地区(如伦敦、香港、纽约、新加坡等)或适用法(governing law)并非普通法的仲裁案件,如很多 ICC 仲裁就属于这种情况,或是越来越多由中国大陆各仲裁机构管理的国际仲裁。简单而言,针对"一事不再审"(res judicata)与"滥用司法程序"(abuse of process)的说法在这些国际仲裁中能否适用与怎样适用是很混乱与不肯定的,这在本章稍早的 9.1.6 段介绍的 Shanghai Fusheng Soya - Food Co. Ltd. v. Pulmuone Holdings Co. Ltd. (2014) HKCFI 894 先例就有所显示。造成这种混乱与不肯定的原因有很多,其中最重要的是如下方面:

1. 普通法下的一事不再审与滥用司法程序的说法相当广泛,包括可以约束有利害关系人士(privies),只要依赖的主要事实与法律大致相同就属于同一诉因或争端并约束之后的诉讼。当然即使都是普通法国家,法律多少也会有一定程度的不同,如美国每个州的法律都不相同。

大陆法虽然都有类似的说法,但十分狭窄。大陆法有一个"triple identify test"的说法,[107] 即第一个诉讼与第二个诉讼当事人一致[不会延伸到有利害关系人士(privy 或 privity)]、要求的救济一致并且依赖的事实一致。大陆法的一事不再审也只适用于生效与执行部分(operative part),判决的原因只是用来澄清与协助理解生效与执行部分。"Henderson v. Henderson Rule"在大陆法国家也不适用。部分大陆法国家也认为,争端的禁反言不应该约束之后的诉讼,这也有道理,因为即使是同样的争端,因为背景不同可能会有不同的结果。例如,同样的争端在之前的诉讼中并不重要,有其他更重要与关键的争端,所以诉讼方并没有花太多时间精力处理该次要争端。但之后的诉讼中这个争端十分重要,如果之前的诉讼结果可以约束诉讼方,就对他很不公平。这也会导致节省司法资源的反效果,即诉讼方为了不被禁反言,必须在第一个诉讼中对每个重要或不重要的争端都全力以赴、坚持到底。

2. 国际仲裁中仲裁庭成员有不同的背景(包括来自不同司法体系的国家),所以对能否适用有关的说法有不同的看法。所以,如果诉讼方(无论原告或被告)提出有关一事不再审与/或滥用司法程序的争议,有关的仲裁庭也不容易做出一致的决定。

3. 估计目前很多诉讼方与其律师在这方面还不够警觉,所以在很多可以提出有关说法的情况下没有提出,等于放弃(waive)了抗辩的权利。但随着法律的发展,估计越来越多的诉讼方(尤其是其律师)会开始注意这个问题。但这个问题无法回避,因为现在合约链(chain of contracts)与/或多方合约(multi - party contract)越来越多,

---

[107] 见《French Civil Code》之 article 1351。

根据 ICC 的统计数据,2016 年的仲裁中有 41% 涉及多方合约,这种合约很容易涉及一事不再审与滥用司法程序的争议。

4. 类似仲裁条文的独立性导致很多仲裁条文的适用法争议(即仲裁条文作为独立合约的适用法是主合约的适用法还是仲裁地法律),应该以什么法律决定一事不再审或滥用司法程序的说法会更加复杂,究竟是主合约的适用法,还是之后的仲裁的仲裁地法律,或是做出之前的判决或裁决的所在地法律?目前,国际上针对这个问题没有达成任何共识。

5. 上一段的问题再加上一事不再审与滥用司法程序到底是程序法还是实体法的争议会变得更加复杂。在英国,一事不再审应该属于实体法,[108] 但滥用司法程序应属于程序法。在美国,一事不再审也属于实体法。[109] 在瑞士,一事不再审属于程序法。[110] 在法国,一事不再审属于实体法还是程序法有含糊之处,虽然表面看来普遍接受不构成一事不再审是程序性决定,但也有说法是构成一事不再审是实际性决定(即属于实体法)。如果是实体法,决定一事不再审或滥用司法程序的说法是否适用的是主合约适用法的说服力更大。而如果是程序法,适用仲裁地(或做出之前的判决或裁决的所在地)的法律的说服力更大。

6. 鉴于一事不再审或滥用司法程序的说法在国际仲裁的适用不明确与有争议性,所以,现在有说法是应该发展与采取一套跨国(transnational)的统一法律。这可见国际法协会(International Law Association)的《Interim Report on Res Judicata and Arbitration, Berlin Conference (2004)》与《Final Report on Res Judicata and Arbitration and Resolution No. 1/2006, Toronto Conference (2006)》。[111] 当然这套跨国的统一法律还留待将来的强制性立法(如国际公约)与非强制性规则(如仲裁协会规则或国际律师协会[International Bar Association,简称"IBA"]规则)的发展。但是,即使有这套跨国的统一法律能否超越仲裁所在地的法律适用,在国际仲裁也存在争议。如在 Coppee Lavalin SA NV v. Ken－Ren Chemicals & Fertilisers Ltd. (1994) 2 Lloyd's Rep. 109 先例中,就说英国不接受跨国法律的管辖:"Transnationalism is a theoretical ideal which posits that international arbitration, at least as regards certain types of contractual disputes conducted under the auspices of an arbitral institution arbitration, is a self－contained juridical system, by its very nature separate from national systems of law, and indeed antithetical to them... **I doubt whether in its purest sense the doctrine**

---

[108] 见 Associated Electric and Gas Insurance Services Ltd. v. European Reinsurance Co. of Zurich (2003) 1 WLR 1041 (PC)先例。

[109] 见 National Union Fire Ins. Co. v. Belco Petroleum Corp., 88 F. 3d 129 (2d Cir. 1996); Chiron Corp. v. Ortho Diagnostic System, Inc., 207 F. 3d 1126 (9th Cir. 2000); Citigroup, Inc. v. Abu Dhabi Investment Authority, 13 Civ. 6073 (PKC)等先例。

[110] 见《Swiss Code de Procedure Civile》之 article 59(2)(e)。

[111] 有兴趣的读者可在 http://www.ila－hq.org 下载有关报告。

now commands widespread support... At all events it cannot be the law of England..."(加黑部分是笔者的强调)

7. 另一个问题是,如果双方提出了一事不再审或滥用司法程序的争议,但仲裁庭漏了做出裁决或错判,究竟属于适用法律错误(mistake of law)还是违反公共政策(public policy)? 这个区别在英国或许不太重要,因为根据1996年《仲裁法》,诉讼方可以就法律问题上诉。但在其他大部分国家(包括在《纽约公约》下)都必须是违反公共政策,当事人才能向法院上诉撤销裁决书。有说法是,一事不再审或滥用司法程序的说法是考虑了法院诉讼要有终局性的公共政策。但仲裁是双方同意的程序,仲裁庭的权力来自诉讼双方,仲裁庭只对诉讼双方有职业责任(professional duty)。因此,仲裁庭漏了对一事不再审或滥用司法程序的争议做出裁决或错判,不应属于违反公共政策,即没有监督法院的救济。

一些ICC国际仲裁案件就涉及这方面的问题,在ICC Case No. 10623 of 2001,仲裁庭没有理会仲裁地法院做出的禁令,强调仲裁庭要对诉讼方负责,说:"An international arbitral tribunal is not an organ of the state in which it has its seat in the same way that a court of the seat would be. The primary source of Tribunal's powers is the parties' agreement to arbitrate. An important consequence of this is that the Tribunal has a duty vis a vis the parties to ensure that their arbitration agreement is not frustrated. In certain circumstances, it may be necessary to decline to comply with an order issued by a court of the seat, in the fulfillment of the Tribunal's larger duty to the parties ... The Tribunal owe a duty to the parties to ensure that their agreement to submit disputes to international arbitration is rendered effective even where that creates a conflict with the courts of the seat of the arbitrator, ..."

在ICC Case No. 6233 of 1992,仲裁庭也是以仲裁自主为由避开了一事不再审的说法,说:"the arbitral tribunal is of the opinion that arbitral tribunals, and not State courts, have jurisdiction to interpret arbitral awards. This power is based on the arbitral clause itself, the purpose of which is to bar the jurisdiction of State courts; nothing authorizes the limitation of the effects of the arbitral clause when the subject of the dispute is the interpretation of the award rendered on the basis of this clause."

8. 诉讼方常常会在仲裁地或外国的法院提出仲裁庭没有管辖权的争议,而国际上普遍接受让仲裁暂时中止(stay)的命令并非对管辖权争议(如仲裁条文的有效性)做出了最终与结论性的判决。如果是仲裁地法院做出仲裁庭没有管辖权的判决,仲裁庭也必须接受。但如果是外国法院的判决,是否构成一事不再审令仲裁庭只能接受而不能再认定自己有管辖权并对有关争议做出裁决? 如针对富争议性的提单(bill of lading)是否合并租约仲裁条文,[112]货方如果能在船东开始伦敦仲裁与/或取得止

---

〔112〕 见笔者《提单与其他付运单证》(2016年)一书第四章之2.5段。

诉禁令(anti - suit injunction)前在中国海事法院获得合并无效的判决,看来就会构成一事不再审并约束伦敦仲裁庭。但在现实中,中国海事法院再加上上诉机制很难比英国法院或伦敦仲裁庭更快做出最终与结论性判决。[113] 在 The Republic of Kazakhstan v. Istil Group Inc. (2008) 1 Lloyd's Rep. 382 先例中,巴黎法院做出了诉讼双方不存在有效的仲裁协议的判决。但 Istil 没有理会这个判决,开始了 LCIA 仲裁,仲裁庭认为他们有管辖权并做出裁决,要求哈萨克斯坦政府赔偿一笔钱给 Istil。但这份裁决书被英国法院以违反诉因的禁反言撤销,仲裁庭受巴黎法院双方没有有效仲裁协议的判决的约束。

9. 目前看来国际仲裁中对这种经常会出现的外国法院针对管辖权做出判决是否约束仲裁庭的争议有不同说法。如在 ICC Case No. 3383 of 1979, ICC 仲裁庭认为较早前的判有一条有效的仲裁协议的临时仲裁(ad hoc arbitration)裁决有绝对(absolute)的一事不再审的效果,说:"It is obvious not for this arbitrator to operate as an appeal body over the decisions of other arbitral tribunals - including those preceding the final award on the merits - which, by definition, are rendered in last instance. Considering, therefore, that where the parties have the power... to challenge before the competent authorities arbitral awards which they consider to be flawed, it is not within the powers of another arbitrator to put such awards in question. It is therefore for this arbitrator to simply take notice of the decisions rendered by the ad hoc tribunal ... in particular the decision in which the arbitral tribunal declared itself competent and accepted the mission conferred upon it by the parties pursuant to the arbitration agreement..."但也有不少 ICC 的仲裁案件中认为不受到较早法院对管辖权的判决的约束:ICC Case No. 4862 of 1986; ICC Case No. 5294 of 1988; ICC Case No. 10623 of 2001 等。

10. 中间措施(Interim measure or relief)是另一个可能有很多争议的领域。在 ICC Case No. 4126 of 1984,仲裁庭拒绝做出中间措施,因为该仲裁与法院程序基本相同,环境也没有发生改变,法院之前拒绝做出该中间措施的决定应约束诉讼双方。仲裁庭最终以司法效率(judicial efficiency)与程序经济(procedural economy)的理由拒绝了原告的申请。但其他 ICC 的国际仲裁中也有不同的决定,如 ICC Case No. 6363 of 1991 就不认为会因一事不再审而受之前的法院判决的约束,因为诉讼方不同,说:"A discrepancy between any one of the elements of a current claim and a past judgment comprising a res judicata (i. e. identity of parties, cause and subject matter) is enough to defeat a defence based on res judicata. Enough has been said to show that the (court) decision is res judicata between [C] and [B], but not as between [A] and [B]..."ICC Case No. 7061 of 1997 也是同样的决定,说:"This arbitration tribunal is not bound by the X award; nor are the parties to these arbitration proceedings. There can

〔113〕 如在本章之 9.1.1 段介绍的 The "Jonna V" (2003) 2 Lloyd's Rep. 617 先例。

be no issue estoppel. . . ”

11. 至于实质争议(substantive dispute),如果法院已经做出了判决是否对之后的仲裁构成一事不再审的争议相对较少。这是因为《纽约公约》生效后,很少会发生平行诉讼(concurrent/parallel litigation)的情况。更多的情况是,双方对之前的仲裁裁决能否构成一事不再审约束之后的仲裁裁决或之后的仲裁是否构成滥用司法程序有争议。如本章之7.2.4段介绍的长期合约中价格调整条文(price review clause),第一次产生争议时仲裁庭做出的裁决能否约束之后的仲裁庭(如果仲裁庭成员不同)?这方面十分复杂与不肯定,并带来若干方面的问题。之前的仲裁裁决要构成一事不再审首先要面对的障碍是仲裁的机密性:Ali Shipping Corporation v. Shipyard Trogir (1998)1 Lloyd's Rep. 643 先例。[114] 也就是说,如果之后的仲裁中的诉讼方与之前的仲裁不同(即使关系密切,如大集团下的不同 BVI 公司),之前的仲裁的标的、证据、裁决书等都不能在之后的仲裁披露(除非属于特殊的例外情况)。当然,如果之后的仲裁的诉讼方相同,机密性的障碍就不再存在:Associated Electric and Gas Insurance Services Ltd. v. European Reinsurance Co. of Zurich (2003) 1 WLR 1041 先例。但从仲裁庭的角度,肯定不愿意受之前的仲裁裁决的约束,也不一定认同之前的仲裁裁决。加上反对一事不再审的说法的一方,也一定会提出新的证据(无论是否重要)以显示情况有所不同,之前的仲裁裁决最多是说服性的(persuasive)。而提出一事不再审的一方也没有什么强制手段可以像国家法院严格对待一事不再审的说法一样,约束仲裁庭或撤销仲裁庭不加理会做出的裁决。

在国际层面,对纯粹是先做出裁决的仲裁庭的裁决约束之后的仲裁庭的合法性(legitimacy)还没有一致的看法。否则,只要一方一提出一事不再审的争议,仲裁庭就应该立即以初步争议(preliminary issue)的方式做出决定。因为一旦一事不再审的说法适用,仲裁就没有必要再进行下去。但笔者还没有听说过国际仲裁中有这种做法。

12. 在投资仲裁中,原告可能对同样的事实以不同身份(如公司与股东)开始同步诉讼向东道国(host country)索赔,希望增加胜诉机会甚至获得双重赔偿(double recovery)。在2017年哥伦比亚大学仲裁日(Columbia Arbitration Day)上,其中一位讲者认为可以通过国际性的“一事不再审”(res judicata)(包括诉因的禁反言与争端的禁反言)解决这个问题。

由于篇幅有限,笔者不再对这个越来越复杂与不断发展的新问题进行进一步的介绍。有兴趣的读者可以下载《Interim Report on Res Judicata and Arbitration, Berlin Conference (2004)》与《Final Report on Res Judicata and Arbitration and Resolution No. 1/2006, Toronto Conference (2006)》两篇报告与关注之后的法律发展。只节录《Final Report on Res Judicata and Arbitration and Resolution No. 1/2006, Toronto Confer-

---

[114] 见本章之7.2.5段。

ence（2006）》中对国际性的一事不再审做出的建议：

“1. To promote efficiency and finality of international commercial arbitration, arbitral awards should have conclusive and preclusive effects in further arbitral proceedings.

2. The conclusive and preclusive effects of arbitral awards in further arbitral proceedings set forth below need not necessarily be governed by national law and may be governed by transnational rules applicable to international commercial arbitration.

3. An arbitral award has conclusive and preclusive effects in further arbitral proceedings if:

3.1　it has become final and binding in the country of origin and there is no impediment to recognition in the country of the place of the subsequent arbitration;

3.2　it has decided on or disposed of a claim for relief which is sought or is being reargued in the further arbitration proceedings;

3.3　it is based upon a cause of action which is invoked in the further arbitration proceedings or which forms the basis for the subsequent arbitral proceedings; and

3.4　it has been rendered between the same parties.

4. An arbitral award has conclusive and preclusive effects in the further arbitral proceedings as to:

4.1　determinations and relief contained in its dispositive part as well as in all reasoning necessary thereto;

4.2　issues of fact or law which have actually been arbitrated and determined by it, provided any such determination was essential or fundamental to the dispositive part of the arbitral award.

5. An arbitral award has preclusive effects in the further arbitral proceedings as to a claim, cause of action or issue of fact or law, which could have been raised, but was not, in the proceedings resulting in that award, provided that the raising of any such new claim, cause of action or new issue of fact or law amounts to procedural unfairness or abuse.

6. The conclusive effects of an arbitral award can be invoked in further arbitration proceedings at any time permitted under the applicable procedure.

7. The preclusive effects of an arbitral award need not be raised on its own motion by an arbitral tribunal. If not waived, such preclusive effects should be raised as soon as possible by a party.”

另可节录一家著名的国际律师事务所在一篇针对国际仲裁目前面对一事不再审的不肯定的文章中所说，如下：

“The concept of res judicata straddles the intersection between substantive and procedural law. There is no right or wrong answer, not any established approach as to whether the lex causae or lex arbitri should be adopted by an international arbitration tribunal in its consideration of res judicata issues. It will probably remain within the discretion of the particular tribunal, to be decided after due consideration of all relevant factors to the particular dispute, including the arbitration agreement and earlier decision.

This makes res judicata a potential area of uncertainty for parties and their legal representatives going into arbitration."

这样看来相比法院诉讼,国际仲裁的另一个缺点就是一事不再审的说法是否适用不肯定(虽然目前很少有人提到这一点)。涉及法院诉讼,不论是普通法或大陆法国家的法院,至少一事不再审的说法在何种情况下适用的法律地位是相对肯定,但国际仲裁就很难说了。

这不仅是在仲裁程序中,对裁决书的执行也会有影响与造成混乱。除了在本章之9.1.6段介绍的Shanghai Fusheng Soya－Food Co. Ltd. v. Pulmuone Holdings Co. Ltd先例中,笔者也看到一个最近有关上海国际仲裁中心(SHIAC)的案件。根据报道,争议涉及德国投资商在2005年向上海地产商购买一座购物中心,但上海地产商中途突然通知德国投资商交易终止。根据德国投资商的说法,当时上海房价/地价急升,上海地产商因此终止交易,但上海地产商不认同这个指控。

双方无法达成和解协议,于是上海地产商在2007年根据买卖合约在当时的贸仲上海分会(2012年后脱离贸仲,变为上海国际仲裁中心)开始仲裁(第一个仲裁),而德国投资商也在2008年根据框架协议开始贸仲上海分会仲裁并申请继续履行合约(第二个仲裁)。两个仲裁的仲裁庭相同,并同时在上海开庭。2009年,开完庭后不久,上海地产商撤回了第一个仲裁的仲裁申请与第二个仲裁中的反索赔。之后,上海地产商根据买卖合约开始了第三个贸仲上海分会仲裁。虽然德国投资商有第三个仲裁是对第二个仲裁的重复的疑虑,但还是同意先委任仲裁员组成仲裁庭,但这不影响它在稍后的仲裁程序中提出反对的权利。而第三个仲裁庭成员与第二个仲裁庭成员不同。

2017年5月,第三个仲裁的仲裁庭做出多数裁决书(majority award),要求德国投资商支付3300万美元。但德国投资商声称这与第二个仲裁的仲裁庭在2013年12月做出的裁决书有冲突。在第二个仲裁的裁决书中,仲裁庭判德国投资商胜诉并要求上海地产商支付3000万美元。德国投资商认为两个仲裁涉及同样当事人与同样的争议,第三个仲裁的裁决书违反了"一事不再审"(res judicata),并与中国法下裁决书的终局性的公共政策(public policy)有冲突。于是,德国投资商在上海市第二中级人民法院申请撤销第三个仲裁的裁决书。

上海市第二中级人民法院的判决结果还未知,但在笔者看来,这个案件与Shanghai Fusheng Soya－Food Co. Ltd. v. Pulmuone Holdings Co. Ltd.先例显示了一事不再审说法对仲裁裁决书的执行带来的混乱。

第十章　民事诉讼/仲裁中的弃权与禁反言

“弃权”(waiver)与“禁反言”(estoppel)在民事诉讼与国际仲裁的过程中经常出现,是诉讼律师需要十分警惕的。一旦发生,对诉讼律师来说就可能是噩梦,经常会涉及被委托方指称职业疏忽(professional negligence)。除了会面对宝贵的时间与金钱上的损失(即使有责任保险),律师事务所的名誉也会受损。弃权与禁反言的出现会在方方面面,包括对仲裁或是法院诉讼的取舍、对时效的保护、对仲裁员甚至当事人委任的律师的资格或利益冲突是否提出质疑、管辖权问题、诉讼程序不当的应对、庭审的言行、应否上诉或寻求对裁决书的救济等。如果做出的行动与选择不及时或做错了选择,就会因为构成弃权与禁反言而无法再改正。

由于英国法相对完整与肯定,因此在很多情况下,诉讼或仲裁中最重要的是对事实的认定,这就涉及证据(特别是文件证据)的问题。本章最后一段会重点针对对享有“特免权”(privilege)的证据的弃权与禁反言。如果不小心放弃了特免权,除了可能导致诉讼或仲裁败诉,还有可能在涉及规管(regulatory)时带来刑事后果与/或天文数字的罚款。

1. 对主权豁免权的弃权

“主权或国家豁免权”(sovereign or state immunity)在民事诉讼特别是国际仲裁中是十分重要的课题。一个主权国家,可以包括君主、国家、政府机构、主权财富基金(sovereign wealth fund)等,在面对诉讼或判决书/裁决书的执行时,都会提出主权豁免的抗辩。英国1978年《State Immunity Act》立法中没有对国家(state)的定义,但在《United Nations Convention on Jurisdictional Immunities of States and Their Property》(尚未生效)中对“国家”一词的定义是:“2. For the purposes of the present articles:...(b) “State” means:(i) the State and its various organs of government;(ii) constituent units of a federal State or political subdivisions of the State, which are entitled to perform acts in the exercise of sovereign authority, and are acting in that capacity;(iii) agencies or instrumentalities of the State or other entities, to the extent that they are entitled to perform and are actually performing acts in the exercise of sovereign authority of the State;(iv) representatives of the State acting in that capacity...”

本小段只会对主权豁免权的弃权与禁反言进行简单介绍,有兴趣的读者可看 Schreuer 先生的《State Immunity: Some Recent Developments》(1988 年);《Oppenheim's International Law》(第 9 版,1992 年);Hafner 教授、Kohen 教授与 Breau 教授合著的《State Practice Regarding State Immunities》(2006);Fox 御用大律师的《Law of State Immunity》(第 2 版,2008 年);Brownlie 御用大律师的《Principles of Public International Law》(第 7 版,2008 年)第十六章;《Dicey, Morris & Collins on The Conflict of Laws》(第 15 版,2012 年)第十章等。

1.1 主权豁免权的历史

在早期,主权国家不会参与商业活动。国家主权的传统功能是维护社会秩序与法制、外交与国防。国家主权在这些活动中享有"绝对豁免权"(absolute immunity)。主权豁免是国际公法的分支之一,其基础是"par in parem non habet imperium"(equal has no power over an equal),即一个主权国家不会对另一个平等的主权国家有管辖权。这在之后变为英国普通法的一部分,并反映在了 1978 年的《State Immunity Act》立法中。

针对主权豁免的历史,Denning 勋爵在 Trendtex Trading Corporation v. Central Bank of Nigeria (1977) 1 Lloyd's Rep. 581 (CA)先例说:

"A century ago no sovereign state engaged in commercial activities. It kept to the traditional functions of a sovereign – to maintain law and order – to conduct foreign affairs – and to see to the defence of the country. It was in those days that England – with most other countries – adopted the rule of absolute immunity. It was adopted because it was considered to be the rule of international law at that time. In The 'Parlement Belge' (1880) 5 P. D. 197, 205, Brett L. J. said: 'The exemption of the person of every sovereign from adverse suit is admitted to be a part of the law of nations... [so also] of some property... The universal agreement which has made these propositions part of the law of nations has been an implied agreement.'

The rule was stated by Dicey in his work on Conflict of Laws, and repeated religiously by the judges thereafter. The classic restatement of it was made by Lord Atkin in Compania Naviera Vascongado v. S. S. Cristina (The Cristina) [1938] A. C. 485, 490: 'The courts of a country will not implead a foreign sovereign, that is, they will not by their process make him against his will a party to legal proceedings whether the proceedings involve process against his person or seek to recover from him specific property or damages'."

"二战"后,主权国家开始越来越多参与商业活动,大部分西方国家逐渐将主权的绝对豁免改为有限制的豁免。也就是说,将主权国家的行为分为政府行为(*acta jure imperii* 或 acts of government)与商业行为(*acta jure gestionis* 或 acts of a commercial nature)，前者有主权豁免权，而后者没有。[1] 这在权威书籍《Dicey, Morris & Collins, The Conflict of Laws》(第15版，2012年)之10－004段有更详细的介绍："**History.** In the 19th century and for much of the 20th century the 'absolute' rule of immunity prevailed, whereby foreign States and sovereigns were accorded immunity for all activities, whether governmental or commercial. But the increase in state trading in the 20th century led a number of countries to develop a distinction, generally called the 'restrictive' theory, between acts of government, acta jure imperii, and acts of a commercial nature, acta jure gestionis. Under the restrictive theory, States were immune in respect of acts of government but not in respect of commercial acts. An early attempt to exclude immunity in the case of ships and cargoes owned or operated by States for commercial purposes, the Brussels Convention of 1926, achieved only limited support, and was not ratified by the United Kingdom until 1979. The enormous increase in state trading after the Second World War led the United States Department of State to announce, in 1952, its adherence to the restrictive theory, and the distinction between governmental and commercial acts was applied by the United States courts and was in 1976 enacted in federal legislation.[2] In 1972 a European Convention on State Immunity, severely restricting the scope of immunity, was concluded under the auspices of the Council of Europe, and came into force in 1976."

1.2　对主权豁免权的弃权与禁反言

想依赖禁反言排除主权豁免权的抗辩十分困难。在 Trendtex Trading Corporation v. Central Bank of Nigeria (1977) 1 Lloyd's Rep. 581 (CA)先例中，案情有关尼日利亚因为出产石油一夜暴富，在12个月内进口了2000万吨水泥进行国内的建设，这个数字是前一年的10倍。但港口、道路等配套的基建工程没有跟上，导致三四百条船在 Lagos 港等待卸货。很多船舶等了超过两年无法卸货，最终货物全损。尼日利亚政府命令开了很多信用证的尼日利亚中央银行，不要在信用证下支付给作为受益人的卖方。这导致这些信用证下的受益人之一(即本先例的原告 Trendtex)在英国法院起诉尼日利亚中央银行。而尼日利亚中央银行则依赖主权豁免权申请法院驳回原告的起诉。

针对主权豁免权，Trendtex 提出的争议之一是禁反言。在中央银行通知信用证下的受益人(即 Trendtex)的信中，说："I write to inform you that no confirmation is re-

---

〔1〕 英国1978年的《State Immunity Act》之 section 3 规定："Commercial transactions and contracts to be performed in United Kingdom. (1) A State is not immune as respects proceedings relating to—(a) a commercial transaction entered into by the State; or (b) an obligation of the State which by virtue of a contract (whether a commercial transaction or not) falls to be performed wholly or partly in the United Kingdom."

〔2〕 美国1976年《Foreign Sovereign Immunities Act》。

quired for credits opened by us... We are irrevocably committed to honour our engagements under this credit. Moreover, our correspondent, the Midland Bank Ltd. , has our authority to pay the beneficiary the full value of this letter of credit through your bank on presentation of relevant shipping documents to them in London, provided the documents are in order.... As a government bank and a prime bank, no supplier should have any cause to doubt our ability to pay our bills promptly. The question of our correspondents confirming our letters of credit should, therefore, not arise. We are sending a copy of this letter to our correspondent bank, the Midland Bank Ltd. , London, and you may wish to contact them for any further information you may require about us."

Trendtex 声称上述写法构成"陈述性禁反言"(estoppel by representation),但这不被高院([1976] 1 WLR 868)与上诉庭接受,原因是在上述的信件中,没有任何关于它将来不会依赖主权豁免权的陈述,因此也不会之后被禁止改变立场。高院的 Donaldson 大法官说:"... the letter does not represent that the Central Bank is not in a position to claim sovereign immunity. It represents that (a) the Central Bank is irrevocably committed to honouring its obligations under the letter of credit, (b) the Central Bank is a government bank, (c) the Central Bank is a prime bank and (d) the Central Bank had not then, and would not in the future, be unable to meet its obligations. All these representations were then true and remain true to this day. A commitment is no less irrevocable, because it is not honoured in the event. 'Irrevocable' means at most that the commitment cannot be revoked without a breach of contract. None of them is inconsistent with a claim to sovereign immunity. Indeed, the representation that the Central Bank was a government bank might well have forewarned the plaintiffs."

除了不存在明确无误的陈述外,Donaldson 大法官还说禁反言要适用必须涉及尼日利亚政府,因为主权豁免权是属于它而不是中央银行,但尼日利亚政府并没有参与这个诉讼,说:"... the fact that the estoppel, to be effective, must bind the state of Nigeria as distinct from the Central Bank. An estoppel is a procedural rule preventing a party to proceedings from leading evidence or putting forward a claim which is inconsistent with a binding representation. But the state of Nigeria is not before the court. What has happened is that the court has been put on notice that these proceedings may implead that state. It has thereupon become its duty to consider this possibility. But this would have been its duty however the point came to its notice: see per Kay L. J. in Mighell v. Sultan of Johore [1894] 1 Q. B. 149, 162."

上诉庭推翻了高院的判决,认为中央银行不属于政府机构,即使属于政府机构,该先例只涉及商业活动,因此没有主权豁免权。当时英国 1978 年《State Immunity Act》还没有出台,但普通法就已经有了枢密院的 The "Philippine Admiral" (1976) 1

Lloyd's Rep. 234 先例。[3] 但该先例涉及对物的诉讼（*in rem* action），当时东欧与苏联有大量船队在国际租船市场全面进行商业活动并与独立船东竞争，因此，当时的商业社会对在这方面限制主权豁免权呼声很高。可以说 Trendtex Trading Corporation v. Central Bank of Nigeria 先例是立法前，在对人诉讼中针对主权国家在商业活动没有主权豁免权的最早的先例。

1.3　对主权豁免权的弃权

至于对主权豁免权的弃权，英国已经有了 1978 年《State Immunity Act》立法并对这方面有所规定。该立法是针对主权豁免权的完整法规与主要的法律根源。正如 Goff 勋爵在 R v. Bow Street Metropolitan Stipendiary Magistrate, Ex p Pinochet（No. 3）（2000）1 AC 147 先例所说："There can be no doubt, in my opinion, that the [1978] Act is intended to provide the sole source of English law on this topic [state immunity]."

除了商业活动与特殊的例外，该 1978 年立法针对的对主权豁免权的弃权主要是两方面：

1. section 2(1)规定如果主权国家主动接受英国法院的管辖，则不会被豁免。根据 section 2(2)的规定，主权国家可以在双方产生争议并开始诉讼后弃权，也可以通过事前的书面协议弃权，但仅仅是一条条文说明是受英国法律管辖是不足够。[4] 相关条文可节录如下："(1) A State is not immune as respects proceedings in respect of which it has submitted to the jurisdiction of the courts of the United Kingdom. (2) A State may submit after the dispute giving rise to the proceedings has arisen or by a prior written agreement; but a provision in any agreement that it is to be governed by the law of the United Kingdom is not to be regarded as a submission."

2. section 9 规定如果主权国家同意了仲裁条文或在发生争议后同意递交仲裁解决，就不能在与仲裁有关的法院程序中被豁免。除非仲裁协议中有相反的规定。相关条文可节录如下："(1) Where a State has agreed in writing to submit a dispute which has arisen, or may arise, to arbitration, the State is not immune as respects proceedings in the courts of the United Kingdom which relate to the arbitration. (2) This section has effect subject to any contrary provision in the arbitration agreement and does not apply to any arbitration agreement between States."

根据 section 9(2)，该立法在在国家与国家之间的仲裁协议，如国家之间签订的双边投资协议（BIT）中的仲裁协议不适用。投资仲裁属于另外的范畴，根据《华盛顿公约》之 Article 25(1)，International Centre of Settlement Investment Disputes（简称 ICSID）对投资仲裁有管辖权。

---

[3] 本章稍后的 1.3.1 段对该先例的案情有简单介绍。

[4] 本章之 1.3.3 段有提到放弃主权豁免权条文的例子。

以下会对这两种不同形式的弃权做简单介绍。

1.3.1 对主权豁免权的弃权之一：主权国家参与诉讼

第一种弃权最明显的情况是一方在英国法院开始诉讼，而主权国家在明知其权利的情况下参与诉讼(submit to jurisdiction)，如做出实质的抗辩行为(taken a step in the proceedings relating to the merits)，通常会被视为接受(submitted to)英国法院管辖。这与在本章之3.2.3段提到的在合约有仲裁条文的情况下，被告没有及时在法院提出管辖权争议就会被视为对仲裁的弃权是同样的道理。如果主权国家没有及时提出有主权豁免权，就会被视为对主权豁免权的弃权，毕竟主权豁免权就是对管辖权的争议。

这也可见英国1978年立法之前，欧盟的《European Convention on State Immunity》(1972)(Cmnd 5081)之Article 3(1)："A contracting state cannot claim immunity from the jurisdiction of a court of another contracting state if, before claiming immunity, it takes any step in the proceedings relating to the merits. However, if the state satisfies the court that it could not have acquired knowledge of facts on which a claim to immunity can be based until after it has taken such a step, it can claim immunity based on these facts if it does so at the earliest possible moment."

上述节录的最后一句即本书第三章之3.4.1段所讲的要构成因选择而弃权，弃权方必须知道令他要在两个对立的权利中做出选择的事实(knowledge of the facts which show that it has to choose between two inconsistent courses of conduct)。而因为放弃主权豁免权是非常严肃的事，所以要求比普通的商业诉讼更严格。除了要知道自己的权利外，主权国家必须有意识与清楚明确地放弃。而代表国家弃权的人士必须有明确的授权，而不能只是依赖表见授权(ostensible authority)，[5] 如通过代理人(这包括律师)弃权。[6] 这可节录In re Republic of Bolivia Exploration Syndicate Ltd.

---

[5] 见本书第五章之12.2.4段。

[6] 在Aziz v. Yemen (2005) EWCA Civ 745先例中，上诉庭的Pill大法官说："Section 2(3) should, however, be read in the light of authority of long standing establishing the importance of state immunity and the importance of its not being waived except with appropriate authority. The fact that the step in proceedings alleged to constitute the waiver is taken by solicitors instructed by the Embassy does not conclude the matter. A solicitor acting without authority cannot waive the immunity. The solicitor's actions establish a waiver only if they have been authorised by the state, which includes authority exercised or conferred by the head of the State's diplomatic mission. That would include a step authorised by the head of mission himself or herself. Authority may be conferred on the solicitors either directly or, in my view, indirectly by a member of the mission authorised by the head of mission to do so... **I do not consider that the doctrine of ostensible authority applies either to the solicitors or to Mr Alkhader**(也门大使馆参赞，是他委任英国律师在该先例中应讯)**or that jurisdiction can be created by an estoppel. The state has protection against unauthorised action taken by a solicitor or member of the mission.**"(加黑部分是笔者的强调)

(1914) 1 Ch 139 先例 Astbury 大法官所说:"Even if it were conceivable that a diplomatic agent can waive his privilege, which is really the privilege of his sovereign, he can only do so **intentionally**, **with full knowledge of his rights**, and **with the sanction of his sovereign or legation**."(加黑部分是笔者的强调)

首先是 Baccus S. R. L. v. Servicio Nacional del Trigo (1957) 1 QB 438 先例。案情涉及原告意大利公司以 CIF 向被告西班牙公司购买 26000 吨的裸麦(rye)。估计因为西班牙公司没有付运,导致意大利公司作为买方向西班牙公司提出损失索赔。由于双方在买卖合约中约定的是英国法院有管辖权,所以意大利公司作为原告在英国起诉。而作为被告的西班牙公司就委任了一家英国律师所应讯(acknowledge)。大约 1 年后(期间西班牙公司有申请费用担保等实质性的抗辩行为),西班牙公司提出了它有主权豁免权,原告的告票自始无效(void ab initio),法院应驳回原告的申请。被告 Servicio Nacional del Trigo 是西班牙农业部下成立的公司,因此双方的第一个争议就是被告是否属于"国家"。在上诉庭,以多数意见(Singleton 大法官不同意)判被告属于"国家",有主权豁免权:"... that the defendants were a department of the State of Spain notwithstanding that they were a corporate body and a separate legal entity, and they were, therefore, entitled to claim sovereign immunity."这很明显是商业案件,在 1978 年立法后是很明确不存在任何主权豁免权的问题。但该先例发生在 1956 年,当时英国普通法的地位还是"绝对豁免权"(absolute immunity)。这直到枢密院的 The "Philippine Admiral" (1976) 1 Lloyd's Rep. 234 先例〔7〕与 1978 年的《State Immunity Act》立法后才有所改变。

至于弃权这方面委任英国律师应诉的是被告的西班牙公司的负责人 Ceviro 先生。他向法院声称,他根本不知道主权豁免权这回事(自己承认不懂),即不知道自己的权利,也没有向他的领导即农业部部长请示,这最后被上诉庭接受西班牙公司没有在明知自己权利的情况下弃权与可以享有主权豁免权。Jenkins 大法官说:"Applying those authorities to the present case it seems to me that the evidence here, and in particular the evidence of the ambassador, makes it reasonably plain that Mr. Cavero knew nothing about sovereign immunity, or, at all events, had no idea that by entering an appearance the defendants would be giving up any advantage or, in particular, any right to claim immunity which they might otherwise have. Furthermore, Mr. Cavero's superiors knew nothing about the matter at all until after the acts relied on as submissions

---

〔7〕 案情涉及菲律宾政府以日本对菲律宾的战争赔款建造了 Philippine Admiral 轮,并在之后将船舶卖给了一家私人公司。合约规定直到买方将船价付清前,菲律宾政府都保留船舶的所有权。之后,船舶由买方在国际航运市场营运了 12 年,当时因为买方仍没有付清船价,所以菲律宾政府可以立即重新占有该船舶。而因为买方付不起船舶维修的费用与无法履行租约,修船厂与承租人在香港扣船。菲律宾政府提出了主权豁免权的争议并一直诉到了枢密院。枢密院判是船舶一直作为一艘商船进行商业营运,所以不存在主权豁免权。

to the jurisdiction had taken place. It seems to me, therefore, that what was done here was done by Mr. Cavero without the knowledge of any of his superiors, in ignorance of his rights and without actual authority inasmuch as I think the evidence shows that the authority of the Minister of Agriculture would in fact have been necessary to enable Mr. Cavero to submit to the jurisdiction."

Parker 大法官说:"So far as this case is concerned, it is true that we have not had the benefit of an affidavit from Senor Cavero, but for my part I cannot impute to him knowledge of the effect of entering an unconditional appearance. Quite apart from that, it seems to me that the evidence is clear that although he is the person, the intermediary, to pass on instructions to English solicitors to deal with a case in England, he is bound to consult the appropriate minister as to whether sovereign immunity should be waived or not. It is true this does open up the rather alarming prospect that a foreign sovereign may allow proceedings to continue for years in this country before taking the point; but for my part I think that that is a theoretical difficulty. I do not think any person, even though he be a foreign sovereign, would be likely to be believed if in such an extreme case he were to come forward and assert that he had had no knowledge whatever of the proceedings. So far, however, as this case is concerned, I am satisfied that the point has been properly taken and that there has been no waiver."

这种先例还有很多,但笔者不多介绍,只介绍近期的 Aziz v. Yemen (2005) EWCA Civ 745 先例。[8] 该先例涉及也门驻英国大使馆的雇员 Aziz 先生被大使馆解雇。

---

[8] 1978 年《State Immunity Act》之 section 4 规定主权国家在与个人雇佣合约下没有主权豁免权,说:"A State is not immune as respects proceedings relating to a contract of employment between the States and an individual where the contract was made in the United Kingdom or the work is to be wholly or partly performed there."但该立法之 section 16 针对了一些不适用的情况,说:"(1) This Part of this Act shall not affect any immunity or privilege conferred by the 〈Diplomatic Privileges Act 1964〉 or the 〈Consular Relations Act 1968〉; and (a) section 4 above does not apply to proceedings concerning the employment of the members of a mission within the meaning of the Convention(这是指 1961 年《Vienna Convention on Diplomatic Relations》,而英国的《Diplomatic Privileges Act 1964》是对该公约的立法) scheduled to the said Act of 1964 or of the members of a consular post within the meaning of the Convention(这是指 1963 年《Vienna Convention on Consular Relations》) scheduled to the said Act of 1968...."在 1964 年《Diplomatic Privileges Act》Schedule 1 之 Article 1 针对使馆成员的定义说:"'the members of the mission' are the head of the mission and the members of the staff of the mission; 'members of the staff of the mission' are the members of the diplomatic staff, of the administrative and technical staff and of the service staff of mission.... the 'members of the administrative and technical staff' are the members of the staff of the mission employed in the administrative and technical service of the mission.."在 Arab Republic v. Gamal-Eldin and Another (1996) ICR 13 先例中,上诉庭判是司机(这是该先例中 Gamal-Eldin 先生与 Mohamed El-Aliary 先生的职位)属于使馆的管理与技术人员,所以主权国家享有豁免权,无论相关人员的职位多么低微(in however humble a role)。

于是,Aziz 先生在伦敦劳工审判庭开始诉讼,声称也门大使馆非法解雇(unfair dismissal),也门大使馆的参赞 Alkhader 先生委任了英国律师应诉。之后,也门大使馆提出了主权豁免权的争议。也门大使馆参赞的证词显示他误以为在劳工审判庭开始的并非诉讼程序,而只是调解程序(自己承认搞错),也门大使馆的大使 Alsaeede 博士也做出证词,表示他从来没有授权参与诉讼,也不认识被委任的 Salfiti 律师。而涉及也门大使馆代也门国家放弃主权豁免权,要先向也门外交部取得批准。上诉庭考虑了参赞与大使的证词,将案件发回劳工审判庭重审认定参赞是否有大使的实质授权委任律师。

从该先例可以看出,虽然现在英国的立法规定了主权国家在进行商业活动时不存在主权豁免权,但各个驻外大使馆的活动,特别是在当地法院在应诉时还是存在危险。

1.3.2 对主权豁免权的弃权之二:主权国家签订书面仲裁协议

针对书面仲裁协议,这是广为接受的对主权豁免权的弃权,也是 1989 年立法之 section 9 的规定。道理是很简单,首先仲裁是双方同意的解决争议机制(consensual process),并且因为仲裁庭不是主权国家下的法院,所以不存在一个主权国家审理另一个主权国家的问题,不会因此影响主权国家之间的友好(international comity)与平等。一般商业合约才会有仲裁协议,而已经提到在立法规定下,主权国家参与商业活动没有主权豁免权,因此这种弃权不会给主权国家带来更大困难。但凡事总有例外,笔者在这里介绍其中的两个先例。

第一个是 Tsavliris Salvage (International) Ltd. v. Grain Board of Iraq (2008) 2 Lloyd's Rep. 90 先例。涉及以 Altair 轮从德国的 Rostock 港运 5 万吨小麦去伊拉克的 Umm Qasr 港。这票小麦如果涉及市场上的买卖,就会是商业行为,但也会有情况小麦或其他粮食是国际上的援助,这就不属于商业行为。但在本先例中,争议并不在买卖合约,而是在付运时发生的海上救助,这就不属于商业行为。Altair 轮在接近卸港的航次中搁浅,这导致船东与著名的提供救助服务的 Tsavliris Salvage 公司(原告)订立了 Lloyd's Open Form 格式(LOF)的救助合约。该 LOF 的救助合约规定救助不成功就不用付钱(no cure no pay),而如果成功救助就根据 Lloyd's Standard Salvage and Arbitration Clauses 的仲裁条文去伦敦劳合社仲裁。仲裁员一般是对海事有经验的大律师作为独任仲裁员(sole arbitrator),他们会决定船东与货方各自应该支付的救助奖金的金额。这方面的法律很清楚,船长如果与救助公司签订 LOF,他除了有船东的授权,在紧急代理人(agent of necessity)[9]的说法下也代表货方,订立的合约也约束货方。在 1989 年《国际救助公约》(International Convention on Salvage)之 Article 6.2 也明确了这一点,说:"2. 船长有权代表船舶所有人签订救助合同。船长或船舶所有人有权代表船上财产所有人签订此种合同。"

---

〔9〕 关于紧急代理人,可见笔者《提单与其他付运单证》(2016 年)第三章之 2.8 段。

Altair 轮上的这批小麦属于伊拉克贸易部下的粮食局，而由于救助成功的小麦是直接运到了伊拉克卸港，所以救助人无法行使海事留置权（maritime lien）强制取得救助担保。这也导致在后来的仲裁中，货方没有参与。仲裁庭考虑到货方是伊拉克的政府部门，所以对管辖权十分小心。仲裁庭最后决定他有管辖权，而粮食局因为签了文书的仲裁协议，不能享有主权豁免权。在仲裁庭做出裁决书后，救助公司在法院要求执行并申请冻结令（freezing injunction）。伊拉克粮食局才根据 1996 年《仲裁法》之 section 67 向法院上诉，提出它享有主权豁免权并以此抗拒冻结令。但这不成功，Gross 大法官的判决被总结如下："There was no real doubt that signature of a LOF, on behalf of a party bound by that signature, would amount to a submission to arbitration, serving to exclude state immunity. By virtue of the operation of art. 6. 2 of the 1989 Convention（国际救助公约）, the managers, as agents of the owners, concluded the on behalf of GBI（被告）as owners of the cargo. There could be no sensible dispute that the LOF was agreed in writing. It followed that GBI agreed in writing to arbitration in accordance with cl. I of the LOF and to the other provisions contained in the LOF. The agreement to submit the matters contained in cl. I of the LOF to arbitration was an express agreement, albeit an agreement made through others acting on GBI's behalf. In the circumstances GBI had agreed in writing to submit a dispute to arbitration for the purposes of s. 9(1) of the State Immunity Act 1978 and was not immune in proceedings relating to the arbitration."

第二个 ETI Euro Telecom International NV v. Republic of Bolivia (2008) 2 Lloyd's Rep. 421 先例涉及投资仲裁。原告 ETI 是一家荷兰公司在名为 Entel 的玻利维亚电讯公司私有化期间持有 50% 的股份并管理控制该公司。ETI 声称玻利维亚政府之后采取了行动重新国有化 Entel，这显然会影响 ETI 在该公司的投资的价值。并且玻利维亚政府试图没收（expropriate）ETI 在该公司的权益，但不做出合理的赔偿。ETI 根据荷兰与玻利维亚双边投资协议（bilateral investment treaty，或简称"BIT"）开始了 ICSID 仲裁，索赔因玻利维亚政府的行为造成的损失。ICSID 仲裁程序开始后，玻利维亚政府没有参与，并在之后宣布了将 ETI 在 Entel 的权益国有化的法令。ETI 声称，很明显玻利维亚政府不会做出任何赔偿。

在 ETI 的单方面申请下（ex parte），纽约法院为了协助 ICSID 仲裁做出了对 Entel 在纽约的银行存款的扣押令（attachment order）。之后 ETI 又在英国法院获得了针对 Entel 在伦敦的 5000 万英镑的存款的冻结令。但该冻结令之后在 Entel 与玻利维亚政府的申请下被撤销，ETI 提起上诉。

该先例的判决涉及在 1982 年《Civil Jurisdiction and Judgments Act》、1997 年《Civil Jurisdiction and Judgments Act 1982 (Interim Relief) Order》、1996 年《仲裁法》下，英国法院在仲裁程序中做出冻结令的权利，这里不具体讨论，只介绍上诉庭针对玻利维亚政府能否依赖主权豁免权做出的判决。

虽然本章之1.3段节录的1978年《State Immunity Act》之section 9规定了如果主权国家同意了仲裁条文或在发生争议后同意接受仲裁解决,就不能在与仲裁有关的法院程序中被豁免。但section 13规定法院不可以做出禁令或履约指令,除非有主权国家的书面同意:"(1) No penalty by way of committal or fine shall be imposed in respect of any failure or refusal by or on behalf of a State to disclose or produce any document or other information for the purposes of proceedings to which it is a party. (2) Subject to subsections (3) and (4) below— (a) relief shall not be given against a State by way of injunction or order for specific performance or for the recovery of land or other property; and (b) the property of a State shall not be subject to any process for the enforcement of a judgment or arbitration award or, in an action in rem, for its arrest, detention or sale. (3) Subsection (2) above does not prevent the giving of any relief or the issue of any process with the written consent of the State concerned; and any such consent (which may be contained in a prior agreement) may be expressed so as to apply to a limited extent or generally; but a provision merely submitting to the jurisdiction of the courts is not to be regarded as a consent for the purposes of this subsection."

因此,法院做出冻结令应属于section 13而不是section 9针对的内容。在Svenska Petroleum Exploration AB v. Government of the Republic of Lithuania (2007) 1 Lloyd's Rep. 293先例中,法院判是执行裁决书(enforcement)属于section 9针对的内容,但实际执行(execution)以拿到裁决书中的金额属于section 13针对的内容,说:"The judge held that there was no basis for construing section 9 of the State Immunity Act (particularly when viewed in the context of the provisions of section 13 dealing with execution) as excluding proceedings relating to the enforcement of a foreign arbitral award. We think that is right. Arbitration is a consensual procedure and the principle underlying section 9 is that, if a state has agreed to submit to arbitration, it has rendered itself amenable to such process as may be necessary to render the arbitration effective... proceedings in support of the arbitral process itself as well as proceedings challenging the award fall within section 9(1), but submitted that proceedings to enforce the award do not. We are unable to accept that distinction. The Act itself draws a distinction between proceedings which relate to the arbitration (section 9) and process in respect of property for the enforcement of an award (section 13). In our view an application under section 101(2) of the Arbitration Act 1996 for leave to enforce an award as a judgment is, as subsection (1) recognises, one aspect of its recognition and as such is the final stage in rendering the arbitral procedure effective. Enforcement by execution on property belonging to the state is another matter, as section 13 makes clear."

玻利维亚政府没有书面同意法院可以做出冻结令等命令,因此上诉庭判是玻利维亚政府可以享有主权豁免权。而这笔存款虽然在Entel名下,但因为Entel不是仲裁的当事人,ETI 对 Entel 也不存在独立的诉因,所以法院因为玻利维亚政府享有主权豁免权而无法做出冻结令,也不能对 Entel 做出禁令。

最后介绍的先例也是笔者(杨大明)律师所处理的案件,FG Hemisphere Associates LLC v. Democratic Republic of the Congo (2011) 14 HKCFAR 95;(2011) 14 HKCFAR 395,简称"刚果"案。案情比较简单。Yugoslavian Company 获得了两个对刚果政府的胜诉判决,加起来金额约 3000 万美元。之后 Yugoslavian Company 将裁决书下应支付的所有利益(包括本金与利息)全部转让(assign)给了一间美国公司 FG。[10] FG 在了解到中国铁路中公司有一笔款项预备汇到刚果时,在香港把这笔款项扣下,希望用作清算在仲裁裁决下欠 FG 的债务。刚果政府在香港提出主权豁免权的抗辩。

FG 当中有一个陈述的理由是刚果政府签了仲裁条文,所以放弃了主张主权豁免权。香港终审法院同意刚果政府放弃了对仲裁庭主张主权豁免权,并且无法挑战仲裁庭有权做出裁决。但是刚果政府没有放弃在香港法院挑战任何关于承认仲裁裁决的法律程序(recognition of arbitration award)和在香港法院挑战任何关于向刚果政府的资产执行的法律程序(execution against assets)。[11] 法院判决可节录如下:

"An application for the grant of leave to enforce the award, often referred to as the "recognition" phase of enforcement, therefore involves discretionary adjudicative proceedings in which the impleaded State may claim state immunity.

It is furthermore clear, as stated above, that even where the recognition proceedings are successful, when the applicant subsequently seeks to execute the award (now treated like a judgment of the court), the impleaded State has a further right to object to execution against the targeted property on the ground of state immunity."

联合国下的组织在订立合约时,虽然也会有一条仲裁条文,但会以明示条文表示订立仲裁协议不代表对豁免权弃权。如笔者(杨良宜)在近期就遇到联合国世界粮食计划署(United Nations World Food Programme)的一份租约标准格式中的仲裁条文的最后说:"Nothing in or relating to this Charter Party shall be deemed a waiver, express or implied, of any of the privileges and immunities of the United Nations World Food Programme under international or national law, including, but not limited to, immunity from any form of legal process and from measures of execution."

〔10〕 这涉及第三方资助(third party funding)。近年来第三方资助仲裁是很热门的话题,第三方资助安排通常是指第三方出资者将会支付受资助的当事人(一般是原告)在诉讼或仲裁程序中的法律费用,以获取该判决或仲裁裁决金额的某个百分比或在法律程序所讨回得益中的其他经济利益作为回报。如果受资助的法律程序不成功,出资者将不会获得任何还款/退款。这些第三方出资者常常是财雄势大的风投基金、上市公司,通过资助一些虽然可以获得巨额赔偿但无力支付诉讼费用的原告而赚钱。而这些诉讼的被告常常是一些发展中国家的政府与/或国企。

〔11〕 关于对裁决书实质执行的弃权,可见本章之 1.3.3 段。

1.3.3 对主权豁免权的弃权之三：主权国家书面放弃主权豁免权

在《Dicey, Morris & Collins on The Conflict of Laws》(第15版,2012年)一书10.014至10.015段:"A foreign State is also immune from the processes of execution.〔12〕 The 1978 Act provides that relief shall not be given against a State by way of injunction or order for specific performance or for the recovery of land or other property, and that the property of a State shall not be subject to any process for the enforcement of a judgment or arbitration award or, in an action in rem, for its arrest, detention or sale〔13〕... The immunity from injunctive relief and execution is distinct from immunity from suit and applies even if one of the jurisdictional exceptions applies.〔14〕 Thus even though a State is not immune as respects proceedings relating to a commercial transaction, the State cannot be enjoined from breach of the contract.〔15〕 But the immunity from injunctive relief and execution is subject to two important exceptions. First, such relief may be given or process may be issued with the written consent (which may be contained in a prior agreement) of the State.〔16〕... Secondly, the immunity from process does not prevent the issue of any process in respect of property which is for the time being in use or intended for use for commercial purposes〔17〕..."

1978年《State Immunity Act》之Section 13规定:"(2) Subject to subsections (3) and (4) below— (a) relief shall not be given against a State by way of injunction or order for specific performance or for the recovery of land or other property; and (b) the property of a State shall not be subject to any process for the enforcement of a judgment or arbitration award or, in an action in rem, for its arrest, detention or sale."

1965年《华盛顿公约》之Article 55规定:"Nothing in Article 54 shall be construed as derogating from the law in force in any Contracting State relating to immunity of that State or of any foreign State from execution."

因此,在与主权国家订立合约时为了确保将来胜诉后可以执行有关的判决书或裁决书,必须有条文明确写明对方放弃主权豁免权。Sabah Shipyard (Pakistan) Ltd.

---

〔12〕 主权国家对实质执行程序有主权豁免权。有关实质执行的各种做法,如提供资料命令、清盘、第三债务人命令、押记命令、对资产的执行、接管等,可见笔者的《仲裁法——从开庭审理到裁决书的作出与执行》一书第十四章。

〔13〕 1978年立法规定不应对国家做出禁令、履约指令、收回土地或其他财产的命令,在实质执行法院判决/仲裁裁决书或对物诉讼时,主权国家的财产不能被扣押、扣留或出售。

〔14〕 对禁令的主权豁免权与对诉讼的主权豁免权不同,即使属于法院或仲裁庭有管辖权解决争议的例外情况,主权国家仍有对禁令的主权豁免权。

〔15〕 ETI Euro Telecom International NV v. Republic of Bolivia (2008) 2 Lloyd's Rep. 421先例。

〔16〕 但这有两种例外情况,一是有主权国家的书面同意。

〔17〕 如果财产是作为商业用途使用或准备作为商业用途使用,主权豁免权不适用,如主权国家拥有的一条商船在市场营运中还是可以被扣押或被做出禁令。

v. Pakistan (2003) 2 Lloyd's Rep. 571 先例虽然发生的时间较早,争议双方也与中国无关,但是属于"走出去"的中国企业会面临的典型问题。在该先例中,Sabah Shipyard是马来西亚母公司在巴基斯坦成立的有限公司,唯一的目的就是为了同巴基斯坦政府与国企 KESC 订立合约,设计、建设、营运与维护在卡拉奇的水上浮动发电站。Sabah Shipyard 与 KESC 订立了名为"Power Purchase Agreement"(PPA)的合约,与巴基斯坦政府订立了名为"Implementation Agreement"(IA)的合约。巴基斯坦政府在IA 的规定下,向 Sabah Shipyard 提供了担保合约,其中有一条明示放弃主权豁免权的条文:

"**2.6 Sovereign Immunity**

2.6 The Guarantor(巴基斯坦政府)hereby irrevocably and unconditionally agrees that the **execution**, **delivery**, **and performance by it** of this Guarantee constitute private and commercial acts.

The Guarantor hereby irrevocably and unconditionally agrees that: (i) should any proceedings be brought against the Guarantor or its assets, other than its military aircraft, naval vessels and other defense related assets or assets protected by the diplomatic and consular privileges under the 1978 Immunity Act of the United Kingdom or the 1976 Sovereign Immunities Act of the United States or any analogous legislation (the "Protected Assets") in any jurisdiction in connection with this Guarantee or any of the transactions contemplated by this Guarantee, no claim of immunity from such proceedings will be claimed by or on behalf of the Guarantor on behalf of itself or any of its assets (other than the Protected Assets); (ii) it waives any right of immunity which it or any of its assets (other than the Protected Assets) now has or may in the future have in any jurisdiction in connection with any such proceedings; and (iii) consents generally in respect of the enforcement of any judgment against it in any such proceedings in any jurisdiction to the giving of any relief or the issue of any process in connection with such proceedings [including without limitation, the making, enforcement or execution against or in respect of any of its assets whatsoever (other than the Protected Assets) regardless of its use or intended use]."

之后工程发生延误,双方产生争议。KESC 以 Sabah Shipyard 违约为由在 Sabah Shipyard 提供的信用证(还款担保)下提现。而 Sabah Shipyard 声称延误是由不可抗力造成,履行的时间根据合约规定可以相应延长,KESC 终止合约是违约/毁约(repudiatory breach)。[18] Sabah Shipyard 在新加坡开始仲裁并胜诉,要求 KESC 在 PPA 下与巴基斯坦政府在担保合约下做出支付。巴基斯坦政府在巴基斯坦法院申请禁令,禁止 Sabah Shipyard 在担保合约下要求支付。而 Sabah Shipyard 在英国申请止诉禁

---

〔18〕 这方面可参阅本书第一章的内容。

令(anti - suit injunction),禁止巴基斯坦政府推进在巴基斯坦法院的程序。该先例的一审法院与上诉庭都判是上述节录的明示条文有效,做出对主权豁免权的弃权,其中包括同意法院做出针对主权国家的禁令。

另在 Soleh Boneh International v. Uganda and National Housing Corp (1993) 2 Lloyd's Rep. 208 先例中,以色列承建商(原告)在与同乌干达政府(第一被告)关系密切的 National Housing Corp(第二被告)订立合约,乌干达政府的财政部长向原告做出了第二被告的履约担保。之后,乌干达政府在 1972 年 3 月颁布了法令,令以色列商人在乌干达的经济活动都无法继续进行。原告根据合约中的仲裁条文开始 ICC 仲裁,声称被告违约并索赔损失。根据仲裁条文,仲裁员应由 Federation of Civil Engineering Contractors 的主席委任,但是 Federation of Civil Engineering Contractors 的主席拒绝做出委任,因此 ICC 委任了一位瑞典工程师作为仲裁员。被告虽然声称委任仲裁员的程序无效,但参与了在瑞典进行的仲裁。最后仲裁判原告胜诉,被告要赔偿原告 950 万美元。被告在瑞典法院要求撤销裁决书,双方一直诉到瑞典的最高法院。

在瑞典最高法院做出判决前,原告向英国法院申请执行裁决书,并提出如果英国法院因为瑞典最高院的诉讼要推迟执行(enforcement),应要求被告提出担保(security)。[19] 一审法院推迟了执行,并要求被告做出约 2935 万美元的担保,这等于裁决金额加利息(因为在瑞典的诉讼程序拖了很久,所以利息金额很高)。被告将一审法院的命令上诉到上诉庭,并提出主权管辖权的争议。被告声称根据 1978 年《State Immunity Act》之 Section 13,法院不能向主权国家做出禁令,而一审法院的命令本质是一个禁令。上诉庭认为只是简单要求一方支付一笔钱而没有规定钱的来源与一个金钱的判决(monetary judgment)没有区别,不属于禁令。但一审法院要求被告做出相当于裁决金额加利息的担保太高,最后将法院命令改为:"an order would be made that unless D provided the $5m. within four weeks there would be leave to enforce the award as a judgment, with liberty to reapply in nine months."

2. 时　　效

2.1　开始诉讼的时效

不论在法院诉讼或是仲裁,错过时效对原告是灾难性的。因为对被告而言,这是非常重要、省钱省力、不影响实质性争议与接近完美的抗辩。被告可以在抗辩索赔时,提出要求先对时效做出初步审理(preliminary issue)。如果原告败诉,这个索赔(无论欠钱或损失的事实如何清楚明确与处于有利的法律地位)也就不存在了,根本

---

〔19〕 这种做法可见本书第九章之 2.6 段。

不必花费大量的时间与金钱持续审理其他方面的实质性争议。而如果原告胜诉,即判没有错过时效,被告唯一的损失就是律师费,不会影响下一步的实质性争议。

笔者的《损失赔偿与救济》一书第十七章针对开始诉讼的时效有详论,内容包括不同类别(法律规定与合约规定等)的时效何时开始计算、如何保护时效、法律可以中断时效计算的例外情况、可以重新启动时效的情况等。另在杨良宜的《合约的解释:规则与应用》一书第十二章第3段也对合约中的时效条文进行了详尽的介绍。

如果被告没有及时提出错过时效的抗辩并要求做出初步审理,也可以之后通过修改文书请求(amendment to pleading or defence)提出(错过时效的抗辩必须在文书请求中提出),除非时间上已经太迟,会对原告造成金钱不足以赔偿的损失:见 Ketteman v. Hansel Properties Ltd. (1987) AC 189 先例。在该先例中,Brandon 勋爵提到有关诉讼中允许修改请求的四个要件,如下:"With regard to the principles on which his discretion to allow or refuse the applications to amend should be exercised, the judge referred to the notes to R. S. C., Ord. 20, r. 5, in The Supreme Court Practice 1982 and to the authorities there cited. The effect of these authorities can, I think, be summarised in the following four propositions. **First**, all such amendments should be made as are necessary to enable the real questions in controversy between the parties to be decided. **Secondly**, amendments should not be refused solely because they have been made necessary by the honest fault or mistake of the party applying for leave to make them: it is not the function of the court to punish parties for mistakes which they have made in the conduct of their cases by deciding otherwise than in accordance with their rights. **Thirdly**, however blameworthy (short of bad faith) may have been a party's failure to plead the subject matter of a proposed amendment earlier, and however late the application for leave to make such amendment may have been, the application should, in general, be allowed, provided that allowing it will not prejudice the other party. **Fourthly**, there is no injustice to the other party if he can be compensated by appropriate orders as to costs."(加黑部分是笔者的强调)

修改文书请求会稍后在本章第10段有进一步介绍。

2.2 承认责任

已经承认责任可能会对错过时效的抗辩构成禁反言。在 Wright v. John Bagnall & Sons Ltd. (1900) 2 QB 240 CA 先例中,雇主一直承诺会对雇员进行赔偿,只是金额谈不拢。法院判是雇主不能以必须在6个月内开始诉讼程序的时效作为抗辩。Collins 大法官说:"... there was ample evidence of an agreement that compensation was to be paid, the only question left open being that of amount. If that is the case the respondents are debarred from raising the point that the statutory limitation applied. In my opinion they have debarred themselves from raising this point by treating the matter as open to negotiations during the whole time in which they were paying the appellant, and have allowed the six months to expire while the negotiations were still proceeding, they cannot then turn round and say that the time for claiming compensation has gone by."

在该先例中,Collins 大法官虽然只用了"被禁止"(debarred)一词,而没有提到"禁反言"(estoppel),但原则上一样。之后的 Lubovsky v. Snelling (1944) KB 45 CA 先例也跟从了这一判法。在 Lubovsky v. Snelling 先例中,被告在承认责任的基础上(on the basis of an admission of liability)与原告谈判。法院判被告不能以《Fatal Accidents Act》规定的 1 年时效作为抗辩。

加拿大的 Travellers Indemnity Co. of Canada v. Maracle (1991) 2 SCR 50 先例也是同样的判法,Sopinka 大法官说:"There must be words or conduct from which it can be inferred that the admission was to apply whether the case settled or not, and that the only issue between the parties, should litigation ensue, is the issue of quantum."

但在爱尔兰的 Ryan v. Connolly (2001) 1 IR 627 SC 先例中,法院判是如果被告承认责任后谈判就暂停了,原告仍然需要证明被告有明确无误的陈述使他可以合理依赖与推断无须开始诉讼程序(即构成了陈述性禁反言)。Keane 大法官说:"I can find nothing in the correspondence to indicate that they were... treating the case as one in which they would regard the institution of proceedings as superfluous and would not raise the Statute of Limitations as a defence..."

这判决很有道理,毕竟承认责任后,下一步仍要计算损失,即使承认责任,也不代表对赔偿的金额没有争议。因此,原告如果因为被告承认了责任就不再理会时效,仍然十分危险。被告除了承认责任外,还必须做出一些言行,如向原告保证或承诺不需要开始诉讼程序或指定仲裁员,令原告合理依赖被告的保证或承诺而没有开始诉讼程序以保护时效。

2.3 持续性的和解谈判

如果被告没有承认责任与同意赔偿金额也没有做出不会以时效作为抗辩的陈述或承诺,持续性的和解谈判通常不能构成禁反言。在澳大利亚的 The "Zhi Jiang Kou" (1991) 1 Lloyd's Rep. 493 先例中,Gleeson 大法官说:"I find myself unable to accept that the communications from the solicitors for the appellants contained any promise or representation,[20] express or tacit, or manifested any common assumption,[21] of the kind upon which the respondent now finds it necessary to rely[22]. Indeed I am still not entirely clear as to the exact nature and content of the representation or assumption

---

〔20〕 Gleeson 大法官不认为持续性的和解谈判属于被告的陈述(构成陈述性禁反言)或承诺(构成承诺性禁反言)。

〔21〕 Gleeson 大法官也不认为持续性的和解谈判会令双方产生共同的假设并构成共识性禁反言。即使存在被告不会以时效已过作为抗辩的假设,也只是原告单方面的希望。

〔22〕 因此,原告不能依赖任何禁反言的说法。

said to have been relied upon. It was expressed in argument in this Court as being **a representation that it would not be necessary for the respondent to commence proceedings until settlement had been fully explored**. **A representation of that kind is hardly unequivocal.** What exactly it means as to the nature of the modification of the time bar which is being effected or offered is **far from clear**.〔23〕 In any event, for the solicitors for the appellants to inform the solicitors for the respondent that the former hoped that the latter would not find it necessary **to commence proceedings until settlement negotiations had been fully explored neither states or suggests, nor justifies the conclusion, that nothing further need be said or done about the limitation period**, and that mere inactivity will suffice to produce the result that the contractual provisions will be treated as modified in some unspecified fashion."(加黑部分是笔者的强调)

在 McGee 教授的《Limitation Periods》(第 6 版,2010 年)一书之 21.020 说:"In recent years a series of cases before the Lands Tribunal have raised the question of estoppel in circumstance here the parties have for some time negotiated on the assumption (more or less shared) that no limitation period applied to the claim in question. Whether this assumption was shown to be unfounded, it became necessary to decide whether defendants were as a result of the negotiation estopped from relying on limitation. Inevitably, this was a question of fact in every case, but it may be noted that very few pleas of estoppel have succeeded.〔24〕... The possibility of relying on estoppel (or waiver) was also recognized in Bytheway v. British Steel Corporation Plc. , June 26, 1997, CA, unreported.〔25〕... **As a matter of principle it is submitted that estoppel ought to be recognised as a possible response to a limitation defence, though of course it would be necessary in each case to show why the defendant's conduct (and presumably the plaintiff's response to it) made it inequitable for the defendant to be allowed to plead limitation.** On the other side of the line is Hillingdon London BC v. Arc Ltd. (No. 2) (2000) R. V. R. 283〔26〕,... **It was held that these negotiations did not preclude the**

---

〔23〕 在该先例中,原告希望依赖陈述性禁反言的说法,有关的陈述或承诺是:"We trust, bearing in mind that the amount involved is relatively small, it will not be necessary for your client to commence proceedings until settlement has been fully explored."但 Gleeson 大法官认为这远远称不上清楚无误(clear and unequivocal)的陈述,令原告相信被告放弃了时效已过的抗辩,因此无须及时开始诉讼。

〔24〕 近年来土地审裁处(Land Tribunal)的不少先例都提出了禁反言的争议,原告声称是在诉讼请求不受时效影响的假设(或多或少是共同假设)下与对方进行谈判。被告是否被禁反言不能以时效已过作为抗辩,取决于原告的假设是否毫无根据,这取决于每个先例的不同事实。但要注意的是,禁反言的说法只在少数的先例中成功。

〔25〕 在本章之 2.3.2 段对该先例有详细介绍。

〔26〕 在本章之 2.3.3 段对该先例有详细介绍。

defendant from subsequently pleading limitation. It is a question of fact whether there has been an agreement, or conduct, sufficient to amount to estoppel or waiver... It is clear from the judgment that establishing estoppel in relation to the Limitation Act is likely to be a formidable task and one which can be accomplished only in the most exceptional cases.〔27〕 Such a case, however, is Williams v. Blaenau Gwent County BC (No. 2) (1999) 2 EGLR 195 (Lands Tribunal), where the Lands Tribunal was prepared to find that the parties had proceeded on the necessary shared assumption as to the validity of the claim and that on the facts it would be inequitable to deprive the claimant of the benefit of this assumption.〔28〕"(加黑部分是笔者的强调)

在接下来的段节,笔者将对一些有关先例进行介绍。

2.3.1　先例之一:Co-operative Wholesale Society v. Chester-le-Street DC

在 Co-operative Wholesale Society v. Chester le Street District Council (1998) 3 EGLR 11 先例中,政府在 1986 年对有关土地做出强制征购令(compulsory purchase order)。之后业主与政府一直进行谈判但不成功,业主在 1994 年 8 月 23 日在土地审裁处开始诉讼,并两次同意政府延期提交专家证据的申请。但在 1995 年 1 月 13 日,政府声称根据 1981 年《Compulsory Purchase (Vesting Declarations) Act》之 section 10(3),业主必须在 1992 年 10 月 10 日前开始诉讼,现在显然时效已过,要求法院驳回请求。土地审裁处一审([1997] 73 P & CR 111)判双方谈判中一直有共同假设双方应尽量谈判解决,如果实在不行再交由土地审裁处决定,无须理会时效:"In my judgment the evidence establishes that both parties in this transaction proceeded on the basis of a common assumption that they were negotiating settlement of a valid claim for compensation without regard to the statutory limitation period and on the basis that if agreement could not be achieved the matter would in the last resort be referred to the Tribunal for determination."

---

〔27〕 在 Holding and Management (Solitaire) Ltd. v. Ideal Homes North West Ltd. and Ors (2004) EWHC 2408 (TCC)先例中,H. H. Judge Coulson Q. C. 大法官同意了这个说法。

〔28〕 该先例涉及共识性禁反言,在《Limitation Periods》(第 6 版,2010 年)一书之 21.021 段提到的 The Executors of the Estate of the Right Honourable Herbert Robert Cayzer Baron Rotherwick v. Oxfordshire CC 先例也是涉及共识性禁反言,案情有关双方对诉讼时效有共同的错误理解,之后其中的一方(被告)如果想做出时效已过的抗辩而不会被共识性禁反言,就需要先向原告做出通知纠正这一错误理解。审判庭认为两个月时间让原告可以提起诉讼是合理时间。《Limitation Periods》(第 6 版,2010 年)一书之 21.021 段提到说:"Where an estoppel by convention can be established, it is apparently possible for the defendant to give notice that it will take the limitation point if proceedings are not commenced promptly. Thereafter the claimant must commence proceedings within a reasonable time. In The Executors of the Estate of the Right Honourable Herbert Robert Cayzer Baron Rotherwick v. Oxfordshire CC (March 21, 2000, Lands Tribunal, Unreported), it was held that a reasonable time was two months after the giving of the notice by the defendant."

之后上诉庭维持了一审判决,认为政府被共识性禁反言不能再以时效已过作为抗辩。有关谈判过程中有许多证据显示政府之后再提出这6年时效是不合情理。Russell大法官说:"There was, in my judgment,... ample material upon which he could hold that it would be unconscionable for the Authority to rely upon the six year period of limitation having regard to the way in which they conducted the negotiations, and indeed having regard to their reaction to the reference once it had been made and they sought an extension of time without referring to the fact that the reference was flawed from the outset."

2.3.2 先例之二:Bytheway v. British Steel Corporation Plc.

在Bytheway v. British Steel Corporation Plc. , June 26, 1997, CA, unreported先例中,原告声称在为被告工作期间长期受严重的噪音影响,导致听力出现问题。原告的律师与被告的保险人之间大概有8000个类似案件,双方同意做出统一的安排(scheme),包括被告的保险人对每个案件中受影响的雇员支付一定的赔偿。1990年,原告的律师考虑到双方一直没有针对时效的问题,写信给被告的保险人希望获得正式的确认。1990年11月16日,被告的保险人回信说:"... that in those noise induced hearing loss cases which are being processed under the terms of our 'working arrangement' we are prepared to allow a general extension of time outside the normal limitation periods for the service of a writ.... We are prepared to accept the date of the letter of claim as being the date of issue of a writ[29] in such cases for the purposes of interest... You have written to us in several cases and we do not propose to respond in each individual case. You may take this letter as formal confirmation of our position."

被告在1993年合法退出了这个安排,双方的争议是被告是否被禁止在参加了这个统一安排但还没有获得赔偿的雇员(包括原告)提起的诉讼中以时效已过作为抗辩。

一审法官认为被告的保险人1990年11月16日的回信属于对时效已过的抗辩的弃权,并且直到原本的安排终止后仍然约束被告。上诉庭的Judge大法官总结一审法官的判决说:"Having concluded that the defendants had 'waived' any limitation point in claims notified under the scheme, the judge concluded that the waiver continued to bind the insurers in litigation after its termination. In reaching this conclusion he took

---

〔29〕 保险合约下经常会出现这种被称为"告票条文"(writ clause)的约定。因为保险公司调查需要时间,如在财产险(如船壳险),被保险人(船东)在船舶发生事故后,向保险公司做出弃权通知(notice of abandonment),保险公司通常会拒绝通知,但签回一份有一条告票条文的文件,并随即调查该事故是否构成推定全损。另是双方谈判达成协议也需要时间,与其花费律师费向法院做出告票(所谓的保护性告票[protective writ]),或是委任仲裁员开始仲裁程序以保护时效,保险公司常常会选择同意将收到被保险人赔付请求的一天当做开始诉讼程序的一天,即当做已经保护了时效。这虽然是保险公司的做法,但其实在任何类别的合约下都可以适用。

into account that having pursued his claim under the scheme the plaintiff could not now be restored to the position in which he would have found himself if he had litigated in early 1991 rather than sought an out – of – court resolution of his claim under the scheme. ”

但 Judge 大法官不同意一审法官的判决，因为被告与任何一位雇员都可以随时退出这个统一安排。该统一安排中也没有一条针对时效问题的条文，如自动延长时效。这样，统一安排本质上与其他任何的谈判一样，只是原告或潜在原告人数多一些。被告的保险人后来退出安排是完全合法，谈不上有过错或误导原告。原告本可以要求被告同意延长时效，否则就退出统一安排并开始法律行动以保护时效。因此，被告完全可以在原告提起的诉讼中提出时效已过的抗辩。Judge 大法官说："... the common ground that the scheme could be terminated by either side at any time and without notice. Unfortunately express provision had not been made within the scheme for the consequences of its termination on claims which had been notified and were being processed but which had not been finally settled at the date of termination. It was however accepted that any individual claimant (such as the plaintiff) was personally entitled to withdraw from the arrangements at any time before his claim was settled and it was implicit that the rights in subsequent litigation of any plaintiff who did so would not be prejudiced... In my judgment any detriment suffered by the plaintiff as a result of his willing participation in the scheme and its subsequent termination by the insurers was not consequent on any breach by the insurers of its terms but rather their reliance on their rights under it. The termination of the scheme entitled the participants in it (whether plaintiffs or defendants) to litigate untrammelled by its terms. Any waiver of its rights by either side within and for the purposes of the scheme did not extend to litigation and accordingly the defendants' insurers were entitled to defend the litigation by the plaintiff by relying on the limitation points which would not and could not have been taken if the claim had been settled within the scheme. ”

2.3.3　先例之三：Hillingdon London BC v. ARC Ltd. (No. 2)

在 Hillingdon London BC v. ARC Ltd. (No. 2) (2000) 3 EGLR 97 先例中，政府在 1982 年 4 月对 ARC 的土地做出了强制购买令(compulsory purchase order)，之后直到 1995 年 9 月 5 日，双方一直在进行谈判。1995 年 9 月 6 日，ARC 在土地审裁处开始诉讼。根据 1980 年《Limitation Act》之 section 9，ARC 应在 1988 年 4 月 26 日前开始诉讼，双方争议之一是政府是否被禁反言不能以时效已过作为抗辩。

1989 年 2 月 13 日，ARC 写信给政府希望能对赔偿达成协议。3 月 10 日，政府回信说："I agree with you it should now be possible to resolve the compensation payable to your company due to the Yiewsley by – pass works. If you will submit your claim we will endeavour to reach agreement with you as Mr Douglas has now left for greener pastures."

1991年8月20日,ARC向政府提出了修改的赔偿金额,并建议之后应怎样继续推进。政府把ARC的信件交给了律师,询问这个索赔请求是否时效已过。律师没有给出明确回答,但认为这是个很好的抗辩。1992年1月8日,政府获得了这方面的法律意见。

之后政府并没有向ARC提出时效已过的争议,直到1994年3月18日,政府写了一封注明"无损害"(without prejudice)的信给ARC,说:"Thank you for your letter of 22 February. The Council(政府)is currently considering whether your client's claim is out of time..."

1994年10月19日,政府写信给ARC拒绝了有关的赔偿请求,其中第一个原因就是时效已过。

一审法官认为1989年2月13日与3月10日的信件显示出双方有共识是ARC仍有一个有效的诉讼,而政府在意识到存在时效已过的抗辩后仍继续谈判构成"共识性禁反言"(estoppel by convention)或"承诺性禁反言"(promissory estoppel)或"弃权"(waiver)。

但这判决被上诉庭推翻,Arden大法官首先确认被告可以对时效弃权与禁反言,但仅仅是在时效已过之后继续谈判不足以构成弃权或禁反言,说:"It is clearly established that a party may waive the right to rely on a limitation defence and that parties may enter into an agreement to waive the limitation defence... The courts will enforce any such waiver or agreement duly made. A party may also be estopped in an appropriate case from relying on a limitation defence. However **no authority has been cited to us**, apart from the decision of the judge in this case, **whereby a party has been held disentitled from relying on a limitation defence merely because he has continued to negotiate with another party about the claim after the limitation period had expired** and without anything being agreed about the manner in which the claim was to be resolved if negotiations broke down."(加黑部分是笔者的强调)

针对对1989年2月13日与3月10日的信件的解释,Arden大法官说:"The judge's(一审法官)conclusion was that the only sensible explanation for the letters dated 13 February 1989 and 10 March 1989 was that both parties believed that ARC had a valid claim for compensation. In our judgment the evidence does not support this conclusion. As the judge found, at all material times LBH(政府)took the view that ARC's claim was not supported by appropriate evidence and was not a valid claim This was LBH's position in June 1990 and it remained its position. This case is thus unlike the Co-operative Wholesale Society v. Chester-le-Street DC, above, in which it was clear that the local authority regarded the claim as one which entitled the claimant to some compensation."

而针对政府在意识到存在时效已过的抗辩后仍继续谈判,Arden大法官判是政府从来没有在双方的通信往来中向 ARC 提出这一点。因此，即使存在共同假设，也在这方面没有沟通过（cross the line），[30] 不构成共识性禁反言。Arden 大法官说："A shared assumption is not on the authorities sufficient to establish an estoppel unless it is communicated. It follows that if in this case there was no shared assumption to the effect that ARC had a valid claim that was not time – barred, there could be no communication by LBH that it was making any such assumption. It also follows from what we have said above that the communication required would in any event be not simply that ARC had a valid claim but also that LBH would not take any defence that might be open to it on the basis of a statutory limitation period."

而即使政府的言行构成了共识性禁反言，1994 年 3 月 18 日的信件提出时效已过后，双方不再有这方面的错误假设，回复到了原本的地位，但 ARC 没有在合理的时间内提起诉讼。Arden 大法官说："In our view the letter of 18 March 1994 was an effective warning that if indeed there was a good limitation point LBH considered itself free to take it. From that date it could no longer even be suggested that the parties were proceeding on some shared assumption, and ARC were no longer entitled to rely on there being a common assumption. If a common assumption existed up to this moment in time, ARC were entitled to a reasonable time to re – act to the disappearance of their assumption. In the circumstances of this claim that period might be measured in weeks rather than days, but not in months. Even if that were too harsh a view, once the position had been more firmly clarified in October 1994, a swift response for ARC was required. To take advantage of any estoppel ARC would have to have started proceedings within about 2 months of this date. That period would give sufficient time to establish if there was any room for agreement with LBH and obtain Counsel's opinion itself if it wished. On any basis the delay of a further period of eleven months was too long. We appreciate that the parties had already been dealing with this claim for many years and that it is not unusual for claims to be referred to the Lands Tribunal many years after the local authority has entered the property being acquired but that it probably a good reason for acting quickly rather than a reason for further dilatoriness. The point on delay is not capable of being met by asserting that any prejudice or at least the greater prejudice would be suffered by ARC and not LBH. There was no reason why proceedings could not be started immediately. For these reasons alone in our judgment the appeal must as respects convention estoppel be allowed."

而针对承诺性禁反言，Arden 大法官认为首先政府没有向 ARC 做出明确无误的

[30]　见本书第六章之 3.1.2 段。

陈述或承诺,[31] 也无法证明 ARC 因为依赖(即使有)而蒙受了任何损害(detriment),[32] 所以,让政府以时效已过作为抗辩不会造成任何不公平(unfair)或不合情理(unconscionable)的情况。[33]

2.4　时效已过之后继续谈判

有疑问是如果双方在时效已过之后继续谈判,被告可否被视为放弃了错过时效的抗辩或构成了禁反言?这看来还是取决于被告的特定言行(在每个先例都不同)能否被认为是清楚无误地承诺了将来诉讼时不会以错过时效作为抗辩。时效已过后,被告在谈判中的言行构成弃权或禁反言的可能性更低,这在上一小段介绍的 Hillingdon London BC v. ARC Ltd.(No. 2)(2000)3 EGLR 97 先例已经显示得很清楚。正如上诉庭的 Arden 大法官所说,仅仅是双方在时效已过之后继续谈判的事实是不足够。在 Seechurn v. ACE Insurance SA(2002)2 Lloyd's Rep. 390 上诉庭先例[34],Ward 大法官说:"The correspondence was typical of the attempts to negotiate a settlement of a claim with all the usual trust and counter trust of potential litigants striving to come to terms without losing too much face; **that was not enough to found estoppels**... If the **necessary promise had been established**, there would have been no difficulty in accepting that **it was intended to be acted on and relied on** with the result that Mr Seechurn(原告)**suffered the detriment** of losing his right to approach the judgment seat, it would then have been **inequitable and unconscionable for the defendant to plead the time bar**... As to the period as the claim became statute barred, the **nature of promise** did not change; there was **an expression of willingness to consider the claim** provided the requested medical examinations were undertaken and the same warning that the defendant would apply to stay the proceedings pending such examinations; no clear promise to surrender the defendant's legal right could be established; and to **assert that the door to compromising the claim was still open was not impliedly to promise that a limitation point would not be taken if negotiations failed**.... After the limitation period expired it was difficult to see how the claimant could have altered his position to his detriment..."(加黑部分是笔者的强调)

Steyn 勋爵在 Super Chem Products Ltd. v. American Life & General Insurance Co. Ltd.(2004)UKPC 2 的枢密院先例也提到,被告在时效已过后继续谈判的另一个重要原因是不知道原告是否已委任律师在有管辖权的法院做出了保护性告票(protective writ),只是没有送达给被告而已。一旦被告拒绝继续谈判,原告就会送达已备妥

[31] 见本书第四章第 6 段。

[32] 见本书第四章第 7 段。

[33] 见本书第四章第 8 段。

[34] 具体的案情可见本书第四章之 11.7 段。

的告票并推进诉讼。这显然是双方都想避免的情况,否则就根本不会有较早的谈判。Steyn 勋爵说:“... the mere fact that a party has continued to negotiate... about a claim after the limitation period has expired, **without anything being agreed about what happens if the negotiations break down, cannot give rise to a waiver or estoppels**... there is nothing to show that the insurers knew whether a protective writ had been issued or not. It is therefore impossible to say that their silence signified that they would not be relying on the time bar.”(加黑部分是笔者的强调)

2.5　同意延长时效的陷阱或危险

关于时效的著名先例有不少涉及租约与提单合约方面,这也可以理解,因为这些类别的合约经常会规定很短的时效。如著名的 Centrocon Arbitration Clause,原来的版本只有 3 个月的时效。而在海上货物运输合约中更普遍[35]的是 1924 年《海牙规则》规定的从卸货/交货开始起算的 1 年时效。这要比许多岸上不同类别的合约通常有立法规定的 6 年时效要短得多。而当事人对时效的了解也有不同,如岸上涉及土地的争议,可能一方(普通老百姓)或双方都对时效的严重性没有太大警觉。所以一旦错过时效,原告需要从双方的谈判中挑出一些能够支持弃权或禁反言的言行(无论是陈述性禁反言或是承诺性禁反言或是共识性禁反言),以对抗被告时效已过的抗辩。但航运业内人士普遍对时效有所了解,特别是提单合约下的货损货差,往往是由船东互保协会(P&I Club)处理案件,有关人员都会有律师背景,理解时效的重要性。而另一方当事人是货方(或代位求偿的保险人),他们或索赔代理往往也精通这方面的法律。在双方的和解谈判中(一般货损货差都以和解了事),货方在距离 1 年时效还有好几个月时,就会明示要求代表船东(潜在的被告)的船东互保协会确认延长时效。如果船东互保协会有所迟疑或推三阻四,货方即会委任(或已经委任)律师做出保护性告票(protective writ)。而接下来如果谈不拢,就把告票送达(无论是对人诉讼还是对物诉讼)。现在很多提单合约会合并一条仲裁条文,货方也是以同样的手法保护时效。毕竟航运业内人士都不会简单以为双方在谈判就是对时效的弃权或禁反言。这些说法即使可以成立,也会涉及昂贵的诉讼(禁反言的争议经常涉及对事实的认定),结果也不肯定。所以双方通过协议,即潜在的被告同意延长时效就省钱省事与安全得多。但在这复杂的国际商业社会,又会出现另一类的问题,即这协议是否有效延长了时效。这在本章稍后分段介绍的几个著名先例中有所显示。

2.5.1　先例之一:The “Astraea”

在 The “Astraea” (1971) 2 Lloyd’s Rep. 494 先例中,承租人与船东订立了程租合约行走一个从澳大利亚装港到印度 Bombay 卸港的航次。租约使用的是 Austwheat 标准格式,其中第 31 条文有关共同海损(general average)的理算与分摊,说:

---

〔35〕《海牙规则》在提单合约中强制适用,而租约也往往通过一条首要条文(clause paramount)合并《海牙规则》。

"General Average, if any, shall be settled in London according to the York-Antwerp Rules, 1950."

而第34条文是仲裁条文,其中有针对抵达卸港后12个月的时效,说:"Any dispute arising under this charter... shall... be settled by Arbitration... each party appointing an Arbitrator... Any claim must be made in writing and claimant's Arbitrator appointed within twelve months of the Vessel's arrival at final port of discharge, otherwise all claims shall be deemed to be waived."

1965年5月5日,船舶在距离Bombay卸港50海里的地方搁浅,船壳与机械在试图重新浮起的过程中受损。船舶在1965年5月16日抵达卸港。之后双方针对共同海损一直有通讯往来。1969年3月11日,船东要求承租人支付根据共同海损理算(general average adjustment)支付相应的金额。但承租人声称因为船东没有及时指定仲裁员并开始仲裁,现在租约约定的时效已过,船东应被视为放弃了索赔的权利。船东在1971年5月3日开始诉讼,要求法院宣告船东对共同海损分摊的索赔没有因为仲裁条文被禁止,因为:(1)这不属于第34条文中规定的在租约下产生的争议(dispute arising under this charter);(2)第31条文是针对共同海损的特定条文,所以解决共同海损的问题应由第31条文而不是解决其他租约争议的第34条文管辖;(3)被告的行为构成禁反言,不能依赖该仲裁条文。

但法院没有支持船东的申请,Roskill大法官判是:(1)共同海损的争议属于租约下产生的争议;(2)第31条文中的"settle"一词指"理算"(adjusted),而第34条文中的"settle"一词指"决定"(determined),与理算无关的共同海损争议的裁定(adjudicate)应受第34条文管辖;(3)因此在1966年5月16日,船东诉讼请求都超过时效而被视为弃权;(4)承租人没有任何行为(包括在时效已过后很长一段时间与船东仍有通讯往来)可被视为足以构成禁反言的陈述或承诺。结果是船东败诉。

2.5.2 先例之二:The "Ion"

在The "Ion" (1980) 2 Lloyd's Rep. 245先例中,案情也涉及货损货差。有关租约的仲裁条文没有规定时效,但因为租约合并了《海牙规则》,所以受1年时效的影响。租约中还合并了"Inter-Club Agreement"。[36] 船舶从日本前往4个中东不同港口卸货,最后在迪拜卸货的时间是1977年6月30日。船东与承租人对货损货差的责任保险加入了不同的船东互保协会,承租人的互保协会在1978年2月5日通知船东的互保协会有货物短缺的索赔,承租人赔给货方后,会来要求船东补偿与分摊。之后双方有持续的通信往来,1978年4月18日,船东的互保协会写信给承租人的互保协会,说:"We refer to our letters of the 22nd February and 16th March and would advise that our Members have no objection to the claims Nos. 1 to 23 being settled in accordance with the Inter-Club Agreement. We have not yet received their advices concerning claims

---

〔36〕 有关船东互保协会内部协议的课题,可见杨大明的《期租合同》一书第二十五篇之25.3段。

24 and 25, referred to in your letter of the 3rd April, but as soon as we hear from them in this regard we will ensure that you are advised accordingly."

承租人作为原告声称船东在信件中承认了责任与根据 Inter-Club Agreement 分摊货物短缺的损失。但 Mocatta 大法官认为当时距离时效还有两个多月,不能构成对时效已过抗辩的禁反言,说:"In my judgment, that allegation cannot be supported. April 18 was over two months before the expiry of the scheduled year. Accordingly, in my opinion, it was incapable of establishing the estoppel sought."

笔者认为,这里的原因是此时距离时效还有两个多月,并且这两个多月中双方也一直有通信往来,因此很难说承租人是依赖了船东的言行(4 月 18 日的信件)而错过了时效并因此蒙受了损害。

另一封稍后的重要信件是船东的互保协会在 1978 年 7 月 4 日写给承租人的互保协会,说:"We refer to your letter of the 16th June (which contained nine shortage claims, making a total of 37) and would advise you that our Members are prepared to abide by the terms and conditions of the Inter-Club Agreement in as far as they are involved for any cargo claims which may have to be settled in respect of the above."

Mocatta 大法官判是与上一封信不同,此时 1 年的时效已过(从交货时开始计算),而船东在信中承认了所有货物短缺的责任并愿意根据 Inter-Club Agreement 分摊损失。承租人声称这封信构成弃权与禁反言,但 Mocatta 大法官认为禁反言的说法不适用。Mocatta 大法官引用了 Sunmer 勋爵在 Atlantic Shipping & Trading Co. v. Louis Dreyfus (1922) 10 Lloyd's Rep. 707 先例的说法:"... Waiver applies to an election as to something in futuro; it is not a term by which to describe the answer to a right, which is complete in proesenti."

但 Mocatta 大法官认为这封信构成了承诺性禁反言,令船东不能再以时效已过作为抗辩,说:"I find it difficult to believe that this long correspondence should be treated by the Court as having no legal effect at all. It is particularly to be noted that this letter of July 4 is written after June 30, that is to say, after the one-year permitted period,... It is true that the letter makes no express mention of a time bar, but, written when it was and in the language used, covering 'any cargo claims which may have to be settled in respect of the above', I accept the view that **there was here a representation capable of amounting to an equitable or promissory estoppel**... It seems to me that this letter, written as it was after the expiry of the one-year period permitted by the Hague Rules, did contain an implied representation by the owners, or on their behalf, that they would not enforce their strict right against the charterers, in that they would not rely upon the time bar."(加黑部分是笔者的强调)

一般来说,时效已过之后的陈述或承诺通常不会被依赖并蒙受损害。笔者认为承租人依赖了该 7 月 4 日的信件,18 个月没有开始诉讼。如果不是因为依赖了该信件,承租人也可以根据1950年《仲裁法》之section 27,[37]以过度困难(undue hardship)为由要求高院延长时效。当时时效只过了几天,获得法院延期的机会显然比18个月后要高得多,这也就是承租人因为依赖而蒙受的损害。

2.5.3 先例之三:The "Henrik Sif"

在The "Henrik Sif" (1982) 1 Lloyd's Rep. 456先例,[38]货方从期租承租人处获得了延长时效的同意,但没有获得船东的同意。当货方开始诉讼后,期租承租人在答辩书中否认自己是提单合约下的承运人(carrier)或托管人(bailee),不是提单合约的当事人或托管关系的对象,不应该承担责任。而货方则声称承租人没有提醒他自己不是承运人,[39]无法同意延长时效,反而同意延长时效造成货方的误解。货方依赖了承租人同意延长时效的言行而错过了时效,因此承租人不能再说自己不是提单承运人。法院支持了货方的立场,判是期租承租人被禁反言,不允许证明不是提单承运人,Webster大法官说:"(期租承租人) was... under a duty to alert(货方) to the true facts... a reasonable man would... have expected him, acting honestly and responsibly, to have informed in one way or another that he was seeking extensions of time from the wrong party. In my judgment... the plaintiffs have established the estoppels by silence... on which they rely."

正如本书第四章之5.2段所讲,该先例被批评得很厉害。但也有其他类似事实的先例判是被告的言行构成了陈述性禁反言(或其他类别的禁反言)。在Smith v. Central Asbestos Co. Ltd. (1973) AC 518 (HL)先例中,部分原告被被告的经理告知在法律上他们不能同时申请公司的伤残抚恤金(disability pension)与索赔损失。因此,上诉庭([1972] 1 QB 244)与最高院都判是原告没有及时采取行动是因为被告雇员的言行,所以让被告以时效已过作为抗辩是不公平与不合情理,被告被禁反言。

该先例与The "Henrik Sif"先例的重要区别之一是在The "Henrik Sif"先例中,货方与期租承租人之间不存在法律关系,但承诺性禁反言需要双方已经存在法律关系。[40] 而在Smith v. Central Asbestos Co. Ltd先例中,原告与被告之间明显存在法律关系。如果The "Henrik Sif"先例的案情有所不同,期租承租人(Trade Lines)是提单下的承运人(即与货方已经存在合约关系),并有意或无意误导货方船东才是承运人,如果这令货方因为混乱(向船东索赔)而错过时效,再回头向期租承租人索赔时,期租承租人就会因为被禁反言而不能以时效已过作为抗辩。

---

〔37〕 这课题可见《仲裁法——从1996年英国仲裁法到国际商务仲裁》第四章之2.2.3段。

〔38〕 另可见本书第四章之5.2段的详细介绍。

〔39〕 这课题可参阅笔者《提单与其他付运单证》(2016年)一书第三章。

〔40〕 见本书第四章第5段。

2.5.4　先例之四:The "August Leonhardt"

在 The "August Leonhardt"(1985) 2 Lloyd's Rep. 28 上诉庭先例,[41] 船东的互保协会(B)在承租人也同意的前提下(provided charterers agree likewise)同意延长货方索赔的时效。承租人和船东加入的是同一个互保协会。货方的律师(A)错误理解互保协会同时代表船东和承运人做出同意延长时效。之后船东以较早的同意是有条件,但该条件并没有被满足(没有取得承租人的同意)为由声称没有成功延长时效。法院判是互保协会的言行不构成禁反言,互保协会在同意延长时效时经常会加上这种前提或先决条件,是货方律师自己不小心有了误解。Kerr 大法官说:"...(B) had no idea that (A) was acting under a mistake and... there was nothing unreasonable in [B's] conduct or state of mind in acting or thinking as he did... Colloquially speaking [A] and [B] were clearly under a mutual mistake... [A] relied on his assumption by not issue a writ. But he did not do so in reliance on anything said or done by [B] which might have been capable of giving rise to an estoppels."

2.5.5　先例之五:The "Stolt Loyalty"

在 The "Stolt Loyalty"(1993) 2 Lloyd's Rep. 281 先例中,[42] 真正/注册船东(Soframar)与光船船东(Stolt Loyalty Inc.)的互保协会都是 Gard。货方的代表律师(Clyde & Co)向 Gard 互保协会要求延长时效。Gard 提供了保函,其中包括针对 Soframar 与 Stolt Loyalty Inc. 的责任(如有)。Clyde & Co 发电传问"船东"是否确认延长时效,说:"T/L DUE TO EXPIRE ON OR ABOUT 26.3.88. PLS CONFIRM BY RETURN THAT **OWNERS** GRANT T/E AS REQUESTED."

Clarke 大法官认为这里的"OWNERS"一词应解释为包括真正船东 Soframar 与光船船东 Stolt Loyalty Inc.,说:"It would be a strained construction of that part of the telex to conclude that Clyde & Co. were asking for an extension of time in respect of their clients' claims against Soframar (whom everyone knew were almost certainly not liable) but not in respect of the claims against Stolt Loyalty (whom everyone knew almost certainly were liable if the ship was responsible at all for the alleged contamination). I accept the argument advanced on behalf of the plaintiffs that construction of the word 'owners' makes no commercial or indeed legal sense in the circumstances."

Gard 回复 Clyde 说它代表"船舶船东"延长时效:"... Meantime, we have received authority to grant you an extension on behalf of the **Shipowners**..."

Gard 声称这里的船东只是指 Saframar,而不是 Stolt Loyalty Inc.,因为 Saframar 才是"船舶船东"。在光租合约下,由于船长与船员不是真正的船舶船东雇佣,所以

[41]　另可见本书第六章之 7.1 段的详细介绍。

[42]　另可见本书第五章之 10.3.4 段的详细介绍。

船舶船东不会是提单合约下的承运人(carrier),[43]因此,Clyde 如果只获得 Saframar 对延长时效的同意毫无作用。但 Clarke 大法官不同意 Gard 的说法,认为强调"船东"与"船舶船东"有所不同,只是文字游戏,说:"... when the letter is construed objectively in its context and against the background circumnstances including in the particular the terms of the offer to which it was responding the word 'shipowners' has the same meaning as 'owners' in the offer telex. It follows that it had the effect of extending time in respect of claims against those concerned as owners or shipowners for whom Gard acted, namely Soframar and Stolt Loyalty."

即使船东只是指 Soframar, Gard 与 Stolt Loyalty Inc. 没有说清楚也构成禁反言,[44]Clarke 大法官说:"... if they were hoping to send a reply they owed a duty to send a full reply. Instead they **deliberately** allowed Clyde & Co. to continue in the mistaken belief that Clyde & Co. had asked for all relevant extensions of time. They **encouraged** Clyde & Co. to continue to make the same mistake... The letter **did produce or at least encourage an expectation** in the mind of (Clyde & Co) that she need take no further action... Moreover that is precisely what it was intended to do. In those circumstances it would... be **unconscionable** to allow the demise charterers to... rely upon the one year time bar. It follows that the demise charterers are stopped from contending that the extension was not granted by the demise charterers, or... from relying upon the time bar... There is no problem here of the kind which existed in The 'August Leonhardt' because the letter from Gard did indeed cross the line between the parties and it was that letter which induced Clyde & Co. to continue in their mistaken belief that they had asked for all relevant extensions of time from those concerned on the side of the ship."

针对 Gard 指是 Clyde 忘记了光船承租人的存在的争辩,Clarke 大法官也不同意,说:"It seems to me that the fact that Gard failed to point out the mistake and deliberately allowed Clyde & Co. to labour under the illusion that all was well (as indeed they hoped that they would) was one of the causes of the fact that Miss Cresswell(Clyde 的律师) was not alerted to her mistake and therefore of her continued belief that she had done all that was necessary.... It is in my opinion sufficient if Gard's action or inaction was one of the causes even if it was not the only cause: see the Amalgamated Investment & Property Co. Ltd. v. Texas Commerce International Bank Ltd. (1982) 1 QB 84 per Mr Justice Goff at p. 104..."

2.6 一般性建议与指引

最后笔者可节录 Mustill & Boyd 的《Commercial Arbitration》(第2版,1989年)一

---

〔43〕 这课题可见笔者《提单与其他付运单证》一书第三章第5段。

〔44〕 关于有责任说清楚,可见本书第五章第10段。

书之第208至209页,针对商业仲裁下(对法院诉讼也适用)对时效的弃权与禁反言做出了一般性建议与指引:

"**Lapse of time, Waiver and estoppels.** A defendant who would otherwise be entitled to rely on a time – limit may lose this defence if his conduct is such as to constitute a waiver or an estoppel. This difficult branch of the law is not specifically concerned with arbitration procedure, and we therefore do not deal with it in detail. Since, however, the question is occasionally raised in the course of an arbitration, it may be helpful to state the following propositions.

First, the conduct of the defendant is more likely to found a waiver or an estoppel if it occurs before, rather than after, the time limit has expired. If the defendant so behaves as to induce the claimant to believe that the defendant will not rely on the time limit, it may not be difficult to persuade the Court that the defendant cannot thereafter complain that the formalities were not completed in time. But if the claimant has already let the time run out, without the defendant having misled him in anyway, it will be much less easy for the claimant to complain that the defendant's subsequent conduct in some way makes it unfair for him to raise the time bar.

Second, the continuation of negotiations between the parties whilst the limitation period is running does not in itself create any waiver or estoppel in favour of the claimant.[45] Nor does mere silence on the part of the defendant during this period suffice to destroy the defendant's right to rely on the time-barred. The defendant is entitled to lie low and watch the claim become time-barred. This being so, if the claimant wishes to negotiate, but sees the end of the limitation period approaching, he should either extract an explicit promise from the defendant to keep the time running during the negotiations, or comply with the necessary formalities before the time expires... If the defendant acts in a way which is only consistent with the claim remaining in existence,[46] he may thereby waive the right to say that the claim has already been totally defeated by the lapse of time. Thus, for example, if the contract expressly entitles the defendant to call upon the plaintiff to produce documents or evidence in support of his claim, and the defendant avails himself of this right, he may thereafter be prevented from saying that as a result of a time-bar there was no longer any claim to prove.

Where the clause is of the claim-barring type, the arbitrator has jurisdiction to decide

---

〔45〕 典型的例子就是 Williams and Mordey v. WH Muller & Co. (London) Ltd. (1924) 18 Lloyd's Rep. 50 先例。

〔46〕 如被告同意赔偿:The "M Eregli" (1981) 2 Lloyd's Rep. 169 先例。

whether it has been waived[47] although, since it is a matter of law, the Court will have the final word on the matter if the question comes before the Court by way of appeal."

简单而言,以上所讲是被告的言行如果构成弃权或禁反言,就会失去原本时效已过的抗辩。被告的言行的当然要清楚无误(clear and unequivocal),如在 The "Zhi Jiang Kou" (1991) 1 Lloyd's Rep. 493 先例中,有关的陈述或承诺是:"We trust, bearing in mind that the amount involved is relatively small, it will not be necessary for your client to commence proceedings until settlement has been fully explored."

但 Gleeson 大法官认为这仍称不上是清楚无误的陈述,笔者认为严格一点解释的确是没有对时效或任何其他抗辩理由(如需要证明损失)的弃权,也不能构成禁反言。这句话的效力比不上简单的一句说"直到我们无法达成和解前,你不用担心时效"或"直到我们无法达成和解前,你也不必花钱调查与保留证据"。

首先,如果被告的言行发生是在时效已过之前会比在时效已过之后更容易构成弃权或禁反言。道理不难理解,如果被告的言行发生在时效已过之前,原告依赖了被告的言行而没有及时开始诉讼,[48]很容易说服法院或仲裁庭被告不能以时效已过作为抗辩。但如果原告在没有被告言行误导的情况下,任由时效过去,就很难说服法院或仲裁庭被告之后的言行令他以时效已过作为抗辩会造成不公平。毕竟,原告没有因为依赖被告的言行而蒙受任何损害。

其次,在时效已过之前持续谈判本身不会构成弃权或禁反言。被告保持沉默任由原告错过时效也不会令他无法以时效已过作为抗辩。如果原告眼见时效即将届满但仍想继续谈判,或者要求被告明确与无条件同意延长时效,或者先完成开始诉讼的必要程序保护时效,再继续谈判。如果被告的言行只能解释为认为诉讼请求仍然存在,就可能构成对时效已过的抗辩的弃权。例如,如果合约中明示规定被告有权要求原告披露文件或证据支持自己的诉讼请求,而被告在时效已过之后行使了这个权利,被告就会因这个言行而被禁反言,不能再声称时效已过,否则原告就不再有任何诉讼请求需要证明。

最后,仲裁庭有管辖权决定被告的言行是否构成弃权或禁反言,但因为这是一个法律问题,仲裁的败诉方可以根据 1996 年英国《仲裁法》之 section 69 上诉到法院。

3. 对仲裁或是法院诉讼的取舍

3.1 仲裁条文 vs《世界人权宣言》

《世界人权宣言》(Universal Declaration of Human Rights)第 10 条规定:"人人完

---

[47] 见 Cerrito v. North Eastern Timber Importers (1952) 1 Lloyd's Rep. 330 先例。

[48] 涉及法院诉讼就是委任律师做出保护性告票(protective writ),而如果合约中有仲裁条文,则是委任仲裁员开始仲裁。但在双方谈判失败前,都不必继续推进诉讼或仲裁,所以不会花费太多费用,也不影响双方继续和解谈判。

全平等地有权由一个独立而无偏倚的法庭进行公正的和公开的审讯,以确定他的权利和责任并判定对他提出的任何刑事指控(Everyone is entitled in full equality to a fair and public hearing by an independent and impartial tribunal, in the determination of his rights and obligations and of any criminal charge against him)。”

英国针对人权的立法 1998 年《Human Rights Act》之 article 6 与《欧洲人权公约》之 article 6 中,也明示了获得公平审判是重要的人权。除非是根据公序良俗、国家安全、保护妇女儿童权益等情况,否则当事人都有在合理期间内获得公开庭审的机会。但对于这一至高无上的人权,也是可以弃权的,在《欧洲人权公约》或者是《Human Rights Act 1998》下,当事人可以清楚无误的方式(unequivocal manner)[49]弃权。因此除非有强有力的公共利益的要求,否则公开庭审并非是必须的:见 Hakansson and Sturesson v. Sweden (1990) 13 EHRR 1; Pauger v. Austria (1997) 25 EHRR 105 等先例。

因为订立的仲裁条文后,双方所有的争议都要交由仲裁庭解决,这等于双方都失去了由独立而无偏倚的法庭进行公正与公开的审讯有关争议,以确定他的权利和责任的权利的机会。因此不愿意参与仲裁的一方,会以仲裁条文违反人权公约(在英国就是 1998 年《Human Rights Act》与《欧洲人权公约》)作为抗辩。在 Stretford v. The Football Association (2007) 2 Lloyd's Rep. 31 (CA)先例中,上诉庭的 Clarke 大法官以双方当事人弃权(放弃人权公约的公开审讯权利)的解释支持仲裁条文的有效性,说:“In our judgment the cases support the general proposition that, where parties have voluntarily or (as some of the cases put it) freely entered into an arbitration agreement they are to be treated as waiving their rights under article 6.”

更近期的 Entico Corporation Ltd. v. United Nations Educational Scientific and Cultural Association (2008) 1 Lloyd's Rep. 673 先例也跟从了以上的说法。即双方自愿订立仲裁协议并不违反人权公约,英国以外的很多国家也有同样判法。

3.2　中止法院程序

仲裁协议是当事人约定通过仲裁而非法院程序的方式,解决特定争议(或通常是有关主合约的所有争议)的合约。仲裁条文类似于专属管辖权条文(exclusive jurisdiction clause),当事人有责任与向对方做出承诺不通过其他方式解决实质争议:AES Ust-Kamenogorsk v. Ust-Kamenogorsk JSC (2013) UKSC 35 先例。

3.2.1　《纽约公约》下法院必须终止法院程序

在 1958 年《纽约公约》下,约一百六十个签约的国家或地区的法院都有责任在

---

〔49〕 如果实践中是除非当事人明示要求公开庭审,否则不进行公开庭审的话,没有提出明示要求就会被认为是以清楚无误的方式弃权了:见 Zumtobel v. Austria (1993) 17 EHRR 116 先例。尤其是在涉及的并非公共问题而是非常技术性与私人的争议时,更容易证明实践中是这样的做法:见 Schuler-Zraggen v. Switzerland (1993) 16 EHRR 405 先例。

一方当事人漠视仲裁条文并开始法院程序时,[50]中止(stay)法院程序并强制该当事人根据约定的仲裁条文进行仲裁。《纽约公约》的 Article Ⅱ(3)说:"The court of a Contracting State, when seized of an action in a matter in respect of which the parties have made an agreement within the meaning of this article, shall, at the request of one of the parties, refer the parties to arbitration, unless it finds that the said agreement is null and void, inoperative or incapable of being performed."

法院在做出中止法院诉讼程序命令后,通常会要求违反仲裁条文的原告补偿因此损失的诉讼费用:A v. B (Costs) (2007) 1 Lloyd's Rep. 358;Kyrgyz Mobil Tel and Ors v. Fellows International Holdings & Ors (2005) EWHC 1329 等先例。

如果没有人提出反对,即使法院注意到有关合约中有仲裁条文,也不会自动否定自己对诉讼有管辖权:如 McKellar and Westerman Ltd. v. Rosemary Dawn Eversfield (1994) ADRLJ 140 先例。

往往是有人反对与申请中止法院程序,法院才需要做出决定是否中止法院程序,将争议交由双方约定的仲裁庭解决。反对的不会是开始法院诉讼程序的原告,而会是被告。

《纽约公约》下要求签约国法院强制性中止法院程序,而法院在这点上是没有自由裁量权的。但也存在仅有的例外如下:(1)仲裁条文空与无效(null and void)、不能实行(inoperative)、不能履行(incapable of being performed)。这在笔者《仲裁法——从1996年英国仲裁法到国际商务仲裁》一书第一章有详细介绍。比较麻烦的是因为各个国家的法律不同,有时会导致面对同样写法/文字的仲裁条文,有些法院认为有效而有些认为无效的情况。在笔者《提单与其他付运单证》(2016年)一书第四章之2.4段提到,英国法院承认租约提单(charterparty bill of lading)合并的租约伦敦仲裁条文有效,而部分中国法院不承认。这样,如果中国收货人与/或代位求偿的保险人在中国法院开始诉讼程序时,船东不会选择申请中止中国法院程序,而会在英国法院申请"止诉禁令"(anti – suit injunction),即让英国法院掌握对仲裁条文的解释权。(2)如果法院程序中的被告参与了有关实质争议的法院程序,会被认定是放弃了以仲裁解决争议的权利(waiver of right to arbitration)。

3.2.2 什么是参与了有关实质争议的法院程序

因此在英国1996年《仲裁法》之 Section 9(3)说:"An application may not be made by a person before taking the appropriate procedural step (if any) to acknowledge the legal proceedings against him or after he has **taken any step in those proceedings to answer the substantive claim.**"(加黑部分是笔者的强调)

---

〔50〕 这样做法会有多种原因,如错误认为仲裁条文无效,故意违反仲裁条文以获取在熟悉的法院进行诉讼等技术上的优势,约定的仲裁条文对自己不利(如另一方是印度公司,但合约同意了在印度仲裁)等。

香港的《仲裁条例》之 Section 20(1)与(5)是与《联合国国际贸易法委员会国际商事仲裁示范法》(简称"联合国示范法")之 Article 8 有类似说法:"A court before which an action is brought in a matter which is the subject of an arbitration agreement shall, if a party so requests not later than when submitting his first statement on the substance of the dispute, refer the parties to arbitration ... If the court refers the parties in an action to arbitration, it must make an order staying the legal proceedings in that action."

香港的《仲裁条例》/《联合国示范法》只针对了递交答辩书这一行为作为有否参与法院实质争议的准则,一旦有此行为,即认定是对仲裁的弃权。而英国《仲裁法》中的参与任何有关实质争议的法院程序可以包括很多行为,即前者相对来说更局限,但后者(英国《仲裁法》)则较难掌握有关的行为会否导致对仲裁弃权。

英国已经有不少先例针对什么是被告参与了有关实质争议的法院程序与什么不是。如向法院申请为了仲裁而中止(stay)法院程序明显不是参与了法院程序,而是针对有关争议向法院提出管辖权异议:Finnish Marine Insurance Co. Ltd. v. Protective National Insurance Co. (1989) 2 Lloyd's Rep. 99 先例。

被告向法院申请披露文件,或是申请命令要求原告披露实质索赔中的文件或细节,属于参与法院程序: Parker, Gaines & Co. Ltd. v. Turpin (1918) 1 KB 358 先例。当然,向法院提交书面答辩、答辩书更明确是对以仲裁解决争议的弃权。

在 Ahad v. Uddin (2005) EWCA Civ 883 先例中,案情有关 Ahad(第一原告)、Ahmed(第二原告)与 Uddin(被告)订立合伙人协议,一同成立与经营一间餐厅。Ahad 是大厨,Ahmed 有一间食品杂货店,所以负责提供物料,而 Uddin 就负责管理。很快大家就有了分歧。Ahad 与 Ahmed 开始法院程序起诉 Uddin 违反合伙人协议并索赔损失,Uddin 也递交了答辩书。虽然合伙人协议中有一条仲裁条文,但 Uddin 没有申请中止法院程序。之后双方的分歧加大,Ahad 做出通知将 Uddin 逐出合伙人并解除了合伙人关系。这重要事实的改变导致 Ahad 需要修改(amend)早前的起诉书的内容,此时 Uddin 才后知后觉提出有仲裁条文存在并申请中止法院程序。一审法院与上诉庭都拒绝了申请,由于针对原起诉书中的诉求与争议,Uddin 递交答辩书已经是对以仲裁解决争议弃权,令法院获得了解决该争议的管辖权。如果新起诉书中的修改部分事实上属于原争议,法院仍然有管辖权。但如果修改部分涉及的是新的诉因,被告就有权根据仲裁条文申请法院中止针对该新诉因的法院程序。

在更近期的 Nokia Corporation v. HTC Corporation (2012) EWHC 3199 (Pat)先例中,被告参加了案件管理会议(case management meeting,或简称"CMC")并同意了递交文书请求(pleading)与披露文件的时间表。1 个月后,被告申请中止法院程序,但被法院拒绝。Floyd 大法官说被告参与案件管理会议并同意时间表是明确无误接受了由法院解决所有的争议。但 Floyd 大法官也接受如果被告在案件管理会议前就清楚表示保留仲裁的权利,[51]情况会有不同:"Whilst the position would have been entirely different if HTC(被告)had reserved their position at any stage prior to the CMC, as is illustrated in some of the cases referred to, this is not such a case. The present case is one in which the step taken is entirely unequivocal and for those reasons I propose to refuse the stay under section 9."

在 Patel v. Patel (1999) 1 All ER (Comm) 923 先例中,被告申请撤销缺席判决(default judgment)与允许他抗辩并提出反索赔的批准。之后被告提出中止法院程序的申请,上诉庭推翻了一审法院的判决,认为整体来看,被告申请允许他抗辩并提出反索赔的批文不属于参与了有关实质争议的法院程序。

在上诉庭的 Capital Trust v. Radio Design (2002) 2 All ER 159 先例中,判被告在指明"如果中止法院程序的申请不成功"(in the event that its application for a stay was unsuccessful)的前提下,要申请原告的诉讼请求在瑞典法下没有机会成功(no real prospect of succeeding)的简易判决(summary judgment),也并非参与有关实质争议的法院程序。

要在各种不同案情下做出什么是或什么不是参与法院程序的判断,Denning 勋爵在 Eagle Star Insurance Co. Ltd. v. Yuval Insurance Co. Ltd. (1978) 1 Lloyd's 357 (CA)先例中认为,考验的标准是被告参与诉讼程序的特定言行在本质上是否默示确认了法院程序的正确性以及被告愿意由法院而非仲裁解决争议,说:"... in order to deprive a defendant of his recourse to arbitration a 'step in the proceedings' must be one which impliedly affirms the correctness of the proceedings and the willingness of the defendant to go along with a determination by the courts of law instead of arbitration."

在该先例中,Denning 勋爵认为被告申请将原告送达的一份有严重缺陷的告票与索赔请求撤销(strike－out)不属于参与了有关实质争议的诉讼程序,说:"Applying this principle, the defendants here were presented with a writ indorsed with a statement of claim which was very defective. They applied, quite properly, to strike it out. This was not an affirmation of the correctness of the proceedings. Quite the contrary, it was a disaffirmation of them. It was not a 'step in the proceedings' such as to debar the defendants from applying for a stay."

后来在 Patel v. Patel 先例中,上诉庭也有类似的考验标准:"Two requirements must be satisfied. First, the conduct of the applicant must be such as to demonstrate an election to abandon his right[52] to stay, in favour of allowing the action to proceed. Second, the act in question must have the effect of invoking the jurisdiction of the court."

---

〔51〕 这课题可见本书第四章之6.5段。

〔52〕 见本书第三章之3.4段。

这个考验标准也被之后的很多先例跟从：见 Kuwait Airways v. Iraq Airways（1994）1 Lloyd's Rep. 276；Capital Trust v. Radio Design；Bilta（UK）Ltd. v. Nazir（2010）EWHC 1086（Ch）等先例。另在近期的 Sierra Fishing Co. v. Farran（2015）1 Lloyd's Rep. 514 先例中，也有详细针对。

笔者（杨大明）早前在一份英文法律刊物上发表有关"第一步"的定义。[53] 里面提到 LMLN No. 609 伦敦仲裁，当中被告一直没有理会与参与仲裁程序，但过了一段时间，当仲裁庭下了命令要求被告提供抗辩时，才写信给仲裁庭要求时间延长（time extension），让被告可以决定是否对仲裁庭的管辖权提出异议。仲裁庭最终认为这个申请已经足够符合"第一步"的定义。这个决定在文章中受到笔者的批评，笔者说："If s. 73(1) does indeed apply to challenges under s. 31(1), then this would appear to be a more satisfactory basis for deciding that the defendants had waived their right to object to the tribunal's jurisdiction in London Arbitration 4/03. Therefore, for the reasons already discussed in this paper, it is submitted that 'the first step in the proceedings to contest the merits' must be one that involves a certain degree of formality. Otherwise it could potentially make litigants wary of engaging the tribunal even on routine matters. This would hardly be constructive."

上述节录的先例中的考验标准看来也是反映笔者以上的看法，即所走的一步必须是清楚表现放弃争议管辖权的争议。

3.2.3　被告对以仲裁解决争议的弃权

法院程序中的原告违反仲裁协议，给被告带来是否要申请法院中止（stay）程序的选择权（election）。被告可以根据合约中的仲裁条文向法院申请中止，或者可以选择继续参与涉及实质争议的法院程序（taking a step in the proceedings）解决争议。如果选择后者，即参与法院程序解决争议，就可以说是被告选择放弃了以仲裁方式解决争议的权利，并认可将解决有关争议的管辖权交给法院。正如 Goff 勋爵在 The "Messiniaki Tolmi"（1984）1 Lloyd's Rep. 266 先例中所说："Now a person voluntarily submits to the jurisdiction of the Court if he voluntarily recognizes, or has voluntarily recognized, that the Court has jurisdiction to hear and determine the claim which is the subject matter of the relevant proceedings. In particular, he makes a voluntary submission to the jurisdiction if he takes a step in the proceedings which in all the circumstances amounts to a recognition of the Court's jurisdiction in respect of the claim which is the subject matter of those proceedings."

另一个例子是笔者（杨大明）处理的一宗前段时间比较重要的案件——华天龙案（The "Hua Tian Long"［2010］3 HKC 557）。案情涉及广州打捞局的一艘重吊驳

---

〔53〕《What is "the First Step in the Proceedings to Contest the Merits" under the Arbitration Act 1996?》（The Journal of the Chartered Institute of Arbitrators Volume 70 No. 4 November 2004）。

船华天龙号在成功协助香港特区政府打捞沉船以清理航道后,在开航前被原告(马来西亚的承租人)在香港法院开始对物诉讼(in rem)的法院程序并扣船。承租人指控华天龙的船东(广州打捞局)没有履行双方之前订立的租约,但广州打捞局称双方只是在谈判,并没有合约关系。承租人要求的索赔金额非常庞大,要求广州打捞局提供上亿元以上的诉前担保,才同意放船。虽然声称存在的租约中有新加坡仲裁条文,但代表广州打捞局的笔者(杨大明)考虑到广州打捞局是半官方的机构,想要依赖香港特区法律中的"君主豁免权"(crown immunity),[54]因此没有向法院申请中止法院诉讼程序,如果去新加坡仲裁,就会失去这个抗辩。最后笔者在这方面在香港一审胜诉,判广州打捞局可享有君主豁免权,但也因为广州打捞局在委托笔者前的律师已经代表打捞局为了放走华天龙号提供担保给法院并带来延误,因此判广州打捞局因为延误与其他言行导致弃权与/或禁反言。但即使如此,由于一审判决可以上诉,仍是逼使马来西亚承租人达成广州打捞局满意的和解协议。

最后需要注意的是,依赖仲裁条文向法院申请中止法院程序并获得成功的被告,不得事后出尔反尔在仲裁程序中指称有关争议不在仲裁条文的管辖范围内:见 Macaura v. Northern Assurance Co. Ltd. (1925) AC 619;South British Insurance Co. Ltd. v. Gauci Bros & Co. (Egypt) (1928) AC 352 等先例。

3.3 "Scott v. Avery"条文

简单而言,合约中的"Scott v. Avery"条文会让被告在法院程序中有一个抗辩,要求法院推迟诉讼直到仲裁庭做出裁决书。"Scott v. Avery"条文兴起于英国法院对自己管辖权外的仲裁仍然抱有显著敌意的年代。"Scott v. Avery"条文为执行一条有效的仲裁条文而不与法院管辖权起冲突提供了一种解决方案。然而在法院大力支持仲裁与《纽约公约》普遍被认同的现在,已经不再有这样做的意义了。对于熟悉现在仲裁业务的人士来说,中止法院程序等待仲裁结果的情况并不罕见,毕竟当事人在有效的仲裁协议下有通过仲裁而非法院诉讼解决争议的合约责任。而如果在中止法院程序后,发生了导致仲裁条文空与无效(null and void)、不能实行(inoperative)或不能履行(incapable of being performed)的事件,[55]一方当事人(一般是原告)可以

---

〔54〕 君主豁免权的问题已经在笔者《仲裁法——从开庭审理到裁决书的作出与执行》一书第十三章之9.2段介绍。简单而言,"一国两制"下带来一个香港特有的新问题,就是主权豁免权外的君主豁免权。香港以前作为英国的殖民地,依从英国法律,不能在香港法院对英国皇室提出任何的诉讼,无论是商业或非商业,理由包括像"国王不会做错事情"(the King can do no wrong)。虽然君主豁免权与主权豁免都属于豁免的特权,而且内容是相通的,但是两者的基础却非常不同。主权豁免是基于国与国之间的平等地位,但君主豁免是基于不平等的君臣地位。随着时间过去,也有立法对这一绝对豁免权做出一定程度的放宽,在香港就是《Crown Proceedings Ordinance》。在香港特区回归中国之后,《Crown Proceedings Ordinance》并没有被废除,这带来一定程度的不明朗,在 The "Hua Tian Long" (2010) 3 HKC 557 先例第一次明确。君主豁免的范围非常有限。

〔55〕 如双方在仲裁协议中指定的仲裁员突然死亡或失去能力,又或是被告后来对仲裁协议做出违约/毁约的言行并被原告接受等。

向法院申请撤销中止命令,恢复针对有关争议的法院程序:见 Trunk Flooring Ltd. v. HSBC Asset Finance (UK) Ltd. (2015) NICA 68 等先例。

"Scott v. Avery"条文常见于海事、保险、大宗货买卖[56]领域,而在其他很多商业合约中很少见。《Russell on Arbitration》(第24版,2015年)一书之2-023段这样描述"Scott v. Avery"条文:"The parties to a contract may agree that no action shall be brought upon it until an arbitration award has been made, or (what amounts to the same thing) may agree that the only obligation arising out of a particular term of the contract shall be to pay whatever sum a tribunal may award... It does not prevent litigation being initiated on a contract containing a clause of this type, but the condition precedent is a defence to the action."

在 Alexander Scott v. George Avery (1856) 5 HL Cas 811 贵族院先例(正因该先例中,此类条文才得名为"Scott v. Avery"条文)中,被保险人的船舶参与船东互保协会(P & I Club),协会规则规定仲裁庭对有关的争议做出裁决前,所有成员都不能在保单下开始法院诉讼(no member shall be entitled to maintain any action in law or suit in equity on his policy until the matter had been considered by arbitrators)。而即使在仲裁庭做出裁决后,也只能向法院起诉裁决书中的金额(only for such sum as the arbitrators may award)。

对于此类条文会否因排除法院管辖权而不合法或违反公共政策[57]的争议,贵族院明确表示不会,并强调了此类条文的功效:"What pretence can there be for saying that there is anything contrary to public policy in allowing parties to contract that they shall not be liable to any action until their liability has been ascertained by a domestic and private tribunal, upon which they themselves agree! Can the public be injured by it? It seems to me that it would be a most inexpedient encroachment upon the liberty of the subject if he were not allowed to enter into such a contract... Is there anything contrary to public policy in saying that the company shall not be harassed by actions, the costs of which might be ruinous, but that any dispute that arises shall be referred to a domestic tribunal, which may speedily and economically determine the dispute? I can see not the slightest ill consequences that can flow from such an agreement, and I see great advantage from it."

也就是说,此类条文可被解释为获得仲裁裁决书是开始法院诉讼的先决条件(condition precedent),而并非是排除法院管辖权(这在当时是违反公共政策)。

---

〔56〕 见 B v. S (2011) EWHC 691 (Comm)先例与 Merkin 与 Flannery 的《Arbitration Act 1996》(第5版,2014年)一书第54页。

〔57〕 在 Czarnikow Ltd. v. Roth Schmidt & Co. (1922) 12 Lloyd's Rep. 195 先例中,上诉庭判仲裁协议约定裁决是最终(final)是无效与违反公共政策,这在《国际商务仲裁》一书第二章之1.2.2段有介绍。

"Scott v. Avery"条文是针对约定的事项，对行使在法院开始诉讼程序的权利设置先决条件，从效果上来看可以分为两个方面。第一方面的效果是合约当事人有进行仲裁的责任，在仲裁庭做出裁决书前，不得在法院开始对合约下有关争议的诉讼。第二个方面的效果是"Scott v. Avery"条文会约定即使原告要在法院司法程序中寻求救济，被告的责任只是支付裁决书中被裁定的金额：Scott v. Liverpool Corpn (1858) 3 De G & J 334；Braunstein v. Accidental Death Insurance Co. (1861) 1 B & S 782；Elliott v. Royal Exchange Assurance Co. (1867) LR 2 Exch 237；Wright v. Ward 24 LT 439；Viney v. Bignold (1887) 20 QBD 172；Scott v. Mercantile Accident & Guarantee Insurance (1892) 66 LT 811；Caledonian Insurance Company v. Andrew Gilmour (1893) AC 85；Spurrier v. La Cloche (1902) AC 446；Central Electricity Generating Board v. Halifax Corpn (1963) AC 785 等先例。

法院会将此类合约条文作为中止法院程序的实质性理由，[58]或作为仲裁庭做出裁决书前被告在任何法院程序中的抗辩理由。[59] 原告只能通过仲裁主张自己的权利，因为一旦被告向法院显示有关合约中有"Scott v. Avery"条文，几乎肯定能够获得法院中止法院程序的命令，否则在之后的法院诉讼中，被告面对任何索赔都可以"Scott v. Avery"条文中的先决条件没有被满足作为抗辩。

3.4 错误选择仲裁或诉讼的言行构成禁反言

上面几段针对的都是在有仲裁条文的情况下错误选择诉讼的情况。如果被告没有向法院申请中止法院程序，就会构成对以仲裁解决争议的"弃权"（waiver）。相反，如果是在应该以法院诉讼解决争议时，因为错误理解合约条文而选择了仲裁，也有可能构成弃权与/或禁反言。

在上诉庭的 The "Amazonia" (1990) 1 Lloyd's Rep. 236 上诉庭先例中，虽然租约合并的澳大利亚 1924 年《海上运输法》强制要求在澳大利亚法院解决有关货损货差的争议，但当事人一致参与伦敦仲裁的行为构成"共识性禁反言"（estoppel by convention）。该先例的案情在本书第六章之 7.5 段有详细介绍，这里不再重复。在该先例中，法院判二船东在开始仲裁时不知道根据有关立法要在澳大利亚法院解决争议，而弃权一般是需要弃权方知道自己的权利与有关的情况，[60] 即二船东参与伦敦仲裁的行为不会构成弃权。但二船东与承租人之间的交往与互动，令双方产生租约中的伦敦仲裁条文是有效的共同错误理解，并最终同意 Donald Davies 先生作为独任仲裁员。如果这时二船东从这个共同错误理解中脱身，会令承租人蒙受损害（时效已过无法开始法院诉讼，更不用说已经产生的律师费用），是不公平与不合情理的（unconscionable），因此构成共识性禁反言。

---

〔58〕 见 Dennehy v. Bellamy (1938) 2 All ER 262 先例。

〔59〕 见 Golding v. London & Edinburgh Insurance Co. Ltd. (1932) 43 Lloyd's Rep. 487 先例。

〔60〕 见本书第三章之 3.4.1 段。

类似 The“Amazonia”先例的弃权与/或禁反言也会在其他情况发生。如《鹿特丹规则》[61]第 75 条针对仲裁地点的选择,说:

“Article 75 Arbitration agreements

1. Subject to this chapter, parties may agree that any dispute that may arise relating to the carriage of goods under this Convention shall be referred to arbitration.

2. The arbitration proceedings shall, at the option of the person asserting a claim against the carrier, take place at:(a) Any place designated for that purpose in the arbitration agreement; or (b) Any other place situated in a State where any of the following place is located: (i) The domicile of the carrier; (ii) The place of receipt agreed in the contract of carriage; (iii) The place of delivery agreed in the contract of carriage; or (iv) The port where the goods are initially loaded on a ship or the port where the goods are finally discharged from a ship...

5. The provisions of paragraphs 1, 2... of this article are deemed to be part of every arbitration clause or agreement, and any term of such clause or agreement to the extent that it is inconsistent therewith is void.”

这样,提单合约(不论是租约或班轮提单)合并或规定了一条伦敦仲裁条文,货方或代位求偿的保险人在发生货损货差后启动了该伦敦仲裁程序,但事后发觉《鹿特丹规则》通过立法在有关的航次强制适用,因此他可以在卸港开始仲裁提起索赔,避开伦敦仲裁条文,而这样对他更有利。但由于较早前已经做出了选择,而《鹿特丹规则》的适用是他应该可以知道的,这就会构成弃权。加上如果已经在较早启动的伦敦仲裁中,双方已有了互动,就会同时构成禁反言。

4. 涉及仲裁员资格的弃权与禁反言

4.1　仲裁员资格

因为仲裁是双方约定的争议解决办法,在订约自由的大原则下,当事人完全可以自由约定仲裁员必须拥有怎样的资格(qualification)。当事人可以通过明示约定仲裁员必须符合的资格与专业水平来控制仲裁员质量。但如果订得不现实,会导致将来发生争议后,难以找到符合资格的仲裁员。现在中国公司/企业也经常会在仲裁协议中约定仲裁员必须懂得中英双语(bilingual),这可以减少诉讼的费用(如翻译的费用)与提高仲裁员对中国文化有一定了解的机会。这在笔者的《仲裁法——从 1996 年英国仲裁法到国际商务仲裁》一书第三章之 2.3 段有详细介绍,这里不再重复。

当事人在委任仲裁员时应特别注意仲裁员资格的问题,必须严格符合仲裁条文

〔61〕　该国际公约在笔者《提单与其他付运单证》(2016 年)一书第四章之 2.5.7 段有介绍。

的规定,否则就会无可争议地导致仲裁庭的管辖权有问题与可能令裁决书被撤销。一般在机构仲裁(institutional arbitration),如国际商会(ICC)仲裁,因为有仲裁机构的监督与仲裁员在委任前要做出更多的宣告,仲裁员(无论是当事人自己委任或机构委任)资格不符的情况发生得较少。而在临时仲裁(ad hoc arbitration),这种情况就较常见。另外,也有情况是仲裁条文中对仲裁员资格要求过高,导致原告找不到符合资格的仲裁员。在时效届临时,委任了明知不符合仲裁条文规定的资格的仲裁员,看被告会否放弃挑战仲裁员资格的权利。

4.2 对仲裁员不符合资格的弃权与禁反言

在 Mustill 与 Boyd 的《Commercial Arbitration》(第 2 版,1989 年)第 256 页总结了若干情况,包括当事人自己委任不符合资格的仲裁员、对方委任不符合资格的仲裁员与第三人委任不符合资格的仲裁员,会带来的弃权与/或禁反言的说法。

1. 当事人自己委任不符合资格的仲裁员:"**Waiver and Estoppel.** . . . The following specific points may be made in relation to disqualification-1 Where a party appoints someone as 'his own' arbitrator and thereafter continues with the arbitration, he implied represents to his opponent that the person appointed has the qualifications required by the contract. He cannot at a subsequent stage object to the award on the ground that the arbitrator was not in fact qualified."

如果仲裁程序中的当事人自己委任了实际上并不符合资格的仲裁员,在败诉后再质疑仲裁庭的资格/管辖权就会面对弃权与禁反言的抗辩:见 Jungheim Hopkins & Co. v. Foukelmann (1909) 2 KB 948; Oakland Metal Co. Ltd. v. Benaim & Co. (1953) 2 Lloyd's Rep. 192 等先例。

在 Oakland Metal Co. Ltd. v. Benaim & Co 先例中,案情涉及锌锭的 CIF 买卖,买卖双方有了争议后,去伦敦仲裁机构仲裁。原告自己委任了一位并非仲裁机构名单上的仲裁员,即不符合该仲裁机构规则要求的资格。最后仲裁庭判原告败诉,于是原告以仲裁员不符合资格为由希望撤销裁决书。但高院没有支持原告的申请,其中提到弃权的问题说如果原告不知道仲裁员不符合资格,就不会构成弃权:"Inasmuch as the plaintiffs had no knowledge of the want of qualification of the arbitrators there has been no waiver here."

但即使原告不知道仲裁员不符合资格,仍会构成"陈述性禁反言"(estoppel by representation),Parker 大法官说:"if a person puts forward an arbitrator and tells the other side, in effect: 'Here is a man whom we appoint who is qualified to act on our behalf,' and the matter proceeds to award, I do not see why, as a matter of principle, that person is not estopped from setting up the non – qualification of his arbitrator. . . they thereby induced the defendant to go on with the arbitration and to incur expense . . . In this case the plaintiffs put forward Mr. Brenner's(原告委任的仲裁员)name under circumstances in which any reasonable person would accept him as an arbitrator qualified to act... and the plaintiffs thereafter, by proceeding with the arbitration and by sending forward their case, were representing and continuing to represent that Mr. Brenner was so qualified. In those circumstances they cannot thereafter be heard to say that he did not have the necessary qualification."

如果原告因为仲裁员资格约定得太高而找不到合适的仲裁员,笔者建议可以考虑几种做法。做法之一是在有管辖权的法院开始诉讼,在被告提出中止法院程序时,指仲裁条文是不能实行(inoperative)或不能履行(incapable of being performed),看能否以努力后仍无法找到符合资格的仲裁员的证据说服法院。另一个做法是委任一个不符合资格的仲裁员,试图鱼目混珠,看被告会否对这方面弃权。而如果在委任了不符合资格的仲裁员后又及时找到了符合资格的仲裁员,可以做出第二份仲裁通知(notice of arbitration),但说明是对第一个仲裁无损害(without prejudice)。这样可以保护时效,防止对方挑战第一个仲裁的仲裁员资格成功时时效已过,无法再启动另一个有效的仲裁进行索赔。

2. 对方委任不符合资格的仲裁员:

"2. Where a party knows that the person appointed by his opponent lacks the necessary qualifications, but nevertheless continues with the arbitration, he thereby waives his right to object, unless he makes a protest in such a way as to enable him to continue on a 'without prejudice' basis.

3. Where, however, the party if ignorant that his opponent's nominee is unqualified, he does not waive his objection in taking part in the reference.

4. An agent (e. g. lawyer) with the necessary authority may bind his principal to accept the appointment of an arbitrator who lacks the necessary qualifications."

如果一方当事人发现对方委任的仲裁员不符合资格,可以向法院申请赶走(removal)仲裁员,这可见英国 1996 年《仲裁法》之 section 24:[62] "A party to arbitral proceedings may (upon notice to the other parties, to the arbitrator concerned and to any other arbitrator) apply to the court to remove an arbitrator on any of the following grounds—...(b) that he does not possess the qualifications required by the arbitration agreement..."

如果一方当事人当时并不知道对方委任的仲裁员不符合资格,在仲裁庭做出他败诉的裁决书后才发现,他可以申请撤销裁决:Earl of Darnley v. London Chatham & Dover Railway (1867) LR 2 HL 43 先例。毕竟弃权方必须知道自己的权利与有关的

---

〔62〕 英国 1996 年《仲裁法》之 Section 24 针对了在仲裁程序中可以向英国法院申请将仲裁员赶走的四种情况,包括本小段介绍的仲裁员不符合合约规定的资格,仲裁员失去能力,本章第 6 段介绍的仲裁员有偏见或利益冲突与本章第 7 段介绍的仲裁员处理程序有严重不正常。这在本章之 7.3.6 段会有进一步介绍。

情况才可以弃权。这种情况也不会构成禁反言，因为他没有做出任何言行可以令对方依赖并蒙受损害，更说不上有任何不公平与不合情理(unconscionable)之处。

但如果知道对方委任的仲裁员不符合资格，仍继续参与仲裁，就会构成对挑战仲裁员资格与撤销裁决书的弃权，除非他做出了抗议或是在"无损害"的前提下继续参与仲裁。但在本书第四章之6.5段已经提到这种"无损害"说法的保护性有限，现实中往往也不可行。因为委任仲裁员的一方在对方不同意的情况下，会要求立即解决这一管辖权争议或自动更换一个仲裁员，以防将来取得胜诉的裁决书后，保留权利的一方采取"正面我赢，反面你输"(heads I win, tails you lose)的策略，有第二次机会推倒重来(second bite of the cherry)。另是现在的立法(Mustill 与 Boyd 的《Commercial Arbitration》于1989年出版，早于英国1996年《仲裁法》)或仲裁机构的规则都不允许延误解决这个仲裁员不符合资格的管辖权争议。如在《联合国示范法》之 article 4/香港《仲裁条例》之 section 11："A party who knows that any provision of this Law from which the parties may derogate or any requirement under the arbitration agreement has not been complied with and yet proceeds with the arbitration without stating his objection to such non－compliance without undue delay or . . . **shall be deemed to have waived his right to object.**"

另在《联合国示范法》之 article 13/香港《仲裁条例》之 section 26 规定异议的程序和时间要求是在仲裁庭成立后或知道有关情况后15天内提出(within 15 days after becoming aware of the constitution of the arbitral tribunal or after becoming aware of any circumstance)。ICC 仲裁规则之 article 14 也说明必须在30日内挑战仲裁员资格。

而在1996年英国《仲裁法》之 section 73 (1)也规定："If a party to arbitral proceedings takes part, or continues to take part, in the proceedings without making, either forthwith or within such time as is allowed by the arbitration agreement or the tribunal or by any provision of this Part, any objection—(a) that the tribunal lacks substantive jurisdiction... he may not raise that objection later, before the tribunal or the court, unless he shows that, at the time he took part or continued to take part in the proceedings, he did not know and could not with reasonable diligence have discovered the grounds for the objection."

这重要的立法条文在本章之7.3.1至7.3.5段有详细介绍，在此只强调该立法条文的本意是一旦发现了任何可以挑战或质疑仲裁员的理由，必须马上提出与行动，不允许单方面延误解决这一争议，防止当事人采取"正面我赢，背面你输"(heads I win, tails you lose)的策略。在这样的立法下，一方当事人不能在知道对方委任的仲裁员不符合资格后，以"无损害"或"保留权利"的说法单方面延误行动。

至于代理人(如律师)可以代表委托人接受对方委任的不合资格的仲裁员也不难理解，即使该代理人没有实际授权，也往往有表见授权(ostensible authority)。

3. 第三人委任不符合资格的仲裁员："5. Where an umpire is to be appointed by

the two arbitrators, their authority to make an appointment is defined by the arbitration agreement under which they themselves were appointed. Neither before they disagree nor afterwards, do they have ostensible authority to bind their appointing parties by choosing an umpire who lacks the necessary qualifications..."

如果双方当事人都不知情的情况下,仲裁机构委任的仲裁员或两位仲裁员委任的公断人(umpire)[63]/首席仲裁员不符合规定,裁决书就应当被撤销。在 Rahcasssi Shipping Co. SA and Blue Star Line Ltd. (1969) 1 QB 173 先例中,仲裁条文明示要求仲裁员与公断人必须是商业人士而非律师(commercial men and not lawyers),产生争议后,仲裁员疏忽大意委任了一位大律师(barrister)作为公断人,而当事人在公断人被委任之时并不知道公断人的律师身份。公断人做出的两份裁决书均对原告不利,于是事后知情的原告向监督的英国法院申请撤销裁决。Roskill 大法官判做出的裁决书因为公断人资格不符并没有管辖权而无效,予以撤销。

5. 管辖权异议

上一段介绍的仲裁员不符合仲裁条文规定的资格只是对管辖权有异议的一种,其他还包括争议方声称主合约与仲裁条文无效,有关的争议根据当地法律不能以仲裁解决(non-arbitrable)等。这在笔者《仲裁法——从 1996 年英国仲裁法到国际商务仲裁》一书第五章有详论,这里不再重复。对管辖权异议一般需要在最晚不迟于首次参与任何有关实质争议的法院程序(1996 年英国《仲裁法》),或者递交书面抗辩意见(香港《仲裁条例》)时提出。至于什么是参与了有关实质争议的法院程序已经在本章之 3.2.2 段有介绍。

在"Kompetenz-Kompetenz"与独立原则(separation principle)的说法下,仲裁庭有权对自己的管辖权做出初步裁决,而败诉一方如果不满意,可以上诉到法院做出最后

---

〔63〕 公断人是波罗的交易所(Baltic Exchange)海事仲裁的一贯做法。当双方原本委任的两位仲裁员有分歧时(即使他们已经对大部分争议达成了一致,但有一个小分歧),他们就应该把这事实通知委任他们的双方当事人,然后委任一位公断人。这位公断人有权作为独任仲裁员(sole arbitrator)做出裁决书。原本的两位仲裁员就职责履行完毕(*functus officio*)。虽然他们可以尝试说服公断人,但后者可以不理会,完全自由地做出裁决,包括两位仲裁员已经是同意的部分。这做法与三人仲裁庭的首席仲裁员(Chairman)在其他两位仲裁员有分歧时有决定票(deciding vote)有区别。因为公断人对案件的看法可以与前两位仲裁员都不一样,即使是他们同意的部分。但作为一个三人仲裁庭的首席仲裁员,明显不能不理会两位仲裁员已经同意了的部分,因为这已经是多数意见。例如,如果第一位仲裁员觉得没有违约,第二位仲裁员觉得有违约而应该做出履行指令(specific performance),而公断人觉得有违约但只应该用金钱赔偿(monetary damages),公断人完全可以自由决定用金钱对违约做出赔偿。这方面可见笔者《仲裁法——从 1996 年英国仲裁法到国际商务仲裁》一书第三章之 2.2.3 段。

的判决。只有顺利组成仲裁庭，才能让它对自己是否有管辖权做出决定（初步裁决），为了鼓励被告参与组成仲裁庭而不会有任何误解（这种误解很容易产生），立法明示规定委任仲裁员并不意味着就放弃了提出管辖权异议的权利。[64]

如《联合国示范法》之 article 16/香港《仲裁条例》之 section 34 (2)规定："A plea that the arbitral tribunal does not have jurisdiction shall be raised not later than the submission of the statement of defence. A party is not precluded from raising such a plea by the fact that he has appointed, or participated in the appointment of, an arbitrator..."也可见 1996 年英国《仲裁法》之 Section 31(1)："An objection that the arbitral tribunal lacks substantive jurisdiction at the outset of the proceedings must be raised by a party not later than the time he takes his first step in the proceedings to contest the merits of any matter in relation to which he challenges the tribunal's jurisdiction. A party is not precluded from raising such an objection by the fact that he has appointed or participated in the appointment of an arbitrator ..."

6. 涉及仲裁员不持偏见与没有利益冲突的弃权与禁反言

在本书第九章之 2.2 段已经提到要构成"一事不再审"(res judicata)一定要先有符合自然公正(natural justice)的公平审讯(fair trial)的一审，这也适用在仲裁。本段介绍的仲裁员不持偏见(unbiased)与没有利益冲突(no conflict of interest)是自然公正的第一个方面，已经在笔者的《仲裁法——从 1996 年英国仲裁法到国际商务仲裁》一书第七章与第八章有详细介绍，这里只针对涉及这方面的弃权与禁反言。而自然公正的另一方面，即程序正当，将在下一段介绍。

6.1 公平审讯的大原则

6.1.1 委任有偏见或利益冲突的仲裁员的后果

在 Mustill 与 Boyd 的《Commercial Arbitration》(第 2 版，1989 年)一书第 249 页说："There are statements in some of the older cases and works of reference which could, if read literally, be understood to mean that a person with an interest in the outcome of a dispute is disqualified from acting as an arbitrator in respect of the dispute, in the sense that a purported appointment of him would be nugatory. This is not correct. Interest is just one example of a fact from which a reasonable person would often infer that there was a risk of the arbitrator suffering from bias; i. e. from a predisposition to decide for or against one party, without proper regard to the true merits of the dispute. Interest in ap-

---

〔64〕 也可见 The "World Era" (1992) 1 Lloyd's Rep. 45 先例。

propriate cases justify the Court in revoking the appointment of the arbitrator, or refuse to stay an action brought in contravention of an agreement to submit the dispute to him for arbitration, or of setting aside any award which he has made. Nevertheless, unless something of this sort occurs, the appointment is effective, the reference is properly constituted, and the award is binding on the parties."

首先,以前一些古老的先例的看法是只要仲裁员有偏见或利益冲突,对他的委任就是空与无效的(nugatory)。这个说法与仲裁员不符合仲裁条文约定的资格是一回事。但这本权威的书籍就认为这个说法是错误的。换言之,即使委任了一位有偏见或利益冲突的仲裁员,所带来的后果并非是对他的委任是空的。但如果利益冲突足够严重,就会导致监督法院的干预,包括把仲裁员赶走、[65]拒绝中止法院程序让有偏见或利益冲突的仲裁员处理有关的实质争议、将已经做出的裁决书撤销。[66] 除非法院做出了这些救济,否则这个委任有效,仲裁员做出的裁决书也是有效与约束争议双方,可以构成"一事不再审"(res judicata)。

在这个说法下,因为对有偏见或利益冲突的仲裁员的委任有效,所以原告是有效保护了时效,这与仲裁员不符合资格的委任不同。而另一方面,因为仲裁员的资格取决于双方的约定,法律没有强制要求,因此争议双方完全可以改变仲裁协议中规定的不令人满意或不可行的资格,或对挑战仲裁员资格"弃权"(waiver)与被"禁反言"(estoppel)。而仲裁员有偏见或偏私或有利益冲突是违反了自然公正的大原则,这也违背了法治的根本原则:见 R v. Inner London Coroner Ex p Dallaglio (1994) 4 All ER 139 等先例。

6.1.2 不能以订约自由影响法院干涉的权利

正因为违反自然公正涉及的是公共政策的问题,不能通过当事人之间的订约自由予以排除。如很多仲裁机构(如 ICC)规则中写明对于仲裁庭的异议,仲裁机构做出的决定是最终与有决定性,这在英国法下不被认可。在 AT & T Corp v. Saudi Cable Co. (2000) 2 Lloyd's Rep. 127 先例中,Woolf 勋爵指出:"Turning to the express provision of the **ICC Rules** which provides that a decision of the ICC Court should be final, **I do not accept** the view of Longmore J that **the finality provision means that the English courts have no power to review the decision of the ICC Court. The finality provision does not operate to exclude the English court's jurisdiction under s. 23 of the 1950 Act.** Accordingly, Longmore J was entitled to consider whether there had been 'misconduct' by breaching the terms of the arbitration agreement. When doing so the court, if required to interpret the ICC Rules, would naturally pay the closest attention to

---

〔65〕 见英国 1996 年《仲裁法》之 section 24。另可见 Veritas Shipping Corp. v. Anglo Canadian Cement Ltd. (1966) 1 Lloyd's Rep. 76 等先例。

〔66〕 见英国 1996 年《仲裁法》之 section 68。

any interpretation of the ICC Rules adopted by the ICC Court, but the English courts retain their jurisdiction to determine whether the ICC Rules have been breached when entertaining an application to remove for alleged misconduct."(加黑部分是笔者的强调)

该先例适用的仍是英国1950年《仲裁法》,而到了英国1996年《仲裁法》,Section 24(法院将仲裁员赶走的权力)与Section 68(以严重不正常[serious irregularity]为由将裁决书撤销)更是在Schedule 1中被列明为强制性(mandatory)立法条文,不得以订约自由排除。

另一种对订约自由的限制是如果双方在仲裁协议中预先同意指定的某一类别的仲裁员或某一位仲裁员,但后来客观看来是有偏见或利益冲突,法院仍然可以干涉,将仲裁员赶走,不承认双方早前的约定。1950年英国《仲裁法》之Section 24(1)规定:"Where an agreement between any parties provides that disputes which may arise in the future between them shall be referred to an arbitrator named or designated in the agreement, and after a dispute has arisen any party applies, on the ground that the arbitrator so named or designated is not or may not be impartial, for leave to revoke the authority of the arbitrator or for an injunction to restrain any other party or the arbitrator from proceeding with the arbitration, **it shall not be a ground for refusing the application that the said party at the time when he made the agreement knew, or ought to have known, that the arbitrator**, by reason of his relation towards any other party to the agreement or of his connection with the subject referred, **might not be capable of impartiality**."(加黑部分是笔者的强调)

在加拿大的Charbonneau v. Les Indus. A. C. Davie Inc. ,(1989) R. J. Q. 1255 (Quebec S. Ct.)先例中,虽然在与农业部订立的合约中约定了农业部部长作为仲裁员,但这不被法院承认。类似的还有约定其中一方的雇员、股东、董事局成员等作为仲裁员不被承认的美国先例:Cross & Brown Co. N Nelson, 167 N. Y. S. 2d. 573 (N. Y. App. Div. 1957); Bill Graham v. Scissor - Tail, Inc. , 623 P. 2d 165 (Cal. S. Ct. 1990); Bennish v. North Carolina Dance Theater, 422 S. E. 2d 335 (N. C. App. 1992)等。

6.1.3　弃权与禁反言的说法可以适用在适合的情况

订约自由受到局限,而另一个法律的原则,即弃权与禁反言,是否受到保证自然公正的公共政策的影响看来是稍有不同。典型被认可的弃权之一是仲裁员已经披露了或双方都知道可能存在的偏见或利益冲突,但受到影响的一方没有反对,看来甚至明确选择接受并配合继续推进仲裁。但到败诉后又出尔反尔,试图在法院以仲裁员有偏见或利益冲突为由撤销裁决书,显然胜诉方会提出弃权与禁反言的争议。毕竟胜诉方因为依赖败诉方较早时看来是接受的言行,继续投入时间、精力与金钱推进仲裁,在裁决书做出后让败诉方有第二次机会推翻重来,是不公平与不合情理的(unconscionable)。可以说,胜诉方成功的机会也很大,因为这与另一个重要理由有一定程度上的冲突,即当事人不能采取"正面我赢,反面你输"(heads I win, tails you lose)

的策略并延迟诉讼的终局性。所以在普通法[67]或大陆法[68]都认为大部分仲裁员的利益冲突都可以被弃权。

至于当事人没有选择挑战仲裁员的原因有很多,可能是对有关的风险不以为意,或是不知道自己有权挑战仲裁员,或是以为自己已经提前弃权[69](但这不一定有效)。在 Weissfisch v. Julius (2006) EWCA 218 先例中,双方在订立仲裁条文时同意放弃挑战仲裁员的权利,说:"The parties expressly waive any rights they may have to challenge the appointment of the Arbitrator on any ground, including on the grounds that he:(a) endeavoured to help the relevant parties settle matters amicably, and/or (b) was engaged in the mediation of their disputes, and/or (c) has been legal advisor... over the course of many years to Amir Weissfisch, Rami Weissfisch and companies owned (or formerly owned) by Amir Weissfisch, Rami Weissfisch and the APW Trust..."

但即使是比较深思熟虑的明示弃权,也不保证将来情况不会发生逆转,或一方后悔与改变心意,以仲裁员有偏见或利益冲突为由要求赶走仲裁员或撤销裁决书。但显然会面对对方以弃权与禁反言对抗。

6.1.4 弃权与禁反言不能适用的情况

虽然上一段提到相当部分仲裁员的利益冲突都可以被弃权,但因为涉及自然公正的公共政策,必须要有底线。在 Gary Born 的《International Commercial Arbitration》(2009 年)一书第 1578 页就提到如果仲裁员受贿(bribery/corruption)或是实际上是为他自己的事情或争议做法官,当事人能否弃权就存在疑问:"... where an arbitrator is guilty of outright corruption or is effectively 'judge in his or her own cause', it is doubtful that objections to his or her independence may ordinarily be waived."

这一地位也反映在了《IBA Guidelines on Conflict of Interest in International Arbi-

---

[67] 见 Rustal Trading Ltd. v. Gill & Duffus SA (2000) 1 Lloyd's Rep. 14 (QB); ASM Shipping Ltd. of India v. TTMI Ltd. of England (2007) 1 Lloyd's Rep. 136 (CA)等先例。在 Ghirardosi v. Minister of Highways of British Columbia (1966) SCR 367 先例中,加拿大最高院判如果当事人在开始仲裁前就已经知道有关的情况但没有反对,之后就不能再要求撤销裁决书:"an award will not be set aside if the circumstances alleged to disqualify an arbitrator were known to both parties before the arbitration commenced and they proceeded without objection."另在加拿大的 Canadian Airline Pilots Assoc. v. Canadian Pacific Airlines, 57 DLR 2d 417 (BC Court of Appeal 1966)先例中,不列颠哥伦比亚省上诉庭也说如果原告在完全知道所有的情况的前提下接受了有偏见或利益冲突的仲裁员,就不能出尔反尔之后再反对:"plaintiffs had full knowledge of partiality which they accepted and cannot later object."

[68] 如瑞士的 Judgment of 9 February 1998, 16 ASA Bull. 634 (Swiss Federal Tribunal) (1997) 判决,联邦法院判当事人必须及时挑战仲裁员:"party must challenge arbitrator without undue delay."另是德国的 Judgment of 12 July 2005, 2006 Schieds VZ 55 (Hanseatisches Oberlandesgericht Hamburg)判决,法院也有类似的说法:"challenge was precluded as it had not been raised without undue delay, as required in Arbitration Rules of the German Maritime Arbitration Association."

[69] 关于提前弃权在本书第三章之 3.5.3 段有介绍。

tration》(简称“IBA 利益冲突指引”)。在《IBA 利益冲突指引》中,对千变万化的情况中的部分进行一定分类。将不会被认为是有偏见或利益冲突的情况归类是“绿色清单”(green list);可能被认为但需要依赖每一个案件的不同事实进行判断的归类为“橙色清单”(orange list);会被认为是有偏见或利益冲突的情况归类为“红色清单”(red list)。对于红色清单中的内容,则进一步分类为“可弃权的红色清单”(Waivable Red List)与“不可弃权的红色清单”(Non-waivable Red List)。

不可弃权的红色清单基本上就是两种。第一种是所谓的为他自己的事情做法官(judge in his or her own cause)。这里针对的是其中一方当事人与仲裁员身份的问题,如仲裁员是一方当事人的法律代表、雇员、经理或董事等。在 Veritas Shipping Corp. v. Anglo Canadian Cement Ltd. (1966) 1 Lloyd's Rep. 76 先例中,被告委任的仲裁员是公司的董事长。这样即使原告因为某些原因没有在较早前挑战仲裁员资格,也不会影响在做出裁决书后申请撤销。第二种是仲裁员与其中一方当事人或对裁决结果有重大经济利益(substantial finance interest)。这涉及更多的情况,如仲裁员是一方当事人的老板或主要股东,仲裁员收费与裁决结果挂钩等。在 Rand v. Readington, 13 N. H. 72 (N. H. Super. 1842)先例中,胜诉方欠仲裁员钱,并表示会将在裁决书下收到的金额还给仲裁员。毫无疑问,该裁决书最后被撤销。

但看来英国法律在不可弃权这方面的地位还不是十分明朗,在《Russell on Arbitration》(第 24 版,2015 年)之 7 - 133 段,说:“A further issue in relation to the loss of the right to object is whether there are any non - waivable grounds for challenging an arbitrator under English law. The traditional and current prevailing view is that there are no non - waivable grounds in English law[70], contradicting with the approach taken by the IBA Guidelines on Conflicts of Interest in International Arbitration which includes a 'non-waivable' red-list. The traditional view was challenged in Weissfisch v. Julius (2006) EWCA 218 where a party disputed the effectiveness of the waiver it had given in circumstances where the arbitrator had acted for both parties to the arbitration and in fact had advised them on the dispute which was submitted to arbitration. The point was not decided as part of the injunction application then before the Court of Appeal.”

在 Weissfisch v. Julius (2006) EWCA 218 先例中,有关的明示弃权已经在上一段节录。而明示弃权涉及的情况,如曾经做过调解员(mediator)或做出过法律意见,相对《IBA 利益冲突指引》不可弃权的红色清单中的情况严重程度是差得多。所以,即使上诉庭对有关争议做出了决定,也不是十分对口。

6.2 仲裁员的披露

在本书第三章之 3.4.1 段提到要构成弃权,弃权方必须知道(knowledge)有关的事实与他的权利。换句话说,当事人必须是在了解会导致仲裁员有偏见或利益冲突

---

〔70〕 见 Smith v. Kvaerner Cementation (2006) EWCA 242 先例。

的事实情况后,做出了不提出反对或异议的选择(election)。如果当事人在当时并不知道有关的事实,也就不会构成弃权。虽然有些会导致仲裁员可能有偏见或利益冲突的事实,当事人可以通过公共领域(public domain)的渠道知道,但当事人没有责任自己做出调查。再说大部分会导致仲裁员可能有偏见或利益冲突的事实只有他自己知道,也就需要他做出披露。当然仲裁员无须也无法对自己也不知道的事实进行披露,但如果仲裁员的披露不完整,即使当事人同意了对仲裁员的委任,也只是对已经披露出来的内容提出反对或异议的弃权。如果是后来才发觉的偏见或利益冲突,当事人仍然可以提出反对或异议,不存在弃权。如果仲裁员已经做出了恰当的披露,当事人又对仲裁员审理或继续审理案件没有提出反对或异议,该当事人就不能事后提出已经披露的事实会有导致偏见或利益中途的危险,这对另一方当事人不公平。

国际仲裁普遍接受仲裁员或将来可能被委任的仲裁员有披露的责任。如在《联合国示范法》之 article 12(1)规定:"when a person is approached in connection with his possible appointment as an arbitrator, he shall disclose any circumstances likely to give rise to justifiable doubts as to his impartiality or independence."这也表示依据《联合国示范法》立法的国家或地区,包括香港特区的《仲裁条例》,也要求仲裁员有披露的法定责任。

《IBA 利益冲突指引》之 General Standard (3)(a)说:"If facts or circumstances exist that may, in the eyes of the parties, give rise to doubts as to the arbitrator's impartiality or independence, the arbitrator shall disclose such facts or circumstances to the parties, the arbitration institution or other appointing authority (if any, and if so required by the applicable institutional rules) and the co-arbitrators, if any, prior to accepting his or her appointment or, if thereafter, as soon as he or she learns of them."

大部分仲裁机构的仲裁规则中也有同样的要求,如 ICC、伦敦仲裁院(LCIA)、香港国际仲裁中心(HKIAC)、新加坡国际仲裁中心(SIAC)等。因此,如果仲裁协议中规定由这些仲裁机构管理或合并了这些仲裁规则,仲裁员就有进行披露的合约责任。

但有趣的是在英国法(立法与普通法)下,仲裁员没有进行披露的责任。英国 1996 年《仲裁法》没有任何明示规定,草拟立法的 Saville 勋爵与他的团队认为,正式的披露责任是很繁重与很可能会导致延误组成仲裁庭。针对普通法地位,《Russell on Arbitration》(第 22 版,2003 年)之 4-036 段说:"early disclosure of prior interests that may give rise to impartiality is advisable but not expressly required by statute."

在最新版的《Russell on Arbitration》(第 24 版,2015 年)之 4-131 段说:"... A failure to disclose of itself does not give rise to the necessary justifiable doubts. The only obligation is to disclose matters which amount to apparent (or actual) bias, i.e. where there is a real possibility of bias. Whilst arbitrators may choose to make a wider disclosure out of an abundance of caution they are under no obligation to do so, let alone under an obligation the breach of which could entitle the aggrieved party to challenge them."

而紧密跟进英国法律地位(包括英国1996年《仲裁法》)的伦敦海事仲裁员规则中,仲裁员也同样没有披露的责任。

在英国普通法下,即使仲裁员有披露的合约责任但漏了披露,看来也不重要,重要的是有关事实是否客观来看会导致仲裁员有偏见或利益冲突。在AT & T Corp v. Saudi Cable Co. (2000) 2 Lloyd's Rep. 127先例中,案情涉及ICC仲裁。原告(AT & T)与被告(Saudi Cable)订立了一个价值高达46亿美元的合约。而原告在订立合约前最主要的竞争对手是名为Nortel的加拿大公司,双方为此合约也闹得不愉快。之后原告与被告产生争议并开始ICC仲裁,原告与被告各自委任了仲裁员,并同意由一名著名的加拿大律师担任首席仲裁员。他根据ICC规则做出了披露,但其中不包括他是Nortel的非执行董事,后来解释是他秘书无心之失。之后,仲裁庭做出两个原告败诉的判决,原告就想以仲裁员有偏见或利益冲突为由撤销裁决书。上诉庭判重点不是仲裁员是否做出披露,而是有关事实是否客观来看会导致仲裁员有偏见或利益冲突。如果不会,仲裁员没有披露不影响裁决书的有效性。在该先例中,上诉庭认为首席仲裁员是Nortel的非执行董事的事实不会导致他有偏见或利益冲突,确认仲裁庭的裁决书的有效性。

另在更近期的A v. B (2011) 2 Lloyd's Rep. 591先例中,案情涉及LCIA仲裁,双方同意一名御用大律师X作为独任仲裁员。A、B双方的代表律师事务所都曾经委任过X,其中B的代表律师事务所在一个与该仲裁完全无关的Y诉讼中委任了X作为代表大律师。Y诉讼一直处于"休眠"状态(双方当事人特别是原告没有推进,有可能双方在试图和解),直到该先例涉及的LCIA仲裁过程中,又"苏醒"并继续推进。B的代表律师事务所在Y诉讼与该仲裁中的律师团队没有重叠,而X直到做出裁决书前不久才警觉要向双方披露有关他在Y诉讼中被B的代表律师事务所委任。之后,X做出的裁决书中判B大部分胜诉。A败诉后上诉到法院,声称仲裁员延误披露可能导致他有偏见或利益冲突的事实有问题,要求撤销裁决书。但这不被法院接受,认为关键还是有关事实是否足以撤销裁决书,并认为根据该先例的事实是不足够:"In those circumstances, I do not consider that the failure by X to disclose until December 2010 his involvement as counsel in the Y litigation can give rise to a real possibility of apparent or... unconscious bias where there would otherwise be none. As the passage from the judgment of the Court of Appeal in Taylor v. Lawrence (2003) QB 528 quoted above demonstrates, the test as to when it is appropriate to disclose potential conflicts or other matters of embarrassment is lower than the test of apparent bias. In other words, it may be appropriate in a borderline case to disclose at an early stage, because, if there is an objection, then even if there is no apparent bias, the judge or arbitrator may still want to consider whether to withdraw."

英国看来是与一些其他国家或地区的法律地位不同,没有惩罚没有披露或没有完全披露的仲裁员的机制。而在一些其他国家或地区,没有披露本身就可以是挑战仲裁员的理由,即使没有披露的事实如果单独来看不足以将仲裁员赶走:如美国的 Forest Elec. Corp. v. HCB Contractors, 1995 WL 37586 (E. D. Pa. 1995)先例。另在《IBA 利益冲突指引》之 article 4(1)规定:“Failure to make such [a required] disclosure creates an appearance of bias, and may of itself be a ground for disqualification even though the non – disclosed facts or circumstances would not of themselves justify disqualification.”

6.2.1 持续地披露

由于仲裁程序的推进需要时间,短则半年、一年,长则几年。有可能在仲裁开始时,不存在可能导致仲裁员有偏见或利益冲突的事实,但在仲裁过程中途出现。这样,仲裁员就需要向双方当事人做出披露。这一持续披露的责任,在《联合国示范法》之 section 12(1)也有规定,如下:“an arbitrator, from the time of his appointment **and throughout the arbitral proceedings**, shall without delay disclose any such circumstances to the parties ...”(加黑部分是笔者的强调)

在《IBA 利益冲突指引》与主要的国际仲裁机构规则中都有类似的写法。

这种持续性披露会带来很多问题与麻烦。像笔者(杨良宜)这种独立仲裁员还好,因为不存在合伙人,可以自己控制,在仲裁期间尽量避免任何会带来利益冲突的事情。但一家大型国际律师事务所可能在全球很多国家都有分所,有几千个律师。其中一位合伙人在某两个跨国公司的争议中担任仲裁员,虽然在接受委任前会做出利益冲突调查,没有发现存在利益冲突。但他是很难保证在仲裁进行的过程中,他所在的律师事务所中任何一个分所的任何一位律师不会接这两个跨国公司任何一间分公司或关联公司的业务。如果发生了却不做出披露,即使这笔生意与该合伙人作为仲裁员审理的案件无关,也有是否存在利益冲突的争议,难保败诉方会试图撤销裁决书。而要国际律师事务所对这些生意都以利益冲突为由不接显然也不现实,只是合伙人之一的仲裁员也控制不了。而一旦做出披露,如果是在仲裁早期还好,双方还可能比较合作,同意对有关的利益冲突弃权。如果是在仲裁的中后期,仲裁结果相对明朗与更容易预测,感觉自己会败诉的一方会以此机会拖延程序或寻求转机,要将仲裁员赶走。这样不仅导致大量时间与金钱的浪费,也会导致仲裁员对在之前已经做了的工作的收费有问题。

为了避免被委任为仲裁员后可能产生的利益冲突的问题,很多是执业律师的仲裁员在接受委任时会要求争议双方“提前弃权”(advanced waiver)。关于提前弃权在本书第三章之 3.5.3 段有介绍,这里不再重复。

6.2.2 披露的程度

《联合国国际贸易法委员会仲裁规则》(2013 年版,简称《联合国仲裁规则》)之 article 11 对披露程度的要求与《联合国示范法》一致,都是很广泛:“When a person is approached in connection with his or her possible appointment as an arbitrator, he or she shall disclose any circumstances **likely to give rise to justifiable doubts** as to his or her impartiality or independence."(加黑部分是笔者的强调)

也就是说,只要有可能会导致偏见或利益冲突,仲裁员就要做出披露。而要赶走仲裁员,仅仅是"可能"并不足够,必须"确实存在"对仲裁员不持偏见与没有利益冲突的合理怀疑。《联合国仲裁规则》之 article 12(1)规定:"Any arbitrator may be challenged if circumstances exist that give rise to justifiable doubts as to the arbitrator's impartiality or independence."

两者之间的差距也不难理解,就像《IBA 利益冲突指引》橙色清单(orange list)中的情况,仲裁员要做出披露,但不一定要辞职,当事人也不一定能以此将仲裁员赶走,这要根据每个案件的不同事实而定。

广泛要求披露的程度不容易掌握,对很多资深的仲裁员都会带来很大的工作量与造成很大困扰。毕竟这些人士有多年的工作经验,与很多从业人士(无论是其他仲裁员、律师或是公司法务)都会打过交道,曾经或正在共事,有千丝万缕的联系。如果要求全部做出披露,就会涉及大量繁琐的工作。另是很多资深的仲裁员的记录也不会太完整,就算记录了当事人与律师事务所处理过的过往案件,也往往不会记录有哪些个别人士如律师参与,完整披露也做不到。所以很多仲裁员,如没有披露习惯的伦敦海事仲裁员的做法是尽量客观看待对有关的案件是否会有偏见或利益冲突,如果会,就不接受委任或辞职;如果不会,也无须做出披露。毕竟,英国没有披露的法律责任。在 ICC 仲裁中,如果做出了披露,而当事人反对,ICC 为了避免麻烦,就很有可能重新委任仲裁员。根据每年 ICC 公布的调查数据,这种情况确实存在。如果在委任时,当事人反对,ICC 重新委任仲裁员的比例高达 70%;而在已经委任了仲裁员后,当事人反对,ICC 将仲裁员赶走的比例只有 10%。

6.2.3 全面与完整披露

在本章之 6.2 段已经提到弃权必须是明确与清楚无误的,并且弃权时必须是对有关的事实有全面了解(full knowledge)。[71] Bingham 勋爵在 Millar v. Dickson (2002) 1 WLR 1615 先例中,针对这个所谓的"对司法权力的弃权"(judicial waiver)说:"In most litigious situations the expression 'waiver' is used to describe voluntary, informed and unequivocal election by a party not to raise a right or raise an objection which it is open to that party to claim or to raise. In the context of entitlement to a fair hearing by an independent and impartial tribunal, such is in my opinion the meaning to be given to the expression."

Hope 勋爵也说(并在之后被 Sumukan Ltd. v. Commonwealth Secretariat [2008] 1 Lloyd's Rep. 40 先例引用):"unless the person is in full possession of all the facts, an alleged waiver of the right to an independent and impartial tribunal must be rejected as

〔71〕 是否有全面了解依赖于每个案件的具体事实:见 Smith v. Kvaerner Cementation (2006) 3 All ER 593 等先例。

not being unequivocal."

在 Smith v. Kvaerner Cementation（2006）3 All ER 593 先例中，案情与仲裁员/法官没有完整与全面披露关系不大，而是涉及当事人的代表大律师没有告知当事人可以做出的选择与每个不同选择的后果。但这仍属于当事人在做出决定时对有关的事实没有全面了解，所以无法构成弃权。

在该先例中，在一个汽车事故造成的人身伤害案件中，特委法官（recorder）与双方当事人大律师均为同一间大律师事务所（barrister chambers）的成员，而特委法官是该事务所的主任。在开庭前，特委法官披露说自己曾经代表与被告属于同一集团的其他公司，并且还有正在进行的诉讼。原告大律师向原告建议说，即使是由该特委法官进行审理，也会是完全公平的审理。而且一旦提出反对或异议，很可能造成不必要的延误，再加上由原告大律师熟悉的法官进行审理也有不少间接好处，因此，原告大律师强烈建议不提出反对或异议。原告也接受了这个建议。

直到开庭结束，原告才意识到由该特委法官进行审理的不妥。而特委法官最后是判原告未能证明司机是得到被告（汽车的车主）同意的情况下驾驶车辆造成事故，也因此未能成功向被告索赔。原告就认为自己是被陷害了，想以特委法官有偏见为由撤销判决。但这就涉及原告没有及时反对或提出异议是否构成"弃权"（waiver）的争议。

上诉庭的 Phillips 勋爵看来是对大律师给予作为原告的客户强烈建议不要对特委法官提出反对或异议持批判态度。要构成有效的弃权，当事人必须了解所有的有关事实、自己可以做出的选择与每个选择的后果，并有公平的机会自由选择。在该先例中，虽然特委法官已经将可能导致偏见的事实告知原告，但除此之外，也应当在一开始就告诉原告他有哪些选择，并在之后确认原告心甘情愿让自己审理案件。另一方面，如果根据事实情况确实可能有偏见，原告大律师应当将所有可能的后果向客户做出解释，包括一旦开庭延期会造成的影响，法官需要发司法誓言（judicial oath）以及受过训练要客观地看待案件等事实。但原告大律师不应向客户阐述自己对于特定法官的个人看法。更重要的是，是否选择提出异议是客户的选择。因此，由于该先例中的大律师反复敦促、鼓励客户选择放弃异议，客户继续仍由该特委法官审理案件的选择被认定为并不是自由地做出的决定。而且客户在做出该决定时，也并没有获悉所有的有关信息。原告并不知道如果他坚持反对要换另一位法官，他的案件多快可以获得审理。因此，原告的行为并没有构成弃权，仍然可以就该特委法官的潜在偏见的指控提出异议。

该先例的判法非常有争议性，在 Charles Hollander QC 与 Simon Salzedo 的《Conflict of Interest》（第 3 版，2008 年）一书之 10－013 段就批评说："But to say that the waiver was not made freely on the basis of counsel's advice is perhaps a surprising conclusion. After all, inexperienced litigants nervous about appearing in court often will need to be guided by counsel's professional view and, it is suggested, would sometimes benefit from counsel giving the client a steer... And whilst it would have been much better for the judge to have made enquiries as to possible alternative arrangements and how long it would take before the case could be tried before another judge,... often that cannot be ascertained with any certainty at short notice. **It is also perhaps surprising that the failure of the recorder to make these enquiries and explain the position in this regard was treated as preventing the waiver being made on full facts.**"（加黑部分是笔者的强调）

6.2.4 披露的优点与缺点

披露的缺点可从两方面看。对当事人来说，一旦仲裁员做出了披露，他就要面临是否提出反对、异议的选择。当事人当然有权确保自己能够得到符合自然公正的公平审判，但轻重不容易掌握。当事人作为非法律专业人士有时会过于紧张，对一些小事也反应过度，做出无谓的挑战。而如果挑战仲裁员不成功，当事人就会担心自己得罪了仲裁员。因此，为了避免仲裁员因为被挑战而对当事人产生偏见，美国仲裁协会（AAA）不会对仲裁员做出他被挑战的通知（也禁止当事人通知仲裁员），如果AAA认为仲裁员有偏见或利益冲突，就会简单将仲裁员赶走。但这样，仲裁员就没有机会对有关的挑战向AAA与当事人做出解释。Gary Born 的《International Commercial Arbitration》（2009年）一书第1555页也说，AAA的做法并不令人满意。在笔者（杨良宜）看来，仲裁员有机会对有关的挑战做出解释很重要。近期笔者有一份裁决书被部分撤销，就是败诉方抓住长达150页的裁决书中的一段说仲裁庭超出了管辖权。因为当时新的香港《仲裁条例》还没有生效，败诉方没有通知仲裁庭，笔者直到看到裁决书被部分撤销的判决才知道有关情况。而法院对整个仲裁程序不了解，只听败诉方的一面之词（尤其是上诉时胜诉方的代表大律师并非仲裁时的代表大律师）。如果笔者作为其中一员的仲裁庭[72]有机会向法院做出全面解释，很有可能法院会做出不同判决。

而从仲裁员的角度来看，本章之6.2.3段已经提到披露的程度不容易掌握，要多花很多时间与金钱。并且仲裁员如果是在被委任前进行披露，而最后又因为当事人的反对而没有获得委任，为了披露所花费的时间与金钱都无法收取费用，造成很大的浪费。而如果是在仲裁过程中被挑战，虽然仲裁机构一般不会要求仲裁员做进一步的披露或是要做出书面或口头的证人证言（不会是类似诉讼的程序）。但如果当事人要求披露，仲裁员是否应该配合？很多仲裁员为了避免麻烦，很可能选择不接受委任或辞职，而这对提出挑战的当事人也不一定是好事。

笔者（杨良宜）就曾经遇到在被委任为首席仲裁员前向当事人披露在过去的三

---

〔72〕 其他两位仲裁庭成员是大律师，在有关的 China Property Development (Holdings) Ltd. v. Mandecly Ltd. & Ors, CACV 92 and 93/2015 先例中，香港法院很奇怪地把它认为犯错的三位仲裁员名字公布。

年内,曾经三次在外方当事人的不同案件中担任仲裁员。结果另一方中方当事人就很紧张,要求笔者解释仲裁涉及的争议与仲裁结果。因为仲裁的机密性,笔者只能说其中一个仲裁还没有结果而另两个双方和解。但中方当事人仍不放心,继续追问笔者其他无法作答的信息。有关的通讯往来有厚厚的两个案卷,最后笔者实在觉得麻烦,放弃了担任这个仲裁的首席仲裁员。外方当事人是国际著名的贸易公司,每年都有很多仲裁、法院诉讼的案件,在过去三年曾经三次在一些金额不大的海事案件中作为仲裁员不算什么。后来笔者听说是委任了一位美国仲裁员替代,而最后中方当事人惨败。虽然笔者作为仲裁员不会偏袒任何一方,也难保不会判中方败诉,但仲裁庭中有一个对中方文化背景有了解的首席仲裁员,对中方当事人显然会是好事。

但披露的好处也很明显,否则国际仲裁也不会普遍接受仲裁员有披露的责任。虽然仲裁员的责任变大,要多花时间、精力与金钱做出调查与披露,但这相比事前不披露,之后被一方查出来要赶走仲裁员甚至被败诉方申请撤销裁决书而浪费的费用是"小巫见大巫"。另是通过披露会令双方当事人对在仲裁庭面前推进程序更安心。正如 Davidson v. Scottish Ministers (2004) UKHL 34 先例所说:"a proper disclosure at the beginning is in itself a badge of impartiality."

6.3　及时提出反对、异议

未能及时提出反对或异议[73]在 1996 年英国《仲裁法》之 Section 73(1)下可以构成弃权行为。这重要的立法条文将在本章之 7.3 段详细介绍,在此只先节录该立法条文如下:"**Loss of right to object.** (1) If a party to arbitral proceedings takes part, or continues to take part, in the proceedings without making, either forthwith or within such time as is allowed by the arbitration agreement or the tribunal or by any provision of this Part, any objection—(a) that the tribunal lacks substantive jurisdiction, (b) that the proceedings have been improperly conducted, (c) that there has been a failure to comply with the arbitration agreement or with any provision of this Part, or (d) that there has been any other irregularity affecting the tribunal or the proceedings, he may not raise that objection later, before the tribunal or the court, unless he shows that, at the time he took part or continued to take part in the proceedings, he did not know and could not with reasonable diligence have discovered the grounds for the objection."

根据 1996 年英国《仲裁法》之 Section 73(1),如果当事人知道或通过尽职调查可以知道提出反对或异议的事实基础,但又继续参与仲裁程序,该当事人就会丧失提出抗议的权利。又如在本章之 4.2 段提到的《联合国示范法》之 article 13/香港《仲裁条例》之 section 26 规定对于仲裁员的不偏私与独立性有足够理由质疑的应当在

---

〔73〕 除了本段针对的仲裁员不持偏见与没有利益冲突,还包括约定的仲裁条文没有得到履行(如是本章之 4.2 段针对的委任的仲裁员不符合合约规定的资格),本章第 5 段针对的管辖权异议,或本章第 7 段针对的严重不正常(serious irregularities)的异议。

仲裁庭成立后或知道有关情况后 15 天内提出(within 15 days after becoming aware of the constitution of the arbitral tribunal or after becoming aware of any circumstance [give rise to justifiable doubts as to his impartiality or independence])。

在英国 Thyssen Canada Ltd. v. Mariana Maritime SA (2005) 1 Lloyd's Rep. 640 先例中,Cooke 大法官说:"The effect of section 73 is that an objection to a serious irregularity may not be raised by a party after participating in the proceedings without taking the objection, unless that party can show that at the time of participation the grounds for the objection were not known to him and he could not with reasonable diligence have discovered them.[74] The approach to this section appears from the decision of Moore – Bick J in Rustal v. Gill & Duffus [2000] 1 LLR 14 page 20 – 21. If the respondent can show that the applicant took part in or continued to take part in the arbitration proceedings without objection, after the grounds of objection arose, the burden passes to the applicant to show that he did not know and could not with reasonable diligence have discovered those grounds at the time.[75] Moreover, the expression 'continues to take part in the proceedings' in section 73 is broadly worded and is designed to ensure that a party who believes he has grounds for objecting on the basis of serious irregularity should raise that objection as soon as he is, or reasonably ought to be, aware of it.[76] He is not permitted to allow the proceedings to continue without alerting the Tribunal and the other party to a serious irregularity, which, in his view, renders the whole arbitral process invalid.[77] As Moore-Bick J points out, this is not only to avoid a waste of time and expense but is based upon a more fundamental point of fairness and justice. It cannot be right for a party to participate in proceedings, which he believes to be fundamentally irregular, with the intention of taking advantage of any decision in his favour, whilst keeping up his sleeve an objection to an irregularity, which he will only produce in the event of an unfavourable decision.[78]"

在美国 AAOT Foreign Economic Association (VO) Technostroyexport v. Interna-

---

[74] Sumukan Ltd. v. Commonwealth Secretariat (2007) EWHC 188 (Comm)先例就涉及这样的情况。

[75] 如果对方可以证明反对或提出异议的一方在有关的事实出现后,仍参与或继续参与仲裁程序,反对或提出异议的一方就有证明他当时不知道也无法通过尽职调查知道有关的事实的举证责任。

[76] 另是 section 73 用的"继续参与程序"是很广泛的说法,目的就是为了确保当事人在发现令他有理由反对或提出异议的有关事实时,尽快反对或提出异议。

[77] 他不能一边继续参与程序而不向仲裁庭与对方当事人提出他认为存在可令仲裁裁决书无效的严重不正常的情况。

[78] 正如 Moore – Bick 大法官指出,这不仅可以避免浪费时间与金钱,而且涉及基本的公平公正的原则。一方当事人不能在出现他认为严重不正常的情况后,如果裁决结果对他有利,他就当什么都没发生过。如果裁决结果对他不利,他就以严重不正常为由,申请撤销裁决。

tional Dec and Trade Sers Inc. 139 F 3d 980（2nd Cir 1999）先例中判："Where a party has knowledge of facts possibly indicating bias or partiality on the part of an arbitrator he cannot remain silent and later object to the award of the arbitrators on that ground. His silence constitutes a waiver of the objection."

澳大利亚高院在 Vakauta v. Kelly（1989）HCA 44 先例中，Toohey 大法官判（这也在之后的 Johnson v. Johnson［2000］HCA 48 先例中被认可与引用）："There is no reason why, in authority or in principle, a litigant who is fully aware of the circumstances from which ostensible bias might be inferred, should not be capable of waiving the right later to object to the judge continuing to hear and dispose of the case."

总结而言，根据近期的先例来看，英国法律下的地位是如果当事人一早知道提出反对或异议的事实基础的存在，但直到裁决书做出后才提出，就很有可能无法依赖了：见 Rustal v. Gill & Duffus（2000）1 Lloyd's Rep. 14；ASM Shipping Ltd. of India v. TTMI Ltd. of England（2005）EWHC 2238（Comm）；Sinclair v. Woods of Winchester Ltd.（2005）EWHC 1631（QB）等先例。

这带来一个问题，就是想提出反对或异议的当事人可否通过泛泛的保留权利（reserve rights），而不在时限内提出正式的反对或异议？

曾经 The "Oranie" and The "Tunisie"（1966）1 Lloyd's Rep. 477 先例中判如果参与程序但做出特定的保留权利声明，而这又被接受的话，并不会构成弃权。但该先例是在 1996 年《仲裁法》生效前，在当时的年代适用的是 1950 年《仲裁法》，其中没有类似 1996 年立法的 Section 73，而且对仲裁的理念与支持也很不一样。

但是在 ASM Shipping Limited v. Bruce Harris & Ors 先例中，船东的律师事务所（Zaiwalla & Co）根据英国《仲裁法》之 Section 24 申请撤销两位仲裁员（Bruce Harris 先生与已经过世的 A. G. Scott 先生），但由于申请的延误造成弃权从而未能成功。而船东律师则提出在之前有过对反对或异议权利的保留，对此 Andrew Smith 大法官说："The first question is when, for the purposes of section 73, the owners made their objection to Mr. Harris and Mr. Scott continuing as arbitrators. Mr. Zaiwalla submitted that at the hearing on 18 November 2005 the owners, as he put it, 'put down a marker' as to their position. Mr. Beloff（船东的代表大律师）certainly warned that the owners might in the future object to the two arbitrators continuing with the reference, but I do not consider that he went further than that. It is not sufficient for the purpose of section 73 that a party indicates that an objection might be made. He must make his objection. Similarly, in my judgment it did not suffice for Zaiwalla & Co. to write on 24 November 2005 that they believed that 'the Arbitrators would consider it wise to... step down'. An objection under section 73 must be stated in properly specific terms..."

看来，立法明示必须（shall）在一个时限内，即参与了涉及实质争议的程序（taken a step in the proceedings）前提出反对或异议，一旦过了这个时限，也就没有可保留的权利了。

7. 涉及仲裁程序不正常的弃权与禁反言

1996年英国《仲裁法》之Section 33(1)(a)体现了《联合国示范法》之Article 18的精神,要求仲裁员有公平、不偏私与避免程序不正常的责任。这责任也是自然公正(natural justice)的第二方面要求。这与本章第6段针对的自然公正的第一个方面的关系是,即使仲裁员不持偏见与没有利益冲突,但仍可能由于不懂、经验不足等多种原因导致他处理的仲裁程序严重不正常(serious irregularity)。

如果有合理理由怀疑存在程序严重不正常的情况,在1996年英国《仲裁法》之Section 24(1)下就可以向法院申请赶走仲裁员,如果已经做出裁决书,则在1996年英国《仲裁法》之Section 68下可以向法院对裁决书的效力提出挑战,并申请把裁决书撤销。

7.1 中间程序命令不受法院制约

仲裁[尤其是临时仲裁(ad hoc arbitration)]与法院不同,本身就没有特定的中间程序。即使是机构仲裁,如是ICC仲裁,虽然对部分中间程序有明示要求,如要有审理范围书(Terms of Reference)、案件管理会议(Case Management Meeting)与程序时间表(Procedural Timetable),但对其他大部分中间程序都没有针对。对于这些没有规定的中间程序应该怎样进行,只要能够保证满足自然公正的要求,完全可以由仲裁庭自行决定,因此有一个出名的说法是"arbitrator is the master of procedure"。法院不会干涉仲裁的中间程序命令(interlocutory rulings),除非程序有严重不正常(serious irregularity)会影响自然公正。

在Fletamentos v. Effjohn (1997) 2 Lloyd's Rep. 302先例中,一审的Morison大法官判中间程序命令也受到法院权力制约:"it could not be the policy of the law to require a party to an arbitration who could justly complain about procedural unfairness, which fell short of misconduct, to continue to invest in the arbitral process and then to challenge the award when he could have had the unfairness put right before the substantive hearing' s. 22(1) of the 1950 Act was apt to interlocutory rulings;..."

Morison大法官认为根据1950年英国《仲裁法》之Section 22(i),自已有审核并在必要时将仲裁员的中间程序命令发回重审的权利。而且Morison大法官倾向于只有在做出裁决书的阶段,法院才有审核这些中间程序公平与否的权力。

但是这判决之后被推翻,Waller大法官指出Morison大法官的看法是错误的,法院从来都没有审核中间程序命令的权力(以裁决书形式做出的命令除外)。过往先例中建立的地位是,法院并没有一般或泛泛地监督仲裁程序、审核中间程序命令的权力,Section 22下的权力仅限于对裁决书的救济。Waller大法官说:"... the Judge seemed to take the view that he had the power to review, and, if necessary, remit the interlocutory ruling to the arbitrators if there had been some form of the procedural mishap. He thought that he had that power under s. 22(1) of the 1950 Act. He may have been tempted into that view... that it was only at an award stage that the Court would have the power to review the fairness of any interlocutory directions not in the form of an award... I am bound to say that I do not believe that the Judge's view as being right. I have always understood the position to be that there are no circumstances which could give rise to a power to review an interlocutory direction not made in the form of an award. Basically the position is, as I understand the authorities, that **the Court has never had some general power to supervise arbitration and review interlocutory decisions... the power to review and remit under s. 22 applies to awards...**"(加黑部分是笔者的强调)

7.2　严重不正常的中间程序的例子

有关严重不正常的中间程序有很多不同的例子,这在笔者《仲裁法——从1996年英国仲裁法到国际商务仲裁》一书第九章有针对,这里不再重复。只简单将一些经常产生争议的情况归类,至于是否属于严重不正常并能成功申请救济,要根据每个先例的不同情况。

1. 仲裁员的误解:见 Peter Cassidy Seed Co. v. Osuustukkukauppa IL (1954) 2 Lloyd's Rep. 586;The "Yperagia" (1977) 1 Lloyd's Rep. 29;The "Aros" (1978) 1 Lloyd's Rep. 456;Jayaar Impex Ltd. v. Toaken Group Ltd. (1996) 2 Lloyd's Rep. 437;The "Linardos" (1994) 1 Lloyd's Rep. 28;Schenker Eurocargo AG v. Transtetno Matliyat Licati Ve Sanayi As (January 1998, unreported);Ledwood Construction v. Kier Construction (1996) 68 Con. L. R. 96;Petroleos de Portugal v. BP Oil International Ltd. (1999) 1 Lloyd's Rep. 854 等先例。

2. 当事人未能有完全的机会提交证据或做出争辩:见 The "Aristides Xilas" (1975) 2 Lloyd's Rep. 402;The "Ciechocinek" (1977) 2 Lloyd's Rep. 134;Shield Properties & Investments v. Anglo – Overseas Transport Co. (No. 1) (1985) 273 E. G. 69;Compagnie National Algerienne de Navigation v. Hecate Shipping Co. (1985) 2 Lloyd's Rep. 588;Control Securities Plc. v. Spencer (1989) 1 EGLR 136;Indian Oil Corp v. Coastal (1990) 2 Lloyd's Rep. 407;Breakbulk Marine v. Dateline(1992, unreported);Krohn & Co. (Import – Export) GmbH & Co. KG v. PT Tulung Agung Indah (1992) 1 Lloyd's Rep. 377;Estates Governors of Alleyn's College v. Williams (1994) EGLR 127;Naporano Iron & Metal Co. v. Sivas Iron & Steelworks Inc. (1997) 2 Lloyd's Rep. 359 等先例。

3. 仲裁庭(或一方当事人)不应在没有通知并让双方(对方)有合理机会争辩的情况下,提出或依赖新的观点,导致裁决书令双方(或对方)当事人感到意外:见 The "Vimeira" (No. 1) (1984) 2 Lloyd's Rep. 66 (CA); Gbangbola v. Smith & Sherriff

Ltd（1998）3 All ER 730（TCC）; The“Pamphilos”（2002）2 Lloyd's Rep. 681; Warborough Investments v. Robinson（2003）EWCA Civ 751; Westland Helicopters Ltd. v. Al – Hejailan（2004）2 Lloyd's Rep. 523; Cameroon Airlines v. Transnet Ltd.（2004）EWHC 1829（Comm）; Vee Networks Ltd. v. Econet Wireless International Ltd.（2005）1 Lloyd's Rep. 192; ABB AG v. Hochtief Airport GmbH（2006）2 Lloyd's Rep. 1; London Underground Ltd. v. Citylink Telecommunications Ltd.（2007）EWHC 1749（TCC）; The“Magdalena Oldendorff”（2008）1 Lloyd's Rep. 7; Terna Bahrain Holding Co. WLL v. Al Shamsi（2013）1 Lloyd's Rep. 86; Ameropa SA v. Lithuanian Shipping Co. of Lithuania（2015）EWHC 3847（Comm）等先例。

4. 仲裁员在任何一方不在场的情况下与证人（事实证人或专家证人）交谈或听取证据：Hussmann（Europe）Ltd. v. Al Ameen Development & Trade Co.（2000）2 Lloyd's Rep. 83; Norbrook Laboratories Ltd. v. A Tank & Moulson Chemplant Ltd.（2006）2 Lloyd's Rep. 485 等先例。

5. 未能更正已由当事人指出的错误：见 Danae Air Transport SA v. Air Canada（1999）2 Lloyd's Rep. 547 先例。

6. 拒绝做出文件披露命令：见 Bromley Park Garden Estates Ltd. v. Mallen（2009）EWHC 609（Ch）先例。

7. 未能在裁决书中考虑、处理与针对当事人提出的所有重要争议/争端：见 Metropolitan Property Realizations Ltd. v. Atmore Investments Ltd.（2008）EWHC 2925（Ch）; Soeximex SAS v. Agrocorp International Pte Ltd.（2012）1 Lloyd's Rep. 52；香港的 A v. B（2015）HKCFI 1077[79]等先例。

8. 仲裁员对没有提交的争议/争端做出决定：见 A K Kablo Imalat San ve Tic AS v. Intamex SA（2011）EWHC 2970（Comm）先例。

9. 依赖受到"特免权"（privilege）保护的文件：见 Double K Oil Products 1996 Ltd. v. Neste Oil Oyj（2010）1 Lloyd's Rep. 141 先例。

10. 仲裁员没有提醒一方当事人他可能漏提某个争辩：The“Magdalena Oldendorff”; The“Amplify”（2012）1 Lloyd's Rep. 206; Terna Bahrain Holding Company Wll v. Al Shamsi 等先例。

11. 仲裁员在没有预先通知双方并获得双方同意的情况下，匆匆根据文件做出裁决书：Pacol Ltd. v. Joint Stock Co. Rossakhar（2000）1 Lloyd's Rep. 109; BTC Bulk Transport Corp v. Glencore International International AG（2006）EWHC 1957（Comm）等先例。

12. 仲裁员没有给当事人盘问对方证人的机会：见 Compania Sud Americana de Vapores SA v. Nippon Yusen Kaisha（2010）1 Lloyd's Rep. 436 先例。

---

[79] 在该香港先例中，有关裁决书没有针对时效的争议，如果有针对，判法会不一样。

13. 其他。

7.3　及时提出反对

7.3.1　普通法弃权与英国 1996 年《仲裁法》之 Section 73(1)的区别

如果一方当事人没有根据英国 1996 年《仲裁法》之 Section 73(1)及时提出反对或异议,常常会被称为对提出反对或异议的弃权,但这与普通法弃权不同。可先节录 Section 73(1),如下:"If a party to arbitral proceedings **take part**, **or continues to take part**, in the proceedings without making, either **forthwith** or within such time as is allowed by the arbitration agreement or the tribunal or by any provision of this Part, any object -...(b) that the proceedings have been improperly conducted...(d) that there has been any other irregularities affecting the tribunal or the proceedings. He may not **raise that objection** later, before the tribunal or the court, **unless** he shows that at the time, he took part or continued to take part in the proceedings, he **did not know and could not with reasonable diligence have discovered** the grounds for the objection."(加黑部分是笔者的强调)

在普通法弃权,弃权方必须在完全知道自己的权利后做出清楚无误的言行。[80] 在 Locabail (UK) Ltd. v. Bayfield Properties Ltd. (2000) QB 451 先例中,上诉庭说:"It is however clear that any waiver must be **clear and unequivocal**, and made with **full knowledge** of all the facts relevant to the decision whether to waive or not."(加黑部分是笔者的强调)

而在 Section 73(1)立法条文下的"弃权"实际上比《联合国示范法》之 Article 4 [要求的是不得过度延误(undue delay)]以及普通法下的地位更广泛。一方面该立法下,反对方不需要完全知道自己的权利,而只需要在尽职调查下可以知道。在权威的《London Maritime Arbitration》(第 4 版,2017 年)一书之 11.49 段,说:"Section 73 is a far-ranging provision **which goes further than the common law doctrine of waiver and estoppel** which were used under the previous law to prevent injustice in such circumstances. Under section 73 (unlike the common law doctrine of waiver) **a party may lose the right to object even where he lacks knowledge of the grounds of objection** unless he can show that he could not have discovered those matters with reasonable diligence. The burden is upon the objection party seeking to object to establish that he was not aware of the ground of objection, and could not have discovered those it with reasonable diligence."(加黑部分是笔者的强调)

另 Merkin 与 Flannery 的《Arbitration Act 1996》(第 5 版,2014 年)一书之 20.50 段所说,Section 73(1)不再要求反对方清楚无误的行为:"In a number of cases decided before the passing of the 1996 Act, the existence or otherwise of waiver rested upon the

---

〔80〕 见本书第三章第 3.4.1 段。

question of whether the applicant had acted in a fashion which unequivocally indicated his intention not to raise any objection to the breach. **The need for unequivocal conduct has been removed by the 1996 Act**."(加黑部分是笔者的强调)

普通法弃权已经十分危险,更不用说更为广泛的 Section 73(1)下的"弃权"。加上立法超越普通法地位,因此有理由与权利提出反对或异议的一方必须小心,严格依照立法条文行事。在本章接下来的段节,将会介绍其中的若干主要要求。

7.3.2 什么属于知道或可以合理发现?

英国 1996 年《仲裁法》之 Section 73(1)最后一部分是一个但书(proviso),即除非(unless)当事人并不知道或者是尽职调查之下也无法发现(did not know and could not with reasonable diligence have discovered)有关反对的事实,否则就会构成对提出反对的"弃权"。当事人想要之后在法院提出反对并依赖这个但书,必须做出宣誓(affidavit),并提供相关证据证明他在继续参与仲裁程序时并不知道或者是尽职调查之下也无法发现:JSC Zestafoni v. Ronly Holdings Ltd. (2004) 2 Lloyd's Rep. 335 先例。[81]

《Russell on Arbitration》(第 24 版,2015 年)一书之 7 - 132 段针对"知道"的程度,说:"To be caught under this section [s. 73] the applicant must have had knowledge of the essential facts constituting the irregularity or had grounds to believe that there was an irregularity.[82] The section does not therefore operate to catch a party who in a general sense had vague grounds to believe that some irregularity may have occurred, unless the circumstances were such as to put that party on a duty of further enquiry..."

在实践中,如果程序严重不正常是发生在裁决书中(如没有针对所有重要争议/争端),败诉方在收到裁决书后提出反对并要求撤销裁决书,应该没有问题。但如果是在仲裁庭做出裁决书前的中间程序曾发生严重不正常的事件,很难说反对方在当时不知道或者是尽职调查下也无法发现。这样,反对方在裁决书之后再以程序严重不正常为由要求撤销裁决书,就会面对在 Section 73(1)下"弃权"的抗辩。

当然,归根究竟还是要依赖于每个案件中的具体事实进行判断。在 Nestor Maritime SA v. Sea Anchor Shipping Co. Ltd. (2012) 2 Lloyd's Rep. 144 先例中,油轮的买方指称卖方有"误述"(misrepresentation)行为,并在仲裁中胜诉。具体的争议有关重要结构部分钢铁厚度的测量问题,关键性的证据是一份买方在事后于 2007 年 9 月获得的检验报告。相比于卖方在 2005 年获得的、也是在油轮买卖中被买方依赖的检验报告,2007 年的检验报告对买方有利的多。而最后是仲裁庭更接受这份 2007 年的检验报告,据此推断卖方提供的 2005 年检验报告不可能正确,因此对买方有误述并判买方胜诉。

---

〔81〕 虽然该先例是针对管辖权而不是程序严重不正常。

〔82〕 见 Sumukan Ltd. v. Commonwealth Secretariat (2007) EWHC 188 (Comm)先例。

卖方之后根据 1996 年英国《仲裁法》之 Section 68 与 Section 69 向法院要求救济，以裁决书的做出涉及欺诈为由申请撤销。卖方也提供了大量证据说明 2007 年的检验报告的有关数字并非真实，以证明买方以虚假证据取得胜诉的裁决书。Eder 大法官针对此欺诈的申请判买方胜诉，理由是卖方存在弃权行为。Eder 大法官说即使确实存在对 2007 年检验报告这份关键性证据的欺诈行为，如果在仲裁程序中卖方尽职调查的话，完全应该是在仲裁程序中就对这份报告的内容产生怀疑与发现有关情况的。Eder 大法官说："In my view, Mr Hill QC(买方代表大律师) is right for the reasons he gives that if there had been the fraud which is now alleged, it could have been discovered with reasonable diligence; that contrary to the sellers' submissions, there were here 'grounds to suspect' that the measurements were fabricated; and that, at the very least, the sellers have not satisfied the burden on them under section 73 to show that the alleged fraud could not with reasonable diligence had been discovered..."

7.3.3 怎样属于及时?

前述节录条文中加黑的"即刻"(forthwith)的字样是被解释为迅速行事(acting promptly)或是没有不必要延误(without necessary delay)，这需要根据每个具体案件的情况进行具体讨论：见 Wicketts & Sterndale v. Brine Builders (2011 unreported) 先例。

在 Margulead Ltd. v. Exide Technologies (2004) EWHC 1019 (Comm) 先例中，Colman 大法官说是在这个语境下，"即刻"意味着合理可能的尽快，显然这就包括尽快咨询与取得法律意见(如果需要)，反正是要根据每个案件不同的事实考虑合理与否。Colman 大法官说："In this context 'forthwith' means as soon as reasonably possible. That clearly involves raising an objection immediately following the arbitrator's procedural ruling. In a case where there is knowledge or reasonable means of knowledge of the grounds for objection, the point must be raised at the hearing. To wait until after publication of the award or indeed until after continuing to participate in the hearing as in this case will be fatal to the right to mount a Section 68 application."

因此在当事人知道或应当知道应该提出反对或异议的事实存在时，无论是在仲裁程序的哪个步骤包括是在开庭审理期间，都应当提出反对，否则就有了提出反对或异议的权利被"弃权"的风险。这在本段提到的很多先例都有明确，如在 O'Donoghue v. Enterprise Inns Plc. (2008) EWHC B15 (Ch) 先例中，仲裁庭于 2008 年 1 月 8 日以意义不大且与产生的费用不成比例为理由，做出不开庭审理的决定，即让仲裁庭以递交的文件审理。原告作为仲裁的当事人没有提出反对，之后虽然也没有采取积极的进一步参与程序的行为(也没有必要，只需要等待裁决书被做出)，但是做出了裁决书发觉败诉之后才提出了反对或异议。该先例中就判即使原告的这些反对是确有理由的，也因为 1996 年英国《仲裁法》之 Section 73(1) 而无法在法院获得救济。至于香港特区先例可见 Gao Haiyan v. Keeneye Holdings Ltd. (2012) 1 HKLRD 627 先例中，一审的 Reyes 大法官判："A party to an arbitration who wishes to rely on non – compliance with the rules governing an arbitration shall do so promptly and shall not proceed with the arbitration as if there has been compliance with a relevant rule, keeping the point of non – compliance up one's sleeve for later use."

该先例被上诉到上诉庭，上诉庭虽然在其他方面否定了一审的判法，但是支持了上一段节录内容中的看法，上诉庭依赖 Locabail（UK）Ltd. v. Bayfield Properties Ltd.（2000）QB 451 的判法说："it is not open to a litigant to wait and see how his claims turn out before pursuing his complaint of bias."

7.3.4 怎样才算反对？

怎样的反对才能令当事人不会失去在 Section 73(1)下提出反对或异议的权利？马上向法院申请赶走仲裁员或撤销裁决书显然是明确地提出反对或异议办法，这也是当事人在看到裁决书后才发现有关的严重不正常（如仲裁员没有针对所有争议）时唯一的反对办法。

但如果是发生在裁决书做出之前的中间程序，当事人就会有很多种提出反对或异议的办法，从最轻微的在通讯往来中向对方与/或仲裁员表示抗议，到最强烈的根据英国 1996 年《仲裁法》之 Section 24 在法院申请将仲裁员赶走。怎样才属于 Section 73 下足够的反对？

相比直接向法院申请赶走仲裁员，先向仲裁庭提出反对一般是更好的选择。仲裁庭可能可以自己解决有关的问题，如被挑战的仲裁员提出辞职。

但在 Section 73(1)下，只是在通讯往来中泛泛地提出反对或异议不足够。反对方必须清楚无误地提醒对方与仲裁庭，他认为有关的事实令他有理由向法院提出反对。因此在 Rustal Trading Ltd. v. Gill & Duffus SA（2000）1 Lloyd's Rep. 14（Comm）先例中，反对方在给仲裁庭的信件中提出对仲裁员能否公平公正地做出裁决有疑问是不足够。

在 ASM Shipping Ltd. v. Harris & Ors（2008）1 Lloyd's Rep. 61 先例中，Andrew Smith 大法官说："The first question is when, for the purposes of section 73, the owners made their objection to Mr. Harris and Mr. Scott（这两位是仲裁员）continuing as arbitrators. Mr. Zaiwalla（原告代表律师）submitted that at the hearing on 18 November 2005 the owners, as he put it, 'put down a marker' as to their position. Mr. Beloff（仲裁开庭时代表原告的大律师）certainly warned that the owners might in the future object to the two arbitrators continuing with the reference, but I do not consider that he went further than that. It is not sufficient for the purpose of section 73 that a party indicates that an objection might be made. He must make his objection. Similarly, in my judgment it did not suffice for Zaiwalla & Co（原告代表律师事务所）to write on 24 November 2005 that they believed that 'the Arbitrators would consider it wise to... step down'. **An objection under section 73 must be stated in properly specific terms.** I do not consider that the owners made their objection to the two arbitrators continuing until 29 December 2005.[83]”（加黑部分是笔者的强调）

再如，在 Hussmann（Europe）Ltd. v. Al Ameen Development & Trade Co.（2000）2 Lloyd's Rep. 83 先例中，原告在开庭第一天提出了对仲裁庭管辖权的反对，并在获得了更多信息之后，在开庭时修改原本的仲裁通知与文书请求。Thomas 大法官判这也属于足够的反对。

由此可见，提出反对的一方只是保留他提出反对或异议的权利没有用。已经在本书第四章之 6.5.5 段已经提到，以“无损害”、“抗议”等说法保留权利有时作用有限。当事人不能以保留权利规避合约与法律的明示或默示规定，即不能以保留权利规避 Section 73“即刻”的要求。另是如果总体来看，当事人的行为（即继续参与仲裁程序）与保留权利不符，保留权利仍是无效。

7.3.5　什么是继续参与仲裁程序？

Section 73（1）下继续参与仲裁程序与本章之 3.2.2 段提到的参与法院程序导致不能再成功申请中止（stay）稍有不同，前者看来更严格。

在 ASM Shipping Ltd. of India v. TTMI Ltd. of England（2005）EWHC 2238 先例中，当事人在已经知悉仲裁员存在偏见的前提下，依然提交了证人证言等。但在取得了裁决书后发现自己败诉，于是提出反对想要撤销裁决书，法院判根据 Section 73（1）这已经太迟。Morison 大法官说：

“ASM were faced with a straight choice: come to the court and complain and seek to removal as a decision maker or let the matter drop. They could not get themselves into a position whereby if the award was in their favor they would drop their objection but make it in the event that the award went against them. A ‘heads we win and tails you lose’ position is not permissible in law as section 73 makes clear.

The threat of objection cannot be held over the head of the tribunal until they made their decision and could be seen as an attempt to put unfair and undue pressure upon him.”

如果当事人一直没有参与仲裁程序，可以在仲裁庭做出裁决书后，以仲裁员不符合资格或仲裁庭没有管辖权等要求撤销裁决书，这种情况下英国 1996 年《仲裁法》之 Section 72 适用。但如果当事人已经参与了仲裁程序，即使在后来发现了严重不正常的情况后，再没有采取积极的行动参与仲裁程序，只是消极沉默与不行动，这仍不足够。当事人必须有一些积极的言行，表示不再参与仲裁程序。如在 Rustal Trading Ltd. v. Gill & Duffus SA（2000）1 Lloyd's Rep. 14 先例中，高院的 Moore -

〔83〕 2005 年 12 月 29 日，Zaiwalla 先生在给仲裁庭的信件中明确说：“the two arbitrators should not continue with the reference as they were part of the tribunal of which one member was found by the court to have had apparent bias, ... indicated a strong hint of the Court's desire that the Arbitrators should resign.”根据该先例的判法，这样的反对才足够明确与有效。

Bick 大法官判除非当事人明示自己不再参与仲裁程序，否则都将视为该当事人仍然参与直到仲裁程序结束，往往也就是做出最后裁决书为止。即使当事人是在庭审结束后到裁决书做出前发现了令他可以提出反对或异议的事实，而在这段时间他无须采取任何积极的行动参与诉讼程序（只需要等待仲裁庭做出裁决书），他仍需要尽快行动提出反对与表示不再参与仲裁程序，否则就会在 Section 73（1）下"弃权"。Moore – Bick 大法官说："Unless a party makes it clear that he is withdrawing from the proceedings, he continues to take part in them until they reach their conclusion, normally in the publication of a final award. I can see no reason why a party who discovers grounds of objection after the conclusion of the hearing and before the publication of the award should not be required to voice it promptly, even at that stage, if he wishes to pursue it later on by challenge to the award."

在 Sierra Fishing Co. v. Farran（2015）1 Lloyd's Rep. 514 先例中，Popplewell 大法官解释说如果想提出反对或异议的当事人一直有参与仲裁程序，在不想再参与时就必须明确表示才足以改变他原本的地位："A party does not take part in an arbitration for the purposes of section 73 unless and until he invokes the jurisdiction of the tribunal in respect of the merits of the dispute or invokes the jurisdiction of the tribunal to determine its own jurisdiction over the merits of the dispute: Broda Agro Trading v. Toepfer [2011] 1 Lloyds Rep. 243, Sovarex v. Romero Alvarez [2011] 2 Lloyd's Rep. 320 at paragraphs [12] – [25]. However once a party has taken part in proceedings, he may 'continue to take part' by silence or inactivity in the face of a right to object which subsequently becomes available to him: Rusal v. Gill & Duffus [2000] 1 Lloyd's Rep. 14 at pp. 20 – 21. **If the status quo is that a party has already taken part, and is therefore participating in an arbitration in which he has invoked the exercise of the tribunal's jurisdiction, he may have to do something positive to change the status quo if he is properly to be regarded as not having continued to take part in the reference.** But in the absence of a prior taking part, mere silence and inactivity will not be sufficient; nor will any activity which is neutral or equivocal as to whether the party invokes or accepts the exercise by the tribunal of jurisdiction over him. In this respect there is no relevant distinction to be drawn between section 72, which preserves the right to challenge the jurisdiction of the tribunal for a person who has not taken part in the proceedings, and section 73 which is concerned with the loss of the right to object more generally."（加黑部分是笔者的强调）

7.3.6 Section 73 的优劣分析

总结而言，英国 1996 年《仲裁法》之 Section 73（1）的主要目的就是避免"正面我赢，背面你输"（heads I win, tails you lose）情况，防止仲裁的胜诉方浪费大量时间与金钱拿到一份最后被撤销的裁决书。因此，在 Section 73（1）下的"弃权"比普通法的弃权更广泛。从另一方面看，在 Section 73（1）针对的情况（包括程序严重不正常）发生后，一方依赖了另一方没有提出反对或异议而是继续参与仲裁程序的言行，花费大量时间与金钱推进仲裁程序。如果在仲裁庭做出裁决书后，另一方因为自己败诉出尔反尔，显然会令胜诉方蒙受损害。当然，因为有了 Section 73（1），所以无须再考虑"禁反言"（estoppel）是否适用的问题。

但对于当事人来说，是否必须即刻（forthwith）提出反对或异议也会左右为难。仲裁庭做出裁决书后才发现有问题，唯一的办法就是根据 Section 67 或 Section 68 向法院要求撤销裁决书，只要权衡这一申请需要的费用与成功的可能性，不存在延误导致在 Section 73 下"弃权"的问题。由于裁决书已经做出，通常就不必再担心得罪仲裁员。但如果是在仲裁程序半途发现有关的情况，就不仅仅需要权衡提出反对并根据 Section 24 向法院申请将仲裁员赶走的费用与继续仲裁程序所可能浪费的费用，而且需要留意事实上法院将仲裁员赶走的情况是非常少见的。在 Brake v. Ptley Wood Farm（Scotland）EWHC 1439（Ch）先例中，Kerr QC 大法官说只有在极端的案件中才会赶走仲裁员："Removal of an arbitrator is an extreme step and is only likely to occur in the rarest of cases."

在《Russell on Arbitration》（第 24 版，2015 年）一书之 7 – 118 段，说："In the arbitration context, on rare occasions where the arbitrator's conduct justifies it and when objection is raised promptly, an arbitrator will be removed as a result of his conduct of the proceedings. The bar for a successful challenge on this ground is very high..."另在 7 – 122 段，说："As discussed above, allegations relating to the conduct of proceedings by arbitrators very rarely succeed..."

在实践中这样极端的案件毕竟非常少见，向法院申请赶走仲裁员尽管是避免出了裁决书再提出会带来的"弃权"问题，但如果不成功（这种机会是极高的），提出反对或异议的一方就会有是否招致仲裁员的反感与在继续进行的仲裁程序有微妙的不利变化的担忧。根据 Section 24，可以向法院申请赶走仲裁员有四种理由。如果是仲裁员不符合合约规定的资格[84]或失去能力[85]还好，毕竟这是事实问题，说不上是对仲裁员的冒犯。但如果是提出仲裁员有偏见或利益冲突，[86]或是程序有严重不正常，[87]为了申请成功就免不了要对事实添油加醋去攻击与丑化仲裁员。如果最后没

---

〔84〕 这是 Section 24（1）（b）："...（b） that he does not possess the qualifications required by the arbitration agreement; ..."

〔85〕 这是 Section 24 （1）（c）："... （c） that he is physically or mentally incapable of conducting the proceedings or there are justifiable doubts as to his capacity to do so;..."

〔86〕 这是 Section 24 （1）（a）："...（a） that circumstances exist that give rise to justifiable doubts as to his impartiality;..."

〔87〕 这是 Section 24 （1）（d）："...（d） that he has refused or failed— （i） properly to conduct the proceedings, or （ii） to use all reasonable despatch in conducting the proceedings or making an award, ..."

有成功赶走仲裁员，就免不了担心仲裁员心态产生变化，但这个担忧对部分仲裁员来说也并非杞人忧天。

因此在笔者看来，在中间程序中试图赶走仲裁员会带来的严重后果，也使得不少确实存在不当行为的仲裁员逃避了其应承担的后果，并为部分仲裁员“壮胆”(robust line)不怕乱来。[88] Section 73(1)虽然在政策上支持了仲裁，减少法院对仲裁的干预，避免了对仲裁程序的拖延与保证了裁决书的终局性，但是以牺牲了部分当事人的利益为代价。

8. 送　　达

已经在本书第九章之3.3.2.2段提到，通知被告诉讼与送达告票对确保自然公正(natural justice)与公平审讯(fair trial)十分重要，被告必须有充分的时间准备抗辩。如果这方面做不到，诉讼程序是否符合自然公正就根本无从谈起，因为被告没有参与的机会。

涉及英国法院的程序下文书送达的要求，在《Civil Procedural Rule》(简称“CPR”)之r 6.2(1)有针对。法院的送达也会涉及弃权与/或禁反言的问题，如本书第六章之7.6段介绍的 Allison v. Limehouse & Co. (1992) 2 AC 105 先例。

在仲裁中，将仲裁通知书(notice of arbitration)通过有效方式(effective means)妥善地送达给被告也非常重要。这在英国1996年《仲裁法》之 section 76(3)-(5)有针对，简单而言，如果通知书被寄给被告最后知道的地址或是公司法人的注册或主要办公地点，就会被视为有效送达。随着通讯方式的发展，普通法也确认了有效送达方式包括传真[89]与电子邮件[90]。

在英国 CPR 与1996年《仲裁法》下都没有限制订约自由，因此，如果合约中规定告票或仲裁通知必须送达给某位人士或代表(通常会是一家英国的律师所)，就必须严格跟从。

另要注意的是，有不少仲裁条文(通过合并《联合国仲裁规则》或机构仲裁规则)要求开始仲裁的当事人在通知中写明有关索赔的多项具体内容，如果内容有所欠缺，也会导致仲裁通知无效。

有效的送达会在被告刻意回避或真正有困难的情况下变得困难与昂贵。在近期

---

[88] 见 Interprods Ltd. v. De La Rue International Ltd. (2014) EWHC 68 先例之“*robust but fair*”的仲裁员决定，或见 Jackson v. Thompsons Solicitors (A Firm) (2015) EWHC 218 (QB) 先例之“*terse and even abrupt*”。

[89] 见 The “Sargasso” (1994) 1 Lloyd’s Rep. 162; The “Petr Shmidt” (1995) 1 Lloyd’s Rep. 202 等先例。

[90] 见 Bernuth Lines Ltd. v. High Sea Shipping Ltd. (2005) EWHC 3020 先例。

的 Sun Tian Gang v. Hong Kong & China Gas (Jilin) Ltd. (2016) HKCFI 1611 香港先例中,笔者(杨良宜)是仲裁员之一,由于原告确认送达仲裁通知与所有有关的文件给身在大陆的被告(一位自然人),但被告一直没出现,于是仲裁庭做出了缺席裁决(default award)。但在原告执行时,被告出现并证明他在仲裁期间入狱,根本没有收到仲裁通知。作为监督法院的香港法院批判原告律师没有将不肯定已经送达仲裁通知的消息告知仲裁庭,并撤销了裁决书。这样,原告不得不重新开始另一个仲裁。

笔者(杨良宜)也见过一位仲裁员过分小心,虽然仲裁通知已经寄到了被告的办公地址与合约中约定的邮箱,但因为被告一直不出现,该仲裁员拒绝合作推进仲裁程序。因为笔者与首席仲裁员都不认为送达有问题,并准备以多数意见推进仲裁。于是,该仲裁员自己在原告提供的文件里搜寻所有被告工作人员或可能有关的人士的电子邮件地址,大范围转发仲裁通知、仲裁庭命令等。本来是否有效送达是原告的责任,而不是仲裁庭需要过度担心的问题。笔者不支持该仲裁员的做法的另一个考虑是大范围转发会有部分是无关人士,即使是工作人员,也可能早已离职,因此该仲裁员的做法违反了仲裁的机密性(confidentiality),而且也不保证能够送达被告。

如果有关的告票或仲裁通知没有根据法律或合约规定有效送达,或是仲裁通知的内容没有完全符合要求,但被告在无效送达后仍积极参与法院诉讼/仲裁,即使只是短暂参与,仍会是有足够言行构成弃权或禁反言(如"共识性禁反言"[estoppel by convention])令他不能之后质疑送达无效。正如 Bridge 勋爵在 Allison Ltd. v. Limehouse & Co 先例中所说:"If one party, knowing that another wishes to serve process upon him, requests or authorizes the other to do so in a particular way which is outside the Rules and the other does so, then, unless the Rules themselves prohibit consensual service the party so served cannot be heard to say that the service was not valid."

在 Martinez v. Hogeweide (1998) 156 DLR (4th) 757 (Alta CA)先例中,案情并非涉及原告没有及时与有效送达告票,而是没有及时送达起诉书,但道理一样。在该先例由于在与被告(保险人)进行和解谈判,所以原告迟延了送达起诉书。7 个月后,被告要求原告送达起诉书,但原告仍然延迟了 3 个月。被告就指称原告送达起诉书超过了时限。法院判虽然和解谈判的存在构成"承诺性禁反言"(primissory estoppel),但由于原告在收到被告要求送达起诉书后仍然有足够的时间,但没有尽快送到,所以不能依赖承诺性禁反言延长有关时间:"Those principles only require that the respondent be given enough time to undo the harm which would accrue without the estoppels. Had the revocation come after the statement of claim expired, or only three days before it expired, doubtless the time to serve would have to be extended by estoppels... not so here."

9. 抗辩的权利

从基本的人权与自然公正的角度考虑，被告都必须有抗辩的权利。合理与公正的法律也一定会尽量保护这个权利。如在英国法下，原告如果财政有问题，就会被要求提供费用担保(security for costs)才允许推进他的索赔请求，但被告有财政问题，就不能要求他提供费用担保才允许他进行抗辩。

这个看来至高无上的权利仍可以通过弃权与禁反言而失去。典型与经常会出现的情况之一就是由于被告明示或默示放弃抗辩的权利，导致法院或仲裁庭最后做出缺席判决或裁决。

但也经常会出现被告在诉讼开始时缺席，但后来参与诉讼。如在本书第九章之3.3.1段介绍的Strachan v. The Gleaner Co. Ltd. and Another (2005) UKPC 33 PC先例中，被告在法院做出了责任方面的缺席判决后，才改变主意参与了计算赔偿金额的诉讼程序。反正在仲裁中，这种情况也不少见。笔者(杨良宜)与绝大多数有经验的仲裁员都不会以任何理由拒绝被告的参与，只要不是太晚甚至是裁决书已经做出而变为职责已履行完毕(*functus officio*)。一般情况下，原告也不会阻止，因为拿到一个被告想抗辩(虽然没有按照程序时间表)但被否决的裁决书会是执行困难。

剥夺被告抗辩的权利也很难有说得通的合法理由，因为弃权与禁反言的说法都很难在这种情况下成立。首先是弃权，只要仲裁程序还没完结，很难说被告在哪个时间点做出不进行抗辩的决定就是最终的选择。更说得通的仍会是禁反言，但即使被告曾经明示或默示他不会做出抗辩，也不会是永久剥夺他的权利。在衡平法救济中，如果被告回心转意想抗辩，也应该让他回复到原本的法律地位。而且也很难说原告怎样依赖被告的言行改变了原本的地位并蒙受损害。如果让被告抗辩引起程序上的不便与浪费，如开庭时间要押后，仲裁庭也可以通过费用上的惩罚对原告进行补偿。

10. 文书请求中对事实的陈述与后续修改

简单而言，无论是法院诉讼或是仲裁程序，第一步都是交换文书请求(exchange of pleadings)，包括起诉书(statement of claim)、答辩书与反索赔(statement of defence and counterclaim)等。文书请求的目的是让双方了解对方的指控与立场，划好战线再推进下一步程序，所以，一般要求必须包括支持己方的指控的主要事实(material facts)。如被告要以“陈述性禁反言”(estoppel by representation)作为抗辩理由，除了写上原告被陈述性禁反言，还要写明原告在什么通讯往来中明示或默示做出了怎样的陈述,被告怎样依赖有关的陈述改变了立场,蒙受了怎样的损害。在国际仲裁中,一般还需要提供相应的文件证据支持。有了这些主要的事实,对方才知道要怎样准备进行反击,如搜寻相反的证据、提供证人证言等。

但文书请求中对事实的陈述并不代表在本书第五章针对的陈述(representation),即在合约谈判时向对方做出的陈述,或是陈述性禁反言的陈述。后一类陈述如果不正确或不全面,就会是误述并有法律的后果。但文书请求中的"事实"只代表当事人自己想要指出的事实以支持他的指控或立场。Parke B 大法官在 Boileau v. Rutin (1848) 2 Exch 665 先例中指出:"... pleadings... are not to be treated as positive allegations of the truth of the facts... for all purposes, but only as statements of the case of the party, to be admitted or denied by the opposite party, and if denied to be proved, and ultimately submitted for judicial decision.[91]"

Simon 勋爵在 United Australia Ltd. v. Barclays Bank Ltd. (1941) AC 1 贵族院先例中说:"There is nothing conclusive about the form in which the writ is issued, is about the claims made in the statement of claim. A plaintiff may at any time before judgment be permitted to amend.[92]"

Manson 大法官在 Laws v. Australian Broadcasting Tribunal (1990) 170 CLR 70 先例中则说:"The suggestion that unverified pleadings should be treated in the same way as any other form of admission fails... to take account of the function and object of pleadings, when they are not required to be verified, in outlining the party's case and defining the issue to be tried. Especially is this so in the case of... defences. A defendant is entitled to put a plaintiff to proof his or her cause of action and to raise alternative matters of defence which may possibly answer the plaintiff's claim, without asserting in an absolute sense the truth or correctness of the particular matters pleaded."

也正因如此,未经证实(证实是指在开庭后被法院或冲裁庭认定,除非对方承认)的文书请求(无论是指称的事实或指控)是允许做出修改或是提出与之前不同的说法或立场。

在上诉庭的 Clarapede & Co. v. Commercial Union Association (1883) 32 WR 262 早期先例中,Brett 大法官就明确了只要不会对方当事人造成不公平,都应该允许对文书请求的修改。如果对方当事人的损失只是用金钱就可以弥补是不会构成不公平,只有会造成对方无可弥补的损害时,法院才会拒绝修改申请。Brett 大法官说:"The rule of conduct of the court in such a case is that, however negligent or careless may have been the first omission, and however late the proposed amendment, the amend-

[91] 文书请求不应被视为对事实真相的说明,而是一方当事人对他的立场的描述,对方当事人完全可以承认、不承认或否认,如果对方不承认,就要进一步做出证明并通过司法程序做出认定。

[92] 告票或起诉书中的事实陈述并不是结论性的。原告在做出判决前任何时候都可以修改。

ment should be allowed if it can be made without injustice to the other side. There is no injustice if the other side can be compensated by costs, but if the amendment will put them into such a position that they must be injured, it ought not to be made."

因此,实践中的做法一般都会允许修改文书请求(即使迟至已经在庭审过程中),但同时也会命令申请修改一方赔付对方因此造成的费用损失。一般仲裁中的做法就是申请修改一方给一个修改的草稿(draft)。如果对方不反对,就可以正式做出修改,只是会要承担对方费用损失,这一般是对方做出相应修改要花费的律师费,但如果申请修改太晚,会造成必须推迟开庭,就会有一大笔浪费的费用。而如果对方反对,就需要仲裁庭决定是否批准修改。仲裁庭一般不会拒绝修改,这也配合了一方以错误理由终止合约事后可以正确理由补救[93]的说法,也没有理由不让双方当事人在最后审理前要求法院或仲裁庭考虑他认为最正确与有利的立场,并做出判决或裁决。但如果属于如下情况,仲裁庭会拒绝批准修改:(1)申请修改一方想借机拖延,而非真想做出修改。(2)会引入时效已过的诉因。在 CPR r 17.4 中就指出,如果要修改的内容涉及超出索赔时效的新诉因,除非是此条立法中指出的几种例外情况,否则一般情况下是不允许的。另也可见本书第九章之 6.2.3 段介绍的 Paragon Finance Plc. v. D B Thakerar & Co. (1998) EWCA Civ 1249 先例。(3)会引入超出了仲裁庭管辖权的争议。(4)会给对方造成不能简单以金钱弥补的损害。

在这样的背景下,也就一般谈不上在文书请求及之后的修改(或撤销曾经做出的承认)涉及"禁反言"(estoppel)了。即使对方当事人依赖了(如据此与第三人达成和解协议)在起诉书/答辩书中的提出的事实(其实不应如此看待与依赖),也不会造成禁反言。

10.1 不能以金钱弥补的损害的定义

在上诉庭的 Cropper v. Smith (1884) 26 Ch D 700 先例中,Bowen 大法官认为判断是否造成不能以金钱弥补的损害,关键在于是否有办法使对方当事人回复到类似一开始就已经提出修改后版本文书请求的地位。除非是很过分的故意行为,否则一开始没有提出修改后版本文书请求是否属于意外、不小心的行为并非特别重要。这与禁反言的说法十分相似,但 Bowen 大法官指出他很少遇到有修改文书请求会造成无法通过金钱弥补损失(支付浪费的费用)的情况。Bowen 大法官说:"The question (of prejudice) seems to me to be this, can you by the imposition of any terms place the other side in as good a position for the purpose of having the right determined as they were in at the time when the mistake of judgment was committed? It does not seem to me material to consider whether the mistake of judgment was accidental or not, if not intended to overreach...I have very seldom, if ever, been unfortunate enough to come across an instance, where a person has made a mistake in his pleadings which has put the other

---

〔93〕 见本书第一章第5段。

side to such a disadvantage as that it cannot be cured by costs."

在之后的 Ketteman v. Hansel Properties Ltd. (1987) AC 189 先例中，看来对这个原则进行了一定程度上的修正。因为有时无法用金钱弥补的方式保证对对方当事人公平，所以太迟提出的修改申请可以被拒绝。法官需要权衡诉讼给对方当事人带来的麻烦，面对新争议会给对方当事人带来的焦虑与虚假的希望等。贵族院说："late amendments may be refused... Because justice cannot always be measured in terms of money... a Judge is entitled to weight in the balance the strain the litigation imposed on litigants... the anxieties occasioned by facing new issues, the raising of false hopes."

金钱不能弥补的损害的例子之一是延误提出修改申请导致对方当事人失去了请自己证人抗辩修改内容的机会(如证人可能去世等)。如在一个仲裁中，仲裁程序开始两年后才开庭审理。但在开庭前，被告提出需要修改抗辩请求，要加上一个指控(allegation)说原告的董事总经理曾经向被告做出口头承诺不追偿一笔债务，但该原告的董事总经理在不久前去世。这样，原告自然大力反对修改了，因为被告有证人(不论真实或伪证)，但原告就根本没有证据了。问题是这若是两年前就在原来的文书请求中提出，原告可以调查并有充分时间向当时在世的董事总经理拿到一份文书的证人证言，这份文件在证人去世的情况下一样可以作为非常有力的证据，完全可以接纳(admissible)。因此，仲裁庭就拒绝了修改申请，因为对原告造成了金钱不能弥补的损害。

10.2 因禁反言而不能修改或改变诉讼立场

一般来说，即使是代表大律师在庭审中做出的承认，只要及时与没有构成禁反言，就可以撤回或改变。这见 H Clark (Doncaster) Ltd. v. Wilkinson (1965) 1 Ch 694 上诉庭先例中，Denning 勋爵所说："an admission made by Counsel... can be withdrawn unless the circumstances are such as to give rise to an **estoppels.**"

在笔者(杨良宜)最近参与的一个北京仲裁，在一开始的质证环节中，被告律师对原告的文件都一一表示接受。但之后检查原件时发现其中一份文件没有原件，于是拒绝接受该文件。原告律师就表示该文件之前已经被接受，被告律师不能出尔反尔再质疑该文件。被告律师做出的反应是否认曾经表示接受，但这不是好的应对办法。因为一来有庭审记录，二来事情刚刚发生，仲裁员记得很清楚。被告律师正确的做法还是表示即使他已经接受了该文件，但只要是及时撤回与没有构成禁反言，就没有理由不允许纠正过去的错误接受。显然被告律师是即时，并且原告律师也不可能因为依赖而蒙受任何损害，因此被告律师完全可以纠正错误的接受。

而在稍早提到诉讼双方对对方的指控不能视为对事实的陈述，所以不存在陈述性禁反言。而即使在双方的文书请求中同意了某些重要事实，但因为都接受这在将来有被对方修改的可能，所以，这种同意或理解不会构成共识性禁反言。因此成功构成禁反言的案件不多，例子之一是在本书第六章之 7.7 段介绍的 G S Fashions Ltd. v. B & Q Plc. (1995) 1 WLR 1088 先例。

在古老的 Steward v. The North Metropolitan Tramways Co. (1885) 16 QBD 178 先例中,原告以被告(一家电车公司)疏忽对电车不当使用并造成损害为由提出索赔。被告之后申请修改文书请求,看来是想将矛头与责任转到当地政府头上,指维护电车的责任属于当地政府。但修改申请被拒绝,理由是针对当地政府已经错过了有关时效。Pollock B 大法官说:"... the action would be wholly displaced by the proposed amendment, and I think it ought not to be allowed... If a defendant chooses to conduct his defence to a certain point on certain lines, and lead the plaintiff into a certain position, the defendant has no right to change his front. That is only acting on the well known **doctrine of estoppels**... the defendants are estopped from saying that they are not the proper defendants."

在上诉庭,Esher 勋爵也认为,如果被告在一开始的文书请求中就提出现在想要修改的内容,原告可能根本不会推进与被告之间的诉讼,而转而向有关的当地政府寻求救济。但现在已经超过了有关的索赔时效,已经无法再向当地政府寻求救济了。如果修改申请被允许,原告在此时已经无法回复到初始的地位了,也就是无法通过费用或其他方式做出弥补了。Esher 勋爵说:"If the defendants had in the first instance pleaded as they now ask to be allowed to plead, the plaintiff could have discontinued his action against the defendants and then have given notice of action and brought an action against the [local authority]; but now, more than six months having elapsed, he can no longer sue [the local authority]. If therefore the amendments were allowed, the plaintiff could not be put in the same position, or compensated by costs or otherwise."

另一个例子是在 The "Kyoan Maru" (1980) 2 Lloyd's Rep. 233 先例中,Kyoan Maru 轮从新加坡/马来西亚运输的锡/橡胶/木材前往日本、北美等地,但遭受全损。货主针对四名被告提出了索赔。第三被告是该船的注册船东,在答辩书中承认自己签发了有关提单以及自己是承运人(carrier)。[94] 但之后第三被告申请修改文书请求,指称早前的承认是错误的,理由是船舶实际上被光船租赁(bareboat charter)给第一被告,第一被告才是承运人。货方就提出自己会因此受到损害,因为自己在过去并没有特别针对第一被告,而现在第一被告已经破产,自己并没有取得任何担保。法院判确实存在损害并导致"禁反言"(estoppel)。Sheen 大法官同意虽然一般来说这种修改都会被允许,使得法院可以对双方之间争议的真正问题做出决定。显然案件不能基于真实的事实做出裁判的话是非常不理想的。无论修改申请是在多迟的阶段提出,只要不会对对方造成不公正的结果就应当予以允许。当然通常这时是要做出费用命令以弥补对方的损失。但在该先例中,如果第三被告在一开始的答辩书中就写清楚了现在拟修改的部分,原告完全有机会在当时从第一被告处取得恰当的诉前担保。然而如果在现阶段仍然允许第三被告修改文书请求的话,原告就会由于此出尔

[94] 这一个课题可见笔者《提单与其他付运单证》(2016 年)一书第三章。

反尔的行为而蒙受无法弥补的损害。Sheen 大法官说:“I start with the premise that generally speaking all such amendments to the pleadings ought to be allowed as well enable the real question in issue between the parties to be decided. It is obviously undesirable for cases to be decided on a basis other than the true facts. However late the proposed amendment, that amendment should be allowed if it can be made without injustice to the other side. Usually an appropriate order for costs will be sufficient to avoid injustice... If the original defence had been in the form of the proposed amended defence, the plaintiffs would have pursued any opportunity to obtain security from the 1st defendants and would in all probability have been successful and if leave were granted to the third defendants to amend the defence at this stage, the plaintiffs would be prejudiced in a way which could not be compensated by any order of this Court.”

11. 原告懈怠诉讼

贵族院在 Birkett v. James (1978) AC 297 先例确认了法院可以原告懈怠诉讼(want of due prosecution)为由撤销索赔请求的做法。如果能够满足两个先决条件,一审法院就有裁量权撤销原告的索赔请求:(1)原告自己不正常(inordinate)与不可原谅(inexcusable)的延误去推进索赔请求;(2)这个延误导致有很大的风险令有关案件不可能公平审理或可能导致被告严重的受损。这种受损一般是指失去证据,但也会有其他受损的情况,如被告原本可以找第三人补偿,但因为延误失去了这个机会(第三人破产等)。另是对证明受损的要求不高,一般只要原告有不正常与不可原谅的延误,就可以假设有关证人的记忆会变得模糊从而失去证据。

仲裁也有大量这类案件,原告及时启动仲裁以保护时效,但一保护了时效,就不继续推进仲裁程序。这导致不少仲裁员在有些案件被委任后,好几年都没有进一步的消息,问题是仲裁员能否像法院一样以原告懈怠诉讼为由撤销仲裁的索赔请求?1979 年到 1980 年年初,英国有大量针对这方面的案例,最终在贵族院的 Bremer Vulkan Schiffbau und Maschinenfabrik v. South India Shipping Corporation Ltd. (1981) 1 Lloyd's Rep. 253 先例后有了定论,即仲裁员没有像法院以原告懈怠诉讼为由撤销索赔请求的权利,因为仲裁员的管辖权与职责相比法院是不同的。由于这个课题已经在杨良宜《国际商务仲裁》(1997 年)一书第八章第 3 段有介绍,不再重复。这是普通法无法解决的问题,而现实中又有这个必要,所以最终还是通过立法赋予仲裁庭撤销索赔请求的权利。在英国 1996 年《仲裁法》之 section 41(3)说:“If the tribunal is satisfied that there has been inordinate and inexcusable delay on the part of the claimant in pursuing his claim and that the delay— (a) gives rise, or is likely to give rise, to a substantial risk that it is not possible to have a fair resolution of the issues in that claim, or

(b) has caused, or is likely to cause, serious prejudice to the respondent, the tribunal may make an award dismissing the claim."

另在香港特区《仲裁条例》之 section 59 也有类似的规定。

虽然有了这样的规定,但操作时还是有问题,很大的问题之一是来自“弃权”(waiver)与“禁反言”(estoppel)。这是因为在原告不正常与不可原谅的延误期间,无论三年还是五年,双方还是间断有互动。这样,就会出现被告申请撤销索赔请求时,原告抗辩说即使有不正常与不可原谅的延误,但被告之前的某些言行构成了弃权或禁反言。这可以 Roebuck v. Mungovin (1994) 1 Lloyd's Rep. 481 先例为例。案情涉及 1984 年 8 月 3 日发生的交通意外。1986 年 4 月 2 日,原告(受害方)向被告发出告票索赔人身伤害损失,并在 4 月 23 日递交了索赔请求。被告在 7 月 24 日递交了答辩书,其中承认了责任[95]但对损失金额有争议。但由于索赔请求里对索赔的金额没有足够的细节,所以被告也同时向原告提出提供进一步详情(further and better particulars)的要求。在接下来接近四年的时间里,双方只是间断在这方面纠缠。到了 1990 年 5 月 3 日,被告的律师还写信给原告的律师要求损失计算的进一步详情。同年 11 月 12 日,被告律师还写了另一封内容类似的信件。1991 年 7 月 29 日,被告申请法院以原告懈怠诉讼为由撤销索赔请求。

一审法院认为,整个延误看来的确是不正常与不可原谅,并令被告在做出抗辩方面受损。至于原告在该先例中延误的原因,根据报道出来的判决看,应该是原告中途换了律师。笔者估计也有其他方面的问题,如有些人身伤害很难在短时间内给出详情,其中可能涉及专家证据与需要进一步观察。而且根据本书第九章第 6 段介绍的“单一诉讼规则”(single action rule),原告必须将所有的人身伤害一次过提出,否则在“吸收原则”(doctrine of merger)或“一事不再审”(res judicata)的说法下,就无法对之后才发觉的额外损失获得赔偿。

但原告提出抗辩,指被告 1990 年 5 月 3 日与 11 月 12 日的信件构成弃权与/或禁反言。一审法院不接受这个抗辩,认为这两封信件只是要求原告提供进一步详情,而这是原告应该提供的,不会构成弃权与禁反言。

这方面的法律已经有较早前的 Lyell's case (1991) 1 WLR 683 上诉庭先例针对。Lyell's case 先例是判即使两个前提条件都能满足,但被告做出一些言行构成弃权或禁反言,法院就不能撤销索赔请求。之后的 Culbert v. Stephen G. Westwell & Co. Ltd. (1993) P. I. Q. R. P. 54 先例对这方面的法律又有了进一步的澄清。如果被告在做出了构成弃权或禁反言的言行后,原告继续不正常与不可原谅的延误,被告仍然可以再次申请以原告懈怠诉讼为由撤销索赔请求。但他必须能够证明后一段延误对他造成了额外损害。但这个要求并不现实,因为证明额外损害十分困难。延误诉讼通常的损害是诉讼拖了太久导致证据失去,证人的记忆随着时间推移,无可避免变得

---

〔95〕 一般在这种交通意外的侵权中,只要有疏忽,责任没有什么可争辩之处。

模糊。如果主要证人之一是在后一段延误死亡,被告还可以证明额外的损害。但如果只是记忆变得模糊,就很难证明主要证人在第一段的延误是记得清清楚楚,后一段延误记忆才变得模糊。

这样的法律地位看来有问题,弃权与禁反言本质上是衡平法的救济,怎会在被告一时的言行构成弃权与/或禁反言后,就永远剥夺了被告根据原告懈怠诉讼要求法院撤销索赔请求的权利？毕竟后一段延误有可能比第一段延误时间更长。

在 Roebuck v. Mungovin 先例中,上诉庭推翻了一审的判决,认为被告在 1990 年 5 月 3 日与 11 月 12 日的信件构成了"陈述性禁反言"(estoppel by representation)。有关的信件显示被告会继续参与诉讼,而原告依赖被告的陈述继续这一诉讼并有一些费用产生。因此,上诉庭根据 Lyell's case 先例的说法判被告不能以原告的延误(无论是前一段还是后一段或是整体延误)申请撤销原告的索赔请求。

但贵族院又推翻了上诉庭的判决,回复到了一审的判法。贵族院也借这个机会推翻了 Lyell's case 先例的说法,认为即使有弃权与禁反言,也只是一审法院在行使是否撤销索赔请求的裁量权(discretion)时的考虑之一。至于考虑的分量,根据每个先例的事实都有所不同。极端之一是该先例中的情况,原告延误的时间很长,而相比之下被告的言行(两封要求提供损失的进一步详情的信件)微不足道,原告即使依赖也不会有太多费用产生,就不会有太重的分量,法院很可能会撤销索赔请求。另一个极端是被告数年来一直积极回应原告,令原告产生了巨额费用,被告的言行就会有较重的分量,法院可能不会撤销索赔请求。Browne-Wilkinson 勋爵说:"I therefore reach the conclusion that Lyell's case should be overruled. Where a plaintiff has been guilty of inordinate and inexcusable delay which has prejudiced the defendant, subsequent conduct by the defendant which induces the plaintiff to incur further expense in pursuing the action does not, in law, constitute an absolute bar preventing the defendant from obtaining a striking-out order. Such conduct of the defendant is, of course, a relevant factor to be taken into account by the judge in exercising his discretion whether or not to strike out the claim, the weight to be attached to such conduct depending upon all the circumstances of the particular case. At one extreme, there will be cases like the present where the defendant's actions are minor (as compared with the inordinate delay by the plaintiff) and cannot have lulled the plaintiff into any major additional expenditure: in such a case a judge exercising his discretion will be likely to attach only slight weight to the defendant's actions. At the other extreme one can conceive of a case where, the plaintiff having been guilty of inordinate delay, the defendant has for years thereafter continued with the action thereby leading the plaintiff to incur substantial legal costs: in such a case the judge may attach considerable weight to the defendant's activities. But it is for the judge in each case in exercising his discretion to decide what weight to attach in all the circumstances of the case to the defendant's actions and I trust that in the future there will be few occasions on which the Court of Appeal will be invited to review his decision on the point."

12. 对法律业务特免权的弃权

本书其他章节介绍的"弃权"(waiver)与"禁反言"(estoppel)主要针对的是合约法下的弃权与禁反言。但在程序法中,只要涉及权利,也适用弃权与禁反言,如诉讼中当事人可以通过弃权放弃权利,也会由于禁反言失去权利。本段主要多针对一种至关重要的法律权利:文件证据的"特免权"(privilege)。

12.1 特免权

文件的"特免权"(privilege)在两个方面都是非常重要的:(1)在一般国际诉讼、仲裁案件中,诉讼双方都会有提供证据的权利与义务。而且今天国际诉讼、仲裁案件中的趋势是对透明度(transparency)越来越重视,只要是与争议有关(relevance),就可能被要求披露。而对于自己并不占有、也无法获得,但处于对方占有、控制之下的文件,就需要在披露程序(disclosure/discovery)中要求对方提供。即使披露这些文件会对对方造成不利,或对方声称这些文件属于商业机密,也往往不得不在法院或仲裁庭的强制命令下做出披露。当然类似的,对方也会在披露程序中要求己方提供这些对己方不利的文件。(2)今天法律非常复杂(而且有越来越复杂与繁多的趋势),社会中的方方面面(无论是婚姻家庭、劳工、金融、税务、经贸合作、竞争、公司治理、商标专利、技术开发与发展、健康与卫生、贪污、国防、反恐与战争等)都依赖专业人士给予法律意见。当事人要了解自己的权利与义务,保护自己依法享有的权利,避免有悖法律法规、规章制度的规定,就需要寻求专业人士的意见。

而对"走出去"的中国公司/企业来说,更重要的是今天面对的各个国家与地区政策、法律法规、规章制度之多与惩罚之严厉是前所未见的,需要严格与小心地保证合规。一方面是因为这些政策、法律法规、规章制度通常是强制性规定,不遵守就会面临巨额罚款、停业整顿等各种类型的处罚措施。另一方面则是这些政策、法律法规、规章制度常常不仅仅是针对公司/企业本身,还会针对公司/企业的股东、董事、高管等人士。而在这些政策、法律法规、规章制度之下,往往也要求被监管人在特定情况下披露文件,有的情况下会授权有关机构直接(甚至是"破门而入")没收、查封被监管人的文件。尤其重要的是,在这些政策、法律法规、规章制度之下,还会涉及严重的后果,如可能会涉及刑事罪行与/或天文数字的罚款[96]等问题。当然政府部门进行调查与监管时往往更倾向于罚款而非起诉公司/企业的董事、高管等,而罚款的金

〔96〕 据说美国在各类监管、法规之下,获得收益超过8%的GDP。在这样巨大的经济利益诱惑下,监管只会加强而不会放松。

额一定程度上取决于被监管的公司/企业的配合程度。公司/企业如果主动披露文件会被视为配合调查,因此权衡利弊后,被监管的公司/企业不一定会抗拒披露。数据显示美国律政司(US Department of Justice)或美国证券交易委员会(US Securities and Exchange Commission)在1977年《Foreign Corrupt Practices Act》[97]下对公司/企业罚款从100万美元到8亿美元(2008年对德国西门子公司的罚款)不等。在决定罚款金额时,很多因素都会被考虑在内,包括支付罚款的能力与对调查与监管的配合程度。因此公司/企业更需要依法办事,而不能泛泛的仅凭自己的主观看法"小心"办事。重要决定的做出必须全面寻求专业人士的法律意见。"走出去"的公司/企业更应该每一步都尽量寻求称职、熟悉有关方面的专业律师意见,也能有法律依据,从而有信心与做出相对正确的判断。法律也不是非黑即白,因此律师给出的法律意见往往不会说死,也不会担保正确。要走出去的公司即使获取了法律意见,仍然要平衡有关的法律风险与商业利益才做出决定。这样法律意见的特免权就显得尤为重要。

被要求披露的一方或被监管人一般而言对文件的披露是抗拒的,因为可能内容对自己不利或涉及隐私或属于公司法人不愿意公开的商业机密。否则是早已经主动披露,或是事后统一披露。抗拒披露表面看来是不让对方取得有关的文件,无法看到也无法知悉文件的内容。但实际上更多的情况或案件中,要求披露的对方都知悉或估计/猜测到有关文件的存在与内容是对其有利的。对方在获得披露后,就会采取进一步的行动,如提交给法院。法院或有关机构就会根据这些文件证据做出判决或决定,如罚款或其他处罚、惩罚。因此,当事人之间常会就有关文件是否可以披露产生激烈的争论与花费大量金钱/诉讼费用让法院做出定论。

法律意见特免权保护的不仅仅是法律意见本身,还包括所有有关的通信往来,为了获取意见提供给律师的资料(如根据此文件向律师咨询是否违反监管法律法规、规章制度,是否违法,以及如何应对等)等文件。这些文件与法律法规、规章制度下的调查有密切关联性,如果不对机密性做出特别保护,恐怕在做出重大商业或诉讼决定时就根本不会寻求律师意见(一旦曝光就太危险),法治社会也就无法运作了。

但对于符合诉讼证据披露要求(如关联性、合法性等)的文件,或是符合了政策、法律法规、规章制度中允许强制文件披露(或是没收、查封范畴)的文件而言,能够抗拒披露的合法理由是非常有限的。对于想要继续发展经营的公司/企业,尤其是想要走出去、走向国际化的中国公司/企业来说,没有完好保存的文件记录是很难做到的,反而更容易产生问题。如是在本国或外国进行监管的有关机构进行调查时,有完整与对自己有利的文件资料完全应该提供给这些有关机构。如果被调查的公司或企业无法提供完整与对自己有利的文件证据进行解释,或是协助用以进行和解谈判,只能导致更严密与严苛的调查,使得所有漏洞都无所遁形,而且这样面对任何指控(即使该指控并不正确)都无法反证。另是从公司管理的角度看,也不能完全没有文件证

---

〔97〕 这只不过是数量众多的监管法规中的一个。

据,明显的例子就是新上任的高管在没有文件证据帮助的情况下肯定无所适从,不知道上一任在任内从事的活动与对将来的计划等。很多跨国公司/企业都有清晰与完整的文件管理政策(coherent document management policy),包括教育员工关于制造文件的风险并要经常考虑这份文件或通信往来将来有向法院或监管部门披露的风险;所有的文件包括通讯工具的聊天记录要在公司服务器备份;要控制机密性文件(特别是可以享有特免权的文件)的流通,避免将来因为失去机密性而无法依赖特免权。公司/企业的法务部门非常重要与繁杂的工作之一就是搜查公司文件,保留对自己有利或至少没有重大不利的文件,销毁对自己不利又可有可无的文件。至于对自己不利但又十分重要的文件,有些公司/企业会转存至海外或律师事务所。这样,至少进行监管的有关机构要搜查与获取有关的文件就相对困难。另在本章之 12.3.1 段会介绍什么是法律意见特免权中的"客户"(client),这在英国法律下相对局限。所以,为了避免在客户定义外的雇员从律师处取得的敏感法律意见由于无法依赖特免权而需要披露,对公司/企业造成伤害,就要小心处理。比较好的做法是针对某个商业交易、项目、报告或其他商业活动,一开始就决定一组人可以作为"客户"对律师进行询问与取得法律意见。一旦做出了这个决定,就要留下文书证据甚至可以告知律师,以防将来就这些与律师沟通的人士是否属于"客户"产生争议以及被挑战特免权。

一份文件常常会是机密性的(confidentiality),但这不足以保护文件免于在诉讼或政策、法律法规、规章制度下的调查中披露。只有在公共政策(public policy)的支持下认为特定类型文件的机密性需要特别保护,使之上升为特免权的地位,才能免于披露。所谓特免权,在 B v. Auckland District Law Society (2003) 2 AC 736 先例中被 Millett 勋爵描述为"a right to resist the compulsory disclosure of information"。换句话说,如果需要制作与保留一份对自己不利的文件,就需要确保有特免权的保护,才能使得这份文件免于披露、永远保持机密性或即使其他人士知道文件内容,也不能依赖。

针对特免权而言,也存在不同的类型。如:

1."法律业务特免权"(legal professional privilege)保护律师与客户之间有关提供法律意见或是为了诉讼目的的通信往来(包括调查取证)等文件免于披露。这最重要,也是比较广泛的特免权类型。包括"法律意见特免权"(legal advice privilege)与"诉讼特免权"(litigation privilege)两种不同的类型。有关的还有"联合特免权"(joint privilege)以及"共同利益特免权"(common interest privilege)。将在本章之下一段对此问题再稍作详细介绍。

2."无损害特免权"(without prejudice privilege),在普通法或英国法的证据规则下,有一条基本的证据规则,双方当事人为了正在进行或可能进行的案件做出和解谈判,如果没有达成和解协议,该谈判内容属于不可采纳(inadmissible)的,可以拒绝披露给法院。涉及的公共政策是鼓励当事人之间尽量试图和解有关争议,放心谈判,即使谈不拢,也不会造成任何损害。谈判中所说的话(如是承认责任或愿意赔偿的金额)都不会被对方利用以影响法院判决。

3. "自证其罪特免权"(self-incrimination privilege),即不能强迫被告人或犯罪嫌疑人自证其罪(刑事犯罪),涉及的公共政策是无罪推定。

4. 其他。还有一些也被称为特免权的情况,如"公共利益特免权"(public interest privilege)即针对特别的案情,法院在对公共利益进行衡量(balance)后认为有必要对特定公共利益进行保护,因此允许拒绝披露;又如是"外交特免权"(diplomatic privilege)等。

特免权作为一种权利的存在,当然也可以被享有该权利的人士所放弃,如 Cotton 大法官在 Lyell v. Kennedy (1884) 27 Ch D 1 先例中说:"There was this contention raised, which I have not forgotten: that the defendant had waived his privilege and therefore could not claim it at all. That, in my opinion, was entirely fallacious. He had done this, he had said, 'Whether I am entitled to protect them or not, I will produce certain of the documents for which I had previously claimed privilege - I will waive that, and I will produce them', but that did not prevent him relying on such protection with regard to others which he did not like to produce. It is not like the case of a man who gives part of a conversation and then claims protection for the remainder, and we think there is no ground for the contention that there has been here a waiver of privilege."

而在接下来的段落中将主要讨论有关最复杂、最常出问题,也是争议最多的法律业务特免权的弃权问题,在近年来也有无数先例涉及这方面。

12.2　法律业务特免权

法律业务特免权(legal professional privilege)是特别重要与常见的特免权类型。在诸多类型的特免权中,法律业务特免权也是涉及最多争议(尤其是近年有很多高院与上诉庭有关法律业务特免权的先例)的类型,复杂程度是其他类型的特免权无可比拟的。法律业务特免权也常常涉及"弃权"(waiver)的问题与争议,相对来说绝少见由于"禁反言"(estoppel)导致无法行使特免权的情况,毕竟在本章之 12.2.2 段会介绍特免权属于重要的实体性权利(substantive right)、基本人权与绝对性权利(absolute right),除非是立法条文明示或有必要的默示,才会导致特免权被超越。[98]

---

[98] 见 R (Morgan Grenfell & Co. Ltd) v. Special Commissioner of Income Tax (2003) 1 AC 563 (HL); B v. Auckland District Law Society (2003) 2 AC 7369 (PC)等先例。明示立法的例子可见英国 1986 年《Insolvency Act》之 Section 291(1)(b):"Where a bankruptcy order has been made, the bankrupt is under a duty...(b) to deliver up to the official receiver all books, papers and other records of which he has possession or control and which relate to his estate and affairs (including any which would be privileged from disclosure in any proceedings)."必要的默示的例子可见 Re L (1997) AC 16 贵族院先例中,判 1989 年《Children Act》有必要的默示在"care proceedings"中排除诉讼特免权对文件的限制。其他明示立法排除特免权(针对自证其罪特免权)有 2006 年《Fraud Act》之 Section 13,1968 年《Theft Act》之 Section 31, 1981 年《Senior Court Act》之 Section 72,1987 年《Criminal Justice Act》之 Section 2, 1985 年《Company Act》之 Section 434,1987 年《Banking Act》之 Section 42 等。虽然这些立法条文明示排除了特免权,但其中也有规定获得的证据不可以在之后的刑事诉讼中被使用。

而禁反言作为衡平法救济的一种,只有在对方依赖并蒙受损害时才造成权利方被禁反言,而要有足够严重的依赖性损害以至于特免权丧失的情况应该是不多的。[99]

12.2.1 法律业务特免权的公共政策考虑

需要建立法律业务特免权有其背后的公共政策考虑。法律是对多方利益做出平衡的综合考量,因此即使是有很好的常识/意识(common sense)的人士客观与冷静地进行判断,也难免有偏差。显然公共政策希望大家的言行都按照定下的规则行事,法律的复杂性要求与鼓励公司/企业法人或自然人在做出任何重要言行前寻求法律意见,才能依法办事,也因此有了保护法律业务特免权的必要。

Anderson v. Bank of British Columbia (1876) 2 Ch D 644 早期先例对法律业务特免权的目的与意义进行了总结,说:"The object and meaning of the rule is that: that as, by reason of the complexity and difficulty of our law, litigation can only be properly conducted by professional men, it is absolutely necessary that a man, in order to prosecute his rights or to defend himself from an improper claim, should have resource to the assistance of professional lawyers, and it being so absolutely necessary, it is equally necessary, to use a vulgar phrase, that he should be able to make a clean breast of it to the gentleman whom he consults with a view to the prosecution of his claim, or the substantiating of his defence against the claim of others; that he should be able to place unrestricted and unbounded confidence in the professional agent, and that the communications he so makes to him should be kept secret, unless with his consent (for it is his privilege and not the privilege of the confidential agent), and he should be enabled properly to conduct his litigation. That is the meaning of the rule.[100]"

同样或类似的说法也可见 Wheeler v. Le Marchant (1881) 1 LR 17 Ch D 675 先例:"It is a rule established and maintained solely for the purpose of enabling a man to obtain legal advice with safety."

较近期的 Ventouris v. Mountain (1991) 1 Lloyd's Rep. 441 先例也有类似的说

---

[99] 《Documentary Evidence》(2015 年,第 12 版)一书之 23－18 段说:"Where a waiver of privilege occurs accidentally, perhaps in the course of evidence where a witness answers a question in a way not so far as necessary for the just determination of his claim expected, or even if it occurs accidentally in the sense that the consequences of a particular line of questioning are not appreciated until too late, it is unattractive for the other party to try to jump on the error **unless he has suffered prejudice**..."(加黑部分是笔者的强调)

[100] 建立法律业务特免权的目的与意义在于由于法律十分复杂与困难,诉讼必须依赖专业人士才能够恰当地进行。任何人士想要通过诉讼维护自己的权利、向他人提出索赔,或是抗辩针对自己的索赔,都需要寻求专业律师的帮助。与寻求律师同样重要的是,寻求律师帮助的人士需要能够赤裸裸地展示给律师所有的情况,律师也才能根据这些情况提供全面与相对正确的法律意见。但要这样做,必须是能够知道自己与律师之间的通信往来有着绝对与不受限制的机密,除非经过自己同意,否则必须被严守秘密不得泄露。

法："The doctrine of legal professional privilege is rooted in the public interest, which requires that hopeless and exaggerated claims and unsound and spurious defences be so far as possible discouraged, and civil disputes so far as possible settled without resort to judicial decision. To this end it is necessary that actual and potential litigants, be they claimants or respondents, should be free to unburden themselves without reserve to their legal adviser, and their legal advisers be free to give honest and candid advice on a sound factual basis, without fear that these communications may be relied on by an opposing party if the dispute comes before the court for decision.[101]"

12.2.2　绝对性、实体性权利与基本人权

因此在今天，法律业务特免权也已经被确定不单纯是在诉讼程序中可以拒绝披露的证据规则，而是属于实体性权利（substantive right），在任何情况下都可以依赖并拒绝将文件交出。

同时法律业务特免权也处于绝对性权利（absolute right）的地位，即使与其他公共利益发生冲突也不会被超越：见贵族院的 R v. Derby Magistrates, Ex p B（1996）AC 487 与枢密院的 B v. Auckland District Law Society（2003）2 AC 736 等先例。不妨节录 Taylor 勋爵在 R v. Derby Magistrates, Ex p B 贵族院先例（该先例中有说法试图以避免错判谋杀案件为由，超越法律业务特免权的保护，但不成功）中所说："The principle which runs through all [the cases] is that a man must be able to consult his lawyer in confidence, since otherwise he might hold back half the truth. The client must be sure that what he tells his lawyer in confidence will never be revealed without his consent. Legal professional privilege is thus much more than an ordinary rule of evidence, limited in its application to the facts of a particular case. It is a fundamental condition on which the administration of justice as a whole rests."

除非是立法中有明示（express）或是必要的默示（necessary implication），否则不能超越特免权：R v. Derby Magistrates, Ex p B；B v. Auckland District Law Society；R（Morgan Grenfell & Co. Ltd）v. Special Commissioner of Income Tax（2003）1 AC 563 等先例。

近期的 ENRC v. Dechert LLP（2016）EWCA Civ 375 上诉庭先例中，显示了什么是立法中必要的默示。英国 1974 年《Solicitors Act》之 Section 70 规定客户质疑律师收费时，高院有进行核算（assessment）的权力。要核算就免不了需要看律师与客户之间的通信往来等文件，否则无法根据合理性等标准做出核算。而这些文件显然本

[101] 公共利益要求尽可能地减少希望不大/过分夸大的诉讼、索赔，或是无意义的抗辩，尽可能让争议方无须经过司法程序就能解决争议。要达到这样的目的，就有必要使当事人可以毫无保留地向法律意见提供者寻求建议（如败诉的可能性、和解中赔偿金额的考量），也无须担忧自己与法律意见提供者所说的话或提到的事实被对方当事人知悉与在法院诉讼中依赖。

是受到特免权保护的。1974 年《Solicitors Act》授予法院核算权力时,也就是有必要的默示可以超越这些文件上的特免权,文件必须被披露不可。该先例中客户被 Serious Fraud Office(SFC)调查,被怀疑很多海外业务涉及欺诈。客户委任律师事务所(Dechert)来应对调查。Dechert 要收取高达 1630 万英镑的费用,客户即向高院申请对律师收费做出核算。而要做出核算不可避免地要全面披露客户与 Dechert 之间的通信往来以显示律师的工作与收费是否匹配。但这些文件一旦在公开法院被披露,就可能被 SFC 在调查中所依赖,甚至导致后续刑事指控等。法院认定在这种情况下,在核算程序中的文件披露一方面是属于本章之 12.5.3 段提到的"限定弃权"(limited waiver),即限定目的只是为了核算而做出的弃权,在核算程序以外的任何其他情况中,仍然保有特免权;另一方面,允许在 CPR 下可以不公开审理进行核算,避免公开审理导致丧失机密性无法再依赖特免权的保护。

而且法律业务特免权也已经被确认为属于基本人权(fundamental human right)。不妨节录 R (Morgan Grenfell Ltd) v. Special Commissioners of Income Tax 贵族院先例中 Hoffmann 勋爵所说:"... LPP(Legal Professional Privilege,法律业务特免权)is a fundamental human right long established by the common law. It is the necessary corollary of the right of any person to obtain skilled advice about the law. Such advice cannot be effectively obtained unless the client is able to put all the facts before the adviser without fear that they may afterwards be disclosed and used to his prejudice."

英国也加入了《欧洲人权公约》(European Convention on Human Rights, ECHR),以及有了引入该公约的立法 1998 年《Human Rights Act》(简称"HRA")。在《欧洲人权公约》或是 HRA 下并没有明示针对特免权的条文,但是通过欧洲人权法院(ECtHR; Cour européenne des droits de l'homme)的不少先例都明确了在《欧洲人权公约》下对特免权的保护:[102] 见 S v. Switzerland (1992) 14 EHHR 670;Brennan v. United Kingdom (2001) 34 EHRR 507;Öcalan v. Turkey (2005) 41 EHRR 985 等欧洲人权法院先例。

---

〔102〕 值得注意的是,在《欧洲人权公约》或 HRA 下,欧洲人权法院的很多先例都有判法是虽然允许进行弃权,但对弃权有特别严格的要求,如在 Hakansson and Stureson v. Swededn (1990) 13 EHRR 1 先例中,欧洲人权法院指出:"... admittedly neither the letter nor the spirit of this provision(指的有关公平裁判的条文,也是被刚刚提到的诸多欧洲人权法院先例依赖以支持特免权保护的条文之一)prevents a person from waiving of his own free will, either expressly or tacitly, the entitlement to have his case heard in public... However, a waiver must be made in an **unequivocal manner and must not run counter to any important public interest.**"(加黑部分是笔者的强调)。类似判法还可见 Deweer v. Belgium (1980) 2 EHRR 439;Le Compte Can Leuven and De Meyere v. Belgium (1981) 4 EHRR 1;Pfeifer and Plankl v. Austra (1992) 14 EHRR 692 ;Bulut v. Austria (1996) 24 EHRR 84 等欧洲人权法院的先例。这严格的要求看来比英国法院的先例中,尤其是针对附带弃权(collateral waiver)的先例更严格,但目前还没有权威性先例针对英国法院部分判决是否违反《欧洲人权公约》的问题。

12.2.3　法律意见特免权与诉讼特免权

法律业务特免权可以分为"法律意见特免权"(legal advice privilege)与"诉讼特免权"(litigation privilege)两大类。前者保护客户(client)向法律意见提供者(legal adviser)寻求法律意见,而后者保护主要目的在于诉讼(litigation)或可能的诉讼制作的文件。

简单而言,相比于诉讼特免权,法律意见特免权针对的文件范围较窄,[103]但认定较为稳定。这与今天越来越繁重的合规义务,政策、法律法规、规章制度下的调查有密切关系。在这些情况下,公司/企业往往不会希望有律师提供的意见(无论最后的商业决定是否遵循意见,或是意见本身就有瑕疵、模棱两可等)被披露给有关机构,造成严重后果(如公司董事高管被刑事起诉或公司被要求支付巨额罚款)。

而诉讼特免权针对的文件范围较宽泛,包括主要针对诉讼或可能发生的诉讼制作的有关文件。也因此不仅仅是与律师之间的文件、通信往来等,在与其他第三人之间(如律师向证人、专家调查取证等,做出的文件与通信往来等)也会产生诉讼特免权。

无论是在诉讼外(如合规义务,政策、法律法规、规章制度下的调查)中,还是在诉讼中(如向大律师、外国律师获取法律意见),都有必要获取法律意见。而对诉讼特免权来说,也会有不少政策、法律法规、规章制度下的调查涉及诉讼或是可能发生的诉讼。因此往往出现争议时,会将法律意见特免权与诉讼特免权共同提出以对抗披露要求。

12.2.4　联合特免权与共同利益特免权

法律业务特免权还涉及一些特别的情况。如"联合特免权"(joint privilege),即多方当事人联合委托律师,或在委托当事人时虽然没有写明但实际多方当事人存在联合利益(joint interest),多方当事人就对文件享有联合特免权。包括保险人(insurer)与被保险人(insured)、再保险人(reinsurer)之间;[104]信托人(trustee)与受益人(beneficiary)之间;[105]母公司与子公司之间;[106]公司与其董事之间;[107]合伙人之间[108]等。在文件产生时,多方当事人就可以联合依赖特免权拒绝披露。

又如"共同利益特免权"(common interest privilege),即享有特免权保护的文件

---

〔103〕只涉及客户与法律意见提供者之间针对法律意见的文件。法律意见提供者一般也就是律师,包括本国律师与外国律师,英国在2007年《Legal Service Act》后,则还会包括一些其他特定人士。英美法还包括公司法务部,但欧洲一些主要国家的看法不同。

〔104〕见 Winterthur Swiss Insurance Company v. AG (Manchester) Limited (2006) EWHC 839 等先例。

〔105〕见 O' Rourke v. Darbishire (1920) AC 581; Schmidt v. Rosewood Trust Ltd. (2003) 2 AC 709; Breakspear v. Auckland (2008) EWHC 220 (Ch)等先例。

〔106〕见 Surface Technology Plc. v. Young (2002) FSR 387 先例。

〔107〕见 Sonic Tape plc's Patent (1987) RPC 251 等先例。

〔108〕见 Pearse v. Pearse (1846) 1 De G &Sm12; Re Pickering (1884) 25 Ch D 247; BBGP Managing General Partner Limited v. Babcock & Brown Global Partners (2010) EWHC 2176 (Ch)等先例。

已经制作与产生,而事后由可以依赖特免权拒绝披露的当事人A将文件交给在当时与他有共同利益(common interest)的当事人B,当事人B在收到文件后就可以依赖共同利益特免权拒绝披露文件:见 Buttes Gas and Oil Co. v. Hammer (No. 3) (1981) QB 233 CA 等先例。所谓共同利益,在 Buttes Gas and Oil Co. v. Hammer (No. 3)先例中被 Denning 勋爵描述为当事人之间是有紧密联系以至于需要将所有人当成同一间事务所的合伙人或同一公司的不同部门(treat all the persons interested as if they were partners in a single firm or departments in a single company)。

而在近年则是有说法在这方面的解释会有所放宽,如在 Formica Ltd. v. Export Credits Guarantee Department (1995) 1 Lloyd's Rep. 692 先例中,Colman 大法官说:"... the essential question in each case is whether the nature of their mutual interest in the context of their relationship is such that the party to whom the documents are passed received them subject to a duty of confidence which the law will protect in the interests of justice."

具体而言,共同利益特免权类似联合利益特免权,可能会发生在保险人与被保险人之间;[109]保险人与再保险人之间;[110]母公司与子公司之间;[111]公司与董事、股东之间;[112]委托人与代理人之间[113]等。

同时也有说法是共同利益特免权可以在当事人B与当事人A对受到特免权保护的文件存在共同利益时,当事人B有要求当事人A向其披露该文件的权利:见 CIA Barca de Panama SA v. George Wimpey & Co. Ltd. (1980) 1 Lloyd's Rep. 598 先例与 Formica Ltd. v. Export Credits Guarantee Department 先例。

12.2.5 国际上的不同看法

而在其他国家对特免权的保护在某些方面会有所不同。如澳大利亚的判法中会强调要保证公平(fairness),在加拿大则有先例涉及特免权在与其他公共利益发生冲突时需要进行权衡(balance),[114]又如在《欧洲人权公约》下也有不同看法。而对于想要走出去的公司/企业来说,寻求专家法律意见必须找到正确的对象,能对每个国家或地区的政策、法律法规、规章制度有针对性地了解,才能得到相对正确与有实用价值的法律意见。在这一点上,相对来说跨国的律师事务所会更有优势,毕竟这些跨国律师事务所有能力以"一揽子"的方式给国际上的跨国公司提供世界多个国家或地区的法律意见。

---

〔109〕 见 Guinness Peat Properties Ltd. v. Fitzroy Robinson Partnership (1987) 1 WLR 1027 先例。

〔110〕 见 Svenska Handelsbanken v. Sun Alliance and London Insurance Plc. (1995) 2 Lloyd's Rep. 84; Commercial Union Assurance Co. Plc. v. Mander (1996) 2 Lloyd's Rep. 640 等先例。

〔111〕 见 USP Strategies Plc. v. London General Holdings Ltd. (2004) EWHC 373 (Ch)先例。

〔112〕 见 Sutton v. GE Capital Commercial Finance Ltd. (2004) 2 BCLC 662 先例。

〔113〕 见 The "World Era" (No. 2) (1993) 1 Lloyd's Rep. 363 等先例。

〔114〕 见 Jones v. Smith (1999) 1 SCR 455 先例。

12.3　谁可以对特免权弃权

在本书第三章第3段已经介绍过,弃权行为只能由权利人做出。而在针对特免权的情况下,能够对特免权弃权的也只能是享有特免权的人士。如是只有有关的国家或权威机关享有外交特免权,[115]当然有关的大使可以代表弃权。[116]又如是对自证其罪特免权来说,显然是被告人或犯罪嫌疑人或其配偶。对无损害特免权来说,则只能由和解谈判的所有当事人共同弃权,而不能单方面弃权。[117]

而对于重要的法律业务特免权来说,情况则会稍有复杂。复杂之处并不是对谁享有特免权存在疑问,因为这个问题的回答是明确的:寻求法律意见的客户或是可能作为诉讼当事人(原告与被告)参与诉讼的人士。

在 Ventouris v. Mountain (1991) 1 Lloyd's Rep. 441 先例中,Bingham 大法官就说"法律业务特免权"从字面上来看好像是律师拥有特免权,但这字面看法其实是误导,实际上这个特免权属于客户(client):"The expression 'legal professional privilege'(这里提到的是法律业务特免权,但实际上是针对了法律意见特免权)is unhappy, because it falsely suggests a privilege enjoyed by the legal profession when in truth it is not the legal profession but the client who enjoys the privilege."

Hoffmann 勋爵在 R (Morgan Grenfell & Co. Ltd) v. Special Commissioner of Income Tax (2003) 1 AC 563 先例中也有类似的说法并指出:"If the client chooses to divulge the information, there is nothing the lawyer can do about it."

权威书籍中的类似说法可见《Phipson on Evidence》(第18版,2013年)一书之23－20段:"The rule is established for the client's benefit, not for the lawyer. Privilege can therefore be waived by client but not lawyer. The lawyer is under a professional obligation to assert the privilege until it is waived by the client. Thus, the lawyer has no locus to assert the privilege in his own right or commence proceedings in his own name for that purpose. The lawyer cannot invoke the privilege or use it for his own benefit if the client waives it. Nor can the person to whom the lawyer communicates under the cloak of litigation privilege claim to rely on it.[118]"

换句话说,只有寻求法律意见的客户或可能作为诉讼当事人的人士才享有特免权,其他人士既然不享有特免权,也就无法对特免权做出弃权,如是实际提供证人证

---

[115] 见 R v. Madan (1961) 2 QB 1 (CA)先例。

[116] 见 R v. AB (1941) 1 KB 454 先例。

[117] 见 Walker v. Wilshire (1889) 23 QBD 335 (CA); Somatra Ltd. v. Sinclair Roche & Temperley (2000) 1 Lloyd's Rep. 311 等先例。

[118] 法律业务特免权是为了保护客户的利益而非律师的利益,因此是客户而非律师可以做出弃权行为。律师则是有专业义务,在客户做出弃权之前不得披露这些文件给任何其他人士。因此,律师没有以自己名义依赖特免权或通过诉讼程序保护特免权的地位。而且如果客户对特免权做出了弃权,律师也无从继续依赖特免权,同样的在诉讼特免权下,调查取证的对象也不得再依赖这些特免权。

言的证人不能弃权：见 Schneider v. Leigh (1955) 2 QB 195; R v. R (1994) 1 WLR 758; Donnelly v. Weybridge Construction Ltd. (2006) EWHC 721 先例等等。[119]

虽然实践中最常见的是由律师依赖法律业务特免权而拒绝披露文件，但需要区分的是律师实际上只是为了客户的利益以及依赖客户的特免权拒绝，并非是自己享有法律业务特免权：见 R v. Central Criminal Court Ex p. Francis and Francis (1989) AC 346 先例。从另一个角度看，只要客户执意弃权，无论是律师还是其他人士都无权阻止：见 Re International Power Industries NV (1985) BCLC 128 先例。

笔者（杨良宜）就曾经遇到一位声名显著的英国律师在一个香港仲裁案件（笔者是仲裁庭的成员）中，在与其欧洲客户的通信中对诉讼对方当事人（中国公司）的律师（中国香港律师）采用了强烈的批判性、歧视性、人身攻击的文字/措辞（如愚蠢、不称职等）。然而该香港仲裁的结果是欧洲客户败诉，导致该欧洲客户拒绝支付英国律师希望收取的数百万港币剩余费用。根据仲裁裁决，该仲裁中存放于香港国际仲裁中心（HKIAC）的预付款有一部分要退还给欧洲客户，但由于前述与英国律师之间的争议，英国律师成功在香港法院获得了对这笔余款的冻结令，以满足应付未付的律师费用。欧洲客户非常不满意，发函给所有有关人士（包括仲裁庭、HKIAC、对方当事人及其律师），大骂其英国律师，指是英国律师的误导才使得自己以为可以胜诉，并披露了与英国律师的通信往来，包括刚刚提到的批判性、歧视性的文字/措辞。这下看来英国律师就可能面临中国香港律师的诽谤之诉或其他法律行动了，而且没有任何办法阻止有权对特免权弃权的欧洲客户这样披露文件。此案件的教训是即使有任何批判性、歧视性的想法，最好也不要以文字记录了。

12.3.1　谁是拥有法律意见特免权的客户

在近期的 Three Rivers DC v. Bank of England (No. 5) (2003) QB 1556 上诉庭先例中，由于 Longmore 大法官倾向于严格地限制法律意见特免权的范围，认为受到法律意见特免权保护的“客户”（client）并不包括公司的一般雇员，即公司的一般雇员与独立第三人在身份上并没有不同，从而导致谁是寻求法律意见的客户范围存在疑问。控制对客户的定义，不包括普通公司雇员，也是可以理解的，毕竟跨国公司雇员数以万计。要知道客户可以弃权，如果任何知情的普通雇员都能弃权的话，会给公司带来严重后果。

在该先例中，由于 BCCI 银行倒闭事件，英国政府任命 Bingham 勋爵开展对英格兰银行的质询，而英格兰银行为了应对调查成立调查应对小组（名为“Bingham Inquiry Unit”，或简称“BIU”），由 BIU 专门委任律师、与外界沟通等，因此被认定只

---

[119]　这里只针对法律业务特免权。在诉讼中，当事人提交给法院或仲裁庭的证人证言，虽然法律业务特免权在该诉讼中被弃权，但只要机密性没有丧失（如不是公开的开庭审理等），该证人证言仍然有可以无需披露给其他人士、类似无损害特免权的权利，如是不得被对方当事人用在其他有关联的诉讼中：见 Prudential Assurance Co. Ltd. v. Fountain Page Ltd. (1991) 1 WLR 756 先例。

有这个调查小组的成员与律师的通信往来才属于“客户”与“法律意见提供者”之间的通信往来,其他人士即使是英格兰银行的行长(governor)也没有这个地位(与律师之间的通信往来不受特免权保护、无法对特免权做出弃权)。

不妨节录 Astex Therapeutics Limited v. Astrazeneca AB (2016) EWHC 2759 先例中,Marsh 大法官对 Three Rivers DC v. Bank of England (No. 5)先例判法的总结:“The Court of Appeal concluded that the Bank is not entitled to privilege in any of the four categories summarised above and expressed the view that if the Governor (英格兰银行行长) himself of the Bank of England had noted down what he remembered in relation to the supervision of BCCI with the intention of giving it to the BIU for transmission to Freshfields(英格兰银行的律师), such a document would not be subject to legal advice privilege. Longmore LJ(做出判决的 Longmore 大法官) accepted the submission by Mr Pollock (英格兰银行对手委任的大律师) that on the evidence before the court... the BIU, which was established to deal with inquiries and to seek and receive Freshfields' advice, is for the purposes of this application, the client rather than any single officer however eminent he or she may be. It follows that no separate consideration need be given to the position of ex - employees who are, obviously, in no better position for the purpose of any claimed privilege.'[120]”

英国对于客户的狭窄定义在目前也只是来自于 Three Rivers DC v. Bank of England (No. 5)先例中,但也已经在之后的一些高院先例中被跟从:见 Astex Therapeutics Limited v. Astrazeneca AB; The RBS Rights Issue Litigation (2016) EWHC 3161 (Ch); SFC v. Eurasian Natural Resources Corporation Ltd. (2017) EWHC 1017(QB)先例。

而事实上各个国家对客户的定义也有不同看法,例如:

1. 美国有不少早期的案件都试图将美国法下的“attorney-client privilege”设定所谓的“control group”的测试标准,将“客户”限定在公司内的这个“control group”之内。但这在美国最高院的 Upjohn Co. v. United States, 449 US 383 (1981)先例中已经被明确否定。在美国,公司雇员与律师的通信往来受到特免权保护,相比英国法地位要广泛得多。

2. 新加坡则是已经有先例明确反对 Three Rivers DC v. Bank of England (No. 5)先例的判法:见 Skandanavia Enskilda Banken AB (Publ), Singapore Branch v. Asia

---

〔120〕 上诉庭的看法是银行没有对文件的特免权,同时指出即使是英格兰银行行长回忆并记录对 BCCI 的监管情况,希望通过 BIU 交给律师事务所(Freshfields)出具法律意见,这份文件也不会受到法律意见特免权的保护。Longmore 大法官对此认可,认为只有向(由英国政府成立并由 Bingham 勋爵负责的)调查 BCCI 银行倒闭的质询作出回应以及与律师沟通的 BIU 才属法律意见特免权的“客户”范畴,无论其他人士在英格兰银行内的工作有多重要的职位都毫无关系。

Pacific Breweries (Singapore) Pte Ltd. and others (2007) 2 SLR 367 先例。

3. 澳大利亚则看来有扩大法律意见特免权适用的趋势，将文件的主要目的(dominant purpose)是否为了获取法律意见作为判断标准：见 Pratt Holdings Pty Ltd. v. Commissioner of Taxation (2004) FCAFC 122 先例。

4. 香港上诉庭的 Citic Pacific Limited v. Secretary for Justice and Commissioner of Police (2015) HKCA 293 先例没有跟从英国判法，而是判只要是主要目的在于获取法律意见的内部机密文件(internal confidential documents of the client's organisation which are produced for the dominant purpose that they or their contents be used to obtain legal advice)，都可以受到法律意见特免权的保护。该先例涉及 2008 年金融危机时，中信泰富(Citic Pacific)于 2008 年 9 月 7 日意识到自己签订的一些远期外汇合约(foreign currency forward contract)可能导致巨大亏损，因此采用银行借贷、向国内公司寻求财政支援等方式希望度过危机。然而作为香港上市公司，根据香港股票交易市场的交易规则，一旦发现有任何对股票价值产生影响的情况，就需要尽可能快地(as soon as is reasonably practicable)披露。但在 2008 年 9 月 16 日，中信泰富子公司在关联交易公告中还提到中信泰富董事并不知悉集团经济情况有重大变更。直到 2008 年 10 月 20 日，才公布利润亏损预警公告，指出远期外汇合约可能导致 147 亿港币以上的损失。信息一发布，就在市场上掀起轩然大波，股票市值跌幅超过 50%。香港证券交易委员会(Securities and Futures Commission, SFC)即根据政策、法律法规、规章制度的要求，对中信泰富展开调查。在 SFC 要求下，中信泰富也愿意配合与同意将一些文件交给了 SFC。警方商业犯罪组也申请到法院命令，从中信泰富搜查与控制了数百页文件与一百多个硬盘中的电子文档，并希望从 SFC 获取中信泰富的文件。该先例就是中信泰富针对被警方搜查与控制的文件(书面与电子文件)，以法律业务特免权为由要求法院限制警方对文件的使用、退还这些文件等。一审([2012] 3 HKLRD G1)跟从了 Three Rivers DC v. Bank of England (No. 5)先例的判法，认定只有集团法务部门以及特定的几个高管与律师之间的通信往来才受到特免权保护，而其他人士与外部律师之间的通信往来不受到法律意见特免权保护。该先例中，争议焦点之一是秘书部某雇员(虽然也有律师资格)与外部律师(Clifford Chance)之间的通信往来被一审法院判不受到特免权保护。这些通信往来对中信泰富来说至关重要，如前述争议焦点中的法律意见就是针对如何草拟对股东与公众的公告。如果这些文件不享有特免权保护，中信泰富与其高管在面对 SFC、香港警方调查时会有严重后患，但对中信泰富而言，非常幸运的是上诉庭否定了一审判决，认为这些文件也受到特免权保护。

12.3.2　谁可以对联合特免权弃权

对于法律业务特免权来说，如果委托律师的客户只是单个主体，显然应当由单个主体享有特免权。而如果是有多个客户联合委托(joint retain)或是在委托时存在联合利益(joint interest)，导致文件受到的是“联合特免权”(joint privilege)或称“联合利益特免权”(joint interest privilege)的保护,特免权就由这多个客户联合享有,要弃权也要一起同意才行:见 The “Sagheera”(1997)1 Lloyds Rep. 160 先例。在 The “Sagheera”先例中,船东与船东互保协会(P&I Club)联合委托了律师事务所对 Sagheera 轮的爆炸沉没事件进行调查,显然就存在了船东与船东互保协会这两个客户对律师进行的联合委托,Rix 大法官对此时互相之间关系的描述是:“Parties who grant a joint retainer to solicitors of course retain no confidence as against one another: if they subsequently fall out and sue one another, they cannot claim privilege. But against all the rest of the world, they can maintain a claim for privilege for documents otherwise within the ambit of legal professional privilege; and because their privilege is a joint one, it can only be waived jointly, and not by one party alone. These principles are, I believe, well established: see for instance Rochefoucauld v. Boustead (1896) 65 L. J. Ch. 794, Cia Barca de Panama S. A. v. George Wimpey Y Co. Ltd. ,[1980] 1 Lloyd’s Rep. 598, In Re Koninsberg (A Bankrupt),[1989] 1 W. L. R. 1257.[121]”

又如是 The “Sagheera”先例中提到的 Rochefoucauld v. Boustead (1896) 65 LJ Ch 794 先例中,两个自然人联合委托律师,并因此产生了受到特免权保护的文件。后来有一个诉讼将这两个自然人都列为共同被告,其中一个自然人想对受特免权保护的文件弃权。法院认定另一个自然人联合享有特免权,而且并没有同意做出弃权,因此文件不得被披露。这种情况的产生也很好理解,毕竟有的情况中,法律意见的内容只是对其中一位联合委托人不利,而对其中另一位来说可能是中性甚至有利的。换句话说,法律业务特免权既然是由客户所享有,即使要对法律业务特免权弃权的行为,也应当由客户做出。如果是多方联合委托,应由多方联合做出弃权行为才有效。

实践中常常出现问题的,公司、合伙企业或信托等对律师做出委托并取得法律意见的情况。因为此时公司的股东或其他高管、合伙企业中的其他合伙人、信托中的受益人究竟是否也同时享有特免权会存在疑问,如股东、高管、董事、合伙人、受益人等是否享有联合特免权。

在本章之 12.1 段已经提到,现在这个问题变得特别尖锐,在可能涉及被监管的领域时,可能或已经开始被调查时,公司都应当委托熟悉有关监管的律师给出如何应对有关机构监管的法律意见。

股东、高管、董事、合伙人或受益人如果与公司一起联合委托律师,如在与律师签订的委托合约(retainer)中,明示将公司高管与股东等的名字作为联合委托人,而且索取的法律意见或者所针对的已经开始或可能开始的诉讼与公司以及股东等有关,

---

〔121〕 多个当事人与其联合委托的律师,互相之间是不存在机密性的,如果多个当事人关系破裂,互相起诉对方,也不能依赖特免权拒绝披露文件。但是对任何其他第三人来说,这多个当事人与联合委托的律师的通信(或文件)仍然受到特免权的保护。由于特免权是联合享有,也只能被联合弃权,而不能被一方当事人单独放弃。这些理论在过往的先例中已经被广泛接受与认可。

公司与股东显然是联合享有法律业务特免权(类似 The "Sagheera"先例中 Rix 大法官所指的"joint retainer"的情况)。这实际上也是典型的联合特免权产生的情况。问题在于一般情况下,委托律师常常只是以公司的名义,而不会明示包括公司其他有关人士。

"法律业务特免权"(legal professional privilege)与委托合约或其他合约如何签订与内容并没有关系。而是要具体看事后产生的有关文件是否可以符合"法律意见特免权"(legal advice privilege)或"诉讼特免权"(litigation privilege)保护的范畴。换句话说,要看有关人士是否属于向律师(或者其他法律意见提供者)索取法律意见的客户,或律师给出的文件是否主要目的是有关人士的诉讼或可能的诉讼。

因此,即使在委托合约或其他合约上没有写明,只要是客观事实符合了判断标准,在律师出具文件时公司与股东存在联合利益(joint interest),公司的股东等人士也同样可以联合享有法律业务特免权。如在 Gouraud v. Edison (1888) 57 LJ Ch 498 先例中就涉及股东与公司的争议。对于一些曾经由律师发出给股东的文件,公司指称股东是代表公司与律师进行通讯,因此,特免权属于公司享有,也可以依赖特免权拒绝披露,但被 Chitty 大法官否定。在 Chitty 大法官看来,该先例中在委托律师之时,股东与公司之间存在类似合伙人之间或信托人与受益人之间的联合利益,因此,律师出具文件的特免权本就由公司与股东联合享有。

在笔者看来,这实际上也意味着,虽然律师只是给出一份法律意见,甚至针对的是同一个问题,但由于公司(或合伙企业、信托等)与股东、高管、董事、合伙人或受益人之间的联合利益,导致这个法律意见的"客户"并不仅仅是公司,还包括了股东、高管、董事、合伙人或受益人。换句话说,会根据事实认定股东、高管、董事、合伙人或受益人也是这个法律意见的对象,因而联合享有特免权。也因此在实际上达到了与联合委托律师有同样的效果,包括在产生了联合特免权的情况下,股东、高管、董事、合伙人或受益人在与公司(或合伙企业、信托等)之间就不能依赖特免权拒绝披露,更重要的看来还包括了(或合伙企业、信托等)与股东、高管、董事、合伙人或受益人在面临第三人的披露要求时,都可以依赖特免权拒绝披露。

但什么时候可以认定为存在联合利益是比较模糊的,如较近期的 R (on the application of Ford) v. Financial Services Authority (2011) EWHC 2583 (Admin)先例中高院的 Burnett 大法官先总结了 Bankim Thanki QC 的《Law of Privilege》一书与 Hodge Malek QC 编辑的《Phipson on Evidence》(2010 年的第 17 版)一书的说法(事实上该先例中这两位作者/编辑分别是申请人与被申请人的代表大律师),以及注意到这两本权威书籍都没有就该先例中这种委托合约只写上公司名字的情况引用任何先例。Burnett 大法官指出:"In short, joint interest privilege can arise in two circumstances. First, when two or more legal persons jointly retain the same lawyer. Secondly when, even though there is no joint retainer, the parties have a joint interest in the subject matter of the communication in issue at the time that it comes into existence. As Mr

Thanki puts it in his book：'... the document must have come into being for the furtherance of the joint purpose or interest.' It is common ground that such an interest may arise between a company and its directors. Whilst the broad principle there articulated was not in issue, it is striking that neither counsel has cited any English authority which establishes the criteria against which this second aspect of joint interest privilege should be considered.[122]"

该先例也是典型的公司内部人士需要法律业务特免权保护的情况。公司(Keydata)受到曾经的英国金融服务监管局(Financial Services Authority,简称 FSA,2013年以后 FSA 的职务被"Financial Conduct Authority"与英格兰银行的"Prudential Regulation Authority"取代)调查。因此。Keydata 委托律师事务所(Irwin Mitchell)应对该调查。而在这个委托下产生的通信往来(如发给律师事务所的指示、律师事务所给出的回复意见等)就可能会受到法律业务特免权的保护,双方对此也没有重大争议。而 9 个月之后,FSA 又扩大了调查范围,一并调查了两位公司董事与一位公司的合规主任(compliance officer)。问题出在后来 Keydata 进入破产接管(administration)程序,接管人(administrator)普华永道(Price Waterhouse Coopers,简称 PWC)为了合作与配合调查,将与律师事务所之间的通信往来提供给了 FSA。FSA 依赖这些文件的内容,向公司董事与合规主任发出调查报告与警告通知(warning notice)。看来下一步会是刑事起诉,因此,董事们与合规主任指称 FSA 的行为不合法,因为公司董事、合规主任可以依赖联合特免权拒绝披露这些文件,FSA 不得依赖这些文件。

该先例中的 FSA 提出应采纳美国做法,即一旦律师由公司单独委托,只有公司才享有法律意见特免权,无论是公司内部的人士与该法律意见的关系有多紧密,或律师是否事实上也向该内部人士个人提供意见,都不得享有同样的特免权。但这也被 Burnett 大法官明确拒绝。

根据美国最高院的 Commodity Futures Trading Commission v. Weintraub 471 US 345, 195 S Ct 1989, 1991 85 L Ed 2d 372 (1985)先例,美国法下不允许在没有联合委托的情况下产生联合特免权。因为这样的做法会阻碍破产法要揭开公司内部欺诈行为的目标,也阻碍了对可能的公司内部不当行为的调查,因此是违反美国公共政策的:"... important policy considerations to circumscribe the availability of joint advice privilege which might result in corporate officers being able to prevent a corporation (or its successor) from waiving privilege. It would 'defeat the Bankruptcy Code's goal of

[122] 简单而言,联合利益特免权产生主要在两种情况。第一种是当两个或更多的法律主体联合委托了同样律师。第二种则是尽管没有联合委托,但这些法律主体在有关通讯进行时有联合利益。Bankim Thanki QC 在其书中指出该文件必须是为了促进联合的目的或利益而制作。普遍看法是在公司与其董事之间就可能会产生这种联合利益。双方对大原则并无争议,但是双方大律师均没有援引任何英国先例中,以说明在何种情况之下会符合第二种联合利益。

uncovering insider fraud' and prevent the investigation of possible misconduct by officers."

但本章之12.2.2段已经提到,在英国法下并没有这样的公共政策或说法:R v. Derby Magistrates, Ex p B (1996) 1 AC 487贵族院先例中明确了特免权不会被其他公共利益所超越的绝对性权利的地位。

Keydata的公司董事、合规主任则提出,在对律师事务所做出委托时,他们合理地相信(reasonably believed)此时寻求的法律意见是为了Keydata与公司董事、合规主任的联合利益(事实上,FSA在事后也确实针对这些人士进行调查)。而Burnett大法官则不同意这样的看法,Burnett大法官指出在考虑什么事实可以构成联合利益特免权时,需要考虑大量的事实,主观的"合理地相信"不能作为判断的依据:"The same principles apply to joint legal privilege but because the interests of persons other than the individual claiming privilege are in play their position must be taken into account when determining whether the joint privilege exists. I do not accept that the test whether the individual concerned 'reasonably believed' that he was the client of the lawyer provides a satisfactory test for joint interest privilege... In searching for the true factual position at the time that the contentious communication was made it is necessary to distinguish between advice being given to an individual as client from advice which is being given to another, but in which the first individual is interested because it impacts upon his personal position. It is the former that supports a claim for joint privilege, not the latter. It is also necessary to recognise that if joint privilege exists it affects the rights of all those who share that joint privilege and also the professional obligations of the lawyers. For this reason statements of subjective belief by an individual claiming joint privilege without more are likely to be of little value. Joint privilege should not arise casually or accidentally. For joint privilege to arise it is necessary for the facts to demonstrate that all those sharing the privilege and the lawyers concerned knew, or from the objective evidence ought to have known, that they enjoyed legal professional privilege with the others. Evidence of an understanding by the lawyer of potential conflicts of interest may provide some evidential support for joint privilege, but it is not a necessary ingredient. It is not unknown for conflicts of interest to arise but those advising to be slow to appreciate their significance. In my judgment, apart from those cases in which there is no legal distinction between those claiming joint privilege... an individual claiming joint privilege with others in a communication with a lawyer, when there is no joint retainer, will need to establish the following facts by evidence: i) That he communicated with the lawyer for the purpose of seeking advice in an individual capacity; ii) That he made clear to the lawyer that he was seeking legal advice in an individual capacity, rather than only as a representative of a corporate body; iii) That those with whom the joint privilege was claimed knew or ought to have appreciated the legal position; iv) That the lawyer knew or ought to have appreciated that he was communicating with the individual in that individual capacity; v) That the communication with the lawyer was confidential."

以上节录内容说的是,联合特免权影响的是所有分享联合特免权的人士以及提供有关法律意见的律师。因此,希望依赖联合特免权保护的人士仅仅提供对自己主观意图的陈述(合理地相信)意义不大。联合特免权不会随便地或是偶然地产生,而是需要有事实显示分享联合特免权的人士以及有关的律师都知道,或是根据客观的证据显示应当知道,他们之间会适用法律业务特免权。如果有证据证明律师在提供法律意见时还考虑过该人士与公司之间的利益冲突问题,这对证明联合特免权的存在有一定支持,但也非必要条件。毕竟有利益冲突出现但律师很迟才发现问题的情况也存在。在没有联合委托合约的情况下,如果要指称由于联合利益的存在而产生联合特免权,要通过证据证明:(1)该人士与律师沟通目的是作为个体的自己寻求法律意见;(2)该人士也向律师表明了自己是以个体身份而非公司代表人身份寻求法律意见;(3)公司应该也知道或应当知道此法律地位;(4)律师知道或应当知道该人士是以个体身份与律师沟通的;(5)该人士与律师的沟通是有机密性的。

显然要满足这五个要求并不容易,因此相比通过明示的联合委托,要依赖个别案件的事实证明联合利益,从而可以有联合特免权的存在是困难重重。

在该先例中,双方都各自提供了大量的文件证据,包括很多当时的文件(通信往来、会议记录、委托合约)以及证人证言等。Burnett 大法官在综合考虑之后认为,前述几项要求能够从提供的证据的字里行间显示出来,因此认为 Keydata 的公司董事、合规主任都是律师提供法律意见的对象,可以享有联合特免权。FSA 也就不能依赖这些特免权文件,之前发出的警告通知无效,而且也不能依赖这些文件做出进一步的其他行动(如刑事起诉等)。

总结而言,对于公司的董事、高管等人士,在涉及合规问题需要委托律师时,虽然在委托书或当时文件并没有对这些人士名字的明确记录,也仍然可以通过事实的背景依赖类似 R (on the application of Ford) v. Financial Services Authority 先例中的默示联合特免权拒绝披露文件。但从这个先例可以看到,要认定联合利益并不容易,而且法院也不会轻易认定联合利益的存在。

而且这样做存在着很大的难度与不确定性,要这样证明当时的事实背景也是非常耗费时间、精力与金钱的行为。更为危险的是,如果在法院就特免权问题作出决定前,有关机构已经根据文件出具报告,一旦公开就有丧失机密性的可能性,也就再也不能依赖特免权拒绝披露了。因此为了肯定,最好还是如同 Burnett 大法官指出的一样,在委托书中就明确记录需要保护的人士(如列明董事、高管的姓名或职位等),或者是在出现需要时以书面记录在各方之间澄清。

而关于联合利益导致的联合特免权,与本章话题有关的是针对弃权来说,联合利益与联合委托导致的联合特免权是否会存在不同。[123] 在权威书籍如《Documentary Evidence》(第 12 版,2015 年)一书之 19 - 02 段说,如果是联合委托的情况,其中一个客户不能单方面对特免权做出弃权。但如果是联合利益,看来更好的看法是没有这个要求:"Where there is a joint privilege, it cannot be waived against third parties unilaterally by only one joint client. However, where there is merely a joint interest, the better view is that no such issue arises."

又如《Law of Privilege》(第 2 版,2011 年)之 6. 08 段则是说:"As with a joint retainer, the privilege is not lost simply because the parties subsequently fall out.[124] Given the extent to which the existence of a joint interest might fetter the actual client's rights in relation to privileged advice, a joint interest ought not to be lightly inferred.[125] Nor have the courts worked through all the consequences of the existence of a joint interest. The concept is less well developed or defined in the case law than joint retainer.[126] It is questionable, for example whether a client is necessarily precluded from waiving privilege in advice he has obtained simply because someone else (of necessity a stranger to the relevant lawyer-client relationship) can assert a joint interest in the advice.[127] For instance, while companies and shareholders might have a joint interest in legal advice, it is doubtful whether the courts would say privilege in legal advice obtained by the company could not be waived by the company unless all its shareholders consented. Would a large multinational corporation be required to obtain the consent of all its shareholders before wai-

---

〔123〕 在刚刚提到的 R (on the application of Ford) v. Financial Services Authority (2011) EWHC 2583 (Admin)先例中,由于当事人之间同意了接管人(普华永道)代表公司做出的弃权行为(注意这里是接管人代表公司做出弃权行为,与之类似但不同的是,破产受托人不能代表破产的自然人做出弃权行为,见本章之 12. 3. 4 段)不影响董事、合规主任可以依赖特免权拒绝披露:"It is accepted that PwC's waiver of privilege on behalf of the company did not impact upon the claimant's privilege. It follows that the FSA may not rely upon the content of those communications in the regulatory proceedings against Keydata or the executives."因此,在该先例中没有对联合利益导致的联合特免权如何弃权的争议。

〔124〕 不会由于联合当事人后来意见不合,就令联合委托导致的联合特免权丧失。如对一个当事人来说,弃权也影响不大而同意弃权,但另一个当事人由于是监管对象,一旦披露就会有麻烦,因此极力反对。

〔125〕 联合利益导致的联合特免权要能够根据事实向法院证明,并不容易被法院接受。

〔126〕 对联合利益导致的联合特免权,普通法下如何处理有关弃权的问题,也不完全清楚与没有针对性的先例。

〔127〕 如果委托合约下的客户想要放弃特免权,是否会被不知名、也从未参与有关客户与律师之间交往的第三人指称有联合利益从而阻碍当事人弃权?

ving privilege in advice the company had obtained? This seems highly unlikely.[128]"

这方面不清楚的地位仍然有待后续普通法进一步发展。但在笔者看来,尽管虽然会发生《Law of Privilege》(第2版,2011年)之6.08段提到的跨国公司与大量股东的例子,但现在对联合利益导致的联合特免权处于收紧趋势,法院不会轻易认定联合利益的存在;而另一方面,如果确实根据案情的综合事实,有理由认为实际上律师出具的法律意见的对象,或是涉及诉讼或可能诉讼的人士包括公司这些大量股东,也没有理由不对这些股东的权利进行保护。换句话说,法院完全可以不认定联合利益的存在,但一旦认定了联合利益存在并导致联合特免权,应当视为与联合委托合约导致的联合特免权有同样地位。尤其是联合利益导致的联合特免权在各方面权利都与联合委托导致的联合特免权相同,如果一定要在弃权方面做出不同看待,就有前后不一致的嫌疑了。但不可否认的是,联合利益导致的联合特免权的确在特定情况中如果不允许实际委托律师的人士(如公司法人)单方面弃权,会导致严重的不公平与大量的费用浪费,而针对这些特别的情况,则可以作为个别的例外情况看待。

12.3.3　共同利益特免权

在本章之12.2.4段已经提到"共同利益特免权"(common interest privilege),即已经受到法律业务特免权保护的文件,被原享有特免权的当事人A(或常被称为"primary privilege holder")将文件保持机密性地[如在信函或文件抬头表明"机密"(confidential)或条文约定不得传阅给第三人等]交出给当事人B(或常被称为"incidental party"),而在交出之时,当事人B对文件有共同利益(common interest),当事人B就可以依赖共同利益特免权,拒绝将文件交出给其他人士。

共同利益特免权常常并不被认为是单独的类型,而纯粹是对特免权弃权的抗辩,或是"anti-waiver device"。这样说法的原因是,常有指称当事人A将文件交给当事人B的行为会导致特免权的弃权,而通过共同利益的说法,可以抗辩这并非是弃权行为:见澳大利亚的State of South Australia v. Peat Marwick Mitchell (1995) 65 SASR 72先例。但在笔者看来,这样的说法并不能很好地解释为何当事人B可以对其他人士以共同利益特免权为由拒绝披露,在一些权威书籍中也没有支持这样的看法。

在较近期的Commercial Union Assurance Co. Plc. v. Mander (1996) 2 Lloyd's Rep. 640先例中,Moore - Bick大法官对共同利益特免权的说法引用了Buttes Gas and Oil Co. v. Hammer (No.3) (1981) QB 223上诉庭先例中所举的例子进行解释:"Take the example given by Lord Justice Donaldson in Buttes v. Hammer (No.3) of tenants in a block of flats. One tenant, acting entirely for his own benefit, obtains legal

---

[128] 如一家大型跨国公司,会有以十万、百万计的股东。如果公司与股东对有关的法律意见确有联合利益,是否说除非是获得这十万、百万的股东的同意,否则公司就无法对法律意见弃权?这要求是不现实的。

advice concerning a dispute with the landlord over a provision in the lease which affects other tenants in a similar way. If he chooses to give a copy of the document containing that advice in confidence to another tenant who is willing to co-operate with him in pursuing a claim their common interest would be sufficient for the document to remain privileged in the latter's hands. I do not, however, see any basis upon which the second tenant could have insisted on seeing the advice if the first tenant did not wish to show it to him, even though they had a common interest in the subject matter.[129]"

共同利益特免权在一定程度上看来与"联合特免权"(joint privilege)存在类似之处。也因此在 Winterthur Swiss Insurance Company v. AG (Manchester) Limited (2006) EWHC 839 (Comm)先例中(有关案情介绍请见本章之12.6.1.2段),Aikens大法官认为对谁可以弃权的问题来说,联合特免权(特别是联合委托律师导致的联合特免权)也与共同利益特免权是一致的:"If the correct analysis is that NIG (原告子公司) is entitled to access to the post – ATE Policy documents by virtue of its 'common interest privilege as a sword', then although Winterthur(原告) would be entitled to discovery as against the Panel Solicitors, it would be met by the claim that the post — ATE Policy documents are subject to privilege, which is a 'common interest privilege' in favour of both the TAG Claimants and NIG. **Moreover, if legal professional privilege is held jointly, then it cannot be waived by one person alone. In my view that rule must apply equally to common interest privilege as much as to 'joint privilege'** where, eg. two parties jointly obtain advice from a lawyer."(加黑部分是笔者的强调)

但联合利益导致的联合特免权与共同利益导致的共同利益特免权存在不少不同之处。如联合特免权要求在委任时存在联合利益,而共同利益特免权是要求在文件被交出时存在共同利益。又如,共同利益特免权需要本享有特免权的人士主动与有意地将文件交出。更显然的不同是,共同利益特免权针对的是已经存在特免权的文件。因此,要将联合利益特免权一概与共同利益特免权类似看待,也显然存在不妥之处。也因此有说法是共同利益特免权的弃权看来只要是"primary privilege party"或者说是原享有特免权的当事人做出弃权就可以导致弃权的后果。毕竟本享有特免权的人士主动与有意将文件(如一份对自己有利的专家报告)披露给其他人士分享,如果弃权还要征得所有收到文件的人士同意,如在集体诉讼案件中,成千上万的人士可能都收到一份文件,如果漏了通知其中一个就导致无法弃权,就说不过去了。正如《Law of Privilege》(第2版,2011年)一书之6.53段所说:"It ought to follow that

---

〔129〕 以租客与业主之间租约条文解释的争议为例,一个租客仅为了自己的利益向律师寻求法律意见,而这份格式租约实际上也被业主用在与其他租客的租赁中。如果寻求了法律意见的租客,在事后将一份法律意见的副本在保有机密性的前提下交给其他愿意协助向业主施压、为了他们的共同利益提起诉讼的租客,这会足以使得这份文件在接受文件的租客手上仍然享有特免权保护。

common interest privilege can be waived by the primary privilege holder. This is the logical conclusion if, as Moore-Bick J concluded in Mander's case(Commercial Union Assurance Co. Plc. v. Mander 先例), common interest privilege involves the voluntary disclosure of information. It would be an undue fetter on the primary privilege holder to say that he cannot waive privilege without the consent of all those parties with whom he has chosen to share his advice."

而在澳大利亚的一些先例中,则是强调了公平原则的适用,看是否会造成其他享有共同利益特免权人士的不公平,正如 Farrow Mortgage Services Pty Ltd. v. Webb (1996) 39 NSWLR 601 先例中新南威尔士上诉庭说:"... In the case of common interest privilege, as distinct from joint privilege, I do not think it will always be necessary that all interested parties concur for the privilege to be waived. If in principle legal professional privilege vested in a party is not lost by dissemination of the contents of confidential documents to other with a common interest, I think that fairness, in many cases, will require that the privilege not be lost because one of those parties, be it the provider or the recipient, is minded to waive it. Once parties with a common interest have exchanged or provided one or another the contents of communications with legal advisers about the subject of their common interest, **the question of whether the privilege is lost with its waiver by one must be determined by asking whether the waiver has made it unfair for the other parties with a common interest to maintain the privilege**... This requires account to be taken of such matters as the circumstances in which the privileged communication took place and came to be exchanged and provided to others."(加黑部分是笔者的强调)

类似的说法也可见较近期的 Patrick v. Capital Finance Corporation (Australia) Pty Ltd. (2004) 211 ALR 272 澳大利亚联邦法院先例。在这样的判法下,无论是否是"primary privilege holder",要真正做出弃权必须是在不造成对其他共同利益特免权享有的人士不公平的情况下。

总结而言,谁可以对共同利益特免权做出弃权的问题也存在很多不明确之处,仍然有待后续先例的厘清与确认。而在笔者看来,谁可以对共同利益特免权做出弃权的问题并不能一概而论,确实需要结合事实来看待。在大部分情况中,如本段前文中提到的 Commercial Union Assurance Co. Plc. v. Mander 先例中,Moore - Bick 大法官介绍的有关租客的例子,如果开始诉讼的租客从大律师处获取了一份法律意见,并交给其他租客过目与参考,事后在诉讼中租客要披露这份法律意见,其他租客没有理由拒绝。但也有不少的情况中,确实由于存在共同利益的多方当事人的行为会互相影响,如在保险人与被保险人之间,如果一方将本受法律业务特免权保护的专家报告等文件披露出去,会导致另一方处于极度不利与不公平的地位,从而可能被法院做出不同判决。但在英国有关特免权的先例中,毕竟与澳大利亚先例不同,不会纯粹依赖公平原则的适用，因此在笔者看来，绝大多数情况下仍然将以“primary privilege holder”可以弃权作为主导思想。

12.3.4 权利的转让与继承

法律业务特免权只能是向律师寻求法律意见的客户，或是面对诉讼或可能的诉讼当事人所享有。一般情况下，特免权的权利并不会转让给其他人所享有，但在有的合约权利被转让时，会有受让人（assignee）可以依赖特免权拒绝披露的情况。

可能的情况之一是不动产产权（title）转让，在实际转让前，如果转让人（assignor）针对不动产的问题获取了法律意见，受让人看来可以依赖此特免权拒绝披露的：见Crescent Farm（Sidcup）Sports Ltd. v. Sterling Offices Ltd.（1972）Ch 553先例。该先例中，一个土地买卖合约中约定，如果在土地交易后的20年内，买方准备出售标的土地的话，卖方享有优先回购的权利。但之后买方将土地出售给了分买方。而卖方则以买方没有给予充分行使优先回购权为由，指称属于违约行为，从而提出损失索赔；同时也以分买方与买方之间存在“共谋”（conspiracy）为由，将分买方也列为被告。在诉讼程序中，卖方就申请分买方披露文件，包括买方曾经告知分买方在买卖前咨询与获取的法律意见等。Goff大法官认为，分买方作为土地产权的继承者获得了这些文件，因此原产权人（买方）享有的特免权等利益也由继承者享有：“it is clearly established that legal professional privilege of a predecessor in title does ensure for the benefit of his successor.”

自然人、公司/企业法人不再存在（如个人的死亡，公司的破产、解散），作为自然人、公司法人等本可以享有的特免权并不一定就此消失，而可能会由死者的继承人（如死者的妻子）、公司的清盘人、破产管理人等继续依赖以拒绝文件披露或决定弃权。

继承的情况在较古老的Calcraft v. Guest（1898）1 QB 759先例中就有涉及。原告家族拥有一片捕鱼区/拥有区域的捕鱼权，在1787年与捕鱼区/捕鱼权有关关的一个刑事案件中，原告的先祖获取了一些受法律特免权保护的文件。一百多年后，被告涉嫌侵犯（trespass）原告经继承得来的捕鱼区/捕鱼权，在诉讼中，被告希望依赖这些一百多年前的文件。但法院拒绝了被告的要求，因为原告通过继承捕鱼区/捕鱼权的产权（title），所有有关的财产、权利都被原告继承了，包括一百多年前文件的特免权保护。该先例也显示了无论过了多久，法律业务特免权仍然可以继续存在（once privileged，always privileged）。

个人破产也会有文件被转移的问题。在Re Konigsberg（1989）1 WLR 1257先例中，夫妻将原本共同所有的一处房产转移为由妻子单独所有，联合委托了律师协助交易。其后丈夫破产，有破产受托人（trustee）被委托管理与处置丈夫的财产。破产受托人怀疑丈夫与妻子的交易实属转移财产逃避债务的行为，因此在与妻子的诉讼中，希望依赖在房产转移中律师出具的文件，但妻子以特免权为由拒绝披露。在该先例中，法院认定对律师的委托是夫妻联合做出，由夫妻联合享有特免权。在丈夫破产后,破产受托人会接替(step in the shoes)丈夫的立场,虽然不能对特免权做出弃权(有关联合委托律师导致联合特免权,向第三人弃权需要所有享有联合特免权的人士共同做出的问题已经在本章之12.3.2段介绍),但联合特免权不能在联合委托人之间适用,因此,破产受托人可以将文件披露出来,交给法院参考和依赖。

在近期的Avonwick Holdings Limited v. Shlosberg (2016) EWCA Civ 1138先例中,则考虑了有关破产信托人对特免权进行弃权的问题。该先例中,S先生(Shlosberg)为了某投资项目,通过自己的W公司(Webinvest)进行集资。主要有两笔资金来源,一笔是从A公司(Avonwick)获得的借贷(同时S先生以个人名义提供担保),另一笔则是从S先生自己家族信托控制的C公司(Castle)获得借贷。获得集资后,再由W公司将款项借贷给Machitski先生的G公司(Globoid)着手投资项目操作。即有两笔贷款,贷款(1):A公司与C公司借贷给W公司;贷款(2):W公司将金钱交给G公司着手投资。

贷款(2)到期后,G公司在借贷到期后未能按时还款,W公司即通过仲裁途径索赔,并与G公司达成和解协议,获得赔偿。G公司之后宣告破产。接着贷款(1)期满,W公司也未能向A公司与C公司还款。债权人A公司即向W公司以及借贷的担保人S先生索赔,并获得胜诉。在此诉讼中,A公司委任了律师事务所Dechert,W公司与S先生联合委托了律师事务所Fladget。而在此诉讼的披露程序中,W公司与G公司的和解协议内容被披露,结果发现G公司的赔偿金额实际上没有赔付给W公司,而主要是赔付给W公司另一笔集资借贷债务的债权人C公司。W公司实际上是个空壳,不会也无能力赔付A公司的胜诉金额。因此,A公司申请W公司与担保人S先生破产。相应的有破产受托人(trustee)被委托管理S先生的财产,以及有破产清算人(liquidator)管理W公司的财产。在个人破产或公司清算的案件中,破产受托人、破产清算人常常与主要债权人委托同一律师事务所以便处理案件,该先例中的破产受托人也委托了A公司的律师事务所Dechert。W公司与S先生联合委托的律师事务所Fladgate也将大量的文件交给了破产受托人。

另一方面,A公司还以和解协议中涉及"共谋"(conspiracy)的经济侵权(economic tort)为由,向实际收到G公司赔偿金额的C公司开始索赔。W公司及其破产清算人加入成为共同原告,G公司、S先生等人士被作为共同被告。在此程序中,S先生的破产受托人试图依赖自己从Fladgate处收到的文件,并指出如果涉及文件特免权保护,自己作为破产受托人要做出弃权。一开始,联合委托律师事务所的S先生拒绝这些文件被使用,并向法院申请禁令限制使用。

在本章之12.3.2段已经提到谁可以对联合特免权弃权的问题。在W公司与S先生联合对Fladgate进行委托并抗辩A公司的索赔时,与Fladgate之间的通信往来显然受到联合特免权的保护,如果要弃权,也只能是W公司与S先生共同弃权。而该先例中的问题是,W公司的破产清算人以及管理S先生财产的破产受托人显然都有弃权的意图,尤其是对于S先生的破产受托人而言,是否可以对本由S先生享有的拒绝披露的权利做出弃权呢？

上诉庭给出的答案是否定的，认为法律业务特免权存在基本人权的属性，归属于S先生个人所有。在本章之12.2.2段已经提到，R v. Derby Magistrates, Ex p B (1996) AC 487与R (Morgan Grenfell & Co. Ltd) v. Special Commissioner of Income Tax (2003) 1 AC 563等先例之下，法律业务特免权是绝对性权利，除非有立法条文明示或必要的默示超越了特免权，否则不会被轻易超越。英国《破产法》虽然允许破产受托人控制与处置破产人的财产权(property)，但仅仅是破产受托人可以查看或使用受特免权保护的文件用以处置财产，而不能做出弃权。不妨节录上诉庭的Terence Etherton大法官在Avonwick Holdings Limited v. Shlosberg先例的判决如下："... The submission has a practical attraction. Indeed, Mr Marshall(S先生的代表大律师) accepted that the trustee can use privileged documentation and the information contained in it for the statutory purpose of getting in and realising the bankrupt's estate. He submitted, and the Judge concluded, however, that the trustee can only use such documentation and information in a way that would not amount to a waiver of privilege. I agree... It is not, however, necessarily implicit that the trustee can waive the bankrupt's legal professional privilege in taking steps against third parties for the benefit of the bankrupt's estate, desirable as that might be from the point of view of the creditors..."

根据这样的说法，也为本段前文中提到的Re Konigsberg先例中的破产受托人得以依赖破产人的权利查看与获取受特免权保护的文件从另一个角度提供了解释。

值得注意的是，这里所针对的只是在自然人破产时的破产受托人的问题。而针对公司破产时的管理人(adminstrator)或清算人(liquidator)与个人破产时的破产受托人的独立身份有所不同。公司的破产管理人或清算人是公司的代理人，因此可以以公司的名义做出弃权行为。Terence Etherton大法官说："They concern documents obtained by administrative receivers and liquidators, who are agents of the company. A trustee in bankruptcy is not an agent of the bankrupt."这在本章之12.3.2段提到的R (on the application of Ford) v. Financial Services Authority (2011) EWHC 2583 (Admin)先例中也已经有所明确。

而在笔者看来，自然人与公司法人在破产后对文件特免权的弃权有不同的对待，理由也很清楚。前者涉及人权，但后者并没有这方面问题。毕竟破产受托人对某些文件的特免权弃权，有可能导致破产的自然人需要承担潜在的刑事责任等问题[这还涉及"自证其罪特免权"(self-incrimination privilege)]。

12.3.5 诉讼中律师的表见授权

律师实际上并非自己拥有特免权拒绝披露，而是为了客户以及依赖客户对文件的特免权可以拒绝将文件披露。随之而来的问题是，虽然律师无法弃权，但在诉讼中，如果律师确实将本享有特免权的文件披露出来，能否被认为是客户的弃权行为呢？

不应该被披露的文件被不小心或错误地披露出来并不罕见,可能是在文件派送时将要送给己方大律师的文件送给了对方律师或大律师。而更多的情况是在披露文件时,一方疏忽披露了一些享有特免权的文件。在诉讼中,律师往往会有当事人的一般授权与特别授权做出诉讼行为,这些行为的后果也要由客户承担。站在对方当事人的角度,如果享有特免权的文件被对方律师交给自己,就可以认为对方的律师有授权这样做,至少可以认为存在"表见授权"(apparent / ostensible autority)的弃权。

不小心或错误地披露一方如果发觉得早,通常的救济办法是要求对方将文件退回(如送错)并承诺不使用这些文件。如果对方不合作,就可以向法院申请禁令,不让对方使用这些文件。法院只要认为他没有弃权,通常会做出禁令,不让对方利用这个机会得益:Goddard v. Nationwide Building Society (1987) QB 670; English and American Insurance Co. Ltd. v. Herbert Smith & Co. (1988) FSR 232, Ch D 等先例。但也有先例认为,如果被披露的有特免权的文件已经被对方检查与复印,就已经太迟,对方可以使用复印的文件作为证据:Clacraft v. Guest (1898) 1 QB 759 CA; Re Briamore Manufacturing Ltd. (In Liquidation) (1986) 1 WLR 1429 Ch D 等先例。但对这种可能造成严重后果的无心之失,也有几种例外情况令对方即使检查与复印了有关文件也无法使用,包括"欺诈"(fraud)与明显错误(obvious mistake)。[130] 由于禁令是一种衡平法救济,如果法院认为不应该让对方在明知道没有弃权的情况下利用这个错误取巧,就会做出救济。

而在 CPR 之后,对这种犯错的情况又多了一重保护,CPR r. 31.30 规定:"Where a party inadvertently allows a privileged document to be inspected, the party who has inspected the document may use it or its contents only with permission of the court."

有关 CPR 后英国在这方面的法律地位,不妨简单节录 Al Fayed v. Commissioner of Police for the Metropolis (2002) EWCA Civ 780 上诉庭先例中,Clarke 大法官总结过往先例后得出的说法:

"i) **A party giving inspection of documents must** decide before doing so **what privileged documents he wishes to allow the other party to see and what he does not**.

ii) Although the privilege is that of the client and not the solicitor, a party clothes **his solicitor with ostensible authority (if not implied or express authority) to waive privilege** in respect of relevant documents.

iii) A solicitor considering documents made available by the other party to litigation owes no duty of care to that party and is in general entitled **to assume that any privilege** which might otherwise have been claimed for such documents **has been waived**.

---

[130] 见 Guinness Peat Properties Ltd. v. Fitzroy Robinson Partnership (1987) 1 WLR 1027 (1987) 1 WLR 1027; Derby v. Weldon (No. 8) (1991) 1 WLR 73 CA; International Business Machines Corp v. Phoenix International Computers Ltd. (1995) 1 All E. R. 413 Ch D 等先例。

iv) In these circumstances, where a party has given inspection of documents, including privileged documents which he **has allowed the other party to inspect by mistake, it will in general be too late for him to claim privilege in order to attempt to correct the mistake by obtaining injunctive relief**.

v) However, the court has jurisdiction to intervene to prevent the use of documents made available for inspection by mistake where justice requires, as for example in the case of inspection **procured by fraud**.

vi) In the absence of fraud, all will depend upon the circumstances, but the court may grant an injunction if the documents have been made available for inspection as a result of **an obvious mistake**.

vii) A mistake is likely to be held to be obvious and an injunction granted where the documents are received by a solicitor and: a) the solicitor appreciates that a mistake has been made before making some use of the documents; or b) it would be obvious to a reasonable solicitor in his position that a mistake has been made; and, in either case, there are no other circumstances which would make it unjust or inequitable to grant relief.

viii) Where a solicitor gives detailed consideration to the question whether the documents have been made available for inspection by mistake and honestly concludes that they have not, that fact will be a relevant (and in many cases an important) pointer to the conclusion that it would not be obvious to the reasonable solicitor that a mistake had been made, but is not conclusive; the decision remains a matter for the court.

ix) In both the cases identified in vii) a) and b) above there are many circumstances in which it may nevertheless be held to be inequitable or unjust to grant relief, but all will depend upon the particular circumstances.

x) Since the court is exercising an equitable jurisdiction, there are no rigid rules."（加黑部分是笔者的强调）

在诉讼中，如果确实是自己的律师不小心或错误地将本享有特免权保护的文件交给了对方，无可避免的是对方会已经知悉了文件中的内容。当然有否影响还是要看被不小心或错误地交出的是什么文件。如果是一份不利的专家报告，本来不准备披露出来给法院，在有禁令的情况下限制该文件的使用就可以防止对方向法院或仲裁庭披露。但如果披露的文件是律师针对庭外和解或对整个案件策略的意见，就会让对方知悉自己的底牌，即使法院出具禁令，也于事无补了。当然如果会造成严重不公平的情况，法院除了可以做出禁止对方使用文件的禁令，也可以做出禁止律师事务所继续代表对方当事人的禁令。在 Ablitt v. Mills & Reeve, The Times, October 25, 1995, QB 先例中，原告代表大律师错将一些文件交给了对方的代表律师 Mills & Reeve。Mills & Reeve 的律师意识到了这个错误，并查询了律师协会的指引。指引中提到律师应该寻求当事人的指令是否要查看这些文件，并警告当事人使用有关文件上的信息会导致法院做出禁止使用文件的禁令并要承担有关费用。律师根据指引寻求当事人的指令，而可以想到当事人希望利用这个机会，要求律师查看。Mills & Reeve 的律师在查看后将文件（包括做的笔记）归还给原告并保证不会在诉讼中使用这些文件，但拒绝停止代理当事人。Blackburne 大法官认为指引有误，让当事人利用送错的文件取巧并让 Mills & Reeve 继续代理当事人会造成严重的不公平。毕竟 Mills & Reeve 的律师在看过有关文件后，清楚知道了原告律师对案件的看法与他们给原告的建议。因此，Blackburne 大法官做出了禁止 Mills & Reeve 继续代理当事人的禁令。

12.3.6　诉讼中证人披露的文件

特免权会丧失的情况并非只有弃权，典型的就是丧失机密性（confidentiality）也会导致不能再依赖特免权：见本章之 12.8 段。丧失机密性但没有弃权的情况，会是不小心、没有弃权意图地将文件公布于公众领域（public domain）等。这两者也有必要进行区分，毕竟很多情况下，法院的救济方式都有所不同，在本章上一段也提到了明显错误（obvious mistake）时可以向法院申请禁令限制文件的使用与传播。同样重要的是在诉讼中时，如果是当事人的弃权，就有可能由于“附带弃权”（collateral waiver）[131]被要求全面披露更多其他文件；如果不是弃权，充其量也只是证人在公开审理中披露的部分文件丧失（loss）机密性、无法再依赖特免权保护而已。这就涉及一个也有争议的话题，即在诉讼中（如在接受反盘问时），证人会披露受特免权保护的文件或资料，如提到较早前获得的律师或专家证人报告的内容等。这就带来了问题，如果证人将受到特免权保护的文件做出披露，是否可以认为是当事人做出弃权？

从原则上来说，如果证人有当事人的授权，证人披露文件的行为属于当事人的弃权。而如果证人并没有当事人的授权，则不会属于当事人的弃权。

但在实践认定中，是否存在当事人的授权问题并不容易判断。如果当事人是公司/企业，而证人本身就是公司/企业的雇员、股东、董事、高管等，证人在开庭时做出披露，可能就会被认为有授权（即使没有实际授权，也有表见授权）。但如果当事人是自然人，或者证人并非当事人的公司/企业的雇员、股东、董事、高管等，就更复杂了。如法院或仲裁庭会询问该证人一方当事人是否追认（ratify）对证人的授权。如果追认，在附带弃权下，该当事人就有需要披露更多文件的危险。

在《Documentary Evidence》（第 12 版，2015 年）之 23 – 14 到 23 – 15 段针对这个问题说：“... If he is the plaintiff or defendant, or an officer of a corporate party, he will have waived privilege by his answer and no question of authority should arise. If he is a person giving instructions in the litigation, he will have authority to waive privilege. But if he is a witness who does not fall into such a category, it is suggested that his answer cannot constitute a waiver. Privilege has not voluntarily been waived by the Party or his

[131]　这将会在本章之 12.7 段进行讨论。

agent. But if the court proceeds on this basis, this may work unfairly to the other side. A's witness gives evidence about a privileged document without A's authority in the course of his evidence... So what does the court do in such circumstances where the party calling the witness has purported to waive the privilege of the party to litigation? One possibility would be that the court treats the witness as having apparent authority to waive privilege. Alternatively the court could invite the party to elect whether to 'ratify' the waiver of privilege (and thus give collateral disclosure) or not to rely on the material waiver at all."

12.4 对特免权弃权的类型

一般来说,对特免权的弃权主要存在如下情况:

1."明示弃权"(express waiver)或"有意/故意的弃权"(intentional waiver)。即当事人主动愿意、有意识地同意将文件交出的情况,往往在这种情况下,除非涉及"附带弃权"(collateral waiver),否则是较少产生争议的。当事人会对特免权进行明示弃权或故意弃权,是因为很多时候这样做是有必要的或有利的,如从当时文件的当事人与其律师之间的讨论能够证明当事人在当时才知道或应当知道有关事实,所以,根据有关时效的英国1980年《Limitation Act》立法,仍然处于诉讼时效内:见Law Society v. Sephton & Co.(2006)UKHL 22;MAC Hotels Limited v. Rider Levett Bucknall UK Limited(2010)EWHC 767(TCC)等先例。有关明示弃权或故意的弃权将会在本章之12.5段进行详细介绍。

同时明示弃权还会涉及"选定对象弃权"(selective waiver)与"限定弃权"(limited waiver),在这些情况下将不是完全对特免权弃权,而只是对特定对象弃权或是为了特定目的弃权,在此弃权范围以外的情况仍然可以依赖特免权保护文件免于披露。选定对象弃权将在本章之12.5.2段进行介绍,限定弃权将在本章之12.5.3段进行介绍。

2."默示弃权"(implied waiver)或"无意的弃权"(unintentional waiver)。即当事人并没有弃权意图,但由于当事人的行为导致被法院认定为属于默示弃权,不能再依赖特免权拒绝披露文件。典型的例子是当事人以律师的"职业疏忽"(professional negligence)为由,向自己的前律师索赔损失:见Lillicrap v. Nalder & Son(1993)1 WLR 94先例;Paragon Finance Plc. v. Freshfields(1999)1 WLR 1183等先例。本章之12.2.2段提到的ENRC v. Dechert LLP(2016)EWCA Civ 375先例也是另一种客户与前律师之间默示弃权的例子。有关默示弃权或无意的弃权将在本章之12.6段进行详细介绍。

3."附带弃权"(collateral waiver)。附带弃权并不严格是一种弃权的类型,有的说法中也将附带弃权认为是对弃权范围的认定。所谓附带弃权,主要是指在诉讼中,当事人对一份文件的特免权做出弃权,但出于公平的考虑,会被法院认定这会是对一系列有关同一问题文件的特免权做出弃权。也有说法是"挑选樱桃规则"(cherry picking rule),不能随意对针对同样"issue in question"/"transaction"的内容[132]进行挑选,挑对自己有利的部分弃权,对不利的部分继续依赖特免权,从而造成不公平(unfairness)或误导(misleading)。类似的还会涉及针对同样主题的一份文件,不能只挑其中对自己有利的部分进行弃权与披露。附带弃权的危险之处在于,当事人在披露某一份文件时是考虑对自己有利,但在附带弃权的说法下会被对方越挖越多,要将其他对自己严重不利的文件也披露出来,带来意想不到的严重后果。有关"挑选樱桃规则"以及附带弃权的问题将在本章之12.7段进行详细介绍。

12.5 弃权类型之一:明示或故意的弃权

典型的"明示弃权"(express waiver)或"故意的弃权"(intentional waiver)在诉讼中很多情况都会发生。包括在文书请求/状书、证人证言、文件披露等程序中主动将享有特免权保护的文件引用与交出。

在非诉中也有明示弃权或故意的弃权,如面对政府监管部门的文件披露要求时,主动、自愿将本受到特免权保护的文件交出。尤其是在今天越来越多的政策、法律法规、规章制度之下,各类有关监管部门都会向公司、个人要求披露文件。

明示弃权或故意弃权还可以是一般地弃权,如主动将受特免权保护的文件出版或是让公众可以获取与阅读,或召开新闻发布会将文件的内容公之于众。当然也有说法是此时不一定属于弃权行为,而只是由于丧失文件享有特免权的基础——机密性(confidentiality),从而不能再以特免权为由拒绝披露了。

12.5.1 需要明示弃权或故意弃权的情况

明示弃权或故意的弃权通常是有必要的。不妨以近期的MAC Hotels Limited v. Rider Levett Bucknall UK Limited (2010) EWHC 767 (TCC)先例为例。案情是原告(MAC)在2001年因开发房地产建造酒店等设施的需要,委托了项目经理、测量师等专业人士提供建议。在2003年9月份完工后,发现最后实际工程花费大大超出预计。

原告先开始针对承建商(constructor)索赔,在文件披露程序中通过申请披露得到的文件,发现承建商存在包括"欺诈"(fraud)在内的一系列违约或不法行为。2009年12月,原告以新的诉因(cause of action),包括项目经理管理不善、测量师建议不妥、未能发现承建商的欺诈等行为是存在疏忽为由,向这些专业人士提出索赔。

原告首先需要面对的严重问题是,项目在2003年9月前已经完工,至2009年12月已经超过6年,以违约作为诉因索赔的时效已逝。原告想到的办法是,根据1980年《Limitation Act》之Section 14A[针对诉因产生时并不知情的疏忽侵权诉讼(negligence actions where facts relevant to cause of action are not known at date of accrual)的情况],对诉因产生时并不知情的疏忽侵权诉讼,时效是从被侵权人知道或应当知道

[132] 如在某次与律师会面时,律师交给客户的多份文件(是否涉及同一主题都有可能),就会被法院认定为是同一"issue in question"/"transaction",不能在其中挑拣一些进行披露。

有关的情况之日起的 3 年。因此,原告就要证明自己作为被侵权人是在 2006 年 12 月后才知道或应当知道这些情况的存在。为了达此目的,原告提交了多份证人证言来显示原告的调查进程,指称自己直到 2009 年年初才发现欺诈等情形。这些证人证言中包括参与调查的律师,这就涉及受特免权保护的客户与律师之间的通信往来等。这样,就需要对这些通信往来等文件的特免权弃权以支持时效方面的争议;当然,虽然此举能够保护时效,但在附带弃权的说法下,也可能导致其他更多文件内容需要被披露,而这些文件可能是对原告不利的。

在该先例中,Havelock - Allan QC 大法官认可了 Benkim Thanki QC 的《Law of Privilege》(2006 年)一书中的说法,而同样的文字也出现在新版《Law of Privilege》(第 2 版,2013 年)一书之 5. 95 段,不妨节录如下:“... a claimant's plea that he could not with reasonable diligence have discovered the relevant matter will not of itself entail a waiver of privilege. However a claimant may find it hard to maintain that the limitation period should not begin to run from a period in which he was in receipt of legal advice unless he is prepared to waive privilege in that advice.”

12.5.2 选定对象弃权

在本章之 12.3.3 段已经提到了有关“共同利益特免权”(common interest privilege)的问题,即对于一份受到特免权保护的文件而言,享有特免权的人士 A 在不对特免权弃权与不丧失机密性的前提下,将该份文件交给了另一位人士 B:(1)在文件被交给 B 时,A 与 B 享有共同利益(common interest),B 就也可以依赖共同利益特免权,拒绝将这份文件披露给其他第三人。(2)如果 A 与 B 之间并没有共同利益,B 也没有明示或默示的义务保有文件的机密性,如果 B 被法院或有关监管机构传召作为证人,并被要求披露文件,是没有任何理由拒绝披露文件的。B 在这种情况下,也可以随意将文件交给他人甚至给公众传阅,导致由于文件失去机密性,A 不能拒绝披露。(3)如果 A 与 B 之间并没有共同利益,但 B 有明示或默示的保密义务,英国法下同时也承认与认可“选定对象弃权”(selective waiver)的说法,在这种情况下,A 不丧失对任何其他第三人依赖特免权拒绝披露的权利,可以在诉讼中拒绝法院或有关监管机构向 B 要求披露文件。

在近期的 USP Strategies Plc. v. London General Holdings Ltd. (2004) EWHC 373 (Ch)先例中,由于税制改革的变动,各大零售消费品公司等原本广泛应用的消费品保险计划不再适合,于是纷纷开始开发新的保修计划(warranty scheme)。该先例中的原告就是一间向各大公司出售与设计基于海外信托的保修计划的公司。

1998 年,原告通过自己的律师草拟了一份名为 CAA(collections account agreement)的保修计划文件,并将这份文件销售给 Scotish Power(一家英国著名能源供应商,同时也有部分电器消费品出售),供其在销售中使用。而该先例中的被告是当时 Scotish Power 的管理人(administrator)。

2000 年,原告向另一家公司 Powerhouse(另一家英国著名的电子产品零售商,但已经于2006年倒闭)销售类似的保修计划文件,但发现被告也参与直接竞争,并且将原告提供给 Scotish Power 的 CAA 文件作为被告的产品投标。原告因此在另案中以侵犯知识产权为由提出索赔。

在此诉讼中涉及的主要争议是,被告在投标前曾经寻求 CAA 是否适合 Powerhouse 使用的法律意见,并在与 Powerhouse 签署了保密协议的前提下,将这份法律意见交给 Powerhouse 参考。原告指称在此过程中,CAA 文件的内容被泄漏给了 Powerhouse,导致原告在与 Powerhouse 的谈判中处于严重不利地位,不得不大幅降价,才获得了竞标成功。因此,原告要求被告披露与 Powerhouse 之间的通信往来。而被告则以该通信往来中包含了律师出具的法律意见为由,对通信往来的部分做出了遮盖。

英国高院指出,受到法律特免权保护的信息即使是被交给特定第三人传阅,只要保有了机密性,不影响这份文件对其他所有人士仍然受到特免权保护免于披露,并不会因为被交给特定第三人传阅而导致特免权丧失(loss)。可以节录 Mann 大法官所说如下:

"Where privileged advice is disclosed to a third party the privilege is capable of attaching to the third party communication because that communication is evidence of the privileged advice within the formulation in Three Rivers. It does not matter whether that third party communication is of the whole of the advice... or a paraphrase of or extract from the advice. '... a passage from Style & Hollander on Documentary Evidence: 'If A shows a privileged document to his six best friends, he will not be able to assert privilege if one of the friends sues him because the document is not confidential as between him and the friend. But the fact six other people have seen it does not prevent him claiming privilege as against the rest of the world.'[133]

I think that it follows from that that A would be able to restrain each of the friends from disclosing to the outside world what they were told on the basis that it remained privileged. The friends could not give secondary evidence of the privileged material - it would be 'evidence of [privileged] communications', or their evidence would be 'evidencing such communications' within the formulation in Three Rivers. By the same token, if a client summarises or extracts advice in a letter to a third party, that written communication is capable of retaining or attracting the privilege which attached to the original advice, subject to waiver. It, too, is something which evidences a privileged communication."

---

〔133〕 这是在《Documentary Evidence》一书旧版本中举的例子,即如果 A 将受特免权保护的文件交给 6 个好友传阅,这份文件的机密性在他们之间就不再存在了,因此,如果之后 6 个好友中的 1 个起诉 A, A 无法依赖特免权拒绝披露文件。但这不影响 A 对其他人士仍然可以依赖特免权的保护。这个例子在 Gotha v. Sothebys (1998) 1 WLR 114 先例中就已经被 Staughton 大法官所肯定。而 USP Strategies Plc. v. London General Holdings Ltd. (2004) EWHC 373 (Ch)先例中的 Mann 大法官在做出认可的情况下,还补充说 A 还可以限制 6 个好朋友不得向其他人士披露该文件的内容。

12.5.3 限定弃权

12.5.3.1 限定弃权是为了特定目的的弃权

对于特免权的弃权,英国法下存在所谓的"限定弃权"(limited waiver)的说法,即为了特定的目的有限定放弃特免权,但并不完全对特免权弃权。在为了特定目的有限定地弃权时,只要不是由于丧失机密性等其他原因不能依赖特免权,就仍然可以在此目的以外的情况中依赖特免权拒绝披露。

最典型的限定弃权是当事人与律师之间有关费用的核算,由于涉及律师的费用,因此,不可避免地有大量受特免权保护的文件需要被披露,以证明工作与收费的合理性,而不少先例都确认与认可在此类诉讼中可以限定弃权,即只是为了此诉讼的目的,有限定地与临时性地向法院弃权:见 Pamplin v. Express Newspapers (1985) 1 WLR 689; Goldman v. Hesper (1988) 3 All ER 97; Bourns Inc. v. Raychen Corp (1999) 3 All ER 154; ENRC v. Dechert LLP (2016) EWCA Civ 375 等先例。

不妨节录 Bourns Inc. v. Raychen Corp 先例中 Aldous 大法官说:"There is good reason to encourage voluntary disclosure of relevant documents in taxation proceedings. A party who claims payment may have to elect whether to pursue that claim in the light of knowledge that it might require disclosure of privileged documents. If he decides to pursue such a claim with the result that natural justice requires disclosure, he should not lose his right of confidentiality more than justice requires. **Justice only requires that right to be lost for the taxation proceedings**"(加黑部分是笔者的强调)

因此,在后续其他诉讼中,仍然可以依赖特免权拒绝披露这些文件。当然如果后一个诉讼实际上是对同一个诉讼的延续(如上诉等),地位就不同了:见 Balu v. Dudley Primary Care Trust (2010) EWHC 1208 (Admin)先例。

也有其他类型诉讼中的限定弃权。如 British Coal Corp v. Dennis Rye (1988) 1 WLR 1113 上诉庭先例中,在前一个刑事案件中,该先例中的原告(British Coal Corp)向检控方提供了受特免权保护的文件,用以针对该先例中的被告(Dennis Rye)的刑事控告,并有部分文件确实被依赖。[134]

而在该先例的民事诉讼中,被告想要依赖前述由原告提供给检控方的文件。上诉庭 Neill 大法官指出,原告在前一个诉讼中披露的文件完全可以只是限定弃权,不用在后一个诉讼中进行披露:"In my judgment the answer to this question is plainly 'No.' Let it be assumed that all the documents have come into the possession of the defendants with the implied consent of the plaintiff and that it could be established that they would have supplied the Category B documents even without an order of the court. Nevertheless it is clear that the plaintiff made the documents available for a limited purpose

---

[134] 如果在前一个刑事案件中将受特免权保护的文件交给控方,但没有被依赖的话,在后一个诉讼案件中仍然是受到特免权保护的:见 Taylor v. Serious Fraud Office (1999) 2 AC 177 先例。

only, namely to assist in the conduct first of a criminal investigation and then of a criminal trial. This action of the plaintiff, looked at objectively as it must be, cannot be construed as a waiver of any rights available to them in the present civil action for the purpose of which the privilege exists."

另一方面,在今天有不少的政策、法律法规、规章制度赋予某些机关、部门对个人、公司/企业等进行调查(investigation)、质询(inquiry)等的权力与职责,而不少的政策、法律法规、规章制度还会赋予这些机关、部门向个人、公司/企业等要求披露文件的权力。

本章之 12.2.2 段已经介绍过只有立法明示或必要默示时,才可以超越特免权,因此,个人、公司/企业等面对调查或质询等完全可以依赖特免权拒绝披露文件。但有不少的情况中,这些文件虽然受特免权保护可以免于披露,但个人、公司/企业等会因其有利于自己的原因而主动披露。而在英国法下,也允许在这种情况下做出限定弃权:见 B v. Auckland District Law Society (2003) 2 AC 736 枢密院先例。

12.5.3.2　限定弃权与特免权丧失

如果在前后两个法律程序(proceedings)中涉及的是不同当事人,毫无疑问的是,只要在前一个程序中披露的受特免权保护的文件没有导致特免权的丧失,如法院程序中,采用了不公开庭审或法院发出限制该文件被使用与披露的命令等,又如在调查、质询等程序中没有将有关信息公开给公众,在后一个程序中就仍然可以享有特免权保护:见 Goldstone v. Williams (1899) 1 Ch 47;Minnesota Mining and Manufacturing v. Remnicks (UK) (1991) FSR 97;Bourns Inc. v. Raychen Corp (1999) 3 All ER 154 等先例。

如果前后两个法律程序中涉及的是相同当事人,就有疑问是在前一程序中受特免权保护的文件被披露,在当事人之间而言就可能没有机密性了,也就不能依赖特免权拒绝披露、在法律程序中对方当事人可以依赖这些文件。但这样看来对披露人来说实在不公平,因为第二个程序的严重性可能会比第一个高得多,如前一个是对当事人的调查与质询程序,而后一个可能是法院的刑事诉讼程序。因此,法院通过一些先例建立的判法是,即使是相同的当事人,在前一个法律程序中限定弃权的受特免权保护的文件,未必能在下一个程序中被对方当事人依赖与使用:见 Pamplin v. Express Newspapers (1985) 1 WLR 689; Goldman v. Hesper (1988) 3 All ER 97; Bourns Inc. v. Raychen Corp; B v. Auckland District Law Society (2003) 2 AC 736 等先例。对于特定目的的弃权的限定弃权来说,弃权只是为了这个特定目的,而此特定目的以外的其他用途中,仍然可以依赖特免权进行弃权。

在《Documentary Evidence》(第 12 版,2015 年)一书之 24 – 10 段提到这个问题说:"Where A discloses material to B in one set of proceedings, if the analysis is that the documents are no longer confidential as between those parties so that privilege can no longer be claimed as between those parties in subsequent litigation, such a result might be unfair to the disclosing party. Thus, the courts have made it clear that a waiver of privilege in one set of proceedings may not always bar an assertion of privilege in subsequent proceedings against the same party, so long as the documents have not come into the public domain. But the authorities are still developing."

在较为近期的 B v. Auckland District Law Society 枢密院先例中,新西兰的奥克兰律师协会由于接到对律师的投诉,对律师开展调查。律师在接受调查过程中自愿披露了一部分受到特免权保护的文件,但在提供文件的当时就明确通过文字记载了愿意这样做并不对特免权完全弃权,说:"on the express basis that, in doing so, privilege is not waived."之后律师协会开始了对律师的诉讼,并要依赖这些文件。问题就是律师是否有权以特免权为由,限制律师协会对文件的依赖与使用呢?

律师协会认为在文件被交出以后,在他们之间就不再有特免权的问题了:"The society's argument, put colloquially, is that privilege entitles one to refuse to let the cat out of the bag; once it is out of the bag, however, privilege cannot help to put it back."

枢密院对此的看法是,该说法并没有针对特免权的弃权问题,而实际上是针对了特免权丧失(loss)的问题。特免权的丧失与特免权的弃权之间可以说并没有直接关系,对特免权弃权并不一定导致特免权丧失,如"选定对象弃权"(selective waiver)或"限定弃权"(limited waiver),只是针对特定人士或特定目的暂时放弃特免权保护;而特免权丧失也不一定是由于对特免权的弃权行为,如丧失机密性、文件被披露给公众都导致特免权丧失,但这些未必涉及当事人的弃权。

因此,枢密院区分了特免权的丧失与特免权的弃权。限定弃权只会发生在当事人认为弃权行为并不会造成特免权丧失的情况,而当前的法律也尽量地在这个基础上予以保护。该先例中的文件由于涉及法律意见而享有特免权保护。律师将文件交出给律师协会,不改变该份文件仍然涉及法律意见与应当受到特免权保护。换句话说,文件的特免权并没有丧失(如文件并没有丧失机密性等),在限定弃权的目的以外的其他程序中,仍然可以继续保护文件免于披露。Millett 勋爵说:

"The question is not whether privilege has been waived, but whether it has been lost. It would be unfortunate if it were. It must often be in the interests of the administration of justice that a partial or limited waiver of privilege should be made by a party who would not contemplate anything which might cause privilege to be lost, and it would be most undesirable if the law could not accommodate it.

The society argued that, once the documents were produced to Mr Ennor(律师协会在调查过程中委任的代表大律师), they ceased to be privileged. Their Lordships consider that this is playing with words. It confuses the nature of the documents with the rights to which the arrangements with Mr Ennor gave rise. The documents are privileged because they were created for the purpose of giving or receiving legal advice. If they are not produced voluntarily, production cannot be compelled. If they are produced voluntarily, the right to withhold production no longer attaches to them. In that sense the privilege may be said to be lost. But they are the same documents, and it is not inappropriate to describe them as privileged. Their inherent characteristics are the same. The policy which protected them from unauthorised disclosure is the same. The cat is still a cat. It can be put back in the bag."

在笔者看来，尽管这从表面看与机密性是特免权基础的说法有冲突，但有强烈的公共利益、公共政策的理由保护文件的特免权。毕竟特免权不仅仅是在当事人之间行使，而可以面对世界上所有人士拒绝披露。即使是在前一个法律程序中，当事人之间机密性丧失，但只要保持了对世界上所有其他人士的机密性，看来就没有理由在后一个程序中要求将这份文件披露出来。毕竟后一个法律程序可能是公开的法院程序（如此先例中对律师提起的诉讼），一旦披露，岂不是导致文件的机密性就此对世界上所有其他人士也丧失了？

12.5.3.3　没有明示限制也可以默示限定弃权

在本章上一段提到的 B v. Auckland District Law Society (2003) 2 AC 736 枢密院先例中，有非常清楚的明示记载了弃权只是为了特定的目的。随之而来的疑问是，是否限定弃权都需要这样的明示说法呢？在 Berezovsky v. Hine (2011) EWCA Civ 1089 上诉庭先例中，就考虑了这个问题。

该先例的案情比较复杂，俄罗斯的 B 先生（Berezovsky）与另一位 P 先生（Patarkatsishvili）在俄罗斯有很成功与规模庞大的投资活动，后来为了政治避难，分别逃到英国。B 先生与 P 先生在英国也各自开始了政治庇护申请（asylum claim）。后来，B 先生与其他人士就前述共同投资的产业发生争议并开始诉讼。由于两人的关系一直非常密切，P 先生也对 B 先生投资产业争议的诉讼提供支持。B 先生也将在这个诉讼中获取的一份草拟证人证言（draft witness statement）通过律师发送给 P 先生。

不幸的是，P 先生突然死亡，B 先生与 P 先生的遗产继承人之间关系破裂，对共同投资产业也产生争议并开始诉讼。B 先生指称，在俄罗斯时 P 先生曾经口头承诺所有投资对半分，但 P 先生的遗产继承人否认。由于 P 先生已经死亡，这相当于是 B 先生的一面之词。

但 B 先生较早发送给 P 先生的草拟证人证言估计在这方面有不利于 B 先生的内容。P 先生的遗产继承人就想要依赖前述的草拟证人证言。毫无争议的是草拟证人证言显然会受到法律业务特免权保护。但 B 先生（通过律师）将草拟证人证言交给 P 先生是否会造成弃权，弃权是否存在限定就是争议焦点之一。

一审法院已经认定的事实是在草拟证人证言被交出给 P 先生时，没有任何明示限定，因此一审法院判 B 先生不能抗拒 P 先生遗产继承人的披露要求，但这被上诉庭否定。上诉庭的 Neuberger 勋爵认为，弃权是否有限制是需要结合案件的案情，对于被指称的弃权行为进行综合的考虑："... where privilege is waived, the question whether the waiver was limited, and, if so, the parameters of the limitation, must be determined by reference to all the circumstances of the alleged waiver, and, in particular, what was expressly or impliedly communicated between the person sending, and the person receiving, the documents in question, and what they must or ought reasonably have understood."

而在该先例中,上诉庭认可与同意一审法院对事实的认定,认为将草拟证人证言发送给P先生,主要是为了两个目的:一是让P先生在其自己的政治庇护申请中使用;二是希望P先生对证人证言的内容进行审核与复查,避免B先生与P先生在各自的政治庇护申请中的说法,以及B先生在投资产业争议诉讼中的说法自相矛盾。也因此上诉庭在综合考虑后,认定这两个目的就是对草拟证人证言交给P先生的默示目的限定,任何这两个目的以外的情况,B先生仍然可以依赖特免权拒绝披露。

这会扩大限定弃权的适用,毕竟有不少的明示或有意弃权,都不会明示限定文件使用目的。这样,如果事实上是弃权的当事人事后反悔,可以指称根据事实可以认定较早的披露是限定弃权与限制文件使用。

对于接收文件的人士来说,这就带来不肯定。毕竟不同案件的事实千变万化,在没有(也很难有)详细的指引下,难以知道披露是否目的限定与何种目的。有限的说法除了刚刚节录的Neuberger勋爵所说要全面考量当时文件的内容,还要考量文件披露人、文件接受人的状况,以及他们对披露行为的理解是怎样的,包括B v. Auckland District Law Society枢密院先例中所说的,做出弃权的当事人在弃权当时并不希望披露行为导致特免权丧失:"... a partial or limited waiver of privilege should be made by a party who would not contemplate anything which might cause privilege to be lost."

Berezovsky v. Hine先例的判法在Citic Pacific Limited v. Secretary for Justice (2012) 2 HKLRD 701香港先例中被跟从。该先例涉及的背景与本章之12.3.1段介绍的Citic Pacific Limited v. Secretary for Justice and Commissioner of Police (2015) HKCA 293先例相同,但针对的是不同文件。该先例中,主要涉及中信泰富(Citic Pacific)交给香港证券交易委员会(Securities and Futures Commission,或称SFC)的一些文件被警方要求披露。中信泰富在知悉后马上开展行动,向法院申请禁令,要求归还本受特免权保护的文件或限制使用。最主要的理由就是自己将文件交给SFC只是限定弃权。

上诉庭的Hartmann大法官首先认可了在香港也适用与跟从英国限定弃权的说法。接着Hartmann大法官跟从Berezovsky v. Hine先例中,判在该先例中将文件交给SFC时只有SFC的调查行为,交出文件的目的也只是回应SFC的要求。而且由于特免权的绝对性权利与基本人权属性,法院不会轻易认为存在对特免权的完全弃权。不妨节录部分判决内容如下:"... In my view, it is understandable that Citic, a publicly listed company of very considerable substance actively trading its shares on the market, would wish to co-operate with the SFC, more especially by way of providing information on how it was that there had been a perceived delay in making the ‘decision’ to publish its profit warning. The SFC was the regulatory body responsible for maintaining the orderly and transparent conduct of the securities and futures industry: see s 5(1)(a) of the Ordinance. It is clear that, from the point of view of Citic, the continued trading of its shares and the hoped for recovery in the value of those shares was essential to its continued viability. . . . bearing in mind that a full waiver of privilege by Citic is not lightly to be inferred, the probabilities, in my view, indicate that what reasonably ought to have been understood on 27 October 2008 when the first five documents were given to the SFC for inspection was that Citic was prepared to waive its privilege in those documents for the only purpose then known to Citic, namely, the SFC investigation, but would inevitably have adopted a very different approach in respect of the issue of privilege if faced with a criminal investigation."

最后可节录《Documentary Evidence》(第 12 版,2015 年)之 24 - 17 段的内容作为本段的小结:". . . The justification for extending the principle so that it is no longer limited to express limitations but where the court is obliged to consider, and perhaps even seeks out, implied restrictions, is certainly not completely obvious. At least where there is an express restriction, the receiving party may prefer not to receive the document at all if it is to be received subject to restriction. Or if the proposed restriction is rejected by the receiving party, the document might then after negotiation still be provided, with the restriction varied or removed entirely. But there is no similar opportunity for the receiving party in cases such as Berezovsky and Citic."

将"明示限定"延伸到"默示限定"的必要性与原因并不明显。对于"明示限定"的限定弃权来说,如是在 B v. Auckland District Law Society 先例中,律师协会在取得文件并注意到有"明示限定"时,如果觉得限定的特定目的不足够、不能接受,就可以拒绝这种程度的披露。这会带来双方的讨价还价,带来对特定目的的改变,或者甚至是不再有限定。但对于"默示限定"的限定弃权来说,文件接收方就根本没有这样的机会。而且他在接收文件时,也不能明确知道限定的目的是什么,如果将有关文件用在其他用途,就可能面对披露方的禁令。

12.5.3.4　其他国家与地区的不同看法

然而在其他国家与地区的法律中,也有不同的看法。如在美国法下不认可"限定弃权"(limited waiver)。在 US Permian Corporation v. United States 665 F2d 1214 (DC Cir 1981)先例中,公司为了应对调查,向美国证券交易委员会披露了受特免权保护的文件,法院认定这样的披露会导致对特免权的完全放弃。这在美国法下也被称为"Premian 规则"。

澳大利亚在 Nework Ten Ltd. v. Capital Television Holdings Ltd. (1995) 35 NSWLR 275 先例中曾经认可了限定弃权的说法。但之后在 Goldberg v. Ng (1995)

185 CLR 83 先例中,案情也涉及客户向律协投诉律师,律师面对律协的调查披露了一些自己享有并受到特免权保护的文件。客户之后在法院开始对律师的民事诉讼,并想要依赖前述受特免权保护的文件。律师指出自己向律师协会披露这些文件是以特定目的做出的披露,属于限定弃权。但这被澳大利亚高院所否定,理由是律协的调查程序与之后的民事诉讼程序是有非常紧密联系的,如果允许律师在调查中依赖这些文件进行抗辩,但在民事诉讼中又以特免权为由不允许客户依赖这些文件,是不公平(unfair)的。这也与澳大利亚有关特免权的问题中非常强调公平(fairness)有关,这实际上与英国法的地位存在一定程度的不同。

12.6 弃权类型之二:默示弃权

12.6.1 联合委托律师

有说法是如果是多方当事人联合委托(joint retain)了律师,他们各自与律师之间通信往来的特免权在互相之间是被"默示弃权"(implied waiver):见 CIA Barca de Panama SA v. George Winpey & Co. Ltd. (1980) 1 Lloyd's Rep. 598; Brown v. Guardian Royal Exchange Assurance Plc. (1994) 2 Lloyd's Rep. 325; Paragon Finance Plc. v. Freshfields (1999) 1 WLR 1183; TSB Bank Plc. v. Robert Irving & Burns (2000) 2 All ER 826 等先例。

也有说法是在这种情况下。不能依赖特免权并非是弃权行为,而是由于这些文件在这些联合委托律师的当事人之间,或者是存在联合利益(joint interest)的当事人之间,从一开始就没有机密性可言,也就根本谈不上存在特免权保护的问题,更谈不上后来的对特免权的弃权了。或者说,被认为对特免权的默示弃权主要是起诉前律师的行为,有关起诉前律师的默示弃权问题将在本章之 12.6.2 段进行探讨。

12.6.1.1 联合委托律师

一般而言,如果是多方当事人联合委托了律师,在联合委托人之间不能以特免权为由,不予披露与律师之间的通信往来。联合委托律师常常发生,尤其是在保险领域。投保了责任险的被保险人在遇到被第三人索赔时,在通知了保险人后,惯常做法都是由保险人委托律师对抗第三人的索赔。但在对抗过程中,可能在保险人与被保险人之间出现利益冲突,导致保险人拒绝理赔部分或全部保额[如发现涉及被保险人的欺诈、或违反保单的承诺性担保(promissory warranty)]。这时保险人就会撤回对被保险人的帮助,而在原委托律师的两个客户之间就需要厘清利益冲突。在 San Diego Federal Credit Union v. Cumis Insurance Society Inc. , 208 Cal Rptr 494 (1984) 美国先例中,加利福尼亚州的上诉庭说:"In the usual tripartite relationship existing between insured, insurer and counsel, there is a single common interest shared among them. Dual representation by counsel is beneficial since the shared goal of minimising or eliminating liability to a third party is the same. A different situation is presented, however, when some or all of the allegations in the complaint do not fall within the scope of coverage under the policy. In such a case, the standard practice of an insurer is to defend under a reservation of rights where the insurer promises to defend but states it may not indemnify the insured if liability is found. In this situation there may be little commonality of interest. Opposing poles of interest are represented on the one hand by the insurer's desire to establish in the third party suit the insured's ' liability rested on intentional conduct' and thus no coverage under the policy, and on the other hand the insured's desire to obtain a ruling... such liability emanated from the non intentional conduct within his insurance coverage... [Counsel] was bound to investigate all conceivable bases on which liability might attach. These investigations and client communications may provide information relating directly to the coverage issue. Furthermore, counsel may form an opinion about the insured's credibility. As between counsel's two clients, there is no confidentiality regarding communications intended to promote common goals. But confidentiality is essential where communication can affect coverage. Thus, the lawyer is forced to walk an ethical tightrope and not communicate relevant information which is beneficial to one or the other of his clients."

如果多方当事人分别与律师订立委托合约,或在多方当事人之间存在利益冲突,显然在多方当事人之间都可以依赖特免权拒绝披露。而恰恰常出现争议的是,一开始多方当事人联合委托律师但后来分道扬镳的情况。The "Sagheera" (1997) 1 Lloyds Rep. 160 先例就是典型的例子,案情涉及 Sagheera 轮在中东海域爆炸并沉没。由于战争险(war risk)与船壳险(hull and machinery)分开投保,因此面对这个全损事件,船东及时地分别告知了承保战争险的保险人(船东互保协会)与承保了船壳险的保险人。但如果爆炸是由于该水域中的水雷导致,应该由战争险保险人理赔;而如果是由船舶自身的原因导致爆炸,如锅炉压力太大,则应由船壳险保险人理赔。因此必须先调查事实与搜集取证,否则连索赔对象是谁都搞不清楚。

在这样的背景下,船东与战争险保险人(船东互保协会)联合指定了一家英国律师事务所进行调查事实与搜集取证。这种做法也常见,毕竟事实或真相只有一个,这样的做法也可以节省开支。而且船东与互保协会一般关系友好,在事故刚发生时也没有明显的利益冲突。只有在实际利益冲突产生,如船东希望根据调查事实与搜集取证向船东互保协会要求理赔,但船东互保协会又拒绝理赔的情况(如对事实或证据的解释或看法不同),才会分道扬镳,各自指定不同的律师事务所。

12.6.1.2 合约中的明示条文

有时候在当事人之间的合约中,会有明示条文约定,导致不能在当事人之间以特免权为由拒绝披露文件。如在 Brown v. Guardian Royal Exchange Assurance Plc. (1994) 2 Lloyd's Rep. 325 先例中,一位律师(Brown 先生)向 Guardian Royal Exchange(GRE)投保了职业责任险(1986 年《Solicitors Indemnity Rules》强制要求律师购买职业责任险)。Brown 先生之后被客户指称在不动产交易中存在疏忽并索赔,因此 Brown 先生将案件通知了保险人 GRE。

在 GRE 的保单中，明示约定经过保险人同意可以委托律师或其他专家，在 Clause 8(c)进一步约定受委托的律师或专家出具的报告需要同时交一份给保险人：“... (c) Except in case of urgency the Brokers will not instruct solicitors or other expert advisers without first obtaining the Insurers' authority, it being understood that the Insurers will not unreasonably withhold such approval in any case where the Insured or the Brokers consider this step to be advisable. Where solicitors or other expert advisers are so employed their fees and expenses will be for the account of the Insurers who may require the solicitors' reports to be submitted directly to them.”

在该先例也是在 GRE 同意之下，一家律师事务所(RPC)被委任为 Brown 先生的代理律师。

之后 GRE 认为 Brown 先生可能涉及“欺诈”(fraud)或“不诚实”(dishonest)行为。这是保单下可以不予赔付的，因此，GRE 拒绝向 Brown 先生做出理赔与保护，RPC 也不再代理 Brown 先生。Brown 先生因此向 GRE 开始推进有关保险合约的仲裁。GRE 在该仲裁中则要求 Brown 先生披露所有与 RPC 之间有关本案件的通信往来，Brown 先生则以法律业务特免权为由，拒绝披露。双方当事人之后一致同意对此披露问题由法院判决。

Brown 先生与 RPC 之间的有关通信往来是受到法律业务特免权保护的。而如果不考虑保单中前述节录的条文，在保险人 GRE 没有联合委托或在委托时没有联合利益，Brown 先生也没有事后将这些文件交给 GRE，就不会有对特免权的弃权，因此，一审的法院做出的认定是这些文件会因法律业务特免权而免于披露。但案件被上诉后被改判，认为虽然这些文件确实享有法律业务特免权的保护，但由于前述节录条文，在 Brown 先生与 GRE 之间不能依赖特免权拒绝披露。上诉庭的 Hoffmann 大法官指出：

“The answer in my view depends entirely upon the construction of clause 8. It says that the insurers are entitled to reports. Two questions arise. First, reports as to what? In my judgment, reports as to everything which the solicitors have learned about the claim. There is nothing in the language of the clause which would justify restricting the scope of the reports... I do not see how RPC could have given the insurers an intelligible report on the prospects of the claim succeeding without at the same time expressing a view on whether Mr Brown had been fraudulent, negligent or neither. In my view the effect of the policy was that anything which Mr Brown said to RPC was to be treated as having been said to the insurers and Mr Brown must be taken to have known this.

The second question is whether the right to ask for a report continued after the termination of the clause 8 retainer. The judge thought that it did not. But this construction produces very arbitrary results. The right of the insurers to know what happened while they were paying the solicitors' bill will depend upon the accident of how regularly reports are made or whether the insurers happened to send a representative to a conference. In the present arbitration, Mr Brown is saying that the insurers are not entitled to any of the documents generated throughout the time that RPC were acting for him, although the insurers would, if they had asked at the time, undoubtedly have been entitled to see whatever was in existence before RPC ceased to act. In my view the more natural construction of clause 8 is that the insurers are entitled at any time to reports on whatever transpired during the subsistence of the retainer. I would therefore allow the appeal."

上诉庭的 Neill 大法官更是提出 Clause 8 是对特免权的默示弃权(waiver of privilege implicit in clause 8):"The policy and the instructions given to RPC established a tripartite arrangement on the following lines:(1) RPC became Mr. Brown's solicitors for the purpose of defending the claim. As far as the outside world was concerned the relationship was the usual one between a solicitor and his client and their communications were protected by legal professional privilege. (2) At the same time a separate relationship of solicitor and client came into existence between RPC and the insurers. The insurers became liable to pay RPC's fees and in return RPC became liable to report to the insurers about the progress of the case. (3) By accepting the benefit of legal representation made available in accordance with the terms of the policy Mr. Brown waived his rights quoad the insurers to claim legal professional privilege in relation to communications about the claim between himself and RPC during the period that representation under the policy continued."

类似的情况还可见 Winterthur Swiss Insurance Company v. AG (Manchester) Limited (2006) EWHC 839 (Comm)先例。该先例涉及近期比较重大的影响数百个律师的事件。起因是在当时英国开始有限制地接受按条件收费(conditional fee),同时收紧了民事诉讼法律援助的条件,因此出现了一些提供诉讼费用支援服务的公司。该先例中的一名原告就是一家从事诉讼费用事后保险(after the event/ATE insurance)的保险公司(The National Insurance & Guarantee Corporation Limited,或称 NIG),委托该先例中的被告之一[AG(Manchester)Ltd 或 The Accident Group Limited,或称 TAG]作为自己的代理人,并授权 TAG 承保(underwriting)或从事保险理赔,向公众推销与提供"不胜诉不收费"(no win no fee)的法律费用保险服务,主要销售对象是人身伤害案件中的受害人。即由受害人将案件交给 TAG 以及律师等人士评估,如果认为情况合适,就会与受害人签署事后保险保单(或称 ATE Policy),由 NIG 提供资金资助诉讼,在索赔成功后,NIG 再从胜诉金额中分得一部分利益。在每个具体案件中的评估人士除了 TAG、与 TAG 有关的其他公司以外,还固定包括了一家专门从事此类诉讼的律师事务所(Rowe Cohen),以及从 TAG 搜罗的总数为 800 人左右的律师列表中挑选出 1 个律师进行评估。

到 2005 年,使用此服务的索赔共有 64741 起,但由于对败诉率的估计不足,导致了严重亏损。NIG(及其母公司 Winterthur Swiss Insurance Company)认为是做出评估的 TAG、Rowe Cohen 以及在律师列表中有关的 626 名律师的评估存在疏忽,并以此为由向他们提出索赔。

与本段内容有关的是,在 NIG 承保的保单下之第 6 条是:"In this regard, the Assured shall do and concur in doing and permit to be done all such acts and things as may be necessary or required by [the insurer] for the purpose of enforcing any rights and remedies or of obtaining relief or indemnity from other parties to which [the insurer] shall be or would become entitled or subrogated upon their paying for any case or loss under the Policy, whether such acts and things shall be or become necessary or required before or after the Assured's indemnification by [the insurer]."

原告的代表大律师 Charles Hollander QC 提出的替代争议之一是,根据此条文,被保险人明示同意了会与保险人合作,帮助保险人向有疏忽的律师提出索赔,包括承诺披露在被保险人与律师之间受到特免权保护的通信往来。

而做出判决的 Aikens 大法官也认为此条文的作用是被保险人不能再依赖特免权的保护,而且 Aikens 大法官明确认为实际上这是面对保险人 NIG 要求提供有关文件的情况下,自动对特免权弃权的合约承诺:"But I have held that NIG is also entitled to have access to the post – ATE Policy documents because of the contractual right to access contained in Condition 6 of the ATE Policies, which are contracts with the TAG Claimants. It is important to recall the **very wide terms of Condition 6**, which place an obligation on the TAG Claimant... **In my view, that wording gives NIG the right to require the TAG Claimant to waive any privilege that it may have in documents if that is necessary or required by NIG for the purpose of enforcing claims against third parties** if it is entitled to bring such claims upon paying an indemnity under the policy. As the TAG Claimant has no choice, then I think that **the wording of the Condition 6 is, effectively, an automatic waiver of privilege by the TAG Claimant**, provided that it is necessary or required by NIG for the purposes defined in the clause. That conclusion is, I think, consistent with the decision in Brown v. GRE, 84 which holds that **an insured cannot use 'litigation privilege' to prevent the insurer from using his contractual right of access to the documents.**"(加黑部分是笔者的强调)

在《Disclosure》(第 4 版,2012 年)一书中也认可这种情况是弃权的一种,如在 16.04 段引用了前述的 Brown v. Guardian Royal Exchange Assurance Plc. 等先例中,说:"An insured claiming under an insurance policy involving legal advice or action on his behalf paid for by the insurer may find that the terms of the policy operate to waive his privilege as against the insurer..."

而需要区分的是,这里的明示条文是在有权弃权的人士与保险人之间的保单条文,而如果并不是有权弃权的人士订立的合约,就没有此效果。如在 Quinn Direct Insurance Ltd. v. Law Society (2010) EWCA Civ 805 上诉庭先例中,律师(South Bank Solicitors,或称 SBS)向保险人(Quinn)投保了职业责任保险(professional liability insurance),保单中也有类似本段前文中介绍的明示条文。SBS 由于在执业过程中的会计问题,被律师协会调查与介入(intervene)管理。也有相当多的前客户向 SBS 提出索赔,因此需要向保险人要求理赔,但保险人以 SBS 涉及欺诈或不诚实行为为由,拒绝理赔。保险人也向(已经介入管理 SBS 的)律师协会要求披露所有 SBS 控制与占有的文件。但在这种情况下,由于这些文件的特免权由 SBS 的前客户享有,也只能由前客户弃权。但前客户并非保险合约的当事人或合约方,也就不受保险合约明示条文的约束。所以只要前客户不弃权,就无须披露。不妨简单节录上诉庭判决所说如下:"It is clear that neither the Law Society nor the client of SBS is a party to the Policy. Accordingly Quinn can have no contractual claim to production of the privileged documents it seeks based on clause 6.2 a) 4) or any other provision of the Policy unless the client has consented either expressly or by implication from its claim against SBS. It follows that the refusal of the Law Society in the exercise of its public functions, to disclose the documents sought by Quinn can only be challenged by Quinn on public law grounds, namely that the Law Society is acting unlawfully in refusing to comply with Quinn's request. As I have pointed out, the request for production is a blanket request in respect of all documents but is only material in relation to privileged documents where privilege has not been waived by the client of SBS because no claim against SBS and by SBS under the Policy has been made. The Law Society claims to be not only entitled to withhold production of them but to be bound to withhold them to preserve client confidentiality in accordance with its primary concern to protect the interests of the former clients of SBS and in accordance with the Code of Conduct."

12.6.1.3　联合委托律师弃权与利益冲突的产生

在本章之 12.6.1.1 段已经提到了在联合委托律师后,常会出现问题的是在多方当事人分道扬镳后,他们之间能否依赖特免权拒绝披露的问题。这在较近期的 TSB Bank Plc. v. Robert Irving & Burns (2000) 2 All ER 826 上诉庭先例进行了讨论,并给出了一种解释的途径。

该先例中的被告(Robert Irving & Burns,或称 RIB)是测量师(surveyor)与估价师(valuer)事务所,对某间酒店为了此先例中的原告进行了估价。1989 年,先是由一位合伙人 Braier 先生进行估价,但后来 Braier 先生离开不再担任合伙人,之后于 1990 年由 Burns 先生重新对酒店进行估价。该先例中的原告(TSB Bank Plc.,或称 TSB)根据估价向酒店的业主提供了某些金融融资产品。但事后发现酒店的实际价值远远低于估价,因此,TSB 以 RIB 存在职业疏忽为由开始向 RIB 索赔损失。RIB 曾经向保险人(Colonia Baltica Insurance Ltd,或称 Colonia)投保了职业疏忽(professional negligence)保险。值得注意的是,保单第 1 条允许保险人完全接手针对被保险人的诉讼,说:"... at any time to take over and conduct in the name of the insured or the said firm, as the case may be, the defence or settlement of the claim."保单第4条则要求被保险人给予完全的协助:"... Where notice has been given in accordance with General Condition 2 or 3 the Insured shall give such full co-operation to Insurers as they shall reasonably require."Colonia 因此参与并委托了律师(RPC)与大律师调查此事。在本章之12.6.1.2段已经提到,在这样明示条文的约定之下,RIB 与保险人 Colonia 之间不能以特免权为由拒绝披露。

在该先例中,由于索赔金额庞大,而且在保单中有条文写明"with effect from 15th July 1996 this policy excludes any claim arising out of work undertaken by Michael Braier",因此,保险人一开始就向律师与大律师咨询是否有机会指称 RIB 的估价涉及 Braier 先生的意见,从而从这个保单脱身,避免理赔。律师与大律师也就有关情况向 Burns 先生进行了询问与调查,但得出的结论看来是否定的,RIB 与保险人因此一致开始联合就原告银行对职业疏忽的指控与索赔进行抗辩。

但在诉讼程序中,由于发现抗辩成功的机会微乎其微,保险人又开始重新考虑自己从保单脱身的可能性。为了达到这个目标,在 RIB、保险人 Colonia、律师 RPC 以及大律师一起参与的会议上,保险人指示大律师近乎以反盘问的方式向 Burns 先生询问有关情况,毫无防备的 Burns 先生的回答中虽然没有与其以前的说法自相矛盾,但不小心提及自己被 Braier 先生的报告所"蒙蔽"(blinded)。事后法院对这个情况的认定是,律师与大律师等于设计了陷阱:"... The skilled cross-examination of Mr. Burns about matters adverse to his interest with a view to founding a repudiation of cover, in a situation where Mr. Burns was entitled to and did repose trust and confidence in his solicitors and counsel, and had received no warning of any sort as to the peril in which he was placed..."

会议结束后,保险人即指出自己在保单下不再有理赔义务,因为 Braier 先生的估价报告是被明示排除出保单以外。RIB 因此将保险人作为第三人拉入此诉讼。而保险人提出 RIB 已经自己承认了估价涉及被 Braier 先生"蒙蔽"的情况,同时要依赖有关会议的文件,如会议纪要等内容。RIB 即向法院申请禁令,限制使用会议中的文件以证明 Burns 先生的说法,理由之一就是这些文件受到法律业务特免权的保护。

上诉庭的判法是,首先根据本章之12.6.1.2段提到的 Brown v. Guardian Royal Exchange Assurance Plc. (1994) 2 Lloyd's Rep. 325 先例的说法,联合委托律师与大律师的保险人(Colonia)以及被保险人(RIB)之间对特免权弃权,这个说法被该先例中双方当事人接受。上诉庭 Morritt 大法官进一步指出,一旦之后在保险人与被保险人之间出现利益冲突,前述对特免权的弃权就会被局限(limit):"... Thus the choice is between the automatic discharge of the retainer at the point of deception and **a limit on the waiver implied at the outset of a joint retainer so as to exclude communications made after an actual conflict of interest has emerged**. In principle I prefer the latter."

(加黑部分是笔者的强调)

上诉庭的 Tuckey 大法官更是指出:“the waiver of privilege implicit in the joint retainer extends to communications made by the insured to the solicitors where there is merely a possible conflict of interest. Without such a waiver I can see that it would be very difficult for a solicitor ever to accept a joint retainer in a case such as this. Many solicitors do and it is in the interests of both insurers and insureds that they should continue to be able to do so. **It is only where, as here, there is an actual conflict of interest that the waiver comes to an end** and even then it will continue if, after notification of the conflict, the insured decides not to instruct separate solicitors.”(加黑部分是笔者的强调)

根据上诉庭的这个判法,如果联合委托律师的当事人之间出现利益冲突(如该先例中的保险人想要依赖保单条文拒绝理赔),对律师来说,应当发现利益冲突并及时告知当事人,否则就可能属于职业疏忽。而原本的默示弃权会在利益冲突发生时即告终。

然而对该先例的判法不少权威书籍有不同看法。在《Law of Privilege》(第 2 版,2011 年)之 6.06 段评论说:“In TSB Bank Plc. v. Robert Irving & Burns... considered that there was an implied waiver of privilege where two parties (insurer and insured) jointly retained a solicitor. They went on to hold, by way of exception, that no such waiver arose in between the parties. This was said to be on the basis that there is a ‘limit on the waiver implied at the outset of a joint retainer so as to exclude communications made after an actual conflict of interest has emerged’. However, there is no obvious basis for such an exception and this case only serves to highlight the difficulty of characterizing joint privilege in terms of waiver.”

在《Documentary Evidence》(第 12 版,2015 年)一书之 24 - 04 段[同样的说法也出现在《Phipson on Evidence》(第 18 版,2013 年)一书之 26 - 28 段]中更是直接认为该先例的判法存在错误之处:

“It is suggested that the Court of Appeal in TSB v. Robert Irving and Burns may have misinterpreted Brown v. Guardian Royal Exchange Assurance. It understood this as providing authority for there being a waiver of privilege between two clients who jointly instruct a solicitor. The issue in Brown was whether insurers were entitled to inspect the assured's privileged documents which came into existence during the period when insurers were acting for the assured. The Court of Appeal held that under the terms of the policy they were so entitled and that was the basis of the decision. Hoffmann LJ in Brown cited the argument put to the court: ‘... that no privilege could exist between parties who instructed a solicitor in a matter as to which they have a joint or common interest or who jointly instruct a solicitor in a matter in which they have different interests and communicate with him in his joint capacity.' He held it was unnecessary to look further than construing the terms of the policy, and decided the case on that basis. In TSB v. Robert Irving and Burns Morritt LJ treated the waiver of privilege issue as being something on which the whole court in Brown had agreed upon, which it is suggested is incorrect.

If TSB v. Robert Irving and Burns was put on the basis, as is submitted is the proper analysis, that there was never any confidence between the two clients where they jointly instruct a solicitor, and thus no privilege between them, the basis for the decision (that there was a waiver of a waiver where the conflict of interest arose and thus privilege is reinstated) does not work. On the somewhat unusual facts of the case, there was a strong public policy justification for the decision. It is apparent that the court sought to reach a result which did not permit the insurer to take advantage of the conduct of its lawyers which had led to the admissions made by the insured. But there seems no reason why the court could not have reached the same result by relying on equitable fraud."

在 Brown v. Guardian Royal Exchange Assurance 先例中,法院仅仅是根据保单明示条文认定文件可以被披露,但并没有一致认定属于默示弃权。反而更合理的分析或解释是在联合委任律师的当事人之间,从一开始就由于不存在机密性原因而互相之间不能依赖特免权拒绝披露。TSB Bank Plc. v. Robert Irving & Burns 先例中上诉庭的判法看来是为了禁止保险人依赖这种明显不公平的方式(律师 RPC 以反盘问的技巧向 Burn 先生套取承认被 Braier 先生的估价报告所蒙蔽),但要达到同样的效果,无须这样判决,完全可以依赖"衡平法欺诈"(equitable fraud)等说法。

至少目前的法律地位可以明确的是,对联合委任律师的当事人来说,互相之间显然不能依赖特免权拒绝披露。同时一旦出现利益冲突,被联合委任的律师就应当马上结束联合委任,不再制造受联合特免权保护的文件。

12.6.2 默示弃权:起诉(前)律师

最典型的对特免权的默示弃权,就是向自己的前律师提出索赔时,就放弃了自己与前律师之间曾经通信往来的特免权保护。这是公平(fairness)的要求:见上诉庭的 Lillicrap v. Nalder & Son (1993) 1 WLR 94 先例与 Paragon Finance Plc. v. Freshfields (1999) 1 WLR 1183 先例等。显然,当事人不能只披露对其诉讼有利的文件,而对那些对自己不利的文件就不予以披露给法庭审查。而针对客户起诉前律师的诉讼来说,不能一方面依赖与律师之间的文件攻击前律师,另一方面又不允许前律师依赖有关材料抗辩(毕竟律师无法对有特免权的文件弃权)。

在近期的 Medcalf v. Mardell (2003) 1 AC 120 贵族院先例(该先例会在本章之 12.6.2.3 段介绍,但并非是客户向前律师索赔的问题)中,将这个地位描述为"法律的默示"(implied by law)。

向前律师以其疏忽、过错为由在法院提出索赔时,是当事人作为原告自愿请求法院裁判其与律师之间原本享有机密性的特殊关系。对于公正裁判所必要的文件(any communication passing between them so far as necessary for the just determination of the claim）就会被法院认定允许披露，即使是特免权，也会被认定为默示弃权：见 Paragon Finance Plc. v. Freshfields 先例。在本章之 12.3 段也已经提到了律师虽然不享有特免权，但有义务依赖客户享有的特免权，不向其他人士（包括法院）披露与客户之间的机密通信往来。而客户向律师在公开法院起诉，也可以看作不再限制律师在此诉讼中披露与依赖这些文件。

之后在 NRG v. Bacon & Woodrow（1995）2 Lloyd's Rep. 77 先例中，Colman 大法官则是说："Waiver of privilege would operate if it could be established and the communications between the plaintiff and his solicitor were likely to be evidentially relevant to an issue and it would be unfair if the defendant did not have access to them in order to assist his defence. But, as I have already explained, the foundation of the waiver is not merely that the assertion of privilege leads to the inaccessibility of evidence relevant to a defence. **It is the inconsistency of the plaintiff on the one hand opening the professional relationship to the inspection of the Court and on the other hand seeking to enforce confidentiality so as to exclude communications to which the professional relationship between the same parties has given rise.**"（加黑部分是笔者的强调）

而且在笔者看来，在客户与律师之间的通信往来等文件，虽然客户可以依赖特免权拒绝披露这些文件给其他第三人，但在客户与律师之间来说，这些文件并不存在真正意义之上的机密性，毕竟这本就是在他们之间互相交流的文件。因此在客户与律师之间来说，也没有道理依赖特免权来拒绝披露。

12.6.2.1　起诉前律师的弃权范围

在 NRG v. Bacon & Woodrow（1995）2 Lloyd's Rep. 77 先例与 Paragon Finance Plc. v. Freshfields（1999）1 WLR 1183 上诉庭先例之后，英国法下对默示弃权的说法做出了确认，即只有在客户向其前律师进行索赔时，出于公平与不能前后矛盾，才导致与前律师之间委托合约下通信往来的特免权被弃权。因此在 Lillicrap v. Nalder & Son（1993）1 WLR 94 先例后，虽然有一些不同判法的先例中，如 Kershaw v. Whelan（1996）1 WLR 358；Hayes v. Dowding（1996）PNLR 578 与 Oceanic Finance Corporation Ltd. v. Norton Rose（unreported, 26 March 1997）先例等，在有了 Paragon Finance Plc. v. Freshfields 上诉庭先例后，再无需考虑这些前述不同判法的先例了。

默示弃权在一些情况中会延伸到与该前律师过往更早委托合约下通信往来的特免权，[135] 但不会延伸到与新律师（另一家律师事务所，如在该争议中客户重新委任的律师事务所，还可能是代表客户向前律师索赔的律师事务所）之间通信往来的特免权。

---

〔135〕 见 Lillicrap v. Nalder & Son（1993）1 WLR 94 先例。

默示弃权不仅仅限于职业疏忽案件,在诉讼费用案件等诉讼[136]中都会涉及,标准是考量客户是否将与前律师之间机密的委托关系置于争议之中(subject the confidential relationship to dispute)。而对律师向客户索赔的案件,暂时看来地位并不完全清楚,Hakendorf v. Countess of Rosenborg (2004) EWHC 2821 QB 先例(案情将在本章之 12.6.2.2 段介绍)中的理由存在一定的问题,是否会被后续先例所跟从,也存在疑问。

而默示弃权的范围是让律师做出必要的抗辩(so far as necessary for the just determination of the claim):见 Paragon Finance Plc. v. Freshfields 先例。根据 ENRC v. Dechert LLP (2016) EWCA Civ 375 上诉庭先例的判法,默示弃权可能会是"限定弃权"(limited waiver),但这方面也存在一定的疑问,可能需要后续先例做出澄清,有兴趣的读者可见 Charles Hollander QC 的《Documentary Evidence》(第 12 版,2015 年)一书之 24-22 至 24-27 段。

默示弃权也不会仅仅由于申请披露的文件涉及重要事实(material fact)或对想法的陈述(statement of mind)就被允许披露。虽然曾经在 Hayes v. Dowding 先例中判默示弃权可以延伸到诉讼当事人与第三人的通信往来,但在 NRG v. Bacon & Woodrow 先例与 Paragon Finance Plc. v. Freshfields 上诉庭先例后,已经肯定只有与被起诉的前律师之间的通信往来,才会由于向前律师索赔而被认定为是对特免权的默示弃权。根据 Paragon Finance Plc. v. Freshfields 上诉庭先例的判法,只要双方当事人不涉及有关的律师,或诉讼争议不涉及与律师之间的委托合约关系,与律师之间通信往来就不会被默示弃权。在近期的一些先例中也跟从与确认了 Paragon Finance Plc. v. Freshfields 先例的判法:见 Farm Assist Limited v. Secretary of State for Environment, Food and Rural Affairs (2008) EWHC 3079 (TCC);Digicel (St Lucia) Ltd. v. Cable & Wireless Plc. (2009) EWHC 1437 (Ch) 等先例。

12.6.2.2 律师就委托合约起诉客户的疑问

反过来也有律师需要向前客户索赔的情况,如客户未能依照委托合约的要求向律师支付费用。这方面的案件并不少见,但其中显然会出现的问题是,法律业务特免权是由客户所享有的,这在本章之 12.3 段已经进行了简单介绍。法律业务特免权会保护的文件覆盖了所有在委托合约下的工作内容,而要证明律师收费的合理性,是需要依赖这些显示了工作内容的文件的。

在 Paragon Finance Plc. v. Freshfields (1999) 1 WLR 1183 上诉庭先例中,也提到与肯定了在客户将与律师之间的机密关系置于争议中(subject the confidential relationship in dispute)时会导致默示弃权。这样律师要向客户索赔,是否会受制于法律业务特免权的保护而无法将文件披露给法院以证明自己的收费呢?

在 Hakendorf v. Countess of Rosenborg (2004) EWHC 2821 QB 先例中,认为律

---

〔136〕 如本章之 12.2.2 段已经提到的 ENRC v. Dechert LLP (2016) EWCA Civ 375 先例。

师向客户的诉讼也属于默示弃权。该先例中的被告(妻子)正与其丈夫进行离婚诉讼。而原告则是一家律师事务所的律师,在前述诉讼中受妻子的委托,代表妻子参与了一段时期的诉讼。原告律师指称妻子拖欠律师费,并且存在可能没有足够财产支付律师费的问题,因而还向法院申请了对妻子的财产冻结令,在该申请中就依赖了一些与妻子之间的通信往来。为此,妻子就指称原告律师的行为违反了双方的委托合同,在她没有做出弃权行为时就将受到法律业务特免权保护的文件披露了出去。

Tugendhat 大法官判原告律师的行为并没有破坏法律业务特免权,不妨节录部分判决如下:

"Further, it seems to me that a communication by a solicitor to the court, made for the purpose of proceedings properly brought by the Solicitor, will not of itself constitute a breach of legal professional privilege... If I were wrong about this, it seems to me that justice requires that I should not discharge the order on that account(作为被告的妻子希望撤销财产冻结令). A solicitor is entitled, in suing for her fees, to the same rights as other litigants, in particular to access to justice, equality of arms and a fair hearing. I do not see how these can be achieved if she cannot use the information which the Solicitor put before the court in this case.

If I were wrong about that, and if I had to resolve the question of principle, I would also decide that in favour of the Solicitor. If, as happened in this case, a former client acts so as to entitle the Solicitor to relief... or gives the Solicitor grounds for applying for a Freezing Order, while challenging a bill in whole or in part, it seems to me that there may well be a situation analogous to that in Paragon Finance. In other words the former client cannot put the former solicitor in that position, and at the same time deny the solicitor the use of materials relevant to the action, which the law plainly permits the solicitor to take."

律师在索赔自己的服务费用时,与其他所有索赔诉讼一样都有权获得公正、公平的审理,而该先例中的情况如果律师不能依赖这些受特免权保护的文件,就谈不上公平、公正。在 Paragon Finance Plc. v. Freshfields 上诉庭先例中,前客户不能一边向律师索赔,一边又不允许律师依赖有关的文件,Hakendorf v. Countess of Rosenborg 先例中也是类似地不能允许前客户(妻子)禁止律师依赖文件。

但 Hakendorf v. Countess of Rosenborg 先例的判法与 Paragon Finance Plc. v. Freshfields 先例的判法还是有一定不同。毕竟弃权行为,无论是明示弃权还是默示弃权,都涉及客户的言行,但有关先例中,妻子并没有任何额外的言行。也因此该先例的判法被一些权威书籍认为是错误的。如在《Phipson on Evidence》(第 18 版,2013 年)一书之 26 – 40 段说:"It is suggested that the reasoning, and the analogy with Paragon cannot be correct, as the client has done nothing and has not waived privilege impliedly or otherwise. But why should the solicitor not use privileged materials for this purpose where they are not confidential between him and the client? If, for example, privileged materials were used for an application by the solicitor to the court to come off the record, as is not uncommon, that surely could not be problematic. It is hard to see how the client can assert his privilege against the solicitor in such circumstances in relation to documents that may have been confidential against the rest of the world but could not be regarded as confidential between those parties. The contrary argument, which seems difficult, would involve setting up some sort of implication that the privileged materials would not be used against the client."

类似的质疑也可见《Documentary Evidence》(第12版,2015年)一书之24－23段:"It would be necessary to argue that the client in instructing the solicitor gives the solicitor implied consent to open up the privileged relationship for the purposes of proceedings against the client. Generally, the case law has not gone this far. However, there may well be circumstances where the solicitor is entitled to use the privileged material against the client. An example would be if the solicitor seeks to make an application to court to come off the record... There is one authority which goes significantly further although it has been criticised and, as the law currently stands, appears to be wrongly decided. In Hankendorf v. Countess of Rosenborg... As the doctrine of implied waiver presently stands, this decision is out of step because the client has taken no positive... step to bring into play the doctrine of implied waiver..."

笔者也同意 Hakendorf v. Countess of Rosenborg 先例的判法确实存在问题,无论是之前的先例还是 Paragon Finance Plc. v. Freshfields 先例的默示弃权说法,都是建立在客户通过言行先将机密关系置于争议之中的情形。这与该先例中的情况是有较大不同的。

更合理的解释可能是在客户委托律师时,就默示同意(implied agreement)律师针对这受特免权保护的关系开始诉讼程序,并在其中依赖必要的文件。这些诉讼程序除了向前客户索赔费用,还会如"come off the record",即律师向法院申请自己不再代理客户,客户的文件也不用再送达给自己。律师会有需要终止代理的合理情况,如客户倒闭或不支付费用,或双方之间关系破裂,甚至客户失踪再也没有进一步的指示等。这时候,律师要主动申请终止代理关系,客户一定是不会予以配合的。要能够通过誓章(affidavit)向法院说明自己的情况以求取得法院的命令,律师就必须要或多或少披露一些受特免权保护的文件。

12.6.2.3 对方当事人向律师索赔浪费的费用时,没有默示弃权允许披露受特免权保护的文件

已经介绍过如果是客户向律师索赔,并将他们之间的机密关系置于争议中,就会有对特免权的默示弃权:见 Paragon Finance Plc. v. Freshfields (1999) 1 WLR 1183 上诉庭先例。这无论是在职业疏忽案件或是在诉讼费用案件中,都是一致的:见 EN-

RC v. Dechert LLP（2016）EWCA Civ 375 上诉庭先例。

但如果不是客户向律师索赔，而是对方当事人向律师索赔浪费的费用（wasted costs）时，就不会有这样的默示弃权。在这个时候，一旦作为当事人的客户不放弃特免权，律师就不能依赖这些被特免权保护的文件进行抗辩，也事实上就无法在诉讼中对抗对方当事人了。

这个窘境在 Ridehalgh v. Horsefield（1994）Ch 205 上诉庭先例中就已经被很好地描述："The respondent lawyers are in a different position. The privilege is not theirs to waive. In the usual case where a waiver would not benefit their client they will be slow to advise the client to waive his privilege, and they may well feel bound to advise that the client should take independent advice before doing so. The client may be unwilling to do that, and may be unwilling to waive if he does. So the respondent lawyers may find themselves at a grave disadvantage in defending their conduct of proceedings, unable to reveal what advice and warnings they gave, what instructions they received. In some cases this potential source of injustice may be mitigated by reference to the taxing master, where different rules apply, but only in a small minority of cases can this procedure be appropriate. Judges who are invited to make or contemplate making a wasted costs order[137] must make full allowance for the inability of the respondent lawyers to tell the whole story. Where there is room for doubt, the respondent lawyers are entitled to the benefit of it. It is again only when, with all allowances made, a lawyer's conduct of proceedings is quite plainly unjustifiable that it can be appropriate to make a wasted costs order."

更典型的是近期的 Medcalf v. Mardell（2003）1 AC 120 贵族院先例中，在该先例的诉讼程序中，当事人（Mardell 先生）的代表大律师指称对方当事人（Medcalf 先生）存在"欺诈"（fraud）等不诚实的行为。后来该诉讼程序中的各方当事人达成和解协议，但是在和解协议中明确保留了 Medcalf 先生针对代表 Mardell 先生的代表大律师申请浪费费用命令的权利。

而 Medcalf 先生确实事后提出根据英国的《Bar Council Rule of Conduct》之 606（c）条的规定，大律师在没有合理可信的资料（reasonably credit material）时，不得建

---

〔137〕浪费费用命令（wasted costs order）是法院做出惩罚当事人的律师，而非当事人的命令。涉及法院认为当事人的律师对当事人在诉讼中不合情理的行为有责任的情况，所以应由律师而非当事人赔偿有关费用。Donaldson 大法官在 Gupta v. Comer（1991）2 WLR 494 先例中说，这必须是律师有严重的疏忽："a serious dereliction of duty as a solictiror, either by himself or his clerks 'gross negligence' or 'a gross neglect'."这种情况发生的不少，只简单举几个例子。在 R. v. Secretary of State for the Home Department, ex p. Abbassi, The Times, April 6, 1992, CA 先例中，上诉庭判律师（包括大律师）要个人支付一个毫无意义的上诉（frivolous appeal）导致的浪费费用。在 Re F., The Times, August 25, 1984 先例中，一方当事人的律师在撤销了单方申请后忘了通知对方，Balcombe 大法官判律师要赔偿有关的费用。

议客户指称对方有欺诈行为："A practising barrister must not devise facts which will assist in advancing his lay client's case and must not draft any originating process pleading affidavit witness statement or notice of appeal containing...（c）any allegation of fraud unless he has clear instructions to make such allegation and has before him reasonably credible material which as it stands establishes a prima facie case of fraud... provided that nothing in this paragraph shall prevent a barrister drafting a pleading affidavit or witness statement containing specific facts matters or contentions included by the barrister subject to the lay client's confirmation as to their accuracy."

Medcalf 先生指称代表 Mardell 先生的大律师违此规则、提出了有关欺诈行为的争议，造成了 Medcalf 先生面对欺诈行为的严重指控产生了额外的诉讼费用等损失，于是向法院申请浪费费用命令，要求大律师赔偿这些损失。

很显然的是，Mardell 先生的代表大律师如果想要对自己是否有合理可信的资料进行举证以显示自己不是凭空提起严重指控，就需要披露与 Mardell 先生的通信往来。毕竟无论是委托合约下的指示还是证据，都会是来自于 Mardell 先生。但是在本章之 12.3 段已经提到法律业务特免权是属于客户的，在该先例中即是 Mardell 先生，如果 Mardell 先生不愿意对其做出弃权，或是根本不予理睬（毕竟案件本身已经和解），大律师无权弃权。

而在该先例中，Mardell 先生完全拒绝披露任何受到特免权保护的通信往来（包括提供给律师的文件资料等），因此，在全部诉讼过程中大律师对这方面问题无法提供任何证据。

对于这样的窘境，英国曾经试图在民事司法改革带来的民事诉讼规则（CPR）中进行修正，但考虑到法律业务特免权的特别地位，最后也仍然决定即使是在浪费费用命令程序中，也仍然要严格保护法律业务特免权，没有通过立法进行超越。

12.7　弃权类型之三或弃权范围：附带弃权/挑选樱桃规则

如果有一批文件都受到特免权保护，如与律师之间的通信往来，或者有一份文件中涉及受特免权保护的多项内容，对这些文件而言，从原则上来说，当事人完全可以选择披露一部分而不披露其他部分，或是选择对部分内容做出遮盖（如获取了多份专家报告，只交出一份专家报告，但对其余几份不是太有利的专家报告不予交出与弃权）。正如 Cotton 大法官在 Lyell v. Kennedy（1884）27 Ch D 1 先例中所提到的所谓"the cardinal quotation"的说法："There was this contention raised, which I have not forgotten, that the defendant had waived his privilege, and therefore could not claim it at all. That, in my opinion, was entirely fallacious. He had done this, he had said 'Whether I am entitled to protect them or not I will produce certain of the documents for which I had previously claimed privilege — I will waive that and I will produce them' but that did not prevent him relying on such protection with regard to others which he did not like to produce. It is not like the case of a man who discloses part of a conversation and then claims protection for the remainder, and we think there is no ground for the contention that there has been here a waiver of privilege."

类似的说法也可见 Paragon Finance Plc. v. Freshfields（1999）1 WLR 1183 上诉庭先例中 Bingham 大法官所说："While there is no rule that a party who waives privilege in relation to one communication is taken to waive privilege in relation to all..."

而如果涉及诉讼中的特定情况，一旦当事人只披露部分文件内容会造成不公平或误导，可以适用"挑选樱桃规则"（cherry-picking rule）与"附带弃权"（collateral waiver）的说法，即当事人对部分文件内容做出的弃权，会实际造成对更广大受特免权保护文件内容的弃权。

在 Great Atlantic Insurance Co. v. Home Insurance Co.（1981）2 Lloyd's Rep. 138 上诉庭先例中，就是典型的涉及披露部分文件，是否可以对文件中针对同一主题的剩余部分以特免权为由拒绝披露的问题。这个问题在实践中也常常遇到。一方面是不少文件事实上确实会针对很多不同的主题，如一份会议记录，可能实际上包括了整个会议中的所有内容；又如一份邮件，常常也会针对不同的主题在进行讨论。这显然也不限于同一份文件中的"挑选樱桃"。也有情况是披露的文件的"issue in question"/"transaction"下存在多份其他未披露的文件。

无论是同一份文件中针对同一主题的内容，还是属于同一"issue in question"/"transaction"的不同文件，常常会同时都受到特免权保护，或者都不受到特免权保护。在文件都不受到特免权保护的情况下，显然都必须要披露了。而如果文件均受到特免权保护，一旦当事人披露其中一份文件中的部分，或是一套文件中的几份，造成的问题就是剩余的内容是否需要被披露呢？

对于此说法最著名的是 Nea Karteria Maritime Co. Ltd. v. Atlantic & Great Lakes Steamship Corporation（No. 2）（1981）Com LR 138 先例中，Mustill 大法官所说："Where a person is **deploying in court** material which would otherwise be privileged, the opposite party and the court must have the opportunity of satisfying themselves that what the party has chosen to release from privilege **represents the whole of the material relevant to the issue in question**. To allow an individual item to be plucked out of context would be to risk injustice through its real weight or meaning being misunderstood."（加黑部分是笔者的强调）

而所谓的"挑选樱桃"的说法则可见 Dunlop Slazenger International Ltd. v. Joe Bloggs Sports Ltd.（2003）EWCA Civ 901 上诉庭先例中，Waller 大法官对 Mustill 大法官以上说法的理解与描述："...Mustill J（as he then was）in Nea Karteria（Nea Karteria Maritime Co. Ltd. v. Atlantic & Great Lakes Steamship Corporation［No. 2］先例）... I would describe that as the cherry picking aspect.... To answer the question whether waiver of part of a privileged communication waives the complete information, it is that dictum of Mustill J（as he then was）which applies. A party is not entitled to cherry pick, and a party to whom privileged information is provided is entitled to have the full contents of what has been supplied in order to see that cherry picking is not taking place. If this material... had been evidence given at a trial, there really would be no answer to the point that the full information should be provided in order to make certain that cherry picking is not taking place."

换句话说,根据公平原则与 Great Atlantic Insurance Co. v. Home Insurance Co 先例的判法,对同一份文件中的部分内容放弃特免权,可能会造成对这份文件的全部内容弃权。判断标准是文件中的这些内容是否属于同一主题。

而对于一套文件来说,会由于对部分文件放弃特免权,导致对全部文件的特免权弃权。而何时会造成一套文件被附带弃权,则主要以 Nea Karteria Maritime Co. Ltd. v. Atlantic & Great Lakes Steamship Corporation (No. 2)先例中 Mustill 大法官的说法(上述节录的加黑部分)作为判断标准,即只有弃权的文件被置于诉讼中(deploying in court),或者说文件在诉讼中被依赖(reliance),才会存在附带弃权的问题;[138] 另一方面则是所有属于同一"issue in question"/"transaction"的文件[139]才会不能"挑选樱桃"或是导致附带弃权。

12.8 丧失机密性与弃权

机密性(confidentiality)是特免权存在的必要非充分条件,如果一份文件没有机

---

[138] 关于何时文件被置于诉讼中(deploying in Court)在过往先例中并没有明确、说法一致的判断标准。Great Atlantic Insurance Co. v. Home Insurance Co. (1981) 2 Lloyd's Rep. 138 上诉庭先例中的说法是"too late to turn the clock back"。在 R v. Secretary of Statement for Transport Ex p Factortame (1997) 9 Admin LR 591 先例中,则指出了很关键的一点在于文件有没有、会不会在诉讼中作为证据被依赖(rely),毕竟如果根本不打算依赖这份文件,也谈不上造成不公平或误导的后果。该先例中的英国政府承诺不会依赖被披露出来的文件,也因此并没有触发附带弃权,类似的先例可见 Fisher v. HMRC (2012) UKFTT 335 先例。在近期的 Brennan v. Sunderland City Council (2009) ICR 479 先例中,也对何时构成依赖有所指引:要考虑披露的究竟是什么,是文件大意、梗概还是原文节录,或仅仅是提到该份文件的存在;以及如何做出的披露,是在文书请求中提到,还是在开庭时依赖文件进行陈述、证明,总之,写得越清楚,就越容易被视为依赖。

[139] 有关附带弃权的范围,在 Nea Karteria Maritime Co. Ltd. v. Atlantic & Great Lakes Steamship Corporation (No. 2) (1981) Com LR 138 先例提到的是同一"issue in question",在 General Accident Fire and Life Corp v. Tanter (1984) 1 WLR 100 先例中,Hobhouse 大法官提到的是同一"transaction"(to which that evidence goes)。但事实上,这两种说法不存在实质上的不同:见 Fulham Leisure Holdings v. Nicholson Graham & Jones (2006) 2 All ER 599 先例。具体而言,附带弃权的范围究竟如何,会是非常依赖每个个案的事实不同而有所不同的。需要提及的是,无论是"issue in question"还是"transaction",都不是指文件的主题,而是针对文件披露的内容与目的。简单而言,尽管有不能"挑选樱桃"与附带弃权的说法存在,但这些原则的适用是有限的。而且从法院先例的判法来看,有倾向限制这些完全依赖公平原则的说法。另一方面,归根结底还是在诉讼程序中不能允许一方当事人选择性地披露文件导致不公平或误导:Ramac Holdings Ltd. v. Brachers (2002) All ER 180;MMI Research Ltd. v. Cellxion (2007) EWHC 2456 (Ch);Dore v. Leicestershire CC (2010) EWHC 34 (Ch);Holyoake v. Candy (2017) EWHC 387 (Ch)。

密性,也就肯定不会受到特免权的保护。这在不少先例中都有提及,在 Goldstone v. Williams (1899) 1 Ch 47 先例中,针对过往诉讼中的一份被记录在案的证词(deposition)是否受到特免权保护因而可以免于披露产生争议。Stirling 大法官指出该先例中由于该份证词被用在过往的公开诉讼程序中,已经可以被公众所获取,就不能再享有特免权的保护。

类似的也可见 British American Tobacco (Investments) Ltd. v. United States (2004) EWCA Civ 1064 上诉庭先例。该先例涉及的案件是据称美国有史以来涉及金额最大的案件,有关美国政府针对各大烟草公司的诉讼。这样的诉讼中涉及大量文件,因此虽然诉讼开始于美国,但在世界各地都展开了对这些烟草公司文件的披露要求。在这些披露要求下,各个烟草公司最常用的对抗方法就是以特免权为由拒绝披露,也因此在世界各地都开始了就文件披露的诉讼。

该上诉庭先例涉及的是非常针对性的问题。在美国进行的诉讼程序中,对部分争议达成双方同意判决(consent judgment),烟草公司与美国政府一致认可法院在之后决定是否将文件开放给公众。而之后尽管烟草公司极力反对,法院仍然发出命令,将文件披露给了公众。在此上诉庭先例中的争议焦点就是,假设这些涉及的文件原可以享有特免权保护,但在美国法院发出命令后,在英国是否仍然享有特免权保护呢?

上诉庭认定在这种情况下,烟草公司并不存在"弃权"(waiver)的行为,毕竟享有法律业务特免权的烟草公司并没有放弃特免权的意图,这也是一般弃权的要求:见本书第三章之 3.1 段。但同时上诉庭也指出,此时由于文件实际上已经被开放给公众,因此。由于机密性的丧失而不再享有特免权保护了。

由于文件在法院公开审理中被透露从而丧失机密性的先例很多,如 City of Gotha v. Sotheby's (1998) 1 WLR 114 上诉庭先例;USP Strategies Plc. v. London General Holdings Ltd. (2004) EWHC 373 (Ch)先例;Burkle Holdings Ltd. v. Laing (No. 2) (2005) EWHC 2022 (TCC)先例等。

对于"联合特免权"(joint privilege)/"联合利益特免权"(joint interest privilege)或者"共同利益特免权"(common interest privilege)而言,近期的 Singla v. Stockler & Anor (2012) EWHC 1176 (Ch)先例也指出,由于文件在多方当事人之间并不存在机密性,从而在他们之间并不能拒绝文件的披露。

在多数情况下,丧失机密性(loss of confidentiality)的问题可以基本等同于特免权弃权或丧失(loss)的问题。如在本章之 12.6.2 段已经提到的客户起诉律师的情况,就实际上一方面是在客户与律师之间不存在机密性,另一方面是起诉前律师行为属于默示的行为弃权:见 Paragon Finance Plc. v. Freshfields (1999) 1 WLR 1183 等先例。

但有时,丧失机密性与对特免权弃权的行为的区分有必要,也是重要的。尤其是针对本章之 12.7 段介绍的"附带弃权"(collateral waiver)/"挑选樱桃规则"(cherry picking rule)，只有先在法院诉讼程序中做出了弃权行为才会触发附带弃权，如果文件只是丧失机密性而并非被弃权，受影响的就只是丧失机密性的文件，不会产生附带弃权而需要披露更多文件了。

典型的例子就是本段前文中提到的 Goldstone v. Williams 先例。在本章之 12.6.2段提到的 NRG v. Bacon & Woodrow (1995) 2 Lloyd's Rep. 77 先例也涉及这个问题。该先例是 NRG 在一次收购交易中委任了一些专业人士提供建议，在过程中也将一些受特免权保护的文件交给这些专业人士。事后 NRG 向这些专业人士以职业疏忽(professional negligence)为由提出索赔。在诉讼中，专业人士就提出要求披露更多其他所有文件。在法院被判虽然有一些受特免权保护的文件由于事前被交出而丧失特免权，从而不能拒绝披露，但其他文件并没有丧失特免权。而且事前将文件"限定对象弃权"(selective waiver)并不是一般与广泛的弃权，因此也不会存在附带弃权的说法。

这也符合了本章之 12.5.3.2 段介绍 B v. Auckland District Law Society (2003) 2 AC 736 枢密院先例中所说，不妨重复节录该段判词如下："The documents are privileged because they were created for the purpose of giving or receiving legal advice. If they are not produced voluntarily, production cannot be compelled. If they are produced voluntarily, the right to withhold production no longer attaches to them. In that sense the privilege may be said to be lost. But they are the same documents, and it is not inappropriate to describe them as privileged. Their inherent characteristics are the same. The policy which protected them from unauthorised disclosure is the same. The cat is still a cat. It can be put back in the bag."

公司的文件管理(document management)中，对受特免权保护的文件要小心对待。即使是公司内部人士，也不能随意互相传阅，以免丧失机密性。即使有必要交给特定公司员工或外部人士(如 NRG v. Bacon & Woodrow 先例中委任的外部专业人士)，也应当明确表示文件属于机密性、不得随意传阅给第三人，或是写明为了特定目的而交出，以达到"选定对象弃权"(selective waiver)或"限定弃权"(limited waiver)，避免一般、广泛的弃权或由于丧失机密性而丧失特免权。

第十一章　合约更改、弃权、禁反言在银行法中的适用

囿于篇幅,本章是唯一针对商业活动中特定范畴业务进行探讨的章节。当然,本章也只是针对银行业务的部分内容简单介绍,而不能面面俱到。

本章将简单介绍五个领域的银行业务:[1]银行与储户(bank and customer)、贷款融资合约(loan facility)、担保合约(security/guarantee/surety)、[2]银团贷款融资合约(syndicated loan)以及信用证(letter of credit/documentary credit)。

1. 银行与储户

储户(customer)[3]是银行最重要的业务,双方就一般银行业务的交往中的言行也经常会带来涉及"弃权"(waiver)与"禁反言"(estoppel)的争议。

这方面主要有两种情况:(1)储户在签发支票或对银行做出其他指令(mandate)时因疏忽(negligence)或不作为(inaction)而被禁反言;(2)银行因自身的错误而被禁反言。

就第一种情况而言,因为储户在开立支票或做出其他对银行的指令时,对银行负有合理小心的义务,他是通过开立支票与做出指令授权银行用他存在银行账户中的钱做出支付。这时,如果储户存在疏忽或不作为,如在支票上多写了一个"0",或书写时前后留出太多的空白位置而给支票的收款人篡改的机会,又或者储户发现有不

---

〔1〕 银行业务没有确定的定义,是随着时间的变化而不断调整的,见 Woods v. Martins Bank Ltd. (1959) 1 Q. B. 55; United Dominions Trust Ltd. v. Kirkwood (1966) 2 Q. B. 431 等先例。

〔2〕 本章讨论的是与贷款融资合约相关的担保(security)、一般保证(guarantee)、连带保证(surety)等。一般来说,担保侧重于指以具体的财产作为保证,一般保证中,保证人对主合约中的债务承担的是次要的责任,即在主债务人违约不履行时,才需要就主合约的债务承担责任。而连带保证中,保证人对主合约债务是与主债务人承担并列的首要责任,债权人可以不经主债务人而直接向连带保证人要求承担债务。由于本章的内容不涉及具体区分这三种合约在法律上的异同,所以将会被统称为"担保合约"。

〔3〕 重要的银行业务是指银行为储户开立支票账户或存款账户并为储户开立的支票做出支付。近年来,因为电子支付的广泛使用,支票的使用已经大幅度减少。

妥的情况但没有及时告知银行等，储户就会被禁反言，而不能在事后有损失再要求银行承担后果。在 Brown v. Westminster Bank Ltd.（1964）2 Lloyd's Rep. 187 先例中，储户给了银行一系列的指令，后来发现最后一个指令是被伪造的，不过因为之前储户已经做出清楚无误的陈述说他所有的指令都是有效的，所以储户被禁反言。另可节录《Chitty on Contracts》（第 32 版，2015 年）之 34－343 段如下："**Estoppel.** The customer may, by his conduct, be precluded from asserting that the banker exceeded his mandate by paying a cheque. Thus, if the customer assured his banker, before payment of the cheque, that his signature was genuine, he would later on be precluded from asserting that it had been forged. In Greenwood v. Martins Bank（1933）AC 51,〔4〕 a husband was aware that his wife had forged and cashed his cheques, but did not disclose this fact to his bankers for a long period. In the meantime the wife forged further cheques and, when threatened by him with exposure, committed suicide. It was held that the husband was estopped〔5〕 from pleading the forgery of any of these cheques and that, as his silence had lulled his bankers into security, he could not recover from them the amount paid on any of the forgeries. It was further held that the detriment sustained by the bank was its inability, resulting from the customer's silence, to proceed against the wife. In a case like Greenwood v. Martins Bank Ltd. the customer must have actual knowledge of the forgery, or have deliberately turned a blind eye, for an estoppel that the customer had knowledge of circumstances which would cause a hypothetical reasonable customer to discover the fraud, is not enough."

就第二种情况而言，如银行在储户的存折上写上了错误的存款余额或银行错将不属于储户的钱存入储户的账户〔6〕或给储户的钱有误（或第三人）。这里可以简单节录《Chitty on Contracts》（第 32 版，2015 年）之 34－356 段所说如下："**Reclaiming money from payee.** In certain cases a bank, which paid money without a mandate or under some other mistake of fact, may wish to claim it back from the payee. Usually such an action is brought for the unjust enrichment of the payee, based on the fact that the money had been paid under a mistake of fact or in circumstances involving a total failure of consideration. . . . **Westdeutsche Landesbank Girozentrale v. Islington LBC**（1996）**AC 669**〔7〕 **establishes that the same principle entitles a bank to recover an amount paid by it to a customer** in pursuance of an enforceable agreement. In the instant case

---

〔4〕 该先例在本书第五章之 10.1.4 段已有介绍。

〔5〕 这种因为有责任说清楚（duty to speak）而导致的禁反言，在本书第五章第 10 段有详论。

〔6〕 见 Akrokerri（Atlantice）Mines Ltd. v. Economic Bank（1904）25 KB 465；Holland v. Manchester and Liverpool District Banking Co.（1909）25 TLR 286；United Overseas Bank v. Jiwani（1977）1 All ER 733 等先例。

〔7〕 该先例在本书第五章之 8.3.1 段有提及。

the action was brought to recover the balance of an amount initially paid by the bank to the local authorities in pursuance of an interest rate swap agreement which was ultra vires the authority's powers. It is, however, clear that no amount would be recoverable in such an action if it was paid out by the bank after it had come to realize that the agreement was void, or at least took the risk that it was void."(加黑部分是笔者的强调)

针对这种情况,银行的错误会构成"陈述性禁反言"(estoppel by representation)。当然,储户也需要证明他有依赖并改变了地位(change of position),如将错给的钱已经部分或全部花掉。这与本书第五章第4段介绍的弄错事实下付钱的情况相似或道理一样。

2. 贷款融资合约

2.1　贷款融资合约的更改

贷款融资合约作为商业活动中融资经常要用到的合约,其本身的"更改"(variation)与其他商业合约的更改没有实质性的不同。所以,在本书第三章第2段中介绍的合约更改原则均适用在贷款融资合约中,包括要有一份持续有效的合约、双方同意与要有约因/对价等,在此不再赘述。关于贷款融资合约的更改会对与其相关的由贷款人(lender)提供担保的担保合约产生怎样的影响,这可见本章之3.4段。

2.2　贷款融资合约的弃权

2.2.1　知道有关权利以及相关事实

在贷款融资合约下,被指称弃权的一方通常是提供贷款的银行或其他金融机构。这样,根据本书第三章对弃权说法的介绍,要构成弃权首先需要贷款人证明银行知道其违反贷款融资合约的行为以及自己在贷款融资合约下的权利,而银行仍然通过言行接受或不反对贷款人的违约,才能构成弃权。

在贷款融资合约下,贷款人与银行在谈判与履行贷款融资合约期间会有着紧密与持续的交往。如果涉及的贷款金额巨大,谨慎的银行一定会对贷款人的背景与财务状况进行尽职调查。如果贷款被批准,银行还会为贷款人开立专门的账户用以履行贷款融资合约,包括发放贷款、监督贷款的使用情况、决定是否要兑现贷款人签发的票据或帮其垫付账单以及定期监控贷款利息与本金的偿还情况。而且贷款融资合约中还会有条文规定贷款人要对贷款融资的款项进行专款专用,并为此款项的使用与流转设立专门的财务记录以供银行随时查阅或询问。

另外,银行也会对贷款融资合约的内容及条文知道的非常清楚,甚至会是由银行提供惯用的标准格式合约。在贷款融资合约中,往往会有对贷款人违约事项(event of default)规定的十分详细的条文,这可见杨良宜所著的《船舶融资与抵押》一书第五章之4.2.1段中列举的有关船舶融资贷款合约中的条文。违约包括在贷款时对银行做出不准确的陈述、保证,如报高船价但在履行时才被发现;贷款人清盘、破产;贷款人延误还款;船舶没有投保保险,船舶没有进行正常的维修保养,船舶被扣押时没有安排及时放船与其他危及担保的行为以及其他各种违约行为。贷款融资合约也针对这一系列的违约行为有救济的条文,如马上清还贷款、占有与变卖作为担保的财产以及要求履行相关的担保合约。这带来的后果就是令贷款融资合约终止。在这种条文下,银行在进行监督时,会对发生的任何违约与它在合约下的权利都十分清楚。本章在此不详细展开讨论针对某一具体贷款融资合约的违约,而只是针对在所有贷款融资合约下最常见并且银行一定会知道的延误支付本金与利息的违约。

针对银行知道自己的权利与相关的事实这一要件,贷款人唯一可能会面对的障碍就是银行的代理人或雇员知道相关违约事实是否能够被认为也是银行自己知道。例如,在本章稍后第4段中介绍的银团贷款融资合约中,代理行知道违约还款的事实是否可以被认定是整个银团知道?

针对这一问题,一般的代理法规则适用。不过在什么时间与什么情况下代理人或雇员知道可以被认定为是雇主也知道,并不是简单的问题。法院会根据不同案件的事实来具体分析,并且会将得出的结论只是局限的适用于特定的案情。[8] 正因为如此,普通法并没有能够从众多的不同案件中提炼出的具有普适性的原则。

结合贷款融资合约的情况,银行自己常常会通过信贷员(loan officer)或贷款审核委员会(loan review committee)来负责包括推销贷款融资项目、为贷款人提供贷款融资政策的咨询、审查贷款人的申请、批准贷款以及跟进贷款融资合约的执行情况等工作。在不存在欺诈的情况下,信贷员作为银行的雇员代表银行来处理贷款融资事宜,对贷款人来说,信贷员知道有关违约情况就可以推定银行也知道。因为在实务操作中,信贷员也的确会向贷款人表示可以代表银行处理有关贷款融资业务的一切事宜,而且根据银行的内部规定,信贷员也需要将收到的信息以及知道的情况马上转告相关的负责人。所以,除非在一些非常特别的情况下银行能够证明知道有关情况的人士没有参与过相关的业务[9]或者对特定的交易没有涉足,也一点不了解,[10] 又或者知悉情况的人士不是以法律认可的身份接收到的消息。[11] 这些特别的情况在贷款实务中并不多见,特别是在通讯发达与技术先进的今天,一些年代久远的案件的

---

〔8〕 如在代理合约中代理有责任将信息及时传递给雇主的情况下,代理知道将会被推定为雇主也是知道的。

〔9〕 见 Re Carew's Estate Act (No. 2) (1862) 31 Beavan 39; 54 E. R. 1051 先例。

〔10〕 在 Re Peruvian Rlys Co. v. Thames and Mersey Marine Insurance Co. (1867) 2 Ch App 617 先例中,Fletcher 先生在两家公司担任董事,在一单交易中,这两家公司都有参与,Fletcher 先生在一家公司有参与并知道相关的信息,但在另一家公司中并不参与具体的业务,所以不能被认定另一家公司知道。

〔11〕 Societe Generale de Paris v. Tramways Union Co. (1884) 14 QBD 424 先例中,通知必须要正式送达给具有授权接收文书的公司秘书才能生效。公司秘书在以个人身份参加亲戚葬礼时,通过亲戚的律师获知的情况不能被认为是他所在的公司也知道。

案情不大可能会再发生。根据本书第五章之 12.2 段所讲的“表见授权”(apparent/ostensible authority)的说法,银行事后即使拿出内部的通讯内容进行抗辩,指称对该雇员“真正授权”(actual authority)有所限制,但该抗辩在面对不知情的贷款人的时候是站不住脚的。所以,如果银行对信贷员或贷款审查委员会有任何权利的限制,需要事先就明示告知贷款人,以保证将来在信贷员或贷款审查委员会有“越权”(ultra vires)的情况出现时,可以免除责任。

在大部分的情况下,信贷员与贷款审核委员会作为银行的雇员,都会有银行的授权去处理贷款人履约的事项,包括有对贷款人违反贷款融资合约的行为做出弃权的权利等。但如果信贷员或贷款审核委员会没有银行的明示授权,并且根据具体的案情也不能构成表见授权,[12]就不能直接根据信贷员与贷款审核委员会的弃权行为就推定银行的弃权。

这可以类比 The “Laconia” (1977) 1 Lloyd’s Rep. 315 (HL)先例中船东的银行对承租人汇款的接受不可以被认为是船东对汇款的接受一样。[13] 与贷款融资合约下银行会持续按照约定收到贷款人分期偿还的利息与本金类似,航运中期租合约下船东也会持续收到承租人支付的船舶租金。而该船舶租金往往又像岸上房屋的租金一样,均是预先支付。该贵族院先例涉及期租合约,期租合约下承租人有准时与足额预先支付租金的义务,如果出现承租人不准时支付租金的情况,根据租约标准条文 NYPE 46,船东有权撤船并终止期租合约。在该先例中,承租人迟延支付租金,收款银行收到了该迟付的租金,但船东随后指示银行退还该迟付的租金并撤船。承租人指称银行接受租金的行为被视为船东也接受,从而船东构成了对撤船权利的弃权。该案经过仲裁、高院、上诉庭,一直打到贵族院,贵族院判是船东在实务中不会在银行还没有收到租金之前就指示银行拒绝接受迟付的款项,因为有可能船东在承租人做出支付之前,就已经选择撤船,这样也就不会有承租人进一步的支付了。并且银行作为船东的代理人也没有代表其客户接受迟付租金并弃权的授权,所以,船东不构成弃权。Salmon 勋爵说:“I doubt whether even if the processing of the payment order had been completed and the owners’ account had been credited with the full amount of the payment order before that amount was returned to the Midland Bank on the following day, a finding of waiver could have been justified... Certainly it was not within the banker’s express or implied authority to make commercial decisions on behalf of their customers by accepting or rejecting late payments of hire without taking instructions. They did take instructions and were told to reject the payment. They did so and returned it to the charterers on the following day which on any view must have been within a rea-

〔12〕 如贷款人知道与他联系的人士不具有能够放弃合约权利的事实。例如,该人士告诉贷款人这件事你不要让我老板(银行)知道。

〔13〕 关于支付租金的课题,可见杨大明《期租合同》一书第十八篇。

sonable time. If the bank had kept the payment for an unreasonable time, the charterers might well have been led to believe that the owners had accepted payment. This would have amounted to a waiver of their right to withdraw the vessel. But nothing of the kind happened in the present case."

2.2.2 贷款融资合约下弃权的构成

在银行知道自己在贷款融资合约下的权利与贷款人履约情况的情况下,如果银行接受或不予反对贷款人未能以合约规定的方式偿还本金或利息(贷款人在贷款融资合约下主要或唯一的义务,也经常会发生违约)的行为(通常是没有按照合约中规定的偿还机制或还款地点[14]进行还款),就很可能被认为是银行有清楚无误的陈述(unequivocal representation),暂时或永久地放弃了他在贷款融资合约下本应有的权利,包括选择执行贷款融资合约中对违约的救济措施,如提前终止贷款融资合约要求贷款人马上清还所有本金与利息等。

在这里需要注意区分的是,贷款人提出不按照贷款融资合约的约定履行的要约(offer)与真正不按照合约履约的违约行为这两种情况。在前者,如果这一要约对贷款银行也有好处(即可以成立约因/对价,如贷款人提供其他更多的担保),贷款银行同意了这一要约,就构成对合约的更改[一般就是贷款重整(rescheduling of loan)或延期偿付(moratorium)]。在对银行没有好处的情况下,银行接受该要约则是银行"单方面弃权"(pure and unilateral waiver)/"因宽限而弃权"(waiver by forbearance),如贷款人的要约或要求暂时停止支付利息与/或本金并被银行接受。这弃权也可以通过合理通知去恢复银行在合约中的权利。而在后者,如果同时面对已经发生的违约履行,银行就有了执行或不执行合约救济(包括提前终止合约)的选择权。如果银行选择了不执行该违约的救济,就构成了"因选择而弃权"(waiver by election)。

正如本书第三章之3.4段中所讲,因选择而弃权要求弃权方做出一些行为或通过口头或书面来表明弃权的立场,而现实中通过行为表示的更多。在贷款融资合约中,最典型的行为就是银行接受不符合合约约定(延误或不足数)的还款,包括利息与本金。在贷款融资合约中,通常提供贷款的银行在合约的条文下都拥有在贷款人违反合约的情况下,要求贷款人提前归还贷款本金与利息的权利。但由于归还的行为多是分期进行,这令银行的权利也是随着利息与本金的每次到期而产生的,所以,在没有其他任何言行表示的情况下,银行接受贷款人延误偿还已经到期的利息的行为并不构成在将来下一次延误时对要求提前归还贷款权利的弃权。如果利息是约定提前支付,银行对利息的接受,将会被视为对在该利息所涵盖的时间内的权利的弃权。又或者银行接受利息支付的行为可以被视为双方关系继续存在的确认(affirm)或构成禁反言。

针对已经欠下的利息或是债务,贷款人要支付给银行天经地义,银行弃权与否都

[14] 在早期通讯与技术不发达的时代才会遇到,可见 Gyles v. Hall (1726) 2 P Wms 378 先例。

不影响这笔钱是需要清还,所以,银行接受这笔钱的支付充其量也是中性的行为。但针对将来的利息或要支付的钱,只不过合约规定要预付,像期租合约下的船舶租金,如果接受,就有了矛盾。因为如果不弃权,也就是银行提前终止合约或船东撤船,一终止合约或撤船,就表示将来要支付的利息或租金永远不会发生了,如果接受了预付的金额,就代表放弃了终止合约与撤船的权利。

针对上述所讲,在 Sean Wilken QC 与 Karim Ghaly 先生所著的《The Law of Waiver, Variation, and Estoppel》(第3版,2012年)一书之17.11段是说:"The most likely form of unequivocal representation by the lending bank will be the acceptance of payments under the facility. It follows that the acceptance of interest payments by the lending bank may be evidence that it has waived its rights. However, it must be remembered that the lending bank will be responding to a breach that would entitle it to call in and determine the facility. Calling in the facility accelerates the repayment of interest and principal by the borrower but will have no effect on obligations of the borrower which have already accrued. It follows that, as the lending bank is waiving its right to call in the facility, the unequivocal representation must relate to the future obligations of the borrower[15]. Therefore, the acceptance of accrued interest will not, without more, found a waiver nor will the acceptance of interest payments after the facility has been called in[16]. It is **only** if the lending bank accepts interest payment **in advance**, **or** as **confirmation of a continuing future relationship** between itself and the borrower, that **a waiver will definitely occur**."(加黑部分是笔者的强调)

在 Keene v. Biscoe (1878) L. R. 8 Ch. D. 201 先例中,受押人(mortgagee)同意如果抵押贷款人(mortgagor)能够准时与足额的偿还利息,本金可以维持2年再清还。6个月的利息到期时,受押人要求抵押贷款人支付,但抵押人没有支付,受押人遂要求抵押人支付利息和本金,虽然在到期三天后,抵押人支付了6个月的利息,受押人也收到了该笔付款。法院判受押人即使随后接受了该笔付款,但从来没有对他收回本金的权利弃权。Fry 大法官说:"Then did the receipt of the £ 10 waive the Plaintiff's right to payment which had already accrued? I see nothing in it to have that effect. Where a right has accrued it can be waived, but to amount to waiver **there must be something done which is inconsistent with the continuance of that right**. Now, the right here was to immediate payment of £ 400 and interest, and the receipt of a portion

---

〔15〕 银行要求贷款人提前归还贷款会加快贷款人还贷的速度,但这并不影响贷款人在贷款融资合约下已经产生的义务(已经产生的利息或需要归还的本金)。所以,如果银行放弃了要求贷款人提前还贷的权利,该清楚无误的陈述所构成的放弃也只是针对要求贷款人提前归还将来才产生的利息与需要归还的本金。

〔16〕 由此,银行接受贷款人偿还已经产生的利息,并不会构成对要求贷款人提前还贷权利的放弃,即使该接受是发生在提出要求贷款人提前还贷之后,也不会带来任何弃权的后果。

of that sum is in no way inconsistent with that demand. I cannot conceive any case more different from that of receipt of rent after a forfeiture. In that case non-payment of rent has given rise to a right of forfeiture, but if the landlord afterwards receives any rent, that puts an end to his right of forfeiture; for if, after knowing the circumstances, he accepts rent, he in fact says that though he might have avoided the lease he has chosen not to do so; he has chosen to say that the lease shall subsist, and he cannot then say that it shall not subsist. The receipt of money as rent is inconsistent with the determination of the lease. But I see no inconsistency here."(加黑部分是笔者的强调)

虽然沉默不能够构成弃权,但银行在做出是否弃权的选择时,要注意不要拖延太久,因为会有危险被法律剥夺了这个权利。[17]

2.2.3 保留权利条文(reservation of rights clause)/不弃权条文(non-waiver clause)

银行面对贷款人违约时需要小心,因为双方在贷款融资合约履行的过程中会有很多通信往来,而这些通信往来中会有一些言行在之后被解释为银行确认双方关系继续存在或者与要求提前归还贷款的立场相反。这时,为了保护自己的权利不被解释为已经弃权,银行需要在通信往来中很小心,如在贷款人迟付利息时,发出一份措辞小心的要求函(如要求尽快支付),并在其中利用"保留权利"(reserve right)等字眼来保护自己的权利,以避免贷款人将来指该要求函与选择执行违约的救济相互矛盾,构成对救济权利的弃权。又或者在贷款融资合约中拟定一个措辞周全的"不弃权条文"(non - waiver clause)。这方面在本书第三章之 3.5 与 3.5.1 段以及第四章之 6.5.2段与 6.5.3 段有详论。尽管"保留权利"的字眼能够令银行在对贷款人违约有过一次弃权之后仍然保留将来能够要求行使权利,但该对已经发生违约可选择救济的权利的保护作用很可能只是暂时性的。如果银行仍然继续与贷款人保持联系并拖延要求贷款人提前还款(银行这种矛盾也可以理解),该保护作用就会失去。因为法院还是会全面解释银行所有的言行,从而总体来看是否构成弃权或禁反言。"保留权利"或"不弃权条文"只会作为部分的证据,而不对判断是否构成对选择救济权利的弃权具有决定性的作用。

在 Sean Wilken QC 与 Karim Ghaly 先生所著的《The Law of Waiver, Variation, and Estoppel》(第 3 版,2012 年)一书之 17.14 段说:"However... the lending bank must not act inconsistently with that reservation of rights. If the bank does so, the general rule will apply and the reservation will have no effect. It is submitted that banks must exercise particular caution in this respect. A bank will normally have close contact with the borrower and the more contact the bank has with the borrower, the more opportunity it will have for acting inconsistently with the reservation of rights, and therefore, the less

〔17〕 这在本书第三章之 3.2 段有针对。

protection that reservation of rights will offer. Further, the lending bank will usually be faced with a stark choice-to accept the breach or call in the facility. When the bank does not call in the facility, it will be difficult to avoid the bank's subsequent actions being construed as some form of unequivocal representation that it has waived its rights... Therefore, it is submitted that a reservation of rights may only offer the bank temporary protection and the prudent bank should decide what action it wishes to take as soon as may be practicable."

接着在 17.20 段说:"A 'non-waiver' clause can be inserted into the facility. That clause will offer some protection but will be strictly construed against the bank.[18] In any event, the bank should react to all defaults by the borrower as quickly as possible, reaching a conclusion as to whether to call in the facility or continue with the transaction. If the bank decides to accept repayments under the facility, then, unless it has taken unusual steps to protect its position, it should be prepared to be held to have waived its rights."

2.2.4 弃权的后果

对于"因选择而弃权"(waiver by election),银行一旦做出选择,就是最终与不能撤回的(final and irrevocable)。这可见本书第三章之 5.2.1 段节录的 Rix 大法官在 Kosmar Villa Holidays Plc. v. Trustees of Syndicate 1243 (2008) EWCA Civ 147 先例中的判词,在此不再重复。

而对于"因宽限而弃权"(waiver by forbearance),银行可以选择在将来通过合理通知恢复自己在贷款融资合约下的权利,即要求贷款人按照合约履行,否则会选择执行或行使合约下救济的权利。这个课题在本书第四章有详论。

3. 担 保 合 约

对于提供贷款的银行或者其他金融机构来说,在贷款融资合约下,贷款人提供的担保(security)至关重要。贷款人提供的担保包括财产(包括不动产)的担保[如抵押(mortgage)、押记(charge)或者质押(pledge)],还有惯常做法是要求如公司董事或母公司或任何其他第三人提供个人担保(personal guarantee)。在没有不动产作为担保的贷款融资合约中,一份个人担保合约可能就是贷款融资合约下唯一的担保。

担保合约本质上是一份合约,它的性质可以节录《Chitty on Contracts》(第 32 版,2015 年)之 45-001 段说明如下:"A contract of suretyship is in essence a contract by which one person (the surety) agrees to answer for some liability of another (the princi-

---

[18] 见 R v. Paulson (1921) 1 AC 271 先例中 Atkinson 勋爵的判词。

pal debtor) to a third person (the creditor). The contract may be constituted by a personal engagement on the part of the surety, or by a charge on property without any personal liability, or by both."

对于提供贷款的银行或金融机构来说,在贷款融资合约的履行出问题也就是贷款人不还钱时,确保一份担保合约的有效与具有强制执行力是非常重要的。而担保合约因历史原因在更改方面与其他合约有很大不同,其本身的更改以及担保合约所针对的主合约(包括本章第 2 段介绍的贷款融资合约)的更改都会给担保合约的强制执行力带来问题,以下详细介绍。

3.1 担保合约的更改

探讨担保合约的更改主要讨论以下问题:(1)不符合 1677 年《The Statute of Frauds》第 4 条对书面形式的要求;(2)对担保合约单方面的更改,而担保人是不知情与没有同意;(3)对主合约(贷款融资合约)的更改。以下将分别介绍这三种情况,对担保合约的有效性有不同程度的影响。

3.2 不符合书面形式的更改

3.2.1 立法对担保合约有特殊的形式要求

对于担保合约的达成与更改适用 1677 年《The Statute of Frauds》第 4 条的规定(以下简称"1677 年立法")。该条文节录如下:"No action shall be brought... whereby to charge the defendant upon any special promise to answer for the debt, default or miscarriages of another person... unless the agreement upon which such action shall be brought or some memorandum or note thereof shall be in writing and signed by the party to be charged therewith or some other person thereunto by him lawfully authorized."

根据该第 4 条的规定,要为他人的债务(debt)[19]、违约(default)[20]或错误(miscarriage)[21]负责的合约一定要以书面形式做出,并且有要负责的人的或有其授权的人士的签字才有效。该书面形式的要求是为了令合约的达成更加肯定。该立法的用意在于防止某些类别合约的达成是根据一些不肯定的证据或根据一些当事人并没有真正订约意图的随意口头说说。[22] 根据该 1677 年立法,最初有五种不同类别的合约的订立与更改是一定要以书面达成,才有法律约束力。这五种合约为:(1)遗嘱执行人用自己的钱偿还遗产执行所带来的债务的合约(contracts by the executor of a will to pay a debt of the estate with his own money);(2)担保合约(contracts in which one party becomes a surety (acts as guarantor) for another party's debt or other obliga-

---

〔19〕 指过去的合约责任,可见 Castling v. Aubert (1802) 2 East 325 先例。

〔20〕 被认为很可能已经包括将来的责任甚至非合约责任,可见 Kirkham v. Marter (1819) 2 B. & Ald. 613 先例。

〔21〕 指所有其他形式的民事责任,可见 Kirkham v. Marter (1819) 2 B. & Ald. 613 先例。

〔22〕 见 Blackburn 勋爵在 Steel v. McKinlay (1879 – 80) L. R. 5 App. Cas. 754 中所说:"by evidence of loose talk, when it never was really meant to make such a contract."

tion)；(3)以婚姻为对价的合约(contracts in consideration of marriage)；(如一位男士对一位女士说你和我结婚我才将财产给你)(4)转让土地权益的合约(contracts for the transfer of an interest in land)；(5)一年内无法履行完毕的合约(contracts that cannot be performed within one year)。

虽然随着立法的发展，根据1954年生效的《Law Reform (Enforcement of Contracts) Act》，该1677年立法已经被大部分废除(repeal)，但立法者一致同意该第4条对书面形式的要求仍然应该适用在担保合约。保留该书面形式的要求在担保合约主要考虑是希望这种单方面受益的合约[被担保人单方面受益，而对担保人(surety/guarantor)来说毫无利益可言]的当事人是经过深思熟虑并以书面清楚的对权利义务做出约定才达成的合约。这样，如果不对合约达成的形式做出规定，就有危险令狡猾的人士有可乘之机，根据一些并不是十分肯定的证据而声称没有经验的相对方已经同意作为担保人就某些债务或责任与狡猾的人士达成了担保合约。

在近期仍能见到支持该立法本意的司法判例，其中在Autocar Equipment Ltd. v. Motemtronic Ltd. and Searle (unreported) CAT No. 656 of 1996, June 20，Henry大法官说："I have made it clear that in my judgement the mischief aimed at by Section 4 of the Statute of Frauds 1677 remains as valid as ever it did... This matter seems to me to be one of practical importance. Where there is an oral promise to answer eventually for the legal default of another the precise wording of that oral promise will often be difficult to ascertain, and often an uncertainty will lie over it even after the Court has found what the words used were. The result may often be commercially improbable and the requirement of a written note or memorandum should operate to make sense of the agreement."

3.2.2　担保合约的更改要遵守1677年立法的规定

担保合约的更改(variation)，尤其是针对重要条文的更改，本质上是达成一份新的合约。如果想要更改后的担保合约也具有法律强制力(enforceable)，也需要满足1677年立法的规定。

如果担保合约只是被口头更改，[23]带来的结果是更改的部分不具有法律强制力，而原担保合约仍然有效。这样，担保合约下的债权人(在与贷款融资合约有关的情况下，通常是提供贷款的银行)将无法根据更改后的内容起诉担保人。这可见Barclays Bank v. Caldwell, (unreported), July 25, 1986先例中，其中涉及担保合约与一份写在回签书信(side letter)[24]中的附带协议(collateral agreement)。该回签书信只有银行的代表单方签署。银行申请将回签书信中的附带协议的内容合并进担保

〔23〕 该口头更改包括后来所讲的口头协议并不仅是口头说说的内容，也包括记录下来但没有签字的内容。总之，不符合1677年立法第4条对形式的规定。

〔24〕 这种文件用于对主合约的更改、补充以及澄清。通常来说，这是一份具有法律效力的文件，但并不绝对。

合约,但这被 Harman 大法官拒绝,他认为这两份文件不能放在一起看待,因为这属于对担保合约的更改,但却不满足形式上的要求。

3.2.3 区分口头协议是对原担保合约的更改还是废除的重要性

接下来将介绍部分早期的先例来显示这方面法律的发展与建立。

首先是早期上诉庭的 Williams v. Moss' Empires (1915) 3 KB 242 先例。案情涉及原告是音乐表演艺术家,被告是剧院老板。两者签订合约,被告聘请原告在他的剧院进行表演并给原告发工资,合约有效期是 1911 年 7 月 31 日到 1915 年 3 月。因为合约的履行超过 1 年,所以 1677 年立法适用。1914 年 7 月第一次世界大战爆发,受战争影响,演员工会与剧院达成协议,按照新的更低的方式计算所有现存表演合约中演员的报酬。后来原告不同意演员工会可以代表自己同意这样的更改,并向被告索赔新的工资金额与原合约中更高工资金额的差别。一审法院在事实上判是原告与被告在 1914 年 8 月有达成口头协议,按照新的较低的计薪方式来计算原告的工资。但一审法院认为,该口头协议是对原合约的更改,因为原合约是适用 1677 年立法,对其更改也要以书面做出,而不能以口头协议达成,从而口头协议不能被强制执行而判原告胜诉。被告就该口头协议是否能够具有法律强制力的问题上诉。其中 Shearman 大法官与 Sankey 大法官均判被告胜诉,原因是该口头协议构成了新的合约并替代了原合约,但因有效期不足 1 年(1914 年 8 月至 1915 年 3 月),从而不适用 1677 年立法与不需要满足书面的要求,所以新合约有效与具有法律强制力。

Shearman 大法官说:"Those cases show that whenever the parties **vary a material term** of an existing contract **they are in effect entering into a new contract**, the terms of which must be looked at in their entirety, and if the new contract is one which is required to be in writing but is not in writing, then it must be wholly disregarded and the parties are relegated to their rights under the original contract. But if on the other hand there is nothing in the terms of the new contract which necessitates a written contract, then, although the original contract was one which was bound to be in writing, the new parol contract can be enforced because although it is not in writing it is nevertheless an effective contract. In the present case it was competent for the parties in August, 1914, to enter into a new verbal contract to vary the terms of the original contract which would expire in March, 1915, and which, therefore, in August, 1914, had less than a year to run. The new contract does not fall within any of the provisions of the Statute of Frauds and therefore need not be in writing. It is a binding and enforceable contract, and, in my opinion, affords a defence to the plaintiff's claim in this action. The appeal must therefore be allowed."(加黑部分是笔者的强调)

Sankey 大法官也说:"A contract which in compliance with the Statute of Frauds is in writing may be rescinded by a new agreement. The new agreement may be one which in order to be enforceable is required to be in writing, or it may be one which is valid though it is not in writing. If it is one which is required to be in writing and is not in writing, it is unenforceable and cannot be treated as evidence that the original contract has been rescinded, and the original contract, therefore, remains in force. But if the new agreement is in writing, or, if verbal, is one which need not be in writing, the new agreement is valid and the original contract is rescinded."

在随后贵族院的 Morris v. Baron (1918) AC 1 先例中,又进一步确立了符合立法的规定而以书面对合约进行更改才有效,否则原合约仍然有效,并且不受口头更改的影响。该先例还区分出对原合约的"更改"(variation)才需要以书面形式做出,但如果新合约是令原合约"废除"(rescission),则不需要书面的形式。该先例所针对的立法是 1893 年《Sale of Goods Act》第 4 条,[25] 这第 4 条的写法与 1677 年立法一致,如下:"Section 4 Contract of sale for ten pounds and upwards (1) A contract for the sale of any goods of **the value of ten pounds or upwards** shall not be enforceable by action unless the buyer shall accept part of the goods so sold, and actually receive the same, or give something in earnest to bind the contract, or in part payment, or unless some note or memorandum **in writing** of the contract be made and **signed by the party** to be charged or his agent in that behalf."(加黑部分是笔者的强调)

Morris v. Baron 先例的案情是原告是精纺织物的生产商,他作为卖方,与被告的买方订立买卖 500 块布匹的合约。原告交付了 223 块布匹,被告没有支付货款,双方产生争议。原告向被告要求支付货款,被告则声称原告延误交付余下 277 块布匹带来了损失。双方都向对方提起诉讼,在诉讼过程中,双方达成了口头协议(parol agreement)。该口头协议规定原告向被告赔偿 30 英镑作为延误交付货物的赔偿,被告则在 3 个月内向原告支付尚未支付的货款以及拥有是否继续要求交付余下货物的选择权。但后来被告在 3 个月内并没有支付货款,却坚持要求原告先交付余下货物。于是原告又根据该口头合约开始了诉讼。在贵族院,法院确认了口头协议要有法律强制力需要以书面做出,否则原合约仍然有效。并且判口头协议如果是对原合约的更改才需要以书面做出,而如果新的口头协议是意在废除原合约并完全替代原合约,则不需要是以书面做出。

这带来要区分双方后来的口头协议究竟是对原合约的更改还是对原合约的废除的重要性。Dunedin 大法官在谈到判断新协议时,对原合约的更改还是废除原合约是要看双方当事人在口头协议所表达的意图说:"The difference between variation and rescission is a real one, and is tested, to my thinking, by this: In the first case there are no such executory clauses in the second arrangement as would enable you to sue upon that alone if the first did not exist; in the second you could sue on the second arrangement alone, and the first contract is got rid of either by express words to that effect, or because, the

〔25〕 当今的 1979 年英国《Sale of Goods Act》已经没有这一条文了。

second dealing with the same subject matter as the first but in a different way[26], it is impossible that the two should both be performed.[27] When I say you could sue on the second alone, that does not exclude cases where the first is used for mere reference, in the same way as you may fix a price by a price list, but where the contractual force is to be found in the second by itself.[28]"

在 British & Beningtons Ltd. v. North Western Cachar Tea Co. Ltd. (1922) 13 Lloyd's Rep. 67 先例中,案情也是有关之后达成的口头协议究竟是对原买卖合约的更改还是废除。贵族院的 Atkinson 勋爵确认了口头协议可以废除原合约,说:"A written contract may be rescinded by parol either expressly or by the parties entering into a parol contract entirely inconsistent with the written one, or, if not entirely inconsistent with, inconsistent with it to an extent that goes to the very root of it."

Sumner 勋爵也同意 Morris v. Baron 先例的判法,即判断新协议是对原合约的更改还是废除是要看当事人在口头协议中的意图,说:"It was, however, argued before your Lordships that... the old contracts were discharged because a varied contract is not the old contract, and as you cannot have a new and varied contract and an old and unvaried contract, regulating the same thing at the same time, the old contract, like other old things, must be disregarded. As a matter of formal logic, this may possibly be so, but such was not the view taken by this House in Morris v. Baron, since, if their Lordships had thought that any variation whatever would make a new contract and discharge the old one, they would have said so expressly... **The variation may be a new contract**, so as to make writing, duly signed, indispensible to its admissibility, for this is a matter of form and of the words of the statute, **but the discharge of the old contract must depend on intention, tested in the manner settled in Morris v. Baron**."(加黑部分是笔者的强调)

这在更近期的枢密院 United Dominions Corporation (Jamaica) Ltd. v. Michael Mitri Shoucair (1968) 3 WLR 893 先例中,Devlin 勋爵针对法律的地位也说:"The disadvantage of this view (the view that a variation, even if unenforceable, created a new contract in placement of the original contract) is that **a minor variation** may destroy the effect of the whole of the transaction between the parties.[29] The alternative view... is based on the intention of the parties. They cannot have that which presumably they

---

〔26〕 更改后的合约与更改前的合约是针对同一件事的不同做法。

〔27〕 不可能这两种做法同时被履行。

〔28〕 依赖更改后的合约提起诉讼不代表不能参考原合约的条文,但有约束力的还是更改后的合约。

〔29〕 这种即使更改不具有强制力但仍然能够产生新合约的观点的不妥之处在于,这会带来微小的更改也能摧毁双方当事人的整个交易的后果。

wanted, that is, the old agreement as amended;[30] so the court has to make up its mind which comes nearer to their intention – to leave them with an unamended agreement or without any agreement at all. [31] **The House** answered this question by rejecting the strict view propounded by Sankey J. and **distinguishing between rescission and variation. If the new agreement reveals an intention to rescind the old, the old goes, and if it does not, the old remains in force and unamended.**[32]"(加黑部分是笔者的强调)

该枢密院先例有关牙买加的《Moneylending Law》(该立法与英国1927年的《Moneylenders Act》一样)。该立法第8条规定贷款年利率在10%的贷款融资合约的达成需要满足形式与程序上的一些要求,包括:(1)一份包含所有贷款融资合约条文的合约备忘录;[33](2)贷款人在贷款之前,在该合约备忘录上签名;(3)该合约备忘录的副本在贷款融资合约达成后的7日内要送达一份给贷款人。该先例中,原告一开始贷款55000英镑给被告,因为合约中规定年利率为9%,所以不需要满足上述对形式与程序的要求。但该合约中没有针对在贷款存续期间出现增加利率或者银行贷款利率上升而令合约利率也需要跟着上升的情况。之后,在贷款融资合约履行期间,牙买加的银行贷款利率上升了2%,所以原告写信给所有的贷款人,包括被告,利率从9%调整为11%。但在该信函中原告并没有将原来的贷款融资合约内容包括进去,所以因不符合第8条第(1)款的规定而在形式上无法强制执行。原告选择在起诉被告时只是主张9%的利率,从而绕开《Moneylending Law》。但牙买加上诉法院与最高院都主张原贷款融资合约或抵押尽管本身没有违反法律的规定,但已经被废除而再不是双方之间真正的合约了。真正已经变为利率11%的合约,而该合约因为不符合法律对于形式的要求而不能被强制执行。

Devlin勋爵就认为该利率的改变是根本不能显示双方当事人是有意图消灭原贷款融资合约的债务与有关抵押,所以牙买加上诉庭判原合约已经被废除不正确,说:"It would be impossible to contend that a temporary variation in the rate of interest reveals any intention to extinguish the debt and the mortgage."

3.2.4　不符合书面要求的口头协议可以被担保人用来抗辩

在加拿大的Re A Debtor (No. 517 of 1991) (1991) The Times, 25 November先例中,法院判决尽管有1677年立法的规定,担保人在面对被担保人起诉时,可以口头

---

〔30〕 另一种观点是基于双方的订约意图。但他们也无法获得他们想要的结果,就是被更改的原合约(因为更改无效)。

〔31〕 所以法院要决定哪种更接近双方的意图,是原合约(更改无效),还是没有合约。

〔32〕 贵族院在Morris v. Barron先例选择了后一种较为宽松的观点,通过区分当事人的意图是更改或是废除原合约。如果更改后的合约显示出双方要废除原合约的意图,原合约就无效,如果没有显示出这种意图,原合约就有效,但不包括更改部分。

〔33〕 根据1677年立法,这是在当事人达成合约的现场所作的非正式记录。它必须登载合同的全部要件与合同的实质部分。

协议的内容作为抗辩(defence)。换言之,不符合书面要求的担保协议或更改只是不可强制执行,即不能作为诉因(cause of action)提起诉讼。该先例的简单案情涉及担保人为其关联公司 IHL 的一笔债务做出担保。但担保人指称他与债权人公司的代表达成了口头协议,对履行担保合约的方式做出了改变,即只需要将涉及的金额转给其关联公司 IHL,就已经可以被视为履行了他在担保合约下的义务,而他也计划这样做。Ferris 大法官说:"notwithstanding s. 4 of the Statute of Frauds 1677, an oral agreement varying the mode of performance of a guarantee **could be relied on by way of defence**, although the absence of a written memorandum would make it impossible to found a cause of action on it. The debtor had guaranteed performance of a monetary debt by an associated company, IHL, but alleged that he had made an oral agreement with a representative of the creditor company that monies advanced by him through another company to IHL should count in reducing or extinguishing his liability under the guarantee."

Ferris 大法官认为 1677 年立法只是令那些不符合形式要求的担保合约变为不可强制执行(unenforceable),但该立法并不是令合约无效(void),这可见 Maddison v. Alderson (1883) 8 App Cas 467 先例。

这表示被担保人(银行或金融机构)以担保合约向担保人起诉索赔,担保人可以以后来不符合书面要求的口头协议中对他有利的条文,如被担保人同意减低担保金额,作为抗辩。

3.2.5 弃权/禁反言不受 1677 年立法的影响

看来 1677 年立法对形式的要求并不影响弃权/禁反言的适用,法院会在适当的案件以弃权/禁反言来绕过 1677 年立法带来在本章之 3.2.2 段详及的困难与不肯定:见 Ogle v. Earl Vane (1868) LR 3 QB 272; Hickman v. Haynes (1875) LR 10 CP 598; Levy & Co. v. Goldberg (1922) 1 KB 688; Besseler Waecheter Glover & Co. v. South Derwent Coal Co. Ltd. (1938) 1 KB 40; Credit Suisse v. Allerdale BC (1995) 1 Lloyd's Rep. 315 等先例。

笔者只介绍较近期的两个先例。第一个是 Besseler Waecheter Glover & Co. v. South Derwent Coal Co. Ltd 先例。该先例涉及对一份国际货物买卖合约的更改,更改的内容针对货物的付运条文(shipment clause)。根据当时生效的 1893 年《Sale of Goods Act》第 4 条的规定,如果合约标的货物的价值在 10 英镑或以上,对合约的订立必须要以书面形式做出。而根据本章之 3.2.2 段所讲,对该合约的更改也需要以书面形式做出。但涉及国际货物买卖合约经常会在无法准时付运时,买卖双方同意延长付运期间(需要对信用证也做出相应的更改),双方不会警觉这种更改要符合书面形式的要求。Goddard 大法官判双方延误付运只是为了各自利益自愿做出宽限,而并非对原买卖合约的更改,所以原合约不受影响。

第二个先例是 Credit Suisse v. Allerdale BC,针对的是"禁反言"(estoppel)的适用。该先例的案情很复杂,包括很多不同的争议,这里只针对与本段介绍的内容有关的部分。Allerdale 区议会为了重新发展旧火车站区域，成立了一间名为 Allerdale Development Co. Ltd. 的公司。原告银行向该公司贷款，由 Allerdale 区议会作为担保人提供担保。之后，审计认为区议会成立公司并提供担保是越权，即担保合约无效。后来该公司发生经济困难，银行要求公司还款。该公司无力还款，宣布破产，银行在担保合约下要求区议会还款。区议会拒绝还款，双方开始诉讼。

针对区议会是否越权的问题，高院与上诉庭（[1996] 2 Lloyd's Rep. 241）都判是区议会越权，即担保合约无效。另一个重要争议是 Allerdale Development Co. Ltd. 公司与银行曾经对主合约进行更改，从 450 万本金加上 150 万利息，变为 500 万本金加上 100 万利息，这是否会导致区议会无须再承担还款责任？[34] 虽然 Colman 大法官做出担保合约无效的判决意味着无须再对其他争议/争端做出判决，但因为双方花费了大量时间与金钱争辩，所以 Colman 大法官仍然进行了针对。(1)假如担保有效，区议会作为担保人是否同意了对主合约的更改？Colman 大法官认定是区议会同意了对主合约的更改。(2)假如区议会没有同意对主合约的更改，是否弃权或被禁反言不能再声称担保合约因为主合约的更改而终止？银行主要依赖的是"共识性禁反言"（estoppel by convention），但 Colman 大法官认为双方不存在任何共识，关于这方面的判决在本书第六章之 3.3.1 段有节录，这里不再重复。至于银行希望依赖的"承诺性禁反言"（promissory estoppel），Colman 大法官判区议会的言行不够清楚无误。因此，银行关于禁反言的争辩失败。(3)假如 Colman 大法官对以上两个争议的判决都错误，即区议会没有同意对主合约的更改，并且言行足以构成禁反言，1677 年立法会否排除禁反言的适用？区议会的争辩是，一旦主合约在没有担保人同意的情况下更改，担保合约就自动终止，除非担保人书面签署，否则不会"复生"，银行是不能以禁反言的说法产生新的担保合约。

Colman 大法官没有支持区议会的争辩，说并不会产生新的担保合约。如果被担保人（原告银行）在没有担保人（区议会）同意的情况下更改主合约，在法律下担保合约就被终止，被担保人不能在该担保合约下要求担保人承担责任。但如果担保人同意了主合约的更改，就不能说在法律下担保合约已经被终止。而即使担保人没有同意主合约的更改，如果法院认为担保人的言行或他与被担保人之间的交往显示了让他拥有担保合约无效的法律权利不合情理，即构成了禁反言，担保人就不能声称担保合约无效。被担保人就可以在原担保合约下起诉担保人，而原担保合约有书面与签署，也就是满足 1677 年立法的要求。Colman 大法官说："Can it therefore be said that if the guarantor would otherwise be estopped from asserting that he had been discharged from liability by the variation of the principal debt or the giving of time, the creditor should be precluded from raising his estoppel by reason of the fact that by doing so he would be evading the application of the Statute of Frauds? In such a case the creditor is

---

〔34〕 这看来会涉及主合约的更改会否影响担保合约的问题，这方面可见本章之 3.3 段。

asserting that by reason of the guarantor's conduct it is unconscionable that the guarantor should be permitted to rely on the equity which would otherwise be a good defence to the creditor's claim. In other words the defence in reliance on the equity is not available because having regard to the course of dealing between the creditor and the guarantor it is unconscionable that it should be. That leaves the original guarantee in place to be sued on by the creditor. The agreement which the creditor then sues upon is the guarantee and that is in writing. Accordingly there is, in my judgment, no basis upon which it can be said that the Statute of Frauds is thereby evaded and that the policy of the law ought to be to prevent such evasion by disallowing reliance on the estoppel."

而即使原担保合约变为新的担保合约，也不影响禁反言的适用。区议会依赖的是 Kok Hoong v. Leong Cheong Kweng（1964）AC 993 先例，该先例涉及的立法是《Moneylenders Act》，Radcliffe 勋爵说到一般的大原则是当事人不能在有立法规定的情况下以禁反言回避（a party could not set up an estoppel in the face of a statute）。在 Kok Hoong v. Leong Cheong Kweng 先例中，Radcliffe 勋爵提到了一些保护未成年人的立法。如果一个未成年人在买东西时说自己是成年人，之后又没有付钱，卖方不能以"陈述性禁反言"（estoppel by representation）为由否定买方以未成年的抗辩，说："An infant who has obtained goods from a tradesman by representing himself to be of full age cannot be estoppel from setting up his infancy, if sued for the price of the goods."

但 Colman 大法官认为 1677 年立法只是规范程序（regulating procedural）而不是禁止性（prohibitory）的立法，所以不影响禁反言的适用，说："Had I been of the view that in seeking to recover against the Council（区议会）as guarantor after variation of the loan agreement not consented to by the Council was an action brought by the bank on a different contract from the original guarantee, my conclusion would have been that the Statute of Frauds did not preclude reliance by the bank on the estoppel. . . . In as much as s. 4 does not strike at the essential validity of a contract of guarantee I should have held that it did not supersede the Court's ability to treat as unconscionable, and therefore to disallow, reliance on discharge of an original guarantee where there has been a giving of time or variation of the principal debt not assented to by the guarantor. Having said that, I note that in Bank of Scotland v. Wright [1991] B. C. L. C. 244 Mr Justice Brooke left open the applicability of estoppel by convention going to the scope of a guarantee having regard to the requirements of the Statute of Frauds."

3.2.6　在非担保合约下以明示条文规定更改要以书面做出的近期先例

在一些非担保合约的简式合约中，会见到以明示条文规定在合约达成后对合约的更改要以书面形式做出。这种条文的文字会是"Variation to this contract must be agreed, set out in writing and signed on behalf of both parties before they take effect"，该种条文也被称为"anti-oral variation clause"（看来想要达到与 1677 年立法相同的效

果）。订立这种条文的主要用意也是防止合约太容易被更改。在 MWB Business Exchange Centres Ltd. v. Rock Advertising Ltd.（2016）EWCA Civ 553 这一近期的上诉庭先例中，涉及的合约内就有一条 anti-oral variation clause。一审法院判订约双方受到该明示条文的约束，所以后来的口头协议无效。但上诉庭推翻了一审法院的判决，并判在订约自由的大原则下，双方当事人可以同意他们之后任何形式（口头或行为）的更改。该先例目前上诉至最高院，还没有最后的定论。这方面与 MWB Business Exchange Centres Ltd. v. Rock Advertising Ltd 先例在本书第三章第 1 段中也有提到。

针对该书面形式的要求，在《提单与其他付运单证》（2016 年）一书第七章之 1.3 段与《合约的解释：规则与应用》一书第二章第 4 段均有提到电子签名有效性的问题，在 C& S Associates UK Limited v. Enterprise Insurance Company PLC（2015）EWHC 3757（Comm）先例说，如果有书面与签署的要求，双方电子邮件往来中的电子签名（往往是在邮件末尾打出的名字）就已经可以满足书面形式的要求。

3.3　在担保人没有同意的情况下单方面更改担保合约

本段将针对未经双方同意，单方面（unilateral）更改担保合约。这种单方面的更改如果对原担保合约是实质性的更改，将会导致原合约自动终止。这可见 Pigot Case（1614）11 Co. Rep. 26b；Lombard Finance v. Brookplain Trading Ltd. and Others（1991）1 WLR 271 等先例。

3.3.1　Pigot Case 原则

Pigot Case（1614）11 Co. Rep. 26b 是被很多后来案例所接受与跟从的权威但过时〔35〕与严苛〔36〕的先例，该案例确立的大原则是如果一个对契约（deed）〔37〕的更改不是经合约双方同意，该更改会令契约无效。案情是 Pigot 先生欠 Winchcombe 先生一笔钱，1611 年 3 月 2 日，双方就该笔欠款签订了一份还款的契约。之后，Winchcombe 先生升任 Oxford 郡的郡长。一个不知名但应该是好意的人士〔38〕在还款契约上 Winchcombe 先生名字的后面以及欠款金额的前面加上"Oxford 郡郡长"的字样。之后因为欠款未还，双方开始诉讼，在 1614 年案件审讯时，Pigot 先生依赖先例主张，该经更改的还款契约已经不是三年前自己签署的那份。法院接受了该说法，Coke 勋爵说："when any deed is altered in a point material, by the plaintiff himself, or by any stranger, without the privity of the obligee, be it by interlineation, addition, rasing, or by drawing of a pen through a line, or through the midst of any material word, that the

〔35〕在当时的年代，契约是非常罕见与重要的，因为纸张或羊皮卷非常昂贵，而且大部分英国人还仍是文盲。

〔36〕见 Co－operative Bank Plc. v. Tipper（1996）4 All ER 366 先例。

〔37〕这是相对于简式合约（simple contract）而言。契约没有约因/对价的要求，但有形式的要求。这可参阅本书第 4 章之 12.1.2 段。

〔38〕这可以是没有得到双方授权的律师或涉及这一交易的中间人或双方当事人的雇员等。

deed thereby becomes void... So if the obligee himself alters the deed by any of the said ways, although it is in words not material, yet the deed is void: but if a stranger, without his privity, alters the deed by any of the said ways in any point not material, it shall not avoid the deed.[39]"

该先例确立了三条规则:(1)契约被受益的一方做出任何的更改,就会变为无效。在担保合约中,就是被担保人的银行对合约的更改。(2)契约被陌生人更改,该更改如果重要,契约无效。(3)如果陌生人对契约的更改是不重要的更改,契约仍然有效。

上述Coke勋爵所说被称为Pigot Case原则,该原则基于两个方面的考虑:(1)经过更改的契约已经不是双方签署时的文件;(2)要避免欺诈。如在担保合约的担保金额上多加一个"0",就很有可能是欺诈或有不正当的意图。

在Master v. Miller (1791) 4 Durn. &E. 320先例中,Gross大法官就上述两个考虑有清楚的说明:"a man shall not take the chance of committing a fraud, and when that fraud is detected recover on the instrument as it was originally made. In such a case the law intervenes, and says that the deed thus altered no longer continues the same deed, and that no person can maintain an action upon it ... and the principle of those cases is that any alteration in a material part of any instrument or agreement avoids it, because it thereby ceases to be the same instrument. And this principle is founded on great good sense, because it tends to prevent the party in whose favour it is made from attempting to make any alteration in it."

Pigot Case原则随后被认为是适用在所有的书面文件,无论该书面文件是否是一份合约,这可见Suffell v. Bank of England (1882) 9 Q. B. D. 555先例与Aldous v. Cornwell (1868) LR 3 QB 573先例,这两个先例涉及的文件都是银行的本票(promissory note)。

之后,Aldous v. Cornwell先例与Bishop of Crediton v. Bishop of Exeter (1905) 2 Ch. 455先例确立了一直沿用至今的Pigot Case原则,即任何更改只适用在重要(material)更改的情况,而不重要的更改并不会让担保人逃避合约义务。

3.3.2 区分更改是否重要的指引

至于判断更改是否重要需要满足哪些条件,在Raiffeisen Zentralbank Osterreich AG v. Crossseas Shipping Ltd. &Others (2000) 1 WLR 1135先例中有明确指引。案

〔39〕 被原告单方面或陌生人/第三人在没有经过债权人同意的情况下,通过在字里行间加字、增加内容、涂掉内容、用笔在一行文字或重要的字词上加标记等方式,对任何一份契约(deed)做出重要与实质性的更改,该契约变为无效;但如果契约债权人自己做出更改,即使该更改不是重要与实质性,也都会令契约无效;如果是陌生人/第三人自己对契约做出更改,如果更改的不是重要的内容,契约仍然有效。

情是第四被告是肯尼亚居民，他与原告银行签订了一份就500万美元提供担保的担保合约，该合约明示接受英国法院管辖，第37条规定委任一位代理人负责接收英国法院的告票与其他法院文件。这种条文在担保合约与其他合约中都是经常出现。在有英国法院专属管辖权条文(exclusive jurisdiction clause)时，为了避免因送达去外国(service out of jurisdiction)[40]带来的时间延误与费用的浪费，对外国当事人，合约会要求双方委任在英国的代理人接收法律文件，通常会是英国的律师事务所或一家有关系的公司。

当第四被告签署该份担保合约时，第37条中委任代理人的名称以及地址都是空白。原告银行的职员后来才将该代理人即本案第一被告的名称、地址、电传与传真信息填入空白处(因为在之前的担保合约，第四被告也是这么填写的)，但第四被告并不知情。当原告银行向第四被告提出要履行担保合约时，第四被告抗辩说银行单方面加入的内容构成对担保合约的重要更改，从而令合约变为没有法律强制力。法院不接受第四被告的抗辩。Potter大法官说一个更改要被视为重要，需要满足两个考验(test)，即：(1)更改的内容是否会影响文书或担保合约的本质(whether the alteration affects the very nature and character of the instrument/guarantee)；(2)更改会给担保人或债务人的权利与义务带来潜在的影响('potentially prejudicial' to the guarantor or obligor's rights or obligations)。

这个区分更改是否重要的指引被Bank of Scotland v. Henry Butcher & Co. & Others (2003) EWCA Civ 67先例跟从。该先例是苏格兰银行给客户Hopkins先生透支了一笔钱，作为Hopkins先生业务的营运资本。Hopkins先生后来与一家名为Henry Butcher & Co. 的公司设立了一家合资公司，后者为Hopkins先生提供咨询服务。Henry Butcher & Co的四位合伙人就Hopkins先生透支的金额与苏格兰银行签订了一份担保合约。后来该担保合约有了更改，把Hopkins透支的金额局限在一个特定的账户。但该更改只是由Henry Butcher & Co公司其中两位合伙人签字。后来，Hopkins先生违约没有支付透支的钱，苏格兰银行向Henry Butcher & Co公司四位合伙人执行担保合约，两位没有在更改后的担保合约上签字的合伙人认为更改没有经过他们的同意，所以该担保合约对他们是无效的。

案件上诉到上诉庭，上诉庭法官判该担保合约有效，Mundy大法官说：

"**Does the alteration to the guarantee after execution invalidate it**?... It is important for this purpose to bear in mind the nature of the alteration,... Mr Hurst's(被告的代表律师) argument is founded on well - known authority of venerable antiquity: Pigot's Case... That, as the judge recognised, is authority for what is trite law, that any material alteration of a document such as a guarantee undertaken after its execution and without the approval of all the parties to the document renders it void.

---

〔40〕 有关告票的送达，可参阅本书第九章之3.3.2.2段与第十章第8段。

But the precise ambit of that doctrine is now to be found in very recent authority in this court: the judgment of Potter LJ (with whom Thorpe and Henry LJJ agreed) in Raiffeisen Zentralbank Osterreich AG v. Crossseas Shipping Ltd. accepting counsel's analysis of the large number of cases to which the court had been referred, Potter LJ identified two categories of materiality for the purpose of the rule in Pigot's Case: (i) The first where there is an alteration which affects the very nature and character of the instrument... (ii) The other where the alteration is 'potentially prejudicial' to the obligor's legal rights or obligations:... Now the present case plainly does not fall into the first category, so I can concentrate, as did the judge in the court below, on the second category... With all respect to Mr Hurst I simply fail to understand how the alteration in the present case can possibly have been either actually or potentially prejudicial to the guarantors. On the contrary, it was plainly for their benefit, for its purpose and effect was to confine the previous scope of the guarantee and to substitute for a guarantee of Mr Hopkins's general indebtedness his indebtedness on a single account. Mr Hurst's argument is devoid of merit and must be rejected."

几百年来这方面的争议主要都是针对更改是否重要,对称职律师来说,任何情况下都是可以找出争辩的地方,如从该更改在性质上是否重要以及会产生的影响等方面下手。法院会根据不同案情的背景/语境来做出判决。如在 Raiffeisen Zentralbank Osterreich AG v. Crossseas Shipping Ltd. & Others 先例中,第四被告就主张自己会受到的影响是,如果银行没有为自己填写上英国的代理人,将来发生争议需要诉讼时,就会需要法院将文件送达到肯尼亚,这会带来时间的延误与麻烦。如果争议金额不大,银行很可能在做出权衡之后,就不开始诉讼了。但这一争辩不被法院接受,法院判这更改不重要。

3.3.3 区分更改是否重要的先例介绍:Lombard Finance Ltd. v. Brookplain Trading Ltd. and Others

笔者在此再多介绍一个 Lombard Finance Ltd. v. Brookplain Trading Ltd. and Others (1991) 1 WLR 271 先例。在该先例中,原告 Lombard Finance Ltd 公司与第一被告 Brookplain Trading Ltd 公司签署了一份贷款融资合约,第二被告 Richardson 先生和第三被告 Faull 先生作为第一被告的董事,为第一被告与原告之间的贷款融资合约签署了一份担保合约,对第一被告按时还款承担担保责任。之后第一被告没有偿还贷款,原告将三被告一起诉至法院。第二与第三被告抗辩说担保合约存在未经他们同意的单方更改,所以变为无效与没有强制执行力。该声称的单方更改是针对担保合约中第一被告的名称。一开始,第一被告的名称被写错成"Brookplain Trading Company Ltd",多了一个"company"。后来该"company"一字被划掉,并且旁边还加上了一些非常潦草的字,看起来像是代表针对该更改双方同意而做的签名确认。第二和第三被告指称他们根本不知道这一更改,而这些潦草的字不是他们所签,是原告伪造的签名。

一审法院在笔迹专家的帮助下对笔迹进行了鉴定,但是最后法院也无法对更改究竟是原告伪造的还是真的由第二与第三被告签署的问题有结论性的认定。一审法院说:"In the face of the evidence of the expert who was called to give evidence concerning his findings in analysing those initials in particular and analysing other writings on the form, I am not able to find and do not find that those initials were made by these defendants. It is very difficult, in the case of part of that in any event, to find there were initials at all because they do not seem to have any particular shape. That is the evidence of the expert which makes me accept that they were initials at all. The document itself was, on a temporary basis only, in the possession of the two defendants. It was then restored to the plaintiffs' agents and to the plaintiffs. So it is inevitable, in my judgment, if I cannot be satisfied on the balance of probabilities that they (Mr. Richardson and Mr. Faull) made the alteration or it was made and they initialled it, that it must have happened whilst it was in the possession of the plaintiffs or one of the plaintiffs' agents. Just how that happened cannot be resolved. It would be a matter of speculation on my part to make any decision how that happened. . . . Well it is possible there has been a forgery but it is not possible to adjudicate on that with any certainty. Let me assume that there has been a forgery, taking the matter at its worst, although I cannot adjudicate as to whether there has been because one cannot decipher precisely what that squiggle is around the word 'Company' which has been deleted. There is an argument there has been a forgery but I cannot readily adjudicate on that argument. . ."

之后到上诉庭,上诉庭支持一审法院,判担保合约有效与可强制执行的结果。上诉庭认为首先将"company"划掉的更改不是重要与实质性的更改。即使不划掉这个字,也没有潦草的签名,这一笔误将来也会根据其他的证据与当事人的订约意图被认定为是"明显错误"(obvious mistake)〔41〕被更改过来 。Dillon 大法官说:". . . the rule in Pigot's Case has for at least a century been held to be applicable only where the alteration made was a material alteration. That is established by Aldous v. Cornwell (1868) L. R. 3 Q. B. 573 and Bishop of Crediton v. Bishop of Exeter [1905] 2 Ch. 455. This particular alteration by the deletion of the word 'Company' is not in my judgment a material alteration. Even if the word 'Company' had never been struck out, the guarantee could have been enforced against Mr. Richardson and Mr. Faull, because plainly the company referred to in the guarantee must have been the company of which Mr. Richardson and Mr. Faull were said to be directors and that was Brookplain Trading Ltd. There could not have been any other company with the name Brookplain Trading Company Ltd.

〔41〕 可见杨良宜《合约的解释:规则与应用》一书第三章之 13.2 段。

It is therefore a mere immaterial misdescription which can be cured by evidence."

关于伪造签名这一指控,虽然没有证据支持,但即使假设这一伪造是由原告公司一位不知名人士在保管这份担保合约时所为,上诉庭认为这伪造并不令担保合约无效与无强制力。Dillon 大法官在他的判词中依赖了一个有关提单的先例 Kwei Tek Chao v. British Traders and Shippers Ltd. (1954) 1 Lloyd's Rep. 16。[42] 该先例中,提单被倒签,众所周知,倒签提单明显是伪造的行为,被告是把货物以 FOB 向分卖方买过来,并以 CIF 转卖给原告。在被告不知情的情况下,被告交出给原告的提单被倒签。原告在卸港向船舶提货时,已经知道提单被倒签的事实,但没有拒货。过了一段时间后,原告才起诉被告,要求退还所有货价。这被 Devlin 大法官拒绝,并说明没有先例是只要一份文件涉及伪造就会全部自动变为无效,在该先例中,倒签的部分只影响提单的一个方面,只有伪造部分会败坏(corrupt)整个核心内容时,文件才会无效。

Dillon 大法官在 Lombard Finance Ltd. v. Brookplain Trading Ltd. and Others 先例说:"... The case concerned a bill of lading. An incorrect date of shipment had been inserted in the bill of lading without authority, not on behalf of the sellers of the goods in question, for they had no knowledge of it. The goods were delivered. By the time they were delivered there had been a fall in the market price. The buyers sued the sellers for the return of the price that they had paid on the documents, claiming that the forged bill of lading was the foundation of the contract that true, accurate and genuine bills of lading should be presented and that the bills of lading were a nullity, being forged, and so the consideration had wholly failed.... Devlin J. then said, and I respectfully agree: 'But such general dicta must be related to the circumstances in which they are made. If somebody forges the signature to a document, that document is wholly fictitious from beginning to end, and it is of course null and void as soon as forgery is proved; but I do not think that that is any authority for the view that any material alteration' — I interject, a fortiori any immaterial alteration — 'to a document destroys it and renders it null and void.... I think that **the true view is that one must examine the nature of the alteration and see whether it goes to the whole or to the essence of the instrument or not. If it does, and if the forgery corrupts the whole of the instrument or its heart, then the instrument is destroyed; but if it corrupts merely a limb, the instrument remains alive, though no doubt defective**.' In the present case the alteration does not go to the whole or to the essence of the instrument. It is an immaterial alteration. Therefore I do not see why the forgery should be treated as corrupting the whole of the instrument so as to destroy it."(加黑部分是笔者的强调)

---

〔42〕 该案例在杨大明《国际货物买卖》一书第二章之 5.4.2 段有介绍。

3.3.4 小结

虽然有以上的指引，但这个指引仍然无法针对现实中出现的各种情况，所以仍然存在不确定性与会产生诉讼。除了有十分接近案情的权威先例做指引或极端的情况，如对担保金额或利息的更改，可以说是法律地位明确，更多的仍然是可以争辩的情况。如在 Co-operative Bank Plc. v. Tipper（1996）4 All ER 366 先例中，担保合约中某处将担保人的名字搞错为主债务人的名字，这错误根据上下文也很容易就看出，银行单方面用铅笔对名称做出的更改只是针对明显错误，但仍然需要通过诉讼，才能执行担保合约。这也可以理解，对于明显错误，一般来讲很倾向于随手改掉，甚至该更改只是为了银行内部用途。

这给银行或金融机构以及他们的代表律师带来的启示可以是对任何担保合约中的更改，即使是针对非常明显的错误，也是要在取得双方同意的基础上再进行。担保人在争议还没有出现时通常会合作，很快就同意，但等到银行或金融机构向担保人要求执行担保合约时，担保人恐怕就不会这么好说话了。

3.4 更改主合约对担保合约的影响

这种情况会给担保合约的有效性带来灾难性的影响。对担保合约的影响在本书第六章之 7.14 段介绍的 Triodosbank NV v. Dobbs（2005）2 Lloyd's Rep. 588 先例有提到。主合约在订约双方同意下被实质更改，但没有事前取得担保人同意或明示许可，针对主合约的担保合约失效。理由很简单，如果第三方的担保人同意为建造一架飞机的主合约提供担保，但主合约被双方更改为建造一艘轮船，就不能假设担保人仍然愿意为交易提供担保。

3.4.1 Holme v. Brunskill 原则

Holme v. Brunskill（1877）3 QBD 494 先例的案情是原告同意将农场、部分山上的草场以及 700 只羊租给租户，被告为租户提供担保，担保租户在租约结束时归还的羊群在数量和质量上都状况良好，不能比租约开始时降低。在租约履行期间，原告与租户就租约内容进行了更改，涉及租户归还了一部分土地给原告，剩下的土地租金相应减低。在租约结束时，租户归还的羊群在数量、质量以及价值上均有所下降，原告于是向被告要求履行担保合约做出支付。被告主张因为租约有未经他同意的更改，所以担保合约变为无效，法院支持了该被告的主张。

由此，该先例确立的原则〔43〕是担保人在为主合约的债务或违约提供担保后，如果在其不知情或未同意的情况下，主合约的当事人对主合约进行更改（除非更改是很明显不重要与非实质性的，或更改会给担保人带来好处），担保人在担保合约下对主合约债务或违约提供担保的责任就有权决定是否自动终止。Cotton 大法官说："The true rule in my opinion is, that if there is any agreement between the principals with reference to the contract guaranteed, **the surety ought to be consulted**, and that if

〔43〕 该原则在 Rees v. Berrington（1817）1 Ves. Jr. 298 之后就已经在适用了。

he has not consented to the alteration, although in cases where it is **without inquiry evident that the alteration is unsubstantial, or that it cannot be otherwise than beneficial to the surety**, the surety may not be discharged; yet, that if it is not self – evident that the alteration is unsubstantial, or one which cannot be prejudicial to the surety, **the court will not**, in an action against the surety, **go into an inquiry as to the effect of the alteration, or allow the question**, whether the surety is discharged or not, to be determined by the finding of a jury as to the materiality of the alteration or on the question whether it is to the prejudice of the surety, but will hold that in such a case **the surety himself must be the sole judge** whether or not he will consent to remain liable notwithstanding the alteration, and that if he has not so consented he will be discharged."（加黑部分是笔者的强调）

在更近期的 Bank of Baroda v. Patel (1996) 1 Lloyd's Rep. 391 先例中，Potter 大法官提到 Holme v. Brunskill 的原则是担保合约法律的著名原则说："It is a well – known principle of surety law that any variation of the terms of agreement between the creditor and the principal debtor which could prejudice the surety will, unless he consents thereto, discharge the guarantor from liability, unless the contract of suretyship provides to the contrary... Thus, if the action of the bank is properly to be regarded as a variation of the terms of the contract and there is no clause in the guarantee apt to cover such an eventuality, that is, at least prima facie, an end of the matter"

《Chitty on Contracts》(第 32 版，2015 年）之 45 – 104 段总结 Holme v. Brunskill 先例的法律地位："**Variation of contract between creditor and debtor.** It is a well established and strictly applied principle that any variation in the terms of the agreement between the creditor and the debtor which could prejudice the surety will, unless he consents thereto, discharge him from liability, unless the contract of suretyship provides to the contrary.〔44〕It is immaterial that the variation has not in fact prejudiced the surety, or that the likelihood that it may do so is remote.〔45〕 If the variation could prejudice the surety it alters the nature of the risk which he has undertaken and he is entitled to decide whether he wishes to continue bound or not.〔46〕 But if it is self – evident that the varia-

---

〔44〕 除非担保合约有明示条文针对，有一个著名与严格的法律原则就是债权人与债务人对他们的合约条文有所更改并会影响担保合约，就必须获得担保人的同意，否则担保人就再也没有责任，除非他做出不同的决定。

〔45〕 至于更改是否实质对担保人造成影响或可能会造成影响是十分遥远，这是无关的。

〔46〕 如果更改因会改变担保人愿意负责的风险的本质而可能影响担保人，担保人就有权独自决定是否受担保合约的约束。在现实中，担保合约对担保人而言是不会有任何好处的。担保人不乘机终止担保合约是不大可能的。

tion is unsubstantial or could not prejudice the surety he will not be discharged.〔47〕The principle is applied very strictly so that even the most trifling variation may discharge the surety.〔48〕.... On the other hand, a guarantor who has entered into a fidelity bond to answer for the contract of a servant has been held not discharged by trifling variations in the contract of employment, such as an increase in salary〔49〕, or an alteration of the length of notice required to terminate the employment〔50〕, since it was held that such variations could not have prejudiced the surety. So also a purported variation of the agreement between the creditor and debtor which is, for some reason, ineffective in law will not discharge the surety since he cannot be prejudiced thereby〔51〕. A common law a deed could not be varied by a parol agreement, and therefore such a variation did not affect the surety〔52〕, but the position was different in equity and the rules of equity now prevail."

3.4.2　严厉的 Holme v. Brunskill 原则的合理性

Holme v. Brunskill (1877) 3 QBD 494 先例做出了一个十分严厉的考验,即主合约的更改在不需要进一步调查(without further inquiry)的情况下就可以被认为是显而易见的不重要(unsubstantial)或担保人的利益不受影响(non - prejudicial)(正像是 Frank v. Edwards [1852] 8 Exch. 214 或 Egbert v. National Crow Bank [1918] AC 903 先例),否则,还是一样会令担保合约无效。

确实,在更加古老的 Samuell v. Howarth (1817) 3 Mer. 272 先例中,Eldon 勋爵说到即使是名义上的更改也会担保合约终止:"that if there be an alteration of the rights of the surety, though only nominal, and for his benefit, he is discharged."

这个看起来十分严厉的原则的合理性,可见 Blackburn 大法官在 Polak and Another v. Everett (1876) 1 QBD 669 先例中所说:"It has been established for a very long time, ... to the present day, without a single case going to the contrary, that on the principles of equity a surety is discharged when the creditor, without his assent, gives time to the principal debtor〔53〕, because by so doing he deprives the surety of part of the right he would have had from the mere fact of entering into the suretyship, namely, to use the name of the creditor to sue the principal debtor, and if this right be suspended for

---

〔47〕如果更改是"显而易见"的不重要或不会令担保人受影响,担保合约不能被终止。

〔48〕这个原则的适用非常严格,所以,很细微的更改都会令担保合约终止。

〔49〕见 Frank v. Edwards (1852) 8 Exch. 214 先例。

〔50〕见 Sanderson v. Aston (1873) LR 8 Exch 先例。

〔51〕见 Egbert v. National Crow Bank (1918) AC 903 先例(违反立法的规定提高利率)。

〔52〕见 Davey v. Prendergress (1821) 5 B & Ald. 187 先例。

〔53〕如果债权人在主合约给了债务人多一些时间做出支付或履行但没有获得担保人的同意,根据衡平法就会令担保人可终止担保合约。

a day or an hour, not injuring the surety to the value of one farthing, and even positively benefiting him, nevertheless, by the principles of equity, it is established that this discharges the surety altogether. **The reason given for** this, as stated in Samuell v. Howarth by Lord Eldon, **is because the creditor, by so giving time to the principal, has put it out of the power of the surety to consider whether he will have recourse to his remedy against the principal or not, and because he in fact cannot have the same remedy against the principal as he would have had under the original contract.**〔54〕 And he adds: 'The creditor has no right, it is against the faith of his contract, to give time to the principal, even though manifestly for the benefit of the surety, without the consent of the surety.' The principle being, as I understand it, that as it is very undesirable that there should be any dispute or controversy about whether it is for his benefit or not, there shall be **the broad principle, that if the creditor does intentionally violate any rights the surety had when he entered into the suretyship, even though the damage be nominal only, he shall forfeit the whole remedy**.〔55〕"(加黑部分是笔者的强调)

3.4.3 Holme v. Brunskill 原则带来的危险

Holme v. Brunskill 原则的危险性在于太容易让担保人逃避担保合约下的责任。虽然理论上来说,如果主合约的更改不重要与对担保人的利益无损害,担保人是不能逃避责任的,但在 Holme v. Brunskill 原则下,该不重要与无损害必须是“显而易见与不需要调查的”(readily apparent, without inquiry)。如果这不重要与无损害并不是这么显而易见,担保人有权独自决定是否应该继续承担担保责任。而从人的本性上来说,担保人在绝大多数情况下都不可能愿意再受担保合约的约束。

当然能取得担保人的同意令担保合约与主合约同步进行更改是最理想的情况,但要证明担保人的同意也不容易。如 Moat Financial Services v. David Wilkinson, Barbara Wilkinson (2005) EWCA Civ 1253 先例就涉及一家有限公司 Cartmells 向原告的金融公司贷款融资,被告(该公司的两位董事也是夫妇二人)为该贷款提供了个人担保,包括在他们居住的房子上登记押记(charge)。随着公司业务的发展壮大,Cartmells 公司打算将贷款金额从原先的 10 万英镑提高到 25 万英镑,于是被告向原告签发了一封信函,要求提高贷款金额并在该信函中就新的贷款做出详细的安排。后来 Cartmells 公司破产,原告在个人担保合约下向被告追讨贷款的本金和利息。被告认为主合约更改而令担保合约无效。法院根据信函中的内容以及主合约与担保合

〔54〕 Eldon 勋爵在另一个先例提到的就是债权人如果多给了债务人时间,就会剥夺了担保人对债务人要求补偿的权利,他再也不能根据与债务人之间的合约要求债务人做出同样的补偿或同样行使在对债权人做出支付后代位取得的对债务人要求偿还的权利。

〔55〕 这个原则认为追究究竟这个更改是否对担保人有利并不理想,所以大原则是只要债权人有意识的违反任何在担保合约下对担保人的权利,即使带来的影响是极微小的,担保人都可以终止担保合约。

约下根本是同一批人而判担保合约不仅有效,并且随着主合约的更改而更改。这是少数主合约更改担保合约也更改的情况。

看来,担保人同意对贷款融资合约中的更改的立场一定要能够被证明,最好是有明确的书面证据以避免将来担保人有任何否认。如果担保人只是知道或应该知道这更改,而没有很充分的证据证明他也同意这更改,仍然可以令担保人逃避担保的责任。没有先例要求担保人如果知道,就有责任向被担保人说清楚(duty to speak)与做出警告。这可见 Polak and Another v. Everett (1876) 1 QBD 669 先例中 Blackburn 大法官说:"... we must take it to be the fact that though the defendant (the guarantor) was well aware of this release being executed, he was not an assenting party to it. Then it is argued that knowledge on the part of the surety that there is going to be a release of a part of the security is enough without assent. I cannot see any authority for that. In Pickard, v. Sears (1837) 6 Ad. & El. 469, it was held that he who stands by and sees another alter his position on the faith of a fact which he can contradict, cannot afterwards take advantage of that alteration. But the rule was corrected in Freeman v. Cooke (1848) 2 Ex. 654, where it was said that if a man stands by and allows another to act without objecting, when, from the usage of trade or otherwise, there is a duty to speak[56], his silence would preclude him as much as if he proposed the act himself. But to say that a person, who, being a surety, becomes aware that the creditor is going to give time or do something else which, if done without his assent, may discharge him, is bound to warn the creditor against doing it, is a thing for which no authority whatever has been cited."

这里根据不同案情,也会有例外。Wittmann (UK) Limited v. Willdav Engineering S. A. (2007) EWCA Civ 824 先例涉及一间名为 Automold 的公司向原告购买汽车零件,其母公司 Willdav 即本案的被告,为 Automold 向本案的原告提供担保,在买卖合约履行期间,Automold 相继又取得三间财务公司的贷款融资来资助购买汽车零件。期间,买卖合约中货物所有权条文有了更改。后来 Automold 破产,货款没有清偿,原告在担保合约下向被告起诉清还。被告以主合约有他没有同意的更改而令担保合约失效作为抗辩。这在一审被法院否定,上诉庭也支持一审的判决。原因是根据本案特别的案情,母公司与子公司是由同一位 Keech 先生经营,所以,Automold 同意买卖合约的更改也等于母公司同意该更改。上诉庭的 Moore - Bick 大法官说:"The judge, as I have said, found that Mr. Keech controlled the affairs of both Willdav and Automold. It is not surprising, therefore, that she found that Willdav, through Mr. Keech, had consented to the restructuring of the contractual arrangements. In those circumstances it may seem surprising that Willdav should now be contending that the guarantee does not extend to Automold's outstanding obligations; indeed, Mr. Wilson (原告

〔56〕 这一课题可见本书第四章之 6.4 段与第五章第 10 段。

的代表大律师) submitted that this was a classic example of a guarantor's consenting to a variation of the underlying contract which would otherwise operate to discharge him."

该严厉的 Holme v. Brunskill 原则是否公平或者具有正当合理性,Blackburn 大法官也在 Polak and Another v. Everett 先例中表达了质疑:"Whether that was a good or a Just principle originally, is a matter which it is far too late to think about now. I must own I have had considerable doubts about the justice of that principle, but ... it has been undisputed law, and nothing but the legislature can interfere to alter it."

3.4.4 主合约下的弃权对担保合约的影响

已经在本章之 3.2.5 段提到,法院通过弃权/禁反言绕过 1677 年立法带来的复杂情况,而达到担保合约实质上被更改了的效果。所以,针对对担保合约条文的弃权/禁反言在理论上不会有任何困难,而且也不必再满足 1677 年立法的形式要求。这样,本书第三章中谈到的弃权内容均适用在担保合约。在主合约的履行中,发生弃权的情况相比于更改会更多,毕竟更改需要更多的要件(如约因/对价)才能成立。正如 Eldon 勋爵或 Blackburn 大法官举的例子,银行允许贷款人多一些时间还款。这种宽限经常发生,因为如果贷款人在到期还款的那天请求银行宽限一下,等第二天有一笔资金到位后再还款,银行很少会不同意甚至提前终止整个贷款融资合约,尤其是在该客户是银行的长期客户并一直都信誉良好的情况下。在这一天之内,银行也很难为这一天的宽限与更改去取得为贷款融资合约提供担保的担保人的同意。这样,银行会有危险将来在贷款人无法偿还贷款时,也会被担保人指称主合约有未经他同意的弃权而失去其在担保合约下的权利。

在可以适用弃权的情况下,主合约的条文也能达到同样被更改的效果。有说法是担保人不能接受对主合约的更改,是因为更改是永久性并且贷款人/债务人主动参与其中会令担保人利益受损害的风险变大。对于弃权(因宽限而弃权)的情况,担保人会假设这种并非双方同意的行为危险性相对来说较低,而弃权构成对合约改变通常又只是暂时性的,弃权方可以通过合理的通知而回复到合约地位。

这方面可节录 Sean Wilken QC 与 Karim Ghaly 先生所著的《The Law of Waiver, Variation, and Estoppel》(第 3 版,2012 年)一书之 17.23 段说:"In contrast to the established view that a material variation of the principal contract discharges the guarantor, it is unclear whether a waiver of the terms of the principal contract has the same effect. It might be said that, as both variation and waiver modify the obligations set out in the principal contract, the guarantor should be discharged in either event. Thus, where the effect of the waiver has been to alter substantially the day – to – day operation of the guarantee, the Courts have held that the alteration is tantamount to being a variation of the contract and has the effect of discharging the guarantor. This approach makes practical sense but, first, avoids the issue and, second, tends to confuse the doctrine of waiver and variation."

不确定与不清楚的地位可见 Bank of Baroda v. Patel (1996) 1 Lloyd's Rep. 391

先例。该先例是原告的银行(Bank of Baroda)根据一般贷款融资合约与授信合约对进出口贸易商 ANY 公司提供预支款项与贷款。其中授信合约中有如下条文:"Above facilities are repayable on demand and are to be secured by the following: (1) General undertaking in relation to Documentary Credit (form enclosed)... (3) Personal guarantee of both the Directors and of Mr. N. C. Patel (form enclosed)... (5) ECGD Cover (Comprehensive). At the time of sending shipping documents to us for advance, you should confirm to us, every quarter, that ECGD premium has been paid by you up to date..."

针对上述第(5)点中提到的 ECGD Cover,其中 ECGD 代表 Export Credits Guarantee Department,这是英国的政府机构,为英国贸易公司提供出口保险,包括赔偿出口商在出口商品之后取不回的货款。

针对第(3)点中提到的 Patel 先生作为 ANY 公司的董事所做出的个人担保,可节录担保合约中的重要条文如下:"1. The guarantor will pay... on demand all monies which now are or shall at any time or times hereafter be due or owing or payable to you [the Bank] or any account whatsoever by the Principal [ANY] either solely or jointly with any other person firm or company together with all interest, costs, commission and other banking charges and expenses which you may in the course of your business as bankers charge against the Principal and all costs, charges and expenses which you may incur in enforcing or obtaining payment of the sums of money due to you from the Principal ... 6. This Guarantee and your rights under it shall not be affected or prejudiced by your holding or taking any other or further securities or by your varying releasing or omitting or neglecting to enforce any such securities or by your varying or determining any credit to the Principal or by your renewing bills of exchange, promissory notes or other negotiable instruments or giving time for payment or granting any other indulgence to or making any other arrangements with or accepting any composition from the Principal or any ... persons ... liable on any bills of exchange, promissory notes or other negotiable instruments or securities held or to be held by you..."

在授信业务持续履行期间,ANY 与银行有一个共识是 ANY 就一些买卖没有取得 ECGD 的保险。银行并没有就此提出反对,也持续提供授信服务。在银行一份内部的记录中,显示银行曾经在 ANY 的要求下放弃了该要求取得 ECGD 保险的权利。因为没有保险的保障,ANY 要自己承担风险,相应的他对银行的责任变大,这当然也对作为担保人的 Patel 先生带来影响。后来 ANY 破产,银行开始追讨欠款与要求 Patel 先生履行担保合约。

在庭审中,银行的代表律师争辩说,第一,授信合约没有被更改,银行只是放弃了在一条对他有利的条文下的权利，[57] 即要求 ANY 就从银行预支的款项投保 ECGD 保险；第二，担保合约中第 6 条文的内容允许银行对此权利放弃而不会免除 Patel 先生作为担保人在担保合约下的义务。

Potter 大法官针对上述两点判定：第一，实务中，弃权与更改会带来同样的结果；第二，担保合约中第 6 条文只是很常见的泛泛针对银行在针对某些特定事件更改、弃权或不作为的情况而不应该被解释为也可以针对在该先例中银行放弃要求 ANY 投保 ECGD 保险的行为。所以，银行败诉。Potter 大法官说：

"First, whether or not, in other contexts, it might properly be dubbed a waiver rather than a variation, the operation of the facility by the bank at the request of ANY without ECGD cover in respect of particular transactions, when both parties were well aware of the terms of the facility, amounts in broad terms to be an agreement so to operate it and in effect as a variation of the terms of the facility. Even were that not so, I consider that operation of the facility in that manner should be regarded as conduct by the bank as creditor to the prejudice of its surety sufficient to discharge the defendant from liability.

I do not think that cl. 6 is apt to assist the bank in this respect. It is a type of clause frequently encountered in bank guarantees relating to the treatment of collateral securities held by the bank. The complaint of the defendant in this case is that the bank failed to obtain the security (if ECGD cover is appropriately so described), when the facility letter in connection with which the guarantee was given required that it should be obtained."

3.4.5 担保合约以明示条文允许更改或弃权

这种在担保合约中以条文明示允许主合约的当事人之间能够就某些事项在不经担保人同意的情况下对主合约做出更改或是弃权，而不会影响担保合约。这种条文现在十分常见，而且也是能够使银行或金融机构的利益得到保护的最好方法。在大多数现代的担保合约中，都会见到这样的明示条文，这种条文通常在主合约进行更改或弃权时被解释为已经被明示授权无需经担保人的同意才能进行，从而保护担保合约的有效性。这在许多先例中有涉及，如：Cowper v. Smith (1838) 4 M & W 519; Perry v. National Provincial Bank of England (1910) 1 Ch 464; Moschi v. Lep Air Services Ltd. and ors. (1973) AC 331; Wood Hall Ltd. v. Pipeline Authority & Anor (1979) 24 ALR 385 等先例。

在《Chitty on Contracts》(第 32 版，2015 年)之 45 – 112 段也提到在目前的担保合约中，可以见到很多主合约更改或债权人宽限债务人履约等行为不会让担保人免除担保责任："The effect of the rules discussed in the preceding paragraphs is so technical and inconvenient that in practice any well – drawn contract of surety will nowadays expressly permit variation of the obligations or the giving of time, without discharging the

---

〔57〕 这个课题可见本书第三章之 3.3.4 段。

surety. At common law, such an agreement takes effect according to its terms[58], but in cases of doubt or uncertainty will be construed in favour of the surety[59]. . . ”

这种条文可以随便节录如 Trafalgar House Construction (Regions) Ltd. v. General Surety & Guarantee Co. Ltd. (1996) AC 199 先例中,工程合约中担保人(有两位)为分承建商向总包商做出的履约担保的内容如下:

“General Surety & Guarantee Co. Ltd.

By this bond we K. D. Chambers Ltd. whose registered office is at 1 London Road Sittingbourne Kent (hereinafter called ‘the subcontractor’) and General Surety & Guarantee Co. Ltd. whose registered office is at Hawthorn Hall Hall Road Wilmslow Cheshire SK9 5BZ (hereinafter called ‘the surety’) are held and firmly bound unto A. Monk Building and Civil Engineering Ltd. (hereinafter called ‘the main contractor’) in the sum of £ 101,285 · 00 (one hundred and one thousand two hundred and eighty five pounds) for the payment of which sum the subcontractor and the surety bind themselves their successors and assigns jointly and severally by these presents.

Sealed with our respective seals and dated this twenty seventh day of November 1989.

Whereas:

(1) The main contractor has entered with the Maidstone Borough Council for the construction of a leisure centre at Mote Park Maidstone Kent (hereinafter referred to as ‘the main contract works’)

(2) The subcontractor by subcontract agreement evidenced by subcontract order no. SC1839/C5495 dated 31 October 1989 made between the main contractor of the one part and the subcontractor of the other part has entered into a subcontract (hereinafter referred to as ‘the said subcontract’) for the construction and completion of the subcontract works (being part of the main contract works) as therein mentioned in conformity with the provisions of the said subcontract

Now the condition of the above written bond is such that if the subcontractor shall duly perform and observe all the terms provisions conditions and stipulations of the said subcontract on the subcontractor’s part to be performed and observed according to the true purport intent andmeaning thereof or if on default by the subcontractors the surety shall

---

[58] 见 British Motor Trust Co. Ltd. v. Hyams (1934) 50 TLR 230; Perry v. National Provincial Bank (1910) 1 Ch 464; Trade Indemnity Co. v. Workington Harbour and Dock Board, etc. (1937) AC 1, 21; Trafalgar House Construction (Regions) Ltd. v. General Surety & Guarantee Co. Ltd. (1996) AC 199, 205; Aviva Insurance Ltd. v. Hackney Empire Ltd. (2012) EWCA Civ 1716 等先例。

[59] 这可见在上一段解释的 Bank of Baroda v. Patel (1996) 1 Lloyd’s Rep. 391 先例。

satisfy and discharge the damages sustained by the main contractors thereby up to the amount of the above written bond then this obligation shall be null and void but otherwise shall be and remain in full force and effect **but no alteration in terms of the said subcontract made by agreement between the main contractor and the subcontractor or in the extent or nature of the subcontract works to be constructed and completed thereunder and no allowance of time by the main contractor under the said subcontract nor any forbearance or forgiveness in or in respect of any matter or thing concerning the said subcontract on the part of the main contractor shall in any way release the surety from any liability under the above written bond**.

Any proceedings against the surety to recover any claim hereunder must be served within six months after 4 February 1991 or such other date as may be certified by the Architect as the date of practical completion of the main contract works.

The common seal of . . . "(加黑部分是笔者的强调)

另在 Aviva Insurance Ltd. v. Hackney Empire Ltd. (2012) EWCA Civ 1716 先例中担保合约的相关条文如下:"Now the conditions of the above-written bond are such that if: (a) the contractor shall subject to condition (c) hereof duly perform and observe all the terms provisions conditions and stipulations of the said contract on the contractor's part to be performed and observed according to the true purport intent and meaning thereof or if (b) on default by the contractor the surety shall satisfy and discharge the damages sustained by the employer thereby up to the amount of the above-written bond or if (c) the architect defined in the said contract shall pursuant to the provisions thereof issue a certificate of practical completion then upon the date stated therein (hereinafter called 'the relevant date') this obligation shall be null and void but otherwise shall remain in full force and effect **but no alteration in the terms of the said contract made by agreement between the employer and the contractor or in the extent or nature of the works to be constructed and completed thereunder and no allowance of time by the employer or the architect under the said contract nor any forbearance or forgiveness in or in respect of any matter or thing concerning the said contract on the part of the employer or the said architect shall in any way release the surety from any liability under the above-written bond.**" [加黑部分是所谓的"宽容条文"(indulgence clause)。]

在订约自由下,这种不同写法的明示条文在每个不同案情的案件也会有争议。如在本章之 3.4.3 段提到的 Wittmann (UK) Limited v. Willdav Engineering S. A. (2007) EWCA Civ 824 先例中,有关 Automold 公司取得三间财务公司的贷款融资来资助购买汽车零件,从而令主合约的买卖合约有了更改,这带来争议是该更改是否在母公司 Willdav 提供的担保合约下的明示条文有针对与允许,担保合约中的明示条文如下：

"3 Guarantor's liability

3.1　The Guarantor shall not be discharged by time or any other concessions given to the Company or any third party by Wittmann or by anything Wittmann may do or omit to do or **by any other dealing or thing** which, but for this provision, would or might discharge the Guarantor.

3.2　This Guarantee shall:...

3.2.2　be a continuing guarantee, shall not be discharged **by any intermediate settlement of the Indebtedness** and shall remain in effect until the Indebtedness is discharged in full.

3.2.3　remain in force notwithstanding (and the Guarantor's obligations under this Guarantee shall not be impaired, affected or discharged by) any failure, defect, illegality or unenforceability of or in any of the Company's obligations in respect of the Indebtedness."(加黑部分就是有争议的文字)

4. 银 团 贷 款

在介绍合约更改、弃权与禁反言的说法如何适用在银团贷款这种业务之前，首先介绍银团贷款的概念与操作。银团贷款又被称为辛迪加贷款(syndicated loan)，是指由两家或两家以上的银行基于同一份贷款融资合约，按约定的时间与比例，通过代理行(agent bank)或牵头行(lead bank)向贷款人提供的贷款或授信业务。银团贷款经常出现在一些高风险、金额巨大、贷款期限长的项目中，包括交通、电力、通讯、船舶建造等行业新建项目贷款以及大型设备租赁、企业并购融资等业务中，从而满足贷款人长期、大额的资金需求。银团贷款是国际银行业中一种重要的信贷模式。银团贷款的做法已经有一段历史，笔者知悉的标准格式合约(贷款人与银团之间与/或银团成员之间)是 Loan Market Association(简称"LMA")[60]制定的一份 145 页的标准格式合约，这是一份主要用在欧洲、中东与非洲的银团贷款融资合约。此外，欧美的一些大银行(通常是代理行或牵头行)在自己经验的基础上找称职律师帮助订立与不断改进自己内部使用的合约版本。这些合约版本通常都会加入一条保密条文(confidential clause)，所以在一般公共领域很难找到这样的合约样本。BIMCO 也正在致力于订立银团贷款的标准格式合约，虽然有关的格式合约主要是用在船舶与/或海洋工程的融资，但估计做出适当的更改(logical amendments)后可以适用在其他项目的银团贷款。

---

〔60〕 1996 年成立的机构，目前有来自六十多个国家的六百多个成员。成员主要是商业银行、投资银行、金融机构与律师所等。这些标准格式是提供给成员使用。

银团贷款融资合约也是一般的商业合约，多家银行成员（participating banks）之间或银团与贷款人之间交往多起来，言行就会导致合约更改、弃权与禁反言的说法适用，以下只针对银团贷款的实务中会产生的部分问题。

4.1　贷款融资合约下的更改或弃权

既然是由多于一家的银行来进行此项银团贷款业务，为了节约与实际可行，不可避免的是由银团中的全部成员委任一家银行（一般也会是牵头行）来负责统一安排贷款的相关事项，包括发放贷款、贷款的还本付息，贷款管理，在银行成员之间进行信息沟通，监督贷款人在有关工程的履行情况，处理贷款人违约事宜等事项。所以，在绝大多数的银团贷款融资合约中，都会规定一家代理行，并约定该代理行的权利与责任范围，包括在何种情况下可以对贷款人的违约行为弃权，如果事事都需要和银团中所有的成员单独沟通并取得他们的同意，势必会加大交易的成本与带来严重的延误。

很多时候，银团贷款融资合约都会允许代理行对贷款人（borrower）一些不严重的违约行为独自决定是否弃权，或者就一些轻微的违约行为在经过具有一定比例投票权的成员［可称为多数融资银行（majority bankers）[61]］批准之后向贷款人做出更改或弃权。至于其他重大的弃权或更改，就必须要代理行取得所有银团成员批准后才能做出。

如果在银团贷款融资合约中，没有就代理行是否有权利代表所有成员就贷款人的某些违约行为弃权进行规定，一般代理法的原则[62]就适用在代理行是否可以默示授权（implied authority）去约束其他的银团成员。如果银团成员已经将管理与监督该贷款运作的权利授权给代理行，在面对贷款人而言，很有可能该代理行就会被认为是具有这种对贷款人违约弃权的权利。这里就涉及表见授权（apparent/ostensible authority），在本书第五章之12.2段有详论。

可节录LMA标准格式有关贷款融资合约下的更改与对贷款人违约的弃权的条文，如下：

"35. Amendments and Waivers

35.1　Required consents

Subject to Clause 35.2 (All Lender matters) and Clause 35.3 (Other exceptions) any term of the Finance Documents[63] may be amended or waived only with the consent

---

〔61〕在LMA的标准格式中，针对多数融资银行的定义是："'Majority Lenders' means a Lender or Lenders whose Commitments aggregate more than [662/3]% of the Total Commitments (or, if the Total Commitments have been reduced to zero, aggregated more than [662/3]% of the Total Commitments immediately prior to the reduction)."

〔62〕这在《提单与其他付运单证》(2016年)第三章第2段有详论。

〔63〕在LMA的标准格式中的定义是："'Finance Documents' means this Agreement, any Fee Letter, any Accession Letter, any Resignation Letter and any other document designated as such by the Agent and the Company."

of the Majority Lenders and the Obligors[64] and any such amendment or waiver will be binding on all Parties.

The Agent may effect, on behalf of any Finance Party[65], any amendment or waiver permitted by this Clause 35.(除了35.2条文列举的需要所有银行同意的事项与35.3条文列举的其他例外情况,对贷款融资合约下的更改与对贷款人违约的弃权只需要多数融资银行同意。)...

35.2 All Lender matters

... [An] amendment or waiver of any term of any Finance Document that has the effect of changing or which relates to:

(a) the definition of 'Majority Lenders' in Clause1.1 (Definitions);

(b) an extension to the date of payment of any amount under the Finance Documents;

(c) a reduction in the Margin or a reduction in the amount of any payment of principal, interest, fees or commission payable;

(d) [a change in currency of payment of any amount under the Finance Documents;]

(e) an increase in any Commitment, an extension of any Availability Period or any requirement that a cancellation of Commitments reduces the Commitments of the Lenders rateably under the relevant Facility;

(f) a change to the Borrowers or Guarantors other than in accordance with Clause25 (Changes to the Obligors);

(g) any provision which expressly requires the consent of all the Lenders;

(h) Clause2.3 (Finance Parties' rights and obligations), [Clause 5.1(Delivery of a Utilisation Request),] Clause 8.1 (Illegality), [Clause 8.2 (Change of control),] [Clause 8.8 (Application of prepayments),] Clause 24 (Changes to the Lenders), Clause 25 (Changes to the Obligors), [Clause 28 (Sharing among the Finance Parties),] this Clause 35, Clause 39 (Governing law) or Clause 40.1 (Jurisdiction);

(i) the nature or scope of the guarantee and indemnity granted under Clause18 (Guarantee and indemnity); or...

shall not be made without the prior consent of all the Lenders.

(以上列举的事项是需要银团全部成员同意才能在贷款融资合约下更改与弃权的事项)

---

〔64〕 在LMA的标准格式中的定义是:"'Obligors' means a Borrower or a Guarantor."

〔65〕 在LMA的标准格式中的定义是:"'Finance Party' means the Agent, the Arranger or a Lender."

35.3 Other exceptions

An amendment or waiver which relates to the rights or obligations of the Agent[66] or the Arranger[67] [or a Reference Bank] (each in their capacity as such) may not be effected without the consent of the Agent, the Arranger [or that Reference Bank], as the case may be.(例外情况也是需要银团全部成员同意的)"

4.2 银团成员对牵头银行的禁反言

在银团贷款的合约中,通常会有"没有依赖条文"(non – reliance clause),[68]该条文主要是指银团成员在决定提供贷款并订立该合约时,没有依赖任何代理行或牵头行的陈述又或是牵头行提供的所有信息不构成陈述(representation)。[69] 毕竟很多银团贷款的成立都是首先由牵头行与客户达成贷款融资协议,然后再物色其他愿意分担该贷款融资项目的银行,并邀请他们组成银团。这样,如果将来贷款收不回来,银团的成员就会向牵头行追讨,理由往往是后者提供的信息不准确,并导致他们同意加入银团。牵头行为了避免将来的风险与诉讼的麻烦,往往会在设立银团的贷款融资合约中加入该没有依赖条文。与普通消费者不同,银行作为十分有经验与强势的商业机构在签订合约时,对任何金融项目的风险的调查与评估都是可以独立负责的,所以,这种条文也不会有不公平之处。

这种条文在本质上可以构成"陈述性禁反言"(estoppel by representation)或"合约性禁反言"(contractual estoppel),因而具有强制执行力。将来如果有争议产生,依赖该条文的代理行或牵头行必须确保该条文的措辞是清楚无误的,并且他因为依赖该条文而带来了损害(detriment)。这方面的权威先例是 Lowe v. Lombank (1960) 1 WLR 196,该先例在本书第八章第 2 段有详细介绍。

这种条文也因为可以构成合约性禁反言而具有强制执行力。这一比较新颖的说法是对之前 Lowe v. Lombank 先例中认为一份针对事实的声明不可以构成合约义务这一严格说法的放宽。因为合约性禁反言本质上并不是禁反言,[70]所以,不需要有依赖并蒙受损害等要件。这样,合约明确写出双方都认可的对有关合约订立的事实基础,法律也需要对这种双方的共识给予法律效力。

在 Raiffeisen Zentralbank Osterreich AG v. The Royal Bank of Scotland Plc.

---

[66] 指代理行。

[67] 指牵头行。

[68] 见 Raiffeisen Zentralbank Osterreich AG v. The Royal Bank of Scotland Plc. (2010) 1 Lloyds Rep. 123; Springwell Navigation Corporation v. JP Morgan Chase Bank and Others (2008) EWHC 1793 (Comm); Titan Steel Wheels Ltd. v. The Royal Bank of Scotland Plc. (2010) 2 Lloyd's Rep. 92 等先例。这个课题可参阅本书第八章第 3 段与第 4 段与《合约的解释:规则与应用》第十三章第 2 段。

[69] 关于误述导致合约的产生,可见本书第五章之 1.1.1 段。

[70] 这可见本书第八章的内容。

(2011) 1 Lloyd's Rep. 123 先例中,被告苏格兰皇家银行与 Enron 公司[71]签订贷款融资合约,借贷的金额是 1.385 亿英镑。被告随后就牵头为该笔贷款设立银团贷款,多家银行加入,原告的银行也是银团中的成员之一,分摊 1000 万英镑的贷款份额。后来 Enron 公司破产,原告收不回贷款金额,于是根据银团贷款融资合约向被告提起索赔的诉讼。本案的重要争议就是被告在设立银团贷款时,是否存在"误述"(misrepresentation)与"诱导"(inducement)与是否能构成合约性禁反言。有关的没有依赖条文成功保护了被告的牵头行,该条文可节录如下:

"... This Information Memorandum (the 'Memorandum') has been prepared from Information supplied by the Company [EEL being defined as the Company].

The contents of this Memorandum have not been independently verified. **No representation, warranty or undertaking (express or implied) is made, and no responsibility is accepted as to the adequacy, accuracy, completeness or reasonableness of this Memorandum or any further information, notice or other document** at any time supplied in connection with the Facility.

This Memorandum is being provided for information purposes only and is not intended to provide the basis of any credit decision or other evaluation and should not be considered as a recommendation that any recipient of this Memorandum should participate in the Facility. **Each potential participant should determine its interest in participating in the Facility based upon such investigations and analysis as it deems necessary for such purpose.**

No undertaking is given to assess or keep under review the business, financial condition, prospects, creditworthiness, status or affairs of the Company, the Borrower or any other person now or at any time during the life of the Facility or (except as specifically provided in the Facility Agreement) to provide any recipient or participant in the Facility with any information relating to the Company, the Borrower or otherwise ...

This Memorandum is being made available to potential participants on the strict understanding that it is confidential. Recipients shall not be entitled to use any of the information contained in this Memorandum other than for the purpose of deciding whether or not to participate in the Facility. Recipients are reminded that this Memorandum is subject to the confidentiality undertaking signed by them."(加黑部分是笔者的强调)

---

[71] Enron 公司的倒闭是轰动国际的新闻。Enron 公司位于美国休斯敦,业务涉足能源、电力、贸易、航运等领域。在高峰时期,《福布斯》连续六年将其评为最具创造力的公司。2000 年,有 1000 亿美元的营收。2001 年,Enron 公司爆出有系统做假账的丑闻,并于随后破产。该事件也带来美国国会通过针对美国公司账目的立法,为 Enron 公司提供审计服务的会计师事务所 Arthur Anderson 受该丑闻的影响也倒闭,从而令原来世界闻名的五大国际会计师事务所变为四家。

5. 信　用　证

众所周知,信用证(letter of credit)是国际贸易中最重要的支付手段之一,其被形容为国际贸易的血液与确保国际贸易顺利开展的基石。由于信用证的国际性,为了建立一套统一的做法而使信用证在国际上使用的更加顺畅,总部在法国巴黎的国际商会(International Chamber of Commerce,简称ICC)很早就开始了工作,在1930年拟订了一套《商业跟单信用证统一惯例》,并于1933年正式公布。随着信用证使用的广泛与深入,国际商会随后在1951年、1962年、1974年、1978年、1983年、1993年对该《商业跟单信用证统一惯例》进行了多次修订,称为《跟单信用证统一惯例》(UCP)。该UCP被各国银行与贸易界广泛采用,成为信用证业务的国际惯例。2006年10月25日,国际商会又对1993年《UCP 500》进行了修订,并于2007年7月1日正式开始生效《UCP 600》。目前,几乎所有信用证中都有明示条文合并UCP600。因此,关于信用证关系的法律是以UCP为基础,在UCP不能适用时,普通法才会适用。

随着信用证在国际贸易中的广泛使用,原来用作国际支付的汇票(bill of exchange/draft)已经很少独立作为支付的方法。虽然在17、18世纪有大量的先例针对汇票操作中的弃权与禁反言的言行,但自从英国1882年《Bill of Exchange Act》之后(目前世界上很多国家也有针对汇票的专门立法)制定了明确的立法条文针对这些问题,针对汇票的普通法案例已很少见到。所以,在本章也不深入的介绍。

信用证的显著特点如下:(1)信用证是一种独立的、有保障的支付手段,本质上也是合约。(2)信用证虽然是作为买卖合约或其他类别的基础合约或主合约的支付手段,是因为有基础合约的存在才存在,但因为信用证是要保障支付才被创立,所以,它又独立于基础合约。基础合约下关于货物的任何争议都不能影响信用证下银行在收到符合要求的单证〔72〕后的支付,唯一的例外是存在信用证下受益人(beneficiary)知道或参与的欺诈,〔73〕通常就是以明知道是假的单证向银行结汇。(3)信用证的独立性带来在信用证合约下所有当事人均是针对单证行事。单证在不同的当事人之间流转,不同的当事人之间有不同的权利与义务。(4)信用证涉及的合约关系中最主要的有四重:第一重是买卖双方之间的买卖合约,相对于信用证本身来说,又被称为基础合约(underlying contract);第二重是开立信用证时,买方/开证人与开证行(issuing bank)之间的合约关系;第三重是开证行与保兑行(confirming bank)/通知行(advising bank)之间的合约关系,本质上是委托代理合约关系,保兑行/通知行是开证行

〔72〕 这单证在国际货物买卖是指“付运单证”(shipment documents),其中最重要的一份单证是装船提单,以证明有关货物已经装船并在运往卸港/目的地途中。

〔73〕 见贵族院的United Merchants (Investments) Ltd. v. Royal Bank of Canada (1983) 1 AC 168先例。

在卖方/受益人所在地委托的代理行以接受卖方提交单证、审理单证、传递单证并代为做出支付;第四重是保兑行/通知行与卖方/受益人之间的合约关系,该合约关系是在保兑行/通知行将信用证通知给卖方的时候成立,在该合约关系下,卖方要向保兑行/通知行提交单据,而保兑行/通知行经过审单之后,需要对卖方支付信用证中的款项。在这个合约关系中,保兑行是连同开证行对受益人承担连带(joint and several)付款的责任,而通知行只是作为开证行的代理人,不承担任何个人付款的责任。(5)银行不会涉及买卖双方之间因买卖合约而产生的争议,对于银行来说,唯一要做的就是审核信用证条文中规定的单证来确定单证是否与信用证条文的规定相符,以令支付条件成熟。所以,信用证的开立首先要严格符合买卖合约的规定,其次是提交的单证要严格符合信用证的规定。

在明确了上述信用证的特点之后,接下来分析更改、弃权与禁反言说法的适用。

5.1　信用证的更改

在探讨此问题之前,首先要明确信用证虽然本质上也是一份合约,但由于信用证同时也是一种支付手段,其中涉及多方当事人与多重合约关系,并拥有其特殊的操作方法,所以其更改也是和其他商业合约有很大不同之处。信用证的更改其实更多与更习惯被称为修改,其英文对应的词也不是泛泛的"variation",而是特定的"amendment"。本章对信用证的修改也称更改。

针对信用证的更改,任何一份信用证往往都会涉及上述所讲的四重基本合约关系,所以对于信用证的更改往往是"牵一发而动全身"。首先,信用证是在开证人的申请下才开立,所以信用证要更改先是开证人向开证行做出申请。与此同时,卖方/受益人要在信用证下获得支付,必须严格按照信用证的规定来履行,主要就是提交符合信用证要求的单证。因此,任何信用证的更改都会给其履约带来影响,从而令信用证的更改与受益人利益攸关。另外,信用证的更改可能会影响保兑行决定是否仍然愿意保兑该信用证。至于其他信用证会涉及的当事人,在信用证更改这个问题上,多是起到一个信息传递的作用。根据上述分析不难看出,在 UCP600 中对信用证更改的问题有 Article 10 来针对。大原则是信用证一旦按照买卖合约的约定开出并通知给受益人,没有受益人的同意,信用证不能单方面被更改。因为开立信用证的通知已经在开证行与受益人之间构成了一份有约束力的合约而不能够被单方面修改。普通法对此也在 Bunge Corp v. Vegetable Vitamin Foods (Pte) Ltd. (1985) 1 Lloyd's Rep. 613 先例中确认当开证行发出的开立信用证的通知被受益人收到的那刻起,信用证就被认为正式开立了(相当于确定了合约),而开证行也会从该时刻起受信用证条文的约束。

在实务中,信用证的更改多是由于买方/开证人开立的信用证不符合买卖合约的约定,卖方要求买方进行更正。或者后来情况发生变化,如发生不可抗力事件导致延期付运,买卖双方同意更改信用证。具体操作通常就是在开证人的申请下,开证行做出更改信函(amending letter)给受益人/卖方:Tamari & Sons Ltd. and Another v.

"Colprogeca"（1969）2 Lloyd's Rep. 18 先例。而如果买卖合约涉及货物的分批付运，也可以在后来批次付运的货物时再开出准确的信用证，正如在 Bunge Corp v. Vegetable Vitamin Foods（Pte）Ltd 先例中，涉及了 4 票付运的棕榈油，Neill 大法官说："it is also accepted that any defects there may have been in the letter of credit which was opened in March could have been corrected in letters of credit opened in April and May for the purposes of shipments in May and June respectively."

当然这个补救只可以在买卖合约下明示或者默示信用证开出的最后期限内做出，否则会是买方/开证人的毁约/违约（repudiatory breach）。[74]

5.1.1 UCP600 的规定

UCP600 Article 10 是这样规定：

"Article 10 Amendments

a. Except as otherwise provided by article 38, a credit can neither be amended nor cancelled without the agreement of the issuing bank, the confirming bank, if any, and the beneficiary.

b. An issuing bank is irrevocably bound by an amendment as of the time it issues the amendment. A confirming bank may extend its confirmation to an amendment and will be irrevocably bound as of the time it advises the amendment. A confirming bank may, however, choose to advise an amendment without extending its confirmation and, if so, it must inform the issuing bank without delay and inform the beneficiary in its advice.

c. The terms and conditions of the original credit (or a credit incorporating previously accepted amendments) will remain in force for the beneficiary until the beneficiary communicates its acceptance of the amendment to the bank that advised such amendment. The beneficiary should give notification of acceptance or rejection of an amendment. If the beneficiary fails to give such notification, a presentation that complies with the credit and to any not yet accepted amendment will be deemed to be notification of acceptance by the beneficiary of such amendment. As of that moment the credit will be amended.

d. A bank that advises an amendment should inform the bank from which it received the amendment of any notification of acceptance or rejection.

e. Partial acceptance of an amendment is not allowed and will be deemed to be notification of rejection of the amendment.

f. A provision in an amendment to the effect that the amendment shall enter into force unless rejected by the beneficiary within a certain time shall be disregarded."

虽然有上述 UCP600 的明示条文规定，但适用起来仍然带来问题。面对买方单

---

〔74〕 针对违约/毁约，在本书第一章有详细介绍。

方面申请更改信用证的情况，卖方如果不同意，则更改无效。但卖方要如何应对这种单方面的更改呢？很多卖方不知道如何应对并因担心将来在交单时被银行拒单而做出不明智的选择。正确的做法是卖方可以向银行或买方提出抗议，反对该更改并表示将会坚持按照原信用证的规定履行，包括按照原信用证合约的规定准备单证。而卖方也的确可以在做出表示之后按照原信用证行事。如果银行或买方坚持按照更改后的信用证行事，卖方可以马上通过开始诉讼或仲裁，向银行根据信用证合约或向买方根据买卖合约索赔由此带来的损失。通常银行会很快做出让步，因为在这种法律地位明确的情况下，卖方通常会很快取得简易判决（summary judgement），银行也就无谓去纠缠。

卖方在面对更改通知时如果保持沉默，则根据 Article 10（c）的规定，仍然表示更改的内容不被接受。更改通知相当于开证行做出的订立新合约的要约（offer），该要约一定要被通过语言或行动明示接受，才能达成新的合约。所以，保持沉默不能被视为接受。Article 10（f）还进一步确保任何明示改变 Article 10（c）的条文是无效的。例如，在更改信函中如果有条文说明受益人不在一定的时间内拒绝，就被视为接受该更改。

由此，卖方在面对更改信函时，可以选择提交符合原信用证的单证，这是以行动拒绝更改。也可以提交符合更改后的信用证的单证，这是以行动表示接受更改。

Article 10（e）针对的是在一份更改信函中存在多个更改的情况，如果卖方只是接受部分而拒绝另外的部分，根据合约达成（formation of contract）的基本原理，即要约不能被部分接受，部分接受等于没有接受任何要约一样，所有对信用证的更改均不能生效。但该部分接受可以构成一个反要约（counter－offer）。如果银行接受了该反要约，信用证的更改是按照卖方同意的部分进行了更改。

根据上述提到的，更改也会影响保兑行，其中 Article 10（b）就有针对。根据 Article 10（b）的内容，开证行一旦发出更改信函，就不能再撤回，即使该更改信函还没有因被受益人接受而生效。保兑行往往又是通知行，如果它在将该更改信函通知给受益人时没有提出任何问题，可以认为保兑行也是受该更改信函的约束，并对更改后的信用证加上自己的保兑责任。但保兑行也完全可以在收到更改信函并转给受益人时，向开证行与受益人提出其保兑不针对更改后的内容。这时，如果受益人接受更改，也要考虑会有后果是保兑行的身份就变为通知行，而更改后的信用证变为没有保兑的信用证（unconfirmed letter of credit）。

5.1.2 笔者处理的与信用证更改有关的仲裁案件

案情涉及中国卖方与英国买方进行一笔钢材的买卖。英国买方按照买卖合约开出信用证并通知给中国卖方。中国卖方也按照合约的约定，备货并安排货物的付运。后来英国买方就货物付运时间单方面对信用证进行了更改，并将更改的信用证再次通知给中国卖方。买卖合约中规定的货物付运时间为 7 月 1 日到 7 月 31 日之间，而更改后的信用证对货物付运时间变为 7 月 20 日至 7 月 31 日，该更改明显不符合买卖合约的规定。而此时货物也在 7 月 13 日就已经装船付运了。可以想得到是,这段时间的钢材市场在下跌,看来这是英国买方在设计让中国卖方落入陷阱。

如果中国卖方了解自己在买卖合约与信用证下的权利,最正确的做法是首先对英国买方更改信用证的行为不予同意或认可,而按照原来的信用证向开证行提交单证并要求付款。因为原信用证已经通知了给中国卖方/受益人而令受益人与银行成立了合约关系,而根据 UCP600 Article 10(a)条的规定,没有受益人的同意,信用证不能被更改,即开证人单方面的更改也无效,开证行仍然要按照原信用证来履约。

但是很遗憾,中国卖方却选择了既不合法也不明智的方法应对。由于中国卖方不了解自己在 UCP600 下所拥有的权利,误以为更改后的信用证有效,所以,即使在已经安排了货物付运并将货物装船信息告知英国卖方的情况下,虽然不同意信用证的更改,但为了能在新的信用证下顺利结汇,而将装船提单上货物的装船日期也按照新的信用证的规定做出相应修改,把 7 月 13 日改为 7 月 20 日。先不说该修改提单的行为是否会被认为是以行动同意了信用证的更改,该修改首先明显不符合事实上货物装船的日期,等于造假,并且更加不明智的地方在于,中国买方早已将真实的装船日期告知英国卖方。这样,英国卖方即刻在开证行所在地荷兰法院向法院申请了止付禁令。欺诈作为唯一能够阻止信用证支付的例外情况,加上有之前中国卖方发给英国买方的真实装船通知可作为证明,荷兰法院立刻接受该申请并对开证行做出了止付禁令。后来,中国卖方因为货物已经付运不得不在途中转卖,英国买方又在转卖地美国扣押货物,希望借此向中国卖方再敲一笔。虽然最后货物转卖,但价格已经比原买卖合约的价格低了很多。

虽然在该仲裁中,笔者所在的仲裁庭是判中国卖方胜诉,但原因是英国卖方违约开立不符合买卖合约的信用证在先。即使涉及欺诈,中国卖方也没有在买卖合约中欺骗英国买方,而是将真实的装船通知一早就告知英国买方。但中国卖方因为制作假提单在信用证合约关系下欺骗荷兰开证行,也令他们胜之不武,但信用证是与买卖合约不同与独立的合约。

后来中国卖方将裁决书拿到英国执行时也遇到了非常大的阻力。因为英国买方以中国卖方的欺诈行为违反英国的公共政策为由,大力抗拒裁决书的认可与执行。[75] 据知,目前英国高院虽然判决笔者的裁决书应该被执行[Sinocore International Co. Ltd. v. RBRG Trading (UK) Ltd. (2017) EWHC 25 (Comm)先例][76],但该案仍在上诉中而并没有最终的结论。由此可见,中国卖方即使在仲裁中胜诉,但执行

---

〔75〕 这个课题可见本书第九章之 3.3.2.3 段。

〔76〕 笔者当时在草拟裁决书时就预见到这一欺诈的因素会令裁决书的执行出问题,所以在该份 76 页的裁决书中,裁定原因占了大部分(60 页),而在该裁决原因中又用了大量篇幅区分买卖合约下的违约与信用证下的欺诈。如果裁决书中只有决定但没有给出太多的原因,在英国法欺诈大于一切(fraud unravels all)的公共政策下,如果稍微和欺诈有关系,就有危险被拒绝执行。

裁决书也充满了变数。

5.2　信用证下的弃权

由于信用证的履约只是针对单证文件，所以弃权的问题主要也是针对单证是否与信用证相符的问题。任何单证与信用证条文的不符点都可以作为弃权的对象。而且在信用证下的弃权通常都是“因选择而弃权”（waiver by election），单方面弃权/“因宽限而弃权”（waiver by forbearance）的说法较难说得通。因为在信用证的多重关系下，因宽限而弃权无法在各种关系中得到解释。如提交的单证有不符点，银行与开证人就要做出是否接受的选择。但如果涉及宽限，如让受益人在信用证规定的最后期限后仍可以提交单证并获得支付，一般会通过信用证的更改，而不会以应宽限而弃权的方式。

关于因选择而弃权，在贷款融资合约中已经详细探讨过弃权方需要知道有关的权利以及要做出清楚无误的陈述等问题，而且在信用证关系下，要满足这些构成要件也不存在太大问题。另也有 UCP600 的条文专门针对审单以及由此带来弃权与禁反言的问题，所以在此不再展开讨论。

接下来，就以信用证下不同当事人之间所存在的合约关系来探讨弃权的问题。

5.2.1　买方与卖方之间

在买卖合约下，买方准时与开立严格符合买卖合约约定的信用证是条件条文以及是卖方履约付运货物的先决条件。买方一旦违反，卖方可以终止买卖合约并索赔损失。由此，买卖双方之间对信用证的弃权，表现在对开立信用证的时间、开立信用证的内容上等，而这些都是基于买卖合约的履行，买卖双方之间的关系非常受市场波动的影响。这可见杨大明所著的《国际货物买卖》一书第十章之 4.5.3 段与 4.7 段的内容，其中有详细的讨论。在本书第四章之 6.5.5.2.2 中介绍的 Nichimen v. Gatoil (1987) 2 Lloyd Rep. 46 先例也是这方面的问题。

由于本章主要讨论信用证合约本身，在此不再展开来讲这一方面（买卖合约下针对信用证承诺的履行）的弃权。在此介绍笔者（杨大明）近期处理过的两个真实案件。

第一个案件是在北京仲裁委员会的案件（虽然在普通法国家仲裁也会带来类似的结果），案情也是非常典型的，涉及铁矿石的国际买卖。买方有责任开信用证，但没有准时开到。当时市场价格大跌，所以开证比较麻烦，原本预备开证的银行不愿意。结果卖方把货物转卖，并向买方索赔损失。买方当中依赖的争辩之一是这次交易前有另外两次，买方都迟延开出信用证，卖方都没有异议，也没有马上把货物转卖，所以这次都不应该有这样的权利。这种是典型的争辩，但不容易成功，这次也不例外，因为合约有了明确的规定信用证要在某个时间之前开出。就算之前的交往有个别情况买方虽然迟开信用证但卖方没有按照合约执行权利，除非个是长期多次与惯常发生，否则一、两次的宽限不代表日后对同样的违约也要宽限。

第二个案件涉及的也是货物买卖合约，货物是钢板。买卖合约对货物质量的要求（包括货物可不可以有锈迹）作出了规定。买方在合约下有开信用证的责任，而买方也开了。信用证对单证中显示生锈没有作出特别的要求，至于开出的信用证与买卖合约并不一致，卖方没有提出反对，看来是对买方的违约放弃了他的权利。

在该案件中，装货时这些钢板有个别锈迹（钢板通常生产出来开始生锈是一个自然的过程，所以一定会有锈迹，只是程度问题），因此，提单上也做出了这样的说明。结果卖方在信用证下向议付行提交提单时，被视为不符点，所以银行不愿支付。这是因为除非有特别说明，否则按照 UCP600 之 Article 27，信用证的默认立场是需要提单都是清洁的。因此，卖方无法在信用证下取得货款。虽然卖方提交的提单不是清洁提单，但这并不构成弃权或禁反言，即卖方不能被禁止在买卖合约下向买方追回货款。因为货物有无符合合约下要求的质量，是看买卖合约的条文，而不是看提单是否清洁。而在这一票，钢材锈迹的程度是符合买卖合约的规定。而且信用证结不了汇的原因也不是钢材的质量有问题，而是买方开出的信用证不符合买卖合约的规定。

至于较早卖方对买方开出不符合买卖合约规定的信用证的弃权或禁反言是卖方不能在他的违约（如没有做出付运）时就这一点声称是买方违约在先，因为买方没有准时与准确的开出符合买卖合约的信用证。

5.2.2　买方与开证行之间

买方与开证行之间的关系主要表现在两个方面：一是买方作为开证申请人（applicant）向开证行申请开立信用证，即给开证行开立信用证的指示；二是在收到卖方/受益人的交单后，如果单证存在不符点（discrepancy），开证行向买方询问是否接受不符点，即放弃拒单的权利。

有统计显示在英国与美国的信用证业务中，有 60% ~70% 的信用证交单在第一次交单时都存在不符点。在 Bankers Trust Co. v. State Bank of India（1991）2 Lloyd's Rep. 443 先例中，证人证言中提到在单证存在不符点的情况下，90% 的开证行都会向申请人询问是否要接受这些不符点。而有很多结汇也正是由于买方对不符点的弃权才顺利完成。尽管如此，因为 UCP600 中 Article 16（b）[77] 规定开证行完全可以根据自己的判断决定是否要向开证人询问是否接受不符点。所以，在开证行对开证人的资信不太有信心时，完全可以不询问开证人而借机拒绝支付信用证下的款项。

信用证的开立一定要符合开证人的指示，这在 Equitable Trust Co. of New York v. Dawson Partners Ltd.（1926）27 Lloyd's Rep. 49 先例中被告要求原告开立一份保兑信用证，并通过原告在雅加达有业务关系的联络行 HSBC 保兑信用证。被告的开证申请是要求提交的单证中有一份质量证明是由两位以上的专家签发并由商会签署（a certificate of quality to be issued by experts who are sworn brokers, signed by the

〔77〕 以下段节有节录。

Chamber of Commerce)。但在信息传递的过程中,由于银行之间使用的电报代码没有区分单数与复数,所以 HSBC 收到的信用证信息中"expert"一词没有"s"。在卖方交单时,HSBC 也接受了由一位专家签发的质量证明。后来,原告对 HSBC 进行了偿付(reimburse)并要求被告进一步对自己进行偿付,被告因为单证不符而拒绝进行偿付。

在信用证下,开证行与买方/开证人除了开立的这份信用证之外,往往还会有其他的业务关系,包括开证行同时与开证人之间有一份长期的贷款融资合约或者对开证人提供授信业务以支持其贸易活动的开展。这时,开证行除了要求开证人提供担保(如个人担保或其他财产作为担保)外,还会就具体的信用证要求提单的指示方(notifying party)不是买方而是开证行自己,以获得装船货物的第一手所有权,并能优先控制货物。[78] 所以,实务中也经常见到在买方不能支付货款给开证行时,开证行自己以提单持有人(holder)的身份向船长提取货物,并作为货物的所有人把货物进行转卖等的处理。显然这种要求完全对开证行有利,也可以被单方面放弃:[79] Guaranty Trust v. Van Den Bergh (1925) 22 Lloyd's Rep. 447 (CA)先例。案情是位于菲律宾马尼拉的出口公司卖一票油给美国买方。美国买方向本案的原告银行申请开立一份不可撤销信用证(irrevocable letter of credit)。即使原告对美国买方的资信存在怀疑,不过在该先例中,在被告为美国买方提供履约担保之后,原告仍然为美国买方开立了信用证。原告为了加强对自己的保护,信用证的条文规定提单要将原告作为提单的指示方,即船东在原告的指示下才能确定把货物交付给谁,从而原告对货物享有第一手的所有权。由于原告发给菲律宾卖方的电报内容不清楚,卖方取得的提单上的指示方仍为美国买方。在收到单证后,原告接受了单证,并对卖方做出了支付。在原告向美国买方要求偿付该笔货款时,美国买方经济陷入困难,无法支付该笔货款。原告于是向被告要求履行担保合约下的支付责任,但被告抗辩说,提单以买方作为指示方不符合信用证的规定。该案上诉到上诉庭,Scrutton 大法官判原告胜诉。理由是该以原告银行为提单指示方的要求纯粹是对原告有利的条文,因此原告可以单方面放弃该条文。Scrutton 大法官说:"A bill of lading to the order of the... [buyers]... was much better for them than a bill of lading to the order of the Trust; and if the Trust had chosen to waive that provision... I do not think... [the buyers]... could have complained."

5.2.3　开证行与受益人之间

这是信用证合约下弃权将会主要涉及的领域,因为受益人交单而开证行审单是信用证下主要的履约内容,而弃权主要针对的对象就是单证中的不符点。这就引出单证一定要与信用证规定相符的原则。该原则的严格性可见很多先例:Skandinaviska

---

〔78〕 在《提单及其他付运单证》第二章之 3.1.5.4 段有针对这个课题。

〔79〕 这个课题可见本书第三章之 3.3.4 段。

Kreditaktie Bolaget v. Barclays Bank (1925) 22 Lloyd's Rep. 523；Bank Melli Iran v. Barclays Bank (Dominion, Colonial & Overseas) (1951) 2 Lloyd's Rep. 367；Soproma SpA v. Marine & Animal By – Products Corp (1966) 1 Lloyd's Rep. 367；The "Lena" (1981) 1 Lloyd's Rep. 68；Banque v. Rayner (1982) 2 Lloyd's Rep. 476；Seaconsar v. Bank Markazi (1993) 1 Lloyd's Rep. 236；Glencore International A. G. and Another v. Bank of China (1996) 1 Lloyd's Rep. 135；Kredietbank Antwerp v. Midland Bank Plc. (1999) CLC 1108 等。

例如，在 Glencore International A. G. and Another v. Bank of China 的上诉庭先例中，Bingham 大法官说："There was, and in the light of authority extending over many years could be, no argument about the overriding legal principle. The duty of the issuing bank is, and is only, to make payment against documents which comply strictly with the terms of the credit."

在现实中，会有情况是单证有不符点并且被银行拒绝支付，但买方还是提取与占有了货物。这可解释为买方是在买卖合约下接受了单证的不符点，毕竟付运单证（主要是指提单）就是货物的物权凭证（document of title）。但买方的接受不能被视为银行在信用证合约下也同样接受了不符点，毕竟是另外一个独立的合约关系。所以还没有支付的货款，卖方可向买方追讨但不能向银行追讨。这在 Uzinterimpex JSC v. Standard Bank Plc. (2008) 2 Lloyd's Rep. 456 先例中，承运人将货物在卸港无单放货给了买方，作为信用证下受益人的卖方要求银行做出支付。Moore – Bick 大法官说："In the case of a documentary sale it is necessary, as that case shows, to distinguish between the seller's right to obtain payment from the bank under the letter of credit and his right to obtain payment from the buyer where for some reason the mechanism provided by the letter of credit fails. As the decision in Sffron v. Societe Miniere Cafrika (1958) 100 CLR 231 demonstrates, acceptance of the goods by the buyer may render him liable for the price and may to that extent involve a waiver on his part of discrepancies in the documents that would otherwise have entitled him to reject them, but it is not sufficient to render the bank liable under the letter of credit to pay the seller against documents that do not conform to its requirements."

曾经有对不符点单证的接受不能被认为下次就同一不符点的弃权。Cape Asbestos Co. Ltd. v. Lloyds Bank Ltd. (1921) WN 274 先例是有关可撤销信用证（revocable letter of credit）的著名先例。该先例的原告是货物的卖方，被告是通知行。信用证经由被告通知给原告，原告履行了部分货物的付运，被告接受了单证并承兑了汇票。后来，开证行撤销了信用证并告知被告，不过被告没有将这一消息通知给原告，原告在不知情的情况下付运了剩余的货物，再次交单时，汇票被拒绝承兑。本先例的案情中也有与 Guaranty Trust v. Van Den Bergh (1925) 22 Lloyd's Rep. 447 (CA) 先例类似的地方是信用证规定提单是以银行为指示方，但原告两次提交的单证中提单均是以买方为指示方，这与信用证不符。原告指称被告在第一次交单后，接受了单证并承兑汇票，所以在第二次交单时也放弃了拒绝单证的权利。Bailhache 大法官不认为被告第一次接受单证并承兑汇票的行为就代表其放弃了在第二次交单时有拒绝同样不符点的权利。他说："That case（Panoustos 先例）was an authority for the proposition that where an act had to be done by the buyer of goods, such, for instance, as the opening of a confirmed banker's credit, and he did not perform that act, and the seller nevertheless went on delivering the goods with knowledge that the act had not been performed, the seller could not suddenly cancel the contract and refuse to make further deliveries without giving the buyer reasonable notice of his intention so as to give the buyer an opportunity of putting himself right. That case was no authority for the proposition, that where an act had to be done periodically, as, for instance, the delivery of a bill of lading in such a case as the present, the fact that it had been done irregularly in the past justified the assumption that the irregularity would be waived in the future. The Panoustos case had only reference to an act which had to be done once and for all, and not to an act which had to be done periodically."

但如果重复多次接受同一不符点，可能会构成双方之间的习惯做法（course of dealing），这时如果弃权方想要回复到原来的地位，就要对违约方做出合理的通知，否则会构成"共识性禁反言"（estoppel by convention）。

5.2.4　UCP600 的相关规定

对于在银行审单中会遇到弃权的问题是在 UCP600 中有明确的规定如下：

"Article 16 Discrepant Documents, Waiver and Notice

a. When a nominated bank acting on its nomination, a confirming bank, if any, or the issuing bank determines that a presentation does not comply, it may refuse to honour or negotiate.

b. When an issuing bank determines that a presentation does not comply, it may in its sole judgement approach the applicant for a waiver of the discrepancies. This does not, however, extend the period mentioned in sub – article 14 (b).

c. When a nominated bank acting on its nomination, a confirming bank, if any, or the issuing bank decides to refuse to honour or negotiate, it must give a single notice to that effect to the presenter.

The notice must state:

i. that the bank is refusing to honour or negotiate; and

ii. each discrepancy in respect of which the bank refuses to honour or negotiate; and

iii. a) that the bank is holding the documents pending further instructions from the presenter; or

b) that the issuing bank is holding the documents until it receives a waiver from the applicant and agrees to accept it, or receives further instructions from the presenter prior to agreeing to accept a waiver; or

c) that the bank is returning the documents; or

d) that the bank is acting in accordance with instructions previously received from the presenter.

d. The notice required in sub – article 16 (c) must be given by telecommunication or, if that is not possible, by other expeditious means no later than the close of the fifth banking day following the day of presentation.

e. A nominated bank acting on its nomination, a confirming bank, if any, or the issuing bank may, after providing notice required by sub – article 16 (c) (iii) (a) or (b), return the documents to the presenter at any time.

f. If an issuing bank or a confirming bank fails to act in accordance with the provisions of this article, it shall be precluded from claiming that the documents do not constitute a complying presentation.

g. When an issuing bank refuses to honour or a confirming bank refuses to honour or negotiate and has given notice to that effect in accordance with this article, it shall then be entitled to claim a refund, with interest, of any reimbursement made."

UCP600 只是针对开证行对单证不符点弃权的情况。如果单证不是第一时间交给开证行(issuing bank),而是交给指定行(nominating bank)或保兑行(confirming bank)时,原则上这些银行也有权决定是否拒绝单证,并且也不应该禁止这些银行向与自己有合约关系的开证行询问是否可以接受不符点。不过这会带来操作上的困难,如指定行或保兑行向开证行询问是否可以接受不符点,开证行还要进一步向买方/开证人询问同样的问题。这一过程非常耗时,很有可能无法在 UCP600 Article 16 (d)规定的 5 个银行工作日的审单日期内完成。而且开证人只是开证行的客户而与指定行或保兑行没有关系,所以后者与信用证相关的货物买卖没有任何利益,也根本不关心货物买卖的交易是否能顺利完成。所以,对于指定行或保兑行来说,最好的做法就是一看到不符点就马上拒单,从而给受益人更多的时间能够修正不符点以在信用证规定的提交单证有效期内再次交单。

针对上述节录的 UCP600 的 Article 16,举一个近期的先例说明其适用。这是 Fortis Bank SA/NV and another v. Indian Overseas Bank (2010) 2 Lloyd's Rep. 641 先例。该先例的案情是 Stemcor 作为卖方,向印度买方 SESA 出售共 15000 吨废钢,并订立五个 CFR 买卖合约。之,后 SESA 向其银行 IOB 在这五个买卖合约下申请并开出了共五个以 Stemcor 为受益人的信用证。货物付运后,Stemcor 向信用证下的保兑行 Fortis Bank 结汇。在前三个信用证下,Fortis Bank 向 Stemcor 做出了支付。在后两个信用证下,Fortis Bank 将付运单证交给 IOB 看是否愿意接受。在货物付运时,废钢的市场价格大幅下跌,导致 SESA 不愿意接受货物并严令 IOB 不做出支付,借口是付运单证存在不符点。这也导致 IOB 拒绝偿还 Fortis Bank 已经支付了的前三个信用证下的款项,也拒绝接受在后两个信用证下的付运单证。但 IOB 没有根据 Fortis Bank 的要求立刻退还付运文件,而是直到一个多月后才退还。因此,Fortis Bank 与 Stemcor 作为共同原告起诉 IOB,要求 IOB 补偿 Fortis Bank 已经在前三个信用证下支付给 Stemcor 的款项,与要求 IOB 在后两个信用证下支付给 Stemcor。该先例的重要争议之一是银行是否有默示的责任在根据 UCP600 之 Article 16(c)(iii)(c)中规定的以付运单证存在不符点为由拒绝支付时,退还付运单证的行为要合理及时(reasonable promptness)的做出?如果存在这样的默示责任,那该一个多月的延误是否违反了这一默示的责任?因为如果违反了这一责任,根据 Article 16(f)的规定,有权提出付运单证存在不符点的银行因被视为弃权而不能再以不符点拒单。

在较早前已有 Hamblen 大法官做出第一个简易判决([2010] 1 Lloyd's Rep. 227),认定信用证要求的付运单证中存在不符点。之后 Hamblen 大法官做出第二个判决([2010] 2 Lloyd's Rep. 641),认定 Article 16(c)(iii)(c)下存在一个默示责任是要求开证行在退还单证时要合理及时的做出。IOB 没有合理及时地退还付运单证的行为是对以不符点拒单权利的弃权,UCP600 Art 16(f)适用。

Hamblen 大法官说:"I also accept that given that it is established banking practice to act promptly in such circumstances, and given the obvious importance of priority processing of documents following a return notice or instruction, a reasonable promptness. If so, then the same analysis must apply to the like obligation which I have held to exist in UCP600. I am therefore satisfied that the obligation to act in accordance with the disposal statement made involves, in relation to a statement that documents are being returned or held pending or in accordance with instructions, an obligation to return the documents and comply with instructions to return them with reasonable promptness... Whatever the exact period of time embraced by the obligation to return the documents with reasonable promptness, it is clear that IOB's delay in doing so for a number of weeks following its 'return' notices involved a failure to do so in accordance with the provisions of article 16 and hence the preclusion under article 16(f) applies."

5.3　禁反言

5.3.1　审单银行先前提出的不符点是否禁反言不能之后再提出其他的不符点

在上述节录的 UCP600 的 Article 16(f)中规定,开证行或保兑行如果没有按照第 16 条的规定行事,就会丧失声称单证不符并拒单的权利。该权利的丧失既可以是因为弃权,也可以被解释为因为"禁反言"(estoppel)。UCP600 的规定与英国普通法在这方面的地位不同。如果 UCP600 不适用,而适用普通法的话,要注意的是普通法下的原则是开证行不会因为起初依赖某个特定不符点拒单而被"禁反言"(estoppel)在随后依赖其他不符点拒单的权利。

在普通法下的先例是 Kydon Cia Naviera SA v. National Westminster Bank Ltd.

The Lena (1981) 1 Lloyd's Rep. 68。该先例是买卖一艘船舶,支付方式是使用信用证,信用证适用 UCP(1962 版)。卖方即原告在结汇时总共有五次交单,每次都因有不符点而被拒单,直到最后信用证有效期过期。在银行与卖方的多次通信往来中,卖方指称开证行根据"陈述性禁反言"(estoppel by representation)与"承诺性禁反言"(promissory estoppel)不能依赖其拒单通知中没有提到过的不符点而作为拒单的理由。当时版本的 UCP 的条文还比较简陋,其中 Article 8 的相关说法节录如下:"(c) If, upon receipt of the documents, the issuing bank considers that they appear on their face not to be in accordance with the terms and conditions of the credit, that bank must determine, on the basis of the documents alone, whether to claim that payment, acceptance or negotiation was not effected in accordance with the terms and conditions of the credit... (e) If such claim is to be made notice to that effect, stating the reasons therefor, must, without delay, be given by cable or other expeditious means to the bank from which the documents have been received (the remitting bank) and such notice must state that the documents are being held at the disposal of such bank or are being returned thereto."

由于条文中没有针对拒单通知要如何写以及是否需要一次将所有不符点写出,所以这一争议要根据普通法的原则解决。法院认为,既然 UCP 中没有写明是否要一次过将全部的不符点写明,根据普通法的说法,银行提出不符点的行为不能被认为是清楚无误的陈述或承诺而构成将来对其他不符点的禁反言,Parker 大法官说:"The question to be determined is, therefore, whether the circumstances are such as to create a factual or promissory representation with regard to any or all of the objections now raised and if so whether the plaintiffs acted upon such representation so as to preclude the defendants from now raising such matters. ... To hold that they thereby made any representation would in my view involve a radical departure from the accepted legal position and would seriously undermine the whole system of documentary credits, for banks would be obliged, for their own protection and the protection of their customers, always to scrutinize with the utmost care every document presented from beginning to end, notwithstanding that they may find in the first few lines of the first document at which they looked one or more good and sufficient reasons for refusal to pay. It is true that there were here successive presentations and that on Dec. 16 the bank were asked to state whether, but for the injunction, they would pay, but I do not consider that this is sufficient. Suppose (1) there are five documents and the bank reject for three specified defects in document No. 1; (2) that the beneficiary rectifies the three defects and presents again. It is clear that the bank is not by this alone estopped from raising other defects. If on this presentation it finds further defects either in the initial document or the next document it can reject again, and again it will not be estopped. It is for the beneficiary to see that the documents are all in order and he has no cause for complaint if the bank rejects as soon as they find one or more defects or if they reject again on finding further defects, and so on."

Parker 大法官随后又提出虽然原则上银行不会被禁反言，但在一些特殊的情况下，[80]有可能会满足构成禁反言的要件，说："The final presentation in this case might, however, stand in a different position. The bank were specifically asked to state defects as a matter of urgency and they then listed a number of what they considered to be defects, some of them being wholly untenable. It might therefore be said that on this occasion the circumstances were special. The credit was on the point of expiring and the plaintiffs were on the face of it seeking a final opportunity to put things right ..."

最后，Parker 大法官认为即使可以认定在特殊的情况下是作出了满足禁反言要件的陈述或承诺，但在本案中，原告并没有对此作出依赖，加上银行针对最后这一次的交单的回信不能被认为是有任何承诺付款的意思，所以最后判原告败诉。

看来依赖普通法的禁反言的确很困难，毕竟很少会有特殊的情况可以是符合禁反言的要件。这仅是一个陈述或承诺，即使是清楚无误，也远远不足够。还要满足其他的要件，即受益人要依赖(rely)这种陈述或承诺，如果让银行可以出尔反尔，会对受益人造成损害(detriment)。还有一个重要的要件是不公平与不合情理(unfair and unconscionable)，可以想得到针对后来提出的不符点银行作为对有关交易没有利益关系都能有合情合理的理由，而不是故意无中生有。所以，在信用证结汇时，很难想到有情况能同时满足这些要件。

但如果允许银行一次又一次的根据不同的不符点而拒单，从受益人的角度来讲是十分不利的，因为这不仅很容易就令受益人没有时间修正不符点而错过信用证或单证的有效期，[81]银行也可以轻易从信用证作出支付的义务/责任下脱身。所以，目前 UCP600 Article 16c(ii)中明确写明在拒付通知中要将每个银行不接受的不符点都写出，如果不按照该规定，Article 16(f)就会令银行丧失拒单的权利。这样是把极度小心与清楚审单的责任与没有做到的风险从受益人/卖方转移给了审单的银行，也通过合并 UCP 改变了普通法的默示地位。

5.3.2　其他涉及禁反言的先例

在上诉庭的 European Asian Bank AG v. Punjab & Sind Bank (No.2) (1983) 1 WLR 642 先例中，[82]原告 European Asian Bank 是当时一间位于德国但在远东地区包括新加坡有大量业务的银行。1979 年 7 月 14 日，一家位于印度新德里的公司 Jain 向一家新加坡公司 Bentrex 以 C&F 孟买的买卖合约购买 300 吨香料，货价为 225 万美元。付款方式为远期的不可撤销信用证在提单签发后的 180 日到期支付。7 月 20

[80]　这个特殊情况可见 Hing Yip Hing Fat Co. Ltd. v. The Daiwa Bank Ltd. (1991) HKCFI 139 先例。

[81]　单证会因 UCP600 之 Article14(c) 过了 21 天而变为失效的单证(stale document)。另买卖合约与信用证会有明示条文更短的交单时间，如装船提单在提单日期的 5 天后失效。

[82]　本先例在本书第五章之 6.3 段已经有谈及，在此更加详细的介绍。

日,Jain 向本案被告 Punjab 银行申请在 7 月 21 日开立信用证,被告于 7 月 21 日将其与 Jain 之间的通信转给 Algemene Bank Nederland(ABN)在新加坡的分行,并指示其通过本案原告将开立信用证的通知发给卖方 Bentrex。ABN 随后于 8 月 4 日保兑了(confirm)该信用证。8 月 7 日,Bentrex 向原告提交付运单证并附随开出一张 225 万美元根据原告指示支付的汇票。原告背书了该汇票,并将其与所有付运单证一起交出给被告的银行。8 月 16 日,Jain 在被询问是否接受提单(bill of lading)是由代理签发而非信用证规定的由船东签发的不符点之后,并没有提出异议并承兑了汇票。同日,被告与原告通信,告知原告单证被接受,付款日为 1980 年 2 月 3 日(accepted by the party to fall due on 3.2.1980)。8 月 20 日,原告向 Bentrex 支付了信用证贴现后(discount)的款项。

1979 年 9 月 8 日,Jain 得知装载有此票货物的船舶在航行途中沉没,船上的所有货物也都在此次沉船事故中灭失。1980 年 2 月 2 日,原告向信用证中写上的位于纽约华尔街的偿付银行的 Irving Trust Co.(reimbursement bank)查询用于支付该笔货款的金额是否已经到账。该银行告知原告,其根本没有此信用证记录,不知道为什么会在没有同意或其授权下被被告写上为偿付银行。于是原告以议付行(negotiating bank)的身份直接向被告开证行要求做出偿付,被告却通知原告,因为卖方存在欺诈根本没有把有关货物付运,Jain 向印度法院成功取得一份止付禁令,令该信用证被合法(印度法律下)阻止支付。从而原告在英国向被告提起诉讼并要求简易判决(summary judgement)。原告声称自己是议付行,并要求作为开证行的被告向他偿付 225 万美元。

双方的争议是原告是否在该信用证下是议付行,有权作出支付并要求开证行偿付。在该信用证中是有两条相互矛盾的条文,如下:"(6) Letter of credit should be advised through Europeanasian Bank, 50 Collyer Quay, Singapore and should be divisionable and **unrestricted for negotiation**...(9) We hereby engage with the drawers, endorsers and bona fide holders of drafts drawn under and in compliance with the terms of the credit that such drafts shall be duly honoured on presentation delivery of documents as specified above STP **negotiations under this credit are restricted to Algemene Bank Nederland NV 2 Cecil Street Corner'd Almeida Street, P.O. Box 493, Singapore**."(加黑部分是笔者的强调)

以上第(6)条文是说信用证由 Europeanasian Bank 做出通知,信用证是可分割与议付不受限制的。而第(9)条文则说信用证项下的汇票是只可以由 Algemene Bank Nederland 进行议付。这两条的内容显然有矛盾。基于法官或仲裁员在解释合约时要尽量令合约中每一句话都有合理的解释与能够与其他内容相互协调的大原则,[83] 上诉庭的 Goff 大法官从第(6)条文中"divisionable"一词作为入手点,对这两条条文

〔83〕 见杨良宜《合约的解释:规则与应用》第三章。

进行协调的解释。他认为第(6)条文的内容是针对信用证转让的情况。根据当时适用的UCP290第46条文,"divisionable"一词代表信用证是"可转让"(transferrable)的。[84] 而可转让即意味着卖方可以此信用证向上一个分卖方做出支付。而通常卖方不愿意让买方得知上一个分卖方的身份,或者该上一个分卖方的身份在信用证开出的时候并不明确,在这种情况下,不受限制的议付将会更符合实际情况的要求。所以,"unrestricted for negotiation"更适合被理解为"unrestricted for negotiation for the purposes of transfer by the beneficiary"。与此同时,第(9)条文对议付做出限制则是针对受益人对信用证贴现的情况,对议付行做出限制的原因很可能是开证行和该议付行有业务上的往来,所以愿意将该商业上的好处给予该有业务往来的银行。该解释令这两条条文都有效并更加合理。根据上述对信用证条文的解释,此案中,并不存在信用证转让的问题,所以原告并非是合资格的议付行。

这就导致原告要求被告偿付就不能依赖信用证的条文,而需要依赖一般法律的禁反言(estoppel)的说法。这涉及被告在8月16日的回复是否对承认原告的议付行地位与行为构成禁反言。Goff大法官基于被告在8月16日与18日两份回复以及被告一直保留单证而没有退还给原告的行为,判被告构成对原告的禁反言而需要向原告作出偿付。两份回复节录如下:"We are pleased to inform you that the above documents are accepted by the party to fall due on 3. 2. 1980." "... the documents are accepted by drawee to mature on 3. 2. 80."

Goff大法官说:"It is true that the communications in question should be read as meaning that the documents had been accepted by Jain to fall due, or mature, on February 3, 1980. But we have no doubt that this was intended to indicate to the plaintiffs that, the defendants' customers having accepted the documents as being in order, they (the defendants) acknowledged that payment under the letter of credit would be made to the plaintiffs as negotiating bankers on the date of maturity. As a matter of commerce, the plaintiffs could not have had the slightest interest in whether Jain, a trading company of whom they knew nothing, were promising to pay on the draft at maturity. After all, it was obvious that the plaintiffs, as negotiating bankers, would be discounting the letter of credit and so paying out a very large sum of money on the faith of these messages. As negotiating bankers, they would be relying on the undertaking of the issuing bank under the letter of credit. That was the only matter that they were interested in. Their inquiry dated August 13 was plainly directed to that. There could have been no question of the

---

〔84〕 虽然根据该条的规定,"divisionable"一词并不合适。"A credit can be transferred only if it is expressly designated as 'transferable' by the issuing bank. Terms such as 'divisible', 'fractionable', 'assignable', and 'transmissible' add nothing to the meaning of the term 'transferable' and shall not be used."

plaintiffs attempting to negotiate drafts accepted by Jain：commercially, they were not saleable documents. In any event, consistently with the obvious conclusion that all the plaintiffs were concerned with was the liability of the defendants under the letter of credit, the defendants retained all the documents, including the drafts, which were never returned to the plaintiffs. In all the circumstances, we have no doubt that, on a true construction of the relevant documents, **the defendants did indeed unequivocally represent to the plaintiffs that they, the defendants recognised that the plaintiffs were entitled to act as negotiating bankers under the letter of credit and that the documents were in order so** that there was, on the face of the documents, a liability upon the defendants to pay the plaintiffs the sum due under the letter of credit on the due date. In our judgment, there is no triable issue on this point."(加黑部分是笔者的强调)

最后再介绍的是,如果银行在收到单证之前就知道并同意单证中会有与信用证某些条文的不符,如不符点,但信用证没有作出更改(amendment)。之后在受益人交单时会被"承诺性禁反言"(promissory estoppel),而不能再以该不符点作为拒付的理由。

这可见 Floating Dock Ltd. v. The Hong Kong and Shanghai Banking Corporation (1986) 1 Lloyd's Rep. 65 先例。该先例是有关浮船坞的买卖,浮船坞要从夏威夷被拖带至中国宁波港交货给买方,付款方式是信用证。买卖合约与信用证有条文规定该浮船坞抵达宁波港的时间为 1985 年 1 月 29 日。后来该浮船坞实际上在 1985 年 2 月 7 日才抵达宁波港。受益人即卖方在知道此延误之后,委任律师与银行作为代表于 1985 年 2 月 4 日在伦敦召开会议,在该会议中,买方接受延误交货。法院在认定事实时,是判在该会议上银行知道该延误的事实,也知道将来提交的单证中显示浮船坞抵达宁波港的时间肯定晚于 1985 年 1 月 29 日。但后来信用证没有正式作出更改,但在卖方交单时,银行以这个不符点拒单。这样,就带来禁反言的争议。Evans 大法官判根据该先例的案情,银行构成了禁反言,他分析说卖方作为受益人对银行的言行有依赖并有损害,继续将浮船坞拖带至宁波港,他说:"**Treating the matter as one of estoppels**, it remains necessary for the plaintiffs to establish that they **relied upon the agreement or upon an implied representation** arising therefrom, in the sense indicated, and that they **suffered some detriment** form so doing. The evidence is clear that Mr. Farley(受益人/卖方代表)and the plaintiffs did rely upon it, for they advised and instructed respectively that the tug should proceed towards Ningpo, where they arrived on Feb. 7. ... In my judgement the fact of reliance is established..."(加黑部分是笔者的强调)

案 例 目 录

图书在版编目(CIP)数据

合约的履行、弃权与禁反言 / 杨良宜，杨大明，杨大志著. -- 北京 ：法律出版社，2018(2024.12 重印)
ISBN 978 - 7 - 5197 - 2028 - 5

Ⅰ. ①合… Ⅱ. ①杨… ②杨… ③杨… Ⅲ. ①国际商法 Ⅳ. ①D996.1

中国版本图书馆 CIP 数据核字(2018)第 037406 号

合约的履行、弃权与禁反言
HEYUE DE LÜXING、QIQUAN YU JINFANYAN

杨良宜
杨大明 著
杨大志

责任编辑 吴 昉
装帧设计 凌点工作室

出版发行 法律出版社
编辑统筹 法律教育出版分社
责任校对 郑怡萍
责任印制 刘晓伟
经　　销 新华书店

开本 710 毫米 × 1000 毫米 1/16
印张 74.5 **字数** 1505 千
版本 2018 年 3 月第 1 版
印次 2024 年 12 月第 3 次印刷
印刷 三河市龙大印装有限公司

地址：北京市丰台区莲花池西里 7 号(100073)
网址：www. lawpress. com. cn
投稿邮箱：info@ lawpress. com. cn
举报盗版邮箱：jbwq@ lawpress. com. cn

销售电话：010 - 83938349
客服电话：010 - 83938350
咨询电话：010 - 63939796

书号：ISBN 978 - 7 - 5197 - 2028 - 5
定价：148.00 元

凡购买本社图书，如有印装错误，我社负责退换。电话：010 - 83938349